Principles of Economics

Second European Edition

Two week loan
Benthyciad pythefnos

Principles of Economics

Second European Edition

Moore McDowell
Rodney Thom
Robert Frank
and
Ben Bernanke

London Boston Burr Ridge, IL Dubuque, IA Madison, WI New York San Francisco
St. Louis Bangkok Bogotá Caracas Kuala Lumpur Lisbon Madrid Mexico City
Milan Montreal New Delhi Santiago Seoul Singapore Sydney Taipei Toronto

Principles of Economics
Moore McDowell, Rodney Thom, Robert Frank and Ben Bernanke
ISBN-13 978-0-07-712169-3
ISBN-10 0-07-712169-4

**McGraw-Hill
Higher Education**

Published by McGraw-Hill Education
Shoppenhangers Road
Maidenhead
Berkshire
SL6 2QL
Telephone: 44 (0) 1628 502 500
Fax: 44 (0) 1628 770 224
Website: www.mcgraw-hill.co.uk

British Library Cataloguing in Publication Data
A catalogue record for this book is available from the British Library

Library of Congress Cataloguing in Publication Data
The Library of Congress data for this book has been applied for from the Library of Congress

Acquisitions Editor: Natalie Jacobs
Development Editor: Hannah Cooper
Editorial Assistant: Tom Hill
Marketing Manager: Vanessa Boddington
Senior Production Editor: James Bishop

Text design by Wearset Ltd, Boldon, Tyne and Wear
Cover design by Paul Fielding
Printed and bound in Singapore by Markono Print Media Pte Ltd

ISBN-13 978-0-07-712169-3
ISBN-10 0-07-712169-4

DEDICATION

For Nuala – MMcD
For Susan – RT

Brief Table of Contents

Detailed Table of Contents

Preface

Writers of introductory textbooks in economics are obliged to make choices. This is hardly surprising, since the fact that people must make choices, sometimes difficult ones, is in the end what economics is about. The first choice in the case of a textbook concerns the approach taken to getting ideas across to different types of students. This in turn reflects the reasons for which students are taking the economics course for which the text is being used and the abilities of the target student body, especially where mathematics is an issue. The second concerns the breadth of the subject matter the text covers. Here the choice is between an attempt to cover all the bases adequately or make sure that the more important bases are covered more fully. Inevitably what is published represents the necessity to compromise. Again, this is hardly surprising, since it, too, mirrors how choices are analysed in economics. Trade-offs are at the heart of rational decision-making.

In many, perhaps most, introductory courses the instructor is dealing with two types of student and, therefore, has two different goals. The first group comprises students whose interest in economics is a general one as part of a broad educational curriculum. Some of these students may never take another economics course. For them the imperative is to give them a good understanding of basic economics principles that will enable them to understand more clearly the world in which they will live, and to retain these insights. The second group comprises students whose objectives or whose programmes envisage progressing to a degree where economics is a major component. For this group the aim of an introductory course will be to provide a firm foundation for going further with the discipline.

Very few undergraduate students of economics proceed to a PhD and become professional economists. However, an understanding of basic economics is of immense value in everyday life. We believe that this obvious fact should inform how economics is taught at the introductory level. It is why, in revising the text, we have tried to adhere to the philosophy that informed the original text of Robert Frank and Ben Bernanke. In Europe, as in the USA, an abiding concern of the academic economist, and one that informed the design of the original text, was this: to judge by what is retained afterwards, many students finish introductory courses without having really learned and understood the most important basic economic principles. The problem is that these courses frequently try to teach students far too much. The Frank and Bernanke proposition is encapsulated in the following paragraphs taken from the third US edition preface.

> Our basic premise is that a small number of basic principles do most of the heavy lifting in economics, and that if we focus narrowly and repeatedly on those principles, students can actually master them in just a single semester.... We rely ... on a well-articulated list of seven core principles, which we reinforce repeatedly by illustrating and applying each principle in numerous contexts...

Scarcity

1. *The Scarcity Principle* Having more of one good thing usually means having less of another.

Cost–Benefit Analysis

2. *The Cost–Benefit Principle* Take no action unless its marginal benefit is at least as great as its marginal cost.

Incentives Matter

3. *The Incentive Principle* Cost–benefit comparisons are relevant not only for identifying the decisions that rational people should make, but also for predicting the actual decisions they do make.

4. ***The Principle of Comparative Advantage*** Everyone does best when each concentrates on the activity for which he or she is relatively most productive.

5. ***The Principle of Increasing Opportunity*** *Cost* Use the resources with the lowest opportunity cost before turning to those with higher opportunity costs.

6. ***The Efficiency Principle*** Efficiency is an important social goal because when the economic 'pie' grows larger, everyone can have a larger slice.

7. ***The Equilibrium Principle*** A market in equilibrium leaves no unexploited opportunities for individuals but may not exploit all gains achievable through collective action.

The text encourages students to become 'economic naturalists'. This means using basic economic principles to understand and explain what you see in the world around you, and to resolve some apparent paradoxes. For example, we don't fit child safety restraints in planes, but we do in cars. Do we not care about children in planes? An economic naturalist understands that infant safety seats are required in cars but not in airplanes because of the high marginal cost of space in planes relative to cars and the lower benefit in terms of reduced risk of injury or death.

Our objective in adapting the original Frank and Bernanke text was to move it somewhat from the first objective above towards the second objective, reflecting academic programme structures in countries other than the USA. However, in doing so we have always been guided by the need to preserve the major advantage the original text had over other texts we had seen. Although we have added some additional theoretical analysis (for example, an expanded use of simple game theory) our focus in this edition remains as it was in the first edition. This was the importance of getting ideas across in a fashion that captures the reader's attention and makes a lasting contribution to basic understanding of the economics underpinnings of ordinary life. Not only is this important in terms of the first objective above, but we believe that it is very important that students who progress with economics should develop a sense of economic intuition as well as mastering technical aspects of the discipline.

Changes in the second edition

Guided by extensive reviewer feedback, our main goal in preparing our second edition has been to reorganize the presentation to accommodate the broadest range of student preparation consistent with the objectives we have already described. For example, while continuing to emphasize verbal and graphical approaches in the main text, we offer several appendices and boxes that allow for more detailed and challenging algebraic treatments of the same material. Among the hundreds of specific refinements we made, the following merit explicit mention.

• We have continued to try to make formal analysis of various parts of economics available while permitting an instructor to avoid using them, and to use simpler approaches where desired. Thus, while including in some cases the formal analysis in the main text, rather than in chapter appendices, the material is presented in a way that permits the reader to proceed around it if this is appropriate.

Microeconomics

• More and clearer emphasis on the core principles
• Integration of the material on the workings of markets into a single chapter

- Extended treatment of the principle of comparative advantage and specialisation, and its links to economic growth and the gains from trade based on specialisation and exchange
- Inclusion, on an optional basis, of rigorous analysis of consumer demand and of profit maximization
- Improved material on the elements of game theory and on the economics of information
- Theoretical and case study analysis of how firms (and regulators) operate in oligopolistic markets
- We have chosen to restrict the material content by removing the section on trade and integration that ended the microeconomics part of the previous edition. In doing this we are responding to suggestions from instructors who adopted the text, most of whom regarded this section as being outside the scope of their course. These chapters will continue to be available on the text website for instructors who prefer to use them and drop other material.
- There are two major changes in the chapter organisation of the material in the micro part of the new edition. These have been made in response to feedback from adopters of the text.
  - The first is the bringing together of the basic elements of market analysis into one (rather long) chapter, rather than treating them as separate subjects.
  - The second is the decision to treat the elements of game theory and strategic choice separately from consideration of oligopoly. Introducing students to the basic concepts of game theory is an important element in any modern text, because of the powerful addition it offers to an economist's understanding of how the world works. It should not be seen as being just part of the analysis of how firms behave in small-number markets, important though it is in that context.

Macroeconomics

- Modular presentation: Part 7, Macroeconomics: Data and Issues, is a self-contained group of chapters that covers measurement issues relating to GDP, the price level and the labour market. This allows instructors to proceed to either the long run (Part 8, The Economy in the Long Run) or the short run (Part 9, The Economy in the Short Run) first with no loss of continuity.
- A revised presentation of long-run growth and productivity: Chapter 19 uses the Solow growth model to analyse key relationships between growth, labour productivity and technical progress.
- A more comprehensive treatment of the Keynesian model: Part 9, The Economy in the Short Run, presents a three-part treatment of Keynesian macroeconomics. Chapters 21 and 22 deal with the real and monetary sectors which are then integrated to construct the IS-LM model in Chapter 23. Chapters 24 and 25 use the IS-LM model to discuss fiscal and monetary policies in a non-inflationary environment.
- Refinements in the presentation of aggregate demand and aggregate supply: Chapters 26 and 27 work together to give students a thorough understanding of both the theory and application of the AD–AS model. In Chapter 26, we develop the reasoning behind the AD curve and the AS curve. In particular:
  - A central bank policy rule is integrated into the IS-LM model to derive a downward-sloping AD curve which links short-run equilibrium output to the rate of inflation.

- Based on the occurrence of unanticipated changes in the rate of inflation the AS curve is now an upward-sloping curve with inflation on the vertical axis. This provides the advantage of placing inflationary expectations at the centre of the story of how the economy's self-correcting mechanism works and how monetary policy affects inflation and output in short-run and long-run equilibrium.
    - We provide students with a series of examples that show how the AD and AS curves work together to determine short-run equilibrium and how the economy adjusts to long-run equilibrium.
    - In Chapter 27, we apply the AD–AS model to macroeconomic policy. We distinguish between real and nominal shocks and ask whether or not the central bank should accommodate shocks. Finally, we use what students have learned to address important current topics such as central bank independence and inflation targeting.
- Flexible coverage of international economics: Chapter 28 presents a self-contained discussion of exchange rate determination that can be used whenever an instructor thinks it best to introduce this important subject. The chapter also integrates trade and capital flows into the IS-LM model and presents a discussion of stabilisation policy in the open economy.

Approach

A key feature of the text is what we call 'economic naturalism'. By using examples and and posing problems we seek to provide answers to questions that should encourage readers to look at the world through the eyes of an economist. Here are a few examples.

In Micro:

Why do airline ticket prices rise when most people fly, while strawberry prices fall when people eat more strawberries?

Why did Americans reduce the size of cars bought to a greater degree than did Europeans in response to increases in the world price of oil?

Why do supermarket checkout lines all tend to be roughly the same length?

In Macro:

Why do Europeans save more than Americans?

Why did the ECB increase interest rates seven times between April 1999 and October 2002?

Does a strong currency imply a strong economy?

Why this rather than another text? In addition to the pedagogic approach already described, we believe that this text differs significantly from others in respect of the emphasis on modern economic analysis.

- **Modern microeconomics:** Economic surplus is more central to the presentation of economics in this than in any other text. This concept underlies the argument for economic efficiency as an important social goal. Instead of dwelling on the problem of equity versus efficiency in policy making, we stress that efficiency (maximizing surplus) permits the achievement of other goals. We analyse rational decision making in a way that identifies the common decision pitfalls identified by 2002 Nobel Laureate Daniel Kahneman and others – such as the tendency to ignore implicit costs, the tendency not to ignore sunk costs, and the tendency to confuse average and marginal costs and benefits. We introduce the student to the elements of game theory, and show how powerful an approach it can be to explaining otherwise baffling problems. We introduce the Coase theorem, and use it to explain and to question aspects of legal and regulatory policy. The text also introduces students to the economics of information, something that is widely ignored as an area of economics in its own right in many other texts.

- **Modern macroeconomics**: Recent developments have renewed interest in cyclical fluctuations without challenging the importance of such long-run issues as growth, productivity, the evolution of real wages, and capital formation. Our treatment of these issues is organized as follows:
  ○ **A two-chapter treatment of long-run issues**, followed by a modern treatment of short-term fluctuations and stabilization policy, emphasizing the important distinction between short- and long-run behaviour of the economy.
  ○ Consistent with both media reporting and public perception we **treat the interest rate rather than the money supply** as the primary instrument of central bank policy.
  ○ A **more realistic treatment of aggregate demand and aggregate supply** which relates output to inflation rather than to the price level, sidestepping the necessity of a separate derivation of the link between the output gap and inflation.

- This book places a **heavy emphasis on globalization**, starting with an analysis of its effects on real wage inequality and progressing to such issues as the benefits of trade, the causes and effects of protectionism, the role of capital flows in domestic capital formation, the link between exchange rates and monetary policy, and the sources of speculative attacks on currencies.

The challenge

The world is a more competitive place now than it was when we started teaching in the 1970s. In arena after arena, business as usual is no longer good enough. Football players used to drink beer and go fishing during the off season, but they now lift weights and ride exercise bicycles. Academics at the start of their careers used to chill out or work on their houses on weekends, but the current crop can now be found most weekends at their computers. The competition for student attention has grown similarly more intense. There are many tempting courses in the typical college curriculum and even more tempting diversions outside the classroom. Students are freer than ever to pick and choose.

Yet many of us seem to operate under the illusion that most students arrive at college with a burning desire to become economics majors. And many of us do not yet seem to have recognized that students' cognitive abilities and powers of concentration are scarce resources. To hold our ground, we must become not only more selective in what we teach, but also more effective as advocates for our discipline. We must persuade students that we offer something of value. A well-conceived and well-executed introductory course in economics can teach our students more about society and human behaviour in a single term than virtually any other course in the university. This course can and should be an intellectual adventure of the first order. Not all students who take the kind of course we envisioned when writing this book will go on to become economics majors, of course. But many will, and even those who do not will leave with a sense of admiration for the power of economic ideas.

Guided Tour

This feature applies economic perspectives to real-world situations, encourages you to think like an economist.

matically people could
having each individua
After the collapse of th
the Soviet-backed regi
lites since the late 1940
formally operated or c

central planning the
allocation of economic
resources is determined by a
political and administrative
mechanism that gathers
information as to technology,
resource availability and end
demands for goods and
services

are commonly subject
collective provision vi
example. Hence, mode

Key terms

These are highlighted and defined in the relevant chapters providing ease of reference.

Maths boxes

These are relatively placed boxes to enable you to dip in and out of additional maths content as you require.

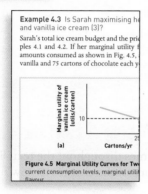

Example 4.3 Is Sarah maximising he and vanilla ice cream (3)?

Sarah's total ice cream budget and the pri ples 4.1 and 4.2. If her marginal utility f amounts consumed as shown in Fig. 4.5, vanilla and 75 cartons of chocolate each y

Figure 4.5 Marginal Utility Curves for Tw current consumption levels, marginal utili flavour

Examples

Examples throughout the text apply the theory discussed to practical contexts.

Recaps

This feature highlights key facts to aid your learning, reminding you what you have learned, or what you should already know.

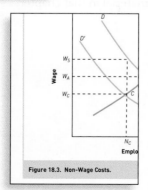

from sales is smaller than
should then cease product
equal to its fixed costs. Bu
    More formally, if P deno
ber of units produced and
we use VC to denote the fi
in the short run if $P \times Q$ is

Short-run shu

Exercise 5.4 In Example 5.2, suppose
profit corresponding to
firm's best option is to ce

Average variable co

Suppose that the firm is u
is, suppose that $P \times Q < V$

Exercises

Exercises feature throughout the chapters, to enable you to practise the techniques you have been taught and apply the methodology to real-world situations.

Review questions

Review questions and activities test your understanding. Problems occur in difficulty in order to build skills and put into practice

Figure 18.3. Non-Wage Costs.

Figures and tables

Each chapter provides a number of figures and tables to help you visualise the various economic models, and to illustrate and summarise important concepts.

Economic naturalist boxes

This feature applies economic perspectives to real-world situations, encouraging you to 'think like an economist'.

> **Economic naturalist 3.1 Why** interruptions in electricity su the beginning of 2008?
>
> In January and February, 2008, South South Africa] began to experience repe ity, simply ran out of capacity to meet ship, and posed a serious threat to t political stability. By definition, there w this can only mean cutting supply to c prices (and possibly in some cases turr outstripped capacity expansion. The la nues by the electricity supplier. In ad Africa was supplying Zimbabwe with therefore, were not facing prices that Inevitably, demand growth and expans unwillingness to see cost-reflective pr supply energy to competing users, and economic disruption, ensued.

Maths boxes

These strategically placed boxes allow you to dip in and out of additional maths content as you wish.

WHY NATIONS BECOME RICH

Box 19.1 The steady-state gr

The Solow model relates changes in *the labour force N* and technical prog ΔY = the change in total output and ΔY from €100 million to €103 million ther year, capital, labour and technology i my's growth rate? To answer this qu defined as the change in output per u

Rearranging gives:

Which is the change in output resultir

Recaps

This feature highlights key themes throughout the text, linking what you have learned in previous sections of the chapter to new material.

> opportunities. For now, lowing core principle:
>
> **The Equilibrium Pri** market in equilibrium not exploit all gains ac
>
> **RECAP** Markets and social we
>
> When the supply and demand curves f with the production and consumption c produce and consume the quantity o surplus.
>
> **Measuring the i** **and demand: ela**
>
> Conventionally, most pc on the basis of penalising of those drugs at the inc

Review questions and problems

Each chapter ends with a set of Review questions and Problems, ranging in difficulty to consolidate learning of the material in that chapter.

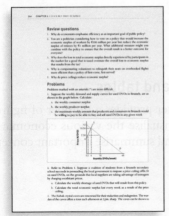

Summary

This briefly reviews and reinforces the main topics you will have covered in each chapter to ensure you have acquired a solid understanding of the key topics.

Technology to Enhance Learning and Teaching

Please visit www.mcgraw-hill.com/textbooks/mcdowell today!

Online Learning Centre (OLC)

After completing each chapter, log on to the supporting Online Learning Centre website. Take advantage of the study tools offered to reinforce the material you have read in the text, and to develop your knowledge of economics in a fun and effective way.

Resources for students include:

- Multiple-choice quizzes
- Graphing tool
- In-chapter solutions
- Glossary

Also available for lecturers:

- Lecture outlines
- Solutions to questions
- Naturalist exercises
- Artwork
- Testbank
- PowerPoint slides
- UK data section

Connect

ECONOMICS

Students can connect to knowledge, connect to learning, connect to their futures

McGraw-Hill Connect Economics™ is a web-based assignment and assessment platform that gives you the power to create assignments, practice tests and quizzes online, while saving you time!

Connect Economics provides the problems directly from the end-of-chapter material in your McGraw-Hill textbook, so you can easily create assignments and tests and deliver them to your students. Connect Economics grades assignments automatically, provides instant feedback to students, and securely stores all student results. Detailed results let you see at a glance how each student performs, and easily track the progress of every student in your course.

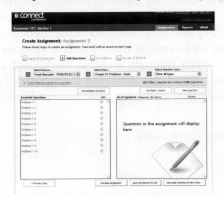

Create Assignments

With 4 easy steps, set up assignments using end-of-chapter questions from your McGraw-Hill textbook and deliver it to your students . . . all online.

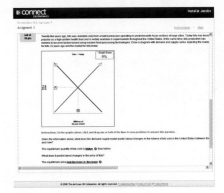

Students Take Assignments & Receive Instant Feedback

Connect Economics helps you close the feedback loop on students' homework and reduce the time you spend grading. Once an assignment is completed, students can see immediately how they've performed and receive feedback on each question.

View Grades & Reports

Track each student's progress in your Connect Economics Grade Reports. Student results on each assignment automatically feed to the grade reports so you can track student or class progress on any concept. Learning objective tags help you track course outcomes and aid in Assurance of Learning.

Contact your local McGraw-Hill representative to learn more about Connect Economics. Visit www.mhhe.com / support.

Test bank available in McGraw-Hill EZ Test Online

A test bank of over 2500 questions is available to lecturers adopting this book for their module. A range of questions is provided for each chapter, including multiple choice, true or false, and short answer or essay questions. The questions are identified by type, difficulty and topic to help you to select questions that best suit your needs and are accessible through an easy-to-use online testing tool, **McGraw-Hill EZ Test Online**.

McGraw-Hill EZ Test Online is accessible to busy academics virtually anywhere – in their office, at home or while travelling – and eliminates the need for software installation. Lecturers can choose from question banks associated with their adopted textbook or easily create their own questions. They also have access to hundreds of banks and thousands of questions created for other McGraw-Hill titles. Multiple versions of tests can be saved for delivery on paper or online through WebCT, Blackboard and other course management systems. When created and delivered though EZ Test Online, students' tests can be marked immediately, saving lecturers time and providing prompt results to students.

To register for this **FREE** resource, visit www.eztestonline.com.

Custom Publishing Solutions: Let us help make our **content** your **solution**

At McGraw-Hill Education our aim is to help lecturers to find the most suitable content for their needs delivered to their students in the most appropriate way. Our **custom publishing solutions** offer the ideal combination of content delivered in the way that best suits lecturer and students.

Our custom publishing programme offers lecturers the opportunity to select just the chapters or sections of material they wish to deliver to their students from a database called Primis at www. primisonline.com.

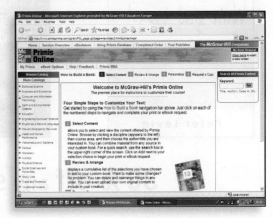

Primis contains over two million pages of content from:

- textbooks
- professional books
- case books – Harvard Articles, Insead, Ivey, Darden, Thunderbird and BusinessWeek
- Taking Sides – debate materials

across the following imprints:

- McGraw-Hill Education
- Open University Press
- Harvard Business School Press
- US and European material

There is also the option to include additional material authored by lecturers in the custom product – this does not necessarily have to be in English.

We will take care of everything from start to finish in the process of developing and delivering a custom product, to ensure that lecturers and students receive exactly the material needed in the most suitable way.

With a Custom Publishing Solution, students enjoy the best selection of material deemed to be the most suitable for learning everything they need for their courses – something of real value to support their learning. Teachers are able to use exactly the material they want, in the way they want, to support their teaching on the course.

Please contact your local McGraw-Hill representative with any questions; alternatively, contact Warren Eels e: warren_eels@mcgraw-hill.com.

Make the Grade!

 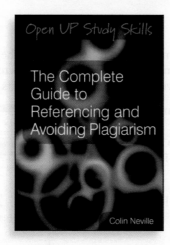 

30% off any Study Skills book!

Our Study Skills books are packed with practical advice and tips that are easy to put into practice and will really improve the way you study. Topics include:

- techniques to help you pass exams
- advice to improve your essay writing
- help in putting together the perfect seminar presentation
- tips on how to balance studying and your personal life

www.openup.co.uk/studyskills

Visit our website to read helpful hints about essays, exams, dissertations and much more.

Special offer! As a valued customer, buy online and receive 30% off any of our Study Skills books by entering the promo code **getahead**

Acknowledgements

Our thanks go to the following reviewers for their comments at various stages in the text's development:

Javad Amid, Uppsala University
Ali Ataullah, Loughborough University
Dr. Maria Brouwer, Amsterdam School of Economics
Graham Cookson, King's College London
Rob Gillanders, University College Dublin
Keith Gray, Coventry University
Dr. Robert Hamilton, Loughborough University
Anthony Heyes, Royal Holloway, University of London
Richard Ledward, Staffordshire University
Oliver Marnet, Aberystwyth University
Johanna Palmberg, Jönköping International Business School
Keith Pilbeam, City University London
Odile Poulsen, University of East Anglia
Philip Reiss, Maastricht University
Dr. Gerard Turley, National University of Ireland, Galway
Cornelis Van Walbeek, University of Cape Town
Perihan Yavash, Coventry University

We would also like to thank all those who contributed to the development of the first edition, and those who offered their feedback in the form of survey responses, as this feedback has also been very useful to us in the development of this new edition.

We must also gratefully acknowledge the help we have received from several colleagues in UCD. John Sheehan and Kevin Denny have used the earlier editions in giving micro principles courses, and Frank Walsh and Ivan Pastine have used them for macro principles and all have assisted us with comments and suggestions. We are deeply indebted to Sarah Parlane for her careful reviewing and amendment of some of the proposed new material in the second edition. Brendan Walsh and David Madden have supplied a steady stream of suggestions and comments on proposed economic naturalists, always witty, sometimes constructive. And Cormac O Grada kept us straight on Giffen Goods.

Over the last few years, in dealing with this and the first edition, we have been ably, cheerfully, and forgivingly supported by some very professional and pleasant people at McGraw-Hill. In recent times those most closely involved have been Natalie Jacobs and Hannah Cooper. We are greatly indebted to them for help and for keeping our noses to the grindstone without too much pain. In the past, Emily Jefferson, Caroline Prodger and Mark Kavanagh gave us great support. To all of these, our sincere thanks.

Acknowledgements

Our thanks go to the following reviewers for their comments at various stages in the text's development:

Javed Amid, Uppsala University
Ali Ataullah, Loughborough University
Dr. Maria Brouwer, Amsterdam School of Economic
Graham Cookson, King's College London
Rob Gillanders, University College Dublin
Keith Gray, Coventry University
Dr. Robert Hamilton, Loughborough University
Anthony Heyes, Royal Holloway, University of London
Richard Ledward, Staffordshire University
Oliver Marnet, Aberystwyth University
Johanna Palmberg, Jönköping International Business School
Keith Pilbeam, City University London
Odile Poulsen, University of East Anglia
Philip Reiss, Maastricht University
Dr. Gerard Turley, National University of Ireland, Galway
Cornelia Van Wheelen, University of Cape Town
Perihan Yavash, Coventry University

We would also like to thank all those who contributed to the development of the first edition, and those who offered their feedback in the form of survey responses, as this feedback has also been very useful to us in the development of this new edition.

We must also gratefully acknowledge the help we have received from several colleagues in UCD. John Sheehan and Kevin Denny have used the earlier editions in giving intro to principles courses, and Frank Walsh and Ivan Pastine have used them for macro principles and all have assisted us with comments and suggestions. We are deeply indebted to Sarah Parlane for her careful reviewing and amendments of some of the proposed new material in the second edition. Brendan Walsh and David Madden have supplied a steady stream of suggestions and comments on proposed economic naturalists, always with, sometimes consultative, And Cormac O Grada kept us straight on Giffen Goods.

Over the last few years, in dealing with this and the first edition, we have been ably, cheerfully, and forgivingly supported by some very professional and pleasant people at McGraw-Hill. In recent times those most closely involved have been Natalie Jacobs and Hannah CooperWe are greatly indebted to them for help and for keeping our noses to the grindstone without too much pain. In the past, Emily Jefferson, Caroline Prodger and Mark Kavanagh gave us great support. To all of these, our sincere thanks.

Every effort has been made to trace and acknowledge ownership of copyright and to clear permission for material reproduced in this book. The publishers will be pleased to make suitable arrangements to clear permission with any copyright holders whom it has not been possible to contact.

Part 1
Introduction

For many students reading this text it will be their first economics text. Others, of course, will have had some exposure to economics before. In either case it is important to understand that economics is not a collection of settled facts, to be copied down and memorised. Mark Twain said that nothing is older than yesterday's newspaper, and the same can be said of yesterday's economic statistics. Indeed, the only prediction about the economy that can be made with confidence is that there will continue to be large, and largely unpredictable, changes.

If economics is not a set of durable facts, then what is it? Fundamentally, it is a way of *thinking about the world*. Over many years economists have developed some simple but widely applicable principles that can help us to understand almost any economic situation (and a multitude of situations that at first sight might not appear to be concerned with economics), from the relatively simple ones such as economic decisions that individuals make every day to the workings of highly complex markets, such as international financial markets. The principal objective of this book, and of this course, is to help you learn these principles and how to apply them to a variety of economic questions and issues.

The three chapters of Part 1 lay out the basic economic principles that will be used throughout the book. Chapter 1 introduces the notion of scarcity – the unavoidable fact that, although our needs and wants are boundless, the resources available to satisfy them are limited. The chapter goes on to show that deciding whether to take an action by comparing the cost and benefit of that action is a useful approach for dealing with the inevitable trade-offs that scarcity creates. Chapter 1 then discusses several important decision pitfalls and concludes by introducing the concept of *economic naturalism*. Chapter 2 goes beyond individual decision making to consider trade, among both individuals and countries. An important reason for trade is that it permits people (or countries) to specialise in the production of particular goods and services, which in turn enhances productivity and raises standards of living. Finally, Chapter 3, a long chapter, looks at how markets work. It presents an overview of the concepts of supply and demand, perhaps the most basic and familiar tools used by economists. It also looks at one of the core concepts in economics, elasticity, the proportionate response of a dependent variable to a change in an independent or causative variable, and how this is measured.

1

Thinking Like an Economist

One of the first things you will learn from studying economics is that thinking (and then speaking) like an economist can make you very unpopular. Partly this is because economists seem to take a lot of pleasure in puncturing other people's balloons (that is, demonstrating that what their victims hold to be self-evident is far from being true). However, a more important aspect of economics as a discipline is that it teaches you to think about problems, and solutions to problems, in a way that others find challenging to their way of thinking.

Consider the following policy issue. It is taken as almost an article of faith by teaching professionals that it is desirable to reduce class sizes, particularly at the primary (elementary) level, in order to improve educational outcomes. Children, it is said, do better in terms of educational achievement, controlling for other factors, if they are taught in smaller classes. Flowing from this is the consistent pressure on governments in many countries to channel funds to schools to enable class sizes to be reduced.

Most people, parents included, would agree with the proposition that reducing class sizes would improve the education children receive. Apart from the fact that teachers continually argue along these lines, everyday experience supports the concept of better classroom experience and consequent educational outcomes being linked to smaller class sizes. Each child, at the very least, can expect to receive more attention in a smaller class than in a larger one.

An economist considering this issue would be likely to ask some hard questions. The first would be 'What evidence exists to support the proposition that smaller classes, all other things being equal, improve educational outcomes?' In order to answer this, the economist would ask what accepted metric exists that permits objective evaluation of outcomes and comparison of results. If you can't measure outcomes and make comparisons over time or across schools on a common, accepted basis, the proposition cannot be demonstrated to be correct. If the accepted metric demonstrates outcome differences statistically related to class size the economist would agree that there is support for the proposition. If not, the economist would be likely to point out that the pressure for smaller classes may reflect the fact that teachers may have a vested interest in pushing for smaller classes as a means of reducing the pressure of work.[1]

So far, we can see that the economist's approach is, first, based on confronting a hypothesis with evidence before conditionally accepting it. This, of course, is exactly what physicists, geologists, astronomers and cosmologists do. It is why economics can credibly seek to be regarded as a science, too. People, unfortunately, tend to respond to this in exactly the same way as most people did a few hundred years ago when informed that the Earth was not flat: common sense supported the flat Earth hypothesis. It is plainly silly even to question the class size hypothesis. People do not like being told that their 'common sense' is incorrect. Bad news for economists.

Incentives
Matter

Second, notice that an economist will always look at motivation. The economist argues that people tend to behave in a self-interested fashion. They respond to incentives. They will combine to press for changes that improve their economic welfare. They may even persuade themselves that what they are seeking is to everyone else's advantage. They are, however, unlikely to combine to press for changes that will reduce their economic welfare. Trades unions do not seek lower wages for their members if unemployment rises. But imputing self-interest to people who are making arguments based on hypotheses about the general good is certain to cause outrage. More bad news for economists.

There are, of course, exceptions to this. Individual altruism exists. Despite some cynical investigatory efforts, most people would accept that Mother Teresa of Calcutta sought primarily to improve the lot of the poor in Calcutta, not to become an international celebrity. People do combine to achieve ends that do not coincide with group self-interest. They may in some cases be spectacularly wrong-headed in the remedies they support (for example, urging motorists to switch to bio-fuels), but most environmentalists seeking to avert global warming are not doing so in order to earn a living.

Returning to the class size issue, the next thing we ask as economists is what it would cost to reduce class sizes, and whether the cost incurred is warranted by the expected benefits. That, of course, may require putting some monetary value on levels of educational achievement. While the public reaction consequences of doing this would be more apparent if we were talking about healthcare interventions, it is easy to see how this question is dismissed by reference to Oscar Wilde's observation about knowing the price of everything and the value of nothing. But the economist's question is motivated by the fact that there is a social cost involved in putting more money into healthcare or education: the value of the things that can't be done as a consequence.

Cost–Benefit
Analysis

Finally, the economist is likely to suggest that we should stop reducing class sizes in any case well before further reductions have no effect on outcomes. The economist will talk about marginal, or incremental, costs, and marginal, or incremental, benefits. The economist will suggest that additional funding to reduce class sizes or to reduce road deaths or to improve the health status of the population should not continue beyond the point where marginal costs equal marginal benefits, even if total benefits could be increased. Try that out on a road safety lobbyist! An acceptable level of deaths on the roads?

---

1 Economists interested in this question have to depend on the research undertaken by educational experts – in particular, educational psychologists. They, too, have been active in questioning this conventional wisdom about reducing class sizes, following a similar research methodology. A highly readable survey of the issues and problems, which argues for very limited evidence of significant gains unless class sizes are reduced below 20, is Bennett, N., 'Annotation: Class Size and the Quality of Educational Outcomes', *Journal of Child Psychology and Psychiatry*, 36(6), 1998, pp. 797–804.

Economics: studying choice in a world of scarcity

No matter how rich a country is and, for most of us, at any rate, as individuals no matter how rich we are, *scarcity* is a fundamental fact of life. There is never enough time, money or energy to do everything we want to do or have everything we would like to have. Scarcity simply means we must choose, and sometimes make hard choices. **Economics** is the study of how people make choices under conditions of scarcity, and of the results of those choices for society.

economics the study of how people make choices under conditions of scarcity and of the results of those choices for society

Scarcity ⬤

If you were a parent with a young child going into the educational system you might definitely prefer schools with a class size of 20 rather than a class size of 30, everything else being equal. But suppose you had to pay fees, and the fees in a small-class school were significantly higher than in a large-class size school. Your income is limited. If you choose the first school you will have to give up something as a result. Your choice will in the end come down to the relative importance of competing demands on that income. Your resources are limited. Therefore you must choose. If you had a menu of schools with different class sizes to choose from, with fees reflecting class size, you could choose any one of them. In doing so you are trading off other things you might do with your income against perceived benefits from class size.

That such trade-offs are widespread and important is one of the core principles of economics. We call it the **Scarcity Principle**, because the simple fact of scarcity makes trade-offs necessary. Another name for the scarcity principle is the **No-Free-Lunch Principle** (which comes from the observation that even lunches that are given to you are never really free – somebody, somehow, always has to pay for them).

Scarcity Principle (also called the No-Free-Lunch Principle) although we have boundless needs and wants, the resources available to us are limited, so having more of one good thing usually means having less of another; hence the cliché, 'There ain't no such thing as a free lunch', sometimes reduced to the acronym TANSTAAFL

Inherent in the idea of a trade-off is the fact that choice involves compromise between competing interests. Economists resolve such trade-offs by using *cost–benefit analysis*, which is based on the disarmingly simple principle that an action should be taken if, and only if, its benefits exceed its costs. We call this statement the **Cost–Benefit Principle**, and it, too, is one of the core principles of economics.

Cost–Benefit Principle an individual (or a firm, or a society) should take an action if, and only if, the extra benefits from taking that action are at least as great as the extra costs

With the Cost–Benefit Principle in mind, let us think about our class-size question again. Imagine that classrooms come in only two sizes – 100-seat lecture halls and 20-seat classrooms – and that your university currently offers introductory economics courses to classes of 100 students.

Question: Should administrators reduce the class size to 20 students?

Answer: Reduce if, and only if, the value of the improvement in instruction outweighs its additional cost.

This rule sounds simple, but to apply it we need some way to *measure* the relevant costs and benefits – a task that is often difficult in practice. If we make a few simplifying assumptions, however, we can see how the analysis might work. On the cost side, the primary expense of reducing class size from 100 to 20 is that we will now need five teachers instead of just one. We'll also need five smaller classrooms rather than a single big one, and this too may add slightly to the expense of the move. For the sake of discussion, suppose that the cost with a class size of 20 turns out to be €1,000 per student more than the cost per student when the class size is 100. Should administrators switch to the smaller class size? If they apply the cost–benefit principle, they will realize that the reduction in class size makes sense only if the *value of attending the smaller class is at least €1,000 per student greater than the value of attending the larger class.*

Would you (or your family) be willing to pay an extra €1,000 for a smaller economics class? If not, and if other students feel the same way, then sticking with the larger class size makes sense. But if you and others would be willing to pay the extra tuition fees, then reducing the class size to 20 makes good economic sense.

Notice that the 'best' class size, from an economics point of view, will generally not be the same as the 'best' size from the point of view of an educational psychologist. The difference arises because the economics definition of 'best' takes into account both the benefits *and* the costs of different class sizes. The psychologist ignores costs and looks only at the learning benefits of different class sizes.

In practice, of course, different people will feel differently about the value of smaller classes. People with high incomes, for example, tend to be willing to pay more for the advantage, which helps to explain why average class size is smaller, and tuition fees higher, at private schools whose students come predominantly from high-income families.

Scarcity and the trade-offs that result also apply to resources other than money. Bill Gates is one of the richest men on Earth. His wealth was once estimated at over €100 billion – more than the combined wealth of the poorest 40 per cent of Americans. Gates has enough money to buy more houses, cars, holidays and other consumer goods than he could possibly use. Yet Gates, like the rest of us, has only 24 hours each day and a limited amount of energy. So even he confronts trade-offs, in that any activity he pursues – whether it be building his business empire or redecorating his mansion – uses up time and energy that he could otherwise spend on other things. Indeed, someone once calculated that the value of Gates' time is so great that pausing to pick up a €100 note from the road simply wouldn't be worth his while.

Applying the Cost–Benefit Principle

rational person someone with well-defined goals, who tries to fulfil those goals as best she can

In studying choice under scarcity, we shall usually begin with the premise that people are **rational**, which means they have well-defined goals and try to fulfil them as best they can. The Cost–Benefit Principle illustrated in our class-size example is a fundamental tool for the study of how rational people make choices.

As in the class-size example, often the only real difficulty in applying the cost–benefit rule is to come up with reasonable measures of the relevant benefits and costs. Only in rare instances will exact money measures be conveniently available. But the cost–benefit framework can lend structure to your thinking even when no relevant market data are available.

To illustrate how we proceed in such cases, the following example asks you to decide whether to perform an action whose cost is described only in vague, qualitative terms.

Example 1.1 Should you walk to the centre of town to save €10 on a €25 computer game?

Imagine you are about to buy a €25 computer game at the nearby college book shop when a friend tells you that the same game is on sale at a city centre store for only €15. If the store in question is a 30-minute walk away, where should you buy the game?

The Cost–Benefit Principle tells us that you should buy it from the store in the city centre if the benefit of doing so exceeds the cost. The benefit of taking any action is the money value of everything you gain by taking it. Here, the benefit of buying elsewhere is exactly €10, since that is the amount you will save on the purchase price of the game. The cost of taking any action is the money value of everything you give up by taking it. Here, the cost of buying in the city centre is the money value you assign to the time and trouble it takes to make the trip. But how do we estimate that money value?

One way is to perform the following hypothetical auction. Imagine that a stranger has offered to pay you to do an errand that involves the same walk to the centre of town (perhaps to drop off a letter for her at the post office). If she offered you a payment of, say, €1,000, would you accept? If so, we know that your cost of walking to the centre of town and back must be less than €1,000. Now imagine her offer being reduced in small increments until you finally refuse the last offer. For example, if you would agree to walk there and back for €9.00 but not for €8.99, then your cost of making the trip is €9.00. In this case, you should buy the game in the town centre, because the €10 you'll save (your benefit) is greater than your €9.00 cost of making the trip.

But suppose, alternatively, that your cost of making the trip had been greater than €10. In that case, your best bet would have been to buy the game from the nearby college book shop. Confronted with this choice, different people may choose differently, depending on how costly they think it is to make the trip into town. But although there is no uniquely correct choice, most people who are asked what they would do in this situation say they would buy the game from the city-centre store.

Economic surplus

Suppose again that in Example 1.1 your 'cost' of making the trip to the city centre was €9. Compared with the alternative of buying the game at the college store, buying it elsewhere resulted in an **economic surplus** of €1, the difference between the benefit of making the trip and its cost. In general, your goal as an economic decision maker is to choose those actions that generate the largest possible economic surplus. This means taking all actions that yield a positive total economic surplus, which is just another way of restating the Cost–Benefit Principle.

economic surplus the economic urplus from taking any action is the benefit of taking that action minus its cost

Note that the fact that your best choice was to buy the game in the city doesn't imply that you *enjoy* making the trip, any more than choosing a large class means that you prefer large classes to small ones. It simply means that the trip is less unpleasant than the prospect of paying €10 extra for the game. Once again, you've faced a trade-off – in this case, the choice between a cheaper game and the free time gained by avoiding the trip.

Opportunity cost

Of course, your mental 'auction' could have produced a different outcome. Suppose, for example, that the time required for the trip is the only time you have left to study for a difficult test the next day. Or suppose you are watching one of your favourite movies on cable, or that you are tired and would love a short nap. In such cases, we say that the **opportunity cost** of making the trip – that is, the value of what you must sacrifice to walk to the city centre and back – is high, and you are more likely to decide against making the trip.

opportunity cost the opportunity cost of an activity is the value of the next best alternative that must be forgone in order to undertake the activity

Increasing
Opportunity
Cost

In this example, if watching the last hour of the cable TV movie is the most valuable opportunity that conflicts with the trip to the city centre, the opportunity cost of making the trip is the money value you place on pursuing that opportunity – that is, the largest amount you'd be willing to pay to avoid missing the end of the movie. Note that the opportunity cost of making the trip is not the combined value of *all* possible activities you could have pursued, but only the value of your *best* alternative – the one you would have chosen had you not made the trip.

Throughout the text we will pose exercises like Exercise 1.1. You will find that pausing to answer them will help you to master key concepts in economics. Because doing these exercises isn't very costly (indeed, many students report that they are actually fun), the Cost–Benefit Principle indicates that it's well worth your while to do them.

Exercise 1.1   You would again save €10 by buying the game in the city rather than at the college store, but your cost of making the trip is now €12, not €9. How much economic surplus would you get from buying the game in the city? Where should you buy it?

The role of economic models

Economists use the Cost–Benefit Principle as an abstract model of how an idealised rational individual would choose among competing alternatives. (By 'abstract model' we mean a simplified description that captures the essential elements of a situation and allows us to analyse them in a logical way.) A computer model of a complex phenomenon such as climate change, which must ignore many details and include only the major forces at work, is an example of an abstract model.

Non-economists are sometimes harshly critical of the economist's cost–benefit model on the grounds that people in the real world never conduct hypothetical mental 'auctions' before deciding whether to make trips to town. But this criticism betrays a fundamental misunderstanding of how abstract models can help to explain and predict human behaviour. Economists know perfectly well that people don't conduct hypothetical mental 'auctions' when they make simple decisions. All the Cost–Benefit Principle really says is that a rational decision is one that is explicitly or implicitly based on a *weighing of costs and benefits*.

Most of us make sensible decisions most of the time, without being consciously aware that we are weighing costs and benefits, just as most people ride a bike without being consciously aware of what keeps them from falling off. Through trial and error, we gradually learn what kinds of choices tend to work best in different contexts, just as bicycle riders internalise the relevant laws of physics, usually without being conscious of them. Even so, learning the explicit principles of cost–benefit analysis can help us make better decisions, just as knowing a little physics can help in learning how to ride a bicycle or drive a car.

A model is to an economist in many ways what a laboratory experiment is to a physical scientist. If you climbed the Leaning Tower of Pisa to test Newton's theory of gravity by dropping a feather and a kilogram of lead, you might conclude that gravity affects metals to a greater degree than it does organic material. The lead fell faster and hit the ground first. A physicist would demonstrate that this is not the case by creating a vacuum and repeating the experiment. We live in a real world where air pressure and resistance affect how objects fall. We create a simplified world to test the gravity hypothesis by removing the pressure and resistance effects. Would you agree with someone who said that there is little value in talking about the workings of gravity because in the real world we don't live in a vacuum?

RECAP Cost–benefit analysis

Scarcity is a basic fact of economic life. Because of it, having more of one good thing almost always means having less of another (the Scarcity Principle). The Cost–Benefit Principle holds that an individual (or a firm, or a society) should take an action if, and only if, the extra benefit from taking the action is at least as great as the extra cost. The benefit of taking any action minus the cost of taking the action is called the *economic surplus* from that action. Hence the Cost–Benefit Principle suggests that we take only those actions that create additional economic surplus.

Four important decision pitfalls[2]

Rational people will apply the Cost–Benefit Principle most of the time, although probably in an intuitive and approximate way rather than through explicit and precise calculation. Knowing that rational people tend to compare costs and benefits enables economists to predict their likely behaviour. As noted earlier, for example, we can predict that students from wealthy families are more likely than others to attend colleges that offer small classes. (Again, while the cost of small classes is the same for all families, the benefit of small classes, as measured by what people are willing to pay for them, tends to be higher for wealthier families.)

Pitfall 1: measuring costs and benefits as proportions rather than absolute money amounts

As Example 1.2 makes clear, the Cost–Benefit Principle proves helpful in another way. Example 1.2 demonstrates that people are not born with an infallible instinct for weighing the relevant costs and benefits of many daily decisions. Indeed, one of the rewards of studying economics is that it can improve the quality of your decisions.

Example 1.2 Should you walk 3 km to save €10 on a €1,000 laptop?

You are about to buy a €1,000 laptop computer at the nearby college store when a friend tells you that the same computer is on sale at a city centre store for only €990. If the latter is half an hour's walk away, where should you buy the computer?

Assuming that the laptop is light enough to carry without effort, the structure of this example is exactly the same as that of Example 1.1 – the only difference being that the price of the laptop is dramatically higher than the price of the computer game. As before, the benefit of buying in town is the money you'll save, namely €10. And since it's exactly the same trip, its cost must also be the same as before. So if you are perfectly rational, you should make the same decision in both cases. Yet when real people are asked what they would do in these situations, the overwhelming majority say they would walk to town to buy the game but would buy the laptop at the college store. When asked to explain, most of them say something like: 'The trip was worth it for the game because you save 40 per cent, but not worth it for the laptop because you save only €10 out of €1,000, or 1 per cent.'

From a standard economics perspective this is faulty reasoning. The benefit of the trip to town is not the *proportion* you save on the original price. Rather, it is the *absolute money amount* you save. Since the benefit of walking to the city to buy the laptop is €10 – exactly the same as for the computer game – and since the cost of the trip must

---

2 The examples in this section reflect the work of Daniel Kahneman and the late Amos Tversky. Kahneman was awarded the 2003 Nobel Prize in Economics for his efforts to integrate insights from psychology into economics.

also be the same in both cases, the economic surplus from making both trips must be exactly the same. And this means that a rational decision maker would make the same decision in both cases. Yet, as noted, most people choose differently.

Exercise 1.2   Which is more valuable, saving £100 on a £2,000 plane ticket from London to Tokyo or saving £90 on a £200 plane ticket from London to Paris?

The pattern of faulty reasoning in the decision just discussed is one of several decision pitfalls to which people are prone. In the discussion that follows, we will identify three additional decision pitfalls. In some cases, people ignore costs or benefits that they ought to take into account, while on other occasions they are influenced by costs or benefits that are irrelevant.

Pitfall 2: ignoring opportunity costs

Sherlock Holmes, Arthur Conan Doyle's legendary detective, was successful because he saw details that most others overlooked. In *Silver Blaze*, Holmes is called on to investigate the theft of an expensive racehorse from its stable. A Scotland Yard inspector assigned to the case asks Holmes whether some particular aspect of the crime requires further study. 'Yes,' Holmes replies, and describes 'the curious incident of the dog in the night-time'. 'The dog did nothing in the night-time,' responds the puzzled inspector. But as Holmes realised, that was precisely the problem. The watchdog's failure to bark when Silver Blaze was stolen meant that the watchdog knew the thief. This clue ultimately proved the key to unravelling the mystery.

Just as we often don't notice when a dog fails to bark, many of us tend to overlook the implicit value of activities that fail to happen. As discussed earlier, however, intelligent decisions require taking the value of *forgone opportunities* properly into account.

The opportunity cost of an activity, once again, is the value of the next best alternative that must be forgone in order to engage in that activity. If buying a computer game in the town means not watching the last hour of a movie, then the value to you of watching the end of that movie is an opportunity cost of the trip. Many people make bad decisions because they tend to ignore the value of such forgone opportunities. To avoid overlooking opportunity costs, economists often translate questions like 'Should I walk to the pub?' into ones like 'Should I walk to the pub or watch the end of the movie on TV?'

Example 1.3   How should you use your father's frequent-flyer points?

It is May (or November in the southern hemisphere). You are interested in going to the United States for the summer, where you hope to work and make next year's pocket money. You expect to make €600 after all costs in the United States. The round-trip airfare to New York is €800. Your father tells you that he has accumulated sufficient frequent-flyer points to buy you the return ticket. However, you now hear that your sister is to be married in Nairobi in September. Your attendance is non-negotiable. The cost of a package return ticket to Nairobi and accommodation is €700. You could use the points instead to cover the cost of the Nairobi trip. Which should you use the points for? The Cost–Benefit Principle tells us that you should go to New York if the benefits of the trip exceed its costs. If it were not for the complication of the frequent-flyer points, solving this problem would be a straightforward matter of comparing your benefit from the summer in the United States with all the relevant costs. And since your airfare exceeds the net amount you expect to earn you would not go to New York.

But what about the possibility of using your frequent-flyer coupon to make the trip? Using it for that purpose might make the flight to New York seem free, suggesting you would reap an economic surplus of €600 by making the trip. But doing so would also mean you would have to pay €700 for your airfare and accommodation costs for Nairobi. So the opportunity cost of using your coupon to go to New York is really €700. If you use the points to go to New York, the trip still ends up being a loser, because the cost, €700, exceeds the benefit by €100. In cases like these, you are much more likely to decide sensibly if you ask yourself: 'Should I use the frequent-flyer points for this trip or save it for an upcoming trip?'

We cannot emphasise strongly enough that the key to using the concept of opportunity cost correctly lies in recognising precisely what taking a given action *prevents us from doing*. Exercise 1.3 illustrates this point by modifying the details of Example 1.3 slightly.

Exercise 1.3   The same as Example 1.3, except that now your frequent-flyer coupon expires before September, so your only chance to use it will be for the New York trip. Should you use your coupon?

Pitfall 3: failure to ignore sunk costs

The opportunity cost pitfall is one in which people ignore costs they ought to take into account. In another common pitfall, the reverse is true: people are influenced by costs they ought to ignore. The only costs that should influence a decision about whether to take an action are those that we can *avoid by not taking the action*. As a practical matter, however, many decision makers appear to be influenced by sunk costs – costs that are beyond recovery at the moment a decision is made. For example, money spent on a non-transferable, non-refundable airline ticket is a sunk cost.

sunk cost a cost that is beyond recovery at the moment a decision must be made

Because sunk costs must be borne *whether or not an action is taken*, they are irrelevant to the decision of whether to take the action. The sunk cost pitfall (the mistake of being influenced by sunk costs) is illustrated clearly in Example 1.4.

Example 1.4 How much should you eat at an all-you-can-eat restaurant?

The Rajput, an Indian restaurant in Berlin, offers an all-you-can-eat lunch buffet for €15. Customers pay €15 at the door, and no matter how many times they refill their plates, there is no additional charge. One day, as a goodwill gesture, the owner of the restaurant tells 20 randomly selected guests that their lunch is on the house. The remaining guests pay the usual price. If all diners are rational, will there be any difference in the average quantity of food consumed by people in these two groups?

Having eaten their first helping, diners in each group confront the following question: 'Should I go back for another helping?' For rational diners, if the benefit of doing so exceeds the cost, the answer is yes; otherwise it is no. Note that at the moment of decision about a second helping, the €15 charge for the lunch is a sunk cost. Those who paid it have no way to recover it. Thus, for both groups, the (extra) cost of another helping is exactly zero. And since the people who received the free lunch were chosen at random, there is no reason to suppose that their appetites or incomes are different from those of other diners. The benefit of another helping thus should be the same, on average, for people in both groups. And since their respective costs and benefits of an additional helping are the same, the two groups should eat the same number of helpings, on average.

Psychologists and economists have experimental evidence, however, that people in such groups do not eat similar amounts.[3] In particular, those for whom the luncheon charge is not waived tend to eat substantially more than those for whom the charge is waived. People in the former group seem somehow determined to 'get their money's worth'. Their implicit goal is apparently to minimise the average cost per bite of the food they eat. Yet minimising average cost is not a particularly sensible objective. It brings to mind the man who drove his car on the highway at night, even though he had nowhere to go, because he wanted to boost his average fuel economy. The irony is that diners who are determined to get their money's worth usually end up eating too much, as evidenced later by their regrets about having gone back for their last helpings.

The fact that the cost–benefit criterion failed the test of prediction in this example does nothing to invalidate its advice about what people *should* do. If you are letting sunk costs influence your decisions, you can do better by changing your behaviour.

Pitfall 4: failure to understand the average–marginal distinction

Often we are confronted with the choice of whether or not to engage in an activity (for example, whether or not to shop in the city). But, in many situations, the issue is not whether to pursue the activity at all, but rather the *extent* to which it should be pursued. We can apply the Cost–Benefit Principle in such situations by repeatedly asking the question 'Should I increase the level at which I am currently pursuing the activity?'

marginal cost the increase in total cost that results from carrying out one additional unit of an activity

marginal benefit the increase in total benefit that results from carrying out one additional unit of an activity

In attempting to answer this question, the focus should always be on the benefit and cost of an *additional* unit of activity. To emphasise this focus, economists refer to the cost of an additional unit of activity as the **marginal cost** of the activity. Similarly, the benefit of an additional unit of the activity is the **marginal benefit** of the activity.

When the problem is to discover the proper level at which to pursue an activity, the cost–benefit rule is to keep increasing the level as long as the marginal benefit of the activity exceeds its marginal cost. As Example 1.5 illustrates, however, people often fail to apply this rule correctly.

Example 1.5 Should the European Space Agency (ESA) expand the Ariane programme from four launches per year to five?

average cost the total cost of undertaking *n* units of an activity divided by *n*

average benefit the total benefit of undertaking *n* units of an activity divided by *n*

Suppose it has been estimated by the economists working for the ESA that the gains from the programme are currently €12 billion per year (an average of €3 billion per launch) and that its costs are currently €10 billion per year (an average of €2.5 billion per launch). On the basis of these estimates, the ESA sends its chief economist to Brussels to persuade the Commission to provide increased EU funding to expand the launch vehicle programme. Should the Commission agree?

To discover whether expanding the programme makes economic sense, we must compare the marginal cost of a launch with its marginal benefit. The economists' estimates, however, tell us only the **average cost** and **average benefit** of the programme – which are, respectively, the total cost of the programme divided

---

3 See, for example, Thaler (1980).

by the number of launches and the total benefit divided by the number of launches. Knowing the average benefit and average cost per launch for all satellites launched thus far is simply not useful for deciding whether to expand the programme. Of course, the average cost of the launches undertaken so far *might* be the same as the cost of adding another launch. But it might also be either higher or lower than the marginal cost of a launch. The same statement holds true regarding average and marginal benefits.

Suppose, for the sake of discussion, that the benefit of an additional launch is in fact the same as the average benefit per launch thus far, €3 billion. Should the ESA add another launch? Not if the cost of adding the fifth launch would be more than €3 billion. And the fact that the average cost per launch is only €2.5 billion simply does not tell us anything about the marginal cost of the fifth launch.

Suppose, for example, that the relationship between the number of satellites launched and the total cost of the programme is as described in Table 1.1. The average cost per launch (column (3)) when there are four launches would then be €10 billion / 4 = €2.5 billion per launch. But note that, in column (2) of Table 1.1, adding a fifth launch would raise costs from €10 billion to €15 billion, making the marginal cost of the fifth launch €5 billion. So if the benefit of an additional launch is €3 billion, increasing the number of launches from four to five would make absolutely no economic sense.

Number of launches (1)	Total cost (€ billion) (2)	Average cost (€ billion) (3)
0	0	0
1	2.0	2.0
2	4.25	2.125
3	6.75	2.25
4	10.0	2.50
5	15.0	3.0

Table 1.1 **Total Cost and Satellite Launches**

Example 1.6 illustrates how to apply the Cost–Benefit Principle correctly in this case.

Example 1.6 How many space vehicles should the ESA launch?

The ESA must decide how many vehicles to launch. The benefit of each launch is estimated to be €3 billion, and the total cost of the programme again depends on the number of launches, in the manner shown in Table 1.1. How many vehicles should be launched?

The ESA should continue to launch satellites as long as the marginal benefit of the programme exceeds its marginal cost. In Example 1.6, the marginal benefit is constant at €3 billion per launch, regardless of the number of launches. The ESA should thus keep launching as long as the marginal cost per launch is less than or equal to €3 billion (Table 1.2).

Applying the definition of marginal cost to the total cost entries in column (2) of Table 1.1 yields the marginal cost values in column (4) of Table 1.2. (Because marginal cost is the change in total cost that results when we change the number of launches by

Number of launches (1)	Total cost (€ billion) (2)	Average cost (€ billion) (3)	Marginal cost (€ billion) (4)
0	0	0	
			2.0
1	2.0	2.0	
			2.25
2	4.25	2.125	
			2.5
3	6.75	2.25	
			3.25
4	10.0	2.5	
			5.0
5	15.0	3.0	

Table 1.2 **Marginal Cost and Satellite Launches**

one, we place each marginal cost entry midway between the rows showing the corresponding total cost entries.) Thus, for example, the marginal cost of increasing the number of launches from one to two is €2.25 billion, the difference between the €4.25 billion total cost of two launches and the €2 billion total cost of one launch.

As we see from a comparison of the €3 billion marginal benefit per launch with the marginal cost entries in column (4) of Table 1.2, the first three launches satisfy the cost–benefit test, but the fourth and fifth launches do not. The ESA should thus launch three space satellites. The Commission should actually reduce its funding.

Exercise 1.4   If the marginal benefit of each launch had been not €3 billion but €4.5 billion, how many satellites should the ESA have launched?

The cost–benefit framework emphasises that the only relevant costs and benefits in deciding whether to pursue an activity further are *marginal* costs and benefits – measures that correspond to the *increment* of activity under consideration. In many contexts, however, people seem more inclined to compare the *average* cost and benefit of the activity. As Example 1.5 has made clear, increasing the level of an activity may not be justified, even though its average benefit at the current level is significantly greater than its average cost.

Exercise 1.5 further illustrates the importance of the average–marginal distinction.

Exercise 1.5   Liverpool, fresh from their 2005 triumph over AC Milan, and assuming they will make the cut in 2006, decide to beef up team management in preparation and hire a new assistant manager. He notices that one player, Steven Gerrard, scores on average a higher percentage of his penalty shots than any other player on the squad. Based on this information, the assistant suggests to the manager that the star player should take *all* the shots. That way, he reasons, the team will score more points and win more games. On hearing this suggestion, the manager fires his assistant for incompetence. What was wrong with the assistant's idea?

Examples 1.2–1.5 make the point that people *sometimes* choose irrationally. We must stress that our purpose in discussing these examples is not to suggest that people *generally* make irrational choices. On the contrary, most people appear to choose sensibly most of the time, especially when their decisions are important or familiar ones. The economist's focus on rational choice thus offers not only useful advice about making better decisions, but also a basis for predicting and explaining human behaviour.

We used the cost–benefit approach in this way when discussing how rising faculty salaries have led to larger class sizes. And, as we shall see, similar reasoning helps to explain human behaviour in virtually every other domain.

RECAP Four important decision pitfalls

1 **The pitfall of measuring costs or benefits proportionally** Many decision makers treat a change in cost or benefit as insignificant if it constitutes only a small proportion of the original amount. *Absolute money amounts*, not proportions, should be employed to measure costs and benefits.

2 **The pitfall of ignoring opportunity costs** When performing a cost–benefit analysis of an action, it is important to account for all relevant *opportunity costs*, defined as the values of the most highly valued alternatives that must be forgone in order to carry out the action. A resource (such as a frequent-flyer coupon) may have a high opportunity cost, even if you originally got it 'for free', if its best alternative use has high value. The identical resource may have a low opportunity cost, however, if it has no good alternative uses.

3 **The pitfall of not ignoring sunk costs** When deciding whether to perform an action, it is important to ignore *sunk costs* – those costs that cannot be avoided even if the action is not taken. Even though a ticket to a concert may have cost you €100, if you have already bought it and cannot sell it to anyone else, the €100 is a sunk cost and should not influence your decision about whether to go to the concert.

4 **The pitfall of using average instead of marginal costs and benefits** Decision makers often have ready information about the total cost and benefit of an activity, and from this it is simple to compute the activity's average cost and benefit. A common mistake is to conclude that an activity should be increased if its average benefit exceeds its average cost. The Cost–Benefit Principle tells us that the level of an activity should be increased if, and only if, its *marginal* benefit exceeds its *marginal* cost.

Some costs and benefits, especially marginal costs and benefits and opportunity costs, are important for decision making, while others, such as sunk costs and average costs and benefits, are essentially irrelevant. This conclusion is implicit in our original statement of the Cost–Benefit Principle (an action should be taken if, and only if, the extra benefits of taking it exceed the extra costs). Yet so important are the pitfalls of using proportions instead of absolute money amounts, of ignoring opportunity costs, of taking sunk costs into account, and of confusing average and marginal costs and benefits that we enumerate these pitfalls separately as one of the core ideas for repeated emphasis.

The *Not-All-Costs-and-Benefits-Matter-Equally Principle* is that some costs and benefits (for example, opportunity costs and marginal costs and benefits) matter in making decisions, whereas others (for example, sunk costs and average costs and benefits) don't.

microeconomics the study of individual choice under scarcity, and its implications for the behaviour of prices and quantities in individual markets

macroeconomics the study of the performance of national economies and the policies that governments use to try to improve that performance

Economics: micro and macro

By convention, we use the term **microeconomics** to describe the study of individual choices and of group behaviour in individual markets. **Macroeconomics**, by contrast, is the study of the performance of national economies and of the policies that governments use to try to improve that performance. Macroeconomics tries to understand the determinants of such things as the national unemployment rate, the overall price level and the total value of national output.

Our focus in this chapter is on issues that face the individual decision maker, whether that individual confronts a personal decision, a family decision, a business decision, a government policy decision, or indeed any other type of decision. Further on, we shall consider economic models of groups of individuals, such as all buyers or all sellers in a specific market. Later still, we shall turn to broader economic issues and measures.

No matter which of these levels is our focus, however, our thinking will be shaped by the fact that although economic needs and wants are effectively unlimited, the material and human resources that can be used to satisfy them are finite. Clear thinking about economic problems must therefore always take into account the idea of *trade-offs* – the idea that having more of one good thing usually means having less of another. Our economy and our society are shaped to a substantial degree by the choices people have made when faced with such trade-offs.

The approach of this text

Choosing the number of students to register in each class is just one of many important decisions in planning an introductory economics course. Another decision, to which the scarcity principle applies just as strongly, concerns which of many different topics to include on the course syllabus. There is a virtually inexhaustible set of topics and issues that might be covered in an introductory course, but only limited time in which to cover them. There is no free lunch: covering some topics inevitably means omitting others.

All textbook authors are necessarily forced to pick and choose. A textbook that covered all the issues ever written about in economics would take up more than a whole floor of your university library. It is our firm view that most introductory textbooks try to cover far too much. A relatively short list of the discipline's core ideas can explain a great deal of the behaviour and events we see in the world around us. So rather than cover a large number of ideas at a superficial level, our strategy is to focus on this short list of core ideas, returning to each entry again and again, in many different contexts. This strategy will enable you to internalise these ideas remarkably well in the brief span of a single course. And the benefit of learning a small number of important ideas well will far outweigh the cost of having to ignore a host of other, less important ideas.[4]

So far, we've already encountered three core ideas: the Scarcity Principle, the Cost–Benefit Principle and the principle that not all costs and benefits matter equally. As these core ideas re-emerge in the course of our discussions, we shall call your attention to them. And shortly after a *new* core idea appears, we shall highlight it by formally restating it.

A second important element in the philosophy of this text is our belief in the importance of active learning. In the same way that you can learn Spanish only by speaking and writing it, or tennis only by playing the game, you can learn economics only by *doing* economics. And because we want you to learn how to do economics, rather than just to read or listen passively as the authors or your instructor does economics, we shall make every effort to encourage you to stay actively involved.

---

4 The famous Australian economist, W. Max Corden, a charming and brilliant teacher as well as a prolific and innovative researcher, was fond of saying to graduate students at a seminar series at Nuffield College, Oxford, that if you couldn't explain something by using the basic tools and concepts of supply and demand it probably wasn't worth explaining in the first place.

For example, instead of just telling you about an idea, we shall usually first motivate the idea by showing you how it works in the context of a specific example. Often, these examples will be followed by exercises for you to try, as well as applications that show the relevance of the idea to real life. Try working the exercises *before* looking at the answers.

Think critically about the applications: Do you see how they illustrate the point being made? Do they give you new insight into the issue? Work the problems at the end of the chapters, and take extra care with those relating to points that you do not fully understand. Apply economic principles to the world around you. (We shall say more about this when we discuss economic naturalism below.) Finally, when you come across an idea or example that you find interesting, tell a friend about it. You'll be surprised to discover how much the mere act of explaining it helps you understand and remember the underlying principle. The more actively you can become engaged in the learning process, the more effective your learning will be.

Economic naturalism

With the rudiments of the cost–benefit framework under your belt, you are now in a position to become an 'economic naturalist', someone who uses insights from economics to help make sense of observations from everyday life. People who have studied biology are able to observe and marvel at many details of nature that would otherwise have escaped their notice. For example, during a walk in the woods in early April the novice may see only trees whereas the biology student notices many different species of trees and understands why some are already in leaf while others still lie dormant. Likewise, the novice may notice that in some animal species males are much larger than females, but the biology student knows that such a pattern occurs only in species in which males take several mates. Natural selection favours larger males in those species because their greater size helps them prevail in the often bloody contests among males for access to females. By contrast, males tend to be roughly the same size as females in monogamous species, in which there is much less fighting for mates.

In similar fashion, learning a few simple economic principles enables us to see the mundane details of ordinary human existence in a new light. Whereas the uninitiated often fail even to notice these details, the economic naturalist not only sees them, but becomes actively engaged in the attempt to understand them. Let us consider a few examples of questions that economic naturalists might pose for themselves.

Economic naturalist 1.1 illustrates a case in which the *benefit* of a product depends on the number of other people who own that product. As the next example demonstrates, the *cost* of a product may also depend on the number of others who own it.

Economic naturalist 1.1 Why do many hardware manufacturers include more than €1,000 worth of 'free' software with a computer selling for only slightly more than that?

The software industry is different from many others in the sense that its customers care a great deal about product compatibility. When you and your classmates are working on a project together, for example, your task will be much simpler if you all use the same word-processing program. Likewise, an executive's life will be easier at tax return time if her financial software is the same as her accountant's.

The implication is that the benefit of owning and using any given software program increases with the number of other people who use that same product. This unusual relationship gives the producers of the most popular programs an enormous advantage and often makes it hard for new programs to break into the market.

Recognising this pattern, the Intuit Corporation offered computer makers free copies of *Quicken*, its personal financial management software. Computer makers, for their part, were only too happy to include the program, since it made their new computers more attractive to buyers. *Quicken* soon became the standard for personal financial management programs. By giving away free copies of the program, Intuit 'primed the pump', creating an enormous demand for upgrades of *Quicken* and for more advanced versions of related software. Thus *TurboTax* and *Macintax*, Intuit's personal income tax software, have become the standards for tax-preparation programs.

Inspired by this success story, other software developers have jumped on to the bandwagon. Most hardware now comes bundled with a host of free software programs. Some software developers are even rumoured to *pay* computer makers to include their programs!

Economic naturalist 1.2 Why don't car manufacturers make cars without heaters?

Virtually every new car sold in Europe today has a heater. But not every car has a CD player yet, although this is changing. The car's heating system costs more than the cost of a CD player. Why the difference?

One might be tempted to answer that although everyone *needs* a heater, people can get along without CD players. Yet heaters are of little use in hot climates, and car rental companies that keep their cars for six months or less, and buy a lot of cars, could well rent cars without heaters (they rent cars without air conditioning!). What is more, cars produced as recently as in the 1960s did *not* all have heaters.

Although heaters cost extra money to manufacture and may not be of much use to all purchasers, they do not cost *much* money and are useful on at least a few days each year in most parts of the continent. As time passed and people's incomes grew, manufacturers found that people were ordering fewer and fewer cars without heaters. At some point it actually became cheaper to put heaters in all cars, rather than bear the administrative expense of making some cars with heaters and others without. No doubt a few buyers would still order a car without a heater if they could save some money in the process. But catering for these customers is just no longer worth it.

Similar reasoning explains why certain cars today cannot be purchased without a CD player. Buyers of the 2003 BMW 745i, for example, got a CD player whether they wanted one or not. Most buyers of this car, which sells for anything up to approximately €100,000, depending on the country in Europe, have high incomes, so the overwhelming majority of them would have chosen to order a CD player had it been sold as an option. Because of the savings made possible when *all* cars are produced with the same equipment, it would have actually cost BMW more to supply cars for the few who would want them without CD players.

Buyers of the least expensive makes of car have much lower incomes on average than BMW 745i buyers. Accordingly, most of them have more pressing alternative uses for their money than to buy CD players for their cars, and this explains why some inexpensive makes continue to offer CD players only as options.

The insights afforded by Economic naturalist 1.2 suggest an answer to the following strange question.

Economic naturalist 1.3 Why do the keypad buttons on drive-in automatic teller machines (ATMs) have Braille dots?

Drive-in ATMs are uncommon in Europe, but are frequently found in North America. Curiously, the keypads have Braille dots. Braille dots are also found in America and Europe on, for example, the buttons in lifts (elevators) and similar places. Their usefulness in drive-in ATM points where the driver uses the ATM from the car is a little unclear. Braille keypads enable blind people to participate more fully in the normal flow of daily activity. But even though blind people can do many remarkable things, they cannot drive automobiles on public roads. Why, then, do the manufacturers of automatic teller machines install Braille dots on the machines at drive-in locations?

The answer to this riddle is that once the keypad moulds have been manufactured, the cost of producing buttons with Braille dots is no higher than the cost of producing smooth buttons. Making both would require separate sets of moulds and two different types of inventory. If the patrons of drive-in machines found buttons with Braille dots harder to use, there might be a reason to incur these extra costs. But since the dots pose no difficulty for sighted users, the best and cheapest solution is to produce only keypads with dots.

Economic naturalist 1.3 was suggested by Cornell student Bill Tjoa, in response to the following assignment.

Exercise 1.6 In 500 words or fewer, use cost–benefit analysis to explain some pattern of events behaviour you have observed in your own environment.

There is probably no more useful step you can take in your study of economics than to perform several versions of the assignment in Exercise 1.6. Students who do so almost invariably become lifelong economic naturalists. Their mastery of economic concepts not only does not decay with the passage of time; it actually grows stronger. We urge you, in the strongest possible terms, to make this investment!

A cautionary note: economists and economics

We have argued that economics has a legitimate claim to be considered as a science. Any scientist will have personal views as to how the world might be improved, and these will usually reflect the body of knowledge that constitutes the science concerned as well as the scientist's own ethical views. To take global warming as an example, a climatologist can use the results of the empirical and theoretical investigation of climate change to predict the consequences of different levels of greenhouse gases on average temperatures over the next century. In so doing the climatologist is engaging in *positive* scientific analysis. The next question that will be asked of the climatologist will be: what can be done about this? The answer should be something like the following: if you wish to reduce climate change by such and such an amount you will have to reduce emissions by so much per annum. Notice that the response avoids the question of what *ought* to be done. As a scientist, our climate change scientist is still engaging in positive science: his answer (assuming the truth is being told) does not reflect his values, but reflects only the conclusions of his science. A key test of this is whether in principle his answer can be falsified. Can it be demonstrated objectively that he is wrong? Can evidence that supports his response be found?

Suppose, however, the climatologist had answered: we must ban all use of private cars. While it may be true that banning car use would reduce emissions, the climatologist is choosing (implicitly) a level of emissions reductions and a mechanism to achieve it. These reflect the chooser's priorities and willingness to impose costs on others and the value placed on reductions in climate change. The climatologist is, of course, entitled to his views on these matters, but is no longer speaking simply as a scientist. His response is not a positive one, but a *normative* one. The response reflects the respondent's value judgements as well as the conclusions of the underlying science. As such it cannot be falsified. The Latin tag, *de gustibus non est disputandum*, applies. This means that conclusions based on tastes or values cannot to that extent be subjected to scientific verification of falsification.

Economists are often called on to advise on economic policy. They are also frequently asked to comment in the media on economic events and developments. In so far as their involvement is as described initially in the case of the climatologist (using economics to demonstrate cause and effect, and options that are open, and consequences of proposed actions) economists are engaging in positive economics. Once they stray beyond this, they are making normative statements, and these statements are normative economics statements. The critical test is whether there is an express or implied 'ought' in the statement. If there is, the statement may be economics in the sense of a conclusion as to economic policy, but it is normative economics, not positive economics.

In practice, it may be difficult for a non-economist to see when an economist is speaking positively or normatively (and this applies to climatologists, too), so that the listener may believe that what is said is in some sense objectively true while in reality it reflects the values of the speaker as much as the science involved. Scientists, including economists, frequently use (abuse?) their scientific knowledge to advance their ethical views on the basis that their statements reflect the conclusions of science: 'I am Sir Oracle and when I ope my lips let no dog bark' (Shakespeare: *Merchant of Venice*, I (i)). Apply the ought test!

Accordingly, we should distinguish between economics statements and propositions that are 'value-free' and those that are based on a value system. The former constitute 'positive' economics and can be accepted or rejected without reference to the value system of the speaker or the listener. The latter constitute 'normative' economics. The trick is to distinguish between them.

Summary

■ Economics is the study of how people make choices under conditions of scarcity and of the results of those choices for society. Economic analysis of human behaviour begins with the assumption that people are *rational* – that they have well-defined goals and try to achieve them as best they can. In trying to achieve their goals, people normally face trade-offs: because material and human resources are limited, having more of one good thing means making do with less of some other good thing.

■ Our focus in this chapter has been on how rational people make choices among alternative courses of action. Our basic tool for analysing these decisions is *cost–benefit analysis*. The Cost–Benefit Principle says that a person should take an action if, and only if, the benefit of that action is at least as great as its cost. The benefit of an action is defined as the largest money amount the person would be willing to pay in order to take the action. The cost of an action is defined as the money value of everything the person must give up in order to take the action.

■ Often the question is not whether to pursue an activity but rather how many units of it to pursue. In these cases, the rational person pursues additional units as long as the marginal benefit of the activity (the benefit from pursuing an additional unit of it) exceeds its marginal cost (the cost of pursuing an additional unit of it).

■ In using the cost–benefit framework, we need not presume that people *choose rationally* all the time. Indeed, we identified four common pitfalls that plague decision makers in all walks of life: a tendency to treat small proportional changes as insignificant, a tendency to ignore opportunity costs, a tendency not to ignore sunk costs, and a tendency to confuse average and marginal costs and benefits.

■ *Microeconomics* is the study of individual choices and of group behaviour in individual markets, while *macroeconomics* is the study of the performance of national economies and of the policies that governments use to try to improve economic performance.

■ *Statements may be positive or normative*: positive economics consists in the conclusions of economics that are independent of the ethical value system of the economist. Normative economics consists in statements in economics that reflect or are based on the ethical value system of the economist, implicitly, explicitly or by omission.

Review questions

1. A friend of yours on the tennis team says: 'Private tennis lessons are definitely better than group lessons.' Explain what you think he means by this statement. Then use the Cost–Benefit Principle to explain why private lessons are not necessarily the best choice for everyone.

2. True or false: Your willingness to drive to town to save €30 on a new appliance should depend on what fraction of the total selling price €30 is. Explain.

3. Why might someone who is trying to decide whether to see a movie be more likely to focus on the €9 ticket price than on the €20 she would fail to earn by not babysitting?

4. Many people think of their air travel as being free when they use frequent-flyer coupons. Explain why these people are likely to make wasteful travel decisions.

5. Is the non-refundable tuition payment you made to your university this year a sunk cost? How would your answer differ if your university were to offer a full tuition refund to any student who dropped out of school during the first two months of the semester?

connect **Problems**

Problems marked with an asterisk (*) are more difficult.

1. The most you would be willing to pay for having a freshly washed car before going out on a date is €6. The smallest amount for which you would be willing to wash someone else's car is €3.50. You are going out this evening, and your car is dirty. How much economic surplus would you receive from washing it?

2. To earn extra money in the summer, you grow tomatoes and sell them at the farmers' market for 30 cents per kg. By adding compost to your garden, you can increase your yield as shown in the table below. If compost costs 50 cents per kg and your goal is to make as much money as possible, how many kilograms of compost should you add?

Kg of compost	Kg of tomatoes
0	100
1	120
2	125
3	128
4	130
5	131
6	131.5

3. Residents of your city are charged a fixed weekly fee of €6 for garbage collection. They are allowed to put out as many bins as they wish. The average household disposes of three bins of garbage per week under this plan. Now suppose that your city changes to a 'tag' system. Each bin to be collected must have a tag affixed to it. The tags cost €2 each and are not reusable. What effect do you think the introduction of the tag system will have on the total quantity of garbage collected in your city? Explain briefly.

4. Once a week, Smith purchases a six-pack of cola and puts it in his refrigerator for his two children. He invariably discovers that all six cans are gone on the first day. Jones also purchases a six-pack of cola once a week for his two children but, unlike Smith, he tells them that each may drink no more than three cans. If the children use cost–benefit analysis each time they decide whether to drink a can of cola, explain why the cola lasts much longer at Jones' house than at Smith's.

5. Tom is a mushroom farmer. He invests all his spare cash in additional mushrooms, which grow on otherwise useless land behind his barn. The mushrooms double in weight during their first year, after which time they are harvested and sold at a constant price per kilogram. Tom's friend Dick asks Tom for a loan of €200, which he promises to repay after one year. How much interest will Dick have to pay Tom in order for Tom to recover his opportunity cost of making the loan? Explain briefly.

6. Suppose that in the last few seconds you devoted to Question 1 in your physics exam you earned 4 extra points, while in the last few seconds you devoted to Question 2 you earned 10 extra points. You earned a total of 48 and 12 points, respectively, on the two questions, and the total time you spent on each was the same. If you could take the exam again, how – if at all – should you reallocate your time between these questions?

7. Martha and Sarah have the same preferences and incomes. Just as Martha arrived at the theatre to see a play, she discovered that she had lost the €10 ticket she had purchased earlier. Sarah had also just arrived at the theatre planning to buy a ticket to see the same play when she discovered that she had lost a €10 note from her purse. If both Martha and Sarah are rational and both still have enough money to pay for a ticket, is one of them more likely than the other to go ahead and see the play anyway?

8.* You and your friend Joe have identical tastes. At 2 pm, you go to the local Ticketmaster outlet and buy a €30 ticket to a football match to be played that night 50 km away. Joe plans to attend the same game, but because he cannot get to the Ticketmaster outlet, he plans to buy his ticket at the game. Tickets sold at the game cost only €25, because they carry no Ticketmaster surcharge. (Many people nonetheless pay the higher price at Ticketmaster, to be sure of getting good seats.) At 4 pm, an unexpected snowstorm begins, making the prospect of the 50 km drive much less attractive than before (but assuring the availability of good seats). If both you and Joe are rational, is one of you more likely to attend the game than the other?

9.* For each long-distance call anywhere in the continental United States, a new phone service will charge users 30 cents per minute for the first 2 minutes and 2 cents per minute for additional minutes in each call. Tom's current phone service charges 10 cents per minute for all calls, and his calls are never shorter than 7 minutes. If Tom's dorm switches to the new phone service, what will happen to the average length of his calls?

10.* The meal plan at university A lets students eat as much as they like for a fixed fee of €500 per semester. The average student there eats 250 kg of food per semester. University B charges €500 for a book of meal tickets that entitles the student to eat 250 kg of food per semester. If the student eats more than 250 kg, he or she pays €2 for each additional kilogram; if the student eats less, he or she gets a €2 per kg refund. If students are rational, at which university will average food consumption be higher? Explain briefly.

Appendix A
Working with equations, graphs and tables

Although many of the examples and most of the end-of-chapter problems in this book are quantitative, none requires mathematical skills beyond rudimentary high-school algebra and geometry. In this brief appendix we shall review some of the skills you will need for dealing with these examples and problems.

One important skill is to be able to read simple verbal descriptions and translate the information they provide into the relevant equations or graphs. You will also need to be able to translate information given in tabular form into an equation or graph, and sometimes you will need to translate graphical information into a table or equation. The following examples illustrate all the tools you will need.

Using a verbal description to construct an equation

We begin with an example that shows how to construct a long-distance telephone billing equation from a verbal description of the billing plan.

Example 1A.1 Your long-distance telephone plan charges you €5 per month plus 10 cents per minute for long-distance calls. Write an equation that describes your monthly telephone bill.

An **equation** is a simple mathematical expression that describes the relationship between two or more **variables**, or quantities that are free to assume different values in some range. The most common type of equation we shall work with contains two types of variable: **dependent variable** and **independent variable**. In this example, the dependent variable is the money amount of your monthly telephone bill, and the independent variable is the variable on which your bill depends – namely, the volume of long-distance calls you make during the month. Your bill also depends on the €5 monthly fee and the 10 cents per minute charge. But, in this example, those amounts are **constants**, not variables. A constant, also called a **parameter**, is a quantity in an equation that is fixed in value, not free to vary. As the terms suggest, the dependent variable describes an outcome that depends on the value taken by the independent variable.

Once you have identified the dependent variable and the independent variable, choose simple symbols to represent them. In algebra courses, X is typically used to represent the independent variable and Y the dependent variable. Many people find it easier to remember what the variables stand for, however, if they choose symbols that are linked in some straightforward way to the quantities that the variables represent. Thus, in this example, we might use B to represent your monthly *bill* in money terms and T to represent the total *time* in minutes you spent during the month on long-distance calls.

equation a mathematical expression that describes the relationship between two or more variables

variable a quantity that is free to take a range of different values

dependent variable a variable in an equation whose value is determined by the value taken by another variable in the equation

independent variable a variable in an equation whose value determines the value taken by another variable in the equation

constant (or parameter) a quantity that is fixed in value

Having identified the relevant variables and chosen symbols to represent them, you are now in a position to write the equation that links them:

$$B = 5 + 0.10T \tag{1A.1}$$

where B is your monthly long-distance bill in money terms and T is your monthly total long-distance calling time in minutes. The fixed monthly fee (5) and the charge per minute (0.10) are parameters in this equation. Note the importance of being clear about the units of measure. Because B represents the monthly bill, we must also express the fixed monthly fee and the per-minute monetary charge, which is why the latter number appears in Eq. (1A.1) as 0.10 rather than 10. Equation (1A.1) follows the normal convention in which the dependent variable appears by itself on the left-hand side while the independent variable or variables and constants appear on the right-hand side.

Once we have the equation for the monthly bill, we can use it to calculate how much you will owe as a function of your monthly volume of long-distance calls. For example, if you make 32 minutes of calls, you can calculate your monthly bill by simply substituting 32 minutes for T in Eq. (1A.1):

$$B = 5 + 0.10(32) = 8.20 \qquad (1A.2)$$

Your monthly bill when you make 32 minutes of calls is thus equal to €8.20.

Exercise 1A.1 Under the monthly billing plan described in Example 1A.1, how much would you owe for a month during which you made 45 minutes of long-distance calls?

Graphing the equation of a straight line

Example 1A.2 shows how to portray the billing plan described in Example 1A.1 as a graph.

Example 1A.2 Construct a graph that portrays the monthly long-distance telephone billing plan described in Example 1A.1, putting your telephone charges, in money per month, on the vertical axis, and your total volume of calls, in minutes per month, on the horizontal axis.

The first step in responding to this instruction is the one we just took, namely to translate the verbal description of the billing plan into an equation. When graphing an equation, the normal convention is to use the vertical axis to represent the dependent variable and the horizontal axis to represent the independent variable. In Fig. 1A.1, we therefore put B on the vertical axis and T on the horizontal axis. One way to construct the graph shown in Fig. 1A.1 is to begin by plotting the monthly bill values that correspond to several different total amounts of long-distance calls. For example, someone who makes 10 minutes of calls during the month would have a bill of $B = 5 + 0.10(10) = $ €6. Thus, in Fig. 1A.1 the value of 10 minutes per month on the horizontal axis corresponds to a bill of €6 per month on the vertical axis (point A). Someone who makes 30 minutes of long-distance calls during the month will have a monthly bill of $B = 5 + 0.10(30) = $ €8, so the value of 30 minutes per month on the horizontal axis corresponds to €8 per month on the vertical axis (point C). Similarly, someone who makes 70 minutes of long-distance calls during the month will have a monthly bill of $B = 5 + 0.10(70) = $ €12, so the value of 70 minutes on the horizontal axis corresponds to €12 on the vertical axis (point D). The line joining these points is the graph of the monthly billing in Eq. (1A.1).

vertical intercept in a straight line, the value taken by the dependent variable when the independent variable equals zero

As shown in Fig. 1A.1, the graph of the equation $B = 5 + 0.10T$ is a straight line. The parameter 5 is the **vertical intercept** of the

slope in a straight line, the ratio of the vertical distance the straight line travels between any two points (**rise**) to the corresponding horizontal distance (**run**)

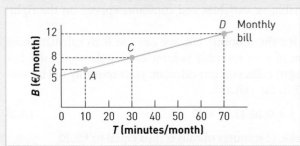

Figure 1A.1 The Monthly Telephone Bill in Example 1A.1. The graph of the equation $B = 5 + 0.10T$ is the straight line shown. Its vertical intercept is 5, and its slope is 0.10.

line – the value of B when $T = 0$, or the point at which the line intersects the vertical axis. The parameter 0.10 is the **slope** of the line, which is the ratio of the **rise** of the line to the corresponding **run**. The ratio rise/run is simply the vertical distance between any two points on the line divided by the horizontal distance between those points. For example, if we choose points A and C in Fig. 1A.1, the rise is $8 - 6 = 2$ and the corresponding run is $30 - 10 = 20$, so rise/run $= 2/20 = 0.10$. More generally, for the graph of any equation $Y = a + bX$, the parameter a is the vertical intercept and the parameter b is the slope.

Deriving the equation of a straight line from its graph

Example 1A.3 shows how to derive the equation for a straight line from a graph of the line.

Example 1A.3 Figure 1A.2 shows the graph of the monthly billing plan for a new long-distance plan. What is the equation for this graph? How much is the fixed monthly fee under this plan? How much is the charge per minute?

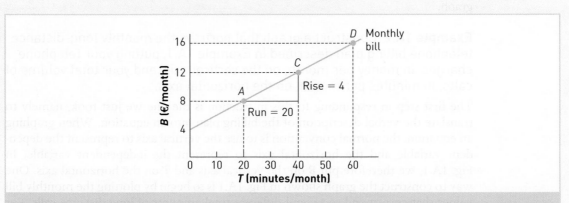

Figure 1A.2 Another Monthly Long-Distance Plan. The vertical distance between points A and C is $12 - 8 = 4$ units, and the horizontal distance between points A and C is $40 - 20 = 20$, so the slope of the line is $4/20 = 1/5 = 0.20$. The vertical intercept (the value of B when $T = 0$) is 4. So the equation for the billing plan shown is $B = 4 + 0.20T$.

The slope of the line shown in Fig. 1A.2 is the rise between any two points divided by the corresponding run. For points A and C, rise $= 12 - 8 = 4$, and run $= 40 - 20 = 20$, so the slope equals rise/run $= 4/20 = 1/5 = 0.20$. And since the horizontal intercept of the line is 4, its equation must be given by

$$B = 4 + 0.20T \tag{1A.3}$$

Under this plan, the fixed monthly fee is the value of the bill when $T = 0$, which is €4. The charge per minute is the slope of the billing line, 0.20, or 20 cents per minute.

Exercise 1A.2 Write the equation for the billing plan shown in the graph below. How much is its fixed monthly fee? Its charge per minute?

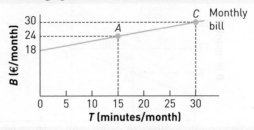

Changes in the vertical intercept and slope

Examples 1A.4 and 1A.5 and Exercises 1A.3 and 1A.4 provide practice in seeing how a line shifts with a change in its vertical intercept or slope.

Example 1A.4 Show how the billing plan whose graph is in Fig. 1A.2 would change if the monthly fixed fee were increased from €4 to €8.

An increase in the monthly fixed fee from €4 to €8 would increase the vertical intercept of the billing plan by €4 but would leave its slope unchanged. An increase in the fixed fee thus leads to a parallel upward shift in the billing plan by €4, as shown in Fig. 1A.3. For any given number of minutes of long-distance calls, the monthly charge on the new bill will be €4 higher than on the old bill. Thus 20 minutes of calls per month costs €8 under the original plan (point A) but €12 under the new plan (point A′). And 40 minutes costs €12 under the original plan (point C), €16 under the new plan (point C′); and 60 minutes costs €16 under the original plan (point D), €20 under the new plan (point D′).

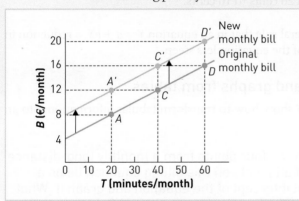

Figure 1A.3 The Effect of an Increase in the Vertical Intercept. An increase in the vertical intercept of a straight line produces an upward parallel shift in the line.

Exercise 1A.3 Show how the billing plan whose graph is in Fig. 1A.2 would change if the monthly fixed fee were reduced from €4 to €2.

Example 1A.5 Show how the billing plan whose graph is in Fig. 1A.2 would change if the charge per minute were increased from 20 cents to 40 cents.

Because the monthly fixed fee is unchanged, the vertical intercept of the new billing plan continues to be 4. But the slope of the new plan, shown in Fig. 1A.4, is 0.40, or twice the slope of the original plan. More generally, in the equation $Y = a + bX$, an increase in b makes the slope of the graph of the equation steeper.

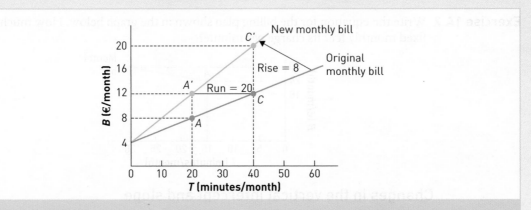

Figure 1A.4 The Effect of an Increase in the Charge per Minute. Because the fixed monthly fee continues to be €4, the vertical intercept of the new plan is the same as that of the original plan. With the new charge per minute of 40 cents, the slope of the billing plan rises from 0.20 to 0.40.

Exercise 1A.4 Show how the billing plan whose graph is in Fig. 1A.2 would change if the charge per minute were reduced from 20 cents to 10 cents.

Exercise 1A.4 illustrates the general rule that in an equation $Y = a + bX$, a reduction in b makes the slope of the graph of the equation less steep.

Constructing equations and graphs from tables

Example 1A.6 and Exercise 1A.5 show how to transform tabular information into an equation or graph.

Example 1A.6 Table 1A.1 shows four points from a monthly long-distance telephone billing equation. If all points on this billing equation lie on a straight line, find the vertical intercept of the equation and graph it. What is the monthly fixed fee? What is the charge per minute? Calculate the total bill for a month with 1 hour of long-distance calls.

Long-distance bill (€/month)	Total long-distance calls (minutes/month)
10.50	10
11.00	20
11.50	30
12.00	40

Table 1A.1 **Points on a Long-Distance Billing Plan**

One approach to this problem is simply to plot any two points from Table 1A.1 on a graph. Since we are told that the billing equation is a straight line, that line must be the one that passes through any two of its points. Thus, in Fig. 1A.5 we use *A* to denote the point from Table 1A.1 for which a monthly bill of €11 corresponds to 20 minutes per month of calls (row 2) and *C* to denote the point for which a monthly bill of €12 corresponds to 40 minutes per month of calls (row 4). The straight line passing through these points is the graph of the billing equation.

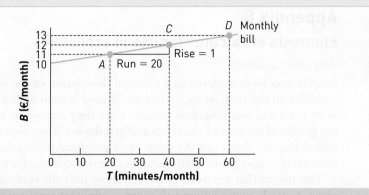

Figure 1A.5 Plotting the Monthly Billing Equation from a Sample of Points. Point *A* is taken from row 2, Table 1A.1, and point *C* from row 4. The monthly billing plan is the straight line that passes through these points.

Unless you have a steady hand, however, or use extremely large graph paper, the method of extending a line between two points on the billing plan is unlikely to be very accurate. An alternative approach is to calculate the equation for the billing plan directly. Since the equation is a straight line, we know that it takes the general form $B = f + sT$, where f is the fixed monthly fee and s is the slope. Our goal is to calculate the vertical intercept f and the slope s. From the same two points we plotted earlier, A and C, we can calculate the slope of the billing plan as $s = \text{rise}/\text{run} = 1/20 = 0.05$.

So all that remains is to calculate f, the fixed monthly fee. At point C on the billing plan, the total monthly bill is €12 for 40 minutes, so we can substitute $B = 12$, $s = 0.05$ and $T = 40$ into the general equation $B = f + sT$ to obtain

$$12 = f + 0.05(40) \tag{1A.4}$$

or

$$12 = f + 2 \tag{1A.5}$$

which solves for $f = 10$. So the monthly billing equation must be

$$B = 10 + 0.05T \tag{1A.6}$$

For this billing equation, the fixed fee is €10 per month, the calling charge is 5 cents per minute (€0.05/minute), and the total bill for a month with 1 hour of long-distance calls is $B = 10 + 0.05(60) = €13$, just as shown in Fig. 1A.5.

Exercise 1A.5 The table below shows four points from a monthly long-distance telephone billing plan.

Long-distance bill (€/month)	Total long-distance calls (minutes/month)
20.00	10
30.00	20
40.00	30
50.00	40

If all points on this billing plan lie on a straight line, find the vertical intercept of the corresponding equation without graphing it. What is the monthly fixed fee? What is the charge per minute? How much would the charges be for 1 hour of long-distance calls per month?

Appendix B
Elements of calculus for use in economics
Why use calculus?

Graphs may be considered as a pictorial description of the relationship between the variables on the axes. As such, they are limited in their ability to treat the relationship in an exact and unambiguous fashion, since they depend on the accuracy with which the graphical account of the relationship is drawn. They also suffer from the unavoidable restriction that even the most exact graphical description is in reality limited to portraying properly the relationship between two variables in a tractable fashion.

This means that a normal graph can show only the relationship between two variables, X and Y, while holding all other factors that might affect the relationship constant. Take, for example, the well-established relationships between temperature, price and consumption of ice cream. Any competent marketing study would easily show that in any location the quantity of ice cream sold on a given day will be inversely related to the unit price at which it is sold. Or, as an economist would put it, the demand curve for ice cream has a negative slope (Fig. 1B.1). Here, following the convention in economics, and in defiance of the mathematical tradition, the consumption of ice cream, the dependent or endogenous variable, is shown on the horizontal axis, while the unit price, the independent, causative or exogenous variable, is shown on the vertical axis.

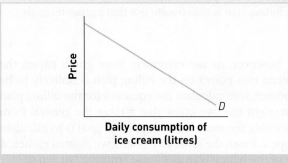

Figure 1B.1 The Demand Curve for Ice Cream. The effect of unit price on consumption.

The marketing analyst would also produce data indicating that, at any given unit price, the quantity sold would rise with the ambient temperature. Less is sold in winter than in summer, when it is raining than when the sun is splitting the pavement. That relationship is shown by using temperature (in degrees) on the vertical axis and consumption on the horizontal (Fig. 1B.2).

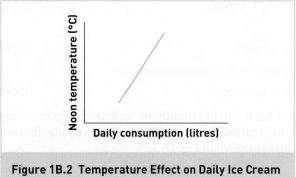

Figure 1B.2 Temperature Effect on Daily Ice Cream Consumption.

Exercise 1B.1 If you were given the information that produced Fig. 1B.2, and wanted to show how the temperature–consumption relationship is affected by a price change, what would you do?

Neither Fig. 1B.1 nor Fig. 1B.2 can deal satisfactorily with the problem that both price and temperature may vary between days, something that makes it difficult to separate the price and temperature effects. As an expedient, when using graphic analysis we assume we know each of the effects from prior information, and adjust one for any change in the other. Thus, if we know the price–consumption relationship (the

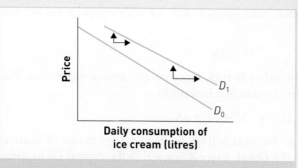

Figure 1B.3 The Demand Curve for Ice Cream. A rise in temperature increases consumption at any price.

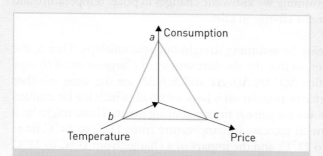

Figure 1B.4 The Surface *abc* shows the Price and Temperature Effects on Consumption, Holding Other Things Constant.

demand curve), we can shift it to make allowance for a change in temperature (Fig. 1B.3).

In this case, we show a hypothetical demand curve for choc ices at a holiday resort (a) when the noon temperature is 18°C, and (b) when it is 27°C. Suppose, however, we wanted to establish what a small change in price and temperature would do to sales. In practice this approach would not be very helpful, since we would need to be very exact in moving the demand curve to take the temperature effect into account. We could, of course, try to draw a three-dimensional graph, using some form of perspective, as shown in Fig. 1B.4, but measuring the impact of changes using this approach is extremely difficult other than in an inexact fashion.

Even if we did adopt this approach, we could not deal with the following problem. Sales will also be affected by the number of visitors to the holiday resort. Our demand curve shift approach and our three-dimensional graph approach will both be incapable of allowing for a change in the final factor, the number of potential consumers.

Dealing with the problem

If we use simple mathematical notation, the basis of the problem and its solution become clear. Use Q to represent the volume of sales (in litres – or, if we prefer, in number of choc ices). Let P represent the unit price (e.g. €0.75 per choc ice). Let T be the temperature at noon, and let N be the number of potential customers.

We are saying that Q is a *function* of P, T and N, which we can write as:

$$Q = Q(P,T,N)$$

Furthermore, let us suppose that market analysis has established for each independent variable its impact on Q. To make this tractable we will suppose that we know that these are as follows:

$$Q = a - bP$$

This, if graphed, would give us a demand curve such as in Fig. 1B.1. The 'coefficient' b tells us by how much Q changes (sales rise or fall) as P changes. It is the slope of the straight line demand curve.[5]

We will also suppose that the temperature and population effects are known and are equally simple:

$$Q = cT$$

---

5 Actually, in geometric terms it is the *inverse* of the slope, because slope measures vertical (P) change over horizontal (Q) change, but this need not concern us here.

meaning that, controlling for price, consumption will rise with temperature in a predictable fashion and

$$Q = dN$$

meaning that, controlling for the other factors, more people means more sales. Putting these together, we can write the whole relationship as

$$Q = a - bP + cT + dN$$

Any change in Q from one day to the next will be due to a change in one or more of the independent variables. Use the Greek letter Δ (capital delta, capital D) to mean 'change in':

$$\Delta Q = - b\Delta P + c\Delta T + f\Delta N$$

Now, assuming all this, and assuming we know the changes in price, temperature and population, we can determine the change in sales.

All very simple? Alas, no.

We have made it all very easy by assuming straight-line relationships. That is, the slopes in each case are constant, so that the absolute impact of a large or small change in P, T and N is given; the ratios $\Delta Q/\Delta P$, $\Delta Q/\Delta T$ and $\Delta Q/\Delta N$ are the same whether the change in temperature, price or population is large or small, which is a bit implausible, and regardless of where we measure it from a starting point. There might be a different impact on sales from an increase in temperature from $11°C$ to $14°C$ from that of a change from $19°C$ to $22°C$, and the impact of a change from $19°C$ to $22°C$ ($3°C$) in one day might be considerably higher than three times the impact of a change from $19°C$ to $20°C$.

Using straight-line relationships is fine for explanatory purposes in a classroom, or as a rough approximation to likely effects, but real life is more complex, and proper measurement of such effects cannot depend on this method. However, it does point us towards the solution.

Return to the simple demand curve of Fig. 1B.1. It could be written, as already noted, $Q = a - bP$. The value of b tells us the change (in litres) of sales for a change (in cents) of price. Suppose it was in fact $Q = 2,000 - 10 P$. In this case $\Delta Q/\Delta P = -10$, which is true whether P is 5 cents or 15 cents, and whether the starting price is 75 cents or 65 cents.

In this case, holding the other factors constant we could set down in a table the level of sales at various prices (Table 1B.1), and the relationship, if graphed, would give us our straight-line demand curve. At a price of zero and for a given number in the resort, and for a given temperature (ice cream is free) people would consume 2,000 litres a day. At a price of €2 a bar, no ice cream would be sold.

Now, suppose the demand curve was not a straight line, which is more than possible. Suppose it was curved, as in Fig. 1B.5.

Then, remembering what the slope of the curve means (the rate at which sales change as price changes), we see that (a) it changes as we move down the curve, and (b) the impact of a change in price depends on where we start from. To add to our woes, there is no reason to believe that the temperature effect or the population effect is linear (a straight line) either.

Price (cents per choc ice)	Volume sold (litres)
0	2,000
10	1,900
50	1,500
75	1,250
100	1,000
150	500
200	0

Table 1B.1 **Sales at Various Prices**

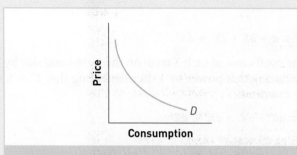

Figure 1B.5 A 'Curved' Demand Curve.

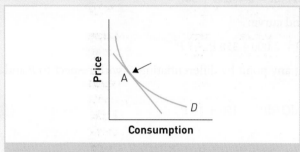

Figure 1B.6 A 'Curved' Demand Curve. The slope at *A* is found by drawing the tangent to the curve at *a* and getting the slope of the tangent.

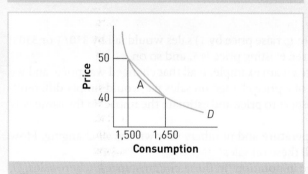

Figure 1B.7 Differentiating.

How do we deal with this?

At its simplest, and using a graph, we would measure the slope by getting the slope of a tangent to the curve at the relevant point (Fig. 1B.6). This is unsatisfactory, since we would need to provide the value of the tangent slope at every point on the curve ... and there is an infinite number of such points; so, operationally, we would have to calculate a large number of tangent slopes in order to make good predictions of price change effects on consumption (or weather or population effects).

The solution: use calculus – differentiating

Go back to the definition of a slope: it is the rate of change of sales (in this example) with respect to the change in price (ignoring the other effects). It is $\Delta Q/\Delta P$. In Fig. 1B.7, starting from a price of 50, if we lower price to 40 we see that sales will rise to 1,650. $\Delta Q/\Delta P$ is 150/10, or 15:1. That is an approximation to, but only an approximation to, the sales increase from any reduction of between 1 cent and 10 cents starting from 50, and not very different from that of a reduction from, say, 48 cents to 47 cents. But it is only an approximation, and will not accurately predict the impact of reducing price by 1 cent at any point in this interval. For that, it would appear we need either tangent values or something else.

We start by noting that if at any point *A* on the curve if ΔP is very small, $\Delta Q/\Delta P$ will be close to the value of the slope at that point.

If we keep making ΔP smaller and smaller around *A*, the slope of the straight line approaches that of the tangent at *A*, and eventually coincides with it. The slope of the tangent is the slope of the curve between two points that are infinitely close to each other (coincide). Or the slope of the tangent is given by $\Delta Q\Delta P$ when ΔP and ΔQ are extremely small ($\Delta P \rightarrow 0$).

For any expression $y = y(x)$ the value of $\Delta y/\Delta x$ as $\Delta x \rightarrow 0$ is written dy/dx, and is described as the 'first derivative' of *y* with respect to *x*. Obtaining it is done by 'differentiating' *y* with respect to *x*.

The *differential calculus* is the procedure that enables us to obtain the value of dy/dx from the original expression $y = y(x)$, or to **differentiate** *y* with respect to *x*.

For simple algebraic functions this turns out to be easy to learn (although we will not prove it here: this is not a rigorous text in mathematics).

differentiation finding the slope or rate of change of a function using algebra rather than geometry

Take an expression

$$Y = a + bX + cX^2 + dX^3$$

dY/dX is found by multiplying the coefficient of each X term on the right-hand side by the power of X concerned and reducing that power by 1. Remembering that $X^0 = 1$, and $X^1 = X$ the expression can be rewritten:

$$Y = aX^0 + bX^1 + cX^2 + dX^3$$

$$dY/dX = 0aX^{-1} + 1bX^0 + 2cX^1 + 3dX^2$$

or

$$dY/dX = b + 2cX + 3dX^2$$

So, if we had a non-linear demand curve:

$$Q = 2,000 - 350\,P + 5\,P^2$$

we can find the slope, dQ/dP, at any point by differentiating Q with respect to P and solving:

$$dQ/dP = -350 + 10\,P$$

Exercise 1B.2 Obtain this result by the procedure just outlined.

For $P = 1$, $dQ/dP = -340$; for $P = 5$, $dQ/dP = -300$; for $P = 15$, $dQ/dP = -200$

$$\Delta Q = (dQ/dP)\,\Delta P$$

That is, for a small change in P (e.g. raise price by 1) sales would fall by $350/1$ or 350 if the existing price is 1, by 300 if the existing price is 5, and so on.

Now, let us go back to our ice cream example. If all that changed was price, and we wanted to estimate the impact of a price change on sales we would simply differentiate the expression for Q with respect to price and estimate the impact in the same way as we have just done.

But suppose that price, temperature and numbers in town are all changing. How do we estimate the impact of all these on sales?

We start with a small change in notation. In these circumstances, where sales, Q, are dependent on (in this case) three variables, P, T and N, we shall use dQ to mean change in sales, dP change in price, dT change in temperature and dN change in potential number of customers. We shall use the small Greek letter delta δ (d), to indicate the rate of change obtained by differentiating where Q is being differentiated with respect to just one of the variables that determine it (or 'partially differentiated').

Since (if we have properly specified the demand relationship) we know that changes in Q are due to the impact of the three independent variables, we can state this formally:

$$dQ = (\delta Q/\delta P)dp + (\delta Q/\delta T)dT + (\delta Q/\delta N)dN$$

Exactly the same procedure as before is used to obtain the rates of change values; but if you want to isolate the effect of T, for example, you differentiate with respect to T, and any term in the expression not including T is ignored (or treated as being multiplied by T^0, which is the same thing).

Exercise 1B.3
$$Q = 3{,}000 - 15\,P - 3\,P^2 + 2.5\,T - 6\,T^{\frac{1}{2}} + 15\,N + 20\,N^{\frac{1}{2}}$$

(i)   Write down the expression for dQ/dP.

(ii) What is dQ/dP if $P = 50$? What is dQ/dT if $T = 16$?

(iii) By how much will sales rise if the numbers in town rise from 10,000 to 10,500? (Remember that raising a number to the power of $\frac{1}{2}$ means its square root, and a negative power means the reciprocal of the positive value, i.e. $X^{-1} = 1/X$.)

There are three other useful differentiation rules for economists.

1. Suppose we know that Y is a product of two variables, each of which is a function of X:

$$Y = UV, \text{ where } U = U(X) \text{ and } V = V(X)$$

and we want to find the impact of a change in X on Y.
How do we differentiate Y with respect to X?
The rule is a simple one:

$$dY/dX = U\,dV/dX + V\,dU/dX$$

This is called the *product chain rule*.

Example

$$Y = UV$$
$$U = 10 - 2X \text{ and } V = -5 + 8X$$
$$dU/dX = -2 \text{ and } dV/dX = 8$$
$$dY/dX = (100 - 2X)(8) + (-5 + 8X)(-2) = 90$$

2. Suppose that $Y = U/V$, where U and V are both functions of X.
The rule is:

$$dY/dX = [(V\,dU/dX) - (U\,dV/dX)]/V^2$$

This is the *divisor chain rule*.

Example

$$Y = U/V$$
$$U = 10 + 2.\,X \text{ and } V = 5 + 8.\,X$$
$$dY/dX = 2(5 + 8.\,X) - 8(10 + 2X)(8)]/(5 + 8X)^2$$
$$= 70/(25 - 80\,X + 64\,X^2)$$

3. Finally, suppose that the relation between Y and X is of the form

$$Y = (a + bX)^n = (f(X))^n$$

The rule for deriving dY/dX is:

$$dY/dX = [n(fX)^{n-1}\,][d(f(X)d(X)]$$

This is the *function chain rule*.

Example

$$Y = (10 + 5X)^2$$
$$dY/dX = 2(10 + 5X)5 = 100 + 50X$$

Exercise 1B.4   (i)   Show that the function chain rule is correct in this case by extending the bracket term in the function rule example and differentiating Y with respect to X.

(ii)   Show that the divisor chain rule is correct by turning the terms in the example into a product:

$$Y = (10 + 2X)(5 + 8X)^{-1}$$

Reference

Thaler, R. (1980) 'Towards a positive theory of consumer choice', *Journal of Economic Behaviour and Organization*, 1(1).

To help you grasp the key concepts of this chapter check out the extra resources posted on the Online Learning Centre. There are chapter summaries, self-test questions, an interactive graphing tool, weblinks and a glossary, all for free!

Visit the Online Learning Centre at: www.mcgraw-hill.co.uk/textbooks/mcdowell for information on accessing all of these resources.

Markets, Specialisation and Economic Efficiency

One aspect of the differences in economic life between developed and undeveloped countries is the high degree of specialisation by firms and households in developed countries compared with that in undeveloped countries. At its most obvious level, think about specialisation at the household level. In the richer, advanced economies of the Organization for Economic Cooperation and Development (OECD), the 'club' of advanced economies, it is very close to being a truism that households (wage earners) in general consume goods and services that they do not produce, and produce goods or services that they do not consume. In poorer economies, we observe widespread household production of goods and services to be consumed within the same households. This is obvious where food production for consumption is concerned and households are in the agricultural sector, but it is also a feature of other consumption items in household budgets. For example, clothes making and repairing is commonly part of the 'output' of a household, but is consumed within the household (although it may also be sold to other households).

This aspect of household activity, or, more accurately, its disappearance, will be familiar to anyone born in the decade after the end of the Second World War in what are now the OECD economies. Ask yourself how many of today's young adults have the household skills that their parents or grandparents have or had? What has replaced those skills? The answer is goods and services produced outside the household (clothes, pizzas, cleaning) and bought in out of earnings derived from what the household produces and sells to other economic entities.

We can see the same phenomenon in the organisation of production by firms. This is often referred to as 'vertical disintegration of production'. Within manufacturing this can be seen in the trend towards separate production of 'parts' from the assembly of those parts into 'final goods'. Planes, trains and automobiles spring to mind immediately. Specialist firms produce gear boxes for car manufacturers. Boeing and Airbus subcontract purchases of components to other suppliers, as do manufacturers of railway engines. Vertical disintegration on this model is another instance of specialisation and exchange replacing within-firm production.

There is, then, a positive correlation between income levels and specialisation and exchange across countries and over time within countries. This raises a further question: if there is a causal relationship between specialisation and income levels, which is the cause and which is the effect? Where there is less specialisation the firm or household by definition contains a wider variety of skills. This is common in poorer countries, but rarer in richer ones, where people specialise and hire others to do things for them. Why this difference in skills and employment?

One might be tempted to answer that the people in poorer countries are simply too poor to hire others to perform these services. But as reasonable as this poverty explanation may seem, the reverse is actually the case. The point to be made in this chapter is that people in poorer countries do not provide their own services because they are poor; rather, they are poor largely *because* they provide their own services.

The alternative to a system in which everyone is a jack-of-all-trades is one in which people *specialise* in particular goods and services, and then satisfy their needs by trading among themselves. Economic systems based on specialisation and the exchange of goods and services are generally far more productive than those with less specialisation. Our task in this chapter is to investigate why this is so. In doing so we shall explore why people choose to exchange goods and services in the first place, rather than having each person produce his or her own food, cars, clothing, shelter and the like.

| Comparative Advantage |

The reason that specialisation is so productive is the existence of what economists call *comparative advantage*. A person has a comparative advantage at producing a particular good or service – say, haircuts – if that person is *relatively* more efficient at producing haircuts than at producing other goods or services. We can all have more of *every* good and service if each of us specialises in the activities at which we have a comparative advantage.

This chapter will also introduce the *production possibilities curve* (PPC), which is a graphical method of describing the combinations of goods and services that an economy can produce. The development of this tool will allow us to see much more precisely how specialisation enhances the productive capacity of even the simplest economy.

Back, then, to rich and poor countries. If it is the failure to specialise that is the root cause of poverty, what is to stop people becoming richer simply by specialising? First, the size of the market determines the limits to the benefits from the specialist division of labour. For specialisation to make sense it may be necessary that others specialise at the same time, so as to create a market for the potentially increased supply of goods and services that specialists produce. Inadequate transport infrastructure may drastically limit the size of the potential market. Specialisation may require training or skills that are hard to acquire. It may require capital in the form of dedicated equipment, which is costly to acquire. Thus there is an element of a 'chicken and egg' problem: specialisation increases the value of goods and services being produced (the size of the economy), but the incentive to specialise may depend on the existing size of the economy.

These problems are the concern of what is known as 'development economics' and, interesting as it is, development economics is outside the scope of an introductory text. However, what we are going to look at in this chapter is fundamental to understanding why countries – and people – become better off through specialisation and exchange. To do so, we look at the problem in a simplified and rather abstract fashion, so as to avoid the kind of difficulties just described.

Exchange and opportunity cost

The *Scarcity Principle* reminds us that the opportunity cost of spending more time on any one activity is having less time available to spend on others. As Example 2.1 makes clear, this principle helps explain why everyone can do better by concentrating on those activities at which they perform best *relative* to others.

Example 2.1 Should a doctor prescribe for himself/herself?

There is a widespread view that doctors should not provide services to themselves or their families for ethical or technical diagnosis-based reasons. These may be well founded, but there is a persuasive, and purely economic, argument that leads to the same conclusion, and reinforces the ethical objection to 'self-supply'. This is that it is economically more efficient to restrict one's medical services to supplying them to people outside the family where there exists a market in medical services. This is particularly the case where there are 'routine' and 'difficult' problems facing a practitioner. Some medical problems are strictly routine, and just as a competent lawyer can draw up a simple will for himself, a doctor with a headache will look for the aspirin on his own. When there exists a hierarchy of problems and abilities this changes.

There are two aspects to treating a medical condition. The first is diagnosis; the second is managing treatment. Let us assume a medical consultant can command fees of €2,000 a day, or €250 an hour, as an expert neurologist in treating neurological conditions (and knows everything there is to know about headaches). A spouse or dependant has a bad headache. A competent general practitioner, for, say, €100 a visit lasting an hour, can examine a patient and determine if it is a routine headache or something more serious and prescribe the necessary course of action: treatment or referral to a consultant. Consequently, the consultant, on the basis of his reputation, can charge €150 an hour for a preliminary diagnosis. It would be irrational for the consultant to treat the family member rather than send that person to the GP if it meant giving up an hour at €250 (what he could earn on patients referred to him) to avoid spending €100 on a fee to the GP. The opportunity cost of an hour of the consultant's time exceeds the fee charged by the GP.

If the consultant is better than the GP at diagnosing headache problems he has an **absolute advantage**. This supposition is what allows him to charge €150 per hour for preliminary diagnosis. If he is better at treating headaches than the GP he has an absolute advantage in that function. But if his opportunity cost of preliminary diagnosis (the €250 he loses by not using that hour for treatment) is higher than that of the GP (€100), the consultant has a **comparative advantage** in treatment, while the GP, who is at an *absolute disadvantage* in both functions, has a comparative advantage in preliminary diagnosis.

absolute advantage one person has an absolute advantage over another if an hour spent in performing a task earns more than the other person can earn in an hour at the task

comparative advantage one person has a comparative advantage over another in a task if his or her opportunity cost of performing a task is lower than the other person's opportunity cost

The ratio of the consultant's income from an hour's treatment advice to that earned from an hour's diagnosis is the opportunity cost in time of an hour's treatment advice. It is $250/150 = 1.67$. For the GP, an hour earns him the same in both activities, so the ratio for both is 1.0. His opportunity cost of time spent diagnosing is less than the consultant's.

The point of Example 2.1 is not that people whose time is valuable should never perform their own services. If that were the case most DIY stores would have many fewer customers. The point is that where time and resources are scarce it is economically efficient to specialise along lines dictated by comparative advantage.

The Principle of Comparative Advantage

One of the most important insights of modern economics is that when two people (or two nations) have different opportunity costs of performing various tasks, they can always increase the total value of available goods and services by trading with one another. Example 2.2 captures the logic behind this insight.

Example 2.2 Should Paula update her own web page?

Consider a small community in which Paula is the only professional bicycle mechanic and Beth is the only professional HTML programmer. Paula also happens to be an even better HTML programmer than Beth. If the amount of time each of them takes to perform these tasks is as shown in Table 2.1, and if each regards the two tasks as equally pleasant (or unpleasant), does the fact that Paula can program faster than Beth imply that Paula should update her own web page?

	Time to update a web page (minutes)	Time to complete a bicycle repair (minutes)
Paula	20	10
Beth	30	30

Table 2.1 **Productivity Information for Paula and Beth**

The entries in Table 2.1 show that Paula has an absolute advantage over Beth in both activities. While Paula, the mechanic, needs only 20 minutes to update a web page, Beth, the programmer, needs 30 minutes. Paula's advantage over Beth is even greater when the task is fixing bikes: she can complete a repair in only 10 minutes, compared with Beth's 30 minutes.

But the fact that Paula is a better programmer than Beth does *not* imply that Paula should update her own web page. Beth has a comparative advantage over Paula at programming: she is *relatively* more productive at programming than Paula. Similarly, Paula has a comparative advantage in bicycle repair. (Remember that a person has a comparative advantage at a given task if his or her opportunity cost of performing that task is lower than another person's.)

What is Beth's opportunity cost of updating a web page? Since she takes 30 minutes to update each page – the same amount of time she takes to fix a bicycle – her opportunity cost of updating a web page is one bicycle repair. In other words, by taking the time to update a web page, Beth is effectively giving up the opportunity to do one bicycle repair. Paula, in contrast, can complete two bicycle repairs in the time she takes to update a single web page. For her, the opportunity cost of updating a web page is two bicycle repairs. Paula's opportunity cost of programming, measured in terms of bicycle repairs forgone, is twice as high as Beth's. Thus Beth has a comparative advantage at programming.

The interesting and important implication of the opportunity cost comparison summarised in Table 2.2 is that the total number of bicycle repairs and web updates accomplished if Paula and Beth both spend part of their time at each activity will always be smaller than the number accomplished if each specialises in the activity in which she has a comparative advantage. Suppose, for example, that people in their community demand a total of 16 web page updates per day. If Paula spent half her time updating web pages and the other half repairing bicycles, an eight-hour workday would yield 12 web page updates and 24 bicycle repairs. To complete the remaining four updates, Beth would have to spend two hours programming, which would leave her six hours to repair bicycles. And since she takes 30 minutes to do each repair, she would have time to complete 12 of them. So when the two women try to be jacks-of-all-trades, they end up completing a total of 16 web page updates and 36 bicycle repairs.

	Opportunity cost of updating a web page	Opportunity cost of a bicycle repair
Paula	2 bicycle repairs	0.5 web page update
Beth	1 bicycle repair	1 web page update

Table 2.2 **Opportunity Costs for Paula and Beth**

Consider what would have happened had each woman specialised in her activity of comparative advantage. Beth could have updated 16 web pages on her own, and Paula could have performed 48 bicycle repairs. Specialisation would have created an additional 12 bicycle repairs out of thin air.

When computing the opportunity cost of one good in terms of another, we must pay close attention to the form in which the productivity information is presented. In Example 2.2, we were told how many minutes each person needed to perform each task. Alternatively, we might be told how many units of each task each person can perform in an hour. Work through Exercise 2.1 to see how to proceed when information is presented in this alternative format.

Exercise 2.1 Consider a small community in which Barbara is the only professional bicycle mechanic and Pat is the only professional HTML programmer. If their productivity rates at the two tasks are as shown in the table, and if each regards the two tasks as equally pleasant (or unpleasant), does the fact that Barbara can program faster than Pat imply that Barbara should update her own web page?

	Productivity in programming (per hour)	Productivity in bicycle repair (per hour)
Pat	2 web page updates	1 repair
Barbara	3 web page updates	3 repairs

The principle illustrated by Examples 2.1 and 2.2 is so important that we state it formally as one of the core principles of the course:

The Principle of Comparative Advantage: everyone does best when each person (or each country) concentrates on the activities for which his or her opportunity cost is lowest.

Indeed, the gains made possible from specialisation based on comparative advantage constitute the rationale for *market exchange*. They explain why each person does not devote 10 per cent of his or her time to producing cars, 5 per cent to growing food, 25 per cent to building housing, 0.0001 per cent to performing brain surgery, and so on. By concentrating on those tasks at which we are relatively more productive, we can together produce vastly more than if we all tried to be self-sufficient.

Specialisation and its effects provide ample grist for the economic naturalist. Here is an example from the world of sports.

Economic naturalist 2.1 What has happened to football (soccer)? They just don't seem to be able to score goals like they used to![1]

In 1954 Roger Bannister broke the 4-minute mile barrier. By the end of the century sub-4-minute miles were frequent events at top athletics meeting. The standards of athletes and their performances have steadily improved right across the spectrum of sports, as intensive and scientific training and the application of technology (permitted) and more questionable methods have been increasingly used to improve performance. Most observers would agree that professionalism has greatly improved the skills and performances of sports in general. In recent years this has been abundantly evident in the case of rugby football. But has it happened in soccer? Consider the following. Look at the scoring record in the World Cup since the 1930s. Between 1930 and 1954 the average number of goals scored in World Cup games rose on a trend from 2.88 to 5.36. From 1954 there was a fairly steady decline to 2.21 in 1990. There seems to have been a small recovery since 1990: 2.71 in 1994, 2.67 in 1998 and 2.52 in 2002. In 2006, however, it was down to 2.2.

One suggestion was that it was getting harder to score in recent decades because goalkeepers were getting bigger ... but no one suggested that they were getting smaller between 1930 and 1954. However, something did happen in the mid-1950s. It became more and more common to put most of a team's effort (in the form of the formation in which players took the field) into defence. The old 3–2–5 formation (five attackers) gave way to 4–3–3 and 4–4–2. For some reason, teams began to shift the weight of specialisation from attack to defence, and this has been maintained to the present, with 4–5–1 not being unknown. On that basis the fall in the average score becomes easy to understand, and when account is taken of the fall in the percentage of attackers, the goal score per attacker may even have risen, consistent with the professionalisation story. The lower score rates, then, reflect not a falling skill among attackers but increased specialisation in defence and a consequent increased ability of teams to defend and selection of players for defensive capability. But what might have driven the move to emphasise and specialise in defence? A possible explanation may lie in the increased amounts of money going into football and the consequent potential cost to a club of losing matches and facing relegation. If teams are risk averse they would be expected to respond to this by putting more effort into specialising in defence and less into attack. What do you think?

Sources of comparative advantage

At the individual level, comparative advantage often appears to be the result of inborn talent. For instance, some people seem to be naturally gifted at programming computers while others seem to have a special knack for fixing bikes. But comparative advantage is more often the result of education, training or experience. Thus we usually leave the design of kitchens to people with architectural training, the drafting of contracts to people who have studied law and the teaching of physics to people with advanced degrees in that field.

---

1 We are indebted to a colleague in University College Dublin's Economics School, David Madden, for suggesting the material for Economic naturalist 2.1.

At the national level, comparative advantage may derive from differences in natural resources or from differences in society or culture. The United States, which has a disproportionate share of the world's leading research universities, has a comparative advantage in the design of electronic computing hardware and software. Canada, which has one of the world's highest per capita endowments of farm and forest land, has a comparative advantage in the production of agricultural products. Topography and climate explain why Colorado specialises in the skiing industry while Hawaii specialises as an ocean resort.

Seemingly non-economic factors can also give rise to comparative advantage. For instance, the emergence of English as the de facto world language gives English-speaking countries a comparative advantage over non-English-speaking nations in the production of books, movies and popular music. Even a country's institutions may affect the likelihood that it will achieve comparative advantage in a particular pursuit. For example, cultures that encourage entrepreneurship will tend to have a comparative advantage in the introduction of new products, whereas those that promote high standards of care and craftsmanship will tend to have a comparative advantage in the production of high-quality variants of established products.

Economic naturalist 2.2 Whatever happened to the British shipbuilding industry?

In the nineteenth century and into the twentieth century the United Kingdom was the world's most important designer and producer of merchant shipping and warships. The UK's comparative advantage in shipbuilding was based on the engineering skills developed in the Industrial Revolution, on suitable locations for building and launching ships, and on its iron and steel industry. This was not confined to commercial shipping: British shipyards built battleships for most of the world. Indeed, one of the things that tipped Turkey into siding with Germany and Austria-Hungary in 1914 was the fact that, when war broke out, the Admiralty seized two dreadnoughts (battleships) on the point of completion for Turkey in British yards, renamed them and took them into the Royal Navy.

But all this has changed. By the end of the twentieth century, apart from some highly specialised activities and some strategic production for the Royal Navy, commercial shipbuilding in the United Kingdom had become virtually extinct

Comparative advantage changes. In this case, we can identify a series of factors that led to the decline in the importance of the United Kingdom as a producer as comparative advantage changed. First, the process became more mechanised: welding replaced skilled and specialised labour-intensive riveting as a technique. Steel became available cheaply elsewhere. Labour costs (even though the technology was becoming more capital-intensive) rose in Britain relative to the Far East. Ship designing as a skill was available on at least as high a quality basis outside Britain. British firms could no longer compete because their costs were higher and there were no vital inputs that demanded that British yards be used.

RECAP Exchange and opportunity cost

Gains from exchange are possible if trading partners have comparative advantages in producing different goods and services. You have a comparative advantage in producing, say, web pages, if your opportunity cost of producing a web page – measured in terms of other production opportunities forgone – is smaller than the corresponding opportunity costs of your trading partners. Maximum production is achieved if each person specialises in producing the good or service in which he or she has the lowest opportunity cost (the Principle of Comparative Advantage). Comparative advantage makes specialisation worthwhile even if one trading partner is more productive than others, in absolute terms, in every activity.

Comparative advantage and production possibilities

Comparative advantage and specialisation allow an economy to produce more than if each person tries to produce a little of everything. In this section we gain further insight into the advantages of specialisation by introducing a graph that can be used to describe the various combinations of goods and services that an economy can produce.

The production possibilities curve

We begin with a hypothetical economy in which only two goods are produced: coffee and pine nuts. It is a small island economy, and 'production' consists either of picking coffee beans that grow on small bushes on the island's central valley floor or of picking pine nuts that grow on trees on the steep hillsides overlooking the valley. The more time workers spend picking coffee, the less time they have available for picking nuts. So if people want to drink more coffee, they must make do with a smaller amount of nuts.

production possibilities curve a graph that describes the maximum amount of one good that can be produced for every possible level of production of the other good

If we know how productive workers are at each activity, we can summarise the various combinations of coffee and nuts they can pick each day. This menu of possibilities is known as the **production possibilities curve** (PPC).

To keep matters simple, we begin with an example in which the economy has only a single worker who can divide her time between the two activities.

Example 2.3 What is the PPC for an economy in which Susan is the only worker?

Consider a society consisting only of Susan, who allocates her production time between coffee and nuts. She is short and has nimble fingers, two qualities that make her more productive at picking coffee than at picking nuts. She can pick 2 kg of nuts or 4 kg of coffee in an hour. If she works a total of 6 hours per day, describe her PPC – the graph that displays, for each level of nut production, the maximum amount of coffee that Susan can pick.

The vertical axis in Fig. 2.1 shows Susan's daily production of coffee, and the horizontal axis shows her daily production of nuts. Let us begin by looking at two extreme allocations of her time. First, suppose she employs her entire workday (6 hours) picking coffee. In that case, since she can pick 4 kg of coffee per hour, she would pick 24 kg per day of coffee and zero kg of nuts. That combination of coffee and nut production is represented by point *A* in Fig. 2.1. It is the vertical intercept of Susan's PPC.

Now suppose, instead, that Susan devotes all her time to picking nuts. Since she can pick 2 kg of nuts per hour, her total daily production would be 12 kg of nuts. That combination is represented

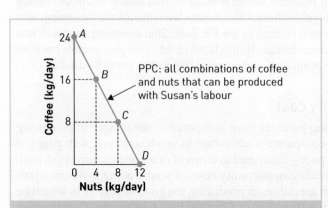

Figure 2.1 Susan's Production Possibilities. For the production relationships given, the PPC is a straight line.

by point D in Fig. 2.1, the horizontal intercept of Susan's PPC. Because Susan's production of each good is exactly proportional to the amount of time she devotes to that good, the remaining points along her production possibilities curve will lie on the straight line that joins A and D.

For example, suppose that Susan devotes 4 hours each day to picking coffee and 2 hours to picking nuts. She will then end up with (4 hours/day) × (4 kg/hour) = 16 kg of coffee per day and (2 hours/day) × (2 kg/hour) = 4 kg of nuts. This is the point labelled B in Fig. 2.1. Alternatively, if she devotes 2 hours to coffee and 4 to nuts, she will get (2 hours/day) × (4 kg/hour) = 8 kg of coffee per day and (4 hours/day) × (2 kg/hour) = 8 kg of nuts. This alternative combination is represented by point C in Fig. 2.1.

Since Susan's PPC is a straight line, its slope is constant. The absolute value of the slope of Susan's PPC is the ratio of its vertical intercept to its horizontal intercept: (24 kg of coffee/day)/(12 kg of nuts/day) = (2 kg of coffee)/(1 kg of nuts). (Be sure to keep track of the units of measure on each axis when computing this ratio.) This ratio means that Susan's *opportunity cost of an additional kilogram of nuts is 2 kg of coffee*.

Note that Susan's opportunity cost (OC) of nuts can also be expressed as the following simple formula:

$$OC_{nuts} = \frac{\text{Loss in coffee}}{\text{Gain in nuts}} \qquad (2.1)$$

where 'loss in coffee' means the amount of coffee given up, and 'gain in nuts' means the corresponding increase in nuts. Likewise, Susan's opportunity cost of coffee can be expressed by this formula:

$$OC_{coffee} = \frac{\text{Loss in nuts}}{\text{Gain in coffee}} \qquad (2.2)$$

To say that Susan's opportunity cost of an additional kilogram of nuts is 2 kg of coffee is thus equivalent to saying that her opportunity cost of a kilogram of coffee is $\frac{1}{2}$ kg of nuts.

The downward slope of the PPC shown in Fig. 2.1 illustrates the Scarcity Principle – the idea that because our resources are limited, having more of one good thing generally means having to settle for less of another (see Chapter 1). Susan can have an additional kilogram of coffee if she wishes, but only if she is willing to give up half a kilogram of nuts. If Susan is the only person in the economy, her opportunity cost of producing a good becomes, in effect, its *price*. Thus the price she has to pay for an additional kilogram of coffee is half a kilogram of nuts; or the price she has to pay for an additional kilogram of nuts is 2 kg of coffee.

Any point that lies either along the PPC or within it is said to be an **attainable point**, meaning that it can be produced with currently available resources. In Fig. 2.2, for example, points A, B, C, D and E are attainable points. Points that lie outside the PPC are said to be **unattainable**, meaning that they cannot be produced using currently available resources. In Fig. 2.2, F is an unattainable point because Susan cannot pick 16 kg of coffee per day *and* 8 kg of nuts. Points that lie within the curve are said to be **inefficient points**, in the sense that existing resources would allow for production of more of at least one good without sacrificing the production of any other good. At E, for example, Susan is picking

attainable point any combination of goods that can be produced using currently available resources

unattainable point any combination of goods that cannot be produced using currently available resources

inefficient point any combination of goods for which currently available resources enable an increase in the production of one good without a reduction in the production of the other

efficient point any combination of goods for which currently available resources do not allow an increase in the production of one good without a reduction in the production of the other

only 8 kg of coffee per day and 4 kg of nuts, which means that she could increase her coffee harvest by 8 kg per day without giving up any nuts (by moving from E to B). Alternatively, Susan could pick as many as 4 additional kilograms of nuts each day without giving up any coffee (by moving from E to C). An **efficient point** is one that lies along the PPC. At any such point, more of one good can be produced only by producing less of the other.

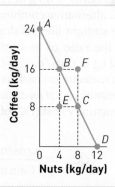

Figure 2.2 Attainable and Efficient Points on Susan's PPC. Points that lie either along the PPC (for example, A, B, C and D) or within it (for example, E) are said to be attainable. Points that lie outside the PPC (for example, F) are unattainable. Points that lie along the PPC are said to be efficient, while those that lie within the PPC are said to be inefficient.

Exercise 2.2   For the PPC shown in Fig. 2.2, state whether the following points are attainable and/or efficient:
a. 20 kg per day of coffee, 4 kg per day of nuts
b. 12 kg per day of coffee, 6 kg per day of nuts
c. 4 kg per day of coffee, 8 kg per day of nuts.

How individual productivity affects the slope and position of the PPC

To see how the slope and position of the PPC depend on an individual's productivity, let us compare Susan's PPC to that of Tom, who is less productive at picking coffee but more productive at picking nuts.

Example 2.4 How do changes in productivity affect the opportunity cost of nuts?

Tom is tall and an agile climber, qualities that make him especially well suited to picking nuts that grow on hillside trees. He can pick 4 kg of nuts or 2 kg of coffee per hour. If Tom were the only person in the economy, describe the economy's PPC.

We can construct Tom's PPC the same way we did Susan's. Note first that if Tom devotes an entire workday (6 hours) to coffee picking, he ends up with (6 hours/day) × (2 kg/hour) = 12 kg of coffee per day and 0 kg of nuts. So the vertical intercept of Tom's PPC is A in Fig. 2.3. If instead he devotes all his time to picking nuts, he gets

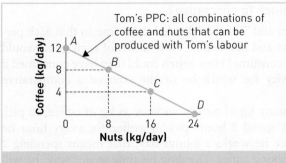

Figure 2.3 Tom's PPC. Tom's opportunity cost of producing 1 kg of nuts is only $\frac{1}{2}$ kg of coffee.

(6 hours/day) × (4 kg/hour) = 24 kg of nuts per day and no coffee. That means that the horizontal intercept of his PPC is D in Fig. 2.3. Because Tom's production of each good is proportional to the amount of time he devotes to it, the remaining points on his PPC will lie along the straight line that joins these two extreme points.

For example, if Tom devotes 4 hours each day to picking coffee and 2 hours to picking nuts, he will end up with (4 hours/day) × (2 kg/hour) = 8 kg of coffee per day and (2 hours/day) × (4 kg/hour) = 8 kg of nuts per day. This is the point labelled B in Fig. 2.3. Alternatively, if he devotes 2 hours to coffee and 4 to nuts, he will get (2 hours/day) × (2 kg/hour) = 4 kg of coffee per day and (4 hours/day) × (4 kg/hour) = 16 kg of nuts. This alternative combination is represented by point C in Fig. 2.3.

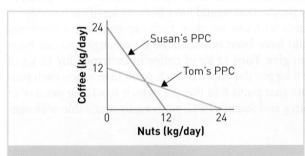

Figure 2.4 Individual PPCs Compared. Tom is less productive in coffee than Susan, but more productive in nuts.

How does Tom's PPC compare with Susan's? Note in Fig. 2.4 that because Tom is absolutely less productive than Susan at picking coffee, the vertical intercept of his PPC lies closer to the origin than Susan's. By the same token, because Susan is absolutely less productive than Tom at picking nuts, the horizontal intercept of her PPC lies closer to the origin than Tom's. For Tom, the opportunity cost of an additional kilogram of nuts is $\frac{1}{2}$ kg of coffee, which is one-quarter Susan's opportunity cost of nuts. This difference in opportunity costs shows up as a difference in the slopes of their PPCs: the absolute value of the slope of Tom's PPC is $\frac{1}{2}$, whereas Susan's is 2.

In this example, Tom has both an absolute advantage and a comparative advantage over Susan in picking nuts. Susan, for her part, has both an absolute advantage and a comparative advantage over Tom in picking coffee.

We cannot emphasise too strongly that the Principle of Comparative Advantage is a *relative* concept – one that makes sense only when the productivities of two or more people (or countries) are being compared. To cement this idea, work through Exercise 2.3.

Exercise 2.3 Suppose Susan can pick 2 kg of coffee per hour or 4 kg of nuts per hour; Tom can pick 1 kg of coffee per hour and 1 kg of nuts per hour. What is Susan's opportunity cost of picking 1 kg of nuts? What is Tom's opportunity cost of picking 1 kg of nuts? Where does Susan's comparative advantage now lie?

The gains from specialisation

Earlier we saw that a comparative advantage arising from disparities in individual opportunity costs creates gains for everyone (see Examples 2.1 and 2.2). Example 2.5 shows how the same point can be illustrated using PPCs.

Example 2.5 How costly is failure to specialise?

Suppose that in Example 2.4 Susan and Tom had divided their time so that each person's output consisted of half nuts and half coffee. How much of each good would Tom and Susan have been able to consume? How much could they have consumed if each had specialised in the activity for which he or she enjoyed a comparative advantage?

Since Tom can pick twice as many kg of nuts in an hour as kg of coffee, to pick equal quantities of each he must spend 2 hours picking coffee for every hour he devotes to picking nuts. And since he works a 6-hour day, that means spending 2 hours picking nuts and 4 hours picking coffee. Dividing his time in this way, he will end up with 8 kg of coffee and 8 kg of nuts per day. Similarly, since Susan can pick twice as many kg of coffee in an hour as kg of nuts, to pick equal quantities of each she must spend 2 hours picking nuts for every hour she devotes to picking coffee. And since she too works a 6-hour day, that means spending 2 hours picking coffee and 4 hours picking nuts. So, like Tom, she will end up with 8 kg of coffee per day and 8 kg of nuts (see Fig. 2.5). Their combined daily production will thus be 16 kg of each good. By contrast, had they each specialised in their respective activities of comparative advantage, their combined daily production would have been 24 kg of each good.

If they exchange coffee and nuts with one another, each can consume a combination of the two goods that would have been unattainable if exchange had not been possible. For example, Susan can give Tom 12 kg of coffee in exchange for 12 kg of nuts, enabling each to consume 4 kg per day more of each good than when each produced and consumed alone. Note that point E in Fig. 2.5, which has 12 kg per day of each good, lies beyond both Tom's and Susan's PPC, yet is easily attainable with specialisation and exchange.

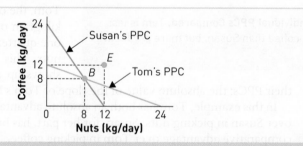

Figure 2.5 Production without Specialisation. When Tom and Susan divide their time so that each produces the same number of kilograms of coffee and nuts, they can produce a total of 16 kg of coffee and 16 kg of nuts each day.

As Exercise 2.4 illustrates, the gains from specialisation grow larger as the difference in opportunity costs increases.

Does it matter how they specialise?

Yes, it does. On the basis of the data used to produce Fig. 2.5 we can show how they should specialise so as to maximise their possible income from coffee and nuts (Fig. 2.6).

Susan has a comparative advantage in nuts, and Tom has a comparative advantage in coffee. Suppose they both devote all their time to nuts. The total they can produce is 36 kg of nuts per day. They decide to reduce nut production in order to produce coffee. Suppose Susan starts to produce coffee (in which she has a comparative advantage). The

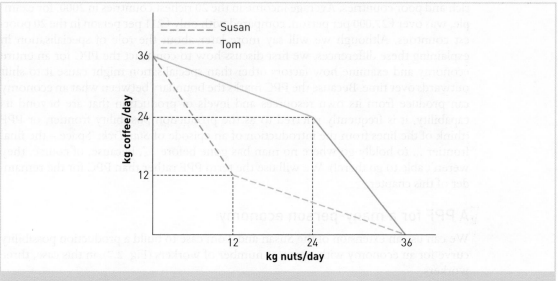

Figure 2.6 Specialisation to Reflect Comparative Advantage. If Susan specialises in coffee, and Tom specialises in nuts the quantities they can produce together are greater than if they specialise the other way. The solid lines constitute their *production possibility frontier* (PPF) or *production possibility curve* (PPC).

combined total of coffee and nuts is given by the solid line. When Susan gives all her time to coffee they are producing 24 kg of nuts (Tom being the nut producer) and 24 kg of coffee (the solid lines). They have specialised to reflect comparative advantage. Suppose, however, they decided to let Tom start producing coffee, while Susan produced nuts. When Tom was fully occupied producing coffee, and Susan producing nuts, they would produce a total of 12 kg of nuts and 12 kg of coffee (the broken lines).

| Increasing Opportunity Cost |

When they specialise according to comparative advantage the combination of coffee and nuts they can produce is given by the solid line production 'frontier'. This lies outside the alternative 'frontier', implying that specialising according to comparative advantage makes possible higher levels of output of both goods ... and higher incomes for the two producers. The solid lines constitute their *production possibility curve* (PPC) or *production possibility frontier* (PPF). If they decided that they wanted to produce 6 kg of coffee it would make more sense to use Susan's time producing coffee rather than to use Tom's, since 6 kg of coffee so produced cost them only 3 kg of nuts, while assigning the job of producing 6 kg of coffee to Tom would cost them 12 kg of nuts.

Exercise 2.4   How do differences in opportunity cost affect the gains from specialisation?

Susan can pick 5 kg of coffee or 1 kg of nuts in an hour. Tom can pick 1 kg of coffee or 5 kg of nuts in an hour. Assuming they again work 6-hour days and want to consume coffee and nuts in equal quantities, by how much will specialisation increase their consumption compared with the alternative in which each produced only for his or her own consumption?

Although the gains from specialisation and exchange grow with increases in the differences in opportunity costs among trading partners, these differences alone still seem insufficient to account for the enormous differences in living standards between rich and poor countries. Average income in the 20 richest countries in 2000, for example, was over €27,000 per person, compared with only €211 per person in the 20 poorest countries. Although we will say more later about the role of specialisation in explaining these differences, we first discuss how to construct the PPC for an entire economy and examine how factors other than specialisation might cause it to shift outwards over time. Because the PPC marks the boundary between what an economy can produce from its own resources and levels of production that are beyond its capability, it is frequently referred to as the production possibility frontier, or PPF (think of the lines from the introduction of an episode of *Star Trek*: 'Space – the final frontier ... to boldly go where no man has gone before ...', because, of course, they weren't able to go there!). We will use the term PPF rather than PPC for the remainder of this chapter.

A PPF for a many-person economy

We can use an extension of the Susan and Tom case to build a production possibility curve for an economy with a greater number of workers (Fig. 2.7), in this case, three workers.

We shall say more in a moment about the reasons for this 'bow' shape. But first note that a bow-shaped PPF means that the opportunity cost of producing nuts increases as the economy produces more of them. This pattern of *increasing opportunity cost* persists over the entire length of the PPF. Note, finally, that the same pattern of increasing opportunity cost applies to coffee. Thus, as more coffee is produced, the opportunity cost of producing additional coffee – as measured by the amount of nuts that must be sacrificed – also rises.

Why is the PPF for the multi-person economy bow-shaped? The answer lies in the fact that some resources are relatively well suited to picking nuts while others are relatively well suited to picking coffee. If the economy is initially producing only coffee and wants to begin producing some nuts, which workers will it reassign? Recall Susan and Tom, the two workers discussed in Example 2.5, in which Tom's comparative advantage was picking nuts and Susan's comparative advantage was picking coffee. We showed that it made sense to ask Susan to start producing coffee before asking Tom to do so. If both workers were currently picking coffee and you wanted to reassign one of them to pick nuts instead, whom would you send? Tom would be the clear choice, because his departure would cost the economy only half as much coffee as Susan's and would augment nut production by twice as much.

The principle is the same in any large multi-person economy, except that the range of opportunity cost differences across workers is even greater than in Example 2.5. As we keep reassigning workers from coffee production to nut production, sooner or later we must withdraw even coffee specialists like Susan from coffee production. Indeed, we must eventually reassign others whose opportunity cost of producing nuts is far higher than hers.

The shape of the PPF shown in Fig. 2.7 illustrates the general principle that when resources have different opportunity costs, we should always exploit the resource with the lowest opportunity cost first. We call this the *Low-Hanging-Fruit Principle*, in honour of the fruit picker's rule of picking the most accessible fruit first.

> **The Principle of Increasing Opportunity Cost** (also called 'The Low-Hanging-Fruit Principle'): in expanding the production of any good, first employ those resources with the lowest opportunity cost, and only afterwards turn to resources with higher opportunity costs.

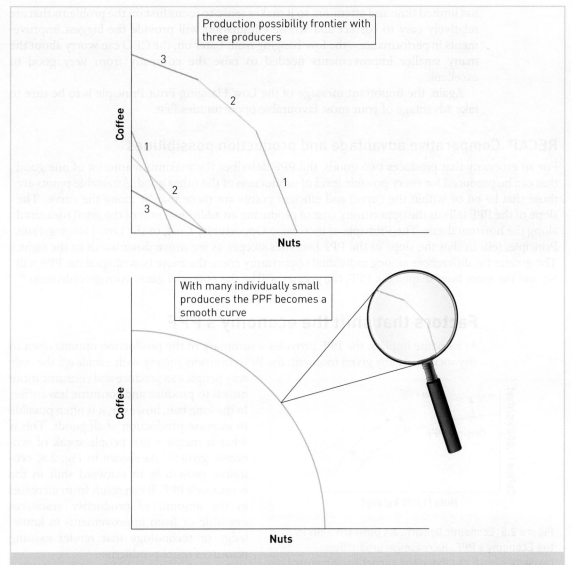

Figure 2.7 The PPF for a Multi-Person Economy. In the upper panel, a three-person economy; in the bottom panel a million-person economy. For an economy with millions of workers, the PPF typically has a gentle outward bow shape.

A note on the logic of the fruit picker's rule

Why should a fruit picker harvest the low-hanging fruit first? This rule makes sense for several reasons. For one, the low-hanging fruit is easier (and hence cheaper) to pick, and if he or she planned on picking only a limited amount of fruit to begin with, they would clearly come out ahead by avoiding the less accessible fruit on the higher branches. But even if they planned on picking all the fruit on the tree, they would do better to start with the lower branches first, because this would enable them to enjoy the revenue from the sale of the fruit sooner.

The fruit picker's job can be likened to the task confronting a new chief executive officer (CEO) who has been hired to reform an inefficient, ailing company. The CEO has limited time and attention, so it makes sense to focus first on the problems that are relatively easy to correct and whose elimination will provide the biggest improvements in performance – the low-hanging fruit. Later on, the CEO can worry about the many smaller improvements needed to raise the company from very good to excellent.

Again, the important message of the Low-Hanging-Fruit Principle is to be sure to take advantage of your most favourable opportunities first.

RECAP Comparative advantage and production possibilities

For an economy that produces two goods, the PPF describes the maximum amount of one good that can be produced for every possible level of production of the other good. Attainable points are those that lie on or within the curve, and efficient points are those that lie along the curve. The slope of the PPF tells us the opportunity cost of producing an additional unit of the good measured along the horizontal axis. The Principle of Increasing Opportunity Cost, or the Low-Hanging-Fruit Principle, tells us that the slope of the PPF becomes steeper as we move downwards to the right. The greater the differences among individual opportunity costs, the more bow-shaped the PPF will be, and the more bow-shaped the PPF, the greater will be the potential gains from specialisation.

Factors that shift the economy's PPF

As its name implies, the PPF provides a summary of the production options open to any society. At any given moment, the PPF confronts society with a *trade-off*: the only way people can produce and consume more nuts is to produce and consume less coffee. In the long run, however, it is often possible to increase production of all goods. This is what is meant when people speak of economic growth. As shown in Fig. 2.8, economic growth is an outward shift in the economy's PPF. It can result from increases in the amount of productive resources available or from improvements in knowledge or technology that render existing resources more productive.

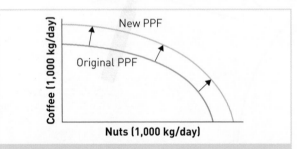

Figure 2.8 Economic Growth: An Outward Shift in the Economy's PPF. Increases in productive resources (such as labour and capital equipment) or improvements in knowledge and technology cause the PPF to shift outwards. They are the main factors that drive economic growth.

What causes the quantity of productive resources to grow in an economy? One factor is *investment* in new factories and equipment. When workers have more and better equipment to work with, their productivity increases, often dramatically. This is surely an important factor behind the differences in living standards between rich and poor countries. According to one study, for example, the value of capital investment per worker in the United States is about $30,000, while in Nepal the corresponding figure is less than $1,000.[2]

Such large differences in capital per worker do not occur all at once. They are a consequence of decades – even centuries – of differences in rates of savings and investment. Over time, even small differences in rates of investment can translate into extremely large differences in the amount of capital equipment available to each

2 Heston and Summers (1991).

worker. Differences of this sort are often *self-reinforcing*: not only do higher rates of saving and investment cause incomes to grow, but the resulting higher income levels also make it easier to devote additional resources to savings and investment. Over time, then, even small initial productivity advantages from specialisation can translate into very large income gaps.

Population growth also causes an economy's PPF curve to shift outwards and thus is often listed as one of the sources of economic growth. But because population growth also generates more mouths to feed, it cannot by itself raise a country's standard of living. Indeed it may even cause a decline in the standard of living if existing population densities have already begun to put pressure on available land, water and other scarce resources.

Perhaps the most important source of economic growth is improvements in *knowledge and technology*. As economists have long recognised, such improvements often lead to higher output through increased specialisation. Improvements in technology often occur spontaneously, but more frequently they are directly or indirectly the result of increases in education.

In Exercise 2.4 we discussed a two-person example in which individual differences in opportunity cost led to a threefold gain from specialisation. Real-world gains from specialisation often are far more spectacular than those in the example. One reason is that specialisation not only capitalises on pre-existing differences in individual skills but also deepens those skills through practice and experience. Moreover, it eliminates many of the switching and start-up costs people incur when they move back and forth among numerous tasks. These gains apply not only to people but also to the tools and equipment they use. Breaking a task down into simple steps, each of which can be performed by a different machine, greatly multiplies the productivity of individual workers.

Even in simple settings, these factors can combine to increase productivity hundreds- or even thousands-fold. Adam Smith, the Scottish moral philosopher who is remembered today as the founder of modern economics, was the first to recognise the magnitude of the gains made possible by the division and specialisation of labour. Consider, for instance, his description of work in an eighteenth-century Scottish pin factory:

> One man draws out the wire, another straightens it, a third cuts it, a fourth points it, a fifth grinds it at the top for receiving the head; to make the head requires two or three distinct operations ... I have seen a small manufactory of this kind where only ten men were employed ... [who] could, when they exerted themselves, make among them about twelve kgs of pins in a day. There are in a kg upwards of four thousand pins of middling size. Those ten persons, therefore, could make among them upwards of forty-eight thousand pins in a day. Each person, therefore, making a tenth part of forty-eight thousand pins, might be considered as making four thousand eight hundred pins in a day. But if they had all wrought separately and independently, and without any of them having been educated to this peculiar business, they certainly could not each of them have made twenty, perhaps not one pin in a day.[3]

The gains in productivity that result from specialisation are indeed often prodigious. They constitute the single most important explanation for why societies that don't rely heavily on specialisation and exchange are rapidly becoming relics.

---

3 This quotation is from Book 1 of Smith's *An Enquiry into the Nature and Causes of the Wealth of Nations*, usually referred to today as *The Wealth of Nations*, originally published in 1776 and frequently said to have launched the discipline of economics (Smith, 1776, book 1).

Why have some countries been slow to specialise?

You may be asking yourself, 'If specialisation is such a great thing, why don't people in poor countries just specialise?' If so, you are in good company. Adam Smith spent many years attempting to answer precisely the same question. In the end, his explanation was that *population density* is an important precondition for specialisation. Smith, ever the economic naturalist, observed that work tended to be far more specialised in the large cities of England in the eighteenth century than in the rural highlands of Scotland:

> In the lone houses and very small villages which are scattered about in so desert a country as the Highlands of Scotland, every farmer must be butcher, baker and brewer for his own family ... A country carpenter ... is not only a carpenter, but a joiner, a cabinet maker, and even a carver in wood, as well as a wheelwright, a ploughwright, a cart and wagon maker.[4]

In contrast, each of these same tasks was performed by a different specialist in the large English and Scottish cities of Smith's day. Scottish highlanders would also have specialised had they been able to, but the markets in which they participated were simply too small and fragmented. Of course, high population density by itself provides no guarantee that specialisation will result in rapid economic growth. But especially before the arrival of modern shipping and electronic communications technology, low population density was a definite obstacle to gains from specialisation.

Nepal remains one of the most remote and isolated countries on the planet. In the mid-1960s, its average population density was less than 30 people per km^2 (Thailand, which has developed much more rapidly than Nepal, had a density of some 140 per km^2 in 1960). Specialisation was further limited by Nepal's rugged terrain. Exchanging goods and services with residents of other villages was difficult, because the nearest village in most cases could be reached only after trekking for several hours, or even days, over treacherous Himalayan trails. More than any other factor, this extreme isolation accounts for Nepal's long-standing failure to benefit from widespread specialisation.

Population density is by no means the only important factor that influences the degree of specialisation. Specialisation may be severely impeded, for example, by *laws and customs* that limit people's freedom to transact freely with one another. The communist governments of North Korea and the former East Germany (GDR) restricted exchange severely, which helps explain why those countries achieved far less specialisation than South Korea and the former West Germany (FRG), whose governments were far more supportive of exchange.

Finally, specialisation (in Smith's example taking the form of the division of labour whereby the process of producing a pin is broken down into separate operations performed by different people) is limited by the *size of the market*. It is worth doing only if a significant quantity of output is to be produced. Hence the 'chicken and egg' problem in a country like Nepal: large-scale production, high productivity and high income depend on division of labour, but division of labour is worthwhile only to the extent that the level of demand for the final products produced by labour warrants it. Because there is little specialisation, Nepal is poor ... but because it is poor there is little incentive to specialise.

---

4 Smith op. cit., book 1, ch. 2.

Can we have too much specialisation?

Of course, the mere fact that specialisation boosts productivity does not mean that more specialisation is always better than less, for specialisation also entails *costs*. For example, most people appear to enjoy variety in the work they do, yet variety tends to be one of the first casualties as workplace tasks become ever more narrowly specialised. Indeed, one of Karl Marx's central themes was that the fragmentation of workplace tasks often exacts a heavy psychological toll on workers:

> All means for the development of production ... mutilate the labourer into a fragment of a man, degrade him to the level of an appendage of a machine, destroy every remnant of charm in his work and turn it into hated toil.[5]

Do the extra goods made possible by specialisation simply come at too high a price? We must certainly acknowledge at least the *potential* for specialisation to proceed too far. Yet specialisation need not entail rigidly segmented, mind-numbingly repetitive work. And it is important to recognise that *failure* to specialise entails costs as well. Those who don't specialise must accept low wages or work extremely long hours.

When all is said and done, we can expect to meet life's financial obligations in the shortest time – thereby freeing up more time to do whatever else we wish – if we concentrate at least a significant proportion of our efforts on those tasks for which we have a comparative advantage.

Comparative advantage and international trade

The same logic that leads the individuals in an economy to specialise and exchange goods with one another also leads nations to specialise and trade among themselves. As with individuals, each nation can benefit from exchange based on comparative advantage, even though one may be generally more productive than the other in absolute terms.

Economic naturalist 2.3 If trade between nations is so beneficial, why are free-trade agreements so controversial?

One of the most heated issues in the 1996 US presidential campaign was President Clinton's support for the North American Free Trade Agreement (NAFTA), a treaty to reduce trade barriers between the United States and its immediate neighbours, Canada and Mexico. The treaty attracted fierce opposition from third-party candidate Ross Perot, who insisted that it would mean unemployment for millions of American workers. It was also widely opposed by trades unions in the United States.

Right from its inception at the beginning of 1957, what is now the European Union (EU) has been legally and politically committed to free trade among its members, and to encouraging free trade on a global basis. However, when the record is examined in relation to trade with non-members, the position is quite different. In the late 1990s the level of protection of EU markets was effectively much higher than might have been suspected from the fact that the maximum official value for the EU's single tariff against imports from outside the Union was only 6 per cent. For foodstuffs, when other protective devices were computed for their tariff equivalent effect, the effective

---

5 Marx (1867, pp. 708–9).

rate of protection was over 32 per cent in 1996. For all goods the effect was 7.7 per cent.[6] (It has to be said that since then there has been a significant reduction in the level of EU protection.)

If free trade and exchange is so beneficial, why does anyone oppose it?

The answer is that while reducing barriers to international trade increases the total value of all goods and services produced in each nation, it does not guarantee that each individual citizen will do better. One specific American concern regarding NAFTA was that it would help Mexico to exploit a comparative advantage in the production of goods made by unskilled labour. Although US consumers would benefit from reduced prices for such goods, many Americans feared that unskilled workers in the United States would lose their jobs to workers in Mexico. In the end, NAFTA was enacted over the vociferous opposition of American labour unions. So far, however, studies have failed to detect significant job losses among unskilled US workers.

The European Union's principal protectionist programme has been aimed at shielding Union farmers from competition from food producers outside the Union. This was the reason for the highly expensive and inefficient Common Agricultural Policy (CAP) that paid EU farmers to produce food that people did not want to consume while excluding more efficient and lower-cost food producers from outside the Union, a policy that was a major barrier to raising Third World incomes. The costs and consequences of the policy have eventually led to its slowly being dismantled, a process that is far from being complete. It was in some measure the decline in the political importance of farming votes and the rise of organised consumer interests that made the old CAP unsustainable. The other factor was that some countries gained from it (France, Ireland and Italy, for example) while others (especially the United Kingdom) lost because they traditionally produced little of their own food requirements.

To explain the link between comparative advantage and trade we start with a country's PPF. In this simplified model (Fig. 2.9) we look at an economy that produces and consumes two goods, guns and butter.

If, somehow, while producing a combination of goods lying along the frontier the economy could consume a combination lying outside the frontier, economic welfare would be increased. Trade permits this. In Fig. 2.10 we suppose that the economy is producing and consuming the volumes of the two goods indicated by point *A*. The

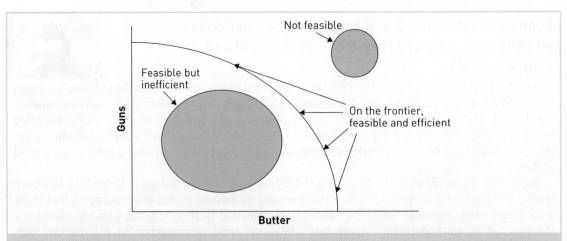

Figure 2.9 Efficient, Inefficient and Impossible Consumption Bundles. Production and consumption within the PPF is inefficient because more of both goods could be produced at no opportunity cost. Consumption of levels of both outside the frontier is not possible from the economy's own resources.

---

6 Jørgensen, Lüthje and Schröder (2001).

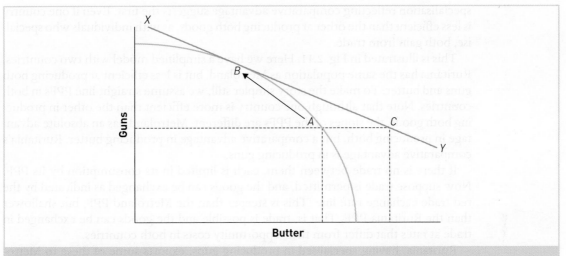

Figure 2.10 Trade and Consumption. When the prices at which a country can trade are different from the opportunity cost of the two goods (the slope of the PPF) the country can increase its total consumption by changing what it produces and exchanging goods at trade prices.

Efficiency

slope of the PPF at *A* tells us the cost (in guns) of more butter, and the cost of more butter in terms of guns. This is the rate at which the economy can exchange guns and butter from its own resources when it is producing at point *A*. Now suppose the economy is offered the chance to buy or sell the two goods on world markets. World prices are such that guns and butter can be exchanged or traded at prices indicated by the slope of the line *XY*. If the economy now increases production of guns and reduces production of butter (moves to point *B*) it can export guns and import butter to arrive at point *C*. At *C* it is consuming the same amount of guns as at *A* but considerably more butter. Hence economic welfare has increased. Even if consumption does not arrive at *C*, welfare has risen since the potential to consume goods has increased relative to the potential in the absence of trade, because the line *XY* lies on or outside the PPF other than at *B*, and outside it at *A*.

This happens when the opportunity cost of one good in terms of the other in the absence of trade differs from the rate at which the goods can be exchanged through trade. In the absence of trade the country's PPF is both its production and consumption possibility frontier. When trade is possible, trade prices determine its consumption possibilities given its production potential.

Scarcity

Note, however, that trade implies contraction in one industry (butter) and expansion of the other (guns). Obviously this has income implications for people in the two industries. Notice also that the overall gain arises if, and only if, there is a shift of resources and a change in the relative sizes of the two industries. This is why most economists reject the concern expressed by the anti-globalist lobby to the effect that opening up markets in the West to exports from poorer countries should not mean contraction of traditional sectors in the poorer countries. This concern is well meaning but wrong-headed. In order for trade to improve economic welfare, it is necessary that resources be shifted to a growing export sector. If the poor country is fully employed, but at a low income and productivity level, expanding export production means a contraction in the activity in the rest of the economy, and typically in traditional production.

If one country gains from being able to trade, do it and its trading partner both gain? Or does trade mean a gain by one at the expense of the other? The logic of specialisation reflecting comparative advantage suggests the first. Even if one country is less efficient than the other at producing both goods, as with individuals who specialise, both gain from trade.

This is illustrated in Fig. 2.11. Here we have a simplified model with two countries. Ruritania has the same population as Metroland, but is less efficient at producing both guns and butter. To make the story simpler still, we assume straight-line PPFs in both countries. Note that although one country is more efficient than the other in producing both goods, the slopes of the PPFs are different. Metroland has an absolute advantage in producing both, but a comparative advantage in producing butter. Ruritania's comparative advantage is in producing guns.

If there is no trade between them, each is limited in its consumption by its PPF. Now suppose trade is permitted, and the goods can be exchanged as indicated by the red trade exchange rate line. This is steeper than the Metroland PPF, but shallower than the Ruritania PPF. That is, trade is possible and the goods can be exchanged in trade at rates that differ from their opportunity costs in both countries.

Ruritania, having specialised in producing guns, exports some of these to Metroland (X on the vertical axis in the left-hand panel) and imports butter from Metroland (M on the horizontal axis). It receives more butter this way than if it had produced the butter by producing fewer guns. Total consumption is at *Cr*, outside Ruritania's PPF. Similarly, Metroland on this basis ends up consuming at *Cm*, also outside its PPF. Both countries have gained from trade.

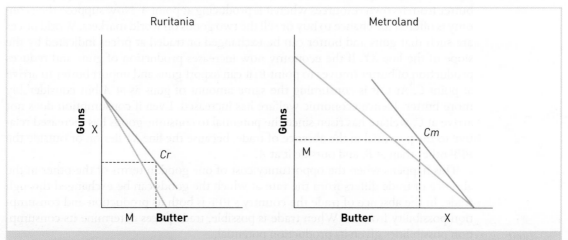

Figure 2.11 Specialisation and the Gain from Trade. When countries specialise according to comparative advantage and trade accordingly both can consume at levels in excess of what would be possible if there were no trade.

RECAP Comparative advantage and international trade

Nations, like individuals, can benefit from exchange, even though one trading partner may be more productive than the other in absolute terms. The greater the difference between domestic opportunity costs and world opportunity costs, the more a nation benefits from exchange with other nations. But expansion in exchange does not guarantee that each individual citizen will do better. In particular, unskilled workers in high-wage countries may be hurt in the short run by the reduction of barriers to trade with low-wage nations.

Summary

- One person has an *absolute* advantage over another in the production of a good if she can produce more of that good than the other person. One person has a *comparative* advantage over another in the production of a good if she is relatively more efficient than the other person at producing that good, meaning that her opportunity cost of producing it is lower than her counterpart's. Specialisation based on comparative advantage is the basis for economic exchange. When each person specialises in the task at which he or she is relatively more efficient, the economic pie is maximised, making possible the largest slice for everyone.

- At the *individual* level, comparative advantage may spring from differences in talent or ability, or from differences in education, training and experience. At the *national* level, sources of comparative advantage include these innate and learned differences, as well as differences in language, culture, institutions, climate, natural resources and a host of other factors.

- The *production possibilities frontier* (PPF), or *production possibilities curve* (PPC), is a simple device for summarising the possible combinations of output that a society can produce if it employs its resources efficiently. In a simple economy that produces only coffee and nuts, a graph of the PPF shows the maximum quantity of coffee production (vertical axis) possible at each level of nut production (horizontal axis). The slope of the PPF at any point represents the opportunity cost of nuts at that point, expressed in kg of coffee.

- All PPFs slope downwards because of the *Scarcity Principle*, which states that the only way a consumer can get more of one good is to settle for less of another. In economies whose workers have different opportunity costs of producing each good, the slope of the PPF becomes steeper as consumers move downwards along the curve. This change in slope illustrates the Principle of Increasing Opportunity Cost (or the Low-Hanging-Fruit Principle), which states that, in expanding the production of any good, a society should first employ those resources that are relatively efficient at producing that good, only afterwards turning to those that are less efficient.

- Factors that cause a country's PPF to shift outwards over time include *investment* in new factories and equipment, *population growth*, and improvements in *knowledge and technology*.

- The same logic that prompts individuals to specialise in their production and exchange goods with one another also leads nations to specialise and trade with one another. On both levels, each trading partner can benefit from an exchange, even though one may be more productive than the other, in absolute terms, for each good. For both individuals and nations, the benefits of exchange tend to be larger the larger are the differences between the trading partners' *opportunity costs*.

Review questions

1. Explain what 'having a comparative advantage' in producing a particular good or service means. What does 'having an absolute advantage' in producing a good or service mean?

2. How will a reduction in the number of hours worked each day affect an economy's PPF?

3. How will technological innovations that boost labour productivity affect an economy's PPF?

4. Why does saying that people are poor because they do not specialise make more sense than saying that people perform their own services because they are poor?

5. What factors have helped the United States to become the world's leading exporter of movies, books and popular music?

Problems

Problems marked with an asterisk (*) are more difficult.

1. Ted can wax 4 cars per day or wash 12 cars. Tom can wax 3 cars per day or wash 6. What is each man's opportunity cost of washing a car? Who has a comparative advantage in washing cars?

2. Ted can wax a car in 20 minutes or wash a car in 60 minutes. Tom can wax a car in 15 minutes or wash a car in 30 minutes. What is each man's opportunity cost of washing a car? Who has a comparative advantage in washing cars?

3. Toby can produce 5 litres of apple cider or 2.5 kg of feta cheese per hour. Kyle can produce 3 litres of apple cider or 1.5 kg of feta cheese per hour. Can Toby and Kyle benefit from specialisation and trade? Explain.

4. Nancy and Bill are auto mechanics. Nancy takes 4 hours to replace a clutch and 2 hours to replace a set of brakes. Bill takes 6 hours to replace a clutch and 2 hours to replace a set of brakes. State whether anyone has an absolute advantage at either task and, for each task, identify who has a comparative advantage.

5. Consider a society consisting only of Helen, who allocates her time between sewing dresses and baking bread. Each hour she devotes to sewing dresses yields 4 dresses, and each hour she devotes to baking bread yields 8 loaves of bread. If Helen works a total of 8 hours per day, graph her PPF.

6. Refer to Problem 5. Which of the points listed below is efficient? Which is attainable?

    a. 28 dresses per day, 16 loaves per day.

    b. 16 dresses per day, 32 loaves per day.

    c. 18 dresses per day, 24 loaves per day.

7. Suppose that in Problem 5 a sewing machine is introduced that enables Helen to sew 8 dresses per hour rather than only 4. Show how this development shifts her PPF.

8. Refer to Problem 7 to explain what is meant by the following statement: 'An increase in productivity with respect to any one good increases our options for producing and consuming all other goods.'

9. Susan can pick 4 kg of coffee in an hour or 2 kg of nuts. Tom can pick 2 kg of coffee in an hour or 4 kg of nuts. Each works 6 hours per day.

    a. What is the maximum number of kg of coffee the two can pick in a day?

    b. What is the maximum number of kg of nuts the two can pick in a day?

    c. If Susan and Tom were picking the maximum number of kg of coffee when they decided that they would like to begin picking 4 kg of nuts per day, who would pick the nuts, and how many kg of coffee would they still be able to pick?

    d. Now suppose that Susan and Tom were picking the maximum number of kg of nuts when they decided that they would like to begin picking 8 kg of coffee per day. Who would pick the coffee, and how many kg of nuts would they still be able to pick?

e. Would it be possible for Susan and Tom to pick a total of 26 kg of nuts and 20 kg of coffee each day? If so, how much of each good should each person pick?

10.* Refer to the two-person economy described in Problem 9.

a. Is the point (30 kg of coffee per day, 12 kg of nuts per day) an attainable point? Is it an efficient point? What about the point (24 kg of coffee per day, 24 kg of nuts per day)?

b. On a graph with kg of coffee per day on the vertical axis and kg of nuts per day on the horizontal axis, show all the points you identified in Problem 9, parts (a)–(e), and in Problem 10(a). Connect these points with straight lines. Is the result the PPF for an economy consisting of Susan and Tom?

c. Suppose that Susan and Tom could buy or sell coffee and nuts in the world market at a price of €2 per kg for coffee and €2 per kg for nuts. If each person specialised completely in the good for which he or she had a comparative advantage, how much could they earn by selling all their produce?

d. At the prices just described, what is the maximum amount of coffee Susan and Tom could buy in the world market? The maximum amount of nuts? Would it be possible for them to consume 40 kg of nuts and 8 kg of coffee each day?

e. In light of their ability to buy and sell in world markets at the stated prices, show on the same graph all combinations of the two goods it would be possible for them to consume.

References

Heston, A. and R. Summers (1991) 'The Penn World Table (Mark 5): An Expanded Set of International Comparisons, 1950–1988', *Quarterly Journal of Economics*, May, pp. 327–68.

Jørgensen, J.G., T. Lüthje and P.J.H. Schröder (2001) 'Trade: The Work-Horse of Integration', Chapter 6 in J.D. Hansen (ed.), *European Integration – An Economic Perspective* (Oxford: Oxford University Press).

Marx, K. (1867) *Das Kapital* (New York: Modern Library).

Smith, A. (1776) *An Enquiry into the Nature and Causes of the Wealth of Nations* (New York: Everyman's Library).

Online LearningCentre

To help you grasp the key concepts of this chapter check out the extra resources posted on the Online Learning Centre. There are chapter summaries, self-test questions, an interactive graphing tool, weblinks and a glossary, all for free!

Visit the Online Learning Centre at: www.mcgraw-hill.co.uk/textbooks/mcdowell for information on accessing all of these resources.

3

Markets, Supply, Demand and Elasticity

If we added up the stocks of food held in supermarkets, convenience stores and restaurants in any large city we would realise that, at any point in time, what is available would meet likely demand for a couple of days at the most. Little or no food is actually produced within the city. But, by and large, city populations (in the developed world, at least) eat well. This requires that, in the case of a large city, thousands of tonnes of food must be delivered to an enormous number of locations in the city every day.

Few who sit down to eat in a restaurant, or buy a sandwich in a sandwich bar, spend much time thinking about the quite extraordinary coordination of people and resources needed to make sure that what they are about to eat is actually available. If they did, it ought to strike them as truly remarkable that somehow it all seems to happen without being centrally controlled. No central agency is actually making and executing decisions that result in our being able to eat what we eat when we eat it. Yet someone has to decide how much of each type of food gets delivered to *each* of the many restaurants, hospitals, supermarkets and grocery stores in a large city, how and when it is delivered, and how delivery systems are made available.

It is not simply a question of transport logistics, delivering the various commodities as and when demanded. There is also the question of how the different quantities of the enormous number of products consumed come to be produced in the first place. The reality is that in each case, and in respect of each delivery, and of each kilogram or litre being produced, some individual somewhere is making a decision that determines what is produced and where it goes. In the end it is the individual decisions, made by people without any detailed knowledge about who needs what, where and when, that somehow produce the end result whereby what we wish to buy of quantity and variety is available when and where we look for it.

Thousands of individuals must decide what role, if any, they will play in this collective effort. Some people – just the right number – must choose to drive food-delivery trucks rather than trucks that deliver concrete. Others must become the mechanics who fix these trucks rather than carpenters who build houses. Others must become farmers rather than architects or bricklayers. Still others must become chefs in upmarket restaurants, or flip burgers at McDonald's, instead of becoming plumbers or electricians.

Yet despite the almost incomprehensible number and complexity of the tasks involved, somehow the supplying of the city manages to get done remarkably smoothly. Yes, from time to time a supermarket will run out of stuffed olives, or you may sometimes be told that someone else has just ordered the last serving of roast duck, but if episodes like these stick in your memory, it is only because they are so rare. For the most part, the city's food delivery system functions so smoothly that it attracts virtually no notice.

But if we look at some other aspects of what we need to live, things are not always as smoothly organised. Think about finding an apartment to rent. In many European and North American cities there are perennial problems affecting the rental housing market. People discover that there are chronic problems in finding accommodation. There is a shortage of rented accommodation, and in some cases this shortage has been increasing rather than declining. We may be able to buy the kind of food we want when and where we want it, but we may find it very difficult to find accommodation. Why?

It is an interesting problem. Housing services and food are both basic requirements of life, and both are needed in any large city. But in the case of the food industry, goods and services are available in wide variety, and people (at least those with adequate income) are generally satisfied with what they receive and the choices available to them. In contrast, in the rental housing industry, chronic shortages and chronic dissatisfaction are rife among both buyers and sellers. Why this difference?

Or think about another basic service: healthcare. The market for healthcare services is one in which, in some European countries, things do not appear to work as smoothly as in the case of food supplies in major conurbations. This is far from uniform in terms of the length of waiting times (a measure of ability to 'consume' the service when demanded). Look at Table 3.1.[1] During the 1990s there were several attempts to reorganise the delivery of UK health services, because the tax-financed National Health Service (NHS) was not seen as delivering care as required when required and at reasonable cost.

Adequate availability of and access to healthcare is seen as a basic requirement in modern societies, but despite the steady growth in spending per head on healthcare in

	Hip replacement	Knee replacement
Australia	163	201
Denmark	112	112
Finland	206	274
Norway	133	160
Netherlands	96	85
Spain	123	148
England	244	281

Table 3.1 **Mean In-patient Waiting Times, days, 2000, for two elective surgery procedures**
Source: Siciliani and Hurst (2003/7)

---

1 The authors of this study make clear that there are serious problems in defining waiting periods that have to be dealt with in making cross-country comparisons. These figures should be treated as indicating relative performance rather than being taken as highly reliable point estimates.

countries in Western Europe and America, in some, but not all, countries this spending does not call forth the level and type of care that people regard as desirable, while in others it does. Complaints about the availability and quality of healthcare seem to be much less common in France or Germany than they are in Britain or Ireland. Why?

Going back to the market for rented accommodation, the problem is that it is highly regulated, generally in favour of 'tenants' rights' and building standards. By and large these regulations result in tenants having to pay less than the market rent, and/or have tenancy rights that are onerous on the landlords. Tighter building regulations impose costs on providers of accommodation. These have the effect of restricting supply when demand rises, so shortages appear. In contrast, by and large, producers and sellers of food are not restricted as to the prices they offer, and face a less restrictive regulatory regime in terms of customer rights and physical planning of retail outlets. The allocation of food is essentially in the hands of market forces – the forces of supply and demand.

The allocation mechanism used in the case of healthcare in systems like Britain's NHS is based on centralised decision-making to a large degree, with weak incentives facing suppliers to expand services when demand increases. Rationing is central to resource allocation in tax-financed healthcare systems.

Although intuition might suggest otherwise, both theory and experience suggest that the seemingly chaotic and unplanned outcomes of market forces can in most cases do a better job of allocating economic resources than can (for example) a government agency, even if the agency has the best of intentions.

In this chapter we shall explore how markets allocate food, housing and other goods and services, usually with remarkable efficiency despite the complexity of the tasks. To be sure, markets are by no means perfect, and our stress on their virtues is to some extent an attempt to counteract what most economists view as an under-appreciation by the general public of their remarkable strengths. But in the course of our discussion we shall see why markets function so smoothly most of the time, and why bureaucratic rules and regulations rarely work as well in solving complex economic problems.

To convey an understanding of how markets work is a major goal of this book, and in this chapter we provide only a brief introduction and overview. As the course proceeds we shall discuss the economic role of markets in considerably more detail, paying attention to some of the problems of markets as well as their strengths.

What, how and for whom? Central planning versus the market

No society – regardless of how it is organised – can escape the need to answer certain basic economic questions. For example, how much of our limited time and other resources should we devote to building housing, how much to the production of food, and how much to providing other goods and services? What techniques should we use to produce each good? Who should be assigned to each specific task? And how should the resulting goods and services be distributed among people?

In the many different societies for which records are available, issues such as these have been decided in essentially one of two ways. One approach is for all relevant economic decisions to be made *centrally*, by an individual or small number of individuals on behalf of a larger group. For example, in many agrarian societies throughout history, families or other small groups consumed only those goods and services that they produced for themselves, and a single clan or family leader made most important production and distribution decisions. On an immensely larger scale, the economic organisation of the former Soviet Union (and other communist countries) was also largely centralised. A centrally controlled bureaucratic structure established production targets for the country's farms and factories, based on an overall plan for achieving targets (including detailed instructions concerning who was to produce what), and set up guidelines for the distribution and use of the goods and services produced.

Neither form of centralised economic organisation is much in evidence today. When implemented on a small scale, as in a self-sufficient family enterprise, centralised decision-making is certainly feasible. For the reasons discussed in Chapter 1, however, the jack-of-all-trades approach was doomed once it became clear how dramatically people could improve their living standards by specialisation – that is, by having each individual focus his or her efforts on a relatively narrow range of tasks. After the collapse of the Soviet Union between 1989 and 1991, and the overthrow of the Soviet-backed regimes in the East European countries that had been Soviet satellites since the late 1940s, there remained in 2008 only three countries worldwide that formally operated or claimed to operate communist societies with **central planning**:

central planning the allocation of economic resources is determined by a political and administrative mechanism that gathers information as to technology, resource availability and end demands for goods and services

Cuba, North Korea and China. The first two of these appear to be on their last legs, economically speaking, and China has by now largely abandoned any attempt to control production and distribution decisions from the centre. The major remaining examples of centralised allocation and control now reside in the bureaucratic agencies that administer programmes such as New York City's rent controls or Britain's NHS – programmes that are themselves becoming increasingly rare.

There are no *pure* free-market economies. Modern industrial countries are characterised by a mixture of structures that deliver goods and services to end users. Where markets do the job, they are commonly subject to various forms of regulation. In the case of some services, collective provision via state structures is common. Public transport is an obvious example. Hence, modern economies are more properly described as *mixed economies*, meaning that goods and services are allocated by a combination of free markets, regulation and other forms of collective control. Still, it makes sense to refer to such systems as free-market economies, or at least market economies, because people are for the most part free to start businesses, to shut them down or to sell them. And, within broad limits, the distribution of goods and services is determined by individual preferences backed by individual purchasing power.

In country after country, markets have replaced centralised control for the simple reason that they tend to assign production tasks and consumption benefits much more effectively. This has not been without controversy. For example, the UK experiment in privatising rail transport has been the subject of considerable criticism, and indeed has effectively been partially reversed. The fact that the process of extending the role of the market, including privatisation, has been far from problem-free has resulted in some cynicism about economists and their ability to agree on policy measures. Nor has the operation of markets been without serious problems in all cases. The US 'sub-prime lending crisis' of 2007–08, which threw world financial markets into serious difficulties, was an example of a market that failed to operate efficiently because the true risk level involved in this lending was not clear to those who ended up financing it.

Despite these reservations, there is broad agreement among economists about markets, with the great majority accepting the superior performance of markets as means for *allocating* society's scarce resources.[2] In most cases, the experience of privatisation and reliance on markets has shown this belief to be correct. An obvious case in point is the passenger airline business, which from the 1930s to the 1980s was highly regulated, with severe restrictions on entry and competition between operators, and (in Europe and most of the world outside the USA) was largely in the hands of state-owned operators with monopoly rights. No one seriously disputes the proposition that the privatisation and deregulation of the air traffic sector across Europe, long called for by transport economists, has revolutionised the choices and costs facing people who want to fly. Ryanair is the standing proof of markets working where state provision and restricted competition have failed.

To see why this is the case, we must explore how goods and services are allocated in private markets, and why intervention to restrict the operations of markets often does not produce the desired results.

Buyers and sellers in markets

Beginning with some simple concepts and definitions, we shall explore how the interactions among buyers and sellers in markets determine the prices and quantities of the various goods and services traded in those markets. We begin by defining a **market**: the market for any good consists of all the buyers and sellers of that good. So, for example, the market for pizza on a given day in a given place is just the set of people (or other economic agents/actors, such as firms) potentially able to buy or sell pizza at that time and location.

market the market for any good consists of all buyers or sellers of that good

In the market for pizza, sellers comprise the individuals and companies that sell – or might, under the right circumstances, sell – pizza. Similarly, buyers in this market include all individuals who buy – or might buy – pizza. What would someone have to pay to buy a slice of pizza? Not very much, is the answer: depending on location and quality you would expect to be able to buy a slice for less than €3 or its equivalent in most countries in Europe.

Where does the market price of pizza come from? More generally, we may ask: 'Why are some goods cheap and others expensive?' Aristotle had no idea. Nor did Plato, nor Copernicus, nor Newton. On reflection, it is astonishing that, for almost the entire span of human history, not even the most intelligent and creative minds on Earth had any real inkling of how to answer that seemingly simple question. Even Adam Smith suffered confusion on this issue.

Smith and other early economists (including Karl Marx) thought that the market price of a good was determined by its *cost of production*. But although costs do affect prices, they cannot explain why one of Pablo Picasso's paintings sells for so much more than one of Jackson Pollock's, or why a Juan Gris sells for more than a Francis Bacon.

Stanley Jevons and other nineteenth-century economists tried to explain price by focusing on the value people derived from consuming different goods and services. It certainly seems plausible that people will pay a lot for a good they value highly. Yet willingness to pay cannot be the whole story, either. Deprive a person in the desert of water, for example, and he will be dead in a matter of hours, and yet water sells for

---

2 Substantial differences remain, of course, as to the distributional consequences of using markets to allocate resources, and these result in some economists in some circumstances opting for the use of regulated or collective provision of goods and services rather than relying on markets. In addition, as will become clear in Chapter 11, below, there is a significant class of economic activities where the market does not operate 'efficiently' as an allocation mechanism.

just a few cents per litre. By contrast, human beings can get along perfectly well without gold, and yet early in 2008 gold fetched €600 an ounce.

Cost of production? Value to the user? Which is it? The answer, which seems obvious to today's economists, is that both matter. Writing in the late nineteenth century, the British economist Alfred Marshall was among the first to show clearly how *costs* and *value* interact to determine both the prevailing market price for a good, and the amount of it that is bought and sold. Our task in the pages ahead will be to explore Marshall's insights and gain some practice in applying them. As a first step, we introduce the two main components of Marshall's groundbreaking analysis: the *demand curve* and the *supply curve*.

The demand curve

demand curve a schedule or graph showing the quantity of a good that buyers wish to buy at each price

In the market for pizza, the **demand curve** for pizza is a simple schedule or graph that tells us how many slices people would be willing to buy at different prices. By convention, economists usually put price on the vertical axis of the demand curve and quantity on the horizontal axis.

A fundamental property of the demand curve is that it is *downward-sloping* with respect to price. For example, the demand curve for pizza tells us that, as the price of pizza falls, buyers will buy more slices. Thus the daily demand curve for pizza in Manchester or Milan on a given day might look like the curve seen in Fig. 3.1. (Although economists usually refer to demand and supply 'curves', we often draw them as straight lines in examples.)

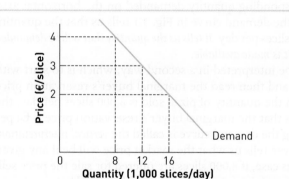

Figure 3.1 The Daily Demand Curve for Pizza. The demand curve for any good is a downward-sloping function of its price.

The demand curve in Fig. 3.1 tells us that when the price of pizza is low – say, €2 per slice – buyers will want to buy 16,000 slices per day, whereas they will want to buy only 12,000 slices at a price of €3, and only 8,000 at a price of €4. The demand curve for pizza – as for any other good – slopes downwards for many reasons. Some of these reasons have to do with the individual consumer's reactions to price changes. Thus, as pizza becomes more expensive, a consumer may switch to chicken sandwiches, hamburgers or other foods that substitute for pizza. This is called the **substitution effect** of a price change. In addition, a price increase reduces the quantity demanded because it reduces a consumer's purchasing power. It affects the consumer's overall ability to consume. For example, if you have to commute by car to work, and fuel prices rise, you are in a sense poorer. Higher commuting costs reduce what is left from your income to spend on other things. Being poorer, you are likely to spend less on (among other things) fuel for weekend leisure use of your car. This is called the **income effect** of a price change.

substitution effect the change in the quantity demanded of a good that results because buyers switch to substitutes when the price of the good changes

income effect the change in the quantity demanded of a good that results because of a change in real income of purchasers arising from the price change

Another reason that the demand curve slopes downwards is that consumers differ in terms of how much they are willing to pay for

> **buyer's reservation price** the largest money amount the buyer would be willing to pay for a unit of a good

the good. The Cost–Benefit Principle (see Chapter 1) tells us that a given person will buy the good if the expected benefit to be received from it exceeds its cost. The benefit is the **buyer's reservation price**, the highest money amount he (or she) would be willing to pay for the good. The cost of the good is the actual amount that the buyer actually must pay for it, which is the market price of the good. In most markets, different buyers have different reservation prices. Thus if a good is sold at a high price, it will satisfy the cost–benefit test for fewer buyers than when it sells for a lower price.

To put this same point another way, the fact that the demand curve for a good is downward-sloping reflects the fact that the reservation price of the marginal buyer declines as the quantity of the good bought increases. Here the marginal buyer is the person who purchases the last unit of the good that is sold. If buyers are currently purchasing 12,000 slices of pizza a day in Fig. 3.1, for example, the reservation price for the buyer of the 12,000th slice must be €3. (If someone had been willing to pay more than that, the quantity demanded at a price of €3 would have been more than 12,000 to begin with.) By similar reasoning, when the quantity sold is 16,000 slices per day, the marginal buyer's reservation price must be only €3.

We defined the demand curve for any good as a schedule telling how much of it consumers wish to purchase at various prices. This is called the *horizontal interpretation* of the demand curve. Using the horizontal interpretation, we start with price on the vertical axis and read the corresponding quantity demanded on the horizontal axis. Thus, at a price of €4 per slice, the demand curve in Fig. 3.1 tells us that the quantity of pizza demanded will be 8,000 slices per day. *It tells us the quantity that will be demanded as a function of the price at which it is made available.*

The demand curve can also be interpreted in a second way, which is to start with quantity on the horizontal axis and then read the marginal buyer's reservation price on the vertical axis. Thus, when the quantity of pizza sold is 8,000 slices per day, the demand curve in Fig. 3.1 tells us that the marginal buyer's reservation price is €4 per slice. This second way of reading the demand curve is called the *vertical interpretation*. This means that the demand curve tells us what the market price will be if any given amount is made available (in this case, if 8,000 slices are offered for sale the price sellers will receive is €4). *It tells us the market price as a function of the available amount.*

Maths Box 3.1 A technical note: demand curves and inverse demand curves

The demand curve tells us quantity demanded by consumers as a function of the price at which it is offered for sale. Graphically, we can also use it to find the market clearing price for a given amount being offered for sale, as stated above. However, if we actually write down the expression for the demand curve, $Q = f(P)$, in order to quantify the relationship it will, for example, be of the form

$$Q = 200 - 10P$$

If we want to quantify the impact of quantity on price paid we need to use the inverse of this, $P = g(Q)$, and the inverse demand curve in this example would be

$$P = 20 - 0.1Q$$

There are times when the inverse demand curve is used in economics, but for the purposes of this chapter, and for calculations of price elasticity of demand below, we will confine ourselves to using the demand curve, not the inverse demand curve.

Exercise 3.1   In Fig. 3.1, what is the marginal buyer's reservation price when the quantity of pizza sold is 10,000 slices per day? For the same demand curve, what will be the quantity of pizza demanded at a price of €3.50 per slice?

The supply curve

> **supply curve** a curve or schedule showing the quantity of a good that sellers wish to sell at each price

In the market for pizza, the **supply curve** is a simple schedule or graph that tells us, for each possible price, the total number of slices that all pizza vendors would be willing to sell at that price. What does the supply curve of pizza look like? The answer to this question is based on the logical assumption that suppliers should be willing to sell additional slices as long as the price they receive is sufficient to cover their opportunity costs of supplying them. Thus, if what you could earn by selling a slice of pizza is insufficient to compensate you for what you could have earned if you had spent your time and invested your money in some other way, you will not sell that slice. Otherwise, you will.

Sellers are expected to differ with respect to their opportunity costs of supplying pizza. For those with limited education and work experience, the opportunity cost of selling pizza is relatively low (because such individuals typically do not have a lot of high-paying alternatives). For others the opportunity cost of selling pizza is of moderate value, and for still others – like rock stars and professional athletes – it is prohibitively high. In part because of these differences in opportunity cost among people, the daily supply curve of pizza will be *upward-sloping* with respect to price. As an illustration see Fig. 3.2, which shows a hypothetical supply curve on a given day.

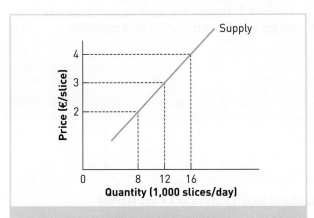

Figure 3.2 The Daily Supply Curve of Pizza.
At higher prices, sellers generally offer more units for sale.

The fact that the supply curve slopes upwards may be seen as a consequence of the *Low-Hanging-Fruit Principle*, discussed in Chapter 1. This principle tells us that as we expand the production of pizza, we turn first to those whose opportunity costs of producing pizza are lowest, and only then to others with higher opportunity costs. It also reflects the fact that if a given producer faces increasing opportunity costs for producing more of a product, it will be necessary to pay more per unit to get more produced.

Like the demand curve, the supply curve can be interpreted either horizontally or vertically. Under the *horizontal interpretation*, we begin with a price, then go over to the supply curve to read the quantity that sellers wish to sell at that price on the horizontal axis. For instance, at a price of €2 per slice, sellers in Fig. 3.2 wish to sell 8,000 slices per day. *It tells us the quantity that producers will supply as a function of the price they expect to receive.*

Under the *vertical interpretation*, we begin with a quantity, then go up to the supply curve to read the corresponding marginal cost on the vertical axis. Thus, if sellers in Fig. 3.2 are currently supplying 12,000 slices per day, the opportunity cost of the marginal seller is €3 per slice. In other words, the supply curve tells us that the marginal cost of producing the 12,000th slice of pizza is €3. (If someone could produce a 12,001st slice for less than €3, (s)he would have an incentive to supply it, so the quantity of pizza supplied at €3 per slice would not have been 12,000 slices per day to begin with.) By similar reasoning, when the quantity of pizza supplied is 16,000 slices per day, the marginal cost of producing another slice must be €4. The **seller's reservation price** for selling an additional unit of a good is the *marginal cost* of producing that good. It is the smallest money amount at which the seller would not be financially worse off by selling an additional unit. Under the vertical interpretation the supply curve tells us the sellers' reservation price for any given quantity. *It tells us the amount that will have to be paid to deliver any quantity as a function of quantity.*

> **seller's reservation price** the smallest money amount for which a seller would be willing to sell an additional unit, generally equal to marginal cost

Exercise 3.2   In Fig. 3.2, what is the marginal cost of a slice of pizza when the quantity of pizza sold is 10,000 slices per day? For the same supply curve, what will be the quantity of pizza supplied at a price of €3.50 per slice?

Example 3.1 Samples of points on the demand and supply curves of a pizza market are provided in Table 3.2. Graph the demand and supply curves for this market, and find its equilibrium price and quantity.

Demand for pizza Price (€/slice)	Supply of pizza Quantity demanded (1,000 slices/day)	Price (€/slice)	Quantity supplied (1,000 slices/day)
1	8	1	2
2	6	2	4
3	4	3	6
4	2	4	8

Table 3.2 **Points along the Demand and Supply Curves of a Pizza Market**

The points in Table 3.2 are plotted in Fig. 3.2 and then joined to indicate the supply and demand curves for this market. These curves intersect to yield an *equilibrium price* of €3.50 per slice and an *equilibrium quantity* of 5,000 slices per day. This means a price at which the amount demanded equals the amount being supplied (see below).

RECAP Demand and supply curves

The *market* for a good consists of the actual and potential buyers and sellers of that good. For any given price, the *demand curve* shows the quantity that demanders would be willing to buy, and the *supply curve* shows the quantity that suppliers of the good would be willing to sell. Suppliers are willing to sell more at higher prices (supply curves slope upwards) and demanders are willing to buy less at higher prices (demand curves slope downwards).

Market equilibrium

> **equilibrium** a system is in equilibrium when there is no tendency for it to change

The concept of **equilibrium** is employed in both the physical and social sciences, and it is of central importance in economic analysis. In general, a system is in equilibrium when all forces at work

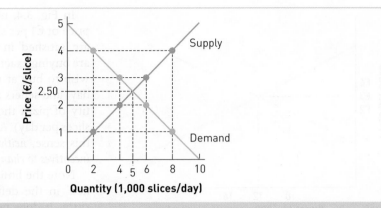

Figure 3.3 Graphing Supply and Demand, and Finding the Equilibrium Price and Quantity. To graph the demand and supply curve, plot the relevant points given in Table 3.2 and then join them with a line. The equilibrium price and quantity occur at the intersection of these curves. At higher prices, sellers generally offer more units for sale.

within the system are cancelled by others, resulting in a *stable, balanced* or *unchanging* situation. In physics, for example, a ball hanging from a spring is said to be in equilibrium when the spring has stretched sufficiently that the upward force it exerts on the ball is exactly counterbalanced by the downward force of gravity. The ball does not move. *Its position does not change.* Equilibrium in this sense is a *static* concept. Now consider a falling object. It accelerates and then its speed becomes a constant. This happens when the force of gravity is just offset by the increase in the resistance as it falls through the air. It reaches its terminal velocity. *Its position in space changes at a constant rate.* This is a *dynamic equilibrium.* In economics, a market for a good or service is said to be in equilibrium when no participant in the market has any reason to alter his or her behaviour, so that there is no tendency for production or price in that market to change. This is a *static equilibrium*. If we think about *inflation* – the phenomenon of generally increasing prices for all goods and services – we will realise that the average rate at which prices rise over time is variable. Inflation measures the average rate of increase of prices. The causes of inflation are considered in macroeconomics. When these are such that inflation is constant (the average of prices is rising at a constant rate) we have a *dynamic equilibrium* in prices.

If we want to determine the final position of a ball hanging from a spring, we need to find the point at which the forces of gravity and spring tension are balanced and the system is in equilibrium. Similarly, if we want to find the price at which a good will sell (which we will call the **equilibrium price**) and the quantity of it that will be sold (the **equilibrium quantity**), we need to find the equilibrium in the market for that good. The basic tools for finding the equilibrium in a market for a good are the supply and demand curves for that good. For reasons that we shall explain, the equilibrium price and equilibrium quantity of a good are the price and quantity at which the supply and demand curves for the good intersect. For the hypothetical supply and demand curves shown earlier for the pizza market, the equilibrium price will therefore be €3 per slice and the equilibrium quantity of pizza sold will be 12,000 slices per day, as shown in Fig. 3.4.

equilibrium price and **equilibrium quantity** the values of price and quantity for which quantity supplied and quantity demanded are equal

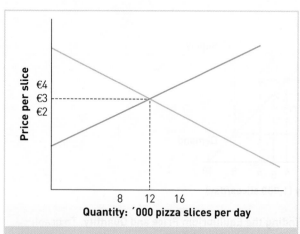

Figure 3.4 The Equilibrium Price and Quantity of Pizza. The equilibrium quantity and price of a product are the values that correspond to the intersection of the supply and demand curves for that product. See Example 3.1, above.

market equilibrium occurs in a market when all buyers and sellers are satisfied with their respective quantities at the market price

In Fig. 3.4, note that at the equilibrium price of €3 per slice, both sellers and buyers are 'satisfied' in the following sense: buyers are buying exactly the quantity of pizza they wish to buy at that price (12,000 slices per day) and sellers are selling exactly the quantity of pizza they wish to sell (also 12,000 slices per day). And since they are satisfied in this sense, *neither buyers nor sellers face any incentives to change their behaviour.*

Note the limited sense of the term 'satisfied' in the definition of **market equilibrium.** It does not mean that sellers would not be pleased to receive a price higher than the equilibrium price. Rather, it means only that they are able to sell all they wish to sell at that price. Similarly, to say that buyers are 'satisfied' at the equilibrium price doesn't mean that they would not be happy to pay less than the equilibrium price. Rather, it means only that they are able to buy exactly as many units of the good as they wish to at the equilibrium price.

Note also that if the price of pizza in our market were anything other than €3 per slice, either buyers or sellers would be frustrated. Suppose, for example, that the price of pizza were €4 per slice, as in Fig. 3.5.

At that price, buyers wish to buy only 8,000 slices per day, but sellers wish to sell 16,000. And since no one can force someone to buy a slice of pizza against their wishes, this means that buyers will buy only the 8,000 slices they wish to buy. So when the

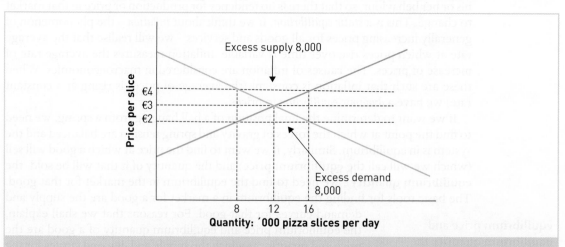

Figure 3.5 Excess Supply and Excess Demand. When price exceeds the equilibrium price, there is excess supply, or surplus, the difference between quantity supplied and quantity demanded. When the price is less than the equilibrium price there is excess demand, or a shortage, the difference between quantity demanded and quantity supplied.

excess supply the amount by which quantity supplied exceeds quantity demanded when the price of a good exceeds the equilibrium price

excess demand the amount by which quantity demanded exceeds quantity supplied when the price of a good lies below the equilibrium price

Equilibrium

price exceeds the equilibrium price, it is sellers who end up being frustrated. At a price of €4, they are left with an **excess supply** of 8,000 slices per day.

Conversely, suppose that the price of pizza were less than the equilibrium price – say, €2 per slice. As shown in Fig. 3.5, buyers want to buy 16,000 slices per day at that price, whereas sellers want to sell only 8,000. And since sellers cannot be forced to sell pizza against their wishes, this time it is the buyers who end up being frustrated. At a price of €2 per slice in this example, they experience an **excess demand** of 8,000 slices per day.

An extraordinary feature of private markets for goods and services is their automatic tendency to gravitate towards their respective equilibrium prices and quantities. The mechanisms by which this happens are implicit in our definitions of excess supply and excess demand. Suppose, for example, that the price of pizza in our hypothetical market was €4 per slice, leading to excess supply, as shown in Fig. 3.5. Because sellers are frustrated in the sense of wanting to sell more pizza than buyers wish to buy, sellers have an incentive to take whatever steps they can to increase their sales. The simplest strategy available to them is to cut their price slightly. Thus, if one seller reduced his price from €4 to, say, €3.95 per slice, he would attract many of the buyers who had been paying €4 per slice for pizza supplied by other sellers. Those sellers, in order to recover their lost business, would then have an incentive to match the price cut. But notice that if all sellers lowered their prices to €3.95 per slice, there would still be considerable excess supply. So sellers would face continuing incentives to cut their prices. This pressure to cut prices will not go away until price falls all the way to €3 per slice.

If price starts out less than the equilibrium price – say, €2 per slice – it is buyers who are frustrated. Someone unable to buy as much pizza as desired at a price of €2 per slice has an incentive to offer a higher price, hoping to obtain pizza that would otherwise have been sold to other buyers.[3] And sellers, for their part, will be only too happy to post higher prices as long as queues of frustrated buyers remain.

 The upshot is that price has a tendency to gravitate to its equilibrium level under conditions of either excess supply or excess demand. And when price reaches its equilibrium level, both buyers and sellers are 'satisfied' in the technical sense of being able to buy or sell precisely the amounts of their choosing.

We emphasise that market equilibrium does not necessarily produce an ideal outcome for all market participants. Thus, in Example 3.1 above, market participants are satisfied with the amount of pizza they buy and sell at a price of €3.50 per slice, but for a poor buyer this may signify little more than he can afford. This means that he can't buy additional pizza without sacrificing other more highly valued purchases.

Indeed, buyers with extremely low incomes often have difficulty purchasing even basic goods and services, which has prompted governments in almost every society to attempt to ease the burdens of the poor. Yet the laws of supply and demand cannot simply be repealed by an act of the legislature. In the next section we will see that when legislators attempt to prevent markets from reaching their equilibrium prices and quantities, they often do more harm than good.

---

3 Unrealistic? Maybe in a pizza parlour where demand exceeds supply, but think about tickets for a rock concert. In any case, the seller has an incentive to raise the price.

Economic naturalist 3.1 Why did South Africa experience interruptions in electricity supply at the end of 2007 and the beginning of 2008?

In January and February, 2008, South Africa (and neighbouring countries that imported power from South Africa) began to experience repeated and economy-wide power cuts as Eskom, the power utility, simply ran out of capacity to meet demand. This caused serious economic disruption and hardship, and posed a serious threat to the economic expansion on which South Africa depended for political stability. By definition, there was excess demand for electricity, and, since it cannot be resold, this can only mean cutting supply to customers. This arose because the authorities had controlled prices (and possibly in some cases turned a blind eye to non-payment of bills) so that demand growth outstripped capacity expansion. The latter takes time, and is also constrained by the access to revenues by the electricity supplier. In addition to domestic demand growth it now appears that South Africa was supplying Zimbabwe with power for which it did not pay. Domestic and other users, therefore, were not facing prices that reflected the opportunity cost of providing them with power. Inevitably, demand growth and expansion constraints led to an inability to supply. In effect political unwillingness to see cost-reflective prices had the consequence that the country became unable to supply energy to competing users, and rationing by blackout, with the costs associated with serious economic disruption, ensued.

Rent controls reconsidered

Most European countries have rent controls of some sort, but there are substantial differences in the type and extent of these controls across countries. In the USA, rent controls are a municipal or state matter, not something decided by central government. Not all US cities have rent controls. New York is one of the best-known cases, having had extensive controls in place since the middle of the Second World War. The experience of New York and the contrasting experiences of cities without controls have resulted in virtual unanimity among American economists that the controls should be abolished. But they linger on. Rent controls represent an attempt to use the law to suspend the market because legislators feel that they are protecting some people who would be badly hurt by having to pay higher rents. The intention may be good, but, as we shall see, the consequences are usually (a) bad, and (b) the opposite to what was sought in bringing in the legal restrictions on rents.

The case against controls can easily be analysed by using the concepts of the supply curve and the demand curve.

Suppose that in the city of New York demand and supply curves for one-bedroom apartments are as shown in Fig. 3.6. This market, left alone, would reach an equilibrium monthly rent of $1,600, at which 2 million one-bedroom apartments would be rented. Both landlords and tenants would be 'satisfied', in the sense that they would not wish to rent either more or fewer units at that price. This would not necessarily mean, of course, that all is well and good. Many potential tenants, for example, might simply be unable to afford a rent of $1,600 per month and thus be forced to remain homeless (or to move out of the city to a cheaper location).

Now suppose that the demand for apartments to rent increases (people moving into the city? incomes rising?). The new conditions mean that the demand curve shifts to the right: at any rent, more people want accommodation; the market clearing price for any given amount rises. The consequence would be (a) a rise in the rents paid for apartments, to $2,000 per month, and (b) an increase in the number of apartments available to rent, to 3 million.

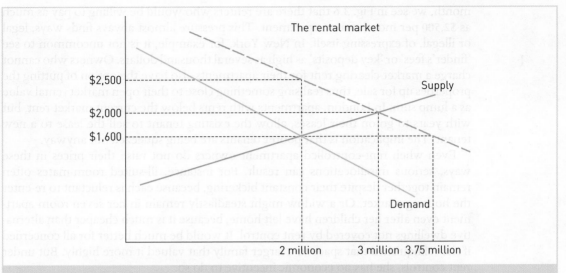

Figure 3.6 An Unregulated Housing Market is hit by Rent Controls. The initial equilibrium monthly rent is $1,600, and 2 million apartments will be rented. Demand rises. The new equilibrium is a supply of 3 million apartments at a rent of $2,000. Fixing the rent at $1,600 results in excess demand of 1.75 million apartments.

Suppose that, following tenants' complaints about rising rents, the city authorities legislated to set the price back to $1,600. Their stated aim in enacting this law was that no person should have to remain homeless because decent housing was unaffordable.

But note in Fig. 3.6 that when rents for one-bedroom apartments are prevented from rising above $1,600 per month, landlords are willing to supply only 2 million apartments per month, 1 million fewer than at the new equilibrium monthly rent of $2,000.[4] At this price tenants would now seek to rent 3.75 million apartments. (For example, many people who would have decided to live across the Hudson River in New Jersey rather than pay $2,000 a month in New York will now choose to live in the city.) So when rents are prevented from rising above $1,600 per month, we see an excess demand for one-bedroom apartments of 1.75 million units each month. Put another way, the rent controls result in a housing shortage of 1.75 million units each month.

If the housing market were completely unregulated, rents would rise sharply, as would the supply of accommodation. With a legal ceiling on rents many other ways exist, however, in which the pressures of excess demand can make themselves felt. For instance, owners will quickly learn that they are free to spend less on maintaining the quality of their rental units. After all, if there are scores of renters knocking at the door of each vacant flat, a landlord has considerable room to manoeuvre. Leaking pipes, peeling paint, broken central heating and other problems are less likely to receive prompt attention – or, indeed, any attention at all – when rents are set well below market-clearing levels.

Nor are reduced availability of apartments and poorer maintenance of existing apartments the only difficulties. With an offering of only 2 million apartments per

---

4 You might think this is unrealistic. After all, the number of one-bedroom apartments can't easily be reduced. Actually, this isn't really the case, since they can be converted to other uses, or they can be sold to people who want to own rather than rent.

month, we see in Fig. 3.6 that there are renters who would be willing to pay as much as $2,500 per month for an apartment. This pressure almost always finds ways, legal or illegal, of expressing itself. In New York, for example, it is not uncommon to see 'finder's fees' or 'key deposits' as high as several thousand dollars. Owners who cannot charge a market-clearing rent for their apartments also have the option of putting the properties up for sale, thus realising something close to their open market rental value as a lump sum. In London, apartments with rents below the current market rent, but with years to go on their leases, allow the existing tenant to sell the lease to a new tenant. The implication is that poorer tenants are being squeezed out anyway.

Even when rent-controlled apartment owners do not raise their prices in these ways, serious misallocations can result. For instance, ill-suited room-mates often remain together despite their constant bickering, because each is reluctant to re-enter the housing market. Or a widow might steadfastly remain in her seven-room apartment even after her children have left home, because it is much cheaper than alternative dwellings not covered by rent control. It would be much better for all concerned if she relinquished that space to a larger family that valued it more highly. But under rent controls, she has no economic incentive to do so.

There is also another more insidious cost of rent controls. In markets without rent controls, landlords cannot discriminate against potential tenants on the basis of race, religion, sexual orientation, physical disability or national origin without suffering an economic penalty. Refusal to rent to members of specific groups would reduce the demand for their apartments, which would mean having to accept lower rents. When rents are artificially pegged below their equilibrium level, however, the resulting excess demand for flats enables landlords to engage in discrimination with no further economic penalty.

Rent controls are not the only instance in which governments have attempted to repeal the law of supply and demand in the interest of helping the poor. During the late 1970s, for example, several governments on both sides of the Atlantic tried to hold the prices of oil products (petrol, central heating oil, etc.) below their equilibrium levels out of concern that higher prices imposed unacceptable hardships on low-income households. This was at a time when supply interruptions in global oil markets (the so-called 'second oil shock') had sent prices up from about €15 per barrel to over €30 per barrel. As with controls in the rental housing market, unintended consequences of price controls in the market made the policy an extremely costly way of trying to aid the poor. For example, petrol shortages resulted in long queues at the pumps – a waste not only of valuable time, but also of petrol as cars sat idling or moving slowly up to the pumps for extended periods.

In their opposition to rent controls and similar measures, are economists revealing a total lack of concern for the poor? Although this claim is sometimes made by those who don't understand the issues, or who stand to benefit in some way from government regulations, there is little justification for it. Economists simply realise that there are *much more effective ways to help poor people than to try to give them apartments and other goods at artificially low prices*. One straightforward approach would be to give the poor additional income and let them decide for themselves how to spend it.

Pizza price controls?

The sources of the contrast between widespread incidence of rent-controlled housing markets and largely unregulated food markets can be seen more vividly by trying to imagine what would happen if concern for the poor successfully lobbied a city

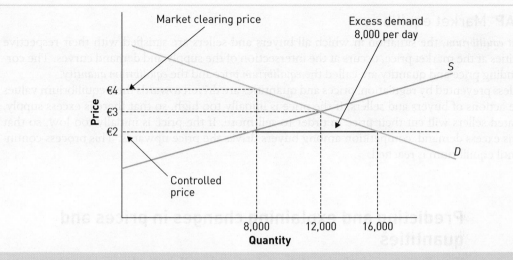

Figure 3.7 Price Controls in the Pizza Market. A price ceiling below the equilibrium price of pizza would result in excess demand for pizza. Supply is less than demand, and the market clearing price, given this supply, is higher than the equilibrium price as well as the controlled ceiling price.

price ceiling a maximum allowable price, specified by law

administration to implement price controls on pizza. Suppose, for example, that the supply and demand curves for pizza are as shown in Fig. 3.7, and that the city imposes a **price ceiling** of €2 per slice, making it unlawful to charge more than that amount. At €2 per slice, buyers want to buy 16,000 slices per day, but sellers want to sell only 8,000.

At a price of €2 per slice, every pizza restaurant in the city will have long queues of buyers trying unsuccessfully to purchase pizza. Frustrated buyers will behave rudely to cooks, who will respond in kind. Friends of restaurant managers will begin to get preferential treatment. Devious pricing strategies will begin to emerge (such as the €2 slice of pizza sold in combination with a €5 glass of Pepsi Cola). Pizza will be made from poorer-quality ingredients. Rumours will begin to circulate about sources of black-market pizza. And so on.

The very idea of not being able to buy a pizza seems absurd, yet precisely such things happen routinely in markets in which prices are held below the equilibrium levels. For example, prior to the collapse of communist governments, it was considered normal in those countries for people to queue for hours to buy basic goods, while the politically connected had first choice of those goods that were available. Nor is this confined to the world of socialist planning. At one point during the 1970s a shortage of potatoes in Western Europe sent potato prices soaring. Potatoes had a high weighting in the procedure by which inflation was measured in Belgium. (This reflected the Belgian passion for *pommes frites*.) The Belgian government sought to hold down the consumer price index (CPI, the measure of inflation) by freezing the price of potatoes. The intervention was a great success, if 'success' is measured by what happened to the CPI. Unfortunately, available supplies of potatoes disappeared as they were exported to the Netherlands, France and Germany where prices were not controlled. So, the price index didn't rise ... because people couldn't get their hands on potatoes (other than in black-market transactions). *Pommes frites* simply disappeared from menus. The controls were rapidly abandoned.

> **RECAP** Market equilibrium
>
> *Market equilibrium*, the situation in which all buyers and sellers are satisfied with their respective quantities at the market price, occurs at the intersection of the supply and demand curves. The corresponding price and quantity are called the *equilibrium price* and the *equilibrium quantity*.
>
> Unless prevented by regulation, prices and quantities are driven towards their equilibrium values by the actions of buyers and sellers. If the price is initially too high, so that there is excess supply, frustrated sellers will cut their price in order to sell more. If the price is initially too low, so that there is excess demand, competition among buyers drives the price upwards. This process continues until equilibrium is reached.

Predicting and explaining changes in prices and quantities

If we know how the factors that govern supply and demand curves are changing, we can make informed predictions about how prices and the corresponding quantities will change. But when describing changing circumstances in the marketplace, we must take care to recognise some important terminological distinctions. For example,

change in the quantity demanded a movement along the demand curve that occurs in response to a change in price

change in demand a shift in the entire demand curve

we must distinguish between the meanings of the seemingly similar expressions **change in the quantity demanded** and **change in demand**. When we speak of a 'change in the quantity demanded', this means the change in the quantity that people wish to buy that occurs in response to a change in price. For instance, Fig. 3.8(a) depicts an increase in the quantity demanded that occurs in response to a reduction in the price of tuna. When the price falls from €5 to €4 per can, the quantity demanded rises from 2,000 to 4,000 cans per day. By contrast, when we speak of a 'change in demand', this means a *shift in the* entire *demand curve*. For example, Fig. 3.8(b) depicts an increase in demand, meaning that at every price the quantity demanded is higher than before.

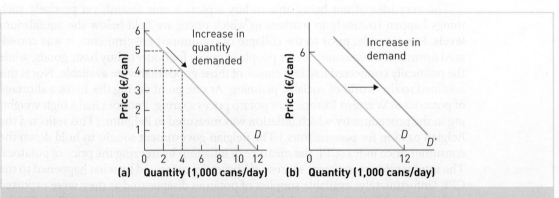

Figure 3.8 An Increase in the Quantity Demanded versus an Increase in Demand.
(a) An increase in quantity demanded describes a downward movement along the demand curve as price falls. (b) An increase in demand describes an outward shift of the demand curve.

In summary, a 'change in the quantity demanded' refers to a movement *along* the demand curve, and a 'change in demand' means a *shift* in the entire curve. In the apartment rental example above, 'demand increased' (the demand curve shifted to the right). If no controls were in place there would have been 'an increase in the quantity supplied' (a movement along the supply curve).

change in supply a shift in the entire supply curve

change in the quantity supplied a movement along the supply curve that occurs in response to a change in price

A similar terminological distinction applies on the supply side of the market. A **change in supply** means a shift in the entire supply curve, whereas a **change in the quantity supplied** refers to a movement along the supply curve.

Alfred Marshall's supply and demand model is one of the most useful tools of the economic naturalist. Once we understand the forces that govern the placements of supply and demand curves, we are suddenly in a position to make sense of a host of interesting observations in the world around us.

Shifts in demand

To get a better feel for how the supply and demand model enables us to predict and explain price and quantity movements, it is helpful to begin with a few simple examples. Example 3.2 illustrates a shift in demand that results from events outside the particular market itself.

Complements two goods are complements in consumption if an increase in the price of one causes a leftward shift in the demand curve for the other (or if a decrease causes a rightward shift)

Example 3.2 What will happen to the equilibrium price and quantity of tennis balls if court-rental fees decline?

Let the initial supply and demand curves for tennis balls be as shown by the curves S and D in Fig. 3.9, where the resulting equilibrium price and quantity are €1 per ball and 40 million balls per month, respectively. Tennis courts and tennis balls are what economists call **complements**, goods that are more valuable when used *in combination* than when used alone. Tennis balls, for example, would be of little value if there were no tennis courts on which to play. As tennis courts become cheaper to use, people will respond by playing more tennis, and this will increase their demand for tennis balls. A decline in court-rental fees will thus shift the demand curve for tennis balls rightwards to D'. (A 'rightward shift' of a demand curve can also be described as an 'upward shift'. These distinctions correspond, respectively, to the horizontal and vertical interpretations of the demand curve.)

Note in Fig. 3.9 that for the illustrative demand shift shown, the new equilibrium price of tennis balls, €1.40, is higher than the original price, and the new equilibrium quantity, 58 million balls per month, is higher than the original quantity.

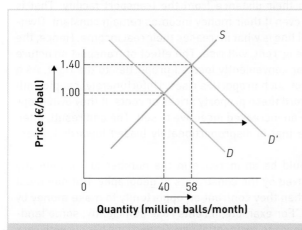

Figure 3.9 The Effect on the Market for Tennis Balls of a Decline in Tennis Court Rental Charges.
When the price of a complement falls, demand shifts right, causing equilibrium price and quantity to rise.

substitutes two goods are substitutes in consumption if an increase in the price of one causes a rightward shift in the demand curve for the other (or if a decrease causes a leftward shift)

To summarise, economists define goods as **substitutes** if an increase in the price of one causes a rightward shift in the demand curve for the other. By contrast, goods are complements if an increase in the price of one causes a leftward shift in the demand curve for the other. The concepts of substitutes and complements enable you to answer questions such as that posed in Exercise 3.3.

Exercise 3.3   How will a decline in air fares between Britain and France affect cross-Channel ferry fares and the price of hotel rooms in resort communities in France?

Demand curves are shifted not just by changes in the prices of substitutes and complements but also by other factors that change the amounts that people are willing to pay for a given good or service. One of the most important such factors is income.

Economic naturalist 3.2 When a city's public transport authority opens or upgrades a rapid transit rail line, why are the users of the upgraded facility often disproportionately those with higher incomes?

Improved public rail transport facilities, usually heavily subsidised by taxpayers, offer transport services to everyone at the same price. But the users of the improved facilities tend to be disproportionately people with higher than average incomes. Far from benefiting everyone equally, they tend to benefit the better-off more. This was hardly the intention of the decision makers when they opted to spend money improving rail services. So, what happens? More efficient public transport reduces travel costs for people inversely in relation to their distance from the transport facility. That is equivalent to an increase in their real incomes even if their money incomes remain constant. Ownership of, or a lease on, property close to the rail line is what increases their real income. Hence, the market price of such property, whether for sale or rent, will rise. The effect of transport structure investment is thus to shift the demand curve for conveniently located properties to the right. As a result, both the equilibrium price and quantity of such properties rises. Unfortunately, people with lower incomes find it increasingly difficult to afford these property prices or rents. If they own property near the upgraded line, poorer people face an increased incentive to sell. The end result, often referred to as 'gentrification', is a user profile that is disproportionately biased towards higher-income households.

It might seem natural to ask how there could be an increase in the number of conveniently located properties, which might appear to be fixed by the constraints of geography. But one must never underestimate the ingenuity of sellers when they confront an opportunity to make money by supplying more of something that people want. For example, if rents rose sufficiently, some landlords might respond by converting warehouse space to residential use. Or perhaps people with cars who do not place high value on living near a station might sell their properties, thereby making them available to people eager to rent them or buy them. (Note that these responses constitute movements *along* the supply curve of conveniently located property, as opposed to *shifts* in that supply curve.)

normal good one whose demand curve shifts rightwards when the incomes of buyers increase and leftwards when the incomes of buyers decrease

inferior good one whose demand curve shifts leftwards when the incomes of buyers increase and rightwards when the incomes of buyers decrease

When incomes increase, the demand curves for most goods will behave like the demand curve for conveniently located property and, in recognition of that fact, economists have chosen to call such goods **normal goods**.

Not all goods are normal goods, however. In fact, the demand curves for some goods actually shift leftwards when income goes up, and such goods are called **inferior goods**.

When would having more money tend to make you want to buy less of something? In general, this will happen in the case of goods for which there exist attractive substitutes that sell for only slightly higher prices. Properties in an unsafe, inconveniently located neighbourhood are an example. Most residents would choose to move out of such neighbourhoods as soon as they could afford to, which means that an increase in income would cause the demand for such property to shift leftwards.

Ground or minced beef with high fat content is another example of an inferior good. For health reasons, most people prefer grades of meat with a low fat content, and when they do buy high-fat meats it is usually a sign of budgetary pressure. When people in this situation receive higher incomes, they usually switch quickly to leaner grades of meat.

Preferences, or tastes, are another important factor in determining whether a given good will meet the cost–benefit test. Steven Spielberg's film *Jurassic Park* appeared to kindle a powerful, if previously latent, preference among children for toy dinosaurs. When this film was first released, the demand for such toys shifted sharply to the right. And the same children who couldn't find enough dinosaur toys suddenly seemed to lose interest in toy designs involving horses and other modern animals, whose respective demand curves shifted sharply to the left.

Expectations about the future are another factor that may cause demand curves to shift. If Apple Macintosh users hear a credible rumour, for example, that a cheaper or significantly upgraded model will be introduced next month, the demand curve for the current model is likely to shift leftwards.

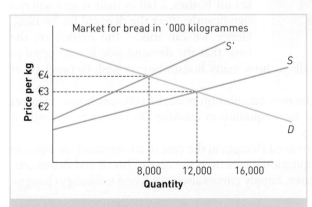

Figure 3.10 The Effect on the Bread Market of an Increase in the Demand for Ethanol as a Fossil Fuel Replacement. When input prices rise, supply shifts left, causing equilibrium price to rise and equilibrium quantity to fall.

Shifts in the supply curve

The preceding examples involved changes that gave rise to shifts in demand curves. Next, we shall look at what happens when supply curves shift. Because the supply curve is based on costs of production, anything that changes production costs will shift the supply curve, and hence will result in a new equilibrium quantity and price.

Example 3.3 What will happen to the equilibrium price and quantity of bread and other foodstuffs as governments encourage production of renewable energy via ethanol?

Suppose the initial supply and demand curves for a product like bread are as shown by the curves *S* and *D* in Fig. 3.10, resulting in an equilibrium price and quantity of €3 per kg and weekly sales in a medium-sized town of 12,000 kg. As demand for ethanol rises, producers increase their purchases of cereal inputs for fermentation to produce ethanol. This means that the prices for cereal products will rise (good news for farmers, who strongly support environmental policies that emphasise replacing fossil fuels elsewhere, but are less enthusiastic about higher fertiliser costs or requirements to reduce methane emissions from cattle). Food producers face higher raw material prices for things like bread. A rise in input prices shifts the supply curve for those products up and to the left. The result is higher prices for the bread, etc., that are produced from these inputs. In the long run, this is expected to spill over to other food products as land and other inputs are switched by farmers to producing raw material for ethanol production and away from producing food.

Example 3.4 What will happen to the equilibrium price and quantity of new houses if the wage rate of carpenters falls?

Suppose that the initial supply and demand curves for new houses are as shown by the curves S and D in Fig. 3.11, resulting in an equilibrium price of €120,000 per house and

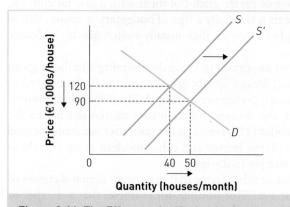

Figure 3.11 The Effect on the Market for New Houses of a Decline in Carpenters' Wage Rates.
When input prices fall, supply shifts right, causing equilibrium price to fall and equilibrium quantity to rise.

an equilibrium quantity of 40 houses per month. A decline in the wage rate of carpenters reduces the marginal cost of making new houses, and this means that, for any given price of houses, more builders can profitably serve the market than before. Diagrammatically, this means a rightward shift in the supply curve of houses, from S to S' in Fig. 3.11. (A 'rightward shift' in the supply curve can also be described as a 'downward shift'.)

Does a decrease in the wage rate of carpenters have any effect on the demand curve for houses? Because it is safe to assume that carpenters form a very small percentage of the total potential demand side of the market for houses, a fall in their wages will not significantly affect the demand for housing. Hence we can model the market on the basis that the demand side is unaffected in this case. The demand curve tells us how many houses buyers wish to purchase at each price.

We see from Fig. 3.11 that the new equilibrium price, €90,000 per house, is lower than the original price, and the new equilibrium quantity, 50 houses per month, is higher than the original quantity.

Examples 3.3 and 3.4 both involved changes in the cost of an *ingredient*, or *input*, in the production of the good in question – cereals in the case of bread and carpenters' labour in the production of houses. Supply curves also shift when *technology* changes. Exercise 3.4 is a case in point.

Exercise 3.4   Why do professors expect students to undertake more revisions of any work submitted for credit today than they demanded from students 30 years ago?

Changes in input prices and technology are two of the most important factors that give rise to shifts in supply curves. In the case of agricultural commodities, *weather* may be another important factor, with favourable conditions shifting the supply curves of such products to the right, and unfavourable conditions shifting them to the left. (Weather may also affect the supply curves of non-agricultural products through its effects on the national transportation system.) Expectations of future price changes may also shift current supply curves, as when the expectation of poor crops as the result of a current drought causes suppliers to withhold supplies from existing stocks in the hope of selling at higher prices in the future. Changes in the number of *sellers* in the market can also cause supply curves to shift.

Four simple rules

For supply and demand curves that have the conventional slopes (upward-sloping for supply curves, downward-sloping for demand curves), the preceding examples and exercises illustrate the four basic rules that govern how shifts in supply and demand affect equilibrium prices and quantities. These rules are summarised in Fig. 3.12 (a)–(d).

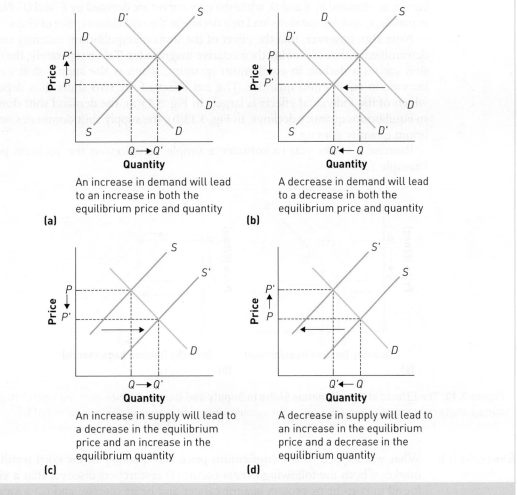

(a) An increase in demand will lead to an increase in both the equilibrium price and quantity

(b) A decrease in demand will lead to a decrease in both the equilibrium price and quantity

(c) An increase in supply will lead to a decrease in the equilibrium price and an increase in the equilibrium quantity

(d) A decrease in supply will lead to an increase in the equilibrium price and a decrease in the equilibrium quantity

Figure 3.12 Four Rules Governing the Effects of Supply and Demand Shifts.

The qualitative rules summarised in Fig. 3.13 hold for supply or demand shifts of any magnitude, provided that the curves have their conventional slopes. But as Example 3.5 demonstrates, when both supply and demand curves shift at the same time, the direction in which equilibrium price or quantity changes will depend on the *relative magnitudes* of the shifts.

Example 3.5 How do shifts in both demand and supply affect equilibrium quantities and prices?

What will happen to the equilibrium price and quantity in the corn tortilla chip market if both of the following events occur: (1) researchers prove that the oils in which tortilla chips are fried are harmful to human health; and (2) the price of corn harvesting equipment falls?

The conclusion regarding the health effects of the oils will shift the demand for tortilla chips to the left, because many people who once bought chips in the belief that they were healthful will now switch to other foods. The decline in the price of harvesting equipment will shift the supply of chips to the right, because additional farmers will now find it profitable to enter the corn market. In Fig. 3.13(a) and 3.13(b), the original supply and demand curves are denoted by S and D, while the new curves are denoted by S' and D'. Note that, in panels (a) and (b), the shifts lead to a decline in the equilibrium price of chips.

Note also, however, that the effect of the shifts on equilibrium quantity cannot be determined without knowing their relative magnitudes. Taken separately, the demand shift causes a decline in equilibrium quantity, whereas the supply shift causes an increase in equilibrium quantity. The net effect of the two shifts thus depends on which of the individual effects is larger. In Fig. 3.13(a), the demand shift dominates, so equilibrium quantity declines. In Fig. 3.13(b), the supply shift dominates, so equilibrium quantity goes up.

Exercise 3.5 asks you to consider a simple variation on the problem posed in Example 3.5.

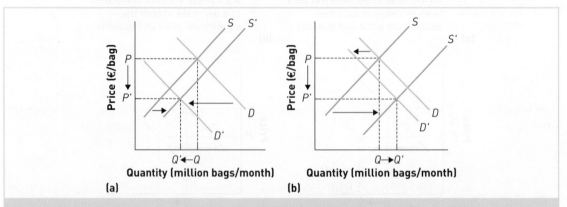

Figure 3.13 The Effects of Simultaneous Shifts in Supply and Demand. When demand shifts left and supply shifts right, equilibrium price falls, but equilibrium quantity may either rise (b) or fall (a).

Exercise 3.5   What will happen to the equilibrium price and quantity in the corn tortilla chip market if both the following events occur: (1) researchers discover that a vitamin found in corn helps protect against cancer and heart disease; and (2) a swarm of locusts destroys part of the corn crop in the US Midwest?

RECAP Factors that shift supply and demand

- **Factors that cause an increase (rightward or upward shift) in demand:**

  1. a decrease in the price of complements to the good or service
  2. an increase in the price of substitutes for the good or service
  3. an increase in income (for a normal good)
  4. an increased preference by demanders for the good or service
  5. an increase in the population of potential buyers
  6. an expectation of higher prices in the future.

When these factors move in the opposite direction, demand will shift left.

- **Factors that cause an increase (rightward or downward shift) in supply:**

  1. a decrease in the cost of materials, labour or other inputs used in the production of the good or service
  2. an improvement in technology that reduces the cost of producing the good or service
  3. an improvement in the weather (especially for agricultural products)
  4. an increase in the number of suppliers
  5. an expectation of lower prices in the future.

When these factors move in the opposite direction, supply will shift left.

Economic naturalist 3.3 Why do the prices of some goods (such as airline tickets from Europe to the United States) go up during the months of heaviest consumption, while others (such as the price of strawberries) go down?

Seasonal price movements for airline tickets are primarily the result of *seasonal variations in demand*. Thus ticket prices on the North Atlantic routes are highest during the summer months because the demand for tickets is highest during those months, as shown in Fig. 3.14(a), where the *w* and *s* subscripts denote winter and summer values, respectively.

By contrast, seasonal price movements for strawberries are primarily the result of *seasonal variations in supply*. In the winter months strawberries offered for sale in Europe are for the most part produced under glass or are imported into Europe. The costs involved are higher than in the summer months, when seasonal factors permit production in the open across a large part of Europe. Costs are lower: the supply curve shifts to the right. The price of strawberries is lowest in the summer months because their supply is highest during those months, as seen in Fig. 3.14(b).

Markets and social welfare

Markets represent a highly effective system of *allocating resources*. When a market for a good is in equilibrium, the equilibrium price conveys important information to potential suppliers about the value that potential demanders place on that good. At the same time, the equilibrium price informs potential demanders about the opportunity cost of supplying the good. This rapid, two-way transmission of information is the reason that markets can coordinate an activity as complex as supplying London or Paris with food and drink, even though no one person or organisation oversees the process.

But are the prices and quantities determined in market equilibrium socially optimal, in the sense of maximising total economic surplus? That is, does equilibrium in

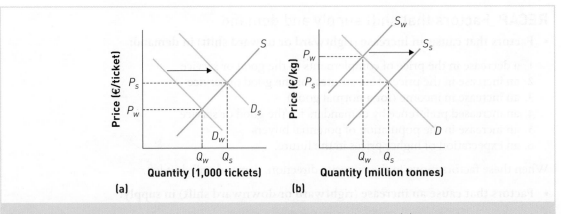

Figure 3.14 Seasonal Variation in the Air Travel and Strawberry Markets. (a) Prices are highest during the period of heaviest consumption when heavy consumption is the result of high demand. (b) Prices are lowest during the period of heaviest consumption when heavy consumption is the result of high supply.

unregulated markets always maximise the difference between the total benefits and total costs experienced by market participants? As we shall see, the answer is 'it depends': a market that is out of equilibrium, such as the market for rented housing in cities with rent control laws, always creates opportunities for individuals to arrange transactions that will increase their individual economic surplus. As we shall see, however, a market for a good that is in equilibrium makes the largest possible contribution to total economic surplus only when its supply and demand curves fully reflect the costs and benefits associated with the production and consumption of that good.

Cash on the table

In economics, we assume that all exchange is purely voluntary. This means that a transaction cannot take place unless the buyer's reservation price for the good exceeds the seller's reservation price. When that condition is met and a transaction takes place, both parties receive an economic surplus. The **buyer's surplus** from the transaction is the difference between her reservation price and the price actually paid. The **seller's surplus** is the difference between the price received and the seller's reservation price. The **total surplus** from the transaction is the sum of the buyer's surplus and the seller's surplus. It is also equal to the difference between the buyer's reservation price and the seller's reservation price.

buyer's surplus the difference between the buyer's reservation price and the price he or she actually pays

seller's surplus the difference between the price received by the seller and his or her reservation price

total surplus the difference between the buyer's reservation price and the seller's reservation price

Suppose that there is a potential buyer whose reservation price for an additional slice of pizza is €4 and a potential seller whose reservation price is only €3. If this buyer purchases a slice of pizza from this seller for €3, the total surplus generated by this exchange is €4 − €2 = €2, of which €4 − €3 = €1 is the buyer's surplus and €3 − €2 = €1 is the seller's surplus.

A regulation that prevents the price of a good from reaching its equilibrium level unnecessarily prevents exchanges of this sort from taking place, and in the process reduces total economic surplus. Consider again the effect of price controls imposed in the market for pizza. The demand curve in Fig. 3.15 tells us that if a price ceiling of €2

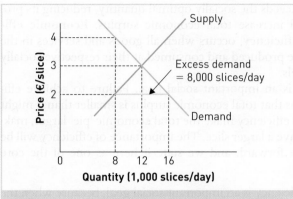

Figure 3.15 Price Controls in the Pizza Market.
A price ceiling below the equilibrium price of pizza would result in excess demand for pizza.

'cash on the table' economic metaphor for unexploited gains from exchange

Equilibrium

per slice were imposed, only 8,000 slices of pizza per day would be sold. At that quantity, the vertical interpretations of the supply and demand curves tell us that a buyer would be willing to pay as much as €4 for an additional slice and that a seller would be willing to sell one for as little €3. The difference – €2 per slice – is the additional economic surplus that would result if an additional slice were produced and sold. As noted earlier, an extra slice sold at a price of €3 would result in an additional €1 of economic surplus for both buyer and seller.

When a market is out of equilibrium, it is always possible to identify *mutually beneficial exchanges* of this sort. When people have failed to take advantage of all mutually beneficial exchanges, we often say that there is 'cash on the table' – the economist's metaphor for unexploited opportunities. When the price in a market is below the equilibrium price, there is cash on the table, because the reservation price of sellers (marginal cost) will always be lower than the reservation price of buyers. In the absence of a law preventing buyers paying more than €2 per slice, restaurant owners would quickly raise their prices and expand their production until the equilibrium price of €3 per slice were reached. At that price, buyers would be able to get precisely the 12,000 slices of pizza they want to buy each day. All mutually beneficial opportunities for exchange would have been exploited, leaving no more cash on the table.

Buyers and sellers in the marketplace have an uncanny ability to detect the presence of cash on the table. It is almost as if unexploited opportunities gave off some exotic scent triggering neuro-chemical explosions in the olfactory centres of their brains. The desire to scrape cash off the table and into their pockets is what drives sellers in each of any large city's thousands of individual food outlets to work diligently to meet their customers' demands. That they succeed to a far higher degree than participants in the city's rent-controlled housing market is plainly evident. Whatever flaws it might have, the market system moves with considerably greater speed and agility than any centralised allocation mechanisms yet devised. But as we emphasise in the following section, this does not mean that markets *always* lead to the greatest good for all.

Smart for one, dumb for all

socially optimal quantity the quantity of a good that results in the maximum possible economic surplus from producing and consuming the good

The **socially optimal quantity** of any good is the quantity that maximises the total economic surplus that results from producing and consuming the good. From the Cost–Benefit Principle (Chapter 1), we know that we should keep expanding production of the good as long as its marginal benefit is at least as great as its marginal cost. This means that the socially optimal quantity is that level for which the marginal cost and marginal benefit of the good are the same.

When the quantity of a good is less than the socially optimal quantity, boosting its production will increase total economic surplus. By the same token, when the quantity

> **economic efficiency** (also called **efficiency**) occurs when all goods and services are produced and consumed at their respective socially optimal levels

of a good exceeds the socially optimal quantity, reducing its production will increase total economic surplus. **Economic efficiency**, or **efficiency**, occurs when all goods and services in the economy are produced and consumed at their respective socially optimal levels.

Efficiency is an important social goal. Failure to achieve efficiency means that total economic surplus is smaller than it might have been. Movements towards efficiency make the total economic 'pie' larger, making it possible for everyone to have a larger slice. The importance of efficiency will be a recurring theme as we move forward, and we state it here as one of the core principles:

> **The Efficiency Principle:** efficiency is an important social goal, because when the economic 'pie' grows larger, everyone can have a larger slice.

Is the market equilibrium quantity of a good efficient? That is, does it maximise the total economic surplus received by participants in the market for that good? When the private market for a given good is in equilibrium, we can say that the cost *to the seller* of producing an additional unit of the good is the same as the benefit *to the buyer* of having an additional unit. If all costs of producing the good are borne directly by sellers, and if all benefits from the good accrue directly to buyers, it follows that the market equilibrium quantity of the good will equate the marginal cost and marginal benefit of the good. And this means that the equilibrium quantity also *maximises total economic surplus*.

Sometimes the production of a good entails costs that fall on people *other than those who sell the good*. This will be true, for instance, for goods whose production generates significant levels of environmental pollution (a topic we shall explore in much greater detail in Chapter 11). As extra units of these goods are produced, the extra pollution harms other people besides sellers. In the market equilibrium for such goods, the benefit *to buyers* of the last good produced is, as before, equal to the cost incurred by sellers to produce that good. But since producing that good also imposed pollution costs on others, we know that the *full* marginal cost of the last unit produced – the seller's private marginal cost plus the marginal pollution cost borne by others – must be higher than the benefit of the last unit produced. So in this case the market equilibrium quantity of the good will be larger than the socially optimal quantity. Total economic surplus would be higher if output of the good were lower. Yet neither sellers nor buyers have any incentive to alter their behaviour.

Another possibility is that people *other than those who buy* a good may receive significant benefits from it. For instance, when someone purchases a vaccination against measles from her doctor, she not only protects herself against measles, but she also makes it less likely that others will catch this disease. From the perspective of society as a whole, we should keep increasing the number of vaccinations until their marginal cost equals their marginal benefit. The marginal benefit of a vaccination is the value of the protection it provides for the person vaccinated *plus* the value of the protection it provides for all others. Private consumers, however, will choose to be vaccinated only if the marginal benefit *to them* exceeds the price of the vaccination. In this case, then, the market equilibrium quantity of vaccinations will be smaller than the quantity that maximises total economic surplus. Again, however, individuals would have no incentive to alter their behaviour.

Situations like those just discussed provide examples of behaviours that we may call 'smart for one, dumb for all'. In each case, the individual actors are behaving rationally.

They are pursuing their goals as best they can, and yet there remain unexploited opportunities for gain from the point of view of the whole society. The difficulty is that these opportunities cannot be exploited by individuals acting alone. In subsequent chapters we shall see how people can often *organise collectively* to exploit such opportunities. For now, we simply summarise this discussion in the form of the following core principle:

The Equilibrium Principle (also called the 'No-Cash-On-The-Table' Principle): a market in equilibrium leaves no unexploited opportunities *for individuals*, but may not exploit all gains achievable through *collective action*.

RECAP Markets and social welfare

When the supply and demand curves for a good reflect all significant costs and benefits associated with the production and consumption of that good, the *market equilibrium price* will guide people to produce and consume the quantity of the good that results in the largest possible economic surplus.

Measuring the impact of price changes on supply and demand: elasticity

Conventionally, most police forces and legal systems in Europe and America operate on the basis of penalising the supply of illegal drugs much more severely than the use of those drugs at the individual level. This aspect of legal systems in the countries involved has been reinforced in recent years by reducing penalties for, and even in some cases 'decriminalising', drug use, while increasing the penalties for supplying those drugs to users. This policy has been criticised by some economists on the grounds that it fails to take into account the impact of policy on supply and demand, and the consequences of that impact. There have been some serious challenges to this criticism and the implied desirability of shifting the emphasis to penalising users. However, what is of interest to us here is the fact that the critics of standard policy have grounded their criticism on a particular tool of economic analysis of markets, the concept of *elasticity*.

From our perspective, therefore, it will serve as a good example of how economics can be used to analyse policy problems that might be thought to be outside the area of interest of economists, while introducing the concept of elasticity. The starting point is a view that 'controlled substances' that are addictive are unlike many other goods that people consume. The difference lies in the response to price change. In the short run at least, the quantity demanded of these addictive goods is only weakly responsive to changes in their prices. The measure of the change in quantity demanded in response to a change in price in this context is called the price *elasticity* of demand. The assertion that the quantity demanded is relatively non-responsive to the price in the case of, say, heroin may be rephrased as saying that '*the price elasticity of demand for heroin is low*', or '*the demand for heroin is price inelastic*'. Critics of conventional policy object to the structure of that policy because a low value for price elasticity of demand for addictive substances has serious implications for criminal behaviour in a broader context. Specifically, they argue that it results in increased crime against persons and property.

This is not surprising. Many illicit drug users commit crimes to finance their addiction. This connection between drugs and crime has led to calls for more vigorous

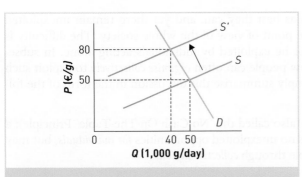

Figure 3.16 The Effect of Extra Border Patrols on the Market for Illicit Drugs. Extra patrols shift supply leftwards and reduce the quantity demanded, but they may actually increase the total amount spent on drugs.

efforts to stop the smuggling of illicit drugs. But can such efforts reduce the likelihood that your laptop computer will be stolen in the next month? If attempts to reduce the supply of illicit drugs are successful, their effect will be to increase the market price of drugs. (From our basic supply and demand analysis, we can see that this increase in price is caused by a leftward shift in the supply curve for drugs; see Fig. 3.16). The law of demand (demand curves slope down) tells us that drug users will respond by consuming a smaller quantity of drugs. But, argue the critics of conventional policy, the amount of crime drug users commit depends not on the *quantity* of drugs they consume, but rather on their *total expenditure* on drugs. Depending on the specific characteristics of the demand curve for illicit drugs, a price increase might reduce total expenditure on drugs, but it could also raise total expenditure.

Given that addicts can finance increased expenditure on drugs only if they increase their incomes to provide the funds, a drugs shortage can lead to a rise in crimes that yield income to the perpetrators. In addition, addicts who are 'pushers' will have an incentive to sell more to finance their own consumption. The empirical basis for this argument is to be found in econometric analysis of some US municipal crime statistics in the 1980s.

Central to the case being made is the issue of what we call *price elasticity of demand*. The concept refers to the responsiveness of quantity demanded to a change in price. If this is low, a reduction in supply, as we will see, leads to an increase in price and spending even though the amount of drugs being consumed must by definition fall. Critics of conventional policy argue that this is the case, and, therefore, that crime increases as addicts attempt to finance an increasingly expensive habit. Therefore, they argue, it is better to go after consumers than to concentrate on interrupting supply. It follows that being able to measure price responsiveness is important, and not just for commercial transactions. It can, as in this case, be important for many aspects of policy formulation.

In the first part of this chapter we saw how shifts in supply and demand curves enabled us to predict the *direction of change* in the equilibrium values of price and quantity. An understanding of price elasticity will enable us to make even more precise statements about the *effects of such changes*. In the illicit drug example just considered, the decrease in supply was expected to lead to an increase in total spending. In many other cases, a decrease in supply will lead to a reduction in total spending. For example, if there was a shortage of apples leading to a fall in the supply of cider in Europe most observers might not expect total spending on cider to rise as its price rose. Why this difference?

The underlying concept used to measure this effect is that of *price elasticity of demand*. We shall explore why some goods have higher price elasticity of demand than others, and the implications of that fact for how total spending responds to changes in price. We shall also discuss the *price elasticity of supply* and examine the factors that explain why it takes different values for different goods.

Price elasticity of demand

When the price of a good or service rises, the quantity demanded falls. But to predict the effect of the price increase on total expenditure, we must also know how much quantity falls. The quantity demanded of some goods, such as salt, is not very sensitive to changes in price. Indeed, even if the price of salt were to double, or to fall by half, most people would hardly alter their consumption of it at all. For other goods, however, the quantity demanded is extremely responsive to changes in price.

Price elasticity defined

price elasticity of demand
percentage change in quantity demanded that results from a 1 per cent change in price

The **price elasticity of demand** for a good is a measure of the responsiveness of the quantity demanded of that good to changes in its price. Formally, the price elasticity of demand for a good is defined as the percentage change in the quantity demanded that results from a 1 per cent change in its price. For example, if the price of beef falls by 1 per cent and the quantity demanded rises by 2 per cent, then the price elasticity of demand for beef has a value of −3. The minus sign follows from the mathematical result that dividing a positive number by a negative number, or a negative number by a positive number, yields a negative number.

Although the definition just given refers to the response of quantity demanded to a 1 per cent change in price, it can also be adapted to other variations in price, provided that they are relatively small. In such cases, we calculate the price elasticity of demand as the percentage change in quantity demanded divided by the corresponding percentage change in price. Thus, if a 2 per cent reduction in the price of pork led to a 6 per cent increase in the quantity of pork demanded, the price elasticity of demand for pork would be

$$\frac{\text{Percentage change in consumption}}{\text{Percentage change in price}} = \frac{6\,\text{per cent}}{-2\,\text{per cent}} = -3 \tag{3.1}$$

elastic demand is elastic with respect to price if the price elasticity of demand is greater than 1

inelastic demand is inelastic with respect to price if the price elasticity of demand is less than 1

unit elastic demand is unit elastic with respect to price if the price elasticity of demand equals 1

Strictly speaking, as long as demand curves slope downwards, the price elasticity of demand will always be negative (or zero), because price changes are always in the opposite direction from changes in quantity demanded. So, for convenience, we can drop the negative sign and speak of price elasticities in terms of absolute value. The demand for a good is said to be **elastic** with respect to price if the absolute value of its price elasticity is greater than 1. It is said to be **inelastic** if the absolute value of its price elasticity is less than 1. Finally, demand is said to be **unit elastic** if the absolute value of its price elasticity is equal to 1 (see Fig. 3.17).

Example 3.6 What is the elasticity of demand for pizza?

When the price of pizza is €1 per slice, buyers wish to purchase 400 slices per day, but when price falls to €0.97 per slice, the quantity demanded rises to 404 slices per day. At the original price, what is the price elasticity of demand for pizza? Is the demand for pizza elastic with respect to price?

In response to a 3 per cent reduction in the price of pizza, the quantity demanded increases by 1 per cent. The price elasticity of demand for pizza is thus (1 per cent)/(3 per cent) = 1/3. So when the initial price of pizza is €1, the demand for pizza is not elastic with respect to price; it is less than 1; it is inelastic.

Exercise 3.6   Suppose the price of a weekly ski pass in Klosters is €160, and the ski lift operator sells 10,000 weekly passes at that price. On the advice of an economist, the price is lowered to €152, and weekly sales rise to 12,000 passes, which was predicted by the economist. What did the economist estimate the price elasticity of demand to be when the price was €160? Was demand elastic or inelastic?

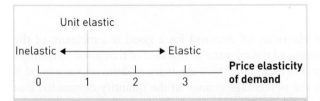

Figure 3.17 Elastic and Inelastic Demand. Demand for a good is called elastic, unit elastic or inelastic with respect to price if the price elasticity is greater than 1, equal to 1, or less than 1, respectively.

Determinants of price elasticity of demand

If you want to know what determines price elasticity of demand for a good or service you must first remember that a rational consumer will purchase a unit of good or service only if the purchase passes the cost–benefit test. For instance, consider a good (such as a flat-screen LED TV set for your flat) that you buy only one unit of (if you buy it at all). Suppose that, at the current price, you have decided to buy it. Now imagine that the price goes up by 10 per cent. Will a price increase of this magnitude be likely to make you change your mind? The answer will depend on factors such as those described below.

Substitution possibilities

When the price of a product you want to buy goes up significantly, you are likely to ask yourself, 'Is there some other good that can do roughly the same job, but for less money?' If the answer is yes, then you can escape the effect of the price increase by simply switching to the substitute product. But if the answer is no, you are more likely to stick with your current purchase.

These observations suggest that the price elasticity of demand will tend to be higher for products for which *close substitutes* are readily available. Salt, for example, has no close substitutes, which is one reason that the demand for it is highly inelastic. Note, however, that while the quantity of salt people demand is highly insensitive to price, the same cannot be said of the demand for any *specific brand* of salt. After all, despite what salt manufacturers say about the special advantages of their own labels, consumers tend to regard one brand of salt as a virtually perfect substitute for another. Thus, if one producer were to raise the price of its salt significantly, many people would simply switch to some other brand.

The vaccine against rabies is a product for which there are essentially no attractive substitutes. A person who is bitten by a rabid animal and does not take the vaccine faces a certain and painful death. So most people in that position would pay any price they could afford rather than do without the vaccine.

Budget share

Suppose the price of key rings were suddenly to double. How would that affect the number of key rings you buy? If you're like most people, it would have no effect at all. Think about it – a doubling of the price of a 25-cent item that you buy only every few years is simply nothing to worry about. By contrast, if the price of the new TV set you were about to buy suddenly doubled, you would definitely want to check out possible substitutes. You might also consider holding on to your current TV for a little longer. *The larger the share of your budget an item accounts for* the greater is your incentive to look for substitutes when the price of the item rises. High-unit-price items therefore tend to have higher price elasticities of demand.

Time

Motor fuel prices have risen sharply in recent years. If you were going to change your car, and fuel prices rose sharply, it is reasonable to suppose you might select a new car that has better fuel economy figures. As a result, the fuel price rise would result in a significant fall in your consumption of fuel. However, if you, for whatever reason, did not contemplate replacing your car for a couple of years your fuel usage would not fall as sharply, being affected only by your usage of the car, and not by its fuel economy. Hence, in the short run, motorists' responses to fuel price changes will be weaker than in the long run. Short-run price elasticity of demand will be lower than long run. This applies to any good the consumption of which is 'habit formed', meaning that past decisions affect current demand.

As this example illustrates, substitution of one product or service for another takes time. Some substitutions occur in the immediate aftermath of a price increase, but many others take place years or even decades later. For this reason, the price elasticity of demand for any good or service will be higher in the *long run* than in the *short run*.

RECAP Factors that influence price elasticity

The price elasticity of demand for a good or service tends to be larger when *substitutes* for the good are more readily available, when the good's share in the consumer's budget is *larger* and when consumers have more time to *adjust* to a change in price.

Some representative elasticity estimates

As the entries in Table 3.3 show, the price elasticities of demand for different products often differ substantially – in this sample, ranging from a high of 3.8 for green peas to a low of 0.18 for theatre and opera tickets. This variability is explained in part by the determinants of elasticity just discussed. Patrons of theatre and opera, for example, often tend to have high incomes, implying that the shares of their budgets devoted to these items are likely to be small. What is more, theatre and opera patrons are often highly knowledgeable and enthusiastic about these art forms; for many of them, there are simply no acceptable substitute forms of entertainment (and, of course, listening to *Rigoletto* on a CD does not yield the satisfaction of seeing others and being seen at Covent Garden!).

Looking at Table 3.3, why is the price elasticity of demand almost 16 times larger for green peas than for theatre and opera performances? The answer cannot be that income effects loom any larger for green peas than for theatre tickets. Even though the average consumer of green peas earns much less than the average theatre or opera patron, the share of a typical family's budget devoted to green peas is surely very small. What differentiates green peas from theatre and opera performances is that there are so many more close substitutes for peas than for opera and theatre. The lowly green pea, which is mostly found in the canned goods or frozen foods sections of supermarkets, just does not seem to have inspired a loyal consumer following.

Good or service	Price elasticity
Green peas	3.80
Restaurant meals	1.63
Automobiles	1.35
Electricity	1.20
Beer	1.19
Movies	0.87
Air travel (foreign)	0.77
Shoes	0.70
Coffee	0.25
Theatre, opera	0.18

Table 3.3 **Price Elasticity Estimates for Selected Products**
Sources: These short-run elasticity estimates are taken from Houthakker and Taylor (1970), Taylor (1975), Elzinga (1971), Fisher (1996)

Using price elasticity of demand

An understanding of the factors that govern price elasticity of demand is necessary not only to make sense of consumer behaviour, but also to design effective public policy. Consider, for example, the debate about how taxes affect smoking among teenagers. An understanding of the factors that govern price elasticity of demand is necessary not only to make sense of consumer behaviour, but also to design effective public policy. Consider, for example, the debate about how taxes affect smoking among teenagers. One weapon in the armoury of governments to curb smoking is taxing cigarettes so as to increase their price. Higher taxes have been (not surprisingly) resisted by the tobacco industry, which has consistently maintained that peer pressure is what encourages teenagers to smoke. The main reason teenagers smoke is that their friends smoke; price, they claimed, had little effect. So forget higher taxes if you want to deter people from smoking. Demand, they argue, is very price inelastic.

They are almost certainly right that peer pressure and other social factors are a significant factor in sustaining demand for tobacco. But that does not imply that a higher tax on cigarettes would have little impact on adolescent smoking rates (i.e. that demand is extremely price inelastic). For at least some teenage smokers, a higher tax would make smoking unaffordable. And even among those who could afford the higher prices, at least some would choose to spend their money on other things rather than pay the higher prices.

Given that the tax would affect at least *some* teenage smokers, the industry's argument begins to unravel. If the tax deters even a small number of smokers directly through its effect on the price of cigarettes, it will also deter others indirectly, by reducing the number of peer role models who smoke. There will be a ripple-out effect. The mere fact that peer pressure may be the primary determinant of teenage smoking therefore does not imply that higher cigarette taxes will have no significant impact on the number of teenagers who smoke or the amount of tobacco they consume.

That this price effect is actually supported by evidence of the effects of restrictions on smoking actually undermines their case. Prohibiting smoking in some circumstances is analytically equivalent to a location- and/or time-specific extremely high price. To the extent that people do not fully (if at all) replace smoking not done where prohibited by an equivalent increase in smoking where permitted, this high pseudo-price will reduce smoking. In 2004 Ireland introduced a workplace ban on smoking, an initiative that has been followed in many countries in Europe and elsewhere since then. The Irish ban does appear to have had the desired effect of reducing the total consumption of tobacco. This implies that demand is not as price inelastic as you might think.

A graphical interpretation of price elasticity

For small changes in price, the price elasticity of demand is the proportion by which quantity demanded changes divided by the corresponding proportion by which price changes. This formulation gives us a simple expression for the price elasticity of demand for a good based on minimal information about its demand curve.

To illustrate, let P be the current price of the good and Q the quantity demanded at that price. Let ΔP be a small change in the current price and ΔQ the resulting change in quantity demanded (see Fig. 3.18). The expression $\Delta P/P$ is then the proportionate change in price; and $\Delta Q/Q$ is the corresponding proportionate change in quantity. The formula for price elasticity can then be written as:

$$\text{Price elasticity} = \varepsilon = \frac{\Delta Q/Q}{\Delta P/P} \qquad (3.2)$$

Suppose, for example, that 20 units were sold at the original price of 100, and that when the price rose to 105, quantity demanded fell to 15 units. Neglecting the negative sign of the quantity change, we would then have $\Delta Q/Q = 5/20$ and $\Delta P/P = 5/100$, or $\varepsilon = (5/20)/(5/100)$; elasticity is 5.

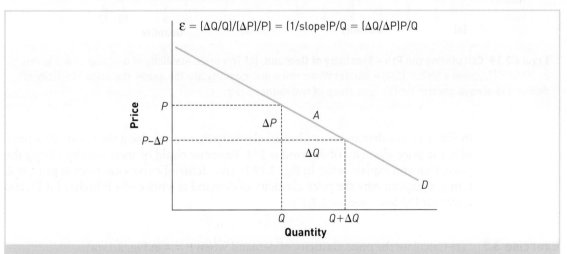

Figure 3.18 A Graphical Interpretation of the Price Elasticity of Demand. The price elasticity of demand at any point along a straight-line demand curve is the ratio of price to quantity at that point times the reciprocal of the slope of the demand curve.

One attractive feature of this formula is that it has a straightforward graphical interpretation. Thus, if we want to calculate the price elasticity of demand at point A on the demand curve shown in Fig. 3.18, we can begin by rewriting the right-hand side of Eq. (3.2) as $(P/Q) \times (\Delta Q/\Delta P)$. And since the slope of the demand curve is equal to $\Delta P/\Delta Q$,

$\Delta Q / \Delta P$ is the reciprocal of that slope: $\Delta Q / \Delta P = 1/\text{slope}$. So the price elasticity of demand at point A, denoted ε_A, has the following simple formula:

$$\varepsilon_A = \frac{P}{Q} \cdot \frac{1}{\text{Slope}} \qquad (3.3)$$

To demonstrate how convenient this graphical interpretation of elasticity can be, suppose we want to find the price elasticity of demand at point A on the demand curve in Fig. 3.19. The slope of this demand curve is the ratio of its vertical intercept to its horizontal intercept: $20/5 = 4$. So $1/\text{slope} = 1/4$. (Actually, the slope is -4, but we again ignore the minus sign for convenience, since the price elasticity of demand always has the same sign.) The ratio P/Q at point A is $8/3$, so the price elasticity at point A is equal to $(P/Q) \times (1/\text{slope}) = (8/3) \times (1/4) = 2/3$. This means that when the price of the good is 8, a 3 per cent reduction in price will lead to a 2 per cent increase in quantity demanded.

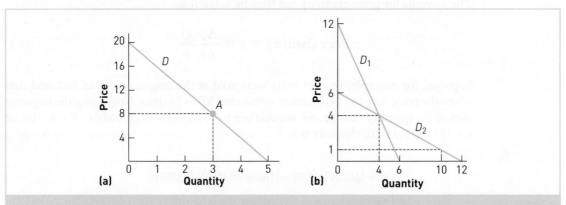

Figure 3.19 Calculating the Price Elasticity of Demand. (a) The price elasticity of demand at A is given by $(P/Q) \times (1/\text{slope}) = (8/3) \times (1/4) = 2/3$. (b) When price and quantity are the same, the price elasticity of demand is always greater for the less steep of two demand curves.

In Fig. 3.19(a) a demand curve has an elasticity that varies along the curve. At a price of 8, the price elasticity of demand is 2/3. Revenue could be increased by raising the price. Can you explain why? In Fig. 3.19(b) two demand curves intersect at price = 4. Can you explain why the price elasticity of demand at a price of 4 is higher for D_2 and lower for D_1? See Exercise 3.7.

Exercise 3.7   (1) Calculate the price elasticity of demand when $P = 4$ in Fig. 3.19(a).
(2) For the demand curves D_1 and D_2 shown in Fig. 3.19(b), calculate the price elasticity of demand when $P = 4$. What is the price elasticity of demand on D_2 when $P = 1$?

Exercise 3.7(2) illustrates the general rule that if two demand curves have a point in common, the steeper curve must be the less elastic of the two with respect to price at that point. But note carefully that this does not mean that the steeper curve is less elastic at every point.

Price elasticity changes along a straight-line demand curve

Price elasticity has a different value at every point along a straight-line demand curve. The slope of a straight-line demand curve is constant, which means that 1/slope is also constant. But the price–quantity ratio, P/Q, declines as we move down the demand curve. The elasticity of demand thus declines steadily as we move downwards along a straight-line demand curve.

This pattern makes sense. After all, a price movement of a given absolute size is small in percentage terms when it occurs near the top of the demand curve but large in percentage terms when it occurs near the bottom of the demand curve. The opposite percentage effect applies in the case of a given quantity change. Price elasticity will be halfway down the demand curve. Why?

The graphical interpretation of elasticity makes it easy to see why. Consider, for example, the price elasticity of demand at point A on the demand curve D shown in Fig. 3.20(a). At that point, the ratio P/Q is equal to $6/3 = 2$. The slope of this demand curve is the ratio of its vertical intercept to its horizontal intercept, $12/6 = 2$. So $(1/\text{slope}) = 1/2$ (again, we neglect the negative sign for simplicity). Inserting these values into the graphical elasticity formula yields $\varepsilon_A = (P/Q) \times (1/\text{slope}) = (2) \times (1/2) = 1$. This result holds not just for the particular demand curve shown, but also for any other straight-line demand curve (Fig. 3.20(b)). Since P/Q declines as we move downwards along a straight-line demand curve, price elasticity of demand must be less than 1 at any point below the midpoint.[5]

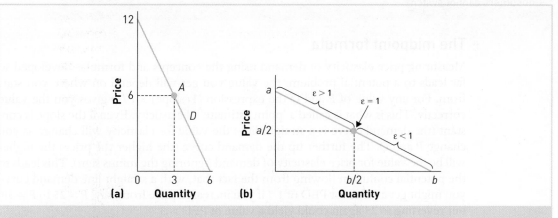

Figure 3.20 Elasticity at the Midpoint of a Straight-line Demand Curve.

Two special cases

There are two important exceptions to the general rule that elasticity declines along straight-line demand curves. Note that the horizontal demand curve in Fig. 3.21(a) has a slope of zero, which means that the reciprocal of its slope is infinite. Price elasticity

---

5 This has to be the case: a point A halfway up the demand curve must refer to a price halfway between zero and the top point of the demand curve. That is, the horizontal line from A to the vertical axis bisects the vertical axis between the origin and the top point of the demand curve. It is a simple theorem from school geometry that the vertical line between A and the horizontal axis must then bisect the horizontal axis between the origin and the bottom point of the demand curve. Hence, the arithmetic result above must always follow with a straight-line demand curve because at this point $P/Q = \Delta P/\Delta Q$.

perfectly elastic demand
demand is perfectly elastic with respect to price if price elasticity of demand is infinite

perfectly inelastic demand
demand is perfectly inelastic with respect to price if price elasticity of demand is zero

of demand is thus infinite at every point along a horizontal demand curve. Such demand curves are said to be **perfectly elastic**.

In contrast, the demand curve in Fig. 3.21(b) is vertical, which means that its slope is infinite. The reciprocal of its slope is thus equal to zero. Price elasticity of demand is thus exactly zero at every point along the curve. For this reason, vertical demand curves are said to be **perfectly inelastic**.

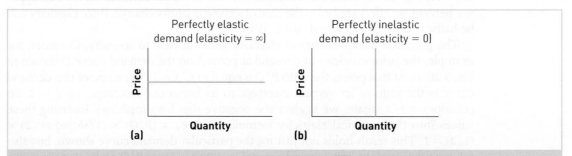

Figure 3.21 Perfectly Elastic and Perfectly Inelastic Demand Curves. The horizontal demand curve (a) is perfectly elastic, or infinitely elastic, at every point. Even the slightest increase in price leads consumers to switch to substitutes. The vertical demand curve (b) is perfectly inelastic at every point. Consumers cannot switch.

The midpoint formula

Measuring price elasticity of demand using the concepts and formulas developed so far leads to a potential problem: the value you get will depend on where you start from. For any value of P and Q the expression $(1/\text{slope}) \times P/Q$ gives you the value correctly. This is what is called a 'point estimate' of elasticity. Even if the slope is constant (the demand curve is a straight line) the value for elasticity will change as you change P and Q. The further up the demand curve (the higher the price) the higher will be the value for price elasticity of demand (ignoring the minus sign). This leads to the potential confusion flowing from the fact that, with a straight-line demand curve you might get a value for PED of 1.5 if you increased price from, say, $P = 25$ to $P = 30$, but reverting to 25 again could yield a value of PED = 3.

Imagine that you are advising a seller as to what would be the consequence of a price change, where what is at stake is choosing a price within a range between $P = 25$ and $P = 30$, and allowing that price to move up and down in the range as costs change. The seller needs to know what he can expect from allowing prices to move. Using economics terminology, he asks you: 'What is the price elasticity of demand for this good?', and will not be impressed if all you can say is that it depends…

What is needed is a reliable 'average' value that will yield a reliable 'average' answer to the question: 'What is the price elasticity of demand for my product?', which really means 'What will happen to my total sales revenue if price changes by so much in that range?'

The answer to the problem lies in generating an estimate using what is known as the 'midpoint formula'.

Strictly speaking, the original question ('What is the price elasticity of demand for this good?') was not well posed. To have elicited a uniquely correct answer, it should have been 'What is the price elasticity of demand at point *A*?' or 'What is the price elasticity of demand at point *B*?' But the seller wants a single answer that will hold up at least approximately regardless of where the price is in the range. To deal with this problem, we use a convention, which we call the *midpoint formula*, for answering ambiguous questions like that originally posed. If the two points in question are (Q_A, P_A) and (Q_B, P_B), this formula is given by

$$\varepsilon = \frac{\Delta Q / \left[(Q_A + Q_B)/2 \right]}{\Delta P / \left[(P_A + P_B)/2 \right]} \qquad (3.4)$$

The midpoint formula thus sidesteps the question of which price–quantity pair to use by using averages of the new and old values. The formula reduces to

$$\varepsilon = \frac{\Delta Q / (Q_A + Q_B)}{\Delta P / (P_A + P_B)} \qquad (3.5)$$

We will not employ the midpoint formula again in this text. Hereafter, all questions concerning elasticity will employ the measure discussed earlier, which is called *point elasticity*.

Maths Box 3.2 Technical note

Demand curves, of course, are not always (or even mostly) straight lines. Hence, the slope of the curve will vary along the curve. Hence, when we want to estimate the price elasticity of demand a formulation using the $(\Delta Q/Q)/(\Delta P/P)$ approach will of necessity be an approximation. To deal with this properly we have to use calculus. As a result, in estimating real-world elasticities economists will normally use the first derivative of the demand curve, dP/dQ, as the measure of slope, and define elasticity as

$$\varepsilon = (-)\,(dQ/dP)\cdot(P/Q) \qquad (3.6)$$

For the rest of the discussion in this chapter we shall stay with the $(\Delta Q/Q)/(\Delta P/P)$ approach.

Exercise 3.8   Suppose that you encounter a question like the following in a standardised test in economics (a multiple-choice test): 'At a price of 3, quantity demanded of a good is 6, while at a price of 4, quantity demanded is 4. What is the price elasticity of demand for this good?' How would you answer it?

RECAP Calculating price elasticity of demand

The price elasticity of demand for a good is the percentage change in the quantity demanded that results from a 1 per cent change in its price. Mathematically, the elasticity of demand at a point along a demand curve is equal to $(P/Q) \times (1/\text{slope})$, where P and Q represent price and quantity and $(1/\text{slope})$ is the reciprocal of the slope of the demand curve at that point. Demand is elastic with respect to price if the absolute value of its price elasticity exceeds 1; inelastic if price elasticity is less than 1; and unit elastic if price elasticity is equal to 1.

Elasticity and total expenditure

Sellers of goods and services will often have a strong interest in being able to answer questions like 'Will consumers spend more on my product if I sell more units at a lower price or fewer units at a higher price?' As it turns out, the answer to this question depends critically on the price elasticity of demand. To see why, let us first examine how the total amount spent on a good varies with the price of the good.

The total daily expenditure on a good is simply the daily number of units bought times the price for which it sells. The market demand curve for a good tells us the quantity that will be sold at each price. We can thus use the information on the demand curve to show how the total amount spent on a good will vary with its price.

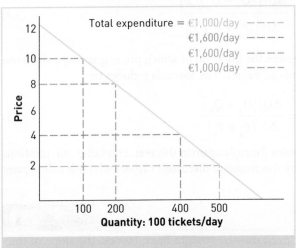

Figure 3.22 The Demand Curve for Cinema Tickets.
An increase in price from €2 to €4 per ticket increases total expenditure on tickets; an increase from €8 to €10 reduces expenditure from €1,600 to €1,000.

To illustrate, let us calculate how much cinema-goers will spend on tickets each day if the demand curve is as shown in Fig. 3.22 and the price is €2 per ticket. The demand curve tells us that at a price of €2 per ticket, 500 tickets per day will be sold, so total expenditure at that price will be €1,000 per day. If tickets sell not for €2 but for €4 apiece, 400 tickets will be sold each day, so total expenditure at the higher price will be €1,600 per day.

Total expenditure = Total revenue: the euro amount that consumers spend on a product ($P \times Q$) is equal to the euro amount that sellers receive.

In this example a rise in price resulted in a rise in total sales revenue. But this does not have to be the case (if it were the case sellers could always increase revenue by raising prices, which is obviously not true, since at some price nothing will be sold). The law of demand tells us that when the price of a good rises, people will buy less of it. The two factors that govern total revenue – price and quantity – will thus always move in opposite directions.

So, a rise in price from €8 per ticket to €10 per ticket will cause total expenditure on tickets to go down. Thus people will spend €1,600 per day on tickets at a price of €8, but only €1,000 per day at a price of €10.

The general rule illustrated by Fig. 3.22 is that a price increase will produce an increase in total revenue whenever it is greater, in percentage terms, than the corresponding percentage change in quantity demanded. Conversely, a fall in price will increase total revenue when, in percentage terms, it is less than the corresponding increase in quantity sold.

This rule can be illustrated by using another graphical representation of the impact of price changes on total sales revenues. In this case we plot price on the horizontal axis and total expenditure by purchasers (sales revenues of the seller) on the vertical axis. In Fig. 3.23 this is done using the information implicit in the demand curve in Fig. 3.22.

To do this, first in table form we derive the total sales revenues values at the prices on the vertical axis of Fig. 3.22. Ideally, we could get values from Fig. 3.22 for a larger number of prices, sufficient to give us a more or less continuous set of values for price and sales revenue or expenditure by purchasers. We then plot these as in Fig. 3.23.

Note that in Fig. 3.23, as the price per ticket increases from €0 to €6, total expenditure increases. But as the price rises from €6 to €12, total expenditure decreases. Total expenditure reaches a maximum of €1,800 per day at a price of €6.

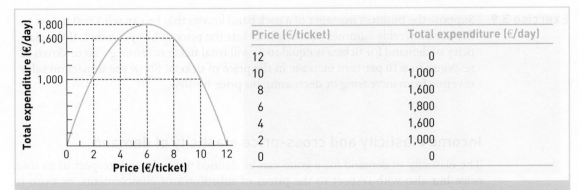

Price (€/ticket)	Total expenditure (€/day)
12	0
10	1,000
8	1,600
6	1,800
4	1,600
2	1,000
0	0

Figure 3.23 Total Expenditure as a Function of Price. For a good whose demand curve is a straight line, total expenditure reaches a maximum at the price corresponding to the midpoint of the demand curve.

This pattern holds true in general. For a straight-line demand curve, total expenditure is highest at the price that lies *on the midpoint of the demand curve*. Total sales revenue, therefore, is maximised where price elasticity of demand is unity. This latter result holds true even if the demand curve is not a straight line, although the point at which elasticity is unity will not usually be halfway between the top and bottom of the demand curve in this case.

The relationship between elasticity and the effect of a price change on total revenue is summarised in Table 3.4, where the symbol ε is used to denote elasticity.

If demand is …	A price increase will …	A price reduction will …
elastic (ε > 1)	reduce total expenditure $P \times Q = PQ$	increase total expenditure $P \times Q = PQ$
inelastic (ε < 1)	increase total expenditure $P \times Q = PQ$	reduce total expenditure $P \times Q = PQ$

Table 3.4 **Elasticity and the Effect of a Price Change on Total Expenditure**

When price elasticity is greater than 1, changes in price and changes in total expenditure always move in opposite directions.

For a product whose price elasticity of demand is less than 1, price changes and total expenditure changes always move in the same direction.

Exercise 3.9   Suppose the business manager of a rock band knows that he can sell 5,000 tickets to the band's weekly summer concerts if he sets the price at €20 per ticket. If the elasticity of demand for tickets is equal to 3, will total ticket revenue go up or down in response to a 10 per cent increase in the price of tickets? Show the impact on sales revenue from increasing or decreasing his price by 10%.

Income elasticity and cross-price elasticity of demand

The elasticity of demand for a good can be defined not only with respect to its own price but also with respect to the prices of substitutes or complements, or even to income. For example, the elasticity of demand for peanuts with respect to the price of cashews – also known as the **cross-price elasticity of demand** for peanuts with respect to cashew prices – is the percentage by which the quantity of peanuts demanded changes in response to a 1 per cent change in the price of cashews. The **income elasticity of demand** for peanuts is the percentage by which the quantity demanded of peanuts changes in response to a 1 per cent change in income.

cross-price elasticity of demand the percentage by which the quantity demanded of the first good changes in response to a 1 per cent change in the price of the second

income elasticity of demand the percentage by which quantity demanded changes in response to a 1 per cent change in income

Unlike the elasticity of demand for a good with respect to its own price, these other elasticities may be either *positive* or *negative*, so it is important to note their algebraic signs carefully. The income elasticity of demand for inferior goods, for example, is negative, whereas the income elasticity of demand for normal goods is positive. When the cross-price elasticity of demand for two goods is positive – as in our peanuts/cashews example – the two goods are *substitutes*. When it is negative, the two goods are *complements*. The elasticity of demand for tennis racquets with respect to court-rental fees, for example, is less than zero.

RECAP Cross-price and income elasticities

When the elasticity of demand for one good with respect to the price of another good is positive, the two goods are *substitutes*; when this cross-price elasticity of demand is negative, the two goods are *complements*. A *normal* good has positive income elasticity of demand and an *inferior* good has negative income elasticity of demand.

The price elasticity of supply

On the buyer's side of the market, we use price elasticity of demand to measure the responsiveness of quantity demanded to changes in price. On the seller's side of the market, the analogous measure is **price elasticity of supply**. It is defined as the percentage change in quantity supplied that occurs in response to a 1 per cent change in price. For example, if a 1 per cent increase in the price of peanuts leads to a 2 per cent increase in the quantity supplied, the price elasticity of supply of peanuts would be 3.

price elasticity of supply the percentage change in quantity supplied that occurs in response to a 1 per cent change in price

The mathematical formula for the price elasticity of supply at any point is the same as the corresponding expression for the price elasticity of demand:

$$\text{Price elasticity of supply} = \frac{\Delta Q / Q}{\Delta P / P} \qquad (3.7)$$

where P and Q are the price and quantity at that point, ΔP is a small change in the initial price and ΔQ is the resulting change in quantity.

As with the corresponding expression for price elasticity of demand, Eq. (3.7) can be rewritten as $(P/Q) \times (\Delta Q/\Delta P)$. And since $(\Delta Q/\Delta P)$ is the reciprocal of the slope of the supply curve, the right-hand side of Eq. (3.7) is equal to $(P/Q) \times (1/\text{slope})$ – the same expression we saw for price elasticity of demand. Price and quantity are always positive, as is the slope of the typical supply curve, which implies that price elasticity of supply will be a positive number at every point.

Consider the supply curve shown in Fig. 3.24(a). The slope of this supply curve is $1/10$, so the reciprocal of this slope is 10. Using the formula, this means that the price elasticity of supply at a supply price of 4 is $(4/20) \times (10) = 2$. The corresponding expression at $P = 5$, $(5/30) \times 10$ yields elasticity 1.67. Elasticity is positive, and declining as P rises because Q rises faster than P along the curve. Elasticity approaches the value for the reciprocal of the slope as P, Q increase. There is an exception to this, which occurs when the supply curve passes through the origin (Fig. 3.24(b)). In this case, the elasticity of supply is positive, but is constant, having the same value at every point on the curve. This is because the value, Q/P, is the same at every point on the curve when it passes through the origin. It is also the same as the reciprocal of the slope. Not only is it constant and positive, therefore, but it is equal to 1.[6] Note the contrast between this result and our earlier finding that price elasticity of demand declines as we move downwards along any straight-line demand curve.[7]

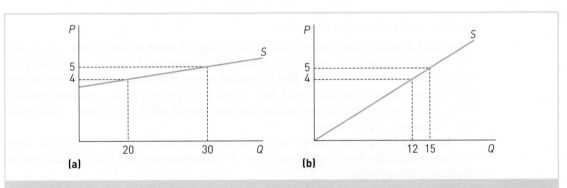

(a)   (b)

Figure 3.24 Calculating the Price Elasticity of Supply Graphically. Price elasticity of supply is $(P/Q) \times (1/\text{slope})$. The price elasticity of supply is equal to 1 at any point along a straight-line supply curve that passes through the origin.

On the buyer's side of the market, two important polar cases were demand curves with infinite price elasticity and zero price elasticity. As Example 3.7 illustrates, analogous polar cases exist on the seller's side of the market.

---

6 Passing through the origin means that there is no minimum expected price other than zero below which there will be no production at all. This is not always the case.

7 Technical note: As with the demand curve, strictly speaking the slope value is based on the first derivative of the supply curve, not on $\Delta P/\Delta Q$. The latter is only an approximation if the supply curve is not a straight line.

Example 3.7 What is the elasticity of supply of land within the territory of Hong Kong?

Land in Hong Kong sells in the market for a price, just like steel or wheat or cars or any other product. And the demand for land in Hong Kong is a downward-sloping function of its price. For all practical purposes, however, its supply is completely fixed, at least in the short run … from time to time the administration in Hong Kong has added a bit by land-fills. No matter whether its price is high or low, the same amount of it is available in the market. The supply curve of such a good is a *vertical* straight line, and its price elasticity is zero at every price. Supply curves of that type are said to be **perfectly inelastic**.

perfectly inelastic supply supply is perfectly inelastic with respect to price if elasticity is zero

perfectly elastic supply supply is perfectly elastic with respect to price if elasticity of supply is infinite

Whenever additional units of a good can be produced by using the same combination of inputs, purchased at the same prices, as have been used so far, the supply curve of that good will be a horizontal straight line. Such supply curves are said to be **perfectly elastic**.

Exercise 3.10 What is the elasticity of supply of lemonade? Suppose that the ingredients required to bring a paper cup of lemonade to market and their respective costs are as shown in the table. Derive the supply curve graphically.

Ingredient	Cents
Paper cup	2.0
Lemon	3.8
Sugar	2.0
Water	0.2
Ice	1.0
Labour (30 seconds @ €6/hour)	5.0

Determinants of supply elasticity

Example 3.7 and the material for Exercise 3.10 suggest some of the factors that govern the elasticity of supply of a good or service. The lemonade case was one whose production process was essentially like a cooking recipe. For such cases, we can exactly double our output by doubling each ingredient. If the price of each ingredient remains fixed, the marginal cost of production for such goods will be constant – and hence their horizontal supply curves.

The Hong Kong land example is a contrast in the extreme. The inputs that were used to produce land in Hong Kong – even if we knew what they were – could not be duplicated at any price.

The key to predicting how elastic the supply of a good will be with respect to price is to know the terms on which *additional units* of the inputs involved in producing that good can be acquired. In general, the more easily additional units of these inputs can be acquired, the higher price elasticity of supply will be. The factors described below (among others) govern the ease with which additional inputs can be acquired by a producer.

Flexibility of inputs

To the extent that production of a good requires inputs that are also useful for the production of other goods, it is relatively easy to lure additional inputs away from their current uses, making supply of that good relatively elastic with respect to price. Thus the fact that lemonade production requires labour with only minimal skills means that a large pool of workers could shift from other activities to lemonade production if a profitable opportunity arose. Brain surgery, by contrast, requires highly trained and specialised labour, which means that even a large price increase would not increase available supplies, except in the very long run.

Mobility of inputs

If inputs can easily be transported from one site to another, an increase in the price of a product in one market will enable a producer in that market to summon inputs from other markets. For example, the supply of agricultural products is made more elastic with respect to price by the fact that thousands of farm workers are willing to migrate northwards during the growing season. The supply of entertainment is similarly made more elastic by the willingness of entertainers to hit the road. Circus performers, lounge singers, comedians and even exotic dancers often spend a substantial fraction of their time away from home. For instance, according to a 1996 *New York Times* article, the top exotic dancers 'basically follow the action, so the same entertainers who worked the Indianapolis 500 now head to Atlanta for the Olympics'.

For most goods, the price elasticity of supply increases each time a new highway is built, or when the telecommunications network improves, or indeed when any other development makes it easier to find and transport inputs from one place to another.

Ability to produce substitute inputs

The inputs required to produce finished diamond gemstones include raw diamond crystal, skilled labour, and elaborate cutting and polishing machinery. In time, the number of people with the requisite skills can be increased, as can the amount of specialised machinery. The number of raw diamond crystals buried in the earth is probably fixed in the same way that Hong Kong land is fixed, but unlike Hong Kong land, rising prices will encourage miners to expend the effort required to find a larger proportion of those crystals. Still, the supply of natural gemstone diamonds tends to be relatively inelastic because of the difficulty of augmenting the number of diamond crystals.

The day is close at hand, however, when gemstone makers will be able to produce synthetic diamond crystals that are indistinguishable from real ones. Indeed, there are already synthetic crystals that fool even highly experienced jewellers. The introduction of a perfect synthetic substitute for natural diamond crystals would increase the price elasticity of supply of diamonds (or, at any rate, the price elasticity of supply of gemstones that look and feel just like diamonds).

Time

Because it takes time for producers to switch from one activity to another, and because it takes time to build new machines and factories and train additional skilled workers, the price elasticity of supply will be higher for most goods in the long run than in the short run. In the short run, a manufacturer's inability to augment existing stocks of equipment and skilled labour may make it impossible to expand output beyond a certain limit. But if a shortage of managers was the bottleneck, new MBAs can graduate in only two years. Or if a shortage of legal staff is the problem, new lawyers can be trained in three years. In the long run, firms can always buy new equipment, build new factories and hire additional skilled workers.

The conditions that gave rise to the perfectly elastic supply curve for lemonade in Exercise 3.10 are also satisfied for many other products in the long run. If a product can be copied (in the sense that any company can acquire the design and other technological information required to produce it), and if the inputs needed for its production are used in roughly fixed proportions and are available at fixed market prices, then the long-run supply curve for that product will be horizontal. But many products do not satisfy these conditions, and their supply curves remain steeply upward-sloping, even in the very long run.

Economic naturalist 3.4 Why are US motor fuel prices so much more volatile than car prices?

New car prices are much less volatile than motor fuel prices, but neither is much use without the other. This is true in Europe as well as in America. In the USA, however, the volatility of fuel prices is greater than in Europe because European prices have a large fixed tax (excise) element in them, while taxes on motor fuels are low and/or ad valorem in America for the most part. In early 2005, while petrol cost €0.95–€1.20 per litre in Europe, it was only €0.27–€0.35 in the United States (at the time, €1 = $1.3). As shown here, for example, the highest daily fuel prices in California's two largest cities were three times higher than the lowest daily prices during 2001–03. Why this enormous difference in volatility as between cars and fuel?

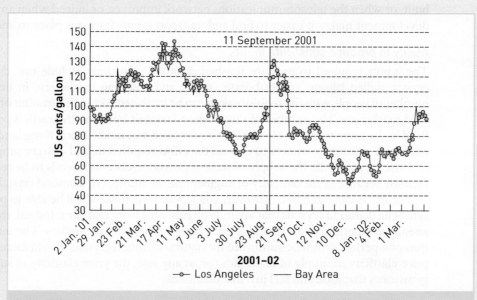

Figure 3.25 Fuel Prices in Two California Cities.
Source: Oil Price Information Service (http://www.opisnet.com)

Two factors stand out as explanations. One is that the short-run price elasticity of demand for fuel is much smaller than the corresponding elasticity for cars. The other is that supply shifts are much more pronounced and frequent in the fuel market than in the car market.

Why are the two markets different? Consider first the difference in price elasticities of demand. In the short run, car ownership and commuting patterns are almost completely fixed, so even if the price of fuel were to change sharply, the quantity we demand will not change by much. In contrast, if there is a sudden dramatic change in the price of cars, we can always postpone or accelerate our next car purchase.

To see why the supply curve in the petrol market experiences larger and more frequent shifts than the supply curve in the car market, we need only examine the relative stability of the inputs employed by sellers in these two markets. Most of the inputs used in producing cars – steel, glass, rubber,

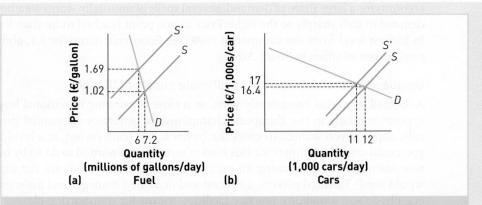

Figure 3.26 Greater Volatility in Fuel Prices than in Car Prices. Fuel prices are more volatile prices because supply shifts are larger and more frequent in the fuel market (a) than in the car market (b), and also because supply and demand are less elastic in the short run in the fuel market.

plastics, electronic components, labour, etc. – are reliably available to car makers. In contrast, the key input used in making petrol – crude oil – is subject to profound and unpredictable supply interruptions.

This is so in part because much of the world's supply of crude oil is controlled by the Organization of Petroleum Exporting Countries (OPEC), a group of oil-exporting countries that has sharply curtailed its oil shipments to the United States on several occasions in the past. Even in the absence of formal OPEC action, however, large retail supply curtailments often occur in the oil market – for example, whenever producers fear that political instability might engulf the major oil-producing countries of the Middle East. When Hurricane Katrina devastated New Orleans and the US Gulf Coast in August 2005, putting a significant proportion of US oil production capacity out of use for several months, prices rose by several dollars a barrel. Precautionary and speculative stock demand is a major component of changes in demand from day to day where oil products are concerned.

Note the sharp spike in petrol prices that occurred just after the terrorist attacks on the World Trade Center and the Pentagon on 11 September 2001. Fears of an impending oil supply interruption were perfectly rational. And such fears alone can trigger a temporary supply interruption as people try to build up stocks. The consequence is oil being diverted from sale to end users into inventories. The same phenomenon led to a surge in oil prices from around $30 per barrel at the end of 2003 to over $40 per barrel by May 2004, as a consequence of fears of supply disruptions associated with unrest in the Middle East arising from the British- and US-led occupation of Iraq. But, once the fear of war recedes, the supply curve of petrol reverts with equal speed to its earlier position. Given the low short-run price elasticity of demand for petrol, that's all it takes to generate the considerable price volatility we see in this market.

The fallback in prices in 2004 turned out to be temporary, as steadily increasing demand, especially from China and India, underpinned a much more durable upward movement in prices, which reached over $60 per barrel in 2005 and $100 at the end of 2007, although they fell back to the $85–$95 range early in 2008, but were back over $130 by the summer of that year. The price of a barrel then fell again to $40 by the end of 2008.

Price volatility is also common in markets in which demand curves fluctuate sharply and supply curves are highly inelastic. One such market was California's unregulated market for wholesale electricity during the summer of 2000. The supply of electricity generating capacity was essentially fixed in the short run. And because air conditioning accounts for a large share of demand, several spells of unusually warm weather caused demand to shift sharply to the right. Price at one point reached more than four times its highest level from the summer of 1999 (see Economic naturalist 3.1, above, for a similar state of affairs in South Africa).

Unique and essential inputs: the ultimate supply bottleneck

A football team that consistently wins, or is close to winning its national league, and appears regularly in the European championship, generates substantial profits as a rule. Suppose you wanted to enter the business as a team owner, at a level at which you could credibly compete for this kind of money, and wanted to do so by building a new team (not by purchasing an existing top-level club). What are the inputs you would need? Talented players, a shrewd and dedicated manager and assistants, trainers, physicians, a stadium, practice facilities, means for transporting players to away games, a marketing staff, and so on. Whereas some of these inputs can be acquired at reasonable prices in the marketplace, many others cannot. Indeed, the most important input of all – highly talented players – is in extremely limited supply. This is so because the very definition of talented player is inescapably relative – simply put, such a player is *one who is better than most others*.

Given the huge payoff that accrues to a championship team, it is no surprise that the bidding for the most talented players has become so intense. If there were a long list of superbly talented strikers, each of star quality, Real Madrid would not have had to pay €20 million plus to Manchester United for David Beckham, and then pay Beckham as much as €5 million a year. But, of course, the supply of such players is extremely limited.

Another source of supply bottlenecks arises from the existence of fixed numbers of places in a football league. It is conceivable that you could produce more and better players by spending more on them. But you can't produce more places at the top of the league. A place in the UK Premiership is an essential input to play against other Premiership clubs. The same applies to Serie A in Italy. There are many hungry football teams in Britain, France, Italy, Spain . . . that would like nothing better than to play in the Champions' League. Every team in England would like to get into the Premiership. But no matter how much each is willing to spend, only two or three can succeed in any year. Similar restrictions apply in the Champions' League. The supply of places in the Premiership or the Champions' League is perfectly inelastic with respect to price, even in the very long run.

Sports champions are by no means the only important product whose supply elasticity is constrained by the inability to reproduce unique and essential inputs. In the movie industry, for example, although the supply of movies starring Jim Carrey is not perfectly inelastic, there are only so many films he can make each year. Because his films consistently generate huge box office revenues, scores of film producers want to sign him for their projects. But because there isn't enough of him to go around, his salary per film is more than $20 million.

In the long run, *unique and essential inputs* are the only truly significant supply bottleneck. If it were not for the inability to duplicate the services of such inputs, most goods and services would have extremely high price elasticities of supply in the long run.

Summary

Supply and demand

- Focusing solely on differences in *costs of production* cannot adequately explain the difference in prices of goods or services. For example, this approach cannot explain why a conveniently located house sells for more than one that is less conveniently located. The same applies to focusing only on willingness to pay. This approach cannot explain why the price of a life-saving appendectomy is less than that of a surgical facelift.

- Alfred Marshall's model of supply and demand explains why, in order to explain variations in price, we must examine the *interaction of cost and willingness to pay*. Goods differ in price because of differences in their respective supply and demand curves.

- The demand curve is a downward-sloping line that tells what quantity buyers will demand at any given price. The supply curve is an upward-sloping line that tells what quantity sellers will offer at any given price. *Market equilibrium* occurs when the quantity buyers demand at the market price is exactly the same as the quantity that sellers offer. The equilibrium price–quantity pair is the one at which the demand and supply curves intersect. In equilibrium, market price measures both the value of the last unit sold to buyers and the cost of the resources required to produce it.

- When the price of a good lies above its equilibrium value, there is an *excess supply* of that good. This motivates sellers to cut their prices, and price continues to fall until the equilibrium price is reached. When price lies below its equilibrium value, there is *excess demand*. Frustrated buyers are motivated to offer higher prices, and the upward pressure on prices persists until equilibrium is reached.

- The market system, relying only on the tendency of people to respond in self-interested ways to market price signals, manages to coordinate the actions of literally billions of buyers and sellers worldwide. If prices and purchases are free to adjust, excess demand or supply tends to be small and temporary.

- The efficiency of markets in *allocating resources* does not eliminate social concerns about how goods and services are distributed among different people. Concern for the well-being of the poor has motivated many governments to intervene in a variety of ways to alter the outcomes of market forces. Sometimes these interventions take the form of laws that peg prices below their equilibrium levels. Such laws almost invariably generate harmful, if unintended, consequences, including shortages and black markets.

- If the difficulty is that the poor have too little money, the best solution is to discover ways of boosting their incomes directly.

- The basic *supply and demand model* is a primary tool of the economic naturalist. Changes in the equilibrium price of a good, and in the amount of it traded in the marketplace, can be predicted on the basis of shifts in its supply or demand curves. The following four rules hold for any good with a downward-sloping demand curve and an upward-sloping supply curve.
  – An increase in demand will lead to an increase in equilibrium price and quantity.
  – A reduction in demand will lead to a reduction in equilibrium price and quantity.
  – An increase in supply will lead to a reduction in equilibrium price and an increase in equilibrium quantity.
  – A decrease in supply will lead to an increase in equilibrium price and a reduction in equilibrium quantity.

■ Incomes, tastes, population, expectations, and the prices of substitutes and complements are among the factors that shift *demand schedules (curves)*. *Supply schedules (curves)*, in turn, are primarily governed by such factors as technology, input prices, expectations, the number of sellers – and, especially for agricultural products, the weather.

■ When (but only when) the supply and demand curves for a good reflect all significant costs and benefits associated with the production and consumption of that good, the market equilibrium price will guide people to produce and consume the quantity of the good that results in the largest possible economic surplus.

Elasticity

■ The price elasticity of demand is a measure of how strongly buyers respond to *changes in price*. It is the percentage change in quantity demanded that occurs in response to a 1 per cent change in price. The demand for a good is called elastic with respect to price if its price elasticity is more than 1; inelastic if its price elasticity is less than 1; and unit elastic if its price elasticity is equal to 1.

■ Goods that occupy only a small share of the typical consumer's budget and have few or no good substitutes, tend to have low price elasticity of demand. Goods such as new cars of a particular make and model, which occupy large budget shares and have many attractive substitutes, tend to have high price elasticity of demand. Price elasticity of demand is higher in the long run than in the short run because people often need time to *adjust to price changes*.

■ The *price elasticity of demand* at a point along a demand curve can also be expressed as the formula $\varepsilon = (\Delta Q/Q)/(\Delta P/P)$. Here, P and Q represent price and quantity at that point and ΔP and ΔQ represent small changes in price and quantity. For straight-line demand curves, this formula can also be expressed as $\varepsilon = (P/Q) \times (1/\text{slope})$. These formulations tell us that price elasticity *declines in absolute terms* as we move down a straight-line demand curve.

■ A cut in price will increase total spending on a good if demand is elastic but reduce it if demand is inelastic. An increase in price will increase total spending on a good if demand is inelastic but reduce it if demand is elastic. *Total expenditure* on a good reaches a maximum when price elasticity of demand is equal to 1.

■ Analogous formulae are used to define the elasticity of demand for a good with respect to *income* and the *prices of other goods*. In each case, elasticity is the percentage change in quantity demanded divided by the corresponding percentage change in income or price.

■ *The price elasticity of supply* is defined as the percentage change in quantity supplied that occurs in response to a 1 per cent change in price. The mathematical formula for the price elasticity of supply at any point is $(\Delta Q/Q)/(\Delta P/P)$, where P and Q are the price and quantity at that point, ΔP is a small change in the initial price and ΔQ is the resulting change in quantity. This formula can also be expressed as $(P/Q) \times (1/\text{slope})$, where $(1/\text{slope})$ is the reciprocal of the slope of the supply curve.

■ The price elasticity of supply of a good depends on how difficult or costly it is to acquire *additional units* of the inputs involved in producing that good. In general, the more easily additional units of these inputs can be acquired, the higher the price elasticity of supply will be. It is easier to expand production of a product if the inputs used to produce that product are similar to the inputs used to produce other products, if inputs are relatively mobile, or if an acceptable substitute for existing inputs can be developed. And, like the price elasticity of demand, the price elasticity of supply is greater in the long run than in the short run.

Review questions

1. Distinguish between the meaning of the expressions 'change in demand' and 'change in the quantity demanded'.

2. Last year a government official proposed that motor fuel price controls be imposed to protect the poor from rising motor fuel prices. What evidence could you consult to discover whether this proposal was enacted?

3. Explain the distinction between the horizontal and vertical interpretations of the demand curve.

4. Give an example of behaviour you have observed that could be described as 'smart for one, dumb for all'.

5. Why does a consumer's price elasticity of demand for a good depend on the fraction of the consumer's income spent on that good?

6. Why does the elasticity of demand for a good with respect to its own price decline as we move down along a straight-line demand curve?

7. Why do economists pay little attention to the algebraic sign of the elasticity of demand for a good with respect to its own price, yet pay careful attention to the algebraic sign of the elasticity of demand for a good with respect to another good's price?

8. Why is supply elasticity higher in the long run than in the short run?

connect Problems

1. How would each of the following affect the EU market supply curve for wheat?
    a. A new and improved crop rotation technique is discovered.
    b. The price of fertiliser falls.
    c. The EU Commission offers new subsidies to farmers growing wheat.
    d. A tornado sweeps through northern France in July.

2. Indicate how you think each of the following would shift demand in the indicated market.
    a. Incomes of buyers in the market for Spanish sun holidays increase.
    b. Buyers in the market for pizza read a study linking hamburger consumption to heart disease.
    c. Buyers in the market for CDs learn of an increase in the price of audio cassettes.
    d. Buyers in the market for CDs learn of an increase in the price of CDs.

3. What will happen to the equilibrium price and quantity of olives in Italy if the wage paid to olive pickers rises?

4. How will an increase in immigration affect the equilibrium price of land?

5. What will happen to the equilibrium price and quantity of beef if the price of chicken feed increases?

6. How will a new law mandating an increase in required levels of automobile insurance affect the equilibrium price and quantity in the market for new automobiles?

7. Suppose the current issue of *Le Monde* reports an outbreak of mad cow disease in the Dordogne as well as the discovery of a new breed of chickens that gain more weight than existing breeds that consume the same amount of food. How will these developments affect the equilibrium price and quantity of chicken sold in France?

8. What will happen to the equilibrium price and quantity of apples if apples are discovered to help prevent colds and a fungus kills 10 per cent of existing apple trees?

9. The schedule below shows daily purchases of bags of *pommes frites* bought in Leuven in Belgium, at a variety of prices.

Price of *pommes frites* (€/pack) day	Number of bags purchased per day
6	0
5	3,000
4	6,000
3	9,000
2	12,000
1	15,000
0	18,000

a. Graph the daily demand curve for bags of *pommes frites* in Leuven.

b. Calculate the price elasticity of demand at the point on the demand curve at which the price is €3.

c. If all outlets increased the price from €3 to €4, what would happen to total sales revenues?

10. Is the demand for a particular brand of car, such as a Ford or a Volkswagen, likely to be more or less price elastic than the demand for all cars? Explain.

11. A 2 per cent increase in the price of milk causes a 4 per cent reduction in the quantity demanded of chocolate syrup. What is the cross-price elasticity of demand for milk with respect to the price of chocolate syrup? Are the two goods complements or substitutes?

12. What are the respective price elasticities of supply at *A* and *B* on the supply curve shown in the graph below?

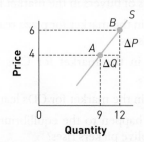

13. At point *A* on the demand curve shown below, by what percentage will a 1 per cent increase in the price of the product affect total expenditure on the product?

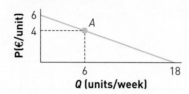

14. In an attempt to induce citizens to conserve energy, the government enacted regulations requiring that all air conditioners be more efficient in their use of electricity. After this regulation was implemented, government officials were then surprised to discover that people used even more electricity than before. Using the concept of price elasticity, explain how this happened.

References

Elzinga, K. (1971) 'The Beer Industry', in W. Adams (ed.), *The Structure of American Industry* (New York: Macmillan).

Fisher, R. (1996) *State and Local Public Finance* (Chicago: Irwin).

Houthakker, H.S. and L. Taylor (1970) *Consumer Demand in the United States: Analyses and Projections*, 2nd edn (Cambridge, MA: Harvard University Press).

Siciliani, L. and J. Hurst (2003) *Explaining Waiting Times for Elective Surgery Across OECD Countries* (OECD Health Working Paper, No. 2003/7).

Taylor, L. (1975) 'The Demand for Electricity: A Survey', *Bell Journal of Economics*, Spring.

Online LearningCentre

To help you grasp the key concepts of this chapter check out the extra resources posted on the Online Learning Centre. There are chapter summaries, self-test questions, an interactive graphing tool, weblinks and a glossary, all for free!

Visit the Online Learning Centre at: www.mcgraw-hill.co.uk/textbooks/mcdowell for information on accessing all of these resources.

Part 2

Competition and the 'Invisible Hand'

Having grasped the basic core principles of economics, you are now in a position to sharpen your understanding of how consumers and firms behave. In Part 2 our focus will be on how things work in an idealised, perfectly competitive economy in which consumers are perfectly informed and no firm has market power.

We begin in Chapter 4 by looking at purchase decisions by consumers. To analyse this we consider what is the basis for rational choices by consumers, and how they should rationally respond to changes in prices, incomes or the types of goods available to them. This enables us to derive testable predictions about the impact of price, income and tastes on behaviour, and provides the theoretical underpinning for the downward-sloping demand curve already discussed in Part 1. In Chapter 5 our focus will shift to the seller's side of the market, where our task will be to see why upward-sloping supply curves are a consequence of production decisions taken by firms whose goal is to maximise profit.

Our agenda in Chapter 6 is to develop more carefully and fully the concept of economic surplus introduced in Part 1 and to investigate the conditions under which unregulated markets generate the largest possible economic surplus. We will also explore why attempts to interfere with market outcomes often lead to unintended and undesired consequences.

Finally, in Chapter 7 we will investigate the economic forces by which the invisible hand of the marketplace guides profit-seeking firms and satisfaction-seeking consumers in ways that, to a surprising degree, serve society's ends. These forces encourage aggressive cost cutting by firms, even though the resulting gains will eventually take the form of lower prices rather than higher profits. We also emphasise, and this sometimes offends public opinion, that in a competitive economy that seeks efficient resource allocation, firm closure (exiting a market) is something that cannot be avoided, and something of which it can be said that efforts to reduce or eliminate it negate the basic reasons for which market economies are said to be efficient. This helps us to see why misunderstanding of competitive forces often results in costly errors, both in everyday decision making and in government policy.

Part 2

Competition and the 'Invisible Hand'

Demand: the Benefit Side of the Market

We start with an apocryphal story. X in Germany is famous for (among other things) its annual beer festival. The city's beer cellars, pubs and other watering holes are full to capacity with locals and visitors for the duration of the festival. According to an urban myth, one year the municipal authorities decided that for the first day of the festival beer should be supplied free of charge in the beer cellars to get the festival off to a good start. The cost of this would be the cost of one day's consumption in the premises concerned, and this was reckoned to be a good investment for the city to attract extra visitors. Arrangements were made with the beer cellars that the city fathers would meet the cost of all the beer consumed in the premises concerned that day. This was done despite the advice of the police that the consequence would be a higher incidence of drunkenness and anti-social behaviour. After all, people faced with the prospect of drinking for free will want to drink more, and the consequences are easy to predict. The city treasury said the plan would bankrupt the city, since at a zero price the amount that would be drunk would be enormous, and the cost to the city of the beer would reflect this. The owners of the other premises complained that they would do no business that day.

At the end of the week the police had to admit that the threatened drunkenness problem did not materialise. The accountants were delighted to report that the cost to the city was not much more than that of normal beer festival bierkeller daily consumption. And the other premises had to admit that their sales hadn't been badly affected after all.

Everyone was surprised, except the son of the Burgermeister (mayor), who was one of the best in the final-year economics class at the university that year. His father had run the free-beer scheme past him before introducing the proposal. The son predicted that there would be some increase in beer consumption, but that the fears of the police were groundless. He explained that there was only so much capacity in the beer cellars, and that he expected that people would be forced to queue to get in to enjoy the free beer. Once in, they could indeed consume more … but by and large each extra stein poured inside the cellar meant one stein fewer consumed by those outside waiting to get in. The queues outside would grow until the time cost of waiting acted as a deterrent to people joining the queue. Faced with this time price they would repair to the pubs that were not offering free beer. In effect, the cellars would supply not much more beer than would normally be the case, but it would be consumed by different individuals than if they sold it. The end result would be that the available drink would be rationed not by a monetary price, but by a *time price* in the queue. Hence, it would not be possible for everyone in X that day to drink as much beer as they might like at a zero price, and those who drank beer 'free' would pay a time price to do so, while others would pay a money price but not have to queue.

When a good or service is scarce, it must somehow be *rationed* among competing users. In most markets, monetary prices perform that task. But, in the case of free beer, waiting time becomes the effective rationing device. Having to stand in a queue is a cost, no less so than having to part with some money.

This story drives home the point that although the demand curve is usually described as a relationship between the quantity demanded of a good and its monetary price, the relationship is really a much more general one. At bottom, the demand curve is a relationship between the quantity demanded and all costs – monetary and non-monetary – associated with acquiring a good.

Our task in this chapter will be to explore the demand side of the market in greater depth than was possible in Chapter 3. There we merely asked you to accept as an intuitively plausible claim that the quantity demanded of a good or service declines as its price rises. This relationship is known as the law of demand, and we shall see how it emerges as a simple consequence of the assumption that people spend their limited incomes in rational ways. In the process, we shall see more clearly the dual roles of *income* and *substitution* as factors that account for the law of demand. We shall also see how to generate market demand curves by adding the demand curves for individual buyers horizontally. Finally, we shall see how to use the demand curve to generate a measure of the total benefit that buyers reap from their participation in a market.

The approach we take is to explain the basic concepts lying behind the idea of the demand curve, and then to use these to derive the proposition that demand curves in general will slope downwards based on logic rather than on simple (and sometimes misleading) notions of common sense. In this chapter we offer first a relatively non-technical explanation based on an assumption concerning consumer behaviour that is referred to as '*diminishing marginal utility*'. This approach suffices for most purposes, but depends on restrictive assumptions concerning people's preferences. So, we then offer a more rigorous and more general analysis of preferences to demonstrate the logical basis for the slope of demand curves, and in doing so introduce a construct that is central to economics analysis after the introductory stage. This construct is the '*indifference curve*'. It is possible to skip this section without losing the thread of the argument in the chapter, but we recommend that you do not take this option if you intend going on to further study in economics.

The law of demand

With our discussion of the 'free' beer offer in mind, let us restate the *law of demand*:

Law of demand: People do less of what they want to do as the cost of doing it rises.

Cost–Benefit
Analysis

By stating the law of demand in this way, we can see it as a direct consequence of the *Cost–Benefit Principle* (Chapter 1), which says that an activity should be pursued if (and only if) its benefits are at least as great as its costs. Recall that we measure the benefit of an activity by the highest price we would be willing to pay to pursue it – namely, our *reservation price* for the activity. When the cost of an activity rises, it is more likely to exceed our reservation price, and we are therefore less likely to pursue that activity.

The law of demand applies to BMWs, cheap key rings and 'free' beer, not to mention compact discs, manicures, medical care and acid-free rain. It stresses that a 'cost' is the sum of *all* the sacrifices – monetary and non-monetary, implicit and explicit – we must make to engage in an activity.

The origins of demand

How much are you willing to pay for the latest Alanis Morissette CD? The answer will clearly depend on how you feel about her music. To Morissette's diehard fans, buying the new release might seem absolutely essential; they'd pay a steep price indeed. But those who don't like Morissette's music may be unwilling to buy it at any price.

Wants (also called 'preferences' or 'tastes') are clearly an important determinant of a consumer's reservation price for a good. But that begs the question of where wants come from. Many tastes – such as the taste for water on a hot day or for a comfortable place to sleep at night – are largely biological in origin. But many others are heavily shaped by culture, and even basic cravings may be socially moulded. For example, people raised in southern India develop a taste for hot curry dishes, while those raised in England often prefer milder foods.

Tastes for some items may remain stable for many years, but tastes for others may be highly volatile. Although books about the *Titanic* disaster have been continuously available since the vessel sank in the spring of 1912, only with the appearance of James Cameron's blockbuster film did these books begin to sell in large quantities. In the spring of 1998, five of the fifteen books on the *New York Times* paperback bestseller list were about the *Titanic* itself or one of the actors in the film. Yet none of these books, or any other book about the *Titanic*, made the bestseller list in 1999. Still, echoes of the film continued to reverberate in the marketplace. In the years since its release, for example, demand for ocean cruises has grown sharply, and several American television networks have introduced shows set on cruise ships.

Peer influence provides another example of how social forces often influence demand. Indeed, it is often the single most important determinant of demand. For instance, if our goal is to predict whether a young man will purchase an illegal recreational drug, our knowing how much income he has is not very helpful. Knowing the prices of whisky and other legal substitutes for illicit drugs also tells us little. Although these factors do influence purchase decisions, by themselves they are weak predictors. But if we know that most of the young man's best friends are heavy drug users, there is a reasonably good chance that he will use drugs as well.

Another important way in which social forces shape demand is in the relatively common desire to consume goods and services that are recognised as the best of their kind. For instance, many people wanted to hear Luciano Pavarotti sing before he retired, not just because of the quality of his voice, but because he was widely regarded as the world's best – or at least the world's best known – tenor.

Consider, too, the decision of how much to spend on an interview suit. As university employment advisers never tire of reminding students at the end of their time in college, when they are looking for a job, making a good first impression is extremely important when you go for an interview. At the very least, that means showing up in a suit that looks good. But 'looking good' is a relative concept. If everyone else shows up in a €200 suit, you'll look good if you show up in a €300 suit. But you won't look as good in that same €300 suit if everyone else shows up in suits costing €1,000. The amount you choose to spend on an interview suit, then, clearly depends on how much others in your circle are spending.

Needs versus wants

In everyday language, we distinguish between goods and services people *need* and those they merely *want*. For example, we might say that someone wants a week's ski holiday in the Austrian Tyrol, but what he really needs is a few days off from his daily routine; or that someone wants a house with a view, but what she really needs is shelter from the elements. Likewise, since people need protein to survive, we might say that a severely malnourished person needs more protein. But it would strike us as odd to say that anyone – even a malnourished person – needs more prime fillet of beef, since health can be restored by consuming far less expensive sources of protein.

Economists like to emphasise that once we have achieved bare subsistence levels of consumption – the amount of food, shelter and clothing required to maintain our health – we can abandon all reference to needs and speak only in terms of wants. This linguistic distinction helps us to think more clearly about the true nature of our choices.

Think about the perennial political problems arising in southern California over the availability of water (much of which is supplied from aquifers in the distant Sierra Nevada mountains). One typical viewpoint that is often expressed in the media is: 'Californians don't have nearly as much water as they need.' Anyone who says this (or agrees with it) will tend to think differently about water shortages than someone who says: 'Californians don't have nearly as much water as they want when the price of water is low.' The first person is likely to focus on regulations to prevent people from watering their lawns, or on projects to capture additional runoff from the Sierra Nevada mountains. The second person is more likely to focus on the low price of water in California. Whereas remedies of the first sort are often costly and extremely difficult to implement, raising the price of water is both simple and effective.

Scarcity ⬤

Cost–Benefit Analysis ⬤

Economic naturalist 4.1 Why has Queensland in Australia a water shortage problem?

South-east Queensland, the so-called Gold Coast, has been the fastest-growing area in Australia in recent years. It has run into serious problems in terms of availability of water to meet rising demand from a growing population. The problem is in fact fairly widespread in Australia, but acute on the Gold Coast. This does not reflect climate change, but rather demand as the country's population increases. This has led in some quarters to calls for limits on immigration in order to slow population growth.

The Queensland State government's response is to undertake massive investment in water infrastructure of the order of Aus$3 billion to increase supply to the Gold Coast communities, of which one-third will have to come from water users through higher water charges, and two-thirds will come from the State Treasury. Note what that means: two-thirds of the cost of providing increased water to the residents of the Gold Coast now and predicted in the future is to be met by a state subsidy. Put another way, at the margin Gold Coast water users in the aggregate will be asked to pay one-third of the cost of the water they consume. At the moment they are paying even less. The price of water is subsidised so that the level of demand is such that marginal benefit is less than marginal cost of supply. The price people will have to pay for water affects decisions to locate homes or businesses in the Gold Coast. If the government persists in meeting extra demand by supplying water at below cost, further development and water shortages (excess demand) will be a permanent feature of the area.

To understand this, suppose that over the last ten years you had contemplated building a holiday home on the Gold Coast, or opening a restaurant or a car wash, but to do so would have meant facing water charges that reflected the long-run marginal cost of providing water of up to three times what was actually being asked. How would that have affected your decision to move to the Gold Coast? Suppose you already had a house there, and water charges had been increased to reflect long-run marginal cost. What do you think would have happened?

In the light of this you might like to consider why, although people complain about the level of water charges, from time to time it has been considered necessary to ban the use of garden hoses in suburban England. You might also ask whether the water shortages in France during the heatwave of the summer of 2005 could have been more appropriately dealt with than by a ban on car washes, pool filling and garden watering.

Translating wants into demand

It is a simple fact of life that although our resources are finite, our appetites for good things are boundless. Even if we had unlimited bank accounts, we'd quickly run out of the time and energy needed to do all the things we wanted to do. Our challenge is to use our *limited resources* to fulfil our desires to the greatest possible degree. And that leaves us with this practical question: 'How should we allocate our incomes among the various goods and services that are available?' To answer this question, it is helpful to begin by recognising that the goods and services we buy are not ends in themselves, but rather means for satisfying our desires.

Measuring wants: the concept of utility

Economists use the concept of *utility* to represent the satisfaction people derive from their consumption activities. The assumption is that people try to allocate their incomes so as to maximise their satisfaction, a goal that is referred to as *utility maximisation*.

Early economists imagined that the utility associated with different activities might some day be subject to precise measurement. The nineteenth-century British economist Jeremy Bentham, for example, wrote of a 'utilometer', a device that could be used to measure the amount of utility provided by different consumption activities. Although no such device existed in Bentham's day, contemporary neuropsychologists now have equipment that can generate at least crude measures of satisfaction.

For Bentham's intellectual enterprise, however, the absence of a real utilometer was of no practical significance. Even without such a machine, he could continue to envision the consumer as someone whose goal was to maximise the total utility he or she obtained from the goods consumed. Bentham's 'utility maximisation model', as we shall see, affords important insights about how rational consumers ought to spend their incomes. To explore how the model works, we begin with an unusually simple problem, that facing a consumer who reaches the front of the queue at a free ice cream stand. How many cones of ice cream should this person, whom we'll call Sarah, ask for? Table 4.1 shows the relationship between the total number of ice cream cones Sarah eats per hour and the total utility, measured in utils per hour, she derives from them. Note that the measurements in the table are stated in terms of cones per hour and utils per hour. Why 'per hour'? Because without an explicit time dimension we would have no idea whether a given quantity was a lot or a little. Five ice cream cones in a lifetime isn't much, but five in an hour would be more than most of us would care to eat.

Cone quantity (cones/hour)	Total utility (utils/hour)
0	0
1	50
2	90
3	120
4	140
5	150
6	140

Table 4.1 **Sarah's Total Utility from Ice Cream Consumption**

As the entries in Table 4.1 show, Sarah's total utility increases with each cone she eats, up to the fifth cone. Eating five cones per hour makes her happier than eating four, which makes her happier than eating three, and so on. But beyond five cones per hour, consuming more ice cream actually makes Sarah less happy. Thus the sixth cone reduces her total utility from 150 utils per hour to 140 utils per hour.

We can display the utility information in Table 4.1 graphically, as in Fig. 4.1. Note in the graph that the more cones per hour Sarah eats, the more utils she gets – but again only up to the fifth cone. Once she moves beyond five, her total utility begins to decline. Sarah's happiness reaches a maximum of 150 utils when she eats five cones per hour. At that point she has no incentive to eat the sixth cone, even though it's absolutely free. Eating it would actually make her worse off.

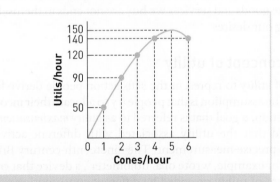

Figure 4.1 Sarah's Total Utility from Ice Cream Consumption. For most goods, utility rises at a diminishing rate with additional consumption.

Table 4.1 and Fig. 4.1 illustrate another important aspect of the relationship between utility and consumption – namely, that the additional utility from additional units of consumption declines as total consumption increases. Thus, whereas one cone per hour is a *lot* better – by 50 utils – than zero, five cones per hour is just a *little* better than four (just 10 utils' worth).

The term **marginal utility** denotes the amount by which total utility changes when consumption changes by one unit. In Table 4.2, column (3) shows the marginal utility values that correspond to changes in Sarah's level of ice cream consumption. For example, the second entry in column (3) represents the increase in total utility (measured in utils per cone) when Sarah's consumption rises from one cone per hour to two. Note that the marginal utility entries in column (3) are placed midway between the rows of the preceding columns. We do this to indicate that marginal utility corresponds to the movement from one consumption quantity to the next. Thus we would say that the marginal utility of moving from one to two cones per hour is 40 utils per cone.

marginal utility the additional utility gained from consuming an additional unit of a good

Cone quantity (cones/hour) (1)	Total utility (utils/hour) (2)	Marginal utility (utils/cone) (3)
0	0	–
1	50	
		40
2	90	
		30
3	120	
		20
4	140	
		10
5	150	
		–10
6	140	

Marginal utility

$$= \frac{\text{Change in utility}}{\text{Change in consumption}}$$

$$= \frac{90 \text{ utils} - 50 \text{ utils}}{2 \text{ cones} - 1 \text{ cone}}$$

$$= 40 \text{ utils/cone}$$

Table 4.2 **Sarah's Total and Marginal Utility from Ice Cream Consumption**

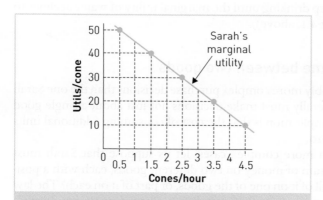

Figure 4.2 Diminishing Marginal Utility. The more cones Sarah consumes each hour, the smaller her marginal utility will be. For Sarah, consumption of ice cream cones reflects diminishing marginal utility.

Because marginal utility is the change in utility that occurs as we move from one quantity to another, when we graph marginal utility we normally adopt the convention of plotting each specific marginal utility value halfway between the two quantities to which it corresponds. Thus, in Fig. 4.2, we plot the marginal utility value of 40 utils per cone midway between one cone per hour and two cones per hour, and so on. (In this example, the marginal utility graph is a downward-sloping straight line for the region shown, but this need not always be the case.)

In so far as there is a tendency for marginal utility to decline as consumption increases, beyond some point consumption is said to be subject to **diminishing marginal utility** (DMU). Observations suggest that this is a pervasive phenomenon, so pervasive that it is sometimes loosely – and wrongly – referred to as the 'law' of diminishing marginal utility. DMU certainly appears to apply not just for Sarah's consumption of ice cream here, but also for most other goods for most consumers. If we have one cake or one Ferrari, we're happier than we are with none; if we have two, we'll be even happier – but not twice as happy – and so on. However, pervasive as it is, it is not a law in the sense of holding true in general. Indeed, some consumption activities even seem to exhibit *increasing* marginal utility. For example, an unfamiliar song may seem irritating the first time you hear it, then gradually become more tolerable the next few times you hear it. Before long, you

diminishing marginal utility the tendency for the additional utility gained from consuming an additional unit of a good to diminish as consumption increases beyond some point

may discover that you *like* the song, and you may even find yourself singing it in the shower. Furthermore, your utility from consumption of a good or expenditure on a good or service may be affected by whether or not other people around you consume it and in what quantities. Thus if everyone you know buys an Apple iPhone 3G, the utility to you of your existing phone may be reduced, and the utility of spending more to get the latest phone may increase. Notwithstanding such exceptions, diminishing marginal utility is a plausible characterisation of the relationship between utility and consumption for many goods. Unless otherwise stated, we shall assume that it holds for the various goods we discuss.

Cost–Benefit Analysis

Incentives Matter

Back for a moment to Sarah. What will she do when she gets to the front of the queue? At that point, the opportunity cost of the time she spent waiting is a *sunk cost*, and is hence irrelevant to her decision about how many cones to order. And since there is no monetary charge for the cones, the cost of ordering an additional one is zero. According to the Cost–Benefit Principle, Sarah should therefore continue to order cones as long as the marginal benefit (here, the marginal utility she gets from an additional cone) is greater than or equal to zero. As we can see from the entries in Table 4.2, marginal utility is positive up to and including the fifth cone but becomes negative after five cones. Thus, as noted earlier, Sarah should order five cones.

In this highly simplified example, Sarah's *utility-maximisation* problem is just like the one she would confront if she were deciding how much water to drink from a public fountain. (*Solution:* Keep drinking until the marginal utility of water declines to zero (see Economic naturalist 4.1, above)).

Allocating a fixed income between two goods

Most of us confront considerably more complex purchase decisions than the one Sarah faced. For one thing, we generally must make decisions not just about a single good but about many. Another complication is that the cost of consuming additional units of each good will rarely be zero.

To see how to proceed in more complex cases, let us suppose that Sarah must decide how to spend a fixed sum of money on two different goods, each with a positive price. Should she spend all of it on one of the goods, or part of it on each? The law of diminishing marginal utility suggests that spending it all on a single good isn't a good strategy. Rather than devote more and more money to the purchase of a good we already consume in large quantities (and whose marginal utility is therefore relatively low), we generally do better to spend that money on other goods that we don't have much of, whose marginal utility will likely be higher.

The simplest way to illustrate how economists think about the spending decisions of a utility-maximising consumer is to work through a scenario like that in Example 4.1.

Example 4.1 Is Sarah maximising her utility from consuming chocolate and vanilla ice cream (1)?

Chocolate ice cream sells for €2 per carton and vanilla sells for €1. Sarah has a budget of €400 per year to spend on ice cream, and her marginal utility from consuming each type varies with the amount consumed as shown in Fig. 4.3. If she is currently buying 200 cartons of vanilla and 100 cartons of chocolate each year, is she maximising her utility?

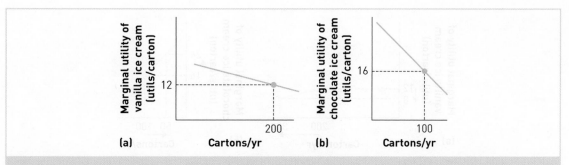

Figure 4.3 Marginal Utility Curves for Two Flavours of Ice Cream (1). At Sarah's current consumption levels, her marginal utility of chocolate ice cream is 25 per cent higher than her marginal utility of vanilla. But chocolate is twice as expensive as vanilla.

Note first that with 200 cartons per year of vanilla and 100 cartons of chocolate, Sarah is spending €200 per year on each type of ice cream, for a total expenditure of €400 per year on ice cream, exactly the amount in her budget. By spending her money in this fashion, is she getting as much utility as possible? Note in Fig. 4.3(b) that her marginal utility from chocolate ice cream is 16 utils per carton. Since chocolate costs €2 per carton, her current spending on chocolate is yielding additional utility at the rate of (16 utils/carton)/(€2/carton) = 8 utils per euro. Similarly, note in Fig. 4.3(a) that Sarah's marginal utility for vanilla is 12 utils per carton. And since vanilla costs only €1 per carton, her current spending on vanilla is yielding (12 utils/carton)/(€1/carton) = 12 utils per euro. In other words, at her current rates of consumption of the two flavours, her spending yields higher marginal utility per euro for vanilla than for chocolate. And this means that Sarah cannot possibly be maximising her total utility.

To see why, note that if she spent €2 less on chocolate (that is, if she bought one carton fewer than before), she would lose about 16 utils;[1] but with the same €2, she could buy two additional cartons of vanilla, which would boost her utility by about 24 utils,[2] for a net gain of about 8 utils. Under Sarah's current budget allocation, she is thus spending too little on vanilla and too much on chocolate.

In Example 4.2, we shall see what happens if Sarah spends €100 per year less on chocolate and €100 per year more on vanilla.

Example 4.2 Is Sarah maximising her utility from consuming chocolate and vanilla ice cream (2)?

Sarah's total ice cream budget and the prices of the two flavours are the same as in Example 4.1. If her marginal utility from consuming each type varies with the amount consumed, as shown in Fig. 4.4, and if she is currently buying 300 cartons of vanilla and 50 cartons of chocolate each year, is she maximising her utility?

---

1 The actual reduction would be slightly larger than 16 utils, because her marginal utility of chocolate rises slightly as she consumes less of it.
2 The actual increase will be slightly smaller than 24 utils, because her marginal utility of vanilla falls slightly as she buys more of it.

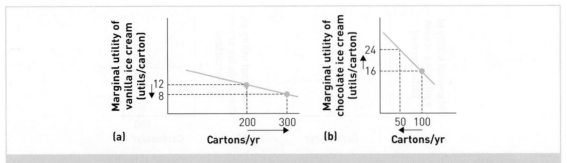

Figure 4.4 Marginal Utility Curves for Two Flavours of Ice Cream (2). When Sarah increases her consumption of vanilla (a), her marginal utility of vanilla falls. Conversely, when she reduces her consumption of chocolate (b), her marginal utility of chocolate rises.

Note first that the direction of Sarah's rearrangement of her spending makes sense in light of Example 4.1, in which we saw that she was spending too much on chocolate and too little on vanilla. Spending €100 less on chocolate ice cream causes her marginal utility from that flavour to rise from 16 to 24 utils per carton (Fig. 4.4(b)). By the same token, spending €100 more on vanilla ice cream causes her marginal utility from that flavour to fall from 12 to 8 utils per carton (Fig. 4.4(a)). Both movements are a simple consequence of the law of diminishing marginal utility.

Since chocolate still costs €2 per carton, her spending on chocolate now yields additional utility at the rate of (24 utils/carton)/(€2/carton) = 12 utils per euro. Similarly, since vanilla still costs €1 per carton, her spending on vanilla now yields additional utility at the rate of only (8 utils/carton)/(€1/carton) = 8 utils per euro. So at her new rates of consumption of the two flavours, her spending yields higher marginal utility per euro for chocolate than for vanilla – precisely the opposite of the ordering we saw in Example 4.1.

Sarah has thus made too big an adjustment in her effort to remedy her original consumption imbalance. Starting from the new combination of flavours (300 cartons per year of vanilla and 50 cartons per year of chocolate), for example, if she then bought two fewer cartons of vanilla (which would reduce her utility by about 16 utils) and used the €2 she saved to buy an additional carton of chocolate (which would boost her utility by about 24 utils), she would experience a net gain of about 8 utils. So, again, her current combination of the two flavours fails to maximise her total utility. This time, she is spending too little on chocolate and too much on vanilla.

Exercise 4.1   Using the prices in Example 4.1, verify that the stated combination of flavours in Example 4.2 costs exactly the amount that Sarah has budgeted for ice cream.

optimal combination of goods the affordable combination that yields the highest total utility

What is Sarah's **optimal combination** of the two flavours? In other words, among all the combinations of vanilla and chocolate ice cream that Sarah can afford, which one provides the maximum possible total utility? Example 4.3 illustrates the condition that this optimal combination must satisfy.

Example 4.3 Is Sarah maximising her utility from consuming chocolate and vanilla ice cream (3)?

Sarah's total ice cream budget and the prices of the two flavours are again as in Examples 4.1 and 4.2. If her marginal utility from consuming each type varies with the amounts consumed as shown in Fig. 4.5, and if she is currently buying 250 cartons of vanilla and 75 cartons of chocolate each year, is she maximising her utility?

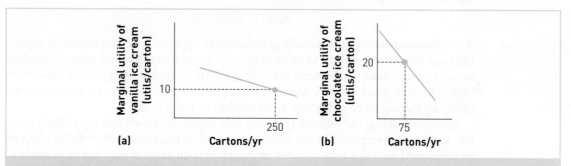

Figure 4.5 Marginal Utility Curves for Two Flavours of Ice Cream (3). At Sarah's current consumption levels, marginal utility per euro is exactly the same for each flavour.

As you can easily verify, the combination of 250 cartons per year of vanilla and 75 cartons per year of chocolate again costs a total of €400, exactly the amount of Sarah's ice cream budget. Her marginal utility from chocolate is now 20 utils per carton (Fig. 4.5(b)), and since chocolate still costs €2 per carton, her spending on chocolate now yields additional utility at the rate of (20 utils/carton)/(€2/carton) = 10 utils per euro. Sarah's marginal utility for vanilla is now 10 utils per carton (Fig. 4.5(a)), and since vanilla still costs €1 per carton, her last euro spent on vanilla now also yields (10 utils/carton)/(€1/carton) = 10 utils per euro. So at her new rates of consumption of the two flavours, her spending yields precisely the same marginal utility per euro for each flavour. Thus, if she spent a little less on chocolate and a little more on vanilla (or vice versa), her total utility would not change at all. For example, if she bought two more cartons of vanilla (which would increase her utility by 20 utils) and one carton of chocolate fewer (which would reduce her utility by 20 utils), both her total expenditure on ice cream and her total utility would remain the same as before. When her marginal utility per euro is the same for each flavour, *it is impossible for Sarah to rearrange her spending to increase total utility*. So 250 cartons of vanilla and 75 cartons of chocolate per year is the optimal combination of the two flavours.

The rational spending rule

Example 4.3 illustrates the *rational spending rule* for solving the problem of how to allocate a fixed budget across different goods. The optimal, or utility-maximising, combination must satisfy this rule.

Rational spending rule: Spending should be allocated across goods so that the marginal utility per euro is the same for each good.

The rational spending rule can be expressed in the form of a simple formula. If we use MU_C to denote marginal utility from chocolate ice cream consumption (again measured in utils per carton), and P_C to denote the price of chocolate (measured in euros per carton), then the ratio MU_C/P_C will represent the marginal utility per euro spent on chocolate, measured in utils per euro. Similarly, if we use MU_V to denote the marginal utility from vanilla ice cream consumption and P_v to denote the price of vanilla, then MU_v/P_v will represent the marginal utility per euro spent on vanilla. The marginal utility per euro will be exactly the same for the two types – and hence total utility will be maximised – when the following simple equation for the rational spending rule for two goods is satisfied:

$$MU_C/P_C = MU_V/P_V$$

The rational spending rule is easily generalised to apply to spending decisions regarding large numbers of goods. In its most general form, it says that the ratio of marginal utility to price must be the same for each good the consumer buys. If the ratio were higher for one good than for another, the consumer could always increase her total utility by buying more of the first good and less of the second.

Strictly speaking, the rational spending rule applies to goods that are *perfectly divisible*, such as milk or petrol. Many other goods, such as bus rides and television sets, can be consumed only in whole-number amounts. In such cases, it may not be possible to satisfy the rational spending rule exactly. For example, when you buy one television set, your marginal utility per euro spent on televisions may be somewhat higher than the corresponding ratio for other goods, yet if you bought a second set the reverse might well be true. Your best alternative in such cases is to allocate each additional euro you spend to the good for which your marginal utility per euro is highest.[3]

Notice that we have not chosen to classify the rational spending rule as one of the core principles of economics. We omit it from this list not because the rule is unimportant, but because it follows directly from the Cost–Benefit Principle. And, as we noted earlier, there is considerable advantage in keeping the list of core principles as small as possible. (If we included 200 principles on this list, there's a good chance you wouldn't remember any of them a few years from now.)

Cost–Benefit
Analysis

Income and substitution effects revisited

In Chapter 3, we saw that the quantity of a good that consumers wish to purchase depends on its own price, the prices of substitutes and complements, and on consumer incomes. We also saw that when the price of a good changes, the quantity of it demanded changes for two reasons: the *substitution* effect and the *income* effect. The substitution effect refers to the fact that when the price of a good goes up, substitutes for that good become relatively more attractive, causing some consumers to abandon the good for its substitutes.

The income effect refers to the fact that a price change makes the consumer either poorer or richer in real terms. Consider, for instance, the effect of a change in the price of one of the ice cream flavours in Example 4.3. At the original prices (€2 per carton for chocolate, €1 per carton for vanilla), Sarah's €400 annual ice cream budget would have enabled her to buy at most 200 cartons per year of chocolate or 400 cartons per year of vanilla. If the price of vanilla rose to €2 per carton, that would reduce not only the maximum amount of vanilla she could afford (from 400 to 200 cartons per year) but also the maximum amount of chocolate she could afford in combination with any given amount of vanilla. For example, at the original price of €1 per carton for vanilla,

---

3 See Problems 6 and 10 at the end of the chapter for examples.

Sarah could afford to buy 150 cartons of chocolate while buying 100 cartons of vanilla; but when the price of vanilla rises to €2, she can buy only 100 cartons of chocolate while buying 100 cartons of vanilla. As noted in Chapter 3, a reduction in real income shifts the demand curves for normal goods to the left.

The rational spending rule helps us see more clearly why a change in the price of one good affects demands for other goods. The rule requires that the *ratio of marginal utility to price* be the same for all goods. This means that if the price of one good goes up, the ratio of its current marginal utility to its new price will be lower than for other goods. Consumers can then increase their total utility by devoting smaller proportions of their incomes to that good and larger proportions to others.

Example 4.4 How should Sarah respond to a reduction in the price of chocolate ice cream?

Sarah's total ice cream budget is again €400 per year and prices of the two flavours are again €2 per carton for chocolate and €1 per carton for vanilla. Her marginal utility from consuming each type varies with the amounts consumed as shown in Fig. 4.6. She is currently buying 250 cartons of vanilla and 75 cartons of chocolate each year, which is the optimal combination for her at these prices (see Example 4.3). How should she reallocate her spending among the two flavours if the price of chocolate ice cream falls to €1 per carton?

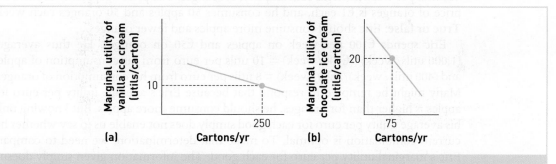

Figure 4.6 Marginal Utility Curves for Two Flavours of Ice Cream (4). At the current combination of flavours, marginal utility per euro is the same for each flavour. When the price of chocolate falls, marginal utility per euro becomes higher for chocolate than for vanilla. To redress this imbalance, Sarah should buy more chocolate and less vanilla.

Because the quantities shown in Fig. 4.6 constitute the optimal combination of the two flavours for Sarah at the original prices, they must exactly satisfy the rational spending rule:

$$MU_C/P_C = (20 \text{ utils}/\text{carton})/€2/\text{carton}) = 10 \text{ utils}/\text{euro}$$

$$= MU_V/P_V = (10 \text{ utils}/\text{carton})/(€/\text{carton})$$

When the price of chocolate falls to €1 per carton, the original quantities will no longer satisfy the rational spending rule, because the marginal utility per euro for chocolate will suddenly be twice what it was before:

$$MU_C/P_C = (20 \text{ utils}/\text{carton})/€1/\text{carton}) = 20 \text{ utils}/\text{euro}$$

$$> MU_V/P_V = (10 \text{ utils}/\text{euro})$$

To redress this imbalance, Sarah must rearrange her spending on the two flavours in such a way as to increase the marginal utility per euro for vanilla relative to the marginal utility per euro for chocolate. And, as we see in Fig. 4.6, that will happen if she buys a larger quantity than before of chocolate and a smaller quantity than before of vanilla.

Exercise 4.2   John spends all his income on two goods: food and shelter. The price of food is €5 per kg and the price of shelter is €10 per m^2. At his current consumption levels, his marginal utilities for the two goods are 20 utils per kg and 30 utils per m^2, respectively. Is John maximising his utility? If not, how should he reallocate his spending?

In Chapter 1 we saw that people often make bad decisions because they fail to appreciate the distinction between average and marginal costs and benefits. As Example 4.5 illustrates, this pitfall also arises when people attempt to apply the economist's model of utility maximisation.

Example 4.5   Should Eric consume more apples?

Eric gets a total of 1,000 utils per week from his consumption of apples and a total of 400 utils per week from his consumption of oranges. The price of apples is €2 each, the price of oranges is €1 each, and he consumes 50 apples and 50 oranges each week. **True or false**: Eric should consume more apples and fewer oranges.

Eric spends €100 per week on apples and €50 on oranges. He thus averages (1,000 utils/week)/(€100/week) = 10 utils per euro from his consumption of apples and (400 utils/week)/(€50/week) = 8 utils per euro from his consumption of oranges. Many might be tempted to respond that because Eric's average utility per euro for apples is higher than for oranges, he should consume more apples. But knowing only his average utility per euro for each good simply does not enable us to say whether his current combination is optimal. To make that determination, we need to compare Eric's marginal utility per euro for each good. The information given simply doesn't permit us to make that comparison.

RECAP Translating wants into demand

The Scarcity Principle (Chapter 1) challenges us to allocate our incomes among the various goods that are available so as to fulfil our desires to the greatest possible degree. The optimal combination of goods is the *affordable combination that yields the highest total utility*. For goods that are perfectly divisible, the rational spending rule tells us that the optimal combination is one for which the marginal utility per euro is the same for each good. If this condition were not satisfied, the consumer could increase utility by spending less on goods for which the marginal utility per euro was lower and more on goods for which the marginal utility per euro was higher.

Applying the rational spending rule

The real payoff from learning the law of demand and the rational spending rule lies not in working through hypothetical examples, but in using these abstract concepts to make sense of the world around you. To encourage you in your efforts to become an economic naturalist, we turn now to a sequence of examples in this vein.

Substitution at work

In the first of these examples, we focus on the role of *substitution*. When the price of a good or service goes up, rational consumers generally turn to less expensive substitutes. Can't afford the monthly repayments for a new car? Then buy a used one, or rent a flat on a bus route or rail line. French cuisine restaurants are too expensive? Then go out for Chinese, or eat at home more often. Cup Final tickets cost too much? Watch the game on television, or read a book. Can't afford a book? Borrow one from your local library, or download some reading matter from the internet. Once you begin to see substitution at work, you will be amazed by the number and richness of the examples that confront you every day.

Economic naturalist 4.2 Why do the wealthy in Manhattan, London, Paris and Rome live in smaller houses than the wealthy in Seattle, the Dordogne, Taunton or Parma?

Microsoft co-founder Bill Gates lives in a 4,000 m² house in Seattle, Washington. The floor area is 0.4 hectares, large even by the standards of Seattle, many of whose wealthy residents live in houses with more than 1,000 m² of floor space. By contrast, persons of similar wealth in Manhattan rarely live in houses or apartments larger than 500 m². Michael Smurfit of the Jefferson Smurfit Corporation lives in a luxurious apartment in Monaco that is a fraction of the size of the mansion of Tony Ryan (one of the original founders of Ryanair) 30 km from the centre of Dublin. Why this difference?

For people trying to decide how large a house to buy, the most obvious difference between Manhattan and Seattle or London and Taunton is the huge difference in housing prices. The cost of land alone is several times higher in Manhattan or London than in Seattle or Taunton, and construction costs are also much higher. Although plenty of New Yorkers could *afford* to build a 4,000 m² mansion, Manhattan housing prices are so high that they simply choose to live in smaller houses and spend what they save in other ways – on lavish summer homes in eastern Long Island, for instance. Rich Londoners and New Yorkers also eat out and go to the theatre more often than their wealthy counterparts in other parts of Britain and the United States.

An especially vivid illustration of substitution occurred during the late 1970s, when fuel shortages brought on by interruptions in the supply of oil from the Middle East led to sharp increases in the price of petrol and other fuels. In a variety of ways – some straightforward, others remarkably ingenious – consumers changed their behaviour to economise on the use of energy. They formed car pools, switched to public transport, moved closer to work, took fewer trips, turned down their central heating thermostats, installed insulation, double glazing and solar heaters, and bought more efficient washing machines and similar appliances. In the United States, many people even moved south to the 'sunshine belt' states, especially Florida, to escape high winter heating bills.

As Economic naturalist 4.3 points out, consumers not only abandon a good in favour of substitutes when it gets more expensive, but they also go back to that good when prices return to their original levels.

Economic naturalist 4.3 After the oil shocks of 1974 and 1979 Europeans did not change significantly the size of car they drove on average. Americans, however, with higher average incomes, switched dramatically from V8 5-litre engine cars to 2-litre four-cylinder cars. Why the difference? And why did they switch back in the 1990s, while there was a much smaller shift in consumption in Europe?

In 1973, the price of petrol was 38 cents per US gallon (approximately 3.5 litres; the Imperial gallon is approximately 4.5 litres). In 1974 the price shot up to 52 cents per gallon in the wake of a major disruption of oil supplies. A second disruption in 1979 drove the 1980 price to $1.19 per gallon. These sharp increases in the price of petrol led to big increases in the demand for cars with four-cylinder engines, which delivered much better fuel economy than the six- and eight-cylinder cars most people had owned. After 1980, however, fuel supplies stabilised, and prices rose only slowly, reaching $1.40 per gallon by 1999. Yet despite the continued rise in the price of petrol, the switch to smaller engines did not continue. By the late 1980s, the proportion of cars sold with six- and eight-cylinder engines began rising again. Why this reversal?

The first key to explaining these patterns is to focus on changes in the **real price** of petrol. When someone decides how big an automobile engine to choose, what matters is not the **nominal price** of petrol, but the price of petrol *relative* to all other goods. After all, for a consumer faced with a decision of whether to spend €1 on a litre of petrol, the important question is how much utility she could get from other things she could purchase with the same money. Even though the price of petrol has continued to rise slowly in nominal, or euro, terms since 1981, it has declined sharply relative to the price of other goods. Even in the aftermath of the Iraq war, petrol prices in Europe were lower in real terms than in 1984. Indeed, in terms of real purchasing power, in America the 1999 price was actually slightly lower than the 1973 price. (That is, in 1999, $1.40 bought slightly more goods and services than 38 cents bought in 1973.) It is this decline in the real price of petrol that accounts for the reversal of the trend towards smaller engines.

real price the euro price of a good relative to the average euro price of all other goods

nominal price the absolute price of a good in euro terms

What about Europe? The second key is to focus on the fact that the *relative increase* in petrol prices was much lower than in the United States. This reflects the fact that high taxes on petrol were and are universal in Europe. In the United States they were and are very low. Hence a doubling of the price of oil typically meant an increase of well under 50 per cent in the price to motorists in Europe, while the increase was close to 100 per cent in the United States. The incentive to shift consumption patterns based on relative price changes was much smaller in Europe. European motorists have, however, shown a willingness to react to higher fuel prices as predicted by economic theory in a way that has not been seen in the United States. They have shifted from smoother and more lively petrol engines to diesels. The 2007–08 price hikes may well lead Americans to imitate the rest of us and shift to diesels, too.

The importance of income differences

The rich are different from you and me. – F. Scott Fitzgerald
Yes, they have more money. – Ernest Hemingway

The most obvious difference between the rich and the poor is that the rich have higher incomes. To explain why the wealthy generally buy larger houses than the poor, we need not assume that the wealthy feel more strongly about housing than the poor. A much simpler explanation is that the total utility from housing, as with most other goods, increases with the amount that one consumes. As Economic naturalist 4.4 illustrates, income influences the demand not only for housing and other goods, but also for quality of service.

Equilibrium

Economic naturalist 4.4 Why should you not be surprised to find longer checkout queues at Aldi or Lidl than at Tesco in Britain or Conad in Italy?

Aldi, Lidl and other discount supermarkets offer a narrower range of goods at lower prices than the older supermarket chains in Britain. They originated in Germany, so it is not surprising that this pattern is repeated in other countries across Europe. People with lower incomes are disproportionately more likely to take advantage of these prices by going to the discount stores. One way that prices are reduced by the discounters is by reducing staffing levels, especially at the checkout. If we make the plausible assumption that people with higher incomes are more willing than others to pay to avoid standing in a queue, we should expect to see shorter queues in the conventional (but higher-priced) supermarkets. Keeping queues short at *any* grocery store means hiring more checkout staff, which means charging higher prices. High-income consumers are more likely than others to be willing to pay for shorter queues.

RECAP Applying the rational spending rule

Application of the rational spending rule highlights the important roles of *income* and *substitution* in explaining differences in consumption patterns – among individuals, among communities and across time. The rule also highlights the fact that *real*, as opposed to nominal, prices and income are what matter. The demand for a good falls when the real price of a substitute falls or the real price of a complement rises.

Indifference curve analysis and the demand curve

This section of the chapter is more technically demanding than the rest of the chapter. It can be skipped as it is not necessary to read it or master its content in order to continue the analysis of demand, but it introduces concepts that are fundamental to further study of economics. It also offers a rigorous basis for the proposition that demand curves slope downwards, and recasts rigorously the concept of consumer rationality.

So far, the analysis used to explain why demand curves slope down and the concept of consumer rationality has explicitly assumed that goods are subject to *diminishing marginal utility* (DMU) for a representative consumer. As a working hypothesis this is fine. There is plenty of evidence in the real world to support the proposition that DMU is a pervasive aspect of individual behaviour. It is also intuitively plausible.

Unfortunately, it doesn't take too much thought for someone to come up with counter-examples – cases where DMU does not, or certainly appears not to, apply. Of course, even in these cases we expect DMU to set in at some stage, but it is clear that it is not in fact a universal aspect of consumer choice. That should raise some doubts as to whether we can establish that demand curves slope downwards in general if we rely on a doubtfully general assumption as to how consumers value goods.

That is not the end of the matter. There is a second problem, which pertains to *measurement*. Earlier we made use of the assumption that we could measure satisfaction in objective units that we called utils. We did this as a pedagogic device, but in fact it is an assumption that is implicit in circumstances that are much more serious than demand theory in an introductory text.

For example, we implicitly appeal to the concept when we argue that society is better off if we transfer wealth from the rich to the poor, because we reckon that the increase in the welfare of the recipients of the transfer exceeds the reduction in the welfare of those who are asked to pay. Philosophically, and empirically, it could obviously be true that the reverse was true in the tax transfer example. Or we might say it is nonsensical to measure satisfaction in objective units anyway. For example, you might be able to answer the question 'Are you happier today than yesterday?' and be quite unable to answer the question 'By how much are you happier today than yesterday?' But DMU implies being able to make that kind of evaluation.

These two considerations lead to the conclusion that a 'proof' of the downward-sloping demand curve and the rational spending criterion that depends on DMU is at best a partial proof, and at worst may be no proof at all.

To deal with this, and also to introduce a tool of analysis that is widely used in economics, we drop any assumption of DMU, and start with a set of assumptions about rational choice.

First, we posit that an individual has a *preference ordering*. By that we mean that we have some means whereby we can in principle define an individual's preferences as to various bundles of goods or services he might consume. We make this as general and unrestrictive as possible.

- **Assumption 1:** The individual's preferences are **complete**. By this we mean that the individual can compare any two bundles of goods and services and say which is preferred or whether one is as good as the other. This is fundamental: the individual can *choose between bundles*.
- **Assumption 2:** The individual's preference ordering over bundles is **ordinal**, rather than **cardinal**. By this we mean that we only require a ranking, but don't require the individual to be able to answer the type of question given above about 'how much happier'. To do that the ranking has to be cardinal. The cardinal numbers are 1, 2, 3 … The ordinal numbers are 1st, 2nd, 3rd … A cardinal ordering enables us to say 'I am 50 per cent happier.' The ordinal ranking is a much less restrictive assumption or requirement.

Cardinal or ordinal? DMU implies that utility is measured cardinally.

- **Assumption 3:** The individual's preferences are **transitive**. By this we mean that if you say you prefer bundle *A* to bundle *B*, and bundle *B* to bundle *C,* you must prefer bundle *A* to bundle *C*.
- **Assumption 4:** The individual's satisfaction level is **monotonically increasing** with respect to any good. This is a technical way of saying that 'more of a good is better', so that, other things being equal, the individual is better off with more of any one good as long as she has the same amount as before of all other goods.
- **Assumption 5:** The individual's preferences are **continuous**. By this we mean that the individual can rank bundles that are very similar, for example containing a small amount more or less of any good or goods.
- **Assumption 6:** We assume that the individual's preferences display a **diminishing marginal rate of substitution**. This will be explained in context later on.

utility function the implication of these assumptions is that the preference ordering can be written as a utility function; this permits trade-offs

Assumptions 1–5 inclusive enable us to say that the individual's preferences over bundles of goods can be written as a **utility function**. Assumption 6 is an assumption about the function. By a utility function we mean that we can write an individual's preferences in the form

$$U_i = U_i(X, Y, ..., Z)$$

where U_i means the individual's utility, and the $X, Y, ..., Z$ are the bundles she is enjoying: her satisfaction is a function of the goods she consumes in the mathematical sense.

The basic feature of all this is that it means that the individual can trade off bundles in terms of their composition while maintaining a given level of satisfaction. While that may seem blindingly obvious, in fact it is not. Frequently, ethical or political choices are made between states of the world in a manner that does not permit trade-offs. An obvious case of this is the question of whether or not, and in what circumstances, abortion should be permitted. The same applies to capital punishment. Suppose both these are prohibited and the government proposes that they should be introduced in limited circumstances, resulting in a small number of cases of both in any year. Opponents of either are not likely to say 'We are against this being permitted, but if, say, everyone was given €1,000 a year more we would accept the proposal.' Instead they rank states of the world on the basis that there is no compensation they would accept that would leave them as happy as before if either were allowed.

The model

The consumer has an income, Y, which is to be spent on two goods, A and B. The unit price of A is P_a and the unit price of B is P_b. Her income is exhausted on the two goods, and from this we derive her *budget constraint* (budget line):

$$Y = P_a A + P_b B$$

where A is the number of units of A consumed and B is the number of units of B consumed. The consumer can consume Y/P_a units of A and Y/P_b units of B or any combination lying on the straight line between these points in Fig. 4.7. The line Y/P_a to Y/P_b

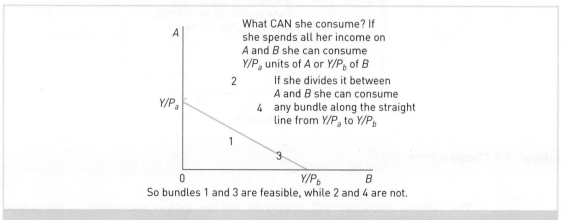

Figure 4.7 **The Consumer's Budget.**

is the budget constraint (budget line). Bundle 1 lies within the constraint: this bundle would not exhaust her income. Bundles 2 and 4 lie outside it: she hasn't enough income to buy either. Bundle 3 lies on the constraint. Only bundles on the constraint will exhaust her income. Given the assumptions above, she will never settle for a bundle lying within the constraint, because she can buy more of one or both and derive a higher level of utility.

If her income rises she can consume more, and bundle 4 becomes feasible (Fig. 4.8).

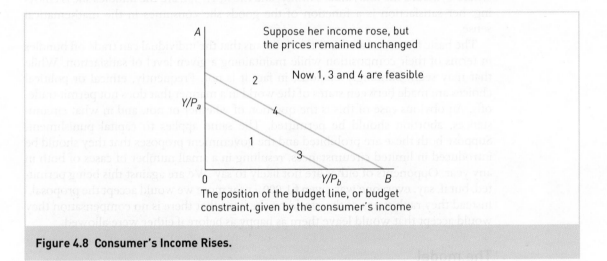

Figure 4.8 Consumer's Income Rises.

If the price of good A fell, her budget constraint would be shifted out on the A axis (Fig. 4.9).

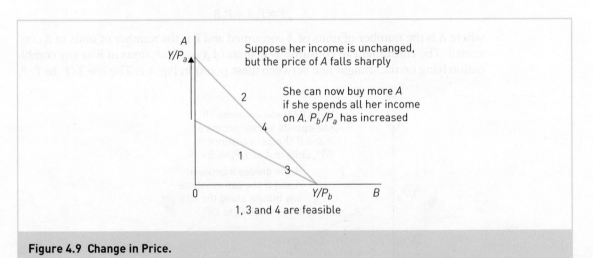

Figure 4.9 Change in Price.

The rational consumer will always be on her budget constraint … but where (Fig. 4.10)?

There is insufficient information so far to answer the question posed in Fig. 4.10. To do so, we have to go back to the *consumer's preferences*. In Fig. 4.11, for any points α, β, γ … the preference assumptions tell us that on a pair-wise comparison the individual can say whether the bundle is preferred to (has higher utility than) the other, is regarded as less desirable than the other (lower utility), or is the same as the other (she is indifferent between the bundles).

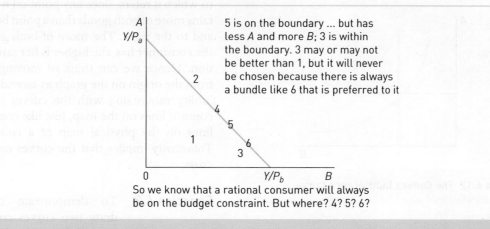

Figure 4.10 Where on the Budget Constraint?

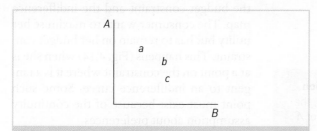

Figure 4.11a Consumer's Preferences.

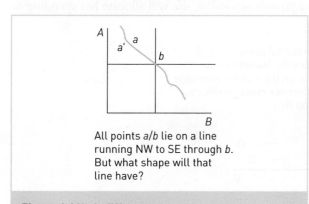

All points a/b lie on a line running NW to SE through b. But what shape will that line have?

Figure 4.11b Indifference.

Formally, for any points a and b in the space shown in Fig. 4.11a, either aPb or bPa or aIb, meaning either a is preferred to b or b is preferred to a or a and b are equally good (the individual is indifferent between them).

If we take any point, it is easy to establish that the points lying above and to the right are preferred, while those lying below and to the left are not as good. The points that are regarded as just as good as the starting point must lie on a line passing from left and above the starting point, passing through it and continuing below and right (Fig. 4.11b).

This is where the final assumption concerning preferences comes in, that of a *diminishing marginal rate of substitution* (DMRS). It means that the less you have of good A the more B you will have to be given to make up for a further reduction in the quantity of A. If this holds true then the line joining points of indifference as in Fig. 4.11b will have to look as in Fig. 4.12. As you move along the indifference curve you trade units of A for B or vice versa while your utility is unchanged

indifference curve a smoothly convex curve; its slope is the consumer's marginal rate of substitution (MRS) between two goods

(hence you are indifferent). The slope of the **indifference curve** shows the marginal rate of substitution. DMRS implies that it is smoothly convex.

There is in principle an infinite number of indifference curves (Fig. 4.13), one for each level of satisfaction, and the further out the curve the higher the level of satisfaction to which it refers, since any point on it contains more of both goods than a point below and to the right. The more of both goods the consumer has, the higher is her satisfaction. Hence we can think of moving out from the origin on the graph as ascending a 'utility mountain', with the curves being contour lines on the map, just like contour lines on the physical map of a country. *Transitivity* implies that the curves cannot cross.

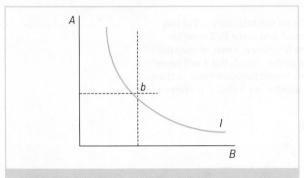

Figure 4.12 The Convex Indifference Curve.

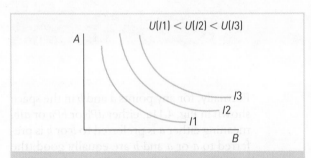

Figure 4.13 Indifference Curves and Satisfaction Levels. The further out an indifference curve is, the higher the consumer's utility from the bundles of *A* and *B* on the curve.

Exercise 4.3 To demonstrate this, draw two curves crossing and show why this is a contradiction in terms.

At this stage we bring the pieces together, the budget constraint and the indifference map. The consumer wants to maximise her utility but has to remain on her budget constraint. This happens (Fig. 4.14) when she is at a point on the constraint where it is a tangent to an indifference curve. Some such point must exist because of the continuity assumption about preferences.

Notice that at this point the slopes of the two lines in Fig. 4.14 are the same. The slope of the indifference curve is the MRS; that of the budget line is P_a/P_b, relative prices. If the individual displays *consumer rationality*, she will allocate her spending so that MRS equals relative price.

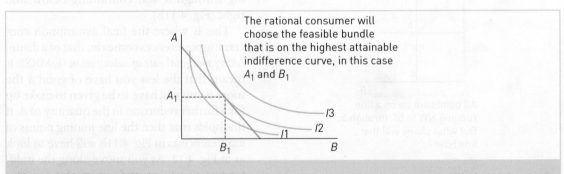

Figure 4.14 Rational Choice.

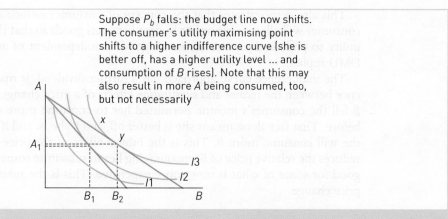

Suppose P_b falls: the budget line now shifts. The consumer's utility maximising point shifts to a higher indifference curve (she is better off, has a higher utility level ... and consumption of B rises). Note that this may also result in more A being consumed, too, but not necessarily

Figure 4.15 Rational Response to a Change in Price.

Consumer rationality: Allocate spending so that MRS equals relative price.

Since the indifference curve traces out the points offering the same level of utility, a move along it leaves utility unchanged. This can be written

$$\Delta U = (dU/dA)\, \Delta A + (dU/dB)\, \Delta B = 0$$

since an increase in A adds satisfaction that is offset by a reduction in B. This equation implies that

$$(dU/dA)\, \Delta A = -(dU/dB)\, \Delta B$$

If we gather terms, we get:

$$\Delta A/\Delta B = -(dU/dB)/(dU/dA)$$

The left-hand side is the slope of the indifference curve, the MRS; the right-hand side is the ratio of marginal utilities.

When the consumer is in equilibrium, maximising utility, the two curves are tangents, and the MRS equals the price ratio. That means that $P_a/P_b = (dU/dB)/(dU/dA)$ (we ignore the sign). That in turn implies that

$$(dU/dA)/P_a = (dU/dB)/P_b$$

which is the familiar MU/P rule we met earlier. So we get the same result without the restrictive assumptions lying behind the DMU assumption.

We can now use the indifference curve model to show that the consumption of a good will rise if its price falls and nothing else changes (i.e. that the demand curve slopes downwards). In Fig. 4.15 we allow the price of B to fall. The budget line swings around its anchor point on the A axis to let the consumer buy more B with the same money income.

When B becomes less expensive the new tangency point is at y, and consumption of B (measured on the horizontal axis) increases. A lower price results in more being demanded, or the demand curve slopes down.

Indifference curve analysis has, therefore, enabled us to conclude that if the price of a good falls, other things being equal, a rational consumer will purchase more of it. This means that the consumer's demand curve slopes down from left to right, which was one of the things that we set out to prove without assuming either DMU or that utility could be measured cardinally.

This also demonstrates that the concept of consumer rationality that states that a consumer will allocate his or her budget between goods so that the ratio of marginal utility to price is the same across all goods is independent of any assumption that DMU applies.

The indifference curve approach has a further dividend. It makes clear the difference between the *income* and *substitution* effects of a price change. When the price of B fell the consumer's income permitted her to consume more of both goods than before. That fact alone means she is better off, and if she is, and if B is a normal good, she will consume more B. This is the *income* effect of the price change. But it also reduces the relative price of B, encouraging her to substitute some of the now cheaper good for some of what is now more expensive. This is the *substitution* effect of the price change.

Income effects

If a good is a 'normal' good, a rise in the consumer's income, prices unchanged, will result in the consumption of the good increases, and a fall in income reduces consumption. This is illustrated in Fig. 4.16. If, however, a rise in income results in a fall in consumption, the good is an inferior good, Fig. 4.17.

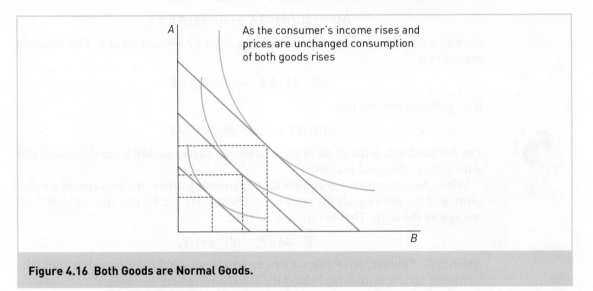

As the consumer's income rises and prices are unchanged consumption of both goods rises

Figure 4.16 Both Goods are Normal Goods.

Substitution effects

If the impact of a change in the price of a good is decomposed into the income effect (the consumer's real income has fallen because the quantity of goods he can buy from a given money income has fallen) and the substitution effect (the impact of relative prices on the consumer's allocation of his income over the goods bought), then we can isolate the substitution effect of a price change by subtracting the income effect. One way to do this is to perform the following thought experiment.

Suppose the consumer faces a significant price increase in an item that is an important component in his consumption basket. Suppose, further, that the government wanted to cushion the consumer's standard of living against the impact of the price change, and gave the consumer an extra weekly income that permitted him/her

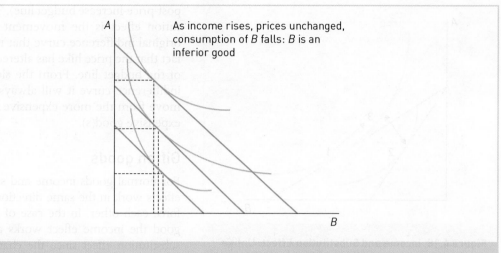

As income rises, prices unchanged, consumption of B falls: B is an inferior good

Figure 4.17 B is an Inferior Good.

Economic naturalist 4.5 Lipstick is an inferior good?

It's easy to think of inferior goods: long-distance bus transport, generic as opposed to branded grocery goods, fast-food meals out (as opposed to serious dining) and so on. But lipstick? A colour piece in the *New York Times* of 1 May 2008 suggested that this is indeed the case. It quoted the CEO of Estée Lauder, Leonard Lauder, on lipstick sales. Against expectations he noted that in the economic downturn post-9/11 lipstick sales rose significantly. He explained buoyant lipstick sales as follows. He hypothesised that lipstick purchases are a way to gauge the economy. 'When it's shaky,' he said, 'sales increase as women boost their mood with inexpensive lipstick purchases instead of $500 sling-backs.' Before you start to consult lipstick sales to predict the behaviour of the economy, you should ask whether this story really does mean that lipstick is an inferior good. If it is, we should expect to see rich women buying less lip gloss and lipstick (although perhaps spending more on quality) than poor women. Any takers?

It was a good story, but there could be another explanation. Suppose that lipstick sales are part of 'indulgence purchases', where the purchase may include a combination of low price (e.g. lipstick) goods and high price (e.g. slingbacks) goods purchased to make you feel good. A recession could well reduce total indulgence spending as incomes fall, but the proportion of the remaining spending going on lipstick (a relatively low-price item) could rise. This would not mean that lipstick is an inferior good in the sense that consumption falls as income rises.

to achieve the same standard of living (utility level) as before. This is illustrated in Fig. 4.18.

The price of B has risen, and the consumer is less well off (is on a lower indifference curve). The government increases his money income by just enough to restore his real income (get him back on to the original indifference curve) (the orange budget line). The consumer moves from bundle 1 (before the price hike) to bundle 2 and then to bundle 3 after his money income is increased. He does not move back to bundle 1. The income effect of the price change is the impact on his consumption of the fact that the price change has lowered his real income. It – the distance between the two indifference curves – has been compensated for by the government and is measured as the increase in money income necessary to compensate the consumer (the shift in the

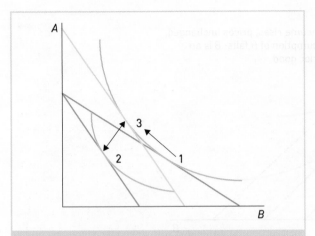

Figure 4.18 Income and Substitution Effect. Unlike the income effect of a price change, the substitution effect always pushes the consumer towards reduced purchases of the good the price of which has risen

post-price-increase budget line). The substitution effect is the movement along the original indifference curve that reflects the fact that the price hike has altered the slope of the budget line. From the slope of the indifference curve it will always involve a move from the more expensive to the less expensive good(s).

Giffen goods

For normal goods income and substitution effects work in the same direction and reinforce each other. In the case of an inferior good the income effect works against the substitution effect since the change in real income from a price change pushes the consumer to purchase more (less) when the price rises (falls). In theory it is possible for the income effect of a price change in the case of an inferior good to swamp the substitution effect. This means that a rise in the price of a good will cause consumption of that good to rise. The impossible appears possible: demand curves could slope upwards.

Fig. 4.19 shows a case of a Giffen Good. The indifference curves are 'bunched' towards the A axis, indicating that B is an inferior good. This effect is so strong that it yields the result that when the price of B falls (rises) the consumption of B by a representative individual falls (rises). If this holds true for a sufficient number of consumers the implication is that, at least for a range of price changes, the observed demand curve will have a positive slope. Can this actually happen? (See Economic naturalist 4.6.)

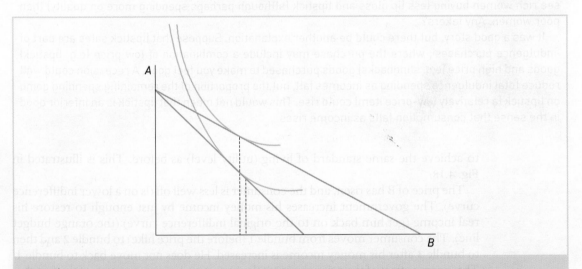

Figure 4.19 A Giffen Good. The Giffen good, or paradox, states that it is possible for a fall in a good's price, other things being held constant, to reduce the quantity demanded. The good has to be an extremely strongly inferior good, so that the income effect of the price change swamps the substitution effect.

Economic naturalist 4.6 Can demand curves slope upwards?

Until 2007 no convincing evidence of an example of a Giffen good had been found. It used to be said that potatoes in Ireland at the time of the Great Famine, 1845–49, were an example of a Giffen good. This was clearly not the case, since fewer, not more, potatoes were consumed by the starving peasantry, which is why a million of them died. Then, in 2007, two American economists, Robert Jensen and Nolan Miller, produced a paper* at the Harvard School of Government, based on analysis of consumption patterns among extremely poor peasants in China, especially in Hunan province. They found evidence that the peasants' dependence on noodles was such that when the price of noodles rose because demand for them in general rose, the quantity of noodles consumed by the peasants actually rose. This was because the higher price of noodles left them so little income to buy other more expensive foodstuffs that they spent the money on noodles. A rising price caused an increase in the quantity demanded among a defined population because the income effect swamped the substitution effect, and the demand curve consequently sloped upwards.

Unless this research is rebutted we must conclude that a Giffen good and an upward-sloping demand curve are both possible.

* Jensen, R. and N. Miller (2007) *Giffen Behaviour: Theory and Evidence* (Harvard School of Government, Faculty Research Working Paper RWP 03-030, December).

Exercise 4.4   Suppose good *B* is an inferior good. Draw an indifference curve diagram that has the effect that a rise in the consumer's money income leads to a fall in consumption of *B*.

RECAP Indifference curve analysis of rational choice

Instead of assuming DMU, we suppose that a consumer's preferences are such that we can say that she has a *utility function*. This enables us to analyse the consumer's behaviour as deriving the maximum utility from the budget at her disposal. Analytically this means choosing the 'best' point on the budget line. That happens when the budget line is tangent to an *indifference curve*, a contour of the utility function. Indifference curves are assumed to be smoothly convex. A change in the price of a good, other things remaining unchanged, means a change in the amount of that good the consumer can buy, and a corresponding change in the slope of the budget line. This gives an unambiguous prediction: a fall (rise) in the price for a good leads to an increase (reduction) in the amount the rational consumer will purchase, which gives us the individual's downward-sloping demand curve. The change in the amount bought can be decomposed into an income and a substitution effect of the price change.

Individual and market demand curves

If we know what each individual's demand curve for a good looks like, how can we use that information to construct the market demand curve for the good? We must *add the individual demand curves together*, a process that is straightforward but requires care.

Horizontal addition

Suppose that there only two buyers – Smith and Jones – in the market for canned tuna, and that their demand curves are as shown in Fig. 4.20(a) and (b). To construct the

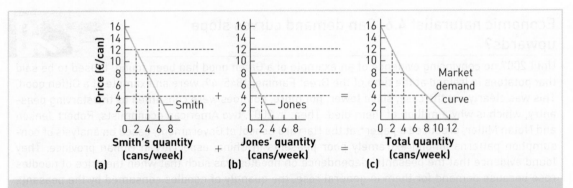

Figure 4.20 Individual and Market Demand Curves for Canned Tuna. The quantity demanded at any price on the market demand curve (c) is the sum of the individual quantities demanded at that price, (a) and (b).

market demand curve for canned tuna, we simply announce a sequence of prices and then add the quantity demanded by each buyer at each price. For example, at a price of €4 per can, Smith demands six cans per week (Fig. 4.20(a)) and Jones demands two cans per week (Fig. 4.20(b)), for a market demand of eight cans per week (Fig. 4.20(c)).

The process of adding individual demand curves in this way to get the market demand curve is known as *horizontal addition*, a term used to emphasise that we are adding *quantities*, which are measured on the horizontal axes of individual demand curves.[4]

Exercise 4.5   The buyers' side of the market for cinema tickets consists of two consumers whose demands are as shown in the diagram below. Graph the market demand curve for this market.

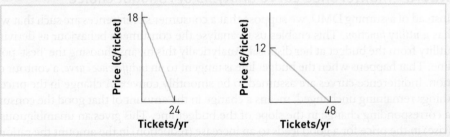

Figure 4.21 illustrates the special case in which each of 1,000 consumers in the market has the same demand curve (Fig. 4.21(a)). To get the market demand curve (Fig. 4.21(b)) in this case, we simply multiply each quantity on the representative individual demand curve by 1,000.

Demand and consumer surplus

In Chapter 1 we first encountered the concept of economic surplus, which in a buyer's case is the difference between the most she would have been willing to pay for a

---

4 Strictly speaking, deriving market demand curves by this method requires that we assume that one individual's consumption of a good at a price is independent of other consumers' consumption of goods at that price.

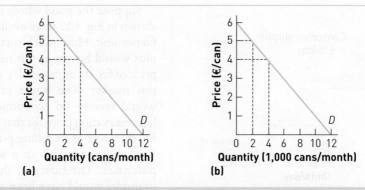

Figure 4.21 The Individual and Market Demand Curves When All Buyers Have Identical Demand Curves. When individual demand curves are identical, we get the market demand curve (b) by multiplying each quantity on the individual demand curve (a) by the number of consumers in the market.

consumer surplus the difference between a buyer's reservation price for a product and the price actually paid

product and the amount she actually pays for it. The economic surplus received by buyers is often referred to as **consumer surplus**.

The term 'consumer surplus' sometimes refers to the surplus received by a single buyer in a transaction. On other occasions it is used to denote the total surplus received by all buyers in a market or collection of markets.

Calculating economic surplus

For performing cost–benefit analysis it is often important to be able to measure the *total consumer surplus* received by all the buyers who participate in a given market. For example, a road linking a mountain village and a port city would create a new market for fresh fish in the mountain village; in deciding whether the road should be built, analysts would want to count as one of its benefits the gains that would be reaped by buyers in this new market.

To illustrate how economists actually measure consumer surplus, we shall consider a hypothetical market for a good with 11 potential buyers, each of whom can buy a maximum of one unit of the good each day. The first potential buyer's reservation price for the product is €11; the second buyer's reservation price is €10; the third buyer's reservation price is €9; and so on. The demand curve for this market will have the 'staircase' shape shown in Fig. 4.22. We can think of this curve as the digital counterpart of traditional analogue demand curves. (If the units shown on the horizontal axis were fine enough, this digital curve would be visually indistinguishable from its analogue counterparts.)

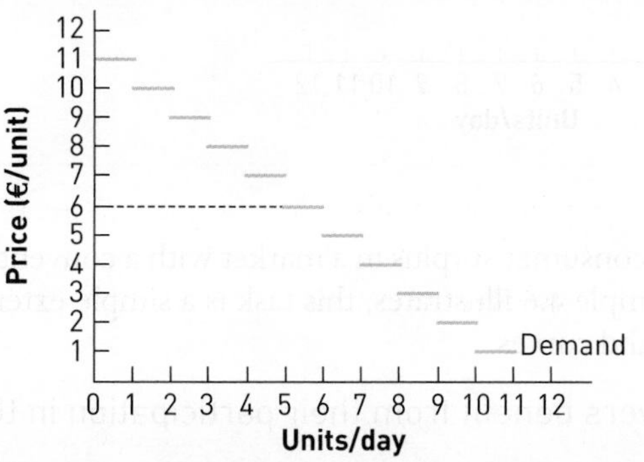

Figure 4.22 A Market with a 'Digital' Demand Curve. When a product can be sold only in whole-number amounts, its demand curve has the 'staircase' shape shown.

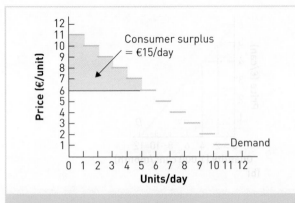

Figure 4.23 Consumer Surplus. Consumer surplus (shaded region) is the cumulative difference between the most that buyers are willing to pay for each unit and the price they actually pay.

Suppose the good whose demand curve is shown in Fig. 4.22 were available at a price of €6 per unit. How much total consumer surplus would buyers in this market reap? At a price of €6, six units per day would be sold in this market. The buyer of the sixth unit would receive no economic surplus, since her reservation price for that unit was exactly €6, the same as its selling price. But the first five buyers would reap a surplus for their purchases. The buyer of the first unit, for example, would have been willing to pay as much as €11 for it, but since she would pay only €6, she would receive a surplus of exactly €5. The buyer of the second unit, who would have been willing to pay as much as €10, would receive a surplus of €4. The surplus would be €3 for the buyer of the third unit, €2 for the buyer of the fourth unit, and €1 for the buyer of the fifth unit.

If we add all the buyers' surpluses together, we get a total of €15 of consumer surplus each day. That surplus corresponds to the shaded area shown in Fig. 4.23.

Exercise 4.6   Calculate consumer surplus for a demand curve like the one just described except that the buyers' reservation prices for each unit are €2 higher than before.

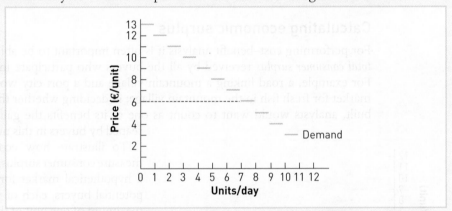

Now suppose we want to calculate consumer surplus in a market with a conventional straight-line demand curve. As Example 4.6 illustrates, this task is a simple extension of the method used for digital demand curves.

Example 4.6 How much do buyers benefit from their participation in the market for milk?

Consider the market for milk whose demand and supply curves are shown in Fig. 4.24, which has an equilibrium price of €2 per litre and an equilibrium quantity of 4,000 litres per day. How much consumer surplus do the buyers in this market reap?

In Fig. 4.24, note first that, as in Fig. 4.20, the last unit exchanged each day generates no consumer surplus at all. Note also that for all milk sold up to 4,000 litres per day,

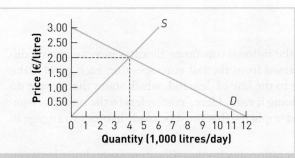

Figure 4.24 Supply and Demand in the Market for Milk. For the supply and demand curves shown, the equilibrium price of milk is €2 per litre and the equilibrium quantity is 4,000 litres per day.

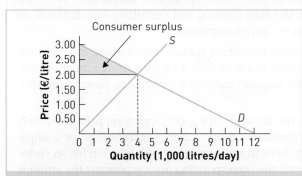

Figure 4.25 Consumer Surplus in the Market for Milk. Consumer surplus is the area of the shaded triangle (€2,000/day).

buyers receive consumer surplus, just as in Fig. 4.24. For these buyers, consumer surplus is the cumulative difference between the most they would be willing to pay for milk (as measured on the demand curve) and the price they actually pay.

Total consumer surplus received by buyers in the milk market is thus the shaded triangle between the demand curve and the market price in Fig. 4.25. Note that this area is a right-angled triangle whose vertical arm is $h =$ €1/litre and whose horizontal arm is $b =$ 4,000 litres/day. And since the area of any triangle is equal to (1/2)(base × height), consumer surplus in this market is equal to

$$(1/2)(4{,}000 \text{ litres/day})(\text{€1/litre}) = \text{€2,000/day}$$

A useful way of thinking about consumer surplus is to ask what is the highest price consumers would pay, in the aggregate, for the right to continue participating in this milk market. The answer is €2,000 per day, since that is the amount by which their *combined benefits exceed their combined costs.*

As discussed in Chapter 3, the demand curve for a good can be interpreted either horizontally or vertically. The horizontal interpretation tells us, for each price, the total quantity that consumers wish to buy at that price. The vertical interpretation tells us, for each quantity, the most a buyer would be willing to pay for the good at that quantity. For the purpose of computing consumer surplus, we rely on the vertical interpretation of the demand curve. The value on the vertical axis that corresponds to each point along the demand curve corresponds to the marginal buyer's reservation price for the good. Consumer surplus is the cumulative sum of the differences between these reservation prices and the market price. It is the area bounded above by the demand curve and bounded below by the market price.

Summary

- If diminishing marginal utility is assumed, the rational consumer allocates income among different goods so that the marginal utility gained from the last euro spent on each good is the same. This rational spending rule gives rise to the law of demand, which states that people do less of what they want to do as the cost of doing it rises. Here, 'cost' refers to the *sum of all monetary and non-monetary sacrifices* – explicit and implicit – that must be made in order to engage in the activity.

- *Indifference curve analysis* states that consumer rationality implies allocating expenditure between two goods so as to equate the marginal rate of substitution between any two goods to their relative price. This implies that demand curves will slope down from left to right, the basic law of demand.

- The ability to substitute one good for another is an important factor behind the law of demand. Because virtually every good or service has at least some substitutes, economists prefer to speak in terms of *wants* rather than needs. We face choices, and describing our demands as 'needs' is misleading because it suggests that we have no options.

- For normal goods, the *income effect* is a second important reason that demand curves slope downwards. When the price of such a good falls, not only does it become more attractive relative to its substitutes, but the consumer also acquires more real purchasing power, and this, too, augments the quantity demanded.

- The demand curve is a schedule that shows the amounts of a good *people want to buy at various prices*. Demand curves can be used to summarise the price–quantity relationship for a single individual, but more commonly we employ them to summarise that relationship for an entire market. At any quantity along a demand curve, the corresponding price represents the amount by which the consumer (or consumers) would benefit from having an additional unit of the product. For this reason, the demand curve is sometimes described as a summary of the benefit side of the market.

- *Consumer surplus* is a quantitative measure of the amount by which buyers benefit as a result of their ability to purchase goods at the market price. It is the area between the demand curve and the market price.

Review questions

1. Why do economists prefer to speak of demands arising out of 'wants' rather than 'needs'?

2. Explain why economists consider the concept of utility useful, even if psychologists cannot measure it precisely.

3. Why does the law of diminishing marginal utility encourage people to spread their spending across many different types of goods?

4. Explain why a good or service that is offered at a monetary price of zero is unlikely to be a truly 'free' good from an economic perspective.

5. Give an example of a good that you have consumed for which your marginal utility increased with the amount of it you consumed.

6. Give examples of cardinal and ordinal measurements.

7. Show how the concept of consumer rationality is the same whether you use DMU or indifference curves to explain demand curves.

8. Show, using indifference curves, how a price rise for one good affects consumption of that good (a) by lowering the consumer's real income, and (b) by altering relative prices of the two goods.

connect **Problems**

Problems marked with an asterisk (*) are more difficult.

1. In which type of restaurant do you expect the service to be more prompt and courteous: an expensive gourmet restaurant or an inexpensive diner? Explain.

2. You are having lunch at an all-you-can-eat buffet. If you are rational, what should be your marginal utility from the last morsel of food you swallow?

3. Martha's current marginal utility from consuming orange juice is 75 utils per centilitre and her marginal utility from consuming coffee is 50 utils per centilitre. If orange juice costs 25 cents per centilitre and coffee costs 20 cents per centilitre, is Martha maximising her total utility from the two beverages? If so, explain how you know. If not, how should she rearrange her spending?

4. Toby's current marginal utility from consuming peanuts is 100 utils per gram and his marginal utility from consuming cashews is 200 utils per gram. If peanuts cost 10 cents per gram and cashews cost 25 cents per gram, is Toby maximising his total utility from the two kinds of nuts? If so, explain how you know. If not, how should he rearrange his spending?

5. Sue gets a total of 20 utils per week from her consumption of pizza and a total of 40 utils per week from her consumption of yoghurt. The price of pizza is €1 per slice, the price of yoghurt is €1 per carton, and she consumes 10 slices of pizza and 20 cartons of yoghurt each week. **True or false:** Sue is consuming the optimal combination of pizza and yoghurt.

6. Anna Lucia lives in Cremona and commutes by train each day to her job in Milan (20 round trips per month). When the price of a round trip goes up from €10 to €20, she responds by consuming exactly the same number of trips as before, while spending €200 per month less on restaurant meals.

   a. Does the fact that her quantity of train travel is completely unresponsive to the price increase imply that Anna Lucia is not a rational consumer?

   b. Explain why an increase in train travel might affect the amount she spends on restaurant meals.

7. For the demand curve shown in the graph, find the total amount of consumer surplus that results in the petrol market if petrol sells for €2 per litre.

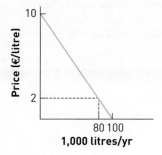

8. Tom has a weekly allowance of €24, all of which he spends on pizza and movie rentals, whose prices are €6 per slice and €3 per rental, respectively. If slices of pizza and movie rentals are available only in whole-number amounts, list all the possible combinations of the two goods that Tom can purchase each week with his allowance.

9.* Refer to Problem 8. Tom's total utility is the sum of the utility he derives from pizza and movie rentals. If these utilities vary with the amounts consumed as shown in the table below, and pizzas and movie rentals are again consumable only in whole-number amounts, how many pizzas and how many movie rentals should Tom consume each week?

Pizzas/week	Utils/week from pizza	Movie rentals/week	Utils/week from rentals
0	0	0	0
1	20	1	40
2	38	2	46
3	54	3	50
4	68	4	54
5	80	5	56
6	90	6	57
7	98	7	57
8	104	8	57

10.* The buyers' side of the market for amusement park tickets consists of two consumers whose demands are as shown in the diagram below.

   a. Graph the market demand curve for this market.

   b. Calculate the total consumer surplus in the amusement park market if tickets sell for €12 each.

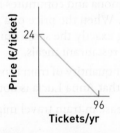

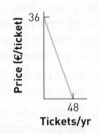

Perfectly Competitive Supply: the Cost Side of the Market

Cars that took more than 50 hours to assemble in the 1970s are now built in less than 8 hours. Similar productivity growth has occurred in many other manufacturing industries. Yet, in many service industries, productivity has grown only slowly, if at all. For example, the Vienna Philharmonic Orchestra performs Beethoven's Fifth Symphony with no fewer musicians today than it did in 1950. And it still takes a barber about half an hour to cut someone's hair, just as it always has.

Given the spectacular growth in manufacturing workers' productivity, it is no surprise that their real wages rose more than fivefold during the twentieth century. But why have real wages for service workers risen just as much? If barbers and musicians are no more productive than they were in the 1890s, why are they now paid five times as much?

An answer is suggested by the observation that the opportunity cost of pursuing any given occupation is the most one could have earned in some other occupation. Most people who become barbers or musicians could instead have chosen jobs in manufacturing. If workers in service industries were not paid roughly as much as they could have earned in other occupations, many of them would not have been willing to work in service industries in the first place.

The trajectories of wages in manufacturing and service industries illustrate the intimate link between the prices at which goods and services are offered for sale in the market and the opportunity cost of the resources required to produce them. Whereas our focus in Chapter 4 was on the buyers' side of the market, our task here is to gain insight into the factors that shape the supply curve, the schedule that tells how many units suppliers wish to sell at different prices.

Although the demand side and the supply side of the market are different in several ways, many of these differences are superficial. Indeed, the behaviour of both buyers and sellers is in an important sense fundamentally the same. After all, the two groups confront essentially similar questions: in the buyer's case, 'Should I buy another unit?' and, in the seller's, 'Should I sell another unit?' What is more, buyers and sellers use the same criterion for answering these questions. Thus a rational consumer will buy another unit if its benefit exceeds its cost; and a rational seller will sell another unit if the cost of making it is less than the extra revenue he can get from selling it (the familiar Cost–Benefit Principle again).

Thinking about supply: the importance of opportunity cost

Many countries or local government areas have regulations that create incentives for people to return bottles and drinks cans, directly or indirectly, to the original seller for recycling. While some people always return their own containers to receive the incentive (usually cash), others pass up this opportunity, leaving their used containers to be recycled by others, or simply get rid of them with other garbage. Returning your containers is *supplying a service*, and its production obeys the same logic as applies to the production of other goods and services. As the following sequence of recycling examples makes clear, the supply curve for a good or service is rooted in the individual's choice of whether to produce it.

Example 5.1 How much time should Harry spend recycling soft drink containers?

Harry is trying to decide how to divide his time between his job as a dishwasher in the student cafeteria at his university, which pays €6 an hour for as many hours as he chooses to work, and gathering soft drink containers around the college to redeem for deposit, in which case his pay depends on both the deposit per container and the number of containers he finds. Earnings aside, Harry is indifferent between the two tasks, and the number of containers he will find depends, as shown in the table below, on the number of hours per day he searches.

Search time (hours/day) (1)	Total number of containers found (2)	Additional number of containers found (3)
0	0	
		600
1	600	
		400
2	1,000	
		300
3	1,300	
		200
4	1,500	
		100
5	1,600	

If the containers may be redeemed for 2 cents each, how many hours should Harry spend searching for containers?

For each additional hour Harry spends searching for soft drink containers, he loses the €6 he could have earned as a dishwasher. This is his *hourly opportunity cost* of searching for soft drink containers. His benefit from each hour spent searching for containers is the number of additional containers he finds (shown in column (3) of the table) times the deposit he collects per container. Since he can redeem each container for 2 cents, his first hour spent collecting containers will yield earnings of 600(€0.02) = €12, or €6 more than he could have earned as a dishwasher.

Incentives Matter

By the Cost–Benefit Principle, then, Harry should spend his first hour of work each day searching for soft drink containers rather than washing dishes. A second hour searching for containers will yield 400 additional containers, for additional earnings of €8, so it, too, satisfies the cost–benefit test. A third hour spent searching yields 300 additional containers, for 300(€0.02) = €6 of additional earnings. Since this is exactly what Harry could have earned washing dishes, he is indifferent between spending his third hour of work each day on one task or the other. For the sake of discussion, however, we shall assume that, when indifferent, he opts to search for containers, in which case he will spend three hours each day searching for containers.

What is the lowest redemption price that would induce Harry to spend at least one hour per day recycling? Since he will find 600 containers in his first hour of search, a 1-cent deposit on each container would enable him to match his €6 per hour opportunity cost. More generally, if the redemption price is p, and the next hour spent searching yields ΔQ additional containers, then Harry's additional earnings from searching the additional hour will be $p(\Delta Q)$. This means that the smallest redemption price that will lead Harry to search another hour must satisfy the equation

$$p(\Delta Q) = €6 \tag{5.1}$$

How high would the redemption price of containers have to be to induce Harry to search for a second hour? Since he can find $\Delta Q = 400$ additional containers if he searches for a second hour, the smallest redemption price that will lead him to do so must satisfy $p(400) = €6$, which solves for $p = 1.5$ cents.

Exercise 5.1 Referring to Example 5.1, calculate the smallest container redemption prices that will lead Harry to search for a third, fourth and fifth hour.

Increasing Opportunity Cost

By searching for soft drink containers, Harry becomes, in effect, a supplier of container-recycling services. In Example 5.1, we saw that Harry's reservation prices for his third, fourth and fifth hours of container search are 2, 3 and 6 cents, respectively. Having calculated these reservation prices, we can now plot his supply curve of container-recycling services. This curve, which plots the redemption price per container on the vertical axis and the number of containers recycled each day on the horizontal axis, is shown in Fig. 5.1. It tells us the number of containers he is willing to recycle at various redemption prices.

Like those we saw in Chapter 3, the supply curve shown in Fig. 5.1 is upward-sloping. There are exceptions to this general rule, but sellers of most goods will offer higher quantities at higher prices than at lower prices.

The relationship between the individual and market supply curves for a product is analogous to the relationship between the individual and market demand curves. The quantity that corresponds to a given price on the market demand curve is the sum of the quantities demanded at that price by all

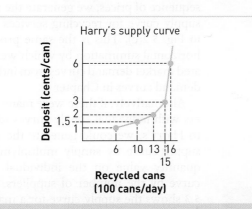

Figure 5.1 An Individual Supply Curve for Recycling Services. When the deposit price increases, it becomes attractive to abandon alternative pursuits to spend more time searching for soft drink containers.

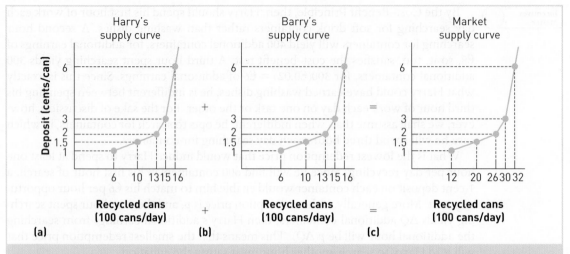

Figure 5.2 The Market Supply Curve for Recycling Services. To generate the market supply curve (c) from the individual supply curves (a) and (b), we add the individual supply curves horizontally.

individual buyers in the market. Likewise, the quantity that corresponds to any given price on the market supply curve is the sum of the quantities supplied at that price by all individual sellers in the market.

Suppose, for example, that the supply side of the recycling services market consists only of Harry and his identical twin, Barry, whose individual supply curve is the same as Harry's. To generate the market supply curve, we first put the individual supply curves side by side, as shown in Fig. 5.2(a) and (b). We then announce a price, and for that price add the individual quantities supplied to obtain the total quantity supplied in the market. Thus, at a price of 3 cents per container, both Harry and Barry wish to recycle 1,500 cans per day, so the total market supply at that price is 3,000 cans per day. Proceeding in like manner for a sequence of prices, we generate the market supply curve for recycling services shown in Fig. 5.2(c). This is the same process of horizontal summation by which we generated market demand curves from individual demand curves in Chapter 4.

Alternatively, if there were many suppliers with individual supply curves identical to Harry's, we could generate the market supply curve by simply multiplying each quantity value on the individual supply curve by the number of suppliers. Figure 5.3 shows the supply curve for a market in which there are 1,000 suppliers with individual supply curves like Harry's. Why do individual supply curves tend to be upward-sloping? One explanation is suggested by the Principle of Increasing Opportunity Cost,

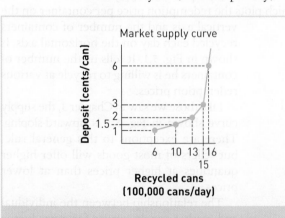

Figure 5.3 The Market Supply Curve with 1,000 Identical Sellers. To generate the market supply curve for a market with 1,000 identical sellers, we simply multiply each quantity value on the individual supply curve by 1,000.

or Low-Hanging-Fruit Principle (Chapter 2). Container recyclers should always look first for the containers that are easiest to find – such as those in plain view in readily accessible locations. As the redemption price rises, it will pay to incur the additional cost of searching further from the beaten path.

If all individuals have identical upward-sloping supply curves, the market supply curve will be upward-sloping as well. But there is an important additional reason for the positive slope of market supply curves: individual suppliers generally differ with respect to their opportunity costs of supplying the product. (The Principle of Increasing Opportunity Cost applies not only to each individual searcher, but also *across* individuals.) Thus, whereas people facing unattractive employment opportunities in other occupations may be willing to recycle soft drink containers even when the redemption price is low, those with more attractive options will recycle only if the redemption price is relatively high.

In summary, then, the upward slope of the supply schedule reflects the fact that costs tend to rise when producers expand production, partly because each individual exploits the most attractive opportunities first, but also because different potential sellers face different opportunity costs.

Production in the short run

To gain a deeper understanding of the origins of the supply curve, it is helpful to consider a small firm confronting the decision of how much to produce. The firm in question is a small company that makes glass bottles from silica, which for simplicity we will assume is available free of charge from a nearby desert deposit. Its electricity comes from solar panels. The only costs incurred by the firm are the wages it pays its employees and the lease payment on its bottle-making machine. The employees and the machine are the firm's only two **factors of production** – inputs used to produce goods and services. In more complex examples, factors of production might also include land, structures, entrepreneurship and possibly others, but for the moment we consider only labour and capital.

factor of production an input used in the production of a good or service

short run a period of time sufficiently short that at least some of the firm's factors of production are fixed

long run a period of time of sufficient length that all the firm's factors of production are variable

law of diminishing returns a property of the relationship between the amount of a good or service produced and the amount of a variable factor required to produce it; it says that when some factors of production are fixed, increased production of the good eventually requires ever larger increases in the variable factor

When we refer to the **short run**, we mean a period of time during which at least some of the firm's factors of production cannot be varied. For our bottle maker, we will assume that the number of employees can be varied at short notice but that the capacity of its bottle-making machinery can be altered only with significant delay. For this firm, then, the short run is simply that period of time during which the firm cannot alter the capacity of its bottle-making machinery. By contrast, when we speak of the **long run**, we refer to a time period of sufficient length that all the firm's factors of production are variable.

Table 5.1 shows how the company's bottle production depends on the number of hours its employees spend on the job each day. It exhibits a pattern that is common to many such relationships. Each time we add an additional unit of labour, output grows; but beyond some point the additional output that results from each additional unit of labour begins to diminish. Note in column (2), for example, that output gains begin to diminish with the third employee. Economists refer to this pattern as the **law of diminishing returns**, and it always refers to situations in which at least

Total number of employees per day (1)	Total number of bottles per day (2)
0	0
1	80
2	200
3	260
4	300
5	330
6	350
7	362

Table 5.1 **Employment and Output for a Glass Bottle Maker**

fixed factor of production an input whose quantity cannot be altered in the short run

variable factor of production an input whose quantity can be altered in the short run

fixed cost the sum of all payments made to the firm's fixed factors of production; the payments that have to be made for the services of an input regardless of whether and how much production actually takes place

variable cost the sum of all payments made to the firm's variable factors of production

total cost the sum of all payments made to the firm's fixed and variable factors of production

marginal cost as output changes from one level to another, the change in total cost divided by the corresponding change in output; by definition it consists of variable costs

some factors of production are fixed. Here, the **fixed factor** is the bottle-making machinery, and the **variable factor** is labour. The law of diminishing returns says simply that successive increases in the labour input eventually yield smaller and smaller increments in bottle output. (Strictly speaking, the law ought to be called the law of *eventually* diminishing returns, because output may initially grow at an increasing rate with additional units of the variable factor.)

Typically, returns from additional units of the variable input eventually diminish because of some form of *congestion*. For instance, in an office with three secretaries and only a single desktop computer, we would not expect to get three times as many letters typed per hour as in an office with only one secretary, because only one person at a time can use the computer.

Some important cost concepts

For the bottle-making firm described in Table 5.1, suppose that the lease payment for the company's bottle-making machine is €40 per day, which must be paid whether the company makes any bottles or not. This payment is both a **fixed cost** (since it does not depend on the number of bottles per day the firm makes) and, for the duration of the lease, a sunk cost. Columns (1) and (2) of Table 5.2 reproduce the employment and output entries (columns (1) and (2)) from Table 5.1, and the firm's fixed cost appears in column (3).

The company's payment to its employees is called **variable cost** because, unlike fixed cost, it varies with the *number of bottles* the company produces. The variable cost of producing 200 bottles per day, for example, is shown in column (4) of Table 5.2 as €24 per day. Column (5) shows the firm's **total cost**, which is the *sum of its fixed and variable costs*. Column (6), finally, shows the firm's **marginal cost**, a measure of how its *total cost changes when its output changes*. Specifically, marginal cost is defined as the change in total cost divided by the corresponding change in output. Note, for example, that when the firm expands production from 80 to 200 bottles per day, its total cost goes up by €12, which gives rise to the marginal cost entry of (€12/day)/(120 bottles/day) = €0.10 per bottle. To emphasise

Employees per day (1)	Bottles per day (2)	Fixed cost (€/day) (3)	Variable cost (€/day) (4)	Total cost (€/day) (5)	Marginal cost (€/bottle) (6)
0	0	40	0	40	
					0.15
1	80	40	12	52	
					0.10
2	200	40	24	64	
					0.20
3	260	40	36	76	
					0.33
4	300	40	48	88	
					0.40
5	330	40	60	100	
					0.60
6	350	40	72	112	
					1.00
7	362	40	84	124	

Table 5.2 **Fixed, Variable and Total Costs of Bottle Production**

that marginal cost refers to the change in total cost when quantity changes, we place the marginal cost entries between the corresponding quantity rows of Table 5.2.

For our bottle-making firm, average variable cost and average total cost values are shown in columns (4) and (6) of Table 5.3. Using the entries in Table 5.3, we plot the

Employees per day (1)	Bottles per day (2)	Variable cost (€/day) (3)	Average variable cost (€/unit of output) (4)	Total cost (€/day) (5)	Average total cost (€/unit of output) (6)	Marginal cost (€/bottle) (7)
0	0	0		40		
						0.15
1	80	12	0.15	52	0.65	
						0.10
2	200	24	0.12	64	0.32	
						0.20
3	260	36	0.138	76	0.292	
						0.33
4	300	48	0.16	88	0.293	
						0.40
5	330	60	0.182	100	0.303	
						0.60
6	350	72	0.206	112	0.32	
						1.00
7	362	84	0.232	124	0.343	

Table 5.3 **Average Variable Cost and Average Total Cost of Bottle Production**

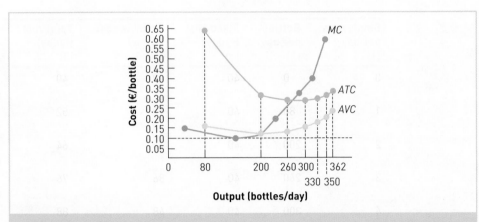

Figure 5.4 The Marginal, Average Variable and Average Total Cost Curves for a Bottle Manufacturer. The *MC* curve cuts both the *AVC* and *ATC* curves at their minimum points. The upward-sloping portion of the marginal cost curve corresponds to the region of diminishing returns.

firm's average total cost, average variable cost and marginal cost curves in Fig. 5.4. (Because marginal cost corresponds to the change in total cost as we move between two output levels, each marginal cost value in Table 5.3 is plotted at an output level midway between those in the adjacent rows.)

Notice, please, several features of the cost curves in Fig. 5.4. For example, the upward-sloping portion of the marginal cost curve (*MC*) corresponds to the region of diminishing returns discussed earlier. Thus, as the firm moves beyond two employees per day (200 bottles per day), the increments to total output become smaller with each additional employee, which means that the cost of producing additional bottles (*MC*) must be increasing in this region.

Note also that the definition of marginal cost implies that the marginal cost curve must intersect both the average variable cost curve (*AVC*) and the average total cost curve (*ATC*) at their respective minimum points. To see why, consider the logic that explains what happens to the average weight of children in an elementary school class when a new student joins the class. If the new (marginal) student is lighter than the previous average weight for the class, average weight will fall, but if the new student is heavier than the previous average, average weight will rise. By the same token, when marginal cost is below average total cost or average variable cost, the corresponding **average cost** must be falling, and vice versa. And this ensures that the marginal cost curve must pass through the *minimum points* of both average cost curves.

average cost total cost for any level of output divided by the number of units of output, often referred to as unit cost; average total cost is the sum of average fixed cost plus average variable cost

Maths Box 5.1 Why a marginal cost curve must cut an average cost curve at its lowest point: a mathematical proof

Recall that average cost is total cost divided by the number of units being produced

$$AC = TC/Q$$

where *Q* is the number of units being produced.

Now consider the slope of average cost, dAC/dQ. Using the rules for differentiation in the maths appendix to Chapter 1 we have

$$dAC/dQ = d(TC/Q)/dQ$$
$$= [Q(dTC/dQ) - TC(dQ/dQ)]/Q^2$$
$$= dTC/dQ - TC/Q$$

dTC/dQ is Marginal Cost, MC; TC/Q is Average Cost, AC.

So, the slope of the AC curve equals the difference between MC and AC, $MC - AC$.

At its bottom point the slope of the AC curve is zero. Therefore $AC = MC$ at this point. To the left the AC curve is falling (it has a negative slope) so MC must be less than AC; to the right of the bottom point it is rising (has a positive slope), so MC must be greater than AC. Therefore MC must cut the AC curve at the bottom point of the AC curve.

Input prices, production capacity and the firm's cost of supply

The firm's costs of supply will reflect any increase or decrease in what it has to pay for inputs. In our glass bottle example, we specifically looked only at the short run, since we held the quantity of capital invested in machinery constant. Over the longer term it is possible for a firm to increase the plant and machinery at its disposal. It is also possible for it to take advantage of technological changes that permit changes in how it produces its output. This will be affected by the prices it faces for its inputs, and this in turn will affect its supply costs.

This means that (a) the law of diminishing returns may not be important in the long run, since both capital and labour employed can be expanded or contracted, and (b) that the firm can in principle choose to adopt new production technologies, including changes that enable it to lower its unit costs. Of particular importance will be an ability to change the proportions in which its production processes use labour and capital (in the form of machinery). Thus, in the short run, a rise in wage costs simply increases its unit costs of production in proportion to the amount of labour necessary to produce a unit of output. But, in the long run, it may be possible for the firm to invest in labour-saving additions to its capital employed, as it moves to a less labour-intensive and more capital-intensive technology of production.

Finally, firms that grow in size (in terms of capacity and output) may find that unit costs fall. In this case the firm is said to be benefiting from *economies of scale*. These may be limited, so that, after some point, further economies of scale cannot be obtained and diseconomies of scale may even set in.

The firm's cost curves that we have derived in relation to the glass bottle example help to illustrate how the diminishing returns problem may be resolved, and show how scale economies (or diseconomies) affect the firm's costs.

Diminishing returns cause the firm's average total cost curve to turn upwards after some point when the advantages of spreading fixed costs over a larger output are offset by falling production efficiencies and rising wage costs arising from using more and more labour with a fixed machinery base. The important thing to note in this context is that the average cost curve reflects costs with a given fixed plant capacity. If the capacity is increased, a new ATC curve applies (or, if you like, the ATC is moved outwards) (Fig. 5.5).

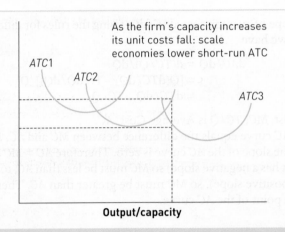

Figure 5.5 Long-run Average Cost and Scale Economies. The glass bottle company's ATC with one, two and three production lines: if it produces the quantity indicated with two production lines it is experiencing diminishing returns at scale 2. But if it can expand to three lines its unit costs will fall. It is taking advantage of scale economies and the diminishing returns problem at scale 2 have been avoided.

Suppose the company can put in a second bottle production line: its ATC is now ATC2. A third line would mean the ATC moves to ATC3. In this case the larger plant (two or three production lines) will have lower unit costs (provided it is producing a larger output). Scale economies are lowering its costs. By expanding its scale of operations from scale 1 to scale 2 it can produce more without running into diminishing returns (although at scale 2 it faces diminishing returns if it expands production without expanding capacity to scale 3, and so on).

(The following section is slightly more technical than what has come before. It can be ignored and you can proceed to the next section, which starts on page 162.) The other way in which a firm can alter its costs in the long run is by changing the technology of production.

production function the technical relation between inputs in a production process and the outputs it produces

To illustrate this, we use the idea of a **production function**, which relates the firm's output to the inputs it uses. We now consider the glass bottle firm's technology choice. It uses the services of two factors of production, labour and capital (L and K), to process its energy and silica inputs to produce bottles. We will assume that the amount of silica and energy required to produce a bottle is fixed and both are available freely. Its output, Q, then depends on its usage of labour and capital services, and can be represented as a function of the input usage:

$$Q = f(K,L)$$

where K and L are the amounts of capital and labour employed in the firm to produce bottles. For ease we will assume that the firm can smoothly substitute capital for labour or labour for capital, and that diminishing returns apply when you change the proportions in which you use capital and labour. On this basis we can graph the combinations of capital and labour that the firm can use to produce a target output (Fig. 5.6). In this case we have a curve, called a production isoquant, for three levels of output per week, 5,000 bottles, 7,000 bottles and 10,000 bottles. The slope of the isoquant shows how many units of K are needed to replace a unit of L while maintaining

marginal product the change in total output from adding one more unit of a factor of production to the total employed while holding all other inputs constant

output. This is given by the ratio of **marginal products** of K and L (the contribution of an extra unit of K or of L to output) at that point, MPk/MPl. Suppose the firm wants to produce 7,000 bottles. Any combination of K and L on the isoquant for 7,000 will suffice to produce the target output. Which will the firm choose? Other things being equal it will choose the lowest cost combination ... but which is that?

The cost of the inputs is $rK + wL$, where r is the hourly rental cost of capital and w is the wage rate for an hour of labour. The key to solving the problem is the relative cost of labour and capital, r/w. Suppose this is $6/12$. Then a line with a slope of $6/12$ (or ½) will tell you all the combinations of labour and capital that can be bought with a given budget for purchasing inputs. In Fig. 5.7, three levels of spending on K and L are set down. Level 1 is too little to produce 7,000 units. Level 3 will do the job ... but is unnecessarily high. Level 2 is the minimum cost budget. The combination of K and L that minimises costs is at A. At this point the relative prices of the two factors are equal to the ratio of their marginal costs, or $MPk/r = MPl/w$. So to find the minimum cost level of factor usage we find that combination at which this equality holds.

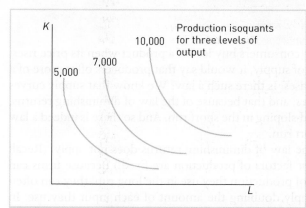

Figure 5.6 Production Isoquants. From the firm's production function we can derive the different quantities of K and L that will produce a given output of bottles per week. The firm wants to produce 7,000, and has to choose a combination lying along the relevant isoquant.

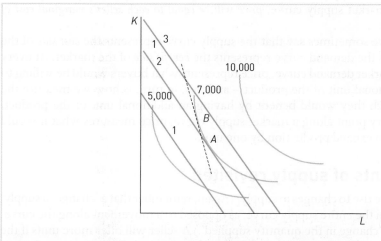

The lowest cost combination of K and L that will produce 7,000 bottles is found where the relative price of K and L equals the ratio of their marginal products at A. If labour costs rise, the firm will substitute capital for labour (B).

Figure 5.7 Efficient Factor Usage. The most efficient usage of factors is where relative factor costs equal the ratio of factor marginal products. A change in factor prices will induce a firm to alter the proportions in which it uses factors of production. Higher labour costs lead to the substitution of capital for labour.

Faced with a rise in the price of one factor (in this case, labour), the firm, given time, will produce any output with a more capital-intensive technique of production, increasing its investment in capital in order to economise on more expensive labour (move from A to B). This helps to offset the impact of higher labour costs on the firm's costs of supply. It also helps explain why we observe more capital-intensive production in richer countries and why labour-intensive production processes migrate to countries with lower incomes per head (and lower wages).

The 'law' of supply

The law of demand tells us that consumers buy less of a product when its price rises. If there were an analogous law of supply, it would say that producers offer more of a product for sale when its price rises. Is there such a law? We know that supply curves are essentially *marginal cost curves*, and that because of the law of diminishing returns, marginal cost curves are upward-sloping in the short run. And so there is indeed a law of supply that applies in the short run.

In the long run, however, the law of diminishing returns does not apply. (Recall that it holds only if at least *some* factors of production are fixed.) Because firms can vary the amounts of *all* factors of production they use in the long run, they can often double their production by simply doubling the amount of each input they use. In such cases costs would be exactly proportional to output, and the firm's marginal cost curve in the long run would be horizontal, not upward-sloping. So for now we shall say only that the 'law' of supply holds in the short run but not necessarily in the long run. For both the long run and the short run, however, the perfectly competitive firm's supply curve is its *marginal cost curve*.[1]

Every quantity of output along the market supply curve represents the summation of all the quantities individual sellers offer at the corresponding price. So the correspondence between price and marginal cost exists for the market supply curve as well as for the individual supply curves that lie behind it. That is, for every price–quantity pair along the market supply curve, *price will be equal to each seller's marginal cost of production*.

This is why we sometimes say that the supply curve represents the *cost side* of the market, whereas the demand curve represents the *benefit side* of the market. At every point along a market demand curve, price represents what buyers would be willing to pay for an additional unit of the product – and this, in turn, is how we measure the amount by which they would benefit by having an additional unit of the product. Likewise, at every point along a market supply curve, price measures what it would cost producers to expand production by one unit.

Determinants of supply revisited

What factors give rise to changes in supply? (Again, remember that a 'change in supply' refers to a shift in the entire supply curve, as opposed to a movement along the curve, which we call a 'change in the quantity supplied'.) A seller will offer more units if the benefit of selling extra output goes up relative to the cost of producing it. And since, as we shall see, the benefit of selling output in a perfectly competitive market is a fixed market price that is beyond the seller's control, our search for factors that influence supply naturally focuses on the cost side of the calculation.

---

1 Subject to the proviso that if price equals marginal cost the firm's total sales revenue has to be greater than its total variable cost, since otherwise it would be better not to produce at all.

Technology

Perhaps the most important determinant of production cost is *technology*. Improvements in technology make it possible to produce additional units of output at lower cost. This shifts each individual supply curve downwards (or, equivalently, outwards) and hence shifts the market supply curve downwards as well. Over time, the introduction of more sophisticated machinery has resulted in dramatic increases in the number of goods produced per hour of effort expended. Every such development gives rise to an outward shift in the market supply curve.

But how do we know that technological change will reduce the cost of producing goods and services? Might not new equipment be so expensive that the producers who use it will have higher costs than those who rely on earlier designs? If so, then rational producers simply will not use the new equipment. The only technological changes that rational producers will voluntarily adopt are those that will reduce their cost of production.

Input prices

Whereas technological change generally (although not always) leads to gradual shifts in supply, changes in the prices of *important inputs* can give rise to large supply shifts literally overnight. For example, the price of crude oil, which is the most important input in the production of motor fuel, often fluctuates sharply, and the resulting shifts in supply cause fuel prices to exhibit corresponding fluctuations.

Similarly, when *wage rates* rise, the marginal cost of any business that employs labour also rises, shifting supply curves to the left (or, equivalently, upwards). When interest rates fall, the opportunity cost of capital equipment also falls, causing supply to shift to the right.

The number of suppliers

Just as demand curves shift to the right when population grows, supply curves also shift to the right as the number of *individual suppliers* grows. For example, if container recyclers die or retire at a higher rate than new recyclers enter the industry, the supply curve for recycling services will shift to the left. Conversely, if a rise in the unemployment rate leads more people to recycle soft drink containers (by reducing the opportunity cost of time spent recycling), the supply curve of recycling services will shift to the right.

Expectations

Expectations about *future price movements* can affect how much sellers choose to offer in the current market. Suppose, for example, that recyclers expect the future price of aluminium to be much higher than the current price because of the growing use of aluminium components in cars. The rational recycler would then have an incentive to withhold aluminium from the market at today's lower price, in order to have more available to sell at the higher future price. Conversely, if recyclers expect next year's price of aluminium to be lower than this year's, their incentive would be to offer more aluminium for sale in today's market.

Changes in prices of other products

Apart from technological change, perhaps the most important determinant of supply is variation in the prices of *other goods and services* that sellers might produce.

Prospectors, for example, search for those precious metals for which the surplus of benefits over costs is greatest. When the price of silver rises, many stop looking for gold and start looking for silver. Conversely, when the price of platinum falls, many platinum prospectors shift their attention to gold.

Revenues from sales: profit-maximising firms in competitive markets

So far, we have looked at the costs the firm faces. However, to determine how much it will produce, or even whether it will stay in production, we must relate costs to revenues from sales, out of which costs will have to be met. This means that, to explore the nature of the supply curve of a product more fully, we must say more about the *goals* of the organisations that supply the product, and the kind of economic environment in which they operate. In virtually every economy, goods and services are produced by a variety of organisations that pursue a host of different motives. The Red Cross supplies blood because its organisers and donors want to help people in need; the local government fixes potholes because the mayor was elected on a promise to do so; karaoke singers perform because they like public attention; and car wash employees are driven primarily by the hope of making enough money to pay their rent and other living expenses.

Profit maximisation

Notwithstanding this rich variety of motives, *most* goods and services that are offered for sale in a market economy are sold by private firms whose main reason for existing is to earn **profit** for their owners. A firm's profit is the difference between the total revenue it receives from the sale of its product and all costs it incurs in producing it. We need to note in passing that this implies that the legal structure of the firm, the property rights it enjoys, and the contracts between the firm and its employees are such as to orientate the firm towards making profits. This is not always the case: in principle, a firm might be owned by the workers (a labour managed enterprise). Many state-owned enterprises across the world operate de facto as labour managed enterprises, and seek to maximise the interests of the employees rather than those of the owners (the taxpayers). Or, as in the insurance sector in many instances, the firm may in effect be owned by its customers rather than by conventional shareholders (mutuals), and behave like a customers' cooperative rather than a profit maximiser. However, most firms can plausibly be considered as aiming at maximising profits, and we will proceed on that assumption.

A **profit-maximising firm** is one whose primary goal is to maximise the amount of profit it earns. The supply curves that economists use in standard supply and demand theory are based on the assumption that the market can plausibly be treated as if the goods or services concerned are sold by profit-maximising firms in **perfectly competitive markets**, which are markets in which individual firms have no influence over the market prices of the products they sell. Because of their inability to influence market price, perfectly competitive firms are often described as **price takers**. Note

profit the total revenue a firm receives from the sale of its product minus all costs – explicit and implicit – incurred in producing it

profit-maximising firm a firm whose primary goal is to maximise the difference between its total revenues and total costs

perfectly competitive market a market in which no individual supplier has significant influence on the market price of the product

price taker a firm that has no influence over the price at which it sells its product

that this does not mean that when economists use supply curves they are always strictly assuming that the markets concerned are perfectly competitive in this sense. For example, economists will frequently use supply and demand curves to analyse what is happening in the oil market, even though, strictly speaking, the major crude oil producers do not display all (or even many) of the characteristics of perfectly competitive producers. In such circumstances what is happening is that the analysis is based on an assumption that the outcome in the market is likely to be close to what would happen in a competitive market.

The following four conditions are often taken to be characteristic of markets that are perfectly competitive.

1. **All firms sell the same standardised product** Although this condition is almost never literally satisfied, it holds as a rough approximation for many markets. Thus the markets for concrete building blocks of a given size, or for apples of a given variety, may be described in this way. This condition implies that buyers are willing to switch from one seller to another if by so doing they can obtain a lower price. In the current context a 33 cl bottle of a particular shape produced by one firm may be assumed to be viewed as the same by a bottling plant as a similar bottle produced by another firm.

2. **The market has many buyers and sellers, each of which buys or sells only a small fraction of the total quantity exchanged** This condition implies that individual buyers and sellers will be price takers, regarding the market price of the product as a fixed number beyond their control. For example, a single farmer's decision to plant fewer hectares of wheat would have no appreciable impact on the market price of wheat, just as an individual consumer's decision to become a vegetarian would have no perceptible effect on the price of beef. In the present case this means that we are looking at the production decision of one of a large number of firms producing virtually identical glass bottles.

3. **Productive resources are mobile** This condition implies that if a potential seller identifies a profitable business opportunity in a market, he or she will be able to obtain the labour, capital and other productive resources necessary to enter that market. By the same token, sellers who are dissatisfied with the opportunities they confront in a given market are free to leave that market and employ their resources elsewhere. There is free entry to and exit from the market.

4. **Buyers and sellers are well informed** This condition implies that buyers and sellers are aware of the relevant opportunities available to them. If that were not so, buyers would be unable to seek out sellers who charge the lowest prices, and sellers would have no means of deploying their resources in the markets in which they would earn the most.

In the real world the market for wheat closely approximates a perfectly competitive market. (The output of one wheat grower in northern France is (usually) indistinguishable from that of his neighbour.) The market for operating systems for desktop computers, however, does not. More than 90 per cent of desktop operating systems are sold by Microsoft, giving the company enough influence in that market to have significant control over the price it charges. For example, if it were to raise the price of its latest edition of Windows by, say, 20 per cent, some consumers might switch to Macintosh computers or install Linux if they own PCs, and others might postpone their next upgrade; but many – perhaps even most – would continue with their plans to buy.

By contrast, if an individual wheat farmer were to try to charge even just 10 cents more than the current market price for a tonne of wheat, he wouldn't be able to sell any of his wheat at all. And since he can sell as much wheat as he wishes at the market price, he has no motive to charge less.

The demand curve facing a perfectly competitive firm

From the perspective of an individual firm in a perfectly competitive market, what does the demand curve for its product look like? Since it can sell as much or as little as it wishes at the prevailing market price, the demand curve for its product is perfectly elastic at the market price. Figure 5.8(a) shows the market demand and supply curves intersecting to determine a market price of P_0. Figure 5.8(b) shows the product demand curve, D_i, as seen by any individual firm in this market: a horizontal line at the market price level P_0.

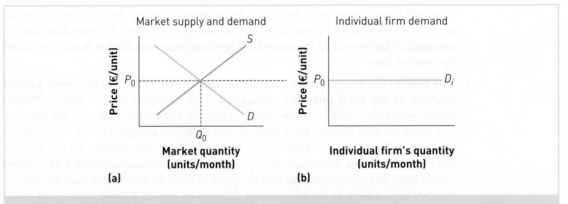

Figure 5.8 The Demand Curve Facing a Perfectly Competitive Firm. The market demand and supply curves intersect to determine the market price of the product (a). The individual firm's demand curve, D_i (b), is a horizontal line at the market price.

imperfectly competitive firm a firm that has at least some control over the market price of its product

Many of the conclusions of the standard supply and demand model also hold for **imperfectly competitive firms** – those firms, like Microsoft, that have at least some ability to vary their own prices. But certain other conclusions do not, as we shall see when we examine the behaviour of such firms more closely in Chapter 8.

Since a perfectly competitive firm has no control over the market price of its product, it needn't worry about choosing the level at which to set that price. As we have seen, the equilibrium market price in a competitive market comes from the intersection of the industry supply and demand curves. The challenge confronting the perfectly competitive firm is to choose its *output level* so that it makes as much profit as it can at that price. As we investigate how the competitive firm responds to this challenge, we shall see once again the pivotal role of our core principle that some costs are more important than others.

A graphical approach to profit maximisation

For our bottle-making firm, average variable cost and average total cost values are shown in columns (4) and (6) of Table 5.3 above. These were used to plot the firm's average total cost, average variable cost and marginal cost curves in Fig. 5.4.

Choosing output to maximise profit

In the following examples and exercises, we shall explore how the company's decision about how many bottles to produce depends on the price of bottles, the wage and the cost of capital.

Example 5.2 If bottles sell for 35 cents each, how many bottles should the company described in Table 5.2 produce each day?

To answer this question, we need simply apply the Cost–Benefit Principle to the question: 'Should the firm expand its level of output?' If its goal is to maximise its profit, the answer to this question will be to expand as long as the *marginal benefit from expanding is at least as great as the marginal cost*. Since the perfectly competitive firm can sell as many bottles as it wishes at the market price of €0.35 per bottle, its marginal benefit from selling an additional bottle is €0.35. If we compare this marginal benefit with the marginal cost entries shown in column (6) of Table 5.2, we see that the firm should keep expanding until it reaches 300 bottles per day (four employees per day). To expand beyond that level it would have to hire a fifth employee, and the resulting marginal cost (€0.40 per bottle) would exceed the marginal benefit.

To confirm that the Cost–Benefit Principle thus applied identifies the profit-maximising number of bottles to produce, we can calculate profit levels directly, as in Table 5.4. Column (3) of Table 5.4 reports the firm's revenue from the sale of bottles, which is calculated as the product of the number of bottles produced per day and the price of €0.35 per bottle. Note, for example, that in the third row of column (3), total revenue is (200 bottles/day) (€0.35/bottle) = €70 per day. Column (5) reports the firm's total daily profit, which is just the difference between its total revenue (column (3)) and its total cost (column (4)). Note that the largest profit entry in column (5), €17 per day, occurs at an output of 300 bottles per day, just as suggested by our earlier application of the Cost–Benefit Principle.

Employees per day (1)	Output (bottles/day) (2)	Total revenue (€/day) (3)	Total cost (€/day) (4)	Profit (€/day) (5)
0	0	0	40	−40
1	80	28	52	−24
2	200	70	64	6
3	260	91	76	15
4	300	105	88	17
5	330	115.50	100	15.50
6	350	122.50	112	10.50
7	362	126.70	124	2.70

Table 5.4 **Output, Revenue, Costs and Profit**

As Exercise 5.2 demonstrates, an increase in the price of the product gives rise to an increase in the profit-maximising level of output.

Exercise 5.2   Same as Example 5.2, except now bottles sell for 62 cents each.

Exercise 5.3 illustrates that a fall in the wage rate leads to a decline in marginal cost, which also causes an increase in the profit-maximising level of output.

Exercise 5.3   Same as Example 5.2, except now employees receive a wage of €6 per day.

Suppose that in Example 5.2 the firm's fixed cost had been not €40 per day but €45 per day. How, if at all, would that have affected the firm's profit-maximising level of output? The answer is 'not at all': each entry in the profit column of Table 5.4 would have been €5 per day smaller than before, but the maximum profit entry still would have been 300 bottles per day.

The observation that the profit-maximising quantity does not depend on fixed costs is not an idiosyncrasy of this example. That it holds true in general is an immediate consequence of the Cost–Benefit Principle, which says that a firm should increase its output if, and only if, the *marginal* benefit exceeds the *marginal* cost. Neither the marginal benefit of expanding (which is the market price of bottles) nor the marginal cost of expanding is affected by a change in the firm's fixed cost.

When the law of diminishing returns applies (that is, when some factors of production are fixed), marginal cost goes up as the firm expands production beyond some point. Under these circumstances, the firm's best option is to keep expanding output as long as *marginal cost is less than price*.

Note that in Example 5.2 if the company's fixed cost had been any more than €57 per day, it would have made a loss at *every* possible level of output. As long as it still had to pay its fixed cost, however, its best bet would have been to continue producing 300 bottles per day. It is better, after all, to experience a smaller loss than a larger one. If a firm in that situation expected conditions to remain the same, though, it would want to get out of the bottle business as soon as its equipment lease expired.

A note on the firm's shutdown condition

It may seem that a firm that can sell as much output as it wishes at a constant market price would *always* do best in the short run by producing and selling the output level for which price equals marginal cost. But there are exceptions to this rule. Suppose, for example, that the market price of the firm's product falls so low that its revenue from sales is smaller than its variable cost at all possible levels of output. The firm should then cease production for the time being. By shutting down, it will suffer a loss equal to its fixed costs. But, by remaining open, it will suffer an even larger loss.

More formally, if P denotes the market price of the product and Q denotes the number of units produced and sold, then $P \times Q$ is the firm's total revenue from sales, and if we use VC to denote the firm's variable cost, the rule is that the firm should shut down in the short run if $P \times Q$ is less than VC for every level of Q:

Short-run shutdown condition: $P \times Q < VC$ for all levels of Q

Exercise 5.4   In Example 5.2, suppose that bottles sold not for €0.35 but only €0.10. Calculate the profit corresponding to each level of output, as in Table 5.4, and verify that the firm's best option is to cease operations in the short run.

Average variable cost and average total cost

Suppose that the firm is unable to cover its variable cost at any level of output – that is, suppose that $P \times Q < VC$ for all levels of Q. It must then also be true that $P < VC/Q$

average variable cost (AVC)
variable cost divided by total
output

for all levels of Q, since we obtain the second inequality by simply dividing both sides of the first one by Q. VC/Q is the firm's **average variable cost (AVC)** – its variable cost divided by its output. The firm's short-run shutdown condition may thus be restated a second way: discontinue operations in the short run if the product price is less than the minimum value of its AVC. Thus:

Short-run shutdown condition (alternative version): $P <$ minimum value of AVC

As we shall see in the next section, this version of the shutdown condition often enables us to tell at a glance whether the firm should continue operations.

average total cost (ATC)
total cost divided by total
output

profitable firm a firm whose
total revenue exceeds its total
cost

A related cost concept that facilitates assessment of the firm's profitability is **average total cost (ATC)**, which is total cost (TC) divided by output (Q): $ATC = TC/Q$. The firm's profit, again, is the difference between its total revenue ($P \times Q$) and its total cost. And since total cost is equal to average total cost times quantity, the firm's profit is also equal to $(P \times Q) - (ATC \times Q)$. A firm is said to be **profitable** if its revenue ($P \times Q$) exceeds its total cost ($ATC \times Q$). A firm can thus be profitable only if the price of its product (P) exceeds its ATC for some level of output.

Keeping track of all these cost concepts may seem tedious. In the next section, however, we will see that the payoff from doing so is that it enables us to recast the profit-maximisation decision in a simple graphical framework.

Economic naturalist 5.1 Why did Swissair collapse because it was losing money, while Alitalia kept flying?

Alitalia, Italy's flag carrier, continually lost money for a decade as a consequence of a cost structure that reflected political pressure (it was state controlled) rather than any commercial reality. It was put up for sale in 2008. Swissair, which went bankrupt in 2001 in the aftermath of 9/11 and had mountains of debt, simply ceased to trade. In the USA, it has been said that the default option for airlines has been to be in 'Chapter 11', a state in which they can continue to trade but their creditors are 'put on ice'. To qualify for Chapter 11 protection a firm must show (a) that it can cover its operating costs, and (b) has a reasonable prospect of becoming sufficiently profitable to pay its creditors more than if they forced it into bankruptcy. In the European case Swissair was unable to pay its creditors and service its debt. It couldn't cover its total costs as passenger demand fell after 9/11. It closed down suddenly … and emerged as a new, smaller airline called, simply, Swiss, which continues to operate today, its assets having been sold as a going concern. Past debts represent sunk costs, and could not be serviced, so shareholders and creditors 'took a cold bath'. In Alitalia's case, in order to keep flying it had, at a minimum, to cover its operating costs, but was unable to do so. It didn't collapse simply because it had another source of revenue as a government-owned airline … access to finance from the taxpayer. This ceased in 2008 when the cash-strapped Italian government decided to sell the airline.

Price = marginal cost: the maximum-profit condition

In Example 5.2, we implicitly assumed that the bottle maker could employ workers only in whole-number amounts. Under these conditions, we saw that the profit-maximising output level was one for which marginal cost was somewhat less than price (because adding yet another employee would have pushed marginal cost higher than price). In Example 5.3, we shall see that when output and employment can be varied continuously, the maximum-profit condition is that price be equal to marginal cost.

Example 5.3 For the bottle maker whose cost curves are as shown in Fig. 5.9, find the profit-maximising output level if bottles sell for €0.20 each. How much profit will this firm earn? What is the lowest price at which this firm would continue to operate in the short run?

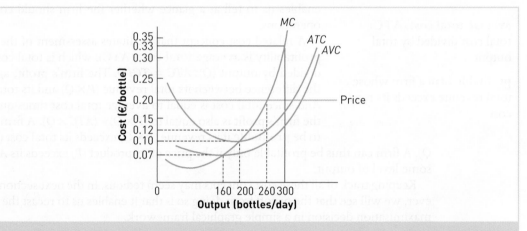

Figure 5.9 Price = Marginal Cost: the Perfectly Competitive Firm's Profit-maximising Supply Rule.
If price is greater than marginal cost, the firm can increase its profit by expanding production and sales. If price is less than marginal cost, the firm can increase its profit by producing and selling less output.

Cost–Benefit
Analysis

The Cost–Benefit Principle tells us that this firm should continue to expand as long as price is at least as great as marginal cost. In Fig. 5.9 we see that if the firm follows this rule, it will produce 260 bottles per day, the quantity at which *price and marginal cost are equal*. To gain further confidence that 260 must be the profit-maximising quantity when the price is €0.20 per bottle, first suppose that the firm had sold some amount less than that – say, only 200 bottles per day. Its benefit from expanding output by one bottle would then be the bottle's market price, here 20 cents. The cost of expanding output by one bottle is equal (by definition) to the firm's marginal cost, which at 200 bottles per day is only 10 cents (see Fig. 5.9). So by selling the 201st bottle for 20 cents and producing it for an extra cost of only 10 cents, the firm will increase its profit by $20 - 10 = 10$ cents per day. In a similar way, we can show that for *any* quantity less than the level at which price equals marginal cost, the seller can boost profit by expanding production.

Increasing
Opportunity
Cost

Conversely, suppose that the firm was currently selling more than 260 bottles per day – say, 300 – at a price of 20 cents each. In Fig. 5.9 we see that marginal cost at an output of 300 is 33 cents per bottle. If the firm then contracted its output by one bottle per day, it would cut its costs by 33 cents while losing only 20 cents in revenue. As a result, its profit would grow by 13 cents per day. The same argument can be made regarding any quantity larger than 260, so if the firm is currently selling an output at which price is less than marginal cost, it can always do better by producing and selling fewer bottles.

We have thus established that if the firm sold fewer than 260 bottles per day, it could earn more profit by expanding; and if it sold more than 260, it could earn more by contracting. It follows that at a market price of 20 cents per bottle, the seller maximises its profit by selling 260 units per week, the quantity for which price and marginal cost are exactly the same.

At that quantity the firm will collect total revenue of $P \times Q = $ (€0.20/bottle) (260 bottles/day) = €52 per day. Note in Fig. 5.9 that at 260 bottles per day the firm's average total cost is $ATC = $ €0.12 per bottle, which means that its total cost is $ATC \times Q = $ (€0.12/bottle)(260 bottles/day) = €31.20 per day. The firm's profit is the difference between its *total revenue and its total cost*, or €20.80 per day. Note, finally, that the minimum value of the firm's AVC curve is €0.07. So if the price of bottles fell below 7 cents each, the firm would shut down in the short run.

Another attractive feature of the graphical method of finding the profit-maximising output level is that it permits us to calculate the firm's profit graphically. Thus, for the firm in Example 5.2, daily profit is simply the difference between price and ATC times the number of units sold: (€0.20/bottle – €0.12/bottle)(260 bottles/day) = €20.80 per day, which is the area of the shaded rectangle in Fig. 5.10.

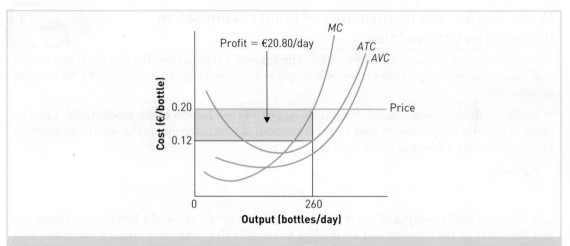

Figure 5.10 Measuring Profit Graphically. Profit is equal to $(P - ATC) \times Q$, which is equal to the area of the shaded rectangle.

Not all firms are as fortunate as the one shown in Fig. 5.10. Suppose, for example, that the price of bottles had been not 20 cents but only 8 cents. Since that price is greater than the minimum value of AVC (see Fig. 5.11), the firm should continue to operate in the short run by producing the level of output for which price equals marginal cost (180 bottles per day). But because price is less than ATC at that level of output, the firm will now experience a loss, or negative profit, on its operations. This profit is calculated as $(P - ATC) \times Q = $ (€0.08/bottle – €0.10/bottle) × (180 bottles/day) = –€3.60 per day, which is equal to the area of the shaded rectangle in Fig. 5.11.

In Chapter 7, we shall see how firms move resources in response to the incentives implicit in profits and losses. But such movements occur in the long run, and our focus here is on production decisions in the short run.

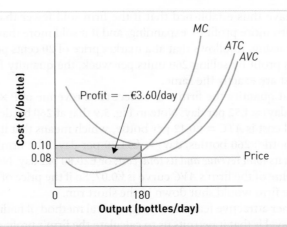

Figure 5.11 A 'Negative Profit'. When price is less than *ATC* as the profit-maximising quantity, the firm experiences a loss, which is equal to the area of the shaded rectangle.

Maths Box 5.2 The mathematics of profit maximisation under perfect competition

The perfectly competitive firm is a *price taker*. The amount it sells has no effect on the price per unit sold it receives. Hence, total sales revenue is simply price (which is given) multiplied by the number of units sold.

Profits total sales revenue minus total costs incurred in production of the product sold. Let *B* be profit. It depends on the level of sales and of costs, both of which depend on the level of production. Hence, profits are a function of the level of production.

Formally,

$$B = B(q)$$

where q is the level of output of the firm. To find the maximum value of a function we obtain the first derivative of the function and set it equal to zero. At this value, it is either a maximum or a minimum. If the second derivative is negative, the value for q is that which maximises the function

$$B = TR(q) - TC(q)$$

and

$$dB/dq = dTR/dq - dTC/dq$$

For a maximum value of *B* it is necessary that this be equal to zero. That means

$$dTR/dq = dTC/dq$$

But dTR/dq and dTC/dq are (in the competitive case) simply price and marginal cost, respectively. Hence this necessary condition says that to maximise profits you produce the level of output that equates price to marginal cost. To be sure that this maximises rather than minimises profits we need to go further. It requires that the second derivative of the expression should be negative.

TC is the sum of fixed plus variable costs. Fixed costs are a constant, *a*. Variable costs, because of diminishing returns, have the form

$$TVC = b \times q + c \times q^2$$

meaning that average variable cost increases with q. Hence, the total cost function is

$$TC = a + b \times q + c \times q^2$$

So the profits function may be written

$$B = p \times q - (a + b \times q + c \times q^2)$$

Differentiating this gives

$$dB/dQ = p - (b + 2c \times q)$$

where p = price and $b + 2cq$ is marginal cost. Setting $dB/dQ = 0$ means price equals marginal cost. Differentiating again gives

$$d^2B/dq^2 = -2c < 0$$

so it is a maximum, and profits are maximised at this point.

RECAP Determinants of supply

Among the relevant factors *causing supply curves to shift* are new technologies, changes in input prices, changes in the number of sellers, expectations of future price changes and changes in the prices of other products that firms might produce.

Applying the theory of supply

Whether the activity is producing new soft drink containers or recycling used ones – or, indeed, any other production activity at all – the same logic governs all supply decisions in perfectly competitive markets (and in any other setting in which sellers can sell as much as they wish to at a constant price): keep expanding output until marginal cost is equal to the price of the product. This logic helps us understand why recycling efforts are more intensive for some products than others.

When recycling is left to private market forces, why are many more aluminium beverage containers recycled than glass ones?

In both cases, recyclers gather containers until their marginal costs are equal to the containers' respective redemption prices. When recycling is left to market forces, the redemption price for a container is based on what companies can sell it (or the materials in it) for. Aluminium containers can easily be processed into scrap aluminium, which commands a high price, and this leads profit-seeking companies to offer a high redemption price for aluminium cans. By contrast, the glass from which glass containers are made has only limited resale value, primarily because the raw materials required to make new glass are so cheap. This difference leads profit-seeking companies to offer much lower redemption prices for glass containers than for aluminium ones.

The high redemption prices for aluminium cans induce many people to track them down, whereas the low redemption prices for glass containers lead most people to ignore them. If recycling is left completely to market forces, then, we would expect to see aluminium soft drink containers quickly recycled, whereas glass containers would increasingly litter the landscape. This is in fact the pattern we do see in countries without recycling laws. (More on how these laws work in a moment.) This pattern is a simple consequence of the fact that the supply curves of container-recycling services are upward-sloping.

The acquisition of valuable raw materials is only one of two important benefits from recycling. The second is that, by removing litter, recycling makes the environment more pleasant for everyone. As Example 5.4 suggests, this second benefit might easily justify the cost of recycling substantial numbers of glass containers.

Example 5.4 What is the socially optimal amount of recycling of glass containers?

Suppose that the 60,000 citizens of Chinon in the Loire Valley in France would collectively be willing to pay 6 centimes for each glass container removed from their local environment. If the local market supply curve of glass container–recycling services is as shown in Fig. 5.12, what is the socially optimal level of glass container recycling?

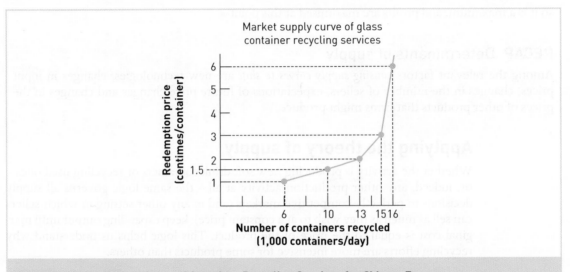

Figure 5.12 The Supply Curve of Container Recycling Services for Chinon, France.

Suppose the citizens of Chinon authorise their Commune to collect tax money to finance litter removal. If the benefit of each glass container removed, as measured by what residents are collectively willing to pay, is 6 centimes, the municipal government should offer to pay 6 centimes for each glass container recycled. To maximise the total economic surplus from recycling, we should recycle that number of containers for which the marginal cost of recycling is equal to the 6 centimes marginal benefit. Given the market supply curve shown in Fig 5.12, the optimal quantity is 16,000 containers per day, and that is how many will be redeemed when the government offers 6 centimes per container.

Although 16,000 containers per day will be removed from the environment in Example 5.4, others will remain. After all, some are discarded in remote locations, and a redemption price of 6 centimes per container is simply not high enough to induce people to track them all down.

Cost–Benefit
Analysis

So why not offer an even higher price, and get rid of *all* glass container litter? For the case in Example 5.4, the reason is that the *marginal cost* of removing the 16,001st glass container each day is greater than the benefit of removing it. Total economic surplus is largest when we remove litter only up to the point that the marginal benefit of litter removal is equal to its marginal cost, which occurs when 16,000 containers per day are recycled. To proceed past that point is actually wasteful.

Many people become upset when they first hear economists say that the socially optimal amount of litter is greater than zero. In the minds of these people, the optimal amount of litter is *exactly* zero. But this position completely ignores the scarcity principle. Granted, there would be benefits from reducing litter further, but there would also be costs. Spending more on litter removal therefore means spending less on other useful things.

If 16,000 containers per day is the optimal amount of litter removal, can we expect the individual spending decisions of private citizens to result in that amount of litter removal? Unfortunately we cannot. The problem is that anyone who paid for litter removal individually would bear the full cost of those services while reaping only a tiny fraction of the benefit. In Example 5.4, the 60,000 citizens of Chinon reaped a total benefit of 6 centimes per container removed, which means a benefit of only $(6/60,000) = 0.0001$ centime per container per person! Someone who paid 6 centimes for someone else to remove a container would thus be incurring a cost 60,000 times greater than his share of the resulting benefit.

In the case of drinks container litter, in short, we have an example in which private market forces do not produce the best attainable outcome for society as a whole. Even people who carelessly toss containers on the ground, rather than recycle them, are often offended by the unsightly landscape to which their own actions contribute. Indeed, this is why they often support laws mandating adequate redemption prices for glass containers.

| Incentives Matter |

People who litter do so not because they don't care about the environment, but because their private incentives make littering misleadingly attractive. Recycling requires some effort, after all; yet no individual's recycling efforts have a noticeable effect on the quality of the environment. The soft drink container-deposit laws that have been enacted in many countries are a simple way to bring individual interests more closely into balance with the interests of society as a whole.

Economic naturalist 5.2 Why have the plastic grocery bags that disfigured the Irish countryside almost entirely disappeared?

Ireland depends heavily on tourism, and 'sells' the image of a green and unspoilt countryside. This is hardly surprising since few people would come to Ireland (or Britain, for that matter) in search of sun, sand and cheap wine: the weather and penal taxes on alcohol rule that out. Unfortunately, during the 1980s and 1990s increased prosperity and other factors led to the prolific use of plastic bags in retailing. A large proportion of these ended up being blown into hedgerows and littering the streets. In 2002, in an attempt to clean up this massive eyesore, the Irish Minister for the Environment persuaded the Minister for Finance to impose a 15 cent per bag tax on plastic bags provided by retail establishments in the budget for 2003 (there were some small exceptions associated with fresh food). There were loud complaints from supermarkets and other grocery and convenience outlets. The government stood its ground. In 2003 the government derived virtually no revenue from the tax ... and plastic bags were about as common as hens' teeth. The impact on the environment was dramatic. Of course, purists in the economics profession were heard to argue that the outcome was sub-optimal since the optimal level of littering is not zero. Do you think anyone listened? If not, what does this tell us about the costs and benefits involved?

Exercise 5.5   If the supply curve of glass container-recycling services is as shown in the diagram below, and each of the city's 60,000 citizens would be willing to pay 0.00005 cents for each glass container removed from the landscape, at what level should the city government set the redemption price for glass containers, and how many will be recycled each day?

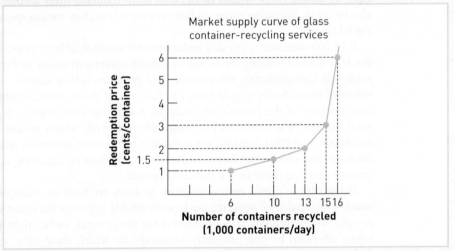

Supply and producer surplus

producer surplus the amount by which price exceeds the seller's reservation price

The economic surplus received by a buyer is called *consumer surplus*. The analogous construct for a seller is **producer surplus**, the difference between the price a seller actually receives for the product and the lowest price for which she would have been willing to sell it (her reservation price, which in general will be her marginal cost).

As in the case of consumer surplus, the term 'producer surplus' sometimes refers to the surplus received by a single seller in a transaction, while on other occasions it describes the total surplus received by all sellers in a market or collection of markets.

Calculating producer surplus

In Chapter 4 we saw that consumer surplus in a market is the area bounded above by the demand curve and bounded below by the market price. Producer surplus in a market is calculated in an analogous way. As Example 5.5 illustrates, it is the area bounded above by the market price and bounded below by the market supply curve.

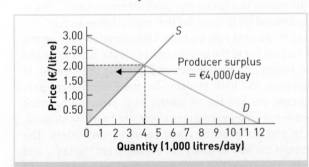

Figure 5.13 Producer Surplus in the Market for Milk. Producer surplus is the area of the shaded triangle. Its value is €4,000 per day

Example 5.5 How much do sellers benefit from their participation in the market for milk?

Consider the market for milk whose demand and supply curves are shown in Fig. 5.13, which has an equilibrium price of

€2 per litre and an equilibrium quantity of 4,000 litres per day. How much producer surplus do the sellers in this market reap?

In Fig. 5.13, note first that for all milk sold up to 4,000 litres per day, sellers receive a surplus equal to the difference between the market price of €2 per litre and their reservation price as given by the supply curve. Total producer surplus received by buyers in the milk market is thus the shaded triangle between the supply curve and the market price in Fig. 5.13. Note that this area is a right-angled triangle whose vertical arm is $h = $ €2/litre and whose horizontal arm is $b = $ 4,000 litres/day. And since the area of any triangle is equal to $(1/2)bh$, producer surplus in this market is equal to

$$(1/2) \, (4{,}000 \text{ litres/day}) \, (\text{€2/litre}) = \text{€4{,}000/day}$$

Producer surplus in this example may be thought of as the highest price sellers would pay, in the aggregate, for the right to continue participating in the milk market. It is €4,000 per day, since that is the amount by which their *combined benefits exceed their combined costs*. It is the difference between what the producer expects to receive for that unit of output and the smallest amount the producer would be willing to accept for that unit of the good.

Summary

- The supply curve for a good or service is a schedule that for any price tells us the *quantity that sellers wish to supply at that price*. The prices at which goods and services are offered for sale in the market depend, in turn, on the opportunity cost of the resources required to produce them.

- Supply curves tend to be upward-sloping, at least in the short run, in part because of the Low-Hanging-Fruit Principle. In general, rational producers will always take advantage of their best opportunities first, moving on to more difficult or costly opportunities only after their best ones have been exhausted. Reinforcing this tendency is the *law of diminishing returns*, which says that when some factors of production are held fixed, the amount of additional variable factors required to produce successive increments in output grows larger.

- For perfectly competitive markets – or, more generally, for markets in which individual sellers can sell whatever quantity they wish at constant price – the seller's best option is to sell that quantity of output for which *price equals marginal cost*, provided price exceeds the minimum value of average variable cost. The supply curve for the seller thus coincides with the portion of his marginal cost curve that exceeds average variable cost. This is why we sometimes say that the supply curve represents the cost side of the market (in contrast to the demand curve, which represents the benefit side of the market).

- An important terminological distinction from the demand side of the market also applies on the supply side of the market. A 'change in supply' means a shift in the entire supply curve, whereas a 'change in the quantity supplied' means a movement along the supply curve. The factors that cause *supply curves to shift* include technology, input prices, the number of sellers, expectations of future price changes and the prices of other products that firms might produce.

- *Producer surplus* is a measure of the economic surplus reaped by a seller or sellers in a market. It is the cumulative sum of the differences between the market price and their reservation prices, which is the area bounded above by market price and bounded below by the supply curve.

Review questions

1. Explain why you would expect supply curves to slope upwards on the basis of the Principle of Increasing Opportunity Cost.

2. Which do you think is more likely to be a fixed factor of production for an ice cream producer during the next two months: its factory building or its workers who operate the machines? Explain.

3. Economists often stress that congestion helps account for the law of diminishing returns. With this in mind, explain why it would be impossible to feed all the people on Earth with food grown in a single flowerpot, even if unlimited water, labour, seed, fertiliser, sunlight and other inputs were available.

4. **True or false:** The perfectly competitive firm should always produce the output level for which price equals marginal cost.

5. Why do we use the vertical interpretation of the supply curve when we measure producer surplus?

connect **Problems**

Problems marked with an asterisk (*) are more difficult.

1. Zoe is trying to decide how to divide her time between her job as a wedding photographer, which pays €27 per hour for as many hours as she chooses to work, and as a fossil collector, in which her pay depends both on the price of fossils and the number of them she finds. Earnings aside, Zoe is indifferent between the two tasks, and the number of fossils she can find depends on the number of hours a day she searches, as shown in the table below.

Hours per day (1)	Total fossils per day (2)
1	5
2	9
3	12
4	14
5	15

  a. Derive a table with price in euro increments from €0 to €30 in column (1) and the quantity of fossils Zoe is willing to supply per day at that price in column (2).

  b. Plot these points in a graph with price on the vertical axis and quantity per day on the horizontal. What is this curve called?

2. A price-taking firm makes air conditioners. The market price of one of its new air conditioners is €120. Its total cost information is given in the table below.

Air conditioners per day	Total cost (€ per day)
1	100
2	150
3	220
4	310
5	405
6	510
7	650
8	800

How many air conditioners should the firm produce per day if its goal is to maximise its profit?

3. The Paducah Slugger Company makes baseball bats out of lumber supplied to it by Acme Sporting Goods, which pays Paducah €10 for each finished bat. Paducah's only factors of production are lathe operators and a small building with a lathe. The number of bats per day it produces depends on the number of employee-hours per day, as shown in the table below.

  a. If the wage is €15 per hour and Paducah's daily fixed cost for the lathe and building is €60, what is the profit-maximising quantity of bats?

  b. What would be the profit-maximising number of bats if the firm's fixed cost were not €60 per day but only €30?

Number of bats per day	Number of employee-hours per day
0	0
5	1
10	2
15	4
20	7
25	11
30	16
35	22

4. In Question 3, how would Paducah's profit-maximising level of output be affected if the government imposed a tax of €10 per day on the company? (**Hint:** Think of this tax as equivalent to a €10 increase in fixed cost.) What would Paducah's profit-maximising level of output be if the government imposed a tax of €2 per bat? (**Hint:** Think of this tax as a €2 per bat increase in the firm's marginal cost.) Why do these two taxes have such different effects?

5. The supply curves for the only two firms in a competitive industry are given by $P = 2Q1$ and $P = 2 + Q2$, where $Q1$ is the output of firm 1 and $Q2$ is the output of firm 2. What is the market supply curve for this industry? (**Hint:** Graph the two curves side by side, then add their respective quantities at a sample of different prices.)

6. Calculate daily producer surplus for the market for pizza whose demand and supply curves are shown in the graph below.

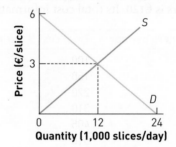

7. For the pizza seller whose marginal, average variable and average total cost curves are as shown in the diagram below, what is the profit-maximising level of output and how much profit will this producer earn if the price of pizza is €2.50 per slice?

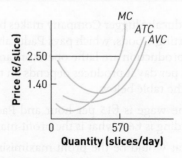

8. For the pizza seller whose marginal, average variable and average total cost curves are as shown in the diagram below, what is the profit-maximising level of output and how much profit will this producer earn if the price of pizza is €0.80 per slice?

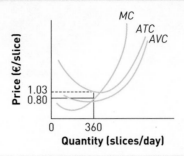

9.* For the pizza seller whose marginal, average variable and average total cost curves are as shown in the diagram below, what is the profit-maximising level of output and how much profit will this producer earn if the price of pizza is €0.50 per slice?

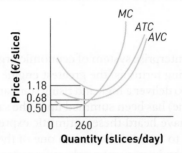

10.* For the pizza seller whose marginal, average variable and average total cost curves are as shown in the diagram below (the same seller as in Problem 9), what is the profit-maximising level of output and how much profit will this producer earn if the price of pizza is €1.18 per slice?

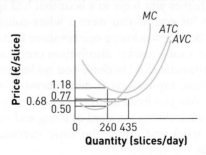

To help you grasp the key concepts of this chapter check out the extra resources posted on the Online Learning Centre. There are chapter summaries, self-test questions, an interactive graphing tool, weblinks and a glossary, all for free!

Visit the Online Learning Centre at: www.mcgraw-hill.co.uk/textbooks/mcdowell for information on accessing all of these resources.

6

Efficiency and Exchange

The free-enterprise system of economic organisation has frequently been described in such glowing terms as 'the greatest engine of progress mankind has ever witnessed'. Its ability to deliver a high and rising standard of living to everyone (even if not equally to everyone) has been summed up in the saying: 'A rising tide lifts all boats.'

If you have heard these optimistic expressions extolling the free market but were struggling to make ends meet in one of the poorer areas of the Paris suburbs largely populated by immigrant workers from North Africa you might be somewhat sceptical. Urban violence, a drab and deteriorating environment, a long and expensive commute to a poorly paid job in the city centre and all the other unpleasant aspects of urban ghettoes would probably be your lot. If you were a 55-year-old unemployed ex-coal miner in County Durham in England in the late 1990s you might have wondered whether you were in a boat that had sprung a leak: there were simply no jobs available for you. If you were a white-collar worker who had lost a job in Seattle because Boeing was losing market share to Airbus, and were now working as a pallet pusher in a supermarket distribution centre and unable to afford adequate treatment for an asthmatic child because you no longer had company health cover, you might regard those expressions as descriptions of an entirely different economic universe from the one you lived in. In all these cases you would have found yourself enduring a poor and declining standard of living and an inability to better your position or find suitable work and afford the basic necessities of a decent existence by society's standards.

For someone in any of these positions a degree of scepticism about the virtues of the system of free markets and private ownership of economic resources that we call 'free enterprise' would be entirely understandable.

Informed students of the market system understand that it could never be expected to avoid all these problems, and others like them, in the first place. *In certain domains –* indeed, in very broad domains – markets are every bit as remarkable as their strongest proponents assert. Yet there are many problems they simply cannot be expected to solve. For example, private markets cannot by themselves guarantee an income distribution that most people regard as fair. Nor can they ensure clean air, uncongested roads or safe neighbourhoods for all. And unemployment can persist even in a booming economy.

Yet markets do enable society to produce sufficient resources to meet all these goals, and more. But the types of problem just described point to an unavoidable conclusion. There are circumstances in which markets do not operate well and the outcome is less than acceptable. As a result, and even in the most successful free-market economies, markets are supplemented by active political coordination and collective provision of goods and services in at least some instances. We will almost always achieve our goals more effectively if we know what tasks private markets can do well, and then allow them to perform those tasks.

Unfortunately, the discovery that markets cannot solve *every* problem seems to have led some critics to conclude that markets cannot solve *any* problems. This misperception is a dangerous one, because it has prompted attempts to prevent markets from doing even those tasks to which they are ideally suited. Our purpose in this chapter will be to explore why many tasks are best left to the market. We shall explore the conditions under which unregulated markets generate the largest possible economic surplus. We shall also discuss why attempts to interfere with market outcomes often lead to unintended and undesired consequences. We shall see why public utilities can more efficiently serve their customers if they set prices in a way that closely mimics the market. And we shall also discuss why the economic burden of a tax does not always fall most heavily on the parties from whom it is directly collected.

Market equilibrium and efficiency

As noted in Chapter 3, the mere fact that markets coordinate the production of a large and complex list of goods and services is reason enough to marvel at them. But economists make an even stronger claim – namely, that markets not only produce these goods, but also produce them as *efficiently* as possible.

efficient (or Pareto efficiency) a situation is efficient if no change is possible that will help some people without harming others

The term **efficient**, as economists use it, has a narrow technical meaning. When we say that market equilibrium is efficient, we mean simply this: *if price and quantity take anything other than their equilibrium values, a transaction that will make at least some people better off without harming others can always be found.* This conception of efficiency is also known as **Pareto efficiency**, after Vilfredo Pareto, the nineteenth-century Italian economist who introduced it.

Why is market equilibrium 'efficient' in this sense? The answer is that when a market is not in equilibrium it is always possible to construct an exchange that helps some without harming others. In a sense, a 'free lunch' exists. Suppose, for example, that the supply and demand curves for milk are as shown in Fig. 6.1, and that the current price of milk is €1 per litre. At that price, sellers offer only 2,000 litres of milk a day. At that quantity, the marginal buyer values an extra litre of milk at €2. This is the price that

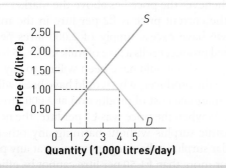

Figure 6.1 A Market in which Price is Below the Equilibrium Level. In this market, milk is currently selling for €1 per litre, €0.50 below the equilibrium price of €1.50 per litre.

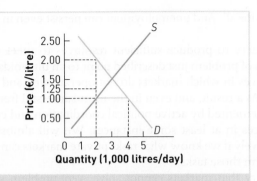

Figure 6.2 How Excess Demand Creates an Opportunity for a Surplus-enhancing Transaction.
At a market price of €1 per litre, the most intensely dissatisfied buyer is willing to pay €2 for an additional litre, which a seller can produce at a cost of only €1. If this buyer pays the seller €1.25 for the extra litre, the buyer gains an economic surplus of €0.75 and the seller gains an economic surplus of €0.25.

corresponds to 2,000 litres a day on the demand curve, which represents what the marginal buyer is willing to pay for an additional litre (another application of the vertical interpretation of the demand curve). We also know that the cost of producing an extra litre of milk is only €1. This is the price that corresponds to 2,000 litres a day on the supply curve, which equals marginal cost (another application of the vertical interpretation of the supply curve).

Furthermore, a price of €1 per litre leads to excess demand of 2,000 litres per day, which means that many frustrated buyers cannot buy as much milk as they want at the going price. Now suppose a supplier sells an extra litre of milk to the most eager of these buyers for €1.25, as in Fig. 6.2. Since the extra litre cost only €1 to produce, the seller is €0.25 better off than before. And since the most eager buyer values the extra litre at €2, that buyer is €0.75 better off than before. In sum, the transaction creates an extra €1 of economic surplus out of thin air!

Note that none of the other buyers or sellers is harmed by this transaction. Thus milk selling for only €1 per litre cannot be efficient. As Exercise 6.1 illustrates, there was nothing special about the price of €1 per litre. Indeed, if milk sells for *any* price below €1.50 per litre (the market equilibrium price), we can design a similar transaction, which means that selling milk for any price less than €1.50 per litre cannot be efficient.

Exercise 6.1   In Fig. 6.1, suppose that milk initially sells for 50 cents per litre. Describe a transaction that will create additional economic surplus for both buyer and seller without causing harm to anyone else.

What is more, it is always possible to describe a transaction that will create additional surplus for both buyer and seller whenever the price lies above the market equilibrium level. Suppose, for example, that the current price is €2 per litre in the milk market shown in Fig. 6.1. At that price, we have excess supply of 2,000 litres per day (see Fig. 6.3). Suppose the most dissatisfied producer sells a litre of milk for €1.75 to the buyer who values it most highly. This buyer, who would have been willing to pay €2, will be €0.25 better off than before. Likewise the producer, who would have been willing to sell milk for as little as €1 per litre (the marginal cost of production at 2,000 litres per day), will be €0.75 better off than before. As when the price was €1 per litre, the new transaction creates €1 of additional economic surplus without harming any other buyer or seller. Since we could design a similar surplus-enhancing transaction at any price above the equilibrium level, selling milk for more than €1.50 per litre cannot be efficient.

The vertical interpretations of the supply and demand curves thus make it clear why only the equilibrium price in a market can be efficient. *When the price realised is either higher or lower than the equilibrium price, the quantity exchanged in the market will always be lower than the equilibrium quantity.*

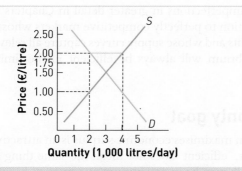

Figure 6.3 How Excess Supply Creates an Opportunity for a Surplus-enhancing Transaction. At a market price of €2 per litre, dissatisfied sellers can produce an additional litre of milk at a cost of only €1, which is €1 less than a buyer would be willing to pay for it. If the buyer pays the seller €1.75 for an extra litre, the buyer gains an economic surplus of €0.25 and the seller gains an economic surplus of €0.75.

If the price is below equilibrium, the quantity sold will be the amount that *sellers offer*. If the price is above equilibrium, the quantity sold will be the amount that *buyers wish to buy*. In either case, the vertical value on the demand curve at the quantity exchanged, which is the value of an extra unit to buyers, must be larger than the vertical value on the supply curve, which is the marginal cost of producing that unit.

So the market equilibrium price is the only price at which buyers and sellers cannot design a surplus-enhancing transaction. The market equilibrium price leads, in other words, to the largest possible total economic surplus. In this specific, limited sense, free markets are said to produce and distribute goods and services efficiently.

Actually, to claim that the observed market equilibrium in terms of prices and quantities is always efficient even in this limited sense is an overstatement. The claim holds only if the following conditions are met.

1. **Buyers and sellers are well informed** If people do not know the quality of a good or service they may find it difficult to evaluate the price they are prepared to pay for it.

2. **Markets are perfectly competitive** A monopolist can use market power to drive a wedge between marginal cost and price, and hence between the cost of producing a good and what people are prepared to pay for it.

3. **The demand and supply curves satisfy certain other restrictions** For example, market equilibrium will not be efficient if the individual marginal cost curves that add up to the market supply curve fail to include all relevant costs of producing the product. Thus, as we saw in Chapter 3, the true cost of expanding output will be higher than indicated by the market supply curve if production generates pollution that harms others. The equilibrium output will then be inefficiently large and the equilibrium price inefficiently low. Likewise, market equilibrium will not be efficient if the individual demand curves that make up the market demand curve do not capture all the relevant benefits of buying additional units of the product. For instance, if a home owner's willingness to pay for ornamental shrubs is based only on the enjoyment she herself gains from them, and not on any benefits that may accrue to her neighbours, the market demand curve for shrubs will understate their value to the neighbourhood. The equilibrium quantity of ornamental shrubs will be inefficiently small, and the market price for shrubs will be inefficiently low.

4. **Transaction costs are low** For example, high tax costs on buying and selling houses can result in demand for existing housing space not being equal to supply; high travel costs can result in excess demand for labour in one part of a city and excess supply persisting in another.

We shall take up such market imperfections in greater detail in Chapters 8–11. For now, we shall confine our attention to perfectly competitive markets whose demand curves capture all relevant benefits and whose supply curves capture all relevant costs. For such goods, market equilibrium will always be efficient in the limited sense described earlier.

Efficiency is not the only goal

The fact that market equilibrium maximises economic surplus is an attractive feature of the market system. However, 'efficient' does not mean the same thing as 'good'. For example, the market for milk may be in equilibrium at a price of €1.50 per litre, yet many poor families may be unable to afford milk for their children at that price. Still others may not even have a place for their children to sleep.

Efficiency is a concept that is based on predetermined attributes of buyers and sellers – their incomes, tastes, abilities, knowledge, and so on. Through the combined effects of individual cost–benefit decisions, these attributes give rise to the supply and demand curves for each good produced in an economy. If we are concerned about inequality in the distribution of attributes such as income, we should not be surprised to discover that markets do not always yield the outcomes we like.

Most of us could agree, for example, that the world would be a better one if all people had enough income to feed their families adequately. The claim that equilibrium in the market for milk is efficient means simply that, *taking people's incomes as given*, the resulting allocation of milk cannot be altered so as to help some people without at the same time harming others.

To this a critic of the market system might respond, 'So what?' As such critics rightly point out, imposing costs on others may be justified if doing so will help those with sufficiently important unmet demands. For example, most people would prefer to provide some funding out of taxes to provide housing for the homeless rather than let the homeless freeze to death. This kind of reasoning led to a decision in the United States in the 1970s to impose price controls on home heating oil when crude oil prices rose sharply after the second oil shock (see below). Many might agree that if the alternative had been to take no action at all, price controls might have been justified in the name of social justice.

But the economists' concept of market efficiency makes it clear that there *must* be a better alternative policy. Price controls on oil prevent the market from reaching equilibrium, and that means forgoing transactions that would benefit some people without harming others. It would have been more efficient to allow heating oil prices to rise, but to give those on low incomes money with which to buy it, rather than reduce prices for everyone and induce a shortage because demand exceeded supply.

Why efficiency should be the first goal

Efficiency is important not because it is a desirable end in itself, but because it enables us to achieve all our other goals to the fullest possible extent. Whenever a market is out of equilibrium, it is always possible to generate additional economic surplus. To gain additional economic surplus is to gain more of the resources we need to do the things we want to do. Whenever any market is out of equilibrium, there is *waste*, and waste is always a bad thing.

RECAP Equilibrium and efficiency

When a market is not in equilibrium – because price is either above the equilibrium level or below it – the quantity exchanged is always *less than the equilibrium level*. At such a quantity, a transaction can always be made in which both buyer and seller benefit from the exchange of an additional unit of output. A market in equilibrium is said to be efficient, or Pareto efficient, meaning that no real-location is possible that will benefit some people without harming others. Total economic surplus in a market is maximised when exchange occurs at the equilibrium price. But the fact that equilibrium is 'efficient' in this sense does not mean that it is 'good'. All markets can be in equilibrium, yet many people may lack sufficient income to buy even basic goods and services. Still, permitting markets to reach equilibrium is important, because when economic surplus is maximised, it is possible to pursue every goal more fully.

The cost of preventing price adjustments

Price ceilings

During 1979, after the second oil shock, the price of home heating oil across America rose by more than 100 per cent. (The percentage increase in Europe was much lower. Why?) Concern about the hardship this sudden price increase would impose on poor families in northern states led the US government to impose a price ceiling in the market for home heating oil. This price ceiling prohibited sellers from charging more than a specified amount for heating oil.

Example 6.1 illustrates why imposing a price ceiling on heating oil, though well intended, was a bad idea.

Example 6.1 How much waste does a price ceiling on heating oil cause?

Suppose the demand and supply curves for home heating oil are as shown in Fig. 6.4, in which the equilibrium price is €1.40 per litre. And suppose that, at that price, many poor families cannot heat their homes adequately. Out of concern for the poor, legislators pass a law setting the maximum price at €1 per litre. How much lost economic surplus does this policy cost society?

First, we can calculate total economic surplus without price controls. If this market is not regulated, 3,000 litres per day will be sold at a price of €1.40 per litre. In Fig. 6.4, the economic surplus received by buyers is the area of the upper shaded triangle. Since the height of this triangle is €0.60 per litre, and its base is 3,000 litres per day, its area is equal to $(1/2)(3,000 \text{ litres}/\text{day})(€0.60/\text{litre}) = €900$ per day. The economic surplus received by producers is the area of the lower shaded triangle. Since this triangle also has an area of €900 per day, total economic surplus in this market will be €1,800 per day.

If the price of heating oil is prevented from rising above €1 per litre, only 1,000 litres per day will be sold, and the total economic surplus will be reduced by the area of the striped triangle shown in Fig. 6.5. Since the height of this triangle is €0.80 per litre, and its base is 2,000 litres per day, its area is $(1/2)(2,000 \text{ litres}/\text{day})(€0.80/\text{litre}) = €800$ per day. Producer surplus falls from €900 per day in the unregulated market to the area of the lower shaded triangle, or $(1/2)(1,000 \text{ litres}/\text{day})(€0.20/\text{litre}) = €100$ per day, which is a loss of €800 per day. Thus the loss in total economic surplus is equal to the loss in producer surplus, which means that the new consumer surplus must be the same as the original consumer surplus. To verify this, note that consumer surplus with the price ceiling is the area of the upper shaded area in Fig. 6.5, which is again

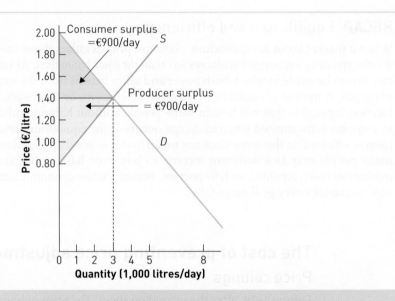

Figure 6.4 Economic Surplus in an Unregulated Market for Home Heating Oil. For the supply and demand curves shown, the equilibrium price of home heating oil is €1.40 per litre, and the equilibrium quantity is 3,000 litres per day. Consumer surplus is the area of the upper shaded triangle (€900 per day). Producer surplus is the area of the lower shaded triangle (also €900 per day).

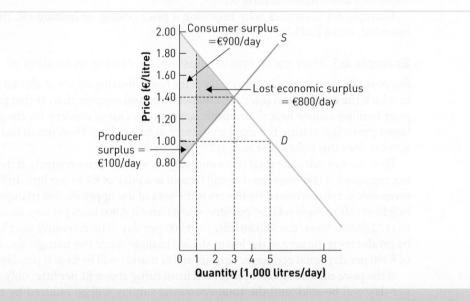

Figure 6.5 The Waste Caused by Price Controls. By limiting output in the home heating oil market to 1,000 litres per day, price controls cause a loss in economic surplus of €800 per day (area of the striped triangle).

€900 per day. (**Hint:** To compute this area in Fig. 6.5, first split it into a rectangle and a triangle.) By preventing the home heating oil market from reaching equilibrium, price controls waste €800 of producer surplus per day without creating any additional surplus for consumers!

Exercise 6.2   In Example 6.1, by how much would total economic surplus have been reduced if the price ceiling had been set not at €1 but at €1.20 per litre?

Efficiency

For several reasons, the reduction in total economic surplus shown in Fig. 6.5 is a conservative estimate of the waste caused by attempts to hold price below its equilibrium level. For one thing, the analysis assumes that each of the 1,000 litres per day that are sold in this market will end up in the hands of the consumers who value them most – in Fig. 6.5, those whose reservation prices are above €1.80 per litre. But since any buyer whose reservation price is above €1 per litre will want to buy at the ceiling price, much of the oil actually sold is likely to go to buyers whose reservation prices are below €1.80. Suppose, for example, that a buyer whose reservation price was €1.50 per litre made it into the queue outside a heating oil supplier just ahead of a buyer whose reservation price was €1.90 per litre. If each buyer had a 20-litre tank to fill, and if the first buyer got the last of the day's available oil, then total surplus would be smaller by €8 that day than if the oil had gone to the second buyer.

A second reason that the reduction in surplus shown in Fig. 6.5 is likely to be an underestimate is that shortages typically prompt buyers to take costly actions to enhance their chances of being served. For example, if the heating oil distributor begins selling its available supplies at 6.00 am, many buyers may arrive several hours early to ensure a place near the front of the queue.

Notwithstanding the fact that price ceilings reduce total economic surplus, their defenders might argue that controls are justified because they enable at least some low-income families to buy heating oil at affordable prices. Yes, but the same objective could have been accomplished in a much less costly way – namely, by giving the poor more income with which to buy heating oil.

It may seem natural to wonder whether the poor, who have limited political power, can really hope to receive income transfers that would enable them to heat their homes. On reflection, the answer to this question would seem to be yes, if *the alternative is to impose price controls that would be even more costly than the income transfers.* After all, the price ceiling as implemented ends up costing heating oil sellers €800 per day in lost economic surplus. So they ought to be willing to pay some amount less than €800 a day in additional taxes in order to escape the burden of controls. The additional tax revenue could finance income transfers that would be far more beneficial to the poor than price controls.

This point is so important, and so often misunderstood by voters and policy makers, that we will emphasise it by putting it another way. Think of the economic surplus from a market as a pie to be divided among the various market participants. Figure 6.6(a) represents the €1,000 per day of total economic surplus available to participants in the home heating oil market when the government limits the price of oil to €1 per litre. We have divided this 'pie' into two slices, labelled R and P, to denote the surpluses received by rich and poor participants. Figure 6.6(b) represents the €1,800 per day of total economic surplus available when the price of home heating oil is free to reach its equilibrium level. This 'pie' is divided among rich and poor participants in the same proportion as the 'pie' in the panel (a).

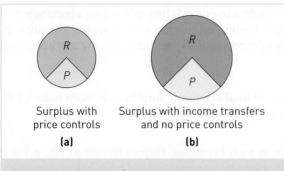

Surplus with price controls

(a)

Surplus with income transfers and no price controls

(b)

Figure 6.6 When the 'Pie' is Larger, Everyone Can Have a Bigger Slice. Any policy that reduces total economic surplus is a missed opportunity to make everyone better off.

The important point to notice is this: *because the pie in panel (b) is larger, both rich and poor participants in the home heating oil market can get a bigger slice of the 'pie' than they would have had under price controls.* Rather than tinker with the market price of oil, it is in everyone's interest to simply transfer additional income to the poor.

Supporters of price controls may object that income transfers to the poor might weaken people's incentive to work, and thus might prove extremely costly in the long run. Difficult issues do indeed arise in the design of programmes for transferring income to the poor. But, for now, suffice it to say that ways exist to transfer income without undermining work incentives significantly. Given such programmes, transferring income to the poor will always be more efficient than trying to boost their living standard through price controls.

Price subsidies

Sometimes governments try to assist low-income consumers by subsidising the prices of 'essential' goods and services. France and Russia, for example, have taken this approach at various times by subsidising the price of bread. But as Example 6.2 illustrates, such subsidies are like price ceilings in that they reduce total economic surplus.

Example 6.2 By how much do subsidies reduce total economic surplus in the market for bread?

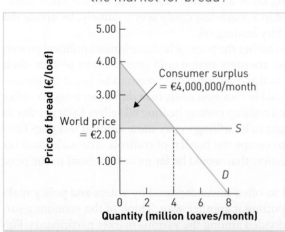

Figure 6.7 Economic Surplus in a Bread Market without Subsidy. For the demand curve shown, consumer surplus (area of the shaded triangle) is €4,000,000. This amount is equal to total economic surplus in the domestic bread market, since no bread is produced domestically.

A small island nation imports bread for its population at the world price of €2 per loaf. If the domestic demand curve for bread is as shown in Fig. 6.7, by how much will total economic surplus decline in this market if the government provides a €1 per loaf subsidy?

With no subsidy, the equilibrium price of bread in this market would be the world price of €2 per loaf, and the equilibrium quantity would be 4,000,000 loaves per month. The shaded triangle in Fig. 6.7 represents consumer economic surplus for buyers in the domestic bread market. The height of this triangle is €2 per loaf, and its base is 4,000,000 loaves per month, so its area is equal to (1/2)(4,000,000 loaves/month) (€2/loaf) = €4,000,000 per month. Because the country can import as much bread as it wishes at the world price of €2 per loaf, supply is *perfectly elastic* in this market. Because the marginal cost of each loaf of bread to

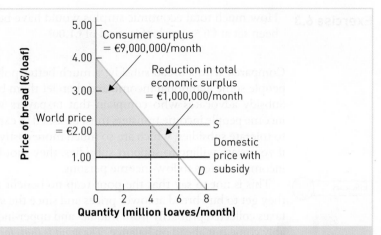

Figure 6.8 The Reduction in Economic Surplus from a Subsidy. Since the marginal cost of bread is €2 per loaf, total economic surplus is maximised at 4,000,000 loaves per month, the quantity for which the marginal buyer's reservation price is equal to marginal cost. The reduction in economic surplus from consuming an additional 2,000,000 loaves per month is €1,000,000 per month, the area of the smaller shaded triangle.

sellers is exactly the same as the price buyers pay, producer surplus in this market is zero. So total economic surplus is exactly equal to consumer surplus, which, again, is €4,000,000 per month.

Now suppose that the government administers its €1 per loaf subsidy programme by purchasing bread in the world market at €2 per loaf and reselling it in the domestic market for only €1 per loaf. At the new lower price, buyers will now consume not 4,000,000 loaves per month but 6,000,000. Consumer surplus for buyers in the bread market is now the area of the larger shaded triangle in Fig. 6.8: $(1/2)(€3/loaf)$ $(6,000,000 \text{ loaves}/\text{month}) = €9,000,000$ per month, or €5,000,000 per month more than before. The catch is that the subsidy was not free. Its cost, which must be borne by taxpayers, is $(€1/loaf)(6,000,000 \text{ loaves}/\text{month}) = €6,000,000$ per month. So even though consumer surplus in the bread market is larger than before, the net effect of the subsidy programme is actually to reduce total economic surplus by €1,000,000 per month.

Another way to see why the subsidy reduces total economic surplus by this amount is to note that total economic surplus is maximised at 4,000,000 loaves per month, the quantity for which the marginal buyer's reservation price is equal to marginal cost, and that the subsidy induces additional consumption of 2,000,000 loaves per month. Each additional loaf has a marginal cost of €2 but is worth less than that to the buyer (as indicated by the fact that the vertical coordinate of the demand curve lies below €2 for consumption beyond 4,000,000). As monthly consumption expands from 4,000,000 to 6,000,000 loaves per month, the cumulative difference between the marginal cost of bread and its value to buyers is the area of the smaller shaded triangle in Fig. 6.8, which is €1,000,000 per month.

This reduction in economic surplus constitutes pure waste – no different, from the perspective of participants in this market, from someone siphoning that much cash out of their bank account each month and throwing it into a bonfire.

Exercise 6.3   How much total economic surplus would have been lost if the bread subsidy had been set at €0.50 per loaf instead of €1.00?

Compared with a bread subsidy, a much better policy would be to give low-income people some additional income and then let them bid for bread on the open market. Subsidy advocates who complain that taxpayers would be unwilling to give low-income people income transfers must be asked to explain why people would be willing to tolerate subsidies, which are so much more costly than income transfers. Logically, if voters are willing to support subsidies, they should be even more eager to support income transfers to low-income persons.

Efficiency

This is not to say that the poor reap no benefit at all from bread subsidies. Since they get to buy bread at lower prices and since the subsidy programme is financed by taxes collected primarily from middle- and upper-income families, poor families probably come out ahead on balance. *The point is that, for the same expense, we could do much more to help the poor.* Their problem is that they have too little income. The simplest and best solution is not to try to peg the prices of the goods they and others buy below equilibrium levels, but rather to give them some additional money.

Economic naturalist 6.1 How governments impoverish their citizens by subsidising oil prices

Between 2005 and early 2008 the price of a barrel of oil (in dollar terms) increased by a factor of 6. Even allowing for the fall in the value of the US dollar this implied an increase in real terms of 400% on the 2005 price. What is interesting, however, is what happened to prices facing consumers. With excise taxes as part of the tax structure there is a tendency for the percentage increase in consumer prices to be lower the higher the excise tax element in the retail price. And excises are not the same across countries. So what happened? The following are dollar prices per US gallon of petrol. Given low gasoline taxes in the USA, the amount by which prices there rose can be treated as the amount caused by the rise in the per barrel price of oil.

	2005	2008	% increase
USA	2.58	4.28	66
United Arab Emirates	1.29	1.70	32
Australia	4.36	6.64	75
South Africa	3.64	5.64	55
India	4.63	5.77	25
United Kingdom	2.27	10.41	359
Singapore	3.23	8.23	155

Source: Global Petrol Prices, www.kshitij.com/research/petrol.shtml

Britain has a policy of increasing the real price of petrol through higher taxes, which makes it an outlier. Look, however, at the figures for the UAE and India. Given what happened to the value of the dollar, plus domestic inflation, consumer prices in real terms actually fell while the real cost of oil quadrupled. This helps explain the surge in demand in India. In the UAE, for an oil exporter, the matter might be less serious. But in both cases the policy of effective subsidy is lowering GNP per head. The cost to the UAE is the money lost by not selling oil consumed at home at world prices minus the consumer surplus on that consumption as in Fig. 6.8. This may be of little importance in a rich country like the UAE ... but in India's case it is a significant cost in terms of income per head. India is paying more for much of its imported oil than the value to Indians of the oil being consumed. The lower price encourages oil consumption, which increases the cost to India of its oil imports as more is imported at higher prices, these being driven in part by subsidised consumption in India. India is not alone. China also subsidises oil consumption. When importing countries subsidise oil consumption they use oil up to a point where the value to users of oil for domestic or commercial use is less than the cost of acquiring the oil abroad. Using less oil would make the country better off, and raise GNP per head.

First-come, first-served policies

Governments are not the only institutions that attempt to promote social goals by preventing markets from reaching equilibrium. Some event promoters, for example, attempt to protect access by low-income purchasers to concerts and sporting events by selling a limited number of tickets below the market-clearing price on a first-come, first-served basis.[1]

The commercial airline industry was an early proponent of the use of the first-come, first-served allocation method, which it employed to ration seats on over-booked flights. Throughout the industry's history, most airlines have routinely accepted more reservations for their flights than there are seats on those flights. Most of the time, this practice causes no difficulty, because many reservation holders don't show up to claim their seats. Indeed, if airlines did not overbook their flights, most flights would take off with many more empty seats, forcing airlines to charge higher ticket prices to cover their costs.

The only real difficulty is that, every so often, more people actually do show up for a flight than there are seats on the plane. Until the late 1970s (i.e. before deregulation increased competition), US airlines dealt with this problem by boarding passengers on a first-come, first-served basis. For example, if 120 people showed up for a flight with 110 seats, the last 10 to arrive were 'bumped', or forced to wait for the next available flight.

The 'bumped' passengers often complained bitterly, and no wonder, since many of them ended up missing important business meetings or family events. As Economic naturalist 6.2 illustrates, there was, fortunately, a simple solution to this problem.

Economic naturalist 6.2 Why does no one complain any longer about being 'bumped' from an overbooked flight?

In 1978, as regulation of the business ended, airlines in the US abandoned their first-come, first-served policy in favour of a new procedure. Since then, their practice has been to solicit volunteers to give up their seats on oversold flights in return for a cash payment or free ticket. Now, the only people who give up their seats are those who volunteer to do so in return for compensation, hence the complete disappearance of complaints about being 'bumped' from overbooked flights. As the airline business has been moving towards deregulation in Europe, the same phenomenon has been observed. Airlines may routinely overbook flights, relying on 'no shows' to balance capacity with demand. When this didn't happen, they in effect 'bought back' seats by offering cash or other compensation. For reasons that are far from clear, the EU Commission has now moved to imposing fixed compensation amounts. This is clearly inefficient. Can you explain why? (See Exercise 6.4 below.)

---

1 That is certainly the stated reason. We shall see in Chapter 8, however, when dealing with pricing strategies of firms with market power, that this form of discounting may also be a discriminatory mechanism that may be expected to increase the sellers' revenues.

Which of the two policies – first-come, first-served or compensation for volunteers – is more efficient? The difficulty with the first-come, first-served policy is that it gives little weight to the interests of passengers with pressing reasons for arriving at their destination on time. Such passengers can sometimes avoid losing their seats by showing up early, but passengers coming in on connecting flights often cannot control when they arrive. And the cost of showing up early is likely to be highest for precisely those people who place the highest value on not missing a flight (such as business executives, whose opportunity cost of waiting in airports is high).

For the sake of illustration, suppose that 37 people show up for a flight with only 33 seats. One way or another, four people will have to wait for another flight. Suppose we ask each of them, 'What is the most you would be willing to pay to fly now rather than wait?' Typically, different passengers will have different reservation prices for avoiding the wait. Suppose that the person who is most willing to pay would pay up to €60 rather than miss the flight; that the person second-most willing to pay would pay up to €59; that the person third-most willing to pay would pay up to €58; and so on. In that case, the person with the smallest reservation price for avoiding the wait would have a reservation price of €24. For the entire group of 37 passengers, the average reservation price for avoiding the wait would be (€60 + €59 + €58 + ... + €24)/37 = €42.

Given the difficulty of controlling airport arrival times, the passengers who get 'bumped' under the first-come, first-served policy are not likely to differ systematically from others with respect to their reservation price for not missing the flight. On average, then, the total cost imposed on the four 'bumped' passengers would be four times the average reservation price of €42, or €168. As far as those four passengers are concerned, that total is a pure loss of consumer surplus.

How does this cost compare with the cost imposed on 'bumped' passengers when the airline compensates volunteers? Suppose that the airline solicits volunteers by conducting an informal auction, increasing its cash compensation offer by €1 increments until it has the desired number of volunteers. As the incentive to stay behind rises, more people will volunteer; those whose reservation prices are the lowest will volunteer first. In this example, offers below €24 would generate no volunteers. An offer of €24 would generate one volunteer; an offer of €25 would generate two volunteers; and so on. A compensation payment of €27 would generate the necessary four volunteers.

What is the net cost of the compensation policy? While the airline pays out (4) (€27) = €108 in compensation payments, not all that amount represents lost economic surplus. Thus the passenger whose reservation price for missing the flight is €24 receives a net gain in economic surplus of €3 – the difference between the €27 compensation payment and her €24 reservation price. Similarly, those whose reservation prices were €25 and €26 receive a net gain of €2 and €1, respectively. The cost of the cash compensation policy net of these gains is thus €108 − €6 = €102, or €66 less than under the first-come, first-served policy.

The compensation policy is more efficient than the first-come, first-served policy because it establishes a market for a scarce resource that would otherwise be allocated by non-market means. Figure 6.9 shows the supply and demand curves for seats under the compensation policy. In this market, the equilibrium price of not having to wait is €26. People who choose not to volunteer at that price incur an opportunity cost of €27 in order not to miss the flight. The four people who do volunteer accept €27 as ample compensation – indeed, more than ample for three of them.

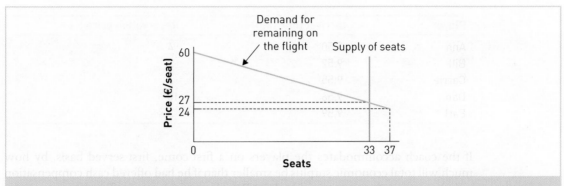

Figure 6.9 Equilibrium in the Market for Seats on Oversold Flights. The demand curve for remaining on the flight is generated by plotting the reservation prices in descending order. The equilibrium compensation payment for volunteers who give up their seats is €27 – the price at which four passengers volunteer to wait and the remaining 33 choose not to wait.

Given all this, it is hard to understand US consumer reaction when the compensation mechanism was introduced. There were strong protests from the Aviation Consumer Action Project (ACAP), a group that portrayed itself as a watchdog for the interests of airline passengers. ACAP's concern was that the shift to a system of compensation payments would mean that poor people would most often end up waiting for the next flight. The new policy, therefore, as far as ACAP was concerned, damaged poor people more than better-off people.

Exercise 6.4   The ACAP objections to the change were inconsistent with what we know about markets. Can you indicate some reasons why ACAP was wrong?

Exercise 6.5   In the light of this, what conclusion should we draw regarding the decision by the EU Commission to intervene in the airline passenger ticket market in Europe, announced in 2004? The Commission proposed that airlines should be obliged to pay any passenger who was 'bumped' a fixed amount, initially set at €250, plus meeting certain costs. This is to replace any 'buy-back' of seats (implicit in what happens in the United States).

Example 6.3 How should a professional tennis coach handle the overbooking problem?

Anticipating a high proportion of 'no shows', a tennis coach routinely books five people for each of his group lesson slots, even though he is able to teach only three people at a time. One day, all five people show up for their lessons at 10 am, the first lesson slot of the morning. Their respective arrival times and the maximum amounts each would be willing to pay to avoid postponing his or her lesson are as given in the table below.

Player	Arrival time (am)	Reservation price (€)
Ann	9.50	4
Bill	9.52	3
Carrie	9.55	6
Dan	9.56	10
Earl	9.59	3

If the coach accommodates the players on a first-come, first-served basis, by how much will total economic surplus be smaller than if he had offered cash compensation to induce two volunteers to reschedule? Which system is more efficient?

The result of using a first-come, first-served policy will be that Dan and Earl, the last two to arrive, will have to postpone their lessons. Since the cost of waiting is €10 for Dan and €3 for Earl, the total cost of the first-come, first-served policy is €13.

Suppose that the coach had instead offered cash compensation payments to elicit volunteers. If he offered a payment of €3, both Bill and Earl would be willing to wait. The total cost of the cash compensation policy would therefore be only €6, or €7 less than under the first-come, first-served policy. So the cash compensation policy is more efficient.

You might feel tempted to ask why the coach would bother to offer cash compensation when he has the option of saving the €6 by continuing with his current policy of first-come, first-served. Or you might wonder why an airline would bother to offer cash compensation to elicit volunteers to wait for the next flight. But we know that it is possible for *everyone* to do better under an efficient policy than under an inefficient one. (When the pie is bigger, everyone can have a larger slice.) Exercise 6.6 asks you to design such a transaction for the tennis lesson example.

Exercise 6.6   Describe a set of cash transfers in Example 6.3 that would make each of the five students and the coach better off than under the first-come, first-served policy. (**Hint:** Imagine that the coach tells his clients that he will stick with first-come, first-served unless they agree to contribute to the compensation pool as he requests.)

In practice, transactions like that called for in Exercise 6.6 would be cumbersome to administer. Typically, the seller is in a position to solve such problems more easily by offering cash payments to elicit volunteers, and then financing those cash payments by charging slightly higher prices. Buyers, for their part, are willing to pay the higher prices because they value the seller's promise not to cancel their reservations without compensation.

 Equilibrium

RECAP   The cost of blocking price adjustments

In an effort to increase the economic welfare of disadvantaged consumers, governments often implement policies that attempt to prevent markets from reaching equilibrium. Price ceilings and subsidies attempt to make housing and other basic goods more affordable for poor families. Private organisations also implement policies that prevent markets from reaching equilibrium, such as allocation on a first-come, first-served basis. Such policies always *reduce total economic surplus* relative to the alternative of letting prices seek their equilibrium levels. It is always possible to design alternative policies under which rich and poor alike fare better.

Marginal cost pricing of public services

The largest possible total economic surplus is achieved in private markets when goods are exchanged at equilibrium prices, where the value of the last unit to the buyer is exactly equal to the seller's marginal cost of producing it. Suppose that the government has decided to become the provider of a good or service, such as water or electricity. If the government's goal is to maximise the resulting total economic surplus, how much should it charge its customers? The theory of *market exchange*, normally applied to perfectly competitive firms that can sell any quantity they choose at a constant market price, helps to answer this question. Consider Example 6.4, in which a local government supplies water to its residents.

Example 6.4 What is the marginal cost of water in Sharm el Sheikh?

Sharm el Sheikh, at the head of the Gulf of Aqaba on the Red Sea, is a thriving tourist resort. Locals and tourists use a great deal of water, which is supplied by the municipal

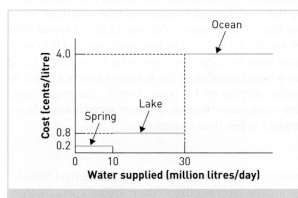

authorities. Suppose the municipal supply company has three potential sources of water: an underground aquifer, a nearby lake and the Red Sea. The aquifer can supply up to 10 million litres per day at a cost of 0.2 cents per litre. The lake can supply an additional 20 million litres per day at a cost of 0.8 cents per litre. Additional water must be distilled using a desalination plant from the sea at a cost of 4.0 cents per litre. Draw the marginal cost curve for water in Sharm el Sheikh.

The *Low-Hanging-Fruit Principle* tells us that the city will use the cheapest source of water first (the spring). Only when the quantity demanded exceeds the spring's capacity will the city turn to the next least expensive source, the lake; and only when the lake's capacity is exhausted will the city supply water from the ocean. The marginal cost curve will thus be as shown in Fig. 6.10.

Figure 6.10 The Marginal Cost Curve for Water.
The current marginal cost of water is the cost of producing an extra litre by means of the most expensive production source currently in use.

Increasing Opportunity Cost

As Example 6.5 illustrates, total economic surplus is maximised when the government charges each customer *exactly the marginal cost* of the water he or she consumes.

Example 6.5 How much should the municipal authority charge for water?

In Example 6.4, suppose that if the price of water were 4.0 cents per litre, citizens of and visitors to Sharm el Sheikh would consume 40 million litres per day. Given the marginal cost curve shown in Fig. 6.10, how much should the city charge a citizen whose water comes from the underground spring? How much should it charge someone whose water comes from the lake?

The citizens of Sharm el Sheikh will enjoy the largest possible economic surplus if the price they pay for water exactly equals the marginal cost of providing it. Since the total amount of water demanded at 4.0 cents per litre exceeds 30 million litres per day, the city will have to supply at least some households with water distilled from the Red Sea, at a cost of 4.0 cents per litre. At 40 million litres per day, the marginal cost of water is thus 4.0 cents per litre, and *this is true no matter where the water comes from*. As long as the city must get *some* of its water from the ocean, the marginal cost of water taken from the underground spring is also 4.0 cents per litre. Water taken from the lake has a marginal cost of 4.0 cents per litre as well.

This statement might seem to contradict the claim that water drawn from the spring costs only 0.2 cents per litre, water drawn from the lake only 0.8 cents per litre. But there is no contradiction. To see why, ask yourself how much the city would save if a family that currently gets its water from the spring were to reduce its consumption by 1 litre per day. The cutback would enable the city to divert that litre of spring water to some other household that currently gets its water from the ocean, which in turn would reduce consumption of ocean water by 1 litre. So if a family currently served by the spring were to reduce its daily consumption by 1 litre, the cost savings would be exactly 4.0 cents. And that, by definition, is the marginal cost of water.

To encourage the efficient use of water, the city should charge every household 4.0 cents per litre for all the water it consumes. Charging any household less than that would encourage households to use water whose marginal benefit is less than its marginal cost. For example, suppose the city charged households who get their water from the spring only 0.2 cents per litre. Those households would then expand their use of water until the benefit they received from the last litre used equalled 0.2 cents. Because that litre could have been used to serve someone who is currently using water distilled from the ocean, for whom the value of the marginal litre is 4 cents, its use would entail a loss in economic surplus of 3.8 cents. Hence charging 4 cents increases surplus (but does involve some redistribution between households relative to when some households are supplied at less than 4 cents).

Exercise 6.7   Suppose that at a price of 0.8 cents per litre of water, the citizens of Sharm el Sheikh would consume a total of only 20 million litres per day. If the marginal cost of water is as shown in Fig. 6.10, how much should the city charge for water? Should that same charge apply to people who get their water from the spring?

RECAP Marginal cost pricing of public services

When a good is provided by a public utility from several sources, the marginal cost of serving a customer is the cost associated with the *least efficient source in use*. A public utility should set price equal to marginal cost if its goal is to maximise economic surplus.

Taxes and efficiency

Who pays a tax imposed on sellers of a good?

Politicians of all stripes seem loath to propose new taxes. But when additional public revenue must be raised, most seem to feel more comfortable proposing taxes paid by sellers than taxes paid by consumers. When pressed to explain why, many respond that businesses can more easily afford to pay extra taxes. Yet the burden of a tax collected from the sellers of a good need not fall exclusively on sellers. Suppose, for example, that a tax of €1 per kg is collected from potato farmers in the market whose demand and supply curves are shown as *D* and *S* in Fig. 6.11.

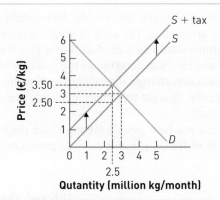

Figure 6.11 The Effect of a Tax on the Equilibrium Quantity and Price of Potatoes. With no tax, 3 million kg of potatoes are sold each month at a price of €3 per kg. With a tax of €1 per kg collected from sellers, consumers end up paying €3.50 per kg (including tax), while sellers receive only €2.50 per kg (net of tax). Equilibrium quantity falls from 3 million kg per month to 2.5 million.

In this market the initial equilibrium price and quantity are €3 per kg and 3 million kg per month, respectively. From the farmers' perspective, the imposition of a tax of €1 per kg is essentially the same as a €1 increase in the marginal cost of producing each kg of potatoes, and hence the tax results in an upward shift in the supply curve by €1 per kg.

As shown in Fig. 6.11, the new equilibrium price (including the tax) will be €3.50, and the new equilibrium quantity will be 2.5 million kg per month. The net price per kg received by producers is one euro less than the price paid by the consumer, or €2.50. Even though the tax was collected entirely from potato sellers, the burden of the tax fell on both buyers and sellers – on buyers, because they pay €0.50 per kg more than before the tax, and on sellers because they receive €0.50 per kg less than before the tax.

The burden of the tax need not fall equally on buyers and sellers, as in the illustration just discussed. Indeed, as Economic naturalist 6.3 illustrates, a tax levied on sellers may end up being paid entirely by buyers.

Economic naturalist 6.3 Does the 'polluter pays' principle make polluters pay?

That the polluter should pay is a widely accepted principle of environmental policy. It informs decisions to charge firms that pollute in proportion to their polluting activities. The producer has to pay the charge, and this is regarded as equitable. Unfortunately it is usually based on a confusion between the *impact* and the *incidence* of a tax. The impact refers to who pays initially; the incidence means who pays in the end. If, for example, an environmental charge is fully passed on to end users of the good, the producer may send a cheque to the government, but the cost of this ends up as higher prices to consumers.

If marginal costs are as in Fig. 6.11 and if we regard environmental charges as a tax, it is obvious that both producers and consumers pay, since producer and consumer surplus are reduced (see Figs 6.13–6.15). There are two sets of circumstances in which the polluting producer pays the charge in its entirety. The first is where a non-polluting good substitute is available, so that the polluter cannot raise his price without experiencing a drastic fall in sales. An example would be imports of the product as a substitute for domestic production. The second is where supply is fixed (the supply curve is a vertical straight line). An example would be a product that is jointly supplied with another product (e.g. hides and meat). The demand for meat determines the quantity of hides. If these are processed and the processing attracts a pollution charge, the tanners and/or the farmers will pay the charge.

If the supply curve is a horizontal straight line (marginal costs are constant), as in Fig. 6.12, consumers end up paying the full cost.

Bear this in mind the next time you hear people talking about the need to make the polluter pay. The real reason is nothing to do with equity, but to provide producers with an incentive to use less polluting processes!

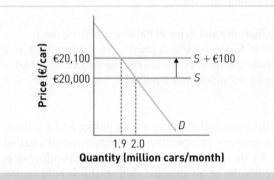

Figure 6.12 The Effect of a Tax on Sellers of a Good with Infinite Price Elasticity of Supply. When the supply curve for a good is perfectly elastic, the burden of a tax collected from sellers falls entirely on buyers.

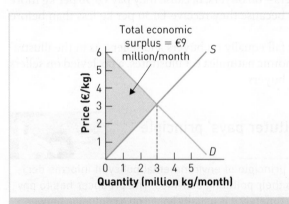

Figure 6.13 The Market for Potatoes without Taxes. Without taxes, total surplus in the potato market equals the area of the shaded triangle, €9 million per month.

Although the long-run supply curve shown in Fig. 6.12 is in one sense an extreme case (since its price elasticity is infinite), it is by no means an unrepresentative one. For, as we discussed in Chapter 3, the long-run supply curve will tend to be horizontal when it is possible to acquire more of all the necessary inputs at constant prices. As a first approximation, this can be accomplished for many – perhaps even most – goods and services in a typical economy.

For goods with perfectly elastic supply curves, the entire burden of any tax is borne by the buyer.[2] That is, the increase in the equilibrium price is exactly equal to the tax. For this empirically relevant case, then, there is a special irony in the common political practice of justifying taxes on business by saying that businesses have greater ability to pay than consumers. To the extent that supply curves are elastic, these taxes end up as higher prices to consumers.

How a tax collected from a seller affects economic surplus

We saw earlier that perfectly competitive markets distribute goods and services efficiently if demand curves reflect all relevant benefits and supply curves reflect all relevant costs. If a tax is imposed on sellers in such a market, will the new market equilibrium still be efficient? Consider again the potato market discussed in Fig. 6.11, whose supply and demand curves are reproduced in Fig. 6.13. In the absence of a tax, 3 million kg of potatoes a month would be sold in this market at a price of €3 per kg, and

---

2 In the example given, the tax was collected from sellers. The same conclusions will apply when a tax is collected from buyers. It raises the supply price by the same amount.

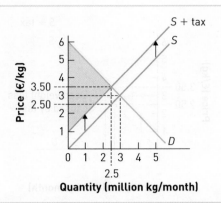

Figure 6.14 The Effect of a €1 per kg Tax on Potatoes. A €1 per kg tax on potatoes would cause an upward shift in the supply curve by €1. The sum of producer and consumer surplus would shrink to the area of the shaded triangle, €6.25 million per month.

the resulting total economic surplus would be €9 million per month (the area of the shaded triangle).

With a tax of €1 per kg collected from potato sellers, the new equilibrium price of potatoes would be €3.50 per kg (of which sellers receive €2.50, net of tax), and only 2.5 million kg of potatoes would be sold each month (see Fig. 6.14). The total economic surplus reaped by buyers and sellers in the potato market would be the area of the shaded triangle shown in Fig. 6.14, which is €6.25 million per month – or €2.75 million less than before.

This drop in surplus may sound like an enormous loss, but it is a misleading figure because it fails to take account of the value of the *additional tax revenue collected*, which is equal to €2.5 million per month (€1 per kg on 2.5 million kg of potatoes). If the government needs to collect no more than a given total amount of tax revenue in order to pay for the services it provides, then the potato tax revenue should enable it to reduce other taxes by €2.5 million per month. So although buyers and sellers lose €2.75 million per month in economic surplus from their participation in the potato market, they also enjoy a €2.5 million reduction in the other taxes they pay. On balance, then, the net reduction in total economic surplus is only €0.25 million.

deadweight loss the reduction in total economic surplus that results from the adoption of a policy

Graphically, the loss in total economic surplus caused by the imposition of the tax can be shown as the small shaded triangle in Fig. 6.15. This loss in surplus is often described as the **deadweight loss** from the tax.

Still, a loss in economic surplus, however small, is something that people would prefer to avoid, and taxes like that just described undoubtedly reduce economic surplus in the markets on which they are imposed. As the long-time US Federal Reserve Board (FRB, the equivalent in the United States of the European Central Bank, or ECB, in the European Union) chairman Alan Greenspan, who retired in 2006, once remarked: 'All taxes are a drag on economic growth. It's only a question of degree.'[3]

A tax reduces economic surplus because it distorts the basic cost–benefit calculation that would ordinarily guide efficient decisions about production and consumption. In the example just considered, the Cost–Benefit Principle tells us that we should

---

3 *Wall Street Journal*, 26 March 1997, p. A1.

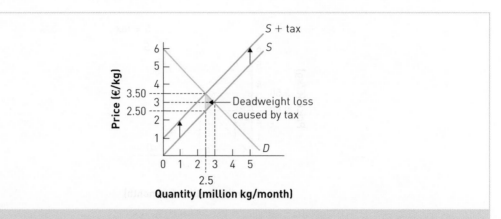

Figure 6.15 The Deadweight Loss Caused by a Tax. For the market shown, the loss in economic surplus caused by a tax of €1 per kg of potatoes equals the area of the small shaded triangle, or €250,000 per month.

expand potato production up to the point at which the benefit of the last kilogram of potatoes consumed (as measured by what buyers are willing to pay for it) equals the cost of producing it (as measured by the producers' marginal cost). That condition was satisfied in the potato market before the tax, but it is not satisfied once the tax is imposed. In Fig. 6.15, for example, note that when potato consumption is 2.5 million kg per month, the value of an additional kilogram of potatoes to consumers is €3.50, whereas the cost to producers is only €2.50, not including the tax. (The cost to producers, including the tax, is €3.50 per kg, but again we note that this tax is not a cost to society as a whole because it offsets other taxes that would otherwise have to be collected.)

Is a tax on potatoes necessarily 'bad'? (When economists say that a policy, such as a tax, is 'bad', they mean – or ought to mean – that it lowers total economic surplus.) To answer this question, we must first identify the *best alternative to taxing potatoes*. You may be tempted to say: 'Don't tax anything at all!' On a moment's reflection, however, you will realise that this is surely not the best option. After all, a country that taxed nothing could not pay for even minimal public services, such as road maintenance, fire protection and national defence. On balance, if taxing potatoes were the best way to avoid doing without highly valued public services, then a small deadweight loss in the potato market would be a small price indeed.

So the real question is whether there are other things we could tax that would be better than taxing potatoes. The problem with a tax on any activity is that if market incentives encourage people to pursue the 'right' amount of the activity (that is, the surplus-maximising amount), then a tax will encourage them to pursue too little of it. As economists have long recognised, this observation suggests that taxes will cause smaller deadweight losses if they are imposed on goods for which the equilibrium quantity is not highly sensitive to changes in production costs.

Taxes, elasticity and efficiency

Suppose that the government put a tax of 50 cents per kg on table salt. How would this affect the amount of salt you and others use? In Chapter 4 we saw that the demand for salt is highly inelastic with respect to price, because salt has few substitutes and occupies only a minuscule share in most family budgets. Because the imposition of a tax on table salt would not result in a significant reduction in the amount of it consumed, the deadweight loss from this tax would be relatively small. More generally, the deadweight loss from a per-unit tax imposed on the seller of a good will be smaller the smaller is the price elasticity of demand for the good.

Figure 6.16 illustrates how the deadweight loss from a tax declines as the demand for a good becomes less elastic with respect to price. In both Figs 6.16(a) and (b), the original supply and demand curves yield an equilibrium price of €2 per unit and an equilibrium quantity of 24 units per day. The deadweight loss from a tax of €1 per unit imposed on the good shown in Fig. 6.16(a) is the area of the shaded triangle in (a), which is €2.50 per day. The demand curve in Fig. 6.16(b), D_2, is less elastic at the equilibrium price of €2 than the demand curve in (a), D_1 (this follows from the fact that P/Q is the same in both cases, whereas $1/\text{slope}$ is smaller in (b)). The deadweight loss from the same €1 per unit tax imposed on the good in Fig. 6.16(b) is the area of the shaded triangle in (b), which is only €1.50 per day.

The reduction in equilibrium quantity that results from a tax on a good will also be smaller the smaller is the elasticity of supply of the good. In Fig. 6.17, for example, the original supply and demand curves for the markets portrayed in (a) and (b) yield an equilibrium price of €2 per unit and an equilibrium quantity of 72 units per day. The deadweight loss from a tax of €1 per unit imposed on the good shown in Fig. 6.17(a) is the area of the shaded triangle in (a), which is €6.50 per day. The supply curve in Fig. 6.17(b), S_2, is less elastic at the equilibrium price than the supply curve in (a), S_1 (again because P/Q is the same in both cases, whereas $1/\text{slope}$ is smaller in (b)). The deadweight loss from the same €1 per unit tax imposed on the good in Fig. 6.17(b) is the area of the shaded triangle in (b), which is only €4.50 per day.

The deadweight loss from a tax imposed on a good whose supply curve is perfectly inelastic will be zero. This explains why many economists continue to favour the tax advocated by Henry George in the nineteenth century. George proposed that all taxes on labour and goods be abolished and replaced by a *single tax on land*. Such a tax, he argued, would cause no significant loss in economic surplus because the supply of land is almost perfectly inelastic.

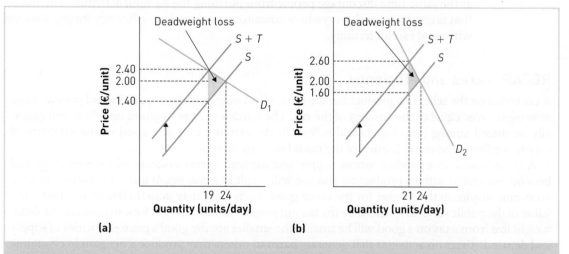

Figure 6.16 Elasticity of Demand and the Deadweight Loss from a Tax. At the equilibrium price and quantity, price elasticity of demand is smaller for the good shown in (b) than for the good shown in (a). The area of the deadweight loss triangle in (b), €1.50 per day, is smaller than the area of the deadweight loss triangle in (a), €2.50 per day.

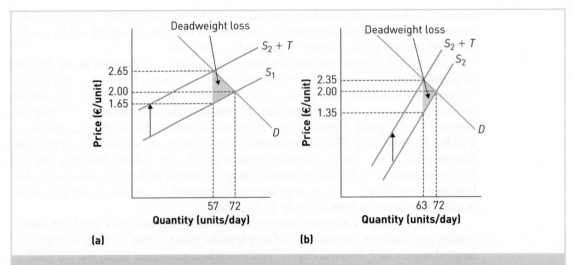

Figure 6.17 Elasticity of Supply and the Deadweight Loss from a Tax. At the equilibrium price and quantity, price elasticity of supply is smaller for the good shown in (b) than for the good shown in (a). The area of the deadweight loss triangle in (b), €4.50 per day, is smaller than the area of the deadweight loss triangle in (a), €6.50 per day.

Taxes, external costs and efficiency

Efficiency

Even more attractive than taxing land, from an efficiency standpoint, is taxing activities that people tend to *pursue to excess*. We have mentioned activities that generate environmental pollution as one example; in Chapter 11 we shall discuss others. Whereas a tax on land does not reduce economic surplus, a tax on pollution can actually increase total economic surplus. Taxes on activities that cause harm to others kill two birds with one stone: they generate revenue to pay for useful public services and at the same time discourage people from pursuing the harmful activities. The notion that taxes always and everywhere constitute an obstacle to efficiency simply does not withstand careful scrutiny.

RECAP Taxes and efficiency

A tax levied on the seller of a product has the same effect on equilibrium quantity and price as a rise in marginal cost equal to the amount of the tax. The burden of a tax imposed on sellers will generally be shared among both buyers and sellers. In the extreme case of a good whose elasticity of supply is infinite, the entire burden of the tax is borne by buyers.

A tax imposed on a product whose supply and demand curves embody all relevant costs and benefits associated with its production and use will result in a *deadweight loss* – a reduction in total economic surplus in the market for the taxed good. Such taxes may nonetheless be justified if the value of the public services financed by the tax outweighs this deadweight loss. In general, the deadweight loss from a tax on a good will be smaller the smaller are the good's price elasticities of supply and demand. Taxes on activities that generate harm to others may produce a net gain in economic surplus, even apart from the value of public services they finance.

Summary

- When the supply and demand curves for a product capture all the relevant costs and benefits of producing that product, then market equilibrium for that product will be *efficient*. In such a market, if price and quantity do not equal their equilibrium values, a transaction can be found that will make at least some people better off without harming others.

- *Total economic surplus* is a measure of the amount by which participants in a market benefit by participating in it. It is the sum of total consumer surplus and total producer surplus in the market. One of the attractive properties of market equilibrium is that it maximises the value of total economic surplus.

- Efficiency should not be equated with *social justice*. If we believe that the distribution of income among people is unjust, we shall not like the results produced by the intersection of the supply and demand curves based on that income distribution, even though those results are efficient.

- Even so, we should always strive for efficiency because it enables us to achieve all our other goals to the fullest possible extent. Whenever a market is out of equilibrium, the economic 'pie' can be made larger. And with a larger pie, everyone can have a larger slice.

- Regulations or policies that *prevent markets from reaching equilibrium* – such as price ceilings, price subsidies and first-come, first-served allocation schemes – are often defended on the grounds that they help the poor. But such schemes reduce economic surplus, meaning that we can find alternatives under which both rich and poor would be better off. The main difficulty of the poor is that they have too little income. Rather than trying to control the prices of the goods they buy, we could do better by enacting policies that raise the incomes of the poor and then letting prices seek their equilibrium levels. Those who complain that the poor lack the political power to obtain such income transfers must explain why the poor have the power to impose regulations that are far more costly than income transfers.

- Even when a good is provided by a *public utility* rather than a private firm, the theory of competitive supply has important implications for how to provide the good most efficiently. The general rule is that a public utility maximises economic surplus by charging its customers the marginal cost of the goods it provides.

- Critics often complain that taxes make the economy less efficient. A tax will indeed reduce economic surplus if the supply and demand curves in the market for the taxed good reflect all the relevant costs and benefits of its production and consumption. But this decline in surplus may be more than offset by the increase in economic surplus made possible by public goods financed with the *proceeds of the tax*. The best taxes are imposed on activities that would otherwise be pursued to excess, such as activities that generate environmental pollution. Such taxes not only do not reduce economic surplus; they actually increase it.

Review questions

1. Why do economists emphasise efficiency as an important goal of public policy?

2. You are a politician considering how to vote on a policy that would increase the economic surplus of workers by €100 million per year but reduce the economic surplus of retirees by €1 million per year. What additional measure might you combine with the policy to ensure that the overall result is a better outcome for everyone?

3. Why does the loss in total economic surplus directly experienced by participants in the market for a good that is taxed overstate the overall loss in economic surplus that results from the tax?

4. Why is compensating volunteers to relinquish their seats on overbooked flights more efficient than a policy of first-come, first-served?

5. Why do price ceilings reduce economic surplus?

connect· Problems

Problems marked with an asterisk (*) are more difficult.

1. Suppose the weekly demand and supply curves for used DVDs in Brussels are as shown in the graph below. Calculate:

   a. the weekly consumer surplus

   b. the weekly producer surplus

   c. the maximum weekly amount that producers and consumers in Brussels would be willing to pay to be able to buy and sell used DVDs in any given week.

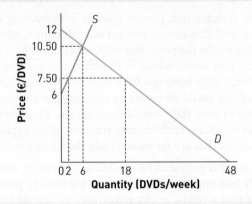

2. Refer to Problem 1. Suppose a coalition of students from a Brussels secondary school succeeds in persuading the local government to impose a price ceiling of €6.50 on used DVDs, on the grounds that local suppliers are taking advantage of teenagers by charging exorbitant prices.

   a. Calculate the weekly shortage of used DVDs that will result from this policy.

   b. Calculate the total economic surplus lost every week as a result of the price ceiling.

3. The Kubak crystal caves are renowned for their stalactites and stalagmites. The warden of the caves offers a tour each afternoon at 2 pm sharp. The caves can be shown to only four people per day without disturbing their fragile ecology. Occasionally, however, more than four people want to see the caves on the same day. The table below lists those who wanted to see the caves on 24 September 2005, together with their respective times of arrival and reservation prices for taking the tour that day.

	Arrival time	Reservation price (€)
Herman	1.48	20
Jon	1.50	14
Kate	1.53	30
Jack	1.56	15
Penny	1.57	40
Fran	1.59	12
Faith	2.00	17

a. If the tour is 'free' and the warden operates it on a first-come, first-served basis, what will the total consumer surplus be for the four people who get to go on the tour on that day?

b. Suppose the warden solicits volunteers to postpone their tour by offering increasing amounts of cash compensation until only four people still wish to see the caves that day. If he gives each volunteer the same compensation payment, how much money will he have to offer to generate the required number of volunteers? What is the total economic surplus under this policy?

c. Why is the compensation policy more efficient than the first-come, first-served policy?

d. Describe a way of financing the warden's compensation payments that will make everyone, including the warden, either better off or no worse off than under the first-come, first-served approach.

4. Suppose the weekly demand for a certain good, in thousands of units, is given by the equation $P = 8 - Q$, and the weekly supply of the good is given by the equation $P = 2 + Q$, where P is the price in euros.

a. Calculate the total weekly economic surplus generated at the market equilibrium.

b. Suppose a per-unit tax of €2, to be collected from sellers, is imposed in this market. Calculate the direct loss in economic surplus experienced by participants in this market as a result of the tax.

c. How much government revenue will this tax generate each week? If the revenue is used to offset other taxes paid by participants in this market, what will be their net reduction in total economic surplus?

5. Is a company's producer surplus the same as its profit? (**Hint:** A company's total cost is equal to the sum of all marginal costs incurred in producing its output, plus any fixed costs.)

6. In Dubrovnik, Croatia, citizens can get their electric power from two sources: a hydroelectric generator and a coal-fired steam generator. The hydroelectric generator can supply up to 100 units of power per day at a constant marginal cost of 1 cent per unit. The steam generator can supply any additional power that is needed at a constant marginal cost of 10 cents per unit. When electricity costs 10 cents per unit, residents of Dubrovnik demand 200 units per day.

a. Draw the marginal cost curve of electric power production in Dubrovnik.

b. How much should the city charge for electric power? Explain. Should it charge the same price for a family whose power comes from the hydroelectric generator as it does for a family whose power comes from the steam generator?

7. The municipal water works of Cortland draws water from two sources: an underground spring and a nearby lake. Water from the spring costs 2 cents per 100 litres to deliver, and the spring has a capacity of 1 million litres per day. Water from the lake costs 4 cents per 100 litres to deliver and is available in unlimited quantities. The demand for water in the summer months in Cortland is $P = 20 - 0.001Q$, where P is the price of water in cents per 100 litres, and Q is quantity demanded in hundreds of litres per day. The demand curve for water in the winter months is $P = 10 - 0.001Q$. If the water works wants to encourage efficient water use, how much should it charge for water in the summer months? In the winter months?

8.* Phil's demand curve for visits to a private-sector health clinic is given by $P = 48 - 8Q$, where P is the price per visit in euros and Q is the number of visits per season. The marginal cost of providing medical services at the clinic is €24 per visit. Phil has a choice between two health policies, A and B. Both policies cover all the costs of any serious illness from which Phil might suffer. Policy A also covers the cost of visits to the clinic, whereas policy B does not. Thus if Phil chooses policy B, he must pay €24 per visit to the clinic.

   a. If the premiums the insurance company charges for policies A and B must cover their respective costs, by how much will the two premiums differ, and what will be the difference in Phil's total expenditure for medical care under the two policies?

   b. Which policy will Phil choose?

   c. What is the most Phil would be willing to pay for the right to continue buying that policy?

9.* The government of Islandia, a small island nation, imports heating oil at a price of €2 per litre and makes it available to citizens at a price of €1 per litre. If Islandians' demand curve for heating oil is given by $P = 6 - Q$, where P is the price per litre in euros and Q is the quantity in millions of litres per year, how much economic surplus is lost as a result of the government's policy?

10.* Refer to Problem 9. Suppose each of the 1 million Islandian households has the same demand curve for heating oil.

   a. What is the household demand curve?

   b. How much consumer surplus would each household lose if it had to pay €2 per litre instead of €1 per litre for heating oil, assuming that there were no other changes in the household budget?

   c. With the money saved by not subsidising oil, by how much could the Islandian government afford to cut each family's annual taxes?

   d. If the government abandoned its oil subsidy and implemented the tax cut, by how much would each family be better off?

   e. How does the resulting total gain for the 1 million families compare with your calculation of the lost economic surplus in Problem 9?

To help you grasp the key concepts of this chapter check out the extra resources posted on the Online Learning Centre. There are chapter summaries, self-test questions, an interactive graphing tool, weblinks and a glossary, all for free!

Visit the Online Learning Centre at: www.mcgraw-hill.co.uk/textbooks/mcdowell for information on accessing all of these resources.

7

Profits, Entry and Exit: the Basis for the 'Invisible Hand'

In New York, in London, indeed in any major city in the 1970s, you would have found a very large population of small secretarial firms offering typing, copying and printing services. In those years, in most American cities, several firms also offered telephone-answering services. Today they have nearly all disappeared or, if they survive, they offer different services. On the other hand, Manhattan offers a large choice of dog-walking service suppliers today; London offers an extraordinary number of yoga and transcendental meditation (TM) instruction services. Both were more or less unheard of in the 1970s.

There has been an explosion in the choice of restaurants available in any big city, but the choice of bookshops has sharply contracted.

Try to have your watch repaired today and you will find that watch repair firms are few and far between. Similarly, it is hard in a modern European city to find a cobbler to mend shoes. In contrast, if you need immediate access to the internet, cyber cafes abound.

The reasons for these changes are in some cases obvious. The PC has revolutionised document preparation, and electronic watches are cheap and disposable. Increased leisure and higher incomes have increased the demand for recreational services. Other changes, however, require deeper study to explain them.

However, what is of interest here is not the underlying cause of these changes, but what actually *happens to bring them about*. That is, the process whereby firms are set up, or disappear, or firms change what they do.

Driving these changes is the business owner's quest for profit. Businesses migrate to industries and locations in which profit opportunities abound, and desert those whose prospects appear bleak. In perhaps the most widely quoted passage from his landmark treatise, *The Wealth of Nations* (1776), Adam Smith wrote:

Incentives Matter

It is not from the benevolence of the butcher, the brewer, or the baker that we expect our dinner, but from their regard of their own interest. We address ourselves not to their humanity, but to their self-love, and never talk to them of our necessities, but of their advantage.

Smith went on to argue that although the entrepreneur 'intends only his own gain', he is 'led by an invisible hand to promote an end which was no part of his intention'. As Smith saw it, even though self-interest is the prime mover of economic activity, the end result is an allocation of goods and services that serves society's collective interests remarkably well. If producers are offering 'too much' of one product and 'not enough' of another, profit opportunities immediately alert entrepreneurs to that fact and provide incentives for them to take remedial action. All the while, the system exerts relentless pressure on producers to hold the price of each good close to its cost of production – and, indeed, to reduce that cost in any ways possible.

The object of this chapter is to provide a deeper insight into the nature of the forces that guide the invisible hand. This involves confronting four questions.

1. What exactly does 'profit' mean, and how is it measured?
2. How does the pursuit of profit serve society's ends, as is asserted by economists who support the use of markets to allocate resources?
3. If competition holds price close to the cost of production, why do so many entrepreneurs become fabulously wealthy?
4. How does public policy affect economic welfare by limiting resource allocation changes?

The central role of economic profit

The economic theory of business behaviour is built on the assumption that the firm's goal is to *maximise its profit*. So we must be clear at the outset about what, exactly, 'profit' means.

Three types of profit

The economist's understanding of profit is different from the accountant's, and the distinction between the two is important to understanding how the 'invisible hand' works.

explicit costs the actual payments a firm makes to its factors of production and other suppliers

accounting profit the difference between a firm's total revenue and its explicit costs

implicit costs the opportunity costs of the resources supplied by the firm's owners

economic profit (or supernormal profit or excess profit) the difference between a firm's total revenue and the sum of its explicit and implicit costs

Accountants define the annual profit of a business as the difference between the revenue it takes in and its **explicit costs** for the year, which are the actual payments the firm makes to its factors of production and other suppliers. Profit thus defined is called **accounting profit**:

$$\text{Accounting profit} = \text{Total revenue} - \text{Explicit costs}$$

Accounting profit is the most familiar profit concept in everyday discourse. It is the one that companies use, for example, when they provide statements about their profits in press releases or annual reports. It is what the tax authorities use to compute corporation tax liabilities.

Economists, by contrast, define profit as the difference between the firm's total revenue and not just its explicit costs, but also its **implicit costs**, which are the opportunity costs of all the resources supplied by the firm's owners. Profit thus defined is called **economic profit**, **supernormal profit** or **excess profit**:

$$\text{Economic profit} = \text{Total revenue} - \text{Explicit costs} - \text{Implicit costs}$$

To illustrate the difference between accounting and economic profit, consider a firm with €400,000 in total annual revenue whose only explicit costs are workers' salaries of €250,000 per year. The owners of this firm have supplied machines and other capital equipment with a total resale value of €1 million. This firm's accounting profit, then, is the difference between its total revenue of €400,000 per year and its explicit costs of €250,000 per year, or €150,000 per year.

To calculate the firm's economic profit, we must first calculate the opportunity cost of the resources supplied by the firm's owners, *the equity capital of the firm*. Suppose that the current annual interest rate on savings accounts is 10 per cent. Had owners not invested in capital equipment, they could have earned an additional €100,000 per year interest by depositing their €1 million in a savings account. So the firm's economic profit is €400,000 per year – €250,000 per year – €100,000 per year = €50,000 per year.

normal profit the opportunity cost of the resources supplied by a firm's owners, equal to accounting profit minus economic profit

Note that this economic profit is smaller than the accounting profit by exactly the amount of the firm's *implicit costs* – the €100,000 per year opportunity cost of the resources supplied by the firm's owners. This difference between a business's accounting profit and its economic profit is called its **normal profit**. Normal profit is simply the opportunity cost of the resources supplied to a business by its owners.

Figure 7.1 illustrates the difference between accounting and economic profit. Figure 7.1(a) represents a firm's total revenues, while Figs. 7.1(b) and (c) show how these revenues are apportioned among the various cost and profit categories.

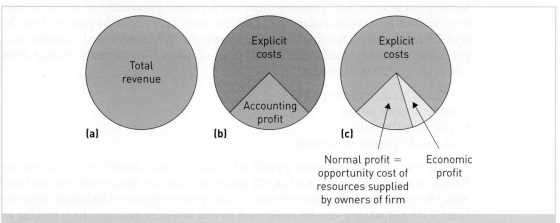

Figure 7.1 The Difference between Accounting Profit and Economic Profit. Accounting profit (b) is the difference between total revenue (a) and explicit costs. Normal profit (c) is the opportunity cost of all resources supplied by firm's owners. Economic profit (c) is the difference between total revenue and all costs, explicit and implicit (also equal to the difference between accounting profit and normal profit).

Examples 7.1 and 7.2 illustrate why the distinction between accounting and economic profit is so important.

Example 7.1 With the changes taking place in the EU's Common Agricultural Policy should we expect the number of farmers to remain unchanged even if the farms appear to remain profitable?

Since the 1990s, successive reforms of the price supports for farm produce available to help farmers in the European Union have been reduced. As a consequence, the prices farmers have been receiving for what they produce have fallen in real terms (i.e. allowing for inflation). As is well known, not only have farm interest groups been complaining vociferously about farm incomes, but it is clear from census data that the numbers in farming have been dropping steadily. At the same time it has often been pointed out that farming remains profitable, and farmers have been paying income taxes, something that would not happen if they were losing money. To understand (and reconcile) these positions, the following two sets of data, in Tables 7.1 and 7.2, will be helpful.

Total revenue (€/year)	Explicit costs (€/year)	Implicit costs (€/year)	Accounting profit (= total revenue – explicit costs) (€/year)	Economic profit (= total revenue – explicit costs – implicit costs) (€/year)	Normal profit (= implicit costs) (€/year)
22,000	10,000	11,000	12,000	1,000	11,000

Table 7.1 **Revenue, Cost and Profit Summary for Example 7.1**

Table 7.1 summarises the following scenario. A wheat farmer in northern France pays €6,000 rent (the going rate) to his elderly uncle for his land and also pays the cost of his various pieces of farm equipment and other inputs. The total for rent and other cost payments comes to €10,000 a year. He supplies only his own labour, and he considers farming just as attractive as his only other employment opportunity, managing a retail store in a nearby town at a salary of €11,000 per year. Apart from the matter of pay, he is indifferent between farming and being a manager. Wheat sells for a constant price per tonne effectively determined by EU price supports. The farmer's revenue from wheat sales is €22,000 per year.

- What is his accounting profit?
- His economic profit?
- His normal profit?
- Should he remain in farming?

As shown in Table 7.1, accounting profit is €12,000 per year, the difference between his €22,000 annual revenue and his €10,000 yearly payment for land, equipment and supplies. His economic profit is that amount less the opportunity cost of his labour. Since the latter is the €11,000 per year he could have earned as a store manager, he is making an economic profit of €1,000 per year. Finally, his normal profit is the €11,000 opportunity cost of the only resource he supplies – namely, his labour. Given that he is otherwise indifferent between the two types of work, he will be better off by €1,000 per year if he remains in farming. He earns an economic profit of €1,000 by remaining on the land.

Exercise 7.1   Suppose the European Union lowers the effective support price, and the value of the annual wheat production on the farm falls to €20,000. What advice would you give the farmer?

economic loss an economic profit that is less than zero

If you work through Exercise 7.1, you will conclude that the farmer now has an economic profit of –€1,000 per year. A negative economic profit is an **economic loss**. If he expects to sustain an economic loss indefinitely, his best bet would be to abandon farming in favour of managing a retail store. Note that he is still earning an accounting profit.

Example 7.2 Does owning the land rather than paying rent to the owner make a difference?

Now suppose that his uncle dies and leaves the land to the farmer. Clearly he is better off, because he doesn't have to pay the uncle €500 a month as rent. Should he now revise his opinion? Would you tell him that he should now stay on in farming because he doesn't have to pay the rent, and has an extra €6,000 at the end of the year?

Cost–Benefit Analysis

The answer is that he should still take the other job, as is shown in Table 7.2. If he continues to farm his own land, his accounting profit will be €16,000 per year, or €6,000 more than before. But his economic profit will still be the same as before – that is, –€1,000 per year – because he should deduct the €6,000 per year opportunity cost of farming his own land, even though he no longer must make an explicit payment to his uncle for it. Why? Because he could rent it to someone else at the going rate. The normal profit from owning and operating his farm will be €17,000 per year – the opportunity cost of the land and labour he provides. But since he earns an accounting profit of only €16,000, he will again do better to abandon farming for the managerial job.

Total revenue (€/year)	Explicit costs (€/year)	Implicit costs (€/year)	Accounting profit (= total revenue – explicit costs) (€/year)	Economic profit (= total revenue – explicit costs – implicit costs) (€/year)	Normal profit (= implicit costs) (€/year)
20,000	4,000	17,000	16,000	–1,000	17,000

Table 7.2 **Revenue, Cost and Profit Summary for Example 7.2**

He would obviously be wealthier as an owner than he was as a renter. But the question of whether to remain a farmer is answered the same way whether he rents his farmland or owns it. He should stay in farming only if that is the option that yields the highest economic profit.

So, as a matter of probability we should expect the numbers on the land to fall, even if the farms remain profitable in an accounting sense, when the real price of what is produced on the land falls. This is because a fall in farm output prices will result in some farmers not making an economic profit from staying in the business.

Exercise 7.2 What would you expect to happen to land values and the numbers engaged in agriculture as a consequence of the introduction of regulations and fiscal incentives to substitute bio-fuel for conventional oil in transport?

RECAP The central role of economic profit

A firm's accounting profit is the difference between its revenue and the sum of all explicit costs it incurs. Economic profit is the difference between the firm's revenue and all costs it incurs – both explicit and implicit. Normal profit is the opportunity cost of the resources supplied by the owners of the firm. When a firm's accounting profit is exactly equal to the opportunity cost of the inputs supplied by the firm's owners, the firm's economic profit is zero. For a firm to remain in business in the long run, it must earn an economic profit greater than or equal to zero.

rationing function of price
to distribute scarce goods to
those consumers who value
them most highly

allocative function of price
to direct resources away from
overcrowded markets and
towards markets that are
underserved

'invisible hand' theory
Adam Smith's theory that
the actions of independent,
self-interested buyers and
sellers will often result in the
most efficient allocation of
resources

Efficiency

The 'invisible hand' theory

Two functions of price

In the free-enterprise system, market prices serve two important
and distinct functions. The first, the **rationing function of price**,
is to distribute scarce goods among potential claimants, ensuring
that those who get them are the ones who value them most.
Thus, if three people want the only antique clock for sale at an
auction, the clock goes home with the person who bids the most
for it.

The second function, the **allocative function of price**, is to
direct productive resources to different sectors of the economy.
Resources leave markets in which price cannot cover the cost of
production and enter those in which price exceeds the cost of
production.

Both the allocative and rationing functions of price underlie
Adam Smith's celebrated theory of the **'invisible hand'** of the
market. Smith believed and taught that the market system
channels the selfish interests of individual buyers and sellers so as to promote the
greatest good for society. The carrot of economic profit and the stick of economic
loss, he argued, were the only forces necessary to ensure not only that existing supplies in any market would be allocated efficiently, but also that resources would be
allocated across markets to produce the most efficient possible mix of goods and
services.

Responses to profits and losses

To understand how the invisible hand works, we begin by looking at how market
forces respond to economic profits and losses. If a firm is to remain in business in the
long run, it must cover all its costs, both explicit and implicit. A firm's normal profit
should be treated as a cost of doing business. Thus the owner of a firm that earns no
more than a normal profit has managed only to recover the opportunity cost of the
resources invested in the firm. By contrast, the owner of a firm that makes a positive
economic profit earns more than the opportunity cost of the invested resources, and
earns more than a normal profit.

Markets in which firms are earning an economic profit tend to attract additional
resources, whereas markets in which firms are experiencing economic losses tend to
lose resources.

To see how this happens, we examine the workings of a hypothetical market for a
product (in this case, wheat) whose short-run supply and demand curves are shown in
Fig. 7.2(a). Figure 7.2(b) depicts the marginal and average total cost curves for a representative farm. The equilibrium price of €2 per tonne is determined by the supply–
demand intersection in (a). The representative farm whose *MC* and *ATC* curves are
shown in (b) then maximises its profit by producing the quantity for which price equals
marginal cost, 130,000 tonnes of wheat per year.

From Chapter 5 we know that average total cost (*ATC*) at any output level is the
sum of all costs divided by output. The difference between price and *ATC* is thus equal
to the average amount of economic profit earned per unit sold. In Fig. 7.2(b), that difference is €0.70 per unit. With 130,000 tonnes per year sold, the representative farm
thus earns an economic profit of €104,000 per year.

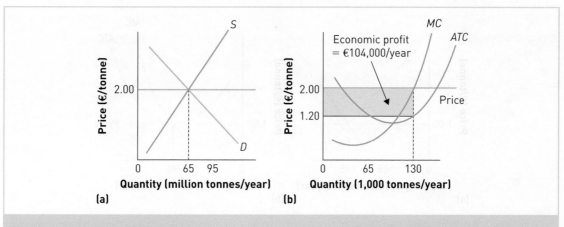

Figure 7.2 Economic Profit in the Short Run in the Wheat Market. At an equilibrium price of €2 per tonne (a), the typical farm earns an economic profit of €104,000 per year (b).

The existence of positive economic profit in the wheat market means that producers in that market are earning more than their opportunity cost of farming. For simplicity, we assume that the inputs required to enter the wheat market – land, labour, equipment and the like – are available at constant prices and that anyone is free to enter this market if he or she chooses. The key point is that since price exceeds the opportunity cost of the resources required to enter the market, others *will* want to enter. As they add their wheat production to the amount already on offer, supply shifts to the right, causing the market equilibrium price to fall, as shown in Fig. 7.3(a). At the new price of €1.50 per tonne, the representative farm now earns much less economic profit than before, only €50,400 per year (Fig. 7.3(b)).

For simplicity, we assume that all farms employ the same standard production method (that is, the farmers are equally efficient, have access to the same technology

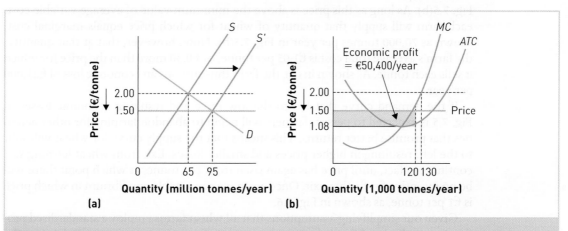

Figure 7.3 The Effect of Entry on Price and Economic Profit. At the original price of €2 per tonne, existing farmers earned economic profit, prompting new farmers to enter. With entry, supply shifts right (from *S* to *S'* in (a)) and equilibrium price falls, as does economic profit (b).

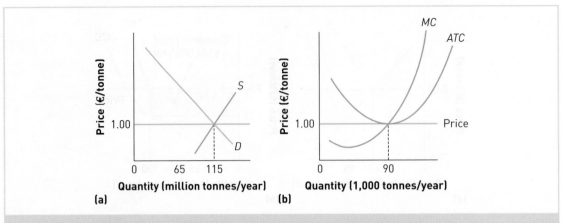

Figure 7.4 Equilibrium when Entry Ceases. Further entry ceases once price falls to the minimum value of *ATC*. At that point all farms earn a normal economic profit. Equivalently, each earns an economic profit of zero.

and pay the same prices for their inputs), so that their *ATC* curves are identical. Entry will then continue until price falls all the way to the minimum value of *ATC*. (At any price higher than that, economic profit would still be positive, and entry would continue, driving price still lower.) Recall from Chapter 5 that the short-run marginal cost curve intersects the *ATC* curve at the minimum point of the *ATC* curve. This means that once price reaches the minimum value of *ATC*, the profit-maximising rule of setting price equal to marginal cost results in a quantity for which price and *ATC* are the same. And, when that happens, economic profit for the representative farm will be exactly zero, as shown in Fig. 7.4(b).

In the adjustment process just considered, the initial equilibrium price had been above the minimum value of *ATC*, giving rise to positive economic profits. Suppose instead that the market demand curve for wheat had intersected the short-run supply curve at a price below the minimum value of each farm's *ATC* curve, as shown in Fig. 7.5(b). As long as this price is above the minimum value of average variable cost, each farm will supply that quantity of wheat for which price equals marginal cost, shown as 70,000 tonnes per year in Fig. 7.5(b). Note, however, that at that quantity, the farm's average total cost is €1.05 per tonne, or €0.30 more than the price for which it sells each tonne. As shown in (b), the farm thus sustains an economic loss of €21,000 per year.

If the demand curve that led to the low price and resulting economic losses in Fig. 7.5 is expected to persist, farmers will begin to abandon farming for other activities that promise better returns. This means that the supply curve for wheat will shift to the left, resulting in higher prices and smaller losses. Exit from wheat farming will continue, in fact, until price has again risen to €1 per tonne, at which point there will be no incentive for further exit. Once again we see a stable equilibrium in which price is €1 per tonne, as shown in Fig. 7.6.

Given our simplifying assumptions that all wheat farms employ a standardised production method and that inputs can be purchased in any quantities at fixed prices, the price of wheat cannot remain above €1 per tonne (the minimum point on the *ATC* curve) in the long run. Any higher price would stimulate additional entry until price again fell to that level. Further, the price of wheat cannot remain below €1 per tonne

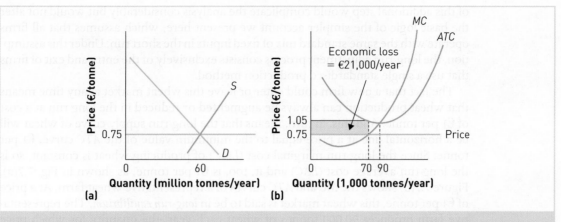

Figure 7.5 A Short-run Economic Loss in the Wheat Market. When price is below the minimum value of *ATC* (a), each farm sustains an economic loss (b).

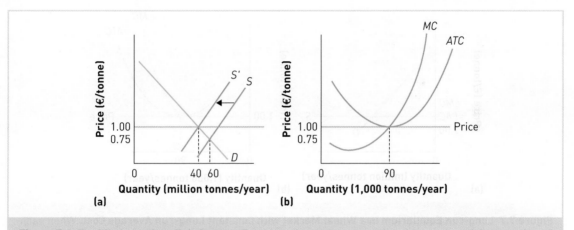

Figure 7.6 Equilibrium when Exit Ceases. Further exit ceases once price rises to the minimum value of *ATC*. At that point all farms earn a normal economic profit. Equivalently, each earns an economic profit of zero.

in the long run, because any lower price would stimulate exit until the price of wheat again rose to €1 per tonne.

Equilibrium

The fact that firms are free to enter or leave an industry at any time ensures that in the long run all firms in the industry will tend to earn zero economic profit. Their goal is not to earn zero profit. Rather, the zero-profit tendency is a consequence of the price movements associated with entry and exit. As the *Equilibrium Principle* – also called the No-Cash-on-the-Table Principle – predicts, when people confront an opportunity for gain, they are almost always quick to exploit it.

What does the long-run supply curve look like in the wheat market just discussed? This question is equivalent to asking: 'What is the marginal cost of producing additional tonnes of wheat in the long run?' In general, adjustment in the long run may entail not just entry and exit of standardised firms, but also the ability of firms to alter the mix of capital equipment and other fixed inputs they employ. Explicit consideration of this additional step would complicate the analysis considerably but would not alter the basic logic of the simpler account we present here, which assumes that all firms operate with the same standard mix of fixed inputs in the short run. Under this assumption, the long-run adjustment process consists exclusively of the entry and exit of firms that use a single standardised production method.

The fact that a new firm could enter or leave this wheat market at any time means that wheat production can always be augmented or reduced in the long run at a cost of €1 per tonne. And this, in turn, means that the long-run supply curve of wheat will be a horizontal line at a price equal to the minimum value of the ATC curve, €1 per tonne. Since the long-run marginal cost (LMC) of producing wheat is constant, so is the long-run average cost (LAC) and it, too, is €1 per tonne, as shown in Fig. 7.7(a). Figure 7.7(b) shows the MC and ATC curves of a representative wheat farm. At a price of €1 per tonne, this wheat market is said to be in *long-run equilibrium*. The representative farm produces 90,000 tonnes of wheat each year, the quantity for which price equals its marginal cost. And since price is exactly equal to ATC, this farm also earns an economic profit of zero.

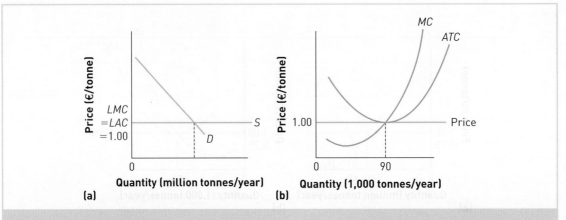

Figure 7.7 Long-run Equilibrium in a Wheat Market with Constant Long-run Average Cost. When each producer has the same ATC curve, the industry can supply as much or as little output as buyers wish to buy at a price equal to the minimum value of ATC (a). At that price, the representative producer (b) earns zero economic profit.

These observations call attention to two attractive features of the invisible hand concept.

1. The first is that the *market outcome is efficient in the long run*. Note, for example, that when the wheat market is in long-run equilibrium, the value to buyers of the last unit of wheat sold is €1 per tonne, which is exactly the same as the long-run marginal cost of producing it. Thus there is no possible rearrangement of resources that would make some participants in this market better off without causing harm to some others. If farmers were to expand production, for example, the added costs incurred would exceed the added benefits; and if they were to contract production, the cost savings would be less than the benefits forgone.
2. The second attractive feature of long-run competitive equilibrium is that the price buyers must pay is no higher than the cost incurred by suppliers. That cost includes a normal profit, the opportunity cost of the resources supplied by owners of the firm.

We must emphasise that Smith's 'invisible hand' does not mean that market allocation of resources is optimal in every way. It simply means that markets are 'efficient' in the limited technical sense discussed in Chapter 6. Thus, if the current allocation differs from the market equilibrium allocation, the 'invisible hand' theory implies that we can reallocate resources in a way that makes some people better off without harming others.

Example 7.3 affords additional insight into how Smith's 'invisible hand' works in practice.

Example 7.3 What happens in a city with 'too many' hair stylists and 'too few' aerobics instructors?

At the initial equilibrium quantities and prices in the markets for haircuts and aerobics classes shown in Fig. 7.8, all suppliers are currently earning zero economic profit. Now suppose that styles suddenly change in favour of longer hair and increased physical fitness. If the long-run marginal cost of altering current production levels is constant in both markets, describe how prices and quantities will change in each market, in both the short run and the long run. Are the new equilibrium quantities socially optimal?

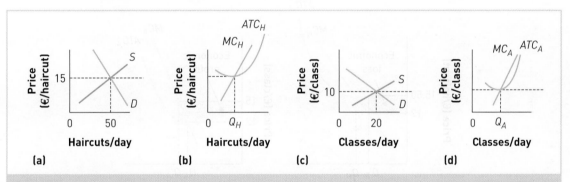

Figure 7.8 Initial Equilibrium in the Markets for (a) Haircuts and (b) Aerobics Classes. MC_H and ATC_H are the marginal cost and average total cost curves for a representative hair stylist, and MC_A and ATC_A are the marginal cost and average total cost curves for a representative aerobics instructor. Both markets are initially in long-run equilibrium, with sellers in each market earning zero economic profit.

The shift to longer hair styles means a leftward shift in the demand for haircuts, while the increased emphasis on physical fitness implies a rightward shift in the demand curve for aerobics classes, as seen in Fig. 7.9. As a result of these demand shifts, the new short-run equilibrium prices change. For the sake of illustration, these new prices are shown as €12 per haircut and €15 per aerobics class.

Because each producer was earning zero economic profit at the original equilibrium prices, hair stylists will experience economic losses and aerobics instructors will experience economic profits at the new prices, as seen in Fig. 7.10.

Because the short-run equilibrium price of haircuts results in economic losses for hair stylists, some hair stylists will begin to leave that market in search of more favourable opportunities elsewhere. As a result, the short-run supply curve of haircuts will shift leftwards, resulting in a higher equilibrium price. Exit of hair stylists will continue until the price of haircuts rises sufficiently to cover the long-run opportunity cost of providing them, which by assumption is €15.

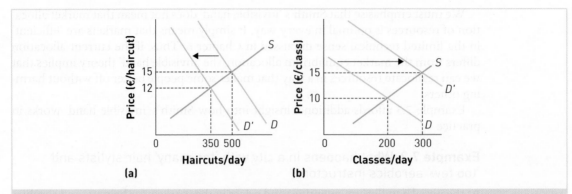

Figure 7.9 The Short-run Effect of Demand Shifts in Two Markets. The decline in demand for haircuts causes the price of haircuts to fall from €15 to €12 in the short run (a), while the increase in demand for aerobics classes causes the price of classes to rise from €10 to €15 in the short run (b).

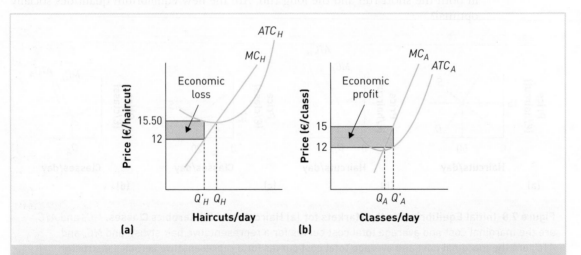

Figure 7.10 Economic Profit and Loss in the Short Run. The assumed demand shifts result in an economic loss for the representative hair stylist (a) and an economic profit for the representative aerobics instructor (b).

By the same token, because the short-run equilibrium price of aerobics classes results in economic profits for instructors, outsiders will begin to enter that market, causing the short-run supply curve of classes to shift rightwards. New instructors will continue to enter until the price of classes falls to the long-run opportunity cost of providing them. By assumption, that cost is €10. Once all adjustments have taken place, there will be fewer hair stylists and more aerobics classes than before. But because marginal costs in both markets were assumed constant in the long run, the prices of the two goods will again be at their original levels.

Of course, those stylists who leave the hair-cutting market will not necessarily be the same people who enter the aerobics teaching market. Indeed, given the sheer number of occupations a former hair stylist might choose to pursue, the likelihood of such a switch is low. Movements of resources will typically involve several indirect steps. Thus a former hair stylist might become a secretary, and a former postal worker might become an aerobics instructor.

We also note that the invisible hand theory says nothing about *how long* these adjustments might take. In some markets, especially labour markets, the required movements might take months or even years. Think of what happened in the coal-mining areas of Britain during the 1980s when coal mining was drastically reduced (and in many areas closed down completely). By way of contrast, consider the consequences of the collapse of MG Rover early in 2005. No one believes that the workers who lost their jobs would for the most part remain unemployed for long. But, even in the worst case (as in coal mining), if the supply and demand curves remain stable, the labour markets will eventually reach equilibrium prices and quantities. And the new prices and quantities will be socially optimal in the same sense as before. Because the value to buyers of the last unit sold will be the same as the marginal cost of producing it, no additional transactions will be possible that benefit some without harming others.

The importance of free entry and exit

The allocative function of price cannot operate unless firms can enter new markets and leave existing ones at will. If new firms could not enter a market in which existing firms were making a large economic profit, economic profit would not tend to fall to zero over time, and price would not tend to gravitate towards the marginal cost of production.

barrier to entry any force that prevents firms from entering a new market

Forces that inhibit firms from entering new markets are sometimes called barriers to entry. In the book publishing market, for example, the publisher (or author) of a book enjoys copyright protection granted by the government. Copyright law forbids other publishers from producing and selling their own editions of protected works. Pharmaceutical companies recoup the costs of R&D by being protected from competition by patents covering new drugs. In many countries the number of retail outlets selling alcohol or tobacco is limited by law.

Barriers to entry may result from practical as well as legal constraints. Some economists, for example, have argued that the compelling advantages of *product compatibility* have created barriers to entry in the computer software market. Since more than 90 per cent of new desktop computers come with Microsoft's Windows operating system (OS) software already installed, rival companies have difficulty selling other operating systems, as a different OS may make it difficult for users to exchange files with friends and colleagues. The bundling of MSWord with Windows, coupled to problems of importing documents prepared with other word-processing (WP) packages into MSWord, has undermined demand for other WP packages, especially Word-Perfect. These compatibility problems, more than all other factors, are widely believed to explain Microsoft's spectacular profit history.

This last effect may be overstated. The emergence of the 'open architecture' free-ware operating system, Linux, has seriously undermined Microsoft's position in the OS market, something that would have been expected by economists of the Chicago School, who have always argued that markets tend to erode positions of market power.

No less important than the freedom to enter a market is the freedom to leave. When the US domestic airline industry was regulated by the federal government, air carriers were often required to serve specific markets, even though they were losing money in them. Similar constraints continue to be imposed by national and EU regulation on a variety of utilities across Europe. They are termed 'universal service obligations' (USOs) in the literature on regulation, and they have the effect of increasing operating costs for suppliers subject to them. When firms discover that a market, once entered, is difficult or impossible to leave, they become reluctant to enter new markets. Barriers to exit thus become barriers to entry. Without reasonably free entry and exit, then, the implications of Adam Smith's 'invisible hand' theory cannot be expected to hold.

All things considered, however, producers enjoy a high degree of freedom of entry in most sectors of the market economies of the West. Recognition of the importance of ease of entry and exit has meant that even where, in countries or sectors, firms enjoy a lower degree of freedom, the consequences (arthritic economies) have led to pressure for change. Because free entry and exit is one of the defining characteristics of perfectly competitive markets, we shall, unless otherwise stated, assume its existence.

The importance of public policy on exit: the 'globalisation' question

It is easy to see why public policy should not create barriers to entry, and the consequences of policy measures that discourage or prohibit entry. When demand increases for the output of an industry and existing firms face barriers to expanding capacity, or new firms face barriers to entry, output cannot adequately expand to meet increased demand, as extra resources, capital and labour cannot be allocated to producing the goods for which demand has increased. Input suppliers will not see demand for their products increase. Resources will not flow into producing the necessary inputs. Prices for the goods for which demand has increased will rise, which means higher profits and wages in the sector. This explains why existing producers will always find reasons for calling for legislation to limit entry … in the public interest, of course.

By and large these arguments are accepted by public opinion and by policy makers in principle, although the latter are prone to finding reasons to refuse to act accordingly from time to time. When, however, the question of exit arises, the situation, in terms of public opinion and policy response, is less receptive. What is different about exit?

When falling demand, or competition from new goods, or competition from foreign suppliers, reduces profits in an industry we have seen what happens: firms, or at least some of them, start to experience losses. This frequently leads to pressure for government intervention to shore up the firms in the industry affected. This can take the form of subventions, restrictions on competition, restrictions on entry to the relevant product market by new suppliers and, most frequently, restrictions on imports from foreign suppliers who are often accused of 'dumping' (i.e. selling at below cost) to undermine traditional suppliers. In Britain, competitive pressure on the motor industry led to government intervention to restructure the British industry in the 1970s and 1980s, culminating in nationalising it. This support to prevent exit merely delayed the exit at huge expense of the entire 'British' industry, which was replaced by more efficient production of cars in Britain by 'foreign' producers. In the USA, competition, especially from Japanese car producers, led to a government bail-out of one firm (Chrysler) in 1980 and attempts to restrict imports from Japan by trade restrictions in order to preserve the business of the Detroit 'Big Three'. The policy failed. By the beginning of the twenty-first century 'American' production of cars had fallen from over 90 per cent of sales in the USA in the early 1970s to less than 50 per cent today, while direct imports and transplanted production of 'foreign' cars accounted for a 50 per cent plus, and growing, market share.

The political reason for the success of such calls for action is obvious: jobs are at stake and votes are up for grabs. It is easy to mobilise public support for measures, often described as temporary, to preserve the industry affected, especially if it is regionally concentrated. What is not understood is that measures that discourage exit effectively 'freeze' the allocation of resources in the economy just when long-term surplus maximisation requires that they move out of the affected sector, that the economy should move along its production possibility frontier, and the sector concerned should contract (or even disappear).

Efficiency

Put another way, measures that discourage exit have the same qualitative effect on economic efficiency as measures that discourage entry. Public perceptions, unfortunately, treat exits as a net cost to the economy (jobs lost, incomes reduced …) arising from increased competition and the public reacts accordingly. This is what underlies much of the rhetoric about the 'costs of globalisation' and the pressure to move away from a world order based on freedom of exchange, trade and specialisation. Much of the opposition to 'globalisation' lies in the perception that opening markets in poorer countries to trade leads to a contraction in output, income and employment in sectors facing increased competition. It is now widely understood that restricting exports from poorer countries by barriers on imports into the countries of the OECD immis-

Comparative Advantage

erises poorer countries, and that without trade access economic growth in those countries will be stunted, extending aid dependence. This has led to calls for asymmetric opening of trade: easier access for poor countries to rich country markets, but restrictions on exports from rich countries to poorer countries (and even from poorer to richer countries) where these disrupt traditional production patterns. Much (and rather ill informed) concern has been expressed in recent years because some African countries are now successfully exporting vegetable products to the countries of the EU while production of foodstuffs for their domestic markets declines, making them more dependent on food imports. The fundamentally flawed basis to this is clear once we think about what increased exports means in the case of poorer countries: the movement of resources out of serving the local market and into serving markets in other countries, movement along the production possibility frontier to increase real income per head.

Scarcity

For incomes per head to rise in poorer counties it is necessary that traditional production patterns are replaced. This is precisely how the richer countries in the world became richer in the first place, by permitting, even encouraging, exit from traditional occupations to permit expansion of new sectors in their economies. In a nutshell, this is what we mean by the concept of the Industrial Revolution of the eighteenth and nineteenth centuries, and the move in the OECD countries from manufacturing to services in the late twentieth and early twenty-first centuries.

RECAP The 'invisible hand' theory

In market economies, the *allocative* and *rationing* functions of prices guide resources to their most highly valued uses. Prices influence how much of each type of good gets produced (the allocative function). Firms enter industries in which prices are sufficiently high to sustain an economic profit and leave those in which low prices result in an economic loss. Prices also direct existing supplies of goods to the buyers who value them most (the rationing function). Industries in which firms earn a positive economic profit tend to attract new firms, shifting industry supply to the right. Firms tend to leave industries in which they sustain an economic loss, shifting supply curves to the left. In each case, the supply movements continue until economic profit reaches zero. In long-run equilibrium, the value of the last unit produced to buyers is equal to its marginal cost of production, leaving no possibility for additional mutually beneficial transactions.

Economic rent versus economic profit

Microsoft chairman Bill Gates is said to be one of the wealthiest men in the world. This, it is widely believed, is largely because the problem of compatibility prevents rival suppliers from competing effectively in the many software markets dominated by his company. This has led to regulatory and judicial confrontations on both sides of the Atlantic as anti-trust policy has been invoked to curb Microsoft's alleged abuses of its market position. Yet numerous people have become fabulously rich even in markets with no conspicuous barriers to entry. If market forces push economic profit towards zero, how can that happen?

economic rent that part of the payment for a factor of production that exceeds the owner's reservation price

The answer to this question hinges on the distinction between economic profit and **economic rent**. When people use the term 'rent' in everyday circumstances they are referring to the payment they might make to a landlord for a flat, or to a car hire company for the use of a car. In economics, however, the term 'rent' has a different meaning, although it is connected to the everyday term in some cases. In economics *'economic rent'* (or simply, *rent*) is that portion of the payment for an input that is above the supplier's reservation price for that input, which is by definition the supply price of that input. Suppose, for example, that a landowner's reservation price for a hectare of land is €100 per year, reflecting its value to the landowner if he used it himself. That is, suppose he would be willing to lease it to a farmer as long as he received an annual payment of at least €100, but for less than that amount he would rather leave it fallow. If competition between would-be farmers resulted in one of them offering him an annual payment (in everyday usage, rents the land from the landowner) not of €100 but of €1,000, the landowner's *economic rent* from that payment would be €900 per year. If the land had no other use as far as the landowner was concerned, and he would be willing to let it for a very small sum, virtually the entire payment received would be an economic rent.

If an economist working for a civil service department is paid €90,000 a year, and if the next best employment available to someone with that skill set and experience in economics was in a university department at a salary of €80,000, €10,000 of the civil servant's salary would be an economic rent.

In our landowner's example, if the supply price of land was €100 per hectare, and large quantities of land were on offer, we would expect rents (in the everyday sense) to be competed down to €100: there would be no *economic* rent earned by landowners. Similarly, in our economist's example, if it were easy for academic economists to leave universities and seek employment in the civil service, we would expect to see the economic rent element in civil service economists' earnings disappear, unless there existed non-pecuniary benefits for academic economists (which has traditionally been the case in much of the English-speaking world).

Economic profit is like economic rent in that it, too, may be seen as the difference between what someone is paid (the business owner's total revenue) and the reservation price for remaining in business (the sum of all costs, explicit and implicit). But whereas competition pushes economic profit towards zero (by increasing supply and driving down price), it has no such effect on the economic rent for inputs if they cannot be replicated easily. For example, although the lease payments for land may remain substantially above the landowner's reservation price, year in and year out, new land cannot come on to the market to reduce or eliminate the economic rent through competition. There is, after all, only so much land to be had.

As Example 7.4 illustrates, economic rent can accrue to people as well as land.

Example 7.4 How much economic rent will a talented chef get?

France prides itself on the quality of its restaurants. There are thousands of them. Most are ordinary and unassuming (even if they might appear to be much better than run-of-the-mill eating establishments in less fortunate countries). And there is a small number of really outstandingly good restaurants, epitomised, perhaps, by La Tour d' Argent in Paris. The key to a restaurant's standing is the skill of the chef. In ordinary restaurants a chef might expect to be paid between €25,000 and €50,000 a year depending on experience and some modest differences in skills. But in establishments like La Tour d'Argent, the master chef could expect a significant multiple of that level of earnings.

Why? Because France takes gastronomy very seriously. Indeed, in early 2003 Bernard Loiseau, the chef-owner of one of the country's most famous hostelries, La Côte d'Or in Saulieu in Burgundy, shook France to its core when he committed suicide after the restaurant was downgraded from 19 to 17 on a 20-point scale by a rating body.

Because French (and other) diners are prepared to pay through the nose to consume the creations of the most talented chefs in France, the restaurants that employ them can charge enormous prices. Consequently, restaurants compete fiercely for talented chefs, and their earnings reflect this competition for the small number of extraordinary *artistes de cuisine*. The bulk of chefs will be paid something like their supply price: what they could earn outside the industry. Their earnings contain little or no economic rent. Master chefs, on the other hand, earning sums of up to €200,000 and more, have the same supply price … and most of their earnings are rent, being derived from the fact they are few in number and supply cannot expand to meet demand.

Since the talented chef's opportunities outside the restaurant industry are no better than an ordinary chef's, why is it necessary to pay the talented chef so much? Suppose the employer were to pay him only €80,000, which they both would consider a generous salary, since it is twice what ordinary chefs earn. The employer would then earn a significant economic profit since his annual revenue would be an order of magnitude higher than that of ordinary restaurants, but his costs would be only €30,000 to €40,000 more.

But this economic profit would create an opportunity for the owner of some other restaurant to bid the talented chef away. For example, if the owner of a competing restaurant were to hire the talented chef at a salary of €90,000, the chef would be €10,000 per year better off, and the rival owner would earn an economic profit. Furthermore, if the talented chef is the sole reason that a restaurant earns a positive economic profit, the bidding for that chef should continue as long as any economic profit remains. This bidding process assumes, of course, that the reason for the chef's superior performance is that he or she possesses some personal culinary skills that cannot be replicated or copied. If instead it were the result of, say, training at a culinary institute in France, then this privileged position would be eroded over time, as other chefs sought similar training.

> **RECAP** Economic rent versus economic profit
>
> Economic rent is the amount by which the payment to a factor of production exceeds the supplier's reservation price. Unlike economic profit, which is driven towards zero by competition, economic rent may persist for extended periods, especially in the case of factors with special talents that cannot easily be duplicated.

The 'invisible hand' in action

To help develop your intuition about how the invisible hand works, we will examine how it can help us gain insight into the patterns we observe in a wide variety of different contexts. In each case, the key idea we want you to focus on is that opportunities for private gain seldom remain unexploited for very long. Perhaps more than any other, this idea encapsulates the essence of that distinctive mind-set known as 'thinking like an economist'.

The 'invisible hand' at the supermarket

As Economic naturalist 7.1 illustrates, the No-Cash-on-the-Table Principle refers not just to opportunities to earn economic profits in cash, but also to any other opportunity to achieve a more desirable outcome.

Economic naturalist 7.1 Why do supermarket checkout queues all tend to be roughly the same length?

Pay careful attention the next few times you go grocery shopping, and you will notice that the queues at all the checkout points tend to be roughly the same length. Suppose you saw one queue that was significantly shorter than the others as you wheeled your trolley towards the checkout area. Which queue would you choose? The shorter one, of course; and, because most shoppers would do the same, the short queue seldom remains shorter for long.

The 'invisible hand' and cost-saving innovations

When economists speak of perfectly competitive firms, they have in mind businesses whose contribution to total market output is too small to have a perceptible impact on market price. As explained in Chapter 5, such firms are often called *price takers*: they take the market price of their product as given and then produce that quantity of output for which marginal cost equals that price.

This characterisation of the competitive firm gives the impression that the firm is essentially a passive actor in the marketplace. Yet, for most firms, that is anything but the case. As Example 7.5 illustrates, even those firms that cannot hope to influence the market prices of their products have very powerful incentives to develop and introduce cost-saving innovations.

Example 7.5 How do cost-saving innovations affect economic profit in the short run? In the long run? And what have markets and incentives to do with this?

Consider the following scenario involving the dissemination of technology. Suppose 40 merchant marine companies operate supertankers that carry oil from the Middle

East to Western Europe. The market is close to perfectly competitive. The cost per trip, including a normal profit, is €500,000. An engineer at one of these companies develops a more efficient propeller design that results in fuel savings of €20,000 per trip. How will this innovation affect the company's accounting and economic profits? Will these changes persist in the long run?

In the short run, the reduction in a single firm's costs will have no impact on the market price of transoceanic shipping services. The firm with the more efficient propeller will thus earn an economic profit of €20,000 per trip (since its total revenue will be the same as before, while its total cost will now be €20,000 per trip lower). As other firms learn about the new design, however, they will begin to adopt it, causing their individual supply curves to shift downwards (since the marginal cost per trip at these firms will drop by €20,000). The shift in these individual supply curves will cause the market supply curve to shift, which in turn will result in a lower market price for shipping and a decline in economic profit at the firm where the innovation originated. When all firms have adopted the new, efficient design, the long-run supply curve for the industry will have shifted downwards by €20,000 per trip, and each company will again be earning only a normal profit. At that point, any firm that did *not* adopt the new propeller design would suffer an economic loss of €20,000 per trip.

The importance of inter-firm competition and the profit motive is central to all this. The failure to disseminate technology in the former Soviet Union (USSR) was a major factor in explaining the failure of the Soviet economy in the long Cold War productivity competition with the West.[1] Despite major achievements in terms of advancing production technologies through research and development (R&D), the USSR's manufacturing capacity fell steadily behind that of the Organization for Economic Cooperation and Development (OECD) in terms of productivity and product quality. One reason for this was that in the planned economy of the Soviet Union, the incentives for managers in state enterprises were related to meeting volume production targets. Innovation, quality and cost considerations were secondary. This reduced the incentive to respond to the possibilities of new technologies compared to those facing managers in Western firms.

The incentive to come up with cost-saving innovations in order to reap economic profit is one of the most powerful forces on the economic landscape. Its beauty, in terms of the invisible hand theory, is that competition among firms ensures that the resulting cost savings will be passed along to consumers in the long run.

The 'invisible hand' in regulated markets

The carrot of economic profit and the stick of economic loss guide resource movements in regulated markets no less than in unregulated ones. Consider the taxi industry, which many cities regulate by licensing taxi cabs and restricting their numbers. These licences are often referred to as 'plates' or 'medallions', because they are issued in the form of a metal disc that must be fixed to the cab, where enforcement officials can easily see it. Cities that regulate cabs in this fashion typically issue fewer medallions than the equilibrium number of taxi cabs in similar markets that are not regulated. Officials then allow the medallions to be bought and sold in the marketplace. As Economic naturalist 7.2 demonstrates, the issuance of taxi medallions alters the equilibrium quantity of taxi cabs but does not change the fundamental rule that resources flow in response to profit and loss signals.

---

1 Iacopetta (2004).

Economic naturalist 7.2 A tale of two cities: regulation and taxi plates in New York and Dublin

Until the early 2000s, New York and Dublin, in common with many cities across the world, both regulated the number of taxis that could operate on their streets. In both cities there was clear evidence of excess demand. People trying to get a taxi could not find one. In both cities prices (fares) were also regulated, and could not adjust to clear the market, or give an incentive to the taxi drivers to respond by working longer hours. The restriction on the number of taxis resulted in higher incomes for taxi drivers and the taxi plates/medallions were traded at substantial prices. People were willing to pay significant amounts of money for permission to work as taxi drivers. In Dublin in 2001, taxi plates/medallions were worth about IRL£90,000 (€115,000). In New York they were traded for more than $200,000 (€200,000).

These prices meant that taxi drivers were earning more than their opportunity cost: the earnings they could make elsewhere. The medallion price is the market capitalisation of the average excess of taxi drivers' annual earnings over their supply price, a form of monopoly profit, a *scarcity rent*. Buying a plate/medallion was an investment decision. If you had funds earning, say 8 per cent, or could borrow at 8 per cent, and a plate yielded €20,000 a year over and above what you could otherwise earn, it would be worth buying at anything up to €250,000 (the sum that would earn you €20,000 at 8 per cent) and, with competition to buy medallions, that is what they would trade for.

At these prices, new drivers do not earn supernormal profits. Why? Because they have had to hand over to previous drivers the capitalisation of those profits. The plates/medallions represent an asset to the holder, with a market value as long as excess demand persists.

In 2002 the Irish government liberalised the taxi regime, reacting to severe public pressure. At that time there were about 2,000 taxis in Dublin. From then on, anyone who wanted to drive a taxi, had a suitable car and had passed certain personal characteristic tests (convictions for certain crimes against the person disqualified you for obvious reasons) could do so on paying an annual licence fee to the city. In 2004, Dublin had 10,000 taxis and, with the exception of some irreducible peak-time problems, taxis could be had on demand. In New York, no such change took place, and people still grumble. In Dublin, the only grumbling is from those who had (unwisely) bought plates/medallions in the run-up to 2002. The market value of a plate fell from €115,000 to zero.

Exercise 7.3   What would happen to the price of a taxi plate if the interest rate was 4 per cent in Economic naturalist 7.2, rather than 8 per cent?

Another regulated market in which the invisible hand was very much in evidence was the regulated commercial airline industry. In the United States, until late 1978, airlines were heavily regulated by the Civil Aeronautics Board (CAB), an agency of the federal government. In Europe it took strong pressure from the European Union from the early 1990s onwards to force national governments to liberalise the market, and the process is still not fully finished.

In the United States, carriers could not provide air services between two cities unless they were given explicit permission to do so. The CAB also prescribed the fares that carriers could charge. In Europe, national regulations not only determined who could fly on what route, and at what fares, but even how many flights they could put on a route. One of the declared objects of these regulatory regimes was to ensure an 'adequate' service on less popular routes. The standard practice was to set fares well above the cost of providing a service on most routes, and then require carriers to use some of the resulting economic profit to pay for service on sparsely travelled routes. But, as Economic naturalist 7.3 illustrates, the regulators failed to reckon with the invisible hand if they thought that high prices on some routes would produce profits to subsidise passengers on other routes.

Economic naturalist 7.3 Why did some US airlines install piano bars on the upper decks of Boeing 747s in the 1970s? Why has deregulation and increased competition resulted in customers paying for food and drink on many airline operators' routes in Europe, while food is not paid for on the Atlantic routes?

The answer to these questions lies in thinking about why food and drink were supplied free of charge under the less competitive regulated regime. The old regime restricted entry to and frequencies on routes and set minimum prices. This enabled planes to fly profitably with many empty seats. But if they could fill those seats, it would be even better. So they sought to compete on 'quality'. In the United States, at one stage this led to the installation of piano bars on the upper decks of Boeing 747s. In Europe, with shorter-haul flights predominant, quality meant hiring more (and more attractive) cabin crew and offering trimmings such as more and better food and drink. These were on offer whether or not people wanted them, and were consumed in quantities reflecting a zero price at point of sale. Their costs ate into the profitability of the airlines and so were 'bundled' into the airlines' fare structures by the regulators.

Competition under deregulation in Europe made paying for food and drink inevitable. Why? If an airline charged a price that covered expected costs of 'free' food and drink it would always be possible for a competitor to offer a lower fare structure that excluded food and drink while selling the latter separately to those who were willing to pay the cost of provision. By 'unbundling' the price of the seat from the price of the food the airlines could increase economic surplus.

So why is food still supplied free on competitive long-haul routes? The answer is that the airlines believe that virtually everyone would want to buy a meal on a six-hour or longer flight. Hence, a 'bundled' price does not oblige people to pay for something they don't want to consume to any significant extent. That limits the potential for competing by 'unbundling'. Add to that the cost of extracting payment and it is easy to see why 'unbundling' is not a cost-effective competitive strategy.

Ironically, one reason for the old regime was to create profits to finance 'social' (i.e. low-density) routes. It is now clear that, for the most part, low fares make previously low-density routes viable where regulation failed to do so. Regulation in this case was a waste of time from the start...as economists preached continuously while governments did not listen.

Exercise 7.4   From what was discussed in Economic naturalist 7.3, can you offer an explanation for the fact that it is now almost universal practice that airlines on North Atlantic routes charge standard-fare passengers for alcoholic drinks but not for soft drinks?

The 'invisible hand' in anti-poverty programmes

As Example 7.6 shows, failure to understand the logic of the invisible hand can lead not only to inefficient government regulation, but also to anti-poverty programmes that are doomed to fail.

Example 7.6 How will an irrigation project affect the incomes of poor farmers?

The World Bank and other development agencies are always under pressure to increase the flows of funds to projects that are designed to increase the incomes of low-productivity agricultural producers in some of the world's poorest countries. The funds flow, all right, but the outcome in terms of the incomes of those working the land frequently turns out to be disappointing. Accusations are then made that either the World Bank is not directing the money to the correct targets, or that the money is being siphoned of by corrupt officials in the recipient countries. No doubt either or both of these may be correct in some cases. However, as the following example is designed to illustrate, part (most?) of the answer may lie in a failure to understand the workings of the invisible hand.

Consider a small and unnamed country somewhere in southern Asia. It has a large population of tenant farmers growing rice, a staple of the local diet. Recently, Western investment has resulted in the establishment of a textile industry turning out T-shirts (factories that have replaced similar establishments in Ireland or France). Suppose unskilled workers must choose between working in a textile factory, earning €4,000 per year and growing rice on a rented parcel of farmland. One worker can farm 80 ha of rise paddy, which rents for €2,500 a year. Such holdings yield a crop that earns €8,000 per year in revenue, and the total non-labour costs of bringing the crop to market are €1,500 per year. The net incomes of rice farmers are thus €4,000 per year – the same as those of textile workers.

The landowners, few in number, receive the rental income from the land, which greatly exceeds the income per head of the peasant farmers who grow the rice. This inequitable distribution of income leads to calls for actions to support the incomes of the large numbers of poor farmers who are handing over a lot of money to the few and very rich landlords. As a result of pressure from Oxfam and other organisations, the World Bank announces that it will fund an irrigation project that would double the output of rice on farms operated by tenant farmers. Rice, of course, is an internationally traded good, so the level of output in this Third World country has no discernible effect on the world (and, therefore, domestic) price of rice. How will the project affect the absolute and relative incomes of tenant farmers in the long run?

Suppose that the irrigation project succeeds in doubling rice yields, which means that each farmer will sell €16,000 worth of rice per year rather than €8,000. If nothing else changed, farmers' incomes would rise from €4,000 per year to €12,000 per year. But the No-Cash-on-the-Table principle tells us that farmers cannot sustain this income level. Think about the impact on the new textile sector. The firms face a given price for the output of the factories. But, to textile workers, there is cash on the table in farming. Seeing an opportunity to triple their incomes, many will want to switch to farming. But since the supply of land is fixed, farm rents will rise as textile workers begin bidding for them. They will continue to rise as long as farmers can earn more than textile workers. The long-run effect of the project, then, will be to raise the rent on rice farms, from €2,500 per year to €10,500 (since at the higher rent the incomes of rice farmers and textile workers will again be the same). Thus the irrigation project will increase the wealth of landowners but will have no long-run effect on the incomes of tenant farmers.

Exercise 7.5   Suppose the government imposes a rent freeze, so that existing farmers do not have to pay more to landlords, and cannot be evicted for not doing so. Can you explain why, after a few years, the World Bank is likely to find the rice still being grown by peasants earning a net €4,000 a year (assuming that nothing else has changed)?

The 'invisible hand' in the stock market

The world's great stock markets (London, Frankfurt, New York and Tokyo are the most important), in which dealers trade in shares (stock) and bonds (fixed interest securities, debt of governments and firms) are among the most competitive markets in the world. Unfortunately, as we shall see, public understanding of how the invisible hand works in these markets is often no better than the state legislator's understanding of how the rice market works.

Calculating the value of a share of stock

A share of stock in a company is a claim to a share of the current and future accounting profits of that company. Thus, if you own 1 per cent of the total number of shares of a company's stock, you effectively own 1 per cent of the company's annual accounting profit, both now and in the future. (We say 'effectively' because companies generally do not distribute their accounting profit to shareholders each year; many reinvest their earnings in the company's operations. Such reinvestment benefits the stockholder by enlarging the company and increasing its future accounting profit.) The price of a share of stock depends not only on a company's accounting profit, however, but also on the market rate of interest, as Example 7.7 illustrates.

Example 7.7 How much will a share of stock sell for?

Suppose we know with certainty that a company's accounting profit will be €1 million this year and every year. If the company has issued a total of 200,000 shares of stock, and the annual interest rate is 5 per cent, at what price will each share sell?

Because there are 200,000 shares of stock, each share entitles its owner to 1/200,000 of the company's annual accounting profit, or €5 per year. Owning this stock is like having a bank deposit that earns €5 per year in interest. To calculate the economic value of the stock, therefore, we need only ask how much an investor would need to deposit in the bank at 5 per cent interest to generate an annual interest payment of €5. The answer is €100, and that is the price that each share will command in the stock market.

Maths Box 7.1 A technical digression: how to calculate present values of future costs and benefits

Earnings to be received in the future are less valuable than earnings received today. Consider a company whose only accounting profit, €14,400, will occur exactly two years from now. At all other times its accounting profit will be exactly zero. How much is ownership of this company worth?

time value of money the fact that a given euro amount today is equivalent to a larger euro amount in the future, because the money can be invested in an interest-bearing account in the meantime; after T years: $PV - M/(1 - r)T$

present value for an annual interest rate r, the present value (PV) of a payment (M) to be received T years from now is the amount that would have to be deposited today at interest rate r to generate a balance of M

To answer this question, we need to employ the concept of the *time value of money* – the fact that money deposited in an interest-bearing account today will *grow in value over time*.

Our goal is to compute what economists call the *present value (PV)* of a €14,400 payment to be received in two years. We can think of this present value as the amount that would have to be deposited in an interest-bearing bank account today to generate a balance of €14,400 two years from today. Let PV denote present value and r the market rate of interest, measured as a fraction. (For example, an annual interest rate of 10 per cent would correspond to $r = 0.10$.) If we put €100 in an account today at 10 per cent annual interest, we will have €100(1.10) = €110 in the account after one year. If we leave €100 in the same account for two years, we will have €100(1.10)(1.10) = €100(1.10)^2 = €121.

More generally, if we put PV in the bank today at the interest rate r, we will have $PV(1 + r)$ one year from now and $PV(1 + r)^2$ two years from now. So to find the present value of a €14,400 payment to be received two years from now we simply solve the equation €14,400 $= PV(1 + r)^2$ and get $PV = $ €14,400$/(1 + r)^2$. If the interest rate is 20 per cent, then $PV = $ €14,400$/(1.2)^2 = $ €10,000. To verify this answer, note that €10,000 deposited at 20 per cent interest today would grow to €10,000 $(1 + 0.2) = $ €12,000 by the end of one year, and that amount left on deposit for a second year would grow to €12,000$(1 + 0.2) = $ €14,400.

More generally, when the interest rate is r, the present value of a payment M to be received T years from now is given by the equation

$$PV = M/(1 + r)^T$$

Exercise 7.6   What is the present value of a payment of €1,728 to be received three years from now if the annual interest rate is 20 per cent?

The efficient markets hypothesis

In practice, of course, no one knows with any certainty what a company's future profits will be. So the current price of a share will depend not on the actual amount of future profits, but on investors' estimates of them. These estimates incorporate information about current profits, prospects for the company's industry, the state of the economy, demographic trends and a host of other factors. As this information changes, investors' estimates of future profits change with it, along with the prices of a share of stock.

efficient markets hypothesis
the theory that the current price of stock in a company reflects all the relevant information about its current and future earnings prospects

How fast does new information affect the price of a stock? With blazing speed, according to the **efficient markets hypothesis**. This hypothesis states that the current price of any company's shares incorporates all available information relevant to the company's earnings. The plausibility of this theory is evident if we think for a moment about what might happen if it were false. Suppose, for example, that at 9.00 am on Monday, 14 October, some investors acquire new information to the effect that the company in Example 7.7 will realise accounting profits not of €1 million per year, but of €2 million. This information implies that the new equilibrium price for each share of its stock should be €200. Now suppose that the price were to remain at its current level (€100) for 24 hours before rising gradually to €200 over the next two weeks. If so, an investor privy to this information could double her wealth in two weeks without working hard, taking any risk, or even being lucky. All she would have to do is invest all her wealth in the stock at today's price of €100 per share.

We may safely assume that there is no shortage of investors who would be delighted to double their wealth without having to work hard or take risks. But in the case just described, they would have to buy shares of the stock within 24 hours of learning of the new profit projections. As eager investors rushed to buy the stock, its price would rise quickly, so that those who waited until the end of the day to buy would miss much of the opportunity for gain. To get the full advantage of the new information, they would have to make their purchases earlier in the day. As more and more investors rushed to buy shares, the window of opportunity would grow narrower and narrower. In the end, the duration of the opportunity to profit from the new information may be just a few minutes long.

In practice, of course, new information often takes time to interpret, and different investors may have different beliefs about exactly what it means. Early information may signal an impending change that is far from certain. As time passes, events may confirm or contradict the implications of the earlier information. The usual pattern is for information to emerge in bits and pieces, and for stock prices to adjust in small increments as each new bit of information emerges. But this does not mean that the price of a stock adjusts gradually to new information. Rather, it means that new information usually emerges gradually. And, as each piece of new information emerges, the market reacts almost instantly.

For example, in the United States in July 1996 a Florida jury awarded a lung cancer patient $750,000 in damages. The price of tobacco stocks plummeted roughly 20 per cent *within minutes*. The award broke a long series of legal precedents in which tobacco companies had not been held liable for the illnesses suffered by smokers. When the verdict was announced, no one knew whether it would be reversed on appeal or whether it would influence future verdicts in such cases. Yet investors who had been monitoring the case carefully knew instantly that massive new financial liabilities had become much more likely.

Despite such persuasive evidence in favour of the efficient markets hypothesis, many investors seem to believe that information about the next sure investment bonanza is as close as their stockbroker's latest newsletter. In most financial centres a large population of salespeople make a living telephoning potential investors to offer the latest tips on how to invest their money. The weekend quality newspapers across Europe have pages devoted to share analysis and advice on whether to buy, hold or sell various shares. The difficulty is that, according to the efficient markets hypothesis, by the time information reaches investors in this way, days, weeks or even months will have gone by, and the information will already have been incorporated into any stock prices for which it might have been relevant. By the time you've read in the newspaper about a share worth buying the reason for buying it will be history.

The *Wall Street Journal* publishes a feature in which a group of leading investment advisers predict which stocks will increase most in price during the coming months. The *Journal* then compares the forecasts with the performance of a randomly selected set of stocks. The usual finding is that the randomly selected portfolios perform little differently from those chosen by the 'experts'. Some of the experts do better than average, others worse. This pattern is consistent with the economist's theory that the invisible hand moves with unusual speed to eliminate profit opportunities in financial markets.

Economic naturalist 7.4 Why isn't a stock portfolio consisting of America's, or Britain's, or Germany's 'best-managed companies' a good investment?

Each year *Fortune* magazine asks executives at America's largest companies to list those US firms, excluding their own, that are managed most efficiently. Imagine that you see the results of this survey and immediately purchase 100 shares of stock in each of the top ten companies on the list. How well might you expect those stocks to perform relative to a randomly selected portfolio?

A stock is said to 'perform well' if its price rises more rapidly than the prices of other stocks. Changes in the price of a company's stock depend not on investors' current beliefs about the company's accounting profit, but on *changes in those beliefs*. Suppose, for the sake of argument, that the 'best-managed' companies had higher accounting profits than other companies at the time of the *Fortune* survey.

Because the prices you paid for their stocks would have reflected those higher earnings, there would be no reason to expect their prices to rise more rapidly than those of other stocks.

But won't the accounting profits of a well-managed company be likely to grow more rapidly than those of other companies? Perhaps; but even if so, beliefs to that effect would also be reflected in current stock prices. Indeed, the stocks of many software, biotechnology and internet commerce companies sell at high prices years before they ever post their first euro of accounting profit.

An understanding of the invisible hand theory might even lead us to question whether a 'well-managed' company will have higher accounting profit than other companies. After all, if an unusually competent manager were known to be the reason a company consistently posted a positive economic profit, other companies could be expected to bid for his services, causing his salary to rise. And the market for his services will not reach equilibrium until his salary has captured all the gains for which his talent is responsible.

We must stress that our point in Economic naturalist 7.4 is *not* that good management does not matter. Good management is obviously better than bad management, for it increases total economic surplus. The point is that the reward for good performance tends to be captured by those who provide that performance. And that is a good thing, in so far as it provides powerful incentives for everyone to perform well.

Economic naturalist 7.5 What happens when good management departs?

In late November 2004, the *Wall Street Journal* and the *Financial Times*, as well as a large number of European daily newspapers, carried the story that the three top executives at Aer Lingus, the Irish state-owned airline that had been tipped for privatisation, had tendered their resignations, to take effect in 2005. The apparent reason was an unwillingness on the part of the Irish government to proceed with the privatisation along the lines favoured by the management team. The team had turned the airline from a loss-making full-service airline into a highly profitable low-cost airline over three years, and the estimated stock market value of the company was about €600 million. By general consent, the effect of the departure of what was seen as one of Europe's most successful aviation management teams was to wipe €200 million (about one-third) off the sale value of the company. The irony is that the government's reluctance to proceed to privatise along the lines being suggested by the management was that it involved a management buy-out. For some reason, the government was not prepared to countenance the concept of a buy-out because it would have meant that the management would have bought the company and made money. For what other reason they would have contemplated buying it is not clear. The government's reluctance to see them making money cost the Irish taxpayer about €200 million, the capitalisation of the additional annual amount that the market reckoned that the team could have earned for the company.

By way of footnote, in March 2005, British Airways announced that it was appointing a new CEO to take up full duties later in the year. His name: Willie Walsh. His previous job: outgoing CEO of Aer Lingus.

RECAP The 'invisible hand' in action

Because individuals and firms are generally eager to improve their position, opportunities for gain seldom remain unexploited for long. Early adopters of *cost-saving innovations* enjoy temporary economic profits. But as additional firms adopt the innovations, the resulting downward supply shift causes price to fall. In the long run, economic profit returns to zero, and all cost savings are passed on to consumers.

The quest for advantage guides resources not only in perfectly competitive markets, but also in heavily regulated markets. Firms can almost always find ways to expand sales in markets in which the regulated price permits an economic profit or withdraw service from markets in which the regulated price results in an economic loss. An understanding of the invisible hand theory is also important for the design of anti-poverty programmes. An irrigation programme that makes land more productive, for example, will raise the incomes of tenant farmers only temporarily. In the long run, the gains from such projects tend to be captured as higher rents to landowners. The efficient markets hypothesis says that the price of a firm's stock at any moment reflects all available information that is relevant for predicting the firm's future earnings. This hypothesis identifies several common beliefs as false – among them that stocks in well-managed companies perform better than stocks in poorly managed ones and that ordinary investors can make large financial gains by trading stocks on the basis of information reported in the news media.

The distinction between an equilibrium and a social optimum

The Equilibrium, or No-Cash-on-the-Table, Principle tells us that when a market reaches equilibrium, no further opportunities for gain are available to individuals. This principle implies that the market prices of resources that people own will even-tually reflect their *economic value*. (As we shall see in later chapters, the same cannot be said of resources that are not owned by anyone, such as fish in international waters.)

The No-Cash-on-the-Table Principle is sometimes misunderstood to mean that there are *never* any valuable opportunities to exploit. For example, the story is told of two American economists on their way to lunch when they spot what appears to be a $100 bill lying on the pavement. When the younger economist stoops to pick up the bill, his older colleague restrains him, saying: 'That can't be a genuine $100 dollar bill.' 'Why not?' asks the younger colleague. 'If it were, someone would have picked it up by now,' the older economist replies.

Equilibrium

The No-Cash-on-the-Table Principle means not that there *never* are any unexploited opportunities, but that there are none when the market is *in equilibrium*. Occasionally a $100 bill does lie on the pavement, and the person who first spots it and picks it up gains a windfall. Likewise, when a company's earnings prospects improve, *somebody* must be the first to recognise the opportunity, and that person can make a lot of money by purchasing the stock quickly.

Still, the No-Cash-on-the-Table Principle is important. It tells us, in effect, that there are only three ways to earn a big payoff: to work especially hard; to have some unusual skill, talent or training; or simply to be lucky. The person who finds a big bank note on the pavement is lucky, as are many of the investors whose stocks perform better than average. Other investors whose stocks do well achieve their gains through hard work or special talent. For example, the legendary investor Warren Buffett, whose portfolio has grown in value at almost three times the stock market average for the past 40 years, spends long hours studying annual financial reports and has a remarkably keen eye for the telling detail. Thousands of others work just as hard yet fail to beat the market averages.

It is important to stress, however, that a market being in equilibrium implies only that no additional opportunities are available *to individuals*. It does not imply that the resulting allocation is necessarily best from the point of view of society as a whole.

Smart for one, dumb for all

Adam Smith's profound insight was that the individual pursuit of self-interest often promotes the broader interests of society. But unlike some of his modern disciples, Smith was under no illusion that this is *always* the case. Note, for example, Smith's elaboration on his description of the entrepreneur led by the invisible hand 'to promote an end which was no part of his intention':

> Nor is it *always* the worse for society that it was no part of it. By pursuing his own interest he *frequently* promotes that of society more effectively than when he really intends to promote it. (Smith, 1776, Book 4, Ch. 2)

As Smith was well aware, the individual pursuit of self-interest often does not coincide with society's interest. In Chapter 3 we cited activities that generate environmental pollution as an example of conflicting economic interests, noting that behaviour in those circumstances may be described as 'smart for one, dumb for all'. As Economic naturalist 7.6 suggests, extremely high levels of investment in earnings forecasts can also be 'smart for one, dumb for all'.

Economic naturalist 7.6 Are there 'too many' smart people working as corporate earnings forecasters?

Stock analysts use complex mathematical models to forecast corporate earnings. The more analysts invest in the development of these models, the more accurate the models become. Thus the analyst whose model produces a reliable forecast sooner than others can reap a windfall by buying stocks whose prices are about to rise. Given the speed with which stock prices respond to new information, however, the results of even the second-fastest forecasting model may come too late to be of much use. Individual stock analysts thus face a powerful incentive to invest more and more money in their models in the hope of generating the fastest forecast. Does this incentive result in the socially optimal level of investment in forecast models?

Beyond some point, increased speed of forecasting is of little benefit to society as a whole, whose interests suffer little when the price of a stock moves to its proper level a few hours more slowly. If *all* stock analysts spent less money on their forecasting models, *someone's* model would still produce the winning forecast, and the resources that might otherwise be devoted to fine-tuning the models could be put to more valued uses. Yet if any one individual spends less, he can be sure the winning forecast will not be his.

The 'invisible hand' went awry in the situation just described because the benefit of an investment to the individual who made it was larger than the benefit of that investment to society as a whole. In later chapters we shall discuss a broad class of investments with this property. In general, the efficacy of the invisible hand depends on the extent to which the individual costs and benefits of actions taken in the marketplace coincide with the respective costs and benefits of those actions to society. These exceptions notwithstanding, some of the most powerful forces at work in competitive markets clearly promote society's interests.

RECAP Equilibrium versus social optimum

A market in *equilibrium* is one in which no additional opportunities for gain remain available to individual buyers or sellers. The No-Cash-on-the-Table Principle describes powerful forces that help push markets towards equilibrium. But even if all markets are in equilibrium, the resulting allocation of resources need not be socially optimal. Equilibrium will not be socially optimal when the costs or benefits to individual participants in the market differ from those experienced by society as a whole.

Summary

■ *Accounting* profit is the difference between a firm's revenue and its explicit expenses. *Economic* profit is the difference between revenue and the sum of the firm's explicit and implicit costs. *Normal* profit is the opportunity cost of the resources supplied to a business by its owners.

■ The quest for economic profit is the 'invisible hand' that drives resource allocation in market economies. Markets in which businesses earn an economic profit tend to attract additional resources, whereas markets in which businesses experience an economic loss tend to lose resources. If new firms enter a market with economic profits, output rises, causing a reduction in the price of the product. Free entry means that prices will continue to fall until economic profits are eliminated. By contrast, the departure of firms from markets with economic losses causes output to contract, increasing the price of the product. Free exit will mean that prices will continue to rise until economic losses are eliminated. In the long run, market forces drive economic profits and losses towards zero.

■ As long as firms' cost curves and market demand curves reflect the full underlying costs and benefits to society of the production of a good or service, the quest for economic profit ensures (a) that existing supplies are allocated efficiently among individual buyers, and (b) that resources are allocated across markets in the most efficient way possible. In any allocation other than the one generated by the market, resources could be rearranged to benefit some people without harming others.

■ *Economic rent* is the portion of the payment for an input that exceeds the reservation price for that input. If a professional football player who is willing to play for as little as €100,000 per year is paid €15 million, he earns an economic rent of €14,900,000 per year. Whereas the invisible hand drives economic profit towards zero over the long run, economic rent can persist indefinitely, because replicating the services of players like Rio Ferdinand is impossible. Talented individuals who are responsible for the superior performance of a business will tend to capture the resulting financial gains as economic rents.

■ Applying the concept of Adam Smith's invisible hand helps explain why regulation of markets can have unintended and wasteful consequences. For instance, when regulation prevents firms from lowering prices to capture business from rivals, firms generally find other ways in which to compete. Thus, if airline regulators set passenger fares above cost, air carriers will try to capture additional business by offering extra amenities and more frequent service. Likewise, many anti-poverty programmes have been compromised by failure to consider how incentives change people's behaviour.

■ A share of stock in a company is a claim to a share of the current and future accounting profits of that company. The price of a share of stock depends not only on its accounting profits, but also on the market rate of interest, since the interest rate affects the present value of future costs and benefits. The total market value of the shares is the market estimate of the present value of the expected profits in the future. When the annual interest rate is r, the present value (PV) of a payment M to be received (or paid) T years from now is the amount that would have to be deposited in a bank account today at interest rate r to generate a balance of M after T years: $PV = M/(1 + r)^T$.

■ According to the efficient markets hypothesis, the market price of a stock incorporates all currently available information that is relevant to that company's future earnings. If this is not the case, people with superior information can consistently make profits in a more or less risk-free fashion.

■ The No-Cash-on-the-Table Principle implies that if someone owns a valuable resource, full information and efficient markets mean that the market price of that resource will fully reflect

▶
> its economic value. The implication of this principle is not that lucrative opportunities never exist, but rather that such opportunities cannot exist when markets are in equilibrium, and that prices will adjust to eliminate them.
>
> ■ The benefit of an investment to an individual sometimes differs from its benefit to society as a whole. Such conflicting incentives may give rise to behaviour that is smart for one but dumb for all. Despite such exceptions, the invisible hand of the market works remarkably well much of the time. One of the market system's most important contributions to social well-being is the pressure it creates to adopt cost-saving innovations. Competition among firms ensures that the resulting cost savings get passed along to consumers in the long run.

Review questions

1. Why do most cities now have more radios but fewer radio repair shops than they did in 1960?
2. How can a business owner who earns 10 million per year from his business credibly claim to earn zero economic profit?
3. Why do market forces drive economic profit but not economic rent towards zero?
4. Why did airlines that once were regulated by government generally fail to earn an economic profit, even on routes with relatively high fares?
5. Why is a payment of 10,000 to be received one year from now more valuable than a payment of 10,000 to be received two years from now?

connect Problems

1. Explain why the following statements are **true** or **false**.
   a. The economic maxim 'There's no cash on the table' means that there are never any unexploited economic opportunities.
   b. Firms in competitive environments make no accounting profit when the market is in long-run equilibrium.
   c. Firms that can introduce cost-saving innovations can make an economic profit in the short run.

2. Explain why new software firms that give away their software products at a short-run economic loss are nonetheless able to sell their stock at positive prices.

3. John Jones owns and manages a cafe whose annual revenue is €5,000. The annual expenses are as in the table below.

Expense	€
Labour	2,000
Food and drink	500
Electricity	100
Vehicle lease	150
Rent	500
Interest on loan for equipment	1,000

a. Calculate John's annual accounting profit.

b. John could earn €1,000 per year as a recycler of aluminium cans. However, he prefers to run the cafe. In fact, he would be willing to pay up to €275 per year to run the cafe rather than to recycle cans. Is the cafe making an economic profit? Should John stay in the business? Explain.

c. Suppose the cafe's revenues and expenses remain the same, but recyclers' earnings rise to €1,100 per year. Is the cafe still making an economic profit? Explain.

d. Suppose John had not had to get a €10,000 loan at an annual interest rate of 10 per cent to buy equipment, but instead had invested €10,000 of his own money in equipment. How would your answers to parts (a) and (b) change?

e. If John can earn €1,000 a year as a recycler, and he likes recycling just as well as running the cafe, how much additional revenue would the cafe have to collect each year to earn a normal profit?

4. A city has 200 advertising companies, 199 of which employ designers of normal ability at a salary of €100,000 a year. Paying this salary, each of the 199 firms makes a normal profit on €500,000 in revenue. However, the 200th company employs Janus Jacobs, an unusually talented designer. This company collects €1,000,000 in revenues because of Jacobs' talent.

a. How much will Jacobs earn? What proportion of his annual salary will be economic rent?

b. Why will the advertising company for which Jacobs works not be able to earn an economic profit?

5. Explain carefully why, in the absence of a patent, a technical innovation invented and pioneered in one tofu factory will cause the supply curve for the entire tofu industry to shift to the right. What will finally halt the rightward shift?

6. The government of the Republic of Self-Reliance has decided to limit imports of machine tools, to encourage development of locally made machine tools. To do so, the government offers to sell a small number of machine-tool import licences. To operate a machine-tool import business costs €30,000, excluding the cost of the import licence. An importer of machine tools can expect to earn €50,000 per year. If the annual interest rate is 10 per cent, for how much will the government be able to auction the import licences? Will the owner of a licence earn an economic profit?

7. Unskilled workers in a poor cotton-growing region must choose between working in a factory for €6,000 a year or being a tenant cotton farmer. One farmer can work a 120-hectare farm, which rents for €10,000 a year. Such farms yield €20,000 worth of cotton each year. The total non-labour cost of producing and marketing the cotton is €4,000 a year. A local politician whose motto is 'Working people come first' has promised that, if he is elected, his administration will fund a fertiliser, irrigation and marketing scheme that will triple cotton yields on tenant farms at no charge to tenant farmers.

a. If the market price of cotton would be unaffected by this policy and no new jobs would be created in the cotton-growing industry, how would the project affect the incomes of tenant farmers in the short run? In the long run?

b. Who would reap the benefit of the scheme in the long run? How much would they gain each year?

8. You have a friend who is a potter. He holds a permanent patent on an indestructible teacup whose sale generates €30,000 a year more revenue than his production costs. If the annual interest rate is 20 per cent, what is the market value of his patent?

9. You have an opportunity to buy an apple orchard that produces €25,000 per year in total revenue. To run the orchard, you would have to give up your current job, which pays €10,000 per year. If you would find both jobs equally satisfying, and the annual interest rate is 10 per cent, what is the highest price you would be willing to pay for the orchard?

10. Ludovico, a renowned chef, owns one of the 1,000 spaghetti restaurants in Sicily. Each restaurant serves 100 plates of spaghetti a night at €5 per plate. Ludovico knows he can develop a new sauce at the same cost as the current sauce, which would be so tasty that all 100,000 spaghetti eaters would buy his spaghetti at €10 per plate. There are two problems: developing the new sauce would require some experimental cost; and the other spaghetti producers could figure out the recipe after one day.

    a. What is the highest experimental cost Ludovico would be willing to incur?

    b. How would your answer change if Ludovico could enforce a year-long patent on her new sauce? (Assume that the interest rate is zero.)

References

Iacopetta, M. (2004) 'Dissemination of technology in planned and market economies', *Contributions to Macroeconomics*, 4(1).

Smith, A. (1776) *An Enquiry into the Nature and Causes of the Wealth of Nations*.

Part 3
Market Imperfections (1): Market Power

We now move away from the world implicitly, and to a lesser extent explicitly, assumed by Adam Smith. In that world, exchange is frictionless, parties to exchanges are fully informed and no one has significant market power. This means investigating what happens when people and firms interact in markets plagued by a variety of imperfections. Not surprisingly, the invisible hand that served society so well in the perfectly competitive world often goes astray in this new environment.

Our focus in Chapter 8 will be on how markets served by only one or a small number of firms differ from those served by perfectly competitive firms. We shall see that, although monopolies often escape the pressures that constrain the profits of their perfectly competitive counterparts, the two types of firm also have many important similarities.

In Chapter 9 we lay the foundation for understanding something of how firms operate in markets where there is neither monopoly nor a very large number of sellers. We do this by introducing the elements of decision making in circumstances where one person's decision affects the behaviour of others. (In perfect or monopolistic competition we look at situations where a firm can make a decision based on the assumption that it will not affect what other firms do.) The basic tool of analysis used here is what has become known as 'game theory'. In this chapter we use game theory in a variety of circumstances to show how it helps explain how decisions are made, and the consequences of those decisions, when the decision makers have to acknowledge interdependence affecting making choices.

In Chapter 10 we look at how firms make decisions in small-number markets where interdependence is the rule of the day. We develop the idea of a firm's reaction, or best response, function as a mechanism to explain what happens in such markets.

Part 3

Market Imperfections (1): Market Power

8

Imperfect Competition and the Consequences of Market Power

Parents, faced with demands from their offspring that they be supplied with the latest fashion trainers, produced by Nike, New Balance, or whatever is in fashion, usually try (and fail) to persuade the youngsters that there is no real difference between the trainers they want and much less expensive brands. The difference in price between the high-fashion brands and the more generic products can hardly be accounted for by differences in costs of production. It is reasonable to assume that the higher-priced fashion brands yield higher profits to the producers than the other brands. This, of course, even if explained, cuts little ice with the average teenager.

As an economist, however, under these circumstances you might expect that producers of training shoes would flood the market with imitations of the high-fashion brands. There is, after all, 'cash on the table'. Indeed, anyone who has travelled in the Far East or North Africa will recount bargain purchases of trainers that are produced locally and are indistinguishable from the branded products sold in the West.

The reason this producer reaction is uncommon in the West is because the producers of Nike and similar products have a *legally enforceable monopoly* on their brands – and, frequently, on the designs of their products. As a result, they can restrict output, safe from competition from replicas, and obtain a higher price for their products based on fashion. Sociologists refer to such goods as 'positional' goods, meaning that they are bought in order to demonstrate *status* or *wealth*.

This particular legal ability to prevent imitations being produced is just one way in which producers of goods can *differentiate* their offerings from those of rivals. By doing so, they put themselves in a position to become **price setters** rather than price takers. They still have to compete for sales with producers of other variants of the good in question. These will offer their own particular brands, or may decide to compete on price by selling more or less generic products.

price setter a firm with at least some latitude to set its own price

imperfectly competitive firms firms that differentiate their products from those of their rivals, with whom they compete

When producers can, for whatever reason, differentiate their products from those of their rivals economists refer to the market concerned as being *imperfectly competitive*, and the firms as being **imperfectly competitive firms**. The key to this type of market is that the output of any producer is not perfectly substitutable for that of another producer. Hence, the purchaser of a unit of the product is not indifferent as to the identity of the producer. If this were not the case, the producer would be a price taker, since if he tried to increase his price, people would simply buy someone else's product.

Our focus in this chapter will be on the ways in which markets served by imperfectly competitive firms differ from those served by perfectly competitive firms. One salient difference is the imperfectly competitive firm's ability, under certain circumstances, to charge more than its cost of production. Nike can sell its latest trainers for €150 a pair (where production costs are perhaps €10). Nike may be the only permitted producer of Nike trainers but, given the intensity of competition from other brands and from generic trainers, its pricing freedom is far from absolute. We shall also see how some imperfectly competitive firms manage to earn an economic profit, even in the long run, and even without government protections such as copyright. And we shall explore why Adam Smith's invisible hand is less in evidence in a world served by imperfectly competitive firms.

Imperfect competition

The concept of a perfectly competitive market should be thought of as an extreme version of competition, in a sense an ideal; the actual markets we encounter in everyday life differ from the ideal in varying degrees. In a classification scheme whose arbitrariness most economists would feel hard-pressed to defend, economics texts usually distinguish among three types of imperfectly competitive market structure.

Different forms of imperfect competition

pure monopoly the only supplier of a unique product with no close substitutes

Pure monopoly, a market in which a single firm is the lone seller of a unique product, is the polar opposite to perfect competition. A real-life example of a full-blown monopolist is not all that easy to find, unless the monopoly is created by law (e.g. a postal monopoly). In the 1980s, anyone in England or Wales who wanted to use electricity had to buy the power supplied by Britain's Central Electricity Generating Board (CEGB). In France there is still only one serious supplier of electricity, Electricité de France.

oligopolist a firm that produces a product for which only a few rival firms produce close substitutes

monopolistically competitive firm one of a large number of firms that produce slightly differentiated products that are reasonably close substitutes for one another

Somewhat closer to the perfectly competitive ideal is *oligopoly*, the market structure in which only a few firms (**oligopolists**) sell a given product. Examples include the market for mobile (cellular) phone services, in which firms like Vodafone, O$_2$ and others are the principal providers. Although there are thousands of retail outlets selling grocery products in most countries, in general the large supermarket chains, of which there are in any country only a few, are accepted as being in a separate market from small convenience stores. As such, they form an oligopoly. An oligopoly, from the Greek, *oligos*, meaning few, is a market in which sales are in the hands of a small number of relatively large suppliers. Closer still to perfect competition is the industry structure known as *monopolistic competition*, which typically consists of a relatively large number of firms that sell the same product with slight differentiations. Examples of **monopolistically competitive firms** include local petrol (gasoline) stations, which differ not so much in what they sell as in their physical locations, or medical services (where these are sold to users).

The essential characteristic that differentiates imperfectly competitive firms from perfectly competitive firms is the same in each of the three cases. So, for convenience, we shall use the term *monopolist* to refer to the price-setting ability of any of the three types of imperfectly competitive firms.

The essential difference between perfectly and imperfectly competitive firms

In advanced economics courses, lecturers generally devote much attention to the analysis of subtle differences in the behaviour of different types of imperfectly competitive firms. Far more important for our purposes, however, will be to focus on the single, common feature that differentiates all imperfectly competitive firms from their perfectly competitive counterparts, namely that whereas the perfectly competitive firm faces a perfectly elastic demand curve for its product, *the imperfectly competitive firm faces a downward-sloping demand curve*.

In the perfectly competitive industry, the supply and demand curves intersect to determine an equilibrium market price. At that price, the perfectly competitive firm can sell as many units as it wishes. It has no incentive to charge more than the market price, because it won't sell anything if it does so. Nor does it have any incentive to charge less than the market price, because it can sell as many units as it wants to at the market price. The perfectly competitive firm's demand curve is thus a horizontal line at the market price, as we saw in Chapter 5.

By contrast, if a local petrol retailer or convenience store – an imperfect competitor – charges a little more than its rivals for some or all of what it sells, some of its customers may desert it. But others will remain, perhaps because they are willing to pay a little extra to continue shopping at their most convenient location. An imperfectly competitive firm thus faces a negatively sloped demand curve. Figure 8.1 summarises this contrast between the demand curves facing perfectly competitive and imperfectly competitive firms.

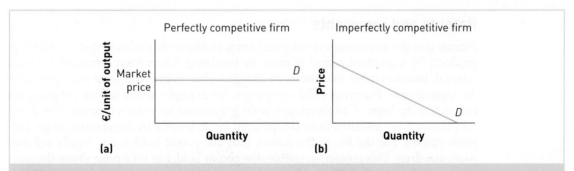

Figure 8.1 The Demand Curves Facing Perfectly and Imperfectly Competitive Firms. (a) The demand curve confronting a perfectly competitive firm is perfectly elastic at the market price. (b) The demand curve confronting an imperfectly competitive firm is downward-sloping.

RECAP Imperfect competition

Perfect competition is an ideal case, at best only approximated in actual industries. Economists study three other types of market structure that differ in varying degrees from perfect competition: *monopoly*, an industry with only one seller of a unique product; *oligopoly*, an industry with only a few sellers; and *monopolistic competition*, an industry in which many firms sell products that are close, but imperfect, substitutes for one another. The demand curve confronting a perfectly competitive firm is perfectly elastic at the market price, while the demand curve confronting an imperfectly competitive firm is downward-sloping.

Five sources of market power

market power a firm's ability to raise the price of a good without losing all its sales

If firms face a downward-sloping demand curve for what they produce they are said to enjoy **market power**. By this is meant that they can select a price at which they offer products to the market, or they can *set the prices* of their products. A common misconception is that a firm with market power can sell any quantity at any price it wishes. It cannot: all it can do is pick a price–quantity combination along its demand curve. If the firm chooses to raise its price, it must settle for reduced sales.

Why do some firms have market power while others do not? Since market power often carries with it the ability to charge a price above the cost of production, such power tends to arise from factors that limit competition. In practice, the following five factors often confer such power: exclusive control over important inputs; patents and copyrights; government licences or franchises; economies of scale; and network economies.

Exclusive control over important inputs

If a single firm controls an input *essential to the production* of a given product, that firm will have market power. For example, to the extent that some commercial tenants are willing to pay a premium for office space in the tallest building in the United States (as of 2003), the Sears Tower, the owner of that building has market power.

Patents and copyrights

Patents give the inventors or developers of new products the exclusive right to sell those products for a specified period of time. By insulating sellers from competition for an interval, patents enable innovators to charge higher prices to recoup their product's *development costs*. Pharmaceutical companies, for example, spend millions of euros on research in the hope of discovering new drug therapies for serious illnesses. The drugs they discover are insulated from competition for an interval by the granting of government patents. For the life of the patent, only the patent holder may legally sell that particular drug. This protection enables the patent holder to set a price above the marginal cost of production. The profits on the sales of the drug are expected to be sufficient (at least) to recoup the cost of the research on the drug. In the same way, copyrights protect the authors of movies, software, music, books and other published works.

Government licences or franchises

In the United States the Yosemite Concession Services Corporation has an exclusive licence from the US federal government to run the lodging and food and drink concession operations at Yosemite National Park in California. One of the government's goals in granting this monopoly was to preserve the wilderness character of the area to the greatest degree possible. And, indeed, the inns and cabins offered by the Yosemite Concession Services Company blend nicely with the valley's scenery. No garish neon signs mar the National Park as they do in places where rival firms compete for tourists' purchases of their services.

A similar rationale applies to the granting of postal service monopoly franchises to (usually state-owned) operators. The goal in this case is the provision of a single-price universal postal delivery service. This, it is felt, would not be possible if the universal service operator faced competition in lucrative urban markets, the profits from which are said to be necessary to cross-subsidise loss-making operations in other parts of the country.

Economies of scale (natural monopolies)

constant returns to scale a production process is said to have constant returns to scale if, when all inputs are changed by a given proportion, output changes by the same proportion

increasing returns to scale a production process is said to have increasing returns to scale if, when all inputs are changed by a given proportion, output changes by more than that proportion; also called **economies of scale**

natural monopoly a monopoly that results from economies of scale

When a firm doubles all its factors of production, what happens to its output? If output exactly doubles, the firm's production process is said to exhibit **constant returns to scale**. If output more than doubles, the production process is said to exhibit **increasing returns to scale**, or **economies of scale**. When production is subject to economies of scale, the average cost of production declines as the number of units produced increases. For example, in the generation of electricity, the use of larger generators lowers the unit cost of production. The markets for such products tend to be served by a single seller, or perhaps only a few sellers, because having a large number of sellers would result in significantly higher costs. Hence, competition between them results in a smaller number of surviving firms. A monopoly that results from economies of scale is called a **natural monopoly**.

A classic example of the impact of scale economies is the evolution of the structure of the passenger and military aircraft markets. In this case, the economies arise not just from the production process but from the enormous costs of designing and marketing new aircraft. In the United Kingdom, the main aircraft-producing country in Europe after the Second World War, there were in the early 1950s at least ten major firms producing military and commercial fixed-wing aircraft. By the early 1970s the industry had just two firms, resulting from mergers and exits: BAC and Hawker Siddeley. By the beginning of the twenty-first century no UK independent producer of large aircraft survived, and virtually the entire British industry (one firm, BAE Systems plc) had become part of a small number of larger multinational operations, being involved with EADS (the producer of Airbus) and Lockheed-Martin (the US producer of the next generation of STOVL strike fighters to replace the Harrier in service in the United States, United Kingdom and other countries). For large commercial passenger planes, there were two European and three North American suppliers as recently as 1980. In 2008 only two remained, Airbus and Boeing, all the others having either merged or exited the industry.

Network economies

Many products become much more valuable to us as more people use them. In the 1980s a 'format war' erupted between Sony's Betamax system for tape-based recording of videos and the Philips/JVC-promoted VHS system. VHS, arguably a technically less advanced system, won simply because it managed through a lower retail price to gain a slight sales edge on the initial version of Betamax, which could not record programmes longer than one hour. Although Betamax later corrected this deficiency, the VHS lead proved insuperable, and this was reflected in the supply of material to rental agencies by the programme providers. This encouraged equipment purchasers to buy VHS format recorders. Once the fraction of consumers owning VHS passed a critical threshold, the reasons for choosing it became compelling – variety and availability of tape rental, access to repair facilities, the capability to exchange tapes with friends, and so on. Between 2005 and 2007 a similar 'format war' occurred between the Blu-ray (Sony) and HD-DVD (Toshiba) systems to replace standard DVD recordings. HD-DVD recordings and equipment cost less, but Blu-ray had a higher storage potential. Lowering the price was not a successful strategy for Toshiba when Sony adopted the strategy of persuading programme providers (major studios) and retailers (e.g. Wal-Mart in the USA) to supply Blu-ray technology product to end users. In 2007 sales of Blu-ray discs exceeded HD-DVD by about 200 per cent. The moving finger was writing. In February 2008, Toshiba announced it was pulling out of developing HD-DVD. The film industry switched away from producing HD-DVD format releases and the format war was over.

The point is that one user's utility from purchasing a system depended on other users' purchases, and on compatibility with suppliers of complementary products. This is what characterises 'network economies': the value of owning a telephone depends on the number of people who purchase a compatible telephone.

A similar network economy helped to account for the dominant position of Microsoft's Windows (and now Vista) operating system, currently installed in more than 90 per cent of all personal computers. Because Microsoft's initial sales advantage gave software developers a strong incentive to write for the Windows format, the inventory of available software in the Windows format is now vastly larger than that for any competing operating system. This 'software gap' and the desire to achieve compatibility for file-sharing gave people a good reason for choosing Windows, even if, as in the case of many Apple Macintosh users, they believed a competing system was otherwise superior.

RECAP Five sources of market power

A firm's power to raise its price without losing its entire market stems from exclusive control of important inputs, patents and copyrights, government licences, economies of scale or network economies. By far the most important and enduring of these are *economies of scale* and *network economies*.

Economies of scale and the importance of fixed costs

As we saw in Chapter 5, variable costs are those that vary with the level of output produced, while fixed costs are independent of output. Strictly speaking, there are no fixed costs in the long run, because all inputs can be varied. But, as a practical matter, start-up costs often loom large for the duration of a product's useful life. Most of the costs involved in the production of computer software, for example, are fixed costs of this sort, one-time costs incurred in writing and testing the software. Once those tasks are done, additional copies of the software can be produced at a very low marginal cost. A good such as software, whose production entails large fixed costs and low variable costs, will be subject to significant economies of scale. Because, by definition, fixed costs don't increase as output increases, the average total cost of production for such goods will decline sharply as output increases.

To illustrate, consider a production process for which total cost is given by the equation $TC = F + MQ$, where F is fixed cost, M is marginal cost (assumed constant in this illustration) and Q is the level of output produced. For the production process with this simple total cost function, variable cost is simply MQ, the product of marginal cost and quantity. Average total cost, TC/Q, is equal to $(F/Q) + M$. As Q increases, average cost declines steadily, because the fixed costs are spread out over more and more units of output.

Figure 8.2 shows the total production cost (panel (a)) and average total cost (panel (b)) for a firm with the total cost curve $TC = F + MQ$ and the corresponding average total cost curve $ATC = (F/Q) + M$. The average total cost curve (panel (b)) shows the decline in per-unit cost as output grows. Though average total cost is always higher than marginal cost for this firm, the difference between the two diminishes as output grows. At extremely high levels of output, average total cost becomes very close to marginal cost (M). Because the firm is spreading out its fixed cost over an extremely large volume of output, the fixed cost per unit becomes almost insignificant.

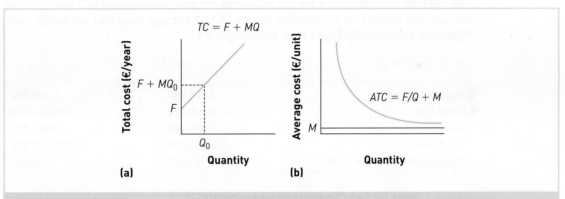

Figure 8.2 Total and Average Total Costs for a Production Process with Economies of Scale. For a firm whose total cost curve of producing Q units of output per year is $TC = F + MQ$, total cost (a) rises at a constant rate as output grows, while average total cost (b) declines. Average total cost is always higher than marginal cost for this firm, but the difference becomes less significant at high output levels.

As Examples 8.1 and 8.2 illustrate, the importance of economies of scale depends on how large *fixed cost* is in relation to *marginal cost*.

Example 8.1 Two video game producers, Nintendo and PlayStation, each have fixed costs of €200,000 and marginal costs of €0.80 per game. If Nintendo produces 1 million units per year and PlayStation produces 1.2 million, how much lower will PlayStation's average total production cost be?

Table 8.1 summarises the relevant cost categories for the two firms. Note in the bottom row that PlayStation enjoys only a 3 cent average cost advantage over Nintendo. Even though Nintendo produces 20 per cent fewer copies of its video game than PlayStation, it does not suffer a significant cost disadvantage because fixed cost is a relatively small part of total production cost.

Cost	Nintendo	PlayStation
Annual production	1,000,000	1,200,000
Fixed cost	€200,000	€200,000
Variable cost	€800,000	€960,000
Total cost	€1,000,000	€1,160,000
Average total cost per game	€1.00	€0.97

Table 8.1 **Costs for Two Computer Game Producers (1)**

But note how the picture changes when fixed cost looms large relative to marginal cost.

Example 8.2 Two video game producers, Nintendo and PlayStation, each have fixed costs of €10,000,000 and marginal costs of €0.20 per video game. If Nintendo produces 1 million units per year and PlayStation produces 1.2 million, how much lower will PlayStation's average total cost be?

The relevant cost categories for the two firms are now summarised in Table 8.2. The bottom row shows that PlayStation enjoys a €1.67 average total cost advantage over Nintendo, substantially larger than in Example 8.1.

Cost	Nintendo	PlayStation
Annual production	1,000,000	1,200,000
Fixed cost	€10,000,000	€10,000,000
Variable cost	€200,000	€240,000
Total cost	€10,200,000	€10,240,000
Average total cost per game	€10.20	€8.53

Table 8.2 **Costs for Two Computer Game Producers (2)**

If the video games the two firms produce are essentially similar, the fact that PlayStation can charge significantly lower prices and still cover its costs should enable it to attract customers away from Nintendo. As more and more of the market goes to PlayStation, its cost advantage will become self-reinforcing. Table 8.3 shows how a shift of 500,000 units from Nintendo to PlayStation would cause Nintendo's average total cost to rise to €20.20 per unit, while PlayStation's average total cost would fall to €6.08 per unit. The fact that a firm could not long survive at such a severe disadvantage explains why the video game market is served now by only a small number of firms.

Cost	Nintendo	PlayStation
Annual production	500,000	1,700,000
Fixed cost	€10,000,000	€10,000,000
Variable cost	€100,000	€340,000
Total cost	€10,100,000	€10,340,000
Average total cost per game	€20.20	€6.08

Table 8.3 **Costs for Two Computer Game Producers (3)**

Exercise 8.1   How big will PlayStation's unit cost advantage be if it sells 2,000,000 units per year, while Nintendo sells only 300,000?

An important worldwide economic trend since the 1970s is that an increasing share of the value embodied in the goods and services we buy stems from *fixed investment in R&D*. For example, in 1984 some 80 per cent of the cost of a computer was in its hardware; the remaining 20 per cent was in its software. With the cost of memory and computing power roughly halving in real terms every couple of years, by 1999 these proportions were reversed. Hardware is cheap ... but software, which is to an even greater degree than hardware the result of fixed investment in R&D, now accounts for most of the cost of a computer. Fixed costs account for about 85 per cent of total costs in the computer software industry, whose products are included in a growing share of ordinary manufactured goods.

Economic naturalist 8.1 Why does Intel sell the overwhelming majority of all microprocessors used in personal computers?

Producing memory and computer processing unit (CPU) chips is relatively cheap. Most of us are blissfully unaware of what is going on inside the computer, so we rationally shouldn't care who makes the bits as long as they work. Under these circumstances it might seem hard to understand why Intel sells about 80 per cent of the microprocessors in PCs. Part of the answer lies in branding and reputation, but that can't be the whole explanation. Knowledgeable purchasers might be expected to prefer, say, an equally powerful chip made by AMD if there is a price difference, while price-conscious, low-intensity home users would also be expected to look for the best value for money.

Intel may be thought of as an innovating chip producer: it is first to market with newer, better chips, the product of its heavy fixed cost investment in R&D. It sells these initially at high prices to high-value users, those with a particular need for more powerful chips. It also sells them at these prices to people who want the best anyway. Then, as (a) other players start to produce competing chips (possibly based on reverse engineering) and as (b) the high-value users have been serviced, it lowers its prices. This gives it a first-mover advantage, based on its R&D, that sustains its market share – which, of course, is also a reflection of its heavy investment (another fixed cost) in brand advertising. If industry sources are correct in forecasting that R&D investment in increasing computing power by improving chip performance is rapidly running into diminishing returns, we would expect to see Intel's share of the chip market start to decline to the extent that it is not based simply on branding.

RECAP Economies of scale and the importance of fixed costs

Research, design, engineering and other fixed costs account for an increasingly large share of all costs required to bring products successfully to market. For products with large fixed costs, marginal cost is lower, often substantially, than average total cost, and average total cost declines, often sharply, as output grows. This cost pattern explains why many industries are dominated by either a *single firm* or a *small number of firms*.

Profit-maximisation for the monopolist

Regardless of whether a firm is a price taker or a price setter, economists assume that its basic goal is to *maximise its profit*. They also assume that, in either case, the operational decision confronting each firm is to select the output level that results in the greatest possible difference between total revenue and total cost. But there are some important differences in how the two types of firm carry out this decision.

For both the perfectly competitive firm and the monopolist, the marginal benefit of expanding output is the additional revenue the firm will receive if it sells one additional unit of output. In both cases, this marginal benefit is called

marginal revenue the change in a firm's total revenue that results from a one-unit change in output

the firm's **marginal revenue**. For the perfectly competitive firm, marginal revenue is exactly equal to the market price of the product. The position for a price-setting firm is different. This is because the amount sold affects the price at which all units are sold.

Marginal revenue for the monopolist

The logic of profit-maximisation is precisely the same for the monopolist as for the perfectly competitive firm. In both cases, the firm keeps expanding output as long as the benefit of doing so exceeds the cost. The calculation of marginal cost is also precisely the same for the monopolist as for the perfectly competitive firm. The only significant difference between the two cases concerns the calculation of *marginal revenue*.

Marginal revenue for a competitive firm is simply the market price. If that price is €6, then the marginal benefit of selling an extra unit is exactly €6. To a monopolist, in contrast, the marginal benefit of selling an additional unit is *strictly less than the market price*. The reason is that while the perfectly competitive firm can sell as many units as it wishes at the market price, the monopolist can sell an additional unit only if it cuts the price – and it must do so not just for the additional unit but for the units it is *currently selling*.

Suppose, for example, that a monopolist with the demand curve shown in Fig. 8.3 is currently selling 2 units of output at a price of €6 per unit. What would be its marginal revenue from selling an additional unit?

This monopolist's total revenue from the sale of 2 units per week is (€6 per unit) (2 units per week) = €12 per week. Its total revenue from the sale of 3 units per week would be €15 per week. The difference – €3 per week – is the marginal revenue from the sale of the third unit each week. Note that this amount is not only smaller than the original price (€6) but smaller than the new price (€5) as well.

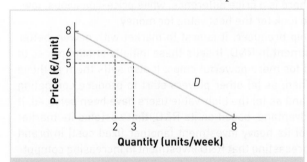

Figure 8.3 The Monopolist's Benefit from Selling an Additional Unit. The monopolist shown receives €12 per week in total revenue by selling 2 units per week at a price of €6 each. This monopolist could earn €15 per week by selling 3 units per week at a price of €5 each. In that case, the benefit from selling the third unit would be €15 – €12 = €3, less than its selling price of €5.

Exercise 8.2   Calculate marginal revenue for the monopolist in Fig. 8.3 as it expands output from 3 to 4 units per week, and then from 4 to 5 units per week.

For the monopolist whose demand curve is shown in Fig. 8.3, a sequence of increases in output – from 2 to 3, from 3 to 4 and from 4 to 5 – will yield marginal revenue of €3, €1 and −€1, respectively. We can display these results in tabular form, as in Table 8.4

Note that in Table 8.4 the marginal revenue values are displayed between the two quantity figures to which they correspond. For example, when the firm expanded its output from 2 units per week to 3, its marginal revenue was €3 per unit. Strictly speaking, this marginal revenue corresponds to neither quantity but to the *movement between* those quantities, hence its placement in Table 8.4. Likewise, in moving from 3 to 4 units per week, the firm earned marginal revenue of €1 per unit so that figure is placed midway between the quantities of 3 and 4 in Table 8.4, and so on.

Quantity	Marginal revenue
2	
3	3
4	1
5	−1

Table 8.4 **Marginal Revenue for a Monopolist (€ per unit)**

To graph marginal revenue as a function of quantity, we plot the marginal revenue for the movement from 2 to 3 units of output per week (€3) at a quantity value of 2.5, because 2.5 lies midway between 2 and 3. Similarly, we would plot the marginal revenue for the movement from 3 to 4 units per week (€1) at a quantity of 3.5 units per week, and the marginal revenue for the movement from 4 to 5 units per week (€1) at a quantity of 4.5. The resulting marginal revenue curve, MR, is shown in Fig. 8.4.

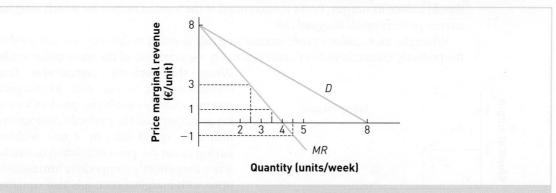

Figure 8.4 Marginal Revenue in Graphical Form. Because a monopolist must cut price to sell an extra unit, not only for the extra unit sold but also for all existing units, marginal revenue from the sale of the extra unit is less than its selling price.

More generally, consider a monopolist with a straight-line demand curve whose vertical intercept is a and whose horizontal intercept is Q_0, as shown in Fig. 8.5. This monopolist's marginal revenue curve will also have a vertical intercept of a, and it will be twice as steep as the demand curve. Thus its horizontal intercept will be not Q_0, but $Q_0/2$, as shown in Fig. 8.5.

Marginal revenue curves can also be expressed algebraically. If the formula for the monopolist's demand curve is $P = a - bQ$, then the formula for its marginal revenue curve will be $MR = a - 2bQ$. This will be demonstrated in the section on the rigorous

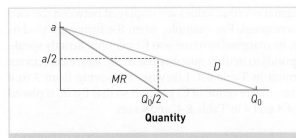

Figure 8.5 The Marginal Revenue Curve for a Monopolist with a Straight-line Demand Curve.
For a monopolist with the demand curve shown, the corresponding marginal revenue curve has the same vertical intercept as the demand curve, and a horizontal intercept only half as large as that of the demand curve.

derivation of the rule for profit-maximisation below. If you have done calculus, this relationship is easy to derive,[1] but even without calculus you can verify it by working through a few numerical examples. First translate the formula for the demand curve into a diagram, and then construct the corresponding marginal revenue curve graphically. Reading from the graph, write the formula for that marginal revenue curve.

The monopolist's profit-maximising decision rule

Having derived the monopolist's marginal revenue curve, we are now in a position to describe how the monopolist chooses the output level that maximises profit. As in the case of the perfectly competitive firm, the Cost–Benefit Principle says that the monopolist should continue to expand output as long as the gain from doing so exceeds the cost. At the current level of output, the benefit from expanding output is the marginal revenue value that corresponds to that output level. The cost of expanding output is the marginal cost at that level of output. Whenever marginal revenue exceeds marginal cost, the firm should expand.

Conversely, whenever marginal revenue falls short of marginal cost, the firm should reduce its output. Profit is maximised at the level of output for which *marginal revenue precisely equals marginal cost*.

When the monopolist's profit-maximising rule is stated in this way, we can see that the perfectly competitive firm's rule is actually a special case of the monopolist's rule. When the perfectly competitive firm expands output by one unit, its marginal revenue exactly equals the product's market price (because the perfectly competitive firm can expand sales by a unit without having to cut the price of existing units). So when the perfectly competitive firm equates price with marginal cost, it is also equating marginal revenue with marginal cost.

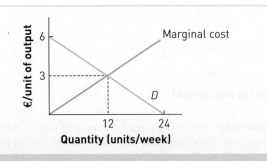

Figure 8.6 The Demand and Marginal Cost Curves for a Monopolist. At the current output level of 12 units per week, price equals marginal cost. Since the monopolist's price is always greater than marginal revenue, marginal revenue must be less than marginal cost, which means this monopolist should produce less.

Example 8.3 What is the monopolist's profit-maximising output level?

Consider a monopolist with the demand and marginal cost curves shown in Fig. 8.6. If this firm is currently producing 12 units per week, should it expand or contract production? What is the profit-maximising level of output?

---

1 Total revenue is average revenue (price) multiplied by Q. $TR = aQ - bQ^2$. Marginal revenue is dTR/dQ: $MR = a - 2bQ$.

In Figure 8.7, we begin by constructing the marginal revenue curve that corresponds to the monopolist's demand curve. It has the same vertical intercept as the demand curve, and its horizontal intercept is half as large. Note that the monopolist's marginal revenue at 12 units per week is zero, which is clearly less than its marginal cost of €3 per unit. This monopolist will therefore earn a higher profit by contracting production until marginal revenue equals marginal cost, which occurs at an output level of 8 units per week. At this profit-maximising output level the firm will charge €4 per unit, the price that corresponds to 8 units per week on the demand curve.

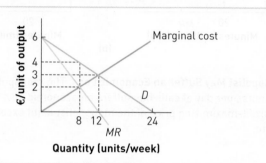

Figure 8.7 The Monopolist's Profit-maximising Output Level. This monopolist maximises profit by selling 8 units per week, the output level at which marginal revenue equals marginal cost. The profit-maximising price is €4 per unit, the price that corresponds to the profit-maximising quantity on the demand curve.

Exercise 8.3   Find the profit-maximising price and level of output for a monopolist with the demand curve $P = 12 - Q$ and the marginal cost curve $MC = 2Q$, where P is the price of the product in euros per unit and Q is output in units per week.

Being a monopolist does not guarantee an economic profit

The fact that the profit-maximising price for a monopolist will always be greater than marginal cost provides no assurance that the monopolist will earn an economic profit. Consider, for example, the long-distance telephone service provider whose demand, marginal revenue, marginal cost and average total cost curves are shown in Fig. 8.8(a). This monopolist maximises its daily profit by selling 20 million minutes per day of calls at a price of €0.10 per minute. At that quantity, $MR = MC$, yet price is €0.02 per minute less than the company's average total cost of €0.12 per minute. As a result, the company sustains an economic loss of €0.02 per minute on all calls provided, or a total loss of (€0.02 per minute)(20,000,000 minutes per day) = €400,000 per day.

The monopolist in Fig. 8.8(a) suffered a loss because its profit-maximising price was lower than its ATC. If the monopolist's profit-maximising price exceeds its average total cost, however, the company will of course earn an economic profit. Consider, for example, the long-distance provider shown in Fig. 8.8(b). This firm has the same demand, marginal revenue and marginal cost curves as the firm shown in Fig. 8.8(a). But because the firm in panel (b) has lower fixed costs, its ATC curve is lower at every level of output than the ATC curve in (a). At the profit-maximising price of €0.10 per minute, the firm in Fig. 8.8(b) earns an economic profit of €0.02 per minute, for a total economic profit of €400,000 per day.

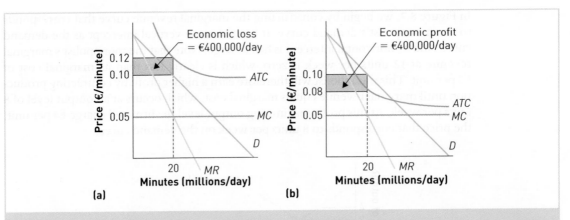

Figure 8.8 Even a Monopolist May Suffer an Economic Loss. The monopolist in (a) maximises its profit by selling 20 million minutes per day of calls but suffers an economic loss of €400,000 per day in the process. Because the profit-maximising price of the monopolist in (b) exceeds *ATC*, this monopolist earns an economic profit.

Maths Box 8.1 Marginal revenue, marginal cost and profit maximisation when a firm has market power: the mathematical approach

This formal derivation of the *MC* = *MR* rule for profit maximisation may be skipped without any loss of continuity.

A monopoly is simply an extreme case of market power. Market power means that the firm can sell more … if it is prepared to let price drop. It can raise price, but will expect to sell less. Consequently, when it sells more, the change in total revenue is not simply the extra sales multiplied by the price achieved for those sales, but must include the change in revenue arising from the previous volume of sales that are now being sold at a lower price, too. This can be expressed formally as follows.

The monopoly (market power) case

Market power (in the limiting case, monopoly) means that the price per unit the firm receives for the amount it puts on the market is a function of the amount being sold:

$$p = p(q)$$

in contrast with perfect competition, where the firm perceives price as given and independent of how much it chooses to sell.

The firm's total cost curve is

$$TC = a + b \times q + c \times q^2$$

and profits are *TR* − *TC*.

The firm's profits function is, therefore, written:

$$B = p(q) \times q - a - b \times q - c \times q^2$$

The first derivative is now

$$dB/dq = p + q(dp/dq) - b - 2c \times q$$

For profits to be maximised, it is necessary that $dB/dq = 0$, meaning that

$$p + q(dp/dq) = b + 2c \times q$$

The left-hand term is the value of dTR/dq (MR) when $TR = p(q)q$. The right-hand side is marginal cost. The expression $q(dp/dq)$ is negative, since dp/dq is the negative slope of the inverse demand curve. Therefore

$$p + q(dp/dq) < p$$

which means that $MR < P$.

Just as the slope of the total cost curve is marginal cost, the slope of the total revenue curve, dTR/dQ, is (by definition), marginal revenue. Hence, the condition for profit maximisation is setting $MR = MC$. The perfect competition case reflects the fact that under perfect competition, where firms have no market power, *price and marginal revenue are the same thing*. When a firm has market power it faces a downward-sloping demand curve. $TR = pq$, $AR = TR/q$; therefore p and AR are the same thing. Since p falls as q increases along the demand curve, AR is falling by definition. Since AR is falling we know that $MR < AR$. Hence, $MR < p$.

Note the implication that in the presence of market power the chosen level of output is one for which $p > MC$, implying loss of surplus relative to the perfectly competitive case.

Example 8.4 To show how this result can be used, take the following example. There is a type of doughnut sold in Germany known as a Berliner.[2] How many Berliners will be sold and at what price each week?

Suppose we know that the demand for Berliners in Berlin (and we suppose there is only one Berliner producer in Berlin) can be stated as:

$$€p = 20,000 - 6q$$

where q is thousands of doughnuts for sale in a week.

Suppose the weekly fixed cost is $€TC = 2,000q$. Then

$$TR = 20,000q - 6q_2; \; TC = 2,000q$$

$$MR = 20,000 - 12q; \; MC = 2,000; \; MR = MC \rightarrow 18,000 = 12q, \text{ or } q = 1,500$$

If $q = 1,500$, $p = 11,000$, and each doughnut sells for €1.10.

RECAP Profit-maximisation for the monopolist

Both the perfectly competitive firm and the monopolist maximise profit by choosing the output level at which marginal revenue equals marginal cost. But whereas marginal revenue equals market price for the perfectly competitive firm, it is always less than market price for the monopolist. A monopolist will earn an economic profit only if price exceeds average total cost at the *profit-maximising level of output*.

---

2 This explains why there were a few chuckles when former US President John F. Kennedy in 1963 expressed his solidarity with the inhabitants of that city, after the Berlin Wall had divided it, in the lapidary phrase '*Ich bin ein Berliner.*'

Why the 'invisible hand' breaks down under monopoly

In our discussion of equilibrium in perfectly competitive markets in Chapters 6 and 7, we saw conditions under which the self-serving pursuits of consumers and firms were consistent with the broader interests of society as a whole. This was what was described as the workings of Adam Smith's 'invisible hand'.

The obvious analytical question that arises from the discussion so far in this chapter is to what extent Smith's conclusions regarding the invisible hand are robust in the sense of what happens if we change assumptions about the market. Smith, after all, was implicitly assuming that markets were 'efficient' in the sense that perfectly competitive markets are (of course, he didn't use the term, which had not been invented, but it is clear what he had in mind). To answer this question, we start with the case of monopoly.

Consider the monopolist in Example 8.3. Is this firm's profit-maximising output level efficient from society's point of view? For any given level of output, the corresponding price on the demand curve indicates the amount that buyers would be willing to pay for an additional unit of output. When the monopolist is producing 8 units per week, the marginal benefit to society of an additional unit of output is thus €4 (see Fig. 8.7). And since the marginal cost of an additional unit at that output level is only €2 (again, see Fig. 8.7), society would gain a net benefit of €2 per unit if the monopolist were to expand production by one unit above the profit-maximising level. Because this economic surplus is not realised, the profit-maximising monopolist is *socially inefficient*.

Efficiency

Recall that the existence of inefficiency means that the economic 'pie' is smaller than it might be. If that is so, why doesn't the monopolist simply expand production? The answer is that the monopolist would gladly do so if only there were some way to maintain the price of existing units and cut the price of only the extra units. As a practical matter, however, that is not always possible.

Consider again the monopolist in Example 8.3, whose demand and marginal cost curves are reproduced in Fig. 8.9. For the market served by this monopolist, what is the socially efficient level of output?

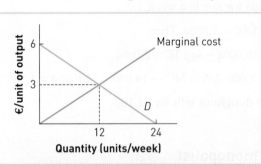

Figure 8.9 The Demand and Marginal Curves for a Monopolist. The socially optimal output level is 12 units per week, the quantity for which the marginal benefit *to the public* is exactly the same as marginal cost.

While the monopolist pays the cost of using resources, usually the price he has to pay represents the opportunity cost of the *resources* he uses. It follows that, at any output level, the cost to society of an additional unit of output is the same as the cost to the monopolist, namely the amount shown on the monopolist's marginal cost curve. However, the marginal benefit to society from another unit being produced is not the same as the marginal benefit to the monopolist. The marginal benefit to *society* (not to the monopolist) of an extra unit of output is simply the amount people are willing to pay for it, which is the amount shown on the monopolist's demand curve. To achieve social efficiency, the monopolist should expand production until the marginal benefit to society equals the marginal cost, which in this case occurs at a level of 12 units per week. Social efficiency is thus achieved at the output level at which the market demand curve intersects the monopolist's marginal cost curve.

Cost–Benefit
Analysis

Unfortunately, the marginal benefit to the monopolist is not what people would be willing to pay for another unit, but the change in his total sales revenues from selling one more unit, or marginal revenue. It is this inequality between the value to society of an extra unit of output (its current price) and the value to the monopolist (its marginal revenue) that is the key factor. His calculus of benefit will lead him to equate marginal cost not with price but with marginal revenue. Since the monopolist's demand curve slopes downwards, to sell more he has to lower unit price (and, remember, price is average revenue). We already know that if any average (in this case price or average revenue) is declining, the marginal curve must lie below it. The marginal revenue curve for a monopolist will always lie below the demand curve if he has to lower price for all units sold to increase sales.

The fact that marginal revenue is less than price for the monopolist results in a *deadweight loss*. For the monopolist just discussed, the size of this deadweight loss is equal to the area of the shaded triangle in Fig. 8.10, which is (1/2)(€2 per unit)(4 units per week) = €4 per week. That is the amount by which total economic surplus is reduced because the monopolist produces too little.

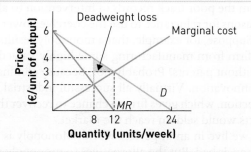

Figure 8.10 The Deadweight Loss from Monopoly. A loss in economic surplus results because the profit-maximising level of output (8 units per week) is less than the socially optimal level of output (12 units per week).

For a monopolist, profit-maximisation occurs when marginal cost equals marginal revenue. Since the monopolist's marginal revenue is always less than price, the monopolist's profit-maximising output level is always below the socially efficient level. Under perfect competition, by contrast, profit-maximisation occurs when marginal cost equals the market price – the same criterion that must be satisfied for social efficiency. This difference explains why the invisible hand of the market is less evident in monopoly markets than in perfectly competitive markets.

Given that monopoly is socially inefficient, why not legislate it out of existence? A cynical response might well be that it would be ironic if parliaments that create monopolies (usually in the public sector) should decide that they are a bad thing in the first place. But it's not as simple as that. Monopolies can (if infrequently) evolve simply through the pressure of competition (which is accepted as a socially beneficial process). In this case, market forces produce concentration of production into a single firm, a natural monopoly, a firm that can produce the output at a lower average resource cost to society than if it were divided between two equally sized firms. Second, many economists believe that monopoly power is inherently transient, and contains within itself the seeds of its own destruction, as its profitability incites competition and innovation to break it down.

Although legal regimes do provide for breaking up monopolies (this is particularly true of the United States), for the most part they provide for its regulation. In part this probably reflects the acceptance that monopolies may derive their existence from scale economies, so that breaking them up would increase total costs of production. It also probably reflects a view that while a monopoly may be a problem, deciding what exactly should replace it may not be a tractable problem for bureaucrats and legislators. Two firms? Three firms? Four firms? …

In the UK experience shipbuilding, steel, aviation, car production and road passenger transport were all the beneficiaries of state intervention to improve industrial efficiency by restructuring via state ownership in the 1970s. In every case the intervention had to be reversed when it was seen to have been a costly failure. It has to be said that the US experience has not been as bad. There, it is the courts, for the most part, or threats of court action, that have driven restructuring of monopolies. Early in the twentieth century the US courts broke up the Rockefeller oil monopoly (Standard Oil). More recently, and more controversially in terms of results, the US Department of Justice used threats of legal action to secure a restructuring of the US telephone sector (in the late 1970s, before mobile phones, by breaking up AT&T).

Apart from the poor track records of intervention to alter market structures, there are other reasons for reluctance to use the coercive power of the state to break monopoly power. Suppose, for example, that a monopoly results from a patent that prevents all but one firm from manufacturing some highly valued product. Would society be better off without patents? Probably not, because eliminating such protection would discourage innovation. Virtually all successful industrial nations grant some form of patent protection, which gives firms a chance to recover the R&D costs without which new products would seldom reach the market.

In short, we live in an imperfect world. Monopoly is socially inefficient and that, needless to say, is bad. But the alternatives to monopoly are not perfect, either.

RECAP Why the monopolist produces 'too little' output

The monopolist maximises profit at the output level for which marginal revenue equals marginal cost. Because its profit-maximising price exceeds marginal revenue, and hence also marginal cost, the benefit to society of the last unit produced (the market price) must be greater than the cost of the last unit produced (the marginal cost). So the output level for an industry served by a profit-maximising monopolist is *smaller* than the socially optimal level of output.

Measuring market power

How pervasive is market power? How much market power does a firm enjoy? Will a merger or acquisition increase the market power of the new firm? To answer questions like these, which are important from a policy perspective, we need to be able to measure market power. A simple approach is to look at the number of firms in a market and to calculate an index of concentration. For example, we could ask what percentage of total sales is in the hands of the largest three or four firms. If they account for most sales in the market, the market is 'concentrated'. A more sophisticated approach is to use what is known as the Hirschman-Hefindahl Index (HHI). This is given by the sum of the squares of the shares of the firms in the market. It has a range of between 10,000 (100 squared) and close to zero. A value of over 2,000 would usually be held to indicate high concentration.

Both these approaches have serious data problems. The first is that we have to define the relevant product market. Is lager in a separate market from ales, or are both in the beer market? The second is that we have to define the relevant geographical market. Is there a French market for cement, or are sales in France merely a portion of sales in a single Europe-wide market? These can be handled, but they pose difficulties at a theoretical and practical level.

Another way to tackle the problem is to use what we have already established about imperfect competition: it gives a firm market power, by which we mean that the demand curve for its product slopes down. The firm will choose the output for which $MC = MR < P$.

We know that competition tends to drive price down towards cost. We also know that the existence of close substitutes means that a firm's sales will be significantly affected by any difference between its price and those of competing firms (the demand curve has a shallow slope) and MR is close to P.

It follows that we can measure a firm's market power, and the market power of a group of firms in a market, by examining the relationship between marginal cost (or a proxy for MC) and price. This gives us the Lerner Index, defined as

$$L = \frac{(P - MC)}{P}$$

In perfect competition, $P = MR = MC$, and $L = 0$. As a firm's market power increases L increases, with a theoretical maximum value of 1 as $(P - MC) \rightarrow 1$.

The Lerner Index has problems, too. In the first place we need to be able to measure price and marginal cost accurately. Second, when the measurement is made the values could reflect temporary rather than permanent aspects on the demand and cost side of the relevant market, thus yielding misleading results. Third, high values for a firm's Lerner Index may result from offering a superior product, or using a more efficient production method (higher demand, lower cost), which does not mean the market as a whole is uncompetitive, or that the firm does not face serious competition.[3]

All of which means plenty of scope for profitable consultancy work for competition policy economists!

Contestability

Market structure may be misleading as a guide to market power in so far as firms have to consider not only the competition they face from other producers in the market already, but also the possibility of entry to the market. Openness to entry can be thought of as reflecting costs of entry. In general, entry to a market is costly in the sense that firms incur costs that they are unlikely to recoup should they exit later. They constitute a sort of 'ticket price' facing a would-be entrant. When these costs are low (in the limiting case, when they are zero) so that a market is open to entry on a hit-and-run basis, it is said to be highly 'contestable'. Contestability can be thought of as the degree of potential competition for existing suppliers from firms that are not in the market.

As with competition from actual suppliers, high contestability implies prices being driven down towards average cost. Indeed, granted certain assumptions, a market with just one supplier (on the face of it, a monopoly) could be characterised by price

---

3 If you want a more complete but understandable account of the problems involved in measuring market power go to the US Federal Trade Commission website at www.ftc.gov/opp/jointvent/classic3.shtm.

and output values approaching those that would obtain under perfect competition. In that case the market would be said to be perfectly contestable. The concept of contestability has given rise to arguments about market power and intervention in markets that play down the issue of structure on the basis that, regardless of structure, it will be sufficient to rely on a high degree of contestability to ensure economic efficiency. When taken in conjunction with the Chicago School view that, in the long run, markets operate as if they are contestable (entry occurs, and/or competition from new products has the same effect as entry), the contestability approach has tended to reduce the concern with which its supporters view concentrated market structures, and made them less supportive of policy measures designed to prevent increased market concentration (merger control regulation).

Perfect contestability requires some demanding assumptions. First, potential entrants must face no difficulties in entering the market and must be able to obtain access to customers on the same basis as incumbent firms. Second, entrants must face exactly the same production etc. costs as incumbents and have access to the same technology. Third, the entrants must be able to assume that entry will not affect prices obtaining other than to the degree that increased supply means a reduction in market clearing prices (this means that there is no need to fear incumbents adopting pricing strategies to punish entrants). If these hold, the market is vulnerable to hit-and-run entry, or is perfectly contestable.[4]

If even a monopoly supplier in a fully contestable market would be constrained to behave more or less as if the market were perfectly competitive, then the need for regulatory activity would be greatly reduced in so far as real-world markets approximated to perfect contestability. While it has been established that some of the claims for the sufficiency of contestability to deliver economic efficiency have been overstated, this approach does contain more than a grain of truth. Low entry barriers and technical ease of entry do constrain incumbent firms in seeking to exploit concentrated market structures. The impact of low-cost airlines on the performance of the established carriers, and the repositioning of those carriers after deregulation, can be seen as a partial vindication of contestability theory. However, the unfortunate reality is that the conditions necessary for full contestability are extremely onerous, and, especially in a short- to medium-term policy context, it is not plausible to argue for withdrawing policy intervention on the grounds that as an empirical matter most markets are sufficiently contestable to ensure economic efficiency regardless of changes in market structures. In addition, for contestability to be a realistic alternative to the standard approach to analysing markets would require treating markets as if they were devoid of uncertainty and the requirement for entrepreneurs to take risky decisions with imperfect information.[5]

Using discounts to expand the market: monopoly power at work for you?

The source of inefficiency in monopoly markets is the fact that the benefit to the monopolist of expanding output is less than the corresponding benefit to society. From the monopolist's point of view, the price reduction the firm must grant existing buyers to expand output is a loss. But from the point of view of those buyers, each euro or dollar of price reduction is a gain – one dollar or euro more in their pockets.

---

4 See Baumol *et al.* (1982).
5 See Brätland (2004).

Note the tension in this situation, which is similar to the tension that exists in all other situations in which the economic 'pie' is smaller than it might otherwise be. As the efficiency principle reminds us, when the economic 'pie' grows larger, everyone can have a larger slice. To say that monopoly is inefficient means that steps could be taken to make some people better off without harming others. If people have a healthy regard for their own self-interest, why doesn't someone take those steps? Why, for example, doesn't the monopolist from the earlier examples sell 8 units of output at a price of €4, and then once those buyers are out the door, cut the price for more price-sensitive buyers? The answer is that frequently that is exactly what he does. Think back to the story in Economic naturalist 8.1, and the strategy of Intel.

Price discrimination defined

price discrimination the practice of charging different buyers different prices for essentially the same good or service

Incentives Matter

Charging different buyers different prices for the same good or service is a practice known as **price discrimination**. Examples of price discrimination include senior citizens' and children's discounts on cinema tickets. DIY superstores in many European countries offer old-age pensioners special deals on certain days. In France and Italy, a standard practice is to offer access to art galleries and museums to the over-60s at a reduced rate. Something that is starting to be used in Europe but is widespread in the United States is the use of cut-out newspaper coupons entitling users to get discounts at supermarkets or other retail outlets. This is a subtle form of price discrimination: the goods are sold at a lower price to those with the time and money constraints that result in their spending time cutting out coupons. Other consumers, more pressed for time or with more money, pay more.

Attempts at price discrimination seem to work effectively in some markets but not in others. Buyers are not stupid, after all; if the monopolist periodically offered a 50 per cent discount on the list price, those who were paying the list price might anticipate the next price cut and postpone their purchases to take advantage of it. In some markets, however, buyers may not know, or simply may not take the trouble to find out, how the price they pay compares with the prices paid by other buyers. Alternatively, the monopolist may be in a position to prevent some groups from buying at the discount prices made available to others. In such cases, the monopolist can price discriminate effectively.

Economic naturalist 8.2 Why do many DIY stores offer discounts on Thursday afternoons?

Males form a larger proportion of purchasers of DIY (do-it-yourself) goods (for use by customers in the repair, maintenance and decoration of their homes and gardens) than most other retail sales. What type of male is able to go shopping on a Thursday afternoon? Predominantly the unemployed and elderly (pensioners) who have, on average, lower incomes. Whenever a firm offers a discount, it aims that discount at buyers who would not purchase the product without it. People with low incomes generally have lower reservation prices than people with high incomes. Believe us: it's not because they feel sorry for 'third agers', it's because they can make higher profits by using a *discriminatory price structure*.

How price discrimination affects output

Curiously, as we shall now see, this use of price discrimination to extract more profits can have the counter-intuitive consequence of making society as a whole better off. The unexpected result of this reasoning arises from the fact that we (reasonably)

assume that higher prices that produce higher profits involve less being offered for sale. But this is not necessarily the case.

Suppose in a small village with a single doctor there are ten households. The doctor is a monopolist, and can set a single price at which he will maximise his profits. Figure 8.10 (p. 259) describes this position. Assume that whatever he says at village meetings about the ethics of public service, he is concerned to maximise his profits. Let us also assume that medical regulations require that he has to post his prices for a month in advance, and sell his services to all and sundry at the posted price. The price is his charge for a visit to his surgery.

Armed with sufficient knowledge as to the villagers' demand for healthcare, he will set the price that maximises his profits (or, equivalently, choose the weekly number of hours he will make available) by setting $MC = MR$, and selecting the relevant price and quantity.

Suppose the ten families (reflecting their incomes, number of children and health status) have differing reservation prices for a weekly visit to the doctor. Rank them from the highest to the lowest, as in Table 8.5.

Family	Reservation price (€ per visit)
1	80
2	75
3	70
4	65
5	60
6	55
7	50
8	45
9	40
10	35

Table 8.5 **Family Reservation Prices**

To make life easy, suppose that the doctor has a constant marginal cost of seeing a patient (this makes the story simpler, but changes nothing). Suppose his MC is 35. We could use this data to derive a village demand curve for a weekly visit (Fig. 8.11).

Under price regulations the profit-maximising doctor will charge a price of €60 and see five families in the week. At this price, village welfare is not maximised. Maximisation of economic surplus would require seeing ten families (where $MC = P$).

The doctor's profits are €(5 × 25) = €125. Families 1–5 have a joint consumer surplus of €(20 + 15 + 10 + 5 + 0) = €50. Total surplus is, therefore, €175.

Now suppose that the regulation determining the doctor's pricing policy is removed, and he is allowed to charge each family its reservation price. He sells the visit to family 1 at €80, to family 2 at €75, and so on (Fig. 8.11). As long as a family is prepared to cover his marginal cost he has an incentive to see the family. He will see all the families, since the reservation price of family 10 is just equal to his MC. Each family pays its reservation price and so keeps no consumer surplus. The doctor has a profit of €(45 + 40 + 35 + 30 + 25 + 20 + 15 + 10 + 5 + 0) = €225. This is the total surplus.

Total surplus is higher; more output is produced; the level of output is the efficient level ($P = MC$). Of course, from the point of view of families 1–5 this is a rough deal,

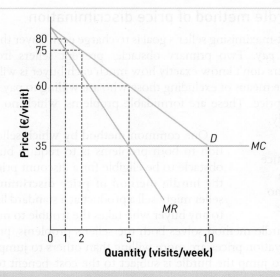

Figure 8.11 Demand Curve for a Weekly Doctor's Visit.

but families 6–10 are better off (because they have chosen to purchase) even though they have no consumer surplus. The entire surplus has been appropriated by the doctor, who at the next village meeting is hailed as a latter-day Robin Hood because he appears to be charging more to the rich to finance supplying the poor.

perfectly discriminating monopolist a firm that charges each buyer exactly his or her reservation price

The doctor in this case is described as a **perfectly discriminating monopolist**. This is a monopolist who can sell each unit he produces at its reservation price. He is engaging in 'first-degree' price discrimination. A firm with market power that can discriminate between groups of purchasers in a market is said to be engaging in 'second-degree' price discrimination. An airline that sells tickets at different prices to different groups reflecting willingness to pay (business and tourist, off-peak and peak-time travel) is an example of a firm practising second-degree price discrimination. A firm that can segment whole markets is a third-degree price discriminator. An example is Levi-Strauss: it has used trade restrictions that have been sanctioned by the European Court of Justice (ECJ) to sell jeans at much lower prices in countries such as India than the prices it charges in the European Union.

In practice, of course, perfect price discrimination can never occur, because no seller knows each and every buyer's precise reservation price. But even if some sellers did know, practical difficulties would stand in the way of their charging a separate price to each buyer. For example, in many markets the seller could not prevent buyers who bought at low prices from reselling to other buyers at higher prices, capturing some of the seller's business in the process. Despite these difficulties, price discrimination is widespread, but it is generally *imperfect price discrimination* – that is, price discrimination in which at least some buyers are charged less than their reservation prices.

However, it remains the case that price discrimination, although redistributive and unpopular, and in some circumstances illegal, has the general property that it is superior in efficiency terms to single price monopoly.

The hurdle method of price discrimination

The profit-maximising seller's goal is to charge each buyer the *highest price that buyer is willing to pay*. Two primary obstacles prevent sellers from achieving this goal. First, sellers don't know exactly how much each buyer is willing to pay. Second, they need some means of excluding those who are willing to pay a high price from buying at a low price. These are formidable problems, which no seller can hope to solve completely.

hurdle method of price discrimination the practice by which a seller offers a discount to all buyers who overcome some obstacle

One common method by which sellers achieve a crude solution to both problems is to require buyers to overcome some obstacle to be eligible for a discount price. This method is called the **hurdle method of price discrimination**. For example, the seller might sell a product at a standard list price and offer a rebate to any buyer who takes the trouble to mail in a rebate coupon.

The hurdle method solves both the seller's problems, provided that buyers with low reservation prices are more willing than others to jump the hurdle. Because the decision to jump the hurdle is subject to the cost–benefit test, such a link seems to exist. As noted earlier, buyers with low incomes are more likely than others to have low reservation prices (at least in the case of normal goods). Because of the low opportunity cost of their time, they are more likely than others to take the trouble to send in rebate coupons. Rebate coupons thus target a discount towards those buyers whose reservation prices are low and who therefore might not otherwise buy the product.

perfect hurdle a threshold that completely segregates buyers whose reservation prices lie above it from others whose reservation prices lie below it, imposing no cost on those who jump the hurdle

A **perfect hurdle** is one that separates buyers precisely according to their reservation prices, and in the process imposes no cost on those who jump the hurdle. With a perfect hurdle, the highest reservation price among buyers who jump the hurdle will be lower than the lowest reservation price among buyers who choose not to jump the hurdle. In practice, perfect hurdles do not exist. Some buyers will always jump the hurdle even though their reservation prices are high. And hurdles will always exclude at least some buyers with low reservation prices. Even so, many commonly used hurdles do a remarkably good job of targeting discounts to buyers with low reservation prices.

Is price discrimination a bad thing?

We are so conditioned to think of discrimination as 'bad' that we may be tempted to conclude that price discrimination must run counter to the public interest. Consider, however, the price coupon example. It is two weeks before Christmas. A supermarket advertises in a local paper, and states that anyone who cuts out and presents to the supermarket manager the coupon in the advertisement will receive a discount of 5 per cent on any oven-ready turkey in the week before Christmas.

On average, the supermarket believes that only those with low opportunity costs of time and a high marginal utility of money income (i.e. the less well-off) will take the trouble to jump the hurdle. Inevitably, some inveterate high-income bargain hunters will do so as well, but an astute supermarket chain will set the hurdle so as to ensure that most of those who jump it have a lower reservation price than those who don't.

By definition, the real income of those who jump the hurdle is improved by doing so: the cost is more than offset by the benefit from paying less for the turkey. Faced with the option of paying more and/or buying a smaller turkey, but not expending effort to jump the hurdle, or jumping, they jump. Their total surplus has increased. That of those who did not jump has not been reduced. The surplus of the supermarket operator must have increased as well … otherwise it would not have made the offer. The acid test is to ask whether a prohibition on coupons would have increased or reduced the total of consumer and producer surplus.

Examples of price discrimination

Once you grasp the principle behind the hurdle method of price discrimination, you will begin to see examples of it all around you. Next time you visit a grocery, hardware store or electrical goods retail outlet, for instance, notice how many different product promotions include cash rebates. Temporary sales are another illustration of the hurdle method. Most of the time, stores sell most of their merchandise at the 'regular' price, but periodically they offer special sales at a significant discount. The hurdle in this instance is taking the trouble to find out when and where the sales will occur and then the cost of waiting before going to the store during that period. This technique works because buyers who care most about price (mainly those with low reservation prices) are more likely to monitor advertisements carefully and buy only during sale periods.

To give another example, book publishers typically launch a new book in hardcover form at a price from €20 to €30, and a year later they bring out a paperback edition priced between €5 and €15. In this instance, the hurdle involves having to wait the extra year and accepting a slight reduction in the quality of the finished product. People who are strongly concerned about price end up waiting for the paperback edition, while those with high reservation prices usually go for the hardback.

Consider the way in which major movies are released. The general rule is that they are released to cinemas first, then to terrestrial and satellite TV for pay-per-view, then to DVD or video for rental, and finally to free-to-air TV. Only movies that are not believed to have initial high reservation prices from a significant number of potential viewers appear in rental outlets first. Basically, this is the same story as in the hardback and paperback book case. The hurdle is willingness to wait to see the movie.

Commercial airlines have perfected the hurdle method to an extent matched by almost no other seller. Their supersaver fares are often less than half their regular economy-class fares. To be eligible for these discounts, travellers must purchase their tickets 7–21 days in advance, and their journey must include a Saturday-night stayover. Vacation travellers can more easily satisfy these restrictions than business travellers, whose schedules often change at the last moment and whose trips seldom involve Saturday stayovers. And – no surprise – the business traveller's reservation price tends to be much higher than the vacation traveller's. Using the technology of online sales they can vary prices continuously over time, and even between purchases at any point in time (if you ask for four tickets from London to Paris you may be quoted a different price from that which would be charged for two tickets).

Or take the example of car manufacturers, who typically offer several different models of what is basically the same car with different external appearances, some technical differences and differences in trim and accessories. In Europe the classic example of this is the VW group. It sells its cars under four brands: VW, Audi, Skoda and Seat. In many cases the different marques are produced in the same factory and, for example, the Seat Toledo shares most of its mechanical and under-the-skin components with the VW Golf. Production costs differ marginally, but by much less than the price to a purchaser. This reflects a strategy of designing and pricing models to appeal to buyer groups with different reservation prices. In the United States, Ford operates the same strategy in differentiating between Ford and Mercury offerings. In

Italy, Fiat does exactly the same thing by using the Fiat, Alfa Romeo and Lancia brands (although in the case of Alfa Romeo, there are performance-enhancing modifications as well as external appearance differences). General Motors in the United States has used this strategy for over 70 years. In 2004 it dropped the Oldsmobile brand, because the demographic segment of the market had shifted away from purchasing this brand.

Recall that the efficiency loss from single-price monopoly occurs because, to the monopolist, the benefit of expanding output is smaller than the benefit to society as a whole. The hurdle method of price discrimination reduces this loss by giving the monopolist a practical means of cutting prices for price-sensitive buyers only. In general, the more finely the monopolist can partition a market using the hurdle method, the smaller the efficiency loss. Hurdles are not perfect, however, and some degree of efficiency will inevitably be lost.

Economic naturalist 8.3 Why does Coca-Cola in two-litre plastic bottles cost twice as much in Australia as on the west coast of the USA?

The price of Coca-Cola in Australia (or any other market outside the USA) has nothing to do with the cost of getting the product to Australia. It is produced in Australia from imported concentrate, which is a low transport cost input. In spring 2008, independent retailers in Sydney, Australia, made a formal complaint to the Australian Competition Commission concerning Coca-Cola prices. They argued that an effective retail duopoly (Coles and Woolworths) had extracted terms from Coca-Cola by which the prices received by Coca-Cola and extracted from customers were substantially higher in Sydney than in Seattle. They argued that independent retailers could not obtain supplies at a price that would enable them to undercut the multiples, and that the retail prices differences could not be explained by cost differences. Price discrimination? It certainly looks like it. In Australia, Coca-Cola accounts for nearly 60 per cent of sales of carbonated soft drinks. It doesn't face serious competition in the Australian market, even from its main international rival, Pepsi Cola. Coke has huge market power and controls sales into Australia through its own distributor. In the USA, although it outsells Pepsi, it faces serious competition from this rival brand. This suggests a lower price elasticity of demand for Coke in Australia than in the USA. It is entirely plausible that it would exploit its market position by increasing prices in Australia, but would have to share the profits with the dominant retail chains who command access to the end market, and protect this arrangement by restricting supply (and charging higher prices) to independent stores. Welfare enhancing? Hardly.

RECAP Using discounts to expand the market

A price-discriminating monopolist is one who charges different prices to different buyers for essentially the same good or service. A common method of price discrimination is the hurdle method, which involves granting a discount to buyers who jump over a hurdle, such as mailing a rebate coupon. An *effective hurdle* is one that is more easily cleared by buyers with low reservation prices than by buyers with high reservation prices. Such a hurdle enables the monopolist to expand output and thereby reduce the deadweight loss from monopoly pricing.

Public policy towards monopolies

Monopoly is problematic not only because of the loss in efficiency associated with restricted output but also because the monopolist as a seller earns an economic profit at the buyer's expense. Many people are understandably uncomfortable about having to purchase from the sole provider of any good or service. For this reason, voters in many societies have empowered government to adopt policies aimed at controlling firms enjoying substantial market power, including natural monopolies.

In the case of natural monopolies, where competition is not commercially feasible, there are several ways to achieve this aim. A government may assume ownership and control of a natural monopoly, or it may merely attempt to regulate the prices it charges. In some cases government solicits competitive bids from private firms to produce natural monopoly services. In still other cases, governments attempt to dissolve natural monopolies into smaller entities that compete with one another. But many of these policies create economic problems of their own. In each case, the practical challenge is to come up with the solution that yields the greatest surplus of benefits over costs. Natural monopoly may be inefficient and unfair but, as noted earlier, the alternatives to it are far from perfect.

The need to achieve social control of natural monopolies was the generally accepted rationale that led to virtually all the network industries in Europe coming into state ownership: railways, postal services, telephone systems, airlines. In many cases the question of whether or not the cost structure of the sector concerned actually had the technical character of a natural monopoly was never rigorously examined. Indeed, there was a sort of circularity of argument in many cases: the state set up state-owned firms or nationalised private firms and amalgamated them, gave them monopoly rights and justified continuing public ownership on natural monopoly grounds.

State ownership and management

Monopoly, including natural monopoly, is inefficient because the monopolist's profit-maximising price is greater than its marginal cost. But even if the natural monopolist *wanted* to set price equal to marginal cost, it could not do so and hope to remain in business. After all, the defining feature of a natural monopoly is *economies of scale in production*, which means that marginal cost will always be less than average total cost. Setting price equal to marginal cost would fail to cover average total cost, which implies an economic loss.

Consider the case of a local cable television company. Once an area has been wired for cable television, the marginal cost of adding an additional subscriber is very low. For the sake of efficiency, all subscribers should pay a price equal to that marginal cost. Yet a cable company that priced in this manner would never be able to recover the fixed cost of setting up the network. This same problem applies not just to cable television companies but to all other natural monopolies. Even if such firms wanted to set price equal to marginal cost (which, of course, they do not, since they will earn more by setting marginal revenue equal to marginal cost), they cannot do so without suffering an economic loss.

One way to attack the efficiency and fairness problems is for the government to take over the industry, set price equal to marginal cost and then absorb the resulting losses out of general tax revenues. This approach has been followed with good results in the state-owned electricity utility industry in France, Electricité de France, whose efficient pricing methods have set the standard for electricity pricing worldwide.

But state ownership and efficient management do not always go hand in hand. Granted, the state-owned natural monopoly is free to charge marginal cost, while the private natural monopoly is not. Yet private natural monopolies often face a much stronger incentive to cut costs than their government-owned counterparts. When the private monopolist figures out a way to cut €1 from the cost of production, its profit goes up by €1. But when the government manager of a state-owned monopoly cuts €1 from the cost of production, the government typically cuts the monopoly's budget by €1 or demands a dividend.

X-inefficiency where market power results in inefficient production rather than higher profits

To the extent that this is a serious issue, we have an example of what economists call **X-inefficiency**, whereby monopoly power results in higher costs being incurred as a means of absorbing the inherent profitability of the monopoly enterprise. It happens to a degree in firms in the private sector with market power, but is a much more serious problem in the public sector because, in the private sector, shareholders can (and do) fire inefficient managers so as to realise profits, while, in the public sector, governments have weak incentives to act decisively to curb waste in public sector firms, and poor information on which to act. Whether the efficiency that is gained by being able to set price equal to marginal cost outweighs the inefficiency that results from a weakened incentive to cut costs is an empirical question.

State regulation of private monopolies

Dissatisfaction with public ownership (costly, slow to innovate, poor responses to changes in demand ...) has led to widespread divestment of state enterprise across Europe and Australasia. However, the consequences have frequently been the creation of privately owned suppliers with substantial market power, bordering on monopoly. As a result, privatisation has been accompanied by increased emphasis on regulation: legal and administrative structures that are entitled to lay down operational requirements and controls (pricing, availability, quality, and so on) for the firms concerned. While this is relatively new in Europe (dating for the most part from the 1980s), it has been the standard US procedure for dealing with natural monopolies and similar circumstances for a very long time. The most common US method of curbing monopoly profits is for government merely to regulate the natural monopoly rather than own it. Most US states, for example, take this approach with electricity utilities, natural gas providers, local telephone companies and cable television companies. The standard procedure in these cases is called **cost-plus regulation**: government regulators gather data on the monopolist's explicit costs of production and then permit the monopolist to set prices that cover those costs, plus a mark-up to assure a normal return on the firm's investment.

cost-plus regulation a method of regulation under which the regulated firm is permitted to charge a price equal to its explicit costs of production plus a mark-up to cover the opportunity cost of resources provided by the firm's owners

While it may sound reasonable, cost-plus regulation has several pitfalls. First, it generates costly administrative proceedings in which regulators and firms quarrel over which of the firm's expenditures can properly be included in the costs it is allowed to recover. This question is difficult to answer even in theory. Consider a firm such as Pacific Telesis, originally the Californian telecommunications operator, but now a communications conglomerate. Its local telephone service is subject to cost-plus regulation but other products and services are unregulated. Many Pacific Telesis employees, from the president down, are involved in both regulated and unregulated activities. How should their salaries be allocated between the two? The company has a strong incentive to argue for greater allocation to the regulated activities, which allows it to capture more revenue from captive customers in the local telephone market.

A second problem with cost-plus regulation is that it blunts the firm's incentive to adopt cost-saving innovations, for, when it does, regulators require the firm to cut its rates. The firm gets to keep its cost savings in the current period, which is a stronger incentive to cut costs than that facing a government-owned monopoly. But the incentive to cut costs would be stronger still if the firm could retain its cost savings indefinitely. Furthermore, in cases in which regulators set rates by allowing the monopolist to add a fixed mark-up to costs incurred, the regulated monopolist may actually have an incentive to *increase* costs rather than reduce them. Outrageous though the thought may be, the monopolist may earn a higher profit by installing gold-plated water taps in the company rest rooms.

Finally, cost-plus regulation does not solve the natural monopolist's basic problem: the inability to set price equal to marginal cost without losing money. Although these are all serious problems, governments seem to be in no hurry to abandon cost-plus regulation.

Another mechanism frequently used is *rate of return* regulation. This lays down the maximum profits a supplier may earn by reference to the capital employed. For example, it could be obliged to set prices on the basis that they permit a 15 per cent return to capital employed. If profits exceed this amount they are either taken away from the firm or it is obliged to reduce prices. *X-inefficiency* is a problem here, too, since a firm can allow other costs to increase since it will lose the profits anyway. More seriously, it can lead to firms investing in capital assets not on the basis of their contribution to net output but simply to permit retention of profits.

For these reasons, recent developments in European regulation have emphasised using *price rules* to sweat productivity out of regulated industries. A classic example of this is the RPI-X approach of the UK regulator in the electricity sector, Ofelec. RPI stands for retail price index, for a long time the main UK measure for inflation. The RPI-X approach sets a rule: your price may rise only at X per cent less than the inflation rate. X is set at a level designed to oblige the firm to implement cost-saving technology as it becomes available, and to rely on productivity gains rather than higher price–cost margins to generate profits.

Such a rule also has its problems, because it can lead to cost cutting at the expense of consumer safety (alleged in the United Kingdom in the case of Railtrack, the entity that was vested with the ownership of the railway infrastructure), and requires the regulator to have accurate knowledge of the potential for cost savings from new technology and productivity improvements that may in fact be difficult to know at all, or knowledge that is in effect confined to the firms being regulated.

Exclusive contracting for natural monopoly

One of the most promising methods for dealing with natural monopoly is for the government to invite private firms to bid for the natural monopolist's market. The government specifies in detail the service it wants – cable television, fire protection, refuse collection – and firms submit bids describing how much they will charge for the service. The lowest bidder wins the contract.

The incentive to cut costs under such an arrangement is every bit as powerful as that facing ordinary competitive firms. Competition among bidders should also eliminate any concerns about the fairness of monopoly profits. And if the government is willing to provide a cash subsidy to the winning bidder, exclusive contracting even allows the monopolist to set price equal to marginal cost.

Contracting has been employed with good results in municipal fire protection and refuse collection. US communities that employ private companies to provide these services often spend only half as much as adjacent communities served by municipal fire and sanitation departments.

Despite these attractive features, however, exclusive contracting is not without problems, especially when the service to be provided is complex or requires a large fixed investment in capital equipment. In such cases, contract specifications may be so detailed and complicated that they become tantamount to regulating the firm directly. And in cases involving a large fixed investment – electricity generation and distribution, for example – officials face the question of how to transfer the assets if a new firm wins the contract. The winning firm naturally wants to acquire the assets as cheaply as possible, but the retiring firm is entitled to a fair price for them. What, in such cases, is a 'fair price'? Fire protection and refuse collection are simple enough, so the cost of contracting out these functions is not prohibitive. But, in other cases, such costs might easily outweigh any savings made possible by exclusive contracting.

This approach is becoming very common in Europe. The highest bridge in Europe, in Tarn in France, was built by a private-sector firm that won the contract to build the bridge and charge a toll. It was opened in December 2004. Motorway construction in Ireland is increasingly being undertaken on the basis of competitive contracting to build and operate (i.e. toll) the roads. A significant proportion of London bus transport is by franchised private operators. In New Zealand, although it remains in state ownership, the postal service is operated by New Zealand Post under a franchise contract with the government.

Vigorous enforcement of anti-trust laws

The nineteenth century witnessed the accumulation of massive private fortunes, the likes of which had never been seen in the industrialised world. This was particularly true in the protected industrial sector of the booming US economy. Public sentiment ran high against the so-called 'robber barons' of the period – the Carnegies, Mellons, Rockefellers and others. In 1890, US Congress passed the Sherman Act, which declared illegal any conspiracy 'to monopolise, or attempt to monopolise … any part of the trade or commerce among the several States'. In 1914, Congress passed the Clayton Act, whose aim was to prevent corporations from acquiring shares in a competitor if the transaction would 'substantially lessen competition or create a monopoly'.

Since the Second World War, but mostly since the requirements of EU membership began to take effect, European countries and the Union have followed the US example by legislation and regulation affecting market structure (mergers and acquisitions (M&A) controls) and the behaviour of firms with substantial market power (in EU language, prohibitions on the 'abuse of a dominant position'). These are built into the grounding treaty provisions of the Union in Articles 81 and 82 of the Treaty of Amsterdam (Articles 85 and 86 of the Rome Treaty it updates).

The generic term most widely used to cover this activity is 'anti-trust laws', recognising their origin in the United States. Anti-trust laws have helped to prevent the formation of *cartels*, or coalitions of firms that collude to raise prices above competitive levels. An early European example of this was the action of the EEC (as it was then) to punish United Brands, the largest banana supplier in Europe, for third-degree price discrimination by segmenting the EEC markets of six states in the 1960s. More recently, the French authorities and the Union imposed heavy fines on the cement producers of Europe, which were found to be operating a cartel. The motor trade in Europe was radically changed in the early 2000s by EU anti-trust actions designed to outlaw vertical distribution agreements operated by manufacturers and retailers that reduced intra-brand and inter-brand competition in the sector.

But such activities have also caused some harm. For example, US federal anti-trust officials spent more than a decade trying to break up the IBM Corporation in the belief that it had achieved an unhealthy dominance in the computer industry. That view was proved comically wrong by IBM's subsequent failure to foresee and profit from the rise of the personal computer. By breaking up large companies and discouraging mergers between companies in the same industry, anti-trust laws may help to promote competition, but they may also prevent companies from achieving *economies of scale*. Similarly, the US and EU cases against Microsoft have been criticised in some quarters as a waste of time, as they assumed that Microsoft's position, undoubtedly bolstered by some dubious practices in 'bundling' and in generating artificial incompatibilities, needed legal action to remedy the situation. And then along comes Linux ...

A final possibility is simply to ignore the problem of natural monopoly: to let the monopolist choose the quantity to produce and sell it at whatever price the market will bear. The obvious objections to this policy are the two we began with – namely, that a natural monopoly is not only inefficient but also unfair. But just as the hurdle method of price discrimination mitigates efficiency losses, it also lessens the concern about taking unfair advantage of buyers.

Consider first the source of the natural monopolist's economic profit. This firm, recall, is one with economies of scale, which means that its average production cost declines as output increases. Efficiency requires that price be set at marginal cost, but because the natural monopolist's marginal cost is lower than its average cost, it cannot charge all buyers the marginal cost without suffering an economic loss.

The depth and prevalence of discount pricing suggests that whatever economic profit a natural monopolist earns will generally not come out of the discount buyer's pocket. Although discount prices are higher than the monopolist's marginal cost of production, in most cases they are lower than the average cost. Thus the monopolist's economic profit, if any, must come from buyers who pay the list price. And since those buyers have the option, in most cases, of jumping a hurdle and paying a discount price, their contribution, if not completely voluntary, is at least not strongly coerced.

So much for the source of the monopolist's economic profit. What about its disposition? Who gets it? A large chunk goes to government via a corporation tax. The remainder is paid out to shareholders, some of whom are wealthy and some of whom are not. However, when we realise that over 80 per cent of shares are held by 'institutions', mostly pension funds, the redistributive consequences of monopoly power become much less clear.

Both the source of the monopolist's economic profit (the list-price buyer) and the disposition of that profit (largely, to fund public services) cast doubt on the claim that monopoly profit constitutes a social injustice on any grand scale. Nevertheless, the hurdle method of differential pricing cannot completely eliminate the fairness and efficiency problems that result from monopoly pricing. In the end, then, we are left with a choice among imperfect alternatives. As the Cost–Benefit Principle emphasises, the best choice is the one for which the balance of benefits over costs is largest. But which choice that is will depend on the circumstances at hand.

RECAP Public policy towards natural monopoly

The natural monopolist sets price above marginal cost, resulting in too little output from society's point of view (the *efficiency* problem). The natural monopolist may also earn an economic profit at buyers' expense (the *fairness* problem). Policies for dealing with the efficiency and fairness problems include state ownership and management, state regulation, exclusive contracting and vigorous enforcement of anti-trust laws. Each of these remedies entails problems of its own.

Summary

- Our concern in this chapter was the conduct and performance of the *imperfectly competitive firm*, a firm that has at least some latitude to set its own price. Economists often distinguish among three different types of imperfectly competitive firms: the pure monopolist, the lone seller of a product in a given market; the oligopolist, one of only a few sellers of a given product; and the monopolistic competitor, one of a relatively large number of firms that sell similar though slightly differentiated products.

- Although advanced courses in economics devote much attention to differences in behaviour among these three types of firm, our focus was on the common feature that differentiates them from perfectly competitive firms. Whereas the perfectly competitive firm faces an infinitely elastic demand curve for its product, the imperfectly competitive firm faces a *downward-sloping demand curve*. For convenience, we use the term *monopolistic* to refer to any of the three types of imperfectly competitive firm.

- Monopolists are sometimes said to enjoy *market power*, a term that refers to their power to set the price of their product. Market power stems from exclusive control over important inputs, from economies of scale, from patents and government licences or franchises, and from network economies. The most important and enduring of these five sources of market power are economies of scale and network economies.

- Unlike the perfectly competitive firm, for which marginal revenue exactly equals market price, the monopolist realises a *marginal revenue that is always less than its price*. This shortfall reflects the fact that, to sell more output, the monopolist must cut the price not only to additional buyers but to existing buyers as well. For the monopolist with a straight-line demand curve, the marginal revenue curve has the same vertical intercept and a horizontal intercept that is half as large as the intercept for the demand curve.

- Whereas the perfectly competitive firm maximises profit by producing at the level at which marginal cost equals the market price, the monopolist maximises profit by equating marginal cost with marginal revenue, which is significantly lower than the market price. The result is an output level that is best for the monopolist but smaller than the level that would be best for society as a whole. At the *profit-maximising* level of output, the benefit of an extra unit of output (the market price) is greater than its cost (the marginal cost). At the *socially efficient* level of output, where the monopolist's marginal cost curve intersects the demand curve, the benefit and cost of an extra unit are the same.

- Market power is reduced to the extent that a market is contestable, meaning that it is open to competition from firms currently not supplying the market. Perfect contestability, involving easy hit-and-run entry, tends to drive price down to cost.

- Both the monopolist and its potential customers can do better if the monopolist can grant discounts to price-sensitive buyers. The extreme example is the *perfectly discriminating monopolist*, who charges each buyer exactly his or her reservation price. Such producers are socially efficient, because they sell to every buyer whose reservation price is at least as high as the marginal cost.

- One common method of targeting discounts towards price-sensitive buyers is the *hurdle method* of price discrimination, in which the buyer becomes eligible for a discount only after overcoming some obstacle, such as mailing in a rebate coupon. This technique works well because those buyers who care most about price are more likely than others to jump the hurdle. While the hurdle method reduces the efficiency loss associated with single-price monopoly, it does not completely eliminate it.

> ■ The various policies that governments employ to mitigate concerns about fairness and efficiency losses arising from natural monopoly include state ownership and management of natural monopolies, state regulation, private contracting and vigorous enforcement of anti-trust laws. Each of these remedies entails costs as well as benefits. In some cases, a *combination* of policies will produce a better outcome than simply allowing natural monopolists to do as they please. But in other cases, a *hands-off* policy may be the best available option.

Review questions

1. What important characteristic do all three types of imperfectly competitive firm share?

2. **True or false:** A firm with market power can sell whatever quantity it wishes at whatever price it chooses.

3. Why do most successful industrial societies offer patents and copyright protection, even though these protections enable sellers to charge higher prices?

4. Why is marginal revenue always less than price for a monopolist but equal to price for a perfectly competitive firm?

5. **True or false:** Because a natural monopolist charges a price greater than marginal cost, it necessarily earns a positive economic profit.

Problems

1. Two car manufacturers, Saab and Volvo, have fixed costs of €1 billion and marginal costs of €10,000 per car. If Saab produces 50,000 cars per year and Volvo produces 200,000, calculate the average production cost for each company. On the basis of these costs, which company's market share do you think will grow in relative terms?

In Problems 2–4, state whether the statements are **true or false**, and explain why.

2. **a.** In a perfectly competitive industry the industry demand curve is horizontal, whereas for a monopoly it is downward-sloping.

   b. Perfectly competitive firms have no control over the price they charge for their product.

   c. For a natural monopoly, average cost declines as the number of units produced increases over the relevant output range.

3. A single-price profit-maximising monopolist:

   a. causes excess demand, or shortages, by selling too few units of a good or service

   b. chooses the output level at which marginal revenue begins to increase

   c. always charges a price above the marginal cost of production

   d. also maximises marginal revenue.

   e. None of the above statements is true.

4. If a monopolist could perfectly price discriminate:

   a. the marginal revenue curve and the demand curve would coincide

   b. the marginal revenue curve and the marginal cost curve would coincide

   c. every consumer would pay a different price

   d. marginal revenue would become negative at some output level

   e. the resulting pattern of exchange would still be socially inefficient.

5. Explain why price discrimination and the existence of slightly different variants of the same product tend to go hand in hand. Give an example from your own experience.

6. What is the socially desirable price for a natural monopoly to charge? Why will a natural monopoly that attempts to charge the socially desirable price invariably suffer an economic loss?

7. TotsPoses, a profit-maximising business, is the only photography business in town that specialises in portraits of small children. George, who owns and runs TotsPoses, expects to encounter an average of eight customers per day, each with a reservation price as shown in the table below.

Customer	Reservation price (€ per photo)
A	50
B	46
C	42
D	38
E	34
F	30
G	26
H	22

a. If the total cost of each photo portrait is €12, how much should George charge if he must charge a single price to all customers? At this price, how many portraits will George produce each day? What will be his economic profit?

b. How much consumer surplus is generated each day at this price?

c. What is the socially efficient number of portraits?

d. George is very experienced in the business and knows the reservation price of each of his customers. If he is allowed to charge any price he likes to any consumer, how many portraits will he produce each day, and what will his economic profit be?

e. In this case, how much consumer surplus is generated each day?

f. Suppose that George is permitted to charge two prices. He knows that customers with a reservation price above $30 never bother with coupons, whereas those with a reservation price of €30 or less always use them. At what level should George set the list price of a portrait? At what level should he set the discount price? How many photo portraits will he sell at each price?

g. In this case, what is George's economic profit, and how much consumer surplus is generated each day?

8. Suppose that a university student cinema is a local monopoly whose demand curve for adult tickets on Saturday night is $P = 12 - 2Q$, where P is the price of a ticket in euros and Q is the number of tickets sold in hundreds. The demand for children's tickets on Sunday afternoon is $P = 8 - 3Q$, and for adult tickets on Sunday afternoon, $P = 10 - 4Q$. On both Saturday night and Sunday afternoon, the marginal cost of an additional patron, child or adult, is €2.

a. What is the marginal revenue curve in each of the three sub-markets?

b. What price should the cinema charge in each of the three sub-markets if its goal is to maximise profit?

9. Suppose you are a monopolist in the market for a specific video game. Your demand curve is given by $P = 80 - Q/2$, and your marginal cost curve is $MC = Q$. Your fixed costs equal €400.

    a. Graph the demand and marginal cost curve.

    b. Derive and graph the marginal revenue curve.

    c. Calculate and indicate on the graph the equilibrium price and quantity.

    d. What is your profit?

    e. What is the level of consumer surplus?

10. Beth is an eight-year-old who old sells homemade lemonade on a street corner in a suburban neighbourhood. Each paper cup of lemonade costs Beth 20 cents to produce; she has no fixed costs. The reservation prices for the ten people who walk by Beth's lemonade stand each day are as listed in the table below.

Person	A	B	C	D	E	F	G	H	I	J
Reservation price (€)	1.00	0.90	0.80	0.70	0.60	0.50	0.40	0.30	0.20	0.10

Beth knows the distribution of reservation prices (that is, she knows that one person is willing to pay €1, another €0.90, and so on), but she does not know any specific individual's reservation price.

    a. Calculate the marginal revenue of selling an additional cup of lemonade. (Start by figuring out the price Beth would charge if she produced only one cup of lemonade, and calculate the total revenue; then find the price Beth would charge if she sold two cups of lemonade; and so on.)

    b. What is Beth's profit-maximising price?

    c. At that price, what are Beth's economic profit and total consumer surplus?

    d. What price should Beth charge if she wants to maximise total economic surplus?

Now suppose that Beth can tell the reservation price of each person. What price would she charge each person if she wanted to maximise profit? Compare her profit to the total surplus calculated in part (c).

References

Baumol, W., J.C. Panzar and R.D. Willig (1982) *Contestable Markets and the Theory of Industry Structure* (New York: Harcourt Brace Jovanovich).

Brätland, J. (2004) 'Contestable markets theory as a regulatory framework: an Austrian post-mortem', *Quarterly Journal of Austrian Economics*, vol. 7, no. 3, pp. 3–28.

Online LearningCentre

To help you grasp the key concepts of this chapter check out the extra resources posted on the Online Learning Centre. There are chapter summaries, self-test questions, an interactive graphing tool, weblinks and a glossary, all for free!

Visit the Online Learning Centre at: www.mcgraw-hill.co.uk/textbooks/mcdowell for information on accessing all of these resources.

Thinking Strategically (1): Interdependence, Decision Making and the Theory of Games

A US newspaper at the end of the 1990s[1] carried a story originating in Hollywood. At a Christmas Eve dinner party in 1997, actor Robert De Niro asked singer Tony Bennett if he would be willing to sing 'Got the World on a String' in the final scene of a film that De Niro would be acting in and which was to be produced by Warner Brothers. He was referring to the project that became the 1999 hit comedy *Analyze This*, in which the troubled head of a crime family, played by De Niro, seeks the counsel of a psychotherapist, played by Billy Crystal. In the script, both the mob boss and his therapist are big fans of Bennett's music. Bennett said he would be interested, and that was that … for a year.

Then his son and agent, Danny Bennett, received a phone call from Warner Brothers to discuss terms. They proposed a fee of $15,000 for Bennett Sr for singing the song. For an hour's work it was a very reasonable offer, and one any singer (or his agent) would be expected to accept in a semi-quaver. Unfortunately, the Warner negotiator let slip that the film was already in the can except for the final scene and the song, and the script clearly led up to this particular song and singer at the ending. Bennett Jr managed to get Warner Brothers up to $200,000. Had they made the offer to Bennett a year earlier, before filming had begun, they would have been €185,000 better off. As they say: in life, timing is everything!

The point of this story is that the payoff to many actions depends not only on the actions themselves but also on when they are taken and how they relate to actions taken by others. In Chapters 5–8, economic decision makers confronted an environment that was essentially fixed. This chapter will focus on cases in which people and especially firms must consider the effect of their behaviour on others. For example, an imperfectly competitive firm will in many circumstances want to weigh the likely responses of rivals when deciding whether to cut prices or to increase marketing expenditure. *Interdependencies* of this sort are the rule rather than the exception in economic and social life. To make sense of the world we live in, then, we must take these interdependencies into account.

An analytical method for handling this type of problem is what is known as game theory. Its origins may be found in a book published in 1944, written by John von

---

1 *New York Times*, 2 May 1999.

Neumann and Oskar Morgenstern, *The Theory of Games and Economic Behavior*.[2] They started from the premise that much economic behaviour can be analysed as a choice of a strategy in situations where people's interests do not coincide, so that *conflict between decision makers* is inevitable. Then, in the early 1950s, John Nash,[3] a mathematician at Princeton, produced a couple of path-breaking papers dealing with the concept of an *equilibrium in a game* – meaning, loosely, an outcome that is stable and predictable given the motives of, and constraints facing, the players. Modern game theory has been built on these foundations, and Nash was subsequently awarded the Nobel Prize in Economics in 1994.

The theory of games

In chess, tennis, or any other game, your payoff from a given move depends on *what your opponent does in response*. In choosing your move, therefore, you must anticipate your opponent's responses, how you might respond and what further moves your own response might elicit.

Consider the following problem that shows how this idea applies in economics. You have decided to open a small supermarket in your home-town neighbourhood, where there is already an established store belonging to a major national chain. The reason is that you have good information that there is 'cash on the table' in the form of profits to be appropriated if you can attract a sufficient number of customers from the incumbent. You do so because you estimate that you can offer a better value-for-money service. You could do this by undercutting the prices of the incumbent. You could do this simply by offering a different choice of goods. You could do this by offering a service that will attract a sufficient number of higher-income shoppers to you who are not satisfied with the one-size-fits-all offerings of the established chain. The market share you hope to achieve makes the proposal profitable. But will you achieve it? That depends on how the incumbent firm reacts.

It could decide that the loss of market share is such that it must respond by lowering prices (increasing value for money). It could decide that there is room in the market for both of you, and it might be happy (if you go upmarket) to leave the upper end of the market (with all the problems of dealing with better-off and more demanding purchasers) to you. It could decide that if you succeed in this venture it is probable that others will imitate you in other local markets, threatening the financial viability of its operations as a whole, and so launch a price war designed to force you out, on the basis that the sight of a corpse hanging from a gibbet deters imitation. Whether or not you enter the market, and the strategy you adopt in the market, will reflect your opinion as to what the other side will do in response to your decision. It's not at all clear that it makes sense to enter just because you see a profitable opportunity in the form of 'cash on the table'. In order to analyse and to predict outcomes in such situations, in which the payoffs to different actors depend on the actions their opponents undertake, economists and other behavioural scientists have devised the mathematical theory of games.

In this chapter we will first introduce the basic elements of game theory, and use them in a variety of hypothetical situations in order to explain some aspects of how people and firms behave. In the next chapter we will use the insights and tools devel-

---

2 Von Neumann and Morgenstern (1944).

3 Nash's sad life (he was diagnosed paranoid schizophrenic) was the subject of the movie *A Beautiful Mind*. For an economist, unfortunately, the movie is marred by its failure to make clear the significance, simple elegance and enormous analytical implications of his exposition of what is now known as the concept of a Nash equilibrium (see p. 281).

oped here to look at competition in markets where the number of firms competing with each other is small, and in which, therefore, decision making has to recognise the pervasive effects of interdependency.

basic elements of a game the players, the strategies available to each player and the payoffs each player receives for each possible combination of strategies

The three elements of a game

Any game has three **basic elements**: the *players*, the list of possible actions (or *strategies*) each player can choose from and the *payoffs* the players receive for each combination of strategies. How these elements combine to form the basis of a theory of behaviour will become clear in the context of Examples 9.1–9.3.

Example 9.1 Should Lufthansa spend more money on advertising?

Suppose that Lufthansa and Alitalia are the only air carriers that serve the Frankfurt–Milan route. Each currently earns an economic profit of €6,000 per flight on this route. If Lufthansa increases its advertising spending in this market by €1,000 per flight and Alitalia spends no more on advertising than it does now, Lufthansa's profit will rise to €8,000 per flight and Alitalia's will fall to €2,000. If both spend €1,000 more on advertising, each will earn an economic profit of €5,500 per flight. This reflects the fact that although the advertising by each will offset the impact of the other's advertising, higher advertising spending by both increases overall demand for tickets. These payoffs are symmetric, so if Lufthansa stands still while Alitalia increases its spending by €1,000, Lufthansa's economic profit will fall to €2,000 per flight and Alitalia's will rise to €8,000. If each must decide independently whether to increase spending on advertising, what should Lufthansa do?

Think of this situation as a game. The players are the two airlines, each of which must choose one of two strategies: to raise spending by €1,000 or to leave it the same.

payoff matrix a table that describes the payoffs in a game for each possible combination of strategies

The payoffs are the economic profits that correspond to the four possible scenarios resulting from their choices. One way to summarise the relevant information about this game is to display the players, strategies and payoffs in the form of a simple table called a **payoff matrix** (see Figure 9.1).

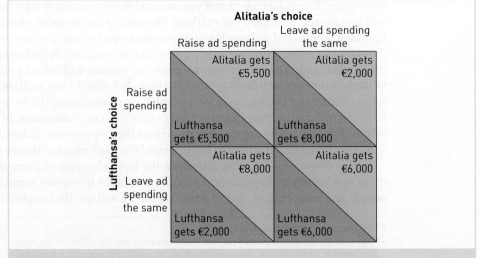

Figure 9.1 The Payoff Matrix for an Advertising Game.

Given the payoff matrix in Figure 9.1, what should Lufthansa do? The essence of strategic thinking is to begin by looking at the situation from the other party's point of view. Suppose Alitalia assumes that Lufthansa will raise its spending on advertising (the top row in Figure 9.1). In that case, Alitalia's best bet would be to follow suit (the left column in Figure 9.1). Why? Because Alitalia's economic profits, given in the upper-left cell of Figure 9.1, will be €5,500 as compared with only €2,000 if it keeps spending level (see the upper-right cell).

Alternatively, suppose Alitalia assumes that Lufthansa will keep spending unchanged (that is, Lufthansa will choose the bottom row in Figure 9.1). In that case, Alitalia would still do better to increase spending, because it would earn €8,000 (the lower left cell) as compared with only €6,000 if it keeps spending level (the lower-right cell). In this particular game, no matter which strategy Lufthansa chooses, Alitalia will earn a higher economic profit by increasing its spending. And since this game is perfectly symmetric, a similar conclusion holds for Lufthansa: no matter which strategy Alitalia chooses, Lufthansa will do better by increasing its spending on ads.

dominant strategy one that yields a higher payoff no matter what the other players in a game choose

dominated strategy any other strategy available to a player who has a dominant strategy

When one player has a strategy that yields a higher payoff no matter which choice the other player makes, that player is said to have a **dominant strategy**. Not all games involve dominant strategies, but both players in this game have one, and that is to increase spending on ads. For both players, to leave ad spending the same is a **dominated strategy** – one that leads to a lower payoff than an alternative choice, regardless of the other player's choice.

Notice, however, that when each player chooses the dominant strategy, the resulting payoffs are smaller than if each had left spending unchanged. When Lufthansa and Alitalia increase their spending on ads, each earns only €5,500 in economic profits as compared with the €6,000 each would have earned without the increase. (We'll say more about this apparent paradox below.)

Nash equilibrium

Nash equilibrium any combination of strategies in which each player's strategy is his or her best choice, given the other players' strategies

A game is said to be in equilibrium if each player's strategy is the best he or she can choose, given the other players' chosen strategies. This definition of equilibrium is sometimes called a **Nash equilibrium**, after the Nobel Laureate John Nash. When a game is in equilibrium, no player has any incentive to deviate from his or her current strategy.

If each player in a game has a dominant strategy, as in Example 9.1, equilibrium occurs when each player follows that strategy. But even in games in which not every player has a dominant strategy, we can often identify an equilibrium outcome. Consider, for instance, the following variation on the advertising game in Example 9.1.

Example 9.2 Should Alitalia or Lufthansa spend more money on advertising?

Once again, suppose that Lufthansa and Alitalia are the only carriers serving the Frankfurt–Milan route, and that the payoffs are as in Figure 9.2. Has Lufthansa a dominant strategy? Has Alitalia? If each firm does the best it can, given the incentives facing the other, what will be the outcome of this game?

In this game, with these payoffs, no matter what Lufthansa does, Alitalia will do better to raise its ad spending, so raising the advertising budget is a dominant strategy for Alitalia. Lufthansa, however, does not have a dominant strategy. If Alitalia raises its spending, Lufthansa will do better to stand still; if Alitalia stands still, however,

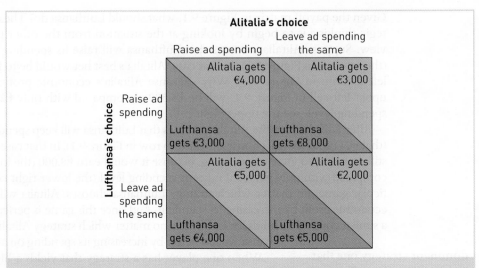

Figure 9.2 Equilibrium When One Player Lacks a Dominant Strategy.

Equilibrium

Lufthansa will do better to spend more. But even though Lufthansa hasn't a dominant strategy, we can still predict what is likely to happen in this game. After all, Lufthansa's managers know what the payoff matrix is, so they can predict that Alitalia will spend more on ads (since that is Alitalia's dominant strategy). Thus the best strategy for Lufthansa, given the prediction that Alitalia will spend more on ads, is to keep its own spending level. If both players do the best they can, taking account of the incentives each faces, this game will end in the lower-left cell of the payoff matrix in Figure 9.2: Alitalia will raise its spending on ads and Lufthansa will not. When both players are positioned in the lower-left cell, neither has any incentive to change its strategy. Therefore the choices corresponding to the lower-left cell in Figure 9.2 satisfy the definition of a Nash equilibrium, a combination of strategies for which each player's choice is the best available option, given the choice made by the other player.

Exercise 9.1   What should Lufthansa and Alitalia do if their payoff matrix is modified as follows?

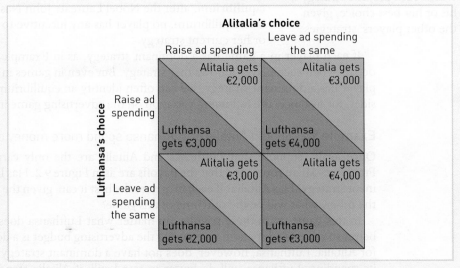

prisoner's dilemma a game in which each player has a dominant strategy and, when each plays it, the resulting payoffs are smaller for each than if each had played a dominated strategy

The prisoner's dilemma

The game in Example 9.1 belongs to an important class of games called the **prisoner's dilemma**. In the prisoner's dilemma, when each player chooses his dominant strategy, the result is unattractive to the group of players as a whole.

The original prisoner's dilemma

Example 9.3 recounts the original scenario from which the prisoner's dilemma drew its name.

Example 9.3 Should the prisoners confess?

Two prisoners, Horace and Jasper, are being held in separate cells for a serious crime that they did in fact commit. The prosecutor, however, has only enough hard evidence to convict them of a minor offence, for which the penalty is one year in jail. Each prisoner is told that if one confesses while the other remains silent, the confessor will be released without prosecution, and the other will spend 20 years in prison. If both confess, they will get an intermediate sentence of five years. (These payoffs are summarised in Figure 9.3.) The two prisoners are not allowed to communicate with one another. Have they a dominant strategy? If so, what is it?

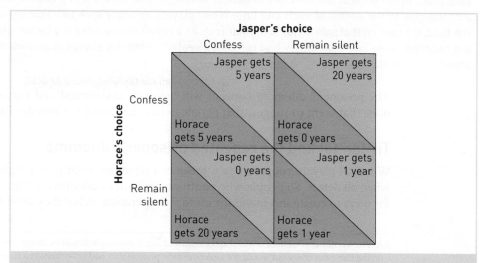

Figure 9.3 The Payoff Matrix for a Prisoner's Dilemma.

Equilibrium ⃝ They have a dominant strategy. It is for each prisoner to confess. No matter what Jasper does, Horace will get a lighter sentence by speaking out. If Jasper confesses, Horace will get five years (upper-left cell in Figure 9.3) instead of 20 (lower-left cell). If Jasper remains silent, Horace will go free (upper-right cell) instead of spending a year in jail (lower-right cell). Because the payoffs are perfectly symmetrical: Jasper will also do better to confess, no matter what Horace does. The difficulty is that, when each follows his dominant strategy and confesses, both will do worse than if each had said nothing. When both confess, they each get five years (upper-left cell) instead of the one year they would have received by remaining silent (lower-right cell). Hence the name of this game: the prisoner's dilemma (or, indeed, prisoners' dilemma).

Prisoner's dilemmas in everyday life

The prisoner's dilemma is one of the most powerful metaphors in all of human behavioural science. Countless social and economic interactions have payoff structures analogous to the one confronted by the two prisoners. Some of those interactions occur between only two players, as in the examples just discussed; many others involve larger groups. But regardless of the number of players involved, the common thread is one of conflict between the narrow self-interest of individuals and the broader interests of larger communities. In Economic naturalist 9.1 we look at the apparently irrational behaviour of fans at some sports games.[4]

Economic naturalist 9.1 Why do people at rugby games stand up on one side in all-seater stadiums and obscure each other's view at critical moments in the game, while soccer fans seem to remain seated when a score is imminent?

The answer lies in how points are scored, but also reflects a prisoner's dilemma in the case of rugby. For those who do not follow the code, which is played with 15 players on each side and an oval ball, the highest points are scored by touching the ball down over the opponent's goal line and this can take place at the edge of the field. In the case of soccer, of course, it's just a case of booting the ball into the goal in the centre of each end line. When players in rugby look like scoring at the edge of the field, the fans on that side all jump to their feet. As a result no one sees any better what is happening near the score line than if they had remained seated … but it's always in someone's interest to stand … so all stand.

The prisoner's dilemma concept will help you understand and answer some questions that seem to suggest that people behave irrationally. Consider Exercise 9.2.

Tit-for-tat and the repeated prisoner's dilemma

When all players cooperate in a prisoner's dilemma, each gets a higher payoff than when all defect. So people who confront a prisoner's dilemma will be on the lookout for ways to create incentives for mutual cooperation. What they need is some way to

---

4 A reviewer of an earlier draft of this chapter suggested that this example should be dropped because some readers on the European continent would not understand the point as they had never been at a rugby game. We understand that the EU Sports Commissioner is to ensure that this instance of cultural deprivation will be rectified by subsidising rugby in Mitteleuropa, but in the meantime we hope that a redraft will make the point clearer.

Exercise 9.2   **Use the prisoner's dilemma model to explain the following three scenarios.**

1. A fire breaks out in the orchestra pit in a theatre during the performance of a play. The next day newspapers comment on the numbers killed and injured in the rush to leave the auditorium, and the numbers who died from smoke inhalation because the doors were jammed by those rushing out, and castigate the audience for panicking and behaving irrationally, when they could all have left the building safely if they had done so row by row.

2. You are invited to a party and return home afterwards with laryngitis developed by having to shout for two hours to make yourself heard. Many other guests suffer similarly. Now if only they had all chosen to speak quietly …

3. It was reported at the end of 2004 that (as many have suspected) the use of mobile phones on planes does not pose a safety hazard. Consequently legal restrictions on their use would in all probability be lifted. In 2008 the EU Commission decided to amend European regulations to permit the use of mobile phones under certain conditions in aircraft. How likely is it that all airlines will completely lift the restriction even if it is no longer legally binding on them to impose it?

repeated prisoner's dilemma a standard prisoner's dilemma that confronts the same players repeatedly

tit-for-tat a strategy for the repeated prisoner's dilemma in which players cooperate on the first move, then mimic their partner's last move on each successive move

Incentives Matter

penalise players who defect. When players interact with one another only once, this turns out to be difficult to achieve. But when they expect to interact repeatedly, new possibilities emerge.

A **repeated prisoner's dilemma** is a standard prisoner's dilemma that confronts the same players not just once but many times. Experimental research on repeated prisoner's dilemmas in the 1960s identified a simple strategy that proves remarkably effective at limiting defection. The strategy is called **tit-for-tat**, and here is how it works. The first time you interact with someone, you cooperate. In each subsequent interaction you simply do what that person did in the previous interaction. Thus, if your partner defected on your first interaction, you would then defect on your next interaction with her. If she then cooperates, your move next time will be to cooperate as well.

The success of tit-for-tat requires a reasonably stable set of players, each of whom can remember what other players have done in previous interactions. It also requires that players have a significant stake in what happens in the future, for it is the fear of *retaliation* that deters people from defecting.

RECAP The prisoner's dilemma

The *prisoner's dilemma* is a game in which each player has a dominant strategy, and in which the payoff to each player when each chooses that strategy is smaller than if each had chosen a dominated strategy. Incentives analogous to those found in the prisoner's dilemmas help to explain a broad range of behaviour in business and everyday life – among them, excessive spending on advertising, cartel instability, standing at concerts and shouting at parties. Cooperation in repeated prisoner's dilemmas can often be sustained by the *tit-for-tat* strategy, in which players cooperate on the first move and mimic their partner's previous move thereafter.

Games in which timing matters

In the games discussed so far, players were assumed to choose their strategies simultaneously, and which player moved first didn't particularly matter. For example, in the prisoner's dilemma, players would follow their dominant strategies even if they knew in advance what strategies their opponents had chosen. But in other situations, such as the negotiations between Warner Brothers and Tony Bennett described at the beginning of this chapter, timing is of the essence.

When players move simultaneously (or can be modelled as doing so) the approach to the game and its outcome based on a simple payoff matrix is inadequate, and what is described as an extensive form of the game becomes necessary. In graphic terms, the payoff matrix is replaced by a decision tree.

The ultimatum bargaining game

To illustrate this, we use a simple example of timing in a game at the level of individual behaviour: the so-called 'ultimatum game'.

Example 9.4 Should Michael accept Tom's offer?

Tom and Michael are subjects in an experiment. The experimenter begins by giving €100 to Tom, who must then propose how to divide the money between himself and Michael. Tom can propose any division he chooses, provided the proposed amounts are whole euros and he offers Michael at least €1. Suppose Tom proposes €X for himself and €(100 – X) for Michael, where X is a whole number no larger than 99. Michael must then say whether he accepts the proposal. If he does, each will get the proposed amount. But if Michael rejects the proposal, each player will get zero, and the €100 will revert to the experimenter. If Tom and Michael know they will play this game only once, and each wants to make as much money for himself as possible, what should Tom propose?

A payoff matrix is not a useful way to summarise the information in this game, because it says nothing about the timing of each player's move. For games in which timing matters, a **decision tree (or game tree)** is more useful. This is called an 'extended' form of the game. This type of diagram describes the possible moves in the sequence in which they may occur, and lists the final payoffs for each possible combination of moves.

The decision tree for the game in Example 9.4 is shown in Fig. 9.4. At A, Tom begins the game by making his proposal. At B, Michael responds to Tom's proposal. If he accepts (the top branch of the tree), Tom will get €X and Michael will get €(100 – X). If he refuses (the bottom branch of the tree), both will get nothing.

decision tree (or game tree) a diagram that describes the possible moves in a game in sequence and lists the payoffs that correspond to each possible combination of moves

ultimatum bargaining game one in which the first player has the power to confront the second player with a take-it-or-leave-it offer

In thinking strategically about this game, the key for Tom is to put himself in Michael's shoes and imagine how he might react to various proposals. This reflects 'interdependence' affecting the player's choice of move. Because he knows that Michael's goal is to make as much money as possible, he knows that Michael will accept his offer no matter how small, because the alternative is to reject it and get nothing. For instance, suppose that Tom proposes €99 for himself and only €1 for Michael (see Fig. 9.5). At B, Michael's best option is to accept the offer. This is a Nash equilibrium, because neither player has any incentive to deviate from the strategy he chose.

This type of game has been called the **ultimatum bargaining**

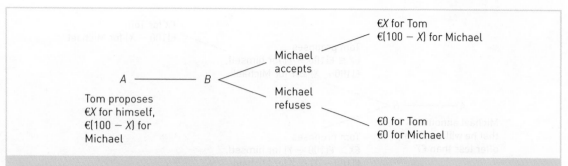

Figure 9.4 Decision Tree for Example 9.4. This decision tree shows the possible moves and payoffs for the game in Example 9.4 in the sequence in which they may occur.

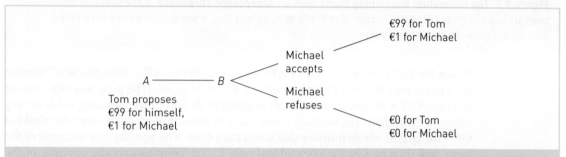

Figure 9.5 Tom's Best Strategy in an Ultimatum Bargaining Game. Because Tom can predict that Michael will accept any positive offer, Tom's income-maximising strategy at *A* is to offer Michael the smallest positive amount possible, €1.

game,[5] because of the power of the first player to confront the second player with a take-it-or-leave-it offer. Michael could refuse a one-sided offer from Tom, but doing so would make him worse off than if he accepted it.

Example 9.5 illustrates the importance of the *timing of moves* in determining the outcome of the ultimatum bargaining game.

Example 9.5 What should Michael's acceptance threshold be?

Suppose we change the rules of the ultimatum bargaining game slightly so that Michael has the right to specify *in advance* the smallest offer he will accept. This means that Michael, rather than Tom, moves first. Once Michael announces this number, he is bound by it. If Tom's task is again to propose a division of the €100, what amount should Michael specify?

This seemingly minor change in the rules completely alters the game. Once Michael announces that €*Y* is the smallest offer he will accept, his active role in the game is over. If *Y* is €60 and Tom proposes €*X* for himself and €(100 – *X*) for Michael, his offer will be rejected automatically if *X* exceeds 40. The decision tree for this game is shown in Fig. 9.6.

---

5 Experiments with the ultimatum game have uncovered something that may not surprise you. When classroom experiments are played using sociology students, literature students and similar groups as test populations, the offers that are made are usually much closer to a 50/50 split than when they are carried out using economics students. In our experience applying this game in class, economics and business students have more 70/30 or 90/10 outcomes than other students. Figure that out! Does economics make you 'rational', or do more 'rational' people take economics?

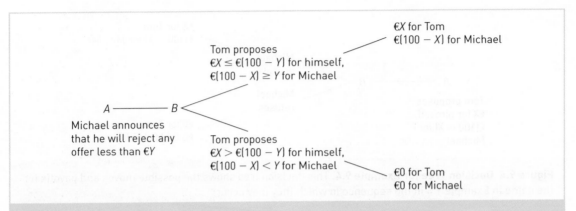

Figure 9.6 The Ultimatum Bargaining Game with an Acceptance Threshold. If Michael can commit himself to a minimum acceptable offer threshold at A, he will fare dramatically better than in the standard ultimatum bargaining game.

When Michael announces that €Y is the smallest offer he will accept, the best Tom can do is to propose €(100 – Y) for himself and €Y for Michael. If he proposes any amount less than €Y for Michael, both will get nothing at all. Since this reasoning holds for any value of Y less than 100, Michael's best bet is to announce an acceptance threshold of €99 – the largest whole number that is less than €100. The equilibrium outcome of the game will then be €99 for Michael and only €1 for Tom, exactly the opposite of the outcome when Tom had the first move.

Credible threats and promises

Why couldn't Michael have threatened to refuse a one-sided offer in the original version of the game? While nothing prevented him from doing so, such a threat would not have been credible. In the language of game theory, a **credible threat** is one that is in the threatener's interest to carry out when the time comes to act. The problem in the original version of the game is that Michael would have no reason to carry out his threat to reject a one-sided offer in the event that he actually received one. Once Tom announced such an offer, refusing it would not pass the cost–benefit test.

credible threat a threat to take an action that is in the threatener's interest to carry out

credible promise a promise that is in the interests of the promisor to keep when the time comes to act

The concept of a credible threat figured prominently in the negotiations between Warner Brothers managers and Tony Bennett over the matter of Bennett's fee for performing in *Analyze This*. Once most of the film had been shot, managers knew they couldn't threaten credibly to refuse Bennett's salary demand, because at that point adapting the film to another singer would have been prohibitively costly. In contrast, a similar threat made before production of the movie had begun would have been credible.

Just as in some games credible threats are impossible to make, in others **credible promises** are impossible.

Example 9.6 Should the business owner open a remote office?

The owner of a thriving business wants to start up an office in a distant city. If she hires someone to manage the new office, she can afford to pay a weekly salary of €1,000 – a premium of €500 over what the manager would otherwise be able to earn – and still earn a weekly economic profit of €1,000 for herself. The owner's concern is that she will not be able to monitor the manager's behaviour. The owner knows that by managing the remote office dishonestly, the manager can boost his take-home pay to €1,500 while causing the owner an economic loss of €500 per week. If the owner believes that all managers are selfish income maximisers, will she open the new office?

The decision tree for the remote office game is shown in Fig. 9.7. At *A*, the managerial candidate promises to manage honestly, which brings the owner to *B*, where she must decide whether to open the new office. If she opens it, they reach *C*, where the manager must decide whether to manage honestly. If the manager's only goal is to make as much money as he can, he will manage dishonestly (bottom branch at *C*), since that way he will earn €500 more than by managing honestly (top branch at *C*).

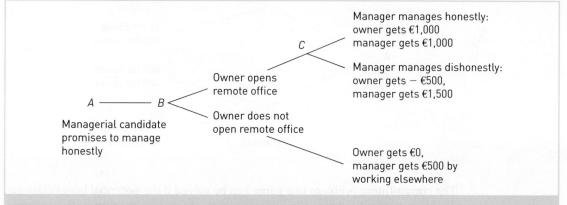

Figure 9.7 Decision Tree for the Remote Office Game. The best outcome is for the owner to open the office at *B* and for the manager to manage the office honestly at *C*. But if the manager is purely self-interested and the owner knows it, this path will not be an equilibrium outcome.

So if the owner opens the new office, she will end up with an economic loss of €500. If she had not opened the office (bottom branch at *B*), she would have realised an economic profit of zero. Since zero is better than –€500, the owner will choose not to open the remote office. In the end, the opportunity cost of the manager's inability to make a credible promise is €1,500: the manager's forgone €500 salary premium and the owner's forgone €1,000 return.

The commitment problem here is that a potential manager of the distant office can promise to behave correctly ... but lacks any mechanism to make the promise credible, since it will pay the candidate for the job to behave opportunistically.

Commitment problems

Games like those in Exercise 9.3 (below), as well as the prisoner's dilemma, the ultimatum bargaining game and the remote office game, confront players with a **commitment problem**, a situation in which they have difficulty achieving the desired outcome because they cannot make credible threats or promises. If both players in the prisoner's dilemma (Example 9.3) could make a binding promise to remain silent, both would be assured of a shorter sentence; hence the logic of the underworld code of *omertà*, under which the family of anyone who provides evidence against a fellow mob member is killed. A similar logic explains the adoption of military arms control agreements, in which opponents sign an enforceable pledge to curtail weapons spending.

commitment problem
a situation in which people cannot achieve their goals because of an inability to make credible threats or promises

Exercise 9.3   Smith and Jones are playing a game in which Smith has the first move at *A* in the following decision tree. Once Smith has chosen either the top or bottom branch at *A* Jones, who can see what Smith has chosen, must choose the top or bottom branch at *B* or *C*. If the payoffs at the end of each branch are as shown, what is the equilibrium outcome of this game? If, before Smith chose, Jones could make a credible commitment to choose either the top or bottom branch when his turn came, what would he do?

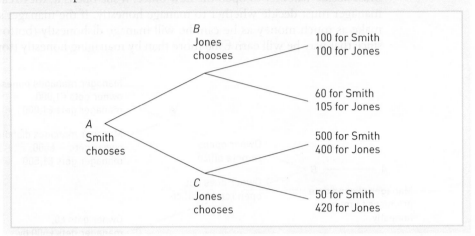

The commitment problem in a game can be solved if the potential beneficiary can find some way of committing himself to a course of action in the future. For example, suppose firm *A* wants to discourage firm *B* from price cutting, and knows that to do so involves acting in a way that makes *B* confident that *A* will not overtly or tacitly engage in price cutting itself. It could sell firm *B* a 'put' option, whereby firm *B* could oblige firm *A* to buy specified quantities of its output at some critical price below today's price. A tacit promise not to cut prices would be made credible by this **commitment device**.

commitment device a way of changing incentives so as to make otherwise empty threats or promises credible

Business owners seem well aware of commitment problems in the workplace and have adopted a variety of commitment devices to solve them. Consider, for example, the problem confronting the owner of a restaurant. She wants her table staff to provide good service so that customers will enjoy their meals and come back in the future. And since good service is valuable to her, she would be willing to pay waiters extra for it. For their part, waiters would be willing to provide good service in return for the extra pay. The problem is that the owner cannot always monitor whether the waiters do provide good service. Her concern is that, having been paid extra for it, the waiters may slack off when she isn't looking. Unless the owner can find some way to solve this problem, she will not pay extra, the waiters will not provide good service, and she, they and the diners will suffer. A better outcome for all concerned would be for the waiters to find some way to commit themselves to good service.

Restaurateurs in many countries have tried to solve this commitment problem by encouraging diners to leave tips at the end of their meals. The attraction of this solution is that the diner is *always* in a good position to monitor service quality. The diner should be happy to reward good service with a generous tip, since doing so will help to ensure good service in the future. And the waiter has a strong incentive to provide good service, because he knows that the size of his tip may depend on it.

The various commitment devices just discussed – the underworld code of *omertà*, the tip for the waiter – all work because they change the material incentives facing the decision makers. But, as Example 9.7 illustrates, sometimes this simple calculus of incentives is not a complete explanation.

Example 9.7 Will Federico leave a tip when dining on the road?

Federico has just finished a €30 dinner at Ristorante Stendhal, just off the Milan–Ancona autostrada near Parma, some 300 km from home. The meal was superb, and the waiter provided good service. If Federico cares only about himself, will he leave a tip?

Once the waiter has provided good service, there is no way for him to take it back if the diner fails to leave a tip. In restaurants patronised by local diners, failure to tip is not a problem, because the waiter can simply provide poor service the next time a non-tipper comes in. And no one wants to appear mean in front of people who might care. But the waiter lacks that leverage with out-of-town diners eating alone. Having already received good service, Federico must choose between paying €30 or €35 for his meal. If he is an essentially selfish person, the former choice may be a compelling one. But if you know that the waiter depends for much of his living on tips you are likely to tip anyway, even if not overgenerously, for the same reason as most people do not engage in shoplifting even when they know they would get away with it: our moral sense overrides our instinct for self-advancement.

RECAP Games in which timing matters

The outcomes in many games depend on the *timing* of each player's move. For such games, the payoffs are best summarised by a *decision tree* rather than a payoff matrix.

The inability to make credible threats and promises often prevents people from achieving desired outcomes in many games. Games with this property are said to confront players with *commitment problems*. Such problems can sometimes be solved by employing *commitment devices* – ways of changing incentives to facilitate making credible threats or promises.

The strategic role of preferences

In all the games we have discussed so far, players were assumed to care only about obtaining the best possible outcome for themselves. Thus each player's goal was to get the highest monetary payoff, the shortest jail sentence, the best chance of survival, and so on. The irony, in most of these games, is that players do not attain the best outcomes. Better outcomes can sometimes be achieved by altering the material incentives selfish players face, but not always.

If altering the relevant material incentives is not possible, commitment problems can sometimes be solved by altering people's psychological incentives. In a society in which people are strongly conditioned to develop moral sentiments – feelings of guilt when they harm others, feelings of sympathy for their trading partners, feelings of outrage when they are treated unjustly – commitment problems arise less often than in more narrowly self-interested societies.

Exercise 9.4   In a moral society, will the business owner open a remote office?

Consider again the owner of the thriving business who is trying to decide whether to open an office in a distant city. Suppose the society in which she lives is one in which all citizens have been strongly conditioned to behave honestly. Will she open the remote office?

Are people fundamentally selfish?

The assumption that people are 'self-interested' in the narrow sense of the term does not always capture the full range of motives that govern choice in strategic settings. Researchers have found that tipping rates in restaurants patronised mostly by out-of-town diners are essentially the same as in restaurants patronised mostly by local diners.

Reflect also on how you would behave in some of the other games we have discussed. In the ultimatum bargaining game, what would you do if your partner proposed €99 for himself and only €1 for you? Would you reject the offer? If so, you are not alone. Two findings of extensive laboratory studies of the ultimatum bargaining game challenge the assumption that most players are narrowly self-interested. First, the most common proposal by the first player in this game is not a 99/1 split, but a 50/50 split. And, second, on the few occasions when the first player does propose a highly one-sided split, the second player typically rejects it. Subjects who reject the offer often mention the satisfaction they experienced at having penalised the first player for an 'unfair' offer.

Indeed, there are many exceptions to the outcomes predicted on the basis of the assumption that people are self-interested in the most narrow sense of the term. People who have been treated unjustly often seek 'revenge' even at ruinous cost to themselves. Every day people walk away from profitable transactions whose terms they believe to be 'unfair'.

In 1982 Argentina, pursuing a claim of sovereignty over the islands, mounted a surprise invasion of the British crown colony of the Falklands Islands (aka the Malvinas). The Argentine junta, in common with many other observers, were surprised by the British decision to spend vast sums, lose lives and risk the core of the Royal Navy's surface fleet to recover the desolate colony. After all, as the Argentine writer Jorge Luis Borges observed, the Falkland War made about as much sense as two bald men fighting over a comb.[6] It looked like a case of other values taking precedence over narrow self-interest. Possibly true: Mrs Thatcher was no ordinary Prime Minister, and rejoiced in the nickname of the 'Iron Lady'. However, at the time, Spain was putting pressure on Britain over Gibraltar (British since 1713), and Britain was facing difficult negotiations with China over the future administration of Hong Kong after its inevitable cession to China. And the UK government was facing internal opposition from the unionised coal miners who were threatening general strikes if the industry was rationalised. In these circumstances, does it seem so economically irrational to demonstrate that you will not be trampled on?

Preferences as solutions to commitment problems

Economists tend to view preferences as ends in themselves. Taking them as given, they calculate what actions will best serve those preferences. This approach to the study of behaviour is widely used by other social scientists and by game theorists, military strategists, philosophers and others. In its standard form, it assumes purely self-interested preferences for present and future consumption goods of various sorts, leisure pursuits and so on. Concerns about fairness, guilt, honour, sympathy and the like typically play no role.

Preferences clearly affect the choices people make in strategic interactions. Sympathy for one's trading partner can make a businessperson trustworthy even when material incentives favour cheating. A sense of justice can prompt a person to incur the costs of retaliation, even when incurring those costs will not undo the original injury.

Incentives
Matter

---

6 Quoted in Barnstone (1993).

It can also induce people to reject one-sided offers, even when their wealth would be increased by accepting them.

Note, however, that although preferences can clearly shape behaviour in these ways, that alone does not solve commitment problems. The solution to such problems requires not only that a person *have* certain preferences, but also that others have some way of *discerning* them. Unless the business owner can identify the trustworthy employee, that employee cannot land a job whose pay is predicated on trust. Unless the predator can identify a potential victim whose character will motivate retaliation, that person is likely to become a victim. And unless a person's potential trading partners can identify him as someone predisposed to reject one-sided offers, he will not be able to deter such offers.

From among those with whom we might engage in ventures requiring trust, can we identify reliable partners? If people could make *perfectly* accurate character judgements, they could always steer clear of dishonest persons. That people continue to be victimised, at least occasionally, by dishonest persons suggests that perfectly reliable character judgements are either impossible to make or prohibitively expensive.

Vigilance in the choice of trading partners is an essential element in solving (or avoiding) commitment problems, for if there is an advantage in being honest and being perceived as such, there is an even greater advantage in only *appearing* to be honest. After all, a liar who appears trustworthy will have better opportunities than one who glances about furtively, sweats profusely and has difficulty making eye contact. Indeed, the liar will have the same opportunities as an honest person but will get higher payoffs because the liar will exploit them to the full.

In the end, the question of whether people can make reasonably accurate character judgements is an empirical one. Experimental studies have shown that, even on the basis of brief encounters involving strangers, subjects are adept at predicting who will cooperate and who will defect in prisoner's dilemma games. For example, in one experiment in which only 26 per cent of subjects defected, the accuracy rate of predicted defections was more than 56 per cent. One might expect that predictions regarding those we know well would be even more accurate.

Do you know someone who would return an envelope containing €1,000 in cash to you if you lost it at a crowded concert? If so, then you accept the claim that personal character can help people to solve commitment problems. As long as honest individuals can identify at least some others who are honest and can interact selectively with them, honest individuals can prosper in a competitive environment.

RECAP The strategic role of preferences

Most applications of the theory of games assume that players are 'self-interested' in the narrow sense of the term. In practice, however, many choices, such as leaving tips in out-of-town restaurants, appear inconsistent with this assumption.

The fact that people seem driven by a more complex range of motives makes behaviour more difficult to predict but also creates new ways of solving commitment problems. *Psychological incentives* can often serve as commitment devices when changing players' material incentives is impractical. For example, people who are able to identify honest trading partners and interact selectively with them are able to solve commitment problems that arise from lack of trust.

Summary

- Economists use the mathematical theory of games to analyse situations in which the payoffs of one's actions depend on the actions *taken by others*. Games have three basic elements: the *players*; the list of *possible actions*, or *strategies*, from which each player can choose; and the *payoffs* the players receive for those strategies. The *payoff matrix* is the most useful way to summarise this information in games in which the timing of the players' moves is not decisive. In games in which the timing of moves does matter, a *decision tree* summarises the information in a much more useful format.

- A *dominant strategy* is one that yields a higher payoff regardless of the strategy chosen by the other player. In some games, such as the prisoner's dilemma, each player has a dominant strategy. The equilibrium occurs in such games when each player chooses his or her dominant strategy. In other games, not all players have a dominant strategy.

- Although the equilibrium outcome of any game is any combination of choices in which each player does the best he can, given the choices made by others, the result is often unattractive from the perspective of players as group. The prisoner's dilemma has this feature. The *incentive structure* of this game helps explain such disparate social dilemmas as excessive advertising, military arms races and failure to reap the potential benefits of interactions requiring trust.

- Individuals can often resolve these dilemmas if they can make *binding commitments* to behave in certain ways. Some commitments, such as those involved in military arms control agreements, are achieved by altering the material incentives confronting the players. Other commitments can be achieved by relying on psychological incentives to counteract material payoffs. Moral sentiments such as guilt, sympathy and a sense of justice often foster better outcomes than can be achieved by narrowly self-interested players. For this type of commitment to work, the relevant moral sentiments must be discernible by one's potential trading partners.

- Building on the idea of payoffs and games enables economists to construct models that indicate the importance of such things as beliefs and modes of competition in understanding how *small-number markets operate*.

- These models yield interesting and plausible conclusions that explain some features of *market behaviour* that are not explained by the simple models of perfect competition or monopolistic competition.

Review questions

1. Explain why a military arms race is an example of a prisoner's dilemma.

2. Why did Warner Brothers make a mistake by waiting until the filming of *Analyze This* was almost finished before negotiating with Tony Bennett to perform in the final scene?

3. Suppose General Motors is trying to hire a small firm to manufacture the door handles for Opel and Holden saloon cars. The task requires an investment in expensive capital equipment that cannot be used for any other purpose. Why might the CEO of the small firm refuse to undertake this venture without a long-term contract fixing the price of the door handles?

4. Would you be irrational to refuse a one-sided offer in an ultimatum bargaining game if you knew that you would be playing that game many times with the same partner?

5. Describe the commitment problem that narrowly self-interested diners and waiters confront at restaurants located on interstate highways. Given that in such restaurants tipping does seem to assure reasonably good service, do you think people are always selfish in the narrowest sense?

connect **Problems**

Problems marked with an asterisk (*) are more difficult.

1. In studying for his economics final, Sam is concerned about only two things: his grade and the amount of time he spends studying. A good grade will give him a benefit of 20; an average grade, a benefit of 5; and a poor grade, a benefit of 0. By studying a lot, Sam will incur a cost of 10; by studying a little, a cost of 6. Moreover, if Sam studies a lot and all other students study a little, he will get a good grade and they will get poor ones. But if they study a lot and he studies a little, they will get good grades and he will get a poor one. Finally, if he and all other students study for the same amount of time, everyone will get average grades. Other students share Sam's preferences regarding grades and study time.

   a. Model this situation as a two-person prisoner's dilemma in which the strategies are to study a little and to study a lot, and the players are Sam and all other students. Include the payoffs in the matrix.

   b. What is the equilibrium outcome in this game? From the students' perspective, is it the best outcome?

2. Consider the following 'dating game', which has two players, A and B, and two strategies, to buy a cinema ticket or a football ticket. The payoffs, given in points, are as shown in the matrix below. Note that the highest payoffs occur when both A and B attend the same event.

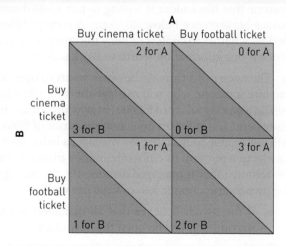

Assume that players A and B buy their tickets separately and simultaneously. Each must decide what to do knowing the available choices and payoffs but not what the other has actually chosen. Each player believes the other to be rational and self-interested.

   a. Does either player have a dominant strategy?

   b. How many potential equilibria are there? (**Hint:** To see whether a given combination of strategies is an equilibrium, ask whether either player could get a higher payoff by changing his or her strategy.)

    c. Is this game a prisoner's dilemma? Explain.

    d. Suppose player *A* gets to buy her ticket first. Player *B* does not observe *A*'s choice but knows that *A* chose first. Player *A* knows that player *B* knows she chose first. What is the equilibrium outcome?

    e. Suppose the situation is similar to part (d), except that player *B* chooses first. What is the equilibrium outcome?

3. Blackadder and Baldrick are rational, self-interested criminals imprisoned in separate cells in a dark medieval dungeon. They face the prisoner's dilemma displayed in the matrix below.

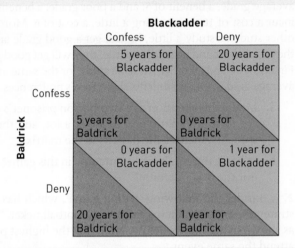

Assume that Blackadder is willing to pay 1,000 ducats for each year by which he can reduce his sentence below 20 years. A corrupt jailer tells Blackadder that before he decides whether to confess or deny the crime, he can tell him Baldrick's decision. How much is this information worth to Blackadder?

4. The owner of a thriving business wants to open a new office in a distant city. If he can hire someone who will manage the new office honestly, he can afford to pay that person a weekly salary of €2,000 (€1,000 more than the manager would be able to earn elsewhere) and still earn an economic profit of €800. The owner's concern is that he will not be able to monitor the manager's behaviour and that the manager will therefore be in a position to embezzle money from the business. The owner knows that if the remote office is managed dishonestly, the manager can earn €3,100 while causing the owner an economic loss of €600 per week.

    a. If the owner believes that all managers are narrowly self-interested income-maximisers, will he open the new office?

    b. Suppose the owner knows that a managerial candidate is a devoutly religious person who condemns dishonest behaviour and who would be willing to pay up to €15,000 to avoid the guilt she would feel if she were dishonest. Will the owner open the remote office?

5. Imagine yourself sitting in your car in a university car park that is currently full, waiting for someone to pull out so that you can park your car. Somebody pulls out, but at the same moment a driver who has just arrived overtakes you in an obvious attempt to park in the vacated spot before you can. Suppose this driver would be willing to pay up to €10 to park in that spot and up to €30 to avoid getting into an argument with you. (That is, the benefit of parking is €10, and the cost of an argument is €30.) At the same time the other driver guesses, accurately, that you too would be willing to pay up to €30 to avoid a confrontation and up to €10 to park in the vacant spot.

    a. Model this situation as a two-stage decision tree in which the other driver's bid to take the space is the opening move and your strategies are (1) to protest and (2) not to protest. If you protest (initiate an argument), the rules of the game specify that the other driver has to let you take the space. Show the payoffs at the end of each branch of the tree.

    b. What is the equilibrium outcome?

    c. What would be the advantage of being able to communicate credibly to the other driver that your failure to protest would be a significant psychological cost to you?

6. Newfoundland's fishing industry has declined sharply due to overfishing, even though fishing companies were supposedly bound by a quota agreement. If all fishing companies had abided by the agreement, yields could have been maintained at high levels.

    a. Model this situation as a prisoner's dilemma in which the players are Company A and Company B, and the strategies are to keep the quota and break the quota. Include appropriate payoffs in the matrix. Explain why overfishing is inevitable in the absence of effective enforcement of the quota agreement.

    b. Provide another environmental example of a prisoner's dilemma.

    c. In many potential prisoner's dilemmas, a way out for a would-be cooperator is to make reliable character judgements about the trustworthiness of potential partners. Explain why this solution is not available in many situations involving degradation of the environment.

7. Consider the following game, called 'matching pennies', which you are playing with a friend. Each of you has a penny hidden in your hand, facing either heads up or tails up (you know which way the one in your hand is facing). On the count of 'three' you simultaneously show your pennies to each other. If the face-up side of your coin matches the face-up side of your friend's coin, you get to keep the two pennies. If the faces do not match, your friend gets to keep the pennies.

    a. Who are the players in this game? What are each player's strategies? Construct a payoff matrix for the game.

    b. Is there a dominant strategy? If so, what?

    c. Is there an equilibrium? If so, what?

8. Consider the following game. Harry has four 20-pence pieces. He can offer Sally from one to four of them. If she accepts his offer, she keeps the coins Harry offered her and Harry keeps the others. If Sally declines Harry's offer, they both get nothing. They play the game only once, and each cares only about the amount of money he or she ends up with.

    a. Who are the players? What are each player's strategies? Construct a decision tree for this ultimatum bargaining game.

    b. Given their goal, what is the optimal choice for each player?

9.* Jill and Jack both have two pails that can be used to carry water down from a hill. Each makes only one trip down the hill, and each pail of water can be sold for €5. Carrying the pails of water down requires considerable effort. Both the children would be willing to pay €2 each to avoid carrying one bucket down the hill and an additional €3 to avoid carrying a second bucket down the hill.

 a. Given market prices, how many pails of water will each child fetch from the top of the hill?

 b. Jill and Jack's parents are worried that the two children don't cooperate enough with one another. Suppose they make Jill and Jack share their revenues from selling the water equally. Given that both are self-interested, construct the pay-off matrix for the decisions Jill and Jack face regarding the number of pails of water each should carry. What is the equilibrium outcome?

References

Barnstone, W. (1993) *With Borges on an Ordinary Evening in Buenos Aires* (Champaign, IL: University of Illinois Press).

Von Neumann, J. and O. Morgenstern (1944) *The Theory of Games and Economic Behavior* (Princeton, NJ: Princeton University Press).

To help you grasp the key concepts of this chapter check out the extra resources posted on the Online Learning Centre. There are chapter summaries, self-test questions, an interactive graphing tool, weblinks and a glossary, all for free!

Visit the Online Learning Centre at: www.mcgraw-hill.co.uk/textbooks/mcdowell for information on accessing all of these resources.

10

Thinking Strategically (2): Competition Among the Few

Competition among the few: interdependence and firm behaviour

Our principal interest in this chapter is the use of the concepts discussed in Chapter 9 to analyse how firms behave in markets in which there are relatively few players. In these circumstances a firm must decide on courses of action (e.g. what price to charge) in the knowledge that its competitors' behaviour will reflect the decisions it takes. This is described as 'interdependence' of decision making. We start by looking at the use of the concept of the prisoner's dilemma as an explanatory model of firm behaviour in interdependent markets.

Cost–Benefit Analysis

Example 10.1 Should Schering Plough or Novartis develop a new tumour-retarding drug?

Suppose two pharmaceutical companies both produce a drug the therapeutic effects of which slow down and may reverse the growth of malignant soft tissue tumours. In each case the success rate is around 70 per cent. Each has reason to believe that a modification to the molecular structure of the active compound in its drug could increase the success rate to around 80 per cent. However, refining the compound and testing it is an expensive process. Current profits from the anti-tumour drugs are the same for both firms (€200 million per annum). The first to market with an improved drug that has passed the testing process will have an unassailable lead over the other in terms of capturing market share and profits, while the loser in this race will see its profits decline as its existing drug loses market share. The same fate awaits a firm if it does not invest and the other does invest: profits decline from their present (no investment) level of €200 million to €25 million. Each has a 50 per cent chance of winning the race. Profits from an improved drug, after allowing for development costs, will be €300 million per annum, so the expected profit for each is 0.5(€300) million, or €150 million if they invest in developing the new drug.

The payoffs to the firms from investing in the required R&D or not investing are laid out in Fig. 10.1.

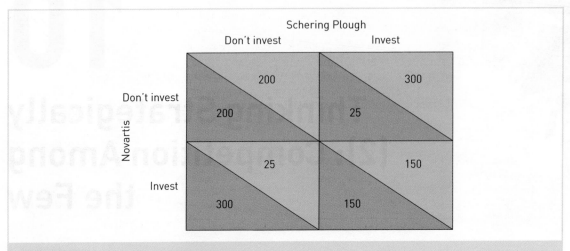

Figure 10.1 A Prisoner's Dilemma in an R&D Game. The dominant strategy in this game is for both to invest, even though each firm's expected profits would be higher if neither invested.

This game is an example of the prisoner's dilemma game introduced in the previous chapter. It casts an interesting light on the behaviour of high-tech firms where R&D is concerned: to maintain profits firms may feel they have to spend competitively on R&D even if to do so reduces profits. If we extend the story to cover the costs of R&D to each firm, a potentially disturbing aspect of this game emerges. The costs will be incurred by both firms, but will be recouped only by the winner of the race to develop the new drug. Suppose R&D costs are the same for both, and amount to €350 million each. Total resources spent to develop the drug are, therefore, €700 million. If the value to society is approximated by the total of the cost of developing the winning

Exercise 10.1 GM and Chrysler must both decide whether to invest in a new assembly system for cars. Games 1 and 2 show how their profits depend on the decisions they might make. Which of these games is a prisoner's dilemma?

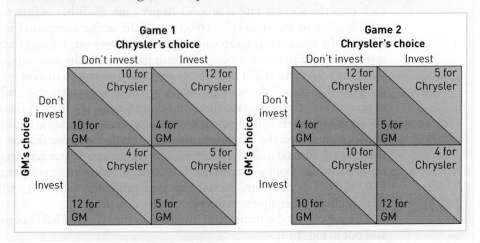

drug and the winning firm's profits from selling it, the total value of the resources spent on drug development (€700 million) exceeds the value to society of the new drug (€650 million). This of course does not happen all the time, but it points to the possibility of 'too much' money being spent on R&D.

Prisoner's dilemmas confronting imperfectly competitive firms

A **cartel** is any coalition of firms or producers that conspires to restrict production for the purpose of earning an economic profit by increasing price and widening the gap between price and cost. The world's best-known (and for some reason widely tolerated) cartel is OPEC, the Organization of Petroleum Exporting Countries, formed in 1960 to control oil production. Its members account for a very large share of the world's oil production. After the surge in oil prices in 2004 from $20 to $55 per barrel, due for the most to precautionary stock-piling because of the situation in Iraq, as oil prices fell back towards $40, and looked as if they would continue to decline, OPEC announced that it intended to cut production in order to maintain prices at or around $40. This was not treated very seriously by most industry observers because over the previous 30 years it had been shown that after initial increases in prices sparked by OPEC production cuts, prices always fell back as OPEC members broke ranks and non-members took advantage of OPEC cuts to raise production. OPEC is not only the best-known cartel, but the best-known example of the problem besetting all cartels: how to get them to work. History shows that cartels are notoriously unstable. As we shall see in Economic naturalist 10.1, the problem confronting oligopolists who are trying to form a cartel is a classic illustration of the prisoner's dilemma.

> **cartel** a coalition of firms that agrees to restrict output for the purpose of earning an economic profit

Why are cartel agreements notoriously unstable?

Start by looking at the situation described in Fig. 10.2. It shows the potential profit of a monopolist in a table water market. Suppose, however, there are two similar producers, Mineral Spring and Aquapure, selling water into this market. If they agree to act in concert, and charge the monopoly price while sharing the profits between them they can make the profits of a potential monopolist, but to do so they have to agree to restrict output to what a real monopolist would put on the market.

In this example we assume that costs are zero, so all revenue is profit. If the firms agree to share the market equally, and stick to this agreement, each will earn profits of €500 per day. Unfortunately, each knows that, since the products are very similar, if it undercuts its 'partner' it can scoop the market as consumers switch to its product. For example, if Aquapure decides to drop its price to €0.90 total sales will rise to 1,100 bottles a day, all produced by Aquapure (Fig. 10.3).

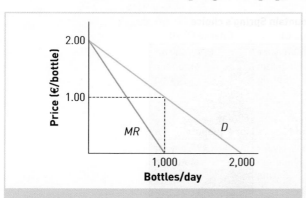

Figure 10.2 The Market Demand for Mineral Water.
Faced with the demand curve shown, a monopolist with zero marginal cost would produce 1,000 bottles per day (the quantity at which marginal revenue equals zero) and sell them at a price of €1.00 per bottle.

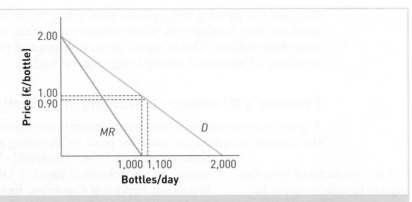

Figure 10.3 The Temptation to Violate a Cartel Agreement. By cutting its price from €1 per bottle to €0.90 per bottle, Aquapure can sell the entire market quantity demanded at that price, 1,100 bottles per day, rather than half the monopoly quantity of 1,000 bottles per day.

Of course, in these circumstances we would expect Mountain Spring to match the price cut, and the outcome would be each firm now selling 550 bottles at €0.90, and joint profits falling from €1,000 to €990: €495 each.

We've been here before; think of this as a game, and set up the payoffs to holding or cutting price (Figure 10.4).

You should recognise the pattern here: it's a prisoner's dilemma game once again as far as choice between €1 and €0.90 is concerned, and each player has an incentive to choose the lower price. Furthermore, you should by now be able to see why this is not the end of the story: at a price of €0.90, each player will have an incentive to choose a lower price, which will drive price down towards zero.

This is why cartels are unstable: once they are in place they create a strong incentive to cheat, and can last if, and only if, the members have an efficient mechanism to police each other's behaviour and enforce observation of the cartel agreement.

Incentives Matter

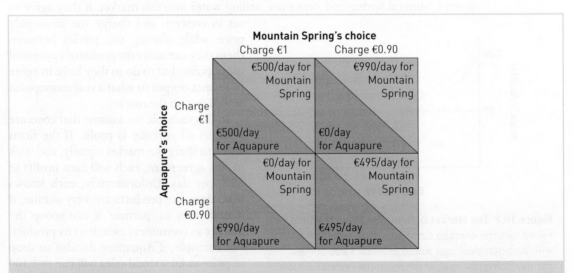

Figure 10.4 The Payoff Matrix for a Cartel Agreement.

Economic naturalist 10.1 So how do cartels actually survive? And how can they be broken?

Two recent episodes in South Africa offer interesting illustrations of cartels at work and how policy makers deal with them. The first is the outbreak of murder and mayhem in the taxi business in South Africa, and the second is the South African Competition Commission's investigation of cartels in the food sector.

The *ancien regime* in South Africa deregulated the taxi business in 1987. This offered a chance for poorer South African blacks to get a foot on the ladder to prosperity by entering the taxi industry, and a rapid expansion of numbers in the business ensued. Competition was fierce, and, to quote the *New York Times* (17 September 2006), after the end of apartheid in 1994 'taxi owners banded into groups, and the groups mushroomed into cartels, using gangland tactics to expand their turf'. Thus, to limit competition within groups and to carve up the wider market without price competition, the organised taxi drivers put in place a highly effective, if unpleasant, mechanism to enforce observation of cartel procedures and to punish deviation and competition from non-members (i.e. members of other cartels). The human cost of cartel enforcement ran into a couple of thousand fatalities. Was the cartelisation successful? One piece of anecdotal evidence strongly supports the profitability of the cartels (and the durability of their policing arrangements). That is the movement of organised crime into the business, with the gang bosses using threats, intimidation and extortion to extract some of the cartel profits from the individual taxi operators in recent years.

In November, 2007 it was announced that Tiger Brands had been fined R98.7 million by the SACC for its involvement in cartels in bread and milling in South Africa. Tiger, having been hauled in to be investigated by the SACC on the grounds of distributor complaint, sought protection under a 'leniency' programme and proceeded to give evidence against other cartel members, in return for a reduced fine of about 5 per cent of turnover. The outcome from the cooperation of Tiger Brands was that in 2008 the SACC announced it was launching an investigation into cartel activity in the food sector as a whole. The interesting thing about this story is the use of a prisoner's dilemma approach to break up cartels, something that is commonplace in competition law enforcement. It goes right back to Horace and Jasper in Chapter 9. The SACC offers a deal: first to squeal gets off lightly, the rest face severe penalties. Without cooperation from a cartel member, it is hard to get the evidence necessary to secure a conviction, but the dominant strategy, it seems, is not to take a chance on someone else giving what they want to the authorities first!

Cartel agreements confront participants with the economic incentives inherent in the prisoner's dilemma, which explains why such agreements have historically been so unstable. Usually a cartel involves not just two firms, but several, an arrangement that can make retaliation against price cutters extremely difficult. In many cases, discovering which parties have broken the agreement is difficult. The instability of cartels is an example of the prisoner's dilemma affecting firm behaviour. However, if it always applied, we would not expect to see any connection between small numbers of producers and higher prices, which, of course, we do see in may cases. So, is there some mechanism available to support cartels by solving the prisoner's dilemma?

Tit-for-tat and the cartel stability problem

In Chapter 9 we considered a 'tit-for-tat' strategy as a solution to the prisoner's dilemma problem when a game is repeated frequently. We saw that the problem is to create an incentive not to defect from a strategy that maximises their joint interests. What is needed is some way to *penalise* players who defect.

Since rival firms in the same industry interact with one another repeatedly, it might seem that the tit-for-tat strategy would ensure widespread collusion to raise prices. And yet, as noted earlier, cartel agreements are notoriously unsuccessful. One difficulty is that tit-for-tat's effectiveness is greatly weakened if there are more than two players in the game. In competitive and monopolistically competitive industries there are generally many firms, and even in oligopolies there are often several. When there are more than two firms, and one defects now, how do the cooperators selectively punish the defector later? By cutting price? That will penalise everyone, not just the defector. Even if there are only two firms in an industry, these firms realise that other firms may enter their industry. So the would-be cartel members have to worry not only about each other, but also about the entire list of firms that might decide to compete with them. Each firm may see this as an impossible task and decide to defect now, hoping to reap at least some economic profit in the short run. What seems clear, in any event, is that the practical problems involved in implementing tit-for-tat have made it difficult to hold cartel agreements together for long.

Stability-enhancing arrangements

Cartel stability can be reinforced by arrangements that provide for the sharing of markets, or costs of abiding by the cartel agreement or sharing profits derived from higher prices. In the European Union the competition authorities imposed substantial fines on firms in the cement industry in 1995 after investigation of complaints of price-fixing conspiracies (a cartel is just that). Central to the operation of the illegal arrangements were devices to create geographical markets for each player.[1] Economic naturalist 10.2 offers an example of how a cartel can be supported by a side arrangement between players.

Economic naturalist 10.2 Why did South African milk producers get into hot water by selling milk to each other?

At the end of 2006 the South African Competition Commission took legal action against the country's eight major milk processors for price fixing through cartel agreements. Four of the largest among them had an arrangement whereby each could sell any 'surplus' milk to the others, who had to take it at agreed prices. There was also a network of other agreements on supply and marketing covering the eight players.

The surplus (and other) arrangements had the effect of reducing the incentive to supply milk 'under the counter' to increase any one player's profits, but undermining the cartel's pricing structure. If any one of the four major players found itself unable to sell milk at the cartel price, the surplus supply agreement meant that the major players would share the cost of taking it off the market. The arrangement meant that the cost to one firm of not selling at below the cartel price was shared between the participating firms. This was held by the SACC to reduce the incentive to cheat, and consequently was a mechanism that assisted price fixing.

---

1 The text of the decision and the facts and reasoning behind it are published as 94/815/EC, 30/11/1994, available on the EU website or in the EU *Official Journal*, OJ L33/1 1995.

Economic naturalist 10.3 Was the OPEC cartel responsible for the surge in oil prices in 2007–08?

In the earlier oil shock episodes (1973–74 and 1979–80) by general agreement the main short-term cause of the price increases was decisions by OPEC members to cut back supply. When prices started to rise sharply in 2007 it was understandable that commentators focused on the refusal of OPEC members to increase supply in the face of rising demand. However, from what we have learned about cartels, an increase in price of the magnitude experienced in 2007–08 should have created an irresistible incentive for some producers to break ranks and pump out more oil, since prices were so much higher than oil production costs. This didn't happen, and oil production was static for three years at around 85–87 million barrels per day.

This suggests that it was demand rising (possibly with an element of speculative purchasing) while short-run marginal costs were high that drove crude oil prices. The high short-run marginal costs reflect the fact that increasing output from existing reserves is not simply a matter of opening the tap a little wider, but frequently involves incurring significant costs. The rising demand reflected growth in consumption in particular in India and China, and the policy in several oil-exporting countries (e.g. Nigeria, Saudi Arabia and Iran) of actually subsidising domestic oil consumption.

RECAP

In small-number markets where firms' decision-making must take into account responses by rivals we can analyse firm behaviour by using the tools of game theory. When we do so, we see that powerful concepts like dominant strategies and the prisoner's dilemma can help us understand how decisions are made. They also help explain why collusion is profitable, but collusive agreements tend to break down in the absence of mechanisms to detect and punish deviations from those agreements.

Timing and commitment problems in oligopolistic markets

In concentrated markets the same issues arise as in simple games at the individual level, which we looked at in Chapter 9. In particular, timing may matter greatly when firms make decisions concerning the dimensions of competition between them. This covers capacity expansion, R&D and product innovation. To illustrate this, and the importance of recognising timing and commitment issues, we look at a real-world example of a major competitive decision in a global industry in which interdependence is a major factor.

Example 10.2 A case study: How did Airbus end up as the only producer of a super-jumbo airliner?

In this example we use a stylised presentation of the main elements of the strategic interaction between the world's two largest aircraft producers when consideration was being given to producing a plane that would carry 50 per cent more passengers than the then largest passenger plane, the B747 jumbo.[2] In the mid-1990s decision makers at Boeing (in Seattle) and Airbus (in Toulouse) were considering whether or not to develop a 'super-jumbo'. The options for Boeing were to develop a new plane

---

2 The presentation we use here is a simplified version of part of an analysis of the issues by two researchers at the Harvard Business School: B. Esty and P. Ghemawat (2002).

or to build a 'stretch' version of the B747 (the jumbo jet). Airbus had a wide-bodied plane (the A300/330/340 series) that competed with Boeing's B767 and B777, but had no plane that competed with the B747 and could be stretched. For Airbus, therefore, a super-jumbo meant a wholly new plane.

Both companies knew that a super-jumbo would be needed to the extent that 'hub and spoke' patterns were characteristic of long-haul travel. Hub-and-spoke refers to the image of a wheel, or rather two wheels. To get from a point on the rim of one to a point on the rim of the other you might connect them directly, or connect the wheel hubs and move from rim to hub to hub to rim. Short-haul flights in smaller planes to major airports are 'spokes', while hub-to-hub covers the long-haul stage of the journey in larger planes (jumbos or super-jumbos). Boeing believed that the market for super-jumbos was considerably smaller than Airbus expected, because point to point (direct 'rim to rim') travel would be more important in long-haul operations, and these demanded smaller planes than super-jumbos. On this basis it was not clear that Boeing should produce a super-jumbo even if Airbus did not. It was highly risky. For Airbus, the complication was that, whether its more optimistic view of the market was correct or not, the established airline preference for using one supplier's planes meant that the demand for Airbus offerings was constrained by its inability to offer a jumbo-type plane.

From Boeing's perspective there was no point in developing a stretch version of the B747 ... unless Airbus went ahead with its own super-jumbo. If, however, Airbus did go ahead, it would have a monopoly of super-jumbos (and Boeing did not think that would be all that profitable). But the fact that airlines prefer to use one supplier in many cases, and that the super-jumbo would reduce demand for B747s, meant that Boeing could find itself losing profitable sales across the range of planes it produced. If, however, Boeing did challenge Airbus in the super-jumbo segment it believed it would (a) lose money directly because neither maker could break even on Boeing's estimate of the likely size of the market, and (b) to some extent Boeing could achieve super-jumbo sales only at the expense of sales of the existing B747 to customers who would like a larger long-haul plane. Boeing's total profits would be badly hit.

Boeing, however, knew that even on Airbus's optimistic view of the size of the market, an entry by Boeing would make it doubtful that either could make a profit from sales of the super-jumbos (unless, of course, they colluded, which was (a) illegal and (b) impossible to police). The best outcome from Boeing's point of view would be for neither to enter the super-jumbo segment of the market. Therefore, if it could persuade Airbus that it would follow Airbus in the event of a launch by Airbus it could deter Airbus from launching, which would maximise Boeing's profits.

Finally, each firm knew the other's opinions of likely market size and market shares and, therefore, had a good idea of what the other side would expect in terms of the impact of the decisions taken on expected profits.

Applying the tools of game theory

This scenario enables us to show how (a) moving from simultaneous decision-making to sequential decision-making helps explain how a game plays out, and (b) the importance of credible commitment in influencing players' actions.

We start with a standard presentation of the payoffs to the various moves in the form presented earlier when we looked at the airline advertising game. Each player has a choice between launching a new plane and not launching (Y and N, respectively). The payoffs are not supposed to be the actual expected values, but represent the relative returns to the different outcomes.

The payoffs are presented in Fig. 10.5 in the familiar two-by-two matrix form that is appropriate when two players are modelled as moving simultaneously. Viewed as a simultaneous movement game the outcome is obvious. In our presentation the structure of payoffs represents that expected for the players by Boeing, and constitute a worst-case scenario for Airbus, which was more optimistic about possible absolute levels of profits, but would accept the relative returns in the different cells. The absolute values are arbitrary.

Boeing has a dominant strategy: do not launch. Airbus knows this although it has no dominant strategy. Consequently, Airbus can confidently choose to launch. Neither side has an incentive to alter its behaviour, given what the other chooses to do. This is a Nash equilibrium. All very simple: this 'normal' form of the game tells us what should (and did) happen. However, real life is a bit more complicated. Airbus chose to launch the A380, and Boeing (in the end) chose to leave the super-jumbo segment of the market to Airbus, and subsequently launched the B787 'Dreamliner'. But it all took some time, and the episode was characterised by uncertainty (at least in terms of public information) as to what Boeing would do. To understand why, we have to look at the game as a game in which timing mattered, and in which Boeing's decision on what it would do depended on what Airbus decided to do, and was committed to doing.

Boeing's moves depend on what Airbus has decided. This in fact puts Boeing in the position where it has to decide what to do (a) if Airbus launches, and (b) if Airbus does not launch. It has to have a strategy (choice of moves) covering both possibilities. Boeing has a choice between four strategies:

1. decide to build a super-jumbo ('yes') regardless of what Airbus has decided ('yes' or 'no'); call this strategy (Yes, Yes)
2. decide not to build a super-jumbo in either case; call this strategy (No, No)
3. decide to build the plane if Airbus builds, and not to build if Airbus does not; call this strategy (Yes, No)
4. decide to build only if Airbus does not build; call this strategy (No, Yes).

So, while Airbus has a choice between two moves (Yes, build; No, don't build), Boeing has in principle four options, depending on its choice of strategy. The table of payoffs in Fig. 10.5 has to be extended as in Fig. 10.6.

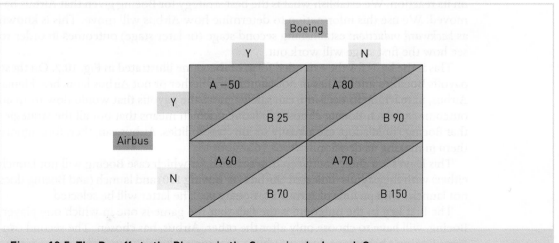

Figure 10.5 The Payoffs to the Players in the Super-jumbo Launch Game.

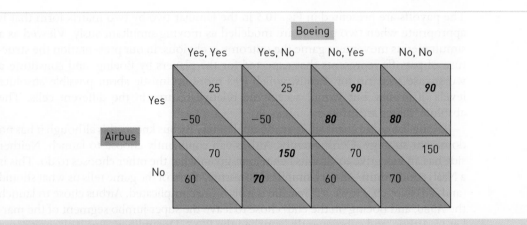

Figure 10.6 Different Strategies Result in Different Nash Equilibria. Boeing's payoffs depend on which of the four strategies it decided on before Airbus moves. There are three Nash equilibria (the cells with bold and italic payoffs).

Now Airbus faces a decision that depends on its information as to what strategy Boeing has adopted. Although Airbus decides first as to whether to build, this decision will in turn depend on what strategy it believes Boeing has adopted (how it will respond to any move by Airbus). This in turn can reflect what Boeing says and does before Airbus decides. Specifically, if Boeing can persuade Airbus that it will do what Airbus does (has a Yes, No strategy) Airbus will choose not to build. So a threat to follow Airbus will result in no super-jumbo being built, and Boeing's profits are maximised. As we will see, such a threat can be interpreted from Boeing's actions ... but Airbus went ahead. Why?

To help answer this question, we can use the extended form of the game, the decision tree. We have used this tool already, in the ultimatum game and in the remote office game in Chapter 9. The game can be seen as having two stages. In the first stage, Airbus chooses between launch and do not launch. In the second stage, Boeing decides on its reaction. We establish what is the best strategy for Boeing given that Airbus has moved. We use this information to determine how Airbus will move. This is known as *backward induction*: establishing second stage (or later stage) outcomes in order to see how the first stage will work out.

This is the basis for the extended form of the game illustrated in Fig. 10.7. On these payoffs Boeing's interest lies in not launching whether or not Airbus launches. Hence Airbus, in reaching its decision, can safely ignore the payoffs that would flow from an outcome in which Boeing chooses to launch, which means that not all the strategies that Boeing could adopt are actually serious possibilities. Airbus can, therefore, ignore them in making its decision.

This leaves it a choice between don't launch (in which case Boeing will not launch either) with the payoffs indicated (Airbus 70, Boeing 150) and launch (and Boeing does not launch) with payoffs of Airbus 80, Boeing 90. The latter will be selected.

The first key to the outcome is the fact that the game is one in which one player, Boeing, will have to choose only after the other, Airbus, has chosen. The second concerns Boeing's behaviour during Airbus's decision making and its implications for the other possible strategies that Boeing might adopt.

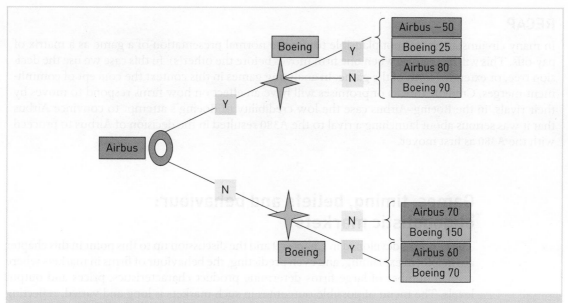

Figure 10.7 The Extended Version of the Game, with Airbus as First Mover.

Credible threats

During this time, Boeing began to plan for a stretched 747, with its engineers doing preliminary design work, while its assembly works began to prepare for construction. At the same time, it started to negotiate with potential airline customers on the configuration of a stretched B747. In short, Boeing's activity was such as to support the proposition that it was willing to go ahead with its challenger. If Airbus believed this, and accepted the payoff structure, its rational response would be to abandon the A380 project, since it would lose money (Airbus – 50). Boeing was making a threat. Although it believed (or stated that it believed) that it was not likely that the market could support profitable sales of two super-jumbos, and possibly even one, it would for various reasons be willing to enter the fray if Airbus proceeded with the A380. This was supported by a view that if Airbus launched, Boeing would launch at relatively low cost by developing an existing model, the B747, rather than introducing a wholly new plane. The object was to ensure that Airbus did not launch, in which case Boeing's profits would be maximised at (Boeing 150).

The problem here is that, on these payoffs, which by assumption were common knowledge, the threat was not credible. No matter what Airbus decided to do, it would never be better for Boeing to launch. This can be seen from the decision tree (extended form) model. Hence, the threat was not credible. In order to be credible a threat or promise must involve a substantial cost to the person who makes it if subsequently it is abandoned.

It remains to be seen whether this will in fact turn out to be a profitable choice, but the point is that (a) at the time it looked profitable, and (b) it was profitable only because Boeing could not credibly threaten to enter if Airbus moved and Airbus could move first.

RECAP

In many circumstances it is not plausible to use the normal presentation of a game as a matrix of pay-offs. This will be the case when one firm moves before the other(s). In this case we use the decision tree, or extended form of the game. In analysing games in this context the concept of commitment merges. Credible threats or promises will have an effect on how firms respond to moves by their rivals. In the Boeing–Airbus case the low credibility of Boeing's attempt to convince Airbus that it was serious about launching a rival to the A380 resulted in the decision of Airbus to proceed with the A380 as first mover.

Games, timing, beliefs and behaviour: oligopolistic markets

The concepts developed in Chapter 9 and the discussion up to this point in this chapter are helpful in explaining, and even predicting, the behaviour of firms in markets where a small number of large firms determine product characteristics, prices and output levels. The menu of possible outcomes in such markets is long and varied, reflecting permutations and combinations of firm strategies, firm beliefs, modes of competition, and numbers and sizes of firms. In this section, we shall look at some basic models that are of use in indicating how differences in structure of markets, firms' beliefs as to other firms' responses, and the manner in which firms compete can affect prices and outputs in those markets.

- **Structure** By 'market structure' we mean the degree of *similarity or difference between* firms (players, in game theory terms) and the *number of firms*. For example, in most parts of Britain or France the everyday grocery trade is shared by a small number of similar-sized large firms (small convenience stores abound, especially in Britain, but they largely sell into another market). On the other hand, retail sales of clothing is divided between a small number of large chain stores (Marks & Spencer, C&A, Debenhams, Galeries Lafayette ...) and a very large number of much smaller outlets.

- **Beliefs** In the prisoner's dilemma, the outcome reflected the *knowledge and beliefs of each of the players about the other*. The outcome depends on the idea that each expects the other to behave independently in a one-off situation to maximise his own utility subject to no external influence or concern about the future. This may (or may not) be plausible in terms of suspects in police custody, but a wider set of beliefs, etc. is plausible in the case of firms interacting in markets.

- **Competition** Firms also differ as to how they *compete*, usually reflecting the products they are engaged in producing. For example, car producers can plausibly be modelled as deciding on a volume of output of a particular type of car, for which they tool up (commit themselves to produce, hoping to be able to sell them). Quantity is the decision competition variable: the firm lets market demand determine how much it realises for a given volume of production, or average revenue, meaning unit price. If firms compete by setting quantities, competition between firms is called 'Cournot competition' (see p. 311). A life assurance producer is best thought of as developing a financial product range, pricing it and waiting to see how many units of the product it can sell. Price is the decision variable, with market demand determining the amount sold. If firms compete by setting prices, competition is called 'Bertrand competition' (again see p. 311).

The oligopolist's 'reaction function'

If we are to understand how firms interact in a market characterised by strong interdependence, we must be able to predict what each will wish to do contingent on the choice of actions of the other or others. This means being able to establish each firm's best response function, or reaction function. This gives us an answer to the question, what will A do in any set of circumstances that reflect what B (or B and C) choose to do?

In the case of the airline advertising game we looked at in Example 9.1 in the previous chapter, the problem is as follows: what is the best thing Alitalia can do, given an action of Lufthansa, and what is the best thing Lufthansa can do, given an action by Alitalia? The choice in this case is a simple one: increase or do not increase spending. But suppose the choice was more complex. For example, suppose both firms could choose between 50 levels of advertising. Then in order to determine (if this is possible) what the outcome would be we would need a much more complex solution method that can be summed up as establishing each side's 'reaction', or 'best response', function. This means identifying the best that each player can do for any value chosen by the other for advertising spending.

The reaction function

In the simple game theory examples used earlier we considered whether a dominant strategy existed for either or both players. In those cases, there were two possible actions by each player, and payoffs derived from these produced a single-equilibrium outcome. It described the best choice of action contingent on what the other player might do. However, where pricing or output decisions are concerned there is a theoretical infinity of choices a firm can make, with related payoffs. Hence we have a range of *best values* for one firm depending on the choices of the other. This leads us to develop the concept of a **reaction function**, or a 'reaction curve'. This will show the preferred action of a given firm as a function of the action of the other firm(s).

reaction function shows the preferred response of a firm in terms of a decision variable as a response to a value of that variable chosen by the other firm(s)

Models of oligopoly

In analysing competition among the few firms in an oligopoly market two basic models are widely used. The difference between them reflects how they compete. This in turn reflects the type of goods that they produce and the technology of production. It can also reflect the time period over which the analysis is undertaken (long-run or short-run analysis). The first of these, and arguably the most important, is what is referred to as the Cournot model. This looks at firms on the basis that they compete by determining how much they will produce (or, perhaps, the capacity they will place on the market in cases such as road or air transport). It dates from pioneering (and, for a long time, forgotten) work in the area by the French economist, Augustin Cournot, in the early part of the nineteenth century. In a Cournot model firms are thought of as taking demand conditions as given, and deciding how much they will supply to the market given what other firms in the market supply or could supply. Examples of oliogopolistic Cournot conditions would include cement production, plate glass production and motor car production. Given demand conditions, price is then determined. The second model is called the Bertrand model, developed by Joseph Bertrand (also French), and considers how firms interact in oligopoly markets where they compete on price. Firms decide on the price at which they will sell, and the quantity sold is determined by demand. Examples include insurance services and supermarkets (at least in the short run).

These models enable us to analyse competition, and the consequences of competition and collusion in markets in which all (or most) production is undertaken by a small number of large firms, and in which the incumbents do not have to worry much (or at all) about possible entry. The menu of possible variants in this analysis is very long. For example, firms may differ in terms of their costs of production, or in scale. The goods they produce may be differentiated by producer, or be highly substitutable. Firms may operate as independent decision makers, or be price or output followers. These will affect the outcome in terms of levels of production/sales, prices and numbers of producers. However, simple models making some basic assumptions actually yield some interesting and robust conclusions concerning the consequences of competition (or its absence) in oligopolistic industries.

In this presentation we will look at the smallest number of firms short of a monopoly, a duopoly, meaning two firms in the market, because it is possible to use graphical analysis with two firms, but not (usually) with a larger number. However, much of what these simple models predict can be extended to markets with more than two firms.

The Cournot Model

We assume two equally sized producers with similar costs of production that supply a market with a good. The products of the two firms are highly substitutable (in the limiting case, identical). Each firm knows what market demand is, and has to decide on its profit maximising level of production. Its main problem is that this will depend on what the other firm is producing. For example, if the first firm happens to be producing whatever level of production would be offered were the market perfectly competitive there is simply no room for any output by the second firm, since it would by definition lose money by producing, as more output would lower market price below average variable cost. If, on the other hand, for some reason the first firm produced nothing at all, the profit-maximising output for the second firm would be the monopoly output.

Since the firms face similar demand and have similar costs, this is symmetrical. Consequently, we know that the output that maximises either firm's profits given the output of the other lies between zero (the other is producing the competitive output) and the monopoly output (the other is producing nothing). To make life simple we will assume that the market demand curve is a straight line, and the firms have constant average and marginal costs.

On this basis we can determine the profit-maximising output for Firm I in a duopoly for any output by Firm II. This is indicated on the horizontal axis in Fig. 10.8. Firm II's output is indicated on the vertical axis. Thus, if Firm II produced the perfectly competitive output (Q_{pc}), with price equal to average cost, and no profits, it would not pay Firm I to produce any output. If Firm II

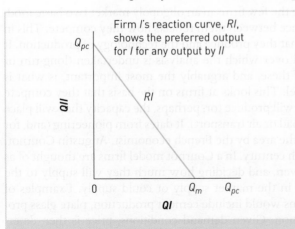

Figure 10.8 Firm *I*'s Reaction Curve, *RI*.

Firm I's reaction curve, RI, shows the preferred output for I for any output by II

chose to produce nothing, leaving the entire market to Firm *I*, the best output for Firm *I* is the monopoly output. With the assumptions just made about demand curves and cost curves, the reaction curve for Firm *I* will be a straight line, as drawn in Fig. 10.8. It runs from the monopoly output on Firm *I*'s axis to the competitive output on Firm *II*'s axis. It shows the profit-maximising output for Firm *I* for any output by Firm *II*. The further out a firm is on its reaction curve the lower are its profits. For either firm, the closer its output is to the monopoly output on its own axis the higher are its profits.

In Figure 10.9 we show the reaction curves for both firms. Notice also the broken lines joining Q_{pc} on each axis and Q_m on each axis. These represent the competitive output and monopoly output divided between the two firms in proportion to the shares indicated by any point on the line. They also, therefore, represent the competitive level of profits (zero) and the monopoly level similarly divided between them. The firm outputs given by the intersection of the two reaction curves involve a level of profits below the monopoly level and above the competitive level shared equally.

The reaction curve shows for each firm the best output for it in terms of its profits given the output of the other. Remember what was defined above in terms of a Nash equilibrium. At the level of output for each indicated by point *X* in Fig. 10.9, neither has any incentive to alter its output. Hence *X* is a Nash equilibrium in quantities, and, in these circumstances, it is a stable equilibrium. If either chooses an output other than that given by point *X* the response by the other will be such that it will increase the first's profits to reverse its decision. Suppose *II* decided to increase its output above the level indicated by *X*, moving towards the monopoly output on its own axis. Unless *I* accommodated this by reducing output along *II*'s curve, in fact *I* would lower output, but by less than this amount. Hence *II*'s profits would fall, so that *II* would have an incentive to reverse the move, going back to *X*.

If both players choose their outputs independently and face the same demand and cost conditions, the result will be the Nash equilibrium output shown by the intersection of the reaction curves at *X*.
If Firm *I* can move first and Firm *II* must follow, the outcome will be at a point like *Y*, *I* with lower profits overall, but higher profits for Firm *I* than at *X*. The lines joining Q_m Q_m and Q_{pc} Q_{pc} represent the monopoly and competitive outputs shared between the firms

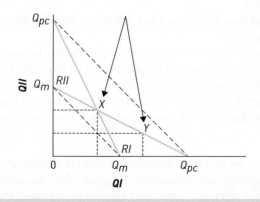

Figure 10.9 Both Players Choose their Outputs Independently.

So, armed with this information (demand and cost conditions, and an assumption that each firm acts independently of the other) we can say what total output and its division (and the associated profits) for each firm would be, and this would be a Nash equilibrium outcome in output levels.

Incentives Matter

Notice something else: this is not the best possible outcome for the two players. The best possible outcome is the monopoly output shared between them. This is shown by the broken line joining the monopoly output levels on the two axes. It involves a lower total output of the good they produce, which, given demand, means higher prices and joint profits than at the Nash equilibrium. We have met this before.

collusion forming a cartel, or equivalent, which increases profits, but also prices to the consumer

competition independent decision making by firms, which means lower prices and higher consumer welfare

leaders and followers firms' beliefs and timing affect the outcome in an oligopolistic market

If they could **collude** and decide jointly on how much to produce, they could do better. This, therefore, is a prisoner's dilemma. Choosing independently means, in effect, **competing**. Colluding means forming a cartel or equivalent.

If they can cooperate (collude rather than compete) they can share the monopoly profits. If they have to choose independently what to do and they can be thought of as deciding what to do simultaneously (as in the prisoner's dilemma), neither can do better than select the output indicated by the intersection of the two reaction curves. The outcome is a Nash equilibrium outcome, since neither firm has an incentive to depart from it.

Suppose, however, that Firm *I* moves first, and believes (correctly) that Firm *II* will follow its move, rather than move independently (a **leader and follower** game). Firm *I* knows that Firm *II* will choose an output on the basis of its reaction curve. That curve becomes the set of outputs for the two firms among which Firm *I* has to choose. The Nash equilibrium is a feasible choice for Firm *I*, but an output level and share that is preferable for Firm *I* exists. It is at a point like *Y* in Fig. 10.9. Total output is higher, and price and industry profits are lower than at the Nash equilibrium. This is shown by the fact that a line drawn through *Y* parallel to the line joining the competitive output on both axes (the total output shared between the two firms as indicated by point *X*) lies nearer to the competitive output line than the Nash equilibrium output line, meaning an output level that is higher and industry profits that are lower than at the Nash equilibrium output. There exists some point like *Y* such that Firm *I*'s output share is sufficiently large to give Firm *I* a higher level of profit despite lower prices than at the Nash equilibrium, meaning of course that Firm *II* does much worse. This is called a Stackelberg equilibrium point.

By changing our assumptions about how firms react to each other, and the timing of moves, we change the predicted outcome.

The Cournot duopoly model indicates that even when there is no collusion between firms a market such as that just looked at, with a small (two) number of large players, will produce an output that is lower than the competitive output, other things being equal. The consequence is that consumer welfare is expected to be reduced by a high degree of concentration of production into a small number of firms. Two questions arise at this stage.

1. In so far as the Cournot model can be taken as indicating a central tendency of concentration of market structure relative to a competitive structure, does increased (reduced) concentration on its own decrease (increase) consumer welfare? Put another way, is the Nash equilibrium output of the firms affected by the degree of concentration? Intuition suggests that this is the case. For once, intuition is

supported by theoretical reasoning. Although proof of this proposition requires some mathematical manipulation of the firms' reaction functions, its conclusion can be stated as follows. If N is the number of equal-sized firms supplying a market where demand and cost conditions are as assumed here, the Nash equilibrium level of market output will be given as

$$Q = \left\{ \frac{N}{(N+1)} \right\} Q_{pc}$$

where Q_{pc} is the output level associated with perfect competition. As N rises, oligopolistic market output, Q, tends to Q_{pc}.

2. As the number of firms falls how does this affect the plausibility of assuming independence of decision making? Independence does not mean assuming that competitors will not react to decisions, although this is the case under perfect competition. It means here not engaging in actions that will result in an output level below the Nash equilibrium, or tacit or overt collusion.[3] There is no simple answer to this question, meaning that a case-by-case approach to the consequences of increased concentration is indicated.

These last two points may be seen as being reflected in the way in which EU competition policy looks at mergers in terms of their effects on economic welfare. This approach is now widely observed outside the EU, and was itself based on the US approach. Mergers are considered in terms of whether they result in a 'significant lessening of competition' (SLC). SLC in turn is seen as being derived from 'unilateral effects' and 'coordinated effects'. The first of these considers whether the merged entity has the power to raise prices profitably simply because it is now bigger relative to the market. A market with a smaller number of larger firms will produce less output and prices will rise as a consequence. The second concerns the impact of the merger on firms' assumptions as to other firms' behaviour and the effect of a firm's decisions on other firms' decisions. As the number of players falls, interdependence of decision making becomes more important, and the potential for coordinated actions that lead to higher prices increases.

RECAP

When a firm has to choose a value for price or quantity that is best for it given any value chosen by its rival(s) the value it selects will be given by its 'best response function' or 'reaction function'. This indicates the best choice for a firm given any choice of the rival(s). Where the reaction curves derived from these functions intersect the outcome is a Nash equilibrium. Hence, given these functions, the outcome of the game is determined, and the firms' outputs or prices are such that neither wishes to change. In this case the firms choose independently, or simultaneously. In the case of Cournot (quantity) competition the reaction curves have a negative slope, and indicate the values for output levels. When one firm can move first, and the other is a follower the result is a Stackelberg equilibrium. In these markets the quantity produced is less than the competitive output but more than the monopoly output.

---

3 This is a controversial point. Tacit collusion is sometimes used to describe the consequence of the recognition of interdependence. However, from a competition policy and law perspective any concentrated market will then exhibit 'tacit collusion', even if all firms act fully independently, which is meaningless in terms of regulation to redress the problem. A more restrictive definition of tacit collusion that is meaningful in terms of legal and regulatory control is that given here: conduct that results in output (price) that is lower (higher) than indicated by a Nash equilibrium.

The Bertrand Model

The previous examples used an assumption of Cournot competition, competition where firms decide on quantity to produce. Suppose, however, that firms compete on *price*. This possibility was analysed by another French mathematician and economist, Joseph Bertrand, who argued in 1883 that the Cournot solution did not generally hold and derived an alternative result where firms decided on prices rather than output levels – this is **Bertrand competition**.

> **Bertrand competition** firms choose a price and accept that quantity sold depends on demand at that price

We saw that under prisoner's dilemma circumstances in the Cournot game the outcome was a level of output between the competitive and the monopoly levels. Now suppose we think about a firm setting a price when its product is identical to that of the other firm, and they each have the same costs. Each firm knows that for any price it chooses that is higher than marginal cost the best response of the other firm is to set a price that is a little lower. If it sets the same price it shares industry profits equally, since it will sell the same amount as the competitor. But a slightly lower price will give it the whole market and all the profits.

You can try this as a problem, but a little thought will result in the following conclusion. Each firm will choose a price at which profits are zero. Price will be set equal to marginal cost, and with constant costs this means zero profits.

This leads to what has been called the *'Bertrand Paradox'*. As long as there are at least two similar firms supplying the market each firm has an incentive to set price lower than that of its rival(s) in order to capture sales profitably, which means that price will be driven down to cost, at which point undercutting no longer makes sense. Increasing the number beyond two, or reducing the number as long as there are at least two has no effect: the game results in a zero price cost margin. Industry structure has no apparent effect on price.

This result points to different conclusions depending on whether firms can best be treated as competing on quantity or price.

But, if we look around, we can see that there are cases where firms can plausibly be treated as competing in terms of setting *prices* (Bertrand as opposed to Cournot competitors), and profits are not zero. The first serious attempt to tackle the Bertrand Paradox conclusion was what is known as the *Edgeworth critique*. The Irish economist and statistician, Francis Ysidro Edgeworth (1845–1926) demonstrated that if the firms face rising marginal costs, or, in the limit, a capacity constraint such that neither can supply the entire market at competitive prices then price will not be driven down to average cost, and firm prices can differ.

We can also see examples of higher prices and profit margins in Bertrand markets when there are fewer competitors. Petrol retailing in local markets is an obvious example of both these market characteristics.

How do we square this with the Bertrand model just described?

There are two bases on which to suggest that the Bertrand Paradox outcome, although formally an equilibrium, is not consistent with what we observe in real-world oligopolies where Bertrand competition is a plausible assumption. The first is that the products of the firms may not be *perfectly substitutable*. If that is so the products will not have to be sold at the same price (different brands of toothpaste are sold on the same supermarket shelves at different prices). When this is the case, it is possible to look at a firm's pricing decision in the same way as we looked at the output decision in the basic Cournot model. We construct a reaction curve for each firm, showing its preferred price given any price set by the competitor (Fig. 10.10).

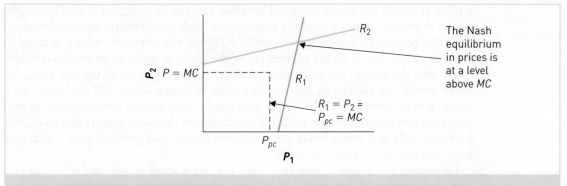

Figure 10.10 The Nash Equilibrium in Prices.

In this case, R_1 shows Firm I's preferred price for its own product given (as a function of) Firm II's price. R_2 is Firm II's reaction curve. Neither will set a price below marginal cost. Assuming constant unit cost and price elasticity of demand symmetry the reaction curves will (conveniently) be straight lines, and a Nash equilibrium in prices is where they intersect. Once again, this price, and the joint profits of the firms, will be lower than if they colluded to set the monopoly price and shared the market. However, the point is that the Nash equilibrium does not mean that prices are set equal to marginal cost. Positive profits can be earned in equilibrium without collusion. Furthermore, if there are more firms/products on offer, meaning that each firm/product faces closer substitutes, a firm's reaction curve becomes steeper, and the Nash equilibrium approaches the perfectly competitive price ($P = MC$). In the absence of cooperative behaviour, the more petrol stations there are in a town the lower we would expect prices to be.

There is a second, and even more important, reason for not expecting prices to fall to marginal cost under Bertrand competition, even if the products of each firm are very similar to those of others. That is the fact that the analysis so far treats the pricing decision as if it were taken just once, and never changed. In fact, of course, firms have to make decisions on price frequently through time. As supply costs move, and/or as demand conditions change, the 'correct' price for a firm to set changes too. We must assume that firms have memories. We must also assume that firms know how to signal how they will respond to price cutting, and how to indicate by their pricing behaviour whether or not they intend competing aggressively or adopting a 'live and let live' approach. Put another way, pricing decisions involve choosing not just a set of prices for your products, but deciding on a *pricing strategy*, or adopting a rule on setting prices as circumstances change.

The consequences of this approach to pricing include a high degree of 'price stickiness' in small-number markets where players can observe accurately what their competitors are doing as far as prices are concerned. It makes sense to analyse the pricing behaviour of firms in these markets in terms of repeated games, pricing rules, signalling and tacit collusion. This approach is also useful because it helps us understand when and why this *tacitly coordinated behaviour* breaks down, and we see price wars breaking out.

Repeated games

Think of a cartel, and ask why a member of it might decide to break ranks. One way to do this is to analyse the cartel as a *repeated game*, in which in each period any player has to choose whether or not to stick by the cartel rules, restrict output and sell at a price at which the firm's marginal revenue exceeds its marginal cost. The single-period dominant strategy (and the consequent Nash equilibrium) suggests breaking the rules, because by breaking them while everyone else obeys the rules you stand to clean up. However, if all the players know the game is going to be repeated indefinitely into the future, the calculation changes. Even if you clean up this week, by undermining the cartel you know that profits in future weeks will be lower. As a result, it is reasonable to believe that you might compare the present value of two profit streams into the future: profits if you undercut the other players this week, but everyone sells at a much lower price into the future, and profits if you – and, you hope, the others – stick by the rules.

Of course, you might reason that since you are a small player, and provided you don't lower prices by too much, the others will prefer to ignore your behaviour – or, better still, may not even be aware of it. Suppose, however, that either by experience, or by some explicit and credible threat, it was clear to you that cheating would not be tolerated, and selective price cuts by large and close competitors were the expected response to any deviation from the rule. How would that affect your choice of strategy? Suppose trade magazines published frequent, reliable and detailed information on who was charging what prices for which goods. Would that encourage you to shave your price?

On the other hand, if it was difficult to observe the quality-adjusted price because the product as sold differs among customers, does that help price fixing? If you had very poor information as to what the market was going to look like in the future, so that future profits are highly uncertain, what effect would that have? Or suppose you were in debt to a financial institution that was charging a high rate of interest on your loan, but the loan could be paid off by a quick killing in the market. High interest rates act as a disincentive to stick by cartel rules.

In practice, of course, we are not usually dealing with an actual cartel. Under competition law in Europe, the United States and other OECD countries, such arrangements are illegal. Participation not only results in being liable to substantial financial penalties, but in some circumstances can result in a prison sentence for those responsible. However, and especially in small-number situations, firms can decide to operate a pricing policy that is based on a recognition that how they behave affects others' behaviour, and vice versa. Recognition of *interdependence of decisions* leads to a situation in which the observed behaviour resembles what might flow from an explicit agreement not to compete aggressively on price. For this reason this behaviour is frequently described as **tacit collusion**.

tacit collusion firms behaving in a manner that resembles what might emerge from a collusive agreement because they recognise their interdependence

Tacit collusion in oligopolistic and imperfectly competitive industries is frequently supported by *pricing* and *signalling* strategies designed to discourage competition and reinforce cooperative behaviour. One common device, which to an uninformed observer looks like aggressive competition on price, is a commitment to match or beat any price by guaranteeing to be the lowest-price seller. This is very widespread as a promotional device but, on closer examination, may in fact operate to support existing prices rather than ensure that buyers face the lowest possible prices. When a large white goods retailer makes such a promise he is signalling credibly to competitors small and large that if they lower prices he will lower his.

Conditions facilitating tacit collusion do not always exist, even where there are few firms and they recognise the fact that their behaviour affects that of the others. First of all, firms may face different cost structures. This can result in significant differences between them in terms of what pricing structure and behaviour maximise

Economic naturalist 10.4 Why was Statoil forced to abandon a rebate scheme that would have helped petrol retailers cut their prices?

In 2002 the Competition Authority in Dublin, Ireland, threatened legal action against a major oil company, Statoil, as a result of an arrangement it had entered into with its retailers in a country town in Ireland.[4] Statoil's scheme involved (a) fixing a maximum price at which petrol could be sold, and (b) offering a rebate to its dealers to enable them to cut their prices if other petrol outlets cut their prices below a marker price. While the first might have been part of a campaign to persuade people that Statoil petrol was a good buy (people notoriously appear not to pay much attention to actual prices per litre), the second element meant that other dealers knew that there was no point reducing price below the marker price since Statoil dealers could costlessly follow them down. This would clearly dampen price competition. Statoil withdrew the scheme.

profits when demand conditions change. For example, the lower a firm's variable costs relative to its fixed costs, the more likely it is to prefer to cut price rather than to cut output if demand weakens.

Pricing may not be transparent, with each unit being sold at a price negotiated with the purchaser on a confidential basis. Tacit collusion on pricing becomes meaningless. This factor on its own is probably the main reason why we see cut-throat competition between Boeing and Airbus.

Differences in product characteristics may mean that firms face different price elasticities of demand. This means they differ in terms of how they view the consequences of a change in prices.

As a result, we do not observe high prices supported by tacit collusion as inevitably following an observation of a small number of large producers in a market. And, even when it does occur, it is frequently undermined by repeated episodes of price wars.

RECAP

Bertrand competition describes markets in which firms compete by choosing a price rather than deciding on how much to produce. In this case a firm will choose a higher (lower) price if its rival(s)'s price is higher (lower). Nash equilibrium occurs where the curves intersect. The Bertrand paradox is resolved if we assume that firms have memories and can predict other firms' behaviour.

When do price wars break out, and how do they end?

In mid-2004 the Chinese Ministry of Information announced that it was stepping up its regulatory supervision of pricing in the telecoms sector in China in order to avoid price wars. Until earlier in the year mobile telephony charges had been set by the Ministry, which was also the regulator. In order to encourage the development of the sector, these price controls were relaxed. As elsewhere in the world, mobile telephony in China was dominated by a small number of players, all large. As soon as price controls were relaxed, a price war broke out, as firms slashed prices to increase market share in what was seen as an expanding market. The government, however, wanted the companies to maintain high profit margins and use them to finance qualitative upgrading of the mobile

---

4 The Competition Authority has described the confrontation and its outcome in Decision E/03/002, which is available on its website: www.TCA.ie.

network. When the government intervened to restrict price cutting, of course, the industry greeted this warmly.[5] Regulation produced higher profits.

One possibility here is that under a tight regulatory regime firms had not been able to learn how others would react to price changes, nor been able to estimate demand elasticities correctly. This would interpret the price war as flowing from poor information as to demand conditions and the degree of interdependence of pricing. Another possibility is that, even with good information, tacit collusion and weak price competition was unlikely under deregulation because of the extraordinary degree of non-transparency of pricing: mobile phone pricing packages are numerous, complex and difficult to compare.

The impact of poor information is a useful starting point. Suppose a firm sees its sales falling, and has poor information as to market conditions. Three possible reasons will arise. The first is that market demand has weakened, and it is sharing the pain with other firms.

The second is that for some reason it has lost competitiveness. The third is that supply has increased as a competitor has increased production. Unfortunately, the firm is not able with any degree of certainty to establish what exactly is going on.

If it had been content not to compete aggressively on price up to this point, it now faces a problem. Suppose its best guess is that there has been a fall in demand. It must choose between (a) tacit collusion on the basis that this is a temporary blip in demand, everyone is in the same boat and price cutting will achieve nothing as it will be imitated; (b) price cutting anyway because the demand reduction may be permanent so that even if everyone is similarly affected there are fewer seats in the boat than potential passengers, and the last to cut prices exits the market. Suppose, however, it suspects that it has lost competitiveness. The options are not to do anything and accept a lower volume of sales (and possibly further falls) or reduce price to make its products more attractive. Finally, it might suspect that the problem is not its own offerings, or demand in the market, but a competitor increasing production. If it does nothing, it accepts a lower market share. If it wishes to protect its market share and signal its intention to do so to anyone who wants to raise theirs, it will respond by reducing price.

What will happen? In all three scenarios, cutting price looks a better bet, even if a case can be made for not cutting price. Betting against a price cut under uncertainty as to what is going on looks unwise. Hence, it is easy to understand why price wars can be triggered by falling demand or by an overestimate of market demand.

Notice, too, that the scenarios point to a further reason for price wars: market disciplining and market 'restructuring'. Responding to price cuts by one supermarket operator by a 'race to the bottom' may not seem to make much sense until you reflect that the expectation that this will happen in future will be reinforced by an aggressive response. It can also be a mechanism to secure a shake-up in an industry, leading to a consolidation among players.

Finally, of course, an episode of price cutting can arise as a consequence of changes on the supply side. New entrants to a market can disturb a collusive equilibrium. Even with tacit collusion, a fall in input costs can result in the collusive equilibrium level of prices falling. Alternatively, a significant fall in one firm's costs that is not enjoyed by other firms can lead to the lower-cost firm seeking to increase share on the back of lower costs.

Do oligopolistic firms always behave in a fashion that looks rational from a game theory perspective? Example 10.3 suggests otherwise.

---

5 The story can be found in the English-language *China Daily*, on its website at www.chinadaily.cn/English/doc/2004-07/03/content_345216.htm.

Economic naturalist 10.5 How the structure of the US tobacco industry was changed by a price war in the 1990s[6]

Philip Morris cut the price of the world's best-selling cigarette, Marlboro, in the spring of 1993 by almost 20 per cent. Price competition from generic and mid-range brands over a period of years had reduced significantly the share of the premium cigarette producers, who at first accommodated the expansion of the cheaper producers and even increased prices in what was a declining market overall. The price cut by Philip Morris hit the mid-range producers hardest, and the main firm producing in this range, American Tobacco, exited the market and sold its business to British American Tobacco. The price war effectively ended when RJR Nabisco decided in November 1993 to raise the price of its premium brands, including the iconic Camel[7]. The move was followed by other producers, including Philip Morris. The generic producers appear to have taken the hint, and by 1995 Philip Morris had regained its lost market share, and both premium and generic cigarette prices were rising together, if slowly. In effect the Marlboro price managed simultaneously to exacerbate and end an ongoing price war, while restoring Philip Morris's position as market leader and consolidating the market.

Example 10.3 The Inverness bus war of 1988–91

After bus deregulation in 1986, many municipal bus companies in Britain found themselves facing competition from private-sector bus companies. In May 1988, one entrant, ITL, started to compete with the incumbent public-sector operator, HSO, in Inverness in the Scottish Highlands, by running minibuses on the routes operated by HSO. HSO responded by increasing its frequency (the volume of service) and, eventually, by replacing some of its conventional buses by minibuses. ITL in August increased its frequencies, and HSO responded in kind. Both firms made substantial losses, and by mid-1989 ITL was effectively bankrupt and had to sell out to a national bus operator. The latter continued to operate in Inverness, and in 1991 HSO withdrew from the town. Britain's Monopolies and Mergers Commission (MMC) investigated the matter and concluded that HSO had engaged in predatory pricing to drive out the entrant. Predatory pricing is selling at below cost to eliminate competition so as to be able to raise prices later and maintain monopoly profits.

In 1993, an academic paper appeared that undermined the MMC's conclusions, and indicated that the unfortunate experience of ITL and HSO was due to a series of miscalculations.[8] The economist authors estimated the Cournot reaction curves for the two firms in the market, and showed that (a) if ITL had entered at a lower level of frequency it could have done so profitably, and (b) that the level at which it entered made it impossible for the incumbent or the entrant to cover costs. Worse, when the losses mounted, and HSO had cut its costs by introducing minibuses, both sides decided to try to establish a leadership position and force the other to cut back capacity. In effect, in terms of Fig. 10.9, both tried to get to a point like Y on the other's reaction curve. If you add the two firms' production at points like Y you will see that total output exceeds the competitive output so that both must make losses. ITL buckled first, but faced with the might of a major national concern operating ITL's services, HSO had to exit the market a couple of years later.

---

6 A full account of the episode on which Economic naturalist 10.5 is based is available in an article by John Kay, *Financial Times*, 5 July 1996.

7 See M. Janovsky (1993) Company news: Increase by RJR may end a price war (*New York Times*, 10 November).

8 Dodgson *et al.* (1993).

Summary

- Analysing competition between firms in small-number markets requires that we accept that the firms, or players, recognise their interdependence. Consequently, decisions on price, output levels, advertising, R&D and other dimensions of competition must reflect an understanding of how other firms will respond.

- This means that, in addition to such factors as costs of production and market demand, decisions will reflect strategic considerations.

- Game theory, as introduced in Chapter 9, provides a basis for analysing strategic decisions by firms in such circumstances. Many competition problems have the features of prisoner's dilemma games.

- Building on the elements of game theory enables us to build models that help us to understand how things like beliefs and modes of competition have an influence on how firms actually behave in *small-number markets*.

- These models yield interesting and plausible conclusions that explain some features of *market behaviour* that are not explained by the simple models of perfect competition or monopolistic competition.

- Timing and the order in which players move are important in understanding what happens, as in the Boeing Airbus game. This means using the decision tree approach to describing a game. In these circumstances, promises, threats and other commitment devices are important elements in predicting outcomes.

- The analysis of competition and industry structures in these circumstances will also reflect how best to model how players compete, namely as Cournot or Bertrand competitors. In general, Cournot-type markets will be more predictably affected by the number of players than Bertrand-type markets.

Review questions

1. Can you explain why cartels offer an example of a prisoner's dilemma problem, and suggest how (ignoring legalities) the problem could be solved for the members of the cartel?

2. Suppose Boeing had entered into a contract with a large airline to produce a stretched B747. How would this have affected Airbus's decision?

3. What differences in firms' cost structures would lead you to treat them as Cournot or Bertrand competitors?

4. Can you show where (approximately) prices would settle if Firm *I* were a leader and Firm *II* a follower in the price-setting game (the equivalent to point *Y* in Fig. 10.9)?

5. Explain why advertising campaigns announcing that 'we will not beaten on price, and will refund twice the difference ...' can be a mechanism to reduce rather than intensify price competition.

connect Problems

1. Two aeroplane manufacturers are considering the production of a new product, a 550-passenger jet. Both are deciding whether to enter the market and produce the new plane. The payoff matrix is as shown below (payoff values are in million euros).

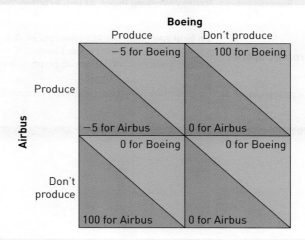

Boeing

	Produce	Don't produce
Produce	−5 for Boeing −5 for Airbus	100 for Boeing 0 for Airbus
Don't produce	0 for Boeing 100 for Airbus	0 for Boeing 0 for Airbus

(Airbus labelled on vertical axis)

The implication of these payoffs is that the market demand is large enough to support only one manufacturer. If both firms enter, both will sustain a loss.

   a. Identify two possible equilibrium outcomes in this game.

   b. Consider the effect of a subsidy. Suppose the European Union decides to subsidise the European producer, Airbus, with a subsidy of €25 million if it enters the market. Revise the payoff matrix to account for this subsidy. What is the new equilibrium outcome?

   c. Compare the two outcomes (pre- and post-subsidy). What qualitative effect does the subsidy have?

2. Can you explain why a competition authority might be more concerned at the emergence of leader-follower behaviour in a market with Bertrand competition than in one with Cournot competition?

3. An incumbent firm can choose between fighting an entrant and accommodating an entrant by yielding some market share to the entrant. Can you create a 2×2 table of payoffs such that the dominant strategy for the incumbent is to accommodate?

4. Suppose the entrant decides that he wishes to signal to the incumbent that he doesn't want a price war. Suppose he believes that a price war would not be in their interests, and also that a small share of a profitable market would be preferable to a large share of a market where prices dropped substantially. To illustrate this, he decides to commit himself to a small scale of entry. Assuming that the entrant moves first, can you create a decision tree that reflects these beliefs?

5. Why might subsidies to R&D by governments reduce economic welfare?

References

Dodgson, J.S., Y. Katsoulakos and C.R. Newton (1993) 'An application of the economic modelling approach to the investigation of predation', *Journal of Transport Economics and Policy*, pp. 153–70.

Esty, B. and P. Ghemawat (2002) *Airbus v Boeing in Super Jumbos: a Case of Failed Pre-emption* (Harvard Business School, Strategy Working Paper, 02-061, February 2002).

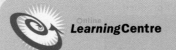

To help you grasp the key concepts of this chapter check out the extra resources posted on the Online Learning Centre. There are chapter summaries, self-test questions, an interactive graphing tool, weblinks and a glossary, all for free!

Visit the Online Learning Centre at: www.mcgraw-hill.co.uk/textbooks/mcdowell for information on accessing all of these resources.

Part 4
Market Imperfections (2): Externalities, Information, Distribution and the Role of the Government in a Market Economy

The current preoccupation with the issues involved in global warming can be thought of as a concern over the failure of a market economic system to 'protect the environment'. It is often seen as revealing a failure of economics to analyse serious economic problems. In fact, although not focused on climate issues, economics has been deeply involved for at least 60 years with the problems that underlie the climate problem. These are the subject matter of Chapter 11, which seeks to examine how markets are inefficient when activities generate costs or benefits that accrue to people not directly involved in those activities. We shall see that if parties cannot easily negotiate with one another, the self-serving actions of individuals usually will not lead to efficient outcomes.

Although the invisible hand theory assumes that buyers and sellers are perfectly informed about all relevant options, this assumption is almost never satisfied in practice. In Chapter 12 we shall explore how basic economic principles can help imperfectly informed individuals and firms make the best use of the limited information they possess.

Why do some people earn so much more money than others? No other single question in economics has stimulated nearly as much interest and discussion. Our aim in Chapter 13 will be to apply simple economic principles in an attempt to answer this question. We shall discuss the human capital model, which emphasises the importance of differences in personal characteristics.

But our focus will be on why people with similar personal characteristics often earn sharply different incomes. Among the factors we shall consider are labour unions, winner-take-all markets, discrimination and the effect of non-wage conditions of employment. In this chapter we shall also explore whether income inequality is something society should be concerned about and, if so, whether practical remedies exist for it. We shall see that government programmes to redistribute income have costs as well as benefits.

In Chapter 14 we shall explore two further aspects of government action in a market economy. The first of these is the function of government as 'regulator': taking legal and administrative steps to change the way in which firms or households behave from what they would do in an unrestricted environment. The second is the role of the government as producer of goods and services. In most Western economies, governments produce goods and services that could easily be (and in many cases are) produced by firms through markets. Why? There are, however, some activities of government as producer that cannot easily be replicated through markets. Why?

11

Externalities and Property Rights

Market efficiency: a reminder

Efficiency

We have stressed in several chapters, but especially in Chapters 5 and 6, that for markets to be an efficient mechanism to allocate a society's economic resources they must (a) exist and (b) be efficient. For the latter a necessary condition is that on both sides of the market prices reflect the value of goods and services to purchasers and the opportunity cost of resources used up in producing them. We have seen that when markets are not competitive (for example, when a supplier has substantial market power) this leads to inefficiency in markets because prices in equilibrium diverge from marginal and average cost. In this chapter we look at another source of market inefficiency. This occurs when prices are established by the usual forces of supply and demand, but some costs or benefits are not reflected in the prices facing consumers or producers.

External costs and benefits

Many activities generate costs or benefits that accrue to people not directly involved in those activities. These effects are generally unintended. They are called **external costs** and **benefits – externalities**, for short. To see how these affect resource allocation, let's start by looking at disease control.

Vaccination (inoculation) is a potent mechanism to control and eradicate infectious diseases by providing immunity against the infective agent. It has wiped out smallpox across the world. Fifty years ago a water-borne virus created an epidemic of poliomyelitis in North America and Europe. The Salk vaccine has almost eradicated polio since then. But in general the success of vaccination relies initially on private decisions to seek protection, usually for children. In recent years, and a matter of controversy, the classic case here was the MMR vaccine that protected against measles, mumps and rubella (German measles). When parents decide to inoculate a newborn child against a variety of infectious diseases they do so because they are concerned for the child's welfare.

external cost (or negative externality) a cost of an activity that falls on people other than those who pursue the activity

external benefit (or positive externality) a benefit of an activity received by people other than those who pursue the activity

externality an external cost or benefit of an activity

Cost–Benefit
Analysis

No inoculation is without some risk, but well-intentioned parents calculate the bene-fits expected for the child and compare them with the possible risks and the costs, if any, of the procedure. In having the child inoculated, however, they confer benefits on other, unidentified parents and children. This is because, in addition to protecting their own child from infection, they also reduce the probability of someone else being infected, as they eliminate part of the transmission vector for the infection. It is rea-sonable to assume that the parents' decision reflects the costs (risk) and benefits (pro-tection) to their own child. They do not calculate the benefits to others flowing from their decision. If the inoculation were financially costly, it is equally reasonable to assume that fewer children would be inoculated, with the consequence that the inci-dence of rubella among pregnant women would increase. Hence we have subsidised or free (and even compulsory in some cases) vaccination programmes to take account of this beneficial spillover effect from decisions to vaccinate.

Box 11.1 Private costs and benefits drive individual economic decisions

The point here is that the *private decision* to take the action reflects the *private calculus of private costs and benefits*. These are *'internalised'* into the decision-making process. What are not internalised are *the costs and benefits to others* of the decision. These are described as *'external effects'* (spillover effects) of the actions they take. These effects are described in economics as *'externalities'*.

In this case, inoculation involves a positive externality: it confers benefits on others at no cost to the decision maker, benefits that do not increase the welfare of the decision maker. Other actions involve negative externalities. They impose costs on others at no cost to the person undertaking the action. An example is a decision to use a car in an urban area during the rush hour. The driver computes into his decision the costs and benefits to him or her of using the car to make a journey at that time. What does not enter into the calculation is that on the journey the driver may delay a large num-ber of motorists, each by a small amount, because the road is already congested.

In general, where there are positive externalities private decision making tends to result in a less than socially optimal (marginal cost = marginal benefit) level of the activity concerned. This is because the resource allocation reflects *marginal private costs* and *marginal private benefits*. The problem is that marginal private benefits are not the same as marginal social benefits. Put another way, the decision maker does not capture all the benefits of his decision. For the same reason, negative externalities imply that 'too much' of the activity occurs, because the decision maker does not face personally all the costs that arise from his actions.

This chapter first focuses on how externalities affect the allocation of resources. Adam Smith's theory of the 'invisible hand' (Chapter 7) applies to an ideal marketplace in which externalities do not exist. In such situations, Smith argued, the self-interested actions of individuals would lead to socially efficient outcomes. We shall see that when the parties affected by externalities can easily negotiate with one another, the 'invisible hand' will still produce an efficient outcome. A corollary of this is that we can think usefully about externalities in terms of the absence of, or poorly defined, tradable property rights.

But, in many cases, such as in the cases of rush-hour traffic and inoculation, negotia-tion is impractical. In those cases, the self-serving actions of individuals simply will not lead to efficient outcomes. Because externalities are widespread, the attempt to forge solutions to the problems they cause is one of the most important rationales not only for the existence of government but for a variety of other forms of collective action as well.

How externalities affect resource allocation

The way in which externalities distort the allocation of resources can be seen clearly in Examples 11.1 and 11.2, and Economic naturalist 11.1.

Example 11.1 Does the honeybee keeper face the right incentives?

Phoebe earns her living as a keeper of honeybees. Her neighbours on all sides grow apples. Because bees pollinate apple trees as they forage for nectar, the more hives Phoebe keeps, the larger the harvests will be in the surrounding orchards. If Phoebe takes only her own costs and benefits into account in deciding how many hives to keep, will she keep the socially optimal number of hives?

For the orchard owners, Phoebe's hives constitute an external benefit, or a *positive* externality. If she takes only her own personal costs and benefits into account, she will add hives only until the added revenue she gets from the last hive just equals the cost of adding it. But since the orchard owners also benefit from additional hives, the total benefit of adding another hive at that point will be greater than its cost. Phoebe, then, will keep too few hives.

Based on this, can you see how there might be 'too many' beehives if they were located near a school or a nursing home?

Cost–Benefit Analysis

Every activity involves *costs* and *benefits*. When all the relevant costs and benefits of an activity accrue directly to the person who carries it out – that is, when the activity generates no externalities – the level of the activity that is best for the individual will be best for society as a whole. But when an activity generates externalities, be they positive or negative, individual self-interest does not produce the best allocation of resources. Individuals who consider only their own costs and benefits will tend to engage too much in activities that generate negative externalities and too little in activities that generate positive externalities. When an activity generates both positive and negative externalities, private and social interests will coincide only in the unlikely event that the opposing effects offset one another exactly.

Efficiency

Economic naturalist 11.1 It pays to know the facts!

The example of bees and orchards in Example 11.1 reflects an example of why markets 'fail' given by the Cambridge (UK) economist, A.C. Pigou, in a textbook written in the 1930s. The point in the example is that neither side *'internalises'* all the benefit of his or her investment decision. All that is considered is the *private benefit* in each case. As a result, there is underinvestment in both orchard and beekeeping. This is because the orchard owner cannot be made to pay for the activities of the bees, and the beekeeper cannot be made to pay for the nectar and pollen derived from the orchard. If payments could be exacted from the beneficiaries, there would be no problem. In fact, as anyone who knew anything about the economics of intensive fruit-growing could have told the Cambridge don, a well-developed market in the services of bees to orchards and vice versa actually does exist. In the USA, the largest managed pollination event in the world is in the almond orchards of California. Around one million hives arrive by truck at the almond orchards each spring. In Australia the threat of infestation of the honeybee population by the Varroa mite resulted in the establishment of a joint action group between beekeepers and the horticultural industry in 2007: Pollination Australia. This is because the services of each to the other are valuable, and as a result beekeepers habitually move large numbers of hives around to serve orchard owners at blossom time, with one or other side paying, depending on supply and demand. Clearly it was unwise to extrapolate from observations derived from the dreary fenland around Cambridge.

The graphical portrayal of externalities

The effects of externalities on resource allocation can be portrayed graphically. Consider first the case of negative externalities. Figure 11.1(a) depicts the supply (Private *MC*) and demand curves for a product whose production involves no external costs or benefits. We may imagine, for example, that the energy that powers the factories in this market comes from non-polluting hydroelectric generators. The resulting equilibrium price and quantity in the market for this product will then be socially optimal, for the reasons discussed in Chapters 3 and 6: the value to buyers of the last unit of the product consumed will be exactly equal to the marginal cost of producing it (€1,300 per tonne in each case), leaving no further possible gains from exchange.

But now suppose that a protracted drought has eliminated hydroelectric power generation, forcing factories to rely instead on electric power produced by coal-burning generators. Now each tonne of output produced is accompanied by an external pollution cost of $XC = €1,000$, as shown in Fig. 11.1(b). Since the external pollution cost falls not on firm owners but on others who live downwind from their factories, Private *MC* is again the supply curve for this product, and its demand curve is again as before, so that the equilibrium price and quantity will be exactly the same as in Fig. 11.1(a), as determined by the intersection of the demand curve (*D*) and the supply curve (Private *MC*). But this time the private market equilibrium is not socially optimal. To see why, note that at $Q_{pvt} = 12,000$ tonnes per year, the value to consumers of the last unit of output produced was only €1,300 per tonne, while the cost of producing that last unit (including the external cost) was €2,300 per tonne. This means that society could gain additional economic surplus by producing fewer units of the product. Indeed, the same conclusion will continue to hold whenever the current output exceeds 8,000 tonnes per year, the output level at which the demand curve intersects Social *MC*. Social *MC*, the socially optimal supply curve of the product, is the result of adding the external cost, *XC*, to every value along Private *MC*. The socially optimal level of output of the good shown in Fig. 11.1(b) is 8,000 tonnes per year, the level that exhausts all possibilities from exchange. For a good whose production generates external costs, the market equilibrium quantity will be higher than the socially optimal quantity.

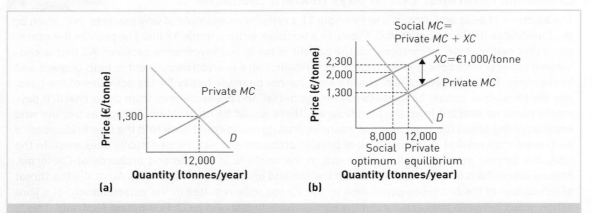

Figure 11.1 How External Costs Affect Resource Allocation. When a market has no external costs or benefits (a), the resulting equilibrium quantity and price are socially optimal. By contrast, when production of a good is accompanied by an external cost (b), the market equilibrium price (€1,300 per tonne) is too low, and the market equilibrium quantity (12,000 tonnes per year) is too high.

What about a good whose production generates external benefits? In Fig. 11.2, Private demand is the demand curve for a product whose production generates an external benefit of XB per unit. The market equilibrium quantity of this good Q_{pvt}, is the output level at which Private demand intersects the supply curve of the product (MC). This time, market equilibrium quantity is smaller than the socially optimal level, denoted Q_{soc}. Q_{soc} is the output level at which MC intersects the socially optimal demand curve (Social demand), which is obtained by adding the external benefit, XB, to every value along Private demand. Note that in Fig. 11.2 in the case of positive externalities the private market equilibrium again fails to exhaust all possible gains from exchange. Thus at Q_{pvt} the marginal cost of producing an additional unit of output is only MB_{pvt}, which is smaller than the marginal benefit of an additional unit by the amount XB. For a good whose production generates external benefits, the market equilibrium quantity will be smaller than the socially optimal quantity.

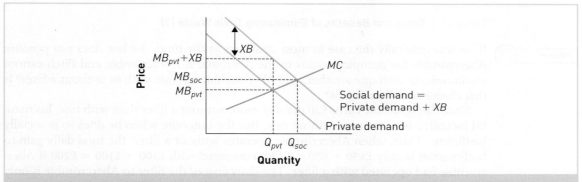

Figure 11.2 A Good Whose Production Generates a Positive Externality for Consumers. The market equilibrium quantity, Q_{pvt}, is smaller than the socially optimal quantity, Q_{soc}, because individual buyers are willing to pay only for the benefits they reap from directly consuming the product.

No matter whether externalities are positive or negative, they *distort the allocation of resources* in otherwise efficient markets. When externalities are present, the individual pursuit of self-interest will not result in the largest possible economic surplus. And when it does not, the outcome is by definition inefficient.

The Coase theorem

To say that a situation is 'inefficient' means that it can be rearranged in a way that would make at least some people better off without harming others. Such situations, as we have seen, are a source of creative tension. The existence of inefficiency, after all, means that there is 'cash on the table' (Chapter 3), which usually triggers a race to see who can capture it. For example, we saw that because monopoly pricing results in an inefficiently low output level, the potential for gain gave monopolists an incentive to make discounts available to price-sensitive buyers. As Examples 11.2 and 11.3 illustrate, the inefficiencies that result from externalities create similar incentives for remedial action.

Example 11.2 Will Abercrombie dump toxins in the river (1)?

In nineteenth-century Lancashire an industrialist named Abercrombie has built a textile factory beside a river. The water supplies power, but is also used in the production process. The process produces a toxic waste by-product from the dyes used. If Abercrombie releases the water untreated back into the river the toxins cause damage to Fitch, a commercial fisherman located downstream. The toxins are short-lived and cause no damage to anyone other than Fitch. At a cost, Abercrombie can filter out the toxins, in which case Fitch will suffer no damage at all. The relevant gains and losses for the two individuals are listed in Table 11.1.

	With filter	Without filter
Gains to Abercrombie	£100/day	£130/day
Gains to Fitch	£100/day	£50/day

Table 11.1 **Costs and Benefits of Eliminating Toxic Waste (1)**

Efficiency

If, as was generally the case in most countries at the time, the law does not penalise Abercrombie for dumping toxins in the river, and if Abercrombie and Fitch cannot communicate with one another, will Abercrombie operate with or without a filter? Is that choice socially efficient?

Since Abercrombie earns £30 per day more without a filter than with one, his natural incentive is to operate without one. But the outcome when he does so is socially inefficient. Thus, when Abercrombie operates without a filter, the total daily gain to both parties is only £130 + £50 = £180, compared with £100 + £100 = £200 if Abercrombie had operated with a filter. The daily cost of the filter to Abercrombie is only £130 – £100 = £30, which is smaller than its daily benefit to Fitch of £100 – £50 = £50. The fact that Abercrombie does not install the filter implies a squandered daily surplus of £20.

Example 11.3 Will Abercrombie dump toxins in the river (2)?

Suppose the costs and benefits of using the filter are as in Example 11.2, except that Abercrombie and Fitch can now communicate with one another at no cost. Even though the law does not require him to do so, will Abercrombie use a filter?

This time, Abercrombie will use a filter. Recall from Chapter 7 the observation that when the economic 'pie' grows larger, everyone can have a larger slice (the efficiency principle). Because use of a filter would result in the largest possible economic surplus, it would enable both Abercrombie and Fitch to have a larger net gain than before. Fitch thus has an incentive to *pay* Abercrombie to use a filter. For example, suppose Fitch offers Abercrombie £40 per day to compensate him for operating with a filter. Both Abercrombie and Fitch will then be exactly £10 per day better off than before, for a total daily net gain of £20.

Because we now assume that they can bargain and enter into some form of contract (requiring well-defined tradable property rights) the externality problem is solved.

Exercise 11.1   In Example 11.3, what is the largest amount, to the nearest euro or pound, by which Fitch could compensate Abercrombie for operating with a filter and still be better off than before?

Ronald Coase, a professor at the University of Chicago Law School, who was born in England and worked there as a professional economist before the Second World War, was the first to see clearly that if people can negotiate with one another at no cost over the right to perform activities that cause externalities, they will always arrive at an efficient solution. This insight, which is often called the **Coase theorem**, is a profoundly important idea, for which Coase was awarded the 1991 Nobel Prize in Economics.[1]

Coase theorem if at no cost people can negotiate the purchase and sale of the right to perform activities that cause externalities, they can always arrive at efficient solutions to the problems caused by externalities

Why, you might ask, should Fitch pay Abercrombie to filter out toxins that would not be there in the first place if it were not for Abercrombie's factory? The rhetorical force of this question is undeniable. Yet Coase points out that externalities are *reciprocal* in nature. The toxins do harm Fitch, to be sure, but preventing Abercrombie from emitting them would penalise Abercrombie, by exactly £30 per day. Why should Fitch necessarily have the right to harm Abercrombie? Indeed, as Example 11.4 illustrates, even if Fitch had that right, he would exercise it only if filtering the toxins proved the most efficient outcome.

Example 11.4 Will Abercrombie dump toxins in the river (3)?

Suppose the law says that Abercrombie may *not* dump toxins in the river unless he has Fitch's permission. If the relevant costs and benefits of filtering the toxins are as shown in Table 11.2, and if Abercrombie and Fitch can negotiate with one another at no cost, will Abercrombie filter the toxins?

	With filter	Without filter
Gains to Abercrombie	£100/day	£150/day
Gains to Fitch	£100/day	£70/day

Table 11.2 **Costs and Benefits of Eliminating Toxic Waste (3)**

Note that, this time, the most efficient outcome is for Abercrombie to operate without a filter, for the total daily surplus in that case will be £220 compared with only £200 with a filter. Under the law, however, Fitch has the right to insist that Abercrombie use a filter. We might expect him to exercise that right, since his own gain would rise from £70 to £100 per day if he did so. But because this outcome would be socially inefficient, we know that each party can do better.

Suppose, for example, that Abercrombie gives Fitch £40 per day in return for Fitch's permission to operate without a filter. Each would then have a net daily gain of £110, which is £10 better for each of them than if Fitch had insisted that Abercrombie use a filter. Abercrombie's pollution harms Fitch, sure enough, but failure to allow the pollution would have caused even greater harm to Abercrombie.

The Coase theorem tells us that regardless of whether the law holds polluters liable for damages, the affected parties will achieve efficient solutions to externalities if they can negotiate costlessly with one another. But note carefully that this does not imply

---

1 Coase's highly readable paper (and one of the most influential of the twentieth century), which enunciated what is now referred to as the Coase theorem, appeared in 1960 (Coase 1960).

that affected parties will be indifferent about whether the law holds polluters responsible for damages. If polluters are liable, they will end up with lower incomes and those who are injured by pollutants will end up with higher incomes than if the law does not hold polluters liable – even though the same efficient production methods are adopted in each case. When polluters are held liable, they must remove the pollution at their own expense. When they are not held liable, those who are injured by pollution must pay polluters to cut back.

Externalities are hardly rare and isolated occurrences. On the contrary, finding examples of actions that are altogether free of them is difficult. And because externalities can distort the allocation of resources, it is important to recognise them and deal intelligently with them. Consider Example 11.5, an externality that arises because of shared living arrangements.

Example 11.5 Will Ann and Betty share an apartment?

Ann and Betty can live together in a two-bedroom apartment in a small university town in Britain for £600 per month, or separately in two one-bedroom apartments, for £400 per month each. If the rent paid were the same for both alternatives, the two women would be indifferent between living together or separately, except for one problem: Ann talks constantly on the telephone. Ann would pay up to £250 per month for this privilege. Betty, for her part, would pay up to £150 per month to have better access to the phone. If the two cannot install a second phone line, should they live together or separately?

Ann and Betty should live together only if the benefit of doing so exceeds the cost. The benefit of living together is the reduction in their rent. Their benefit from living together is £200 per month. Their cost of living together is the least costly arrangement they can make to deal with Ann's objectionable telephone habits. Since Ann would be willing to pay up to £250 per month to avoid changing her behaviour, the £200 rent saving is too small to persuade her to change. But Betty is willing to put up with Ann's behaviour for a compensation payment of only £150 per month. Since that amount is smaller than the total saving in rent, the least costly solution to the problem is for Betty to live with Ann and simply put up with her behaviour.

Table 11.3 summarises the relevant costs and benefits of this shared living arrangement. The Cost–Benefit Principle tells us that Ann and Betty should live together if and only if the benefit of living together exceeds the cost. The cost of the shared living arrangement is not the sum of all possible costs but the least costly accommodation to the problem (or problems) of shared living. Since the £200 per month saving in rent exceeds the least costly accommodation to the phone problem, Ann and Betty can reap a total gain in economic surplus of £50 per month by sharing their living quarters.

An initial reaction to this problem might be that Ann and Betty should not live together, because if the two share the rent equally, Betty will end up paying £300 per month – which when added to the £150 cost of putting up with Ann's phone behaviour comes to £50 more than the cost of living alone. As persuasive as that argument may sound, however, it is mistaken. The source of the error, as Example 11.6 makes clear, is the assumption that the two must share the rent equally.

Example 11.6 What is the highest rent Betty would be willing to pay for the two-bedroom apartment?

In Example 11.5, what is the highest rent Betty would be willing to pay to share an apartment with Ann? Betty's alternative is to live alone, which would mean paying

Benefits of shared living		
Total cost of separate apartments	Total cost of shared apartment	Rent savings from sharing
(2)(£400/month) = £800/month	£600/month	£200/month
Costs of shared living		
Problem	Ann's cost of solving problem	Betty's cost of solving problem	Least costly solution to the problem
Ann's phone usage	Curtailed phone usage: £250/month	Tolerate phone usage: £150/month	Betty tolerates Ann's phone usage: £150/month
Gain in surplus from shared living		
Rent savings (£200/month) −	Least costly accommodation to shared living problems (£150/month) =	Gain in surplus: £50/month

Table 11.3 **The Gain in Surplus from Shared Living Arrangements**

£400 per month, her reservation price for a living arrangement with no phone problem. Since the most she would be willing to pay to avoid the phone problem is £150 per month, the highest monthly rent she would be willing to pay for the shared apartment is £400 − £150 = £250. If she pays that amount, Ann will have to pay the difference, namely, £350 per month, which is clearly a better alternative for Ann than paying £400 to live alone.

Legal remedies for externalities

We have seen that efficient solutions to externalities can be found whenever the affected parties can negotiate with one another at no cost. But negotiation is not always practical. A motorist with a noisy exhaust silencer, for example, imposes costs on others, yet they cannot flag him down and offer him a compensation payment to fix it. In recognition of this difficulty, most governments simply require that cars have working silencers. Indeed, the explicit or implicit purpose of a large share – perhaps the lion's share – of laws is to solve problems caused by externalities. The goal of such laws is to help people achieve the solutions they might have reached had they been able to negotiate with one another.

When negotiation is costless, the task of adjustment generally falls on the party who can accomplish it at the lowest cost. For instance, in Example 11.5, Betty put up with Ann's annoying phone habits because doing so was less costly than asking Ann to change her habits. Many municipal noise abatement orders also place the burden of adjustment on those who can accomplish it at lowest cost. Consider, for example, the restrictions on loud music at parties, which often take effect at a later hour at night on weekends than during the week. This pattern reflects both the fact that the gains from loud music tend to be larger at weekends (more people want to party at weekends) and the fact that the disturbance costs of such music are likely to be higher on week-nights (people cannot have a lie-in the next morning). By setting the noise curfew at different hours on different days of the week, the law places the burden on party-goers during the week and on sleepers during the weekend. Similar logic explains why noise abatement orders sometimes prohibit motorists from using their car horns near hospitals, but permit their use elsewhere.

Exercise 11.2   The exposition of the Coase theorem in Coase's 1960 paper referred to a case heard in the Chancery Division of the High Court in London in 1879.[2] The facts were as follows. A confectioner (Bridgeman) had for years operated a business from his premises on a London street that involved using mortars and pestles to grind and mix ingredients. A doctor, Sturges, who had a practice in an adjoining premises, built a consultation room up against the wall of Bridgeman's premises. The vibrations from the confectionery business interfered with the doctor's ability to listen to people's chests. He sued the confectioner for 'nuisance' (a tort under common law; a tort is an injury to a person or property). What would you have decided in this case (a) if you had never heard of the Coase theorem, and (b) if you were fully aware of the Coase theorem?

Exercise 11.3   Use the idea of externality resolution to explain why there exist the following legal interventions to influence individual behaviour.
    (a) Why is it common to find a requirement that motorists have, and use, snow chains in mountainous regions when there is snow on the ground?
    (b) Why do most urban areas in the developed world have strongly enforced zoning restrictions on occupations and building types?
    (c) Why do governments frequently use taxpayers' money to subsidise non-commercial research by university academics?

The optimal amount of negative externalities is not zero

Curbing pollution and other negative externalities entails both costs and benefits. The Cost–Benefit Principle developed in Chapter 5 applies to public policy in relation to externalities. The best policy is to curtail pollution until the cost of further abatement (marginal cost) just equals the marginal benefit. In general, the marginal cost of abatement rises with the amount of pollution eliminated. (Following the Low-Hanging-Fruit Principle, polluters use the cheapest clean-up methods first and then turn to more expensive ones.) And if diminishing marginal utility applies to environmental action, it suggests that, beyond some point, the marginal benefit of pollution reduction tends to fall as more pollution is removed. As a result, the marginal cost and marginal benefit curves almost always intersect at less than the maximum amount of pollution reduction.

Cost–Benefit
Analysis

    The intersection of the two curves marks instead the *socially optimal level of pollution reduction*. If pollution is curtailed by any less than that amount, society will gain more than it will lose by pushing the clean-up effort a little further. But if regulators push beyond the point at which the marginal cost and benefit curves intersect, society will incur costs that exceed the benefits. The existence of a *socially optimal level of pollution reduction* implies the existence of a socially optimal level of pollution, and that level will almost always be greater than zero.

    This point, a central tenet of the economic approach to policy making, is one that the public at large are not comfortable with. The concept implies that there is an acceptable level of something that people regard as intrinsically unacceptable, and

---

2 Sturges vs Bridgeman, 11 Chancery Division 852, 1879.

leads to clashes between economists and other commentators on public policy issues. How often have you heard the statement that since human life is priceless there is no acceptable level of death on the roads? Actually, it is easy to show that we do put a price on life, even our own. And we do not in reality behave individually as if no road death is tolerable, even our own. However, because, as we saw in Chapter 5, people have been conditioned to think of pollution as bad, many cringe when they hear the phrase 'socially optimal level of pollution'. But to speak of a socially optimal level of pollution is not the same as saying that *pollution is good*. It is merely to recognise that society has an interest in cleaning up the environment, but only up to a certain point. The underlying idea is no different from the idea of an optimal level of dirt in a flat. After all, even if you spent the whole day, every day, vacuuming your flat, there would be *some* dirt left in it. And because you have better things to do than vacuum all day, you probably tolerate substantially more than the minimal amount of dirt. A dirty apartment is not good, nor is pollution in the air you breathe. But in both cases, the clean-up effort should be expanded only until the marginal benefit equals the marginal cost.

RECAP External costs and benefits

Externalities occur when the costs or benefits of an activity accrue to people other than those directly involved in the activity. The *Coase theorem* says that when affected parties can negotiate with one another without cost, activities will be pursued at efficient levels, even in the presence of positive or negative externalities. But when negotiation is prohibitively costly, inefficient behaviour generally results. Activities that generate negative externalities are pursued to excess, while those that generate positive externalities are pursued too little. Laws and regulations are often adopted in an effort to alter inefficient behaviour that results from externalities.

Property rights and the 'tragedy of the commons'

People who grow up in the industrialised nations tend to take the institution of private property for granted. Our intuitive sense is that people have the right to own any property they acquire by lawful means and to do with that property much as they see fit. In reality, however, property laws are considerably more complex in terms of the rights they confer and the obligations they impose. Moreover, the set of property rights created and enforced at law has significant implications in terms of the efficiency with which resources are used.

In 1968 an article was published in *Science* that gave the debate on economics and its impact on real life a memorable phrase that is now a commonplace term in the analysis of property rights and their implications.[3] The term used was the **'tragedy of the commons'**. The 'tragedy' is that when valuable assets are held in common so that their fruits may be shared, the end result is usually that the assets are overexploited and wasted. Common ownership has the same consequences as *no ownership at all*.

'tragedy of the commons' the tendency for a resource that has no price to be used until its marginal benefit falls to zero

In 1975 two American economists from the University of Delaware published a paper demonstrating this point and its consequences.[4] They provided persuasive evidence of the effects of common ownership as opposed to private ownership of oyster fisheries on the US eastern seaboard. Common ownership resulted in lower output

3 Hardin (1968).
4 Agnello and Donnelly (1975).

per head because the oyster beds were overexploited. Another way of putting it was that under common ownership there was insufficient investment in maintaining the productive potential of the beds. Anyone who refrained from harvesting a kilogram of oysters was investing the income forgone in maintaining production potential. But in doing so not only could he not benefit from the increased production in the future resulting from his actions, but he was conferring a 'free lunch' on all the others who were entitled to harvest the oysters. The inevitable consequence was overexploitation of the biomass.

Incentives
Matter

The collapse of fish stocks in north-west European waters in the 1990s led the EU Commission to propose drastic reductions in fishing quotas in 2004. This, too, was a reflection of the consequences of the exacerbation of a tragedy of the commons by the EU's Common Fisheries Policy (CFP). Under the European treaties the deep-sea fishery waters of all EU states must be open to fishing boats from any member state. It was bad enough when member state governments had to face the problem of overfishing of national waters by crews based in the various states. The richest fishing waters of Western Europe are those in what is, formally, the Irish economic zone. Even before full liberalisation of access, Irish drift net fishing in Irish coastal waters reduced Atlantic salmon stocks in Irish rivers to close to extinction, and the government could, or would, do little about the problem. When boats from other states, frequently with exhausted waters at home, overfish Irish waters the Irish ability to police the problem is inadequate and the other states' governments are not unduly concerned. The result has been a fish stock crash. The EU is now acting, belatedly and crudely, to offset this tragedy of the commons problem.

Economic naturalist 11.2 What common factor links poor housing on reservations for Native Americans in the USA and the failure to develop commercial agriculture in Zambia after the collapse of agriculture across the Zambesi in Zimbabwe?

Even in relatively prosperous reservations in the USA there is very little conventional private housing, with the population for the most part living in federally funded accommodation or in trailers. In Zambia, to a casual observer, given the collapse of Zimbabwe under the Mugabe kleptocracy, it is hard to understand why agriculture is so underdeveloped. Africa faces a food shortage, while fertile land in Zambia lies unused or underused.

In both cases a significant explanatory variable is land tenure. Land is held by, and allocated by, the tribe. As a result it is very hard to get a loan (mortgage) to build a conventional house on a reservation, since you can't put up the land it's on as security. Similarly, if land is held tribally, investment in its potential for agriculture is highly problematic, since an investor has no easily established property right in the improvement of the land, and has no long-term right to exploit it.

The problem of unpriced resources

The tragedy of the commons is part of a more general problem that arises when scarce resources are not priced to users, or are underpriced (a zero price is not even a limiting case: in some instances governments have permitted exploitation at a negative price – i.e. have subsidised people to undertake the exploitation; US federal policy in the nineteenth century on encouraging settlement of the west had this characteristic in some respects). To understand the laws that govern the use of property, we must begin by asking why societies created the institution of private property in the first place. Examples 11.7 and 11.8, which show what happens to property that nobody owns, suggest an answer.

Example 11.7 How many cattle will villagers graze on the commons?

A village has five households, each of which has accumulated savings of €100. The village has a commonly owned tract of grazing land. Each villager can use the money to buy a government bond that pays 13 per cent interest per year or to buy a year-old bullock, send it on to the commons to graze, and sell it after one year. The price the villager will get for the two-year-old animal depends on the amount of weight it gains while grazing on the commons, which in turn depends on the number of steers sent on to the commons, as shown in Table 11.4.

The price of a two-year-old steer declines with the number of cattle grazing on the commons, because the more cattle, the less grass available to each. The villagers make their investment decisions one at a time, and the results are public. If each villager decides how to invest individually, how many cattle will be sent on to the commons and what will be the village's total income?

Number of steers on the commons	Price per two-year-old steer (€)	Income per steer (€/year)
1	126	26
2	119	19
3	116	16
4	113	13
5	111	11

Table 11.4 **The Relationship between Herd Size and Steer Price**

If a villager buys a €100 government bond, he will earn €13 interest income at the end of one year. Thus he should buy and graze a bullock on the commons if and only if the animal will command a price of at least €113 as a two year old. When each villager chooses in this self-interested way, we can expect four households to send a steer on to the commons. (Actually, the fourth villager would be indifferent between investing in a steer or buying a bond, since he would earn €13 either way. For the sake of discussion, we shall assume that, in the case of a tie, people choose to be cattle grazers.) The fifth householder, seeing that he would earn only €11 by sending a fifth steer on to the commons, will choose instead to buy a government bond. As a result of these decisions, the total village income will be €65 per year – €13 for the one bondholder and 4 × (€13) = €52 for the four cattle grazers.

Has Adam Smith's invisible hand produced the most efficient allocation of these villagers' resources? We can tell at a glance that it has not, since their total village income is only €65 – precisely the same as it would have been had the possibility of cattle raising not existed. The source of the difficulty will become evident in Example 11.8.

Example 11.8 What is the socially optimal number of cattle to graze on the commons?

Suppose the five households in Example 11.7 confront the same investment opportunities as before, except that this time they are free to make their decisions as a group rather than individually. How many bullocks will they send on to the commons, and what will be their total village income?

This time, the villagers' goal is to maximise the income received by the group as a whole. When decisions are made from this perspective, the criterion is to send a steer on to the commons only if its marginal contribution to village income is at least €13, the amount that could be earned from a government bond. As the entries in column (5) of Table 11.5 indicate, the first bullock clearly meets this criterion, since it contributes €26 to total village income. But the second does not. Sending it on to the commons raises the village's income from cattle raising from €26 to €38, a gain of just €12. The €100 required to buy the second bullock would thus have been better invested in a government bond. Worse, the collective return from grazing a third animal is only €10; from a fourth, only €4; and, from a fifth, only €3.

Number of steers on the commons (1)	Price per two-year-old steer (€) (2)	Income per steer (€/year) (3)	Total cattle income (€/year) (4)	Marginal income (€/year) (5)
1	126	26	26	26
2	119	19	38	12
3	116	16	48	10
4	113	13	52	4
5	111	11	55	3

Table 11.5 **Marginal Income and the Socially Optimal Herd Size**

Efficiency

In sum, when investment decisions are made with the goal of *maximising total village income*, the best choice is to buy four government bonds and send only a single bullock on to the commons. The resulting village income will be €78: €26 from grazing the single animal and €52 from the four government bonds. That amount is €3 more than the total income that resulted when villagers made their investment decisions individually. Once again, the reward from moving from an inefficient allocation to an efficient one is that the economic 'pie' grows larger. And when the 'pie' grows larger, everyone can get a larger slice. For instance, if the villagers agree to pool their income and share it equally, each will get €15.60, or €2.60 more than before.

Exercise 11.4   How would your answers to Examples 11.7 and 11.8 differ if the interest rate were not 13 per cent but 11 per cent per year?

Why do the villagers in Examples 11.7 and 11.8 do better when they make their investment decisions collectively? The answer is that when individuals decide alone, they ignore the fact that sending another steer on to the commons will cause existing steers to gain less weight. Their failure to consider this effect makes the return from sending another steer seem misleadingly high to them.

The grazing land on the commons is a valuable *economic resource*. When no one owns it, no one has any incentive to take the opportunity cost of using it into account. And, when that happens, people will tend to use it until its marginal benefit is zero. This problem, and others similar to it, are examples of the tragedy of the commons. The essential cause of the tragedy of the commons is the fact that one person's use of commonly held property imposes an *external cost* on others by making the property less valuable. The tragedy of the commons also provides a vivid illustration of the Equilibrium Principle (see Chapter 3). Each individual villager behaves rationally by sending an additional steer on to the commons, yet the overall outcome falls far short of the attainable ideal.

The effect of private ownership

As Example 11.9 illustrates, one solution to the tragedy of the commons is to place the village grazing land under private ownership.

Example 11.9 How much will the right to control the village commons sell for?

Suppose the five households face the same investment opportunities as before, except that this time they decide to auction off the right to use the commons to the highest bidder. Assuming that the villagers can borrow as well as lend at an annual interest rate of 13 per cent, what price will the right to use the commons fetch? How will the owner of that property right use it, and what will be the resulting village income?

To answer these questions, simply ask yourself what you would do if you had complete control over how the grazing land were used. As we saw in Example 11.8, the most profitable way to use this land is to send only a single steer to graze on it. If you do so, you will earn a total of €26 per year. Since the opportunity cost of the €100 you spent on the single yearling steer is the €13 in interest you could have earned from a bond, your economic profit from sending a single steer on to the commons will be €13 per year, provided you can use the land for free. But you cannot; to finance your purchase of the property right, you must borrow money (since you used your €100 savings to buy a year-old bullock).

What is the most you would be willing to pay for the right to use the commons? Since its use generates an income of €26 per year, or €13 more than the opportunity cost of your investment in the bullock, the most you would pay is €100 (because that amount used to purchase a bond that pays 13 per cent interest would also generate income of €13 per year). If the land were sold at auction, €100 is precisely the amount you would have to pay. Your annual earnings from the land would be exactly enough to pay the €13 interest on your loan and cover the opportunity cost of not having put your savings into a bond.

Note that when the right to use the land is auctioned to the highest bidder, the village achieves a more efficient allocation of its resources, because the owner has a strong incentive to take the opportunity cost of more intensive grazing fully into account. Total village income in this case will again be €78. If the annual interest on the €100 proceeds from selling the land rights is shared equally among the five villagers, each will again have an annual investment income of €15.60.

The logic of *economic surplus maximisation* helps to explain why the most economically successful nations have all been ones with well-developed private property laws. Property that belongs to everyone belongs, in effect, to no one. Not only is its potential economic value never fully realised, it usually ends up being of no value at all.

Bear in mind, however, that in most countries the owners of private property are not free to do *precisely* as they wish with it. For example, local planning regulations or zoning laws may give the owner of a plot of residential building land the right to build a three-storey house but not a six-storey house. Here, too, the logic of economic surplus maximisation applies, for a fully informed and rational legislature would define property rights so as to create the largest possible total economic surplus. In practice, of course, such ideal legislatures never really exist. Yet one view of the essence of politics is the creation of arrangements that make people better off. If a legislator could propose a change in the planning regime affecting his constituency that would enlarge the total economic surplus for the people in that constituency, he could also propose a scheme that would give each constituent a larger income by sharing out the gain, thus enhancing his chances of re-election.

As an economic naturalist, challenge yourself to use this framework when thinking about the various restrictions you encounter in private property laws: zoning laws that constrain what you can build and what types of activities you can conduct on your land; traffic laws that constrain what you can do with your car; employment and environmental laws that constrain how you can operate your business. Your understanding of these and countless other laws will be enhanced by the insight that everyone can gain when the private property laws are defined so as to create the largest total economic surplus.

When private ownership is impractical

Do not be misled into thinking that the law provides an *ideal* resolution of all problems associated with externalities and the tragedy of the commons. Defining and enforcing efficient property rights entails costs, after all, and sometimes the costs outweigh the gains.

Economic naturalist 11.3 Why are shared milkshakes consumed too quickly?

Sara and Susan are identical twins who love chocolate milkshakes. Their mother buys them each a 25 cl carton each Saturday at the shopping centre. The girls take 10 minutes to finish their milkshakes. Their mother gets 10 minutes' peace. One weekend the mother buys them a 50 cl carton, and two straws (the 50 cl shake costs less than two 25 cl shakes). The carton is empty in 3 minutes. Bad decision on the mother's part. Why? If each has a straw and each knows that the other is self-interested, will the twins consume the milkshake at an optimal rate? Because drinking a milkshake too quickly chills the taste buds, the twins will enjoy their shake more if they drink it slowly. Yet each knows that the other will drink any part of the milkshake she doesn't finish herself. The result is that each will consume the shake at a faster rate than she would if she had half a shake all to herself.

Here are some further examples of the type of tragedy of the commons that is not easily solved by defining private ownership rights.

Harvesting timber on remote public land

On remote public land, enforcing restrictions against cutting down trees may be impractical. Each tree cutter knows that a tree that is not harvested this year will be bigger, and hence more valuable, next year. But he also knows that if he doesn't cut the tree down this year, someone else will. In contrast, private companies that grow trees on their own land have no incentive to harvest timber prematurely and a strong incentive to prevent outsiders from doing so.

Harvesting whales in international waters

Each individual whaler knows that harvesting an extra whale reduces the breeding population, and hence the size of the future whale population. But the whaler also knows that any whale that is not harvested today will be taken by some other whaler.

The solution would be to define and enforce property rights to whales. But the oceans are vast, and the behaviour of whalers is hard to monitor. And even if their behaviour could be monitored, the concept of national sovereignty would make the international enforcement of property rights problematic.

More generally, the animal species that are most severely threatened with extinction tend to be those that are economically valuable to humans but that are not privately owned by anyone. This is the situation confronting whales. Contrast it with the situation confronting chickens, which are also economically valuable to humans but which, unlike whales, are governed by traditional laws of private property. This difference explains why no one worries that Colonel Sanders might threaten the extinction of chickens. It also explains why allowing people to harvest ivory legally from herds that they own may be the best way to protect elephants from poachers in sub-Saharan Africa, and ecotourism is the best hope for the survival of the South-east Asian tiger population.

Controlling multinational environmental pollution

Each individual polluter may know that if he and all others pollute, the damage to the environment will be greater than the cost of not polluting. But if the environment is common property into which all are free to dump, each has a powerful incentive to pollute. If all polluters live under the jurisdiction of a single government, enforcing laws and regulations that limit the discharge of pollution may be practical. But if polluters come from many different countries, solutions are much more difficult to implement. Thus the Mediterranean Sea has long suffered serious pollution, because none of the many nations that border it has an economic incentive to consider the effects of its discharges on other countries. The smaller number of countries involved (and the fact that almost all were members of the then EEC) permitted agreements to be reached to control and reduce the pollution of the River Rhine, which suffered on a similar basis to that of the Mediterranean.

As the world's population continues to grow, the absence of an effective system of international property rights will become an economic problem of increasing significance.

RECAP Property rights and the tragedy of the commons

When a valuable resource has a price of zero, people will continue to exploit it as long as its marginal benefit remains positive. The tragedy of the commons describes situations in which valuable resources are squandered because users are not charged for them. In many cases, an efficient remedy for such waste is to define and enforce rights to the use of valuable property. But this solution is difficult to implement for resources such as the oceans and the atmosphere, because no single government has the authority to *enforce property rights* for these resources.

Positional externalities

Steffi Graf received more than €1.6 million in tournament winnings in 1992; her endorsement and exhibition earnings totalled several times that amount. By any reasonable measure, the quality of her play was outstanding, yet she consistently lost to arch-rival Monica Seles. But in April 1993, Seles was stabbed in the back by a deranged fan and forced to withdraw from the tour. In the ensuing months, Graf's tournament winnings accumulated at almost double her 1992 pace, despite little change in the quality of her play.

Payoffs that depend on relative performance

In professional tennis and a host of other competitive situations, the rewards people receive typically depend not only on how they perform in absolute terms but also on how they perform relative to their closest rivals. David Beckham in soccer, Brian O'Driscoll in rugby, were similar to Monica Seles in tennis. In these situations, competitors have an incentive to take actions that will increase their odds of winning. For example, tennis players can increase their chances of winning by hiring personal fitness trainers and sports psychologists to travel with them on the tour. That is why the Olympics are plagued by the performance-enhancing drugs problem. Yet the simple mathematics of competition tells us that the sum of all individual payoffs from such investments will be larger than the collective payoff. In any tennis match, for example, each contestant will get a sizeable payoff from money spent on fitness trainers and sports psychologists, yet each match will have exactly one winner and one loser, no matter how much players spend. The overall gain to tennis spectators is likely to be small, and the overall gain to players as a group must be zero. To the extent that each contestant's payoff depends on his or her relative performance, then, the incentive to undertake such investments will be excessive, from a collective point of view.

positional externality occurs when an increase in one person's performance reduces the expected reward of another in situations in which reward depends on relative performance

Positional arms races

A **positional externality** means that, whenever the payoffs to one contestant depend at least in part on how he or she performs relative to a rival, any step that improves one side's relative position must necessarily worsen the other's. Just as the invisible hand of the market is weakened by the presence of standard externalities, it is also weakened by positional externalities.

Economic naturalist 11.4 Why do many US grocery stores stay open all night, even in small towns? And why do retailers cheerfully accept legal restrictions on opening hours?

Most European countries have legal or zoning restrictions of some form on hours of opening of retail outlets. Economists have argued that this is clearly anti-competitive. In general in big-city America, and even in small towns, it is possible to find a good number of grocery stores open 24 hours a day. Ithaca, New York, has seven large supermarkets, five of which are open 24 hours a day. In Italy, pharmacies operate on a basis of maintaining service by arranging to close for a day in turn so that there is always at least one pharmacy available. The convenience of all-night shopping could be maintained at lower cost if all but one of the stores were to close during late-night hours. Why do many remain open?

The answer is that it reflects higher costs being incurred as a result of yet another prisoner's dilemma.

Most people do the bulk of their shopping at one supermarket. Other things being equal, more people will choose the store with the most convenient hours. If one closes at midnight while the other decides to stay open until 1 am, the latter will obviously capture all the business from midnight to 1 am. It will also capture some of the business of the other store that would have gone to that store before midnight but now has the choice of shopping after midnight. The optimum strategy is for the second store to stay open too. The extra cost of staying open may well exceed the willingness of people to pay at that time (as they can always choose to shop earlier).

In the situation described in Economic naturalist 11.4, the dominant strategy for each store is to remain open an extra hour, even though each would be better off if both closed at midnight. And, of course, the rivalry does not stop there, for if both stay open until 1 am, each will see an opportunity to better its rival by staying open until 2. As long as the cost of staying open another hour is small relative to the gains received, all stores will stay open 24 hours a day. But though consumers do gain when stores remain open longer, beyond some point the benefit to consumers is small relative to the costs borne by merchants. The problem is that for any individual merchant who fails to match a rival's hours, the costs may be even larger.

In such situations, the public might be well served by an amendment to the antitrust laws that permits stores to cooperate to limit their hours, perhaps through an agreement calling for each store to serve in rotation as the only all-night grocery. Local statutes that limit business hours might serve the same purpose.

Exercise 11.5 Before accepting this as a case for universal restrictions on opening hours, consider what would be the consequence of restricting stores to, say, eight hours a day and no Sunday opening.

positional arms race a series of mutually offsetting investments in performance enhancement that is stimulated by a positional externality

positional arms control agreement an agreement in which contestants attempt to limit mutually offsetting investments in performance enhancement

We have seen that positional externalities often lead contestants to engage in an escalating series of mutually offsetting investments in performance enhancement. We call such spending patterns **positional arms races**.

Positional arms control agreements

Because positional arms races produce inefficient outcomes, people have an incentive to curtail them. Steps taken to reduce positional arms races, such as rules against anabolic steroids, may therefore be thought of as **positional arms control agreements**.

Once you become aware of positional arms races, you will begin to see examples of them almost everywhere. You can hone your skills as an economic naturalist by asking these questions about every competitive situation you observe. What form do the investments in performance enhancement take? What steps have contestants taken to limit these investments? Sometimes positional arms control agreements are achieved by the imposition of formal rules or by the signing of legal contracts. We shall now consider examples of this type of agreement.

Campaign spending limits

In the United States, presidential candidates routinely spend more than $100 million on advertising. Yet if both candidates double their spending on ads, each one's odds of winning will remain essentially the same. Recognition of this pattern led Congress to adopt strict spending limits for presidential candidates. (That those regulations have proved difficult to enforce does not call into question the logic behind the legislation.) Similar restrictions apply to parliamentary elections in many West European countries.

Arbitration agreements

In the business world, contracting parties often sign a binding agreement that commits them to arbitration in the event of a dispute. By doing so, they sacrifice the option of pursuing their interests as fully as they might wish to later, but they also insulate themselves from costly legal battles. In the United Kingdom and Ireland, what is called 'case management' is required by judges in many High Court civil cases. This means obliging the parties to exchange reports and have expert witnesses remove from consideration by the court matters on which there is no dispute, thus avoiding costly court time hearing testimony on which there is agreement between the parties.

Mandatory starting dates for school

A child who is a year or so older than most of her elementary (primary) classmates is likely to perform better, in relative terms, than if she had entered school with children her own age. And since most parents are aware that admission to universities and eligibility for top jobs upon graduation depend largely on *relative* academic performance, many are tempted to keep their children out of kindergarten a year longer than necessary. Yet there is no social advantage in holding *all* children back an extra year, since their relative performance will essentially be unaffected. In many jurisdictions, therefore, the law requires children who reach a determined age by a given date in a year to start school in that year. However, this needs qualification. The use of the feminine pronoun in this case is deliberate, not simply politically correct. Most developmental psychologists will agree that, on average, between the ages of 12 and 18 boys develop mentally more slowly than girls (which is part of the reason teenage girls give boys in their classes such a hard time socially). It follows that if boys and girls take terminal exams and leave school at the same age, girls will do better than boys ... and better than if they were ranked at the same mental age. Requiring boys to start schooling at the same age as girls, then, is equivalent to giving girls as a group a slight edge in competitive exams at 18. Unfortunately, in today's political climate it looks rather unlikely that any government will pick up that hot potato.

Social norms as positional arms control agreements

In some cases, *social norms* may take the place of formal agreements to curtail positional arms races. Here are two familiar examples.

Nerd norms

Some students care more – in the short run, at least – about the grades they get than how much they actually learn. When such students are graded on the curve – that is, on the basis of their performance relative to other students – a positional arms race ensues, because if all students were to double the amount of time they studied, the distribution of grades would remain essentially the same. Students who find themselves in this situation are often quick to embrace 'nerd norms', which brand as social misfits those who 'study too hard'.

Norms against vanity

Cosmetic and reconstructive surgery has produced dramatic benefits for many people, enabling badly disfigured accident victims to recover a more normal appearance. It has also eliminated the extreme self-consciousness felt by people born with strikingly unusual features. Such surgery, however, is by no means confined to the conspicuously disfigured. Increasingly, 'normal' people are seeking surgical improvements to their appearance. Demand has continued to grow steadily. Once a carefully guarded secret, these procedures are now sometimes offered as prizes in charity raffles. In America, undertakers have begun to complain that the non-combustible silicon implants used in breast and buttocks augmentation are clogging their crematoria.

In individual cases, cosmetic surgery may be just as beneficial as reconstructive surgery is for accident victims. Buoyed by the confidence of having a straight nose or a wrinkle-free complexion, patients sometimes go on to achieve much more than they ever thought possible. But the growing use of cosmetic surgery has also had an unintended side effect: it has altered the standards of normal appearance. A nose that once would have seemed only slightly larger than average may now seem jarringly big. The same person who once would have looked like an average 55 year old may now look nearly 70. And someone who once would have tolerated slightly thinning hair or an average amount of cellulite may now feel compelled to undergo hair transplantation or liposuction. Because such procedures shift people's frame of reference, their payoffs to individuals are misleadingly large. From a social perspective, therefore, reliance on them is likely to be excessive. Legal sanctions against cosmetic surgery are difficult to imagine. But some communities have embraced powerful social norms against cosmetic surgery, heaping scorn and ridicule on the consumers of facelifts and tummy tucks. In individual cases, such norms may seem cruel. Yet without them, many more people might feel compelled to bear the risk and expense of cosmetic surgery.

Summary

- *Externalities* are the costs and benefits of activities that accrue to people who are not directly involved in those activities. When all parties affected by externalities can negotiate with one another at no cost, the invisible hand of the market will produce an efficient allocation of resources. According to the *Coase theorem*, the allocation of resources is efficient in such cases because the parties affected by externalities can compensate others for taking remedial action.

- Negotiation over externalities is often impractical, however. In these cases, the self-serving actions of individuals typically will not lead to an efficient outcome. The attempt to forge solutions to the problems caused by externalities is one of the most important rationales for *collective action*. Sometimes collective action takes the form of laws and government regulations that alter the incentives facing those who generate, or are affected by, externalities. Such remedies work best when they place the burden of accommodation on the parties who can accomplish it at the lowest cost. Traffic laws, zoning laws, environmental protection laws and free speech laws are examples.

- Curbing pollution and other negative externalities entails *costs* as well as *benefits*. The optimal amount of pollution reduction is the amount for which the marginal benefit of further reduction just equals the marginal cost. In general, this formula implies that the socially optimal level of pollution, or of any other negative externality, is greater than zero.

- When grazing land and other valuable resources are owned in common, no one has an incentive to take into account the opportunity cost of using those resources. This problem is known as the *tragedy of the commons*. Defining and enforcing private rights governing the use of valuable resources is often an effective solution. Not surprisingly, most economically successful nations have well-developed institutions of private property. Property that belongs to everyone belongs, in effect, to no one. Not only is its potential economic value never fully realised, it usually ends up having no value at all.

- The difficulty of *enforcing* property rights in certain situations explains a variety of inefficient outcomes, such as the excessive harvest of whales in international waters and the premature harvest of timber on remote public lands. The excessive pollution of seas that are bordered by many countries also results from a lack of enforceable property rights.

- Situations in which people's rewards depend on how well they perform in relation to their rivals give rise to *positional externalities*. In these situations, any step that improves one side's relative position necessarily worsens the other's. Positional externalities tend to spawn positional arms races – escalating patterns of mutually offsetting investments in performance enhancement. Collective measures to curb positional arms races are known as *positional arms control agreements*. These collective actions may take the form of formal regulations or rules, such as rules against anabolic steroids in sports, campaign spending limits, and binding arbitration agreements.

Review questions

1. Shoes may be viewed as the result of a positional externality. What incentive problem explains why the freeways in cities such as Los Angeles suffer from excessive congestion?

2. How would you explain to a friend why the optimal amount of freeway congestion is not zero?

3. If a country's government could declare any activity that imposes external costs on others illegal, would such legislation be advisable?

4. Why does the Great Salt Lake, which is located wholly within the state of Utah, suffer lower levels of pollution than Lake Erie, which is bordered by several states and Canada?

connect   Problems

Problems marked with an asterisk (*) are more difficult.

1. Determine whether the following statements are **true or false**, and briefly explain why.

   a. A given total emission reduction in a polluting industry will be achieved at the lowest possible total cost when the cost of the last unit of pollution curbed is equal for each firm in the industry.

   b. In an attempt to lower their costs of production, firms sometimes succeed merely in shifting costs to outsiders.

2. Phoebe keeps a bee farm next door to an apple orchard. She chooses her optimal number of beehives by selecting the honey output level at which her private marginal benefit from beekeeping equals her private marginal cost.

   a. Assume that Phoebe's private marginal benefit and marginal cost curves from beekeeping are normally shaped. Draw a diagram of them.

   b. Phoebe's bees help to pollinate the blossoms in the apple orchard, increasing the fruit yield. Show the social marginal benefit from Phoebe's beekeeping in your diagram.

   c. Phoebe's bees are Africanised killer bees that aggressively sting anyone who steps into their flight path. Phoebe, fortunately, is naturally immune to the bees' venom. Show the social marginal cost curve from Phoebe's beekeeping in your diagram.

   d. Indicate the socially optimal quantity of beehives on your diagram. Is it higher or lower than the privately optimal quantity? Explain.

3. Suppose the supply curve of boom box rentals at a holiday resort in the Mediterranean is given by $P = 5 + 0.1Q$, where P is the daily rent per unit in euros and Q is the volume of units rented in hundreds per day. The demand curve for boom boxes is $20 - 0.2Q$. If each boom box imposes €3 per day in noise costs on others, by how much will the equilibrium number of boom boxes rented exceed the socially optimal number?

4. Refer to Problem 3. How would the imposition of a tax of €3 per unit on each daily boom box rental affect efficiency in this market?

5. Suppose the law says that Jones may *not* emit smoke from his factory unless he gets permission from Smith, who lives downwind. If the relevant costs and benefits of filtering the smoke from Jones' production process are as shown in the table below, and if Jones and Smith can negotiate with one another at no cost, will Jones emit smoke?

	Jones emits smoke (€)	Jones does not emit smoke (€)
Surplus for Jones	200	160
Surplus for Smith	400	420

6. John and Karl can live together in a two-bedroom flat for €500 per month, or each can rent a single-bedroom flat for €350 per month. Aside from the rent, the two would be indifferent between living together and living separately, except for one problem: John leaves dirty dishes in the sink every night. Karl would be willing to pay up to €175 per month to avoid John's dirty dishes. John, for his part, would be willing to pay up to €225 to be able to continue his sloppiness. Should John and Karl live together? If they do, will there be dirty dishes in the sink? Explain.

7. How, if at all, would your answer to Problem 6 differ if John would be willing to pay up to €30 per month to avoid giving up his privacy by sharing quarters with Karl?

8. Barton and Statler are neighbours in an apartment complex in London's Canary Wharf. Barton is a concert pianist and Statler is a poet working on an epic poem. Barton rehearses his concert pieces on the baby grand piano in his front room, which is directly above Statler's study. The matrix below shows the monthly payoffs to Barton and Statler when Barton's front room is and is not soundproofed. The soundproofing will be effective only if it is installed in Barton's apartment.

	Soundproofed	Not soundproofed
Gains to Barton	£100/month	£150/month
Gains to Statler	£120/month	£80/month

a. If Barton has the legal right to make any amount of noise he wants and he and Statler can negotiate with one another at no cost, will Barton install and maintain soundproofing? Explain. Is his choice socially efficient?

b. If Statler has the legal right to peace and quiet and can negotiate with Barton at no cost, will Barton install and maintain soundproofing? Explain. Is his choice socially efficient?

c. Does the attainment of an efficient outcome depend on whether Barton has the legal right to make noise, or Statler the legal right to peace and quiet?

9. Refer to Problem 8. Barton decides to buy a full-sized grand piano. The new payoff matrix is as follows.

	Soundproofed	Not soundproofed
Gains to Barton	£100/month	£150/month
Gains to Statler	£120/month	£60/month

a. If Statler has the legal right to peace and quiet and Barton and Statler can negotiate at no cost, will Barton install and maintain soundproofing? Explain. Is this outcome socially efficient?

b. Suppose that Barton has the legal right to make as much noise as he likes and that negotiating an agreement with Barton costs £15 per month. Will Barton install and maintain soundproofing? Explain. Is this outcome socially efficient?

c. Suppose Statler has the legal right to peace and quiet, and it costs £15 per month for Statler and Barton to negotiate any agreement. (Compensation for noise damage can be paid without incurring negotiation cost.) Will Barton install and maintain soundproofing? Is this outcome socially efficient?

d. Why does the attainment of a socially efficient outcome now depend on whether Barton has the legal right to make noise?

10.* A village has six residents, each of whom has accumulated savings of €100. Each villager can use this money either to buy a government bond that pays 15 per cent interest per year or to buy a year-old llama, send it on to the commons to graze, and sell it after one year. The price the villager gets for the two-year-old llama depends on the quality of the fleece it grows while grazing on the commons. That in turn depends on the animal's access to grazing, which depends on the number of llamas sent to the commons, as shown in the table below. The villagers make their investment decisions one after another, and their decisions are public.

Number of llamas on the commons	Price per two-year-old llama (€)
1	122
2	118
3	116
4	114
5	112
6	109

a. If each villager decides individually how to invest, how many llamas will be sent on to the commons, and what will be the resulting net village income?

b. What is the socially optimal number of llamas for this village? Why is that different from the actual number? What would net village income be if the socially optimal number of llamas were sent on to the commons?

c. The village committee votes to auction the right to graze llamas on the commons to the highest bidder. Assuming villagers can both borrow and lend at 15 per cent annual interest, how much will the right sell for at auction? How will the new owner use the right, and what will be the resulting village income?

References

Agnello, R.J. and L. Donnelly (1975) 'Property rights and efficiency in the oyster industry', *Journal of Law and Economics*, 18.

Coase, R. (1960) 'The problem of social cost', *Journal of Law and Economics*, 4.

Hardin, G. (1968) 'The tragedy of the commons', *Science*, 162.

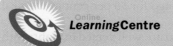
Online **Learning**Centre

To help you grasp the key concepts of this chapter check out the extra resources posted on the Online Learning Centre. There are chapter summaries, self-test questions, an interactive graphing tool, weblinks and a glossary, all for free!

Visit the Online Learning Centre at: www.mcgraw-hill.co.uk/textbooks/mcdowell for information on accessing all of these resources.

12

The Economics of Information

Consider the following problem. You are on your first visit to Istanbul. You visit the famous bazaar, and are tempted to make a purchase. In the bazaar it is expected that purchaser and seller will bargain before any deal is done. No one in his right mind (except perhaps a naive tourist) would agree to pay the seller's initial asking price. This is by custom a considerable amount greater than the seller's reservation price. So what will you offer for the brass ornament or silk scarf, or whatever has caught your eye? It is easy to say that you will not offer more than your own reservation price. But if you can obtain the object at less than your reservation price (that is, at a price greater or equal to the seller's reservation price, but less than yours) while both sides gain you will have done better than if you had paid your reservation price. Typically therefore, you will offer a price below your reservation price. After prolonged haggling either a deal is done or it is not done. We know that it will not be done if your reservation price is below the seller's. But can we be sure it will be done if your reservation price exceeds his?

Before saying it will of course be done, reflect for a moment. What in fact drives your reservation price in this one-on-one bargaining situation? If we think of it simply as the money value you place on the object then the deal will be done. But suppose you believe that another seller in the bazaar might be prepared to accept less than your reservation price – would you agree to hand that amount over to the first seller?

In this second case your willingness to pay reflects other people's valuations. There is nothing unusual about this. If you walk into an antiques shop and see an eighteenth-century Hogarth print that you would like at the price, but a friend whispers to you that an identical print was sold at auction three weeks ago for 50 per cent of the dealer's price would you pay the asking price?

Before saying that you would not, reflect again. If you are well versed in eighteenth-century prints you might well say that the auction price was an aberration, reflecting the tastes of the people in the room that day, and that in general a higher price would be expected. Then you would probably reject the friend's advice and make the purchase. But if you did not have this information it is more probable that you would leave without buying the print.

HOW THE MIDDLEMAN ADDS VALUE   353

Your willingness to pay will, therefore, in some circumstances reflect your own relevant knowledge, and may reflect your beliefs about other people's willingness to pay. Both factors may be summed up as 'information'. You may be well or poorly informed when contemplating a decision to buy or sell. This has significant implications for how markets work.

Adam Smith's invisible hand theory presumes that buyers are fully informed about the myriad ways in which they might spend their money: what goods and services are available, what prices they sell for, how long they last, how frequently they break down, and so on. But of course no one is ever really *fully* informed about anything. And sometimes people are completely ignorant of even the most basic information. Still, life goes on, and most people muddle through somehow.

Consumers employ a variety of strategies for gathering information, some of which are better than others. They read *Which?* magazine, talk to family and friends, visit stores, kick the tyres on used cars, and so on. But one of the most important aspects of choosing intelligently without having complete information is having at least some idea of the extent of one's ignorance. Someone once said that there are two kinds of consumers in the world: those who don't know what they're doing and those who don't know that they don't know what they're doing. The people in the second category are the ones who are most likely to choose foolishly. Auctioneers (and used car salesmen) just love them. They frequently walk away with the prize, but they won the prize only because they were prepared to pay, and did pay, more than anyone else would pay, and did so because they were unable accurately to estimate its value to them, meaning that with better information about the object they would have paid less or not bought at all.

Basic economic principles can help you in identifying those situations in which additional information is most likely to prove helpful. In this chapter, we will explore what those principles tell us about how much information to acquire and how to make the best use of limited information.

How the middleman adds value

One of the most common problems consumers confront is the need to choose among different versions of a product whose many complex features they do not fully understand. As Example 12.1 illustrates, in such cases consumers can sometimes rely on the knowledge of others.

Example 12.1 How should a consumer decide which pair of skis to buy?

On a ski holiday in Zell am See you decide to buy a new pair of skis, but because the technology has changed considerably since you bought your last pair (or, possibly, because all you know is which end is the front) you don't know which of the current brands and models would be best for you. The big ski goods shop beside the main gondola lift has the largest selection, so you go there and ask for advice. The salesperson appears to be well informed; after asking about your experience level and how aggressively you ski, he recommends the Salomon X-Scream 9. You buy a pair for €600, then head back to your chalet near Kaprun and show them to your roommate, who helpfully tells you that you could have bought them on the internet for only €400. How do you feel about your purchase? Are the different prices charged by the two suppliers related to the services they offer? Were the extra services you got by shopping in Zell worth the extra €200?

Internet retailers can sell for less because their costs are so much lower than those of full-service retail stores. Those stores, after all, must hire knowledgeable salespeople, put their merchandise on display, rent expensive retailing space, and so on. Internet retailers and mail-order houses, by contrast, typically employ unskilled telephone clerks, and they store their merchandise in cheap warehouses. But if you are a consumer who doesn't know which is the right product for you, the extra expense of shopping at a speciality retailer is likely to be a good investment. Spending €600 on the right skis is smarter than spending €400 on the wrong ones.

Many people believe that wholesalers, retailers and other agents who assist manufacturers in the sale of their products play a fundamentally different economic role from the one played by those who actually make the products. In this view, the production worker is the ultimate source of economic value added. Sales agents are often disparaged as mere middlemen, parasites on the efforts of others who do the real work.

On a superficial level, this view might seem to be supported by the fact that many people go to great lengths to avoid paying for the services of sales agents. Many manufacturers cater to them by offering consumers a chance to 'buy direct' and sidestep the middleman's commission. But, on closer examination, we can see that the economic role of sales agents is essentially the same as that of production workers. Consider Example 12.2.

Example 12.2 How does better information affect economic surplus?

You have inherited a pair of nineteenth-century silver candlesticks. Needing some money (and perhaps being unable to afford to insure them) you decide to sell them. How do you go about it? In the small town where you live there is no (trustworthy) antiques dealer. Your reservation price is €300. You realise that as an alternative to putting an advertisement in the local newspaper, offering them to the highest bidder, you could decide to auction them off on eBay. The cost of the advertisement would be €20; the commission payable to eBay is 5 per cent of the amount paid by the winning bidder. In each case this represents the costs of providing the service.

Advertising means (you hope) being offered the highest reservation price from the local population. Using eBay means that a much larger number of potential bidders will be aware of what is for sale. Now suppose that the local highest reservation price is €400, while in the much larger population of potential bidders on eBay there are two people with reservation prices of €800 and €900 respectively. In the eBay auction the object is sold to the highest bidder, but at the second highest bidder's highest offer. This is called a second price auction, rather than an English auction, where the highest bidder's highest offer is paid.[1]

---

1 The decision by eBay to use a second price auction is interesting. A well-known result of auction theory is the 'revenue equivalence theorem'. It says that in this type of auction, where goods are bought because they are of value to the individual buying them and are referred to as private value auctions (as opposed to, say an oil lease, where the goods have a common commercial value) the expected sales revenue to the seller (or the auction house) is usually the same whether a first price, English, auction is used or a second price auction. Why does eBay use the rarer second price auction? Obviously, because it thinks that this way it will earn higher commissions, which means that on average it expects higher payments by winning bidders. This suggests that revenue equivalence doesn't hold all the time, something that controlled experiments with auctions supports. In turn, this means that the number of bidders and/or bidders' strategies in auctions like an eBay auction for CDs, or camping equipment or whatever, can at least sometimes be affected by the rules of the auction.

Second price auctions are not common, but they have been used more widely than many economists think. In particular they have been widely used for well over a century in philately (stamp collecting). If you are interested, see a very readable paper: Lucking-Reiley (2000).

Consider now the implications of using eBay rather than the local newspaper in terms of economic surplus. You will receive (net) €760: €460 more than your reservation price. The purchaser will receive surplus of €100 (why?). The total surplus is €560. Had you used the newspaper the total surplus would be (€400 – 300 – 20) or €80. If you sold at €400 the surplus is yours; at a price below €400 it is divided between you and the local bidder. But the total, no matter at what price you sell it, is €80.

eBay in this example is providing a service by making information available (nineteenth-century candlesticks for sale) to people who can make good use of it. A real increase in economic surplus results when an item ends up in the hands of someone who values it more highly than the person who otherwise would have bought it. That increase is just as real and valuable as the increase in surplus that results from manufacturing cars, growing corn, or any other productive activity.

RECAP How the middleman adds value

In a world of incomplete information, sales agents and other middlemen add genuine economic value by increasing the extent to which goods and services find their way to the consumers who value them most. When a sales agent causes a good to be purchased by a person who values it by €20,000 more than the person who would have bought it in the absence of a sales agent, that agent augments total economic surplus by €20,000, an achievement on a par with the production of a €20,000 car.

The optimal amount of information

Without a doubt, having more information is better than having less. But information is generally costly to acquire. In most situations, the value of additional information will decline beyond some point. And because of the Low-Hanging-Fruit Principle, people tend to gather information from the cheapest sources first before turning to more costly ones. Typically, then, the marginal benefit of information will decline, and its marginal cost will rise, as the amount of information gathered increases.

The cost–benefit test

Cost–Benefit
Analysis

Information gathering is an activity like any other. The Cost–Benefit Principle tells us that a rational consumer will continue to gather information as long as its marginal benefit exceeds its marginal cost. Suppose, for the sake of discussion, that analysts had devised a scale that permits us to measure units of information, as on the horizontal axis of Fig. 12.1. If the relevant marginal cost and marginal benefit curves are as shown in the diagram, a rational consumer will acquire I^* units of information, the amount for which the marginal benefit of information equals its marginal cost.

Another way to think about Fig. 12.1 is that it shows the optimal level of ignorance. When the cost of acquiring information exceeds its benefits, acquiring additional information simply does not pay. If

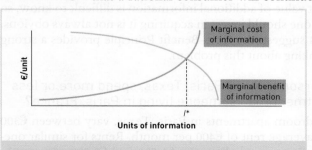

Figure 12.1 The Optimal Amount of Information.
For the marginal cost and benefit curves shown, the optimal amount of information is I^*. Beyond that point, information costs more to acquire than it is worth.

information could be acquired free, decision makers would, of course, be glad to have it. But when the cost of acquiring the information exceeds the gain in value from the decision it will facilitate, people are better off to remain ignorant.

The free-rider problem

Does the invisible hand assure that the optimal amount of advice will be made available to consumers in the marketplace? The next example suggests one reason that it might not.

Economic naturalist 12.1 Why is finding knowledgeable sales assistants to help you often difficult?

People can choose for themselves whether to bear the extra cost of retail shopping. Those who value advice and convenience can pay slightly higher prices, while those who know what they want can buy for less over the web or by mail order. **True or false:** It follows that private incentives lead to the optimal amount of retail service.

The market would provide the optimal level of retail service except for one practical problem, namely that consumers can make use of the services offered by retail outlets without paying for them. After benefiting from the advice of informed salespersons and after inspecting the merchandise, the consumer can return home and buy the same item from an internet retailer or mail-order house. Not all consumers do so, of course. But the fact that customers can benefit from the information provided by retail stores without paying for it is an example of the **free-rider problem**, an incentive problem that results in too little of a good or service being produced. Because retail outlets have difficulty recovering the cost of providing information, private incentives are likely to yield less than the socially optimal level of retail service. So the statement above is false.

free-rider problem an incentive problem in which too little of a good or service is produced because non-payers cannot be excluded from using it

Exercise 12.1   Apart from its possible contribution to free-rider problems, how is increased access to the internet likely to affect total economic surplus?

Two guidelines for rational search

In practice, of course, the exact value of additional information is difficult to know, so the amount of time and effort one should invest in acquiring it is not always obvious. But as Examples 12.3 and 12.4 suggest, the Cost–Benefit Principle provides a strong conceptual framework for thinking about this problem.

Example 12.3 Should a person living in Paris, Texas, spend more or less time searching for an apartment than someone living in Paris, France?

Suppose that rents for one-bedroom apartments in Paris, Texas, vary between €300 and €500 per month, with an average rent of €400 per month. Rents for similar one-bedroom apartments in Paris, France, vary between €1,500 and €2,500 per month, with an average rent of €2,000. In which city should a rational person expect to spend a longer time searching for an apartment?

In both cities, visiting additional apartments entails a cost, largely the opportunity cost of one's time. In both cities, the more apartments someone visits, the more likely it is that he or she will find one near the lower end of the rent distribution. But because rents are higher and are spread over a broader range in Paris, France, the expected saving from further time spent searching will be greater there than in Paris, Texas. And so a rational person will expect to spend more time searching for an apartment in France.

Example 12.3 illustrates the principle that spending additional search time is more likely to be worthwhile for expensive items than for cheap ones. For example, one should spend more time searching for a good price on a diamond engagement ring than for a good price on a stone made of cubic zirconium; more time searching for a low fare from London to Sydney than for a low fare from Paris to Frankfurt; and more time searching for a car than for a bicycle. By extension, hiring an agent – someone who can assist with a search – is more likely to be a good investment in searching for something expensive than for something cheap. For example, people typically engage estate agents to help them find a house, but they seldom hire agents to help them have their car serviced.

Example 12.4 Who should expect to search longer for a good price on a used piano?

Both Tom and Tim are shopping for a used upright piano. To examine a piano listed in the classified ads, they must travel to the home of the piano's current owner. If Tom has a car and Tim does not and both are rational, which one should expect to examine fewer pianos before making his purchase?

The benefits of examining an additional piano are the same in both cases, namely a better chance of finding a good instrument for a low price. But because it is more costly for Tim to examine pianos, he should expect to examine fewer of them than Tom.

Example 12.4 makes the point that when searching becomes more costly, we should expect to do less of it. And as a result, the prices we expect to pay will be higher when the cost of a search is higher.

The gamble inherent in search

Suppose you are in the market for a one-bedroom apartment and have found one that rents for €400 per month. Should you rent it or search further in hopes of finding a cheaper apartment? Even in a large market with many vacant apartments, there is no guarantee that searching further will turn up a cheaper or better apartment. Searching further entails a cost, which might outweigh the gain. In general, someone who engages in further search must accept certain costs in return for unknown benefits. Thus further search invariably carries an element of risk.

In thinking about whether to take any gamble, a helpful first step is to compute its **expected value** – the average amount you would win (or lose) if you played that gamble an infinite number of times. To calculate the expected value of a gamble with more than one outcome, we first multiply each outcome by its corresponding probability of occurring, and then add. For example, suppose you win €1 if a coin flip comes up heads and lose €1 if it comes up tails. Since $\frac{1}{2}$ is the probability of heads (and also the probability of tails), the expected value of this gamble is $(\frac{1}{2})(€1) + (\frac{1}{2})(-€1) = 0$. A gamble with an expected value of zero is called a **fair gamble**. If you played this gamble a large number of times, you wouldn't expect to make money, but you also wouldn't expect to lose money.

expected value of a gamble the sum of the possible outcomes of the gamble

fair gamble a gamble whose expected value is zero

better-than-fair gamble one whose expected value is positive

risk-neutral person someone who would accept any gamble

risk-averse person someone who would refuse any fair gamble

A **better-than-fair gamble** is one with a positive expected value. (For example, a coin flip in which you win €2 for heads and lose €1 for tails is a better-than-fair gamble.) A **risk-neutral person** is someone who would accept any gamble that is fair or better. A **risk-averse person** is someone who would refuse to take any fair gamble.

Exercise 12.2   Consider a gamble in which you win €4 if you flip a coin and it comes up heads and lose €2 if it comes up tails. What is the expected value of this gamble? Would a risk-neutral person accept it?

In Example 12.5 we apply these concepts to the decision of whether to search further for an apartment.

Example 12.5 Should you search further for an apartment?

You have arrived in San Francisco for a one-month summer visit and are searching for a one-bedroom sublet for the month. There are only two kinds of one-bedroom apartment in the neighbourhood in which you wish to live, identical in every respect except that one rents for €400 and the other for €360. Of the vacant apartments in this neighbourhood, 80 per cent are of the first type and 20 per cent are of the second type. The only way you can discover the rent for a vacant apartment is to visit it in person. The first apartment you visit is one that rents for €400. If you are risk-neutral and your opportunity cost of visiting an additional apartment is €6, should you visit another apartment or rent the one you've found?

If you visit one more apartment, you have a 20 per cent chance of it being one that rents for €360 and an 80 per cent chance of it being one that rents for €400. If the former, you'll save €40 in rent, but if the latter, you'll face the same rent as before. Since the cost of a visit is €6, visiting another apartment is a gamble with a 20 per cent chance to win €40 − €6 = €34 and an 80 per cent chance of losing €6 (which means 'winning' −€6). The expected value of this gamble is thus (0.20)(€34) + (0.80)(−€6) = €2. Visiting another apartment is a better-than-fair gamble, and since you are risk-neutral you should take it.

Exercise 12.3   Refer to Example 12.5. Suppose you visit another apartment and discover that it, too, is one that rents for €400. If you are risk-neutral, should you visit a third apartment?

The commitment problem when search is costly

When most people search for an apartment, they want a place to live not for just a month but for a year or more. Most landlords, for their part, are also looking for long-term tenants. Similarly, few people accept a full-time job in their chosen field unless they expect to hold the job for several years. Firms, too, generally prefer employees who will stay for extended periods. Finally, when most people search for mates, they are looking for someone with whom to settle down.

Because in all these cases search is costly, examining every possible option will never make sense. Apartment hunters don't visit every vacant apartment, nor do landlords interview every possible tenant. Job seekers don't visit every employer, nor do employers interview every job seeker. And not even the most determined searcher can manage to date every eligible mate. In these and other cases, people are rational to end their searches, even though they know a more attractive option surely exists out there somewhere.

But herein lies a difficulty. What happens when, by chance, a more attractive option comes along after the search has ceased? Few people would rent an apartment if they thought the landlord would kick them out the moment another tenant came along who was willing to pay higher rent. Few landlords would be willing to rent to a tenant if they expected her to move out the moment she discovers a cheaper apartment. Employers, job seekers and people who are looking for mates would have similar reservations about entering relationships that could be terminated once a better option happened to come along.

This potential difficulty in maintaining stable matches between partners in ongoing relationships would not arise in a world of perfect information. In such a world, everyone would end up in the best possible relationship, so no one would be tempted to renege. But when information is costly and the search must be limited, there will always be the potential for existing relationships to dissolve.

Incentives Matter

In most contexts, people solve this problem not by conducting an exhaustive search (which is usually impossible, in any event) but by committing themselves to remain in a relationship once a mutual agreement has been reached to terminate the search. Thus landlords and tenants sign a lease that binds them to one another for a specified period, usually six months or a year. Employees and firms enter into employment contracts, either formal or informal, under which each promises to honour his obligations to the other, except under extreme circumstances. And in most countries a marriage contract penalises those who abandon their spouses. Entering into such commitments limits the freedom to pursue one's own interests. Yet most people freely accept such restrictions, because they know the alternative is failure to solve the search problem.

RECAP The optimal amount of information

Additional information creates value, but it is also costly to acquire. A rational consumer will continue to acquire information until its marginal benefit equals its marginal cost. Beyond that point, it is rational to remain uninformed.

Markets for information do not always function perfectly. Free-rider problems often hinder retailers' efforts to provide information to consumers.

Search inevitably entails an element of risk, because costs must be incurred without any assurance that search will prove fruitful. A rational consumer can minimise this risk by concentrating search efforts on goods for which the variation in price or quality is relatively high and on those for which the cost of search is relatively low.

Asymmetric information

One of the most common information problems occurs when the participants in a potential exchange are not equally well informed about the product or service that is offered for sale. For instance, the owner of a used car may know that the car is in excellent mechanical condition, but potential buyers cannot know that merely by inspecting

asymmetric information where buyers and sellers are not equally informed about the characteristics of products or services

it or taking it for a test drive. Economists use the term **asymmetric information** to describe situations in which buyers and sellers are not equally well informed about the characteristics of products or services. In these situations, sellers are typically much better informed than buyers, but sometimes the reverse will be true.

As Example 12.6 illustrates, the problem of asymmetric information can easily prevent exchanges that would benefit both parties.

Example 12.6 Selling your car privately

You own a Ford Fiesta, four years old, with 100,000 kilometres (60,000 miles) on the clock. You have always driven it carefully, and have had it serviced regularly, in line with the manufacturer's instructions. It has never been damaged in an accident. In short, you know the car to be in excellent condition. Now, for whatever reason, you have decided to sell it privately. The going price for four-year-old Fiestas is €6,000.

Someone who sees the advertisement in the local paper wants to buy a good four-year-old Fiesta, for which he would pay €8,000 if it is in excellent condition (like yours), but only €6,000 if it is in average condition for that age, and all he has to go on is your description and a bunch of receipts. (He could hire a mechanic to examine the car, but doing so is expensive, and many problems cannot be detected even by a mechanic.) Will he buy your car? Is this outcome efficient?

Because your car looks the same as other four-year-old Fiestas, he is unlikely to be willing to pay €8,000 for it. After all, for only €6,000, he can buy some other car that is in just as good condition, as far as he can tell. The probability is that he will buy another Fiesta. He therefore will buy someone else's car, and yours will go unsold. This outcome is not efficient.

The 'lemons' model

Example 12.6 serves as a useful introduction to what is called the problem of the 'market for lemons'. In colloquial American usage in the late 1960s and early 1970s a 'lemon' was a car that was, or might be, in poor condition in a way that would be unknowable to a buyer. In Britain at the time the equivalent was known as a 'Monday' car: one assembled by a hung-over workforce at British Leyland on a Monday morning – it might look all right, but was almost guaranteed to break down about ten minutes after leaving the showroom.

The problem lies in the economic incentives created by asymmetric information. These suggest that the selection of used cars of any given age being offered for sale will be of lower quality than the average in the total population of used cars of that age. One reason is that people who mistreat their cars, or whose cars were never very good to begin with, are more likely than others to want to sell them. Buyers know from experience that cars for sale on the used car market are more likely to be 'lemons' than cars that are not for sale. This realisation causes them to lower their reservation prices for a used car.

But that's not the end of the story. Once used car market prices have fallen, the owners of cars that are in good condition have an even stronger incentive to hold on to them. This causes the average quality of the cars offered for sale on the used car market to decline still further. It helps explain why new cars depreciate so much once they have been bought. University of California at Berkeley economist George Akerlof, a Nobel laureate, was the first to explain the logic behind this downward

lemons model George Akerlof's explanation of how asymmetric information tends to reduce the average quality of goods offered for sale

spiral.[2] Economists use the term **lemons model** to describe Akerlof's explanation of how asymmetric information affects the average quality of the used goods offered for sale.

As Example 12.7 suggests, the lemons model has important practical implications for consumer choice.

Economic naturalist 12.2 Should you buy your aunt's car?

One of the almost universal pieces of folk wisdom is that you should never buy a car from a close friend or a member of your family. The reasoning is that if things go wrong with the car the impact on relationships can be serious. Actually, a good economic naturalist would probably ignore it. You want to buy a used Honda Accord. Your Aunt Germaine buys a new car every four years, and she has a four-year-old Accord that she is about to trade in. You believe her report that the car is in good condition, and she is willing to sell it to you for €10,000, which is the current 'blue book' value for four-year-old Accords. (The blue book value of a car is the average price for which cars of that age and model sell in the used car market.) Should you buy your aunt's Honda?

Akerlof's lemons model tells us that cars for sale in the used car market will be of lower average quality than cars of the same vintage that are not for sale. If you believe your aunt's claim that her car is in good condition, then being able to buy it for its blue book value is definitely a good deal for you, since the blue book price is the equilibrium price for a car that is of lower quality than your aunt's.

Examples 12.7 and 12.8 illustrate the conditions under which asymmetric information about product quality results in a market in which *only* lemons are offered for sale.

Example 12.7 How much will a naive buyer pay for a used car?

Consider a world with only two kinds of car: good ones and lemons. An owner knows with certainty which type of car she has, but potential buyers cannot distinguish between the two types. A total of 10 per cent of all new cars produced are lemons. Good used cars are worth €10,000 to their owners, but lemons are worth only €6,000. Consider a naive consumer who believes that the used cars currently for sale have the same quality distribution as new cars (i.e. 90 per cent good, 10 per cent lemons). If this consumer is risk-neutral, how much would he be willing to pay for a used car?

Buying a car of unknown quality is a gamble, but a risk-neutral buyer would be willing to take the gamble provided it is fair. If the buyer can't tell the difference between a good car and a lemon, the probability that he will end up with a lemon is simply the proportion of lemons among the cars from which he chooses. The buyer believes he has a 90 per cent chance of getting a good car and a 10 per cent chance of getting a lemon. Given the prices he is willing to pay for the two types of car, his expected value of the car he buys will thus be $0.90(€10,000) + 0.10(€6,000) = €9,600$. And since he is risk-neutral, that is his reservation price for a used car.

Exercise 12.4 How would your answer to the question posed in Example 12.7 differ if the proportion of new cars that are lemons had been not 10 per cent but 20 per cent?

Example 12.8 Who will sell a used car for what the naive buyer is willing to pay?

Refer to Example 12.7. If you were the owner of a good used car, what would it be worth to you? Would you sell it to a naive buyer? What if you owned a lemon?

2 Akerlof (1970).

Since you know your car is good, it is worth €10,000 to you, by assumption. But since a naive buyer would be willing to pay only €9,600, neither you nor any other owner of a good car would be willing to sell to that buyer. If you had a lemon, of course, you would be happy to sell it to a naive buyer, since the €9,600 the buyer is willing to pay is €3,600 more than the lemon would be worth to you. So the only used cars for sale will be lemons. In time, buyers will revise their naively optimistic beliefs about the quality of the cars for sale on the used car market. In the end, all used cars will sell for a price of €6,000, and all will be lemons.

In practice, of course, the mere fact that a car is for sale does not guarantee that it is a lemon, because the owner of a good car will sometimes be forced to sell it, even at a price that does not reflect its condition. The logic of the lemons model explains this owner's frustration. The first thing sellers in this situation want a prospective buyer to know is the reason they are selling their cars. For example, classified ads often announce, 'Just had a baby, must sell my 2002 Lotus' or 'Transferred to Germany, must sell my 2003 Rover 75.' Any time you pay the blue book price for a used car that is for sale for some reason unrelated to its condition, you are beating the market.

The credibility problem in trading

Why can't someone with a high-quality used car simply *tell* the buyer about the car's condition? The difficulty is that buyers' and sellers' interests tend to conflict. Sellers of used cars, for example, have an economic incentive to overstate the quality of their products. Buyers, for their part, have an incentive to understate the amount they are willing to pay for used cars and other products (in the hope of bargaining for a lower price). Potential employees may be tempted to overstate their qualifications for a job. And people searching for mates have been known to engage in deception.

That is not to say that most people *consciously* misrepresent the truth in communicating with their potential trading partners. But people do tend to interpret ambiguous information in ways that promote their own interests. Thus, 92 per cent of factory employees surveyed in one study rated themselves as more productive than the average factory worker.[3]

Notwithstanding the natural tendency to exaggerate, the parties to a potential exchange can often gain if they can find some means to communicate their knowledge truthfully. In general, however, mere statements of relevant information will not suffice. People have long since learned to discount the used car salesman's inflated claims about the cars he is trying to unload. But as the next example illustrates, though communication between potential adversaries may be difficult, it is not impossible.

Example 12.9 How can a used car seller signal high-quality credibly?

You knew your Fiesta to be in excellent condition, and the potential purchaser would have been willing to pay your reservation price if he could be confident of getting such a car. What kind of signal about the car's quality would the purchaser find credible?

Again, the potential conflict between the buyer's and seller's interests suggests that mere statements about the car's quality may not be persuasive. But suppose you offer a warranty, under which you agree to remedy any defects the car develops over the next six months. You can afford to extend such an offer because you know the car is unlikely to need expensive repairs. In contrast, a person who knows his car has a

---

3 Some psychologists call this phenomenon the 'Lake Wobegon effect', after Garrison Keillor's mythical Minnesota town, where 'all the children are above average'.

cracked engine block would never extend such an offer. The warranty is a credible signal that the car is in good condition. It enables the purchaser to buy the car with confidence, to both his and the seller's benefit.

The costly-to-fake principle

costly-to-fake principle to communicate information credibly to a potential rival, a signal must be costly or difficult to fake

The preceding examples illustrate the **costly-to-fake principle**, which holds that if parties whose interests potentially conflict are to communicate credibly with one another, the signals they send must be costly or difficult to fake. If the seller of a defective car could offer an extensive warranty just as easily as the seller of a good car, a warranty offer would communicate nothing about the car's quality. But warranties entail costs that are significantly higher for defective cars than for good cars – hence their credibility as a signal of product quality.

To the extent that sellers have an incentive to portray a product in the most flattering light possible, their interests conflict with those of buyers, who want the most accurate assessment of product quality possible. Note that in the following example, the costly-to-fake principle applies to a producer's statement about the quality of a product.

Incentives Matter

Economic naturalist 12.3 Why do firms insert the phrase 'As advertised on TV' when they advertise their products in magazines and newspapers?

Company *A* sponsors an expensive national television advertising campaign on behalf of its compact disc player, claiming it has the clearest sound and the best repair record of any CD player in the market. Company *B* makes similar claims in a sales brochure but does not advertise its product on television. If you had no additional information to go on, which company's claim would you find more credible? Why do you suppose Company *A* mentions its TV ads when it advertises its CD player in print media?

Accustomed as we are to discounting advertisers' inflated claims, the information given might seem to provide no real basis for a choice between the two products. On closer examination, however, we see that a company's decision to advertise its product on national television constitutes a credible signal about the product's quality. The cost of a national television campaign can run well into millions of euros, a sum a company would be foolish to spend on an inferior product.

For example, in 2002 Pepsi paid Britney Spears €8 million to appear in its two 30-second Super Bowl ads in the USA and it paid more than €3.5 million to Fox TV for broadcasting those ads. National TV ads can attract potential buyers' attention and persuade a small fraction of them to try a product. But these huge investments pay off only if the resulting initial sales generate other new business – either repeat sales to people who tried the product and liked it or sales to others who heard about the product from a friend.

Because ads cannot persuade buyers that a bad product is a good one, a company that spends millions of euros advertising a bad product is wasting its money. An expensive national advertising campaign is therefore a credible signal that the producer *thinks* its product is a good one. Of course, the ads don't guarantee that a product *is* a winner, but in an uncertain world, they provide one more piece of information. Note, however, that the relevant information lies in the expenditure on the advertising campaign, not in what the ads themselves say.

These observations may explain why some companies mention their television ads in their print ads. Advertisers understand the costly-to-fake principle and hope that consumers will understand it as well.

As Economic naturalist 12.4 illustrates, the costly-to-fake principle is also well known to many employers.

Economic naturalist 12.4 Why do many companies care so much about elite educational credentials?

Microsoft is looking for a hardworking, smart person for an entry-level managerial position in a new technical products division in north-west France. Two candidates, Iain and Jean-Pierre, both economists, seem alike in every respect but one: Iain graduated with a starred first from New College, Oxford, while Jean-Pierre graduated with a C1 average from Nanterre. Whom should Microsoft hire?

If you want to persuade prospective employers that you are both hardworking and intelligent, there is perhaps no more credible signal than to have graduated with distinction from a highly selective educational institution. Most people would like potential employers to think of them as hardworking and intelligent. But unless you actually have both those qualities, graduating with the highest honours from a university like Oxford will be extremely difficult. The fact that Jean-Pierre graduated from a much less selective institution and earned only a C1 average is not proof positive that he is not diligent and talented, but companies are forced to play the percentages. In this case the odds strongly favour Iain.

This may help explain why the better UK universities are so concerned about being required to be less selective in their admissions policies in order to improve the chances of youngsters from socially disadvantaged parts of the UK gaining access.

Conspicuous consumption as a signal of ability

Some individuals of high ability are not highly paid. (Remember the best school teacher you ever had.) And some people, such as the multi-billionaire investor Warren Buffett, earn a lot, yet spend very little. Virgin CEO Richard Branson dresses in jeans and open-neck shirts. So does Michael O'Leary of Ryanair. But such cases run counter to general tendencies. In competitive markets, the people with the most ability tend to receive the highest salaries. And, as suggested by the Cost–Benefit Principle, the more someone earns, the more he or she is likely to spend on high-quality goods and services. These tendencies often lead us to infer a person's ability from the amount and quality of the goods he consumes.

If the less able guru loses business because of the suits he wears and the car he drives, why doesn't he simply buy better suits and a more expensive car? His choice is between saving for retirement or spending more on his car and clothing. In one sense, he cannot afford to buy a more expensive car, but in another sense, he cannot afford *not* to. If his current car is discouraging potential clients from hiring him, buying a better one may simply be a prudent investment. But because *all* consultants have an incentive to make such investments, their effects tend to be mutually offsetting.

When all is said and done, the things people consume will continue to convey relevant information about their respective ability levels. The costly-to-fake principle tells us that the Jaguar S-type is an effective signal precisely because the consultant of low ability cannot afford one, no matter how little he saves for retirement. Yet from a social perspective, the resulting spending pattern is inefficient, for the same reason that other positional arms races are inefficient (see Chapter 11). Society would be better off if everyone spent less and saved more for retirement.

The problem of conspicuous consumption as an ability signal does not arise with equal force in every environment. In smaller towns, where people tend to know one another well, an accountant who tries to impress people by spending beyond her means is likely to succeed only in demonstrating how foolish she is. Thus the wardrobe a professional person 'needs' in towns like Inverness or Perugia costs less than the wardrobe the same person would need in Edinburgh or Rome.

Statistical discrimination

In a competitive market with perfect information, the buyer of a service would pay the seller's cost of providing the service. In many markets, however – the market for fire insurance is one example – the seller does not know the exact cost of serving each individual buyer.

In such cases, the missing information has an economic value. If the seller can come up with even a rough estimate of the missing information, she can improve her

Economic naturalist 12.5 Why do Irish males under 25 years of age pay more than Irish females of the same age, and both more than their British equivalents, for car insurance?

The accident death rate on Irish roads is significantly higher than on British roads, which are among the safest in Europe. There are fewer motorways in Ireland, and on some of those that do exist, to save money for the Exchequer (politicians and bureaucrats tend to limit considerations of costs to whatever the Exchequer has to pay), the government chose not to put crash barriers in the central divide when building them. In addition, the cost per accident is higher for a variety of reasons, including a greater resort to judicial decisions involving expensive outings to the High Court. This explains the higher level of motor insurance costs in Ireland. What it does not explain is why Irish (and other) males pay more than females, and why this is even more the case in Ireland than in many other EU countries. One is tempted to say discrimination – a charge that would certainly be laid were rates for women drivers higher. But it has nothing to do with discrimination on gender grounds. It reflects *expected costs*.

The expected cost to an insurance company of insuring any given driver depends on the probability that the driver will be involved in an accident. No one knows what that probability is for any given driver, but insurance companies can estimate rather precisely the proportion of drivers in specific groups who will be involved in an accident in any given year. Irish males under 25 are much more likely than older males and females of any age to become involved in road accidents. (Testosterone seems to have something to do with it. So does alcohol. The combination is lethal.) Young Irish males drink more than their elders, or other EU equivalents, drive more (the population density is lower than in the UK or most of continental Europe and public transport is less universal) and crash more often. Because of high Irish taxes on cars, they also drive smaller and lighter cars than the average in most other countries. The consequences are obvious.

To remain in business, an insurance company must collect enough money from premiums to cover the cost of the claims it pays out, plus whatever administrative expenses it incurs. Consider an insurance company that charges lower rates for young males with clean driving records than for females with blemished ones. Given that the former group is more likely to have accidents than the latter, the company cannot break even unless it charges females more, and males less, than the respective costs of insuring them. But if it does so, rival insurance companies will see cash on the table. They can offer females slightly lower rates and lure them away from the first company. The first company will end up with only young male policy holders and thus will suffer an economic loss at the low rates it charges. That is why, in equilibrium, young males with clean driving records pay higher insurance rates than young females with blemished records.

position. As Economic naturalist 12.5 illustrates, firms often do so by imputing characteristics to individuals on the basis of the groups to which they belong.

statistical discrimination
the practice of making judgements about the quality of people, goods or services based on the characteristics of the groups to which they belong

The insurance industry's policy of charging high rates to young male drivers is an example of **statistical discrimination**. Other examples include the common practice of paying higher salaries to people with college degrees than to people without them. Statistical discrimination occurs whenever people or products are judged on the basis of the groups to which they belong.

Even though everyone *knows* that the characteristics of specific individuals can differ markedly from those of the group to which they belong, competition promotes statistical discrimination. For example, insurance companies know perfectly well that *some* young males are careful and competent drivers. But unless they can identify *which* males are the better drivers, competitive pressure forces them to act on their knowledge that, as a group, young males are more likely than others to generate insurance claims.

Similarly, employers know that many people with only a secondary education are more productive than the average university graduate. But because employers usually cannot tell in advance who those people are, competitive pressure leads them to offer higher wages to graduates, who are more productive, on average, than those with only a secondary education.

Statistical discrimination is the *result* of observable differences in group characteristics, not the cause of those differences. Young males, for example, do not generate more insurance claims because of statistical discrimination. Rather, statistical discrimination occurs because insurance companies know that young males generate more claims. Nor does statistical discrimination cause young males to pay insurance rates that are high in relation to the claims they generate. Among any group of young male drivers, some are careful and competent, and others are not. Statistical discrimination means the more able males will pay high rates relative to the volume of claims they generate, but it also means the less able male drivers will pay low rates relative to the claims they generate. On average, the group's rates will be appropriate to the claims its members generate.

Still, these observations do little to ease the frustration of the young male who knows himself to be a careful and competent driver, or the high-school graduate who knows herself to be a highly productive employee. Competitive forces provide firms with an incentive to identify such individuals and treat them more favourably whenever practical. Insurance companies in Ireland and elsewhere are now introducing programmes to help identify 'careful' drivers from among the young male population. These include voluntary limitations on time of driving (most fatalities occur between 11.00 pm and 5.00 am), drinking and speed, as well as taking advanced driving courses.

Adverse selection

Although insurance companies routinely practise statistical discrimination, each individual within a group pays the same rate, even though individuals within the group often differ sharply in terms of their likelihood of filing claims. Within each group, buying insurance is thus most attractive to those individuals with the highest likelihood of filing claims. As a result, high-risk individuals are more likely to buy insurance than low-risk individuals, a pattern known as **adverse selection**. Adverse selection

adverse selection the pattern in which insurance tends to be purchased disproportionately by those who are most costly for companies to insure

forces insurance companies to raise their premiums, which makes buying insurance even less attractive to low-risk individuals, which raises still further the average risk level of those who remain insured. In some cases, only those individuals faced with extreme risks may continue to find insurance an attractive purchase.

Moral hazard

moral hazard the tendency of people to expend less effort protecting those goods that are insured against theft or damage

Moral hazard is another problem that makes buying insurance less attractive for the average person. This problem refers to the fact that some people take fewer precautions when they know they are insured. Someone whose car is insured, for example, may take less care to prevent it from being damaged or stolen. Driving cautiously and searching for safe parking spaces require effort, after all, and if the losses from failing to engage in these precautions are covered by insurance, some people will become less vigilant.

By offering policies with deductible provisions (excesses), insurance companies help many of their potential clients soften the consequences of problems like moral hazard and adverse selection. Under the terms of an automobile collision insurance policy with, say, a €1,000 excess provision, the insurance company covers only those collision repair costs in excess of €1,000. For example, if you have an accident in which €3,000 in damage occurs to your car, the insurance company covers only €2,000, and you pay the remaining €1,000.

An excess means that the insured is sharing part of the risk with the insurer. For this reason this is sometimes referred to as an example of 'co-insurance'. Carrying more of the risk makes the insured party take more precautions. A system of no-claims bonuses operates in the same way: if you make a claim your costs will increase when the time comes to renew the policy. This reduces the incentive to make a claim rather than carry the full cost of an accident yourself.

How does the availability of such policies mitigate the negative effects of adverse selection and moral hazard? Since the policies are cheaper for insurance companies to provide, they sell for lower prices. The lower prices represent a much better bargain, however, for those drivers who are least likely to file insurance claims, since those drivers are least likely to incur any uncovered repair costs. Policies with deductible provisions also confront careless drivers with more of the extra costs for which they are responsible, giving them additional incentives to take precautions.

These policies benefit insurance buyers in another way. Because the holder of a policy with an excess provision will not file a claim at all if the damage to his car in an accident is less than the deductible threshold, insurance companies require fewer resources to process and investigate claims, savings that get passed along in the form of lower premiums.

RECAP Asymmetric information

Asymmetric information describes situations in which not all parties to a potential exchange are equally well informed. In the typical case, the seller of a product will know more about its quality than the potential buyers. Such asymmetries often stand in the way of mutually beneficial exchange in the markets for high-quality goods, because buyers' inability to identify high quality makes them unwilling to pay a commensurate price.

Information asymmetries and other communication problems between potential exchange partners can often be solved through the use of signals that are costly or difficult to fake. Product warranties are such a signal, because the seller of a low-quality product would find them too costly to offer.

Buyers and sellers also respond to asymmetric information by attempting to judge the qualities of products and people on the basis of the groups to which they belong. A young male may know he is a good driver, but auto insurance companies must nonetheless charge him high rates because they know only that he is a member of a group that is frequently involved in accidents.

Summary

- Virtually every market exchange takes place on the basis of *less than complete information*. More information is beneficial both to buyers and to sellers, but information is costly to acquire. The rational individual therefore acquires information only up to the point at which its marginal benefit equals its marginal cost. Beyond that point one is rational to remain ignorant.

- Retailers and other sales agents are important sources of information. To the extent that they enable consumers to find the right products and services, they add economic value. In that sense they are no less productive than the workers who manufacture goods or perform services directly. Unfortunately, the *free-rider problem* often prevents firms from offering useful product information.

- Several principles govern the *rational search for information*. Searching more intensively makes sense when the cost of a search is low, when quality is highly variable or when prices vary widely. Further search is always a gamble. A risk-neutral person will search whenever the expected gains outweigh the expected costs. A rational search will always terminate before all possible options have been investigated. Thus in a search for a partner in an ongoing bilateral relationship, there is always the possibility that a better partner will turn up after the search is over. In most contexts, people deal with this problem by entering into contracts that commit them to their partners once they have mutually agreed to terminate the search.

- Many potentially beneficial transactions are prevented from taking place by *asymmetric information* – the fact that one party lacks information that the other has. For example, the owner of a used car knows whether it is in good condition, but potential buyers do not. Even though a buyer may be willing to pay more for a good car than the owner of such a car would require, the fact that the buyer cannot be sure he is getting a good car often discourages the sale. More generally, asymmetric information often prevents sellers from supplying the same quality level that consumers would be willing to pay for.

- Both buyers and sellers can often gain by finding ways of communicating what they know to one another. But because of the potential conflict between the interests of buyers and sellers, mere statements about the relevant information may not be credible. For a signal between potential trading partners to be credible, it must be *costly to fake*. For instance, the owner of a high-quality used car can credibly signal the car's quality by offering a warranty – an offer that the seller of a low-quality car could not afford to make.

- Firms and consumers often try to estimate missing information by making use of what they know about the *groups to which people or things belong*. For example, insurance firms estimate the risk of insuring individual young male drivers on the basis of the accident rates for young males as a group. This practice is known as *statistical discrimination*. Other examples include paying college graduates more than high-school graduates and charging higher life insurance rates to 60 year olds than to 20 year olds. Statistical discrimination helps to explain the phenomenon of disappearing political discourse, which occurs when opponents of a practice such as the death penalty remain silent when the issue is discussed publicly.

Review questions

1. Can it be rational for a consumer to buy a Toyota without having first taken test drives in competing models built by Ford, VW, Renault, Honda and others?

2. Explain why a gallery owner who sells a painting might actually create more economic surplus than the artist who painted it.

3. Explain why used cars offered for sale are different, on average, from used cars not offered for sale.

4. Explain why the used car market would be likely to function more efficiently in a community in which moral norms of honesty are strong than in a community in which such norms are weak.

5. Why might leasing a new Porsche be a good investment for an aspiring Hollywood film producer, even though he can't easily afford the monthly payments?

connect Problems

1. State whether the following are **true or false**, and briefly explain why.

   a. Companies spend billions of dollars advertising their products on network TV primarily because the texts of their advertisements persuade consumers that the advertised products are of high quality.

   b. You may not get the optimal level of advice from a retail shop when you go in to buy a lamp for your bike, because of the free-rider problem.

   c. If you need a lawyer, and all your legal expenses are covered by insurance, you should *always* choose the best-dressed lawyer with the most expensive car and the most ostentatiously furnished office.

   d. The benefit of searching for a spouse is affected by the size of the community you live in.

2. Consumers know that some fraction x of all new cars produced and sold in the market are defective. The defective ones cannot be identified except by those who own them. Cars do not depreciate with use. Consumers are risk-neutral and value non-defective cars at €10,000 each. New cars sell for €5,000 and used ones for €2,500. What is the fraction x?

3. Carlos is risk-neutral and has an ancient farmhouse with great character for sale in Slaterville Springs, Montana. His reservation price for the house is €130,000. The only possible local buyer is Whitney, whose reservation price for the house is €150,000. The only other houses on the market are modern ranch houses that sell for €125,000, which is exactly equal to each potential buyer's reservation price for such a house. Suppose that if Carlos does not hire a real estate agent, Whitney will learn from her neighbour that Carlos's house is for sale and will buy it for €140,000. However, if Carlos hires a real estate agent, he knows that the agent will put him in touch with an enthusiast for old farmhouses who is willing to pay up to €300,000 for the house. Carlos also knows that if he and this person negotiate, they will agree on a price of €250,000. If agents charge a commission of 5 per cent of the selling price and all agents have opportunity costs of €2,000 for negotiating a sale, will Carlos hire an agent? If so, how will total economic surplus be affected?

4. Ann and Barbara are computer programmers in Nashville, Tennessee, who are planning to move to Portland, Oregon. Each owns a house that has just been appraised for €100,000. But whereas Ann's house is one of hundreds of highly similar houses in a large, well-known suburban development, Barbara's is the only one that was built from her architect's design. Who will benefit more by hiring an estate agent to assist in selling her house, Ann or Barbara?

5. For each pair of occupations listed, identify the one for which the kind of car a person drives is more likely to be a good indication of how good she is at her job:

    a. primary school teacher; estate agent

    b. dentist; municipal government administrator

    c. engineer in the private sector; engineer in the military.

6. Brokers who sell stocks over the internet can serve many more customers than those who transact business by mail or over the phone. How will the expansion of internet access affect the average incomes of stockbrokers who continue to do business in the traditional way?

7. Whose income do you predict will be more affected by the expansion of internet access:

    a. stockbrokers or lawyers?

    b. doctors or pharmacists?

    c. book-shop owners or the owners of galleries that sell original oil paintings?

8. How will growing internet access affect the number of film actors and musicians who have active fan clubs?

9. Fred, a retired accountant, and Jim, a senior civil servant, are 63-year-old identical twins who collect antique pottery. Each has an annual income of €100,000 (Fred's from a pension, Jim's from salary). One buys most of his pottery at local auctions and the other buys most of his from a local dealer. Which brother is more likely to buy at an auction, and does he pay more or less than his brother who buys from the local dealer?

References

Akerlof, G. (1970) 'The market for lemons', *Quarterly Journal of Economics*, 84.

Lucking-Reiley, D. (2000) 'Vickrey auctions in practice: from nineteenth-century philately to twenty-first-century e-commerce', *Journal of Economic Perspectives*, 14, 3, pp. 183–92.

Online Learning Centre

To help you grasp the key concepts of this chapter check out the extra resources posted on the Online Learning Centre. There are chapter summaries, self-test questions, an interactive graphing tool, weblinks and a glossary, all for free!

Visit the Online Learning Centre at: www.mcgraw-hill.co.uk/textbooks/mcdowell for information on accessing all of these resources.

13

Labour Markets, Income Distribution, Wealth and Poverty

Differences in incomes are sometimes hard to rationalise in terms of differences in the abilities of the people concerned. The returns resulting from winning (and retaining!) an Olympic gold medal in, say, swimming, may be quite substantial in terms of advertising, appearance money, endorsements and so on. The winner may be (and usually is) only very marginally superior as an athlete to the silver and bronze medallists. But, typically, the latter tend to sink from public consciousness, and their lifetime earnings are small fractions of those of gold medallists who do not significantly outrank them in terms of inherent performance ability.

And when we look at the incomes of people with similar abilities in different countries or in different sectors of the same country we can frequently observe substantial differences in what they earn, controlling for the amount of work they undertake. In recent years, for example, Western health sector employers have taken advantage of very large differences in the earnings of trained nurses in countries such as the Philippines and Western Europe to recruit nursing staff from those countries to meet staff shortages in Europe. High-quality economists working in government departments typically earn lower salaries than equally competent analysts working in the financial sector or in consultancy firms.

Why do some people earn so much more than others? No other single question in economics has stimulated as much interest and discussion. In case you think it is simply a matter of whether you live in a rich country or a poor country, the fact is that, say, although the United States is an extremely rich country American citizenship is neither necessary nor sufficient for receiving a high income. Many of the wealthiest people in the world come from extremely poor countries, and many Americans are homeless and malnourished.

Our aim in this chapter will be to employ simple economic principles in an attempt to explain why different people earn different incomes. We shall discuss the human capital model, which emphasises the importance of differences in personal characteristics. But our focus will be on why people with similar personal characteristics often earn sharply different incomes. Among the factors we shall consider are trades unions, discrimination, the effect of non-wage conditions of employment, and winner-take-all markets. We shall explore whether *income inequality* is something society should be concerned about and, if so, whether practical remedies for it exist. As we shall see, government programmes to redistribute income have costs as well as benefits: as always, policy makers must compare an imperfect status quo with the practical consequences of imperfect government remedies.

Our approach is based on the tried and tested technique of applying the analysis of markets to the problem, on the basis that a person's earnings from labour can be thought of as reflecting the price received for an hour of work and the number of hours worked (i.e. sold by the worker and bought by the employer). The same applies to incomes earned from the ownership of productive assets.

The economic value of work

In some respects, the sale of human labour is profoundly different from the sale of other goods and services. For example, although someone may legally relinquish all future rights to the use of her TV set by selling it, in societies with legal systems based on the Western model the law no longer permits people formally to sell themselves into slavery or to trade in people in the sense of selling and buying an absolute right of disposal of a person's services. The law does, however, permit employers to 'rent' our services. And in many ways the rental market for labour services functions much like the market for most other goods and services. Each specific category of labour has a *demand curve* and a *supply curve*. These curves intersect to determine both the *equilibrium wage* and the *equilibrium quantity of employment* for each category of labour.

What is more, shifts in the relevant demand and supply curves produce changes analogous to those produced by shifts in the demand and supply curves for other goods and services. For instance, an increase in the demand for a specific category of labour will generally increase both the equilibrium wage and the equilibrium quantity of employment in that category. By the same token, an increase in the supply of labour to a given occupation will tend to increase the level of employment and lower the wage rate in that occupation.

As in our discussions of other markets, our strategy for investigating how the labour market works will be to go through a series of examples that shed light on different parts of the picture. In Economic naturalist 13.1, we focus on how the equilibrium principle can help us to understand how wages will differ among workers with different levels of productive ability.

Economic naturalist 13.1 If there is no such thing as slavery, how did the media report that Manchester United sold David Beckham to Real Madrid for several millions of pounds sterling?

The answer is that they didn't sell Beckham. Real Madrid had to pay Beckham to come to play for them and pay Manchester United a sum to allow Beckham to terminate his existing contractual obligations to United. Labour contracts frequently have a *time dimension* to them and these impose restrictions on one or both sides in terms of freedom to end the relationship. These are the consequences of explicit contract negotiations between the parties and/or legal requirements imposed by labour law. Beckham entered into a contract with Real Madrid to play for them for a period of time in return for a package that included a lump sum and a scale of salary and bonus payments. United, which might well have initiated the process, accepted payment for relinquishing their existing contractual right to retain Beckham as a player, rights that were contained in a previous contract entered into by Beckham. Beckham simply changed employer. No one bought him. But someone did buy out his *contractual obligations*. Football commentators may understand the game ... but if their use of language reflects their understanding of the economics behind it, they need to take a refresher course.

Example 13.1 How much will the potters earn?

Go into any garden centre or DIY outlet in Europe and you are likely to find glazed earthenware pots for sale. These are mostly made in China and nearby countries in the Far East. In many cases, the pots are made unglazed and then sold to firms that apply the glazing. It is at this stage that the pots become distinctive. As originally produced, the output of one pottery producer is more or less the same as that of any other producer. It is something close to what we would describe as a perfectly competitive industry. Suppose that Peking Pottery Works (PPW) is one of numerous identical companies in China that hire potters who mould clay into standard pots. These companies sell the pots for 1.20 yuan each to a finishing company that glazes and fires them, and then sells them in the retail marketplace. Clay and water, both available free of charge in unlimited quantities, are the only inputs used by the potters. The equipment is owned by the proprietor of PPW, who rents it to the potters for 0.10 yuan per pot to cover his costs and allow him some income for his efforts. Currently only two potters work for PPW, whose only cost other than potters' salaries is a 0.10 yuan handling cost for each pot it delivers to the finisher. Potter Han delivers 100 pots per week and potter Lee delivers 120. If the labour market for potters is perfectly competitive, how much will each be paid?

We begin with the assumption that Han and Lee have decided to work full time as potters, so our focus is not on how much they will work but on how much they will be paid. After taking handling costs and the equipment charge into account, the value of the pots that Han delivers is 100 yuan per week, and that is the amount PPW will pay him. To pay him less would risk having him bid away by a competitor. For example, if PPW paid Han only 90 yuan per week, the company would then enjoy an economic profit of 10 yuan per week as a result of hiring him. Seeing this cash on the table (Chapter 3), a rival firm could then offer Han 91 yuan, thus earning an additional economic profit of 9 yuan per week by bidding him away from PPW. So under the bidding pressure from rival employers, PPW will have difficulty keeping Han if it pays him less than 100 yuan per week. And the company would suffer an economic loss if it pays him more than 100 yuan per week. Similarly, the value of the pots delivered each week by Lee is 120 yuan, and this will be her competitive equilibrium wage.

marginal physical product, or marginal product of labour (MP) the additional output a firm gets by employing one additional unit of labour

value of marginal product of labour (VMP) the money value of the additional output a firm gets by employing one additional unit of labour

In Example 13.1, the number of pots each potter delivered each week was that potter's **marginal physical product** (or **marginal product (MP)**, for short) **of labour**. More generally, a worker's marginal product is the extra output the firm gets as a result of hiring that worker. When we multiply a worker's marginal product by the net price for which each unit of the product sells, we get that worker's **value of marginal product, or VMP of labour**. (In Example 13.1, the 'net price' of each pot was 1.00 yuan – the difference between the 1.20 sale price and the 0.20 handling and equipment charge.) The general rule in competitive labour markets is that a worker's pay in long-run equilibrium will be *equal to* *her VMP, which is the net contribution she makes to the employer's revenue.* Employers would be delighted to pay workers less than their respective VMPs, but if labour markets are truly competitive they cannot get away with doing so for long.

Cost–Benefit
Analysis

In Example 13.1, each worker's VMP was independent of the number of other workers employed by the firm. In such cases, we cannot predict how many workers a firm will hire. PPW could break even with two potters, with ten, or even with 1,000 or more. In many other situations, however, we can predict exactly how many workers a firm will hire. Consider Example 13.2.

Example 13.2 How many workers should WTK AG hire?

Wilhelm Tell Kunstfabrik AG (WTK), located in Zurich, hires workers in a competitive labour market at a wage of Sfr350 per week to make cuckoo clock cases from scrap wood that is available free of charge. If the cases sell for Sfr20 each and the company's weekly output varies with the number of workers hired, as shown in Table 13.1, how many workers should WTK hire?

Number of workers (1)	Total number of clock cases/week (2)	MP (extra clock cases/week) (3)	VMP (Sfr/week) (4)
0	0		
1	30	30	600
2	55	25	500
3	76	21	420
4	94	18	360
5	108	14	280

Table 13.1 **Employment and Productivity in WTK (when clock cases sell for Sfr20 each)**

In Example 13.1 our focus was on wage differences for employees whose productive abilities differed. In contrast, we assume here that all workers are equally productive and the firm faces a fixed market wage for each. The fact that the marginal product of labour declines with the number of workers hired is a consequence of the *law of diminishing returns.* (As discussed in Chapter 5, this law says that when a firm's capital or other productive inputs are held fixed in the short run, adding workers beyond some point results in ever smaller increases in output.) Column (3) of Table 13.1 reports the marginal product for each additional worker, and column (4) reports the value of each successive worker's marginal product – the number of clock cases he or she adds times the selling price of Sfr20. WTK should keep hiring as long as the next worker's VMP is at least Sfr350 per week (the market wage). The first four workers have VMPs larger than Sfr350, so WTK should hire them. But since hiring the fifth worker would add only Sfr280 to weekly revenue, WTK should not hire that worker.

Note the similarity between the perfectly competitive firm's decision about how many workers to hire and the perfectly competitive firm's output decision we considered in Chapter 5. When labour is the only variable factor of production, the two decisions are essentially the same. Because of the unique correspondence between the firm's total output and the total number of workers it hires, deciding how many workers to hire is the same as deciding *how much output to supply.*

The worker's attractiveness to the employer depends not only on how many clock cases she produces, but also on the price of clock cases and on the wage rate. For example, because VMP rises when product price rises, an increase in product price will lead employers to hire more workers. Employers will also increase hiring when the wage rate falls.

Exercise 13.1 In Example 13.2, how many workers should WTK hire if the price of clock cases rises to Sfr26?

Exercise 13.2 How many workers should WTK hire if the wage rate falls to Sfr275 per week?

RECAP The economic value of work

In competitive labour markets, employers face pressure to pay each worker the value of his or her marginal product. When a firm can hire as many workers as it wishes at a given market wage, it should expand employment as long as the value of *marginal product of labour exceeds the market wage*.

The equilibrium wage and employment levels

As we saw in Chapter 3, the equilibrium price and quantity in any competitive market occur at the intersection of the relevant supply and demand curves. The same is true in competitive markets for labour.

The demand for labour

An employer's reservation price for a worker is the most the employer could pay without suffering a decline in profit. As already discussed, this reservation price for the employer in a perfectly competitive labour market is simply VMP, the value of the worker's marginal product. Because of the law of diminishing returns, we know that the marginal product of labour, and hence VMP, declines in the short run as the quantity of labour rises. The individual employer's demand curve for labour in any particular occupation – say, computer programmers – may thus be shown, as in Fig. 13.1(a), as a downward-sloping function of the wage rate. Suppose firm 1 (panel (a)) and firm 2 (panel (b)) are the only two firms that employ programmers in a given community. The demand for programmers in that community will then be the horizontal sum of the individual firm demands (panel (c)).

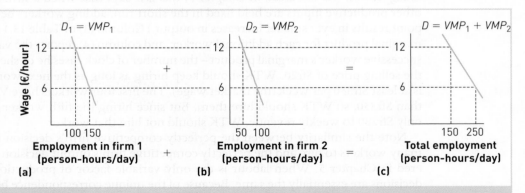

Figure 13.1 The Occupational Demand for Labour. If firm 1 and firm 2 are the only firms that employ labour in a given occupation, we generate the demand curve for labour in that occupation by adding the individual demand curves horizontally.

The supply curve of labour

What does the supply curve of labour for a specific occupation look like? Will more labour be offered at high wage rates than at low wage rates? An equivalent way to pose the same question is to ask whether consumers will wish to consume *less leisure* at high wage rates than at low wage rates. By themselves, the principles of economic theory do not provide an answer to this question, because a change in the wage rate exerts two opposing effects on the quantity of leisure demanded. One is the *substitution* effect, which says that, at a higher wage, leisure is more expensive, leading consumers to consume less of it. The second is the *income* effect, which says that, at a higher wage, consumers have more purchasing power, leading them to consume more leisure. Which of these two opposing effects dominates is an empirical question.

For the economy as a whole during the past several centuries, the working week has been declining and real wages have been rising. This pattern might seem to suggest that the supply curve of labour is downward-sloping, and for the economy as a whole it may be. There is also evidence that individual workers may sometimes work fewer hours when wage rates are high than when they are low. A study of taxi cab drivers in New York City, for example, found that drivers quit earlier on rainy days (when the effective wage is high because of high demand for cab rides) than on sunny days (when the effective wage is lower).[1]

The same effect was observed in Dublin after the taxi market was liberalised in 2001. The consequence of liberalisation was that the expected number of fares per hour (and, therefore, the expected hourly income of a representative taxi driver) fell as a result of liberalisation. Previously, with chronic excess demand, taxi drivers could expect their cars to be full any time they chose to take them on to the streets. Now with a big increase in the number of taxis, drivers had to go looking for fares. The reaction of the taxi drivers was to demand restrictions on entry because they were now 'obliged' (i.e. chose) to work more hours as a consequence of the fall in the expected hourly income.

Whether any individual's labour supply curve is upward-sloping depends on income and substitution effects. When we move to groups of workers this can still be the case, provided that they are shielded from competition from new entrants. These observations notwithstanding, with easy entry to an occupation the supply of labour *to any particular occupation* is almost surely upward-sloping, because wage differences among occupations influence occupational choice. It is no accident, for example, that many more people are choosing jobs as computer programmers now than in 1970. Wages of programmers have risen sharply since the 1970s, which has led many people to forsake other career paths in favour of programming. Curve *S* in Fig. 13.2 represents the supply curve of computer programmers. Its positive slope is typical of the supply curves for most individual occupations.

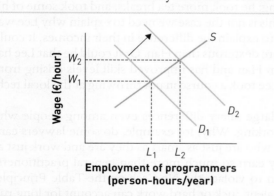

Figure 13.2 The Effect of an Increase in the Demand for Computer Programmers. An increase in the demand for programmers from D_1 to D_2 results in an increase in the equilibrium level of employment (from L_1 to L_2) and an increase in the equilibrium wage (from W_1 to W_2).

---

1 Babcock *et al.* (1997).

Market shifts

As more tasks have become computerised since the 1980s, the demand for programmers has grown, as shown by the shift from D_1 to D_2 in Fig. 13.2. Equilibrium in the market for computer programmers occurs at the intersection of the relevant supply and demand curves. The increase in demand has led to an increase in the equilibrium level of programmers from L_1 to L_2 and a rise in the equilibrium wage from W_1 to W_2.

As discussed in Chapter 8, the market for stocks and other financial assets reaches equilibrium very quickly in the wake of shifts in the underlying supply and demand curves. Labour markets, by contrast, are often much slower to adjust. When the demand for workers in a given profession increases, shortages may remain for months, or even years, depending on how long it takes people to acquire the skills and training needed to enter the profession.

RECAP Equilibrium in the labour market

The demand for labour in a perfectly competitive labour market is the horizontal sum of each employer's VMP curve. The supply curve of labour for an individual labour market is upward-sloping, even though the supply curve of labour for the economy as a whole may be vertical or even downward-sloping. In each labour market, the demand and supply curves intersect to determine the *equilibrium wage and level of employment*.

Explaining differences in earnings

The theory of competitive labour markets tells us that differences in pay reflect differences in the corresponding VMPs. Thus, in Example 13.1, Lee earned 20 per cent more than Han because she made 20 per cent more pots each week than he did. That begs the obvious question: why was Lee able to (and/or chose to) produce more pots than Han? Note that if it simply represented a decision by Han to work less hard there is nothing that really needs explaining: he took more tea breaks, and took some of his real income that way. However, if this is not the case we need to explain why Lee was more productive than Han in order to explain the difference in their incomes. It could simply be talent: Lee is naturally more dexterous than Han. Or it could be that Lee has been working at the job longer than Han and has improved skill levels arising from this experience. Or it could be that Lee took a course in pot throwing at the local technological institute, and Han did not.

We often see (or think we see) large salary differences even among people who appear equally talented and hard-working. Why, for example, do some lawyers earn so much more than those plumbers who are just as smart as they are and work just as hard? And why do surgeons usually earn so much more than general practitioners? These wage differences might seem to violate the No-Cash-on-the-Table Principle, which says that only differences in talent, luck or hard work can account for long-run differences in earnings. For example, if plumbers could earn more by becoming lawyers, why don't they just switch occupations? Similarly, if general practitioners could boost their incomes by becoming surgeons, why didn't they become surgeons in the first place?

human capital theory a theory of pay determination that says a worker's wage will be proportional to his or her stock of human capital

The human capital explanation

Answers to these questions are suggested by **human capital theory**, which holds that an individual's VMP is proportional to his

human capital an amalgam of factors such as education, training, experience, intelligence, energy, work habits, trustworthiness and initiative that affect the value of a worker's marginal product

or her stock of human capital – an amalgam of factors such as education, experience, training, intelligence, energy, work habits, trustworthiness and initiative. According to this theory, some occupations pay better than others because they require larger stocks of human capital. For example, a general practitioner could become a surgeon, but only by undertaking formal training for several more years. An even larger investment in additional education is required for a plumber to become a lawyer.

There are two angles to this account of differences in earnings. On the one hand, other things being equal, the more human capital you possess the higher will be your earnings, because human capital increases your VMP. On the other hand, because human capital is in most cases costly to acquire (money costs of training, time and opportunity costs of earnings forgone) it is relatively scarce and commands a high price. Put another way, the payment received by owners of human capital is the *supply price* of that capital, the social benefit of which is increased labour productivity – and, therefore, income per head – in society as a whole.

Differences in demand can result in some kinds of human capital being more valuable than others. Consider two occupations: tax accountants and computer programmers. Both occupations require demanding technical training. Since the 1970s there has been a steady increase in the demand for skilled programmers in virtually all advanced Western economies. During that period, the demand for the services of US tax accountants has fallen as more and more American taxpayers have used tax-preparation software in lieu of hiring accountants to help them with their taxes. This is less evident in Europe, where online tax returns are a fairly recent development, and where the combination of complex tax codes and high marginal tax rates have supported the use of tax accountants and equivalent professionals in dealing with the tax authorities. In the United States, incomes of computer programmers have risen relative to the incomes of people employed as tax accountants because the training of programmers (the human capital of programmers) now yields a higher return in the labour market.

Trades unions

Two workers with the same amount of human capital may earn different wages if one of them belongs to a **labour union** and the other does not. A labour (or trades)

labour union a group of workers who bargain collectively with employers for better wages and working conditions

union is an organisation through which workers attempt to bargain collectively with employers for better wages and working conditions.

The impact of trades unions in labour markets is something about which there is considerable controversy in economics, a controversy that is reflected in a wider political and social debate about the role of unions and the protection they receive in law from the legal redress sought by those hurt by their actions. At one end of the spectrum there are many, including economists, who believe that unions can have the effect of ensuring levels of real income and working conditions to employees as a whole in excess of those that would be provided in a labour market without unions. Obviously, this view is widely held by members of trades unions and their professional advisers. At the other end are economists who believe that whatever value unions may have had in the early twentieth century, in protecting disorganised workers from exploitation by capitalists enjoying market power in the labour market, has largely disappeared. Instead, they regard unions as affecting labour markets in much the same way that cartels affect product markets. To illustrate, consider a simple economy with two labour markets, neither of which is unionised initially. Suppose the total supply of labour to the two markets is fixed at $S_0 = 200$ workers per day, and that the demand curves are as shown by VMP_1 and VMP_2 in Fig. 13.3(a) and (b). The sum of the two demand curves, $VMP_1 + VMP_2$ (panel (c)), intersects the supply curve to determine an equilibrium wage of €9 per hour. At that wage, firms in market 1 hire 125 workers per day (panel (a)), and firms in market 2 hire 75 (panel (b)).

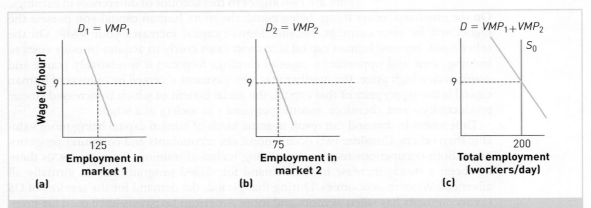

Figure 13.3 An Economy with Two Non-unionised Labour Markets. Supply and demand intersect to determine a market wage of €9 per hour (c). At that wage, employers in market 1 hire 125 workers per day and employers in market 2 hire 75 workers per day. The VMP is €9 in each market.

Now suppose that workers in market 1 form a union and refuse to work for less than €12 per hour. Because demand curves for labour are downward-sloping, employers of unionised workers reduce employment from 125 workers per day to 100 (Fig. 13.4(a)). The 25 displaced workers in the unionised market would of course be delighted to

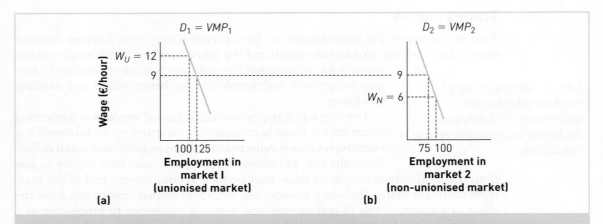

Figure 13.4 The Effect of a Union Wage Above the Equilibrium Wage. When the unionised wage is pegged at W_u = €12/hour (a), 25 workers are discharged. When these workers seek employment in the non-unionised market, the wage in that market falls to W_N = €6/hour (b).

find other jobs in that market at €12 per hour. But they cannot, and so they are forced to seek employment in the non-unionised market. The result is an excess supply of 25 workers in the non-union market at the original wage of €9 per hour. In time, wages in that market decline to $W_N = €6$ per hour, the level at which 100 workers can find jobs in the non-unionised market (Fig. 13.4(b)).

Equilibrium

It might seem that the gains of the unionised workers are exactly offset by the losses of non-unionised workers. On closer inspection, however, we see that pegging the union wage above the equilibrium level actually *reduces* the value of total output. If labour were allocated efficiently between the two markets, its value of marginal product would have to be the same in each. Otherwise, the total value of output could be increased by moving workers from the low-VMP market to the high-VMP market. With the wage set initially at €9 per hour in both markets, the condition for efficient allocation was met, because labour's VMP was €9 per hour in both markets. But because the collective bargaining process drives wages (and hence VMPs) in the two markets apart, the value of total output is no longer maximised. To verify this claim, note that if a worker is taken out of the non-unionised market, the reduction in the value of output there will be only €6 per hour, which is less than the €12 per hour gain in the value of output when that same worker is added to the unionised market.

Exercise 13.3 In Fig. 13.4, how much would the total value of output be increased if the wage rate were €9 per hour in each market?

However, the above analysis implicitly assumes that competitive conditions apply in labour markets in the absence of unions. If this assumption is dropped, and it is assumed instead that potential employers are few in number, then the position changes. In a competitive market employers are *price takers*: any one firm's employment decision has no appreciable impact on wage rates. If they are few in number, employers have market power analogous to a small number of sellers of a product: the individual firm's decisions affect prices. 'Market power' here does not mean harsh Dickensian employers using their position to grind workers into poverty (although that may indeed be the case). It simply means not being price takers. This results in lower wages, lower employment and lower production than if the labour market were competitive. If this is indeed the case, the argument that unions distort resource allocation and worsen the incomes of those outside the unions has to be reassessed.

To illustrate this, consider Fig. 13.5 (panels (a) and (b)). This looks at the position of a single employer of labour in a relevant labour market. The employer is a local 'monopsonist', or sole buyer of a product (labour) being offered by a large number of competing workers.

The employer's demand curve for labour (the *VMP* curve) is, as usual, downward-sloping. He faces an upward-sloping supply curve of labour. The more labour he demands the higher the price (wages) he will have to pay. If the market had been competitive the level of employment and the level of wages would be determined by the intersection of the supply curve and the demand curve (W_c and N_c) (panel (a)). But, if the market is monopsonistic, and the employer wishes to maximise profits this will not happen. Why?

The supply curve of labour represents the *average cost of labour to the employer* (because total labour cost is simply the rectangle formed by the level of employment and the corresponding point on the labour supply curve). For this reason, it is also

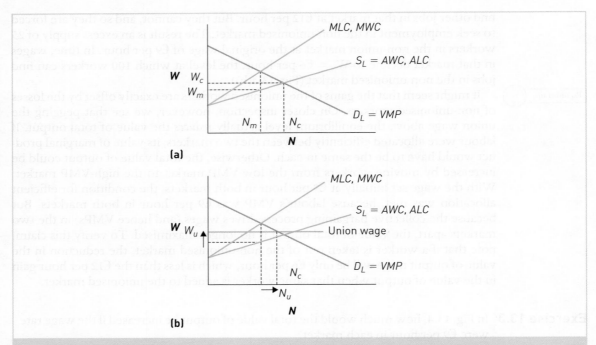

Figure 13.5 How a Union Can Increase Employment when the Employer Has Market Power.

labelled *ALC*. Note that this is increasing as the employer purchases more labour (because he is not a price taker in the labour market). To maximise profits the employer will hire that quantity of labour for which the *marginal* cost of labour, not the average cost of labour, equals the value marginal product. Since *AWC* is upward-sloping, the marginal cost of labour must lie above it: the *MLC* line. That intersects the *VMP* curve to the left of the hypothetical competitive level of employment. The monopsonistic employer will purchase less labour than in the case of a competitive market, N_m. Nor is that the end of the matter: if he seeks only that amount of labour, the market-clearing wage rate is W_m, from the labour supply curve (*ALC*). He not only purchases less labour, but will pay a lower wage than if the market were competitive.

Now suppose a union appears and organises the workers. It then confronts the employer with a demand for $W_u > W_m$, and enters into a contract with the employer (formal or informal) to the effect that provided he pays W_u he may hire as much or as little labour as he likes. If this is conceded (and the alternative is a strike), the employer now faces a fixed *ALC* curve (and when an average is constant, the marginal equals the average). Hence his *MLC* is now a horizontal line from W_u, and, to maximise profits, he will purchase the quantity of labour for which *MLC* = *VMP*. The consequence of the arrival of the union is higher wages and higher employment. Total surplus in the economy is increased because, other things being equal, more labour hired means more goods being produced and lower product prices.

There is, therefore, a respectable case for arguing for exactly the opposite conclusions as to the consequences of unionisation. Is this just another example of two-handed economics resulting in no conclusions? On balance, we think not. Although the second approach is useful in explaining some aspects of the labour market (for example, the role of unions in the public sector in mixed economies, where the employer is protected from competition and is the only employer), the assumption of weak competition among employers (market power) is less plausible than it seems once a longer-term view of labour markets in modern circumstances is adopted. In these circumstances, an assumption that markets are more rather than less competitive is in most circumstances more plausible. This reflects the observation that (especially given sufficient time) markets for final goods and markets for labour are subject to relatively free entry and exit.

Ease of entry into the final goods market reduces the market power of incumbent firms as purchasers of labour: they are likely to find themselves competing for labour more intensively and having to pay 'the going rate'. The monopsonistic market model has an implicit assumption that the employer is the only person to whom the workers can in effect sell their labour. But if workers are mobile between jobs and between locations, this is hard to sustain: mobility forces employers to compete. And if they have to compete then they cannot exploit market power to pay wages that are below competitive levels, which, of course, reduces the incentive to join a union in the first place. In fact, the evidence of declining union membership across the developed world is the strongest argument for the competitive model's basic plausibility in the context of a modern capitalist economy.

Wages paid to workers in a unionised firm are sometimes 50 per cent or more above the wages paid to their non-unionised counterparts. To the alert economic naturalist, this difference prompts a question.

Economic naturalist 13.2 If unionised firms have to pay more, how do they manage to survive in the face of competition from their non-unionised counterparts?

In fact, non-unionised firms sometimes do drive unionised firms out of business. To a considerable degree, the problems of the national flag carrier airlines in Europe reflect the erosion of their markets by the 'no-frills' low-cost airlines epitomised by Ryanair. The latter are in general non-unionised, while the flag carriers are heavily unionised. The flight of the British newspapers from Fleet Street in central London to out-of-town sites such as Wapping in the 1980s was in large measure a flight from unionised to non-unionised production processes in order to survive. Even so, unionised and non-unionised firms often manage to compete head to head for extended periods. If their costs are significantly higher, how do the unionised firms manage to survive?

The observed pay differential actually overstates the difference between the labour costs of the two types of firm. Because the higher union wage attracts an excess supply of workers, unionised employers can adopt more stringent hiring requirements than their non-unionised counterparts. As a result, unionised workers tend to be more experienced and skilled than non-unionised workers. Studies estimate that the union wage premium for US workers with the same amount of human capital is only about 10 per cent.

Another factor is that unions may actually boost the productivity of workers with any given amount of human capital, perhaps by improving communication between management and workers. Similarly, the implementation of formal grievance procedures, in combination with higher pay, may boost morale among unionised workers, leading to higher productivity. Labour turnover is also significantly lower in unionised firms, which reduces hiring and training costs. Studies suggest that union productivity may be sufficiently high to compensate for the premium in union wages. So even though wages are higher in unionised firms, these firms may not have significantly higher labour costs per unit of output than their non-unionised counterparts.

Unionisation is a more plausible explanation of wage differentials in Europe than in the United States. In the United States, unionisation now involves about 14 per cent of the workforce (down from 20 per cent in the early 1980s and 35 per cent in 1954). Furthermore, while the average is around 14 per cent, when public-sector employment is ignored, the average falls to 10 per cent (about 40 per cent of US public-sector employees are in a union). Because the union wage premium is small and applies to only a small fraction of the labour force, US union membership is probably not an important explanation for why workers with similar qualifications often earn sharply different incomes.

In Western Europe the average is higher although, in most countries, falling. In the EU15 in 2001, unionisation was about 30 per cent (measured as 'union density', the percentage of the workforce belonging to a union). Within this average there was enormous variation: at one end, Sweden's union density was close to 90 per cent, while Spain's was 15 per cent. Germany, France, Italy, the United Kingdom and the Netherlands were all within about 5 per cent of the average (not surprising, since they account for most of the EU15's employment). The pattern in Europe resembles that in the United States to this extent: in general, union density is much higher in the public sector … and, of course, the public sector is a larger element in the economies of Western Europe than in those of North America. In the United Kingdom, 60 per cent of public-sector employees are in unions, and over 70 per cent of public-sector 'professionals' (educators, scientists, accountants, and so on) are in a union. Only 20 per cent of private-sector employees are in a union, and this percentage is falling steadily.

The wage and work condition differentials that unionisation helps to explain in some European countries are those between public-sector employees and those in the private sector. Not only is employment in the public sector less volatile, but pension entitlements are notoriously much greater, and in many sectors the relative wages of public-sector workers have risen as a consequence of the exercise of union power in parts of the economy that are sheltered from competition. However, under EU liberalisation programmes, this is likely to be a diminishing influence on relative wages as between public- and private-sector employees.

The impact of unions on wage developments is also likely to be reduced by increased globalisation, especially reflecting the growing importance of foreign direct investment (FDI) in Europe. One reason for the decline in unionisation is the increasing resistance of new employers to union recognition. The Irish experience points this out dramatically. Ireland has received a proportionately much greater share of non-EU FDI into the Union since the 1980s than any other EU15 country. The largest component of this *inward investment* came from US companies. But, while 80 per cent of FDI set-ups from other EU countries in Ireland between 1987 and 1997 involved union recognition (and 20 per cent did not), in the case of US-sourced FDI in Ireland the percentages were 90 per cent non-recognition and 10 per cent recognition.[2]

Compensating wage differentials

If people are paid the value of what they produce, why do panel beaters in a car repair shop earn more than lifeguards on a crowded summer beach? Repairing cars is obviously important, but is it more valuable than saving the life of a drowning child? If your central heating unit breaks down and you call out a repair service, the hourly rate at which the repair technician is paid is likely to be higher than the hourly rate for an intensive care unit staff nurse. Is cleaning a burner more important than monitoring

---

2 Gunnigle and O'Sullivan (2003).

a critically ill post-operative accident victim? In each case, you will almost certainly answer no. However, the amount paid to someone is not simply a matter of the value of what that person does, but, as Example 13.3 illustrates, the wage for a particular job depends not only on the value of what workers produce in that job, but also on how attractive they find the *working conditions* associated with the job.

Example 13.3 Why do some public relations (PR) personnel earn more than others?

You are about to graduate; you plan to pursue a career in PR and have two job offers. One is in a firm that specialises in dealing with the problems of organisations such as Oxfam and Médecins Sans Frontières. The other represents the interests of Imperial Tobacco, British American Tobacco and a couple of the oil majors. Except for the subject matter, working conditions are identical in the two jobs. If each job paid €30,000 per year and offered the same prospects for advancement, which would you choose? When a similar question was recently posed to a sample of final-year under-graduate students at the US Cornell University, almost 90 per cent of them chose the first type of job. When asked how much more they would have to be paid to induce them to switch to the second type of job, their median response was a premium of $15,000 per year. (The offer was in dollars, since they were American students.) At any given salary, most preferred the first type of job, and would take an implicit wage cut to retain it. As Example 13.3 suggests, employers who offer jobs with less attractive working conditions cannot hope to fill them unless they also offer higher salaries.

Other things being equal, jobs with attractive working conditions will pay less than jobs with less attractive conditions. Wage differences associated with differences in working conditions are known as **compensating wage differentials**. Economists have identified compensating differentials for a host of different specific working con-

compensating wage differential a difference in the wage rate – negative or positive – that reflects the attractiveness of a job's working conditions

ditions. Studies have found, for example, that safe jobs tend to pay less than otherwise similar jobs that entail greater risks to health and safety. Studies have also found that wages vary in accordance with the attractiveness of the work schedule. For instance, working night shifts commands a wage premium, and teachers must accept lower wages in part because many of those with children value having hours that coincide with the school calendar.

Discrimination in the labour market

Women and minorities continue to receive lower wage rates, on average, than white males with similar measures of human capital. This pattern poses a profound challenge to standard theories of competitive labour markets, which hold that competitive pressures will eliminate wage differentials not based on differences in productivity. Defenders of standard theories attribute the wage gap to unmeasured differences in human capital, and/or to preferences on the part of different categories of workers, and/or to differences in non-wage costs of employment across different groups of workers. Many critics of these theories reject the idea that labour markets are effectively competitive, and instead attribute the gap to various forms of *discrimination*.

employer discrimination an arbitrary preference by an employer for one group of workers over another

Discrimination by employers

Employer discrimination is the term used to describe wage differentials that arise from an arbitrary preference by an employer for one group of workers over another. An example occurs if two labour force groups, such as males and females, are equally productive, on average, yet some employers (discriminators) prefer hiring males and are willing to pay higher wages to do so. While much of the controversy and analysis has focused on earnings, similar considerations apply to career prospects and promotions, summed up in the case of gender differentials in the concept of the 'glass ceiling', the invisible barrier that is claimed to affect the ability of women to secure career advancement on the same basis as men.

Most consumers are not willing to pay more for a product produced by males than for an identical one produced by females (if indeed they even *know* which type of worker produced the product). If product price is unaffected by the composition of the workforce that produces the product, and if men are paid more than women for comparable work, a firm's profit will be smaller the more males it employs, because males cost more yet are no more productive (on the assumption that discrimination is the cause of the wage gap). Thus the most profitable firms will be those that employ only females.

Arbitrary wage gaps are an apparent violation of the No-Cash-on-the-Table Principle (Chapter 3). The initial wage differential provides an opportunity for employers who hire mostly females to grow at the expense of their rivals. Because such firms make an economic profit on the sale of each unit of output, their incentive is to expand as rapidly as they possibly can. And, to do that, they would naturally want to continue hiring only the cheaper females. But as profit-seeking firms continue to pursue this strategy, the supply of females at the lower wage rate will run out. The short-run solution is to offer females a slightly higher wage. But this strategy works only if other firms do not pursue it. Once they, too, start offering a higher wage, females will again be in short supply. The only stable outcome occurs when the wage of females reaches parity with the wage of males. The wage for both males and females will thus settle at the common value of their VMP.

Equilibrium

Another way of looking at this is to consider the circumstances under which discrimination is feasible, even if not profit maximising. Suppose a firm discriminates by paying, say, fair-haired workers more than dark-haired workers (or, equivalently, hiring less productive fair-haired rather than more productive dark-haired at a common wage). In doing so the employer must, by definition, increase his unit costs. If he faces competition in the market into which he is selling the product of the firm he will be undercut by firms that do not discriminate on hair-colour grounds. Eventually he must cease discrimination or go out of business. Discrimination increases his costs; he forgoes profits in order to discriminate. This is feasible only as long as there are potential profits to be absorbed by the costs of discrimination. Competition from other firms eliminates that source of funds to finance discrimination.

Any employer who wants to voice a preference for hiring males must now do so by paying males a wage in excess of the VMP. Employers can discriminate against females if they wish, but only if they are willing to pay premium wages to males out of their own profits. Not even the harshest critics of the competitive model seem willing to impute such behaviour to the owners of capitalist enterprises … unless, of course, the owners are protected from the consequences of their actions either by government or by the absence of competitive pressure.

customer discrimination the willingness of consumers to pay more for a product produced by members of a favoured group, even if the quality of the product is unaffected

Discrimination by others

If employer discrimination is not the primary explanation of the wage gap in competitive markets, what is? In some instances, **customer discrimination** may provide a plausible explanation.

For example, if people believe that juries and clients are less likely to take female or minority ethnic group lawyers seriously, members of these groups will face a reduced incentive to attend law school, and law firms will face a reduced incentive to hire those who do. Fanciful? Consider Economic naturalist 13.3.

Economic naturalist 13.3 Why are Irish barristers permitted to continue to wear wigs, and English barristers permitted to achieve the status of Queen's Counsel?

In the ceaseless pursuit of modernisation, the Irish government proposed in 1996 to prohibit by legislation the wearing of wigs by barristers in court (an inheritance of the British courts tradition in which barristers appearing in court wear gowns, white collar tabs – a token, according to some, of mourning for Queen Anne, who died in 1714 – dark clothes and horsehair wigs based on those worn by males in the late eighteenth century – think of Kavanagh QC!). A few months later, the government retreated to making the wearing of wigs a matter of choice (up to then it had been a requirement under court rules), and wigs continue to be worn by most barristers. In 2003, the Lord Chancellor of England, who is a member of the cabinet (and who, incidentally, also in pursuit of modernisation, was at the same time proposing the abolition of his own 1,400-year-old office) announced that he intended to abolish the status of Queen's (King's) Counsel (QC or KC), a mark of achievement and expertise among advocacy lawyers, dating from the sixteenth century. A year later the Lord Chancellor dropped the proposal (and subsequently announced that he was also dropping the proposal for his own abolition).

Traditionalists and economists who argued that (a) tradition was important, and (b) in neither case could the traditional practice convincingly be shown to damage end user interests (by raising costs or reducing quality of service by lawyers) made little headway against the modernisers. Then, in the Irish case, women barristers let it be known that they favoured wigs because it put them on a level playing field with their male colleagues. Without wigs, clients would not take them as seriously as they would male lawyers. In England, lawyers from minority racial groups made the same case for QC status. Acquiring QC status was a means of advancing the position of minority advocates and showing that they could deliver a superior service to clients. In both countries, the government immediately changed its mind.

Parental discrimination

Another possible source of persistent wage gaps is discrimination and socialisation within the family. For example, families may provide less education for their female children, or they may socialise them to believe that lofty career ambitions are not appropriate.

Other sources of the wage gap

Part of the wage gap may be explained by compensating wage differentials that spring from differences in preferences for other non-wage elements of the compensation package. Jobs that involve exposure to physical risk, for example, command higher wages, and if men are relatively more willing to accept such risks they will earn more than females with otherwise identical stocks of human capital. (The same difference would result if employers felt constrained by social norms not to assign female employees to risky jobs.)

Elements of human capital that are difficult to measure may also help to explain earnings differentials. For example, productivity is influenced not only by the quantity of education an individual has, which is easy to measure, but also by its *quality*, which is much harder to measure. Part of the observed aggregate black–white differential in US wages may thus be due to the fact that schools in black neighbourhoods have not been as good, on average, as those in white neighbourhoods.

Differences in the courses people take at university or other tertiary-level institutions appear to have similar implications for differences in productivity. For instance, students in maths, engineering or business – both male and female – tend to earn significantly higher salaries than those who study the humanities and do not acquire other professional training after graduating. The fact that males are disproportionately represented in the former group gives rise to a male wage premium that is unrelated to employer discrimination.

As economists have grown more sophisticated in their efforts to measure human capital and other factors that influence individual wage rates, unexplained wage differentials by sex and race have grown steadily smaller, and have even disappeared altogether in some studies.[3] Some work, however, continues to find significant unexplained differentials by race and sex. Debate about discrimination in the workplace will continue until the causes of these differentials are more fully understood.

Winner-take-all markets

Differences in human capital do much to explain observed differences in earnings. Yet earnings differentials have also grown sharply in many occupations within which the distribution of human capital among workers seems essentially unchanged. Consider Economic naturalist 13.4.

Economic naturalist 13.4 Why do Renée Fleming and Angela Gheorghiu earn millions more than sopranos of only slightly lesser ability?

Although the best sopranos have always earned more than others with slightly lesser talents, the earnings gap is sharply larger now than it was in the nineteenth century. Today, top singers such as Fleming and Gheorghiu earn millions of euros per year – hundreds or even thousands of times what sopranos only marginally less talented earn. Given that listeners in 'blind hearings' often have difficulty identifying the most highly paid singers, why is this earnings differential so large?

The answer lies in a fundamental change in the way in which we consume most of our music. That change is the consequence of the technology of recording. As late as the early 1950s, recordings were more or less confined to 78 rpm graphite discs. Then came vinyl LPs, and in the mid-1980s digital recording on CD. These developments made it possible to hear music at least as well as at a live performance, and more cheaply and on demand. But before recording, in the nineteenth century, to hear a professional singer it was necessary to attend a live performance, usually in a concert hall. In any one day, therefore a singer could perform for at most a thousand people. Today a singer can perform instantaneously and simultaneously for hundreds of millions.

Nineteenth-century audiences would have been delighted to listen to the world's best soprano, but no one singer could hope to perform in more than a tiny fraction of the world's concert halls, of which there were a great number (remember the story of the building of an opera house in Manaus in the middle of the Matto Grosso!). As a result, given the demand for good singing, it could be met only by a large number of good singers. Given the total willingness to pay for singing, it would be divided over a large number of singers. Given that the difference between the best and the next best was not large,

---

3 Polackek and Kim (1994).

we would expect the differences in earnings of singers to be limited to what could be extracted from a limited number of live performances. Being better would yield a higher income, but the spread of incomes would be limited. People would still pay to listen to other singers.

Today, in contrast, most of the music we hear comes in recorded form, which enables the best soprano to be literally everywhere at once. As soon as the master recording has been made, Renée Fleming's performance can be burned on to compact discs at the same low cost as for a slightly less talented singer's. Tens of millions of buyers worldwide are willing to pay a few cents extra to hear the most talented performers. This means that the demand for the singing of less talented performers is sharply reduced. Recording companies would be delighted to hire the best singers at modest salaries, for by so doing they would earn an enormous economic profit. But that would unleash bidding by rival recording companies for the best singers. Such bidding ensures that the top singers will earn multimillion-euro annual salaries (most of which constitute economic rents, as discussed in Chapter 7). Slightly less talented singers earn much less, because the recording industry simply does not need them.

winner-take-all labour market one in which small differences in human capital translate into large differences in pay

The market for sopranos is an example of a **winner-take-all labour market**, one in which small differences in ability or other dimensions of human capital translate into large differences in pay. Such markets have long been familiar in entertainment and professional sports. But as technology has enabled the most talented individuals to serve broader markets, the winner-take-all reward structure has become an increasingly important feature of modern economic life, permeating such diverse fields as law, journalism, consulting, medicine, investment banking, corporate management, publishing, design, fashion and even the hallowed halls of academe.

Contrary to what the name seems to imply, a winner-take-all market does not mean a market with literally only one winner. Indeed, hundreds of professional musicians earn multimillion-euro annual salaries. Yet tens of thousands of others, many of them nearly as good, struggle to pay their bills.

The fact that small differences in human capital often give rise to extremely large differences in pay might seem to contradict human capital theory. Note, however, that the winner-take-all reward pattern is completely consistent with the competitive labour market theory's claim that individuals are paid in accordance with the contributions they make to the *employer's net revenue*. The leverage of technology often amplifies small performance differentials into very large ones.

RECAP Explaining differences in earnings among people

Earnings differ among people in part because of differences in their *human capital*, an amalgam of personal characteristics that affects productivity. But pay often differs substantially between two people with the same amount of human capital. This can happen for many reasons: one person may belong to a labour union while the other does not; one may work in a job with less pleasant conditions; one may be the victim of discrimination; or one may work in an arena in which technology or other factors provide greater leverage to human capital.

Trends in inequality

It is widely believed that since the mid-1970s *inequality of outcome* (in terms of the incomes households enjoy) has increased in most advanced world economies. In most market economies most citizens receive most of their income from the sale of their own labour. An attractive feature of the free-market system is that it rewards initiative, effort and risk taking: the harder, longer and more effectively a person works, the more he or she will be paid.

Yet relying on the marketplace to distribute income also entails an important drawback: those who do well often end up with vastly more money than they can spend, while those who fail often cannot afford even basic goods and services. Hundreds of thousands of American families are homeless, and still larger numbers go to bed hungry each night. Many distinguished philosophers have argued that such poverty in the midst of plenty is impossible to justify on moral grounds. It is thus troubling that income inequality has been growing rapidly since the 1970s. The data in Table 13.2 offer an indication of the extent of this problem in the US context.

Quintile (per cent)	1980	1990	2000
Bottom 20	12,756	12,625	14,232
Second 20	27,769	29,448	32,268
Middle 20	41,950	45,352	50,925
Fourth 20	58,200	65,222	74,918
Top 20	97,991	121,212	155,527
Top 5	139,302	190,187	272,349

Table 13.2 **Mean Income Received by Families in Each Income Quintile and by the Top 5 Per Cent of Families, 1980–2000 (2000 dollars)**

The period from the end of the Second World War until the early 1970s was one of balanced income growth in the United States. During that period, incomes grew at almost 3 per cent a year for rich, middle-class and poor Americans alike. In the ensuing years, however, the pattern of income growth has been dramatically different.

In the first row of Table 13.2, for example, notice that families in the bottom 20 per cent of the income distribution saw their real incomes grow by less than 12 per cent from 1980 to 2000 (a growth rate of less than one-half of 1 per cent per year).

The third row of Table 13.2 indicates that the real incomes of families in the middle quintile grew by less than 22 per cent during the same 20-year period (a growth rate of less than 1 per cent per year). In contrast, real incomes jumped more than 58 per cent for families in the top quintile.

Between 1980 and 2000, incomes for families in the top 5 per cent jumped by more than 95 per cent. Even for these families, however, income growth rates were low relative to those of the immediate post-Second World War decades.

The only people whose incomes have grown substantially faster than in that earlier period are those at the very pinnacle of the income ladder. Real earnings of the top 1 per cent of US earners, for example, have more than doubled since 1980, and those even higher up have taken home pay cheques that might have seemed unimaginable in 1980.

It is important to emphasise that being near the bottom of the income distribution in one year does not necessarily mean being stranded there for ever. Many chief executive officers (CEOs) now earning multi-million-dollar pay cheques, for example, were struggling young graduate students in 1980, and were classified in the bottom 20 per cent of the income distribution for that year. We must bear in mind, too, that not all economic mobility is *upward*. Many US blue-collar workers, for instance, had higher real incomes in 1980 than they do today.

Measuring the distribution of income or wealth

Is the US situation different from that in other countries (Sweden or the United Kingdom, for example) and, if so, by how much? By how much has this position changed over, say, a 20-year period? Has income distribution in, say, Britain, changed in the same way as that in the United States? How have any measures adopted to alter the distribution affected their target? To be in a position to answer questions like these we must have an *agreed and objective measure of income distribution*. It must also be *cardinal* rather than simply ordinal. There are in fact several such measures available, but the one that is most widely used and easiest to both understand and compute is what is known as the **Gini coefficient**. It does not, note, 'explain' the level or change in any distribution; it does not evaluate distributions (that in country *X* is worse or better than that in country *Y*); it merely provides a basis for *comparing distributions* on an objective numerical basis.

Gini coefficient a measure of equality of distribution that compares the actual distribution with a benchmark of absolute equality

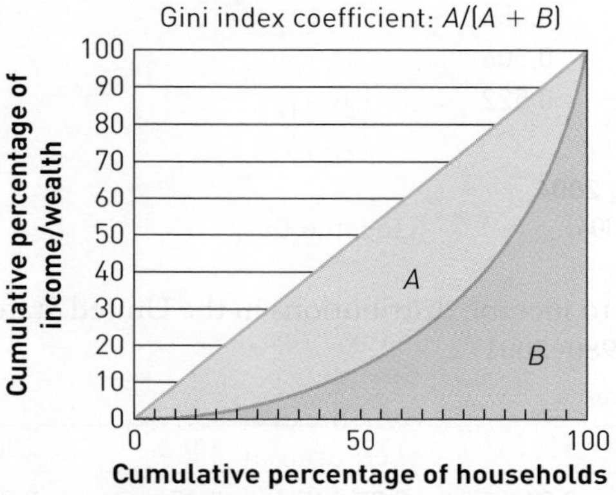

The measure was developed by the great Italian statistician, Corrado Gini (1884–1965), in a monograph published in 1912.[4] It measures the degree to which an observed distribution differs from a hypothetical perfectly equal distribution. It is demonstrated in graph form in Fig. 13.6.

On the vertical axis are given the percentiles of the magnitude being measured; in this case, income, from 0 to 100 per cent. On the horizontal axis are given percentiles of the population over which the distribution is being measured. If the income of the population was perfectly equally distributed, then any 1 per cent of the population would earn 1 per cent of total population income, and any 10 per cent or 20 per cent would earn 10 per cent or 20 per cent of the total.

Figure 13.6 Gini Index: a Measure of Distribution.

Starting, then, with an arbitrary 1 per cent of the population, then 2 per cent, then 3 per cent, and so on, and graphing the percentage of the total income they account for, we would get the 45° straight line in Fig. 13.6. Then, taking the actual distribution, we start with the poorest 1 per cent or 5 per cent on the horizontal axis and plot their share of total income, then that of the bottom 2 per cent (or 5 per cent, depending on the statistics available) and continue until we have accounted for the entire population. The graph we get is called the **Lorenz curve**.[5]

Lorenz curve the graph of the cumulative distribution of income or wealth by percentages of households or individuals from poorest to richest

The Gini coefficient is the ratio of the area between the Lorenz curve (*A*) to the total area under the 45° line (*A* + *B*). It has a value somewhere between 0 (everyone has the same income, perfect equality) and 1 (one person has all the income, perfect inequality). The higher the value, the less equal is the distribution.

---

4 Gini (1912).

5 Max Otto Lorenz (1880–1962) was an American economist. He developed the concept to describe income inequalities in a paper published in 1905 (Lorenz 1905).

Table 13.3 contains data on Gini coefficients for a number of OECD countries in 2004. The results are not all that surprising: the Scandinavian economies, with highly developed 'cradle-to-grave' welfare systems financed out of high taxation, have more equal distributions than countries with more market-orientated economies. The United States has a less equal distribution than the United Kingdom – but not enormously less equal.

Japan	0.249
Sweden	0.250
Germany	0.283
France	0.327
Australia	0.352
Ireland	0.359
United Kingdom	0.360
United States	0.408
Russia	0.456
Nigeria	0.506
Argentina	0.522

Table 13.3 **Gini Coefficients by Country, 2004**
Source: UN, *Human Development Report* (2004).

Table 13.4 shows what has happened to income distributions in the United States and the United Kingdom over the years 1980–2001/2.

Country	1980	1985	1990	1995	2000	2001/2
UK	0.28	0.29	0.36	0.33	0.35	0.33
USA	0.40	0.42	0.43	0.45	0.46	0.47

Table 13.4 **UK and US Gini Coefficients, 1980–2001/2**
Source: US Bureau of the Census; UK National Statistics (2005). UK data refer to household disposable income pre-tax (2002); US data refer to household income, pre-tax (2001).

Table 13.5 shows values for several countries in years between 1993 and 2005. There are some small differences in estimates for the US and UK cases between the values in Tables 13.4 and 13.5, reflecting different original data sources and estimating procedures. The values for the Gini coefficients in this table suggest that, broadly speaking, there has not been much change in the rankings across countries, and that there is some evidence of a trend towards greater equality in the countries with more unequal distributions.

Inequality: a moral problem?

John Rawls, a moral philosopher at Harvard University, constructed a cogent ethical critique of the marginal productivity system, one based heavily on the economic theory of *choice* itself.[6] In thinking about what constitutes a 'just distribution of income', Rawls asks us to imagine ourselves meeting to choose the rules for distributing income.

6 Rawls (1971).

	1993	1994	1995	1996	1997	1998	1999	2000	2001	2002	2003	2004	2005
Neth'ld		.257					.231						
Norway		.238						.251					
Sweden		.221						.252					.237
Swtzld								.280		.224			
Italy	.339		.338			.346		.333					
UK		.339	.344				.343						.345
USA	.355				.372			.368				.372	
Spain			.353					.336					
Poland			.318				.313						
Russia			.447					.434					
Mexico		.495		.477		.492		.491				.458	

Table 13.5 **Gini Coefficients by Country Over Time**
Source: Luxembourg Income Project, based on OECD estimates.

The meeting takes place behind a 'veil of ignorance', which conceals from participants any knowledge of what talents and abilities each has. Because no individual knows whether he is smart or dull, strong or weak, fast or slow, no one knows what rules of distribution would work to his own advantage. Rawls argues that the rules people would choose in such a state of ignorance would necessarily be fair; and, if the rules are fair, the income distribution to which they give rise will also be fair.

What sort of rules would people choose from behind a veil of ignorance? If the national income were a fixed amount, most people would probably give everyone an equal share. That scenario is likely, Rawls argues, because most people are strongly risk averse. Since an unequal income distribution would involve not only a chance of doing well but a chance of doing poorly, most people would prefer to eliminate the risk by choosing an equal distribution. If diminishing marginal utility applies to wealth, a given chance of a given gain over the average income is less valuable than avoiding the same chance of the same loss relative to the average. An individual for whom this is the case is said to be *risk averse*.

Imagine, for example, that you and two friends have been told that an anonymous benefactor donated €300,000 to divide among you. How would you split it? If you are like most people, you would propose an equal division, or €100,000 for each of you. Most of us, most of the time, behave in a risk-averse fashion. The logical extreme of the Rawlsian thought experiment is that people would choose a fully egalitarian outcome if they could not choose (or influence) their position in society. Given this, an egalitarian distribution is ethically superior to an unequal one.

Rawls' logic is appealing ... but is not necessarily convincing, at least in its extreme version. It depends first of all on an assumption that a person's economic welfare depends on his income alone, and that no benefits are derived by anyone from the activities of those who are better off: no pop stars; no patrons of the arts. It also expressly assumes that the size of the cake is independent of the way it is sliced. This is fine for real cakes, but not for the 'cake' of gross national product (GNP). While there are several dissenting voices, most economists would support the proposition that a successful market economy cannot function properly (i.e. maximise the size of the 'cake') without incentives that imply some *inequality of outcome*. If either or both of these factors is built into Rawls' thought experiment it is not at all obvious that a risk-averse individual would choose a highly equal distribution from behind a veil of ignorance.

Efficiency

Whatever the choice made from behind that veil, the attraction of a commitment to a high degree of equality is far from absolute when we consider its impact in the real world. For many, the goal of absolute equality is quickly trumped by other concerns when we set about making the rules for distributing wealth in modern market economies. Wealth, after all, generally doesn't grow on trees – we must produce it. In a large economy, if each person were guaranteed an equal amount of income, few would invest in education or the development of special talents; and the incentive to work would be sharply reduced. In a country without rewards for hard work and risk taking, national income would be dramatically smaller than in a country with such rewards. Of course, material rewards for effort and risk taking necessarily lead to inequality.

Rawls accepts, to be fair, that people would be willing to accept a certain degree of inequality as long as these rewards produced a sufficiently large increase in the total amount of output available for distribution. But how much inequality would people accept? Much less than the amount produced by purely competitive markets, Rawls argues. The idea is that, behind the veil of ignorance, each person would fear ending up in a disadvantaged position, so each would choose rules that would produce a more equal distribution of income than exists under the marginal productivity system. And since such choices *define* the just distribution of income, Rawls argues, fairness requires at least some attempt to reduce the inequality produced by the market system. Most people would agree with this weaker Rawls proposition. After all, most people voluntarily redistribute income through gifts and donations to the poor or disaster relief: look at the global, non-governmental response to the tsunami catastrophe of Christmas 2004 in South-east Asia.

RECAP Why is income inequality a moral problem?

John Rawls argues that the degree of inequality typical of unregulated market systems is unfair because people would favour substantially less inequality if they chose distributional rules from *behind a veil of ignorance*.

Methods of income redistribution

A political consensus that the existing distribution of income is less than optimal leads to policies by government designed to improve the distribution. These take two basic forms. The first is to do something to change the *underlying factors* that produce the observed distribution. The second is to compensate for the *outcome observed*. An example of the first would be to improve the ability of children from poor families to obtain tertiary-level education. An example of the second would be direct payments to households with incomes below some threshold value.

Although we, as a society, have an interest in limiting income inequality, programmes for reducing it are often fraught with practical difficulties. The challenge is to find ways to raise the incomes of those who cannot fend for themselves, without at the same time undermining their incentive to work, and without using scarce resources to subsidise those who are not poor. The manner in which the funds are raised will also be subject to a similar test: to what extent does the raising of the funds reduce the *global income* from which the funds are raised? Of course, some people simply cannot work, or cannot find work that pays enough to live on. In a world of perfect information, the government could make generous cash payments to those people, and withhold support from those who can fend for themselves. In practice, however, the two groups are often hard to distinguish. So we must choose among imperfect alternative measures.

Redistribution takes place through one or both of two channels. In the first place, the design of the *tax structure*, which produces the revenues to finance government spending, can be skewed in such a way that those with greater resources pay more for the services provided to all, or to some. If this is the case the incidence of taxation is 'progressive' (as opposed to 'regressive', when the incidence is heavier on those with fewer resources). In the second place, the *composition of public spending* can be biased towards providing income or services to those with fewer resources. The net redistributive impact of the government reflects the balance of the effects of policies on taxation and spending. In this respect it can be misleading to treat a particular tax or spending item without looking at the overall impact of all taxes and spending structures in order to judge the effectiveness of the government in terms of income redistribution.

Welfare payments and in-kind transfers

In all advanced countries the government tries to alter the distribution of income and wealth by creating entitlements to money payments and the provision of goods and services free of charge or at a price that is below the cost of provision. Economists have long argued the merits of these two approaches. The balance of conclusions is that *money payments* are preferable to provision of what are really benefits in kind.

in-kind transfer a payment made not in the form of cash, but in the form of a good or service

In-kind transfers are direct transfers of goods or services to low-income individuals or families. This includes both free-of-charge provision and provision at below cost. Examples are subsidised public housing, subsidised school meals, education without fees and 'free' medical care. In many European jurisdictions they also include some more dubious features such as benefits to defined groups of people: for example, the elderly benefit from such things as free public transport, exemption from refuse collection charges, reductions in the price of electricity – and even free TV licences. Economists criticise these on two grounds. The first is that (unless you do not trust those on low incomes to spend wisely) it is axiomatically true that it is welfare enhancing for the poor to give them money to spend as they wish rather than to constrain them to consume a predetermined bundle of goods of equal cost. The second is that in-kind transfers tend not to be accurately related to the means of those receiving them. At its most obvious, why should we think that all those over 65 (the elderly) are poor? The same, of course, applies to some monetary payments: most West European countries offer payments to families (in some cases to mothers) on the basis of the number of children they have. This benefits the rich equally with the poor. The motivation is to help poor families with a large number of children. The effect is to transfer real resources to families with children, regardless of their means.

Monetary transfers consist of cash (or equivalent) payments to recipients who are designated by some standard as entitled to the payment. Non-contributory old age pensions are an example of this kind of payment in many European countries. Children's allowances are another. The single most important element in this structure is *unemployment relief*: people who are unable to find work are entitled to a replacement of their earnings by a sum paid by the state. In the United States, such payments are severely limited in terms of the duration of any period of receipt of payments. European countries are mostly much more liberal. Obviously, unemployment is the most important proximate cause of poverty, so entitling the unemployed to cash income support tackles poverty head on. Unfortunately, it can have perverse incentive effects, since it can discourage people from accepting employment. This is why there is growing pressure in Europe to follow the US model and make it limited in duration – and, where it is already limited, to reduce the period further.

Universality and means testing

In the United States, there is a strong bias towards a system of cash or in-kind benefits based on objective means testing. To qualify for Medicaid, households have to demonstrate a level of income that is sufficiently low to qualify for the health cost benefit. The Aid to Families with Dependent Children (AFDC) programme is **means-tested** on a sliding scale. In Europe, there is a stronger emphasis on universalist provision. The UK's universal National Health Service (NHS) is a classic example. Child support payments, a common feature of European social support structures in one form or another, are a further example.

means-tested a benefit programme whose benefit level declines as the recipient earns additional income

On the face of it, it must appear wasteful and illogical to raise taxes in order to make payments to the very people from whom the tax is raised rather than raise less taxation and deliver the funds to those who are less well off. There are, however, two strong counter-arguments supporting a universalist approach. The first is an administrative one, and one that also has an element of social sensitivity in it. This is the argument that (a) it is significantly more costly to devise, administer and modify a social spending programme that is based on establishing recipients' entitlement to receive the transfers involved, and (b) it is kinder and more effective to grant support to people in need of support without requiring them to devote time and resources to proving that they meet the legal requirements of an entitlement. The second argument concerns what is known as the *poverty trap*. If a family that as of now is entitled to, say, a rent subsidy manages to increase its income but in so doing ceases to be eligible for the subsidy, the loss of the subsidy is in effect a tax on the extra income the family has earned. If a social support programme offers resources to people who are unemployed, then it implies a tax on taking up a job offer. Programmes of support to single mothers frequently mean that if the father co-habits with the mother and helps support the family, the support is withdrawn. That does not exactly encourage two-parent families. This kind of thing can lead to a position in which poorer families face an extremely high *effective marginal tax rate* if they take steps that will reduce their poverty and, as a result, have a very weak incentive to take those steps, thus creating for them the 'poverty trap'.

Income tax and redistribution

One obvious way of dealing with the issues just discussed is to apply income tax to any universal social support programme receipts. This has the effect of (a) ensuring that the benefits flow preponderantly to those on lower incomes, and (b) the level of payment can be increased without increasing taxes generally. The potential to use the tax system as the engine for redistribution that this raises has been the subject of debate among both economists and social workers. It has been suggested that it might be possible to replace the whole panoply of income support programmes by a reform of

negative income tax (NIT) a system under which the government would grant every citizen a cash payment each year, financed by an additional tax on earned income

the tax code. The central element in this proposal is what is called **negative income tax (NIT)**.

There are several variants of this concept, but they have in common the idea that income tax takes away a proportion of the payer's income over some threshold, and that the threshold could be used as a basis for paying money to people whose incomes are below that threshold. For example, suppose there is a 25 per cent income tax on family incomes above, say, €10,000 per annum. This would be replaced by a tax of 25 per cent of (income − €10,000). A household with an income of €8,000 would face a tax bill of €0.25(8000 − 10000) = −€500. A negative tax bill is, of course, a receipt. The family would receive a cheque for €500, an NIT payment. In this case everyone, regardless of income, faces the same effective tax rate. If a family with €15,000 earns an extra €1,000, it retains €750 (75 per cent) and pays €250 (25 per cent) in tax. A family with €8,000 that earns an extra €1,000 keeps the whole €1,000, but receives €250 rather than €500. The extra €1,000 leaves it with a net increase of €750 (75 per cent) as it loses the €250 (25 per cent) NIT payment.

The big problem with this type of proposal is the incentive difficulty. Note that in the last example a household with no income at all would receive €2,500. Suppose (rather unrealistically) that this constituted what the government considered to be the **poverty threshold**, the level of income below which a family is 'poor' – i.e. has insufficient income to sustain an acceptable lifestyle. At a marginal effective tax rate of 25 per cent, no one would pay any tax to the Exchequer until they had an income four times the poverty level. A widely used and far from generous poverty threshold is 40 per cent of the average industrial wage. On that basis no one earning less than 160 per cent of the average industrial wage would pay any income tax. In most Western economies that would mean about 60 per cent of households paying no income tax. It doesn't take a genius to work out that you couldn't finance current government spending programmes if only 40 per cent of people paid any income taxes, and then only at 25 per cent for some time after hitting the threshold, unless taxes on the rest were confiscatory, something that would have very serious incentive effects on work effort and risk taking.

poverty threshold the level of income below which a family is 'poor'

Exercise 13.4 Using the data above, what would the tax rate have to be if everyone below and those just above the tax threshold (€10,000) were to face the same effective tax rate while the poverty threshold is set at half the tax threshold?

Finally, the higher the basic payment (the poverty threshold) relative to the income tax threshold, the lower is the incentive to work at all, since work does, you will remember, have an *opportunity cost*: what you can do with the time you spend working if you don't work.

Minimum wages

Very many, but not all, industrialised countries have sought to increase the standard of living of low-wage workers by enacting general minimum wage legislation – laws that prohibit all employers from paying workers less than a specified hourly wage. Of those that haven't, the majority have sectoral or industrial minimum wage provisions, affecting significant numbers of employees. The general minimum wage rate varies from country to country. In 2008, the US federal minimum wage was $6.50/hour, and was scheduled to rise to $7.25/hour in July 2009. Many US states have higher minimum rates than the federal rate. In Europe, minimum wage structures vary by country. In 2008, Norway, Sweden, Finland, Denmark, Switzerland, Germany, Austria, Italy and Cyprus had no general minimum wage laws. In Germany, political pressure to introduce one was strong. Much of the German economy was affected by sectoral minimum rate agreements. The United Kingdom general minimum wage for adult (over 22) workers in 2008 was £5.52/hour. In Ireland, the rate was €8.65; in France it was €8.71; in Spain it was €600/month, or about €4 per hour. Outside Europe, in 2008, while there were widespread sectorally binding minimum rates in force in both countries, neither South Africa nor Australia had a generally applicable minimum wage rate. In New Zealand it was NZ$12 per hour.

At one point, economists were almost unanimous in their opposition to minimum wage laws, arguing that such laws reduce total economic surplus, as do other regulations that prevent markets from reaching equilibrium. Even today, economists as a whole tend to be critical of minimum wage legislation on the grounds that elementary theory (see the discussion of the impact of unions on p. 379) suggests that such interventions in labour markets damage employment prospects and hurt those not covered by the minimum wage. Some economists have now questioned this blanket opposition to minimum wage laws, citing studies that have failed to show significant reductions in employment following increases in minimum wage levels. These studies may well imply that, as a group, low-income workers are better off with minimum wage laws than without them. But as we saw in Chapter 6, any policy that prevents a market from reaching equilibrium causes a reduction in *total economic surplus* – which means society ought in principle to be able to find a more effective policy for helping low-wage workers.

How does a minimum wage affect the market for low-wage labour? In Fig. 13.7, note that when the law prevents employers from paying less than W_{min}, employers hire fewer workers (a decline from L_0 to L_1). Unemployment results. The L_1 workers who keep their jobs earn more than before, but the L_0–L_1 workers who lose their jobs earn nothing. Whether workers together earn more or less than before thus depends on the *elasticity of demand for labour*. If elasticity of demand is less than 1, workers as a group will earn more than before. If it is more than 1, workers as a group will earn less.

| Efficiency |

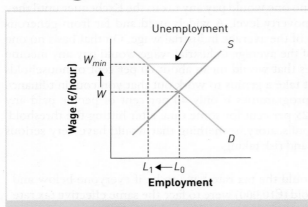

Figure 13.7 The Effect of Minimum Wage Legislation on Employment. If minimum wage legislation requires employers to pay more than the equilibrium wage, the result will be a decline in employment for low-wage workers.

The earned income tax credit

A US fiscal innovation in 1975 is an example of how it is possible to achieve the goals of minimum wage legislation without incurring its costs. First proposed by President Richard Nixon, the earned income tax credit (EITC) was enacted into law in 1975, and has drawn praise from both left and right on the political spectrum. The programme is essentially a *wage subsidy* in the form of a credit against the amount a family owes in federal income taxes. For example, a family of four with total earned income of $13,000 in 2001 would have received an annual tax credit of about $4,000. That is, the programme would have reduced the annual federal income tax payment of this family by roughly that amount. Families who earned less would have received a larger tax credit, and those who earned more would have received a smaller one. Families whose tax credit exceeds the amount of tax owed actually receive a cheque from the government for the difference. The EITC is thus essentially the same as a *negative income tax* (NIT), except that eligibility for the programme is confined to people who work. Like both the NIT and the minimum wage, the EITC puts extra income into the hands of workers who are employed at low wage levels. But unlike the minimum wage, the EITC creates no incentive for employers to lay off low-wage workers.

Contrast that intervention in the labour market with the decision of the Irish government in 2000 to introduce a minimum wage at a level of IRL£4.40 (€5.60). At the time this was the highest minimum wage in the OECD. We can think of the minimum wage as an *off-budget tax* on employers of low-wage workers, the proceeds of which are transferred to the employee rather than to the government. That's why it is expected to reduce demand for low-skill labour. However, at the time anyone on an hourly income of IRL£4.40 faced a marginal tax rate of 20 per cent plus social insurance contributions, giving an effective tax on the employee's marginal pound of about 26 per cent. By introducing the minimum wage on this basis the Irish government was taxing the employment of low-skill labour by employers (reducing the demand for such labour) and then taxing the tax in the hands of the recipient. This bizarre state of affairs, in which the incentives were strongly biased against increasing employment and real income for low-paid workers, continued until the end of 2004 when the government removed all those earning minimum wages from liability to income tax.

Example 13.4 By how much will a minimum wage reduce total economic surplus?

Suppose the demand and supply curves for unskilled labour in the Birmingham labour market are as shown in Fig. 13.8. By how much will the imposition of a minimum wage at £7 per hour reduce total economic surplus? By how much do worker surplus and employer surplus change as a result of adopting the minimum wage?

In the absence of a minimum wage, the equilibrium unskilled wage for Birmingham would be £5 per hour, and employment would be 5,000 person-hours per day. Both employers and workers would enjoy economic surplus equal to the area of the shaded triangles in Fig. 13.8: £12,500 per day.

With a minimum wage set at £7 per hour, employer surplus is the area of the upper shaded triangle in Fig. 13.9, £4,500 per day, and worker surplus is the area of the lower-left shaded area, £16,500 per day. The minimum wage thus reduces employer surplus by £8,000 per day and increases worker surplus by £4,000 per day. The net reduction in surplus is the area of the right-hand shaded triangle shown in Fig. 13.9: £4,000 per day.

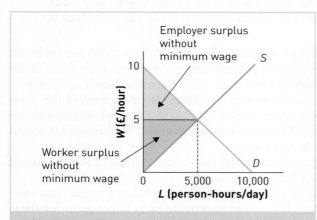

Figure 13.8 Worker and Employer Surplus in an Unregulated Labour Market. For the demand and supply curves shown, worker surplus is the area of the lower shaded triangle, £12,500 per day, the same as employer surplus (upper shaded triangle).

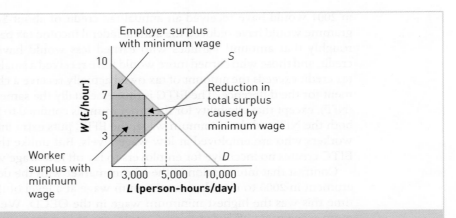

Figure 13.9 The Effect of a Minimum Wage on Economic Surplus. A minimum wage of £7 per hour reduces employment in this market by 2,000 person-hours per day, for a reduction in total economic surplus of £4,000 per day (area of the right-hand shaded triangle). Employer surplus falls to £4,500 per day (area of upper shaded triangle), while worker surplus rises to £16,500 per day (lower-left shaded area).

Exercise 13.5   In Example 13.4, by how much would total economic surplus have been reduced by the £7 minimum wage if labour demand in Birmingham had been perfectly inelastic at 5,000 person-hours per day?

Example 13.5 illustrates the central message of the efficiency principle, which is that if the economic 'pie' can be made larger, everyone can have a larger slice.

Example 13.5 Refer to Example 13.4. How much would it cost the government each day to provide EITC under which workers as a group receive the same economic surplus as they do under the £7 per hour minimum wage? (Assume for simplicity that the EITC has no effect on labour supply.)

With an EITC in lieu of a minimum wage, employment will be 5,000 person-hours per day at £5 per hour, just as in the unregulated market. Since worker surplus in the unregulated market was £4,000 per day less than under the minimum wage, the government would have to offer a tax credit worth £0.80 per hour for each of the 5,000 person-hours of employment to restore worker surplus to the level obtained under the £7 minimum wage. With an EITC of that amount in effect, worker surplus would be the same as under the £7 minimum wage.

If the EITC were financed by a £4,000 tax on employers, employer surplus would be £4,000 greater than under the £7 minimum wage.

We stress that our point is not that the minimum wage produces no gains for low-income workers, but rather that it is possible to provide even larger gains for these workers if we avoid policies that try to prevent labour markets from reaching equilibrium.

Summary

■ A worker's long-run equilibrium pay in a competitive labour market will be equal to the value of her marginal product (VMP) – the market value of whatever goods and services she produces for her employer. The law of diminishing returns says that when a firm's capital and other productive inputs are held fixed in the short run, adding workers beyond some point results in ever-smaller increases in output. Firms that purchase labour in competitive labour markets face a constant wage, and they will hire labour up to the point at which VMP equals the *market wage*.

■ *Human capital theory* says that an individual's VMP is proportional to his stock of human capital – an amalgam of education, experience, training, intelligence and other factors that influence productivity. According to this theory, some occupations pay better than others simply because they require larger stocks of human capital.

■ Wages often differ between individuals whose stocks of human capital appear nearly the same, as when one belongs to a labour union and the other does not. Compensating *wage differentials* – wage differences associated with differences in working conditions – are another important explanation for why individuals with similar human capital might earn different salaries. They help to explain why refuse collectors earn more than lifeguards and, more generally, why individuals with a given stock of human capital tend to earn more in jobs that have less attractive working conditions.

■ Many firms pay members of certain groups – notably minority groups and women – less than they pay other people who seem to have similar employment characteristics. If such *wage gaps* are the result of employer discrimination, their existence implies profit opportunities for firms that do not discriminate. Several other factors, including discrimination by customers and institutions other than firms, may explain at least part of the observed wage gaps.

■ Technologies that allow the most productive individuals to serve broader markets can translate even small differences in human capital into enormous differences in pay. Such technologies give rise to *winner-take-all* markets, which have long been common in sports and entertainment, and which are now becoming common in other professions.

■ Although incomes grew at almost 3 per cent a year for all income classes from the 1950s to the 1980s, the lion's share of income growth in the years since has been concentrated among the *top earners*.

■ Philosophers have argued that at least some *income redistribution* is justified in the name of fairness, because if people chose society's distributional rules without knowing their own personal circumstances, most would favour less inequality than would be produced by market outcomes.

■ Policies and programmes for *reducing poverty* include minimum-wage laws, the EITC, food and housing vouchers, subsidised school lunches, free healthcare, public housing and income supplements. Of these, all but the EITC fail to maximise total economic surplus, either by interfering with work incentives or by preventing markets from reaching equilibrium.

■ The NIT works much like the EITC, except that it includes those who are not employed.

Review questions

1. Why is the supply curve of labour for any specific occupation likely to be upward-sloping, even if, for the economy as a whole, people work fewer hours when wage rates increase?

2. **True or false**: If the human capital possessed by two workers is nearly the same, their wage rates will be nearly the same. Explain.

3. How might recent changes in income inequality be related to the proliferation of technologies that enable the most productive individuals to serve broader markets?

4. Give two self-interested reasons that a top earner might favour policies to redistribute income.

5. Why is exclusive reliance on the negative income tax unlikely to constitute a long-term solution to the poverty problem?

connect ## Problems

Problems marked with an asterisk (*) are more difficult.

1. H2Oclean Ltd supplies domestic kitchen water filters to the retail market in Essex and hires workers to assemble the components. An air filter sells for €26, and H2Oclean can buy the components for each filter for €1. Kevin and Sharon are two workers for H2Oclean Ltd. Sharon can assemble 60 air filters per month, and Kevin can assemble 70. If the labour market is perfectly competitive, how much will each be paid?

2. Stone, Inc. owns a clothing factory, hiring workers in a competitive market to cut denim to make jeans. The fabric costs €5 per pair. The company's weekly output varies with labour usage, as shown in the table below.

Number of workers	Jeans (pairs/week)
0	0
1	25
2	45
3	60
4	72
5	80
6	85

a. If the jeans sell for €35 a pair, and the competitive market wage is €250 per week, how many workers should Stone hire? How many pairs of jeans will the company produce each week?

b. Suppose the Clothing Workers Union now sets a weekly minimum acceptable wage of €230 per week. All the workers Stone hires belong to the union. How does the minimum wage affect Stone's decision about how many workers to hire?

c. If the minimum wage set by the union had been €400 per week, how would the minimum wage affect Stone's decision about how many workers to hire?

d. If Stone again faces a market wage of €250 per week but the price of jeans rises to €45, how many workers will the company now hire?

3. Reacteurs de France, SA (RdF), supplier of engines for France's space exploration programme, hires workers to assemble the components. An engine sells for €30,000, and RdF can buy the components for each engine for €25,000. Belmondo and Halliday are two workers for RdF. Belmondo can assemble 1/5 of an engine per month, and Halliday can assemble 1/10. If the labour market is perfectly competitive and components are RdF's only other cost, how much will each be paid?

4. Carolyn owns a soda factory and hires workers in a competitive labour market to bottle the soda. Her company's weekly output of bottled soda varies with the number of workers hired, as shown in the table below.

Number of workers	Cases/week
0	0
1	200
2	360
3	480
4	560
5	600

a. If each case sells for €10 more than the cost of the materials used in producing it and the competitive market wage is €1,000 per week, how many workers should Carolyn hire? How many cases will be produced per week?

b. Suppose the Soda Bottlers Union now sets a weekly minimum acceptable wage of €1,500 per week. All the workers Carolyn hires belong to the union. How does the minimum wage affect Carolyn's decision about how many workers to hire?

c. If the wage is again €1,000 per week but the price of soda rises to €15 per case, how many workers will Carolyn now hire?

5. Suppose the equilibrium wage for unskilled workers in New Jersey is $7 per hour. How will the wages and employment of unskilled workers in New Jersey change if the state legislature raises the minimum wage from $5.15 per hour to $6 per hour?

6. Jones, who is currently unemployed, is a participant in three means-tested welfare programmes: food vouchers, rent vouchers and day care vouchers. Each programme grants him €150 per month in vouchers, which can be used like cash to purchase the good or service they cover.

a. If benefits in each programme are reduced by 40 cents for each additional euro Jones earns in the labour market, how will Jones' economic position change if he accepts a job paying €120 per week?

b. In the light of your answer to part (a), explain why means testing for welfare recipients has undesirable effects on work incentives.

7. Sue is offered a job re-shelving books in the University of Limerick library from noon until 1 pm each Friday. Her reservation wage for this task is €10 per hour.

a. If the library director offers Sue €100 per hour, how much economic surplus will she enjoy as a result of accepting the job?

b. Now suppose the library director announces that the earnings from the job will be divided equally among the 400 students who live in Sue's residence. Will Sue still accept?

c. Explain how your answers to parts (a) and (b) illustrate one of the incentive problems inherent in income redistribution programmes.

8.* Suppose the demand and supply curves for unskilled labour in the Bremen labour market are as shown in the graph below. By how much will the imposition of a minimum wage of €12 per hour reduce total economic surplus? Calculate the amounts by which employer surplus and worker surplus change as a result of the minimum wage.

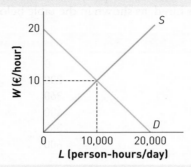

9.* Refer to Problem 8. How much would it cost the government each day to provide an EITC under which workers as a group receive the same economic surplus as they do under the €12 per hour minimum wage? (Assume for simplicity that the EITC has no effect on labour supply.)

References

Babcock, L., C. Camerer, G. Loewenstein and R. Thaler (1997) 'Labor supply of New York City cab drivers: one day at a time', *Quarterly Journal of Economics*, 111.

Gini, C. (1912) *Variabilità e mutabilità: contributo allo studio delle distribuzioni e delle relazioni statistiche* (Bologna: Tipografia di Paolo Cuppin).

Gunnigle, P. and M. O'Sullivan (2003) 'Organized labour in the Celtic tiger: trends in trade union penetration in the Republic of Ireland', paper delivered to the 13th Congress of the International Industrial Relations Association, Berlin.

Lorenz, M.O. (1905) 'Methods of measuring the concentration of wealth', *Publications of the American Statistical Association*, 9, pp. 209–19.

Polackek, S. and M. Kim (1994) 'Panel estimates of the male–female earnings functions', *Journal of Human Resources*, 29, 2, pp. 406–28.

Rawls, J. (1971) *A Theory of Justice* (Cambridge, MA: Harvard University Press).

To help you grasp the key concepts of this chapter check out the extra resources posted on the Online Learning Centre. There are chapter summaries, self-test questions, an interactive graphing tool, weblinks and a glossary, all for free!

Visit the Online Learning Centre at: www.mcgraw-hill.co.uk/textbooks/mcdowell for information on accessing all of these resources.

14

Government in the Market Economy: Regulation and Production of Public Goods and Other Services

In the course of Chapter 8 we looked at the performance of firms that enjoy substantial market power. The limiting case of this is the model of monopoly. Several things emerged from that material. In the first place we saw that market power results in a reduction in economic efficiency in that we cannot generally expect firms to choose outputs and prices that equate price to marginal cost. We also saw that firms will exploit market power to extract profits derived from restricting output, something that transfers real income from consumers to producers.

regulation legal intervention in markets to alter the way in which firms or consumers behave

To respond to this type of problem we saw that we rely on governmental (or, indeed, supranational) intervention in the form of **regulation**. This takes the form of restrictions on how firms operate, and on the structures of markets. It is the basis for regulation in the form of competition policy, and mergers and acquisitions (M&A) policy.

In this chapter we shall be looking at the role of government in the market economy under two headings. The first of these is its role as regulator in a broader context than simply that of competition and mergers policy. The second is the function of government as an agent in the economy in its own right, acting as a producer of goods and services. In this respect we shall in the main be considering the role of government in the provision of what are known as *public goods* and *merit goods*.

Government and regulation

What is common to the general problem of market failure and the narrow question of market power as an instance of market failure is that regulation is seen by economists as a means of correcting that failure. Our starting point is that if governments need to regulate economic activity they need to understand the economics foundations of regulatory intervention. When they don't they (and their critics) can end up pursuing irrational policies. Instead of market failure we have *regulatory failure*. Consider the following responses over concerns about 'security of supply'.

Regulatory blunders: the security of supply neurosis

Whether due to misunderstanding, or whether reflecting underhand actions to protect certain interest groups, governments frequently take regulatory action to protect or improve 'security of supply'. The market, it is said, does not adequately provide security. It is necessary for the state to regulate how markets work in order to improve the situation. Since suppliers make profits by selling things to consumers, and since supply interruptions will undermine those profits, it might be thought that suppliers would be acutely aware of any potential threat, and take steps to provide security. Governments think otherwise, and frequently think somewhat hazily about regulation, taxation and market failure, as three examples, two concerning energy and one concerning food, make clear.

Consider first the arguments used to raise taxes on oil consumption or, equivalently, to subsidise or mandate use of renewables and/or domestic fuel supplies in order to reduce dependence on Middle Eastern oil. The justification is essentially one of correcting market failure. Oil consumers are not factoring into their decisions on oil consumption the implicit cost to the economy as a whole of its vulnerability to supply interruption. Whether or not, or to what extent, this is really the case is a moot point. After all, any large-scale seller or buyer of oil would be perfectly well aware of the consequences to his business of supply interruption, and could be assumed to have factored that into his plans for organising his business, including insuring against interruption. Presumably the same applies to the purchase of energy by households for domestic purposes.

The alleged basis for the European Union's Common Agriculture Policy (CAP) was originally to ensure security of food supplies in Europe. Since the 1960s, Europeans have been paying higher than necessary prices and producing food they couldn't eat, while excluding imports from outside the Union, in order to ensure a secure supply. The fear was that, as in 1914–1918 and 1939–1945, hostilities might prevent imports of foodstuffs to Europe. Just who was going to be around to need the food in the event of the Cold War going hot was not explained.

Security of supply is not a neurosis peculiar to Europe. In 1979, in the wake of the second major oil supply interruption in a decade, the US government actively considered a proposal to reduce American dependence on imported oil by imposing a federal motor fuel tax of 50 cents per US gallon (approximately 15 cents per litre). Fierce opposition to the proposal resulted in its being dropped. It would be pleasant to think that this reflected a clearer understanding of the problem by the electorate than by the government. Unfortunately, the real reason it was dropped was because of economic illiteracy in Congress.

Anticipating objections that the tax would impose an unacceptable hardship on the poor, policy makers proposed to return the revenues from the tax to the people by reducing the payroll tax – the tax on wages that supports the social security system. But critics, mostly in Congress, ridiculed the proposal, stating that if the revenues from the tax were returned to the people, the quantity of motor fuel demanded would remain essentially the same. Their argument tipped the debate, and officials never managed to implement the proposal. The argument was, however, nonsensical. Can you see why? Check back to Chapter 4.

In the context of the huge increase in oil prices in 2007–2008 the issue of supply security became entangled in concerns over global warming. In 2008 this resulted in calls for regulations in the USA and Europe to speed up shifts to renewables in order to reduce the dependence of Western economies on (high-priced) imported oil. There may be a case for regulation to take externalities into account and tackle global warming, but to use it to reduce dependency on imported oil is highly questionable. The fact is, however, that there is no security of supply problem for oil as long as users are prepared to pay the going price and producers want to sell the stuff. If the going price rises, other energy sources will be substituted for oil without the need for regulation. As regards the price of oil, if importing countries really want to drive down the world price of oil, the best thing they can do is collectively to increase taxes on oil consumption. Likely to happen? Not while Western countries such as Britain and the USA continue to produce a substantial proportion of their oil needs themselves, and their oil companies would suffer from a fall in oil prices. In addition, the political reaction of consumers to higher oil taxes makes such decisions unlikely.

However, it is well known that consumers have a weak intellectual grasp of the impact of regulation, so using regulation to reduce consumption may be politically more palatable than using taxes and prices, even though the end result of the regulation will be to reduce consumer real income by at least as much as a tax hike on consumption would.

The regulatory framework

First, let us look at how regulation is implemented. At its basis is some form of legislative intervention that has the effect of modifying individuals' or firms' behaviour in the context of the legal framework of property rights and contract law that underpins the workings of markets. Without an adequate legal framework markets cannot function efficiently. Change that framework and you will change how firms and individuals will behave in terms of market transactions.

That is not to say there are no markets without the legal institutions provided by a state as we know it. A really good example of markets functioning in an almost lawless environment on a wide scale is what has happened in Somalia since the 1980s.[1] There are burgeoning markets in most goods and many relatively technologically complex services in a territory that has no functioning government making and enforcing laws. Instead, local warlords provide a set of enforced property rights, and enforce contracts where necessary ... and take a cut of the action (a sort of informal tax system).

Within states with the full panoply of legal property rights and legal enforcement, markets can function outside the law. Prohibition in the United States gave the world the spectacle of a well-developed market in alcoholic drink entirely outside the law. And, while by definition the law does not provide the basis for exchange in illegal goods and services (such as heroin or prostitution), there are markets for those goods and services, with buyers and sellers. But transactions in these markets are very costly compared with transactions in markets that rely on the legal establishment and enforcement of property rights and contractual relations.

The legal framework lays down the ground rules for *market exchange*. Changes in that framework are the first form of regulation to be considered. For example, governments all over the world lay down by law certain workers' rights that supersede simple contracts between employers and employees (pay rates, statutory notice periods, statutory holiday entitlements, entitlements to redundancy payments, working time restrictions, and so on). Minimum wage legislation is the most obvious case in point. Trades unions are usually exempt from parts of the law on contracts that firms must

---

1 If you are interested, read Cockburn (2002), which has provided the basis for this account of a market without laws.

respect (ever since the 1906 Trades Disputes Act, unions in Britain have enjoyed a degree of protection from actions for breach of contract in relation to their members' activities in pursuing grievances). Germany was notorious for legal restrictions on opening hours for retail establishments that made German cities and towns commercial dead zones at weekends. In Italy, shops must close for a weekly rest period. In France only a very small number of outlets (known as 'tabacs') may sell tobacco. France has also introduced (but subsequently has been forced to modify) a 35-hour working week. In virtually all countries you cannot practise medicine unless you possess a set of qualifications laid down by law. In many countries there are legal restrictions on price cutting. For example, in some EU countries it is prohibited to sell a range of goods at less than the price on the invoice covering their purchase by a retailer.

In these cases we have examples of *direct legislative regulation*. The law defines the permissible range of activities, and the normal procedures for law enforcement are used to make sure the restrictions are respected.

While economists have always been interested in such basic forms of regulation and their consequences, most attention has been paid to the operations of *delegated regulation*. This refers to the system whereby the legislature sets up a body to regulate an industry or market along certain lines proscribed by legislation, and makes the agency so created the legal regulatory body. It in turn issues legally binding regulations and decisions affecting the structure and/or performance of the entities covered in its remit.

Some agencies exist to moderate particular aspects of behaviour across all sectors of the economy. For example, there are two US agencies, the Department of Justice and the Federal Trade Commission, that act to regulate market behaviour by firms to counter abuse of market power. Under EU law all member states must have a 'competition authority' (although not necessarily using exactly that title: in the United Kingdom it has been the Competition Commission since 2000; in France it is the *Conseil de Concurrence*, or Competition Council). Subject to the guidelines set down under national and EU law, it is responsible for the implementation of competition policy within the member states. It polices markets in general to deal with problems such as collusive fixing of prices, and can stop or modify M&As that are larger than a defined threshold size. National competition authorities operate in collaboration with the Competition Directorate of the EU Commission that concerns itself with competition matters having a wider dimension than the member state, and whose findings have binding effects on the decisions of the national authorities. Competition Commissions have been established in virtually all 'advanced' countries, and even in some less so, over the last 30 years.

There are also sector-specific regulatory agencies. These supervise the performance of specific industries. These regulators can, for example, typically determine what prices the firm or firms in a sector may charge. The idea is that these are industries where technical considerations suggest that there will be only one (a natural monopoly) supplier or at best a small number of suppliers (reflecting substantial economies of scale). In the United Kingdom, acronyms like Ofcom are used (in this case, the office that regulates telecommunications).

In this chapter we shall look at regulatory intervention in markets in three areas in order to demonstrate the problems facing regulators and the benefits and costs of well-designed and poorly designed regulation. These are (i) regulation to deal with externality problems in the form of environmental degradation; (ii) health and safety regulation affecting household and labour market behaviour; and (iii) regulation of public utilities (in this case, electricity production and sale). The importance of the issues discussed is twofold.

First, there is the question of *regulatory design and practice*. Regulation is supposed to correct market failure. The benefits of regulation can be thought of as the reduction (or elimination) of the costs associated with market failure. Poor performance by the regulator (if an agency) or design of legal regulation (if it is direct regulation) will result in a smaller reduction in the costs of market failure – or, worse, an exacerbation of those costs.

Second, some questions are raised by *poor regulation*. Why does it happen? How can it be reduced as a problem?

Three case studies

1. Regulation to protect the environment from industrial pollution: using price incentives in environmental regulation

As we saw in Chapter 11, goods whose production generates negative externalities, such as atmospheric pollution, tend to be overproduced whenever negotiation among private parties is costly. Suppose we decide as a society that the best attainable outcome would be to have half as much pollution as would occur under completely unregulated conditions. In that case, how should the clean-up effort be distributed among those firms that currently discharge pollutants into the environment?

The most efficient – and hence best – distribution of effort is the one for which *each polluter's marginal cost of abatement is exactly the same*. To see why, imagine that under current arrangements the cost to one firm of removing a tonne of pollutant from the air is larger than the cost to another firm. Society could then achieve the same total reduction in pollution at lower cost by having the first firm discharge 1 tonne more into the air and the second firm 1 tonne less.

Unfortunately, government regulators seldom have detailed information on how the cost of reducing pollution varies from one firm to another. Traditionally, many pollution control regimes therefore require all polluters simply to cut back their emissions by the same proportion or to meet the same absolute emissions standards. If different polluters have different marginal costs of pollution abatement, however, these approaches will not be efficient. That is now changing, thanks to increased interest in using market devices to improve regulatory control of emissions.

Taxing pollution

Alternative policies can distribute the clean-up more efficiently, even if the government lacks detailed information about how much it costs different firms to curtail pollution. One method is to tax pollution and allow firms to decide for themselves how much pollutant to emit. Example 14.1 illustrates the logic of this approach.

Example 14.1 What is the least costly way to cut pollution by half?

Cost–Benefit Analysis

Each of two firms, Sludge Oil and Northwest Lumber, has access to five production processes, each of which has a different cost and creates a different amount of pollution. The daily costs of the processes and the number of tonnes of smoke emitted are shown in Table 14.1. Pollution is currently unregulated, and negotiation between the firms and those who are harmed by pollution is impossible, which means that each firm uses process A, the least costly. Each firm emits 4 tonnes of pollutant per day, for a total of 8 tonnes of pollutant per day.

Process (smoke)	A (4 tonnes/day)	B (3 tonnes/day)	C (2 tonnes/day)	D (1 tonne/day)	E (0 tonnes/day)
Cost to Sludge Oil (€/day)	100	200	600	1,300	2,300
Cost to Northwest Lumber (€/day)	300	320	380	480	700

Table 14.1 **Costs and Emissions for Different Production Processes**

The government is considering two options for reducing total emissions by half. One is to require each firm to curtail its emissions by half. The other is to set a tax of €T per tonne of smoke emitted each day. How large must T be to curtail emissions by half? What would be the total cost to society under each alternative?

If each firm is required to cut pollution by half, each must switch from process A to process C. The result will be 2 tonnes per day of pollution for each firm. The cost of the switch for Sludge Oil will be €600 per day − €100 per day = €500 per day. The cost to Northwest Lumber will be €380 per day − €300 per day = €80 per day, for a total cost of €580 per day.

Consider now how each firm would react to a tax of €T per tonne of pollutant. If a firm can cut pollution by 1 tonne per day, it will save €T per day in tax payments. Whenever the cost of cutting a tonne of pollutant is less than €T, then each firm has an incentive to switch to a cleaner process. For example, if the tax were set at €40 per tonne, Sludge Oil would stick with process A, because switching to process B would cost €100 per day extra but would save only €40 per day in taxes. Northwest Lumber, however, would switch to process B, because the €40 saving in taxes would be more than enough to cover the €20 cost of switching.

Incentives Matter

The problem is that a €40 per day tax on each tonne of pollutant results in a reduction of only 1 tonne per day, 3 short of the 4 tonne target. Suppose instead that the government imposed a tax of €101 per tonne. Sludge Oil would then adopt process B, because the €100 extra daily cost of doing so would be less than the €101 saved in taxes. Northwest Lumber would adopt process D, because for every process up to and including C, the cost of switching to the next process would be less than the resulting tax saving.

Overall, then, a tax of €101 per tonne would result in the desired pollutant reduction of 4 tonnes per day. The total cost of the reduction would be only €280 per day (€100 per day for Sludge Oil and €180 per day for Northwest Lumber), or €300 per day less than when each firm was required to cut its pollution by half. (The taxes paid by the firms do not constitute a cost of pollution reduction, because the money can be used to reduce whatever taxes would otherwise need to be levied on citizens.)

Exercise 14.1 In Example 14.1, if the tax were €61 per tonne of pollutant emitted each day, which production processes would the two firms adopt?

Efficiency

The advantage of the tax approach is that it concentrates pollution reduction in the hands of the firms that can accomplish it *at least cost*. Requiring each firm to cut emissions by the same proportion ignores the fact that some firms can reduce pollution much more cheaply than others. Note that under the tax approach, the cost of the last tonne of smoke removed is the same for each firm, so the efficiency condition is satisfied.

One problem with the tax approach is that unless the government has detailed knowledge about each firm's cost of reducing pollution, it cannot know how high to set the pollution tax. A tax that is too low will result in too much pollution, while a tax that is too high will result in too little. Of course, the government could start by setting a low tax rate and gradually increasing the rate until pollution is reduced to the target level. But because firms often incur substantial *sunk costs* when they switch from one process to another, that approach might be even more wasteful than requiring all firms to cut their emissions by the same proportion.

Auctioning pollution permits

Another alternative is to establish a target level for pollution and then auction off permits to emit that level. The virtues of this approach are illustrated in Example 14.2.

Example 14.2 How much will pollution permits sell for?

Two firms, Sludge Oil and Northwest Lumber, again have access to the production processes described earlier (which are reproduced in Table 14.2). The government's goal is to cut the current level of pollution, 8 tonnes per day, by half. To do so, the government auctions off four permits, each of which entitles the bearer to emit 1 tonne of smoke per day. No smoke may be emitted without a permit. What price will the pollution permits fetch at auction, how many permits will each firm buy and what will be the total cost of the resulting pollution reduction?

Process (smoke)	A (4 tonnes/day)	B (3 tonnes/day)	C (2 tonnes/day)	D (1 tonne/day)	E (0 tonnes/day)
Cost to Sludge Oil (€/day)	100	200	600	1,300	2,300
Cost to Northwest Lumber (€/day)	300	320	380	480	700

Table 14.2 **Costs and Emissions for Different Production Processes**

If Sludge Oil has no permits, it must use process E, which costs €2,300 per day to operate. If it had one permit, it could use process D, which would save it €1,000 per day. Thus the most Sludge Oil would be willing to pay for a single 1 tonne pollution permit is €1,000 per day. With a second permit, Sludge Oil could switch to process C and save another €700 per day; with a third permit, it could switch to process B and save another €400; and with a fourth permit, it could switch to process A and save another €100. Using similar reasoning, we can see that Northwest Lumber would pay up to €220 for one permit, up to €100 for a second, up to €60 for a third and up to €20 for a fourth.

Suppose the government starts the auction at a price of €90. Sludge Oil will then demand four permits and Northwest Lumber will demand two, for a total demand of six permits. Since the government wishes to sell only four permits, it will keep raising the price until the two firms together demand a total of only four permits. Once the price reaches €101, Sludge Oil will demand three permits and Northwest Lumber will demand only one, for a total quantity demanded of four permits. Compared to the unregulated alternative, in which each firm used process A, the daily cost of the auction solution is €280: Sludge Oil spends €100 switching from process A to process B, and Northwest Lumber spends €180 switching from A to D. This total is €300 less than the cost of requiring each firm to reduce its emissions by half. (Again, the permit fees paid by the firms do not constitute a cost of clean-up, because the money can be used to reduce taxes that would otherwise have to be collected.)

Equilibrium

The auction method has the same virtue as the tax method: it concentrates pollution reduction in the hands of those firms that can accomplish it *at the lowest cost*. But the auction method has other attractive features that the tax approach does not have. First, it does not induce firms to commit themselves to costly investments that they will have to abandon if the clean-up falls short of the target level. And, second, it allows private citizens a direct voice in determining where the emission level will be set. For example, any group that believes the pollution target is too lenient could raise money to buy permits at auction. By keeping those permits locked away in a safe, the group could ensure that they will not be used to emit pollution.

emissions trading a system whereby firms can trade emission reductions, with the result that any given level of emissions reduction is undertaken by those with the lowest costs of achieving reductions

Several decades ago, when economists first proposed the auctioning of pollution permits, or **emissions trading**, outraged reactions were widely reported in the press, and in recent years the proposal has fallen foul of 'green' environmentalists. Most of those reactions amounted to the charge that the proposal would 'permit rich firms to pollute to their heart's content'. Such an assertion betrays a total misunderstanding of the forces that generate pollution. Firms pollute not because they *want* to pollute, but because dirty production processes are cheaper than clean ones. Society's only real interest is in keeping the *total amount of pollution* from becoming excessive, not in who actually does the polluting. And, in any event, the firms that do most of the polluting under an auction system will not be rich firms, but those for whom pollution reduction is least costly.

Comparative Advantage

Economists have argued patiently against these misinformed objections to the auction system, and their efforts have finally borne fruit. The sale of pollution permits is now common in several parts of the United States, and there is growing interest in other countries in such an approach.

Economic naturalist 14.1 Emissions trading in the EU: what can trading deliver?

As an instrument to achieve emissions reductions in line with the targets set at Kyoto the EU Commission published a Green Paper in 2000[2] outlining proposals for the establishment of a price-based mechanism to reduce emissions. This was the creation of an emissions trading regime. It envisaged the establishment of *national quotas* for emissions of carbon dioxide (CO_2), which the national governments would allocate and then permit firms to trade, buying or selling reflecting the costs of reducing emissions and the penalties for not doing so. The proposal provided the basis for a Council Directive in 2003[3] establishing an emissions trading regime and which set down national allocations. The emissions trading regime began to function in January 2005.

Ignoring differences of detail, the essence of the scheme is that which was described in Example 14.2. Faced with legally binding national requirements to reduce emissions (and fines for non-compliance), firms could either reduce emissions or purchase the right not to do so. Given a fixed allocation for each country, and, therefore, for the Union as a whole, this created a market in the right to emit greenhouse gases, with the allocation being subject to reduction to comply with Kyoto targets. By reducing emissions a firm created a *saleable asset* (the reduction) that it could retain or sell.

2 COM/2000/87, available on the Commission website: europa.eu.int/comm/index_en.htm.
3 Council Directive 2003/87/EC.

The implication, as in the examples above, is that a trading system would allocate the reduction in emissions as between firms (and, therefore, as between EU regions) in such a way as to ensure that the costs of reduction would be minimised.

A preliminary and somewhat aggregated estimate undertaken in 2000 suggested that if the EU15 were treated as six zones, and abatement costs in those zones were taken to represent the costs of reducing emissions, the cost of complying with Kyoto could be reduced by 25 per cent by permitting EU-wide emissions trading.[4] The annual cost with EU15-wide trading was estimated at 0.15 per cent of GDP for the EU15 as a whole. If the zones had to meet their targets without trading between zones, but using the most efficient means to reduce emissions within zones, the cost would amount to 0.20 per cent of GDP per annum. Using the most efficient methods within zones is equivalent to using emissions trading within zones.

Further work undertaken at the same time to establish the general cost implications of different approaches to managing emissions through regulation gives an idea of the degree to which different approaches affect the overall economic costs of reaching environmental targets. If we assumed that the target for emissions reduction agreed from achieving lower total liquid fuel usage is accepted and *then* imposed a national average target percentage emissions reduction on all sectors in each country across the EU15, the cost of reducing emissions by sector (as opposed to simply reducing liquid fuel usage) to reach Kyoto targets for CO_2 would be of the order of €20 billion per annum. If, however, we obtained the same total reduction based on permitting emissions trading within countries (i.e. the national target is met, but via trading within each country) the cost would be of the order of €9 billion per annum. This would be reduced further by €3 billion, or one-third, by permitting full EU15-wide trading.[5]

RECAP Using price incentives in environmental regulation

An efficient programme for reducing pollution is one for which the *marginal cost of abatement* is the same for all polluters. Taxing pollution has this desirable property, as does the auction of pollution permits. The auction method also has the advantage that regulators can achieve a desired abatement target without having detailed knowledge of the abatement technologies available to polluters.

2. Using regulation to counteract the exploitation of market power: market failure and regulatory failure – the Californian power crisis

Regulation to control the pricing of electricity has become a familiar part of the EU political and economic landscape since 1990. The proximate cause has been the decisions taken since the early 1990s to liberalise energy markets as part of the programme to create the single market envisaged in the Maastricht Treaty. Prior to this, and in the United Kingdom prior to the ideological revolution associated with the premiership of Margaret Thatcher, the norm in Europe was for state-owned monopoly supply systems to operate in each country or region. Generation, transmission and distribution of electricity was in general vertically integrated, with a single state-controlled entity being responsible for the three functions: producing power, transmitting current to the user and selling the power to the user. By retaining the firms in public ownership, it was believed that any tendency to use a monopoly position to raise prices would be eliminated, since the supplier's management was appointed by the government and

4 Institute for Prospective Technological Studies (IPTS) (2000). The IPTS is a Directorate-General Research Centre.

5 Capros and Mantzos (2000).

was subject to political control. Monopoly was believed to be unavoidable because it was generally accepted that electricity was a local (at least) natural monopoly.

In the United States, in contrast, the norm was for privately owned firms to produce and sell electricity. These firms were regional monopolies and, as in Europe, were in general vertically integrated. However, because they were privately owned it was felt necessary to subject them to regulatory control, in order to ensure that they could not abuse their monopoly position by generating huge profits by means of monopoly restrictions on output leading to higher prices to end users. So, regulation has been a feature of the US energy sector for much longer than in Europe.

From the late 1980s onwards there was growing pressure in California to 'deregulate' the electricity sector. Much of this came from the big power companies and from large commercial purchasers. The latter, under California's existing regulatory regime, had been paying higher prices for power in order to keep down prices to consumers and some politically sensitive commercial and other uses. In other words, these large commercial users were being obliged to *cross-subsidise* consumption of power by other users. In fact, 'deregulation' really meant 're-regulation' to permit increased competition in generation and distribution. Inevitably, this meant what has been referred to as 'rebalancing' of prices to reduce or eliminate cross-subsidisation between types of user, and to make power charges reflect the marginal cost of supplying power. That is what competitive markets do. Deregulation in 1996 was supposed to solve the industry's problems. As far as many in California were concerned, it did nothing, but rather resulted in the power crises of 2001 and 2002. These were put down by critics of deregulation to the short-term-maximising behaviour of the power companies.

However, one problem with the regulatory process is that it, too, is subject to failure. In the Californian case the regulatory regime discouraged power suppliers from investing in new capacity while simultaneously sheltering large numbers of consumers from paying the true cost of the power they were consuming (encouraging consumption of power in circumstances where the marginal willingness to pay was less than the marginal cost of production). This reflected the fact that the regulatory function had been 'captured' by powerful lobby groups. They ensured that prices to large numbers of end users were prevented from rising to reflect scarcity of capacity.

Rising demand (and supply problems arising from falling availability of low-cost power imports from hydroelectric sources in neighbouring states) led to shortages as domestic Californian generating capacity failed to expand to meet demand because price controls discouraged investment in new capacity while encouraging demand growth. The consequences in 2001–02 were a series of shortages leading to rationing and blackouts on a rolling basis.

Regulatory capture is seen by economists as a serious problem because it has the effect of perverting a process designed to reduce market failure so as to introduce further problems akin to those it was supposed to solve. In the Californian case, the regulatory process was captured by populist pressure groups. More often, however, the regulator may be captured by the entity being regulated. When this happens, regulation is used to protect producer interests at the expense of general economic efficiency. Classic cases of regulation protecting producer interest are where legislation permits self-regulation by a trade or profession. In recent years this has led to reforms in regulation procedures in areas such as legal services, accountancy services and some parts of the health services sector. Less obvious, but potentially equally damaging to economic efficiency, are cases where an 'independent' regulator is 'turned' over time by the industry being regulated. This can happen when the regulator depends on the industry being regulated for the information required to perform its functions.

3. Regulation and health and safety: remedying defective incentives

Workplace safety regulations

Most industrialised countries have laws that attempt to limit the extent to which workers are exposed to health and safety risks on the job. These laws often are described as necessary to protect workers against exploitation by employers with market power. Given the working conditions we saw in the early stages of the Industrial Revolution, the idea that such exploitation pervades unregulated private markets has intuitive appeal.

The miserable conditions of factory workers, juxtaposed with the often opulent lifestyle enjoyed by factory owners, seemed to affirm the idea that owners were exploiting workers. But if conditions in the factories were in fact too dangerous, how much safer should they have been?

Consider the question of whether to install a specific safety device – say, a guard rail on a lathe. Many people are reluctant to employ the Cost–Benefit Principle to answer such a question. To them, safety is an absolute priority, so the guard rail should be installed regardless of its cost. Yet most of us do not make personal decisions about our own health and safety that way. No one you know, for example, gets the brakes on his car checked every day, even though doing so would reduce the likelihood of being killed in an accident. The reason, obviously, is that daily brake inspections would be very costly and would not reduce the probability of an accident significantly compared with annual or semi-annual inspections.

The same logic can be applied to installing a guard rail on a lathe. If the amount one is willing to pay to reduce the likelihood of an accident exceeds the cost of the guard rail, it should be installed; otherwise, it should not be. And no matter how highly we value reducing the odds of an accident, we will almost surely settle for less than perfect safety. After all, to reduce the risk of an accident to nearly zero, one would have to enclose the lathe in a thick Plexiglas case and operate it with remote-controlled mechanical arms. Faced with the prohibitive cost of such an alternative, most of us would decide that the best approach is to add safety equipment whose benefit exceeds its cost and then exercise caution while operating the machine.

But will unregulated employers offer the level of workplace safety suggested by the Cost–Benefit Principle? Most nations appear to have decided that they will not. As noted, virtually every industrial country now has comprehensive legislation mandating minimum safety standards in the workplace – laws usually described as safeguards against the exploitation of workers.

Yet explaining safety regulation as an antidote for exploitation raises troubling questions. One difficulty stems from the economist's argument that competition for workers prods firms to provide the socially optimal level of amenities. For example, if an amenity – say, a guard rail on a lathe – costs €50 per month to install and maintain, and workers value it at €100 per month, then the firm must install the device or risk losing workers to a competitor that does. After all, if a competing firm were to pay workers €60 per month less than they currently earn, it could cover the cost of the device with €10 to spare, while providing a compensation package that is €40 per month more attractive than the first employer's.

Critics respond to this argument that in practice there is very little competition in the labour market. They argue that incomplete information, worker immobility and other frictions create situations in which workers have little choice but to accept whatever conditions employers offer. Alternatively, they argue that workers are poorly informed and unable to make 'rational' decisions in relation to health and safety.

Finally, there is an argument to the effect that people will take more risks if someone else pays the costs. If society is committed to paying for medical treatment or to replacing earnings in the case of workplace injuries, this introduces 'moral hazard' and a higher level of injury than if workers and employers had to meet these costs.

The first of these arguments has the following weakness: even if a firm were the only employer in the market, it would still have an incentive to install a €50 safety device that is worth €100 to the worker. Failure to do so would be to leave cash on the table.

The defective information argument, too, is troubling, because competing firms would have a strong incentive to call the devices to the workers' attention. If the problem is that workers cannot move to the competing firm's location, then the firm can set up a branch near the exploited workers. Collusive agreements to restrain such competition should prove difficult to maintain, because each firm can increase its profit by cheating on the agreement.

In fact, worker mobility between firms is high, as is entry by new firms into existing markets; and, as noted in Chapter 10, cartel agreements have always been notoriously unstable. Information may not be perfect, but if a new employer in town is offering a better deal, sooner or later word gets around.

Finally, if, despite these checks, some firms still manage to exploit their workers, we should expect those firms to earn a relatively high profit. But in fact we observe just the opposite. Year in and year out, firms that pay the *highest* wages are the most profitable. And so we are left with a puzzle. The fear of exploitation by employers with market power has led governments to adopt sweeping and costly safety regulations; yet the evidence suggests that exploitation cannot be a major problem. As Example 14.3 suggests, however, safety regulation might prove useful even in a perfectly competitive environment with complete information.

The strongest argument is the third one: regulation is designed to shelter taxpayers from the costs of accidents. There is, however, another interesting argument in favour of regulation, derived from the tools of game theory we developed in Chapter 10.

Example 14.3 Will Don and Michael choose the optimal amount of safety?

Suppose Don and Michael are the only two members of a hypothetical community. They get satisfaction from three things – their income, safety on the job and their position on the economic ladder. Suppose Don and Michael must both choose between two jobs, a safe job that pays €50 per week and a risky job that pays €80 per week. The value of safety to each is €40 per week. Having more income than one's neighbour is worth €40 per week to each; having less income than one's neighbour means a €40 per week reduction in satisfaction. (Having the same income as one's neighbour means no change in satisfaction.) Will Don and Michael make the best job choices possible in this situation?

Viewed in isolation, each person's decision should be to take the safe job. Granted, it pays €30 per week less than the risky job, but the extra safety it offers is worth €40 per week. So aside from the issue of relative income, the value of the safe job is €90 per week (its €50 salary plus €40 worth of safety), or €10 per week more than the risky job.

Once we incorporate concerns about relative income, however, the logic of the decision changes in a fundamental way. Now the attractiveness of each job depends on the job chosen by the other. The four possible combinations of choices and their corresponding levels of satisfaction are shown in Figure 14.1. If each man chooses a safe job, he will get €50 of income, €40 worth of satisfaction from safety and – because each will have the same income – zero satisfaction from relative income. So if each man chooses the safe job, each will get a total of €90 worth of satisfaction. If, instead, each man chooses the risky job, each will get €80 of income, zero satisfaction from safety, and because each has the same income as the other, zero satisfaction from relative income. If we compare the upper-left cell of Figure 14.1 with the lower-right cell, then, we can say unequivocally that Don and Michael would be happier if each took a safe job at lower income than if each chose a risky job with more income.

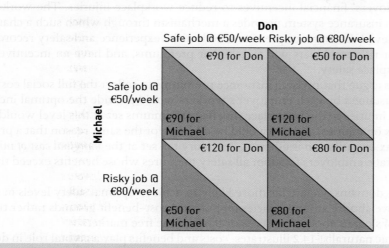

Figure 14.1 The Effect of Concern about Relative Income on Worker Choices Regarding Safety.

But consider how the choice plays out once the two men recognise their *interdependence*. Suppose, for example, that Michael chooses the safe job. If Don then chooses the unsafe job, he ends up with a total of €120 of satisfaction – €80 in salary plus €40 from having more income than Michael. Michael, for his part, ends up with only €50 worth of satisfaction – €50 in salary plus €40 from safety, minus €40 from a having lower income than Don. Alternatively, suppose Michael chooses the risky job. Then Don will again do better to accept the risky job, for by doing so he gets €80 worth of satisfaction rather than €50.

In short, no matter which job Michael chooses, Don will get more satisfaction by choosing the risky job. Likewise, no matter which job Don chooses, Michael will do better by choosing the risky job. Yet when each follows his dominant strategy, they end up in the lower-right cell of the table, which provides only €80 per week of satisfaction to each – €10 less than if each had chosen the safe job. Thus their job–safety choice confronts them with a prisoner's dilemma (see Chapter 10). As in all such situations, when the players choose independently, they fail to make the most of their opportunities.

Exercise 14.2 How would your answer to the question posed in Example 14.3 have differed if the value of safety had been not €40 per week, but €20?

Example 14.3 suggests an alternative explanation for safety regulation, one that is not based on the need to protect workers from exploitation. If Don and Michael could choose collectively, they would pick the safe job and maximise their combined satisfaction. Thus each might support legislation that establishes safety standards in the workplace.

Regulation, however, does not always improve matters. The labour market may not be perfect, but government regulators aren't perfect either.

The issue is not that there is no role for regulation, but that it is not clear that the regulations imposed are not more onerous than are necessary to correct the market failure, whatever it is. For this reason many economists favour programmes that increase employers' financial incentives to reduce workplace injuries. The worker's compensation insurance system provides a mechanism through which such a change might be achieved. If insurance premiums reflect the experience and safety record of the firm, poor risk employers will face higher premiums, and have an incentive to increase workplace safety.

Economists argue that revising insurance premiums to reflect the full social cost of the injuries sustained by each employer's workers would provide the optimal incentive to curtail injuries in the workplace. In effect, premiums set at this level would be an optimal tax on injuries, and this would be efficient for the same reason that a properly chosen tax on pollution is efficient. An injury tax set at the *marginal cost of injury* would encourage employers to adopt all safety measures whose benefits exceed their costs.

As in other domains, we are far more likely to achieve optimal safety levels in the workplace if we choose among policies on practical cost–benefit grounds rather than on the basis of slogans about the merits or flaws of the free market.

As Economic naturalist 14.2 illustrates, costs and benefits play a pivotal role in decisions about whether the government chooses to constrain individual choice in the safety domain, and, if so, how.

Economic naturalist 14.2 Why does the government require safety seats for infants who travel in cars, but not for infants who travel in aeroplanes?

A mother cannot legally drive her six-month-old son to a nearby grocery shop without first strapping him into a government-approved safety seat. Yet she can fly with him from London to Rome with no restraining device at all. Why this difference?

In case of an accident – whether in a car or an aeroplane – an infant who is strapped into a safety seat is more likely to escape injury or death than one who is unrestrained. But the probability of being involved in a serious accident is hundreds of times higher when travelling by car than when travelling by air, so the benefit of having safety seats is greater for trips made by car. Using safety seats is also far more costly on plane trips than on car trips. Whereas most cars have plenty of extra room for a safety seat, parents might need to purchase an extra ticket to use one on an aeroplane. Most parents appear unwilling to pay €600 more per trip for a small increment in safety, for either themselves or their children. So much for the view that human life is priceless!

RECAP Workplace safety regulation

Most countries regulate safety in the workplace, a practice often defended as needed to protect workers from being exploited by employers with market power. Yet safety regulation might be attractive even in perfectly competitive labour markets, because the *social payoff* from investment in safety often exceeds the private payoff. An injury tax set at the *marginal cost of injury* would encourage optimal investment in workplace safety.

Public health and safety

Because public health and law enforcement officials are charged with protecting our health and safety, political leaders are often reluctant to discuss expenditures on public health and law enforcement in cost–benefit terms. But because we live in a world of scarcity, we cannot escape the fact that spending more in these areas means spending less on other things of value.

Illnesses, like accidents, are costly to prevent. The socially optimal expenditure on a health measure that reduces a specific illness is that amount for which the marginal benefit to society of the measure exactly equals its marginal cost. For example, in deciding how much to spend on vaccinating against measles, a rational public health policy would expand the proportion of the population vaccinated until the marginal cost of an additional vaccination was exactly equal to the marginal value of the illnesses thus prevented.

As Economic naturalist 14.3 illustrates, however, the decision whether to be vaccinated looks very different from each individual's perspective.

Economic naturalist 14.3 Why do most governments encourage (and some actually require) vaccination against childhood illnesses?

Recent evidence on the epidemiology of vaccination has finally laid to rest the hypothesis that the combined inoculation of young children by one injection against measles, mumps and rubella (MMR) is linked to autism. While this fear was prevalent there was strong resistance to the MMR vaccination, especially in the United Kingdom but also in other countries in Europe. The government line was consistent: even before the link was shown almost certainly not to exist, the benefits from the MMR injection greatly outweighed the costs, and it continued to encourage people to use the procedure.

This raises an interesting question. Why should the government encourage and subsidise vaccination? Free or highly subsidised vaccination against a variety of illnesses is a common feature of most advanced countries' health and social welfare systems. In some cases, vaccination is effectively compulsory in that access to state-financed education is conditional on a child's having been vaccinated. In the United States, proof of immunisation against diphtheria, measles, poliomyelitis and rubella is now universally required for entry into state schools. Most states also require immunisation against tetanus (49 states), pertussis (whooping cough) (44 states), mumps (43 states) and hepatitis B (26 states). Why these requirements?

Being vaccinated against a childhood illness entails a small but potentially serious risk. The vaccine against pertussis, for example, is believed to cause some form of permanent brain damage in 1 out of every 110,000 children vaccinated. Contracting the disease itself also poses serious health risks, and in an environment in which infections were sufficiently likely to occur, individuals would have a compelling reason to bear the risk of being vaccinated in order to reduce the even larger risk from infection. The problem is that in an environment in which most children were vaccinated, infection rates would be low, making the risk of vaccination loom understandably large in the eyes of individual families. The ideal situation from the perspective of any individual family would be to remain unvaccinated in an environment in which all other families were vaccinated. But as more and more families decided to forgo vaccination, infection rates would mount. Eventually the vaccination rate would stabilise at the point at which the additional risk to the individual family of becoming vaccinated would be exactly equal to the risk from remaining unvaccinated. But this calculation ignores the fact that a decision to remain unvaccinated poses risk not just to the individual decision maker, but also to others who have decided to become vaccinated (since no vaccine affords 100 per cent protection against infection).

Relegating the vaccination decision to individuals results in a sub-optimally low vaccination rate, because individual decision makers fail to take adequate account of the cost that their becoming infected will impose on others. It is for this reason that most states require vaccinations against specific childhood illnesses.

Government in the economy: producing public goods

The second area of government activity that we want to consider is that of the government acting as a producer of goods and services that are either consumed or are inputs into further production. Economists usually consider such outputs under two headings: **merit goods** and **public goods**.

merit goods goods produced under non-market conditions by the state for political reasons

public good a good or service that, to at least some degree, is both non-rival and non-excludable

Merit goods are goods that could be, and frequently are, produced in markets, but for political reasons are produced under non-market conditions by the state. Obvious examples are health services (e.g. the UK NHS), education and housing. All these can be, and are, produced in markets in nearly all countries ... but are also produced by (or for) the state to allocate on a basis other than conventional demand expressed in terms of willingness to pay.

The term 'public goods' is used to describe certain outputs that for technical reasons simply cannot be produced efficiently if production is left to the interaction of the supply and demand sides of a market. By 'efficiently' is meant production resulting in the quantity being produced being that for which marginal benefits equal marginal costs.

The involvement of the state in the provision of merit goods is pervasive, but in the end reflects political rather than economic pressures. Public goods provision, on the other hand, is the consequence of purely economic factors affecting the potential for market provision of certain types of output. As we shall see, the provision of public goods requires collective decisions on whether to produce them, how much to produce and finding the money to pay for provision.

Public goods versus private goods

Government spending in OECD countries is equivalent to 30–50 per cent of GNP, varying between countries. Much of this is, of course, *redistribution*. But typically half or more represents the cost of government direct provision of goods and services (the justice system, for example, or defence forces' salaries). Another tranche represents purchases of the output of private-sector firms (for example, when roads, hospitals or ground attack fighters are produced).

non-rival good a good whose consumption by one person does not diminish its availability for others

non-excludable good a good that it is difficult, or costly, to exclude non-payers from consuming

In many cases these are 'merit' goods: goods whose production could efficiently be left to markets but, for political reasons, usually distributive, are determined by political choices. In the other cases, and in the case of some goods that might be treated as merit goods, the spending is on what are described as 'public' goods. In this treatment of the government as an *economic agent* we will be considering the issue of public goods provision.

Public goods are those goods or services that are, in varying degrees, **non-rival** and **non-excludable**. A non-rival good is one whose consumption by one person does not diminish its availability for others. For example, if the armed forces prevent a hostile nation from invading your city, your enjoyment of that protection does not diminish its value to your neighbours. A good is non-excludable if it is difficult to exclude non-payers from consuming it. For instance, even if your neighbours don't pay their share of the cost of maintaining an army, they will still enjoy its protection.

Another example of a non-rival and non-excludable good is a terrestrial (i.e. not via cable or satellite) TV broadcast of *ER*, *Coronation Street* or *Match of the Day*. The fact that you tune in one evening does not make the programme any less available to others, and once the broadcast has been beamed out over the airwaves it is difficult to prevent anyone from tuning in. Similarly, when the millennium celebrations in many cities across the world involved magnificent fireworks displays, the municipal authorities concerned couldn't charge people for watching given the fact that the display was (and had to be) visible over a wide area. Curiously, private individuals could charge viewers if they owned or provided a limited amount of superior viewing facilities.

In contrast, the typical private good is diminished one-for-one by any individual's consumption of it. For instance, when you eat a sandwich, it is no longer available for anyone else. Moreover, people can easily be prevented from consuming sandwiches if they don't pay.

Exercise 14.3 Which of the following, if any, is non-rival?
  a. The website of the EU Commission at 3 am.
  b. The World Cup soccer championship game watched in person.
  c. The World Cup soccer championship game watched on TV.

Goods that are both highly non-excludable and non-rival are often called **pure public goods**. Two reasons favour government provision of such goods. First, for-profit private companies would have obvious difficulty recovering their cost of production. Many people might be willing to pay enough to cover the cost of producing the good, but if it is non-excludable, the company cannot easily charge for it (an example of the free-rider problem discussed in Chapter 12). And, second, if the marginal cost of serving additional users is zero once the good has been produced, then charging for the good would be inefficient, even if there were some practical way to do so.

pure public good a good or service that, to a high degree, is both non-rival and non-excludable

collective good a good or service that, to at least some degree, is non-rival but excludable

pure private good one for which non-payers can easily be excluded and for which each unit consumed by one person means one unit fewer available for others

This inefficiency often characterises the provision of **collective goods** – non-rival goods for which it is possible to exclude non-payers. Pay-per-view cable television is an example. People who don't pay to get Sky TV may be unable to view some programmes as soon as subscribers. Remember the controversy over whether or not certain football games could be restricted to pay-TV channels? Since the marginal cost to society of those excluded from viewing is literally zero, excluding these viewers is wasteful.

A **pure private good** is one from which non-payers can easily be excluded and for which one person's consumption creates a one-for-one reduction in the good's availability for others. The theory of perfectly competitive supply developed in Chapter 5 applies to pure private goods, of which basic agricultural products are perhaps the best examples.

pure commons good one for which non-payers cannot easily be excluded and for which each unit consumed by one person means one unit fewer available for others

A **pure commons good** is a rival good that is also non-excludable, so called because goods with this combination of properties almost always result in a tragedy of the commons (see Chapter 11). Fish in ocean waters are an example.

The classification scheme defined by the non-rival and non-excludable properties is summarised in Table 14.4. The columns of the table indicate the extent to which one person's consumption of a good fails to diminish its availability for others. Goods in the right-hand column are non-rival, and those in the left-hand column are not. The rows of Table 14.4 indicate the difficulty of excluding non-payers from consuming the good. Goods in the top row are non-excludable, those in the bottom row, excludable. Private goods (lower-left cell) are rival and excludable. Public goods (upper-right cell) are non-rival and non-excludable. The two hybrid categories are commons goods (upper-left cell), which are rival but non-excludable, and collective goods (lower-right cell), which are excludable but non-rival.

		Non-rival	
		Low	High
Non-excludable	High	Commons good (fish in the ocean)	Public good (national defence)
	Low	Private good (wheat)	Collective good (pay-per-view TV)

Table 14.4 **Private, Public and Hybrid Goods**

Collective goods are provided sometimes by government, sometimes by private companies. Most pure public goods are provided by government, but even private companies can sometimes find profitable ways of producing goods that are both non-rival *and* non-excludable. An example is broadcast radio and TV, which covers its costs by selling airtime to advertisers.

The mere fact that a good is a pure public good does not necessarily mean that government ought to provide it. On the contrary, the only public goods the government should even *consider* providing are those whose benefits exceed their costs. The cost of a public good is simply the sum of all the explicit and implicit costs incurred to provide it. The benefit of a public good is measured by asking how much people would be willing to pay for it. Although that sounds similar to the way we measure the benefit of a private good, an important distinction exists. The benefit of an additional unit of a private good, such as a cheeseburger, is the highest sum that any individual buyer would be willing to pay for it. In contrast, the benefit of an additional unit of a public good, such as an additional broadcast episode of *Sesame Street*, is the sum of the reservation prices of all people who will watch that episode.

Even if the amount that all beneficiaries of a public good would be willing to pay exceeds its cost, government provision of that good makes sense only if there is no other less costly way of providing it. For example, whereas city governments often pay for fireworks displays, they almost invariably hire private companies to put on these events. Finally, if the benefit of a public good does not exceed its cost, we are better off without it.

Paying for public goods

Not everyone benefits equally from the provision of a given public good. For example, some people find fireworks displays highly entertaining, but others simply don't care about them and still others actively dislike them. Ideally, it might seem that the most equitable method of financing a given public good would be to tax people in proportion to their willingness to pay for the good. To illustrate this approach, suppose Jones values a public good at €100, Smith values the same good at €200 and the cost of the good is €240. Jones would then be taxed €80, and Smith would be taxed €160. The good would be provided, and each taxpayer in this example would reap a surplus equal to 25 per cent of his tax payment: €20 for Jones, €40 for Smith.

In practice, however, government officials usually lack the information they would need to tax people in proportion to their willingness to pay for specific public goods. (Think about it: if a tax official asked you how much you would be willing to pay to have a new motorway and you knew you would be taxed in proportion to the amount you responded, what would you say?) Examples 14.4–14.6 illustrate some of the problems that arise in financing public goods, and suggest possible solutions to these problems.

Example 14. 4 Will rural roads in Tuscany be upgraded?

One of the picturesque features of the rolling and mountainous countryside in Tuscany, Umbria and Le Marche in Italy is the number of 'white' (i.e. unpaved) roads that wander between fields, vineyards and olive groves to small groups of houses. Unfortunately, although picturesque, they wreck car suspensions, and in the winter are frequently impassable. So why are they not upgraded to tarmac by the households using them?

Two families, the Camerons and the Sarkozys, have holiday villas in Le Marche, side by side at the end of a 2 km white road some distance up the Sibillini from Sarnano. Fed up with replacing shock absorbers, and being unable to use the villas during the ski season, they are considering the question of upgrading the road. A local construction firm, Fratelli Berlusconi, has quoted a price of €10,000 to do the job. Both families feel very strongly about having the road upgraded, but because the Sarkozys earn twice what the Camerons earn they differ as to willingness to pay. For the Sarkozys, richer, with twice the income of the Camerons, and having more visitors, it is worth €8,000. To the Camerons, with less money and being less sociable, it is worth only €4,000. Would either family be willing to foot the bill individually? Is it efficient for them to share the cost?

Neither will pay the full cost individually because each has a reservation price that is *below its cost*. But because the two together value the upgrading of the road at €12,000, sharing the cost would be socially efficient. If they were to do so, total economic surplus would be increased by €2,000. Since sharing the cost is the efficient outcome, we might expect that the Camerons and the Sarkozys would quickly reach agreement to finance the project. Unfortunately, however, the joint purchase and sharing of facilities is often more easily proposed than accomplished. One hurdle is that people must incur costs merely to get together to discuss joint purchases. With only two people involved, those costs might not be significant. But if hundreds or thousands of people were involved, communication costs could be prohibitive.

With large numbers of people, the free-rider problem also emerges (see Chapter 12). After all, everyone knows that the project will either succeed or fail independently of any one person's contribution to it. Everyone thus has an incentive to withhold contributions – or get a free ride – in the hope that others will contribute.

Finally, even when only a few people are involved, reaching agreement on a fair sharing of the total expense may be difficult. For example, the Sarkozys and the Camerons might be reluctant to disclose their true reservation prices to one another because of what it revealed as to their relative incomes.

A solution could be to ask Fratelli Berlusconi to use its local knowledge to get the Comune of Sarnano to do the job. Unfortunately, the Comune is likely to argue that if the road is upgraded at the taxpayers' expense the two families will capture all the benefits while exporting the cost almost entirely to the other taxpayers. In any case, it is not clear to the Comune that the benefits actually exceed the costs. If they do, why do the two families not pay to get the job done? Now, if they were to consider allowing the Comune to tax them to pay for the work, the matter might be looked at again.

These practical concerns may lead us to empower government to buy public goods on our behalf. But, as Example 14.5 makes clear, this approach does not eliminate the need to reach political agreement on how public purchases are to be financed.

Example 14.5 Will the Comune get consent to upgrade the road if it is financed by an 'equal tax' rule?

Suppose the two families could ask the Comune to help broker the road upgrading. And suppose that the regional government's tax policy must follow a 'non-discrimination' rule that prohibits charging any citizen more for a public good than it charges his or her neighbour. Another rule is that public goods can be provided only if a majority of citizens approve of them. What will happen?

> **poll tax** a tax that collects the same amount from every taxpayer
>
> **regressive tax** a tax under which the proportion of income paid in taxes declines as income rises

A tax that collects the same amount from every citizen is called a **poll tax**. A poll tax is an example of a **regressive tax**, one for which the proportion of a taxpayer's income that is paid in taxes declines as the taxpayer's income rises. If the Comune must rely on a poll tax, it must raise €5,000 from each family. But since the upgrading is worth only €4,000 to the Camerons, they will vote against the project, thus denying it a majority.

This is a general problem with poll tax finance, leaving aside considerations of fairness. The point is not confined to the specific public good considered. It applies whenever taxpayers place significantly different valuations on public goods, as will almost always happen whenever people earn significantly different incomes. An equal-tax rule under these circumstances will almost invariably rule out the provision of many worthwhile public goods.

As Example 14.6 suggests, one solution to this problem is to allow taxes to vary by income.

Example 14.6 Will the road be upgraded if the Comune can levy a proportional tax on income?

Incentives Matter

Suppose that the Camerons propose that the revenue be raised by imposing a proportional tax on income. Will the Sarkozys agree?

> **proportional income tax** one under which all taxpayers pay the same proportion of their incomes in taxes

A **proportional income tax** is one under which all taxpayers pay the same percentage of their incomes in taxes. Under such a tax, the Sarkozys would support the proposal because, otherwise, each family would fail to enjoy a public good whose benefit exceeds its share of its cost. Under the proportional tax on income, the Camerons would contribute €3,333 towards the €10,000 cost of the road and the Sarkozys would contribute €6,667. The road would be upgraded, resulting in additional surpluses of €667 for the Camerons and €1,333 for the Sarkozys.

Economic naturalist 14.4 makes the point that just as equal contributions are often a poor way to pay for public goods, they are also often a poor way to share expenses within the household.

Economic naturalist 14.4 Why might a pre-nuptial agreement to share costs equally lead to a divorce?

Suppose David earns €20,000,000 per year while Victoria earns only €1,000,000. Given his income, David as an individual would probably want to spend much more than Victoria would on housing, travel, entertainment, education for their children, and the many other items they consume jointly. What will happen if the couple adopts a rule that each must contribute an equal amount towards the purchase of such items?

This rule would constrain the couple to live in a small (well, smaller) house, take only inexpensive vacations and skimp on entertainment, dining out and their children's education. It is therefore easy to see why David might argue for a change in the agreement. If Victoria's unwillingness to see spending rise could not be overcome, a divorce might be the only way out.

Public goods and jointly consumed private goods are different from individually consumed private goods in the following important way: different individuals are free to consume whatever quantity and quality of most private goods they choose to buy, but *jointly consumed goods must be provided in the same quantity and quality for all persons.*

As in the case of private goods, people's willingness to pay for public goods is generally an increasing function of income. Wealthy individuals tend to assign greater value to public goods than low-income people do, not because the wealthy have different tastes but because they have more money. A poll tax (head tax) would result in high-income persons getting smaller amounts of public goods than they want. By increasing the total economic surplus available for all to share, a tax system that assigns a larger share of the tax burden to people with higher incomes makes possible a better outcome for both rich and poor alike. Indeed, virtually all industrialised nations have at least mildly **progressive tax** systems, which means that the proportion of income paid in taxes actually rises with a family's income.

progressive tax one in which the proportion of income paid in taxes rises as income rises

Progressive taxation and even proportional taxation have often been criticised as being unfair to the wealthy, who are forced to pay more than others for public goods that all consume in common. The irony in this charge, however, is that exclusive reliance on poll taxes, or even proportional taxes, would curtail the provision of public goods and services that are of greatest value to high-income families. Studies have shown, for example, that the income elasticity of demand for public goods such as parks and recreation facilities, clean air and water, public safety, uncongested roads and aesthetically pleasing public spaces is substantially greater than 1. Failure to rely on progressive taxation would result in gross underprovision of such public goods and services.

In the examples considered thus far, the question was whether to provide a particular public good and, if so, how to pay for it. In practice, we often confront additional questions about what *level* and *quality* of a public good to provide.

The demand curve for a public good

To calculate the socially optimal quantity of a public good, we must first construct the *demand curve* for that public good. The process for doing so differs in an important way from the one we use to generate the market demand curve for a private good.

For a private good, all buyers face the same price and each chooses the quantity she wishes to purchase at that price. Recall that to construct the demand curve for a private good from the demand curves for individual consumers, we place the individual demand curves side by side and add them horizontally. That is, for each of a series of fixed prices, we add the resulting quantities demanded on the individual demand curves. In Figure 14.2, for example, we add the individual demand curves for a private good, D_1 and D_2 (panels (a) and (b)), horizontally to obtain the market demand curve for the good D (panel (c)).

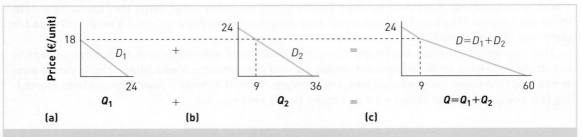

Figure 14.2 Generating the Market Demand Curve for a Private Good. To construct the market demand curve for a private good (c), we add the individual demand curves (a) and (b) horizontally.

For a public good, all buyers necessarily consume the same quantity, although each may differ in terms of willingness to pay for additional units of the good. Constructing the demand curve for a public good thus entails not horizontal summation of the individual demand curves but *vertical* summation. That is, for each of a series of quantity values, we must add the prices that individuals are willing to pay for an additional unit of the good. The curves D_1 and D_2 in Fig. 14.3(c) and (b) show individual demand curves for a public good by two different people. At each quantity, these curves tell how much the individual would be willing to pay for an additional unit of the public good. If we add D_1 and D_2 vertically, we obtain the total demand curve D for the public good (panel (a)).

Exercise 14.4   Bill and Tom are the only demanders of a public good. If Bill's demand curve is $P_B = 6 - 0.5Q$ and Tom's is $P_T = 1 - 2Q$, construct the demand curve for this public good.

In Example 14.7, we see how the demand curve for a public good might be used in conjunction with information about costs to determine the optimal level of public park provision in a city.

Example 14.7 What is the optimal quantity of urban park space?

The city government of a new, planned community must decide how much parkland to provide. The marginal cost curve and the public demand curve for urban parkland are as shown in Fig. 14.4. Why is the marginal cost curve upward-sloping and the demand curve downward-sloping? Given these curves, what is the optimal quantity of parkland?

The marginal cost schedule for urban parkland is upward-sloping because of the Low-Hanging-Fruit Principle (Chapter 2): the city acquires the cheapest parcels of land first, and only then turns to more expensive parcels. Likewise, the marginal willingness-to-pay (WTP) curve is downward-sloping because of the law of diminishing marginal utility. Just as people are generally willing to pay less for their fifth hot dog than for their first, they are also willing to pay less for the 101st ha of parkland than for the 100th ha. Given these curves, A^* is the optimal quantity of parkland. For any quantity less than A^*, the benefit of additional parkland exceeds its cost, which means that total economic surplus can be made larger by expanding the amount of parkland. For example, at A_0, the community would be willing to pay €200,000 for an additional hectare of urban parkland, but its cost is only €80,000. Similarly, for any quantity of parkland in excess of A^*, the community would gain more than it would lose by selling off some parkland.

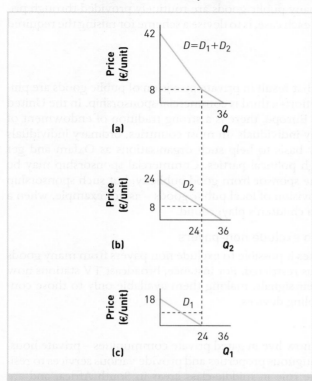

Figure 14.3 Generating the Demand Curve for a Public Good. To construct the demand curve for a public good (a), we add the individual demand curves (c) and (b) vertically.

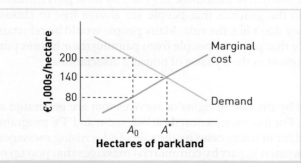

Figure 14.4 The Optimal Quantity of Parkland. The optimal number of hectares of urban parkland is A^*, the quantity at which the public's willingness to pay for additional parkland is equal to the marginal cost of parkland.

Private provision of public goods

One advantage of using the government to provide public goods is that once a tax collection agency has been established to finance a single public good, it can be expanded at relatively low cost to generate revenue for additional public goods. Another advantage is that because government has the power to tax, it can summarily assign responsibility for the cost of a public good without endless haggling over who bears what share of the burden. And in the case of goods for which non-payers cannot be excluded, the government may be the only feasible provider.

Exclusive reliance on government also entails disadvantages, however. Most fundamentally, the government's one-size-fits-all approach invariably requires many people to pay for public goods they don't want, while others end up having to do without public goods they want desperately. For example, many people vehemently oppose the provision of *any* sex education in schools, while others fervently believe that far more such instruction should be provided than is currently offered in most school curricula. In addition, mandatory taxation strikes many people as coercive, even if they approve of the particular public goods being provided.

It is no surprise, then, that governments are not the exclusive providers of public goods in any society. Indeed, many public goods are routinely provided through private channels. The challenge, in each case, is to devise a scheme for raising the required revenues.

Funding by donation

Two well-known mechanisms that result in private provision of public goods are philanthropy and volunteer work effort; a third is commercial sponsorship. In the United States, and to a lesser extent in Europe, there is a strong tradition of endowment of research and the arts by wealthy individuals. In most countries, ordinary individuals offer their time on a voluntary basis to help such organisations as Oxfam and get involved in political life through political parties. Commercial sponsorship may be motivated by the payback to the sponsor from good publicity, but such sponsorship frequently takes the form of provision of local public goods – as, for example, when a firm pays for improvements in a children's playground.

Development of new means to exclude non-payers

New electronic technology makes it possible to exclude non-payers from many goods that in the past could not be thus restricted. For instance, broadcast TV stations now have the ability to scramble their signals, making them available only to those consumers who purchase descrambling devices.

Private contracting

More than 8 million Americans now live in gated private communities – private housing associations that wall off contiguous properties and provide various services to residents. They are increasingly the rule in middle-class areas in South Africa, and are starting to become common in parts of Europe. Many of these associations provide security services, schools and fire protection and in other ways function much like ordinary local governments. Recognising that individual incentives may not be strong enough to assure socially optimal levels of maintenance and landscaping, these associations often bill home owners for those services directly. Many of the rules imposed by these associations are even more restrictive than those imposed by local governments, a distinction that is defended on the grounds that people are always free to choose some other neighbourhood if they don't like the rule. Many people would be reluctant to tolerate a municipal ordinance that prevents people from painting their houses purple, yet such restrictions are common in the by-laws of housing associations.

Sale of by-products

Many public goods are financed by the sale of rights or services that are generated as by-products of the public goods. For instance, as noted earlier, radio and TV programming is a public good that is paid for in many cases by the sale of advertising messages. Internet services are also underwritten in part by commercial messages that pop up or appear in the headers or margins of web pages. Franchising sales of souvenirs can be a means of financing the costs of maintaining heritage sites.

Given the quintessentially voluntary nature of privately provided public goods, it might seem that reliance on private provision might be preferred whenever it proved feasible. But, as Economic naturalist 14.5 makes clear, private provision often entails problems of its own.

Economic naturalist 14.5 Why do commercial TV channels favour programmes like *I'm a Celebrity* ... over Verdi operas?

In a given time slot, a television channel faces the alternative of broadcasting either *I'm a Celebrity ... Get Me Out of Here!* or Verdi's *Rigoletto*. Suppose that if it chooses *Celebrity*, it will win 20 per cent of the viewing audience, but only 18 per cent if it chooses *Rigoletto*. Suppose those who would choose *Celebrity* would collectively be willing to pay €20 million for the right to see that programme, while those who choose *Rigoletto* would be willing to pay €30 million. And suppose, finally, that the time slot is to be sponsored by a detergent company, that has acquired all the advertising airtime. Which programme will the network choose? Which programme would be socially optimal? The detergent maker cares primarily about the number of people who will see its advertisements, and their spending habits, and will thus choose the programme that will attract the largest audience, other things being equal – here, the *Celebrity* show. The fact that those who prefer *Rigoletto* would be willing to pay a lot more to see it is of little concern to the sponsor. But to identify the optimal result from society's point of view, we must take this difference into account. Because the people who prefer opera could pay the other viewers more than enough to compensate them for relinquishing the time slot, *Rigoletto* is the efficient outcome. But unless its supporters happen to buy more soap in total than the *Celebrity* viewers, the latter will prevail.

In short, reliance on advertising and other indirect mechanisms for financing public goods provides no assurance that the goods chosen will maximise economic surplus. This does not mean that it cannot be efficient. Even on the WTP figures already given it could be the case that it is still socially optimal. Suppose the detergent company is prepared to pay €15 million to sponsor the programme because it is a scarce resource that is of value to it, while the highest potential bidder for the slot if *Rigoletto* is played is a wine importer who would pay €3 million. The airtime is allocated to sponsor and audience with a joint willingness to pay €35 million if *Celebrity* is broadcast, as opposed to €33 million in the case of *Rigoletto*. These methods allow viewers to register not just which programmes they prefer but also the strength of their preferences, as measured by how much they are willing to pay. But although pay-per-view TV is more likely to select the programmes the public most values, it is also less efficient than broadcast TV in one important respect. As noted earlier, charging each household a fee for viewing discourages some households from tuning in. And since the marginal social cost of serving an additional household is exactly zero, limiting the audience in this way is inefficient. Which of the two inefficiencies is more important – free TV's inefficiency in choosing among programmes or pay-TV's inefficiency in excluding potential beneficiaries – is an empirical question. In any event, the mix between private and public provision of public goods and services differs substantially from society to society and from arena to arena within any given society. These differences depend on the nature of available *technologies* for delivering and paying for public goods, and also on people's *preferences*.

One way to avoid the inefficiency that arises when advertisers choose programming is to employ pay-per-view methods of paying for television programming.

Example 14.8 By how much is economic surplus reduced by a pay-per-view charge?

If a recently released movie is available on a pay-per-view channel on Thursdays at 10 pm, the demand curve for each episode is given by $P = 20 - Q$, where P is the price per household in euros and Q is the number of households who choose to watch the programme (in millions). If the regulated pay-per-view charge is €10 per household, by how much would economic surplus rise if the same episode were shown instead on 'free' network TV?

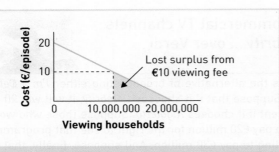

Figure 14.5 The Loss in Surplus from a Pay-per-view Fee. Twice as many households would watch the programme if its price were zero instead of €10. The additional economic surplus is the area of the shaded triangle, or €50 million.

With a fee of €10 per episode, 10 million households will watch (see Fig. 14.5). But if the same episode were shown on network TV, 20 million households would watch. The additional economic surplus reaped by the extra 10 million households is the area of the shaded triangle, €50 million. The marginal cost of permitting these additional households to watch is zero, so the total gain in surplus is €50 million. In general, charging a positive price for a good whose marginal cost is zero will result in a loss in surplus. As we saw in Chapter 7, the size of the loss that results when price is set above marginal cost depends on the *price elasticity of demand*. When demand is more elastic, the loss in surplus is greater. Exercise 14.5 provides an opportunity to see that principle at work.

Exercise 14.5 How would your answer to Example 14.8 have been different if the demand curve had been given instead by $P = 15 - 2Q$?

Summary

■ Governments intervene in the market economy in two ways (other than to redistribute income and wealth): they seek to correct *market failure*, and they produce a range of *goods and services*.

■ Just as markets are prone to market failure, policy makers need to recognise the possibility of *regulatory failure*. This arises when regulation is badly designed, or when the regulatory process is captured by those it seeks to regulate.

■ Regulatory design is exemplified by the issues involved in environmental regulation. An understanding of the forces that give rise to environmental pollution can help to identify those policy measures that will achieve a desired reduction in pollution at the lowest possible cost. Both the taxing of pollution and the sale of transferable pollution rights promote this goal. Each distributes the cost of the environmental clean-up effort so that the *marginal cost of pollution abatement* is the same for all polluters.

■ A perennially controversial topic is the application of the Cost–Benefit Principle to policies involving public health, safety and security. Many critics feel that the use of cost–benefit analysis in this domain is not morally legitimate, because it involves putting a monetary price on human life. Yet the fundamental principle of scarcity applies to human health and safety, just as it does to other issues. Spending more on public health and safety necessarily means spending less on other things of value. Failure to weigh the relevant costs and benefits, then, means that society will be *less likely to achieve its stated goals*.

■ One of government's principal tasks is to provide *public goods*, such as national defence and the criminal justice system. Such goods are, in varying degrees, *non-rival* and *non-excludable*. The first property describes goods for which one person's consumption does not diminish the amount available for others, while the second refers to the difficulty of preventing non-payers from consuming certain goods.

■ Goods that are both highly non-excludable and non-rival are often called *pure public goods*. A collective good – such as pay-per-view cable television – is non-rival but excludable. Commons goods are goods that are rival but non-excludable.

■ Because not everyone benefits equally from the provision of any given public good, charging all taxpayers equal amounts for the provision of public goods will generally not be either feasible or desirable. As in the case of private goods, people's WTP for public goods generally increases with income, and most governments therefore levy *higher taxes on the rich* than on the poor.

■ The criterion for providing the optimal quantity or quality of a public good is to keep increasing quantity or quality as long as the marginal benefit of doing so exceeds the marginal cost. One advantage of using the government to provide public goods is that once a tax collection agency has been established to finance a single public good, it can be expanded at relatively low cost to generate revenue to finance additional public goods. A second advantage is that because government has the power to tax, it can easily assign responsibility for the cost of a public good. And in the case of goods for which non-payers simply cannot be excluded, the *government may be the only feasible provider*.

■ One disadvantage to exclusive reliance on government for public goods provision is the element of coercion inherent in the tax system, which makes some people pay for public goods they don't want, while others do without public goods they do want. Many public goods are provided through private channels, with the necessary funding provided by donations, by sale of by-products, by development of new means to exclude non-payers and in many cases by private contract. A *loss in surplus* results, however, whenever monetary charges are levied for the consumption of a non-rival good.

Review questions

1. Why is vaccination against many childhood illnesses a legal requirement for entry into state-funded schools in the United States?

2. Why do economists believe that pollution taxes and effluent permits are a more efficient way to curb pollution than laws mandating across-the-board cutbacks?

3. Does it make sense to require more sophisticated and expensive safety equipment in large commercial passenger jets than in small private planes?

4. a. Which of the following goods are non-rival?
      Apples
      Stephen King novels
      Street lighting in college grounds
      Public service radio broadcasts

   b. Which of the goods in part (a) are non-excludable?

5. Give examples of goods that are, for the most part:
   a. rival but non-excludable
   b. non-rival but excludable
   c. both non-rival and non-excludable.

6. Why might even a wealthy person prefer a proportional income tax to a poll tax?

7. **True or false:** A tax on an activity that generates negative externalities will improve resource allocation in the private sector and also generate revenue that could be used to pay for useful public goods. Explain.

connect ## Problems

1. Two firms, Sludge Oil and Northwest Lumber, have access to five production processes, each one of which has a different cost and creates a different amount of pollution. The daily costs of the processes and the corresponding number of tonnes of smoke emitted are as shown in the table below.

Process (smoke)	A (4 tonnes/day)	B (3 tonnes/day)	C (2 tonnes/day)	D (1 tonne/day)	E (0 tonnes/day)
Cost to Sludge Oil (€/day)	50	70	120	200	500
Cost to Northwest Lumber (€/day)	100	180	500	1,000	2,000

   a. If pollution is unregulated, which process will each firm use, and what will be the daily smoke emission?

   b. The city council wants to curb smoke emissions by 50 per cent. To accomplish this, it requires each firm to curb its emissions by 50 per cent. What will be the total cost to society of this policy?

2. The city council in Problem 1 again wants to curb emissions by half. This time, it sets a tax of €T per day on each tonne of smoke emitted. How large will T have to be to effect the desired reduction? What is the total cost to society of this policy?

3. Refer to Problem 2. Instead of taxing pollution, the city council decides to auction off four permits, each of which entitles the bearer to emit 1 tonne of smoke per day. No smoke may be emitted without a permit. Suppose that the government conducts the auction by starting at €1 and asking how many permits each firm wants to buy at that price. If the total is more than four, it then raises the price by €1, and asks again, and so on, until the total quantity of demanded permits falls to four. How much will each permit sell for in this auction? How many permits will each firm buy? What will be the total cost to society of this reduction in pollution?

4. The table below shows all the marginal benefits for each voter in a small town whose town council is considering a new swimming pool with capacity for at least three citizens. The cost of the pool would be €18 per week and would not depend on the number of people who actually used it.

Voter	Marginal benefit (€/week)
A	12
B	5
C	2

    a. If the pool must be financed by a weekly poll tax levied on all voters, will the pool be approved by majority vote? Is this outcome socially efficient? Explain.

    b. The town council instead decides to auction a franchise off to a private monopoly to build and maintain the pool. If it cannot find such a firm willing to operate the pool, then the pool project will be scrapped. If all such monopolies are constrained by law to charge a single price to users, will the franchise be sold – and, if so, how much will it sell for? Is this outcome socially efficient? Explain.

5. Two consumers, Smith and Jones, have the following demand curves for broadcasts of recorded opera on Saturdays:

    Smith: $P_S = 12 - Q$
    Jones: $P_J = 12 - 2Q$

where P_S and P_J represent marginal willingness to pay values for Smith and Jones, respectively, and Q represents the number of hours of opera broadcast each Saturday.

    a. If Smith and Jones are the only broadcast listeners, construct the demand curve for opera broadcasts.

    b. If the marginal cost of opera broadcasts is €15 per hour, what is the socially optimal number of hours of broadcast opera?

References

Capros, P. and L. Mantzos (2000) *The Economic Effects of EU-wide Industry-level Emission Trading to Reduce Greenhouse Gases: Results from the PRIMES Energy Systems Model*, Brussels, May.

Cockburn, A. (2002) 'Somalia: a failed state?', *National Geographic Magazine*, July, www.findarticles.com/p/articles/mi_hb3343/is_200207/ai–n8059104.

Institute for Prospective Technological Studies (IPTS) (2000) *Preliminary Analysis of the Implementation of an EU-wide Permit Trading Scheme on CO$_2$ Emissions Abatement Costs: Results from the POLES Model*, Brussels, April.

Part 5

Macroeconomics: Issues and Data

Physical scientists study the world on many different scales, ranging from the inner workings of the atom to the vast dimensions of the cosmos. Although the laws of physics are thought to apply at all scales, scientists find that some phenomena are best understood 'in the small' and some 'in the large'. Although the range of scales they must deal with is much more modest than in physics, economists also find it useful to analyse economic behaviour at both the small-scale, or 'micro' level, and the large-scale, or 'macro' level. This section of the book introduces you to *macroeconomics*, the study of the performance of national economies. Unlike *microeconomics*, which focuses on the behaviour of individual households, firms and markets, macroeconomics takes a bird's-eye view of the economy. So, while a microeconomist might study the determinants of consumer spending on personal computers, macroeconomists analyse the factors that determine aggregate, or total, consumer spending. Experience has shown that, for many issues, the macroeconomic perspective is the more useful.

Chapter 15 begins our discussion of macroeconomics by introducing you to some of the key macroeconomic issues and questions. These include the search for the factors that cause economies to grow, productivity to improve and living standards to rise over long periods of time. Macroeconomists also study shorter-term fluctuations in the economy (called *recessions* and *expansions*), unemployment, inflation, and the economic interdependence among nations, among other topics. Macroeconomic policies – government actions to improve the performance of the economy – are of particular concern to macroeconomists, as the quality of macroeconomic policy making is a major determinant of a nation's economic health.

To study phenomena such as economic growth scientifically, economists must have accurate measurements. Chapters 16, 17 and 18 continue the introduction to macroeconomics by discussing how some key macroeconomic concepts are measured and interpreted. Chapter 16 discusses an important measure of the level of economic activity known as *gross* domestic product (GDP). Besides describing how GDP is constructed in practice, this chapter also discusses the issue of how it is related to the economic well-being of the typical person. Chapter 17 concerns the measurement of *the price level and inflation* and includes a discussion of the costs that inflation imposes on the economy, while Chapter 18 explains how *unemployment* is measured, and discusses several important labour market trends.

15

Macroeconomics: the Bird's-Eye View of the Economy

In 1929 the economies of large industrial countries such as the United Kingdom, France, Germany and the United States slowed dramatically. Faced with declining sales, factories, shipyards, mines, railway companies and other producers of goods and services cut their output levels, which in turn led to mass layoffs: between 1928 and 1932, the British unemployment rate increased from 10 to 22 per cent of the labour force. In some other countries, conditions were even worse. In Germany, which had never fully recovered from its defeat in the First World War, the economy's output declined by 16 per cent and nearly a third of all workers were without jobs. Indeed, the desperate economic situation was a major reason for Adolf Hitler's election as chancellor of Germany in 1933. Introducing extensive government control over the economy, Hitler rearmed the country and ultimately launched the Second World War.

Historians now refer to the years following 1929 as the Great Depression. How could such an economic catastrophe have happened? One often-heard hypothesis is that the Great Depression was caused by wild financial speculation especially in the United States, which provoked the stock market crash of 1929. But though stock prices may have been unrealistically high in 1929, there is little evidence to suggest that the fall in stock prices was a major cause of the Depression. A similar crash in October 1987, when stock prices fell a record 23 per cent in one day – an event comparable in severity to the crash of October 1929 – did not slow the economy significantly. Another reason to doubt that the 1929 stock market crash caused the Great Depression is that, far from being confined to the United States, the Depression was a worldwide event, affecting countries that did not have well-developed stock markets at the time. The more reasonable conclusion is that the onset of the Depression probably caused the stock market crash, rather than the other way round.

What *did* cause the Great Depression? Today most economists who have studied the period blame *poor economic policy making* in both Europe and the United States. Of course, policy makers did not set out to create an economic catastrophe. Rather, they fell prey to the misconceptions of the time about how the economy worked. In other words, the Great Depression, far from being inevitable, might have been avoided if only the state of economic knowledge had been better. From today's perspective, the

Great Depression was to economic policy making what the voyage of the *Titanic* was to ocean navigation.

One of the few benefits of the Great Depression was that it forced economists and policy makers of the 1930s to recognise that there were major gaps in their understanding of how the economy worked. This recognition led to the development of a new sub-field within economics, called *macroeconomics*. Recall from Chapter 1 that macroeconomics is the study of the performance of national economies and the policies governments use to try to improve that performance.

This chapter will introduce the subject matter and some of the tools of macroeconomics. Although understanding episodes such as the Great Depression remains an important concern of macroeconomists, the field has expanded to include the analysis of many other aspects of national economies. Among the issues that macroeconomists study are the sources of long-run economic growth and development, the causes of high unemployment and the factors that determine the rate of inflation. Appropriately enough in a world in which economic 'globalisation' preoccupies businesspeople and policy makers, macroeconomists also study how *national economies interact*. Since the performance of the national economy has an important bearing on the availability of jobs, wages and salaries, prices and inflation, as well as the cost of borrowing and the rate of return on saving, it is clear that macroeconomics addresses bread-and-butter issues that affect virtually everyone.

In light of the Great Depression, macroeconomists are particularly concerned with understanding how macroeconomic policies work and how they should be applied.

macroeconomic policies
government actions designed to affect the performance of the economy as a whole

Macroeconomic policies are government actions designed to affect the performance of the economy as a whole (as opposed to policies intended to affect the performance of the market for a particular good or service, such as sugar or haircuts). The hope is that by understanding more fully how macroeconomic policies affect the economy, economists can help policy makers do a better job – and avoid serious mistakes, such as those that were made during the Great Depression.

The major macroeconomic issues

We defined macroeconomics as the study of the performance of the national economy as well as the policies used to improve that performance. Let us now take a closer look at some of the major economic issues that macroeconomists study.

Economic growth and living standards

Although the wealthy industrialised countries (such as the United States, Canada, Japan and the countries of Western Europe) are certainly not free from poverty, hunger and homelessness, the typical person in those countries enjoys a standard of living better than at any previous time or place in history. By standard of living we mean the degree to which people have access to goods and services that make their lives easier, healthier, safer and more enjoyable. People with a high living standard enjoy more and better consumer goods: sports utility vehicles, camcorders, mobile phones and the like. But they also benefit from a longer life expectancy and better general health (the result of high-quality medical care, good nutrition and good sanitation), from higher literacy rates (the result of greater access to education), from more time and opportunity for cultural enrichment and recreation, from more interesting and

Scarcity

fulfilling career options, and from better working conditions. Of course, the Scarcity Principle will always apply – even for the citizens of rich countries, having more of one good thing means having less of another. But higher incomes make these choices much less painful than they would be otherwise. Choosing between a larger flat and a nicer car is much easier than choosing between feeding your children adequately and sending them to school, the kind of hard choice people in the poorest nations face all the time.

Americans and Europeans sometimes take their standard of living for granted, or even as a 'right'. But we should realise that the way we live today is radically different from the way people have lived throughout most of history. The current standard of living in Europe is the result of many years of *economic growth*, a process of steady increase in the quantity and quality of the goods and services the economy can produce. The basic equation is simple: the more we can *produce*, the more we can *consume*. Also, consumption does not only include cars, DVDs and foreign holidays, etc. It also includes access to the better health and education services that sustained economic growth makes possible.

Figure 15.1 shows how the output of the European and American economies has increased since 1900. (We discuss the measure of output used here, real gross domestic product (GDP), in Chapter 17.) European output is measured as the aggregate or total output of the 12 largest economies in Western Europe. Although output fluctuates at times, the overall trend has been unmistakably upwards. Indeed, in 2006, the output of the European economy was more than 11 times what it was in 1900, while the United States economy was 25 times larger.

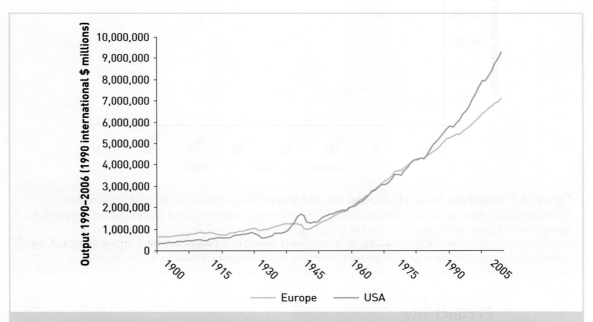

Figure 15.1 Output: Europe and the USA. European (12 largest economies) and American output 1900–2006. The output of the European economy has increased 11-fold since 1990 and that of the United States 25-fold.

Source: OECD (2003) *The World Economy: Historical Statistics* (Paris: OECD Development Centre) and the Conference Board and Groningen Growth and Development Centre (http://www.conference-board.org/economics).

- What caused this remarkable economic growth?
- Can it continue?
- Should it continue?

These are some of the questions macroeconomists try to answer.

Population growth and an increasing labour force are important reasons underlying rapid output growth. Between 1900 and 2006 the population of the 12 largest European economies almost doubled while the US population increased fourfold over the same period. However, because of population growth, increases in *total* output cannot be equated with improvements in the general standard of living. Although increased output means that more goods and services are available, increased population implies that more people are sharing those goods and services. Because population changes over time, output *per person* is a better indicator of the average living standard than total output. Figure 15.2 shows output per person in Europe, the United States and India since 1900. The diagram clearly illustrates the significant differences in living standards between the Western economies and India. Relative to 1900, output per person has increased by about seven times in Europe and the United States, and by four times in India.

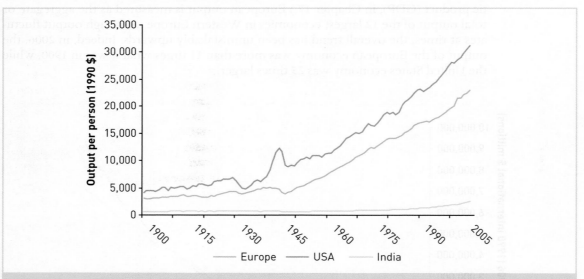

Figure 15.2 Output per Person in Europe, the USA and India. European (12 largest economies), American and Indian output per person 1900–2006. In Europe and the United States output per person has increased sevenfold since 1990 and in India fourfold.

Source: OECD (2003) *The World Economy: Historical Statistics* (Paris: OECD Development Centre) and the Conference Board and Groningen Growth and Development Centre (http://www.conference-board.org/economics).

Productivity

In Chapter 18 we shall see that growth in output per person is closely linked to labour productivity or amount which the typical person can *consume*. Table 15.1 shows how average labour productivity or output per person employed (that is, total output divided by the number of people working) has changed over a period of more than 120 years.

	1870	1913	1950	1973	1990	2006
Western Europe	4,702	8,072	11,551	28,108	37,476	48,635
France	4,051	7,458	11,214	31,910	45,356	54,708
Germany	4,414	7,824	9,231	26,623	34,352	42,345
Italy	3,037	5,412	8,739	25,661	36,124	46,154
United Kingdom	7,614	11,296	15,529	26,956	35,061	49,031
United States	6,683	13,327	23,615	40,727	47,976	63,891
China			1,273	1,745	3,280	10,898
Ratio: US/Europe	1.42	1.65	2.04	1.44	1.28	1.31

Table 15.1 **Output per Person Employed, 1870–2006 (1990 international $)**
Source: OECD (2003) *The World Economy: Historical Statistics* (Paris: OECD Development Centre) and the Conference Board and Groningen Growth and Development Centre, Total Economy Database, November 2007 (http://www.conference-board.org/economics).

Table 15.1 shows that, in 2006, a European worker could produce more than ten times the quantity of goods and services produced by a worker in 1870, while an American worker could also produce almost ten times more, despite the fact that in both economies the working week is now much shorter than it was in 1870. Economists refer to output per employed worker as **average labour productivity**.

average labour productivity
output per person employed

The final row of Table 15.1 shows the ratio of US to European labour productivity. In 1950, US workers were twice as productive as their European counterparts but the ratio declined over the next 50 years and especially between 1950 and 1973, which is sometimes referred to as a *catch-up period*. Economic naturalist 15.1 looks at Europe's catch-up in greater detail.

Exercise 15.1 The last row in Table 15.1 shows that, between 1950 and 1973, average labour productivity in Western Europe increased at a faster rate than in the United States. Calculate the same ratio for each of the countries in Table 15.1. Was the rate of catch-up the same in all European countries?

Average labour productivity and *output per person* are closely related. This relationship makes sense: as we noted earlier, the more we can produce, the more we can consume. Because of this close link to the average living standard, average labour productivity, and the factors that cause it to increase over time, are of major concern to macroeconomists.

Although the long-term improvement in output per worker is impressive, the *rate* of improvement has slowed somewhat since the 1970s. Between 1950 and 1973 output of the average European employed worker increased by about 6 per cent per year. But from 1973 to 1995 the average rate of increase in output per worker was 2.1 per cent per year. Slowing productivity growth leads to less rapid improvement in living standards, since the supply of goods and services cannot grow as quickly as it does during periods of rapid growth in productivity. Identifying the causes of productivity slowdowns and speed-ups is thus an important challenge for macroeconomists.

The current standard of living in Europe is not only much higher than it was in the past but also much higher than in many other nations today.

- How can we explain the long periods of sustained economic growth enjoyed by advanced industrial countries such as the United Kingdom, the United States and Japan?

- Why have many of the world's countries, including the developing nations of Asia, Africa and Latin America as well as some former communist countries of Eastern Europe, not enjoyed the same rates of economic growth as the industrialised countries?
- How can the rate of economic growth be improved in these countries?

Economic naturalist 15.1   Explaining Europe's catch-up, 1950–73

Table 15.1 shows that in the 70 years preceding the Second World War, American labour productivity not only exceeded European productivity, but that the gap between them widened. However, in the decades following the war, the reverse occurred and Europe closed the gap on the United States. Not only did the difference between American and European labour productivity decline between 1950 and 1973, but European output per person increased from 52 to 73 per cent of American output per person. Why did this catch-up occur after 1950? One obvious answer is that the catch-up was the result of reconstructing Europe's war-ravaged economies, paid for in part by the US-financed Marshall Plan. Reconstruction certainly played a role but it is not the only reason for Europe's catch-up period between 1950 and 1973. The American Economist Robert J. Gordon discusses this issue and presents a number of reasons why Europe did so badly before the Second World War and so well afterwards.[1] One of Gordon's hypotheses is that we can understand Europe's catch-up only if we first understand why the United States surged ahead during the nineteenth century and the first half of the twentieth century. In answering this question, Gordon highlights the fact that America was a full political, monetary and economic union long before Europe, and that the creation of an internal, or single, market enabled the United States to exploit the advantages of mass production and key inventions such as electricity and the internal combustion engine. In contrast, Europe was fragmented by nation states, trade barriers and war. As Gordon puts it:

> Looking back at the long history of Europe falling behind the US and then catching up, it is hard to avoid the conclusion that this topic has more to do with politics and history rather than with economics. The sources of US advantage prior to 1913 centre on its internal common market, an achievement of the Founding Fathers, Abraham Lincoln and the Union Army, rather than any particular genius at business or technology, and free internal trade led in turn to exploitation of raw materials and leadership in materials-intensive manufacturing. Postwar Europe gradually rid itself of internal trade barriers and largely caught up to the American productivity frontier as a result.

Gordon's hypothesis raises several interesting questions. First, as the European single market, the common currency and the proposed constitution intensify the pace of economic and political integration, will Europe become 'more like America' and further close the gap on the United States? Second, and somewhat more trivial, Gordon's argument is an obvious boost to the 'what if' theorists. What if the Union Army had been defeated at Gettysburg in July 1863 and the Confederacy emerged victorious in the Civil War of 1861–65? Would America have fragmented into nation states and become 'more like Europe', with internal strife, trade barriers and impediments to the free movement of labour? If so, would the economic and political histories of Europe and America have been dramatically different?

Example 15.1   Productivity and living standards in the United Kingdom and China

The following table gives total output, output per person and average labour productivity for the United Kingdom and People's Republic of China (PRC) in 2006. We use euros to facilitate the comparison.

---

1 Gordon (2004).

Compare total output, output per person and average labour productivity for the United Kingdom and China in 2006. What do the results suggest about comparative living standards?

Standard	UK	China
Total output (billions of €)	1,109	6,634
Output per person	18,302	5,061
Average labour productivity	39,072	8,684

Source: The Conference Board and Groningen Growth and Development Centre (http://www.conference-board.org/economics).

Although the total output of the Chinese economy is approximately six times that of the United Kingdom, output per person and average labour productivity in China are each only about 27 and 22 per cent, respectively, of what they are in the United Kingdom. Thus, though the Chinese economy is much larger than the British economy, there is a large gap in *productivity*. This gap translates into striking differences in *living standards* as measured by output per person. Higher output per person gives British citizens much greater access to consumer goods, healthcare, transportation, education and other benefits of affluence.

Exercise 15.2   The following data give total output, total population and numbers employed for Germany and Turkey in 2006. Find output per person and average labour productivity in each country. How do living standards compare?

	Germany	Turkey
Output (billions of €s)	1,319	453
Population (millions)	83	70
Numbers employed (millions)	39	23

Recessions and expansions

Economies do not always grow steadily – sometimes they go through periods of unusual strength or weakness. Figure 15.3 shows the annualised growth rate for the UK economy from 1960 to 2006. You can easily identify periods of high and low growth. Growth was relatively high in the early 1970s and from the mid-1990s onwards. By contrast, growth was relatively low and in some years negative in the mid-1970s and the early years of the 1980s and 1990s.

Periods of rapid economic growth are called *expansions* and slowdowns in economic growth are called *recessions*; alternating periods of expansion and recession are often referred to as the *business cycle*. During expansionary phases real incomes and employment tend to rise, whereas they tend to fall during recessionary phases. Normally the economy faces inflationary pressures during an expansion and rising unemployment in a recession. The alternating cycle of recessions and expansions raises some questions that are central to macroeconomics.

- What causes these short-term fluctuations in the rate of economic growth?
- Can economic policy moderate the magnitude and duration of expansions and recessions?

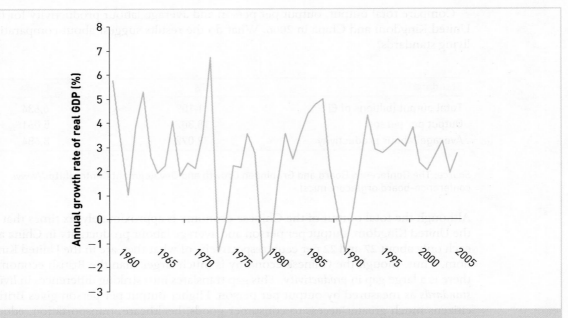

Figure 15.3 UK Growth Rate of Real GDP 1960–2006. Annual percentage change in real gross domestic product.

Unemployment

The *unemployment rate*, defined as the percentage of the workforce who would like to be employed but can't find work, is a key indicator of the state of the labour market. When the unemployment rate is high, work is hard to find and people who do have jobs typically find it harder to get promotions or wage increases. Figure 15.4 shows the unemployment rate in the United Kingdom since 1900. Unemployment rises during recessions – note the dramatic spike in unemployment during the Great Depression, as well as the increases in unemployment during the 1974–75 and 1981–82 recessions. But, even in the so-called 'good times', such as the 1960s and the 1990s, some people are unemployed.

- What are the causes of unemployment and why does it rise so sharply during recessions?
- What are the appropriate economic policies for dealing with unemployment?

Exercise 15.3   Find the most recent unemployment rates for France, Germany and the United Kingdom, and compare them with the most recent unemployment rate for the United States. Useful sources are the home pages of Eurostat (http://epp.eurostat. ec.eu.int), the statistical agency of the European Union, and the Organization for Economic Cooperation and Development (OECD), an organisation of industrialised countries (http://www.oecd.org/).

Inflation

The rate of *inflation* is the rate at which prices in general are increasing over time. Figure 15.5 shows the UK inflation rate in the United Kingdom since 1970. In recent

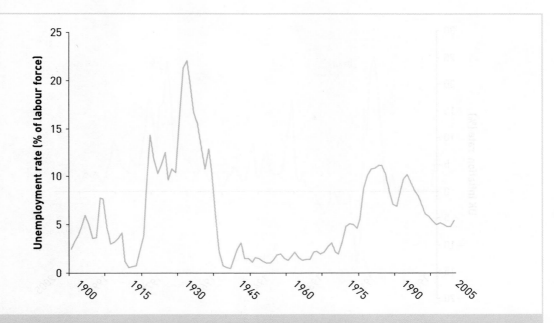

Figure 15.4 The UK Unemployment Rate, 1900–2006. The unemployment rate is the percentage of the labour force that is out of work. The unemployment rate spikes upwards during recessions but is always positive, even during expansions.
Source: British Labour Historical Abstract for 1900 to 1968, *The European Economy* and OECD for 1969 to 2006.

years, inflation has been relatively low in most industrial countries. However, as Figure 15.5 shows, UK inflation exceeded 20 per cent in the mid-1970s (a period of recession!) but was negative in the 1920s and early 1930s. Economists are interested in the causes of inflation and its relationship with the rate of unemployment.

* What are the causes of inflation?
* Why do we sometimes observe inflation and unemployment rising together?
* What are the appropriate economic policies for dealing with unemployment?
* What costs does inflation impose on different sections of the population?

Economic interdependence among nations

National economies do not exist in isolation but are increasingly *interdependent*. This is especially true for Europe, where the introduction of the single market and the common currency (the euro) has dramatically increased the degree of integration and interdependences between EU member states. International trade is a key indicator of interdependences between countries. In 2003, total exports accounted for 34 per cent of aggregate EU output, while imports accounted for 32 per cent. By comparison, the United States exported about 9 per cent of all the goods and services it produced, and imported 14 per cent of the goods and services that Americans used. However, in the case of EU countries it is important to distinguish between *intra-EU* and *extra-EU* trade. Intra-EU trade is exports and imports *between* member states, while extra-EU trade is trade with countries *outside* the Union. British exports to France are intra-EU trade, while imports from Norway are extra-EU trade. In 2003, intra-EU trade accounted for approximately 50 per cent of total EU exports and imports.

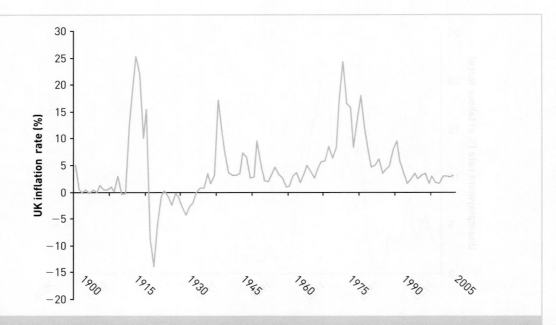

Figure 15.5 The UK Inflation Rate, 1900–2006. The inflation rate fluctuates over time. It was negative during the Great Depression and exceeded 20 per cent during the oil crises in the 1970s.
Source: Inflation and the Value of the Pound, House of Commons Research Paper 99/20 and Office for National Statistics.

Sometimes, international flows of goods and services become a matter of political and economic concern. For example, those who opposed the expansion of the European Union to include countries in Central and Eastern Europe (CEE) complained that low-priced imports from these countries threatened jobs in Western countries. Similar concerns were expressed following the creation of the North American Free Trade Agreement (NAFTA) between the United States, Canada and Mexico. Are free-trade agreements, in which countries agree not to tax or otherwise block the international flow of goods and services, a good or a bad thing?

A related issue is the phenomenon of *trade imbalances*, which occur when the quantity of goods and services that a country sells abroad (its *exports*) differs significantly from the quantity of goods and services its citizens buy from abroad (its *imports*). The difference between exports and imports is often referred to as *net exports*. Figure 15.6 shows British net exports of goods and services since 1960, measured as a percentage of gross domestic product. You can see that the *trading surplus*, or an excess of exports over imports, in the late 1970s and 1980s turned to a *trade deficit* in the 1990s.

- What causes trade deficits and surpluses?
- Are they harmful or helpful?

Exercise 15.4 Using the most recent data on exports and imports for the European Union, find the EU's current trade deficit or surplus. Compare your results with the most recent trade data for the United States. Useful sources are the home pages of Eurostat (http://epp.eurostat.ec.eu.int), the EU statistical agency, and the OECD (http://www.oecd.org/).

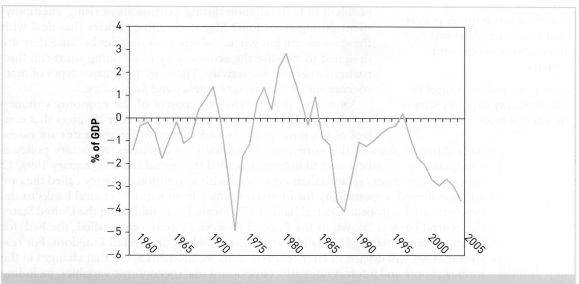

Figure 15.6 UK Net Exports as a Percentage of GDP 1960–2006.

RECAP The major macroeconomic issues

- *Economic growth and living standards* Since 1900 the industrialised nations have experienced remarkable economic growth and improvements in living standards. Macroeconomists study the reasons for this extraordinary growth and try to understand why growth rates vary markedly among nations.

- *Productivity* Average labour productivity, or output per employed worker, is a crucial determinant of living standards. Macroeconomists study the causes of variations in the rate of productivity growth.

- *Recessions and expansions* Economies experience periods of slower growth (recessions) and more rapid growth (expansions). Macroeconomists examine the sources of these fluctuations and the government policies that attempt to moderate them.

- *Unemployment* The unemployment rate is the fraction of the labour force who would like to be employed but can't find work. Unemployment rises during recessions, but there are always unemployed people, even during good times. Macroeconomists study the causes of unemployment, including the reasons why it sometimes differs markedly across countries.

- *Inflation* The inflation rate is the rate at which prices in general are increasing over time. Questions macroeconomists ask about inflation include: Why does inflation vary over time and across countries? Must a reduction in inflation be accompanied by an increase in unemployment (or vice versa)?

- *Economic interdependence among nations* Modern economies are highly interdependent. Related issues studied by macroeconomists include the gains from closer economic integration, the desirability of free trade agreements, and the causes and effects of trade imbalances.

Macroeconomic policy

In this chapter we have asked questions such as 'What are the appropriate economic policies to moderate the magnitude and duration of expansions and recessions over the course of the business cycle?' More specifically, how can policy makers address the

stabilisation policies policies that moderate short-run fluctuations in economic activity

monetary policy control of the economy's money supply or interest rates

problem of high inflation during expansions or rising unemployment during recessions? Macroeconomic policies that deal with these issues are known as **stabilisation policies** because they are designed to stabilise the economy by moderating short-run fluctuations in economic activity. There are two major types of macroeconomic policy: *monetary policy* and *fiscal policy*.

Monetary policy refers to control of the economy's money supply and interest rates. We shall see in later chapters that control of the money supply and control of interest rates are essentially different sides of the same coin. In virtually all countries, monetary policy is conducted by a publicly owned institution called the *central bank*. In January 1999, 12 European countries replaced their currencies with a common currency called the *euro* and transferred responsibility for monetary policy from national central banks to the newly created European Central Bank (ECB) located in Frankfurt. In the United States the central bank is known as the Federal Reserve System, often called 'the Fed' for short, while the Bank of England is the central bank of the United Kingdom. For reasons that we will discuss in later chapters, most economists agree that changes in the money supply and interest rates affect important macroeconomic variables, including aggregate output, unemployment, inflation and exchange rates.

fiscal policy decisions that determine the government's budget, including the amount and composition of government expenditures and government revenues

Fiscal policy refers to decisions that change the government's budget deficit or surplus defined as the difference between government expenditures and revenues. Hence fiscal policy operates through government decisions to spend more or less or to cut or increase rates of taxation. As with monetary policy, economists generally agree that fiscal policy can have important effects on the overall performance of the economy. However, many economists believe that large government deficits (an excess of expenditures over revenues) can lead to instability and are harmful to growth and employment. It is for this reason that European countries have attempted, with limited success, to restrict the size of government deficits by an agreement known as the *Stability and Growth Pact* (SGP).

structural policy government policies aimed at changing the underlying structure, or institutions, of the nation's economy

From a longer-term perspective, governments may also use **structural policies** to change the economy's underlying structure and institutions. Structural policies come in many forms, from minor tinkering to ambitious overhauls of the entire economic system. The move away from government control of the economy and towards a more market-orientated approach in many formerly communist countries, such as Poland, the Czech Republic and Hungary, is a large-scale example of structural policy. Many developing countries have tried similar structural reforms. Supporters of structural policy hope that, by changing the basic characteristics of the economy or by remaking its institutions, they can stimulate economic growth and improve living standards.

Positive versus normative analyses of macroeconomic policy

Macroeconomists are frequently called upon to analyse the effects of a proposed policy. For example, if government is debating the merits of higher taxes on fossil fuels, economists may be asked to prepare an analysis of the likely effects on the overall economy, as well as on specific industries, regions or income groups. An objective

positive analysis addresses the economic consequences of a particular event or policy, not whether those consequences are desirable

normative analysis addresses the question of whether a policy *should* be used; normative analysis inevitably involves the values of the person doing the analysis

analysis aimed at determining only the economic consequences of a particular policy – not whether those consequences are desirable – is called a **positive analysis**. In contrast, a **normative analysis** includes recommendations on whether a particular policy *should* be implemented. While a positive analysis is supposed to be objective and scientific, a normative analysis involves the *values* of the person or organisation doing the analysis: conservative, socialist or middle of the road.

While pundits often joke that economists cannot agree among themselves, the tendency for economists to disagree is exaggerated. When economists do disagree, the controversy often centres on normative judgements (which relate to economists' personal values) rather than on positive analysis (which reflects an objective knowledge of the economy). For example, socialist and conservative economists might agree that a particular tax cut would increase the incomes of the relatively wealthy (positive analysis). But they might vehemently disagree on whether the policy *should* be enacted, reflecting their personal views about whether wealthy people deserve a tax break (normative analysis).

The next time you hear or read about a debate over economic issues, try to determine whether the differences between the two positions are primarily positive or normative. If the debate focuses on the actual effects of the event or policy under discussion, then the disagreement is over positive issues. But if the main question has to do with conflicting personal opinions about the *desirability* of those effects, the debate is normative. The distinction between positive and normative analyses is important, because objective economic research can help to resolve differences over positive issues. When people differ for normative reasons, however, economic analysis is of less use.

Exercise 15.5 Which of the following statements are positive and which are normative? How can you tell?

a. Banning smoking in public places will lead to lower employment in bars and restaurants.

b. Irrespective of its effect on employment, government should ban smoking in public places in order to protect public health.

c. A tax increase would be acceptable if most of the burden fell on those with incomes over €100,000.

d. Government should offer grants to first-time house buyers in order to promote home ownership.

e. Grants to first-time house buyers will lead to higher house prices.

RECAP Macroeconomic policy

Macroeconomic policies affect the performance of the economy as a whole. The three types of macroeconomic policy are monetary policy, fiscal policy and structural policy. *Monetary policy* refers to the determination of the nation's money supply and interest rates. *Fiscal policy* involves decisions about the government budget, including its expenditures and tax collections. *Structural policy* refers to government actions to change the underlying structure or institutions of the economy. Structural policy can range from minor tinkering to a major overhaul of the economic system, as with the formerly communist countries that are attempting to convert to market-orientated systems.

The analysis of a proposed policy can be positive or normative. A positive analysis addresses the policy's likely economic consequences, but not whether those consequences are desirable. A normative analysis addresses the question of whether a proposed policy *should* be used. Debates about normative conclusions inevitably involve personal values and thus generally cannot be resolved by objective economic analysis alone.

Aggregation

In Chapter 1, we discussed the difference between macroeconomics – the study of national economies – and microeconomics – the study of individual economic entities, such as households and firms, and the markets for specific goods and services. The main difference between the fields is one of perspective: macroeconomists take a 'bird's-eye view' of the economy, ignoring the fine details to understand how the system works as a whole. Microeconomists work instead at the 'ground level', studying the economic behaviour of individual households, firms and markets. Both perspectives are useful – indeed, essential – to understand what makes an economy work.

Although macroeconomics and microeconomics take different perspectives on the economy, the basic tools of analysis are much the same. In the chapters to come you will see that macroeconomists apply the same core principles as microeconomists in their efforts to understand and predict economic behaviour. Even though a national economy is a much bigger entity than a household, or even a large firm, the choices and actions of individual decision makers ultimately determine the performance of the economy as a whole. So, for example, to understand saving behaviour at the national level, the macroeconomist must first consider what motivates an individual family or household to save. The core principles introduced in Part 1 prove very useful for attacking such questions.

Exercise 15.6 Which of the following questions would be studied primarily by macroeconomists and which by microeconomists? Explain.

  a. Does increased government spending lower the unemployment rate?
  b. Does Microsoft Corporation's dominance of the software industry harm consumers?
  c. Would charging tuition fees to university students improve the quality of education?
  d. Should the Bank of England aim to reduce inflation still further?
  e. Why is the average rate of household saving higher in France than in the United States?
  f. Does the increase in the number of consumer products being sold over the internet threaten the profits of conventional retailers?

While macroeconomists use the core principles of economics to understand and predict individual economic decisions, they need a way to relate millions of individual decisions to the behaviour of the economy as a whole. One important tool they use to link individual behaviour to national economic performance is **aggregation**, the adding up of individual economic variables to obtain economy-wide totals.

aggregation the adding up of individual economic variables to obtain economy-wide totals

For example, macroeconomists don't care whether consumers drink red or white wine, go to the cinema or rent DVDs, live in rented or owner-occupied housing. These individual economic decisions are the province of microeconomics. Instead, macroeconomists add up consumer expenditures on all goods and services during a given period to obtain *aggregate*, or total, consumer expenditure. Similarly, a macroeconomist would not focus on plumbers' wages versus electricians' wages, but would concentrate instead on the average wage of all workers. By focusing on aggregate variables, such as total consumer expenditures or the average wage, macroeconomists suppress the mind-boggling details of a complex modern economy to see the broad economic trends.

Example 15.2 Aggregation (1): a national crime index

To illustrate not only why aggregation is needed but also some of the problems associated with it, consider an issue that is only partly economic: crime. Suppose policy makers want to know whether *in general* the problem of crime in a country such as the United Kingdom is getting better or worse. How could an analyst obtain a statistical answer to that question?

Police keep detailed records of the crimes reported in their jurisdictions, so in principle a researcher could determine precisely how many bag snatchings occurred last year on the London Underground. But data on the number of crimes of each type in each city and region would produce stacks of computer output. Is there a way to add up, or aggregate, all the crime data to get some sense of the national trend?

Government departments such as the UK Home Office use aggregation to obtain national *crime rates*, which are typically expressed as the total number of crimes reported to the police per 1,000 of the population (www.homeoffice.gov.uk). Although aggregation of crime statistics reveals the 'big picture', it may obscure important details. An aggregate index lumps together relatively minor crimes such as petty theft with more serious crimes involving violence. Most people would agree that violent crimes do far more damage than petty theft, so adding together these two very different types of crime might give a false picture of UK crime. For example, according to Home Office aggregate data for 2003–04 the number of crimes reported by the police was down by 1 per cent on the previous year. Violent crime, however, increased by 12 per cent over the same period, which is probably more significant than the fall in the overall, or aggregate, crime rate. This loss of detail is a cost of aggregation – the price analysts pay for the ability to look at broad economic or social trends.

Example 15.3 Aggregation (2): French exports

France exports a wide variety of products and services to many different countries. French manufacturing firms such as Airbus and Renault sell planes and cars to airlines and households in Europe, Africa, North America and Asia, and French vineyards sell wine all over the world. Suppose macroeconomists want to compare the total quantities of French-made goods sold to various regions of the world. How could such a comparison be made?

Economists can't add jumbo jets, cars and bottles of wine – the units aren't comparable. But they can add the *money values* of each – the revenue Airbus and car manufacturers earn from foreign sales and the euro value of French wine sold abroad. By comparing the euro values of French exports to other countries in a particular year, economists are able to determine which regions are the biggest customers for French-made goods.

RECAP Aggregation

Macroeconomics, the study of national economies, differs from *microeconomics*, the study of individual economic entities (such as households and firms) and the markets for specific goods and services. Macroeconomists take a 'bird's-eye view' of the economy. To study the economy as a whole, macroeconomists make frequent use of *aggregation*, the adding up of individual economic variables to obtain economy-wide totals. For example, a macroeconomist is more interested in the determinants of total French exports, as measured by their total euro value, than in the factors that determine the exports of specific goods such as wine or aircraft. A cost of aggregation is that the fine details of the economic situation are often obscured.

Studying macroeconomics: a preview

This chapter has introduced many of the key issues of macroeconomics. In the chapters to come we shall look at each of these issues in more detail. Chapters 16 and 17 cover the *measurement* of economic performance, including key variables such as the level of economic activity and the rate of inflation. Obtaining quantitative measurements of the economy, against which theories can be tested, is the crucial first step in answering basic macroeconomic questions like those raised in this chapter. Chapter 18 discusses the labour market: wages and unemployment.

In Part 6 we shall study economic behaviour over relatively long periods of time. Chapter 19 examines economic growth and productivity improvement, the fundamental determinants of the average standard of living in the long run. In Chapter 20 we study capital markets and financial intermediation with a focus on saving and investment or the creation of new capital goods, such as factories and machines.

John Maynard Keynes, a celebrated British economist, once wrote that 'In the long run, we are all dead'. Keynes' statement was intended as an ironic comment on the tendency of economists to downplay short-run economic problems on the grounds that 'in the long run', the operation of the free market will always restore economic stability. Keynes, who was particularly active and influential during the Great Depression, correctly viewed the problem of massive unemployment, whether 'short run' or not, as the most pressing economic issue of the time. So why start our study of macroeconomics with the long run? Keynes' comment notwithstanding, long-run economic performance is extremely important, accounting for most of the substantial differences in living standards and economic well-being the world over. Furthermore, studying long run economic behaviour provides an important background for understanding short-term fluctuations in the economy.

We turn to those short-term fluctuations in Part 7. Chapter 21 provides background on what happens during recessions and expansions and introduces the Keynesian model, which focuses on variations in aggregate spending as a key determinant of short-term economic fluctuations. The role played by money and its relation to the rate of inflation is covered in Chapter 22, which also introduces some important central banks such as the European Central Bank, the US Federal Reserve System and the Bank of England. Chapter 23 introduces the IS-LM model by integrating the role of money and interest rates into the Keynesian model, and presents a general equilibrium approach to the simultaneous determination of aggregate output, interest rates and the average price level. Chapter 24 discusses the role of fiscal policy in moderating economic fluctuations, while the second major policy tool for stabilising the economy, monetary policy, is the subject of Chapter 25. Chapter 26 brings inflation into the analysis, and discusses the circumstances under which macroeconomic policy makers may face a short-term trade-off between inflation and unemployment, while Chapter 27 deals with the control of inflation.

The international dimension of macroeconomics is the focus of Part 8. Chapter 28 introduces exchange rates, capital flows and the balance of payments, and we will discuss how exchange rates are determined and how they affect the workings of the economy.

Summary

■ Macroeconomics is the study of the performance of national economies and of the policies governments use to try to improve that performance. The five broad issues macroeconomists study are:
1. sources of economic growth and improved living standards
2. trends in *average labour productivity*, or output per employed worker
3. short-term fluctuations in the pace of economic growth (recessions and expansions)
4. causes of and cures for unemployment and inflation
5. economic interdependence among nations.

■ To help explain differences in economic performance among countries, or in economic performance in the same country at different times, macroeconomists study the implementation and effects of macroeconomic policies. *Macroeconomic policies* are government actions designed to affect the performance of the economy as a whole. Macroeconomic policies include *monetary policy* (the determination of the nation's money supply), *fiscal policy* (relating to decisions about the government's budget) and *structural policy* (aimed at affecting the basic structure and institutions of the economy).

■ In studying economic policies, economists apply both *positive analysis* (an objective attempt to determine the consequences of a proposed policy) and *normative analysis* (which addresses whether a particular policy *should* be adopted). Normative analysis involves the values of the person doing the analysis.

■ Macroeconomics is distinct from microeconomics, which focuses on the behaviour of individual economic entities and specific markets. Macroeconomists make heavy use of *aggregation*, which is the adding up of individual economic variables into economy-wide totals. Aggregation allows macroeconomists to study the 'big picture' of the economy, while ignoring fine details about individual households, firms and markets.

Review questions

1. How did the experience of the Great Depression motivate the development of the field of macroeconomics?
2. In general, how does the standard of living in Europe today compare with the standard of living in other countries? To the standard of living in Europe a century ago?
3. Why is average labour productivity a particularly important economic variable?
4. **True or false:** Economic growth within a particular country generally proceeds at a constant rate. Explain.
5. **True or false:** Differences of opinion about economic policy recommendations can always be resolved by objective analysis of the issues. Explain.
6. What type of macroeconomic policy (monetary, fiscal, structural) might include each of the following actions:
   a. a broad government initiative to reduce the country's reliance on agriculture and promote high-technology industries
   b. a reduction in income tax rates
   c. provision of additional cash to the banking system
   d. an attempt to reduce the government budget deficit by reducing spending
   e. a decision by a developing country to reduce government control of the economy and to become more market-orientated?

Problems

1. In the years to 2050 the Japanese population is expected to decline, while the fraction of the population that is retired is expected to increase sharply. What are the implications of these population changes for total output and average living standards in Japan, assuming that average labour productivity continues to grow? What if average labour productivity stagnates?

2. Is it possible for average living standards to rise during a period in which average labour productivity is falling? Discuss, using a numerical example for illustration.

3. Eurostat is the European agency that collects a wide variety of statistics about the European economy. From the Eurostat home page (http://epp.eurostat.ec.eu.int) find data for the most recent year available on EU exports and imports of goods and services. Is the Union running a trade surplus or deficit?

4. Which of the following statements are positive and which are normative?
   a. If the ECB raises interest rates, demand for housing is likely to fall.
   b. The ECB should be primarily concerned with keeping inflation low irrespective of the rate of unemployment.
   c. Share prices are likely to fall over the next year as the economy slows.
   d. A reduction in the capital gains tax (the tax on profits made in the stock market) would lead to a 10–20 per cent increase in stock prices.
   e. Government should not reduce capital gains taxes without also providing tax breaks for lower-income people.

5. Which of the following would be studied by a macroeconomist? By a microeconomist?
   a. The effect of higher oil prices on employment.
   b. The effect of government subsidies on sugar prices.
   c. Factors affecting average wages in the UK economy.
   d. Inflation in developing countries.
   e. The effects of tax cuts on consumer spending.

References

Gordon, R.J. (2004) 'Two centuries of economic growth: Europe chasing the American frontier', NBER Working Paper, 10662.

OECD (2003) *The World Economy: Historical Statistics* (Paris: OECD Development Centre).

To help you grasp the key concepts of this chapter check out the extra resources posted on the Online Learning Centre. There are chapter summaries, self-test questions, an interactive graphing tool, weblinks and a glossary, all for free!

Visit the Online Learning Centre at: www.mcgraw-hill.co.uk/textbooks/mcdowell for information on accessing all of these resources.

16

Measuring Economic Activity: Gross Domestic Product

The growth of real gross domestic product slowed to 1 per cent last quarter …

Inflation appears subdued as the consumer price index registered an increase of only 0.2 per cent last month …

News reports like these fill the airwaves – some TV and radio stations carry nothing else. In fact, all kinds of people are interested in economic data. The average person hopes to learn something that will be useful in a business decision, a financial investment or a career move. The professional economist depends on economic data in much the same way that a doctor depends on a patient's vital signs – pulse, blood pressure and temperature – to make an accurate diagnosis. To understand economic developments and to be able to give useful advice to policy makers, businesspeople and financial investors, an economist must have up-to-date, accurate data. Political leaders and policy makers also need economic data to help them in their decisions and planning.

Interest in *measuring the economy*, and attempts to do so, date back as far as the mid-seventeenth century, when Sir William Petty (1623–87) conducted a detailed survey of the land and wealth of Ireland. The British government's purpose in commissioning the survey was to determine the capacity of the Irish people to pay taxes to the Crown. But Petty used the opportunity to measure a variety of social and economic variables, and went on to conduct pioneering studies of wealth, production and population in several other countries. A firm believer in the idea that scientific progress depends first and foremost on accurate measurement, he once interrupted a meeting of the British Royal Society (a distinguished association of scientists, of which Petty was a founding member) to correct a speaker who had used the phrase 'considerably bigger'. A rule should be passed barring such vague terms, Petty proposed, so that 'no word might be used but what marks either number, weight, or measure'.[1]

Not until the twentieth century did economic measurement come into its own. The Second World War was an important catalyst for the development of accurate

---

1 This story reported by Charles H. Hull (Hull 1900).

economic statistics, since its very outcome was thought to depend on the mobilisation of economic resources. Two economists, Simon Kuznets in the United States and Richard Stone in the United Kingdom, developed comprehensive systems for measuring a nation's *output of goods and services*, which were of great help to Allied leaders in their wartime planning. Kuznets and Stone each received a Nobel Prize in Economics for their work, which became the basis for the economic accounts used today by almost all the world's countries.

gross domestic product (GDP) the market value of the final goods and services produced in a country during a given period

In this chapter we shall discuss how economists measure a key macroeconomic variable frequently used to analyse the state of the economy – **gross domestic product (GDP)**. Chapters 17 and 18 focus on two other indicators of economic activity: *inflation* and *unemployment*.

Measuring economic activity might sound like a straightforward and uncontroversial task, but that is not the case. Indeed, the basic measure of a nation's output of goods and services, GDP, has been criticised on many grounds. Some critics have complained that GDP does not adequately reflect factors such as the distribution of income and the effect of economic growth on the environment. Because of problems like these, they charge, policies based on GDP statistics are likely to be flawed. By the end of this chapter you will understand how official measures of output are constructed and used, and will have gained some insight into these debates over their accuracy. Understanding the *strengths and limitations of economic data* is the first critical step towards becoming an intelligent user of economic statistics, as well as a necessary background for the economic analysis in the chapters to come.

Gross domestic product: measuring the economy's output

Chapter 15 emphasised the link between an economy's output of goods and services and its living standard. We noted that high levels of output per person, and per worker, are typically associated with a high standard of living. But what, exactly, does 'output' mean? To study economic growth and productivity scientifically, we need to be more precise about how economists define and measure an economy's output.

The most frequently used measure of an economy's output is called GDP, a measure of how much an economy produces in a given period, such as a quarter (three months) or a year. More precisely, GDP is the market value of the *final goods and services* produced in a country during a given period. To understand this definition, let us take it apart and examine each of its parts separately. The first key phrase in the definition is 'market value'.

Market value

A modern economy produces many different goods and services, from toothpaste (a good) to acupuncture (a service). Macroeconomists are not interested in this kind of detail, however; rather, their goal is to understand the behaviour of the economy as a whole. For example, a macroeconomist might ask: Has the overall capacity of the economy to produce goods and services increased over time? If so, by how much?

To be able to talk about concepts such as the 'total output' or 'total production' – as opposed to the production of specific items such as toothpaste – economists need to *aggregate* the quantities of the many different goods and services into a single number. They do so by adding up the *market values* of the different goods and services the economy produces. A simple example will illustrate the process. In the imaginary economy of Orchardia, total production is 4 apples and 6 bananas. To find the total output of Orchardia, we could add the number of apples to the number of bananas and conclude that total output is 10 pieces of fruit. But what if this economy also produced 3 pairs of shoes? There really is no sensible way to add apples and bananas to shoes.

Suppose, though, that we know that apples sell for €0.25 each, bananas for €0.50 each and shoes for €20.00 a pair. Then the market value of this economy's production, or its GDP, is equal to

$$(4 \text{ apples} \times €0.25/\text{apple}) + (6 \text{ bananas} \times €0.50/\text{banana})$$
$$+ (3 \text{ pairs of shoes} \times €20/\text{pair}) = €64.00$$

Notice that when we calculate total output this way, the more expensive items (the shoes) receive a higher weighting than the cheaper items (the apples and bananas). In general, the amount that people are willing to pay for an item is an indication of the *economic benefit* they expect to receive from it (see Chapter 3). For this reason, higher-priced items should count for more in a measure of aggregate output.

Example 16.1 Orchardia's GDP

Suppose Orchardia were to produce 3 apples, 3 bananas and 4 pairs of shoes at the same prices as above. What is its GDP now? Now the Orchardian GDP is equal to

$$(3 \text{ apples} \times €0.25/\text{apple}) + (3 \text{ bananas} \times €0.50/\text{banana})$$
$$+ (4 \text{ pairs of shoes} \times €20/\text{pair}) = €82.25$$

Notice that the market value of Orchardian GDP is higher in Example 16.1 than earlier, even though two of the three goods (apples and bananas) are being produced in smaller quantities than before. The reason is that the good whose production has increased (shoes) is much more valuable than the goods whose production has decreased (apples and bananas).

Exercise 16.1 Suppose Orchardia produces the same quantities of the three goods as originally at the same prices (see the discussion preceding Example 16.1). In addition, it produces 5 oranges at €0.30 each. What is the GDP of Orchardia now?

Exercise 16.2 The following are assumed monthly data on German production of passenger cars and other light vehicles (a category that includes minivans, light trucks and sports utility vehicles). The data are broken down into two categories: German car producers (Volkswagen, BMW, etc.) and foreign-owned plants (such as General Motors). The average selling price is €17,000 for passenger cars and €25,000 for other light vehicles.

Producer	Passenger cars	Other light vehicles
German producers	471,000	714,000
Foreign-owned plants	227,000	63,000

Compare the output of German producers to that of foreign-owned plants in terms of both the total number of vehicles produced and their market values (contribution to GDP). Explain why the two measures give different impressions of the relative importance of production by German-owned and foreign-owned plants.

Market values provide a convenient way to add together, or aggregate, the many different goods and services produced in a modern economy. A drawback of using market values, however, is that not all economically valuable goods and services are bought and sold in markets. For example, the unpaid work of a home maker, although it is of economic value, is not sold in markets and so is not counted in GDP. But paid housekeeping and childcare services, which are sold in markets, do count. This distinction can create some pitfalls, as Examples 16.2 and 16.3 show.

Example 16.2 Women's labour force participation and GDP measurement

The percentage of adult women working outside the home has increased dramatically since the 1960s. In the United Kingdom the percentage of females of working age who are classified as either working or actively seeking work has increased from less than 50 per cent in 1960 to about 70 per cent today. Similar trends have been observed in other European and North American countries This trend has led to a substantial increase in the demand for paid daycare and housekeeping services, as working wives and mothers require more help at home. How have these changes affected measured GDP? The entry of many women into the labour market has raised measured GDP in two ways. First, the goods and services that women produce in their new jobs have contributed directly to increasing GDP. Second, the fact that paid workers took over previously unpaid housework and childcare duties has increased measured GDP by the amount paid to those workers. The first of these two changes represents a genuine increase in economic activity, but the second reflects a transfer of existing economic activities from the unpaid sector to the market sector. Overall, then, the increase in measured GDP associated with increased participation in the labour force by women probably overstates the actual increase in economic activity.

Comparative
Advantage

Economic naturalist 16.1 Why has female participation in the labour market increased by so much?

In a world governed only by economic principles – without social conventions, customs or traditions – home-making tasks such as cleaning, cooking and child rearing would be jobs like any other. As such, they would be subject to the principle of *comparative advantage*: those people (either men or women) whose comparative advantage lay in performing home-making tasks would specialise in them, freeing people whose comparative advantage lay elsewhere to work outside the home. In other words, home-making tasks would be done by those with the lowest opportunity cost in those tasks. In such a world, to see a woman with a medical degree doing housework would be very unusual – her opportunity cost of doing housework would be too high.

But of course we don't live in a world driven only by economic considerations. Traditionally, *social custom* has severely limited the economic opportunities of women (and in some societies it still does). However, social restrictions on women have weakened considerably since 1900, particularly in the industrialised countries, as a result of the increased educational attainment of women, the rise of the feminist movement and other factors. As traditional social restraints on women have loosened, domestic arrangements have moved in the direction dictated by comparative advantage – to an increasing degree, home-making tasks are now performed by paid specialists, while the majority of women (and men) work outside the home.

Although home-making activities are excluded from measured GDP, in a few cases goods and services that are not sold in markets are included in GDP. By far the most important are the goods and services provided by national and local governments. The protection provided by the army and navy, the transportation convenience of highway systems and the education provided by the state-funded school system are examples of publicly provided goods and services that are not sold in markets. As market prices for publicly provided goods and services do not exist, economic statisticians add to the GDP the *costs* of providing those goods and services as rough measures of their economic value. For example, to include public education in the GDP, the statisticians add to GDP the salaries of teachers and administrators, the costs of textbooks and supplies, and the like. Similarly, the economic value of the national defence establishment is approximated, for the purposes of measuring GDP, by the *costs* of defence: the pay earned by soldiers and sailors, the costs of acquiring and maintaining weapons, and so on.

With a few exceptions, like publicly provided goods and services, GDP is calculated by adding up market values. However, not all goods and services that have a market value are counted in GDP. As we shall see next, GDP includes only those goods and services that are the end products of the production process, called *final goods and services*. Goods and services that are used up in the production process are not counted in GDP.

Example 16.3 Mary finds a job

Suppose Mary is a single mother who does not work and depends totally on unemployment and other benefits. As will be explained later in this chapter, payments such as unemployment benefit are not counted as part of GDP because no service is provided in return. Mary will of course spend a lot of time looking after her children but this work is unpaid and not counted as part of GDP. Hence Mary contributes nothing to the official measure of GDP. Suppose Mary finds a job at €500 per week and pays a childminder €200 per week to look after her children. As conventionally measured this adds €700 to GDP – Mary's income plus the childminder's income. However the childminder has taken over Mary's previous unpaid work, which was not counted as part of GDP, and the total supply of 'childminding services' has not increased. Hence while Mary's job represents a genuine increase in GDP, paying the childminder does not; it simply transfers activity from the unpaid to the paid sector.

Final goods and services

final goods or services goods or services consumed by the ultimate user; because they are the end products of the production process, they are counted as part of GDP

intermediate goods or services goods or services used up in the production of final goods and services, and therefore not counted as part of GDP

Many goods are used in the production process. Before a baker can produce a loaf of bread, grain must be grown and harvested, the grain must then be ground into flour and, together with other ingredients, baked into bread. Of the three major goods that are produced during this process – the grain, the flour and the bread – only the bread is used by consumers. Because producing the bread is the ultimate purpose of the process, the bread is called a *final good*. In general, a **final good or service** is the end product of a process, the product or service that consumers actually use. The goods or services produced on the way towards making the final product – here, the grain and the flour – are called **intermediate goods or services**.

Since we are interested in measuring only those items that are of direct economic value, only final goods and services are included in GDP. Intermediate goods and services are *not* included. To illustrate, suppose that the grain from the previous example has a market value of €0.50 (the price the milling company paid for the grain). The grain is then ground into flour, which has a market value of €1.20 (the price the baker paid for the flour). Finally, the flour is made into a loaf of fine French bread, worth €2.00 at the local supermarket. In calculating the contribution of these activities to GDP, would we want to add together the values of the grain, the flour and the bread? No, because the grain and flour are intermediate goods, valuable only because they can be used to make bread. So, in this example, the total contribution to GDP is €2.00, the value of the loaf of bread, the *final product*.

Example 16.4 illustrates the same distinction, but this time with a focus on services.

Example 16.4 The barber and his assistant

Your barber charges €20 for a haircut. In turn, the barber pays his assistant €5 per haircut in return for sharpening the scissors, sweeping the floor and other chores. For each haircut given, what is the total contribution of the barber and his assistant, taken together, to GDP?

The answer to this problem is €20, the price, or market value, of the haircut. The haircut is counted in GDP because it is the *final service*, the one that actually has value to the final user. The services provided by the assistant have value only because they contribute to the production of the haircut; thus they are not counted in GDP.

Example 16.5 illustrates that the same good can be either intermediate or final, depending on how it is used.

Example 16.5 A good that can be either intermediate or final

Farmer Brown produces €100 worth of milk. He sells €40 worth of milk to his neighbours and uses the rest to feed his pigs, which he sells at his local market for €120. What is Farmer Brown's contribution to GDP?

The final goods in this example are the €40 worth of milk and the €120 worth of pigs sold at market. Adding €40 and €120, we get €160, which is Farmer Brown's contribution to GDP. Note that part of the milk Farmer Brown produced serves as an intermediate good and part as a final good. The €60 worth of milk that is fed to the pigs is an intermediate good, and so it is not counted in GDP. The €40 worth of milk sold to the neighbours is a final good, and so it is counted.

capital good a long-lived good, which is itself produced and used to produce other goods and services

A special type of good that is difficult to classify as intermediate or final is a **capital good**. A capital good is a long-lived good, which is itself produced and used to produce other goods and services. Factories and machines are examples of capital goods. Capital goods do not fit the definition of final goods, since their purpose is to *produce other goods*. On the other hand, they are not used up during the production process, except over a very long period, so they are not exactly intermediate goods either. For purposes of measuring GDP, economists have agreed to classify newly produced capital goods as final goods. Otherwise, a country that invested in its future by building modern factories and buying new machines would be counted as having a lower GDP than a country that devoted all its resources to producing consumer goods.

We have established the rule that only final goods and services (including newly produced capital goods) are counted in GDP. Intermediate goods and services, which are used up in the production of final goods and services, are not counted. In practice, however, this rule is not easy to apply, because the production process often stretches over several periods. To illustrate, recall the earlier example of the grain that was milled into flour, which in turn was baked into a loaf of French bread. The contribution of the whole process to GDP is €2, the value of the bread (the final product). Suppose, though, that the grain and the flour were produced near the end of the year 2002 and the bread was baked early the next year, in 2003. In this case, should we attribute the €2 value of the bread to GDP for 2002 or to GDP for 2003?

Neither choice seems quite right, since part of the bread's production process

value added for any firm, the market value of its product or service minus the cost of inputs purchased from other firms

occurred in each year. Part of the value of the bread should probably be counted in the year 2002 GDP and part in the year 2003 GDP. But how should we make the split? To deal with this problem, economists determine the market value of final goods and services indirectly, by adding up the **value added** by each firm in the production process. The value added by any firm equals the market value of its product or service minus the cost of inputs purchased from other firms. As we shall see, *summing the value added by all firms* (including producers of both intermediate and final goods and services) gives the same answer as simply adding together the value of final goods and services. But the value added method eliminates the problem of dividing the value of a final good or service between two periods.

To illustrate this method, let us revisit the example of French bread, which is the result of multiple stages of production. We have already determined that the total contribution of this production process to GDP is €2, the value of the bread. Let us show now that we can get the same answer by summing value added. Suppose that the bread is the ultimate product of three corporations: ABC Grain Company, Inc., produces grain; General Flour produces flour; and Hot'n'Fresh Baking produces the bread. If we make the same assumptions as before about the market value of the grain, the flour and the bread, what is the value added by each of these three companies?

ABC Grain Company produces €0.50 worth of grain, with no inputs from other companies, so ABC's value added is €0.50. General Flour uses €0.50 worth of grain from ABC to produce €1.20 worth of flour. The value added by General Flour is thus the value of its product (€1.20) less the cost of purchased inputs (€0.50), or €0.70. Finally, Hot'n'Fresh Baking buys €1.20 worth of flour from General Flour and uses it to produce €2.00 worth of bread. So the value added by Hot'n'Fresh is €0.80. These calculations are summarised in Table 16.1.

Company	Revenues (€) –	Cost of purchased inputs (€) =	Value added (€)
ABC Grain	0.50	0.00	0.50
General Flour	1.20	0.50	0.70
Hot'n'Fresh	2.00	1.20	0.80
Total			2.00

Table 16.1 **Value Added in Bread Production**

You can see that summing the value added by each company gives the same contribution to GDP, €2.00, as the method based on counting final goods and services only. Basically, the value added by each firm represents the portion of the value of the final good or service that the firm creates in its stage of production. Summing the value added by all firms in the economy yields the total value of final goods and services, or GDP.

You can also see now how the value added method solves the problem of production processes that bridge two or more periods. Suppose that the grain and flour are produced during 2002 but the bread is not baked until 2003. Using the value added method, the contribution of this production process to 2002 GDP is the value added by the grain company plus the value added by the flour company, or €1.20. The contribution of the production process to 2003 GDP is the value added by the baker, which is €0.80. Thus part of the value of the final product, the bread, is counted in the GDP for each year, reflecting the fact that part of the production of the bread took place in each year.

Exercise 16.3   Amy's card shop receives a shipment of Valentine's Day cards in December 2002. Amy pays the wholesale distributor of the cards a total of €500. In February 2003 she sells the cards for a total of €700. What are the contributions of these transactions to GDP in 2002 and 2003?

We have now established that GDP is equal to the market value of final goods and services. Let us look at the last part of the definition: 'produced within a country during a given period'.

Produced within a country during a given period

The word 'domestic' in the term 'gross domestic product' tells us that GDP is a measure of *economic activity* within a given country. Thus, only production that takes place within the country's borders is counted. For example, German GDP includes the market value of *all* cars produced within German borders, even if they are made in foreign-owned plants (recall Exercise 16.2). However, cars produced in the Czech Republic by a German-owned company such as Volkswagen are *not* counted. The market value of these cars is part of Czech GDP.

We have seen that GDP is intended to measure the amount of production that occurs during a given period, such as the calendar year. For this reason, only goods and services that are *actually produced* during a particular year are included in GDP for that year. Example 16.6 and Exercise 16.4 illustrate this.

Example 16.6   The sale of a house and GDP

A 20-year-old house in Manchester is sold to a young family for £200,000. The family uses an estate agent to find the house and pays a 5 per cent commission (or £10,000). The family also has to pay a solicitor a 3 per cent commission (or £6,000) to take care of the legal work. What is the contribution of this transaction to GDP?

Because the house was not produced during the current year, its value is *not* counted in this year's GDP. (The value of the house was included in the GDP 20 years earlier, the year the house was built.) In general, purchases and sales of existing assets, such as old houses or used cars, do not contribute to the current year's GDP. However, the £10,000 fee paid to the estate agent and the £6,000 paid to the solicitor represent the market value of the services the family purchased when buying the house. Since those services were provided during the current year, they are counted in current-year GDP. Hence the transaction contributes £16,000 to current-year GDP.

Exercise 16.4   Joan Smith sells 100 shares in a low-fares airline called FlyEuro.Com for €50 per share. She pays her broker a 2 per cent commission for executing the sale. How does Joan's transaction affect the current-year GDP?

The expenditure method for measuring GDP

GDP is a measure of the quantity of final goods and services *produced* by an economy. But any good or service that is produced will also be *purchased* and used by some economic agent – a consumer buying Christmas gifts or a firm investing in new machinery, for example. For many purposes, knowing not only how much is produced, but who *uses it* and *how*, is important.

Economic statisticians divide the users of the final goods and services that make up the GDP for any given year into four categories: *households, firms, governments* and the *foreign*

RECAP Measuring GDP

Gross domestic product (GDP) equals

- **the market value**
  GDP is an *aggregate* of the market values of the many goods and services produced in the economy. Goods and services that are *not sold in markets*, such as unpaid housework, are not counted in GDP. An important exception is goods and services provided by the government, which are included in GDP at the government's cost of providing them.

- **of final goods and services**
  Final goods and services (which include capital goods, such as factories and machines) are counted in GDP. *Intermediate goods and services*, which are used up in the production of final goods and services, are not counted. In practice, the value of final goods and services is determined by the *value added method*. The value added by any firm equals the firm's revenue from selling its product minus the cost of inputs purchased from other firms. Summing the value added by all firms in the production process yields the value of the final good or service.

- **produced in a country during a given period**
  Only goods and services produced *within a nation's borders* are included in GDP.
  Only goods and services produced during the *current year* (or the portion of the value produced during the current year) are counted as part of the current-year GDP.

sector (that is, foreign purchasers of domestic products). They assume that all the final goods and services that are produced in a country in a given year will be purchased and used by members of one or more of these four groups. Furthermore, the amounts that purchasers spend on various goods and services should be equal to the market values of those goods and services. As a result, GDP can be measured with equal accuracy by either of two methods: (1) adding up the market values of all the final goods and services that are produced domestically, or (2) adding up the total amount spent by each of the four groups on final goods and services and subtracting spending on imported goods and services. The values obtained by the two methods will be the same.

Corresponding to the four groups of final users are four components of expenditure: consumption, investment, government purchases, and net exports. That is, households consume, firms invest, governments make government purchases, and the foreign sector buys the nation's exports. Table 16.2 gives the values for each of these components for the British economy in 2006. Note that total investment is subdivided into investment expenditures by firms, government, households (new dwellings) and inventories. Detailed definitions of the components of expenditure, and their principal sub-components, follow.

consumption expenditure (or consumption) spending by households on goods and services, such as food, clothing and entertainment

Consumption expenditure (or simply **consumption**) is spending by households on goods and services such as food, clothing and entertainment. Consumption expenditure is sub-divided into three sub-categories:

1. *consumer durables* are long-lived consumer goods such as cars and furniture; note that new houses are not treated as consumer durables but as part of investment
2. *consumer non-durables* are shorter-lived goods such as food and clothing
3. *services*, a large component of consumer spending, include everything from haircuts and taxi rides to legal, financial and educational services.

Consumption[1]		828,008
Investment		234,078
Business investment	154,400	
Residential investment	54,483	
Government investment	23,936	
Inventory investment	+1,259	
Government purchases		286,256
Net exports		−46,394
Exports	371,805	
Imports	418,199	
		1,301,948
Net acquisition of valuables		+285
Statistical discrepancy		1,340
Gross domestic product		1,303,573

Table 16.2 **Expenditure Components of UK GDP, 2006 (£ million)**
1. Includes expenditures by non-profit institutions
Source: Monthly Digest of Statistics, January 2008 (Office for National Statistics, London).

investment spending by firms on final goods and services, primarily capital goods and housing

Investment is spending by firms on final goods and services, primarily capital goods and housing. Investment is divided into three subcategories:

1. *business fixed investment* is the purchase by firms of *new capital goods* such as machinery, factories and office buildings (remember that, for the purposes of calculating GDP, long-lived capital goods are treated as final goods rather than as intermediate goods); firms buy capital goods to increase their capacity to produce
2. *residential investment* is construction of *new houses and flats*
3. *inventory investment* is the addition of *unsold goods* to company inventories; in other words, the goods that a firm produces but doesn't sell during the current period are treated, for accounting purposes, as if the firm had bought those goods from itself (this convention guarantees that production equals expenditure); inventory investment can take a negative value if the value of inventories on hand falls over the course of the year.

government purchases purchases by central and local governments of final goods and services; government purchases do *not* include *transfer payments*, which are payments made by the government in return for which no current goods or services are received, nor do they include interest paid on the government debt

People often refer to purchases of financial assets, such as shares, as 'investments'. That use of the term is different from the definition we give here. A person who buys a share issued by British Airways acquires partial ownership of the *existing* physical and financial assets controlled by the company. A share purchase does not usually correspond to the creation of *new* physical capital, however, and so is not 'investment' in the sense we are using the term in this chapter. We shall generally refer to purchases of financial assets, such as stocks and bonds, as 'financial investments', to distinguish them from a firm's investment in new capital goods, such as factories and machines. Indeed, as we shall see in Chapter 22, purchases of financial assets are a means by which households accumulate wealth and are really a form of saving rather than investment.

Government purchases are expenditures by central and local governments on final goods and services, such as computers, fighter planes, consultancy services, and salaries paid to police, civil servants and schoolteachers. Government purchases do *not* include *transfer payments*, which are payments made by the government in return for which no current goods or services are received. Examples of transfer payments (which, again, are *not* included in government purchases) are unemployment benefits, pensions paid to government workers and welfare payments. Interest paid on the government debt is also excluded from government purchases.

net exports exports minus imports

Net exports equal exports minus imports.

- *Exports* are domestically produced final goods and services that are sold abroad.
- *Imports* are purchases by domestic buyers of goods and services that were produced abroad. Imports are subtracted from exports to find the net amount of spending on domestically produced goods and services.

A country's net exports reflect the *net* demand by the rest of the world for its goods and services. Net exports can be negative, since imports can exceed exports in any given year.

The relationship between GDP and expenditures on goods and services can be summarised by an equation. Let

$$Y = \text{GDP, or output}$$
$$C = \text{consumption expenditure}$$
$$I = \text{investment}$$
$$G = \text{government purchases}$$
$$NX = \text{net exports}$$

Using these symbols, we can write that GDP equals the sum of the four types of expenditure algebraically as

$$Y = C + I + G + NX$$

Example 16.7 Measuring GDP by production and by expenditure

To illustrate the equivalence between the production and expenditure methods of measuring GDP, assume that the economy produces one good: automobiles. In a given year 1,000 automobiles are produced, valued at €10,000 each.

Of these, 700 are sold to consumers, 200 are sold to businesses, 50 are sold to the government and 25 are exported abroad. No automobiles are imported. The automobiles left unsold at the end of the year are held in inventory by the auto producers. Find GDP in terms of (a) the market value of production and (b) the components of expenditure. You should get the same answer both ways.

The market value of the production of final goods and services in this economy is 1,000 autos × €10,000 per auto, or €10 million.

To measure GDP in terms of expenditure, we must add spending on consumption, investment, government purchases and net exports. Consumption is 700 autos × €10,000, or €7 million. Government purchases are 50 autos × €10,000, or €0.5 million. Net exports are equal to exports (25 autos at €10,000, or €0.25 million) – imports (0), so net exports are €0.25 million.

But what about investment? Here we must be careful. The 200 autos that are sold to businesses, worth €2 million, count as investment. But notice, too, that the auto companies produced 1,000 automobiles but sold only 975 (700 + 200 + 50 + 25). Hence 25 autos were unsold at the end of the year and were added to the automobile producers' inventories. This addition to producer inventories (25 autos @ €10,000, or

€0.25 million) counts as inventory investment, which is part of total investment. Thus total investment spending equals the €2 million worth of autos sold to businesses plus the €0.25 million in inventory investment, or €2.25 million.

Total expenditure is $C + I + G + NX = $ €7 million + €2.25 million + €0.5 million + €0.25 = €10 million, the same as the market value of production.

Exercise 16.5 Extending Example 16.7, suppose that 25 of the automobiles purchased by households are imported rather than domestically produced. Domestic production remains at 1,000 autos valued at €10,000 each. Once again, find GDP in terms of (a) the market value of production and (b) the components of expenditure.

RECAP Expenditure components of GDP

GDP can be expressed as the sum of expenditures on domestically produced final goods and services. The four types of expenditure that are counted in GDP, and the economic groups that make each type of expenditure, are as shown in the table below.

Who makes the expenditure?	Type of expenditure	Examples
Households	Consumption	Food, clothes, haircuts, new cars
Business firms	Investment	New factories and equipment, new houses, increases in inventory stocks
Governments	Government purchases	New school buildings, new military hardware, salaries of soldiers, teachers and government officials
Foreign sector	Net exports, or exports minus imports	Exported manufactured goods, legal or financial services provided by domestic residents to foreigners

GDP and the incomes of capital and labour

GDP can be thought of equally well as a measure of *total production* or as a measure of *total expenditure* – either method of calculating GDP gives the same final answer. There is yet a third way to think of GDP, which is as the *incomes of capital and labour*.

Whenever a good or service is produced or sold, the revenue from the sale is distributed to the workers and the owners of the capital involved in the production of the good or service. Thus, except for some technical adjustments that we will ignore, GDP also equals labour income plus capital income. *Labour income* comprises wages, salaries and the incomes of the self-employed. *Capital income* is made up of payments to owners of physical capital (such as factories, machines and office buildings) and intangible capital (such as copyrights and patents). The components of capital income include items such as profits earned by business owners, the rents paid to owners of land or buildings, interest received by bondholders, and the royalties received by the holders of copyrights or patents. Both labour income and capital income are to be understood as measured prior to payment of taxes; ultimately, of course, a portion of both types of income is captured by the government in the form of tax collections.

Figures 16.1, 16.2 and 16.3 may help you visualise the three equivalent ways of thinking about GDP: expenditure categories, income categories and gross value added by sector.

Figures 16.1, 16.2 and 16.3 capture the importance of consumption expenditures

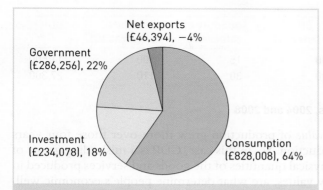

Figure 16.1 GDP by Expenditure Category: United Kingdom 2006 (£ million).

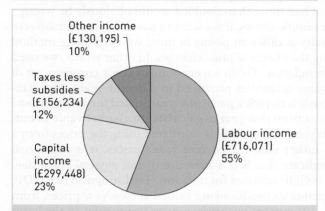

Figure 16.2 GDP by Type of Income: United Kingdom 2006 (£ million). Other income includes operating surplus of the non-corporate sector.

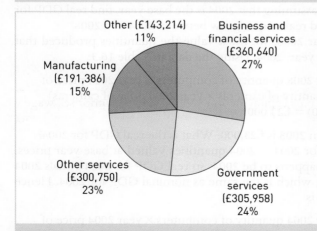

Figure 16.3 GDP by Gross Value Added: United Kingdom 2006 (£ million). Other services includes hotels, restaurants and transport. Other includes agriculture, mining and construction.

(households), labour income (wages and salaries) and the service sectors in the determination of GDP.

Nominal GDP versus real GDP

As a measure of the total production of an economy over a given period, such as a particular year, GDP is useful in comparisons of economic activity in different countries. For example, GDP data for 2008, broken down country by country, could be used to compare aggregate production in France and Germany during that year. However, economists are interested in comparing levels of economic activity not only in different *countries* but *over time* as well. For example, a government running for re-election on the basis of successful economic policies might want to know by how much GDP had increased during its term.

As the following example shows, using GDP to compare economic activity at two different points in time may give misleading answers. Suppose for the sake of illustration that the economy produces only computers and cameras. The prices and quantities of the two goods in two years, 2004 and 2008, are shown in Table 16.3. If we calculate GDP in each year as the market value of production, we find that GDP for 2004 is (10 computers × €1,000/computer) + (15 cameras × €100/camera) = €11,500. GDP for 2008 is (20 computers × €1,200/computer) + (30 cameras × €110/camera) = €27,300. Comparing GDP for 2008 to GDP for 2004, we might conclude that it is 2.4 times greater (€27,300/€11,500).

But look more closely at the data given in Table 16.3. Can you see what is wrong with this conclusion? The quantities of both computers and cameras produced in 2008 are exactly twice the quantities produced in 2004. If economic activity, as measured by actual production of both goods, exactly doubled over the four years, why do the calculated values of GDP show a greater increase?

The answer, as you also can see from Table 16.3, is that *prices* as well as *quantities* rose between 2004 and 2008. Because of the

Year	Quantity of computers	Price of computers (€)	Quantity of cameras	Price of cameras (€)	GDP (€)
2004	10	1,000	15	100	11,500
2008	20	1,200	30	110	27,300

Table 16.3 **Prices and Quantities, 2004 and 2008**

increase in prices, the *market value* of production grew more over those four years than the *physical volume* of production. So, in this case, GDP is a misleading gauge of economic growth, since the physical quantities of the goods and services produced in any given year, not the money values, are what determine people's economic well-being. Indeed, if the quantities produced had remained constant but the prices of computers and cameras had risen 2.4 times between 2004 and 2008, GDP would have risen 2.4 times as well, with no increase in physical production! In that case, the claim that the economy's (physical) output had more than doubled would obviously be wrong.

real GDP a measure of GDP in which the quantities produced are valued at the prices in a base year rather than at current prices; real GDP measures the actual *physical volume* of production

nominal GDP a measure of GDP in which the quantities produced are valued at current-year prices; nominal GDP measures the *current money value* of production

As this example shows, if we want to use GDP to compare economic activity at different points in time, we need some method of excluding the effects of price changes. In other words, we need to *adjust for inflation*. To do so, economists use a common set of prices to value quantities produced in different years. The standard approach is to pick a particular year, called the *base year*, and use the prices from that year to calculate the market value of output in each year. When GDP is calculated using the prices from a base year, rather than the current year's prices, it is called **real GDP**, to indicate that it is a measure of *real physical production*. Real GDP is GDP adjusted for inflation. To distinguish real GDP, in which quantities produced are valued at base-year prices, from GDP valued at current-year prices, economists refer to the latter measure as **nominal GDP**.

Example 16.8 Calculating the change in real GDP

Using data from Table 16.3 and assuming that 2004 is the base year, find real GDP for 2008 and 2004. By how much did real output grow between 2004 and 2008?

To find real GDP for the year 2008, we must value the quantities produced that year using the prices in the base year, 2004. Using the data in Table 16.3:

Year 2008 real GDP = (year 2008 quantity of computers × year 2004 price of computers) + (year 2008 quantity of cameras × year 2004 price of cameras)
= (20 × €1,000) + (30 × €100) = €23,000

The real GDP of this economy in 2008 is €23,000. What is the real GDP for 2004?

By definition, the real GDP for 2004 = 2004 quantities valued at base-year prices. The base year in this example happens to be 2004, so real GDP for 2004 equals 2004 quantities valued at 2004 prices, which is the same as nominal GDP for 2004. Hence real GDP for the base year 2004 is:

Year 2004 real GDP = (year 2004 quantity of computers × year 2004 price of computers) + (year 2004 quantity of cameras × year 2004 price of cameras)
= (10 × €1,000) + (15 × €100) = €11,500

In general, in the base year, real GDP and nominal GDP are the same. We can now determine how much real production has actually grown over the four-year period.

Since real GDP was €11,500 in 2004 and €23,000 in 2008, the physical volume of production doubled between 2004 and 2008. This conclusion makes good sense, since Table 16.3 shows that the production of both computers and cameras exactly doubled over the period. By using real GDP, we have eliminated the effects of price changes and obtained a reasonable measure of the actual change in physical production over the four-year span.

Exercise 16.6 Using Table 16.3, find real GDP in 2004 and 2008 if 2008 is selected as the base year. Compare your result with Example 16.8 in which 2004 is used as the base year.

If you have completed Exercise 16.6 you will have found that real GDP doubles between 2004 and 2008 irrespective of which year is used as the base year. Can we conclude from this that the calculation of real GDP is independent of the year selected as the base year? The answer is no. When production of different goods grows at different rates and when the prices of some goods fall relative to others, the calculation of real GDP may be sensitive to the chosen base year. Example 16.9 provides an illustration.

Example 16.9 Does the choice of the base year matter?

Suppose production and prices of computer and cameras in 2004 and 2008 are as follows:

Year	Quantity of computers	Price of computers (€)	Quantity of cameras	Price of cameras (€)
2004	10	1,000	15	100
2008	40	500	20	100

Calculate real GDP in each year using (a) 2004 as the base year (b) 2008 as the base year. Do the results differ?

Note that, for 2004, these data are the same as those in Table 16.3. However, between 2004 and 2008 computer production increases by more and the price of computers falls by half. Camera production increases at a slower rate and the price of cameras is constant.

(a) Using 2004 as the base year:

$$\text{Year 2004 real GDP} = (10 \times €1,000) + (15 \times €100) = €11,500$$
$$\text{Year 2008 real GDP} = (40 \times €1,000) + (20 \times €100) = €42,000$$

Hence when 2004 is used as the base year real GDP in 2008 is about 3.6 times what it was in 2004 (42,000/11,500).

(b) Using 2008 as the base year:

$$\text{Year 2004 real GDP} = (10 \times €500) + (15 \times €100) = €6,500$$
$$\text{Year 2008 real GDP} = (40 \times €500) + (20 \times €100) = €22,000$$

Hence when 2008 is used as the base year real GDP in 2008 is about 3.4 times what it was in 2004 (22,000/6,500).

Example 16.9 shows that the choice of base year can make a small difference. Using 2004 as the base year suggests that 2008 GDP is 3.6 times that in 2004 as compared to 3.4 when 2008 is used as the base year. This difference is very small and we get much the same result irrespective of which year is used as the base year. However in computing real GDP for European countries economists and statisticians have found that results can be quite sensitive to the choice of base year. This is especially true when the production of some goods has been rising rapidly and their relative prices falling. Over the last 20 years computers are perhaps the best example of this type of good. To cope with this problem economists now use an alternative method of calculating real GDP. This method is known as *chain-linking* and is described in Box 16.1. This method makes the calculation of real GDP less sensitive to the choice of base year. However the two approaches share the basic idea of valuing output in terms of base year prices, and the results obtained are generally similar.

Maths Box 16.1 Chain-linking

Chain-linking uses a technique known as a geometric average to 'link' GDP data from adjacent years. To illustrate, suppose we have prices and quantities for successive years 1 and 2. The chain-linked ratio of GDP between the two years is computed as:

$$\sqrt{(\text{Ratio of real GDPs with year 1 as the base year})}\sqrt{(\text{Ratio of real GDPs with year 2 as the base year})}$$

The first term is the square-root of the real GDP in year 2 relative to real GDP in year 1 with year 1 as the base year. That is:

$$\frac{\text{Year 2 real GDP at year 1 prices}}{\text{Year 1 real GDP at year 1 prices}}$$

The second term is the square-root of the real GDP in year 2 relative to real GDP in year 1 with year 2 as the base year. That is:

$$\frac{\text{Year 2 real GDP at year 2 prices}}{\text{Year 1 real GDP at year 2 prices}}$$

Suppose that the first ratio is 1.06 and the second 1.03. That is, when year 1 is the base year real GDP increases by 6 per cent between the two years but when year 2 is the base year the increase is only 3 per cent. The chain-linked ratio of real GDP between the two years is computed as:

$$\sqrt{1.06}\sqrt{1.03} = 1.0449$$

This implies that real GDP grew by 4.49 per cent between year 1 and year 2. Note that this is very close to the simple arithmetic average: 4.5 per cent.

RECAP Nominal GDP versus real GDP

Real GDP is calculated using the prices of goods and services that prevailed in a base year rather than in the current year. Nominal GDP is calculated using current-year prices. Real GDP is GDP adjusted for inflation; it may be thought of as measuring the physical volume of production. Comparisons of economic activity at different times should always be done using real GDP, not nominal GDP.

Real GDP is not the same as economic well-being

Because the economy's growth rate is measured as the annualised percentage change in real GDP, economic analysts normally view real GDP and its rate of change as key indicators of macroeconomic activity. However, while real GDP may be a good measure of economic activity, it is *not necessarily* the same as economic well-being. Real GDP is an imperfect measure of economic well-being because, for the most part, it captures only those goods and services that are *priced and sold in markets*. Many factors that contribute to people's economic well-being are not priced and sold in markets, and thus are largely or even entirely omitted from GDP. To understand why an increase in real GDP does not always promote economic well-being, let us look at some factors that are not included in GDP but do affect whether people are better off.

Leisure time

When real GDP increases, households can consume more goods and services, which increases their utility and economic well-being. As these goods and services are priced and sold in markets they are counted as part of GDP. However households with higher incomes may also decide to take more leisure time. But leisure is not *priced and sold in markets* and its value is not counted in real GDP. As additional leisure increases household utility it adds to their overall economic well-being. Hence the increase in real GDP may understate the increase in economic well-being.

Increasing Opportunity Cost

Economic naturalist 16.2 Why do people work fewer hours today than their great-grandparents did?

Most Europeans start work later in life, retire earlier and, in many cases, work fewer hours per week than people of 50 or 100 years ago.

The *opportunity cost* of working less – retiring earlier, for example, or working fewer hours per week – is the earnings you forgo by not working. If you can make €400 per week at a summer job, for example, then leaving the job two weeks early to take a trip with some friends has an opportunity cost of €800. The fact that people are working fewer hours today suggests that their opportunity cost of forgone earnings is lower than their grandparents' and great-grandparents' opportunity cost. Why this difference?

Over the past century, rapid economic growth in industrialised countries has greatly increased the *purchasing power* of the average worker's wages (see Chapter 18). In other words, the typical worker today can buy more goods and services with his or her hourly earnings than ever before. This fact would seem to suggest that the opportunity cost of forgone earnings (measured in terms of what those earnings can buy) is greater, not smaller, today than in earlier times. But because the buying power of wages is so much higher today than in the past, Europeans can achieve a reasonable standard of living by working fewer hours than they did in the past. Thus, while your grandparents may have had to work long hours to pay the rent or put food on the table, today the extra income from working long hours is more likely to buy relative luxuries, like nicer clothes or a fancier car. Because such *discretionary purchases* are easier to give up than basic food and shelter, the true opportunity cost of forgone earnings is lower today than it was 50 years ago. As the opportunity cost of leisure has fallen, Europeans have chosen to enjoy more of it.

Non-market economic activities

Not all economically important activities are bought and sold in markets; with a few exceptions, such as government services, non-market economic activities are omitted from GDP. We mentioned earlier the example of unpaid housekeeping services. Another example is volunteer services, such as unpaid work for charity and aid agencies. The fact that these unpaid services are left out of GDP does *not* mean that they are unimportant. The problem is that, because there are no market prices and quantities for unpaid services, estimating their market values is very difficult.

How far do economists go wrong by leaving non-market economic activities out of GDP? The answer depends on the type of economy being studied. Although non-market economic activities exist in all economies, they are particularly important in poor economies. For example, in rural villages of developing countries, people commonly trade services with each other or cooperate on various tasks without exchanging any money. Families in these communities also tend to be relatively self-sufficient, growing their own food and providing many of their own basic services. Because such non-market economic activities are not counted in official statistics, GDP data may substantially understate the true amount of economic activity in the poorest countries.

Closely related to non-market activities is what is called the *underground economy*, which includes transactions that are never reported to government officials and data collectors. The underground economy encompasses both legal and illegal activities – from informal babysitting jobs to organised crime. For instance, some people pay temporary or part-time workers such as house cleaners and painters in cash, which allows these workers to avoid paying taxes on their income. Economists who have tried to estimate the value of such services by studying how much cash the public holds have concluded that these sorts of transactions are quite important, even in advanced industrial economies.

Environmental quality and resource depletion

China has recently experienced tremendous growth in real GDP. But in expanding its manufacturing base, it has also suffered a severe decline in air and water quality. Increased pollution certainly detracts from the quality of life, but because air and water quality are not bought and sold in markets, the Chinese GDP does not reflect this downside of their economic growth.

The exploitation of finite natural resources also tends to be overlooked in GDP. When an oil company pumps and sells a barrel of oil, GDP increases by the value of the oil. But the fact that there is one fewer barrel of oil in the ground, waiting to be pumped some time in the future, is not reflected in GDP.

A number of efforts have been made to incorporate factors such as air quality and resource depletion into a comprehensive measure of GDP. Doing so is difficult, since it often involves placing a euro value on *intangibles*, such as having a clean river to swim in instead of a dirty one. But the fact that the benefits of environmental quality and resource conservation are hard to measure in euros does not mean that they are unimportant.

Quality of life

What makes a particular town or city an attractive place in which to live? Some desirable features you might think of are reflected in GDP: spacious, well-constructed homes, good restaurants and stores, a variety of entertainment and high-quality schools. However, other indicators of the good life are not sold in markets and so may be omitted from GDP. Examples include a low crime rate, minimal traffic congestion, active civic organisations and open space.

Poverty and economic inequality

GDP measures the *total* quantity of goods and services produced and sold in an economy, but it conveys no information about who gets to enjoy those goods and services. Two countries may have identical GDPs but differ radically in the distribution of economic welfare across the population. Suppose, for example, that in one country – call it Equalia – most people have a comfortable middle-class existence; both extreme poverty and extreme wealth are rare. But in another country, Inequalia – which has the same real GDP as Equalia – a few wealthy families control the economy, and the majority of the population lives in poverty. While most people would say that Equalia has a better economic situation overall, that judgement would not be reflected in the GDPs of the two countries, which are the same.

In countries such as the United Kingdom and the United States, absolute poverty has been declining. Today, many families whose income is below today's official 'poverty line' own a television, a car and in some cases their own home. Some economists have argued that people who are considered 'poor' today live as well as many middle-class people did in the 1950s.

But, though absolute poverty seems to be decreasing, *inequality of income* has generally been rising. The chief executive officer of a large corporation may earn hundreds of times what the typical worker in the same firm receives. Psychologists tell us that people's economic satisfaction depends not only on their absolute economic position – the quantity and quality of food, clothing and shelter they have – but on what they have compared with what others have. If you own an old, dilapidated car but are the only person in your neighbourhood to have a car, you may feel privileged. But if everyone else in the neighbourhood owns a luxury car, you are likely to be less satisfied. To the extent that such comparisons affect people's well-being, *inequality* matters as well as absolute poverty. Again, because GDP focuses on total production rather than on the distribution of output, it does not capture the effects of inequality.

GDP is related to economic well-being

You might conclude from the list of factors omitted from the official figures that GDP is a poor measure of economic welfare. Indeed, numerous critics have made that claim. However we must recognise that real GDP per person *does* tend to be positively associated with many things people value, including a high material standard of living, better health and life expectancies, and better education. We discuss next some of the ways in which a higher real GDP implies greater economic well-being.

Availability of goods and services

Obviously, citizens of a country with a high GDP are likely to possess more and better goods and services (after all, that is what GDP measures). On average, people in high-GDP countries enjoy larger, better-constructed and more comfortable homes, higher-quality food and clothing, a greater variety of entertainment and cultural opportunities, better access to transportation and travel, better communications and sanitation, and other advantages. While social commentators may question the value of material consumption – and we agree that riches do not necessarily bring happiness or peace of mind – the majority of people in the world place great importance on achieving material prosperity.

Health and education

Beyond an abundance of consumer goods, a high GDP brings other more basic advantages. Table 16.4 shows the differences between rich and poor countries with regard to some important indicators of well-being, including life expectancy, infant and child mortality rates, measures of nutrition, and educational opportunity. Three groups of countries are compared: (1) developing countries as a group, (2) the least developed countries and (3) the high-income OECD countries. As the first row of Table 16.4

Indicator	All developing countries	Least developed countries	High-income OECD countries
GDP per person ($)	5,282	1,499	33,831
Life expectancy at birth (years)	66.1	54.5	79.4
Infant mortality rate (per 1,000 live births)	57	97	5
Under-5 mortality rate (per 1,000 live births)	83	153	6
Births attended by skilled personnel (%)	60	35	99
Incidence of HIV/AIDS (% in 15–49 age group)	1.2	3.4	0.3
Undernourished people (%)	17	37	Negligible
Combined enrolment rate for primary, secondary and tertiary schools (%)	64.1	48.0	93.9
Adult literacy rate (%)	76.9	53.9	99.0
Total population (millions)	5,215.0	765.7	931.5

Table 16.4 **GDP and Basic Indicators of Well-being**

Source: United Nations, *Human Development Report* (2007–2008), available at http://hdr.undp. org/. All data are for 2005, except incidence of HIV (2003) and undernourished people (1999–2001). GDP data are adjusted to account for local differences in prices of basic commodities and services (adjusted for purchasing power parity, PPP).

shows, these three groups of countries have radically different levels of GDP per person. Most notably, GDP per person in the high-income countries is more than 20 times that of the least developed countries.[2]

How do these large differences in GDP relate to other measures of well-being? Table 16.4 shows that, on some of the most basic measures of human welfare, the developing countries fare much worse than the industrial countries. In round figures a child born in one of the least developed countries has a 10 per cent (97/1,000) chance of dying before its first birthday and about a 15 per cent (153/1,000) chance of dying before its fifth birthday. The corresponding figures for the rich countries are 0.5 per cent (5/1,000) and 0.6 per cent (6/1,000), respectively. A child born in a rich country has a life expectancy of just over 79 years, compared with about 55 years for a child born in one of the least developed countries. Superior nutrition, sanitation and medical services in the richer countries account for these large discrepancies in basic welfare. Skilled health personnel assist at 99 per cent of births in rich countries but only 35 per cent in the poorest countries. The poor also experience much higher rates of illness. For example, the incidence of HIV/AIDS in the least developed countries is 3.4 per cent of the population aged 15–49, about 11 times the rate in rich countries. On another important dimension of human well-being, literacy and education rates, high-GDP countries also have the advantage. As Table 16.4 shows, 99 per cent of adults in rich countries can read and write as compared to 53.9 per cent in the poorest developing countries. The percentage of children enrolled in primary, secondary and tertiary education in rich countries is 93.9 per cent, or almost twice that in the least developed countries.

2 The GDP data in Table 16.4 use US prices to value goods and services in developing nations. Since basic goods and services tend to be cheaper in poor countries, this adjustment significantly increases measured GDP in those countries.

Table 16.4 points to an important conclusion, namely countries with high real GDP per head of the population have higher life expectancy, lower infant mortality, better nutrition, better healthcare and better educational systems, all of which are key indicators of economic well-being. Hence while real GDP may be an imperfect indicator of overall economic welfare, a high real GDP per head is nonetheless vital to improving economic well-being. In short, the higher is real GDP per head the greater are the resources available for investment in health and education, and the greater the country's economic welfare. In Chapter 20 we shall discuss why real GDP per person grows over time and differs between countries.

Economic naturalist 16.3 Why do far fewer children complete high school in poor countries than in rich countries?

One possible explanation is that people in poor countries place a lower priority on getting an education than people in rich countries. But immigrants from poor countries often place a heavy emphasis on education – though it may be that people who emigrate from poor countries are unrepresentative of the population as a whole.

An economic naturalist's explanation for the lower schooling rates in poor countries would rely not on cultural differences but on differences in *opportunity cost*. In poor societies, most of which are heavily agricultural, children are an important source of labour. Beyond a certain age, sending children to school imposes a high opportunity cost on the family. Children who are in school are not available to help with planting, harvesting and other tasks that must be done if the family is to survive. In addition, the cost of books and school supplies imposes a major hardship on poor families. In rich, non-agricultural countries, school-age children have few work opportunities, and their potential earnings are small relative to other sources of family income. The low opportunity cost of sending children to school in rich countries is an important reason for the higher enrolment rates in those countries.

RECAP Real GDP and economic well-being

Real GDP is at best an imperfect measure of economic well-being. Among the factors affecting well-being *omitted from real GDP* are the availability of leisure time, non-market services such as unpaid home making and volunteer services, environmental quality and resource conservation and quality-of-life indicators such as a low crime rate. Also real GDP does not reflect the degree of *economic inequality* in a country. Because real GDP is not the same as economic well-being, proposed policies should not be evaluated strictly in terms of whether or not they increase GDP.

Although GDP is not the same economic well-being, it is positively associated with many things that people value, including a higher material standard of living, better health, longer life expectancies, and higher rates of literacy and educational attainment. This relationship between real GDP and economic well-being has led many people to emigrate from poor nations in search of a better life, and has motivated policy makers in developing countries to try to increase their nations' rates of economic growth.

Summary

■ The basic measure of an economy's output is *gross domestic product (GDP)*, the market value of the final goods and services produced in a country during a given period. Expressing output in terms of market values allows economists to aggregate the millions of goods and services produced in a modern economy.

■ Only *final goods and services* (which include *capital goods*) are counted in GDP, since they are the only goods and services that directly benefit final users. *Intermediate goods and services*, which are used up in the production of final goods and services, are not counted in GDP, nor are sales of existing assets, such as a 20-year-old house. Summing the value added by each firm in the production process is a useful method of determining the value of final goods and services.

■ GDP can also be expressed as the sum of four types of expenditure: *consumption, investment, government purchases* and *net exports*. These four types of expenditure correspond to the spending of households, firms, the government and the foreign sector, respectively.

■ To compare levels of GDP over time, economists must eliminate the effects of inflation. They do so by measuring the market value of goods and services in terms of the prices in a base year. GDP measured in this way is called *real GDP*, while GDP measured in terms of current-year prices is called *nominal GDP*. Real GDP should always be used in making comparisons of economic activity over time.

■ Real GDP per person is an imperfect measure of economic well-being. With a few exceptions, notably government purchases of goods and services (which are included in GDP at their cost of production), GDP includes only those *goods and services* sold in markets. It excludes important factors that affect people's well-being, such as the amount of leisure time available to them, the value of unpaid or volunteer services, the quality of the environment, quality-of-life indicators such as the crime rate, and the degree of economic inequality.

■ Real GDP is still a useful indicator of *economic well-being*, however. Countries with a high real GDP per person not only enjoy high average standards of living; they also tend to have higher life expectancies, low rates of infant and child mortality, and high rates of school enrolment and literacy.

Review questions

1. Why do economists use market values when calculating GDP? What is the economic rationale for giving high-value items more weight in GDP than low-value items?

2. A large part of the agricultural sector in developing countries is subsistence farming, in which much of the food that is produced is consumed by the farmer and the farmer's family. Discuss the implications of this fact for the measurement of GDP in poor countries.

3. Give examples of each of the four types of aggregate expenditure. Which of the four represents the largest share of GDP in the United Kingdom? Can an expenditure component be negative? Explain.

4. Al's shoeshine stand shined 1,000 pairs of shoes last year and 1,200 pairs this year. He charged €4 for a shine last year and €5 this year. If last year is taken as the base year, find Al's contribution to both nominal GDP and real GDP in both years. Which measure would be better to use if you were trying to measure the change in Al's productivity over the past year? Why?

5. Would you say that real GDP per person is a useful measure of economic well-being? Defend your answer.

connect Problems

1. How would each of the following transactions affect the GDP of the United Kingdom?

   a. The UK government pays €1 million in salaries for government workers.

   b. The UK government pays €1 million to social security recipients.

   c. The UK government pays a UK firm €1 million for newly produced computers.

   d. The UK government pays €1 million in interest to holders of UK government bonds.

   e. The UK government pays €1 million to Saudi Arabia for crude oil to add to UK official oil reserves.

2. Intelligence Incorporated produces 100 computer chips and sells them for €200 each to Bell Computers. Using the chips and other labour and materials, Bell produces 100 personal computers. Bell sells the computers, bundled with software that Bell licenses from Microsoft at €50 per computer, to PC Charlie's for €800 each. PC Charlie's sells the computers to the public for €1,000 each. Calculate the total contribution to GDP using the value added method. Do you get the same answer by summing up the market values of final goods and services?

3. For each of the following transactions, state the effect both on French GDP and on the four components of aggregate expenditure.

   a. A French household buys a new car produced in France.

   b. A French household buys a new car produced in the UK.

   c. A French car rental business buys a new car from a French producer.

   d. A French car rental business buys a new car imported from Germany.

   e. The French government buys a new, domestically produced car for the use of a French diplomat, who has been appointed the ambassador to Sweden.

4. Here are some data for an economy. Find its GDP. Explain your calculation.

Consumption expenditures	€600
Exports	75
Government purchases of goods and services	200
Construction of new homes and apartments	100
Sales of existing homes and apartments	200
Imports	50
Beginning-of-year inventory stocks	100
End-of-year inventory stocks	125
Business fixed investment	100
Government payments to retirees	100
Household purchases of durable goods	150

5. The nation of Small-Land produces soccer balls, cases of beer, and painkillers. Here are data on prices and quantities of the three goods in 2000 and 2005:

Year	Balls		Beer		Painkillers	
	Quantity	Price (€)	Quantity	Price (€)	Quantity	Price (€)
2000	100	5	300	20	100	20
2005	125	7	250	20	110	25

Assume that 2000 is the base year. Find nominal GDP and real GDP for both years.

6. The government is considering a policy to reduce air pollution by restricting the use of 'dirty' fuels by factories. In deciding whether to implement the policy how, if at all, should the likely effects of the policy on real GDP be taken into account? Discuss.

References

Hull, C.H. (1900) 'Petty's place in the history of economic theory', *Quarterly Journal of Economics*, 14 May, pp. 307–40.

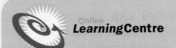

To help you grasp the key concepts of this chapter check out the extra resources posted on the Online Learning Centre. There are chapter summaries, self-test questions, an interactive graphing tool, weblinks and a glossary, all for free!

Visit the Online Learning Centre at: www.mcgraw-hill.co.uk/textbooks/mcdowell for information on accessing all of these resources.

17

Measuring the Price Level and Inflation

There is a story about an economics graduate, let's call her Roberta, who got a job with a Frankfurt-based bank. Five years on Roberta has been promoted several times and is a high earner with a salary of €100,000 per year. Roberta has a comfortable life and lives in a luxury apartment, which costs €20,000 per year in rent. Despite her good fortune Roberta decides that she wants to see the world and asks her employer for two years' unpaid leave. Over the next two years Roberta travels extensively and uses her savings. On returning to Frankfurt she resumes her job at the bank at her old salary of €100,000 per year. However, while Roberta was away Frankfurt has boomed as a financial centre and when she tries to rent her old apartment she finds that the annual rent has doubled to €40,000. She also finds that prices for the other goods and services she likes to buy – haircuts, restaurant meals, theatre tickets, etc. – have also increased substantially. The problem that Roberta faces is that, because of inflation, the *real purchasing power* of her money income has been reduced. Roberta may have had a great time on her travels but at the price of a decline in her real standard of living as measured by the quantities of goods and services her income permits her to buy.

This story illustrates a simple but very important point, which is that the value of money depends entirely on the prices of goods and services one wants to buy. High and sustained inflation – a rapid and ongoing increase in the prices of most goods and services – can radically reduce the buying power of a given amount of money; €100,000 may be a substantial salary at the prices prevailing today but it becomes less attractive if these prices double or treble over a few years.

Inflation can also make a comparison of economic conditions at different points in time quite difficult. When the authors of this book were undergraduates, 'essential' items like pints of beer and cinema tickets might have cost less than one euro (actually, in those far-off days, prices in the United Kingdom and Ireland were measured in non-decimal pounds, shillings and pence). Today the same items might cost five or six times as much. You might conclude from this that students were much better off in 'the good old days', but were they really? Without more information, we can't tell, for though the prices of beer and cinema tickets have gone up, so has the amount of spending money students have to buy these and other items such as books. The real question is whether young people's spending money has increased as much as or more than the prices of the things they want to buy. If so, then they are no worse off today than we were when we were young and a beer cost a shilling.

Inflation also creates uncertainty when we try to look into the future, to ask questions such as: 'How much should I plan to save for retirement?' The answer to this question depends on how much inflation is likely to occur before one retires (and thus how much things like heating, food and clothing will cost). Inflation can pose similar problems for policy makers. For example, to plan long-term government spending programmes they must estimate how much the government's purchases will cost several years in the future. How many times have you read newspaper reports on projects such as a new road or hospital that has run over its budget because inflation was higher than expected at the time the project was planned?

An important benefit of studying macroeconomics is learning how to avoid the confusion inflation interjects into comparisons of economic conditions over time or projections for the future. In this chapter, a continuation of our study of the construction and interpretation of economic data, we shall see how both prices and inflation are measured and how the money value of goods and services can be 'adjusted' to eliminate the effects of inflation. Quantities that are measured in euros or pounds and then adjusted for inflation are called real quantities (recall, for example, the concept of real GDP in Chapter 16).

More important than the complications inflation creates for economic measurement are the costs that it imposes on the economy. In this chapter we shall see why high inflation can significantly impair an economy's performance, to the extent that economic policy makers claim a low and stable rate of inflation as one of their chief objectives. We shall conclude the chapter by showing how inflation is linked to another key economic variable, the rate of interest on financial assets.

The consumer price index: measuring the price level

Suppose you are asked the following question: By how much did the 'cost of living' in Sweden and the United Kingdom increase between 2005 and 2007? The *cost of living* is usually taken to mean the cost of an average or standard basket of goods and services (housing, food, clothing, transport, entertainment, etc.) purchased by a typical household. The basic tool economists use to answer this type of question is the consumer price index (or CPI for short). The CPI is a measure of the cost of living during a particular period. Specifically, the consumer price index (CPI) for any period measures the cost in that period of a standard set, or basket, of goods and services *relative* to the cost of the same basket of goods and services in a fixed year, called the base year.

consumer price index (CPI) for any period, measures the cost in that period of a standard basket of goods and services relative to the cost of the same basket of goods and services in a fixed year, called the *base year*

Although there may be differences in computational methods and in the definition of an average basket of goods and services, the principles underlying the CPI are similar in most countries. To illustrate how a typical CPI is constructed, suppose that the government has designated 2005 as the base year. Assume for the sake of simplicity that in 2005 a typical household's monthly budget consisted of spending on just three items: rent, hamburgers and train tickets. In reality, of course, families purchase hundreds of different items each month, but the basic principles of constructing the CPI are the same no matter how many items are included. Suppose, too, that the family's average monthly expenditures in 2005, the base year, were as shown in Table 17.1.

Item	Cost in 2005 (€)
Rent	500
Hamburgers (60 @ €2.00 each)	120
Train tickets (10 @ €6.00 each)	60
Total expenditure	680

Table 17.1 **Monthly Household Budget of the Typical Family, 2005 (Base Year)**

Now let's fast-forward to the year 2007. Over that period, the prices of various goods and services are likely to have changed; some will have risen and some fallen. Let's suppose that by 2007 the household's rent has risen to €630. Hamburgers now cost €2.50 each, and the price of train tickets has risen to €7.00 each. So, in general, prices have been rising.

By how much did the family's cost of living increase between 2005 and 2007? Table 17.2 shows that if the typical family wanted to consume the *same basket of goods and services* in 2007 as they did in 2005, they would have to spend €850 per month, or €170 more than the €680 per month they spent in 2005. In other words, to live the same way in the year 2007 as they did in the year 2005, the family would have to spend 25 per cent more (€170/€680) each month. So, in this example, the cost of living for the typical family rose 25 per cent between 2005 and 2007.

Item	Cost in 2007 (€)	Cost in 2005 (€)
Rent	630	500
Hamburgers (60 @ €2.50 each)	150	120
Train tickets (10 @ €7.00 each)	70	60
Total expenditure	850	680

Table 17.2 **Cost of Reproducing the 2005 (Base-Year) Basket of Goods and Services in 2007**

In most countries, the government agency responsible for producing the CPI calculates the official CPI using essentially the same method. The first step in deriving the CPI is to pick a *base year* and determine the basket of goods and services that were consumed by the typical family during that year. In practice, the government learns how consumers allocate their spending through a detailed survey, called the Consumer or Household Expenditure Survey, in which randomly selected families record every purchase they make and the price they pay over a given month. Let's call the basket of goods and services that results the *base-year basket*. Then, each month, government employees visit thousands of stores and conduct numerous interviews to determine the current prices of the goods and services in the base-year basket. The CPI in any given year is computed using this formula:

$$\text{CPI} = \frac{\text{Cost of the base-year basket of goods and services in the current year}}{\text{Cost of the base-year basket of goods and services in the base year}}$$

Returning to the example of the typical family that consumes three goods, we can calculate the CPI in 2007 as

$$\text{CPI in 2007} = \frac{€850}{€680} = 1.25$$

In other words, in this example the cost of living in the year 2007 is 25 per cent higher than it was in 2005, the base year. Notice that the base-year CPI is always equal to 1.00, since in that year the numerator and the denominator of the CPI formula are the same. The CPI for a given period (such as a month or year) measures the cost of living in that period *relative* to what it was in the base year.

Often, news reporters multiply the CPI by 100 to get rid of the decimal point. If we were to do that here, the year 2007 CPI would be expressed as 125 rather than 1.25, and the base-year CPI would be expressed as 100 rather than 1.00.

Example 17.1 Measuring the typical family's cost of living

Suppose that in addition to the three goods and services the typical family consumed in 2005 they also bought four sweaters at €30 each. In 2007 the same sweaters cost €50 each. The prices of the other goods and services in 2005 and 2007 were the same as in Table 17.2. Find the change in the family's cost of living between 2005 and 2007. Adding four sweaters at €30 each raises the cost of the 2005 base-year basket to €800. What does this same basket (including the four sweaters) cost in 2007? Rent, the price of hamburgers and the train tickets is €850, as before. Adding the cost of the four sweaters at €50 each raises the total cost of the basket to €1,050. The CPI equals the cost of the basket in 2007 divided by the cost of the basket in 2005 (the base year), or €1,050/€800 = 1.31. We conclude that the family's cost of living rose 31 per cent between 2005 and 2007.

Exercise 17.1 Returning to the three-good example in Tables 18.1 and 18.2, find the 2007 CPI if the household's rent falls from €500 in 2005 to €400 in 2007. The prices for hamburgers and train tickets in the two years remain the same as in Tables 18.1 and 18.2.

| price index a measure of the average price of a given class of goods or services relative to the price of the same goods and services in a base year |

A CPI is not itself the price of a specific good or service; it is a **price index**. A price index measures the average price of a class of goods or services relative to the price of those same goods or services in a base year.

Exercise 17.2 The CPI captures the cost of living for the 'typical' or average family. Suppose you were to construct a personal price index (PPI) to measure changes in your own cost of living over time. In general, how would you go about constructing such an index? Why might changes in your PPI differ from changes in the CPI?

Inflation

The CPI provides a measure of the average *level* of prices relative to prices in the base year. *Inflation*, in contrast, is a measure of how fast the average price level is *changing* over time. The **rate of inflation** is defined as the annual percentage rate of change in the price level – as measured, for example, by the CPI.

rate of inflation the annual percentage rate of change in the price level, as measured, for example, by the CPI

Suppose that the CPI has a value of 1.25 in 2006 and a value of 1.30 in 2007. The rate of inflation between 2006 and 2007 is the percentage increase in the price level, or the increase in the price level (0.05) divided by the initial price level (1.25), which is equal to 4 per cent.

Economic naturalist 17.1 The EU's Harmonised Index of Consumer Prices

National price indices can vary widely in their coverage of goods and services and their methods of construction. For example, some countries such as Ireland include mortgage interest and credit charges, while others treat these costs as financing costs rather than consumer expenditure, and exclude them from their national CPIs. Likewise, some national CPIs are based exclusively on expenditure by domestic residents inside the country, while others include expenditures in other countries. These differences in national price indices make it difficult to derive accurate international comparisons of national inflation rates. In particular, because the Maastricht Treaty charges the European Central Bank (ECB) with the responsibility of maintaining price stability, or low inflation, the Bank requires comparable price indices that can be used to compute the average inflation rate in the euro-zone (those countries using the euro as their currency). In response to this, Eurostat (the EU statistical office) has developed a *Harmonised Index of Consumer Prices* (HICP), which can be used as a comparable measure of inflation in member states. Each member state of the European Union now produces a national HICP using a common methodology. Using country weights that reflect differences in GDP these national HICPs can be aggregated to an EU harmonised price index. Hence changes in the aggregated HICP measure the average rate of inflation in the European Union. In addition to national and EU-wide HICPs, Eurostat also produces HICPs for other groupings. The most important of these is the *Monetary Union Index of Consumer Prices* (MUICP), which is a weighted average of national HICPs in the Eurosystem. The ECB uses the MUICP to monitor price stability, which it now defines as a year-on-year increase of below 2 per cent in the MUICP. Likewise the Bank of England uses the UK HICP (somewhat confusingly known as the CPI) to monitor British inflation. Details on the construction and use of the HICP can be found at the Eurostat website: http://epp.eurostat.ec.eu.int.

Example 17.2 Using the HICP

Let us return to the question posed at the start of this chapter: By how much did the 'cost of living' in Sweden and the United Kingdom increase between 2005 and 2007? The following table gives the HICP for Sweden and the United Kingdom over 2005 to 2007 using 2005 = 100 as the base year.

	HICP	
	Sweden	UK
2005	100.00	100.00
2006	101.50	102.30
2007	103.20	104.70

To find the increase in the cost of living we must compute the inflation rate for each country in each year and over the entire period. For Sweden the inflation rate between 2005 and 2006 is the percentage increase in the HICP or $(101.5 - 100)/100 = 0.0150$, or 1.50 per cent. Likewise, between 2006 and 2007, the Swedish cost of living, as measured by the HICP, rose by $(103.2 - 101.5)/10.5 = 0.0167$, or 1.67 per cent, and over the period 2005 to 2007 the increase is 3.20 per cent. The corresponding figures for the United Kingdom are 2.30 (2005–06), 2.35 (2006–07) and 4.70 (2005–07) per cent.

Because the HICP uses the same methodology across countries it enables us to make valid international comparisons of inflation rates. For example, using comparable price indices we can say that, between 2005 and 2007, British inflation was 4.7 per cent as compared to 3.2 per cent in Sweden. This, however, does not necessarily mean that living costs are higher in the United Kingdom. It simply means that, over this period, prices rose faster in the United Kingdom than in Sweden. To see this, suppose that in 2005 a given basket of goods and services cost €1,000 in the UK and €1,200 in Sweden. Now suppose that by 2007 the same basket cost €1,047 in the United Kingdom and €1,238.40 in Sweden. Using 2005 as the base year the United Kingdom price index is 100 in 2005 and 104.7 (1047/1000) in 2007, an increase of 4.70 per cent. Likewise the Swedish price index is 100 in 2005 and 103.2 (1238.4/1,200) in 2007, an increase of 3.20 per cent. Hence although the United Kingdom price index is higher than the Swedish index in 2007 it does not necessarily follow that that 'cost of living' is higher in the UK.

Exercise 17.3   Using the data in Example 17.2 recalculate the CPI and annual inflation rates using 2007 as the base year. Are the annual inflation rates the same?

Example 17.3 Making comparisons: Europe's most expensive city

Suppose you are thinking about working abroad and decide to investigate living costs for expatriates in a range of European cities. You might compare national or city-based CPIs, but as these may differ in terms of construction and the range of prices used, your results may be misleading. For example, rents for flats may be higher in London than in Paris but if British and French statisticians treat housing costs in different ways their cost-of-living indices may not be comparable. To address this type of problem Mercer HR produces a series of harmonised price indices for capital cities. Using Brussels as the 'base city' (setting the cost of living in Brussels at 100), the table below gives the Mercer 2007 expatriate index of living costs in a range of capital cities, including housing costs.

Brussels	Berlin	Madrid	Rome	Dublin	Paris	London
100	99	106	113	115	117	145

Source: www.mercerHR.com

Hence, in 2007, the cost of living in Madrid was 6 per cent higher than in Brussels. Berlin was the lowest-cost city and London the most expensive. Living costs for expatriates in London were 45 per cent higher than in Brussels.

Deflation

Deflation is a situation in which the average level of prices is falling rather than rising – that is, the rate of inflation is negative. Referring back to Figure 15.5 shows that the United Kingdom experienced deflation during the Great Depression of the 1920s and early 1930s. Example 17.4 gives a more recent case.

Example 17.4 Japanese deflation 2000–04

The table below gives Japanese CPI values for the years 2000–04 (base year 1996 = 100). Find the rates of inflation in each year starting with 2001.

Year	CPI
2000	101.2
2001	101.1
2002	100.5
2003	100.3
2004	100.3

deflation a situation in which the prices of most goods and services are falling over time so that inflation is negative

The Japanese inflation rate between 2000 and 2001 was $(101.1 - 102.2)/101.1 = -0.1$ per cent. Likewise the inflation rates for 2002, 2003 and 2004 were −0.6, −0.2 and 0 per cent, respectively. Hence Japan experienced *negative* inflation, or **deflation**, over these years.

Adjusting for inflation

A price index such as the CPI is an extremely useful tool. Not only does it allow us to measure changes in the cost of living; it can also be used to adjust economic data to *eliminate the effects of inflation*. In this section we shall see how a price index such as the CPI can be used to convert quantities measured at current euro or pound values into real terms, a process called **deflating**. By current euro or pound values we mean measuring the value of a given *quantity* of goods and services in *today's prices*. We will also see that the CPI can be used to convert real quantities into nominal or money terms, a procedure called *indexing*. Both procedures are useful not only to economists but to anyone who needs to adjust payments, accounting measures or other economic quantities for the effects of inflation.

deflating (a nominal quantity) the process of dividing a nominal quantity by a price index (such as the CPI) to express the quantity in real terms

Deflating a nominal quantity

An important use of the CPI is to adjust **nominal quantities** – quantities measured at their current money values – for the effects of inflation. To illustrate, suppose we know that the typical family in a certain metropolitan area had a total income of €50,000 in 2005 and €51,500 in 2007, an increase of 3 per cent. Was this family better off in 2007 than in 2005?

nominal quantity a quantity that is measured in terms of its current euro or pound value

Without any more information than this we might be tempted to say yes because the family's income increased over the two-year period. But prices might also have been rising as fast as or faster than the family's income. Suppose, as was the case in the United Kingdom, the CPI increases from 100 to 104.7 between 2005 and 2007. As the prices increased by 4.7 per cent and the family's income increased by only 3 per cent, we would have to conclude that the family is worse off, in terms of the goods and services they can afford to buy, despite the increase in their *nominal*, or current euro, income.

real quantity a quantity that is measured in physical terms – for example, in terms of quantities of goods and services

We can make a more precise comparison of the family's purchasing power in 2005 and 2007 by calculating its income in those years in *real* terms. In general, a **real quantity** is one that is measured in *physical terms* – for example, in terms of the quantities of goods and services that a given amount of money can buy. As shown in Table 17.3, we can convert a nominal quantity into a real quantity if we divide the nominal quantity by a price index for the period. The calculations in Table 17.3 show that in *real* or purchasing power terms, the family's income actually *decreased* by €812, or 1.6 per cent of its initial real income of €50,000, between 2005 and 2007.

Year	Nominal family income (€)	CPI	Real family income = nominal family income/CPI (€)
2005	50,000	1.000	50,000/1.000 = 50,000
2007	51,500	1.047	51,500/1.047 = 49,188

Table 17.3 **Comparing the Real Values of a Family's Income, 2005 and 2007.** The base year is 2005 = 1.

The problem for this family is that although its income has been rising in nominal terms, it has not kept up with inflation. Dividing a nominal quantity by a price index to express the quantity in real terms is called deflating the nominal quantity. (Be careful not to confuse the idea of deflating a nominal quantity with deflation, or negative inflation. *The two concepts are different.*)

Dividing a nominal quantity by a price index to measure it in *real or purchasing power terms* is a very useful tool. It can be used to eliminate the effects of inflation from comparisons of any nominal quantity – workers' wages, healthcare expenditures, college tuition fees, government expenditure on education – over time. In Table 17.3 dividing the family's nominal income by the CPI gives a measure of the real quantity of goods and services that the family can purchase in each year, the correct measure of its real standard of living. Such real quantities are sometimes referred to as *inflation-adjusted* quantities.

Example 17.5 Winning Wimbledon: how much is it *really* worth?

In 1978 Martina Navratilova won the first of her nine Wimbledon singles titles. Her prize money was £17,100. Navratilova won her last title in 1990 when the prize money was £171,000. Which prize was worth more to Navratilova?

In 1978 the British Retail Price Index, or RPI, was 0.53 and 1.33 in 1990 (1985=1).[1] Dividing the 1978 prize by 0.53, we obtain £32,264, which is the value of the prize money 'in 1985 pounds'. Dividing the 1990 prize by that year's price index, 1.33, gives £128,571 in 1985 pounds. We can now compare the two prizes. In money terms the 1990 prize is 10 times the 1978 prize (171,000/17,100). However, in real terms the difference is much narrower, with the 1990 prize approximately 4 times the 1978 prize. Hence, although adjusting for inflation brings the two figures closer together (since

---

1 The RPI is the United Kingdom's national or domestic price index and should not be confused with the CPI, which is the United Kingdom's name for the HICP. The RPI is a more comprehensive measure and includes goods and services such as mortgage costs, which are excluded from the CPI. It also has a much longer data run.

real wage the wage paid to workers measured in terms of real purchasing power; the real wage for any given period is calculated by dividing the nominal (euro) wage by the CPI for that period

part of increase in the prize money compensates for the increase in prices between 1978 and 1990), in real terms Navratilova's final championship still earned four times her first victory.

Clearly, in comparing wages or earnings at two different points in time, we must adjust for changes in the price level. Doing so yields the **real wage** – the wage measured in terms of real purchasing power. The real wage for any given period is calculated by dividing the money wage by the CPI for that period.

Exercise 17.4 In 2004 Maria Sharapova won the Wimbledon title. Sharapova's prize money was £560,500. In 2004 the RPI was 1.97. How did Sharapova's real earnings compare with Navratilova's 1990 winnings?

Example 17.6 Real wages of British workers

Few very of us are lucky or talented enough to play at Wimbledon, let alone win a singles title. For most individuals and households, weekly or monthly wages constitute their major earnings. According to the British Office for National Statistics the average weekly wage in UK manufacturing industries was £369.40 in 1997 and £539.30 in 2007, an increase of almost 46 per cent. Compare the real wages of British workers in these years.

To find the real wage in 1997 and 2007, we need to know that the CPI was 0.897 in 1997 and 1.047 in 2007 (using 2005 = 1 as the base year). Dividing £369.40 by 0.897, we find that the real wage in 1997 was £411.80. Dividing £539.30 by 1.047 we find that the real wage in 2007 was £515.10, an increase of 25 per cent. Hence the increase in real wages was only 55 per cent of the corresponding increase in nominal wages.

Exercise 17.5 The average weekly wage for women working in UK manufacturing industries was £170.30 in 1990 and £356 in 2003, an increase of 109 per cent. The corresponding money wages for men are £282.20 in 1990 and £486.80 in 2003, an increase of 73 per cent. Using the price data in Example 17.6, how does the real wage in 2003 compare with that in 1990?

Indexing to maintain buying power

A price index can also be used to convert real quantities to nominal quantities. Suppose, for example, that in 2000 average government payments to unemployed workers were €1,000 per month. Let's assume that the government would like the real value of these benefits to remain constant over time so that the average unemployed workers' standard of living is unaffected by inflation. To achieve this objective, at what level should the government set the monthly unemployment benefit in 2007?

The nominal, or money, benefit government should pay in the year 2007 to maintain real purchasing power depends on how much inflation has taken place between 2000 and 2007. Suppose that the CPI has risen 20 per cent between 2000 and 2007. That is, on average the prices of the goods and services consumers buy have risen 20 per cent over that period. For the unemployed to 'keep up with inflation' their benefit in the year 2007 must be €1,200 per month, or 20 per cent more than it was in 2000. In general, to keep purchasing power constant, the money benefit must be increased each year by the percentage increase in the CPI.

indexing the practice of increasing a nominal quantity each period by an amount equal to the percentage increase in a specified price index; indexing prevents the purchasing power of the nominal quantity from being eroded by inflation

The practice of increasing a nominal quantity according to changes in a price index to prevent inflation from eroding purchasing power is called **indexing**. In some countries, government pensions are automatically indexed to inflation. Each year, without any action by government, benefits increase by an amount equal to the percentage increase in the CPI. Some labour contracts are indexed as well so that wages are adjusted for changes in inflation.

Example 17.7 An indexed wage contract

A wage contract provides for a first-year wage of €12.00 per hour and specifies that the *real wage* will increase by 2 per cent in the second year of the contract and by another 2 per cent in the third year. The CPI is 1.00 in the first year, 1.05 in the second year and 1.10 in the third year. Find the money wage that must be paid in the second and third years.

Let W_2 stand for the nominal wage in the second year. Deflating by the CPI in the second year, we can express the real wage in the second year as $W_2/1.05$. The contract says that the second-year real wage must be 2 per cent higher than the real wage in the first year – that is, €12.00 × 1.02 = €12.24. As the year 2 CPI = 1.05 the year 2 real wage is $W_2/1.05$ = €12.24. Multiplying through by 1.05 to solve for W_2, we get W_2 = €12.85, the nominal wage required by the contract in the second year. In the third year, the real wage must be €12.24 × 1.02 = €12.48. As the year 3 CPI = 1.10 the year 3 real wage is $W_3/1.10$ = €12.48. Multiplying through by 1.10 to solve for W_3, we get W_3 = €13.73, the nominal wage required by the contract in the third year.

Exercise 17.6   An accountant retires with an inflation-indexed pension of €2,000 per month. In the three years following his retirement, inflation is 2, 3 and 4 per cent. What is the nominal value of the accountant's pension after three years?

RECAP Methods to adjust for inflation

- *Deflating* To correct a nominal quantity, such as a family's euro income, for changes in the price level, divide it by a price index such as the CPI. This process, called *deflating* the nominal quantity, expresses the nominal quantity in terms of real purchasing power. If nominal quantities from two different years are deflated by a price index with the same base year, the purchasing power of the two deflated quantities can be compared.
- *Indexing* To ensure that a nominal payment, such as a wage or pension, represents a constant level of real purchasing power, increase the nominal quantity each year by a percentage equal to the rate of inflation for that year (a procedure known as *indexing*).

Does the CPI measure 'true' inflation?

You may have concluded that measuring inflation is straightforward, but as with GDP the issue is not free from controversy. Indeed, the question of whether inflation is properly measured has been the subject of serious debate. Because the CPI is one of the most important economic statistics, the issue is far from academic. Policy makers such as the Bank of England and the European Central Bank pay close attention to the latest inflation numbers when deciding what actions to take on interest rates. For example, the Bank of England *may* decide to increase sterling interest rates if the year-on-year rise in the British CPI exceeds its target for inflation, currently 2 per cent. Furthermore, when inflation starts to increase, labour unions may become more aggressive in seeking higher nominal wage increases to safeguard their members' real wages.

When a 1996 report for the American government concluded that changes in the CPI were a poor measure of 'true' inflation, a major controversy ensued. The report, prepared by a commission headed by Michael Boskin, formerly the chief economic adviser to President George H.W. Bush, concluded that the official CPI inflation rate *overstated* the true inflation rate by as much as one to two percentage points a year. In other words, if the official inflation rate is reported to be 3 per cent, the 'true' inflation rate might be 2 per cent, or even 1 per cent.

If this assessment is correct, then indexing pensions and other payments to the official inflation rate could be costing millions of euros more than necessary every year. In addition, an overstated rate of inflation would lead to an underestimation of the true improvement in living standards over time. If the typical family's nominal income increases by 3 per cent per year, and inflation is reported to be 2 per cent per year, economists would conclude that families are experiencing an increase in their real incomes. But if the 'true' inflation rate is really 1 per cent per year, then the family's real income is actually rising.

The Boskin Commission gave a number of reasons why the official inflation rate might overestimate the true rate of inflation. Two are particularly important. First, in practice statisticians cannot always adjust adequately for changes in the *quality* of goods and services. Suppose a new personal computer (PC) has 20 per cent more memory, computational speed and data storage capacity than last year's model. Suppose, too, for the sake of illustration, that its price is 20 per cent higher. Has there been inflation in computer prices? Economists would say no; although consumers are paying 20 per cent more for a computer, they are getting 20 per cent more computer power. The situation is really no different from paying 20 per cent more for a pizza that is 20 per cent bigger. However, because quality change is difficult to measure precisely, and because they have many thousands of goods and services to consider, statisticians often miss or understate changes in quality. In general, whenever statisticians fail to adjust adequately for improvements in the quality of goods or services, they will tend to overstate inflation. This type of overstatement is called *quality-adjustment bias*.

An extreme example of quality-adjustment bias can occur whenever a totally new good becomes available. For example, the introduction of the first effective AIDS drugs significantly increased the quality of medical care received by AIDS patients. In practice, however, quality improvements that arise from totally new products are likely to be poorly captured by the CPI, if at all. The problem is that since the new good was not produced in the base year, there is no base-year price with which to compare the current price of the good. Statisticians use various approaches to correct for this problem, such as comparing the cost of the new drug to the cost of the next-best therapies. But such methods are necessarily imprecise and open to criticism.

The second problem emphasised by the Boskin Commission arises from the fact that the CPI is calculated for a *fixed basket of goods and services*. This procedure does not allow for the possibility that consumers can switch from products whose prices are rising to those whose prices are stable or falling. Ignoring the fact that consumers can switch from more expensive to less expensive goods leads statisticians to overestimate the true increase in the cost of living.

Suppose, for instance, that people like coffee and tea equally well and in the base year consumed equal amounts of each. But then a frost hits a major coffee-producing nation, causing the price of coffee to double. The increase in coffee prices encourages consumers to forgo coffee and drink tea instead – a switch that doesn't make them much worse off, since they like coffee and tea equally well. However, the CPI, which measures the cost of buying the base-year basket of goods and services, will rise significantly when the price of coffee doubles. This rise in the CPI, which ignores the fact that people can *substitute* tea for coffee without being made significantly worse off, exaggerates the true increase in the cost of living. This type of overstatement of inflation is called *substitution bias*.

Example 17.8 Substitution bias

Suppose the CPI basket for 2005, the base year, is as follows.

Item	Expenditure (€)
Coffee (50 cups @ €1/cup)	50.00
Tea (50 cups @ €1/cup)	50.00
Scones (100 @ €1 each)	100.00
Total	200.00

Assume that consumers are equally happy to drink coffee or tea with their scones. In 2005, coffee and tea cost the same, and the average person drinks equal amounts of coffee and tea.

In the year 2007, coffee has doubled in price to €2 per cup. Tea remains at €1 per cup, and scones are €1.50 each. What has happened to the cost of living as measured by the CPI? How does this result compare with the true cost of living?

To calculate the value of the CPI for the year 2007, we must first find the cost of consuming the 2005 basket of goods in that year. At year 2007 prices, 50 cups each of coffee and tea, and 100 scones cost $(50 \times €2) + (50 \times €1) + (100 \times €1.50) = €300$. Since consuming the same basket of goods cost €200 in 2005, the base year, the CPI in 2007 is €300/€200, or 1.50. This calculation leads us to conclude that the cost of the fixed basket has increased 50 per cent between 2000 and 2005.

However, we have overlooked the possibility that consumers can substitute a cheaper good (tea) for the more expensive one (coffee). Indeed, since consumers like coffee and tea equally well, when the price of coffee doubles they will shift entirely to tea. Their new consumption basket – 100 cups of tea and 100 scones – is just as enjoyable to them as their original basket. If we allow for the substitution of less expensive goods, how much has the cost of living really increased? The cost of 100 cups of tea and 100 scones in 2007 is only €250, not €300. From the consumer's point of view, the true cost of living has risen by only €50, or 25 per cent. The 50 per cent increase therefore overstates the increase in the cost of living as the result of substitution bias.

The Boskin Commission's findings have been controversial. While quality-adjustment bias and substitution bias undoubtedly distort the measurement of inflation, estimating precisely how much of an overstatement they create is difficult. (If economists knew exactly how big these biases were, they could simply correct the data.)

Economic naturalist 17.2 Why is inflation in the healthcare sector apparently high?

Government statisticians report inflation rates for different categories of goods and services, as well as for the overall consumer basket. According to the official measures, since the 1980s the prices of medical services have tended to rise much more rapidly than the prices of other goods and services. Why is inflation in the healthcare sector apparently high?

Although inflation rates in the healthcare sector are high, some economists have argued that reported rates greatly overstate the true rate of inflation in that sector. The reason, claim critics, is the quality-adjustment bias. Healthcare is a dynamic sector of the economy, in which ongoing technological change has significantly improved the quality of care. To the extent that official data fail to account for improvements in the quality of medical care, inflation in the healthcare sector will be overstated.

Economists Matthew Shapiro and James Wilcox illustrated the problem with the example of changes in the treatment of cataracts (cloudiness in the lens of the eye that impairs vision).[2] The lens must still be removed surgically, but there have been important improvements in the procedure since the 1970s. First, surgeons can now replace the defective lens with an artificial one, which improves the patient's vision considerably without contact lenses or thick glasses. Second, the techniques for making and closing the surgical incision have been substantially improved. Besides reducing complications and therefore follow-up visits, the new techniques can be performed in the physician's surgery, with no hospital stay (older techniques frequently required three nights in hospital). Thus the new technologies have both improved patient outcomes and reduced the number of hours doctors and nurses spend on the procedure.

Shapiro and Wilcox point out that official measures of healthcare inflation are based primarily on data such as the doctor's hourly rate or the cost of a night in the hospital. They do not take into account either the reduction in a doctor's time or the shorter hospital stay now needed for procedures such as cataract surgery. Furthermore, Shapiro and Wilcox argue, official measures do not take adequate account of improvements in patient outcomes, such as the improved vision that cataract patients now enjoy. Because of the failure to adjust for improvements in the quality of procedures, including the increased productivity of medical personnel, official measures may significantly overstate inflation in the healthcare sector.

The costs of inflation: not always what you think

In the 1970s, when inflation in Europe and North America was considerably higher than it is now, opinion polls often suggested that the public viewed it as 'public enemy number one'. Although European and American inflation rates have been much lower in recent years, workers, employers, financial experts and government are still concerned about inflation, or the *threat of inflation*. Indeed, both the Bank of England and the European Central Bank are required to meet specific inflation targets. Why do people worry so much about inflation? Detailed opinion surveys often find that many people are confused about the meaning of inflation and its economic effects. Before describing the true economic costs of inflation, which are real and serious, let us examine this confusion.

2 Shapiro and Wilcox (1996).

price level a measure of the overall level of prices at a particular point in time as measured by a price index such as the CPI

relative price the price of a specific good or service in comparison to the prices of other goods and services

We need first to distinguish between the **price level** and the **relative price** of a good or service. The price level is a measure of the overall level of prices at a particular point in time as measured by a price index such as the CPI. Recall that the inflation rate is the percentage change in the price level from year to year. In contrast, a relative price is the price of a specific good or service *in comparison* to the prices of other goods and services. For example, if the price of oil is increasing by 10 per cent and the economy-wide inflation rate is 3 per cent, the relative price of oil would be increasing. Conversely, if the price of oil is rising by 3 per cent, while inflation is 10 per cent, the relative price of oil would be falling. That is, oil would become cheaper relative to other goods and services, even though it has not become cheaper in absolute terms.

Public opinion surveys suggest that many people are confused about the distinction between inflation, or an increase in the overall *price level*, and an increase in a specific *relative price*. Suppose that hostilities in the Middle East led to a doubling in crude oil prices. Higher oil prices will feed into prices of other goods and services, and most especially into goods such as petrol and home-heating oil. Upset by large increases in the prices of 'essential' goods such as petrol and heating oil, people might demand that government take action to stop 'this rampant inflation'. But while the increase in petrol and heating oil prices hurts consumers, how does it impact on the economy-wide inflation rate? Because petrol and heating oil are only two items in a consumer's budget, two of the thousands of goods and services that people buy every year, large increases in their prices will have a proportionately lower impact on the inflation rate. As Example 17.9 illustrates, the impact of higher prices for one good depends on the *weight* given to it in computing the CPI. If, for example, petrol accounts for 5 per cent of the CPI basket of goods and services than each 1 per cent increase in petrol prices increases the overall inflation rate by $1 \times 0.05 = 0.05$ per cent.

In this example, inflation is not the real problem. What upsets consumers is the change in the *relative prices* of petrol and oil, particularly compared with the price of labour (wages). By increasing the cost of using a car and heating a home, the increase in the relative price of oil reduces the income that people have left over to spend on other things. The important point is that changes in the average price level (inflation) and changes in the relative prices of specific goods are two quite different issues. The public's tendency to confuse the two is important, because the remedies for the two problems are different. To counteract changes in relative prices, the government would need to implement policies that affect the supply and demand for specific goods. In the case of higher oil prices, for example, the government could try to restore supplies by mediating the peace process in the Middle East or encourage consumers to buy more fuel-efficient cars and heating systems. To counteract inflation, however, the government must resort (as we will see) to changes in macroeconomic policies, such as monetary or fiscal policies. If public pressure forces the government to adopt anti-inflationary policies when the real problem is a relative price change, the economy could actually be hurt by the effort. Example 17.9 shows why economic literacy is important, to both policy makers and the general public.

Example 17.9 Relative prices and inflation

The following table gives a breakdown of British inflation between December 2005 and December 2006.

Commodity group	Percentage change	Weight in CPI basket
Food	4.67	0.103
Alcohol and tobacco	2.79	0.043
Clothing and footwear	−4.09	0.062
Housing, water, electricity, gas and other fuels	11.38	0.115
Furniture and household equipment	0.49	0.068
Health	3.38	0.024
Transport	2.09	0.152
Communication	0.50	0.024
Recreation and culture	−0.30	0.153
Education	14.04	0.018
Restaurants and hotels	3.25	0.138
Miscellaneous goods and services	3.50	0.100
CPI (overall index)	3.00	

The first column gives the broad commodity groups used in the CPI basket, the second column gives the percentage change in the average price of each commodity group and the third column gives the weight attached to each group in computing the CPI. For example, over these 12 months the price of food rose by 4.67 per cent, which accounted for 10.3 per cent (0.103) of the overall inflation rate of 3 per cent. If you multiply each price increase by its respective weight they should, allowing for rounding, sum to the percentage change in the CPI. That is:

$$4.67 \times 0.103 + 2.78 \times 0.043 + ... + 3.50 \times 0.10 \approx 3.0$$

In the cases of two commodity groups, 'Housing, water, electricity, gas and other fuels' and 'Education', prices rose by much more than the overall CPI. In the first the price increase (11.38) was almost 4 times that of the CPI and, in second (14.04), almost 5 times. However, the combined weight attached to these groups in computing the CPI is 26.8 per cent (0.115 + 0.153), which means that 73.6 per cent of the annual inflation rate is accounted for by price increases in other commodity groups. In six of these other groups the price increase was less than the increase in the overall CPI, and in two cases prices actually fell. Hence large price increases in goods such as electricity and gas do not necessarily imply a correspondingly large increase in the rate of inflation. Looking closely at these data we see that in six cases the increase in the price of the commodity group exceeded the rate of inflation, but in the remaining six the price increase was less than the rate of inflation. In the first six the relative price of the goods increased, while in the remaining six the relative price fell.

The true costs of inflation

Having dispelled the common confusion between inflation and relative price changes, we are now free to address the *true economic costs of inflation*. There are a variety of such costs, each of which tends to reduce the efficiency of the economy. Five of the most important are discussed here.

'Shoe-leather' costs

As all shoppers know, *cash is convenient*. Unlike cheques, which are not accepted every-where, and credit cards, for which a minimum purchase is often required, cash can be used in almost any routine transaction. Businesses, too, find cash convenient to hold. Having plenty of cash on hand facilitates transactions with customers, and reduces the need for frequent deposits and withdrawals from the bank.

Inflation raises the cost of holding cash to consumers and businesses. Suppose you are given a present of €1,000 in cash and decide to keep it 'under the mattress' rather than spend it immediately or lodge it in a bank deposit. What happens to the buying power of the €1,000 over time? If inflation is zero so that on average the prices of goods and services are not changing, the buying power of the €1,000 does not change over time. At the end of a year your purchasing power is the same as it was at the beginning of the year. But suppose the inflation rate is 10 per cent. In that case, the purchasing power of the €1,000 will fall by 10 per cent each year. After a year, you will still have €1,000 in cash, but its purchasing power – or the amount of goods and services it can buy – will be reduced to only €900. In general, the higher the rate of inflation, the less cash people will want to hold because of the loss of *purchasing power* that they will suffer.

Technically, currency is a debt owed by the government or central bank to the cur-rency holder. So when currency loses value, the losses to holders of cash are offset by gains to the government or central bank, which now owes less in real terms to currency holders. Thus, from the point of view of society as a whole, the loss of purchasing power is not in itself a cost of inflation, because it does not involve wasted resources. (Indeed, no real goods or services were used up when your €1,000 lost part of its value.) How-ever, when faced with inflation, people are not likely to accept a loss in purchasing power but instead will try to 'economise' on their cash holdings. For example, instead of drawing out enough cash for a month the next time they visit the bank, they will draw out enough to last only a week. The inconvenience of visiting the bank or automated teller machine (ATM) more often to minimise one's cash holdings is a real cost of infla-tion. Similarly, businesses will reduce their cash holdings by sending employees to the bank more frequently, or by installing computerised systems to monitor cash usage. To deal with the increase in bank transactions required by consumers and businesses trying to use less cash, banks will need to hire more employees and expand their operations.

Cost–Benefit Analysis

The costs of more frequent trips to the bank, new cash management systems and expanded employment in banks are real costs. They use up resources, including time and effort, that could be used for other purposes. Traditionally, the costs of economis-ing on cash have been called *shoe-leather costs* – the idea being that shoe leather is worn out during extra trips to the bank. Shoe-leather costs probably are not a significant problem in Europe today, where inflation is only 2–3 per cent per year. But in econo-mies with high rates of inflation, such as Germany in the 1920s when inflation was well over 1,000 per cent, they can become very significant.

'Noise' in the price system

In Chapter 3, we described the remarkable economic coordination that is necessary to provide the right amount and the right kinds of food to residents of large cities every day. This feat is not orchestrated by some food distribution ministry staffed by bureaucrats. It is done much better than a ministry ever could by the workings of free markets, operating without central guidance.

How do free markets transmit the enormous amounts of information necessary to accomplish complex tasks like supplying all varieties of food and other goods to a

| Equilibrium |

large metropolitan city such as London? The answer is through the *price system*. As an example, consider the supply of different types of fresh fish to restaurants in London. Suppose restaurant owners cannot find sufficient quantities of John Dory, a relatively rare and expensive species, and start to bid up its market price. Fish suppliers notice the higher price for John Dory and realise that they can make a profit by supplying more John Dory to the market. That is, an increase in the *relative price* of John Dory is a signal that additional profit can be made by increasing the supply of John Dory. As the price of John Dory rises, consumers will shift to cheaper, more available types of fish and the market for John Dory will reach equilibrium only when there are no more unexploited opportunities for profit, and both suppliers and demanders are satisfied at the market price. Multiply this example a million times and you will gain a sense of how the price system achieves a truly remarkable degree of economic coordination.

However, if the increase in John Dory prices reflects an economy-wide increase in inflation, the price of John Dory *relative to the prices of other goods and services* will not change and there will be no unexploited profit opportunities to bring additional John Dory to the market. Hence the suppliers' problem is to decide if higher John Dory prices are a change in its relative price or just a reflection of rising inflation. If inflation is low and stable the supplier of foodstuffs will immediately recognise the increase in John Dory prices as a signal to bring more to market. However, when inflation is high and volatile, the signals that are transmitted through the price system can become more difficult to interpret, much in the way that static, or 'noise', makes a radio signal harder to interpret. In a volatile inflationary environment it becomes more difficult to discern whether the increase in the price of one good is a true signal of increased demand, and the supplier needs to know what is happening to the prices of other goods and services across the economy. Since this information takes time and effort to collect, the supplier's response to the change in John Dory prices is likely to be slower and more tentative.

In summary, price changes are the market's way of communicating information to suppliers and consumers. An increase in the price of a good or service tells consumers to economise on their use of the good or service and suppliers to bring more of it to market. But when inflation is high and volatile, prices are affected not only by changes in the supply and demand for a product but also by changes in the general price level. Inflation creates static, or 'noise', in the price system, obscuring the information transmitted by prices and reducing the efficiency of the market system. This reduction in the efficiency of the price system imposes real economic costs.

Distortions of the tax system

Most countries operate a progressive income tax system that levies higher rates of tax on higher levels of income. For example, the first €5,000 of income may be taxed at a zero rate, the next €20,000 at 20 per cent and the remainder at 40 per cent. The divisions in the household's income, 0 – €5,000, €5,000 – €25,000 and greater than €25,000, are known as *tax brackets*. Consider an individual called John who earns €50,000 per year. John's tax liability can be summarised as follows:

Tax bracket	Tax rate (%)	Tax paid
First €5,000	0	0
Next €20,000	20	€4,000
Next €25,000	40	€10,000
Total tax liability		€14,000

Hence John pays €14,000, or 28 per cent of his pre-tax income (€50,000), and has an after-tax income of €36,000. Note that the tax system is *progressive* because a household earning €25,000 would pay €4,000 or 16 per cent of its income in tax. Now suppose John's income is indexed to inflation. If inflation is 10 per cent per year his annual income will increase by €5,000 to €55,000 and John's new tax liability will be as follows.

Tax bracket	Tax rate (%)	Tax paid
First €5,000	0	0
Next €20,000	20	€4,000
Next €30,000	40	€12,000
Total tax liability		€16,000

John's tax bill rises to €16,000, or 29 per cent of his pre-tax income (€55,000), but he is now paying a higher proportion of his income in tax even though his real income has remained constant, a phenomenon known as *bracket creep*. This effect is called a *distortion* because John is worse off in real terms even though the rates of income tax have remained unchanged. John's after-tax income rises by 8.3 per cent, €36,000 to €39,000, but with inflation at 10 per cent his real purchasing power has declined. This distortion can be avoided by indexing the income tax brackets to inflation. For example, suppose that the upper ends of the zero and 20 per cent brackets were increased by 20 per cent to €5,500 and €27,500, respectively. John would now pay zero on the first €5,500, 20 per cent on the next €22,000 and 40 per cent on the remaining €27,500, giving a total tax bill of €15,400, or 28 per cent of pre-tax income (€55,000), and his after-tax income rises by 10 per cent, €36,000 to €39,600, keeping its real purchasing power constant.

Although indexing can solve the problem of bracket creep, many provisions of the various tax codes have not been indexed, either because of lack of political support or because of the complexity of the task. As a result, inflation can produce unintended changes in the taxes people pay, which in turn may cause them to change their behaviour in economically undesirable ways.

Example 17.10 Accelerated depreciation

An important provision in the many tax codes for which inflation poses problems is a *depreciation allowance*. Suppose a firm buys a machine with a ten-year productive life for €1,000. With a depreciation allowance the firm can take a percentage of the purchase price as a deduction from its taxable profits in each of the ten years. If the allowance is 10 per cent, then the firm can reduce its taxable profits by €100 in each year of the machine's productive life. For example, if the tax rate on profits is 40 per cent then the firm can reduce its tax bill by €40 per year.

The idea behind this type of provision is that the wearing out of the machine is a *cost of doing business* that should be deducted from the firm's profit. Also, giving firms a tax break for investing in new machinery encourages them to invest and modernise their plants. What happens if capital depreciation allowances are not indexed to inflation? Suppose that, at a time when the inflation rate is high, a firm is considering purchasing a €1,000 machine. The managers know that the purchase will allow them to deduct €100 per year from taxable profits for the next ten years. But that €100 is a fixed amount that is not indexed to inflation. Looking forward, managers will recognise that five, six or ten years into the future, the real value of the annual €100 tax deduction will be much lower than at present because of inflation. They will have less incentive to buy the machine and may decide not to make the investment at all. Indeed, many studies have found that a high rate of inflation can significantly reduce the rate at which firms invest in new factories and equipment.

One way round this distortion is to permit *accelerated* depreciation allowances. For example, suppose the firm is permitted to deduct the full purchase price in year 1. With a 40 per cent tax on profits the firm would be able to reduce the year 1 tax bill by €400 as compared with €40 per year over ten years. Accelerated allowances therefore protect the firm from the effects of higher inflation in the future.

In many countries, tax codes are highly complex, containing hundreds of provisions and tax rates. This lack of indexation means that inflation can seriously distort the incentives provided by the tax system for people to work, save and invest. The resulting adverse effects on economic efficiency and economic growth represent a real cost of inflation.

Unexpected inflation

Unexpected changes in the rate of inflation can impose costs and benefits on parties to fixed nominal contracts. To illustrate, consider a trades union negotiating an annual wage increase with a group of employers. The rate of inflation that is expected over the contract period is bound to be an important consideration to both sides. If the union and the employers expect the inflation rate to be 3 per cent over the coming year then both should be happy to agree a 3 per cent increase in the money or nominal value of wages. From the union's perspective a 3 per cent increase will maintain the real purchasing power of its members' income, and from the employer's point of view 3 per cent is affordable because it expects the average price of its output to increase by the same amount. In short, providing the inflation rate actually turns out to be 3 per cent, then the *real wage* received by employees and the real cost of labour to employers will remain constant. But suppose that due to events that could not have been foreseen when the contract was agreed, inflation turns out to be higher than expected at 5 per cent. In that case the purchasing power of wages will be less than anticipated and employees will experience a decline in living standards. However, employers will gain because prices will be rising faster than wages and the real cost of paying the workers will be less than anticipated. Conversely, if inflation turns out to be lower than expected then employees will gain because the purchasing power of their wages will increase, but employers will lose because prices will be rising at a slower rate than wages and the real cost of paying the workers will be more than anticipated.

To take another example, suppose you take out a €1,000 one-year loan at 5 per cent interest. At the end of the year you will repay the loan plus €50 interest, a total of €1,050. The €50 interest payment is the nominal cost of the loan. The real cost depends on the rate of inflation over the loan period. If you expect inflation to be 3 per cent, then the real value of your liability will be eroded by 3 per cent and the expected real cost of the loan will be approximately 2 per cent. What happens if inflation turns out to be higher than expected, at 5 per cent? In this case, the real cost of the loan will be zero because the actual rate of inflation equals the nominal cost of borrowing: 5 per cent. In this case you will gain in real terms but the lender will lose because the real return on the loan is less than expected. Conversely if inflation turns out to be lower than expected then the real cost will be higher than expected; the borrower will lose and the lenders will earn a higher return than expected.

It is important to note that in each of these examples the effect of unanticipated changes in the rate of inflation is to *redistribute purchasing power* from one group to another. In the first case an unexpected rise in inflation redistributes purchasing power from employees to employers, and in the second from lenders to borrowers. Likewise an unexpected fall in inflation redistributes purchasing power from employers to employees and from borrowers to lenders. Hence, from an economy-wide point of view, the loss in purchasing power by one group is matched by an unanticipated gain to another group. In other words, the effect of unanticipated inflation is not to *destroy* purchasing power but to *redistribute* it.

Although redistributions caused by unanticipated inflation do not directly destroy wealth, but only transfer it from one group to another, they are still bad for the economy. Our economic system is based on *incentives*. For it to work well, people must know that if they work hard, save some of their income and make wise financial investments, they will be rewarded in the long run with greater real wealth and a better standard of living. Some observers have compared a high-inflation economy to a casino, in which wealth is distributed largely by luck – that is, by random fluctuations in the inflation rate. In the long run, a 'casino economy' is likely to perform poorly, as its unpredictability discourages people from working and saving. (Why bother if inflation can take away your savings overnight?) Rather, a high-inflation economy encourages people to use up resources in trying to anticipate inflation and protect themselves against it.

Interference with long-run planning

The fifth and final cost of inflation we shall examine is its tendency to interfere with the long-run planning of households and firms. Many economic decisions take place within a long time horizon. Planning for retirement, for example, may begin when workers are in their twenties or thirties, and firms may develop long-run investment and business strategies that look decades into the future. Clearly, high and erratic inflation can make long-term planning difficult. Suppose, for example, that you want to enjoy a certain standard of living when you retire. How much of your income do you need to save to make your dreams a reality? That depends on what the goods and services you plan to buy will cost 30 or 40 years from now. With high and erratic inflation, even guessing what your chosen lifestyle will cost by the time you retire is extremely difficult. You may end up saving too little and having to compromise on your retirement plans; or you may save too much, sacrificing more than you need to during your working years. Either way, inflation will have proved costly.

In summary, inflation damages the economy in a variety of ways. Some of its effects are difficult to quantify and are therefore controversial. But most economists agree that a low and stable inflation rate is instrumental in maintaining a healthy economy.

RECAP The true costs of inflation

The public sometimes confuse changes in *relative prices* (such as the price of oil) with inflation, which is a change in the *overall level of prices*. This confusion can cause problems, because the remedies for undesired changes in relative prices and for inflation are different.

There are a number of true costs of inflation, which together tend to reduce economic growth and efficiency. These include:

- *shoe-leather costs*, or the costs of economising on cash (for example, by making more frequent trips to the bank or installing a computerised cash management system)
- *'noise' in the price system*, which occurs when general inflation makes it difficult for market participants to interpret the information conveyed by prices
- *distortions of the tax system* – for example, when provisions of the tax code are not indexed
- unexpected *redistributions of wealth*, as when higher-than-expected inflation hurts wage earners to the benefit of employers, or hurts creditors to the benefit of debtors
- interference with *long-term planning*, arising because people find it difficult to forecast prices over long periods.

Hyperinflation

Although there is some disagreement about whether an inflation rate of, say, 5 per cent per year imposes important costs on an economy, few economists would question the fact that an inflation rate of 500 per cent or 1,000 per cent per year disrupts economic performance. A situation in which the inflation rate is

hyperinflation a situation in which the inflation rate is extremely high

extremely high is called **hyperinflation**. Although there is no official threshold above which inflation becomes hyperinflation, inflation rates in the range of 500 to 1,000 per cent per year would surely qualify. Since the 1970s, episodes of hyperinflation have occurred in several Latin American countries (including Argentina and Brazil), in Israel and in several countries attempting to make the transition from communism to capitalism – including Russia, where inflation exceeded 2,000 per cent in 1992. In Europe the classic example of hyperinflation is the case of Germany in the early 1920s. Following its defeat in the First World War, Germany was faced with the dual problem of rebuilding its devastated economy and the burden imposed by the Treaty of Versailles, which required Germany to pay war reparations (or compensation) to France and Britain. Rather than impose ever-higher taxes on its citizens, the German government resorted to printing money, which, as we will see in Chapter 22, ultimately leads to accelerating inflation. For example, in the last quarter of 1923 (October–December) prices were 53,000 per cent higher than in the previous quarter (July–September). Example 17.11 describes a more recent case of hyperinflation.

Example 17.11 Hyperinflation in Zimbabwe

A more recent example of hyperinflation is the case of Zimbabwe. In July 2008 the Reserve Bank of Zimbabwe (www.rbz.co.zw) reported that Zimbabwe's year-on-year inflation rate was a staggering 11,268,758 per cent – that's more than 11 million per cent on a year-to-year basis! While other estimates may differ there is no question that the inflation rate in Zimbabwe is in the millions of per cent per year.

As with most other hyperinflations, the source of Zimbabwe's inflation is printing money to pay for government purchases of goods and services. Rather than finance purchases and public-sector salaries by taxation on non-bank borrowing, the government simply orders the central bank to print more money. For example, in 2007 the money supply increased by 155,606 per cent. Essentially this hyperinflation has rendered the Zimbabwe currency worthless. For example, when Zimbabwe gained its independence in 1980 the Zimbabwe dollar was worth slightly more than the US dollar. However, in May 2008, Zimbabwe's central bank issued a 500-million-dollar note with a value equal to approximately two US dollars. Likewise, in mid-2008, a loaf of bread cost 200 million Zimbabwe dollars, or the cost of 60 new cars in 1998. To stop the hyperinflation the government must stop funding its expenditure by printing money and adopt a different monetary system. Two possibilities are 'dollarisation' and a currency board. Dollarisation means that the Zimbabwe dollar is abolished and replaced with a 'hard' currency such as the US dollar, the euro or South African rand. A currency board means that the Reserve Bank of Zimbabwe can continue to issue Zimbabwe dollars but only if they are backed by an equivalent amount of convertible currencies.

Hyperinflation greatly magnifies the costs of inflation. For example, shoe-leather costs – a relatively minor consideration in times of low inflation – become quite important during hyperinflation, when people may visit the bank two or three times per day to hold money for as short a time as possible. With prices changing daily, or even hourly, markets work quite poorly, slowing economic growth. Massive redistri-

Economic naturalist 17.3 How costly is high inflation?

Economic theory suggests that high inflation rates, especially those associated with hyperinflation, reduce economic efficiency and growth. Most economists believe that the economic costs associated with high inflation outweigh the perceived benefits, yet we continue to see episodes of high inflation throughout the world. In reality, how costly are high inflation rates?

Economists Stanley Fischer, Ratna Sahay and Carlos A. Végh examined the economic performance of 133 market economies over the period 1960–96 and uncovered 45 episodes of high inflation (12-month inflation rates greater than 100 per cent) among 25 different countries.[3] They found that, while uncommon, episodes of high inflation impose significant economic costs on the countries experiencing them. During periods of high inflation, these countries saw real GDP per person fall by an average of 1.6 per cent per year, real consumption per person fall by an average of 1.3 per cent per year, and real investment per person fall by an average of 3.3 per cent per year. During low-inflation years these same countries experienced positive growth in each of these variables. In addition, during periods of high inflation, these countries' trade and government budget deficits were larger than during low-inflation years.

Falling output and consumption levels caused by high inflation reduce the economic well-being of households and firms, and have a disproportionate effect on poor workers, who are least likely to have their wages indexed to the inflation rate and thus avoid a real loss in purchasing power. As pointed out in the previous section, high inflation rates also distort relative prices in the marketplace, leading to a *misallocation of resources* that can have long-term economic consequences. Falling investment in new capital caused by high inflation, for example, leads not only to a slowdown in current economic activity but also to reduced growth rates of future output. Because of these adverse economic effects, policy makers have an incentive to keep inflation rates low.

butions of wealth take place, impoverishing many. Not surprisingly, episodes of hyperinflation rarely last more than a few years; they are so disruptive that they quickly lead to a public outcry for relief.

Inflation and interest rates

So far, we have focused on the *measurement* and *economic* costs of inflation. Another important aspect of inflation is its close relationship to other key macroeconomic variables. For example, economists have long realised that during periods of high inflation *interest rates* tend to be high as well. We shall close this chapter with a look at the relationship between inflation and interest rates, which will provide a useful background to the chapters to come.

Inflation and the real interest rate

Earlier, in our discussion of the ways in which unexpected changes in inflation redistribute wealth, we saw that inflation tends to hurt creditors and help debtors by reducing the value of the money with which debts are repaid. The effect of inflation on debtors and creditors can be explained more precisely using an economic concept called the **real interest rate**. An example will illustrate.

real interest rate the annual percentage increase in the purchasing power of a financial asset; the real interest rate on any asset equals the nominal interest rate on that asset minus the inflation rate

Suppose that there are two neighbouring countries, Alpha and Beta. In Alpha, whose currency is called the alphan, the inflation rate is zero and is expected to remain at zero. In Beta, where the currency is the betan, the inflation rate is 10 per cent and is expected to remain at that level. Bank deposits pay 2 per cent annual interest

3 Fischer *et al.* (2002).

in Alpha and 10 per cent annual interest in Beta. In which country are bank depositors getting a better deal?

You might be tempted to answer Beta, since interest rates on deposits are higher in that country. But if you think about the effects of inflation, you will recognise that Alpha, not Beta, offers the better deal to depositors. To see why, think about the change over a year in the real purchasing power of deposits in the two countries. In Alpha, someone who deposits 100 alphans in the bank on 1 January will have 102 alphans on 31 December. As there is no inflation in Alpha, and goods and services will cost the same at the end of the year as at the beginning, the 102 alphans represent a 2 per cent increase in buying power.

In Beta, the depositor who deposits 100 betans on 1 January will have 110 betans by the end of the year – 10 per cent more than she started with. But the prices of goods and services in Beta, we have assumed, will also rise by 10 per cent. Thus the Beta depositor can afford to buy precisely the same amount of goods and services at the end of the year as she could at the beginning; she gets no increase in buying power. So the Alpha depositor has the better deal.

Economists refer to the annual percentage increase in the *real* purchasing power of a financial asset as the real interest rate, or the *real rate of return* on that asset. In our example, the real purchasing power of deposits rises by 2 per cent per year in Alpha and by 0 per cent per year in Beta. So the real interest rate on deposits is 2 per cent in Alpha and 0 per cent in Beta. The real interest rate should be distinguished from the more familiar market interest rate, also called the **nominal interest rate**. The nominal interest rate is the annual percentage increase in the nominal, or euro, value of an asset.

nominal interest rate (or market interest rate) the annual percentage increase in the nominal value of a financial asset

As the example of Alpha and Beta illustrates, we can calculate the real interest rate for any financial asset, from a bank deposit to a government bond, by subtracting the rate of inflation from the market or nominal interest rate on that asset. So, in Alpha, the real interest rate on deposits equals the nominal interest rate (2 per cent) minus the inflation rate (0 per cent), or 2 per cent. Likewise, in Beta, the real interest rate equals the nominal interest rate (10 per cent) minus the inflation rate (10 per cent), or 0 per cent.

We can write this definition of the real interest rate in very simple mathematical terms:

$$r = i - \pi$$

where

r = the real interest rate
i = the nominal, or market, interest rate
π = the inflation rate

Example 17.12 Real interest rates 1970 to 2005

The table below shows interest rates on 20-year British government bonds for selected years between 1970 and 2005. In which of these years did the financial investors who bought these bonds get the best deal? The worst deal?

Financial investors and lenders do best when the *real* (not the nominal) interest rate is high, since the real interest rate measures the increase in their *purchasing power*. We can calculate the real interest rate for each year by subtracting the inflation rate from the nominal interest rate. The results are 2.7 per cent for 1970, −9.6 per cent for 1975, −4.2 per cent for 1980, 4.5 per cent for 1985, 1.7 per cent for 1990, 5 per cent for

Year	Interest rate (%)	Inflation rate (%)
1970	9.2	6.5
1975	14.4	24.0
1980	13.8	18.0
1985	10.6	6.1
1990	11.1	9.4
1995	8.3	3.3
2000	4.7	2.9
2005	4.4	2.8

1995, 1.8 per cent for 2000 and 1.6 per cent for 2005. For purchasers of government bonds, the best of these years was 1995, when they enjoyed a real return of 5 per cent. The worst year was 1975, when their real return was actually negative. In other words, despite receiving 14.4 per cent nominal interest, financial investors ended up losing purchasing power in 1975, as the inflation rate exceeded the interest rate earned by their investments. Once again the effect of inflation is *distributive*. For example, in 1975, when the real rate of interest was close to −10 per cent, the effect of high inflation was to redistribute purchasing power from lenders (bond holders) to borrowers (government).

The concept of the real interest rate helps to explain more precisely why an unexpected surge in inflation is bad for lenders and good for borrowers. For any given nominal interest rate that the lender charges the borrower, the higher the inflation rate, the lower the real interest rate the lender actually receives. So unexpectedly high inflation leaves the lender worse off. Borrowers, on the other hand, are better off when inflation is unexpectedly high, because their real interest rate is lower than anticipated.

Although unexpectedly high inflation hurts lenders and helps borrowers, a high rate of inflation that is expected may not redistribute wealth at all, because expected inflation can be built into the nominal interest rate. Suppose, for example, that the lender requires a real interest rate of 2 per cent on new loans. If the inflation rate is confidently expected to be zero, the lender can get a 2 per cent real interest rate by charging a nominal interest rate of 2 per cent. But if the inflation rate is expected to be 10 per cent, the lender can still ensure a real interest rate of 2 per cent by charging a nominal interest rate of 12 per cent. Thus high inflation, if it is *expected*, need not hurt lenders – as long as the lenders can adjust the nominal interest rate they charge to reflect the expected inflation rate.

The data in Example 17.12 also suggest a positive correlation between inflation and the nominal rate of interest. That is, the years in which inflation is high (1975, 1980 and 1990) are also the years in which the nominal rate of interest, but not necessarily the real rate of interest, is highest. Conversely nominal interest rates tend to be lower in years when inflation is relatively low. This tendency for nominal interest rates to follow inflation rates is called the **Fisher effect**, after the early twentieth-century American economist Irving Fisher, who first pointed out the relationship.

Fisher effect the tendency for nominal interest rates to be high when inflation is high, and low when inflation is low

Exercise 17.7 What is the real rate of return to holding cash? (Hint: Does cash pay interest?) Does this real rate of return depend on whether the rate of inflation is correctly anticipated? How does your answer relate to the idea of shoe-leather costs?

Summary

■ The basic tool for measuring inflation is the *consumer price index*, or CPI. The CPI measures the cost of purchasing a fixed basket of goods and services in any period relative to the cost of the same basket of goods and services in a base year. The *inflation rate* is the annual percentage rate of change in the price level as measured by a *price index* such as the CPI.

■ The official inflation rate, based on the CPI, may *overstate* the true inflation rate for two reasons. First, it may not adequately reflect improvements in the quality of goods and services. Second, the method of calculating the CPI ignores the fact that consumers can substitute cheaper goods and services for more expensive ones.

■ A *nominal quantity* is a quantity that is measured in terms of its current money value. Dividing a nominal quantity, such as a family's income or a worker's wage in euros, by a price index, such as the CPI, expresses that quantity in terms of real purchasing power. This procedure is called *deflating* the nominal quantity. If nominal quantities from two different years are deflated by a common price index, the purchasing power of the two quantities can be compared. To ensure that a nominal payment, such as a pension, represents a constant level of real purchasing power, the nominal payment should be increased each year by a percentage equal to the inflation rate. This method of adjusting nominal payments to maintain their purchasing power is called *indexing*.

■ The public sometimes confuses increases in the *relative prices* for specific goods or services with inflation, which is an increase in the *general price level*. Since the remedies for a change in relative prices are different from the remedies for inflation, this confusion can cause problems.

■ Inflation imposes a number of true costs on the economy, including 'shoe-leather' costs, which are the real resources that are wasted as people try to economise on cash holdings, 'noise' in the price system, distortions of the tax system, unexpected redistributions of wealth, and interference with long-run planning. Because of these costs, most economists agree that sustained economic growth is more likely if inflation is low and stable. *Hyperinflation*, a situation in which the inflation rate is extremely high, greatly magnifies the costs of inflation and is highly disruptive to the economy.

■ The *real interest rate* is the annual percentage increase in the purchasing power of a financial asset. It is equal to the *nominal*, or *market*, *interest rate* minus the inflation rate. When inflation is unexpectedly high, the real interest rate is lower than anticipated, which hurts lenders but benefits borrowers. When inflation is unexpectedly low, lenders benefit and borrowers are hurt. To obtain a given real rate of return, lenders must charge a high nominal interest rate when inflation is high and a low nominal interest rate when inflation is low. The tendency for nominal interest rates to be high when inflation is high, and low when inflation is low, is called the *Fisher effect*.

Review questions

1. Explain why changes in the cost of living for any particular individual or family may differ from changes in the official cost-of-living index, the CPI.

2. What is the difference between the *price level* and the *rate of inflation* in an economy?

3. Why is it important to adjust for inflation when comparing nominal quantities (for example, workers' average wages) at different points in time? What is the basic method for adjusting for inflation?

4. Describe how indexation might be used to guarantee that the purchasing power of the wage agreed to in a multi-year labour contract will not be eroded by inflation.

5. Give two reasons why the official inflation rate may understate the 'true' rate of inflation. Illustrate by examples.

6. 'It's true that unexpected inflation redistributes wealth, from creditors to debtors, for example. But what one side of the bargain loses the other side gains. So from the perspective of the society as a whole, there is no real cost.' Do you agree? Discuss.

7. How does inflation affect the real return on holding cash?

8. **True or false:** If both the potential lender and the potential borrower correctly anticipate the rate of inflation, inflation will not redistribute wealth from the creditor to the debtor. Explain.

connect **Problems**

1. A government survey determines that typical family expenditures each month in the year designated as the base year are as follows:

    20 pizzas, €10 each
    Rent, €600
    Petrol and car maintenance, €100
    Phone service, €50

    In the year following the base year, the survey determines that pizzas have risen to €11 each, rent is €640, petrol and car maintenance have risen to €120 and the phone service has dropped in price to €40.

    a. Find the CPI in the subsequent year and the rate of inflation between the base year and the subsequent year.

    b. The family's nominal income rose by 5 per cent between the base year and the subsequent year. Are they worse off or better off in terms of what their income is able to buy?

2. The table below gives values for the EU HICP for each year from 1990 to 2001. For each year, beginning with 1991, calculate the rate of inflation from the previous year. What happened to inflation rates over the 1990s?

1990	81.7
1991	85.9
1992	89.3
1993	92.4
1994	95.0
1995	97.7
1996	100.0
1997	101.7
1998	103.0
1999	104.3
2000	106.2
2001	108.6

3. Here is a hypothetical income tax schedule, expressed in nominal terms, for 2002.

Family income (€)	Taxes due (% of income)
<20,000	0
20,000–30,000	10
30,000–50,000	20
>50,000	25

The government wants to ensure that families with a given real income are not pushed up into higher tax brackets by inflation. The CPI is 175 in 2002 and 192.5 in 2004. How should the income tax schedule be adjusted for 2004 to meet the government's objective?

4. The typical consumer's food basket in the base year 2000 is as follows:

30 chickens @ €3.00 each
10 hams @ €6.00 each
10 steaks @ €8.00 each

A chicken feed shortage causes the price of chickens to rise to €5.00 each in 2001. Hams rise to €7.00 each, and the price of steaks is unchanged.

    a. Calculate the change in the 'cost-of-eating' index between 2000 and 2001.

    b. Suppose that consumers are completely indifferent between two chickens and one ham. For this example, how large is the substitution bias in the official 'cost-of-eating' index?

5. The table below shows the actual UK per-litre prices for unleaded premium petrol for selected years from 1990 to 2004 with the value of the CPI for those years. Would it be fair to say that most of the changes in petrol prices during this period were due to general inflation, or were factors specific to the oil market playing a role as well?

Year	Price (pence/litre)	CPI (1996 = 100)
1990	38.37	81.1
1995	53.44	97.6
2000	75.38	105.6
2004	76.20	111.2

6. On 1 January 2000, Albert invested €1,000 at 6 per cent interest per year for three years. The CPI on 1 January 2000, stood at 100. On 1 January 2001, the CPI stood at 100. On 1 January 2002, it was 110 and on 1 January 2003, the day Albert's investment matured, the CPI was 118. Find the real rate of interest earned by Albert in each of the three years and his total real return over the three-year period. Assume that interest earnings are reinvested each year and earn interest.

7. Frank is lending €1,000 to Sarah for two years. Frank and Sarah agree that Frank should earn a 2 per cent real return per year.

    a. The CPI is 100 at the time that Frank makes the loan. It is expected to be 110 in one year and 121 in two years. What nominal rate of interest should Frank charge Sarah?

    b. Suppose Frank and Sarah are unsure about what the CPI will be in two years. Show how Frank and Sarah could index Sarah's annual repayments to ensure that Frank gets an annual 2 per cent real rate of return.

8. In the base year for computing the CPI, expenditures of the typical consumer break down as follows:

Item	%
Food and beverages	17.8
Housing	42.8
Clothing	6.3
Transportation	17.2
Medical care	5.7
Entertainment	4.4
Other goods, services	5.8
Total	100.0

Suppose that, since the base year, the prices of food and beverages have increased by 10 per cent, the price of housing has increased by 5 per cent, and the price of medical care has increased by 10 per cent. Other prices are unchanged. Find the CPI for the current year.

References

Fischer, S., R. Sahay and C.A. Végh (2002) 'Modern hyper- and high inflations', *Journal of Economic Literature*, 11, pp. 837–80.

Shapiro, M. and J. Wilcox (1996) 'Mismeasurement in the consumer price index: an evaluation', in B. Bernanke and J. Rotemberg (eds), *NBER Macroeconomics Annual*.

To help you grasp the key concepts of this chapter check out the extra resources posted on the Online Learning Centre. There are chapter summaries, self-test questions, an interactive graphing tool, weblinks and a glossary, all for free!

Visit the Online Learning Centre at: www.mcgraw-hill.co.uk/textbooks/mcdowell for information on accessing all of these resources.

18

The Labour Market: Wages and Unemployment

In Chapter 15 we discussed the remarkable economic growth and increased productivity that has occurred in the industrialised world since 1800. These developments have greatly increased the quantity of goods and services that the economy can produce. But we have not yet discussed how the fruits of economic growth are distributed. Has everyone benefited equally from economic growth and increased productivity? Or is the population divided between those who have caught the 'train' of economic modernisation, enriching themselves in the process, and those who have been left at the station?

To understand how economic growth and change affect different groups, we must turn to the *labour market*. Except for retirees and others receiving government support, most people rely almost entirely on wages and salaries to pay their bills and save for the future. Hence it is in the labour market that most people will see the benefits of the economic growth and increasing productivity. This chapter starts by looking at unemployment, and other labour market indicators are measured. The second part of the chapter describes different types of unemployment and their costs, while the final part focuses on several important labour market trends. We shall see that two key factors contributing to recent trends in wages, employment and unemployment are the *globalisation* of the economy, as reflected in the increasing importance of international trade, and ongoing *technological change*. By the end of the chapter, you will understand better the connection between these macroeconomic developments and the economic fortunes of workers and their families.

The unemployment rate

unemployment rate the number of unemployed people divided by the labour force

In assessing the level of economic activity in a country, economists look at a variety of statistics. Besides real GDP and inflation, one statistic that receives much attention from both economists and the general public is the *rate of unemployment*. The **unemployment rate** is a sensitive indicator of conditions in the labour market. When the unemployment rate is low, jobs are secure and relatively easy to find. Low unemployment is often also associated with improving wages and working conditions, as employers compete to attract and retain workers.

Measuring unemployment

In most countries a government agency publishes regular estimates of the numbers unemployed computed from the results of surveying randomly selected households. Although the precise methods may vary from country to country, most classify the population of working age (normally over 15 or 16 years) into one of three categories.

1. *Employed* A person is employed if he or she worked *full-time or part-time* during the survey period, or is on vacation or sick leave from a regular job.
2. *Unemployed* A person is unemployed if he or she is not employed but is *actively seeking employment*.
3. *Out of the labour force* A person is considered to be out of the labour force if he or she is *not employed or actively seeking employment*. In other words, people who are neither employed nor unemployed (in the sense of looking for work but not being able to find it) are 'out of the labour force'. Full-time students, unpaid home makers, retirees and people unable to work because of disabilities are examples of people who are out of the labour force.

Note the important distinction between unemployed who are *actively seeking employment* and those who are not working and are out of the labour force. The former are people who are not employed but will take a suitable job if offered. The latter are also people who are not employed but are not seeking employment. To find the unemployment rate, we must first calculate the size of the **labour force**. The labour force is defined as the total number of employed and unemployed people in the economy (the first two categories listed above). The unemployment rate is then defined as the number of unemployed people divided by the labour force. Notice that people who are out of the labour force (because they are in school, have retired or are disabled, for example) are not counted as unemployed and thus do not affect the unemployment rate. In general, a high rate of unemployment indicates that the economy is performing poorly.

labour force the total number of employed and unemployed people in the economy

Figure 18.1 shows unemployment rates for the United Kingdom and the EU15 since 1960. Throughout the 1960s and early 1970s European unemployment rates were exceptionally low but increased significantly from 1974–75 onwards. The rise in unemployment since the mid-1970s can be explained by a series of recessions, which affected most Western countries in 1974, 1980, 1990 and 2001. Note that following the recession of 1990–91 British unemployment declined much more rapidly than the European average.

The labour force participation rate

participation rate the percentage of the working-age population in the labour force (that is, the percentage that is either employed or looking for work)

Another useful statistic is the labour force **participation rate** or the percentage of the working-age population in the labour force (that is, the percentage of the labour force that is either employed or looking for work). The participation rate is calculated by dividing the labour force by the working-age population.

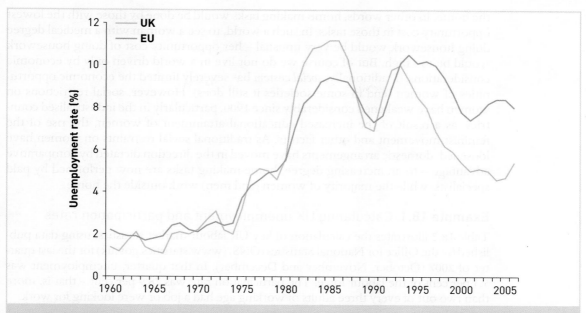

Figure 18.1 Unemployment Rates for UK and EU15 1960–2006. The unemployment rate, or the percentage of the labour force that is unemployed, was around 2 per cent in the 1960s and early 1970s. Throughout the 1960s and early years of the 1970s European unemployment rates were exceptionally low but increased following the recessions at the start of each decade.
Source: OECD, *Economic Outlook.*

Table 18.1 shows male and female participation rates for five countries in 1973, 1990 and 2006. For all countries, male participation rates have declined while female participation has increased.

Country	Male			Female		
	1973	1990	2006	1973	1990	2006
France	85.2	75.0	74.2	50.1	52.7	63.9
Germany	89.1	79.0	81.4	49.6	55.5	68.5
Italy	85.1	75.1	74.6	33.7	44.0	50.8
UK	93.0	88.3	83.2	53.2	67.3	70.3
USA	86.2	85.6	81.9	51.1	67.8	69.3

Table 18.1 Male and Female Participation Rates
Note: The data refer to men and women aged 15–64 years who are classified as either employed or unemployed.
Source: OECD, *Employment Outlook* (www.oecd.org).

Comparative Advantage

Why have female participation rates increased? In a world governed by economic principles without social conventions, customs or traditions, home-making tasks such as cleaning, cooking and child rearing would be jobs like any other. As such, they would be subject to the principle of *comparative advantage*: those people (either men or women) whose comparative advantage lay in performing home-making tasks would specialise in them, freeing people whose comparative advantage lay elsewhere to work outside the home. In other words, home-making tasks would be done by those with the lowest opportunity cost in those tasks. In such a world, to see a woman with a medical degree doing housework would be very unusual – her opportunity cost of doing housework would be too high. But of course we do not live in a world driven only by economic considerations. Traditionally, *social custom* has severely limited the economic opportunities of women (and in some societies it still does). However, social restrictions on women have weakened considerably since 1900, particularly in the industrialised countries, as a result of the increased educational attainment of women, the rise of the feminist movement and other factors. As traditional social restraints on women have loosened, domestic arrangements have moved in the direction dictated by comparative advantage – to an increasing degree, home-making tasks are now performed by paid specialists, while the majority of women (and men) work outside the home.

Example 18.1 Calculating UK unemployment and participation rates

Table 18.2 illustrates the calculation of key UK labour market statistics, using data published by the Office for National Statistics (ONS) (www.statistics.gov.uk) for the last quarter of 2007 (October, November and December). In that quarter, unemployment was 5.3 per cent of the labour force. The participation rate was 78.9 per cent – that is, more than two out of every three adults of working age had a job or were looking for work.

Employed	28.134
Plus:	
Unemployed	1.588
Equals:	
Labour force	29.722
Plus:	
Not in labour force	7.919
Equals:	
Working-age population	37.641
Unemployment rate (%)	5.3
Participation rate (%)	78.9

Table 18.2 **UK Employment Data, Fourth Quarter 2007 (Millions)**
Note: The data refer to people between the ages of 16 and 64 (men) or 59 (women). The unemployment rate is calculated as the number unemployed as a percentage of the labour force. The participation rate is calculated as the labour force as a percentage of the working-age population.

Exercise 18.1 Suppose that in a total working-age population of 1,000, 40 per cent are working and 10 per cent are unemployed but actively seeking employment.

    a. Calculate the unemployment rate for this economy.
    b. Calculate the labour force participation rate for this economy.

Suppose a new government scheme leads 60 people who were neither working nor seeking work to start looking for employment. If the number unemployed falls by 16 find:

    c. the change in the unemployment rate
    d. the change in the labour force participation rate.

frictional unemployment the short-term unemployment associated with the process of matching workers with jobs

structural unemployment the long-term and chronic unemployment that exists even when the economy is producing at a normal rate

cyclical unemployment the extra unemployment that occurs during periods of recession

Types of unemployment and their costs

Unemployment is not a homogeneous concept in the sense that all people classified as being unemployed are out of work for the same reason and for the same duration. Economists have found it useful to classify unemployment into three broad types: **frictional unemployment**, **structural unemployment** and **cyclical unemployment**. Each type of unemployment has different causes and imposes different economic and social costs.

Frictional unemployment

The function of the labour market is to *match available jobs with available workers*. If all jobs and workers were the same, or if the set of jobs and workers were static and unchanging, this matching process would be quick and easy. But the real world is more complicated. In practice, both jobs and workers are highly *heterogeneous*. Jobs differ in their location, in the skills they require, in their working conditions and hours, and in many other ways. Workers differ in their career aspirations, their skills and experience, their preferred working hours, their willingness to travel, and so on.

The real labour market is also *dynamic*, or constantly changing and evolving. On the demand side of the labour market, technological advances, globalisation and changing consumer tastes spur the creation of new products, new firms and even new industries, while outmoded products, firms and industries disappear. Thus CD players have replaced record players, and word processors have replaced typewriters. As a result of this upheaval, new jobs are constantly being created, while some old jobs cease to be viable. The workforce in a modern economy is equally dynamic. People move, gain new skills, leave the labour force for a time to rear children or go back to school, and even change careers.

Because the labour market is heterogeneous and dynamic, the process of matching jobs with workers often takes time. For example, a software engineer who loses or quits her job may take weeks or even months to find another software company that has a job requiring her specific skills. In her search she will probably consider alternative areas of software development or even totally new challenges. She may also want to think about different regions of the country in which software companies are located, or even different countries. During the period in which she is searching for a new job, she is counted as *unemployed*.

Short-term unemployment that is associated with the process of matching workers with jobs is called *frictional unemployment*. The *costs* of frictional unemployment are low and may even be negative – that is, frictional unemployment may be economically beneficial. First, frictional unemployment is short term, so its psychological effects and direct economic losses are minimal. Second, to the extent that the search process leads to a better match between worker and job, a period of frictional unemployment is actually productive, in the sense that it leads to higher output over the long run. Indeed, a certain amount of frictional unemployment seems essential to the smooth functioning of a rapidly changing, dynamic economy.

Structural unemployment

A second major type of unemployment is *structural unemployment*, or the long-term and chronic unemployment that exists even when the economy is producing at a normal rate. Several factors contribute to structural unemployment. First, *a lack of skills, language barriers* or *discrimination* keeps some workers from finding stable, long-term jobs. Migrant farm workers and unskilled construction workers who find short-term or temporary jobs from time to time, but never stay in one job for very long, fit the definition of chronically unemployed.

Second, economic changes sometimes create a long-term mismatch between the skills some workers have and the available jobs. Under the forces of globalisation the European textile and coal-mining industries, for example, have declined over the years, while the computer and financial services industries have grown rapidly. Ideally, textile workers and miners who lose their jobs will be able to find new jobs in computer firms and financial institutions (worker mobility), so that their unemployment will be only frictional in nature. In practice, of course, many ex-textile workers and miners lack the education, ability and training necessary to work in the computer and financial services industries. Since their skills are no longer in demand, these workers may drift into chronic or long-term unemployment.

In most countries structural unemployment is identified with *long-term unemployment*, generally defined as unemployment with more than six months' duration. Table 18.3 gives estimates of long-term unemployment in a range of European countries and the United States for 2006. Clearly long-term unemployment is a greater problem in Europe than in the United States. However, there are also differences between European countries, with long-term unemployment being higher in France and Germany than in Ireland and the United Kingdom. Economic naturalist 18.3 (p. 523) discusses this difference in greater detail.

Duration	% of total unemployment			
	France	Germany	UK	USA
Short-term unemployed	62.6	73.1	40.9	17.6
Long-term unemployed	44.0	57.2	22.1	10.0

Table 18.3 **Long-Term Unemployment, 2006**
Source: OECD, *Employment Outlook*, 2007.

Finally, structural unemployment can result from *structural features of the labour market* that act as barriers to employment. Examples of such barriers include trades unions and minimum wage laws, both of which may keep wages above their market-clearing level, creating unemployment. We shall discuss some of these structural features shortly.

The *costs* of structural unemployment are much higher than those of frictional unemployment. Because structurally unemployed workers do little productive work over long periods, their idleness causes substantial economic losses to both the unemployed workers and to society. Structurally unemployed workers also lose out on the opportunity to develop new skills on the job, and their existing skills wither from disuse. Long spells of unemployment are also much more difficult for workers to cope with psychologically than the relatively brief spells associated with frictional unemployment.

Cyclical unemployment

The third type of unemployment occurs during periods of recession (that is, periods of unusually low production) and is called *cyclical unemployment*. Cyclical unemployment occurs when the economy experiences a decline in the demand for the goods and services it produces – computers, software, textiles, cars, etc. Because fewer goods and services are being bought, producers such as computer and car manufacturers start to cut back on production and lay off workers. Provided that policy makers take the appropriate actions to boost demand, such as cutting interest rates and reducing income taxes, increases in cyclical unemployment are likely to be short-lived. However, if corrective action is not taken, workers who lose their jobs because of a decline in demand may become long-term unemployed. We shall study cyclical unemployment and its remedies in later chapters dealing with recessions and macroeconomic policy.

In principle, frictional, structural and cyclical unemployment add up to the *total unemployment rate*. In practice, sharp distinctions often cannot be made between the different categories, so any breakdown of the total unemployment rate into the three types of unemployment is necessarily subjective and approximate.

Exercise 18.2 How would you classify the following types of unemployment? What, if any, is the appropriate policy response?

    a. Following a sudden downturn in economic activity Michael loses his job as a car salesman.

    b. Following EU enlargement a Scottish shirt factory shifts production to Poland, making Scottish workers redundant.

    c. After taking a computing course Mandy quits her job as a supermarket checkout operator to search for an occupation that can best reward her newly acquired skills.

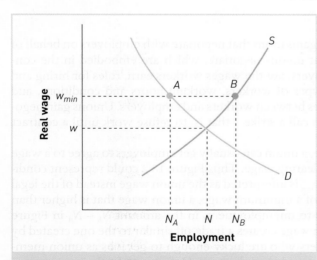

Figure 18.2 A Legal Minimum Wage May Create Unemployment. If the minimum wage w_{min} exceeds the market-clearing wage w for low-skilled workers, it will create unemployment equal to the difference between the number of people who want to work at the minimum wage, N_B, and the number of people that employers are willing to hire, N_A.

Impediments to full employment

In discussing structural unemployment, we mentioned that *structural features* of the labour market may contribute to long-term and chronic unemployment. Let us discuss a few of those features.

Minimum wage laws

Many countries have *minimum wage laws*, which prescribe the lowest hourly wage that employers may pay to workers. Basic supply and demand analysis can be used to illustrate the effects of minimum wages on employment and unemployment. Figure 18.2 shows the demand and supply curves for low-skilled workers, to whom the minimum wage is most relevant. The market-clearing real wage, at which the quantity of labour demanded equals the quantity of labour supplied, is w, and the corresponding level of employment is N. Now suppose there is a legal minimum wage, w_{min}, that exceeds the market-clearing wage w. At the minimum wage, the number of people who want jobs, N_B, exceeds the number of workers that employers are willing to hire, N_A. The result is unemployment in the amount $N_B - N_A$, also equal to the length of the line segment AB. If there were no minimum wage, this unemployment would not exist in competitive labour markets, since the labour market would clear at wage w.

As Figure 18.2 illustrates, minimum wages can lead to higher unemployment. How widespread is this effect? Minimum wages will have the greatest impact when they are set above the competitive or market-clearing wage (w in Figure 18.2) and when they apply to a high proportion of the workforce. Table 18.4 gives some indication of the coverage of minimum wages over a range of countries in 2006. The first row gives the minimum wage as a percentage of average monthly earnings in industry and services, while the second gives the percentage of full-time workers with earnings on the minimum wage. With the exception of France, the minimum wage does not exceed 50 per cent of the average wage and the proportion of workers covered is very low. Hence, on this evidence, minimum wages do not appear to have significant economic effects of the type illustrated in Figure 18.2.

	France	Spain	UK	USA
Minimum wage as a percentage of average monthly earnings in industry and services	56.0	41.4	36.9	30.7
Percentage of full-time workers with earnings on the minimum wage	15.1	0.96	1.9	1.1

Table 18.4 **Minimum Wages, 2006**
Source: Eurostat (http://eurostat.ec.eu.int).

Trades unions

Trades, or labour, unions are organisations that negotiate with employers on behalf of workers. Among the issues that unions negotiate, which are embodied in the contracts they draw up with employers, are the wages workers earn, rules for hiring and firing, the duties of different types of workers, working hours and conditions, and procedures for resolving disputes between workers and employers. Unions gain negotiating power by their power to call a strike – that is, to refuse work until a contract agreement has been reached.

Through the threat of a strike, a union can usually get employers to agree to a wage that is higher than the market-clearing wage. Thus Figure 18.2 could represent conditions in a unionised industry if w_{min} is interpreted as the union wage instead of the legal minimum wage. As in the case of a minimum wage, a union wage that is higher than the market-clearing wage leads to unemployment, in the amount $N_B - N_A$ in Figure 18.2. Furthermore, a high union wage creates a trade-off similar to the one created by a minimum wage. Those workers who are lucky enough to get jobs as union members will be paid more than they would be otherwise. Unfortunately, their gain comes at the expense of other workers who are unemployed as a result of the artificially high union wage.

Are unions good for the economy? That is a controversial, emotionally charged question. Early in the twentieth century, some employers who faced little local competition for workers exploited their advantage by forcing workers to toil long hours in dangerous conditions for low pay. Through bitter and sometimes bloody confrontations with these companies, labour organisations succeeded in eliminating many of the worst abuses. Unions also point with pride to their historic political role in supporting progressive labour legislation, such as laws that banned child labour. Finally, union leaders often claim to increase productivity and promote democracy in the workplace by giving workers some voice in the operations of the firm.

Opponents of unions, while acknowledging that these organisations may have played a positive role in the past, question their value in a modern economy. Today, more and more workers are professionals or semi-professionals, rather than production workers, so they can move relatively easily from firm to firm. Indeed, many labour markets have become national or even international, so today's workers have numerous potential employers. Thus the forces of *competition* – the fact that employers must persuade talented workers to work for them – should provide adequate protection for workers. Indeed, opponents would argue that unions are becoming increasingly self-defeating, since firms that must pay artificially high union wages and abide by inflexible work rules will not be able to compete in a global economy. The ultimate effect of such handicaps will be the failure of unionised firms and the loss of union jobs. Indeed, unions are in decline in many European countries, with the highest incidence of union membership being in the public sector – civil servants, school teachers and the police.

However, in some European countries low union membership does not necessarily imply that unions have become less influential. The reason is that labour laws often require that wages agreed between firms and unions apply to all workers in the industry regardless of whether they are union members. For example, in France union membership covers only about 10 per cent of the non-government workforce but because French law requires non-unionised firms to accept the wages agreed by unionised firms, union bargaining can affect up to 90 per cent of the workforce in certain industries. In contrast, about 35 per cent of the UK workforce belongs to trades unions but because British law does not require that wages agreed in unionised firms should also apply to non-unionised firms, union wage bargaining affects only approximately 40 per cent of the workforce.

Unemployment and welfare benefits

Another structural feature of the labour market that may increase the unemployment rate is the availability of *unemployment and other benefits* paid to people who lose their jobs. In addition to unemployment benefit, unemployed workers may also receive other payments such as housing and child benefit. These benefits provide an important safety net because they help the unemployed to maintain a decent standard of living while they are looking for a job. But because their availability allows the unemployed to search longer or less intensively for a job, they may lengthen the average amount of time the typical unemployed worker is without a job. Most economists would argue that unemployment and other benefits should be generous enough to provide basic support but not so generous as to remove the incentive actively to seek work. Thus, benefits should last for only a limited time, and should be set at levels below the income a worker receives when working.

Table 18.5 compares the benefits received by unemployed workers in three large European economies and the United States. Benefits are measured as the *net replacement ratio*, defined as the ratio of total income received while unemployed to total income earned while working inclusive of all benefits and taxes. Hence if a worker has an after-tax income of €600 per week while working and an income of €300 per week if s/he is made unemployed the net replacement ration is 50 per cent. An important feature of Table 18.5 is that benefits paid to the long-term unemployed are much lower in the United States than in France, Germany or the United Kingdom.

	France	Germany	UK	USA
Short-term unemployed	67	60	41	62
Long-term unemployed	51	48	50	14

Table 18.5 **Net Replacement Ratios (%) 2005.**
Note: The data are for single people earning the average wage.
Source: OECD (www.oecd.org).

Other government regulations

Besides minimum wage legislation, many other government regulations, such as health and safety regulations, limits on working hours, paid maternity leave and statutory holiday entitlements, can affect the labour market. While many of these regulations are beneficial and widely supported they may impose costs on employers and result in lower levels of employment and take-home wages. For example, if workers are paid €100 per day a new government regulation which requires that workers

non-wage costs costs imposed on employers over and above the wage actually paid to employees

get an extra day of paid holiday per year will increase the cost of employing labour by €100 per year because firms have to pay the wage even though nothing is actually produced on the holiday. This type of regulation is often referred to as a **non-wage cost**. Figure 18.3 illustrates the possible effects of non-wage costs.

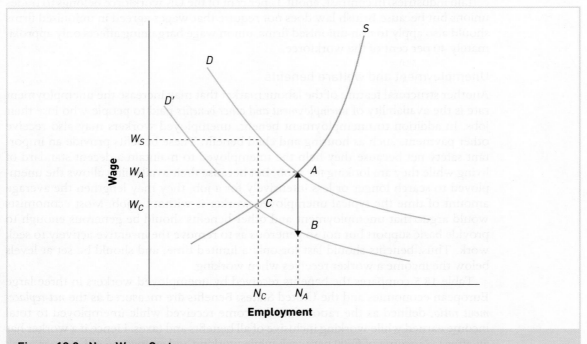

Figure 18.3. Non-Wage Costs.

Cost–Benefit Analysis ⃝ Figure 18.3 shows the demand and supply curves for labour. In the absence of non-wage costs, the equilibrium wage is w_A and employment is N_A. Now assume that government regulations impose a non-wage cost equal to the distance AB on each person employed. As the cost of employing each worker will now be the wage paid plus the non-wage cost, AB firms will reduce the wage they are prepared to pay by the amount of the non-wage costs. That is, the demand for labour curve shifts to D', establishing a new market equilibrium at point C with a lower wage w_C and a lower level of employment N_C. Hence in competitive labour markets non-wage costs lead to lower employment and lower take-home wages. Note that although workers receive a lower take-home wage they may place a value on the extra benefits the government regulations confer on them. Hence we can consider the wage w_S, which equals the take-home wage w_C plus the non-wage cost, as the *social wage* defined as the wage from employment plus the value of the non-wage benefits. As in the case of minimum wages, government regulations may improve the welfare of those lucky enough to retain their jobs but are detrimental to those who lose their jobs, $N_C N_A$ in Figure 18.3.

RECAP Unemployment

Economists distinguish among three broad types of unemployment. *Frictional unemployment* is the short-term unemployment that is associated with the process of matching workers with jobs. *Structural unemployment* is the long-term, or chronic, unemployment that occurs even when the economy is producing at a normal rate. *Cyclical unemployment* is the extra unemployment that occurs during periods of recession. Frictional unemployment may be economically beneficial, as improved matching of workers and jobs may increase output in the long run. Structural and cyclical unemployment impose heavy economic costs on workers and society, as well as psychological costs on workers and their families.

Structural features of the labour market may cause structural unemployment. Examples of such features are legal minimum wages or union contracts that set wages above market-clearing levels; unemployment insurance, which allows unemployed workers to search longer or less intensively for a job; and government regulations that impose extra costs on employers. Regulation of the labour market is not necessarily undesirable, but it should be subject to the *cost–benefit* criterion. Heavy labour market regulation and high unionisation rates in Western Europe help to explain the persistence of high unemployment rates in those countries.

Labour force trends (1): increasing wage inequality

Recent decades have seen a marked increase in the difference between the wages earned by skilled and unskilled workers. In the United States, for example, some studies suggest that the real wages of the least-skilled workers may have actually *declined* since the early 1970s, while the best-educated, highest-skilled workers have enjoyed continuing gains in real wages. Many observers now worry about the possible emergence of a 'two-tier' labour market with well-paid jobs for the well educated and highly skilled, but less and less opportunity for those with low levels of schooling or skills. Economic naturalist 18.1 gives possible reasons for this trend focusing on the effects of globalisation and the impact of technological change.

Economic naturalist 18.1 Why has the gap between the wages of skilled and less skilled workers widened in recent years?

Many commentators have attributed the increasing divergence between the wages of skilled and unskilled workers to two phenomena: globalisation and technological change. We consider each of these in turn.

(1) Globalisation. The term globalisation refers to the fact that the markets for many goods and services are becoming international, rather than national or local in scope. While Europeans have long been able to buy products from all over the world, the ease with which goods and services can cross borders is increasing rapidly. Within the European Union the elimination of tariffs (taxes on imports) and the creation of the single market have dramatically reduced barriers to trade between member states. The North American Free Trade Agreement (NAFTA) has also reduced tariffs on goods and services traded between Canada, Mexico and the United States. Facilitators such as the General Agreement on Tariffs and Trade (GATT) and the World Trade Organization (WTO) have led to increased trade between Europe, North America, Africa and Asia. In addition, factors such as free capital mobility and technological advances such as the internet have promoted globalisation.

The effects of globalisation on the labour market are mixed, however, which explains why some politicians and pressure groups oppose free trade agreements. Liberalising trade often means that consumers switch from domestically produced goods and services to foreign-made products. Consumers would not make this switch unless the foreign products were better, cheaper, or both, so expanded trade clearly makes them better off. But workers and companies in the domestic industries that lose business may suffer from the increase in foreign competition.

The effects of increasing trade on the labour market can be analysed using Figure 18.4. Figure 18.4 contrasts the supply and demand for labour in two different industries, (a) textiles and (b) computer software. Imagine that, initially, there is little or no international trade in these two goods. Without trade, the demand for workers in each industry is indicated by the curves marked $D_{textiles}$ and $D_{software}$ respectively. Wages and employment in each industry are determined by the intersection of the demand curves and the labour supply curves in the industry. Figure 18.4 shows that initially the real wage is the same in both industries, equal to w. Employment is $N_{textiles}$ in textiles and $N_{software}$ in software.

Initially, real wages in the two industries are equal at w. After an increase in trade, (a) demand for workers in the importing industry (textiles) declines, lowering real wages and employment, while (b) demand for workers in the exporting industry (software) increases, raising real wages and employment in that industry.

Comparative Advantage What will happen when this economy is opened up to trade? For example, the enlargement of the European Union to include countries in Central and Eastern Europe (CEEs) has liberalised trade between the more prosperous countries of the old EU15 and new member states such as Poland and Hungary. Under the process of trade globalisation, countries will begin to produce for export those goods or services at which they are relatively more efficient, and to import goods or services that they are relatively less efficient at producing. Suppose the country in this example is a Western country which is relatively more efficient at producing software than at manufacturing textiles. With the opening of trade, the country gains new foreign markets for its software and begins to produce for export as well as for domestic use. Meanwhile, because the country is relatively less efficient at producing textiles, consumers begin to purchase foreign-made textiles, which are cheaper or of higher quality, instead of the domestic product. In short, software becomes an exporting industry and textiles an importing industry.

These changes in the demand for domestic products are translated into changes in the demand

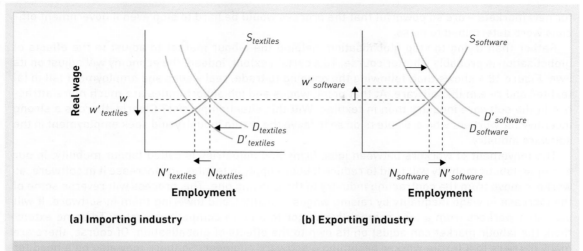

Figure 18.4 The Effect of Globalisation on the Demand for Workers in Two Industries. Initially, real wages in the two industries are equal at *w*. After an increase in trade, (a) demand for workers in the importing industry (textiles) declines, lowering real wages and employment, while (b) demand for workers in the exporting industry (software) increases, raising real wages and employment in that industry.

for labour. The opening of export markets increases the demand for domestic software, raising its relative price. The higher price for domestic software, in turn, raises the value of the marginal products of software workers, shifting the labour demand curve in the software industry to the right, from $D_{software}$ to $D'_{software}$ in Figure 18.4(b). Wages in the software industry rise, from *w* to $w'_{software}$, and employment in the industry rises as well. In the textile industry the opposite happens. Demand for domestic textiles falls as consumers switch to imports. The relative price of domestic textiles falls with demand, reducing the value of the marginal product of textile workers and hence the demand for their labour, to $D'_{textiles}$ in Figure 18.4(a). Employment in the textile industry falls, and the real wage falls as well, from *w* to $w'_{textiles}$.

In sum, Figure 18.4 shows how globalisation can contribute to increasing wage inequality. Initially, we assumed that software workers and textile workers received the same wage. However, the opening up of trade raised the wages of workers in the 'winning' industry (software) and lowered the wages of workers in the 'losing' industry (textiles), increasing inequality.

In practice, the tendency of trade to increase wage inequality may be even worse than depicted here, because the great majority of the world's workers, particularly those in developing countries, have relatively low skill levels. Thus, when industrialised countries such as the United Kingdom, France, Germany and the United States open up trade with developing countries, the domestic industries that are likely to face the toughest international competition are those that use mostly low-skilled labour. Conversely, the industries that are likely to do the best in international competition are those that employ mostly skilled workers. Thus increased trade may lower the wages of those workers who are already poorly paid and increase the wages of those who are well paid.

The fact that increasing trade may exacerbate wage inequality explains some of the political resistance to globalisation, but in general it does not justify attempts to reverse the trend. Increasing trade and globalisation are a major source of improvement in living standards, in both Europe and abroad, so trying to stop the process is counter-productive. Indeed, the economic forces behind globalisation – primarily, the desire of consumers for better and cheaper products and of producers for new markets – are so powerful that the process would be hard to stop even if government officials were determined to do so.

Rather than trying to stop globalisation, helping the labour market to adjust to the effects of globalisation is probably a better course. To a certain extent, indeed, the economy will adjust on its own. Figure 18.4 shows that, following the opening to trade, real wages and employment fall in (a) textiles and rise in (b) software. At that point, wages and job opportunities are much more attractive in the software industry than in textiles. Will this situation persist? Clearly, there is a strong incentive for workers who are able to do so to leave the textile industry and seek employment in the software industry.

The movement of workers between jobs, firms and industries is called labour mobility. In our example, labour mobility will tend to reduce labour supply in textiles and increase it in software, as workers move from the contracting industry to the growing one. This process will reverse some of the increase in wage inequality by raising wages in textiles and lowering them in software. It will also shift workers from a less competitive sector to a more competitive sector. To some extent, then, the labour market can adjust on its own to the effects of globalisation. Of course, there are many barriers to a textile worker becoming a software engineer. So there may also be a need for transition aid to workers in the affected sectors. Ideally, such aids help workers train for and find new jobs. Because trade and globalisation increase the total economic 'pie', the 'winners' from globalisation can afford the taxes necessary to finance retraining for the 'losers' and still enjoy a net benefit from increased trade.

(2) Technological change. The influence of technology on skilled–unskilled wage differentials is broadly similar to the influence of globalisation. The main economic benefit of globalisation is increased specialisation and the efficiency that it brings. Instead of each country trying to produce everything its citizens consume, each can concentrate on producing those goods and services at which it is relatively more efficient.   Suppose that in a given country globalisation results in specialization in skilled industries such as software and that new technology is biased towards skilled workers, which means that it raises their productivity relative to that of unskilled workers, which in turn increases the demand for skilled workers. In terms of Figure 18.4 the demand curve for 'software' or skilled workers will shift further to the right, increasing the skilled wage and the differential relative to unskilled wages.

Because new technologies favour skilled workers and increase wage inequality, should government regulators act to block them? As in the case of globalisation, most economists would argue against trying to block new technologies, since technological advances are necessary for economic growth and improved living standards. The remedies for the problem of wage inequalities caused by technological change are similar to those for wage inequalities caused by globalisation. First among them is worker mobility. As the pay differential between skilled and unskilled work increases, unskilled workers will have a stronger incentive to acquire education and skills, to everyone's benefit. A second remedy is transition aid. Government policy makers should consider programmes that will help workers to retrain if they are able, or should provide income support if they are not.

Exercise 18.3 In some countries, trades unions typically favour tough restrictions on immigration, while employers tend to favour more liberal policies. Why?

Both sides gain from free trade

In Economic naturalist 18.1 we saw that the processes of globalisation, free trade and technological change can lead to greater wage inequality within a *single country*. However, international trade is a *two-way process*. One country's imports are another's exports, and if one country is importing more, its partner country must be exporting more. For example, suppose that Germany is the domestic country in Economic naturalist 18.1. Opening trade with other countries leads to lower wages in the German textile industry because demand shifts from domestic to foreign production, which implies a corresponding increase in the demand for textiles in countries exporting to Germany. What are the effects on wages and employment in these new partner countries? This question is considered in Economic naturalist 18.2.

Exercise 18.4 Suppose that free trade with Poland causes German textile workers to become unemployed. Would you classify the unemployed German textile workers as frictional, structural or cyclical unemployment? What are the appropriate policies to help unemployed textile workers to find new jobs?

Economic naturalist 18.2 EU enlargement: the impact of trade and technological change.

In May 2004 ten new member states, mostly CEE nations (e.g. Estonia, Hungary, Latvia and Poland), joined the European Union. Unlike previous enlargements, which opened EU membership to relatively wealthy countries such as Sweden and the United Kingdom, the countries joining in 2004 had living standards well below the EU average. Slovakian real GDP per person, for example, is about 40 per cent of the EU average. Also, although there are significant differences between the accession countries, a common feature is that, in terms of technology, management skills and the quality of goods and services produced, they generally lag behind their Western partners (e.g. France, Germany and the United Kingdom). Hence we might expect the new members of the Union to benefit in two ways: gains from trade with the West and greater access to superior Western technology.

Figure 18.5 illustrates the possible effects of EU enlargement on real wages and employment in the accession countries. Following on from Economic naturalist 18.1, we shall assume that Germany is the domestic country and Poland is its new partner. We shall also assume that Poland is relatively more efficient in textile production and Germany in the production of the capital goods (e.g. machines) required to produce textiles, and that German-made capital goods are more technologically advanced than their Polish equivalents. As Poland's accession to the European Union opens free trade between Poland and Germany, we would expect Poland to specialise in textile production and Germany in capital goods. Hence Poland will export textiles to Germany and import capital equipment. Figure 18.5 shows the effects on wages and employment in the Polish textile industry. Opening trade increases German demand for Polish textiles, raising their relative prices, which increases the value of the marginal product of Polish textile workers and shifts the labour demand curve to the right from D to D'. As a result, real wages will rise from w to w', and employment from N to N'. If Polish textile manufacturers replace their capital equipment with more technologically advanced machines imported from Germany, the technological improvement will lead to an increase in the productivity and skills of textile workers, shifting the labour demand curve further to the right from D' to D'', with wages rising to w'' and employment to N''.

Hence both sides gain from free trade. Germany gains by importing Polish textiles and switching resources from textile production to goods such as software and capital equipment in which it is

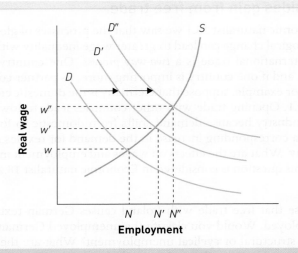

Figure 18.5 EU Enlargement: the Effect on Wages and Employment in Accession Countries. The figure shows the effects of opening Western markets to new member states. Full access to the EU market enables accession countries to specialise in products in which they are relatively efficient. Increased Western demand for these products raises the value of the workers' marginal product, shifting the labour demand curve to the right and leading to higher real wages and employment. Exploiting Western technology and management skills also leads to improved labour productivity, with further gains in real wages and employment.

relatively more efficient. Poland gains because access to the German market enables it to specialise in industries where it is relatively efficient, and to take advantage of German technology, which improves the skills and productivity of Polish textile workers. More generally, as the accession countries now have full access to the single market we can expect to see changes in trade patterns between 'Western' and 'Eastern' Europe, with each group specialising in the areas where they are relatively efficient. The resulting gains, together with the opportunity to import Western technology and management skills, should eventually raise living standards in the CEE countries.

Labour force trends (2): unemployment in Europe and the United States

As shown in Figure 18.6, unemployment has been high in some major European countries since the 1980s. Over the period 1995–2005, for example, the average rate of unemployment was 8.5 per cent in Germany and over 11 per cent in France, as compared to just over 5 per cent in the United States. However, as Figure 18.6 shows, there are important differences between European countries. While unemployment remains high in France and Germany it has declined in Ireland and the United Kingdom. Economic naturalist 18.3 discusses these differences.

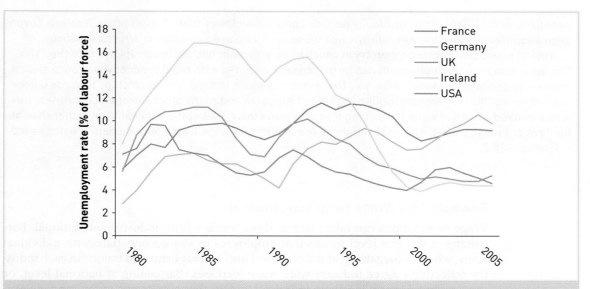

Figure 18.6 Unemployment Rates in Western Europe and the United States, 1980–2006.

Note: Prior to 1991 the German series is for the former West Germany.

Source: OECD, *Main Economic Indicators* (www.oecd.org).

Economic naturalist 18.3 Why are unemployment rates so high in Western Europe?

One explanation for the high unemployment in major European countries is the existence of structural 'rigidities' in their labour markets. Relative to the United States, European labour markets are highly regulated. European governments set rules in matters ranging from the number of weeks of vacation workers must receive to the reasons for which a worker can be dismissed. Minimum wages tend to be relatively high in Europe, and unemployment benefits are much more generous than in the United States. European unions are also far more powerful than those in the United States; in countries such as France, wage agreements are often extended by law to all firms in the industry, whether or not they are unionised. This lack of flexibility in labour markets – which some observers refer to as *Eurosclerosis* – causes higher frictional and structural unemployment.

If European labour markets are so dysfunctional, why has serious European unemployment emerged only since the 1980s? One explanation turns on the increasing pace of *globalisation and skill-biased technological change*. As we have seen, these two factors decrease the demand for less skilled labour relative to the demand for skilled labour. In the United States, falling demand has depressed the wages of the less skilled, increasing wage inequality. But in Western Europe, high minimum wages, union contracts, generous unemployment insurance and other factors may have created a *floor* for the wage that firms could pay or that workers would accept. As the marginal productivity of the less skilled dropped below that floor, firms no longer found it profitable to employ those workers, swelling the ranks of the unemployed. Thus the combination of labour market rigidity and the declining marginal productivity of low-skilled workers may be responsible for the European unemployment problem.

Evidence for the idea that inflexible labour markets have contributed to European unemployment comes from the United Kingdom, where the government of Prime Minister Margaret Thatcher instituted a series of reforms beginning in the early 1980s. Britain has since largely deregulated its labour market so that it functions much more like that in the United States. Figure 18.6 shows that unemployment in Britain has gradually declined and is now lower than in most other Western European countries. Labour market reforms like those in Britain are examples of *structural policies*.

Ireland is another European country in which unemployment has declined rapidly since the 1980s. The decline in Irish unemployment has largely been associated with rapid productivity growth and an increasing demand for labour. Also, like the United Kingdom, Ireland has taken steps towards labour market deregulation. However, unlike the United Kingdom and many other European countries, Ireland has used a form of wage bargaining that sets wage increases at the *national* level rather than at the firm or industry level. The implications of these different wage bargaining models are discussed in Example 18.2.

Example 18.2 Wage bargaining models

Wage negotiations can take place at three levels – firm, industry and national. Bargaining at the *firm* level means that employees or unions negotiate with individual firms, whereas bargaining at *industry* level implies that firms and unions in each industry collectively agree industry-wide wage increases. Bargaining at national level, or *social partnership* as it is known in Ireland, means that employers, unions and government agree economy-wide wage increases. Economic research suggests that employment is best protected when wage increases are set at the firm or national level, and most vulnerable when negotiations take place at industry level.

Consider an airline industry with two firms, FlyEasy and FlyFast. When unions and employers bargain at the firm level each will pay close attention to the effect of their negotiations on their competitors. For example, if FlyFast unions push for higher wage increases than FlyEasy unions, they run the risk that their firm will lose competitiveness and that customers will shift to FlyEasy, resulting in possible job losses at FlyFast. However, if both unions jointly negotiate with the airline industry they know that each firm will retain its competitive position as both FlyEasy and FlyFast will pay the same wage increases. Hence, bargaining at firm level is more likely to exert a moderating influence on wage demands, thus reducing the adverse effects on employment. Likewise, when wage increases are set at the national level, unions, employers and government (the *social partners*) are more likely to pay closer attention to national objectives and the economy's international competitiveness, resulting in more moderate wage increases. In the case of Ireland, the social partners collectively agreed to moderate wage increases in order to address the alarmingly high unemployment rates of the 1980s. As Figure 18.6 shows, countries that use the firm-level (United Kingdom) or national-level (Ireland) models have lower unemployment rates than countries where wage bargaining is at industry level.

Summary

- In most countries the unemployment rate, perhaps the best-known indicator of the state of the labour market, is based on survey data conducted by government agencies. These surveys classify all respondents of working age as employed, unemployed or not in the labour force. The *labour force* is the sum of employed and unemployed workers – that is, people who have a job or are looking for one. The *unemployment rate* is calculated as the number of unemployed workers divided by the labour force. The *participation rate* is calculated as labour force (employed plus unemployed) divided by the total population of working age.

- Recent decades have seen a marked rise in female labour force participation and a decline in male participation.

- There are three broad types of unemployment: frictional, structural and cyclical. *Frictional unemployment* is the short-term unemployment associated with the process of matching workers with jobs in a dynamic, heterogeneous labour market. *Structural unemployment* is the long-term and chronic unemployment that exists even when the economy is producing at a normal rate. It arises from a variety of factors, including language barriers, discrimination, structural features of the labour market, lack of skills, or long-term mismatches between the skills workers have and the available jobs. *Cyclical unemployment* is the extra unemployment that occurs during periods of recession. The costs of frictional unemployment are low, as it tends to be brief and to create more productive matches between workers and jobs. But structural unemployment (which is often long term) and cyclical unemployment (which is associated with significant reductions in real GDP) are relatively more costly.

- *Structural features* of the labour market that may contribute to unemployment include minimum wage laws, which discourage firms from hiring low-skilled workers; labour unions, which can set wages above market-clearing levels; unemployment benefits, which reduce the incentives of the unemployed to find work quickly; and other regulations, which – although possibly conferring benefits – increase the costs of employing workers – for example, when wages negotiated in unionised firms apply to non-unionised firms in the same industry. The labour market 'rigidity' created by government regulations and union contracts is more of a problem in Europe than in the United States, which may account for Europe's high unemployment rates.

- Two reasons for the increasing wage inequality are economic globalisation and *skill-biased technological change*. Both have increased the demand for, and hence the real wages of, relatively skilled and educated workers. Attempting to block globalisation and technological change is counter-productive, however, since both factors are essential to economic growth and increased productivity. To some extent, the movement of workers from lower-paying to higher-paying jobs or industries (*worker mobility*) will counteract the trend towards wage inequality. A policy of providing transition aid and training for workers with obsolete skills is a more useful response to the problem.

- *Wage bargaining*, which can take place at firm, industry and national level, may also have an effect on employment. The evidence suggests that employment is best protected when wages are negotiated at the firm or national level, and most vulnerable when wages are set at the industry level.

Review questions

1. Explain how the rate of unemployment and the labour force participation rate are calculated.

2. **True or false:** A high participation rate implies a low unemployment rate. Explain.

3. List three types of unemployment and their causes. Which of these types is economically and socially the least costly? Explain.

4. What are the two major factors contributing to increased inequality in wages? Briefly, why do these factors raise wage inequality? Contrast possible policy responses to increasing inequality in terms of their effects on economic efficiency.

5. Describe some of the structural features of European labour markets that have helped to keep European unemployment rates high. If these structural features create unemployment, why don't European governments just eliminate them?

6. How would you expect the 2004 enlargement of the European Union to affect wages and employment in the new member states?

Problems

1. The towns of Littlehampton and Bighampton each have a labour force of 1,200 people. In Littlehampton, 100 people were unemployed for the entire year, while the rest of the labour force was employed continuously. In Bighampton every member of the labour force was unemployed for 1 month and employed for 11 months.

    a. What is the average unemployment rate over the year in each of the two towns?

    b. What is the average duration of unemployment spells in each of the two towns?

    c. In which town do you think the costs of unemployment are higher? Explain.

2. In a total population of 10 million people 20 per cent are classified as not being of working age. In the working-age population 40 per cent are classified as employed, 20 per cent are classified as retired or in full-time education and 10 per cent are classified as not seeking employment. For this population calculate:

    a. the labour force

    b. the unemployment rate

    c. the labour force unemployment rate.

3. Using the data in Problem 2 suppose that increased government investment in the infrastructure leads to 250,000 of those classified as unemployed finding employment and reduces the numbers classified as not seeking employment by the same amount. Calculate the changes in:

    a. the labour force

    b. the unemployment rate

    c. the labour force unemployment rate.

4. Here is a report from a not-very-efficient labour force survey taker: 'There were 65 people in the houses I visited, 10 of them had children under 16 and 10 retired; 25 people had full-time jobs, and 5 had part-time jobs. There were 5 full-time home

makers, 5 full-time students over age 16 and 2 people who were disabled and cannot work. The remaining people did not have jobs but all said they would like one. One of these people had not looked actively for work for more than a year, however.' Find the labour force, the unemployment rate and the participation rate implied by the report.

5. The demand for and supply of labour in a certain industry are given by the equations

$$\text{Demand: } N_d = 400 - 2w$$
$$\text{Supply: } N_s = 240 + 2w$$

where N_d is the number of workers employers want to hire, N_s is the number of people willing to work, and both labour demand and labour supply depend on the wage w, which is measured in euros per day.

 a. Find employment and the wage in labour market equilibrium.

 b. Suppose government introduces a minimum wage of €50 per day. Find employment and unemployment. Is anyone made better or worse off by the minimum wage? In answering the last part of the question, consider not only workers but employers and other people in the society, such as consumers and taxpayers.

 c. Repeat part (b) except now assume that a union contract requires that workers be paid €60 per day.

 d. Suppose that the cost of complying with new government regulations on workplace safety reduces labour demand to $N_d = 360 - 2w$. Find the change in numbers employed and the equilibrium wage.

6. For each of the following scenarios, state whether the unemployment is frictional, structural or cyclical. Justify your answer.

 a. Ted lost his job when the steel mill closed down. He lacks the skills to work in another industry and so has been unemployed for over a year.

 b. Alice was laid off from her job at the car plant because the recession reduced the demand for cars. She expects to get her job back when the economy picks up.

 c. Lance is an unskilled worker who works for local removal companies during their busy seasons. The rest of the year he is unemployed.

 d. Gwen had a job as an office clerk but quit when her husband was transferred to another city. She looked for a month before finding a new job that she liked.

 e. Tao looked for a job for six weeks after finishing college. He turned down a couple of offers because they didn't let him use the skills he had acquired at college, but now he has a job in the area that he trained for.

 f. Karen's parents are injured in a road accident. She quits her job as a teacher to become a full-time carer.

7. How would each of the following be likely to affect the real wage and employment of unskilled workers on an automobile plant assembly line?

 a. Demand for the type of car made by the plant increases.

 b. A sharp increase in the price of petrol causes many commuters to switch to public transport.

 c. Because of alternative opportunities, people become less willing to do factory work.

    d. The plant management introduces new assembly line methods that increase the productivity of skilled relative to unskilled workers.

8. Skilled or unskilled workers can be used to produce a small toy. Initially, assume that the wages paid to both types of workers are equal.

    a. Suppose that electronic equipment is introduced that increases the marginal product of skilled workers (who can use the equipment to produce more toys per hour worked). The marginal products of unskilled workers are unaffected. Explain, using words and graphs, what happens to the equilibrium wages for the two groups.

    b. Suppose that unskilled workers find it worthwhile to acquire skills when the wage differential between skilled and unskilled workers reaches a certain point. Explain what will happen to the supply of unskilled workers, the supply of skilled workers, and the equilibrium wage for the two groups. In particular, what are equilibrium wages for skilled workers relative to unskilled workers after some unskilled workers acquire training?

To help you grasp the key concepts of this chapter check out the extra resources posted on the Online Learning Centre. There are chapter summaries, self-test questions, an interactive graphing tool, weblinks and a glossary, all for free!

Visit the Online Learning Centre at: www.mcgraw-hill.co.uk/textbooks/mcdowell for information on accessing all of these resources.

Part 6

The Economy in the Long Run

For millennia the great majority of the world's inhabitants eked out a spare existence by tilling the soil. Only a small proportion of the population lived above the level of subsistence, learned to read and write, or travelled more than a few kilometres from their birthplaces. Large cities grew up, serving as imperial capitals and centres of trade, but the great majority of urban populations lived in dire poverty, subject to malnutrition and disease.

Then, in the 1700s, a fundamental change occurred. Spurred by technological advances and entrepreneurial innovations, a process of economic growth began. Sustained over many years, this growth in the economy's productive capacity has transformed almost every aspect of how we live – from what we eat and wear to how we work and play. What caused this economic growth? And why have some countries enjoyed substantially greater rates of growth than others? As the Nobel Prize winner Robert E. Lucas, Jr put it in a classic article on economic development: 'The consequences for human welfare involved in questions like these are simply staggering: Once one starts to think about them, it is hard to think about anything else.'

The subject of Part 6 is the behaviour of the economy in the long run, including the factors that cause the economy to grow and develop. Chapter 19 begins by tackling the causes and consequences of economic growth. A key conclusion of the chapter is that improvements in average labour productivity are the primary source of rising living standards; hence policies to improve living standards should focus on stimulating productivity. As the creation of new capital goods is an important factor underlying rising productivity, Chapter 20 examines the processes of saving and capital formation.

19

Economic Growth, Productivity and Living Standards

A speaker at a conference on the effects of economic growth and development on society posed the following question: 'Which would you rather be? An ordinary, middle-class French or British citizen today, or the richest person in Europe at the time of Napoleon?'

A member of the audience spoke out immediately: 'I can answer that question in one word: dentistry.'

The answer may have caused laughter but it was a good answer nonetheless. Dentistry in Europe at the time of Napoleon – whether the patient was rich or poor – was a primitive affair. Most dentists simply pulled a patient's rotten teeth, with a shot of brandy for anaesthetic. Other types of medical care were not much better than dentistry. Eighteenth- and early nineteenth-century doctors had no effective weapons against tuberculosis, typhoid fever, diphtheria, influenza, pneumonia and other communicable diseases. Such illnesses, now quite treatable, were major killers in Napoleon's time. Infants and children were particularly susceptible to deadly infectious diseases and even a well-to-do family could often lose two or three children to these illnesses.

Medical care is not the only aspect of ordinary life that has changed drastically since the late 1770s. Today we can use the Channel Tunnel to travel between London and Paris in a matter of hours; in 1800 the same journey could take several days. We can now fly from European capital cities to places such as Beijing, Tokyo and Los Angeles in less than a day; even in 1950 similar journeys could take weeks, or even months.

No doubt you can think of other enormous changes in the way average people live, even over the past few decades. Computer technologies and the internet have changed the ways people work and study in just a few years, for example. Though these changes are due in large part to scientific advances, such discoveries by themselves usually have little effect on most people's lives. New scientific knowledge leads to widespread improvements in living standards only when it is *commercially applied*. Better understanding of the human immune system, for example, has little impact unless it leads to new therapies or drugs. And a new drug will do little to help unless it is affordable to those who need it.

A tragic illustration of this point is the AIDS epidemic in Africa. Although some new drugs will moderate the effects of the virus that causes AIDS, they are so expensive that they are of little practical value in poverty-stricken African nations grappling with the disease. But even if the drugs were affordable, they would have limited benefit without modern hospitals, trained health professionals, and adequate nutrition and sanitation. In short, most improvements in a nation's living standard are the result not just of scientific and technological advances but of an *economic system* that makes the benefits of those advances available to the average person.

In this chapter we shall explore the sources of economic growth and rising living standards in the modern world. We shall begin by reviewing the remarkable economic growth in the industrialised countries, as measured by real GDP per person. Since the mid-nineteenth century (and earlier in some countries), a radical transformation in living standards has occurred. What explains this transformation? The key to rising living standards is a *continuing increase in average labour productivity*, which depends on several factors such as technology, the skills of the labour force, and the legal and social environment in which they work. We shall analyse each of these factors and discuss its implications for government policies to promote growth. We shall also discuss the costs of rapid economic growth and consider whether there may be limits to the amount of economic growth a society can achieve.

The remarkable rise in living standards: the record

The advances in healthcare and transportation mentioned at the beginning of this chapter illustrate only a few of the impressive changes that have taken place in people's material well-being since 1800, particularly in industrialised countries such as France, Germany, the United Kingdom and the United States. To study the factors that affect living standards systematically, however, we must go beyond anecdotes and adopt a specific measure of economic well-being in a particular country and time.

In Chapter 16 we introduced the concept of *real* GDP as a basic measure of the level of economic activity in a country. Recall that real GDP measures the physical volume of goods and services produced during a specific period, such as a quarter or a year. Consequently, real GDP *per person* provides a measure of the quantity of goods and services available to the typical resident of a country at a particular time. Although, as we saw in Chapter 16, real GDP per person is certainly not a perfect indicator of economic well-being, it is positively related to a number of pertinent variables, such as life expectancy, infant health and literacy. Lacking a better alternative, economists have focused on real GDP per person as a key measure of a country's living standard and stage of economic development.

Figure 15.2 (p. 440) showed the remarkable growth in real GDP per person that occurred in Europe and the United States between 1900 and 2003. For comparison, Table 19.1 shows real GDP per person in eight major countries in selected years from 1870 to 2003 (US dollars are used to facilitate comparisons). Figure 19.1 displays the same data graphically for five of the eight countries.

The data in Table 19.1 and Figure 19.1 tell a dramatic story. For example, in the United States (which was already a relatively wealthy industrialised country in 1870), real GDP per person grew more than 11-fold between 1870 and 2000. In Japan, real GDP per person grew more than 25-fold over the same period. Underlying these statistics is an amazingly rapid process of economic growth and transformation, through which, in just a few generations, relatively poor agrarian societies became highly industrialised economies – with average standards of living that could scarcely have

Country (1)	1870 (2)	1913 (3)	1950 (4)	1979 (5)	2003 (6)	Annual % change 1870–2003 (7)	Annual % change 1950–2003 (8)
Australia	5,512	7,236	9,369	17,670	28,312	1.2	2.1
Canada	2,328	5,509	8,906	19,892	29,201	1.9	2.3
France	2,229	4,484	6,146	18,138	26,176	1.8	2.8
Germany	1,152	2,218	4,785	17,222	25,271	2.3	3.2
Italy	2,852	4,018	5,128	16,912	25,458	1.7	3.1
Japan	931	1,763	2,141	16,329	26,636	2.6	4.9
United Kingdom	3,892	5,976	8,709	16,557	26,852	1.5	2.1
United States	2,887	6,852	12,110	22,835	35,488	1.9	2.0

Table 19.1 **Real GDP per Person in Selected Countries, 1870–2003 (in 2000 US Dollars)**
Note: Rebased to 2000 and updated to 2003. 'Germany' refers to West Germany in 1950 and 1979.
Sources: Derived from Maddison (1988, Tables A2, B2–B4) and OECD, *Quarterly National Accounts*.

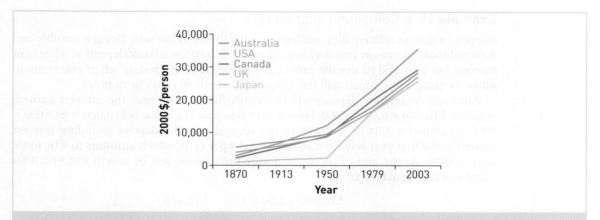

Figure 19.1 **Real GDP per Person in Five Industrialised Countries, 1870–2003.** Economic growth has been especially rapid since the 1950s, particularly in Japan.

been imagined in 1870. As Figure 19.1 shows, a significant part of this growth has occurred since 1950, particularly in Japan.

A note of caution is in order. The further back in time we go, the less precise are historical estimates of real GDP. Most governments did not keep official GDP statistics until after the Second World War; production records from earlier periods are often incomplete or of questionable accuracy. Comparing economic output over a century or more is also problematic because many goods and services that are produced today were unavailable – indeed, inconceivable – in 1870. How many nineteenth-century horse-drawn wagons, for example, would be the economic equivalent of a BMW 328i car or an Airbus jet? Despite the difficulty of making precise comparisons, however, we can say with certainty that the variety, quality and quantity of available goods and services increased enormously in industrialised countries during the nineteenth and twentieth centuries, a fact reflected in the data on real GDP per capita.

Why 'small' differences in growth rates matter

Columns (7) and (8) of Table 19.1 show the annual growth rates of real GDP per person, both for the entire 1870–2003 period and the more recent years, 1950–2003. At first glance these growth rates don't seem to differ much from country to country. For example, for the period 1870–2003, the highest growth rate is 2.6 per cent (Japan) and the lowest is 1.2 per cent (Australia). But consider the long-run effect of this seemingly 'small' difference in annual growth rates. In 1870, in terms of output per person, Australia was the richest of the eight countries listed in Table 19.1, with a real GDP per person nearly six times that of Japan. Yet by 2003 Japan had almost caught up with Australia, the difference in GDP being only 6 per cent as compared to 600 per cent in 1870. This remarkable change in economic fortunes is the result of the apparently small difference between a 1.2 per cent growth rate and a 2.6 per cent growth rate, maintained over 130 years.

The fact that what seem to be small differences in growth rates can have large long-run effects results from what is called the *power of compound interest*.

Example 19.1 Compound interest (1)

Suppose a distant relative dies and leaves you €10,000 in her will. Being a sensible and forward-looking person you decide to save the €10,000 in a bank deposit at 4 per cent interest per year and to use the proceeds to support your lifestyle when you retire in 40 years' time. How much will the €10,000 be worth 40 years from now?

After one year your deposit will be worth the €10,000 plus the interest earned, which is €10,000 × 0.04 = €400. Hence after one year the value is €10,000 + €10,000 × 0.04 = €10,000 × 1.04 or €10,400. In the second year the deposit including interest earned in the first year will earn an additional 4 per cent, which amounts to €10,400 × 0.04 = €416. At the end of the second year the deposit will be worth €10,816. This value can be calculated as:

$$€10,000 \times 1.04 \times 1.04 = €10,816$$

or:

$$€10,000 \times (1.04)^2 = €10,816$$

Hence, after 40 years, the deposit will be worth:

$$€10,000 \times (1.04)^{40} = €48,010.12$$

compound interest the payment of interest not only on the original deposit but also on all previously accumulated interest

This example illustrates the idea of **compound interest**, which is an arrangement in which interest is paid not only on the original deposit but also on all previously accumulated interest, and is distinguished from *simple interest* in which interest is paid only on the *original deposit*. If your account earned 4 per cent simple interest, it would accumulate by only €400 each year (4 per cent of the original €10,000 deposit), for a total value of €10,000 + 40 × €400 = €26,000 after 40 years.

Example 19.2 Compound interest (2)

Refer to Example 19.1. What would your €10,000 deposit be worth after 40 years if the annual interest rate is 5 per cent? What would it be worth if the annual interest rate is 6 per cent?

At 5 per cent interest, the deposit would accumulate to:

$$€10,000 \times (1.05)^{40} = €70,399.89$$

And at 6 per cent interest it would accumulate to:

$$€10,000 \times (1.06)^{40} = €102,857.20$$

Table 19.2 summarises these results and also includes the final value of the deposit at 2 and 3 per cent interest.

Interest rate (%)	Value of €10,000 after 40 years (€)
2	22,080.40
3	32,620.38
4	48,010.12
5	70,399.89
6	102,857.20

Table 19.2 **Compound Interest**

The power of compound interest is that, even at relatively low rates of interest, a small sum, compounded over a long enough period, can greatly increase in value. A more subtle point, illustrated by Examples 19.1 and 19.2, is that small differences in interest rates matter a lot. The difference between a 5 per cent and a 6 per cent interest rate doesn't seem tremendous, but over a long period of time it implies large differences in the amount of interest accumulated on an account. Likewise, the effect of switching from a 4 per cent to a 6 per cent interest rate is enormous, as our calculations show.

Economic growth rates are similar to compound interest rates. Just as the value of a bank deposit grows each year at a rate equal to the interest rate, so the size of a nation's economy expands each year at the rate of economic growth. This analogy suggests that even a relatively modest rate of growth in output per person – say, 1 to 2 per cent per year – will produce tremendous increases in average living standards over a long period. And relatively small *differences* in growth rates, as in the case of Australia versus Japan, will ultimately produce very different living standards. Over the long run, then, the *rate of economic growth* is an extremely important variable. Hence, government policy and other factors that affect the long-term growth rate even by a small amount will have a major economic impact.

Exercise 19.1 Suppose that real GDP per capita in the United Kingdom had grown at 4.9 per cent per year, as Japan's did, instead of the actual 2.1 per cent per year, from 1950 to 2003. How much larger would real GDP per person have been in the United Kingdom in 2003?

Why nations become rich: the crucial role of average labour productivity

What determines a nation's economic growth rate? To get some insight into this vital question, we shall find it useful to express real GDP per person as the product of two terms: *average labour productivity* and the *share of the population that is working*. To do this, let Y equal the economy's total real output, N equal the number of employed workers, and POP the total population. Then real GDP per person can be written as Y/POP; average labour productivity, or output per employed worker, equals Y/N; and the share of the population that is working is N/POP. The relationship between these three variables is

$$\frac{Y}{POP} = \frac{Y}{N} \times \frac{N}{POP}$$

which, as you can see by cancelling out N on the right-hand side of the equation, always holds exactly. In words, this basic relationship is

Real GDP per person = Average labour productivity × Share of population employed

This expression for real GDP per person tells us something very basic and intuitive: the quantity of goods and services that each person can consume depends on (1) how much each worker can produce and (2) how many people (as a fraction of the total population) are working. Furthermore, because real GDP per person equals average labour productivity times the share of the population employed, real GDP per person can *grow* only to the extent that there is *growth* in worker productivity and/or the fraction of the population that is employed.

Which of these two factors, average labour productivity or the share of the population employed, contribute most to the growth of real GDP per person? Referring back to Table 19.1, we see that since 1950 Japan recorded the highest annual percentage change in real GDP per person, and the United Kingdom and the United States the lowest. Figures 19.2, 19.3 and 19.4 graph the behaviour of average labour productivity (left axis) and the share of the population employed (right axis) for each of these

Figure 19.2 Average Labour Productivity and the Share of the Population Employed, Japan 1960–2006.

Source: The Conference Board and Groningen Growth and Development Centre (http://www.conference-board.org/economics).

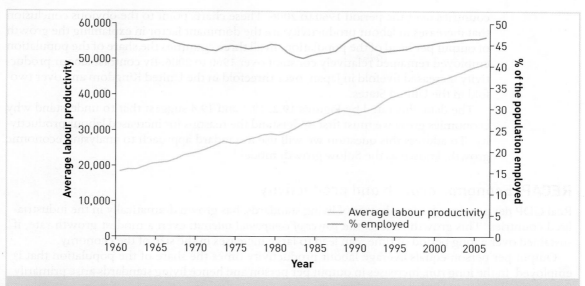

Figure 19.3 Average Labour Productivity and the Share of the Population Employed, United Kingdom 1960–2006.

Source: The Conference Board and Groningen Growth and Development Centre (http://www.conference-board.org/economics).

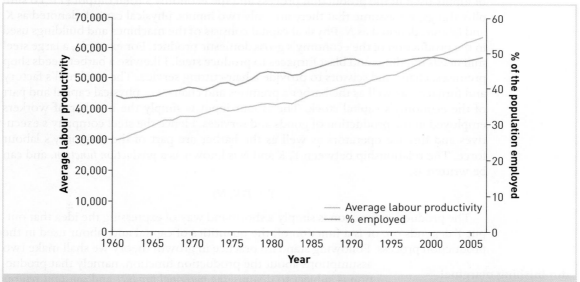

Figure 19.4 Average Labour Productivity and the Share of the Population Employed, United States 1960–2006.

Source: The Conference Board and Groningen Growth and Development Centre (http://www.conference-board.org/economics).

countries over the period 1960 to 2006. These charts point to the obvious conclusion that increases in labour productivity are the dominant factor in explaining the growth of output per head of the population. In all three countries the share of the population employed remained relatively constant over 1960 to 2006. By contrast labour productivity increased fivefold in Japan, over threefold in the United Kingdom and over twofold in the United States.

The data illustrated by Figures 19.2, 19.3 and 19.4 suggest that to understand why economies grow we must first understand the reasons for increased labour productivity. To address this question we will use a standard approach to analysing economic growth, known as the Solow growth model.[1]

RECAP Economic growth and productivity

Real GDP per person, a basic indicator of living standards, has grown dramatically in the industrialised countries. This growth reflects the *power of compound interest*: even a modest growth rate, if sustained over a long period of time, can lead to large increases in the size of the economy.

Output per person equals average labour productivity times the share of the population that is employed. In the long run, increases in output per person and hence living standards arise primarily from increases in average labour productivity.

The Solow growth model

The Solow growth model starts by postulating a relationship between the quantities of inputs used in the production process and the economy's total output (Y). To simplify things, we assume that there are only two inputs, physical capital, denoted as K, and labour, denoted as N. Physical capital consists of the machines and buildings used in the production of the economy's gross domestic product. For example, a large steel mill needs buildings and blast furnaces to produce steel. Likewise a barber needs shop premises, chairs and scissors to provide a hair-cutting service. The steel mill's factory and furnaces, as well as the barber's premises and chairs, are physical capital and part of the economy's capital stock. The labour input is simply the number of workers employed in the production of goods and services. Hence the steel company's executives and furnace operators as well as the barber are part of the economy's labour force. The relationship between Y, K and N is known as a *production function*, and can be written as:

$$Y = F(K, N)$$

The production function is simply a shorthand way of expressing the idea that output Y depends on, or is a function of, the quantities of capital and labour used in the production process. Following standard practice in growth theory we shall make two assumptions about the production function, namely that production is subject to *diminishing marginal product* and *constant returns to scale* to individual inputs.

diminishing marginal product if the amount of labour and other inputs employed is held constant, then the greater the amount of capital already in use, the less an additional unit of capital adds to production

Diminishing marginal product

The marginal product of an input such as capital or labour is defined as the change in total output per unit increase in that input *with the quantities of all other inputs held constant*. Letting the Greek symbol delta Δ denote the phrase 'the change in', $\Delta Y =$ the change

---

1 See Solow (1956).

in output and ΔK = the change in the amount of capital. Holding the labour input constant the marginal product of capital is defined as:

$$MPK = \frac{\Delta Y}{\Delta K}$$

For example, if the $MPK = 5$ then each additional unit of capital such as a new machine increases total output by 5 units. The assumption of diminishing marginal product simply means that the MPK declines as K is increased with N held constant.

Example 19.3 Diminishing marginal product

Table 19.3 illustrates the idea of diminishing marginal product to capital.

Capital number of planes	Number of passengers per flight	Total output	Marginal product of capital
5	200	1,000	
6	180	1,080	80
7	160	1,120	40

Table 19.3 Diminishing Marginal Product
Note: the labour input is held constant.

Increasing Opportunity Cost

Consider an airline operating five planes with 200 passenger seats each. The planes are the airline's capital, and the pilots and flight attendants are its labour force. To keep things simple, assume that the airline operates five flights per day. The airline's capacity to carry passengers depends on the number of seats and the staff available to operate flights. Hence operating at full capacity and with sufficient staff the airline is capable of carrying 1,000 passengers per day, its output Y. Now suppose the airline purchases a sixth plane but does not recruit additional labour. The marginal product of capital is the additional number of passengers the airline can carry by adding the sixth or marginal plane. The airline's problem is that to operate the additional flight it will have to reallocate staff from other planes, thus reducing their capacity to carry passengers. Suppose that after this reallocation each flight can service only 180 rather than 200 passengers. Total output as measured by the number of passengers will increase to 1,080. Hence the marginal product of capital equals 80 additional passengers per day. What happens if the airline adds a seventh plane? To operate an additional flight the airline will again have to reallocate staff. If this reallocation means that each flight can service only 160 passengers then total output will increase to 1,120 and the marginal product of capital will decline to 40 passengers per day.

Constant returns to scale

constant returns to scale if the labour and capital inputs are both increased by equal proportions then total output increases by the same proportion

As defined in Chapter 8 a production process is said to have **constant returns to scale** if, when all inputs are changed by a given proportion, output changes by the same proportion. Under this assumption we can write the production function as:

$$zY = F(zK, zN)$$

z can be any positive number. For example, if K and N are both increased by 5 per cent $z = 1.05$ and Y also increases by 5 per cent. Letting $z = 1/N$ we can write the production function as:

$$\frac{Y}{N} = F\left(\frac{K}{N}, 1\right)$$

This equation simply says that average labour productivity or output per worker (Y/N) increases as the amount of capital per worker (K/N) increases. For simplicity of exposition we shall denote average labour productivity as lower case $y = (Y/N)$ and capital per worker as lower case $k = (K/N)$. Hence under constant returns to scale we can write the production function as:

$$y = f(k) \tag{19.1}$$

Equation 19.1 gives our first insight into answering the question 'What determines the productivity of the average worker in a particular country at a particular time?' Other things being equal, the greater the capital stock per worker (k) the greater is average labour productivity (y). (Note, we can ignore the '1' in the production function as it is a constant.)

Given these assumptions, Figure 19.5 gives a graphical representation of the production function. In Figure 19.5 the $y = f(k)$ curve illustrates the production function and shows how average labour productivity increases with the amount of capital per worker. Note that the assumption of diminishing marginal product means that the production function becomes flatter and the rate of increase of average labour productivity decreases as the capital stock per worker increases.

Equation 19.1 suggests that average labour productivity increases with the amount of physical capital available to the workforce. This conclusion is supported by Figure 19.6, which shows the relationship between average labour productivity (real GDP per worker) and the amount of capital per worker in 15 major countries, including the eight industrialised countries listed in Table 19.1. Figure 19.6 shows a strong relationship between the amounts of capital per worker and productivity, consistent with the theory. Note, though, that the relationship between capital and productivity is somewhat weaker for the richest countries. For example, Germany has more capital

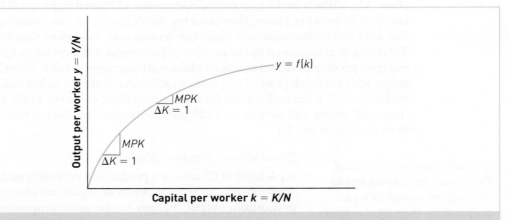

Figure 19.5 The Production Function. The $y = f(k)$ curve is known as the production function and shows how average labour productivity $y = Y/N$ increases with the capital per worker or the capital–labour ratio $k = K/N$. For a constant labour force N the slope of this line measures the marginal product of capital MPK. Given the assumption of diminishing marginal product the slope will become smaller and the curve flatter as the capital–labour ratio increases.

Figure 19.6 Average Labour Productivity and Capital per Worker in 15 Countries, 1990. Countries with large amounts of capital per worker also tend to have high average labour productivity, as measured by real GDP per worker.
Source: Penn World Tables (www.nber.org). Countries included are those listed in Table 19.1, plus all countries with populations of 40 million or more for which data are available.

per worker than the United States, but German workers are less productive than American workers on average. Diminishing returns to capital may help to explain the weakening of the relationship between capital and productivity at high levels of capital. In addition, Figure 19.6 does not account for many other differences among countries, such as differences in economic systems or government policies. Thus we should not expect to see a perfect relationship between the two variables.

Exercise 19.2   Refer to Table 19.3. Assume that the airline has 100 employees and that each plane is valued at €1 million. Find the capital–labour ratio and average labour productivity at each valuation of the capital stock.

As illustrated by Figure 19.5, the production function simply tells us that average labour productivity increases with the amount of capital per worker, or the capital–labour ratio (k). Hence, to determine equilibrium value for average labour productivity we must first ask what determines the equilibrium capital–labour ratio.

Investment and saving

The stock of physical capital increases over time because of investment in new capital goods such as factories, machines and blast furnaces. The Solow model assumes that investment is financed by saving and that saving is a constant fraction of income Y. Letting I denote investment in physical capital and S denote total saving, this assumption can be expressed as:

$$I = S = sY$$

where s = the savings rate. For example if $s = 0.10$ then 10 per cent of income is saved and invested per period. Dividing through by N and letting $i = I/N$, or investment per head of the workforce, and $y = Y/N$, we can write this relationship as:

$$i = sy = sf(k)$$

In long-run equilibrium investment per worker will just be sufficient to keep the capital–labour ratio constant. Hence, to determine the equilibrium value for k, we must ask the question 'How much investment is required to keep the capital–labour ratio constant?' The answer depends on two factors – the rate of depreciation and population growth.[2] Depreciation is that part of the capital stock that wears out and becomes less productive each period. If capital depreciates at a rate d per period then investment per head must be at least dk to keep the capital–labour ratio from falling. However, if the labour force grows at a constant rate n per period, then the economy will require additional investment of nk to keep the capital–labour ratio constant. It follows that in each period the economy requires investment per head to be $(d + n)k$ to maintain a constant capital–labour ratio. Hence we will call $(d + n)k$ *required investment*. For example, if 3 per cent of the capital stock wears out each year and the population grows by 2 per cent, then required investment per person employed must be 5 per cent to keep the capital–labour ratio constant. That is, $(d + n) = 0.05$. We can express the long-run equilibrium condition as:

$$\Delta k = i - (d + n)k = 0$$

Investment per worker i is normally referred to as *gross investment* and the change in the capital–labour ratio Δk as *net investment*. Hence, in long-run equilibrium, gross investment equals required investment, and net investment per worker is zero.

Figure 19.7 illustrates these relationships. The straight line $(d + n)k$ illustrates the amount of investment per worker required to maintain a constant capital–labour ratio while the $i = sf(k)$ curve shows how gross investment per worker increases with saving and output per worker. Note that as investment is assumed to be a constant proportion of income per worker, the investment curve will have the same shape as the production function and, as $y = f(k)$, we can write the investment function as $i = sf(k)$.

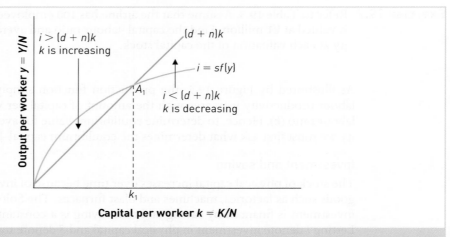

Figure 19.7 The Equilibrium Capital–Labour Ratio. The equilibrium capital–labour ratio is determined at A_1 where gross investment is just sufficient to maintain a constant capital–labour ratio.

---

2 For simplicity we shall assume that the number of people employed N grows at the same rate as the total population *POP*.

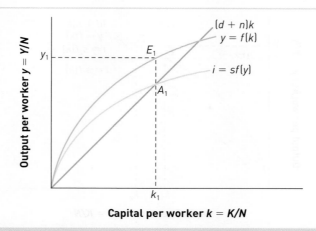

Figure 19.8 Equilibrium Labour Productivity. The equilibrium capital–labour ratio (k_1) determines the equilibrium value of average labour productivity (y_1).

In Figure 19.7 the capital–labour ratio will be constant at the point A_1 where the two curves intersect and $i = (d + n)k$. Hence k_1 is the equilibrium capital–labour ratio. At a capital–labour ratio less than k_1 net gross investment will exceed required investment and k will be increasing. The opposite holds if k is greater than k_1.

We are now in a position to determine the equilibrium value average labour productivity. Figure 19.8 simply adds the production function $y = f(k)$ to Figure 19.7. As in Figure 19.7, the equilibrium capital–labour ratio is determined at point A_1 and the corresponding equilibrium value of average labour productivity is determined by the production function at E_1. Hence, in Figure 19.8, the equilibrium capital–labour ratio is k_1 and equilibrium average labour productivity is y_1. Once the economy reaches this equilibrium, both output per worker and capital per worker will be constant. We refer to a point such as E_1 as a *steady-state* equilibrium because in the absence of any shocks, such as a change in the saving rate, there is no reason why either the capital–labour ratio or labour productivity should change.

However, although output per person employed will be constant in the steady-state the economy's total output Y will be growing at the same rate as the total population. To see this, remember that labour productivity is defined as $y = Y/N$. Hence, as labour productivity is constant in steady-state equilibrium, total output Y must be growing at the same rate as the population N for their ratio y to be constant. This is an important conclusion of the Solow model – in long-run steady-state equilibrium the economy's growth rate is equal to the rate of population growth n. This conclusion is illustrated by Example 19.4, which considers the long-run effect of an increase in the saving rate s.

Example 19.4 An Increase in the Saving Rate

Figure 19.9 illustrates the effects of an increase in the saving rate in the Solow model. At the initial equilibrium point E_1 the capital–labour ratio is k_1 and labour productivity y_1. As we have seen, output per worker will be constant at y_1, but total output will be growing at a rate equal to the rate of population growth n. An increase in the saving rate from s_1 to s_2 will shift the gross investment curve upwards from $s_1 f(k)$ to the

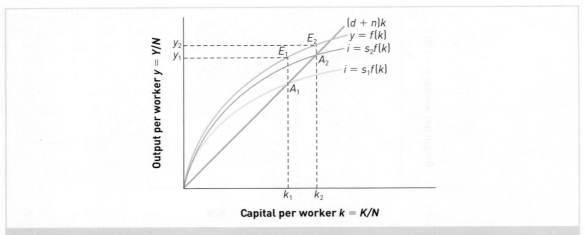

Figure 19.9 An Increase in the Saving Rate. Increasing the saving rate from s_1 to s_2 shifts the investment curve upwards, leading to higher investment. The equilibrium capital–labour ratio increases from k_1 to k_2 and the equilibrium value of average labour productivity from y_1 to y_2. Between E_1 and E_2 labour productivity $y = Y/N$ will be increasing and the growth rate of total output Y will exceed the rate of population growth n. However, once the new equilibrium is established at E_2 labour productivity stabilises at y_2 and the growth rate of total output Y will equal the rate of population growth n.

dashed curve $s_2f(k)$. Gross investment will now exceed required investment and the capital stock will increase until capital per worker reaches k_2, at which point gross investment is just sufficient to keep k constant. The new equilibrium is at point E_2 with output per worker equal to y_2. Between E_1 and E_2 average labour productivity $y = Y/N$ will be increasing, implying that the growth rate of total output Y will exceed the rate of population growth n. However, once the new equilibrium is established at E_2, labour productivity stabilises at y_2 and the growth rate of total output Y will equal the rate of population growth n. Hence, in the long run, the economy's growth rate equals the rate of population growth and is independent of the saving rate.

Exercise 19.3 Using Figure 19.8, illustrate the effect of an increase in the rate of population growth n on (a) average labour productivity (b) the growth rate of aggregate output Y.

Figure 19.9 teaches us an important lesson about economic growth – that capital accumulation alone cannot explain the sustained increases in labour productivity and income per head such as those exhibited by Table 19.1. The reason is the assumption of diminishing marginal product, a property of most production processes. As the economy moves from E_1 to E_2 the capital–labour ratio is increasing, leading to higher labour productivity and higher income per head. However, because of diminishing marginal product, each unit increase in the capital stock results in progressively lower increases in output and average labour productivity. If, with a saving rate equal to s_2, the economy were to grow beyond E_2 then because of diminishing marginal product saving would be insufficient to cover required investment $(d + n)k$ and the capital–labour ratio would fall back to k_2. Hence, to explain the type of sustained increases in income as shown in Table 19.1 or Figure 19.1, we need to add an additional dimension to the Solow model. This is achieved by introducing the idea of *technical progress*.

Explaining economic growth: the role of technical progress

The Solow model has enabled us to reach two important conclusions.

1. Average labour productivity, the key determinant of differences in income per person, depends on the amount of physical capital per head of the workforce. Other things being equal, the more capital that is available to the workforce the higher the level of both labour productivity and income per head of the population.
2. In the long run the economy's steady-state growth rate should equal the rate of population growth.

While the first conclusion is fairly intuitive, and supported by the evidence in Figure 19.6, the second is less so. In fact we know that over relatively long periods of time growth in most industrialised economies tends to exceed the rate of population growth. For example, between 1950 and 2003 the UK population increased by about 20 per cent, or approximately 0.4 per cent per year. Real income, on the other hand, increased by 2.1 per cent per annum over the same period (Table 19.1). How can we explain this difference? To date we have assumed that to achieve higher average labour productivity requires an increase in the amount of capital per worker. Is it possible that average labour productivity can increase even if the capital–labour ratio is constant? The answer is yes, and **technical progress** is key to understanding why. Technical progress enables us to use existing resources more efficiently and to produce a higher output using the same quantities of capital and labour. As a simple illustration, consider the personal computer, or PC. When the first PCs were introduced into homes and offices their major applications were for tasks such as word processing and solving computational problems. By itself this new technology provided a significant boost to productivity. However, the introduction of the internet linked computers across the world and provided another boost to the productivity of capital (computers) and labour (computer operators). Also, the invention and application of new computer chips and operating systems made PCs faster, more efficient and more productive.

technical progress an improvement in knowledge that enables a higher output to be produced from existing resources

Comparative Advantage

Going further back we can think of many other examples where new technologies resulted in significant productivity growth. For example, in the eighteenth century most agricultural produce had to be sold locally due to the lack of efficient national and international transport systems. Today the availability of rapid shipping, rail and road networks and refrigerated transport (technical progress) allows farmers to sell their products virtually anywhere in the world. With a broader market in which to sell, farmers can specialise in those products best suited to local land and weather conditions. Similarly, factories can obtain their raw materials wherever they are cheapest and most abundant, produce the goods they are most efficient at manufacturing and sell their products wherever they will fetch the best price. Both these examples illustrate the *Principle of Comparative Advantage* (Chapter 2): that overall productivity increases when producers concentrate on those activities at which they are relatively more efficient.

In fact, most economists would probably agree that technical progress is the *single most important source of higher productivity* and economic growth in general.

To introduce technical progress into the Solow model we make a small but very significant change to the production function and write equation 19.1 as:

$$y = Af(k) \qquad (19.2)$$

where A denotes technology. If technology improves by g per cent per year then $A = (1 + g)$. For example, if $g = 0.01$ then $A = 1.01$ and average labour productivity will increase by 1 per cent per year even if the capital–labour ratio k is constant. However, in addition to directly increasing labour productivity, improved technology will also result in a higher capital–labour ratio. This is illustrated by Figure 19.10.

In Figure 19.10 the production function is $y_1 = Af(k)$ and the economy is initially in equilibrium at the point E_1. The capital–labour ratio is k_1 and average labour productivity is y_1. Technical progress at rate g per period means that output per worker increases at any given capital–labour ratio. This is illustrated by the upward shift in the production function to $y_2 = (1 + g)Af(k)$. As saving is a constant fraction of income the investment curve will also shift up from i_1 to the dashed curve i_2. At the point C gross investment i will be greater than required investment $(d + n)k$ and the capital–labour ratio will increase. Steady-state equilibrium is restored at the point E_2 with a higher capital–labour ratio k_2 and higher average labour productivity y_2. However, if technology continues to improve at g per cent per period the production function and the investment curve will continue to shift upwards and aggregate output will continue to grow over time.

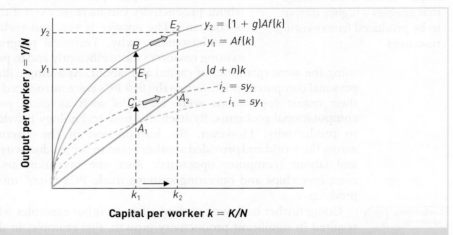

Figure 19.10 Technical Progress in the Solow Model. Starting from the equilibrium position E_1 technical progress at rate g per annum increases average labour productivity at any given capital–labour ratio. This is illustrated by an upward shift in the production function from y_1 to y_2. As output per worker increases (E_1 to B), saving also increases and the savings curve shifts upwards to sy_2. Investment will now exceed depreciation by the distance CA_1 and the capital–labour ratio will start to increase. Equilibrium is restored when investment again equals depreciation at point A_2, giving a new capital–labour ratio of k_2 and a new equilibrium at E_2 with higher labour productivity at y_2. However, if technology continues to improve at g per cent per period the production function and the investment curve will continue to shift upwards and aggregate output will continue to grow over time.

Maths Box 19.1 The steady-state growth equation

The Solow model relates changes in total output Y to changes in the stock of physical capital K, the labour force N and technical progress A. If we let Δ denote the phrase 'the change in' then ΔY = the change in total output and $\Delta Y/Y$ = the economy's rate of growth. If, for example, Y increases from €100 million to €103 million then $\Delta Y/Y = 3/100 = 0.03$, or 3 per cent. Suppose that, in a given year, capital, labour and technology increase by the amounts ΔK, ΔN and ΔA, what is the economy's growth rate? To answer this question recall that the marginal product of capital MPK is defined as the change in output per unit change in the capital stock. That is:

$$MPK = \frac{\Delta Y}{\Delta K}$$

Rearranging gives:

$$\Delta Y = MPK \times \Delta K$$

which is the change in output resulting from a given change in K with all other inputs held constant. Likewise we can define the marginal product of labour MPN as:

$$MPN = \frac{\Delta Y}{\Delta N}$$

Rearranging this equation gives:

$$\Delta Y = MPN \times \Delta N$$

which is the change in output resulting from a given change in N with all other inputs held constant. With technical progress the production function is $Y = AF(K, L)$ and the change in output resulting from a change in technology with K and N constant is:

$$\Delta Y = F(K,N) \times \Delta A$$

Hence if capital, labour and technology increase by the amounts ΔK, ΔN, and ΔA the resulting change in output is:

$$\Delta Y = MPK \times \Delta K + MPN \times \Delta N + F(K,N) \times \Delta A$$

Dividing both sides of this equation by $Y = AF(K, N)$ gives:

$$\frac{\Delta Y}{Y} = \frac{MPK}{Y} \, \Delta K + \frac{MPN}{Y} \, \Delta N + \frac{\Delta A}{A}$$

Multiplying and dividing the first term by K and the second term by N gives:

$$\frac{\Delta Y}{Y} = \left(\frac{MPK \times K}{Y} \right) \frac{\Delta K}{K} + \left(\frac{MPN \times N}{Y} \right) \frac{\Delta N}{N} + \frac{\Delta A}{A} \qquad (1)$$

Assuming that capital owners are paid a real return equal to capital's marginal product, the term $MPK \times K$ equals total capital income (income per unit times the number of units) and the term $(MPK \times K)/Y$ equals capital's share of total output. Likewise, if labour is paid a real wage equal to its marginal product then $(MPN \times N)$ is total labour income and $(MPN \times N)/Y$ equals labour's share of total output. As there are only two inputs in the production function then the shares of capital and labour must sum to one. Hence if capital's share is denoted as α labour's share must be $1 - \alpha$. Substituting for the shares of capital and labour we can write Equation (1) as:

$$\frac{\Delta Y}{Y} = \alpha \frac{\Delta K}{K} + \left(1 - \alpha \right) \frac{\Delta N}{N} + \frac{\Delta A}{A} \qquad (2)$$

Equation (2) says that the economy's growth rate depends on the growth of the capital stock and the labour force weighted by their respective income shares plus the rate of technical progress. However, we know that in steady-state equilibrium the capital–labour ratio $k = K/N$ is constant, implying that K and N are growing at the same rate. That is:

$$\frac{\Delta K}{K} = \frac{\Delta N}{N}$$

Substituting for $\Delta K/K$ in Equation (2) gives:

$$\frac{\Delta Y}{Y} = \frac{\Delta N}{N} + \frac{\Delta A}{A} \tag{3}$$

Equation (3) gives two important results.

1. First, the steady-state growth of total output $\Delta Y/Y$ equals the sum of the rate of labour force or population growth $\Delta N/N$ plus the rate of technical progress $\Delta A/A$.
2. Second, the steady-state growth of income per person $\Delta Y/Y - \Delta N/N$ equals the rate of technical progress $\Delta A/A$.

These results highlight the importance of technical progress. In the absence of technical progress the economy will grow at the rate of population or labour force growth $n = \Delta N/N$ and average labour productivity will be constant. Technical progress is therefore fundamental to understanding why the economy grows over time.

Box 19.1 presents a more technical derivation of the economy's equilibrium growth rate, which can be expressed as:

$$\frac{\Delta Y}{Y} = \alpha \frac{\Delta K}{K} + (1 - \alpha) \frac{\Delta N}{N} + \frac{\Delta A}{A} \tag{19.3}$$

Equation 19.3 may look somewhat complicated, but it has a straightforward and intuitive interpretation. The term $\Delta Y/Y$ is the growth rate of total output defined as the change in Y measured as a proportion or percentage of total output Y. Likewise, the terms $\Delta K/K$, $\Delta N/N$ and $\Delta A/A$ are the growth rates for capital, labour and technical progress respectively. The term α is the share of total income accruing to the owners of capital and $(1 - \alpha)$ is labour's share of total income. We can think of the capital share as profits and the labour share as wages and salaries. Now suppose $\alpha = 0.25$ so that 25 per cent of total income accrues to capital owners with the remaining 75 per cent accruing to labour. If in a given year capital stock were to increase by 3 per cent this would add 0.75 per cent to total output (the percentage increase in the capital stock times the share of income generated by capital). Likewise if the labour force increased by 3 per cent, output would increase by 2.25 per cent to total output (0.75 times 3). Hence equation 19.3 simply says that the growth in total output can be decomposed into three sources – the contribution of capital $\alpha \Delta K/K$, the contribution of labour $(1 - \alpha)\Delta N/N$ and the contribution made by technical progress $\Delta A/A$.

However, we know that in steady-state equilibrium the capital–labour ratio $k = K/N$ is constant, implying that K and N are growing at the same rate. That is:

$$\frac{\Delta K}{K} = \frac{\Delta N}{N}$$

Substituting for $\Delta K / K$ in equation 19.3 gives:

$$\frac{\Delta Y}{Y} = \frac{\Delta N}{N} + \frac{\Delta A}{A} \tag{19.4}$$

Equation 19.4 gives two important results. First, the steady-state growth of total out-put $\Delta Y / Y$ equals the sum of the rate of labour force or population growth $\Delta N / N$ plus the rate of technical progress $\Delta A / A$. Second, the steady-state growth of income per person $\Delta Y / Y - \Delta N / N$ equals the rate of technical progress $\Delta A / A$. These results high-light the importance of technical progress. In the absence of technical progress the economy will grow at the rate of population or labour force growth $n = \Delta N / N$ and average labour productivity will be constant. For example, suppose that in Figure 19.10 technical progress ceases when the economy reaches the point E_2. Average labour productivity would then be constant at y_2 and aggregate output would increase at the rate of population or labour force growth. *Introducing technical progress radically changes these conclusions and enables us to understand the sustained increase in living stan-dards as shown in Table 19.1.* Technical progress is therefore fundamental to under-standing why the economy grows over time.

Human capital

The Solow model helps us to understand why some countries have much higher liv-ing standards than others, and why growth rates may differ over time and across countries. A look back at Figure 19.6 confirms that the amount of capital available to the average worker can explain large differences in income per head between coun-tries. Compare, for example, the capital–labour ratio in rich countries such as the USA, Germany and the UK with the amount of capital per worker in much poorer countries such as India and Nigeria. But differences in the amount of physical capital are not the only reason why Western industrial nations enjoy much higher living stan-dards than many countries in Africa and Asia. Significant differ-ences in **human capital** can also help to explain differences in productivity and living standards.

human capital the accumulation of skills, experience and knowledge by the workforce

Human capital is the accumulation of skills, experience and knowledge by the economy's workforce. Workers with a large stock of human capital are more productive than workers with less training. For example, a secretary who knows how to use a word-processing pro-gram will be able to type more letters than one who doesn't; a motor mechanic who is familiar with computerised diagnostic equipment will be able to fix engine prob-lems that less well-trained mechanics cannot. Letting H denote the stock of human capital we can rewrite the production function as:

$$Y = AF(K, N, H)$$

Assuming constant returns to scale and dividing through by N gives:

$$y = Af(k, h)$$

where $h = H / N$ or the stock of human capital per worker conventionally measured as the average years of education per worker. Other things being equal, the greater the stock of human capital per worker the greater are average labour productivity and living standards.

This conclusion is illustrated by Figure 19.11, which shows two production func-tions assumed to represent the UK and India. Because the UK has a much higher stock

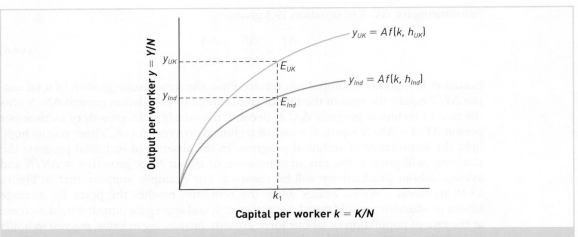

Figure 19.11 Human Capital. If the UK has a higher stock of human capital per worker than India, its output per worker and living standards will be higher even if both countries have the same capital–labour ratio.

of human capital per worker the average labour productivity of its workers will be higher at any given capital–labour ratio. Hence, even if India had the same capital–labour ratio as the UK (which it does not) its average labour productivity and living standards would still be much lower because its workforce is less educated and less skilled than that of the UK.

Economic naturalist 19.1 Why did West Germany and Japan recover so successfully from the devastation of the Second World War?

Germany and Japan sustained extensive destruction of their cities and industries during the Second World War and entered the post-war period impoverished. Yet, within 30 years, both countries had not only been rebuilt but had become worldwide industrial and economic leaders. What accounts for these 'economic miracles'?

Many factors contributed to the economic recovery of the two countries, including the substantial aid provided by the United States to Europe under the Marshall Plan, and to Japan during the US occupation. Most economists agree, however, that high levels of *human capital* played a crucial role in both countries.

At the end of the war, Germany's population was exceptionally well educated, with a large number of highly qualified scientists and engineers. The country also had (and still has today) an extensive apprentice system that provided on-the-job training to young workers. As a result, Germany had a *skilled industrial workforce*. In addition, the area that became West Germany benefited substantially from an influx of skilled workers from East Germany and the rest of Soviet-controlled Europe, including 20,000 trained engineers and technicians. Beginning as early as 1949, this concentration of human capital contributed to a major expansion of Germany's technologically sophisticated, highly productive manufacturing sector. By 1960, West Germany was a leading exporter of high-quality manufactured goods, and its citizens enjoyed one of the highest standards of living in Europe.

Japan also began the post-war period with a skilled and educated labour force. In addition, occupying American forces restructured the Japanese school system and encouraged all Japanese to obtain a good education. Even more so than the Germans, however, the Japanese emphasised on-the-job training. As part of a *lifetime employment system*, under which workers were expected to stay with the same company their entire career, Japanese firms invested extensively in worker training. The payoff to these investments in human capital was a steady increase in average labour productivity, particularly in manufacturing. By the 1980s, Japanese manufactured goods were among the most advanced in the world and Japan's workers among the most skilled.

Although high levels of human capital were instrumental in the rapid economic growth of West Germany and Japan, human capital alone cannot create a high living standard. A case in point is Soviet-dominated East Germany, which had a level of human capital similar to West Germany's after 1945 but did not enjoy the same economic growth. For reasons we shall discuss later in the chapter (see Economic naturalist 19.4), the communist system imposed by the Soviets utilised East Germany's human capital far less effectively than the economic systems of Japan and West Germany.

RECAP The Solow model

The Solow model enables us to reach the following conclusions.

- Average labour productivity, the key determinant of income per head and living standards, is closely related to the amount of physical capital available to the workforce. Other things being equal, the higher the economy's capital–labour ratio the higher will be labour productivity and living standards.
- Differences in living standards can be explained by differences in physical and human capital. Countries with high capital–labour ratios and educated workforces will have higher income per head and enjoy higher living standards than countries with low capital–labour ratios and poorly educated workforces.
- In the absence of technical progress the economy will reach steady-state equilibrium. In this equilibrium average labour productivity will be constant and total output will grow at the same rate as the population.
- Introducing technical progress enables us to better understand long-run increases in labour productivity and living standards. With technical progress the equilibrium growth rate of total output will equal the rate of population growth plus the rate of technical progress.

Total factor productivity

In our discussion of technical progress we introduced the equilibrium growth equation (19.3), which is formally derived in Box 19.1:

$$\frac{\Delta Y}{Y} = \alpha \frac{\Delta K}{K} + (1 - \alpha) \frac{\Delta N}{N} + \frac{\Delta A}{A}$$

To recap, the term $\Delta Y/Y$ is the growth rate of total output defined as the change in Y measured as a proportion or percentage of total output Y, and $\Delta K/K$, $\Delta N/N$ and $\Delta A/A$ are the growth rates for capital, labour and technology respectively. The term α is the share of total income accruing to the owners of capital and $(1 - \alpha)$ is labour's share of total income. Hence equation (19.3) simply says that the growth in total output can be decomposed into three sources – the contribution of capital $\alpha \Delta K/K$, the contribution of labour $(1 - \alpha)\Delta N/N$ and the contribution made by technical progress $\Delta A/A$. Given this interpretation we can rearrange equation (19.3) as:

$$\frac{\Delta A}{A} = \frac{\Delta Y}{Y} - \alpha \frac{\Delta K}{K} - (1 - \alpha) \frac{\Delta N}{N} \tag{19.4}$$

total factor productivity that part of the growth in output which is not accounted for by capital and labour growth

Equation 19.4 gives us an alternative and broader interpretation of the parameter A. Rather than thinking of A as a measure of technical progress only, we can think of it as the contribution to the growth in total output made by factors other than the inputs capital and labour. When viewed in this way, A is often referred to as **total factor productivity**, or TFP, because it is the amount by which output would increase even if the quantities of capital and labour are constant $(\Delta K / K = \Delta N / N = 0)$.[3]

Both technical change and human capital can be thought of as contributing to TFP. Technical progress can directly increase labour productivity while investment in human capital enables the workforce to use the existing capital stock more productively. However, TFP can be influenced by other factors such as entrepreneurship and management skills, and the political and legal environment.

Entrepreneurship and management

The productivity of workers depends in part on the people who help to decide what to produce and how to produce it: entrepreneurs and managers. Entrepreneurs are people who create new economic enterprises. Because of the new products, services, technological processes and production methods they introduce, entrepreneurs are critical to a dynamic, healthy economy. Individuals such as Henry Ford (automobiles), Bill Gates (software) and Richard Branson (airlines) have played central roles in the development of their industries both nationally and internationally – and, not incidentally, amassed huge personal fortunes in the process. These people and others like them have been criticised for some of their business practices, in some cases with justification. Clearly, though, they and dozens of other prominent business leaders have contributed significantly to economic growth. Henry Ford, for example, developed the idea of *mass production*, which lowered costs sufficiently to bring automobiles within reach of the average family. Ford began his business in his garage, a tradition that has been maintained by thousands of innovators ever since.

Entrepreneurship, like any form of creativity, is difficult to teach, although some of the supporting skills, such as financial analysis and marketing, cannot always be learned in college or business school. How, then, does a society encourage entrepreneurship? History suggests that the entrepreneurial spirit will always exist; the challenge to society is to channel entrepreneurial energies in economically productive ways. For example, economic policy makers need to ensure that taxation is not so heavy, and regulation not so inflexible, that small businesses – some of which will eventually become big businesses – cannot get off the ground. Sociological factors may play a role as well. Societies in which business and commerce are considered to be beneath the dignity of refined, educated people are less likely to produce successful entrepreneurs (see Economic naturalist 19.2). Overall, a social and economic environment that allows entrepreneurship to flourish appears to promote economic growth and rising productivity, perhaps especially so in high-technology eras like our own.

---

3 Note that TFP is that part of the growth in output that is left over or unexplained after we account for the contributions of capital and labour. Hence it is calculated as a residual and sometimes referred to as the *Solow residual.* (see Solow 1957).

Economic naturalist 19.2 Why did medieval China stagnate economically?

The Sung period in China (AD 960–1270) was one of considerable technological sophistication; its inventions included paper, waterwheels, water clocks, gunpowder and possibly the compass. Yet no significant industrialisation occurred, and in subsequent centuries Europe saw more economic growth and technological innovation than China. Why did medieval China stagnate economically?

According to research by economist William Baumol,[4] the main impediment to industrialisation during the Sung period was a social system that inhibited entrepreneurship. Commerce and industry were considered low-status activities, not fit for an educated person. In addition, the emperor had the right to seize his subjects' property and to take control of their business enterprises – a right that greatly reduced his subjects' incentives to undertake business ventures. The most direct path to status and riches in medieval China was to go through a system of demanding civil service examinations given by the government every three years. The highest scorers on these national examinations were granted lifetime positions in the imperial bureaucracy, where they wielded much power and often became wealthy, in part through corruption. Not surprisingly, medieval China did not develop a dynamic entrepreneurial class, and consequently its scientific and technological advantages did not translate into sustained economic growth. China's experience shows why scientific advances alone cannot guarantee economic growth; to have economic benefits, scientific knowledge must be *commercially applied* through new products and new, more efficient means of producing goods and services.

Although entrepreneurship may be more glamorous, managers – the people who run businesses on a daily basis – also play an important role in determining average labour productivity. Managerial jobs span a wide range of positions, from the supervisor of the loading dock to the CEO (chief executive officer) at the helm of a large multinational company. Managers work to satisfy customers, deal with suppliers, organise production, obtain financing, assign workers to jobs and motivate them to work hard and effectively. Such activities enhance labour productivity. For example, in the 1970s and 1980s, Japanese managers introduced new production methods that greatly increased the efficiency of Japanese manufacturing plants. Among them was the *just-in-time* (JIT) inventory system, in which suppliers deliver production components to the factory just when they are needed, eliminating the need for factories to stockpile components. Japanese managers also pioneered the idea of organising workers into semi-independent production teams, which allowed workers more flexibility and responsibility than the traditional assembly line.

The political and legal environment

So far, we have emphasised the role of the private sector in increasing average labour productivity. But government, too, has a role to play in fostering improved productivity. One of the key contributions government can make is to provide a *political and legal environment* that encourages people to behave in economically productive ways – to work hard, save and invest wisely, acquire useful information and skills, and provide the goods and services that the public demands.

One specific function of government that appears to be crucial to economic success is the establishment of *well-defined property rights*. Property rights are well defined when the law provides clear rules for determining who owns what resources (through a system of deeds and titles, for example) and how those resources can be used.

---

4 Baumol (1990).

Imagine living in a society in which a dictator, backed by the military and the police, could take whatever he wanted, and regularly did so. In such a country, what incentive would you have to raise a large crop or to produce other valuable goods and services? Very little, since much of what you produced would probably be taken away from you. Unfortunately, in many countries of the world today, this situation is far from hypothetical.

Political and legal conditions affect the growth of productivity in other ways, as well. Political scientists and economists have documented the fact that *political instability* can be detrimental to economic growth. This finding is reasonable, since entrepreneurs and savers are unlikely to invest their resources in a country whose government is unstable, particularly if the struggle for power involves civil unrest, terrorism or guerrilla warfare. For example, one hoped-for benefit of the Northern Ireland peace process was a so-called, but yet to be fully realised, 'peace dividend' in terms of greater investment, higher economic growth and lower unemployment.

However, government can do much more than guaranteeing well-defined property rights and political stability. In particular, government can promote the growth of free and flexible markets that encourage the development of new technologies and products by providing incentives to entrepreneurship, innovation and higher productivity. Economic naturalist 19.3 provides a European example.

Economic naturalist 19.3 The Lisbon Agenda

In March 2000 Europe's political leaders agreed a ten-year strategy designed to promote economic growth and employment in the European Union. Of particular concern was that, relative to the United States, Europe continued to experience a low rate of job creation, higher and more persistent unemployment and lower labour productivity. The aim of the new strategy, which has subsequently become known as the *Lisbon Agenda*, was to transform Europe into 'the most competitive and dynamic knowledge-based economy in the world', a goal to be achieved by a series of *structural reforms* in labour, product and financial markets. At the heart of the Lisbon Agenda is the realisation that to exploit the full benefits of economic integration Europe must provide greater incentives for innovation, job creation and competitiveness by promoting flexible and responsive labour markets and more efficient welfare and tax systems, which encourage job seeking and do not over-penalise successful and innovative high-income earners, and a reduction in the administrative 'red tape' that stifles innovation and entrepreneurship. For example, some estimates suggest that whereas it took just one week to establish a new business in the United States it could take up to 12 weeks, and cost four times more, in Europe. Likewise, in some European countries there are limits on the maximum working week and unions have a legal right to be involved in management decisions such as a decision to close a plant or retail outlet. More generally, high and long-lived unemployment benefits, generous redundancy payments and labour laws that make 'hiring and firing' unduly difficult and expensive are seen as disincentives to job creation, investment and innovation.

Most mid-term reviews of the Lisbon Agenda agree that it has failed to deliver. The fundamental problem is that labour market institutions and welfare systems have evolved in different ways and there is no common, or one-size, model to which all countries can agree. On the one side, countries such as France and Germany favour an approach that promotes social cohesion rather than individualism, whereas others such as Ireland and the United Kingdom have moved towards more flexible systems that place greater emphasis on incentives and economic efficiency. If the Lisbon Agenda is to succeed, Europe must find a way to reconcile these differences.

Land and other natural resources

Besides capital goods, other inputs to production help to make workers more productive, among them land, energy and raw materials. Fertile land is essential to agriculture, and modern manufacturing processes make intensive use of energy and raw materials.

In general, an abundance of natural resources increases the productivity of the workers who use them. For example, a farmer can produce a much larger crop in a land-rich country such as the United States or Australia than in a country where the soil is poor or arable land is limited in supply. With the aid of modern farm machinery and great expanses of land, American farmers are today so productive that even though they constitute less than 3 per cent of the population, they provide enough food not only to feed the country but to export to the rest of the world.

Although there are limits to a country's supply of arable land, many other natural resources, such as petroleum and metals, can be obtained through international markets. Because resources can be obtained through trade, countries need not possess large quantities of natural resources within their own borders to achieve economic growth. Indeed, a number of countries have become rich without substantial natural resources of their own, including Japan, Singapore and Switzerland, as well as Hong Kong. Just as important as possessing natural resources is the ability to *use them productively* – for example, by means of advanced technologies.

Exercise 19.4 A Senegalese worker who emigrates to France is likely to find that his average labour productivity is much higher in France than it was at home. The worker is, of course, the same person he was when he lived in Senegal. How can the simple act of moving to France increase the worker's productivity? What does your answer say about the incentive to emigrate?

RECAP Determinants of average labour productivity

Key factors determining average labour productivity in a country include:

- the quantity of *physical capital*
- the introduction of new technologies – *technical progress*
- the skills and training of workers – *human capital*
- the availability of land and other *natural resources*
- the effectiveness of *management* and *entrepreneurship*
- the broad *social and legal environment*.

The worldwide productivity slowdown – and recovery?

During the 1950s and 1960s most of the major industrialised countries saw rapid growth in real GDP and average labour productivity. In the 1970s, however, productivity growth began to slow down around the world. Slower growth in real GDP and in average living standards followed.

The slowdown in the growth of labour productivity is documented in Table 19.4, which gives data for five major industrialised countries. Note the sharp decline in productivity growth in all five countries during 1973–79 compared with 1960–73. Japan's case was particularly striking: its productivity growth rate fell from 7.6 per cent per year in 1960–73 to 2.7 per cent in 1973–79. In the United States, annual productivity growth fell from 2.3 per cent before 1973 to just 0.6 per cent per year during 1973–79. During the period 1979–2000, productivity growth improved somewhat in the United States and the United Kingdom but, in all five countries, the rate of productivity improvement since 1979 has been much slower than it was prior to 1973.

The sudden decline in worldwide productivity growth around 1973 is puzzling to economists and policy makers alike. What might have caused it? In the 1970s and 1980s many economists thought that the fourfold increase in oil prices that followed the Arab–Israeli war (1973) might have caused the slowdown. However, oil prices (relative to the prices of other goods) eventually returned to pre-1973 levels, but productivity growth did not. Thus oil prices are no longer thought to have played a critical role in the slowdown.

Country	Percentage growth, annual rates		
	1960–73	1973–79	1979–2000
France	4.6	2.3	1.8
Germany	4.0	2.6	2.0
Japan	7.6	2.7	2.0
United Kingdom	2.8	1.3	1.7
United States	2.3	0.6	1.7

Table 19.4 **Average Labour Productivity Growth Rates in Selected Countries, 1960–2000**

One view of the slowdown in productivity since 1973 is that (at least in part) it is not a real phenomenon but the result of *poor measurement of productivity*. According to this argument, many of the productivity improvements that occur in modern services-orientated economies are difficult to capture in economic statistics. For example, the computerisation of inventories allows supermarkets to offer customers a wider variety of products, with less chance that a particular product will be out of stock. ATMs and online banking allow people to make financial transactions 24 hours a day, not just when the bank is open. Many medical procedures can be done far more quickly, safely and painlessly today than just a few years ago. In theory, all these improvements in the quality of services should be captured in real GDP, and hence in productivity measures. In reality, accurate measurement of improvements in quality is difficult, as we saw when discussing biases in the CPI in Chapter 17, and some improvements may be missed. If the productivity slowdown is not real but reflects only poor measurement, then economists need not worry about it.

Another explanation has been called the technological *depletion hypothesis*.[5] According to this hypothesis the high rates of productivity in the 1950s and 1960s reflected an unusual period of 'catch-up' after the Second World War. Although scientific and technical advances continued to be made during the 1930s and 1940s (many of which arose from military research), depression and war prevented them from being adapted to civilian use. During the 1950s and 1960s, the backlog of technological breakthroughs was applied commercially, producing high rates of productivity growth at first and then a sharp decline in new technological opportunities. Once the catch-up period was over, productivity growth slowed. According to this hypothesis, then, the slow-

---

5 Nordhaus (1982).

down in productivity growth since the 1970s reflects a *dearth of technological opportunities* relative to the immediate post-war period. From this perspective, the 1950s and 1960s were the exception, and the period since the 1970s represents a return to more normal rates of productivity growth.

Other explanations of the productivity slowdown include a steady increase in government regulations that have diverted resources from productive uses to protecting the environment and increasing worker safety. Although socially desirable, such regulations typically increase production costs and result in lower productivity. All these theories have some plausibility but, in truth, economists have yet to agree on a comprehensive reason explaining the slowdown.

The costs of economic growth

Both this chapter and Chapter 16 emphasised the positive effects of economic growth on the average person's living standard. But should societies always strive for the highest possible rate of economic growth? The answer is no. Even if we accept for the moment the idea that increased output per person is always desirable, attaining a higher rate of economic growth does impose costs on society.

What are the costs of increasing economic growth? The most straightforward is the cost of creating *new capital*. We know that by expanding the capital stock we can increase future productivity and output. But, to increase the capital stock, we must divert resources that could otherwise be used to increase the supply of consumer goods. For example, to add more robot-operated assembly lines, a society must employ more of its skilled technicians in building industrial robots and fewer in designing video games. To build new factories, more resources must be assigned to factory construction and less to improving the housing stock.

In short, high rates of investment in new capital require people to tighten their belts, consume less and save more – a real *economic cost*.

Should a country undertake a high rate of investment in capital goods at the sacrifice of consumer goods? The answer depends on the extent that people are willing and able to sacrifice consumption today to have a bigger economic 'pie' tomorrow. In a country that is very poor, or is experiencing an economic crisis, people may prefer to keep consumption relatively high, and savings and investment relatively low. The midst of a thunderstorm is not the time to be putting something aside for a rainy day! But in a society that is relatively well off, people may be more willing to make sacrifices to achieve higher economic growth in the future.

Consumption sacrificed to *capital formation* is not the only cost of achieving higher growth. In Europe and the United States in the nineteenth and early twentieth centuries, periods of rapid economic growth were often times in which many people worked extremely long hours at dangerous and unpleasant jobs. While those workers helped to build the economy that we enjoy today, the costs were great in terms of reduced leisure time and, in some cases, workers' health and safety.

Scarcity ⬤

Cost–Benefit Analysis ⬤

Other costs of growth include the cost of the research and development (R&D) that is required to improve technology, and the costs of acquiring training and skill (human capital). The fact that a higher living standard tomorrow must be purchased at the cost of current sacrifices is an example of the *Scarcity Principle* (Chapter 1), that having more of one good thing usually means having less of another. Because achieving higher economic growth imposes real economic costs, we know from the *Cost–Benefit Principle* (Chapter 1) that higher growth should be pursued only if the benefits outweigh the costs.

Promoting economic growth

If a society decides to try to raise its rate of economic growth, what are some of the measures that policy makers might take to achieve this objective? Here is a short list of suggestions, based on our discussion of the factors that contribute to growth in average labour productivity – and, hence, output per person.

Policies that support research and development

The Solow model teaches us that sustained economic growth requires continuous technical progress, which in turn requires investment in research and development (R&D). In many industries, private firms have an adequate incentive to conduct R&D activities. There is no need, for example, for the government to finance research for developing a better underarm deodorant. But some types of knowledge, particularly basic scientific knowledge, may have widespread economic benefits that cannot be captured by a single private firm. The developers of the silicon computer chip, for example, were instrumental in creating huge new industries, yet they received only a small portion of the profits flowing from their inventions. Because society in general, rather than the individual inventors, may receive much of the benefit from basic research, government may need to support basic research. Government also sponsors a great deal of applied research, particularly in military and space applications. To the extent that national security allows, the government can increase growth by sharing the fruits of such research with the private sector. For example, the global positioning system (GPS), which was developed originally for military purposes, is now available in private passenger vehicles, helping drivers find their way.

Policies to increase human capital

Because skilled and well-educated workers are more productive than unskilled labour, governments in most countries try to increase the human capital of their citizens by supporting education and training programmes. In many European countries, governments provide free public education at all levels from primary school to university. Most countries also support active labour market programmes, which provide job training for unskilled youths, disabled workers and older workers whose skills have become obsolete.

Economic naturalist 19.4 Why do almost all countries provide free state education?

All industrial countries provide their citizens with free education through to secondary school and most subsidise college and other tertiary education. Why?

Most Europeans are so used to the idea of free public education that this question may seem odd. But why should the government provide free education when it does not provide even more essential goods and services, such as food or, in some cases, medical care? Furthermore, educational services can be, and indeed commonly are, supplied and demanded on the private market, without the aid of the government.

An important argument for free, or at least subsidised, education is that the private demand curve for educational services does not include all the *social benefits* of education. (Recall the *Equilibrium Principle* (Chapter 3), which states in part that a market in equilibrium may not exploit all the gains achievable from collective action.) For example, the democratic political system relies on an educated citizenry to operate effectively – a factor that an individual demander of educational services has little reason to consider. From a narrower economic perspective, we might argue that individuals do not capture the full economic returns from their schooling. For example, people with high human capital, and thus high earnings, pay more taxes – funds that can be used to finance government services and aid the less fortunate. Because of income taxation, the private benefit to acquiring human capital is less than the social benefit, and the demand for education on the private market may be less than optimal from society's viewpoint. Similarly, educated people are more likely than others to contribute to technological development, and hence to general productivity growth, which may benefit many other people besides themselves. Finally, another argument for public support of education is that poor people who would like to invest in human capital may not be able to do so because of insufficient income.

The Nobel Laureate Milton Friedman, among many economists, suggested that these arguments may justify government grants, called educational *vouchers*, to help citizens purchase educational services in the private sector, but they do *not* justify the government providing education directly, as through the state school system. Defenders of state education, on the other hand, argue that the government should have some direct control over education in order to set standards and monitor quality. What do you think?

Policies that promote saving and investment

Average labour productivity increases when workers can utilise a sizeable and modern capital stock. To support the creation of new capital, government can encourage high rates of saving and investment in the private sector. Many provisions in the tax code are designed expressly to stimulate households to save and firms to invest. For example, households may get tax relief when they save in specially designated schemes and firms can be given tax credits, which reduce their tax bills when they invest in new capital. Private-sector saving and investment are discussed in greater detail in Chapter 20.

Government can contribute directly to capital formation through *public investment*, or the creation of government-owned capital. Public investment includes the building of roads, bridges, airports, dams and, in some countries, energy and communications networks. For example, the construction of highway systems reduces long-haul transportation costs and improves productivity throughout the economy. Today, the web of computers and communication links we call the internet is having a similar effect. Many research studies have confirmed that government investment in the *infrastructure*, the public capital that supports private-sector economic activities, can be a significant source of growth.

The legal and political framework

Although economic growth comes primarily from activities in the private sector, the government plays an essential role in providing the framework within which the private sector can operate productively. We have discussed the importance of secure property rights and a well-functioning legal system, of an economic environment that encourages entrepreneurship and of political stability and the free and open exchange of ideas. Government policy makers should also consider the potential effects of tax and regulatory policies on activities that increase productivity, such as investment, innovation and risk taking. Policies that affect the legal and political framework are examples of *structural macroeconomic policies* (see Chapter 15).

The poorest countries: a special case?

Radical disparities in living standards exist between the richest and poorest countries of the world (see Table 16.4 for some data). Achieving economic growth in the poorest countries is thus particularly urgent. Are the policy prescriptions of this section relevant to those countries, or are very different types of measures necessary to spur growth in the poorest nations?

To a significant extent, the same factors and policies that promote growth in richer countries apply to the poorest countries as well. Increasing human capital by supporting education and training, increasing rates of saving and investment, investing in public capital and infrastructure, supporting R&D and encouraging entrepreneurship, are all measures that will enhance economic growth in poor countries.

However, to a much greater degree than in richer countries, most poor countries need to improve the legal and political environment that underpins their economies. For example, many developing countries have poorly developed or corrupt legal systems, which discourage entrepreneurship and investment by creating uncertainty about property rights. Taxation and regulation in developing countries are often heavy-handed and administered by inefficient bureaucracies, to the extent that it may take months or years to obtain the approvals needed to start a small business or expand a factory. Regulation is also used to suppress market forces in poor countries; for example, the government, rather than the market, may determine the allocation of bank credit or the prices for agricultural products. Structural policies that aim to ameliorate these problems are important preconditions for generating growth in the poorest countries. But probably most important – and most difficult, for some countries – is establishing political stability and the rule of law. Without political stability, domestic and foreign savers will be reluctant to invest in the country, and economic growth will be difficult (if not impossible) to achieve.

Can rich countries help poor countries to develop? Historically, richer nations have tried to help by providing financial aid through loans or grants from individual countries (foreign aid) or by loans made by international agencies, such as the World Bank and the International Monetary Fund (IMF). Experience has shown, however, that financial aid to countries that do not undertake structural reforms, such as reducing excessive regulation or improving the legal system, is of limited value. To make their foreign aid most effective, rich countries should help poor countries achieve *political stability* and undertake the necessary reforms to the *structure of their economies*.

Are there limits to growth?

Earlier in this chapter we saw that even relatively low rates of economic growth, if sustained for a long period, will produce huge increases in the size of the economy. This fact raises the question of whether economic growth can continue indefinitely without depleting natural resources and causing massive damage to the global environment. Does the basic truth that we live in a finite world of finite resources imply that, ultimately, economic growth must come to an end?

The concern that economic growth may not be sustainable is not a new one. An influential book, *The Limits to Growth* (1972),[6] reported the results of computer simulations that suggested that unless population growth and economic expansion were halted,

---

6 Meadows *et al.* (1972).

Economic naturalist 19.5 Promoting growth and cohesion in Europe

For the first 20 years of its existence the group of countries now called the European Union was a club of six relatively rich nations – Belgium, France, Germany, Italy, Luxembourg and the Netherlands. The first enlargement occurred in 1973 when the United Kingdom, Denmark and Ireland joined, to be followed by Greece in 1981, and Spain and Portugal in 1986. One significant feature of these enlargements was the inclusion of four relatively poor countries – Ireland, Greece, Portugal and Spain – with real incomes per person between 55 and 65 per cent of the European average. Up to that point regional policy, or measures to help disadvantaged areas, had mostly been left to individual countries. However, the inclusion of these four poorer countries posed a new problem for the Union. If the process of economic integration was to promote higher living standards then a way had to be found for the benefits to be enjoyed by all members. The Union responded to this challenge by redirecting policy from general growth-promoting policies to a strategy that would favour the poorer members and help them catch up with the richest countries. In the late 1980s and early 1990s the Union introduced a series of measures under the general titles of *Structural and Cohesion Funds,* designed to channel resources towards its more disadvantaged members. Structural Funds could be used in disadvantaged regions in all member states, but the Cohesion Funds could be allocated only to the 'poor four' – Greece, Ireland, Portugal and Spain – who became known as the Cohesion Countries. The purpose of these funds was to promote economic growth and convergence by investing in areas such as infrastructure and human capital.

Figure 19.12 shows the growth of real GDP per person, as a percentage of the EU average, in the four Cohesion Countries since 1980. Compared with Greece, Portugal and Spain, Ireland is the obvious success story, with GDP per person increasing from 64 per cent of the EU average in 1980 to 115 per cent in 2001. One theory suggests that Ireland made better use of Structural and Cohesion Funds by targeting them at key areas such as the transport infrastructure and job training programmes. However, while compared with the other Cohesion Countries, Ireland may have made better use of

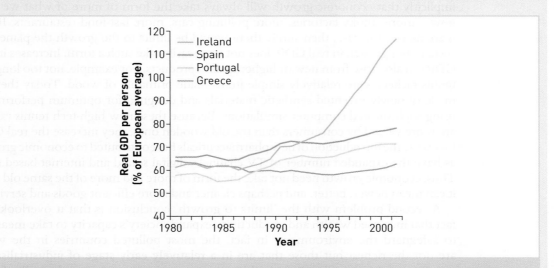

Figure 19.12 Real GDP per Person in the Cohesion Economies, 1980–2001. The figure shows real GDP per person, as a percentage of the EU average, in the four Cohesion Country economies – Greece, Ireland, Portugal and Spain. Only Ireland has managed to reach and even exceed the average level of GDP per person in the European Union. The others still lag well behind.

EU funding, the funds by themselves are only a part, and probably a relatively small part, of the Irish economic miracle, often referred to as the 'Celtic Tiger'. Economists are generally agreed that there is no single factor explaining the phenomenal performance of the Irish economy. Relatively low wages (at least in the 1980s and early 1990s), a young and educated labour force, together with EU funding certainly played significant roles. However, if one factor stands out it is not EU funding but the introduction of the single European market (SEM) in 1993. Unifying the European market provided a direct incentive for American multinationals to invest and produce in Europe. While all EU countries have attracted foreign direct investment (FDI), Ireland had several advantages not enjoyed by the others, namely a low rate of profits tax and the fact that it was an English-speaking country. As a result, Ireland attracted a disproportionate amount of FDI. Large international companies such as Dell, Intel, Microsoft and Monsanto now have major production facilities in Ireland supplying both the EU and US markets. Not only did these companies create employment but, by introducing cutting-edge technology, they improved the skills and productivity of the Irish labour force, which, as we saw at the start of this chapter, is a necessary condition for sustained economic growth.

The 2004 enlargement of the European Union to include countries in Central and Eastern Europe with income levels less than half of the EU average poses an even greater problem. In the future, EU funding will be directed towards these new accession states. However, as the experience of Greece, Ireland, Portugal and Spain shows, Structural and Cohesion Funds, although important, are unlikely to solve the problem by themselves.

the world would soon run out of natural resources, drinkable water and breathable air. This book, and later works in the same vein, raises some fundamental questions that cannot be done full justice here. However, in some ways its conclusions are misleading.

One problem with the 'limits to growth' theory lies in its underlying concept of *economic growth*. Those who emphasise the environmental limits on growth assume implicitly that economic growth will always take the form of more of what we have now – more smoky factories, more polluting cars, more fast-food restaurants. If that were indeed the case, then surely there would be limits to the growth the planet can sustain. But growth in real GDP does not necessarily take such a form. Increases in real GDP can also arise from new or higher-quality products. For example, not too long ago tennis rackets were relatively simple items made primarily of wood. Today they are made of newly invented synthetic materials and designed for optimum performance using sophisticated computer simulations. Because these new high-tech tennis rackets are more valued by consumers than the old wooden ones, they increase the real GDP. Likewise, the introduction of new pharmaceuticals has contributed to economic growth, as have the expanded number of TV channels, digital sound and internet-based sales. Thus, economic growth need not take the form of more and more of the same old stuff; it can mean newer, better, and perhaps cleaner and more efficient goods and services.

A second problem with the 'limits to growth' conclusion is that it overlooks the fact that increased wealth and productivity expand society's capacity to take measures to safeguard the environment. In fact, the most polluted countries in the world are not the richest but those that are in a relatively early stage of industrialisation (see Economic naturalist 19.6). At this stage, countries must devote the bulk of their resources to basic needs – food, shelter, healthcare – and continued industrial expansion. In these countries, clean air and water may be viewed as luxuries rather than basic needs. In more economically developed countries, where the most basic needs are more easily met, extra resources are available to keep the environment clean. Thus continuing economic growth may lead to less, not more, pollution.

A third problem with the pessimistic view of economic growth is that it ignores the power of the market and other social mechanisms to deal with scarcity. During the oil-supply disruptions of the 1970s, newspapers were filled with headlines about the energy crisis and the imminent depletion of world oil supplies. Yet in 2005 the world's known oil reserves were actually *greater* than they were in the 1970s. Today's energy situation is so much better than was expected in the 1970s because the market went to work. Reduced oil supplies led to an increase in prices that changed the behaviour of both demanders and suppliers. Consumers insulated their homes, purchased more energy-efficient cars and appliances, and switched to alternative sources of energy. Suppliers engaged in a massive hunt for new reserves, opening up major new sources in Latin America, China and the North Sea. In short, *market forces* solved the energy crisis.

In general, shortages in any resource will trigger price changes that induce suppliers and demanders to deal with the problem. Simply extrapolating current economic trends into the future ignores the power of the market system to recognise shortages and make the necessary corrections. Government actions spurred by political pressures, such as the allocation of public funds to preserve open space or reduce air pollution, can be expected to supplement market adjustments.

| Equilibrium |

Despite the shortcomings of the 'limits to growth' perspective, most economists would agree that not all the problems created by economic growth can be dealt with effectively through the market or the political process. Probably most important, global environmental problems, such as the possibility of global warming or the ongoing destruction of rainforests, are a particular challenge for existing economic and political institutions. Environmental quality is not bought and sold in markets and thus will not automatically reach its optimal level through market processes (recall the *Equilibrium Principle*, Chapter 3). Nor can local or national governments effectively address problems that are global in scope. Unless international mechanisms are established for dealing with global environmental problems, these problems may become worse as economic growth continues.

Economic naturalist 19.6 Why is the air quality so poor in Mexico City?

Developing countries such as Mexico, which are neither fully industrialised nor desperately poor, often have severe environmental problems. Why?

One concern about economic growth is that it will cause ever-increasing levels of environmental pollution. Empirical studies show, however, that the relationship between pollution and real GDP per person is more like an inverted U (see Figure 19.13). In other words, as countries move from very low levels of real GDP per person to 'middle-income' levels, most measures of pollution tend to worsen, but environmental quality improves as real GDP per person rises even further. One study of the relationship between air quality and real GDP per person found that the level of real GDP per person at which air quality is the worst – indicated by point *A* in Figure 19.13 – is roughly equal to the average income level in Mexico.[7] And indeed, the air quality in Mexico City is exceptionally poor, as any visitor to that sprawling metropolis can attest.

That pollution may worsen as a country industrialises is understandable, but why does environmental quality improve when real GDP per person climbs to very high levels? There are a variety of explanations for this phenomenon. Compared with middle-income economies, the richer economies are more concentrated in 'clean', high-value services such as finance and software production

---

7 Grossman and Krueger (1993).

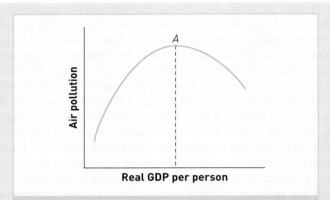

Figure 19.13 The Relationship between Air Pollution and Real GDP per Person. Empirically, air pollution increases with real GDP per person up to a point and then begins to decline. Maximum air pollution (point *A*) occurs at a level of real GDP per person roughly equal to that of Mexico.

as opposed to pollution-intensive industries such as heavy manufacturing. Rich economies are also more likely to have the expertise to develop sophisticated and cost-effective anti-pollution technologies. But the main reason the richer economies tend to be cleaner is the same reason that the homes of rich people are generally cleaner and in better condition than the homes of the poor. As income rises above the level necessary to fulfil basic needs, more resources remain to dedicate to 'luxuries' like a clean environment (the *Scarcity Principle*, Chapter 1). For the rich family, the extra resources will pay for a cleaning service; for the rich country, they will pay for pollution control devices in factories and on cars. Indeed, anti-pollution laws are generally tougher and more strictly enforced in rich countries than in middle-income and poor countries.

Increasing
Opportunity
Cost

RECAP Economic growth: developments and issues

- Labour productivity growth slowed throughout the industrialised world in the early 1970s. One possible explanation for this is that *productivity growth* has become harder to measure; another is the *technological depletion hypothesis*, that technological opportunities occur less frequently today than in the immediate post-war period. Some evidence suggests a recent resurgence in productivity growth in the United States.
- Economic growth has substantial costs, notably the sacrifice of *current consumption* that is required to free resources for creating new capital and new technologies. Higher rates of growth should be pursued only if the benefits outweigh the costs.
- Policies for promoting economic growth include policies to increase *human capital* (education and training); policies that promote *saving and capital formation*; policies that support R&D; and the provision of a *legal and political framework* within which the private sector can operate productively. Deficiencies in the legal and political framework (for example, official corruption or poorly defined property rights) are a special problem for many developing countries.
- Some have argued that *finite resources* imply ultimate limits to economic growth. This view overlooks the fact that growth can take the form of better, rather than more, goods and services; that increased wealth frees resources to safeguard the environment; and that political and economic mechanisms exist to address many of the problems associated with growth. However, these mechanisms may not work well when environmental or other problems arising from economic growth are global in scope.

Summary

- Since 1800 the industrialised nations have seen enormous improvements in living standards, as reflected in large increases in real GDP per person. Because of the power of *compound interest*, relatively small differences in growth rates, if continued over long periods, can produce large differences in real GDP per person and average living standards. Thus, the rate of *long-term economic growth* is an economic variable of critical importance.

- Real GDP per person is the product of *average labour productivity* (real GDP per employed worker) and the share of the population that is *employed*. Growth in real GDP per person can occur only through growth in average labour productivity, in the share of the population that is working, or both. In most countries the main source of the increase in real GDP per person is rising average labour productivity.

- Among the factors that determine labour productivity are the quantity and quality of the *physical capital* that workers use; the talents, education, training and skills of workers, or *human capital*; the availability of land and other *natural resources*; the application of *technology* to the production and distribution of goods and services; the effectiveness of *entrepreneurs* and managers; and the broad *social and legal environment*. Because of *diminishing returns to capital*, beyond a certain point expansion of the capital stock is not the most effective way to increase average labour productivity. Economists generally agree that *technical progress* is the most important single source of improvements in productivity and living standards.

- Since the 1970s the industrial world has experienced a *slowdown* in productivity growth. Some economists have suggested that the 'slowdown' is more the result of an inability to measure increases in the quality of output than of any real economic change. Others have suggested that the exploitation of a backlog of technological opportunities following the Great Depression and the Second World War led to unusually high growth rates in the 1950s and 1960s, a view called the *technological depletion hypothesis*. In this view, the slower growth in US productivity since about 1970 in fact reflects a return to a more normal rate of growth. US productivity growth has picked up since about 1991, however, possibly as the result of new technologies.

- Economic growth has costs as well as benefits. Prominent among them is the need to sacrifice *current consumption* to achieve a high rate of investment in new capital goods; other costs of growing more quickly include extra work effort and the costs of R&D. Thus more economic growth is not necessarily better; whether increased economic growth is desirable depends on whether the benefits of growth outweigh the costs.

- Among the ways in which government can *stimulate economic growth* are by adopting policies that encourage the creation of human capital; that promote saving and investment, including public investment in infrastructure; that support R&D, particularly in the basic sciences; and that provide a legal and political framework that supports private-sector activities. The poorest countries, with poorly developed legal, tax and regulatory systems, are often in the greatest need of an improved legal and political framework, and increased political stability.

- Are there limits to growth? Arguments that economic growth must be constrained by environmental problems and the limits of natural resources ignore the fact that economic growth can take the form of increasing quality as well as increasing quantity. Indeed, increases in output can provide additional resources for cleaning up the environment. Finally, the market system, together with political processes, can solve many of the problems associated with economic growth. On the other hand, global environmental problems, which can be handled by neither the market nor by individual national governments, have the potential to constrain economic growth.

Review questions

1. What has happened to real GDP per person in the industrialised countries since 1900? What implications does this have for the average person?

2. Why do economists consider growth in average labour productivity to be the key factor in determining long-run living standards?

3. What is technical progress? Why is it important to an explanation of sustained economic growth?

4. What is human capital? Why is it economically important? How is new human capital created?

5. Discuss how talented entrepreneurs and effective managers can enhance average labour productivity.

6. What major contributions can the government make to the goal of increasing average labour productivity?

7. What explanations have been offered for the slowdown in productivity growth observed in industrial countries since the early 1970s?

8. Discuss the following statement: 'Because the environment is fragile and natural resources are finite, ultimately economic growth must come to an end.'

connect Problems

1. Richland's real GDP per person is €10,000, and Poorland's real GDP per person is €5,000. However, Richland's real GDP per person is growing at 1 per cent per year and Poorland's is growing at 3 per cent per year. Compare real GDP per person in the two countries after 10 years and after 20 years. Approximately how many years will it take Poorland to catch up with Richland?

2. Refer to Table 19.4 for growth rates of average labour productivity over the periods 1960–73, 1973–79 and 1979–2000. Suppose that growth of average labour productivity in France had continued at its 1960–73 rate until 2000. Proportionally, how much higher would French average labour productivity in 2000 have been, compared with its actual value? (**Note:** You do not need to know the actual values of average labour productivity in any year to solve this problem.) Does your answer shed light on why economists consider the post-1973 productivity slowdown to be an important issue?

3. Data for Canada, Germany and Japan on the ratio of employment to population in 1979 and 2003 are as in the table below. Using data from Table 19.1, find average labour productivity for each country in 1979 and in 2003. How much of the increase in output per person in each country over the 1979–2003 period is due to increased labour productivity? To increased employment relative to population?

Country	1979	2003
Canada	0.44	0.50
Germany	0.33	0.43
Japan	0.47	0.52

4. Is the following statement **True or False**? Explain your answer. 'In steady-state equilibrium, both average labour productivity and the capital–labour ratio will be constant. It follows that the economy's aggregate output Y must also be constant.'

5. In a given economy, average labour productivity is €50,000, the capital–labour ratio is €20,000 and the saving rate is 10 per cent. If the population grows at 0.5 per cent per year and 1.5 per cent of the capital stock depreciates each year, what are the values of (a) gross investment (b) net investment and (c) required investment? What would you predict about the future behaviour of the capital–labour ratio and average labour productivity in this economy?

6. Suppose that due to a programme of government investment in education the average years of schooling increased from 10 to 12. Using Fig. 19.8 explain how this might effect (a) average labour productivity and (b) the growth rate of total output Y.

7. True or false: For advances in basic science to translate into improvements in standards of living, they must be supported by favourable economic conditions. Discuss, using concrete examples where possible to illustrate your arguments.

References

Baumol, W. (1990) 'Entrepreneurship: unproductive and destructive', *Journal of Political Economy*, October, pp. 893–921.

Grossman, G.M. and A.B. Krueger (1993) 'Environmental impacts of a North American Free Trade Agreement', in P. Garber (ed.), *The Mexico–US Free Trade Agreement* (Cambridge, MA: MIT Press).

Maddison, A. (1988) *Phases of Capitalist Development* (Oxford: Oxford University Press).

Meadows, D., D.L. Meadows, J. Randers and W.W. Behrens III (1972) *The Limits to Growth* (New York: New American Library).

Nordhaus, W. (1982) 'Economic policy in the face of declining productivity growth', *European Economic Review*, May–June, pp. 131–58.

Solow, R.M. (1956) 'A contribution to the theory of economic growth', *Quarterly Journal of Economics*, February 1956.

Solow, R.M. (1957) 'Technical change and the aggregate production function', *Review of Economics and Statistics*, 39, pp. 312–20.

Online Learning Centre

To help you grasp the key concepts of this chapter check out the extra resources posted on the Online Learning Centre. There are chapter summaries, self-test questions, an interactive graphing tool, weblinks and a glossary, all for free!

Visit the Online Learning Centre at: www.mcgraw-hill.co.uk/textbooks/mcdowell for information on accessing all of these resources.

20

Capital Markets: Saving, Investment and Capital Formation

Saving and investment are crucial to the economic well-being of both individuals and nations. People need to save to provide for their retirement and for other future needs, such as their children's education or a new home. An individual's or a family's savings can also provide a crucial buffer in the event of an economic emergency, such as the loss of a job or unexpected medical bills. At the national level, investment in new capital goods – factories, equipment and housing – is an important factor promoting economic growth and higher living standards. As we shall see in this chapter, the resources necessary to produce new capital come primarily from a nation's collective saving.

In this chapter we shall look at saving and its links to the formation of new capital. We begin by defining the concepts of saving and wealth, and exploring the connection between them. We shall consider why people choose to save, rather than spend all their income. We then turn to national saving – the collective saving of households, businesses and government. Because national saving determines the capacity of an economy to create new capital, it is the more important measure of saving from a macroeconomic perspective.

A healthy economy not only saves adequately but also *invests those savings in a productive way*. Most decisions to invest in new capital are made by firms. As we shall see, a firm's decision to invest is in many respects analogous to its decision about whether to increase employment; firms will choose to expand their capital stocks when the benefits of doing so exceed the costs.

In market economies, such as those in Western Europe and North America, channelling society's savings into the best possible capital investments is the role of the *financial system*: banks, stock markets, bond markets, and other financial markets and institutions. For this reason, many economists have argued that the development of well-functioning financial markets is a crucial precursor to sustained economic growth. Hence we shall discuss some major financial markets and institutions, and their role in directing saving to productive uses.

We end the chapter by showing how national saving and capital formation are related, using a supply and demand approach.

Saving and wealth

The **saving** of an economic unit, whether a household, a business, a university or a country, may be defined as its *current income* minus its *spending on current needs*. For example, if the Rossi family earns €1,000 per week, spends €900 weekly on living expenses such as rent, food, clothes and entertainment, and deposits the remaining €100 in a bank account, its saving is €100 per week. The **saving rate** of any economic unit is its saving divided by its income. Since the Rossis save €100 from a weekly income of €1,000, their saving rate is €100/€1,000, or 10 per cent.

saving current income minus spending on current needs

saving rate saving divided by income

wealth the value of assets minus liabilities

assets anything of value that one owns

liabilities the debts one owes

The saving of an economic unit is closely related to its **wealth**, or the value of its assets minus its liabilities. **Assets** are anything of value that one *owns*, either *financial* or *real*. Examples of financial assets that you or your family might own include cash, bank accounts, shares in companies and government bonds. Examples of real assets include property, jewellery, consumer durables like cars and valuable collectibles. **Liabilities**, on the other hand, are the debts one *owes*. Examples of liabilities are credit card balances, bank loans and mortgages.

Accountants list the assets and liabilities of a family, a firm, a university or any other economic unit on a *balance sheet*. Comparing the values of the assets and liabilities helps them to determine the economic unit's wealth, also called its *net worth*.

Example 20.1 The Rossis construct their balance sheet

To take stock of their financial position, the Rossis list their assets and liabilities on a balance sheet. The result is shown in Table 20.1. What is the Rossis' wealth?

Assets		Liabilities	
Cash	€100	Mortgage	€200,000
Bank account	1,200	Credit card balance	250
Shares	1,000		
Car (market value)	3,500		
House (market value)	250,000		
Total	€255,800		€200,250
		Net worth	€55,550

Table 20.1 **The Rossis' Balance Sheet**

The Rossis' financial assets are their cash holdings (notes and coin), the balance in their bank account and the current value of their shares. Together their financial assets are worth €2,300. They also list €253,500 in real assets – the sum of the market values of their car and house. The Rossis' total assets, both financial and real, come to €255,800. Their liabilities are the mortgage on their home and the balance due on their credit card, which total €200,250. The Rossis' wealth, or net worth, then, is the value of their assets (€255,800) minus the value of their liabilities (€200,250), or €55,550.

Exercise 20.1   What would the Rossis' net worth be if their mortgage was €270,000 rather than €250,000? Construct a new balance sheet for the household.

Saving and wealth are related, because saving contributes to wealth. To understand this relationship better, we must distinguish between *stocks* and *flows*.

Stocks and flows

Saving is an example of a **flow**, a measure that is defined *per unit of time*. For example, the Rossis' savings are €100 *per week*. Wealth, in contrast, is a **stock**, a measure that is defined *at a point in time*. The Rossis' wealth of €55,550, for example, is their wealth on a particular date.

flow a measure that is defined per unit of time

stock a measure that is defined at a point in time

To visualise the difference between stocks and flows, think of water running into a bath. The amount of water in the bath at any specific moment – for example, 100 litres at 7.15 pm – is a *stock*, because it is measured at a specific point in time. The rate at which the water flows into the bath – for example, 5 litres per minute – is a *flow*, because it is measured per unit of time. In many cases, a flow is the *rate of change* in a stock: if we know that there are 100 litres of water in the bath at 7.15 pm, for example, and that water is flowing in at 5 litres per minute, we can easily determine that the stock of water will be changing at the rate of 5 litres per minute, and will equal 105 litres at 7.16 pm, 110 litres at 7.17 pm, and so on, until the bath overflows.

The relationship between saving (a *flow*) and wealth (a *stock*) is similar to the relationship between the flow of water into a bath and the stock of water in the bath in that the *flow* of saving causes the *stock* of wealth to change at the same rate. Indeed, as Example 20.2 illustrates, every euro that a person saves adds a euro to her wealth.

Example 20.2 The link between saving and wealth

The Rossis save €100 per week. How does this saving affect their wealth? Does the change in their wealth depend on whether the Rossis use their saving to accumulate assets or to reduce their liabilities?

The Rossis could use the €100 they saved this week to increase their assets – for example, by adding the €100 to their bank account – or to reduce their liabilities – for example, by paying off their credit card balance. Suppose they add the €100 to their bank account, increasing their assets by €100. Since their liabilities are unchanged, their wealth also increases by €100, to €55,650 (see Table 20.1).

If the Rossis decide to use the €100 they saved this week to pay off their credit card balance, they reduce it from €250 to €150. That action would reduce liabilities by €100, leaving their assets unchanged. Since wealth equals assets minus liabilities, reducing their liabilities by €100 increases their wealth by €100, to €55,650. Thus, saving €100 per week raises the Rossis' stock of wealth by €100 a week, regardless of whether they use their saving to increase assets or reduce liabilities. In either case the *flow* of saving leads to an increase in the *stock* of wealth.

The close relationship between saving and wealth explains why saving is so important to an economy. Higher rates of saving today lead to faster accumulation of wealth, and the wealthier a nation is, the higher its standard of living. Thus a high rate of saving today contributes to an improved *standard of living* in the future.

Exercise 20.2   Continuing with the Rossis, assume that Table 20.1 is their family balance sheet on 1 January 2004. Assume that the following transactions take place over 2004: (a) the Rossis save €400 per month; (b) the market value of the Rossis' car falls by €1,000; (c) the market value of the Rossis' house increases by 10 per cent; (d) the Rossis' have monthly mortgage payments of €300, of which €100 is interest on the debt and €200 is repayment on the loan. Other items in their balance sheet remain unchanged. Find the Rossis' net worth on 1 January 2005.

Capital gains and losses

Though saving increases wealth, it is not the only factor that determines wealth. Wealth can also change because of changes in the values of the real or financial *assets* one owns. Suppose the Rossis' shares rise in value, from €1,000 to €1,500. This increase in the value of the Rossis' shares raises their total assets by €500 without affecting their liabilities. As a result, the Rossis' wealth rises by €500, from €255,800 to €256,300, and their net worth from €55,550 to €56,050.

capital gains increases in the value of existing assets

capital losses decreases in the value of existing assets

Changes in the value of existing assets are called **capital gains** when an asset's value increases, and **capital losses** when an asset's value decreases. Just as capital gains increase wealth, capital losses decrease wealth. Capital gains and losses are not counted as part of saving, however. Instead, the change in a person's wealth during any period equals the saving done during the period plus capital gains or minus capital losses during that period. In terms of an equation:

$$\text{Change in wealth} = \text{Saving} + \text{Capital gains} - \text{Capital losses}$$

Exercise 20.3 How would each of the following actions or events affect the Rossis' *saving* and their *wealth*?

a. The Rossis deposit €100 in the bank at the end of the week as usual. They also charge €150 to their credit card, raising the balance to €400.

b. The Rossis use €400 from their bank account to pay off their credit card bill.

c. The Rossis' old car is recognised as a classic. Its market value rises from €3,500 to €4,000.

d. A fall in property prices reduces the value of the Rossis' house by €20,000.

We have seen how saving is related to the accumulation of wealth. To understand why people choose to save, however, we need to examine their *motives for saving*.

RECAP Saving and wealth

In general, *saving* is current income minus spending on current needs. *Wealth* is the value of assets – anything of value that one owns – minus liabilities – the debts one owes. Saving is measured per unit of time (for example, euros per week) and thus is a *flow*. Wealth is measured at a point in time and thus is a *stock*. In the same way as the flow of water through the tap increases the stock of water in a bathtub, the flow of saving increases the stock of wealth.

Wealth can also be increased by *capital gains* (increases in the value of existing assets) or reduced by *capital losses* (decreases in asset values).

Why do people save?

Why do people save part of their income instead of spending everything they earn? Economists have identified at least three broad reasons for saving. First, people save to meet certain *long-term objectives*, such as a comfortable retirement. By saving part of their income during their most productive working years, households can support a higher standard of living during their retirement years. In fact, saving, and borrowing, are means by which households can move expenditure on goods and services, or

intertemporal substitution
a means of moving
consumption across time by
substituting consumption in
one year for consumption in
another year

consumption, across time. When a household saves, it is refraining from consumption by spending less than its income. However, as saving increases the household's stock of wealth, it will be possible to spend more on goods and services and consume above income in future years. Put another way, saving means that households are substituting *future* for *current* consumption. Conversely, if a household borrows this year it can consume above its current income. But as borrowing today has to be repaid in subsequent years the household must consume less than its income at some point in the future. Hence borrowing is a means by which households can substitute *present* for *future* consumption. Economists refer to this transfer of consumption across time as **intertemporal substitution**.

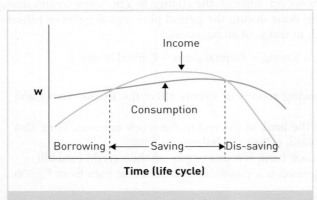

Figure 20.1 Life-Cycle Saving. By saving and borrowing, households can separate their life-cycle consumption path from their income profile.

Figure 20.1 illustrates how intertemporal substitution can enable a household to follow different consumption and income paths over its lifetime. For many households *income from employment* starts at a relatively low level but rises as the working members acquire job skills and experience, and then declines at retirement. This life-cycle profile of earned income is illustrated by the hump-shaped income curve in Figure 20.1. If households could not save or borrow then their life-cycle consumption would follow the same path. However, by borrowing in the early years when income is relatively low and expenditure on housing, children, etc., is high, the household can support a higher level of consumption.

As income rises in the more productive years of its life cycle the household can use its greater resources to repay earlier borrowing and save, or accumulate wealth, to support consumption during its retirement years when the household is running its wealth down, or *dis-saving*. Because this type of saving and borrowing enables the household to separate its consumption path from its life-cycle income profile, economists refer to it as **life-cycle saving**.

life-cycle saving saving to
smooth out the household's
consumption path

precautionary saving saving
for protection against
unexpected setbacks, such as
the loss of a job or a medical
emergency

bequest saving saving done
for the purpose of leaving an
inheritance

A second reason to save is to protect oneself and family against *unexpected setbacks* – the loss of a job, for example, or a costly health problem. Saving for protection against potential emergencies is called **precautionary saving**.

A third reason to save is to accumulate an *estate* to leave to one's heirs, usually one's children but possibly a favourite charity or other worthy cause. Saving for the purpose of leaving an inheritance, or bequest, is called **bequest saving**.

To be sure, people usually do not mentally separate their saving into these three categories; rather, all three reasons for saving motivate most savers to varying degrees. Economic naturalist 20.1 shows how these reasons for saving can explain differences between household saving in Europe and the United States.

Economic naturalist 20.1 Why do Europeans save more than Americans?

Household saving in the United States, which has always been comparatively low, has fallen even further since the 1990s. Figure 20.2 shows recent trends in household saving rates in France, Germany and the United States, and clearly illustrates that Europeans save more than Americans. Why do American households save so little compared with their European counterparts?

Economists do not agree on the reasons for differences between household saving rates in Europe and the United States, although many hypotheses have been suggested. It is possible that higher saving rates in Europe may have as much to do with historical and psychological factors as with economics.

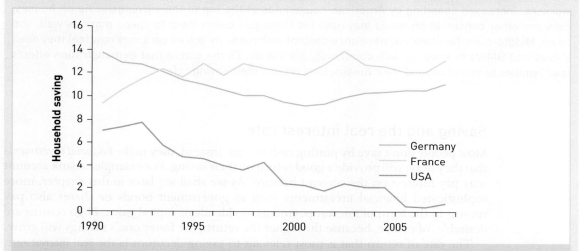

Figure 20.2 Household Saving as a Percentage of Disposable Income, 1990–2007. European household saving is now significantly higher than in the United States.
Source: OECD (www.oecd.org).

The United States has not known sustained economic hardship since the Great Depression of the 1930s. Most European economies, on the other hand, suffered devastation in the Second World War, whereas the American economy prospered. Also, during the Cold War period (1950–89), parts of Western Europe were very much on the 'front line', creating greater uncertainty about the future than in the United States. Although the immediate effects of world wars have faded into memory they may have implanted a much stronger inertia (old habits die hard) in European saving behaviour compared with that of the United States. Perhaps a less prosperous and more volatile history has led to stronger *precautionary* and *bequest* motives for saving in Europe than in the United States.

Life-cycle reasons may also explain part of the differences between European and American household saving behaviour. In Chapter 19 we saw that in the 1990s income per person increased more rapidly in the United States than in Europe. If this rise in the relative US standard of living is viewed as permanent then it reduces the need to save from current income to support future consumption.

Three other factors present in both America and Europe, but more prominent in the United States, may help to explain recent differences in saving rates. First, the pace of *financial innovation* has been much more rapid in the United States than in Europe, giving American households greater access to credit markets and reducing *precautionary* motives for saving. For example, unlike in some European countries, US home owners find it relatively easy to borrow against their home equity (the difference between the market value of a family's home and its mortgage liability). Second, during the 1990s an increasing number of Americans acquired stocks, either directly through purchases or indirectly through their pension and retirement funds. At the same time, share prices rose at record rates. The strongly rising 'bull market', which increased the prices of most shares, enabled many Americans to enjoy significant capital gains and increased wealth without saving much, if anything. Indeed, some economists argued that the low household saving rate of the 1990s is partially *explained* by the bull market; because capital gains increased household wealth by so much, many people saw no need to save. Finally, *demonstration effects* may have depressed US saving from the 1980s. Chapter 20 discussed the phenomenon of increasing wage inequality, which has been much more pronounced in the United States, and has improved the relative position of more American skilled and educated workers. Increased spending by American households at the top of the earnings scale on houses, cars and other consumption goods may have led those just below them to spend more as well, and so on. Middle-class families that were once content with medium-priced cars may now feel they need Volvos and BMWs to keep up with community standards. To the extent that demonstration effects lead families to spend beyond their means, they reduce their saving rate.

Saving and the real interest rate

Most people don't save by putting cash in a tin. Instead, they make *financial investments* that they hope will provide a good return on their saving. For example, a bank account may pay interest on the account balance. As we shall see later in this chapter, more sophisticated financial investments such as government bonds or shares also pay returns in the form of interest payments, dividends or capital gains. High returns are desirable, of course, because the higher the return, the faster one's savings will grow.

The rate of return that is most relevant to saving decisions is the *real interest rate*, denoted *r*. Recall from Chapter 18 that the real interest rate is the rate at which the real purchasing power of a financial asset increases over time. The real interest rate equals the market, or nominal, interest rate (*i*) minus the inflation rate (π).

> Cost–Benefit
> Analysis

The real interest rate is relevant to savers because it is the 'reward' for saving. Suppose you are thinking of increasing your saving by €1,000 this year. If the real interest rate is 5 per cent, then in a year your extra saving will give you extra purchasing power of €1,050, measured in today's money. But if the real interest rate were 10 per cent, your sacrifice of €1,000 this year would be rewarded by €1,100 in purchasing power next year. Obviously, all else being equal, you would be more willing to save today if you knew the reward next year would be greater. In either case the cost of the extra saving – giving up your weekly night out – is the same. But the *benefit* of the extra saving, in terms of increased purchasing power next year, is higher if the real interest rate is 10 per cent rather than 5 per cent.

Example 20.3 By how much does a high savings rate enhance a family's future living standard?

The Spends and the Thrifts are similar families, except that the Spends save 5 per cent of their income each year and the Thrifts save 20 per cent. The two families began to save in 1980 and plan to continue to save until their respective breadwinners retire in the year 2015. Both families earn €40,000 a year in real terms in the labour market, and both put their savings in a fund that has yielded a real return of 8 per cent per year, a return they expect to continue into the future. Compare the amount that the two families consume in each year from 1980 to 2015, and compare the families' wealth at retirement.

In the first year, 1980, the Spends saved €2,000 (5 per cent of their €40,000 income) and consumed €38,000 (95 per cent of €40,000). The Thrifts saved €8,000 in 1980 (20 per cent of €40,000) and hence consumed only €32,000 in that year, €6,000 less than the Spends. In 1981, the Thrifts' income was €40,640, the extra €640 representing the 8 per cent return on their €8,000 savings. The Spends saw their income grow by only €160 (8 per cent of their savings of €2,000) in 1981. With an income of €40,640, the Thrifts consumed €32,512 in 1981 (80 per cent of €40,640) compared with €38,152 (95 per cent of €40,160) for the Spends. The consumption gap between the two families, which started out at €6,000, thus fell to €5,640 after one year.

Because of the more rapid increase in the Thrifts' wealth and hence interest income, each year the Thrifts' income grew faster than the Spends'; each year the Thrifts continued to save 20 per cent of their higher incomes compared with only 5 per cent for the Spends. Figure 20.3 shows the paths followed by the consumption spending of the two families. You can see that the Thrifts' consumption, though starting at a lower level, grows more quickly. By 1995 the Thrifts had overtaken the Spends, and from that point onwards, the amount by which the Thrifts outspent the Spends grew with each passing year. Even though the Spends continued to consume 95 per cent of their income each year, their income grew so slowly that, by 2000, they were consuming nearly €3,000 a year less than the Thrifts (€41,158 a year versus €43,957). And by the time the two families retire, in 2015, the Thrifts will be consuming over €12,000 per year more than the Spends (€55,774 versus €43,698). Even more striking is the difference between the retirement nest eggs of the two families. Whereas the Spends will enter retirement with total accumulated savings of just over €77,000, the Thrifts will have more than €385,000, five times as much.

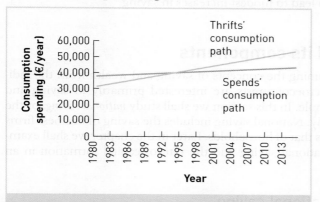

Figure 20.3 Consumption Trajectories of the Thrifts and the Spends. The figure shows consumption spending in each year by two families, the Thrifts and the Spends. Because the Thrifts save more than the Spends, their annual consumption spending rises relatively quickly. By the time of the retirement in the year 2015, the Thrifts 1both consume significantly more each year than the Spends and also have a retirement nest egg that is five times larger.

These dramatic differences depend in part on the assumption that the real rate of return is 8 per cent, a relatively high rate of return from a historical perspective. However, the point of the example, which remains valid under alternative assumptions about the real interest rate and saving rates, is that, because of the power of *compound interest*, a high rate of saving pays off in the long run.

While a higher real interest rate increases the reward for saving and encourages people to save, another force counteracts that extra incentive. Recall that a major reason for saving is to attain specific goals such as a comfortable retirement. If the goal is a specific amount – say, €25,000 for a down payment on a home – then a higher rate of return means that households can save *less* and still reach their goal, because funds that are put aside will grow more quickly. For example, to accumulate €25,000 at the end of five years, at a 5 per cent interest rate a person would have to save about €4,309 per year. At a 10 per cent interest rate, reaching the €25,000 goal would require saving only about €3,723 per year. To the extent that people are *target savers* who save to reach a specific goal, higher interest rates actually decrease the amount they need to save.

In sum, a higher real interest rate has both positive and negative effects on saving – a *positive* effect because it increases the reward for saving and a *negative* effect because it reduces the amount people need to save each year to reach a given target. Empirical evidence suggests that, in practice, higher real interest rates lead to modest increases in saving.

RECAP Why do people save?

Motivations for saving include saving to meet long-term objectives, such as retirement (*life-cycle saving*), saving for emergencies (*precautionary saving*) and saving to leave an inheritance or bequest (*bequest saving*). The amount that people save also depends on macroeconomic factors, such as the real interest rate. A higher real interest rate stimulates saving by increasing the reward for saving, but it can also depress saving by making it easier for savers to reach a specific savings target. On balance, a higher real interest rate appears to lead to modest increases in saving.

National saving and its components

Thus far, we have been examining the concepts of saving and wealth from the individual's perspective. But macroeconomists are interested primarily in saving and wealth for the country as a whole. In this section we shall study *national saving*, or the *aggregate saving* of the economy. National saving includes the saving of business firms and the government, as well as that of households. Later in the chapter we shall examine the close link between national saving and the rate of capital formation in an economy.

The measurement of national saving

To define the saving rate of a country as a whole, we shall start with a basic accounting identity that was introduced in Chapter 17. According to this identity, for the economy as a whole, production (or income) must equal total expenditure. In symbols, the identity is

$$Y = C + I + G + NX$$

where Y stands for either production or aggregate income (which must be equal), C equals consumption expenditure, I equals investment spending, G equals government purchases of goods and services, and NX equals net exports.

To simplify things, we shall assume that net exports (NX) equal zero so that the condition that output equals expenditure becomes

$$Y = C + I + G$$

To determine how much saving is done by the nation as a whole, we can apply the general definition of saving. As for any other economic unit, a nation's saving equals its *current income* less its *spending on current needs*. The current income of the country as a whole is its GDP, or Y – that is, the value of the final goods and services produced within the country's borders during the year.

Identifying the part of total expenditure that corresponds to the nation's spending on current needs is more difficult than identifying the nation's income. The component of aggregate spending that is easiest to classify is investment spending I. We know that investment spending – the acquisition of new factories, equipment and other capital goods, as well as residential construction – is done to expand the economy's future productive capacity or provide more housing for the future, not to satisfy current needs. So investment spending clearly is *not* part of spending on current needs.

Deciding how much of consumption spending by households, C, and government purchases of goods and services, G, should be counted as spending on current needs is less straightforward. Certainly most consumption spending by households – on food, clothing, utilities, entertainment, and so on – is for current needs. But consumption spending also includes purchases of long-lived *consumer durables*, such as cars, furniture and appliances. Consumer durables are only partially used up during the current year; they may continue to provide service, in fact, for years after their purchase. So household spending on consumer durables is a combination of spending on current needs and spending on future needs.

As with consumption spending, most government purchases of goods and services are intended to provide for current needs. However, like household purchases, a portion of government purchases is devoted to the acquisition or construction of long-lived capital goods, such as roads, bridges, schools, government buildings and military hardware. And like consumer durables, these forms of *public capital* are only partially used up during the current year; most will provide useful services far into the future. So, like consumption spending, government purchases are in fact a mixture of spending on current needs and spending on future needs.

Although in reality not all spending by households and the government is for current needs, in practice determining precisely how much of such spending is for current needs and how much is for future needs is extremely difficult. For simplicity's sake, in this book we shall treat *all* of both consumption expenditures (C) and government purchases (G) as spending on current needs. But bear in mind that because consumption spending and government purchases do in fact include some spending for future rather than current needs, treating all of C and G as spending on current needs will understate the true amount of national saving.

national saving the saving of the entire economy, equal to GDP less consumption expenditures and government purchases of goods and services, or $Y - C - G$

If we treat all consumption spending and government purchases as spending on current needs, then the nation's saving is its income Y less its spending on current needs, $C + G$. So we can define **national saving** S as

$$S = Y - C - G \qquad (20.1)$$

Figure 20.4 shows the national saving rates (national saving as a percentage of GDP) for the years 1960–2006 for France, Germany and the United Kingdom, and shows that, since about 1970, European national saving rates have tended to decline. As we shall see next, the reason for this decline is partly related to the behaviour of government rather than private saving.

Private and public components of national saving

To understand national saving better, we shall divide it into two major components: *private* saving, which is saving done by households and businesses, and *public* saving, which is saving done by the government.

To see how national saving breaks down into public and private saving, we work with the definition of national saving, $S = Y - C - G$. To distinguish private-sector income from public-sector income, we must expand this equation to incorporate taxes as well as payments made by the government to the private sector. Government payments to the private sector include both *transfers* and *interest* paid to individuals and

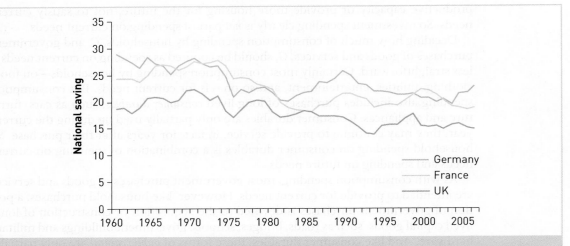

Figure 20.4 National Saving as a Percentage of GDP, 1960–2006. European national savings rates (as a percentage of GDP) have declined since the 1970s.
Source: OECD (www.oecd.org).

transfer payments payments the government makes to the public for which it receives no current goods or services in return

institutions holding government bonds. **Transfer payments** are payments the government makes to the public for which it receives no current goods or services in return. Unemployment benefits, welfare payments and pensions to government workers are transfer payments.

Let T stand for taxes paid by the private sector to the government *less* transfer payments and interest payments made by the government to the private sector. Since T equals private-sector tax payments minus the various benefits and interest payments the private sector receives from the government, we can think of T as net taxes. If we add and then subtract T from the definition of national saving, $S = Y - C - G$, we get

$$S = Y - C - G + T - T$$

Rearranging this equation and grouping terms, we obtain

$$S = (Y - T - C) + (T - G) \tag{20.2}$$

This equation splits national saving S into two parts: *private saving*, or $Y - T - C$, and public saving, $T - G$.

private saving the saving of the private sector of the economy is equal to the after-tax income of the private sector minus consumption expenditures $(Y - T - C)$; private saving can be further broken down into household saving and business saving

Private saving, $Y - T - C$, is the saving of the private sector of the economy. Why is $Y - T - C$ a reasonable definition of private saving? Remember that saving equals current income minus spending on current needs. The income of the private (non-governmental) sector of the economy is the economy's total income Y less net taxes paid to the government, T. The private sector's spending on current needs is its consumption expenditures C. So private-sector saving, equal to private-sector income less spending on current needs, is $Y - T - C$. Letting $S_{private}$ stand for private saving, we can write the definition of private saving as

$$S_{private} = Y - T - C$$

Private saving can be further broken down into saving done by households and business firms. *Household saving*, also called personal saving, is saving done by families and individuals. Household saving corresponds to the familiar image of families putting aside part of their incomes each month, and it is the focus of much attention in the news media. Businesses use the revenues from their sales to pay workers' salaries and other operating costs, to pay taxes and to provide dividends to their shareholders. The funds remaining after these payments have been made are equal to *business saving*. A business firm's savings are available for the purchase of new capital equipment or the expansion of its operations. Alternatively, a business can put its savings in the bank for future use.

public saving the saving of the government sector is equal to net tax payments minus government purchases $(T - G)$

Public saving, $T - G$, is the saving of the government sector, both local and national. Net taxes T are the income of the government. Government purchases G represent the government's spending on current needs (remember that, for the sake of simplicity, we are ignoring the investment portion of government purchases). Thus $T - G$ fits our definition of saving, in this case by the public sector. Letting S_{public} stand for public saving, we can write out the definition of public saving as

$$S_{public} = T - G$$

Using equation (20.2) and the definitions of private and public saving, we can rewrite national saving as

$$S = S_{private} + S_{public} \tag{20.3}$$

This equation confirms that national saving is the *sum of private saving and public saving*. Figure 20.5 shows the national saving broken down into business, household and public saving for Germany and the UK over 1990 to 2007.

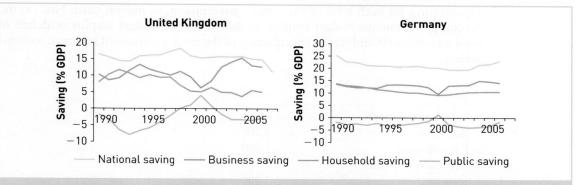

Figure 20.5 UK and German National Saving and its Components (as a Percentage of GDP) 1990–2007.
Source: OECD (www.oecd.org).

Public saving and the government budget

Although the idea that households and businesses can save is familiar to most people, the fact that the *government can also save* is less widely understood. Public saving is closely linked to the government's decisions about spending and taxing. Governments finance the bulk of their spending by taxing the private sector. If taxes and spending in a given year are equal, the government is said to have a *balanced budget*. If in any given year the government's spending exceeds its tax collections, the difference is called the **government budget deficit**. If the government runs a deficit, it must make up the difference by borrowing from the public through issuance of government bonds. Algebraically, the government budget deficit can be written as $G - T$, or government purchases minus net tax collections.

government budget deficit
the excess of government spending over tax collections $(G - T)$

government budget surplus
the excess of government tax collections over government spending $(T - G)$; the government budget surplus equals public saving

In some years, the government may spend less than it collects in taxes. The excess of tax collections over government spending is called the **government budget surplus**. When a government has a surplus, it uses the extra funds to pay off its outstanding debt to the public. Algebraically, the government budget surplus may be written as $T - G$, or net tax collections less government purchases.

If the algebraic expression for the government budget surplus, $T - G$, looks familiar, that is because it is also the definition of public saving, as we saw earlier. Thus, *public saving is identical to the government budget surplus*. In other words, when the government collects more in taxes than it spends, public saving will be *positive*. When the government spends more than it collects in taxes so that it runs a deficit, public saving will be *negative*.

Example 20.4 illustrates the relationships among public saving, the government budget surplus and national saving.

Example 20.4 Government saving

Suppose that in a fictional country called Euroland, government is organised on two levels, central and local. The table below shows last year's data on revenues and expenditures for each level of Euroland's government, in million euro. Find (a) the central government's budget surplus or deficit, (b) the budget surplus or deficit of local governments and (c) the contribution of the total government sector to national saving.

Item	€ million
Central government:	
Receipts	2,000
Expenditures	1,800
Local governments:	
Receipts	1,200
Expenditures	1,150

The central government's receipts minus its expenditures were $2,000 - 1,800 = 200$, so the central government ran a budget surplus of €200 million. Local government receipts minus expenditures were $1,200 - 1,150 = 50$, so local governments ran a collective budget surplus of €50 million. The budget surplus of the entire public sector – that is, the central government surplus plus the local surplus – was $200 + 50 = 250$, or €250 million. So the contribution of the government sector to Euroland's national saving was €250 million.

Exercise 20.4 Continuing Example 20.4, the table below shows the analogous data on government revenues and expenditures five years previously. Again, find (a) the central government's budget surplus or deficit, (b) the budget surplus or deficit of local governments and (c) the contribution of the government sector to national saving.

Item	€ million
Central government:	
Receipts	1,420
Expenditures	1,640
Local governments:	
Receipts	950
Expenditures	875

If you did Exercise 20.4 correctly, you would have found that the government sector's contribution to national saving five years ago was *negative*. The reason is that the central and local governments taken together ran a *budget deficit* in that year, reducing national saving by the amount of the budget deficit.

RECAP National saving and its components

- *National saving*, the saving of the economy as a whole, is defined by $S = Y - C - G$, where Y is GDP, C is consumption spending and G is government purchases of goods and services. National saving is the sum of public saving and private saving: $S = S_{private} + S_{public}$.
- *Private saving*, the saving of the private sector, is defined by $S_{private} = Y - T - C$, where T is net tax payments. Private saving can be broken down further into household saving and business saving.
- *Public saving*, the saving of the government, is defined by $S_{public} = T - G$. Public saving equals the government budget surplus, $T - G$. When the government budget is in surplus, government saving is positive; when the government budget is in deficit, public saving is negative.

Investment and capital formation

From the point of view of the economy as a whole, the importance of national saving is that it provides the funds needed for *investment*. Investment – the creation of new capital goods and housing – is critical to increasing average labour productivity and improving standards of living.

What factors determine whether, and how much, firms choose to invest? Firms acquire new capital goods for the same reason that they hire new workers: they expect that doing so will be profitable. We saw in Chapter 20 that the profitability of employing an extra worker depends primarily on two factors: the cost of employing the worker and the value of the worker's marginal product. In the same way, firms' willingness to acquire new factories and machines depends on the expected *cost* of using them and the expected *benefit*, equal to the value of the marginal product that they will provide.

Example 20.5 Should Manuel buy a motor cycle (1)?

Manuel is currently working in an office earning €15,600 after taxes but is considering buying a motor cycle and going into the courier business delivering letters and small packages around Madrid. He can buy a €4,000 motor cycle by taking out a loan at 6 per cent annual interest. With this cycle and his own labour Manuel reckons he can net €20,000 per year after deduction of costs such as petrol and maintenance. Of the €20,000 net revenues, 20 per cent must be paid to the government in taxes. Assume that the motor cycle can always be resold for its original purchase price of €4,000. Should Manuel buy the motor cycle?

To decide whether to invest in the capital good (the motor cycle), Manuel should compare the financial benefits and costs. With the motor cycle he can earn revenue of €20,000, net of petrol and maintenance costs. However, 20 per cent of that, or €4,000, must be paid in taxes, leaving Manuel with €16,000. Manuel could earn €15,600 after taxes by working at his current job, so the financial benefit to Manuel of buying the motor cycle is the difference between €16,000 and €15,600, or €400; €400 is the value of the *marginal product* of the motor cycle. Why is the motor cycle's marginal product €400? Because by using it to operate his courier service the motor cycle adds €400 to Manuel's income.

Since the motor cycle does not lose value over time, and since running and maintenance costs have already been deducted, the only remaining cost Manuel should take into account is the interest on the loan for the motor cycle. Manuel must pay 6 per cent interest on €4,000, or €240 per year. Since this financial cost is less than the financial benefit of €400, the value of the motor cycle's marginal product, Manuel should buy the motor cycle.

Manuel's decision might change if the costs and benefits of his investment in the motor cycle change, as Example 20.6 shows.

Example 20.6 Should Manuel buy a motor cycle (2)?

With all other assumptions the same as in Example 20.5, decide whether Manuel should buy the motor cycle:

a. if the interest rate is 12 per cent rather than 6 per cent

b. if the purchase price of the motor cycle is €8,000 rather than €4,000

c. if the tax rate on Manuel's net revenues is 21 per cent rather than 20 per cent

d. if the motor cycle maintenance costs are higher so that Manuel's net revenues will be €19,500 rather than €20,000

e. if Manuel can use his savings held in a bank deposit at 5 per cent interest to finance the purchase rather than borrowing the €4,000; what would Manuel's decision be if the deposit rate was 7 per cent?

In each case, Manuel must compare the financial costs and benefits of buying the motor cycle.

a. If the interest rate is 12 per cent, then the interest cost will be 12 per cent of €4,000, or €480, which exceeds the value of the motor cycle's marginal product (€400). Manuel should not buy the motor cycle.

b. If the cost of the motor cycle is €8,000 then Manuel must borrow €8,000 instead of €4,000. At 6 per cent interest, his interest cost will be €480 – too high to justify the purchase, since the value of the motor cycle's marginal product is €400.

c. If the tax rate on net revenues is 21 per cent, then Manuel must pay 21 per cent of his €20,000 net revenues, or €4,200 in taxes. After taxes, his revenues will be

€15,800, which is only €200 more than he could make working at his current job. Furthermore, the €200 will not cover the €240 in interest that Manuel would have to pay. So, again, Manuel should not buy the motor cycle.

d. If the motor cycle is less efficient than originally expected so that Manuel can earn net revenues of only €19,500, Manuel will pay €3,900 in taxes, leaving €15,600 – the same amount he could earn by staying in his office job. So in this case, the value of the motor cycle's marginal product is zero. At any interest rate greater than zero, Manuel should not buy the motor cycle.

e. If Manuel cashes in €4,000 of his savings to buy the motor cycle he gives up interest of 5 per cent, or €200 per year. Since the financial cost is less than the value of the motor cycle's marginal product of €400, Manuel should buy the motor cycle and use his savings rather than take a loan at 6 per cent. With 7 per cent interest on deposits Manuel would give up interest of €280 per year, which is less than the value of the motor cycle's marginal product but greater than the cost of taking a loan. Manuel should buy the motor cycle but finance the purchase with a loan rather than using his savings.

Exercise 20.5 Repeat Example 20.5, but assume that, over the course of the year, wear and tear reduces the resale value of the motor cycle from €4,000 to €3,800. Should Manuel buy the motor cycle?

In Example 20.5 we saw that Manuel will invest in the motor cycle if the value of its marginal product (VMP) is greater than the financing cost of the investment. With the rate of interest at 6 per cent the financing cost of borrowing the €4,000 necessary to buy the motor cycle is €240 ($0.06 \times 4,000$). Hence the investment is profitable so long as the VMP is greater than €240. More generally, if we let PK denote the purchase price of the capital and r denote the real rate of interest then the financing cost is rP_K and the investment will be profitable so long as

$$\text{VMP} > rP_K$$

Dividing both sides of this condition by the capital cost P_K gives

$$\text{VMP}/P_K > r$$

rate of return on an investment equals the value of marginal product expressed as a percentage of the purchase price

The ratio of the VMP to the purchase price is the **rate of return** on the investment. In the case of Manuel's motor cycle $P_K = €4,000$ and the VMP is €400. Hence the rate of return is $400/4,000 = 0.1$, or 10 per cent. As the rate of return exceeds the real rate of interest, 6 per cent, the investment is profitable.

Example 20.7 Should Manuel buy a motor cycle (3)?

Repeat Example 20.5, explaining Manuel's decision by comparing the rate of return on the investment with the financing cost.

a. As the financing cost of 12 per cent exceeds the 10 per cent rate of return Manuel should not buy the motor cycle.

b. As the purchase price is €8,000 the rate of return is $400/8,000 = 0.05$, or 5 per cent, which is less than the 6 per cent financing cost, Manuel should not buy the motor cycle.

c. As the value of the marginal product is only €200 the investment's rate of return is $200/4,000 = 0.05$, or 5 per cent, which is less than the 6 per cent financing cost, Manuel should not buy the motor cycle.

d. As the value of the marginal product is zero the rate of return is also zero. Manuel should not buy the motor cycle.

e. As the rate of return, 10 per cent, is greater than the financing costs of 5 or 7 per cent, Manuel should make the investment.

The examples involving Manuel and the motor cycle illustrate the main factors firms must consider when deciding whether to invest in new capital goods. On the cost side, two important factors are the *price of capital goods* and the *real interest rate*. Clearly, the more expensive new capital goods are, the more reluctant firms will be to invest in them. Buying the motor cycle was profitable for Manuel when its price was €4,000, but not when its price was €8,000.

Why is the real interest rate an important factor in investment decisions? The most straightforward case is when a firm has to borrow to purchase its new capital. The real interest rate then determines the real cost to the firm of paying back its debt. Since financing costs are a major part of the total cost of owning and operating a piece of capital, a higher real interest rate makes the purchase of capital goods less attractive to firms, all else being equal.

Increasing
Opportunity
Cost

Even if a firm does not need to borrow to buy new capital – say, because it has accumulated enough profits to buy the capital outright – the real interest rate remains an important determinant of the desirability of an investment. If a firm does not use its accumulated profits to acquire new capital, most likely it will use those profits to acquire financial assets such as bonds, which will earn the firm the real rate of interest. If the firm uses its profits to buy capital rather than to purchase a bond, it forgoes the opportunity to earn the real rate of interest on its funds. Thus the real rate of interest measures the *opportunity cost* of a capital investment. Since an increase in the real interest rate raises the opportunity cost of investing in new capital, it lowers the willingness of firms to invest, even if they do not literally need to borrow to finance new machines or equipment.

On the benefit side, the key factor in determining business investment is the *value of the marginal product* of the new capital (VMP), which should be calculated net of both operating and maintenance expenses and taxes paid on the revenues the capital generates. The ratio of the value of the marginal product to the capital cost is the *rate of return* to the investment. If the rate of return exceeds the real rate of interest the investment will be profitable. The value of the marginal product and the rate of return are affected by several factors. For example, a technological advance that allows a piece of capital to produce more goods and services would increase the value of its marginal product and rate of return, as would lower taxes on the revenues produced by the new capital. An increase in the relative price of the good or service that the capital is used to produce will also increase the value of the marginal product and, hence, the desirability of the investment. For example, if the going price for courier services were to rise then, all else being equal, investing in the motor cycle would become more profitable for Manuel.

Economic naturalist 20.2 Why has investment in computers increased so much since the 1980s?

Since about 1980, investment in new computer systems has risen sharply. While this trend is present in many countries it is especially true of the United States (see Figure 20.6). Purchases of new computers and software by American firms now exceed 2.5 per cent of GDP and amount to about 15 per cent of all private non-residential investment. Why has investment in computers increased so much?

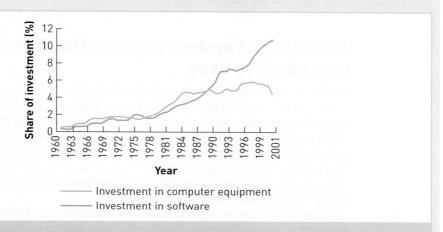

Figure 20.6 Investment in Computers and Software, 1960–2001. Investment in computer equipment and software since 1960 shown as a percentage of private non-residential investment. Computer-related investments by US firms have risen significantly since about 1980, but investment in computer equipment dropped sharply in 2000 and 2001.

Source: Bureau of Economic Analysis (http://www.bea.gov/).

Cost–Benefit Analysis

Investment in computers has increased by much more than other types of investment. Hence, the factors that affect all types of investment (such as the real interest rate and the tax rate) are not likely to be responsible for the boom. The two main causes of increased investment in computers appear to be the declining price of *computing power* and the increase in the value of the *marginal product* of computers. In recent years, the price of computing power has fallen at a precipitous rate. An industry rule of thumb is that the amount of computing power that is obtainable at a given price doubles every 18 months. As the price of computing power falls, an investment in computers becomes more and more likely to pass the *cost–benefit* test.

On the benefit side, for some years after the beginning of the computer boom economists were unable to associate the technology with significant productivity gains. Defenders of investment in computer systems argued that the improvements in goods and services computers create were particularly hard to measure. How does one quantify the value to consumers of 24/7 access to cash or the ability to make airline reservations online? Critics responded that the expected benefits of the computer revolution may have proved illusory because of problems such as user-unfriendly software and poor technical training. However, US productivity has increased noticeably since the 1990s and many people now credit the improvement to investment in computers and computer-related technologies such as the internet. As more firms become convinced that computers do add significantly to productivity and profits, the boom in computer investment can be expected to continue.

RECAP Factors that affect investment

Any of the following factors will increase the willingness of firms to invest in new capital:

1. a decline in the price of new capital goods
2. a decline in the real interest rate
3. technological improvement that raises the marginal product of capital
4. lower taxes on the revenues generated by capital
5. a higher relative price for the firm's output.

The financial system and the allocation of saving to productive uses

We have emphasised the importance of high rates of saving and investment for economic growth and increased productivity. High rates of saving and investment by themselves are not sufficient, however. A case in point is the former Soviet Union (FSU), which had very high rates of saving and investment but often used its resources very inefficiently – for example, by constructing massive but poorly designed factories that produced inferior goods at high cost. A successful economy not only saves but also uses its savings wisely by applying these limited funds to the investment projects that seem likely to be the most productive.

In the Soviet Union, a centralised bureaucracy made decisions about the allocation of saving to alternative uses. Because the bureaucrats in Moscow had relatively poor information and because they allowed themselves to be influenced by non-economic considerations such as political favouritism, they often made poor decisions. In market economies such as the United Kingdom, Germany and the United States, in contrast, savings are allocated by means of a decentralised, market-orientated financial system. In these countries the financial system consists both of financial *institutions*, such as banks, and financial *markets*, such as bond markets and stock markets.

In market economies the financial system improves the allocation of savings in at least two distinct ways. First, the financial system provides *information* to savers about which of the many possible uses of their funds are likely to prove most productive and hence pay the highest return. By evaluating the potential productivity of alternative capital investments, the financial system helps to direct savings to their best uses. Second, financial markets help savers to *share the risks* of individual investment projects. Sharing of risks protects individual savers from bearing excessive risk, while at the same time making it possible to direct savings to projects, such as the development of new technologies, which are risky but potentially very productive as well.

In the following two sections we shall briefly discuss three key components of the financial system: the banking system, the bond market and the stock market. In doing so we can elaborate on the role of the financial system as a whole in providing information about investment projects and in helping savers to share the risks of lending.

The banking system

financial intermediaries firms that extend credit to borrowers using funds raised from savers

The banking system consists of commercial banks, of which there are thousands in Europe. Commercial banks are privately owned firms that accept deposits from individuals and businesses and use those deposits to make loans. Banks are the most important example of a class of institutions called **financial intermediaries**, firms that extend credit to borrowers using funds raised from savers. Other examples of financial intermediaries are building societies and credit unions.

Why are financial intermediaries such as banks, which 'stand between' savers and investors, necessary? Why don't individual savers just lend directly to borrowers who want to invest in new capital projects? The main reason is that, through specialisation, banks and other intermediaries develop a *comparative advantage* in evaluating the quality of borrowers – the information-gathering function that we referred to a moment ago. Most savers, particularly small savers, do not have the time or the knowledge to determine for themselves which borrowers are likely to use the funds they receive most productively. In contrast, banks and other intermediaries have gained expertise in performing the information-gathering activities necessary for profitable lending, including checking out the borrower's background, determining whether the borrower's business plans make sense and monitoring the borrower's activities during the life of the loan. Because banks specialise in evaluating potential borrowers, they can perform this function at a much lower cost, and with better results, than individual savers can on their own. Banks also reduce the costs of gathering information about potential borrowers by *pooling the savings* of many individuals to make large loans. Each large loan needs to be evaluated only once, by the bank, rather than separately by each of the hundreds of individuals whose savings may be pooled to make the loan.

Banks help savers by eliminating their need to gather information about potential borrowers and by directing their savings towards higher-return, more productive investments. Banks help borrowers as well, by providing access to credit that might otherwise not be available. Unlike a large corporation, which typically has many ways to raise funds, a small business that wants to buy a new computer or remodel its offices will have few options other than going to a bank. Because the bank's lending officer has developed expertise in evaluating small business loans, and may even have an ongoing business relationship with the small-business owner, the bank will be able to gather the information it needs to make the loan at a reasonable cost. Likewise, households that want to borrow for projects such as home improvement will find few alternatives to a bank. In sum, banks' expertise at gathering information about alternative lending opportunities allows them to bring together small savers, looking for good uses for their funds, and small borrowers with worthwhile investment projects.

In addition to being able to earn a return on their savings, a second reason that people hold bank deposits is to make it easier to make payments. Most bank deposits allow the holder to write a cheque against them or draw on them using a debit card or ATM card. For many transactions, paying by cheque or debit card is more convenient than using cash. For example, it is safer to send a cheque through the post than to send cash, and paying by cheque gives you a record of the transaction, whereas a cash payment does not.

Bonds and shares

Large and well-established companies that wish to obtain funds for investment will sometimes go to banks. Unlike the typical small borrower, however, a larger firm usually has alternative ways of raising funds, notably through the corporate bond market and the stock market. We first discuss some of the mechanics of bonds and shares, and then return to the role of bond and stock markets in allocating saving.

bond a legal promise to repay a debt, usually including both the principal amount and regular interest payments

principal amount the amount originally lent

coupon rate the interest rate promised when a bond is issued

coupon payments regular interest payments made to the bondholder

Bonds

A **bond** is a legal promise to repay a debt, usually including both the **principal amount**, which is the amount originally lent, and regular interest payments. The promised interest rate when a bond is issued is called the **coupon rate** and the regular interest payments made to the bondholder are called coupon payments. The **coupon payment** of a bond that pays interest annually equals the coupon rate times the principal amount of the bond. For example, if the principal amount of a bond is €1,000,000 and its coupon rate is 5 per cent, then the annual coupon payment made to the holder of the bond is 0.05 times €1,000,000, or €50,000.

Corporations and governments frequently raise funds by issuing bonds and selling them to savers. The coupon rate that a newly issued bond has to promise in order to be attractive to savers depends on a number of factors, including the bond's term, its credit risk and its tax treatment. The *term* of a bond is the length of time before the debt it represents is fully repaid, a period that can range from 30 days to 30 years or more. Generally lenders will demand a higher interest rate to lend for a longer term. *Credit risk* is the risk that the borrower will go bankrupt and thus not repay the loan. A borrower that is viewed as 'risky' will have to pay a higher interest rate to compensate lenders for taking the chance of losing all or part of their financial investment. For example, so-called 'high-yield bonds', less formally known as 'junk bonds', are bonds issued by firms judged to be risky by credit-rating agencies; these bonds pay higher interest rates than bonds issued by companies thought to be less risky.

Bonds also differ in their *tax treatment*. For example, in some countries interest paid on bonds issued by local governments may be exempt from taxes, or taxed at a low rate. Because of this tax advantage, lenders are willing to accept a lower interest rate on these bonds.

Bondholders are not required to hold bonds until *maturity*, the time at which they are supposed to be repaid by the issuer, but are always free to sell their bonds in the *bond market*, an organised market run by professional bond traders. The market value of a particular bond at any given point in time is called the *price* of the bond. As it turns out, there is a close relationship between the price of a bond at a given point of time and the *interest rate* prevailing in financial markets at that time, as illustrated by Example 20.8.

Example 20.8 Bond prices and interest rates

On 1 January 2004, Tanya purchases a newly issued, two-year government bond with a principal amount of €1,000. The coupon rate on the bond is 5 per cent, paid annually. Hence Tanya, or whoever owns the bond at the time, will receive a coupon payment of €50 (5 per cent of €1,000) on 1 January 2005, and €1,050 (a €50 coupon payment plus repayment of the original €1,000 lent) on 1 January 2006.

On 1 January 2005, after receiving her first year's coupon payment, Tanya decides to sell her bond to raise the funds to take a vacation. She offers her bond for sale in the bond market. How much can she expect to get for her 'used' bond if the prevailing interest rate in the bond market is 6 per cent? If the prevailing interest rate is 4 per cent?

As we mentioned, the price of a 'used' bond at any point in time depends on the prevailing interest rate. Suppose first that, on 1 January 2005, when Tanya takes her bond to the bond market, the prevailing interest rate on newly issued one-year bonds is 6 per cent. Would another saver be willing to pay Tanya the full €1,000 principal amount of her bond? No, because the purchaser of Tanya's bond will receive €1,050 in one year, when the bond matures; whereas if he uses his €1,000 to buy a new one-year bond paying 6 per cent interest, he will receive €1,060 (€1,000 principal repayment plus €60 interest) in one year. So Tanya's bond is not worth €1,000 to another saver.

How much would another saver be willing to pay for Tanya's bond? Since newly issued one-year bonds pay a 6 per cent return, he will buy Tanya's bond only at a price that allows him to earn at least that return. As the holder of Tanya's bond will receive €1,050 (€1,000 principal plus €50 interest) in one year, the price for her bond that allows the purchaser to earn a 6 per cent return must satisfy the equation

$$\text{Bond price} \times 1.06 = €1,050$$

Solving the equation for the bond price, we find that Tanya's bond will sell for €1,050/1.06, or just under €991. To check this result, note that in one year the purchaser of the bond will receive €1,050 or €59 more than he paid. His rate of return is €59/€991, or 6 per cent, as expected.

What if the prevailing interest rate had been 4 per cent rather than 6 per cent? Then the price of Tanya's bond would satisfy the relationship bond price × 1.04 = €1,050, implying that the price of her bond would be €1,050/1.04, or almost €1,010. What happens if the interest rate when Tanya wants to sell is 5 per cent, the same as it was when she originally bought the bond? You should show that in this case the bond would sell at its face value of €1,000.

This example illustrates a general principle, that *bond prices and interest rates are inversely related*. When the interest rate being paid on newly issued bonds rises, the price that financial investors are willing to pay for existing bonds falls, and vice versa.

Exercise 20.6 Three-year government bonds are issued at a face value (principal amount) of 100 and a coupon rate of 7 per cent, interest payable at the end of each year. One year prior to the maturation of these bonds, a newspaper headline reads, 'Bad Economic News Causes Prices of Bonds to Plunge', and the story reveals that these three-year bonds have fallen in price to 96. What has happened to interest rates? What is the one-year interest rate at the time of the newspaper story?

Issuing bonds is one means by which a company or a government can obtain funds from savers. Another important way of raising funds, but one restricted to corporations, is by issuing shares to the public.

Shares

A **share (or equity)** is a claim to partial ownership of a firm. For example, if a company has 1 million shares outstanding, ownership of one share is equivalent to ownership of one-millionth of the company. Shareholders receive returns on their shares in two forms. First, shareholders receive a regular payment called a **dividend** for each share they own. Dividends are determined by the firm's management and usually depend on the firm's recent profits. Second, shareholders receive returns in the form of *capital gains* when the price of their share increases.

share (or equity) a claim to partial ownership of a firm

dividend a regular payment received by shareholders for each share that they own

Prices of shares are determined through trading on a stock exchange, such as the London or Frankfurt stock exchanges. A share's price rises and falls as the demand for the share changes. Demand for shares in turn depends on factors such as news about the prospects of the company. For example, the share price of a pharmaceutical company that announces the discovery of an important new drug is likely to rise on the announcement because financial investors expect the company to become more profitable in the future. Example 20.9 illustrates numerically some key factors that affect share prices.

Example 20.9 How much should you pay for a share of EuroFly.com?

You have the opportunity to buy shares in a new low-cost airline called EuroFly.com, which plans to sell cheap flights over the internet. Your stockbroker estimates that the company will pay €1.00 per share in dividends a year from now, and that in a year the market price of the company will be €80.00 per share. Assuming that you accept your broker's estimates as accurate, what is the most that you should be willing to pay today per share of EuroFly.com? How does your answer change if you expect a €5.00 dividend? If you expect a €1.00 dividend but an €84.00 share price in one year?

Based on your broker's estimates, you conclude that in one year each share of EuroFly.com you own will be worth €81.00 in your pocket – the €1.00 dividend plus the €80.00 you could get by reselling the shares. Finding the maximum price you would pay for the share today therefore boils down to asking how much would you invest today to have €81.00 a year from today. Answering this question in turn requires one more piece of information, which is the expected rate of return that you require in order to be willing to buy shares in this company.

How would you determine your required rate of return to hold shares in EuroFly.com? For the moment, let's imagine that you are not too worried about the potential riskiness of the share, either because you think that it is a 'sure thing' or because you are a devil-may-care type who is not bothered by risk. In that case, your required rate of return to hold EuroFly.com should be about the same as you can get on other financial investments, such as government bonds. The available return on other financial investments gives the *opportunity cost* of your funds. So, for example, if the interest rate currently being offered by government bonds is 6 per cent, you should be willing to accept a 6 per cent return to hold EuroFly.com as well. In that case, the maximum price you would pay today for a share of EuroFly.com satisfies the equation

$$\text{Share price} \times 1.06 = \text{€81.00}$$

This equation defines the share price you should be willing to pay if you are willing to accept a 6 per cent return over the next year. Solving this equation yields share price = €81.00/1.06 = €76.42. If you buy EuroFly.com for €76.42, then your return over the year will be (€81.00 − €76.42)/€76.42 = €4.58/€71.42 = 6 per cent, which is the rate of return you required to buy the shares.

If instead the dividend is expected to be €5.00, then the total benefit of holding EuroFly.com shares in one year, equal to the expected dividend plus the expected price, is €5.00 + €80.00, or €85.00. Assuming again that you are willing to accept a 6 per cent return to hold EuroFly.com, the price you are willing to pay today satisfies the relationship share price × 1.06 = €85.00. Solving this equation for the share price yields €85.00/1.06 = €80.19. Comparing with the previous case we see that a higher expected dividend in the future increases the value of EuroFly.com shares today. That's why good news about the future prospects of a company – such as the announcement by a pharmaceutical company that it has discovered a useful new drug – affects its share price immediately.

If the expected future price of the share is €84.00, with the dividend at €1.00, then the value of holding the share in one year is once again €85.00, and the calculation is the same as the previous one. Again, the price you should be willing to pay for the share is €80.19.

These examples show that an increase in the future dividend or in the future expected share price raises the share price today, whereas an increase in the return a saver requires to hold the share lowers today's share price. Since we expect required returns in the stock market to be closely tied to market interest rates, this last result implies that increases in interest rates tend to depress share prices as well as bond prices.

Our examples also took the future share price as given. But what determines the future share price? Just as today's share price depends on the dividend that shareholders expect to receive this year and the share price a year from now, the share price a year from now depends on the dividend expected for next year and the share price two years from now, and so on. Ultimately, then, today's share price is affected not only by the dividend expected this year but by future dividends as well. A company's ability to pay dividends depends on its earnings. Thus, as we noted in the example of the pharmaceutical company that announces the discovery of a new drug, news about future earnings – even earnings quite far in the future – is likely to affect a company's share price immediately.

Exercise 20.7   As in Example 20.9, you expect a share of EuroFly.com to be worth €80.00 per share in one year, and also to pay a dividend of €1.00 in one year. What should you be willing to pay for the share today if the prevailing interest rate, equal to your required rate of return, is 4 per cent? What if the interest rate is 8 per cent? In general, how would you expect share prices to react if economic news arrives which implies that interest rates will rise in the very near future?

In Example 20.9 we assumed that you were willing to accept a return of 6 per cent to hold EuroFly.com, the same return that you could get on a government bond. However, financial investments in the stock market are quite risky in that returns to holding shares can be highly variable and unpredictable. For example, although you expect a share of EuroFly.com to be worth €80.00 in one year, you also realise that there is a chance it might sell as low as €50.00 or as high as €110.00 per share. Most financial investors dislike risk and unpredictability, and thus have a higher required rate of return for holding risky assets like shares than for holding relatively safe assets such as government bonds. The difference between the required rate of return to hold risky assets and the rate of return on safe assets, like government bonds, is called the **risk premium**. Example 20.10 illustrates the effect on share prices of financial investors' dislike of risk.

risk premium the rate of return that financial investors require to hold risky assets minus the rate of return on safe assets

Example 20.10 Riskiness and share prices

Continuing Example 20.9, suppose that EuroFly.com is expected to pay a €1.00 dividend and have a market price of €80.00 per share in one year. The interest rate on government bonds is 6 per cent per year. However, to be willing to hold a risky asset like a share of EuroFly.com, you require an expected return four percentage points higher than the rate paid by safe assets such as government bonds (a risk premium of 4 per cent). Hence you require a 10 per cent expected return to hold EuroFly.com. What is the most you would be willing to pay for the share now? What do you conclude about the relationship between perceived riskiness and share prices?

As a share of EuroFly.com is expected to pay €81.00 in one year and the required return is 10 per cent, we have share price × 1.10 = €81.00. Solving for the share price, we find the price to be €81.00/1.10 = €73.64, less than the price of €76.42 we found when there was no risk premium and the required rate of return was 6 per cent (Example 20.9). We conclude that financial investors' dislike of risk, and the resulting risk premium, lowers the prices of risky assets like shares.

RECAP Factors affecting share prices

- An increase in expected *future dividends* or in the expected *future market price* of a share raises the current price of the share.
- An increase in *interest rates*, implying an increase in the required rate of return to hold shares, lowers the current price of shares.
- An increase in *perceived riskiness*, as reflected in an increase in the risk premium, lowers the current price of shares.

Bond markets, stock markets and the allocation of saving

Like banks, bond markets and stock markets provide a means of channelling funds from savers to borrowers with productive investment opportunities. For example, a company that is planning a capital investment but does not want to borrow from a bank has two other options: it can issue new bonds, to be sold to savers in the bond market, or it can issue new shares in itself, which are then sold in the stock market. The proceeds from the sales of new bonds or shares are then available to the firm to finance its capital investment.

How do share and bond markets help to ensure that available savings are devoted to the most productive uses? As we mentioned earlier, two important functions served by these markets are gathering information about prospective borrowers and helping savers to share the risks of lending.

The informational role of bond and stock markets

Savers and their financial advisers know that to get the highest possible returns on their financial investments, they must find the potential borrowers with the most profitable opportunities. This knowledge provides a powerful incentive to scrutinise potential borrowers carefully.

For example, companies considering a new issue of shares or bonds know that their recent performance and plans for the future will be carefully studied by financial investors and professional analysts working for specialised firms in cities such as London and New York, which are noted for their expertise. If the analysts and other potential purchasers have doubts about the future profitability of the firm, they will offer a relatively low price for the newly issued shares or they will demand a high interest rate on newly issued bonds. Knowing this, a company will be reluctant to go to the bond or stock market for financing unless its management is confident that it can convince financial investors that the firm's planned use of the funds will be profitable. Thus the ongoing search by savers and their financial advisers for high returns leads the bond and stock markets to direct funds to the uses that appear most likely to be productive.

Risk-sharing and diversification

Many highly promising investment projects are also quite risky. The successful development of a new drug to lower cholesterol could create billions of euros in profits for a drug company; but if the drug turns out to be less effective than some others on the market, none of the development costs will be recouped. An individual who lends her life savings to help finance the development of the anti-cholesterol drug may enjoy a handsome return but also takes the chance of losing everything. Savers are generally reluctant to take large risks, so without some means of reducing the risk faced by each saver it might be very hard for the company to find the funds to develop the new drug.

diversification the practice of spreading one's wealth over a variety of different financial investments to reduce overall risk

Bond and stock markets help reduce risk by giving savers a means to *diversify* their financial investments. **Diversification** is the practice of spreading one's wealth over a variety of different financial investments to reduce overall risk. The idea of diversification follows from the adage that 'you shouldn't put all your eggs in one basket'. Rather than putting all of her savings in one very risky project, a financial investor will find it much safer to allocate a small amount of savings to each of a large number of shares and bonds. That way, if some financial assets fall in value, there is a good chance that others will rise in value, with gains offsetting losses. Example 20.11 illustrates the benefits of diversification.

Example 20.11 The benefits of diversification

Hugh has €1,000 to invest and is considering two shares, the Smith Umbrella Company and the Jones Suntan Lotion Company. Suppose the price of each share depends on how good the summer is. If the summer turns out to be cold and wet the price of Smith Umbrella shares will rise by 10 per cent but will remain unchanged if the summer is hot and sunny. Likewise, the price of Jones Suntan shares is expected to rise by 10 per cent if the summer is good but will remain unchanged if it is bad. The chance of a good summer is 50 per cent, and the chance of bad summer is also 50 per cent. How should Hugh invest his €1,000?

If Hugh were to invest all his €1,000 in Smith Umbrella, he has a 50 per cent chance of earning a 10 per cent return, in the event of a bad summer, and a 50 per cent chance of earning zero, if the summer is good.

His average, or expected, return is 50 per cent times 10 per cent plus 50 per cent times zero, or 5 per cent. Similarly, an investment in Jones Suntan yields 10 per cent return half of the time, when it's sunny, and 0 per cent return the other half of the time, when it rains, for an average return of 5 per cent.

Although Hugh can earn an *average* return of 5 per cent in either share, investing in only one share or the other is quite risky, since the actual return he receives varies widely depending on whether there is rain or shine. Can Hugh *guarantee* himself a 5 per cent return, avoiding the uncertainty and risk? Yes, all he has to do is put €500 into each of the two shares. If it rains, he will earn €50 on his Smith Umbrella share and nothing on his Jones Suntan. If it's sunny, he will earn nothing on Smith Umbrella but €50 on Jones Suntan. Rain or shine, he is guaranteed to earn €50 – a 5 per cent return – without risk.

The existence of bond markets and stock markets makes it easy for savers to diversify by putting a small amount of their savings into each of a wide variety of different financial assets, each of which represents a share of a particular company or investment project. From society's point of view, diversification makes it possible for risky but worthwhile projects to obtain funding, without individual savers having to bear too much risk.

Saving, investment and the real rate of interest

Saving and investment are determined by different forces. Ultimately, though, in an economy without international borrowing and lending, *national saving must equal investment*. The supply of savings (by households, firms and the government) and the demand for savings (by firms that want to purchase or construct new capital) are equalised through the workings of *financial markets*. Figure 20.7 illustrates this process. Quantities of national saving and investment are measured on the horizontal axis; the real interest rate is shown on the vertical axis. As we shall see, in the market for saving, the real interest rate functions as the 'price'.

In Figure 20.7 the supply of savings is shown by the upward-sloping curve marked S. This curve shows the quantity of national saving that households, firms and the government is willing to supply at each value of the real interest rate. The saving curve is upward-sloping because empirical evidence suggests that increases in the real interest rate stimulate saving. The demand for saving is given by the downward-sloping curve marked I. This curve shows the quantity of investment in new capital that firms would choose and hence the amount they would need to borrow in financial markets, at each value of the real interest rate. Because higher real interest rates raise the cost of borrowing and reduce firms' willingness to invest, the demand for saving curve is downward-sloping.

Putting aside the possibility of borrowing from foreigners, a country can invest only those resources that its savers make available. In equilibrium, then, desired investment (the demand for savings) and desired national saving (the supply of savings) must be equal. As Figure 20.7 suggests, desired saving is equated with desired investment through adjustments in the real interest rate, which functions as the 'price' of saving. The movements of the real interest rate clear the market for savings in much the same way as the price of apples clears the market for apples. In Figure 20.7, the real interest rate that clears the market for saving is r, the real interest rate that corresponds to the intersection of the supply and demand curves.

The forces that push the real interest rate towards its equilibrium level are similar to the forces that lead to equilibrium in any other supply and demand situation.

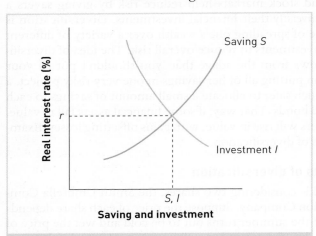

Figure 20.7 The Supply of and Demand for Savings. Savings are supplied by households, firms and the government, and demanded by borrowers wishing to invest in new capital goods. The supply of saving (S) increases with the real interest rate, and the demand for saving by investors (I) decreases with the real interest rate. In financial market equilibrium, the real interest rate takes the value that equates the quantity of saving supplied and demanded.

Equilibrium Suppose, for example, that the real interest rate exceeded r. At a higher real interest rate, savers would provide more funds than firms would want to invest. As lenders (savers) competed among themselves to attract borrowers (investors), the real interest rate would be bid down. The real interest rate would fall until it equalled r, the only interest rate at which both borrowers and lenders are satisfied, and no opportunities are left unexploited in the financial market (recall Chapter 3's *Equilibrium Principle*). What would happen if the real interest rate were *lower* than r?

Changes in factors *other than the real interest rate* that affect the supply of or demand for saving will shift the curves, leading to a new equilibrium in the financial market. Changes in the real interest rate cannot shift the supply or demand curves, just as a change in the price of apples cannot shift the supply or demand for apples, because the effects of the real interest rate on savings are already incorporated in the slopes of the curves. Examples 20.12 and 20.13 will illustrate the use of the supply and demand model of financial markets.

Example 20.12 The effects of new technology

Exciting new technologies have been introduced in recent years, ranging from the internet to new applications of genetics. A number of these technologies appear to have great commercial potential. How does the introduction of new technologies affect saving, investment and the real interest rate?

The introduction of any new technology with the potential for commercial application creates profit opportunities for those who can bring the fruits of the technology to the public. In economists' language, the *technological breakthrough* raises the marginal product and the rate of return of new capital. Figure 20.8 shows the effects of a technological breakthrough, with a resulting increase in the marginal product of capital. At any given real interest rate, an increase in the marginal product of capital makes firms more eager to invest. Thus, the advent of the new technology causes the demand for saving to shift upwards and to the right, from I to I'.

At the new equilibrium point F, investment and national saving are higher than before, as is the real interest rate, which rises from r to r'. The rise in the real interest rate reflects the increased demand for funds by investors as they race to apply the new technologies. Because of the incentive of higher real returns, saving increases as well. Example 20.13 examines the effect of changing fiscal policies on the market for saving.

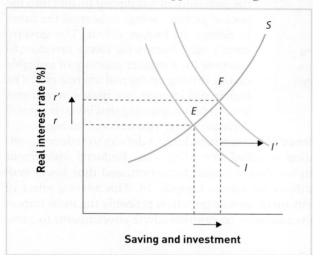

Figure 20.8 The Effects of a New Technology on National Saving and Investment. A technological breakthrough raises the marginal product of new capital goods, increasing desired investment and the demand for savings. The real interest rate rises, as do national saving and investment.

Example 20.13 An increase in the government budget deficit

Suppose the government increases its spending without raising taxes, thereby increasing its budget deficit (or reducing its budget surplus). How will this decision affect national saving, investment and the real interest rate?

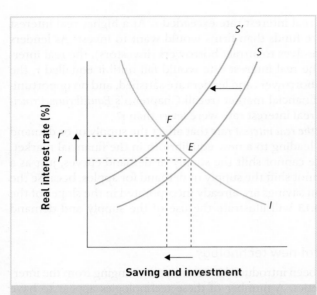

Figure 20.9 The Effects on National Saving and Investment of an Increase in the Government Budget Deficit. An increase in the government budget deficit reduces the supply of saving, raising the real interest rate and lowering investment. The tendency of increased government deficits to reduce investment in new capital is called *crowding out*.

National saving includes both private saving (saving by households and businesses) and public saving, which is equivalent to the government budget surplus. An increase in the government budget deficit (or a decline in the surplus) reduces public saving. Assuming that private saving does not change, the reduction in public saving will reduce national saving as well.

Figure 20.9 shows the effect of the increased government budget deficit on the market for saving and investment. At any real interest rate, a larger deficit reduces national saving, causing the saving curve to shift to the left, from S to S'. At the new equilibrium point F, the real interest rate is higher at r', and both national saving and investment are lower. In economic terms, the government has dipped further into the pool of private savings to borrow the funds to finance its budget deficit. The government's extra borrowing forces investors to compete for a smaller quantity of available saving, driving up the real interest rate. The higher real interest rate makes investment less attractive, assuring that investment will decrease along with national saving.

crowding out the tendency of increased government deficits to reduce investment spending

The tendency of government budget deficits to reduce investment spending is called **crowding out**. Reduced investment spending implies slower capital formation, and thus lower economic growth, as we saw in Chapter 19. This adverse effect of budget deficits on economic growth is probably the most important cost of deficits, and a major reason why economists advise governments to minimise their deficits.

Exercise 20.8 Suppose the general public become less concerned about the future and save less at each rate of interest. How will the change in public attitudes affect the rate of capital formation and economic growth?

At the national level, a high saving rate leads to greater investment in new capital goods and thus higher standards of living. At the individual or family level, a high saving rate promotes the accumulation of wealth and the achievement of economic security. In this chapter we have studied some of the factors that underlie saving and investment decisions.

Summary

- In general, *saving* equals current income minus spending on current needs; the *saving rate* is the percentage of income that is saved. *Wealth*, or net worth, equals the market value of assets (real or financial items of value) minus liabilities (debts). Saving is a *flow*, being measured in euros per unit of time; wealth is a *stock*, measured in euros at a point in time. Just as the amount of water in a bathtub changes according to the rate at which water flows in, so the stock of wealth increases at the saving rate. Wealth also increases if the value of existing assets rises (*capital gains*) and decreases if the value of existing assets falls (*capital losses*).

- Individuals and households save for a variety of reasons, including *life-cycle* objectives; the need to be prepared for an emergency (*precautionary saving*); and the desire to leave an inheritance (*bequest saving*). The amount people save is also affected by the real interest rate, which is the 'reward' for saving. Evidence suggests that higher real interest rates lead to modest increases in saving. Saving can also be affected by psychological factors, such as the degree of self-control and the desire to consume at the level of one's neighbours (demonstration effects).

- The saving of an entire country is *national saving*, S. National saving is defined by $S = Y - C - G$, where Y represents total output or income, C equals consumption spending, and G equals government purchases of goods and services. National saving can be broken up into private saving (or $Y - T - C$) and public saving (or $T - G$), where T stands for taxes paid to the government less transfer payments and interest paid by the government to the private sector. Private saving can be further broken down into household saving and business saving. In most countries, the bulk of national saving is done by the private sector.

- *Public saving* is equivalent to the government budget surplus, $T - G$; if the government runs a budget deficit, then public saving is negative.

- *Investment* is the purchase or construction of new capital goods, including housing. Firms will invest in new capital goods if the benefits of doing so outweigh the costs. Two factors that determine the cost of investment are the price of new capital goods and the real interest rate. The higher the real interest rate, the more expensive it is to borrow, and the less likely firms are to invest. The benefit of investment is the value of the marginal product of new capital, which depends on factors such as the productivity of new capital goods, the taxes levied on the revenues they generate and the relative price of the firm's output.

- Besides balancing saving and investment in the aggregate, financial markets and institutions play the important role of allocating saving to the *most productive investment projects*. The financial system improves the allocation of saving in two ways. First, it provides information to savers about which of the many possible uses of their funds are likely to prove most productive, and hence pay the highest return. For example, *financial intermediaries* such as banks develop expertise in evaluating prospective borrowers, making it unnecessary for small savers to do that on their own. Similarly, share and bond analysts evaluate the business prospects of a company issuing shares or bonds, which determines the price the share will sell for or the interest rate the company will have to offer on its bond. Second, financial markets help savers share the risks of lending by permitting them to *diversify* their financial investments. Individual savers often hold shares through *mutual funds*, a type of financial intermediary that reduces risk by holding many different financial assets. By reducing the risk faced by any one saver, financial markets allow risky but potentially very productive projects to be funded.

- Corporations that do not wish to borrow from banks can obtain finance by issuing bonds or shares. A *bond* is a legal promise to repay a debt, including both the *principal amount* and regular interest payments. The prices of existing bonds decline when interest rates rise. A *share* is a

▶
claim to partial ownership of a firm. The price of a share depends positively on the *dividend* the share is expected to pay and on the expected future price of the share, and negatively on the rate of return required by financial investors to hold the share. The required rate of return in turn is the sum of the return on safe assets and the additional return required to compensate financial investors for the riskiness of shares, called the *risk premium*.

■ In the absence of international borrowing or lending, the supply of and demand for national saving must be equal. The *supply* of national saving depends on the saving decisions of households and businesses and the fiscal policies of the government (which determine public saving). The *demand* for saving is the amount business firms want to invest in new capital. The real interest rate, which is the 'price' of borrowed funds, changes to equate the supply of and demand for national saving. Factors that affect the supply of or demand for saving will change saving, investment and the equilibrium real interest rate. For example, an increase in the government budget deficit will reduce national saving and investment, and raise the equilibrium real interest rate. The tendency of government budget deficits to reduce investment is called *crowding out*.

Review questions

1. Explain the relationship between saving and wealth, using the concepts of flows and stocks. Is saving the only means by which wealth can increase? Explain.

2. Give three basic motivations for saving. Illustrate each with an example. What other factors would psychologists cite as being possibly important for saving?

3. Define *national saving*, relating your definition to the general concept of saving.

4. Why are household saving rates in Europe higher than in the United States?

5. Why do increases in real interest rates reduce the quantity of saving demanded? (**Hint:** Who are the 'demanders' of saving?)

6. Give two ways that the financial system can help to improve the allocation of savings. Illustrate with examples.

7. Judy plans to sell a bond that matures in one year and has a principal value of €1,000. Can she expect to receive €1,000 in the bond market for the bond? Explain.

8. Share prices surge but the prices of government bonds remain stable. What can you infer from the behaviour of bond prices about the possible causes of the increase in share values?

9. Name one factor that could increase the supply of saving and one that could increase the demand for saving. Show the effects of each on saving, investment and the real interest rate.

connect Problems

1. a. Corey has a mountain bike worth €300, a credit card debt of €150, €200 in cash, a Paul McCartney autograph worth €400, €1,200 in a bank account and an electricity bill due for €250. Construct Corey's balance sheet and calculate his net worth. For parts (b)–(d), explain how the event affects Corey's assets, liabilities and wealth.

   b. Corey discovers that his Paul McCartney autograph is a worthless forgery.

   c. Corey uses €150 from his wages to pay off his credit card balance. The remainder of his earnings is spent.

d. Corey writes a €150 cheque on his bank account to pay off his credit card balance.

Of the events in parts (b)–(d), which, if any, correspond to saving on Corey's part?

2. State whether each of the following is a stock or a flow, and explain.

 a. The gross domestic product (GDP)

 b. National saving

 c. The value of the French housing stock on 1 January 2003

 d. The amount of British currency in circulation as of this morning

 e. The government budget deficit

 f. The quantity of outstanding government debt on 1 January 2003

3. Ellie and Vince are a married couple, both with university degrees and jobs. How would you expect each of the following events to affect the amount they save each month? Explain your answers in terms of the basic motivations for saving.

 a. Ellie learns she is pregnant.

 b. Vince reads in the paper about possible layoffs in his industry.

 c. Vince had hoped that his parents would lend financial assistance towards the couple's planned purchase of a house, but he learns that they can't afford it.

 d. Ellie announces that she would like to go to law school in the next few years.

 e. A boom in the stock market greatly increases the value of the couple's retirement funds.

 f. Vince and Ellie agree that they would like to leave a substantial amount to local charities in their wills.

4. Suppose that the government introduces a new special savings scheme (SSS) to encourage households to save more. An individual who deposits part of current earnings in an SSS does not have to pay income taxes on the earnings deposited, nor are any income taxes charged on the interest earned by the funds in the SSS. However, when the funds are withdrawn from the SSS, the full amount withdrawn is treated as income and is taxed at the individual's current income tax rate. In contrast, an individual depositing in a non-SSS account has to pay income taxes on the funds deposited and on interest earned in each year but does not have to pay taxes on withdrawals from the account. Another feature of SSSs that differs from a standard saving account is that funds deposited in an SSS cannot be withdrawn prior to retirement, except upon payment of a substantial penalty.

 a. Greg, who is five years from retirement, receives a €10,000 bonus at work. He is trying to decide whether to save this extra income in an SSS account or in a regular savings account. Both accounts earn 5 per cent nominal interest, and Greg is in the 30 per cent tax bracket in every year (including his retirement year). Compare the amounts that Greg will have in five years under each of the two saving strategies, net of all taxes. Is the SSS a good deal for Greg?

 b. Would you expect the availability of SSSs to increase the amount that households save? Discuss in light of (i) the response of saving to changes in the real interest rate and (ii) psychological theories of saving.

5. For parts (a)–(c) below, use the economic data given to find national saving, private saving, public saving and the national saving rate.

a. Household saving = 200 Business saving = 400
   Government purchases of goods and services = 100
   Government transfers and interest payments = 100
   Tax collections = 150 GDP = 2,200

b. GDP = 6,000 Tax collections = 1,200
   Government transfers and interest payments = 400
   Consumption expenditures = 4,500
   Government budget surplus = 100

c. Consumption expenditures = 4,000 Investment = 1,000
   Government purchases = 1,000 Net exports = 0
   Tax collections = 1,500
   Government transfers and interest payments = 500

6. Ellie and Vince are trying to decide whether to purchase a new home. The house they want is priced at €200,000. Annual expenses such as maintenance, taxes and insurance equal 4 per cent of the house's value. If properly maintained, the house's real value is not expected to change. The real interest rate in the economy is 6 per cent, and Ellie and Vince can qualify to borrow the full amount of the purchase price (for simplicity, assume no down payment) at that rate.

   a. Ellie and Vince would be willing to pay €1,500 monthly rent to live in a house of the same quality as the one they are thinking about purchasing. Should they buy the house?

   b. Does the answer to part (a) change if they are willing to pay €2,000 monthly rent?

   c. Does the answer to part (a) change if the real interest rate is 4 per cent instead of 6 per cent?

   d. Does the answer to part (a) change if the developer offers to sell Ellie and Vince the house for €150,000?

   e. Why do home-building companies dislike high interest rates?

7. The builder of a new cinema complex is trying to decide how many screens she wants. The table below shows her estimates of the number of patrons the complex will attract each year, depending on the number of screens available.

Number of screens	Total number of patrons
1	40,000
2	75,000
3	105,000
4	130,000
5	150,000

After paying the movie distributors and meeting all other non-interest expenses, the owner expects to net €2.00 per ticket sold. Construction costs are €1,000,000 per screen.

   a. Draw up a table showing the value of marginal product for screen 1–screen 5. What property is illustrated by the behaviour of marginal products?

   b. How many screens will be built if the real interest rate is 5.5 per cent?

   c. If the real interest rate is 7.5 per cent?

   d. If the real interest rate is 10 per cent?

   e. If the real interest rate is 5.5 per cent, how far would construction costs have to fall before the builder would be willing to build a five-screen complex?

8. Simon purchases a bond, newly issued by the Amalgamated Corporation, for €1,000. The bond pays €60 to its holder at the end of the first and second years, and pays €1,060 upon its maturity at the end of the third year.

    a. What are the principal amount, the term, the coupon rate and the coupon payment for Simon's bond?

    b. After receiving the second coupon payment (at the end of the second year), Simon decides to sell his bond in the bond market. What price can he expect for his bond if the one-year interest rate at that time is 3 per cent? 8 per cent? 10 per cent?

    c. Can you think of a reason that the price of Simon's bond after two years might fall below €1,000, even though the market interest rate equals the coupon rate?

9. Shares in Brothers Grimm plc, manufacturers of gingerbread houses, are expected to pay a dividend of €5.00 in one year and to sell for €100 per share at that time. How much should you be willing to pay today per share of Grimm:

    a. if the safe rate of interest is 5 per cent and you believe that investing in Grimm carries no risk?

    b. if the safe rate of interest is 10 per cent and you believe that investing in Grimm carries no risk?

    c. if the safe rate of interest is 5 per cent but your risk premium is 3 per cent?

    d. Repeat parts (a)–(c), assuming that Grimm is not expected to pay a dividend but that the expected price is unchanged.

10. For each of the following scenarios, use supply and demand analysis to predict the resulting changes in the real interest rate, national saving and investment. Show all your diagrams.

    a. The legislature passes a 10 per cent investment tax credit. Under this programme, for every €100 that a firm spends on new capital equipment, it receives an extra €10 in tax refunds from the government.

    b. A reduction in military spending moves the government's budget from deficit into surplus.

    c. A new generation of computer-controlled machines becomes available. These machines produce manufactured goods much more quickly and with fewer defects.

    d. The government raises its tax on corporate profits. Other tax changes are also made, such that the government's deficit remains unchanged.

    e. Concerns about job security raise precautionary saving.

    f. New environmental regulations increase firms' costs of operating capital.

LearningCentre Online

To help you grasp the key concepts of this chapter check out the extra resources posted on the Online Learning Centre. There are chapter summaries, self-test questions, an interactive graphing tool, weblinks and a glossary, all for free!

Visit the Online Learning Centre at: www.mcgraw-hill.co.uk/textbooks/mcdowell for information on accessing all of these resources.

8. Simon purchases a bond, newly issued by the Amalgamated Corporation, for £1,000. The bond pays £60 to its holder at the end of the first and second years, and pays £1,060 upon its maturity at the end of the third year.

   a. What are the principal amount, the term, the coupon rate and the coupon payment on Simon's bond?

   b. After receiving the second coupon payment (at the end of the second year), Simon decides to sell his bond in the bond market. What price can he expect for his bond if the one-year interest rate at that time is 3 per cent? 8 per cent?

   c. Can you think of a reason that the price of Simon's bond after two years might fall below £1,000 even though the market interest rate equals the coupon rate?

9. Shares in Brothers Grimm plc, manufacturers of gingerbread houses, are expected to pay a dividend of £5.00 in one year and to sell for £100 per share at that time. How much should you be willing to pay today per share of Grimm?

   a. if the safe rate of interest is 5 per cent and you believe that investing in Grimm carries no risk.

   b. if the safe rate of interest is 10 per cent and you believe that investing in Grimm carries no risk.

   c. if the safe rate of interest is 5 per cent but your risk premium is 3 per cent.

   d. Repeat parts (a)–(c), assuming that Grimm is not expected to pay a dividend but that the expected price is unchanged.

10. For each of the following scenarios, use supply and demand analysis to predict the resulting changes in the real interest rate, national saving and investment. Show all your diagrams.

    a. The legislature passes a 10 per cent investment tax credit. Under this programme, for every £100 that a firm spends on new capital equipment it receives an extra £10 in tax funds from the government.

    b. A reduction in military spending moves the government's budget from deficit into surplus.

    c. A new generation of computer-controlled machines becomes available. These machines produce manufactured goods much more quickly and with lower defects.

    d. The government raises its tax on corporate profits. Other tax changes are also made, such that the government's deficit remains unchanged.

    e. Concerns about job security raise precautionary saving.

    f. New environmental regulations increase firms' costs of operating capital.

Part 7

The Economy in the Short Run

In previous chapters we have seen that over long periods of time the economy's average rate of growth is the crucial determinant of living standards. But short-term fluctuations in the economy's growth rate also affect economic welfare. In particular, periods of slow or negative economic growth, known as *recessions*, may create significant economic hardship and dissatisfaction. Recessions are periods of below-average economic growth and, for many people, especially those who lose their jobs, they are periods in which living standards may actually fall. In Part 7 we shall explore the causes of short-term fluctuations in key economic variables, including output, unemployment and inflation, and the options available to policy makers for stabilising the economy.

Chapter 21 sets the scene for our study of recessions, and expansions and introduces the basic Keynesian model, which focuses on fluctuations in spending, or *aggregate demand*, as the key source of short-run fluctuations in aggregate output and employment. Chapter 22 introduces the concept of the economy's money supply. It explains how money is created and how the economy's stock of money and interest rates are controlled by the central bank. Chapter 23 integrates money and interest rates into the Keynesian model, and presents a general equilibrium approach to the determination of aggregate output, interest rates and the price level known as the IS-LM model. Chapters 24 and 25 explain the role of fiscal and monetary policies in smoothing short-run fluctuations and stabilising the economy. Chapter 26 incorporates inflation into the analysis, and Chapter 27 discusses the policies that can be used to control it. By the end of Part 7 we shall have discussed the major causes of short-term economic fluctuations, as well as the options that policy makers have in responding to them.

21

Short-Term Economic Fluctuations

In Part 6 we discussed the factors that determine long-run economic growth. Over the broad sweep of history, those factors determine the economic success of a society. Indeed, over a span of 30, 50 or 100 years, relatively small differences in the rate of economic growth can have an enormous effect on the average person's standard of living. But even though the economic 'climate' (long-run economic conditions) is the ultimate determinant of living standards, changes in the economic 'weather' (short-run fluctuations in economic conditions) are also important. A good long-run growth record is not much consolation to a worker who has lost her job due to a recession, or to a pensioner whose real standard of living is reduced by inflation. Recessions and periods of sustained inflation are also bad news for governments as their management of the economy is often a key factor in deciding how people vote at elections.

Recessions and expansions

recession a period in which the economy is growing at a rate significantly below normal

As background to the study of short-term economic fluctuations, let us review the historical record of the fluctuations in the British economy. Figure 21.1 shows the path of real GDP in the United Kingdom since 1920. As you can see, the growth path of real GDP is not always smooth; the bumps and wiggles correspond to short periods of faster or slower growth.

The inset in Figure 21.1 shows the Great Depression, which had a devastating impact on all industrial economies between 1929 and 1933. You can also see that the UK economy was volatile in the mid-1970s, the early 1980s and 1990s, with serious recessions in 1974–75, 1980–81 and 1990–91. Most European countries, together with the United States and Japan, experienced recessions around the same times as the United Kingdom. Each of these recessions was preceded by significant increases in oil prices. In the 1970s and early 1980s this was the result of action taken by the Organization of Petroleum Exporting Countries (OPEC), which cut production and raised oil prices in 1973 and again in 1979. In 1990–91 the rise in oil prices was related to Iraq's invasion of Kuwait and the resulting Gulf War.

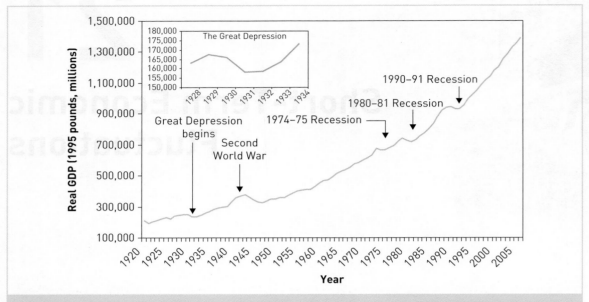

Figure 21.1 Fluctuations in Real UK GDP, 1920–2005. The inset highlights the Great Depression of 1929–32.

expansion a period in which the economy is growing at a rate significantly above normal

boom a particularly strong and protracted expansion

The opposite of a recession is an **expansion** – a period in which the economy is growing at a rate that is significantly *above* normal. A particularly strong and protracted expansion is called a **boom**. In the United Kingdom, strong expansions are evident for most of the 1950s, the mid-1960s, the late 1980s and towards the end of the twentieth century. In fact the expansion of the 1950s prompted the then Prime Minister Harold Macmillan, to fight, and win, the 1959 general election under the slogan 'You have never had it so good.' As can also be seen from Figure 21.1, on average, expansions have endured much longer than recessions.

Expansions and recessions are not limited to a few industries or regions, but are *felt throughout the economy*. Indeed, the largest fluctuations may have a *global impact*. For instance, the Great Depression of the 1930s affected most of the world's economies, and the recessions of 1974–75, 1980–81 and 1990–91 were experienced by Canada, Japan and the United States, as well as most countries in Western Europe. Figure 21.2 shows growth rates of real GDP over the period 1970–2002 for France, Germany and the United Kingdom. You can see that all three countries experienced peaks and troughs at approximately the same time, and especially in the case of the 1974–75 recessions.

Unemployment and *inflation* are key indicators of short-term economic fluctuations. The unemployment rate typically rises sharply during recessions and recovers during expansions. Figure 21.3 shows the UK unemployment rate since 1970 and illustrates that unemployment starts to rise steeply once a recession starts. Recall from Chapter 18 that the part of unemployment that is associated with recessions is called *cyclical unemployment*. Beyond this increase in unemployment, labour market conditions generally worsen during recessions. For example, during recessions real wages grow more slowly, workers are less likely to receive promotions or bonuses, and new

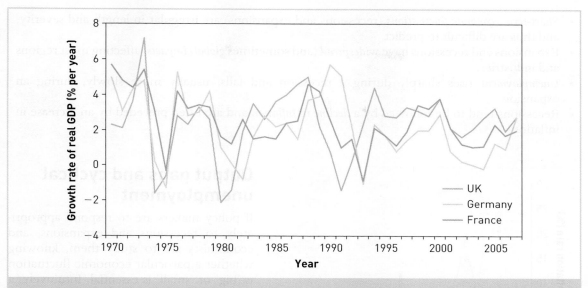

Figure 21.2 Real GDP Growth Rates in Germany, France and the United Kingdom, 1970–2006.

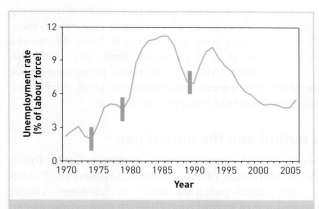

Figure 21.3 UK Unemployment, 1970–2006.
Recessions are indicated by a vertical bar.

entrants to the labour force (such as college graduates) have a much tougher time finding attractive jobs.

Like unemployment, *inflation* follows a typical pattern in recessions and expansions, though it is not so sharply defined. Figure 21.4 shows the UK inflation rate since 1970. In Figure 21.4, vertical bars indicate periods of recession. As you can see, recessions tend to be followed by a decline in the rate of inflation. Furthermore, many – though not all – post-war recessions have been preceded by increases in inflation, as Figure 21.4 shows. The behaviour of inflation during expansions and recessions will be discussed more fully in Chapter 26.

RECAP Recessions, booms and their characteristics

- A *recession* is a period in which output is growing more slowly than normal. An *expansion*, or *boom*, is a period in which output is growing more quickly than normal.
- The beginning of a recession is called the *peak*, and its end (which corresponds to the beginning of the subsequent expansion) is called the *trough*.
- The sharpest recession in the history of most industrial countries was the initial phase of the *Great Depression* in 1929–32. Severe recessions also occurred in the early 1970s, 1980s and 1990s. Each of these recessions followed large increases in world oil prices.

▶ • *Short-term economic fluctuations* (recessions and expansions) are irregular in length and severity, and thus are difficult to predict.
  • Expansions and recessions have *widespread* (and sometimes *global*) *impacts*, affecting most regions and industries.
  • *Unemployment* rises sharply during a recession and falls, usually more slowly, during an expansion.
  • Recessions tend to be followed by a *decline in inflation* and are often preceded by an increase in inflation.

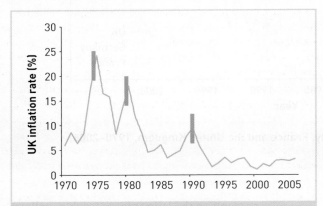

Figure 21.4 UK Inflation Rate, 1970–2006.
Recessions are indicated by a vertical bar.

output gap the difference between the economy's potential output and its actual output at a point in time ($Y^* - Y$)

potential output (or potential GDP or full-employment output) the amount of output (real GDP) that an economy can produce when using its resources, such as capital and labour, at normal rates

Output gaps and cyclical unemployment

If policy makers are to respond appropriately to recessions and expansions, and economists are to study them, knowing whether a particular economic fluctuation is 'big' or 'small' is essential. Intuitively, a 'big' recession or expansion is one in which output and the unemployment rate deviate significantly from their normal or trend levels. In this section we shall attempt to be more precise about this idea by introducing the concept of the **output gap**, which measures how far output is from its normal level at a particular time. We shall also revisit the idea of *cyclical unemployment*, or the deviation of unemployment from its normal level. Finally, we shall examine how these two concepts are related.

Potential output and the output gap

The concept of potential output is a useful starting point for thinking about the measurement of expansions and recessions. **Potential output**, also called **potential GDP** or **full-employment output**, is the amount of output (real GDP) that an economy can produce when using its resources, such as capital and labour, at normal rates. Potential output is not a fixed number but *grows over time*, reflecting increases in both the amounts of available capital and labour and their productivity. We discussed the sources of growth in potential output (the economy's productive capacity) in Chapter 19. We shall use the symbol Y^* to signify the economy's potential output at a given point in time.

Why does a nation's output sometimes grow quickly and sometimes slowly? Logically, there are two possibilities. First, changes in the rate of output growth may reflect changes in the rate at which the country's potential output is increasing. For example, a decrease in the rate of technological innovation might reduce the rate of potential output growth in an industrial economy. Under the assumption that the country is using its resources at normal rates, so that actual output equals potential output, a significant slowdown in potential output growth would tend to result in recession.

Similarly, the introduction of new technologies and increased capital investment could produce higher growth in potential output, and hence an economic boom.

Undoubtedly, changes in the rate of growth of potential output are part of the explanation for expansions and recessions. In the United States, for example, the economic boom of the second half of the 1990s was propelled in part by new information technologies such as the internet, and the severe slowdown in Japan during the 1990s reflected in part a reduction in the growth of potential output, arising from factors such as slower growth in the Japanese labour force and capital stock. When changes in the rate of GDP growth reflect changes in the growth rate of potential output, the appropriate policy responses are those discussed in Chapters 19 and 20. In particular, when a recession results from slowing growth in potential output, the government's best response is to try to promote saving, investment, technological innovation, human capital formation and other activities that support growth.

A second possible explanation for short-term economic fluctuations is that *actual output does not always equal potential output*. For example, potential output may be growing normally, but for some reason the economy's capital and labour resources may not be fully utilised, so that actual output is significantly below the level of potential output. This low level of output, resulting from under-utilisation of economic resources, would generally be interpreted as a recession. Alternatively, capital and labour may be working much harder than normal – firms may put workers on overtime, for example – so that actual output expands beyond potential output, creating a boom.

At any point in time, the difference between potential output and actual output is called the *output gap*. Recalling that $Y^\star$ is the symbol for potential output and that Y stands for actual output (real GDP), we can express the output gap as $Y^\star - Y$. A positive output gap – when actual output is below potential, and resources are not being fully utilised – is called a **recessionary gap**. A negative output gap – when actual output is above potential, and resources are being utilised at above-normal rates – is referred to as an **expansionary gap**.

recessionary gap a positive output gap, which occurs when potential output exceeds actual output ($Y^\star > Y$)

expansionary gap a negative output gap, which occurs when actual output is higher than potential output ($Y > Y^\star$)

Policy makers generally view both recessionary gaps and expansionary gaps as problems. It is not difficult to see why a recessionary gap is bad news for the economy: when there is a recessionary gap, capital and labour resources are not being fully utilised, and output and employment are below normal levels. An expansionary gap is considered a problem by policy makers for a more subtle reason: what's wrong, after all, with having higher output and employment than normal? A prolonged expansionary gap is problematic because, when faced with a demand for their products that significantly exceeds their normal capacity, firms tend to raise prices. Thus an expansionary gap typically results in increased inflation, which reduces the efficiency of the economy in the longer run. (We discuss the genesis of inflation in more detail in Chapter 26.) Figure 21.5 shows estimated output gaps for EU countries in 2006. Note that the gap is measured as the percentage deviation of actual output Y from potential output $Y^\star$, or $(Y^\star - Y)/Y^\star$. Hence a positive value indicates a recessionary gap. Figure 21.5 shows output gaps for EU countries in 2006.

Whenever an output gap exists, whether it is recessionary or expansionary, policy makers have an incentive to try to eliminate the gap by returning actual output to potential. In Chapters 23–25 we shall discuss both how output gaps arise and the tools that policy makers have for *stabilising* the economy – that is, bringing actual output into line with potential output.

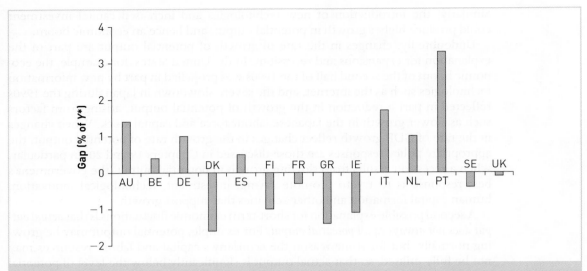

Figure 21.5 Output Gaps for EU Member States, 2006. The gap is measured as the percentage deviation of *Y* from *Y**. A positive value indicates a recessionary gap.
Source: OECD, *Economic Outlook* (www.oecd.org).

The natural rate of unemployment and cyclical unemployment

Efficiency

Whether recessions arise because of slower growth in potential output or because actual output falls below potential, they bring bad times. In either case actual output falls or at least grows more slowly, implying reduced living standards. Recessionary output gaps are particularly frustrating for policy makers because they imply that the economy has the *capacity* to produce more, but for some reason available resources are not being fully utilised. Recessionary gaps are *inefficient* in that they unnecessarily reduce the total economic 'pie', making the typical person worse off.

An important indicator of the low utilisation of resources during recessions is the *unemployment rate*. In general, a *high* unemployment rate means that labour resources are not being fully utilised, so that output has fallen below potential (a recessionary gap). By the same logic, an unusually *low* unemployment rate suggests that labour is being utilised at a rate greater than normal, so that actual output exceeds potential output (an expansionary gap).

To understand the relationship between the output gap and unemployment better, recall from Chapter 18 the three broad types of unemployment: frictional unemployment, structural unemployment and cyclical unemployment. *Frictional unemployment* is the short-term unemployment that is associated with the matching of workers and jobs. Some amount of frictional unemployment is necessary for the labour market to function efficiently in a dynamic, changing economy. *Structural unemployment* is the long-term and chronic unemployment that occurs even when the economy is producing at its normal rate. Structural unemployment often results when workers' skills are outmoded and do not meet the needs of employers – so, for example, steelworkers may become structurally unemployed as the steel industry goes into a long-term decline, unless those workers can retrain to find jobs in growing industries. Finally, *cyclical unemployment* is the extra unemployment that occurs during periods of recession. Unlike cyclical unemployment, which is present only during recessions, frictional

natural rate of unemployment the part of the total unemployment rate that is attributable to frictional and structural unemployment; equivalently, the unemployment rate that prevails when cyclical unemployment is zero, so that the economy has neither a recessionary nor an expansionary output gap

unemployment and structural unemployment are always present in the labour market, even when the economy is operating normally. Economists call the part of the total unemployment rate that is attributable to frictional and structural unemployment the **natural rate of unemployment**. Put another way, the natural rate of unemployment is the unemployment rate that prevails when cyclical unemployment is zero, so that the economy has neither a recessionary nor an expansionary output gap. We will denote the natural rate of unemployment as $u^{\star}$.

Cyclical unemployment, which is the difference between the total unemployment rate and the natural rate, can be expressed as $u - u^{\star}$, where u is the actual unemployment rate and $u^{\star}$ denotes the natural rate of unemployment. In a recession, the actual unemployment rate u exceeds the natural unemployment rate $u^{\star}$, so cyclical unemployment, $u - u^{\star}$, is positive. When the economy experiences an expansionary gap, in contrast, the actual unemployment rate is lower than the natural rate, so that cyclical unemployment is negative. Negative cyclical unemployment corresponds to a situation in which labour is being used more intensively than normal, so that actual unemployment has dipped below its usual frictional and structural levels.

RECAP Output gaps and cyclical unemployment

Potential output is the amount of output (real GDP) that an economy can produce when using its resources, such as capital and labour, at normal rates. The output gap, $Y^{\star} - Y$, is the difference between potential output $Y^{\star}$ and actual output Y. When actual output is below potential, the resulting output gap is called a *recessionary gap*. When actual output is above potential, the difference is called an *expansionary gap*. A recessionary gap reflects a waste of resources, while an expansionary gap threatens to ignite inflation; hence policy makers have an incentive to try to eliminate both types.

The *natural rate of unemployment*, $u^{\star}$, is the sum of the frictional and structural unemployment rates. It is the rate of unemployment that is observed when the economy is operating at a normal level, with no output gap.

Cyclical unemployment, $u - u^{\star}$, is the difference between the actual unemployment rate u and the natural rate of unemployment $u^{\star}$. Cyclical unemployment is positive when there is a recessionary gap, negative when there is an expansionary gap and zero when there is no output gap.

Why do short-term fluctuations occur? A preview and a parable

What causes periods of recession and expansion? In the preceding section we discussed two possible reasons for slowdowns and speed-ups in real GDP growth. First, growth in *potential output* itself may slow down or speed up, reflecting changes in the growth rates of available capital and labour, and in the pace of technological progress. Second, even if potential output is growing normally, *actual output* may be higher or lower than potential output – that is, expansionary or recessionary output gaps may develop. Earlier in this book we discussed some of the reasons why growth in potential output can vary, and the options that policy makers have for stimulating growth in potential output. But we have not yet addressed the question of how output gaps can arise, or what policy makers should do in response. The causes and cures of output gaps will be a major topic of Chapters 21–25. Here is a brief preview of the main conclusions of those chapters.

- In a world in which prices adjusted immediately to balance the quantities supplied and demanded for all goods and services, output gaps would not exist. However, for many goods and services, the assumption that prices will adjust immediately is not realistic. Instead, many firms adjust the prices of their output only periodically. In particular, rather than changing prices with every variation in demand, firms tend to adjust to changes in demand in the short run by varying the quantity of *output* they produce and sell. This type of behaviour is known as 'meeting the demand' at a pre-set price.
- Because in the short run firms tend to meet the demand for their output at pre-set prices, changes in the amount that customers decide to spend will affect output. When total spending is low for some reason, output may fall below potential output; conversely, when spending is high, output may rise above potential output. In other words, *changes in economy-wide spending* are the primary cause of output gaps. Thus government policies can help to eliminate output gaps by influencing total spending. For example, the government can affect total spending directly simply by changing its own level of purchases.
- Although firms tend to meet demand in the short run, they will not be willing to do so indefinitely. If customer demand continues to differ from potential output, firms will eventually adjust their prices to eliminate output gaps. If demand exceeds potential output (an *expansionary* gap), firms will raise their prices aggressively, spurring inflation. If demand falls below potential output (a *recessionary* gap), firms will raise their prices less aggressively or even cut prices, reducing inflation.
- Over the longer run, price changes by firms eliminate any output gap and bring production back into line with the economy's potential output. Thus the economy is 'self-correcting' in the sense that it operates to eliminate output gaps over time. Because of this self-correcting tendency, in the long run actual output equals potential output, so that output is determined by the *economy's productive capacity* rather than by the rate of spending. In the long run, total spending influences only the rate of inflation.

These ideas will become clearer as we proceed through Chapters 21–25. Before plunging into the details of the analysis, though, let us consider an example that illustrates the links between spending and output in the short and long run.

Bill produces gourmet ice cream on his premises on London's Oxford Street and sells it directly to the public. What determines the amount of ice cream that Bill produces on a daily basis? The productive capacity, or potential output, of the shop is one important factor. Specifically, Bill's potential output of ice cream depends on the amount of capital (number of ice cream makers) and labour (number of workers) that he employs, and on the productivity of that capital and labour. Although Bill's potential output usually changes rather slowly, on occasion it can fluctuate significantly – for example, if an ice cream maker breaks down or Bill contracts the flu.

The main source of day-to-day variations in Bill's ice cream production, however, is not changes in potential output but fluctuations in the *demand* for ice cream by the public. Some of these fluctuations in spending occur predictably over the course of the day (more demand in the afternoon than in the morning, for example) the week (more demand on weekends) or the year (more demand in the summer and during the tourist season). Other changes in demand are less regular – more demand on a hot summer day than a cool one. Some changes in demand are hard for Bill to interpret: for example, a surge in demand for strawberry ice cream on one particular Tuesday could reflect a permanent change in consumer tastes, or it might just be a random, one-time event.

How should Bill react to these ebbs and flows in the demand for ice cream? The basic supply and demand model that we introduced in Chapter 3, if applied to the market for ice cream, would predict that the price of ice cream should change with every change in the demand for ice cream. For example, prices should rise on hot sunny days, and they should fall on cold rainy days, when most people would prefer a hot drink to an ice cream cone. Indeed, taken literally, the supply and demand model of Chapter 3 predicts that ice cream prices should change almost moment to moment. Imagine Bill standing in front of his shop like an auctioneer, calling out prices in an effort to determine how many people are willing to buy at each price!

Cost–Benefit Analysis

Of course, we do not expect to see this behaviour by an ice cream parlour owner. Price setting by auction does in fact occur in some markets, such as the market for grain or the stock market, but it is not the normal procedure in most retail markets, such as the market for ice cream. Why this difference? The basic reason is that sometimes the economic benefits of hiring an auctioneer and setting up an auction exceed the costs of doing so, and sometimes they do not. In the market for grain, for example, many buyers and sellers gather together in the same place at the same time to trade large volumes of standardised goods (tonnes of grain). In that kind of situation, an auction is an efficient way to determine prices and balance the quantities supplied and demanded. In an ice cream parlour, by contrast, customers come in by twos and threes at random times throughout the day. Some want shakes, some cones and some sodas. With small numbers of customers and a low sales volume at any given time, the costs involved in selling ice cream by auction are much greater than the benefits of allowing prices to vary with demand.

So how does Bill, the ice cream parlour manager, deal with changes in the demand for ice cream? Observation suggests that he begins by setting prices based on the best information he has about the demand for his product and the costs of production. Perhaps he prints up a menu or makes a sign announcing the prices. Then, over a period of time, he will keep his prices fixed and serve as many customers as want to buy (up to the point where he runs out of ice cream or room in the parlour at these prices). This behaviour is what we call 'meeting the demand' at pre-set prices, and it implies that *in the short run*, the amount of ice cream Bill produces and sells is determined by the demand for his products.

However, *in the long run*, the situation is quite different. Suppose, for example, that Bill's ice cream earns a city-wide reputation for its freshness and flavour. Day after day Bill observes long queues in his ice cream parlour. His ice cream maker is overworked, as are his employees and his table space. There can no longer be any doubt that, at current prices, the quantity of ice cream the public wants to consume exceeds what Bill is able and willing to supply on a normal basis (his potential output). Expanding the ice cream parlour is an attractive possibility, but not one (we assume) that is immediately feasible. What will Bill do?

Certainly one thing Bill can do is raise his prices. At higher prices, Bill will earn higher profits. Moreover, raising ice cream prices will bring the quantity of ice cream demanded closer to Bill's normal production capacity – his potential output. Indeed, when the price of Bill's ice cream finally rises to its equilibrium level, the parlour's actual output will equal its potential output. Thus, over the long run, ice cream prices adjust to their equilibrium level, and the amount that is sold is determined by potential output.

This example illustrates in a simple way the links between spending and output – except, of course, that we must think of this story as applying to the whole economy, not to a single business. The key point is that there is an important difference between the short run and the long run. In the short run, producers often choose not to change their prices, but rather to meet the demand at pre-set prices. Because output is determined by demand, in the short run total spending plays a central role in determining the level of economic activity. Thus Bill's ice cream parlour enjoys a boom on an unusually hot day, when the demand for ice cream is strong, while an unseasonably cold day brings an ice cream recession. But in the long run, prices adjust to their *market-clearing levels*, and output equals potential output. Thus the quantities of inputs and the productivity with which they are used are the primary determinants of economic activity in the long run, as we saw in Chapter 19. Although total spending affects output in the short run, in the long run its main effects are on prices.

Economic naturalist 21.1 Why did the Coca-Cola Company test a vending machine that 'knows' when the weather is hot?

According to the *New York Times* (28 October 1999, p. C1), the Coca-Cola Company has quietly tested a soda vending machine that includes a temperature sensor. Why would Coca-Cola want a vending machine that 'knows' when the weather is hot?

When the weather is hot, the demand for refreshing soft drinks rises, increasing their market-clearing price. To take advantage of this variation in consumer demand, the vending machines that Coca-Cola tested were equipped with a computer chip that gave them the capability to raise prices automatically when the temperature climbs. The company's chairman and chief executive, M. Douglas Ivester, described in an interview how the desire for a cold drink increases during a sports championship final held in the summer heat. 'So it is fair that it should be more expensive,' Mr Ivester was quoted as saying. 'The machine will simply make this process automatic.' Company officials suggested numerous other ways in which vending machine prices could be made dependent on demand. For example, machines could be programmed to reduce prices during off-peak hours or at low-traffic machines.

In traditional vending machines, cold drinks are priced in a way analogous to the way Bill prices his ice cream: a price is set, and demand is met at the pre-set price, until the machine runs out of soda. The weather-sensitive vending machine illustrates how technology may change pricing practices in the future. Indeed, increased computing power and access to the internet have already allowed some firms, such as airline companies, to change prices almost continuously in response to variations in demand. Conceivably, the practice of meeting demand at a pre-set price may some day be obsolete.

On the other hand, Coca-Cola's experiments with 'smart' vending machines also illustrate the barriers to fully flexible pricing in practice. First, the new vending machines are more costly than the standard model. In deciding whether to use them, the company must decide whether the extra profits from variable pricing justify the extra cost of the machines. Second, in early tests many consumers reacted negatively to the new machines, complaining that they take unfair advantage of thirsty customers. In practice, customer complaints and concerns about 'fairness' make companies less willing to vary prices sensitively with changing demand.

Spending and output in the short run

The story of Bill's ice cream shop suggested that when prices are slow to change, spending might be an important factor influencing fluctuations in short-run output. We shall now focus on this link at the aggregate or macro level. To fix our ideas we first consider a parable about two countries called Big-Land and Small-Land. Big-Land is a large economy producing a wide range of goods and services. Small-Land is a much smaller economy and its industry is highly specialised in one good which, for the sake of illustration, we shall assume to be shoes. We shall also assume that most of Small-Land's shoe production is exported and sold to households in Big-Land. Of course, Small-Land will have firms other than shoe manufacturers. The majority of Small-Land's workforce may be employed in shoe factories but they spend their incomes on the many goods and services produced or sold domestically. These would include food sold by supermarkets, clothes, restaurant meals, petrol, haircuts, etc. Even though many of these goods may be produced in Big-Land their distribution and sale creates jobs in Small-Land. Workers who supply these goods earn income, which, of course, is part of Small-Land's GDP. We shall assume that Small-Land's GDP is currently equal to potential GDP, or Y^*.

Now suppose that households in Big-Land become uncertain about the future of Big-Land's economy and decide to increase their regular savings by reducing consumption expenditures. This could be due to factors such as uncertainty about the financial health of Big-Land's banking system or external events such as war in a region important to Big-Land's economy. Whatever the cause, lower spending by consumers in Big-Land means that they will purchase fewer shoes produced in Small-Land. The immediate effect will be that shoe producers in Small-Land will find that sales are less than expected and they will start to accumulate stocks of unsold shoes. Initially they may add this unsold production to their inventories, but if low sales persist they will eventually cut back on production and make some of their workers redundant. As profits and incomes fall, Small-Land's GDP will start to decline, leading to a recessionary gap, $Y^* > Y$.

Unfortunately, this is not the end of the story. Small-Land's government may pay benefits to unemployed shoe workers, but these are likely to be well below what these workers were earning in wages and salaries. With lower incomes, unemployed shoe workers will spend less on food, clothes, restaurant meals, petrol and haircuts, etc. As sales of these goods decline the firms supplying them will scale down their businesses and lay off some of their workers, creating a vicious circle with further declines in spending and more redundancies. In this scenario, the problem is not a lack of productive capacity – Small-Land's factories, shops and restaurants have not lost their ability to produce – but rather *insufficient spending* to support the normal level of production.

The idea that a decline in *aggregate spending* may cause output to fall below its potential level was one of the key insights of *John Maynard Keynes*, a highly influential British economist of the first half of the twentieth century. The goal of this chapter is to present a theory, or model, of how recessions and expansions may arise from fluctuations in aggregate spending, along the lines first suggested by Keynes. This model, which we call the *basic Keynesian model*, is also known as the *Keynesian cross*, after the diagram that is used to illustrate the theory. In the body of the chapter we will emphasise a numerical and graphical approach to the basic Keynesian model.

We shall begin with a brief discussion of the key assumptions of the basic Keynesian model. We shall then turn to the important concept of total, or aggregate, *planned spending* in the economy. We shall show how, in the short run, the rate of aggregate spending helps to determine the level of output, which can be greater than or less than potential output. In other words, depending on the level of spending, the economy may develop an output gap. 'Too little' spending leads to a recessionary output gap, while 'too much' creates an expansionary output gap.

An implication of the basic Keynesian model is that government policies that affect the level of spending can be used to reduce or eliminate output gaps. Policies used in this way are called *stabilisation policies*. Keynes himself argued for the active use of fiscal policy – policy relating to government spending and taxes – to eliminate output gaps and stabilise the economy. In the latter part of this chapter we shall show why Keynes thought fiscal policy could help to stabilise the economy, and we shall discuss the usefulness of fiscal policy as a stabilisation tool.

The basic Keynesian model is not a complete or entirely realistic model of the economy, since it applies only to the relatively short period during which firms do not adjust their prices but instead meet the demand forthcoming at pre-set prices. Furthermore, by treating prices as fixed, the basic Keynesian model presented in this chapter does not address the determination of *inflation*. Nevertheless, this model is an essential building block of leading current theories of short-run economic fluctuations and stabilisation policies. In Chapter 26 we shall extend the basic Keynesian model to incorporate inflation and other important features of the economy.

The Keynesian model's crucial assumption: firms meet demand at pre-set prices

The basic Keynesian model is built on a key assumption. This is that firms do not continuously change their prices as supply and demand conditions change; rather, over short periods, firms tend to keep their prices fixed and *meet the demand* that is forthcoming at those prices. As we will see, the assumption that firms vary their production in order to meet demand at pre-set prices implies that fluctuations in spending will have powerful effects on the nation's real GDP.

> **Key assumption of the basic Keynesian model:** In the short run, firms meet the demand for their products at pre-set prices.

Firms do not respond to every change in the demand for their products by changing their prices. Instead, they typically set a price for some period and *meet the demand* at that price. By 'meeting the demand', we mean that firms produce *just enough to satisfy their customers* at the prices that have been set.

The assumption that, over short periods of time, firms meet the demand for their products at pre-set prices is generally realistic. Think of the stores where you shop. The price of a pair of jeans does not fluctuate from moment to moment according to the number of customers who enter the store or the latest news about the price of denim. Instead, the store posts a price and sells jeans to any customer who wants to buy at that price, at least until the store runs out of stock. Similarly, the corner pizza restaurant may leave the price of its large pizza unchanged for months or longer, allowing its pizza production to be determined by the number of customers who want to buy at the pre-set price.

Firms do not normally change their prices frequently because doing so would be costly. Economists refer to the costs of changing prices as **menu costs**. In the case of the pizza restaurant, the menu cost is literally just that – the cost of printing up a new menu when prices change. Similarly, the clothing store faces the cost of re-marking all its merchandise if the manager changes the prices. But menu costs may also include other kinds of costs – for example, the cost of doing a market survey to determine what price to charge, and the cost of informing customers about price changes.

menu costs the costs of changing prices

Menu costs will not prevent firms from changing their prices indefinitely. As we saw in the case of Bill's ice cream parlour, too great an imbalance between demand and supply, as reflected by a difference between sales and potential output, will eventually lead firms to change their prices. If no one is buying jeans, for example, at some point the clothing store will mark down its prices. Or if the pizza restaurant becomes the local hot spot, with a queue of customers stretching out the door, eventually the manager will raise the price of a large pizza. Like many other economic decisions, the decision to change prices reflects a *cost–benefit* comparison: prices should be changed if the benefit of doing so – the fact that sales will be brought more nearly in line with the firm's normal production capacity – outweighs the menu costs associated with making the change. As we have stressed, the basic Keynesian model developed in this chapter ignores the fact that prices will eventually adjust, and should therefore be interpreted as applying to the short run.

Economic naturalist 21.2 Will new technologies eliminate menu costs?

Thanks to new technologies, changing prices and informing customers about price changes is becoming increasingly less costly. Will technology eliminate menu costs as a factor in price setting? Keynesian theory is based on the assumption that the costs of changing prices, which economists refer to as *menu costs*, are sufficiently large to prevent firms from adjusting prices immediately in response to changing market conditions. However, in many industries, new technologies have eliminated or greatly reduced the direct costs of changing prices. For example, the use of bar codes to identify individual products, together with scanner technologies, allows a grocery store manager to change prices with just a few keystrokes, without having to change the price label on each can of soup or loaf of bread. Airlines use sophisticated computer software to implement complex pricing strategies, under which two travellers on the same flight to London may pay very different fares, depending on whether they are business or vacation travellers, and on how far in advance their flights were booked. Online retailers, such as booksellers, have the ability to vary their prices by type of customer and even by individual customer, while other internet-based companies, such as eBay and Priceline, allow for negotiation over the price of each individual purchase. As described in Economic naturalist 21.1, the Coca-Cola Company experimented with a vending machine that automatically varied the price of a soft drink according to the outdoor temperature, charging more when the weather is hot.

Will these reductions in the direct costs of changing prices make the Keynesian theory, which assumes that firms meet demand at pre-set prices, less relevant to the real world? This is certainly a possibility that macroeconomists must take into account. However, it is unlikely that new technologies will completely eliminate the costs of changing prices any time soon. Gathering information about market conditions needed to set the profit-maximising price – including the prices charged by competitors, the costs of producing the good or service, and the likely demand for the product – will remain costly for firms. Another cost of changing prices is the use of the valuable managerial time and attention needed to make informed pricing decisions. A more subtle cost of changing prices – particularly raising prices – is that doing so may lead regular customers to rethink their choice of suppliers and decide to search for a better deal elsewhere.

Planned aggregate expenditure

planned aggregate expenditure (PAE) total planned spending on final goods and services

In the Keynesian theory discussed in this chapter, output at each point in time is determined by the amount that people throughout the economy want to spend – what we shall refer to as **planned aggregate expenditure (PAE)**. Specifically, planned aggregate expenditure is *total planned spending on final goods and services*.

The four components of spending on final goods and services were introduced in Chapter 16 and are as follows.

1. *Consumer expenditure*, or simply *consumption* (*C*), is spending by households on final goods and services. Examples of consumer expenditure are spending on food, clothes and entertainment, and on consumer durable goods such as cars and furniture.
2. *Investment* (*I*) is spending by firms on new capital goods, such as office buildings, factories and equipment. Spending on new houses and apartment buildings (residential investment) and increases in inventories (inventory investment) are also included in investment.
3. *Government purchases* (*G*) is spending by governments (national and local) on goods and services. Examples of government purchases include spending on new roads, schools and hospitals, military hardware, the services of government employees, such as soldiers, police and government office workers and the salaries paid to politicians. Recall from Chapter 16 that *transfer payments* – such as social security benefits and unemployment insurance – and interest on the government debt are *not* included in government purchases. Transfer payments and interest contribute to aggregate expenditure only at the point when they are spent by their recipients (for example, when a recipient of unemployment benefits uses the funds to buy food, clothing or other consumption goods).
4. *Net exports* (*NX*) equals exports minus imports. Exports are sales of domestically produced goods and services to foreigners; imports are purchases by domestic residents of goods and services produced abroad. Net exports represent the *net demand for domestic goods by foreigners*.

Together, these four types of spending – by households, firms, the government and the rest of the world – sum to total, or aggregate, spending.

Planned spending versus actual spending

In the Keynesian model, output is determined by planned aggregate expenditure. Could *planned* spending ever differ from *actual* spending? The answer is yes. The most important case is that of a firm that sells either less or more of its product than expected. As was explained in Chapter 16, additions to the stocks of goods sitting in a firm's warehouse are treated as *inventory investment* by the firm. That is, when measuring GDP, government statisticians assume that the firm buys its unsold output from itself; they then count those purchases as part of the firm's investment spending.[1]

Suppose, then, that a firm's actual sales are *less* than expected, so that part of what it had planned to sell remains in the warehouse. In this case, the firm's actual investment, including the unplanned increases in its inventory, is greater than its planned investment, which did not include the added inventory. Suppose we let I^P equal the firm's planned investment, including planned inventory investment. A firm that sells less of its output than planned, and therefore adds more to its inventory than planned, will find that its actual investment (including unplanned inventory investment) exceeds its planned investment, so that $I > I^P$.

What about a firm that sells *more* of its output than expected? In that case, the firm will add less to its inventory than it planned, so actual investment will be less than planned investment, or $I < I^P$. Example 21.1 gives a numerical illustration.

---

1 For the purpose of measuring GDP, treating unsold output as being purchased by its producer has the advantage of ensuring that actual production and actual expenditure are equal.

Example 21.1 Actual and planned investment

The Fly-by-Night Kite Company produces €5,000,000 worth of kites during the year. It expects sales of €4,800,000 for the year, leaving €200,000 worth of kites to be stored in the warehouse for future sale. During the year, Fly-by-Night adds €1,000,000 in new production equipment as part of an expansion plan. Find Fly-by-Night's actual investment I and its planned investment I^p if actual kite sales turn out to be €4,600,000. What if they are €4,800,000? What if they are €5,000,000?

Fly-by-Night's planned investment I^p equals its purchases of new production equipment (€1,000,000) plus its planned additions to inventory (€200,000), for a total of €1,200,000 in planned investment. The company's planned investment does not depend on how much it actually sells.

If Fly-by-Night sells only €4,600,000 worth of kites, it will add €400,000 in kites to its inventory instead of the €200,000 worth originally planned. In this case, actual investment equals the €1,000,000 in new equipment plus the €400,000 in inventory investment, so I = €1,400,000. We see that when the firm sells less output than planned, actual investment exceeds planned investment ($I > I^p$).

If Fly-by-Night has €4,800,000 in sales, then it will add €200,000 in kites to inventory, just as planned. In this case, actual and planned investment are the same:

$$I = I^p = €1,200,000$$

Finally, if Fly-by-Night sells €5,000,000 worth of kites, it will have no output to add to inventory. Its inventory investment will be zero, and its total actual investment (including the new equipment) will equal €1,000,000, which is less than its planned investment of €1,200,000 ($I < I^p$).

Because firms that are meeting the demand for their product or service at pre-set prices cannot control how much they sell, their actual investment (including inventory investment) may well differ from their planned investment. However, for households, the government and foreign purchasers, we may reasonably assume that actual spending and planned spending are the same. Thus, from now on we will assume that, for consumption, government purchases and net exports, *actual spending equals planned spending*.

With these assumptions, we can define planned aggregate expenditure by the following equation:

$$PAE = C + I^p + G + NX \qquad (21.1)$$

Equation (21.1) says that planned aggregate expenditure is the sum of planned spending by households, firms, governments and foreigners. We use a superscript p to distinguish planned investment spending by firms, I^p, from actual investment spending, I. However, because planned spending equals actual spending for households, the government and foreigners, we do not need to use superscripts for consumption, government purchases or net exports.

Consumer spending and the economy

The largest component of planned aggregate expenditure – nearly two-thirds of total spending – is consumption spending, denoted C. As already mentioned consumer spending includes household purchases of goods, such as groceries and clothing; services, such as healthcare, concerts and legal fees; and consumer durables, such as cars, furniture and home computers. Thus consumers' willingness to spend affects sales and profitability in a wide range of industries. (Households' purchases of new homes are usually classified as investment, rather than consumption; but home purchases represent another channel through which household decisions affect total spending.)

What determines how much people plan to spend on consumer goods and services in a given period? While many factors are relevant, a particularly important determinant of the amount people plan to consume is their after-tax, or *disposable*, income, defined as income Y minus net taxes T or $(Y - T)$. Other things being equal, households and individuals with higher disposable incomes will consume more than those with lower disposable incomes. Keynes himself stressed the importance of disposable income in determining household consumption decisions, claiming a 'psychological law' that people would tie their spending closely to their incomes. Other factors such as the real rate of interest may also affect consumption expenditures. For now we shall ignore those other factors, returning to some of them later.

A general equation that captures the link between consumption and the private sector's disposable income is

$$C = \bar{C} + c(Y - T) \qquad (21.2)$$

consumption function the relationship between consumption spending and its determinants, in particular disposable (after-tax) income

This equation, which we shall dissect in a moment, is known as the **consumption function**. It relates consumption spending to its determinants, in particular to disposable (after-tax) income.

Let us look at the consumption function, Equation (21.2), more carefully. The right-hand side of Equation (21.2) contains two terms, $\bar{C}$ and $c(Y - T)$. The first term, $\bar{C}$, is a constant term in the equation that is intended to capture factors *other than disposable income* that affect consumption. For example, suppose consumers were to become more optimistic about the future, so that they desire to consume more and save less at any given level of their current disposable incomes. An increase in desired consumption at any given level of disposable income would be represented in the consumption function as an increase in the term $\bar{C}$.

Other factors will of course influence consumption expenditures. Perhaps the most important is changes in the real rate of interest. For example, an increase in the real rate of interest makes saving more attractive and increases borrowing costs, leading to lower consumption at a given level of disposable income. At the end of this chapter we will introduce the real rate of interest into the consumption function and analyse the implications for the determination of equilibrium output. Changes in asset prices may also influence consumption. For example, suppose there is a boom in the stock market or a sharp increase in home prices, making consumers feel wealthier and hence more inclined to spend at a given level of current disposable income. This effect could be captured by assuming that $\bar{C}$ increases. Likewise, a fall in home prices or share prices that made consumers feel poorer and less inclined to spend would be represented by a decrease in $\bar{C}$. Economists refer to the effect of changes in asset prices on households' wealth and hence their consumption spending as the **wealth effect** of changes in asset prices.

wealth effect the tendency of changes in asset prices to affect households' wealth and thus their spending on consumption goods

marginal propensity to consume (MPC), or, c, the amount by which consumption rises when disposable income rises by one euro; we assume that $0 < c < 1$

The second term on the right-hand side of Equation (21.2), $c(Y - T)$, reflects the effect of disposable income, $Y - T$, on consumption. The parameter c, a fixed number, is called the *marginal propensity to consume*. The **marginal propensity to consume (MPC)** is the amount by which consumption rises when disposable income rises. If, for example, $c = 0.75$ then a €100 increase in disposable income induces a €75 increase in consumption with

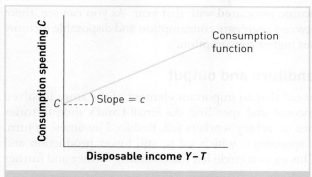

Figure 21.6 A Consumption Function. The consumption function relates households' consumption spending, C, to disposable income, $Y - T$. The vertical intercept of this consumption function is the exogenous component of consumption, $\bar{C}$, and the slope of the line equals the marginal propensity to consume, c.

the remaining €25 being saved. Normally we assume that the marginal propensity to consume is greater than 0 (an increase in income leads to an increase in consumption) but less than 1 (the increase in consumption will be less than the full increase in income). Mathematically, we can summarise these assumptions as $0 < c < 1$.

Figure 21.6 shows a hypothetical consumption function, with consumption spending (C) on the vertical axis and disposable income ($Y - T$) on the horizontal axis. The intercept of the consumption function on the vertical axis equals exogenous consumption $\bar{C}$, and the slope of the consumption function equals the marginal propensity to consume, c.

To see how this consumption function fits reality, compare Figure 21.6 to Figure 21.7, which shows the relationship between aggregate real consumption expenditures and real disposable income in the United Kingdom for the period 1960–2003. Figure 21.7, a type of diagram called a *scatter plot*, shows aggregate real consumption on the vertical axis and aggregate real disposable income on the horizontal axis. Each point on the graph corresponds to a year between 1960 and 2003. The position of each point is determined by the combination of

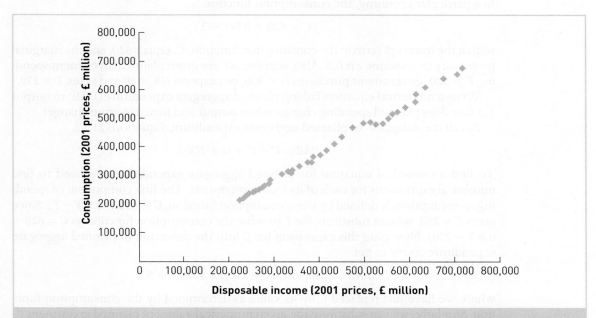

Figure 21.7 The UK Consumption Function, 1960–2003. Each point represents a combination of real consumption and real disposable income for a specific year between 1960 and 2003. Note the strong positive correlation between income and consumption.

consumption and disposable income associated with that year. As you can see, there is indeed a close relationship between aggregate consumption and disposable income: higher disposable income implies higher consumption.

Planned aggregate expenditure and output

Thinking back to Small-Land, recall that an important element of the story involved the links among production, income and spending. As Small-Land's shoe factories reduced production, the incomes of factory workers fell. Reduced incomes, in turn, forced workers to curtail their spending – which led to still lower production and further reductions in income. This vicious circle led the economy further and further into recession.

The logic of the Small-Land story has two key elements: (1) declines in production (which imply declines in the income received by producers) lead to reduced spending; and (2) reductions in spending lead to declines in production and income. In this section we look at the first part of the story: the effects of production and income on *spending*. We return later in this chapter to the effects of spending on production and income.

Why do changes in production and income affect planned aggregate spending? The consumption function, which relates consumption to disposable income, is the basic source of this relationship. Because consumption spending C is a large part of planned aggregate spending, and because consumption depends on output Y, aggregate spending as a whole depends on output. Example 21.2 illustrates this relationship numerically.

Example 21.2 Linking planned aggregate expenditure to output

In a particular economy, the consumption function is

$$C = 620 + 0.8(Y - T)$$

so that the intercept term in the consumption function, $\bar{C}$, equals 620, and the marginal propensity to consume c is 0.8. Also, suppose we are given planned investment spending $I^P = 220$, government purchases $G = 300$, net exports $NX = 20$ and taxes $T = 250$.

Write a numerical equation linking planned aggregate expenditure (PAE) to output Y. How does planned spending change when output and hence income change?

Recall the definition of planned aggregate expenditure, Equation (21.1):

$$PAE = C + I^P + G + NX$$

To find a numerical equation for planned aggregate expenditure, we need to find numerical expressions for each of its four components. The first component of spending, consumption, is defined by the consumption function, $C = 620 + 0.8(Y - T)$. Since taxes $T = 250$, we can substitute for T to write the consumption function as $C = 620 + 0.8(Y - 250)$. Now plug this expression for C into the definition of planned aggregate expenditure above to get

$$PAE = [620 + 0.8(Y - 250)] + I^P + G + NX$$

where we have just replaced C by its value as determined by the consumption function. Similarly, we can substitute the given numerical values of planned investment I^P, government purchases G and net exports NX into the definition of planned aggregate expenditure to get

$$PAE = [620 + 0.8(Y - 250)] + 220 + 300 + 20$$

To simplify this equation, first note that $0.8(Y - 250) = 0.8Y - 200$, then add all the terms that don't depend on output Y. The result is:

$$PAE = (620 - 200 + 220 + 300 + 20) + 0.8Y$$

$$= 960 + 0.8Y$$

The final expression shows the relationship between planned aggregate expenditure and output in this numerical example. Note that, according to this equation, a €100 increase in Y leads to an increase in PAE of $0.8 \times 100 = €80$. The reason for this is that the marginal propensity to consume, c, in this example is 0.8. Hence each €100 increase in income raises consumption spending by €80. Since consumption is a component of total planned spending, total spending rises by €80 as well.

autonomous expenditure the portion of planned aggregate expenditure that is independent of output

induced expenditure the portion of planned aggregate expenditure that depends on output Y

The solution to Example 21.2 illustrates a general point: PAE can be divided into two parts, a part that *depends* on output (Y) and a part that is *independent* of output. The portion of PAE that is independent of output is called **autonomous expenditure**. In Example 21.2, autonomous expenditure is the constant term in the equation for PAE, or 960. This portion of planned spending, being a fixed number, does not vary when output varies. By contrast, the portion of PAE that depends on output (Y) is called **induced expenditure**. In Example 21.2, induced expenditure equals $0.8Y$, the second term in the expression for PAE. Note that the numerical value of induced expenditure depends, by definition, on the numerical value taken by output. Autonomous expenditure and induced expenditure together equal PAE.

RECAP Planned aggregate expenditure

Planned aggregate expenditure (PAE) is total planned spending on final goods and services. The four components of planned spending are consumer expenditure (C), planned investment (I_p), government purchases (G) and net exports (NX). Planned investment differs from actual investment when firms' sales are different from what they expected, so that additions to inventory (a component of investment) are different from what firms anticipated.

The largest component of aggregate expenditure is *consumer expenditure*, or simply consumption. Consumption depends on disposable, or after-tax, income, according to a relationship known as the *consumption function*, stated algebraically as $C = \bar{C} + c(Y - T)$.

The constant term in the consumption function, $\bar{C}$, captures factors *other than disposable income* that affect consumer spending. For example, an increase in housing or stock prices that makes households wealthier and thus more willing to spend – an effect called the *wealth effect* – could be captured by an increase in $\bar{C}$. The slope of the consumption function equals the *marginal propensity to consume*, c, where $0 < c < 1$. This is the amount by which consumption rises when disposable income rises by one euro.

Increases in output Y, which imply equal increases in income, cause consumption to rise. As consumption is part of PAE, planned spending depends on output as well. The portion of PAE that depends on output is called *induced expenditure*. The portion of PAE that is independent of output is called *autonomous expenditure*.

Short-run equilibrium output

Now that we have defined *PAE* and seen how it is related to output, the next task is to see how *output* itself is determined. Recall the assumption of the basic Keynesian

short-run equilibrium output the level of output at which output Y equals planned aggregate expenditure, *PAE*; short-run equilibrium output is the level of output that prevails during the period in which prices are predetermined

model: in the short run, producers leave prices at pre-set levels and simply meet the demand that is forthcoming at those prices. In other words, during the short-run period in which prices are pre-set, firms produce an amount that is equal to PAE. Accordingly, we define **short-run equilibrium output** as the level of output at which output Y equals *PAE*:

$$Y = PAE \qquad (21.3)$$

We can now find the short-run equilibrium output for the economy described in Example 21.2. In that economy *PAE* is given by:

$$PAE = 960 + 0.8Y$$

Using Equation (21.3) to equate Y and *PAE* gives

$$Y = 960 + 0.8Y$$

or

$$Y(1 - 0.8) = 960$$

Dividing both sides by $0.2 = 1 - 0.8$ gives the value for short-run equilibrium output:

$$Y = 960/0.2 = 4,800$$

Hence, in the economy described by Example 21.2, short-run equilibrium output is 4,800.

Because the determination of short-run equilibrium output is important to the subject matter of this chapter and future chapters, we shall develop two general methods that can be used to solve for the equilibrium value of Y. Example 21.3 presents an algebraic approach, while Example 21.4 presents a more intuitive tabular, or numeric, method.

Example 21.3 Solving short-run equilibrium output (the algebraic approach)

We have seen that the economy reaches its short-run equilibrium output when *actual* output Y equals *planned* aggregate expenditure *PAE*:

$$Y = PAE$$

Equation (21.1) says that planned aggregate expenditure is the sum of four components – consumption (C), planned investment (I^P), government purchases (G) and net exports (NX):

$$PAE = C + I^P + G + NX$$

The components of *PAE* can be sub-divided into two types, *induced* (depends on output) and *autonomous* (independent of output). Consumption spending is determined by the consumption function, Equation (21.2), and consists of both induced and autonomous components:

$$C = \bar{C} + c(Y - T)$$

The first term $\bar{C}$ captures factors other than income that affect consumption, and is autonomous. Substituting the consumption function into the definition of *PAE* gives

$$PAE = [\bar{C} + c(Y - T)] + I^P + G + NX$$
$$= [\bar{C} - cT + I^P + G + NX] + cY$$

We have assumed that tax revenues (T), planned investment (I^P), government purchases (G) and net exports (NX) are all autonomous (do not depend on Y). Using an over-bar to denote a given value of an autonomous variable we can define *total autonomous expenditures*, denoted by $\bar{A}$, as

$$\bar{A} = \bar{C} - c\bar{T} - \bar{I} + \bar{G} + \overline{NX}$$

which is the first term in the equation for *PAE*. Hence:

$$PAE = \bar{A} + cY$$

This equation simply divides *PAE* into an autonomous component $\bar{A}$ and an induced component, cY. As equilibrium output is the level of output at which $Y = PAE$ the economy will reach its short-run equilibrium when

$$Y = \bar{A} + cY$$

or

$$Y(1 - c) = \bar{A}$$

Dividing both sides by $(1 - c)$ gives

$$Y = \left(\frac{1}{1 - c}\right)\bar{A} \qquad (21.4)$$

Equation 21.4 gives short-run equilibrium output in terms of total autonomous expenditures $\bar{A}$ and the marginal propensity to consume, c. For given values of total autonomous expenditures and the marginal propensity to consume Equation (21.4) can be used to determine the short-run equilibrium value of the economy's output. In Example 21.2, $\bar{C} = 620$, $\bar{I} = 220$, $\bar{G} = 300$, $\overline{NX} = 20$, $\bar{T} = 250$ and $c = 0.8$ Hence:

$$\bar{A} = [620 - 200 + 220 + 300 + 20] = 960$$

and

$$Y = \left(\frac{1}{1 - 0.8}\right)960 = 4,800$$

which is the same answer as in Example 21.2.

Exercise 21.1 Suppose the economy can be described as follows: consumption function is $C = 860 + 0.6(Y - T)$, $I^P = 900$, $G = 800$, $NX = 200$ and $T = 600$. Using the method described in Example 21.3, find short-run equilibrium output in this economy.

For those who may find algebra difficult, Example 21.4 illustrates an alternative and perhaps more intuitive method to solve for short-run equilibrium output.

Example 21.4 Solving short-run equilibrium output (the numeric approach)

We can find the short-run equilibrium for the economy described in Example 21.2 using Table 21.1. Column (1) of Table 21.1 gives some possible values for short-run equilibrium output. To find the correct value, we must compare each to the value of *PAE* at that output level. Column (2) shows the value of *PAE* corresponding to the values of short-run equilibrium output in column (1). Recall that in Example 21.2, planned spending is determined by the equation $PAE = 960 + 0.8Y$.

Output Y (1)	Planned aggregate expenditure $PAE = 960 + 0.8Y$ (2)	$Y - PAE$ (3)	$Y = PAE$? (4)
4,000	4,160	−160	No
4,200	4,320	−120	No
4,400	4,480	−80	No
4,600	4,640	−40	No
4,800	4,800	0	Yes
5,000	4,960	40	No
5,200	5,120	80	No

Table 21.1 **Numerical Determination of Short-Run Equilibrium Output**

Because consumption rises with output, total planned spending (which includes consumption) rises also. But if you compare columns (1) and (2), you will see that when output rises by 200, planned spending rises by only 160. That is because the *marginal propensity to consume* (MPC) in this economy is 0.8, so that each euro in added income raises consumption and planned spending by 80 cents.

Again, short-run equilibrium output is the level of output at which $Y = PAE$ – or, equivalently, $Y - PAE$, = 0. Looking at Table 21.1, we can see there is only one level of output that satisfies that condition, $Y = 4,800$. At that level, output and *PAE* are precisely equal, so that producers are just meeting the demand for their goods and services.

In this economy, what would happen if output differed from its equilibrium value of 4,800? Suppose, for example, that output were 4,000. Looking at column (2) of Table 21.1, you can see that, when output is 4,000, *PAE* equals 960 + 0.8(4,000), or 4,160. Thus if output is 4,000, firms are not producing enough to meet demand. They will find that as sales exceed the amounts they are producing, their inventories of finished goods are being depleted by 160 per year, and that actual investment (including inventory investment) is less than planned investment. Under the assumption that firms are committed to meeting their customers' demand, firms will respond by expanding their production.

Would expanding production to 4,160 – the level of planned spending firms faced when output was 4,000 – be enough? The answer is no, because of *induced expenditure*. That is, as firms expand their output, aggregate income (wages and profits) rises with it, which in turn leads to higher levels of consumption. Indeed, if output expands to 4,160, planned spending will increase as well, to 960 + 0.8(4,160), or 4,288. So an output level of 4,160 will still be insufficient to meet demand. As Table 21.1 shows, output will not be sufficient to meet planned aggregate expenditure until it expands to its short-run equilibrium value of 4,800.

What if output were initially greater than its equilibrium value – say, 5,000? From Table 21.1 we can see that when output equals 5,000, planned spending equals only 4,960 – less than what firms are producing. So at an output level of 5,000, firms will not sell all they produce, and they will find that their merchandise is piling up on store shelves and in warehouses (actual investment, including inventory investment, is greater than planned investment). In response, firms will cut their production runs. As Table 21.1 shows, they will have to reduce production to its equilibrium value of 4,800 before output just matches planned spending.

Exercise 21.2   Construct a table like Table 21.1 for the economy described in Exercise 21.1 What is short-run equilibrium output in this economy? (**Hint:** Try using values for output above 5,000.)

We have used two approaches to solve for short-run equilibrium output – the algebraic model in Example 21.3 and the numeric model in Example 21.4. Both give the same answer for the economy described in Example 21.2, $Y = 4,800$. Figure 21.8 illustrates this solution graphically. Output Y is plotted on the horizontal axis and planned aggregate expenditure PAE on the vertical axis. The figure contains two lines, one of which is a 45° line extending from the origin. In general, a 45° line from the origin includes the points at which the variable on the vertical axis equals the variable on the horizontal axis. Hence, in this case, the 45° line represents the equation $Y = PAE$. Since short-run equilibrium output must satisfy the equation $Y = PAE$, the combination of output and spending that satisfies this condition must lie somewhere on the 45° line in Figure 21.8.

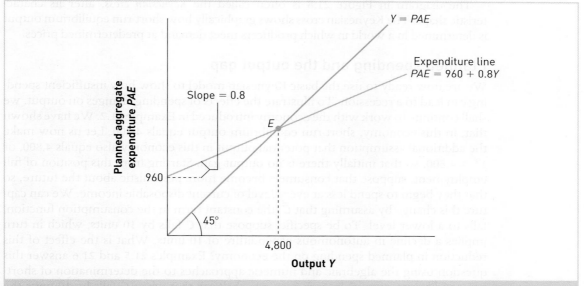

Figure 21.8 Determination of Short-Run Equilibrium Output (Keynesian Cross). The 45° line represents the short-run equilibrium condition $Y = PAE$. The line $PAE = 960 + 0.8Y$, referred to as the 'expenditure line', shows the relationship of PAE to output. Short-run equilibrium output (4,800) is determined at the intersection of the two lines, point E. This type of diagram is known as a 'Keynesian cross'.

The second line in Figure 21.8, less steep than the 45° line, shows the relationship between planned aggregate expenditure PAE and output Y. Because it summarises how planned spending depends on output, we shall call this line the *expenditure line*. In this example, we know that the relationship between PAE and output (the equation for the expenditure line) is

$$PAE = 960 + 0.8Y$$

According to this equation, when $Y = 0$, the value of PAE is 960. Thus 960 is the intercept of the expenditure line, as shown in Figure 21.8. Notice that *the intercept of the expenditure line equals autonomous expenditure*, a result that will always hold. The slope of the line relating aggregate demand to output is 0.8, the value of the coefficient of output in the equation $PAE = 960 + 0.8Y$. Where does the number 0.8 come from? (**Hint:** What determines by how much aggregate spending increases when output rises by a euro?)

Only one point in Figure 21.8 is consistent with *both* the definition of short-run equilibrium output, $Y = PAE$, and the given relationship between planned spending and output, $PAE = 960 + 0.8Y$. That point is the intersection of the two lines, point E. At point E, short-run equilibrium output equals 4,800, which is the same value that we obtained in Examples 21.3 and 23.4. At points to the right of E, output exceeds planned aggregate expenditure. Hence, to the right of point E, firms will be producing more than they can sell, which will lead them to reduce their rate of production. By contrast, to the left of point E, planned aggregate spending exceeds output. In that region, firms will not be producing enough to meet demand, and they will tend to increase their production. Only at point E, where output equals 4,800, will firms be producing enough to just satisfy planned spending on goods and services.

The diagram in Figure 21.8 is often called the *Keynesian cross*, after its characteristic shape. The Keynesian cross shows graphically how short-run equilibrium output is determined in a world in which producers meet demand at predetermined prices.

Planned spending and the output gap

We are now ready to use the basic Keynesian model to show how insufficient spending can lead to a recession. To illustrate the effects of spending changes on output, we shall continue to work with the economy introduced in Example 21.2. We have shown that, in this economy, short-run equilibrium output equals 4,800. Let us now make the additional assumption that potential output in this economy also equals 4,800, or $Y^\star = 4{,}800$, so that initially there is no output gap. Starting from this position of full employment, suppose that consumers become more pessimistic about the future, so that they begin to spend less at every level of current disposable income. We can capture this change by assuming that $\bar{C}$, the constant term in the consumption function, falls to a lower level. To be specific, suppose that $\bar{C}$ falls by 10 units, which in turn implies a decline in autonomous expenditure of 10 units. What is the effect of this reduction in planned spending on the economy? Examples 21.5 and 21.6 answer this question using the algebraic and numeric approaches to the determination of short-run equilibrium output. In each case, we shall see that when $\bar{C}$ falls by 10 units the economy will experience a recessionary gap equal to 50 units.

Example 21.5 A fall in planned spending leads to a recession (the algebraic approach)

From Equation 21.4 we know that short-run equilibrium output is given by:

$$Y = \left(\frac{1}{1-c}\right)\bar{A}$$

In Example 21.2 the marginal propensity to consume is $c = 0.8$ and total autonomous expenditures are

$$\bar{A} = \bar{C} - c\bar{T} - \bar{I} + \bar{G} + \bar{NX}$$
$$= 620 - 200 + 220 + 300 + 20$$
$$= 960$$

which gives an equilibrium value for Y equal to 4,800 ($960/0.2 = 4,800$). If the autonomous component of consumption $\overline{C}$ falls by 10 units, then the new value for total autonomous expenditure will be

$$\overline{A} = \overline{C} - c\overline{T} - \overline{I} + \overline{G} + \overline{NX}$$
$$= 610 - 200 + 220 + 300 + 20$$
$$= 950$$

and the new value for short-run equilibrium output is

$$Y = \left(\frac{1}{1 - 0.8}\right) 950 = 4,750$$

Hence, a 10-unit fall in autonomous expenditure results in a 50-unit fall in equilibrium output ($4,800 - 4,750$). The recessionary gap, $Y^\star - Y$, is 50 units.

Example 21.6 A fall in planned spending leads to a recession (the numeric approach)

Table 21.2 illustrates the numeric approach and is in the same form as Table 21.1. The key difference is that in Table 21.2 planned aggregate expenditure is given by $PAE = 950 + 0.8Y$, rather than by $PAE = 960 + 0.8Y$, as in Table 21.1.

Output Y	Planned aggregate expenditure $PAE = 950 + 0.8Y$	$Y - PAE$	$Y = PAE$?
(1)	(2)	(3)	(4)
4,600	4,630	−30	No
4,650	4,670	−20	No
4,700	4,710	−10	No
4,750	4,750	0	Yes
4,800	4,790	10	No
4,850	4,830	20	No
4,900	4,870	30	No
4,950	4,910	40	No
5,000	4,950	50	No

Table 21.2 **Determination of Short-Run Equilibrium Output after a Fall in Spending**

As in Table 21.1, column (1) shows alternative possible values of output Y, and column (2) shows the levels of planned aggregate expenditure PAE implied by each value of output in column (1). Notice that 4,800, the value of short-run equilibrium output found in Table 21.1, is no longer an equilibrium; when output is 4,800, planned spending is 4,790, so output and planned spending are not equal. As Table 21.2 shows, following the decline in planned aggregate expenditure, short-run equilibrium output is 4,750, the only value of output for which $Y = PAE$. Thus a drop of 10 units in autonomous expenditure has led to a 50-unit decline in short-run equilibrium output. If full-employment output is 4,800, then the recessionary gap shown in Figure 21.9 is $4,800 - 4,750 = 50$ units.

We can also illustrate the effects of the decline in consumer spending on the economy using the Keynesian cross diagram. Figure 21.9 shows the original short-run

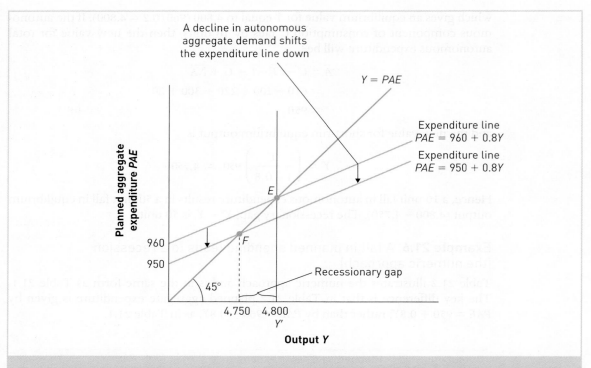

Figure 21.9 A Decline in Planned Spending Leads to a Recession. A decline in consumers' willingness to spend at any current level of disposable income reduces planned autonomous expenditure and shifts the expenditure line down. The short-run equilibrium point drops from *E* to *F*, reducing output and opening up a recessionary gap.

equilibrium point of the model (*E*), at the intersection of the 45° line, along which *Y* = *PAE*, and the original expenditure line, representing the equation *PAE* = 960 + 0.8*Y*. As before, the initial value of short-run equilibrium output is 4,800, which we have now assumed also corresponds to potential output *Y**. But what happens if $\bar{C}$ declines by 10, reducing autonomous expenditure by 10 as well?

Originally, autonomous expenditure in this economy was 960, so a decline of 10 units causes it to fall to 950. Instead of the economy's planned spending being described by the equation *PAE* = 960 + 0.8*Y*, as initially, it is now given by *PAE* = 950 + 0.8*Y*. What does this change imply for the graph in Figure 21.9? Since the intercept of the expenditure line (equal to autonomous expenditure) has decreased from 960 to 950, the effect of the decline in consumer spending will be to shift the expenditure line down in parallel fashion, by 10 units. Figure 21.9 indicates this downward shift in the expenditure line. The new short-run equilibrium point is at point *F*, where the new, lower expenditure line intersects the 45° line.

Point *F* is to the left of the original equilibrium point *E*, so we can see that output and spending have fallen from their initial levels. Since output at point *F* is lower than potential output, 4,800, we see that the fall in consumer spending has resulted in a recessionary gap in the economy. More generally, starting from a situation of full employment (where output equals potential output), any decline in autonomous expenditure leads to a recession. Examples 21.5 and 21.6 show that a decline in autonomous expenditure, arising from a decreased willingness of consumers to spend, causes short-run equilibrium output to fall, and opens up a recessionary gap. The same conclusion applies to declines in autonomous expenditure arising from other sources. Suppose, for example, that firms become disillusioned with new technologies and cut back their planned investment in new equipment. In terms of the model, this reluctance of firms to invest can be interpreted as a decline in planned investment spending I^P. Under our assumption that planned investment spending is autonomous and does not depend on output, planned investment is part of autonomous expenditure. So a decline in planned investment spending depresses autonomous expenditure and output, in precisely the same way that a decline in the autonomous part of consumption spending does. Similar conclusions apply to declines in other components of autonomous expenditure, such as government purchases and net exports, as we shall see in later applications.

Exercise 21.3 Using the economy described in Exercise 21.1, assume that consumers become *more* confident about the future. As a result, $\bar{C}$ rises by 10 units. Find the resulting change in short-run equilibrium output.

The multiplier

In Examples 21.5 and 21.6 we analysed a case in which the initial decline in consumer spending (as measured by the fall in $\bar{C}$) was only 10 units, and yet short-run equilibrium output fell by 50 units. Why did a relatively modest initial decline in consumer spending lead to a much larger fall in output?

The reason the impact on output was greater than the initial change in spending is the 'vicious circle' effect suggested by the Small-Land story earlier in this chapter. Specifically, a fall in consumer spending not only reduces the sales of consumer goods directly; it also reduces the incomes of workers and owners in the industries that produce consumer goods. As their incomes fall, these workers and capital owners reduce their spending, which reduces the output and incomes of *other* producers in the economy. These reductions in income lead to still further cuts in spending. Ultimately, these successive rounds of declines in spending and income may lead to a decrease in *PAE* and output that is significantly greater than the change in spending that started the process.

income–expenditure multiplier the effect of a 1-unit change in autonomous expenditure on short-run equilibrium output; for example, a multiplier of 5 means that a 10-unit decrease in autonomous expenditure reduces short-run equilibrium output by 50 units

The effect on short-run equilibrium output of a 1-unit change in autonomous expenditure is called the **income–expenditure multiplier**, or the *multiplier* for short. To find the value of the multiplier recall that Equation (21.4) determines short-run equilibrium output as

$$Y = \left(\frac{1}{1-c}\right)\bar{A}$$

If the marginal propensity to consume $c = 0.8$ then $1/(1-c)$ equals $1/0.2$ or 5 and each unit change in total autonomous expenditures $\bar{A}$ results in a 5-unit change in Y. For example, if $\bar{A} = 1,000$ then equilibrium $Y = 5,000$. However, if $\bar{A}$ falls by 100 to 900 then equilibrium Y declines by 500 to 4,500. Hence, for each unit change in $\bar{A}$, Y changes by 5 units (500/100). More generally, as a 1-unit change in $\bar{A}$ leads to a change in Y equal to $1/(1-c)$ it follows that the term $1/(1-c)$ is the *multiplier*. The idea that a change in spending may lead to a significantly larger change in short-run equilibrium output is a key feature of the basic Keynesian model. Box 21.1 provides a more rigorous derivation of the multiplier.

Maths Box 21.1 The income–expenditure multiplier  5

This box gives a more complete explanation of the *income–expenditure multiplier* in the basic Keynesian model. In Example 21.5, we saw that a drop in autonomous expenditure of 10 units caused a decline in short-run equilibrium output of 50 units, five times as great as the initial change in spending. Hence the multiplier in this example is 5.

To see why this multiplier effect occurs, note that the initial decrease of 10 in consumer spending (more precisely, in the constant term of the consumption function, $\bar{C}$) in Example 21.5 has two effects. First, the fall in consumer spending directly reduces planned aggregate expenditure by 10 units. Second, the fall in spending also reduces by 10 units the incomes of producers (workers and firm owners) of consumer goods. Under the assumption of Example 21.5 that the marginal propensity to consume is 0.8, the producers of consumer goods will therefore reduce *their* consumption spending by 8, or 0.8 times their income loss of 10. This reduction in spending cuts the income of *other* producers by 8 units, leading them to reduce their spending by 6.4, or 0.8 times their income loss of 8. These income reductions of 6.4 lead still other producers to cut their spending by 5.12, or 0.8 times 6.4, and so on. In principle this process continues indefinitely, although after many rounds of spending and income reductions the effects become quite small.

When all these 'rounds' of income and spending reductions are added, the *total* effect on planned spending of the initial reduction of 10 in consumer spending is

$$10 + 8 + 6.4 + 5.12 + \ldots$$

The three dots indicate that the series of reductions continues indefinitely. The total effect of the initial decrease in consumption can also be written as

$$10[1 + 0.8 + (0.8)^2 + (0.8)^3 + \ldots]$$

This expression highlights the fact that the spending that takes place in each round is 0.8 times the spending in the previous round (0.8), because that is the marginal propensity to consume out of the income generated by the previous round of spending.

A useful algebraic relationship, which applies to any number x greater than 0 but less than 1, is

$$1 + x + x^2 + x^3 + \ldots = \frac{1}{1 - x}$$

If we set $x = 0.8$, this formula implies that the total effect of the decline in consumption spending on aggregate demand and output is $10\left(\dfrac{1}{1 - 08}\right) = 10\left(\dfrac{1}{0.2}\right) = 10 \times 5 = 50$

This answer is consistent with our earlier calculation, which showed that short-run equilibrium output fell by 50 units, from 4,800 to 4,750.

By a similar analysis we can also find a general algebraic expression for the multiplier in the basic Keynesian model. Recalling that c is the marginal propensity to consume out of disposable income, we know that a 1-unit increase in autonomous expenditure raises spending and income by 1 unit in the first round, by $c \times 1 = c$ units in the second round, by $c \times c = c^2$ units in the second round, by $c \times c^2 = c^3$ units in the third round, and so on. Thus the total effect on short-run equilibrium output of a 1-unit increase in autonomous expenditure is given by

$$1 + c + c^2 + c^3 + \ldots$$

Applying the algebraic formula given above, and recalling that $0 < c < 1$, we can rewrite this expression as $1/(1 - c)$. Thus, in a basic Keynesian model with a marginal propensity to consume of c, the multiplier equals $1/(1 - c)$. Note that if $c = 0.8$, then $1/(1 - c) = 1/(1 - 0.8) = 5$, which is the same value of the multiplier we found numerically above.

As we shall see in the following chapters, the size of the multiplier is important in determining the effectiveness of *macroeconomic policies* as a means to stabilise the economy. Hence, it is important to ask what determines the value of the multiplier. Clearly, the marginal propensity to consume (MPC) out of disposable income c is crucial. If the MPC is large, then, as disposable income falls, people will reduce their spending sharply, and the multiplier effect will be large. Conversely, if the MPC is small, households will not reduce their expenditure by as much when income falls, and the multiplier will be smaller. For example, if $c = 0.8$ the multiplier is 5. However if $c = 0.6$ the multiplier is $1/0.4 = 2.5$. As shown in Example 21.7, the openness of the economy to international trade can also affect the value of the multiplier.

Example 21.7 The multiplier and imports

So far, we have assumed that expenditures on imports are autonomous (do not depend on Y). However, imports are part of *domestic expenditures* and may change as Y changes. As incomes increase we would expect households to spend more on goods and services, including those produced in other economies. For example, approximately 33 per cent of total GDP in the European Union was spent on imports and, in small countries such as Belgium and Ireland, the percentage was much higher, at 75 per cent or more. Likewise, part of investment expenditures by firms and government purchases will be spent on imported goods. Note that this is why we have included *net* exports (exports minus imports) in our definition of total planned aggregate expenditures:

$$PAE = C + I^P + G + NX$$

For example, if a Belgian household buys a camera manufactured in Japan, the camera is part of Japan's GDP not Belgium's. However, as expenditure on the imported camera is included in domestic consumption C and net exports NX (exports *minus* imports) it cancels out in our definition of PAE. If the camera costs €500 its purchase increases C by €500 and reduces NX by €500, leaving total expenditure on *domestically* produced goods unaffected. As expenditures on consumption, investment and government purchases all include imports it seems unrealistic to assume that imports are totally autonomous. Suppose we were to relax this assumption and assume that imports vary with Y. We shall see that for a given value of the marginal propensity to consume, this reduces the value of the multiplier.

The last term in the equation for PAE denotes net exports, or exports less imports. Denoting exports as EX and imports as IM we can define net exports as

$$NX = EX - IM$$

and PAE as

$$PAE = C + I^P + G + EX - IM$$

The consumption function

$$C = \bar{C} + c(Y - T)$$

import function the relationship between imports and income

marginal propensity to import the proportion of a change in income that is spent on imports

implies that consumption, which includes expenditure on imports, is an induced expenditure. To treat imports as an induced expenditure we introduce an additional equation, which we shall call the **import function**:

$$IM = mY$$

The parameter m is a constant greater than zero but less than one ($0 < m < 1$) and is known as the **marginal propensity to import**. For example, if $m = 0.4$ a €100 increase in Y leads to (or induces) a €40 increase in expenditure on imports. Likewise, if Y falls by €100, expenditure on imports will fall by €40.

Using the consumption and import functions to substitute for C and IM in the equation for PAE gives

$$PAE = [\bar{C} - c(Y - T)] + I^P + G + EX - mY$$
$$= [C - cT + I^P + G + EX] + (c - m)Y$$

Treating the first term on the right-hand side as total autonomous expenditures, $\bar{A}$, we get

$$PAE = \bar{A} + (c - m)Y$$

As equilibrium output is the level at which $Y = PAE$ the economy will reach its short-run equilibrium when

$$Y = \bar{A} + (c - m)Y$$

or

$$Y(1 - c + m) = \bar{A}$$

Dividing both sides by $(1 - c + m)$ gives equilibrium Y as

$$Y = \left(\frac{1}{1 - c + m}\right)\bar{A} \tag{21.5}$$

The multiplier is the term $1/(1 - c + m)$, which is smaller than the previous value $1/(1 - c)$. For example if $c = 0.8$ and $m = 0.2$, the multiplier is $1/0.4 = 2.5$ as compared with 5 when imports are exogenous ($m = 0$). To explain why treating imports as an induced expenditure reduces the value of the multiplier, suppose that autonomous expenditures fall by 10 units leading to an 8-unit fall in consumption. We have seen that this creates a 'vicious circle' leading to further declines in consumption and, if $m = 0$ and the multiplier is 5, an eventual fall in Y of 50 units. In this case the entire fall in consumption falls on domestic production. However, if $m = 0.2$ the initial decline in consumption can be broken down into 6 units on domestic production and 2 units on imports, and as imports are not part of Y the effect on domestic production is smaller and each round of the 'vicious circle' leads to a smaller decline in economic activity.

It follows that the greater the marginal propensity to import the lower the value of the multiplier. For example, we have seen that when $c = 0.8$ and $m = 0.2$ the multiplier is 2.5. However, if $c = 0.8$ and $m = 0.3$ the value of the multiplier falls to $1/(1 - 0.8 + 0.3) = 2$. In short, the more important are imports in domestic expenditure the lower the multiplier is likely to be. This, as we have seen, is characteristic of several European economies, and especially the smaller ones in which imports account for a high proportion of total expenditure.

Exercise 21.4 Repeat Exercise 21.3 but this time assume that net exports are $NX = 2,600 - 0.4Y$ (imports are an induced expenditure and the marginal propensity to import $m = 0.4$). Explain why your answer differs from that in Exercise 21.3.

The tax multiplier

The income–expenditure multiplier measures the effect of a change in autonomous expenditure on short-run equilibrium output. However, net taxes T are also part of autonomous expenditure. Example 21.8 illustrates how equilibrium output responds to a change in net taxes.

Example 21.8 The tax multiplier

Suppose that, due to a sudden increase in unemployment, government transfer payments were to increase by 10 units. What is the effect on equilibrium output?

Net taxes are defined as tax revenues minus transfer payments, which include unemployment benefits. Hence a 10-unit increase in unemployment benefits means that net taxes will fall by an equal amount. To calculate the impact on Y, recall that Equation (21.4) determines short-run equilibrium output as

$$Y = \left(\frac{1}{1-c} \right) \bar{A}$$

where:

$$\bar{A} = \bar{C} - c\bar{T} + \bar{I} + \bar{G} + \overline{NX}$$

which we can write as

$$\bar{A} = [\bar{C} + \bar{I} + \bar{G} + \overline{NX}] - c\bar{T} \text{ or } \bar{A} = \bar{A}' - c\bar{T}$$

where $\bar{A}' = [\bar{C} + \bar{I} + \bar{G} + \overline{NX}]$. Hence we can express equilibrium output as:

$$Y = \frac{1}{1-c} \bar{A}' - \frac{c}{1-c} \bar{T}$$

With autonomous expenditures constant, a change in net taxes causes a change in equilibrium output equal to $c/(1-c)$ units, or

$$\Delta Y = -\frac{c}{1-c} \Delta \bar{T} \tag{21.6}$$

tax multiplier the effect of a change in net taxes on short-run equilibrium output. Because the marginal propensity to consume is less than 1, the tax multiplier will be smaller than the income–expenditure multiplier

For example, if $c = 0.8$ then $c/(1-c) = 0.8/0.2 = 4$ and a 10-unit decrease in net taxes increases equilibrium Y by 40 units. As the term $c/(1-c)$ gives the change in short-run equilibrium output that results from change in net taxes it is called the **tax multiplier**. Note that because the marginal propensity to consume is less than one $(0 < c < 1)$, the tax multiplier will be smaller than the income–expenditure multiplier, $1/(1-c)$. When, for example, $c = 0.8$ the tax multiplier is 4 but the income–expenditure multiplier is 5.

RECAP Finding short-run equilibrium output

Short-run equilibrium output is the level of output at which output equals planned aggregate expenditure – or, in symbols, $Y = PAE$. For a specific sample economy, short-run equilibrium output can be solved for algebraically, numerically or graphically.

The graphical solution is based on a diagram called the *Keynesian cross*. The Keynesian cross diagram includes two lines: a 45° line that represents the condition $Y = PAE$, and the expenditure line, which shows the relationship of *PAE* to output. Short-run equilibrium output is determined at the intersection of the two lines. If short-run equilibrium output differs from potential output, an *output gap* exists.

Increases in autonomous expenditure shift the expenditure line upwards, increasing short-run equilibrium output; decreases in autonomous expenditure shift the expenditure line downwards, leading to declines in short-run equilibrium output. Decreases in autonomous expenditure that drive actual output below potential output are a source of *recessions*.

Generally, change in autonomous expenditure leads to a larger change in short-run equilibrium output, reflecting the working of the *income–expenditure multiplier*. The multiplier arises because a given initial increase in spending raises the incomes of producers, which leads them to spend more, raising the incomes and spending of other producers, and so on.

As imports are expenditures on foreign output the value of the multiplier will be lower when the economy is open to international trade.

Planned aggregate expenditure and the real interest rate

In previous sections we saw how planned spending is affected by changes in real output Y. Changes in output affect the private sector's disposable income $(Y - T)$, which in turn influences consumption spending – a relationship captured by the *consumption function*. A second variable that has potentially important effects on aggregate expenditure is the real interest rate r. For households, the effect of a higher real interest rate is to increase the reward for saving, which leads households to save more and, at given level of income, *consume less*. Thus, saying that a higher real interest rate *increases* saving is the same as saying that a higher real interest rate *reduces* consumption spending at each level of income. The idea that higher real interest rates reduce household spending makes intuitive sense. Think, for example, about people's willingness to buy consumer durables, such as cars or furniture. Purchases of consumer durables, which are part of consumption spending, are often financed by borrowing from a bank, credit union or finance company. When the real interest rate rises, the monthly finance charges associated with the purchase of a car or a piano are higher, and people become less willing or able to make the purchase. Thus at a given level of disposable income a higher real interest rate reduces people's willingness to spend on consumer goods. Conversely, a lower real rate of interest will stimulate consumption by making saving less attractive and by reducing the real cost of borrowing.

Besides reducing consumption spending, a higher real interest rate also discourages firms from making capital investments. For example, upgrading a computer system may be profitable for a manufacturing firm when the cost of the system can be financed by borrowing at a real interest rate of 3 per cent. However, if the real interest rate rises to 6 per cent, doubling the cost of funds to the firm, the same upgrade may not be profitable and the firm may choose not to invest. Conversely a fall in the real rate of interest will reduce financing costs and make investment more profitable. We should also remember that residential investment – the building of houses and flats – is also part of investment spending. Higher interest rates, in the form of higher mortgage rates, certainly discourage this kind of investment spending as well.

To capture the effect of interest rate changes on planned spending we must modify the equations for consumption (the consumption function) and planned investment. Hence:

$$C = C + c(Y - T) - ar$$
$$I^P = \bar{I} - br$$

The first equation is the consumption function with an additional term, equal to $-ar$. Think of a as a fixed number, greater than zero, that measures the strength of the interest rate effect on consumption. Thus the term $-ar$ captures the idea that when the real interest rate r rises, consumption declines by a times the increase in the interest rate. For example if $a = 200$ a 1 per cent (0.01) increase in the interest rate reduces consumption by 2 units (200×0.01). Likewise, the second equation adds the term $-br$ to the equation for planned investment. The parameter b is a fixed positive number that measures how strongly changes in the real interest rate affect planned investment. For example if $b = 500$ a 1 per cent (0.01) increase in the interest rate reduces consumption by 5 units (500×0.01). We continue to assume that government purchases, taxes and net exports are exogenous variables, so that $G = \bar{G}$, $T = \bar{T}$ and $NX = \overline{NX}$.

To solve for short-run equilibrium output, we start as usual by finding the relationship of planned aggregate expenditure (PAE) to output. The definition of planned aggregate expenditure is

$$PAE = C + I^P + G + NX$$

Substituting the modified equations for consumption and planned investment into this definition, along with the exogenous values of government spending, net exports, and taxes, we get

$$PAE = [\bar{C} + c(Y - \bar{T}) - ar] + [\bar{I} - br] + \bar{G} + \overline{NX}$$

The first term in brackets on the right-hand side describes the behaviour of consumption, and the second bracketed term describes planned investment. Rearranging this equation in order to group together terms that depend on the real interest rate and terms that depend on output, we find

$$PAE = [\bar{C} - c\bar{T} + \bar{I} + \bar{G} + \overline{NX}] - (a + b)r + cY$$

This equation is similar to the previous equation for PAE except that it has an extra term, $-(a + b)r$, on the right-hand side. This extra term captures the idea that an increase in the real interest rate lowers planned spending by reducing consumption and planned investment. To find short-run equilibrium output, we set $Y = PAE$ and solve for Y. Hence:

$$Y = [\bar{C} - c\bar{T} + \bar{I} + \bar{G} + \overline{NX}] - (a+b)r + cY$$

Collecting the terms in Y gives

$$Y = \left(\frac{1}{1 - c}\right)[\bar{C} - c\bar{T} + \bar{I} + \bar{G} + \overline{NX} - (a + b)r]$$

or:

$$Y = \left(\frac{1}{1 - c}\right)[\bar{A} - (a + b)r] \qquad (21.6)$$

where $\bar{A} = [\bar{C} - c\bar{T} + \bar{I} + \bar{G} + \bar{NX}]$. Equation (21.6) defines short-run equilibrium output when consumption and investment vary with the real rate of interest. Example 21.9 illustrates this relationship.

Example 21.9 Short-run equilibrium output and the real rate of interest

Suppose that, in a given economy, $\bar{A} = 1,010$, $c = 0.8$, $a = 400$ and $b = 600$. Find short-run equilibrium output when the real rate of interest $r = 0.3$ and when $r = 0.05$.

With the marginal propensity to consume $c = 0.8$ the income–expenditure multiplier $1/(1 - c) = 5$. Substituting the given values for $\bar{A}$, a and b into Equation (21.6) gives:

$$r = 0.03: Y = 5[1,010 - 1,000 \times 0.03] = 4,900$$

$$r = 0.05: Y = 5[1,010 - 1,000 \times 0.05] = 4,800$$

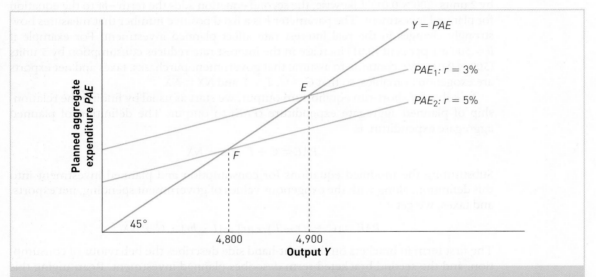

Figure 21.10 Equilibrium Output and the Real Rate of Interest. When the real rate of interest is 3 per cent, short-run equilibrium is at point E and $Y = 4,900$. An increase in the interest rate to 5 per cent reduces planned expenditures at each level of output giving the new expenditure line PAE_2, giving a new equilibrium at F and a lower equilibrium $Y = 4,800$.

Hence, other things being equal, the higher the real rate of interest the lower is short-run equilibrium output. This relationship is shown graphically in Figure 21.10. The line PAE_1 is the planned aggregate expenditure line with the real rate of interest $r = 3$ per cent, or 0.03. Short-run equilibrium is at the point E where the planned expenditure line intersects the 45° line and $Y = PAE$. At the real rate of interest at 5 per cent, consumption and investment expenditures will be lower at each level of Y. Hence with the real rate of interest $r = 5$ per cent, the planned aggregate expenditure line will be lower at PAE_2, giving equilibrium at point F and a lower value for short-run equilibrium output.

Exercise 21.5 Suppose that, in a given economy, $\bar{A} = 1,016$, $c = 0.8$, $a = 500$ and $b = 700$. Find short-run equilibrium output when the real rate of interest $r = 0.03$ and when $r = 0.05$. Compare your answer to Example 21.9.

Summary

- Real GDP does not grow smoothly. Periods in which the economy is growing at a rate significantly below normal are called *recessions*; periods in which the economy is growing at a rate significantly above normal are called *expansions*. A severe or protracted recession, like the long decline that occurred between 1929 and 1932, is called a *depression*, while a particularly strong expansion is called a *boom*. Most European economies experienced recession in the early 1970s, 1980s and 1990s. Each of these recessions was preceded by a rise in oil prices.

- Short-term economic fluctuations are irregular in length and severity, and are thus hard to forecast. Expansions and recessions are typically felt throughout the economy and may even be *global* in scope. *Unemployment* rises sharply during recessions, while *inflation* tends to fall during or shortly after a recession. Durable goods industries tend to be particularly sensitive to recessions and booms, whereas services and non-durable goods industries are less sensitive.

- *Potential output*, also called potential GDP or full employment output, is the amount of output (real GDP) that an economy can produce when it is using its resources, such as capital and labour, at normal rates. The difference between potential output and actual output is the *output gap*. When output is below potential, the gap is called a *recessionary gap*; when output is above potential, the difference is called an *expansionary gap*. Recessions can occur either because potential output is growing unusually slowly or because actual output is below potential. Because recessionary gaps represent wasted resources and expansionary gaps threaten to create inflation, policy makers have an incentive to try to eliminate both types.

- The *natural rate of unemployment* is the part of the total unemployment rate that is attributable to *frictional* and *structural* unemployment. Equivalently, the natural rate of unemployment is the rate of unemployment that exists when the output gap is zero. *Cyclical* unemployment, the part of unemployment that is associated with recessions and expansions, equals the total unemployment rate less the natural unemployment rate.

- The basic Keynesian model shows how fluctuations in planned *aggregate expenditure*, or total *planned spending*, can cause actual output to differ from potential output. Too little spending leads to a *recessionary* output gap; too much spending creates an *expansionary* output gap. This model relies on the crucial assumption that firms do not respond to every change in demand by changing prices. Instead, they typically set a price for some period, then meet the demand forthcoming at that price. Firms do not change prices continually because changing prices entails costs, called *menu costs*.

- *Planned aggregate expenditure* (PAE) is total planned spending on final goods and services. The four components of total spending are consumption, investment, government purchases and net exports. Planned and actual consumption, government purchases and net exports are generally assumed to be the same. *Actual* investment may differ from planned investment, because firms may sell a greater or lesser amount of their production than they expected. If firms sell less than they expected, for example, they are forced to add more goods to inventory than anticipated. And, because additions to inventory are counted as part of investment, in this case actual investment (including inventory investment) is greater than planned investment.

- Consumption is related to disposable, or after-tax, income by a relationship called the *consumption function*. The amount by which desired consumption rises when disposable income rises by one euro is called the *marginal propensity to consume* (MPC, or c). The MPC is always greater than 0 but less than 1 (that is, $0 < c < 1$).

▶ ■ An increase in real output raises planned aggregate expenditure, since higher output (and, equivalently, higher income) encourages households to consume more. PAE can be broken down into two components: autonomous expenditure and induced expenditure. *Autonomous expenditure* is the portion of planned spending that is independent of output; *induced expenditure* is the portion of spending that depends on output.

■ In the period in which prices are fixed, the *short-run equilibrium output* is the level of output that just equals planned aggregate expenditure. Short-run equilibrium can be determined algebraically or numerically by a table that compares alternative values of output and the planned spending implied by each level of output. Short-run equilibrium output can also be determined graphically in a Keynesian cross diagram, drawn with planned aggregate expenditure on the vertical axis and output on the horizontal axis. The Keynesian cross contains two lines: an expenditure line, which relates planned aggregate expenditure to output, and a 45° line, which represents the condition that short-run equilibrium output equals planned aggregate expenditure. Short-run equilibrium output is determined at the point at which these two lines intersect.

■ Changes in *autonomous expenditure* will lead to changes in short-run equilibrium output. In particular, if the economy is initially at full employment, a fall in autonomous expenditure will create a recessionary gap, and a rise in autonomous expenditure will create an expansionary gap. The amount by which a 1-unit increase in autonomous expenditure raises short-run equilibrium output is called the *multiplier*. An increase in autonomous expenditure not only raises spending directly; it also raises the incomes of producers, who in turn increase their spending, and so on. Hence the multiplier is greater than 1; that is, a 1 euro increase in autonomous expenditure tends to raise short-run equilibrium output by more than 1 euro. Because imports may vary with income, the value of the multiplier will be lower when the economy is open to international trade. This is an important feature of the smaller European economies.

■ Changes in the real rate of interest affect planned spending. For example, an increase in the real rate of interest will reduce consumption and investment by making saving more attractive and increasing the real cost of borrowing. Other things being equal, the higher the real rate of interest the lower is equilibrium output.

Review questions

1. Define *recession* and *expansion*. What are the beginning and ending points of a recession called? Which have been longer on average, recessions or expansions?

2. How is each of the following likely to be affected by a recession: the natural unemployment rate, the cyclical unemployment rate and the inflation rate?

3. Define *potential output*. Is it possible for an economy to produce an amount greater than potential output? Explain.

4. **True or false:** When output equals potential output, the unemployment rate is zero. Explain.

5. What is the key assumption of the basic Keynesian model? Explain why this assumption is needed if one is to accept the view that aggregate spending is a driving force behind short-term economic fluctuations.

6. Give an example of a good or service whose price changes very frequently and one whose price changes relatively infrequently. What accounts for the difference?

7. Define *planned aggregate expenditure* (PAE) and list its components. Why does planned spending change when (a) output changes (b) the real rate of interest changes?

8. Explain how planned spending and actual spending can differ. Illustrate with an example.

9. Sketch a graph of the consumption function. Discuss the economic meaning of (a) a movement from left to right along the graph of the consumption function; and (b) a parallel upward shift of the consumption function. Give an example of a factor that could lead to a parallel upward shift of the consumption function.

10. Sketch the Keynesian cross diagram. Explain in words the economic significance of the two lines graphed in the diagram. Given only this diagram, how could you determine autonomous expenditure, induced expenditure, the marginal propensity to consume and short-run equilibrium output?

11. Define the *multiplier*. In economic terms, why is the multiplier greater than 1?

12. Define the *marginal propensity to import*. Why does a high value for the marginal propensity to import imply a low value for the multiplier?

connect Problems

1. Acme Manufacturing is producing €4,000,000 worth of goods this year and expects to sell its entire production. It is also planning to purchase €1,500,000 in new equipment during the year. At the beginning of the year the company has €500,000 in inventory in its warehouse. Find actual investment and planned investment if

   a. Acme actually sells €3,850,000 worth of goods

   b. Acme actually sells €4,000,000 worth of goods

   c. Acme actually sells €4,200,000 worth of goods.

Assuming that Acme's situation is similar to that of other firms, in which of these three cases is output equal to short-run equilibrium output?

2. Data on before-tax income, taxes paid and consumption spending for the Simpson family in various years are given in the table below.

Before-tax income (€)	Taxes paid (€)	Consumption spending (€)
25,000	3,000	20,000
27,000	3,500	21,350
28,000	3,700	22,070
30,000	4,000	23,600

   a. Graph the Simpsons' consumption function and find their household's marginal propensity to consume.

   b. How much would you expect the Simpsons to consume if their income was €32,000 and they paid taxes of €5,000?

   c. Homer Simpson wins a lottery prize. As a result, the Simpson family increases its consumption by €1,000 at each level of after-tax income. ('Income' does not include the prize money.) How does this change affect the graph of their consumption function? How does it affect their marginal propensity to consume?

3. An economy is described by the following equations:

$$C = 1,800 + 0.6(Y - T)$$
$$I^P = 900$$
$$G = 1,500$$
$$NX = 100$$
$$T = 1,500$$
$$Y^* = 9,000$$

   a. Using the algebraic method, find the short-run equilibrium value for output in this economy.

   b. What is the value of the multiplier in this economy?

   c. Find autonomous expenditure and induced expenditure in this economy.

   d. Is the economy experiencing an output gap? If so, what is its value?

   e. Find the effect on short-run equilibrium output of a decrease in planned investment from 900 to 800.

   f. Find the effect on short-run equilibrium output of an increase in autonomous consumption from 1,800 to 1,900.

4. For the economy described in Problem 3:

   a. construct a table like Table 21.1 to find short-run equilibrium output; consider possible values for short-run equilibrium output ranging from 8,200 to 9,000

   b. show the determination of short-run equilibrium output for this economy using the Keynesian cross diagram.

5. For the economy described in Problem 3, suppose that net exports are given by $NX = 950 - mY$. If the marginal propensity to import is $m = 0.1$:

   a. find the value for short-run equilibrium output

   b. find the value for the multiplier; why does it differ from the answer in Problem 3?

   c. Repeat parts (e) and (f) in Problem 3. Why do your answers differ?

To help you grasp the key concepts of this chapter check out the extra resources posted on the Online Learning Centre. There are chapter summaries, self-test questions, an interactive graphing tool, weblinks and a glossary, all for free!

Visit the Online Learning Centre at: www.mcgraw-hill.co.uk/textbooks/mcdowell for information on accessing all of these resources.

22

Money and Interest Rates

The final section of Chapter 21 introduced the idea that planned aggregate expenditures depend on the real rate of interest as well as disposable income. However, Chapter 21 does not explain how the interest rate is determined. For instance, in Example 21.9, we calculated the short-run equilibrium level of output for assumed values of the interest rate but did not explain why at a particular time the rate of interest is 3 per cent or 5 per cent or any other value. Hence in this chapter we extend the Keynesian model to include the macroeconomic determinants of the rate of interest. We shall see that in the Keynesian model the rate of interest is determined by the interaction of the demand for and supply of money, and the equilibrium rate of interest is the rate that clears the market for money by equating the demand for money to the money supply.

Money and its uses

What is money and why do people use money? Money has three principal uses: a *medium of exchange*, a *unit of account* and a *store of value*.

Money serves as a **medium of exchange** when it is used to purchase goods and services, as when you pay cash for a newspaper. This is perhaps money's most crucial

medium of exchange an asset used in purchasing goods and services

barter the direct trade of goods or services for other goods or services

function. Think about how complicated daily life would become if there were no money. Without money, all economic transactions would have to be in the form of **barter**, which is the direct trade of goods or services for other goods or services. Barter is highly inefficient because it requires that each party to a trade has something that the other party wants, a so-called *double coincidence of wants*. For example, under a barter system, a musician could get her dinner only by finding someone willing to trade food for a musical performance. Finding such a match of needs, where each party happens to want exactly what the other person has to offer, would be difficult to do on a regular basis. In a world with money, the musician's problem is considerably simpler. First, she must find someone who is willing to pay money for her musical performance.

Then, with the money received, she can purchase the food and other goods and services that she needs. In a society that uses money, it is not necessary that the person who wants to hear music and the person willing to provide food to the musician be one and the same. In other words, there need not be a double coincidence of wants for trades of goods and services to take place.

Comparative Advantage

By eliminating the problem of having to find a double coincidence of wants in order to trade, the use of money in a society permits individuals to specialise in producing particular goods or services, as opposed to having every family or village produce most of what it needs. *Specialisation* greatly increases economic efficiency and material standards of living, as we discussed in Chapter 2 (the *Principle of Comparative Advantage*). This usefulness of money in making transactions explains why savers hold money, even though money generally pays a low rate of return. Cash, for example, pays no interest at all, and the balances in chequing accounts usually pay a lower rate of interest than could be obtained in alternative financial investments.

unit of account a basic measure of economic value

Money's second function is as a *unit of account*. As a **unit of account**, money is the basic yardstick for measuring *economic value*. In the countries that use the euro as their currency virtually all prices – including the price of labour (wages) and the prices of financial assets, such as government bonds – are expressed in euros. In the United States these prices are measured in dollars and in the United Kingdom in pounds sterling. Expressing economic values in a common unit of account allows for easy comparisons. For example, milk can be measured in litres and coal in tonnes, but to judge whether 1,000 litres of milk is economically more or less valuable than a tonne of coal, we express both values in money terms. The use of money as a unit of account is closely related to its use as a medium of exchange; because money is used to buy and sell things, it makes sense to express prices of all kinds in money terms.

store of value an asset that serves as a means of holding wealth

As a **store of value**, its third function, money is a way of holding wealth. For example, the miser who stuffs cash into his mattress or buries gold coins under the old oak tree at midnight is holding wealth in money form. Likewise, if you regularly keep a balance in your chequing account, you are holding part of your wealth in the form of money. Although money is usually the primary medium of exchange or unit of account in an economy, it is not the only store of value. There are numerous other ways of holding wealth, such as owning bonds, shares or property.

Measuring money

How much money, defined as financial assets usable for making purchases, is there in the economy at any given time? This question is not simple to answer because in practice it is not easy to draw a clear distinction between those assets that should be counted as money and those that should not. Euro, dollar and sterling notes and coins are certainly a form of money, and a Van Gogh painting certainly is not. However, in some countries, brokerage firms now offer accounts that allow their owners to combine financial investments in stocks and bonds with cheque-writing and credit card privileges. Should the balances in these accounts, or some part of them, be counted as money? It is difficult to tell.

Economists skirt round the problem of deciding what is and isn't money by using several alternative definitions, which vary in how broadly the concept of money is defined. In the Eurosystem the European Central Bank (ECB) uses three definitions. The first is a relatively 'narrow' definition of the amount of money in the economy

M1 sum of currency outstanding and balances held in chequing accounts

M2 all the assets in M1 plus some additional assets that are usable in making payments but at greater cost or inconvenience than the use of currency or cheques

M3 all assets in M2 plus marketable securities with a high degree of liquidity and price certainty

called **M1**. M1 is the sum of currency outstanding and balances held in deposits on which the holder can write cheques and withdraw cash from ATMs, etc. Deposits of this type are called 'overnight' deposits. The second definition is a broader measure of money, called **M2**, and includes all the assets in M1 plus some additional deposits that are usable in making payments, but at greater cost or inconvenience than the use of currency or cheques. These deposits normally require advance notice of withdrawal and may carry a penalty if withdrawn early. The final, and broadest, definition is money called **M3**, which comprises all assets in M2 and certain marketable instruments issued by financial institutions. These instruments have high liquidity, which means they can easily be sold, without significant risk of capital loss and are considered to be close substitutes for the type of the deposit included in M1 and M2. Table 22.1 lists the components of M1, M2 and M3, and also gives the amount of each type of asset outstanding as of November 2007. Similar data for the United Kingdom and the United States can be found at www.bankofengland.co.uk and www.federalreserve.gov.

We shall see that in formulating monetary policy most central banks such as the ECB and the Bank of England tend to concentrate on broad definitions of the money supply such as M2 and M3. However, for illustrative purposes, it is sufficient to think of money as the sum of currency outstanding and balances in overnight accounts, or M1.

M1	**3,859.7**
Currency	618.8
Overnight deposits	3,240.9
M2	**7,307.4**
M1	3,859.7
Deposits with up to 2 years' maturity	1,914.3
Deposits requiring up to 3 months' notice of withdrawal	1,533.4
M3	**8,620.3**
M2	7,307.4
Marketable instruments	1,312.9

Table 22.1 **Components of M1, M2 and M3 (November 2007)**
Notes: Billion euros adjusted for seasonal variation. In M1, currency refers to cash and overnight deposits are deposits that can immediately be converted into currency. M2 includes all components of M1 plus deposits with maturity up to two years or redeemable at up to three months' notice. M3 comprises all assets in M2 plus money market instruments such as repurchase agreements, money market fund shares/units and debt securities with maturity of up to two years.
Source: Tables S12 and S13 ECB, *Monthly Bulletin* (February 2008) (www.ecb.int).

RECAP Money and its uses

Money is any asset that can be used in making purchases, such as currency or a chequing account. Money serves as a *medium of exchange* when it is used to purchase goods and services. The use of money as a medium of exchange eliminates the need for *barter* and the difficulties of finding a 'double coincidence of wants'. Money also serves as a *unit of account* and a *store of value*.

The ECB uses three measures of money: M1, M2 and M3. M1, a more narrow measure, is made up primarily of currency and balances held in chequing accounts. The broader measures, M2 and M3, include all the assets in M1 plus some additional assets usable in making payments.

The demand for money

Like other assets, such as shares, bonds and property, money is a store of value or a way of *holding wealth*. Anyone who has some wealth must determine the *form* in which they wish to hold that wealth. For example, if Louis has wealth of €10,000, he could, if he wished, hold all €10,000 in cash. Or he could hold €5,000 of his wealth in the form of cash and €5,000 in government bonds. Or he could hold €1,000 in cash, €2,000 in a chequing account, €2,000 in government bonds and €5,000 in rare stamps. Indeed, there are thousands of different real and financial assets to choose from, all of which can be held in different amounts and combinations, so Louis' choices are virtually infinite. The decision about the forms in which to hold one's wealth is called the **portfolio allocation decision**.

> **portfolio allocation decision** the decision about the forms in which to hold one's wealth

What determines the particular *mix of assets* that Louis or another wealth holder will choose? All else being equal, people generally prefer to hold assets that they expect to pay a high *return* and do not carry too much *risk*. They may also try to reduce the overall risk they face through *diversification* – that is, by owning a variety of different assets. Many people own some real assets, such as a car or a home, because they provide services (transportation or shelter) and often a financial return (an increase in value, as when the price of a home rises in a strong housing market).

Here we do not need to analyse the entire portfolio allocation decision, but only one part of it – namely, the decision about how much of one's wealth to hold in the form of *money*. To simplify things, we shall assume that assets classified as money carry a zero nominal rate of interest and that the average real return on all other forms of holding wealth is what we have called the real rate of interest r, defined as the nominal rate of interest i minus the rate of inflation π. That is $r = i - \pi$. What do we mean by *the* nominal interest rate? There are of course many different assets, each with its own interest rate. So can we really talk about *the* nominal interest rate? The answer is that, while there are many different assets, each with their own corresponding interest rate, the rates on those assets tend to *rise and fall together*. This is to be expected, because if the interest rates on some assets were to rise sharply while the rates on other assets declined, financial investors would flock to the assets paying high rates and refuse to buy the assets paying low rates. So, although there are many different interest rates in practice, speaking of the general level of interest rates usually does make sense. In this book, when we talk about *the* nominal interest rate, what we have in mind is some average measure of interest rates. This simplification is one more application of the macroeconomic concept of *aggregation*, introduced in Chapter 15.

The amount of wealth an individual chooses to hold in the form of money is that individual's **demand for money**. So if Louis decided to hold his entire €10,000 in the form of cash, his demand for money would be €10,000. But if he were to hold €1,000 in cash, €2,000 in a bank account, which can be used to finance transactions, and €7,000 in government bonds, his demand for money would be only €3,000 – that is, €1,000 in cash plus the €2,000 in his bank account.

> **demand for money** the amount of wealth an individual chooses to hold in the form of money

Macroeconomic determinants of the demand for money

How much money should individuals and firms choose to hold? Or, what are the determinants of the demand for money? In any household or business, the demand for money will depend on a variety of individual circumstances. For example, a high-volume retail business that serves thousands of customers each day will probably choose to have more money on hand than a legal firm that bills clients and pays employees monthly. But while individuals and businesses vary considerably in the amount of money they choose to hold, three macroeconomic factors affect the demand for money quite broadly: the nominal interest rate, real output and the price level.

- *The nominal interest rate i*: the opportunity cost of holding wealth in the form of money is the real return to monetary assets relative to real return on alternative assets such as government bonds. The real return to any asset is the nominal rate of interest on that asset minus the rate of inflation or $i - \pi$. As we are assuming that monetary assets pay zero nominal interest, the real return to money is simply $(0 - \pi)$ and for interest-bearing assets such as government bonds the real return $(i - \pi)$. Hence the opportunity cost of holding money is the real return on alternative assets minus the real return to money or $(i - \pi) - (0 - \pi) = i$ *the nominal rate of interest*. Other things being equal, the higher the prevailing nominal interest rate the greater the opportunity cost of holding money, and hence the less money individuals and businesses will demand. Example 22.1 illustrates the relationship between the demand for money and the nominal interest rate.

Example 22.1 How much money should Kim's restaurants hold?

Kim owns several successful restaurants. Her accountant informs her that, on a typical day, her restaurants are holding a total of €50,000 in cash on the premises. The accountant points out that if Kim's restaurants reduced their cash holdings, Kim could use the extra cash to purchase assets such as interest-bearing government bonds.

The accountant proposes two methods of reducing the amount of cash Kim's restaurants hold. First, she could increase the frequency of cash pickups by her armoured car service. The extra service would cost €500 annually but would allow Kim's restaurants to reduce their average cash holding to €40,000. Second, in addition to the extra pickups, Kim could employ a computerised cash management service to help her keep closer tabs on the inflows and outflows of cash at her restaurants. The service costs €700 a year, but the accountant estimates that, together with more frequent pickups, the more efficient cash management provided by the service could help Kim reduce average cash holdings at her restaurants to €30,000.

How much money should Kim's restaurants hold if the nominal interest rate on government bonds is 6 per cent? How much if the interest rate on government bonds is 8 per cent?

Kim's restaurants need to hold cash to carry out their normal business, but holding cash also has an *opportunity cost*, which is the interest those funds could be earning if they were held in the form of government bonds instead of zero-interest cash. As the interest rate on government bonds is 6 per cent, each €10,000 by which Kim can reduce her restaurants' money holdings yields an annual benefit of €600 (6 per cent of €10,000).

If Kim increases the frequency of pickups by her armoured car service, reducing the restaurants' average money holdings from €50,000 to €40,000, the benefit will be the additional €600 in interest income that Kim will earn. The cost is the €500 charged by the armoured car company. Since the benefit exceeds the cost, Kim should purchase the extra service and reduce the average cash holdings at her restaurants to €40,000.

Should Kim go a step further and employ the cash management service as well? Doing so would reduce average cash holdings at the restaurants from €40,000 to €30,000, which has a benefit in terms of extra interest income of €600 per year. However, this benefit is less than the cost of the cash management service, which is €700 per year. So Kim should *not* employ the cash management service and instead should maintain average cash holdings in her restaurants of €40,000.

If the interest rate on government bonds rises to 8 per cent, then the benefit of each €10,000 reduction in average money holdings is €800 per year (8 per cent of €10,000) in extra interest income. In this case, the benefit of employing the cash management service, €800, exceeds the cost of doing so, which is €700. So Kim should employ the service, reducing the average cash holdings of her business to €30,000. Example 22.1 shows that a higher nominal interest rate on alternative assets reduces the quantity of money demanded.

- *Real income or output Y:* an increase in aggregate real income or output – as measured, for example, by real GDP – raises the quantity of goods and services that people and businesses want to buy and sell. When the economy enters a boom, for example, people do more shopping and stores have more customers. To accommodate the increase in transactions, both individuals and businesses need to hold more money. Thus higher real output raises the demand for money. Conversely, the lower is real income the lower the demand for money.
- *The price level P:* an increase in the average price level P increases the cost of buying a given basket of goods and services. Hence households and firms will require higher money balances to finance a given volume of transactions. A higher price level is associated with a higher demand for money. Conversely, a fall in the price level reduces the demand for money.

Example 22.2 shows that an increase in real income or a rise in the price level increases the quantity of money demanded

Example 22.2 The Simpsons' demand for money

The Simpsons have a disposable income of €1,000 per week. They spend 70 per cent, or €700, on consumption and save €300 per week. Each Monday the Simpsons deposit €700 of their weekly income in a bank account and spend €100 per day using a debit card.

(a) What is the Simpsons' demand for money as measured by their average daily deposit balance?
(b) What is the Simpsons' demand for money if, at constant prices, their disposable income increases to €1,200 and they spend €120 per day?
(c) Starting with a weekly income of €1,000, suppose the CPI rises by 10 per cent and the Simpsons' disposable income also rises by 10 per cent, to €1,100. If the Simpsons continue to spend 70 per cent of their income at an even rate throughout the week, what is their demand for money?

The following table gives the Simpsons' money balances at the start of each day.

Day	Daily money holding		
	Income: €1,000 (2)	Income: €1,100 (3)	Income: €1,200 (4)
Monday	700	770	840
Tuesday	600	660	720
Wednesday	500	550	600
Thursday	400	440	480
Friday	300	330	360
Saturday	200	220	240
Sunday	100	110	120
Average money holding per day	400	440	480

(a) With a real disposable income of €1,000 per week (column 2) the Simpsons spend €700 per week at €100 per day. Their money holding is €700 at the start of day one (Monday), €600 at the start of day two (Tuesday) and €100 at the start of day seven (Sunday). Hence, over the week, their average money holdings are $(700 + 600 + \ldots + 100)/7 = €400$.

(b) When the Simpsons' real income increases to €1,200 per week (column 4) they continue to spend 70 per cent, or €840, on consumption at €120 per day, and their money holdings decline from €840 at the start of day one to €120 at the start of day seven, giving an average money holding of $(840 + 720 + \ldots + 120)/7 = 480$. Hence without any change in their consumption behaviour (they continue to spend 70 per cent of real disposable income) the Simpsons' demand for money increases with their real income. The reason is straightforward: the higher is real income the higher is consumption expenditure, requiring a higher average money balance.

(c) When the Simpsons' disposable income increases to €1,100 (column 3) per week they continue to spend 70 per cent, or €770, on consumption at €110 per day, and their money holdings decline from €770 at the start of day one to €110 at the start of day seven, giving an average money holding of $(770 + 660 + \ldots + 110)/7 = 440$. Hence without any change in their consumption behaviour (they continue to spend 70 per cent of real disposable income) the Simpsons' demand for money increases with the price level. Note that, in this example, the CPI increases from 1.0 to 1.1 and the Simpsons' real expenditure is constant (700 before the price rise and $770/1.1 = 700$ after) but their demand for money increases because of the rise in the CPI. Also note that the real value of the average money balance remains constant – 400 before the price rise and $440/1.1 = 400$ after. Hence the increase in P increases the *nominal* demand for money but not the *real* demand for money.

Exercise 22.1 Refer back to Example 22.1. How much cash should Kim's restaurants hold if the interest rate fell from 6 per cent to 4 per cent?

The money demand curve

We have seen that the demand for money depends on three factors – the nominal rate of interest i, real income Y and the price level P. For constant values of Y and P, the relationship between the demand for money and the rate of interest can be represented graphically by the **money demand curve**. As illustrated by Figure 22.1, the money demand curve relates the aggregate quantity of money demanded MD to the nominal interest rate i. Because an increase in the nominal interest rate increases the opportunity cost of holding money, which reduces the quantity of money demanded, the money demand curve slopes down.

money demand curve shows the relationship between the aggregate quantity of money demanded M and the nominal interest rate i; because an increase in the nominal interest rate increases the opportunity cost of holding money, which reduces the quantity of money demanded, the money demand curve slopes down

If we think of the nominal interest rate as the 'price' (more precisely, the opportunity cost) of money and the amount of money people want to hold as the 'quantity', the money demand curve is analogous to the demand curve for a good or service. As with a standard demand curve, the fact that a higher price of money leads people to demand less of it is captured in the downward slope of the demand curve. Furthermore, as in a standard demand curve, changes in factors other than the price of money (the nominal interest rate) can cause the demand curve for money to shift. For a given nominal interest rate, any change that makes people want to hold more money will shift the money demand curve to the right, and any change that makes people want to hold less money will shift the money demand curve to the left. We have already identified two macroeconomic factors other than the nominal interest rate that affect the economy-wide demand for money: *real income* and the *price level*. Because an increase in either of these variables increases the demand for money, it shifts the money demand curve rightwards, as shown in Figure 22.2. Similarly, a fall in real income or the general price level reduces money demand, shifting the money demand curve leftwards.

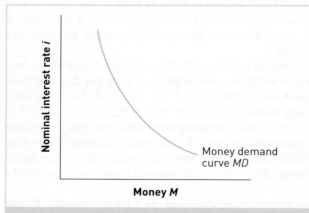

Figure 22.1 The Money Demand Curve. The money demand curve relates the economy-wide demand for money to the nominal interest rate. Because an increase in the nominal interest rate raises the opportunity cost of holding money, the money demand curve slopes down.

The money demand curve may also shift in response to other changes that affect the cost or benefit of holding money, such as technological and financial advances. For example, the introduction of ATMs and the use of debit cards reduced the amount of money that people chose to hold and thus shifted the economy-wide money demand curve to the left.

RECAP Money demand

For the economy as a whole, the demand for money is the amount of wealth that individuals, households and businesses choose to hold in the form of *money*. The opportunity cost of holding money is measured by the *nominal interest rate i*, which is the return that could be earned on alternative assets such as bonds. The benefit of holding money is its usefulness in transactions.

Increases in real GDP (Y) or the price level (P) raise the nominal volume of transactions and thus the economy-wide demand for money. The demand for money is also affected by technological and financial innovations, such as the introduction of ATMs, that affect the costs or benefits of holding money.

The money demand curve relates the economy-wide demand for money to the nominal interest rate. Because an increase in the nominal interest rate raises the opportunity cost of holding money, the money demand curve slopes downwards.

Changes in factors other than the nominal interest rate that affect the demand for money can shift the money demand curve. For example, increases in real GDP or the price level raise the demand for money, shifting the money demand curve to the right, whereas decreases shift the money demand curve to the left.

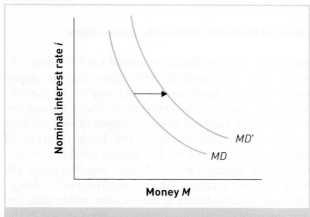

Figure 22.2 A Shift in the Money Demand Curve.
At a given nominal interest rate, any change that makes people want to hold more money – such as an increase in the general price level or in real GDP – will shift the money demand curve to the right.

The money supply: commercial banks and the creation of money

What determines the amount of money in the economy? If the economy's supply of money consisted entirely of currency, the answer would be simple: the supply of money would just be equal to the value of the currency created and circulated by the government. However, as we have seen, in modern economies the money supply consists not only of currency but also of deposit balances held by the public in commercial (that is, private) banks. The determination of the money supply in a modern economy thus depends in part on the *behaviour of commercial banks and their depositors*.

To see how the existence of commercial banks affects the money supply, we shall use the example of a fictional country, the Republic of Euroland. Initially, we assume, Euroland has no commercial banking system. To make trading easier and eliminate the need for barter, the government establishes a central bank and orders it to put 1 million identical paper notes, called euros, denoted €, into circulation. The central bank prints the euros and distributes them to the populace. At this point, the Euroland money supply is €1 million.

However, the citizens of Euroland are unhappy with a money supply made up entirely of paper euros, since the notes may be lost or stolen. In response to the demand for safe keeping of money, some Euroland entrepreneurs set up a system of commercial banks. At first, these banks are only storage vaults where people can deposit their euros. When people need to make a payment they can either physically withdraw their euros or, more conveniently, write a cheque or use a debit card drawn on their account. Cheques and debit cards give the banks permission to transfer euros from the account of the person making the payment to the account of the person receiving the payment. With a system of payments based on cheques and debit cards, the paper euros need never leave the banking system, although they flow from one bank to another as a depositor of one bank makes a payment to a depositor in another bank. Deposits do not pay interest in this economy; indeed, the banks can make a profit only by charging depositors fees for safeguarding their cash and using cheques or debit cards.

Let us suppose for now that people prefer bank deposits to cash, and deposit all their euros with the commercial banks. With all euros in the vaults of banks, the balance sheet of all of Euroland's commercial banks taken together is as shown in Table 22.2.

The *assets* of the commercial banking system in Euroland are the paper euros sitting in the vaults of all the individual banks. The banking system's *liabilities* are the deposits of the banks' customers or the money owed by the banks to the depositors.

Assets		Liabilities	
Currency	€1,000,000	Deposits	€1,000,000

Table 22.2 **Consolidated Balance Sheet of Euroland Commercial Banks: Initial**

bank reserves cash or similar assets held by commercial banks for the purpose of meeting depositor withdrawals and payments

100 per cent reserve banking a situation in which banks' reserves equal 100 per cent of their deposits

Cash or similar assets held by banks are called **bank reserves**. In this example, bank reserves, for all the banks taken together, equal €1,000,000 – the currency listed on the asset side of the consolidated balance sheet. Banks hold reserves to meet depositors' demands for cash withdrawals or to pay cheques drawn on their depositors' accounts. In this example, the bank reserves of €1,000,000 equal 100 per cent of banks' deposit liabilities, which are also €1,000,000. A situation in which bank reserves equal 100 per cent of bank deposits is called **100 per cent reserve banking**.

Bank reserves are held by banks in their vaults, rather than circulated among the public, and thus are *not* counted as part of the money supply. However, bank deposit balances, which can be used in making transactions, *are* counted as money. So, after the introduction of 'safe-keeper' banks in Euroland, the money supply, equal to the value of bank deposits, is €1,000,000, which is the same as it was prior to the introduction of banks.

After a while, to continue the story, the commercial bankers of Euroland begin to realise that keeping 100 per cent reserves against deposits is not necessary. True, a few euros flow in and out of the typical bank as depositors receive payments or write cheques, but, for the most part, the stacks of paper euros just sit there in the vaults, untouched and unused. It occurs to the bankers that they can meet the random inflow and outflow of euros to their banks with reserves that are less than 100 per cent of their deposits. After some observation, the bankers conclude that keeping reserves equal to only 10 per cent of deposits is enough to meet the random ebb and flow of withdrawals and payments from their individual banks. The remaining 90 per cent of deposits, the bankers realise, can be lent out to borrowers to earn interest.

So the bankers decide to keep reserves equal to €100,000, or 10 per cent of their deposits. The other €900,000 they lend out at interest to firms who want to use the money to make improvements to their businesses. After the loans are made, the balance sheet of all of Euroland's commercial banks taken together has changed, as shown in Table 22.3.

reserve–deposit ratio bank reserves divided by deposits

After the loans are made, the banks' reserves of €100,000 no longer equal 100 per cent of the banks' deposits of €1,000,000. Instead, the **reserve–deposit ratio**, which is bank reserves divided

Assets		Liabilities	
Currency (= reserves)	€100,000	Deposits	€1,000,000
Loans	€900,000		

Table 22.3 **Consolidated Balance Sheet of Euroland Commercial Banks after One Round of Loans**

fractional-reserve banking system a banking system in which bank reserves are less than deposits so that the reserve–deposit ratio is less than 100 per cent

by deposits, is now equal to 100,000/1,000,000, or 10 per cent. A banking system in which banks hold fewer reserves than deposits so that the reserve–deposit ratio is less than 100 per cent is called a **fractional-reserve banking system**.

Notice that €900,000 has flowed out of the banking system (as loans to firms) and is now in the hands of the public. But firms use these funds to pay for improvements to their businesses and the €900,000 will be paid to building contractors. As we have assumed that private citizens prefer bank deposits to cash for making transactions these contractors will redeposit the €900,000 in the banking system. After these deposits are made, the consolidated balance sheet of the commercial banks is as in Table 22.4.

Assets		Liabilities	
Currency (= reserves)	€1,000,000	Deposits	€1,900,000
Loans	€900,000		

Table 22.4 **Consolidated Balance Sheet of Euroland Commercial Banks after Euros are Redeposited**

Notice that bank deposits, and hence the economy's money supply, now equal €1,900,000. In effect, the existence of the commercial banking system has permitted the creation of new money. These deposits, which are liabilities of the banks, are balanced by assets of €1,000,000 in reserves and €900,000 in loans owed to the banks.

The story does not end here. On examining their balance sheets, the bankers find that they once again have 'too many' reserves. With deposits of €1,900,000 and a 10 per cent reserve–deposit ratio, they need only €190,000 in reserves. But they have €1,000,000 in reserves – €810,000 too many. Since lending out their excess euros is always more profitable than leaving them in the vault, the bankers proceed to make another €810,000 in loans. Eventually these lent-out euros are redeposited in the banking system, after which the consolidated balance sheet of the banks is as shown in Table 22.5.

Assets		Liabilities	
Currency (= reserves)	€1,000,000	Deposits	€2,710,000
Loans	€1,710,000		

Table 22.5 **Consolidated Balance Sheet of Euroland Commercial Banks after Two Rounds of Loans and Redeposits**

Now the money supply has increased to €2,710,000, equal to the value of bank deposits. Despite the expansion of loans and deposits, however, the bankers find that their reserves of €1,000,000 *still* exceed the desired level of 10 per cent of deposits, which are €2,710,000. And so yet another round of lending will take place.

Exercise 22.2   Determine what the balance sheet of the banking system of Euroland will look like after a third round of lending to firms and redeposits of euros into the commercial banking system. What is the money supply at that point?

The process of expansion of loans and deposits will end only when reserves equal 10 per cent of bank deposits, because as long as reserves exceed 10 per cent of deposits the banks will find it profitable to lend out the extra reserves. Since reserves at the end of every round equal €1,000,000, for the reserve–deposit ratio to equal 10 per cent, total deposits must equal €10,000,000. Further, since the balance sheet must balance, with assets equal to liabilities, we know as well that at the end of the process loans to cheese producers must equal €9,000,000. If loans equal €9,000,000, then bank assets, the sum of loans and reserves (€1,000,000), will equal €10,000,000, which is the same as bank liabilities (bank deposits). The final consolidated balance sheet is as shown in Table 22.6.

Assets		Liabilities	
Currency (= reserves)	€1,000,000	Deposits	€10,000,000
Loans	€9,000,000		

Table 22.6 **Final Consolidated Balance Sheet of Euroland Commercial Banks**

The money supply, which is equal to total deposits, is €10,000,000 at the end of the process. We see that the existence of a fractional-reserve banking system has multiplied the money supply by a factor of 10, relative to the economy with no banks or the economy with 100 per cent reserve banking. Put another way, with a 10 per cent reserve–deposit ratio, each euro deposited in the banking system can 'support' 10 euros' worth of deposits.

In this example deposits will expand through additional rounds of lending as long as the actual ratio of reserves to deposits exceeds the ratio desired by banks. When the actual reserve ratio equals the desired reserve ratio the expansion stops. So, ultimately, deposits in the banking system satisfy the following relationship:

$$\text{Desired reserve} - \text{deposit ratio} = \frac{\text{Bank reserves}}{\text{Bank deposits}}$$

This equation can be rewritten to solve for bank deposits:

$$\textit{Bank deposits} = \frac{\textit{Bank reserves}}{\textit{Desired reserve} - \textit{deposit ratio}}$$

or, letting D denote bank deposits, RES denote bank reserves and rr denote the banks' desired reserve–deposit ratio we can write the above equation as:

$$D = \frac{1}{rr} RES \tag{22.1}$$

In Euroland, since all the currency in the economy flows into the banking system, bank reserves equal €1,000,000. The reserve–deposit ratio desired by banks rr is 0.10. Therefore, using Equation (22.1), we find that bank deposits equal 1/0.10 times €1,000,000, or €10,000,000, the same answer we found in the consolidated balance sheet of the banks, Table 22.6.

Exercise 22.3 Find deposits and the money supply in Euroland if the banks' desired reserve–deposit ratio is 5 per cent rather than 10 per cent. What if the total amount of currency circulated by the central bank is 2,000,000 euros and the desired reserve–deposit ratio remains at 10 per cent?

The money supply with both currency and deposits

In the example of Euroland we assumed that all money is held in the form of deposits in banks. However, in reality firms and households keep only part of their money holdings in deposits and hold the rest in the form of currency. To see what difference this makes let M = the money supply, CUR = currency in circulation with the non-bank public and D = bank deposits. The stock of money can be defined as:

$$M = CUR + D \qquad (22.2)$$

As in the case of Euroland we shall continue to assume that banks hold reserves in the form of currency. However, given the amount of currency issued by the central bank, currency holdings by the non-bank public will reduce the supply of reserves available to the banking system. For example, if the central bank has issued €1 million euros in currency and the public decide to hold €0.2 million then only €0.8 million is available to the banking system as reserves. To see how this affects the determination of the money supply we shall refer to the sum of currency held by the non-bank public (CUR) and bank reserves (RES) as the **monetary base**, sometimes referred to as the **stock of high-powered money**, defined as:

the monetary base or stock of high-powered money the potential quantity of reserves available to commercial banks, defined as the sum of bank reserves and currency held by the non-bank public

$$H = CUR + RES \qquad (22.3)$$

To keep things simple, we shall assume that the public hold a constant fraction cr (or currency ratio) of deposits in currency. That is:

$$CUR = crD \qquad (22.4)$$

From Equation (22.1) we know that bank reserves are fraction rr of deposits. Hence we can write Equation (22.3) as:

$$H = crD + rr\,D$$
$$= (cr + rr)D$$

Rearranging to solve for deposits gives:

$$D = \frac{1}{cr + rr}H \qquad (22.5)$$

Substituting Equations (22.4) and (22.5) into Equation (22.2) gives:

$$M = \frac{cr}{cr + rr}H + \frac{1}{cr + rr}H$$

or:

$$M = \left(\frac{1 + cr}{cr + rr} \right) H \tag{22.6}$$

the money multiplier the effect of a €1 change in the monetary base of the money supplier

In Equation (22.6) the term $(1 + cr)/(cr + rr)$ is known as the **money multiplier** because it measures the response of the money supply to each euro change in the monetary base. Example 22.3 illustrates how this changes the story of money creation in Euroland.

Example 22.3 The money supply with currency and deposits

Suppose that in Euroland the public hold 5 per cent of deposits in the form of currency, the banks' desired reserve ratio is 10 per cent and the monetary base is €3 million. Find Euroland's money supply. How is the money supply divided between currency held by the public and bank deposits? How is the monetary base divided between bank reserves and non-bank currency holdings?

Using Equation (22.6) the money multiplier is $1.05/0.15 = 7$ and the money supply is $7 \times 3 = $ €21 million. Deposits are determined by Equation (22.5) $D = H/(cr + rr) = 3/0.15 = $ €20 million. As the public's currency–deposit ratio is 5 per cent, currency held outside the banking system is $0.05 \times 20 = $ €1 million. Bank reserves would be $RES = rrD = 0.1 \times 20 = $ €2 million and the public's currency holdings would be $CUR = crD = 0.05 \times 20 = $ €1 million.

Exercise 22.4   Refer to Example 22.3. What would happen to the money supply if the non-bank public decides to economise on currency holdings and reduce their currency–deposit ratio to 2 per cent? How would the money supply be divided between deposits and non-bank currency holdings?

RECAP Commercial banks and the creation of money

Part of the money supply consists of deposits in private commercial banks, hence the behaviour of commercial banks and their depositors helps to determine the money supply.

Cash or similar assets held by banks are called *bank reserves*. In modern economies, banks' reserves are less than their deposits, a situation called *fractional-reserve banking*. The ratio of bank reserves to deposits is called the *reserve–deposit ratio*; in a fractional-reserve banking system, this ratio is less than 1. The portion of deposits not held as reserves can be lent out by the banks to earn interest. Banks will continue to make loans and accept deposits as long as the reserve–deposit ratio exceeds its desired level.

This process of deposit creation stops only when the actual and desired reserve–deposit ratios are equal. At that point, total bank deposits equal bank reserves divided by the desired reserve–deposit ratio, and the money supply equals the currency held by the public plus bank deposits.

The amount of reserves available to the banks is determined by the amount of currency or reserve assets issued by the central bank and the non-bank public's currency holdings. Increased currency holdings by the public reduce the supply of reserves available to the banks and, via the money multiplier, lead to a lower money supply.

Controlling the money supply: central banks and open-market operations

Central banks are institutions established by government for the purpose of regulating the banking system and conducting monetary policy. The central bank of the Eurosystem is the European Central Bank, located in Frankfurt, and the corresponding central banks of the United Kingdom and the United States are the Bank of England and the Federal Reserve System. All central banks have a primary responsibility for formulating monetary policy, which involves decisions about the appropriate size of the money supply. Referring back to Equation (22.6) it is clear that a central bank can control the money supply if it can control the monetary base defined as the sum of bank reserves plus currency holdings by the non-bank public. Or, given the non-bank public's currency holdings, the central bank can control the money supply if it can control the supply of reserves available to the commercial banks. For example, given the amount of currency held by the public, and the commercial banks desired reserve ratio, Equation (22.6) tells us that the central bank can engineer a decrease or increase in the money supply if it can decrease or increase the supply of reserves.

open-market operations (OMOs) open-market purchases and open-market sales

In general central banks can change the supply of reserves available to commercial banks by conducting **open-market operations (OMOs)** in government bonds and other financial assets. To illustrate, suppose that the central bank wants to increase bank reserves, with the ultimate goal of increasing bank deposits and the money supply. To accomplish this the central bank buys financial assets, usually government bonds, from the public. To simplify the actual procedure a bit, think of the central bank as paying for the bonds by issuing cheques drawn on itself, which are then deposited with the commercial banks. Given the non-bank public's currency holdings this will lead to an increase in the reserves of the commercial banking system. The increase in bank reserves will lead in turn, through the process of lending and redeposit of funds described earlier, to an expansion of bank deposits and the money supply. The central bank's purchase of government bonds from the public is called an **open-market purchase**.

open-market purchase the purchase of government bonds from the public by the central bank for the purpose of increasing the supply of bank reserves and the money supply

To reduce bank reserves and hence the money supply, the central bank reverses the procedure. It sells some of the government bonds that it holds (acquired in previous open-market purchases) to the public. Assume that the public pays for the bonds by writing cheques on their accounts in commercial banks. Then, when the central bank presents the cheques to the commercial banks for payment, reserves equal in value to the government bonds sold by the central bank are transferred from the commercial banks to the central bank. The central bank retires these reserves from circulation, lowering the supply of bank reserves and, hence, the overall money supply. The sale of government bonds by the central bank to the public for the purpose of reducing bank reserves and hence the money supply is called an **open-market sale**. Open-market purchases and sales together are called *open-market operations*.

open-market sale the sale by the central bank of government bonds to the public for the purpose of reducing bank reserves and the money supply

Example 22.4 Increasing the money supply by OMOs

In Example 22.3 the public hold 5 per cent of deposits in the form of currency, banks' desired reserve ratio is 10 per cent and the monetary base is €3 million. If the central bank purchases €0.2m worth of government bonds from the non-bank public, by how much would Euroland's money supply increase? By how much would bank reserves and non-bank currency holdings increase?

The open-market purchase increases the monetary base by €0.2 million. Using Equation (22.6) the money supply will increase by the money multiplier times the increase in the monetary base, or $7 \times 0.2 = €1.4$ million. Hence the money supply increases from €21 to €22.4 million. Using Equation (22.5) deposits would increase by 1.3 to $3.2/0.15 = €21.3$ million. Bank reserves would increase by 0.13 to $0.1 \times 21.3 = €2.13$ million, and the public's currency holdings would increase by 0.07 to $0.05 \times 21.3 = €1.07$ million.

Exercise 22.5   Continuing Example 22.4, suppose that instead of an open-market purchase of €0.2 million, the central bank conducts an open-market sale of €0.5 worth of government bonds. What happens to bank reserves, bank deposits and the money supply?

The money supply curve

We have seen that, by using open-market operations, the central bank can determine the economy's money supply at any level it wishes. More precisely, unlike the demand for money the supply of money does not depend on the rate of interest. This result is illustrated by Figure 22.3, which has the quantity of money on the horizontal axis and the nominal rate of interest on the vertical axis. In Figure 22.3 the initial money supply curve is MS_1 and is drawn as a vertical (or perfectly inelastic) line to illustrate the idea that the money supply does not depend on the nominal rate of interest i.

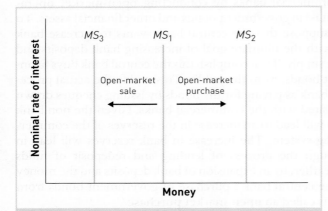

Figure 22.3 The Money Supply Curve. The central bank sets the money supply at MS_1. An open-market purchase increases the money supply and shifts the money supply curve to MS_2. An open-market sale reduces the money supply and shifts the money supply curve to MS_3.

An open-market purchase by the central bank increases the monetary base at any given rate of interest, shifting the money supply curve to the right from MS_1 to MS_2. Conversely, an open-market sale by the central bank reduces the monetary base at any given rate of interest, shifting the money supply curve to the left from MS_1 to MS_3.

Equilibrium in the market for money

Equilibrium

Figure 22.4 shows the demand for and the supply of money in a single diagram. The nominal interest rate is on the vertical axis, and the nominal quantity of money (in euros) is on the horizontal axis. As we have seen, because a higher nominal interest rate increases the opportunity cost of holding money, the money demand curve slopes downwards. Because we are assuming that the central bank fixes the supply of money, we have drawn the *money supply curve* as a vertical line that intercepts the horizontal axis at the quantity of money chosen by the bank, denoted M. Note that, unlike the demand for money, the money supply is fixed at M at all rates of interest.

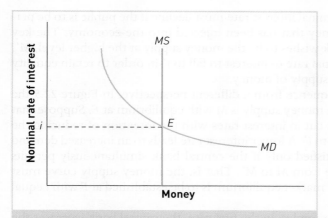

Figure 22.4 Money Market Equilibrium. Equilibrium in the market for money occurs at point E, where the demand for money by the public equals the amount of money supplied by the central bank. The equilibrium nominal interest rate, which equates the supply of and demand for money, is i.

As in standard supply and demand analysis, equilibrium in the market for money occurs at the intersection of the supply and demand curves, shown as point E in Figure 22.4. The equilibrium amount of money in circulation, M, is simply the amount of money the central bank chooses to supply. The equilibrium nominal interest rate i is the interest rate at which the quantity of money demanded by the public, as determined by the money demand curve, equals the fixed supply of money made available by the central bank.

How the central bank controls the nominal interest rate

The public and the financial media usually talk about central bank policy in terms of decisions about the nominal interest rate rather than the money supply. Indeed, policy makers themselves usually describe policy in terms of setting a value for the interest rate rather than fixing the money supply at a particular level. For example, policy decisions by the ECB or the Bank of England are always announced in terms of interest rate changes and not as decisions to expand or contract the money supply. However, we can now show that *controlling the money supply and controlling the interest rate is essentially the same thing*.

Figure 22.4 showed that the nominal interest rate is determined by equilibrium in the market for money. Let us suppose that the central bank decides that it wishes to lower the interest rate. To lower the interest rate, the central bank must increase the supply of money, which can be accomplished by an open-market purchase and increasing the amount of reserves it makes available to the banking system.

Figure 22.5 shows the effects of an increase in the money supply. If the initial money supply is M, then equilibrium in the money market occurs at point E and the equilibrium nominal interest rate is i. Now suppose the central bank increases the money supply to M'. This increase in the money supply shifts the vertical money supply curve to the right, which shifts the equilibrium in the money market from point E to point F. Note that at point F the equilibrium nominal interest rate has

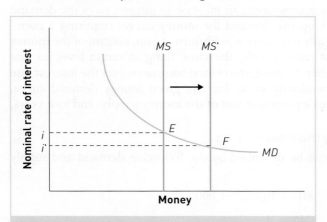

Figure 22.5 Controlling the Rate of Interest. The central bank can lower the equilibrium interest rate by increasing the supply of money. For the given money demand curve, an increase in the money supply from M to M' shifts the equilibrium point in the money market from E to F, lowering the equilibrium nominal interest rate from i to i'.

declined, from i to i'. The nominal interest rate must decline if the public is to be persuaded to hold the extra money that has been injected into the economy. The key point is that if the central bank wishes to fix the money supply at the higher level, M', then it must permit the nominal rate of interest to fall to i' in order to retain equality between the demand for and supply of money.

Now consider the same sequence from a different perspective. In Figure 22.5 the initial interest rate is i and the money supply is M with equilibrium at E. Suppose that the central bank announces a cut in interest rates with the intention of reducing the average nominal interest rate to i'. A lower interest rate leads to an increased demand for money, which can be satisfied only if the central bank simultaneously permits the money supply to increase from M to M'. That is, the money supply curve must shift to MS' if the new money market equilibrium is to be established at F with i equal to i'.

Now compare these two examples. In the first case, the central bank increases the money supply from M to M'. For the public to willingly hold the higher money balances the interest rate must fall from i to i'. In the second case the central bank reduces the interest rate from i to i'. To satisfy the increased demand for money, the money supply must increase from M to M'. Hence, saying that the central bank sets the money supply at M' is exactly the same as saying that it sets the average interest rate at i'. It follows that there is no contradiction between these two ways of describing monetary policy – controlling the *money supply* or setting interest rates. Any value of the money supply implies a specific level for *nominal interest rates*, and vice versa.

A similar scenario unfolds if the central bank decides to raise interest rates. To raise interest rates, it must *reduce* the money supply. A reduction of the money supply is accomplished by reducing the amount of reserves it makes available to commercial banks. With fewer reserves available the banks must contract lending, leading to a fall in deposits and a lower money supply. For the money market to restore equilibrium, the rate of interest must rise to reduce the demand for money in line with supply. Alternatively, if the central bank announces an increase in interest rates the demand for money will fall (we move up the demand for money curve) requiring a corresponding fall in the money supply to restore equilibrium. Again, control of the money supply and control of interest rates is really the same thing. A target level for one implies a given level for the other. In short, the central bank *cannot* set the interest rate and the money supply independently since, for any given money demand curve, a particular interest rate implies a particular size of the money supply, and vice versa.

Example 22.5 Controlling the interest rate

Suppose the money market can be described by the following demand and supply equations.

$$MD = 10,000 - 1,000i$$

$$MS = M$$

If the central bank sets M at €9,950 find the equilibrium rate of interest. What happens to the equilibrium rate of interest if the central bank increases the money supply to €9,960? Alternatively, by how much would the central bank have to increase the money supply if it wishes to reduce the interest rate by 0.01, or 1 per cent?

The money market will be in equilibrium when $MD = MS$. Hence in equilibrium $10,000 - 1,000i = 9,950$. Solving for the equilibrium interest rate gives: $i = (10,000 - 9,950)/1,000 = 0.05$, or 5 per cent. If the central bank increases the money supply by

€10 to €9,960 the equilibrium condition becomes $10,000 - 1,000i = 9,960$. Solving for the equilibrium interest rate gives: $i = (10,000 - 9,960)/1,000 = 0.04$ or 4 per cent. Hence increasing the money supply by €10 reduces the interest rate by 1 per cent. Alternatively, if the central bank announces a 1 per cent cut in interest rates from 5 to 4 per cent, the demand for money would increase from 9,950 to $MD = 10,000 - 1,000(0.04) = 9,960$. Hence, to restore equilibrium, the central bank would have to permit a €10 increase in the money supply. Controlling the interest rate and controlling the money supply is the same thing – they are different sides of the same coin.

The European Central Bank

On 1 January 1999, 11 member states of the European Union adopted a common currency called the *euro*. These countries were Austria, Belgium, Finland, France, Germany, Ireland, Italy, Luxemburg, the Netherlands, Portugal and Spain. Greece joined in January 2001, Slovenia in January 2007, and Cyprus and Malta in January 2008. The United Kingdom, Sweden and Denmark decided to opt out of the euro and retain their national currencies. Together the countries using the euro as their currency form the **Eurosystem**, or the euro area. In effect the participating countries agreed to eliminate their national currencies (francs, guilders, lira, etc.) and replace them with the new common currency. At the same time, control of monetary policy in each country passed from their national central banks to the newly established **European Central Bank (ECB)** based in Frankfurt. The ECB is at the centre of a new central banking system known as the **European System of Central Banks (ESCB)**, which consists of the ECB and the national central banks (NCBs) of all EU member states, including those of the non-participating countries. However, while the non-participating central banks, such as the Bank of England, are part of the ESCB, they play no role in its decision-making process. To distinguish between those member states that use the euro as their common currency and those who have retained their national currencies, the ECB uses the term *Eurosystem* to refer to the former.

Eurosystem those EU member states that use the euro as their currency and for whom the ECB is their central bank

European Central Bank (ECB) the central bank of the Eurosystem, which comprises all countries using the euro as their currency

European System of Central Banks (ESCB) the ECB and the national central banks of all member states, including those who do not use the euro as their currency

The ECB is responsible for the *formulation and implementation of a single monetary policy* throughout the entire euro area and for the supervision and regulation of the banking and financial system. It has two key decision-making bodies: the Executive Board and **Governing Council**. The Executive Board consists of the President and Vice-President of the ECB, plus four others appointed on the recommendation of the EU's Ecofin Council (the council of finance ministers) after consultation with the European Parliament (EP) and the heads of government of the participating member states. The Governing Council consists of all members of the Executive Board, plus the governors of the NCBs participating in the Eurosystem. The President and Vice-President are normally former governors of NCBs; the other members of the Executive Board are selected on the basis of their experience in financial matters and appointed for a non-renewable eight-year term. NCB governors must be appointed by their governments for a minimum term of five years.

Governing Council the ECB's supreme decision-making body

The Governing Council is the supreme decision-making body of the ECB. It formulates monetary policy for the entire Eurosystem and has a monopoly on decisions relating to interest rates and the supply of reserves to the banking system. The Executive Board prepares information relevant to meetings of the Governing Council and is responsible for implementing policy decisions. A full description of both bodies and their membership can be found on the ECB website (www.ecb.int).

ECB independence

The statutes governing the ESCB are contained in the Treaty on European Union (1993), which is often referred to as the Maastricht Treaty or TEU. Articles 107 and 108 of the Treaty stipulate three key provisions designed to establish the crucial principle of central bank independence: (1) the ECB, the NCBs and members of their decision-making bodies are prohibited from taking instructions from EU institutions and national governments; (2) EU institutions and governments are likewise prohibited from attempting to influence members of ECB decision-making bodies; (3) the ESCB is prohibited from lending to national governments and EU institutions. We should also note that the statutes of the ECB can be altered only by revising the Maastricht Treaty, which requires unanimity among all member states and in some cases a national referendum. These provisions ensure that ECB decisions on monetary policy are free from political influence and that voting members of the Governing Council can act in what they perceive to be the best interests of the Eurosystem rather than as political representatives of national governments.

How the ECB controls interest rates

How do policy decisions by the ECB's Governing Council lead to changes in retail interest rates across the Eurosystem? Why, for example, does an ECB announcement that in order to offset inflationary pressures the Council has decided to 'increase interest rates' by 0.25 per cent lead to corresponding increases in interest rates on deposit, mortgages and car loans, etc.? The ECB does not control these retail interests directly. In fact the Governing Council has direct control of only one interest rate, known as the **main refinancing rate**, which is the interest rate at which the ECB is willing to lend reserves to commercial banks in the Eurosystem. How do changes in the ECB's refinancing rate lead to changes in retail interest rates across the Eurosystem?

main refinancing rate the interest rate that commercial banks pay to borrow reserves from the ECB

inter-bank market a wholesale market on which commercial banks can borrow from or lend to each other

A specialised market, known as the overnight **inter-bank market**, provides the link between the ECB's refinancing rate and the interest rates that firms and households earn on saving or pay to borrow. The overnight inter-bank market is a wholesale market on which commercial banks can borrow from or lend to each other on an overnight basis. For example, consider a commercial bank that on a given day is experiencing a shortage of reserves. One way in which the bank can make up the shortage is by borrowing from another bank that has a surplus of reserves. Such transactions take place on the inter-bank market and the interest rate at which these transactions take place is known as the overnight inter-bank rate. The overnight rate is best thought of as a wholesale rate or the interest rate at which banks deal with each other and, as in other markets, changes in wholesale prices normally lead to corresponding changes in retail prices. In this case the overnight rate is the 'wholesale' price, and if prices rise or fall on the wholesale market the changes are normally passed on to consumers in the form of higher or lower prices. Hence changes in the overnight interest rate normally lead to changes in the interest rates that commercial banks charge on loans or offer to depositors.

marginal lending facility a facility that enables commercial banks to borrow reserves from the ECB

deposit facility a facility that enables commercial banks to deposit excess reserves with the ECB

The ECB influences the overnight inter-bank rate by offering commercial banks alternatives to the inter-bank market. These alternatives are known as the ECB's **marginal lending facility** and the **deposit facility**. To illustrate, consider a bank that wishes to borrow on an overnight basis to meet a liquidity shortage. The bank can borrow on the inter-bank market or it can use the ECB's marginal lending facility. If it chooses the former, the interest rate it pays is the prevailing inter-bank rate. If it chooses the latter, the ECB will charge an interest rate equal to its main refinancing rate plus 1 per cent. As the bank knows that it can borrow from the ECB at the refinancing rate plus 1 per cent it will never borrow on the inter-bank market at a higher rate. Hence the marginal lending facility puts a ceiling on the inter-bank rate. If, for example, the refinancing rate set by the Governing Council is 3 per cent, commercial banks know that they can borrow from the ECB at 4 per cent and will not borrow on the inter-bank market at a higher rate. Alternatively, consider a bank with excess reserves. This bank has the choice of lending on the inter-bank market or using the ECB's deposit facility. If it chooses the latter, the ECB will accept the deposit and pay an interest rate equal to its main refinancing rate minus 1 per cent. As the bank knows that it can lend to the ECB (make a deposit) at the refinancing rate minus 1 per cent it will never lend on the inter-bank market at a lower rate. Hence the deposit facility sets a floor for the inter-bank rate. If, for example, the refinancing rate set by the Governing Council is 3 per cent commercial banks know that they can earn 2 per cent by using the ECB's deposit facility and will not lend on the inter-bank market at a lower rate.

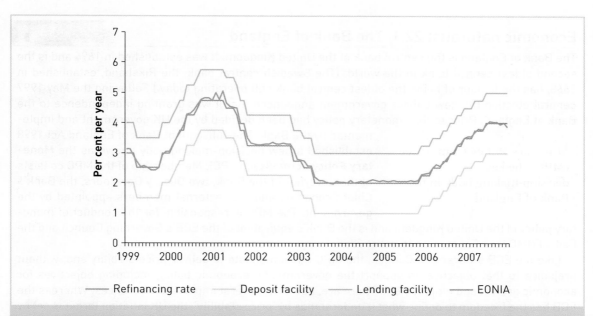

Figure 22.6 ECB Interest Rates and EONIA, January 1999–December 2007. The refinancing rate is the interest rate that commercial banks pay to borrow reserves from the ECB. It is set by the ECB's Governing Council and is the key interest rate in the Eurosystem. The deposit and lending facility rates set floor and ceiling for the overnight inter-bank rate (EONIA).

As changes in the ECB's refinancing rate lead to changes in the interest rates that the ECB charges or offers on its lending and deposit facilities they also lead to changes in the inter-bank rate. For example, if the Governing Council announces a rise in the refinancing rate, commercial banks know that they can earn higher interest by lending excess liquidity to the ECB, thus forcing a corresponding rise in the inter-bank rate and, as wholesale rates rise higher, retail rates will follow. As different countries in the Eurosystem operate their own inter-bank markets, the ECB targets an average overnight interest rate known as the *European Over-Night Index Average*, or **EONIA**.

EONIA European Over-Night Index Average, a weighted average of overnight rates on the Eurosystem's inter-bank markets

Figure 22.6 illustrates these key interest rates over the period January 1999 to December 2007. It is clear from this figure that the inter-bank wholesale rate follows the ECB's refinancing rate very closely.

RECAP The European Central Bank

The European Central Bank (or ECB), is the central bank of the Eurosystem, which consists of those countries using the *euro* as their common currency. The ECB is responsible for the formulation and implementation of monetary policy throughout the Eurosystem. Under the provisions of the Maastricht Treaty the ECB is a highly independent central bank and is free from political influence by EU institutions and national governments. Its key decision-making body, the Governing Council, determines monetary policy in the interests of the Eurosystem as a whole rather than in the interests of individual countries. The ECB has, however, a primary mandate for maintaining *price stability*, which it now defines as a medium-term inflation rate below but close to 2 per cent per year.

Economic naturalist 22.1 The Bank of England

The Bank of England is the central bank of the United Kingdom. It was established in 1694 and is the second oldest central bank in the world. (The Swedish central bank, the Riksband, established in 1668, has the honour of being the oldest central bank still operating today.) Following the May 1997 general election the new Labour government announced that it was granting independence to the Bank of England. Prior to this, monetary policy had been decided by the UK government and implemented by the Bank. The subsequent Bank of England Act 1998 established a new decision-making body known as the **Monetary Policy Committee (MPC)**. Membership of the MPC consists of the Governor of the Bank, two Deputy Governors, the Bank's Chief Economist and four external members appointed by the government. The MPC is responsible for the conduct of monetary policy in the United Kingdom and is the Bank's equivalent of the ECB's Governing Council and the Fed's FOMC (see Economic naturalist 22.2).

Monetary Policy Committee (MPC) the key decision-making body in the Bank of England

Like the ECB's Governing Council, the MPC has a mandate to deliver price stability and, without prejudice to that objective, to support the government's economic policy, including objectives for economic growth and employment. There are, however, several important differences. Whereas the ECB has the freedom to define what it understands by 'price stability', the UK inflation target is set by the government rather than the MPC. Given this inflation target, currently 2 per cent, the MPC has the freedom to decide on the monetary policy required to fulfil its mandate. The MPC is also required to publish a quarterly Inflation Report containing a detailed analysis of monetary and price developments in the United Kingdom and the economic justification for the Bank's policy decisions. Also, unlike meetings of the Governing Council, the minutes and voting record of the MPC are published and available, along with the its Inflation Reports, on the Bank's website: www.bankofengland.co.uk.

In the previous section we saw how interest rate decisions by the ECB's Governing Council lead to changes in retail interest rates across the Eurosystem. In the United Kingdom the Bank of England's Monetary Policy Committee plays a similar role. Open market operations by the Bank of England are known as repurchase agreements, or *repos*. To illustrate how repos work, consider a situation in which a commercial bank wishes to borrow reserves from the Bank of England. The Bank will provide this liquidity by buying assets – usually UK government bonds – from the commercial bank, which agrees to repurchase the assets on a fixed date. The difference between the selling and repurchase prices is the interest rate the bank pays for the loan. To take an illustrative example, suppose the Bank of England buys £100 worth of bonds from the commercial bank, which then agrees to repurchase the bonds in two weeks' time at an agreed price of £105. Hence the commercial bank has borrowed £100 at a cost of £5. The interest on the loan is 5/100, or 5 per cent and is generally known as the *repo rate*. It is this interest, or the repo price, that is set by the Monetary Policy Committee. If the Committee decides to increase the repo rate it makes borrowing more expensive for the commercial banks and will lead to higher retail rates. Hence the repo rate is equivalent to the ECB's refinancing rate. Figure 22.7 graphs the two-week repo rate and the average overnight sterling inter-bank rate for the period 1999 to 2007.

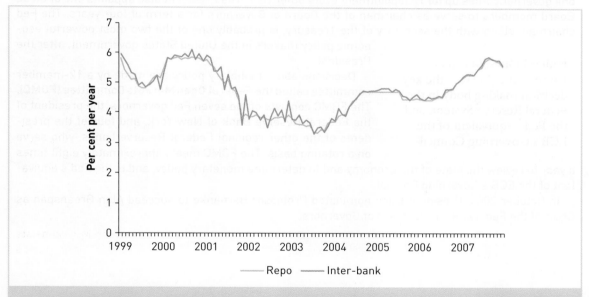

Figure 22.7 Repo Rate and the Average Overnight Sterling Inter-Bank Rate, January 1999–December 2007.

It is clear from Figure 22.7 that the inter-bank wholesale rate follows the Bank of England's repo rate very closely.

Economic naturalist 22.2 The Federal Reserve System

The Federal Reserve System (or the Fed) is the central bank of the United States. The Fed was created by the Federal Reserve Act, passed by Congress in 1913, and began operations in 1914. Like all central banks, the Fed is a publicly owned agency. Like the ECB, the Fed is also a highly independent central bank, but unlike the ECB the Fed does not have a primary mandate for price stability. While the Federal Reserve Act requires the Fed to promote public goals such as economic growth, low inflation and the smooth operation of financial markets, these objectives are not ranked.

The Federal Reserve Act also established a system of 12 regional Federal Reserve banks, each associated with a geographical area called a Federal Reserve District. Congress hoped that the establishment of Federal Reserve banks around the country would ensure that different regions were represented in the national policy-making process. In fact, the regional Feds regularly assess economic conditions in their districts and report this information to policy makers in Washington. Regional Federal Reserve banks also provide various services, such as cheque-clearing, to the commercial banks in their district. These regional Federal Reserve Banks are the Fed's equivalent of the ESCB's NCBs.

At the national level, the leadership of the Federal Reserve System is provided by its *Board of Governors*. The Board of Governors, together with a large professional staff, is located in Washington, DC, and is the Fed's equivalent of the ECB in Frankfurt. The Board consists of seven governors, who are appointed by the President of the United States to 14-year terms. The terms are staggered so that one governor comes up for reappointment every other year. The President also appoints one of these Board members to serve as chairman of the Board of Governors for a term of four years. The Fed chairman, along with the secretary of the Treasury, is probably one of the two most powerful economic policy makers in the United States government, after the President.

Federal Open Markets Committee (FOMC) the key decision-making body in the Federal Reserve System, and the Fed's equivalent of the ECB's Governing Council

Decisions about monetary policy are made by a 12-member committee called the **Federal Open Markets Committee (FOMC)**. The FOMC consists of the seven Fed governors, the president of the Federal Reserve Bank of New York, and four of the presidents of the other regional Federal Reserve banks, who serve on a rotating basis. The FOMC meets approximately eight times a year to review the state of the economy and to determine monetary policy, and is the Fed's equivalent of the ECB's Governing Council.

In October 2005, President Bush nominated Professor Bernanke to succeed Alan Greenspan as Chair of the Federal Reserve Board of Governors.

Summary

- *Money* is any asset that can be used in making purchases, such as currency and chequing account balances. Money has three main functions: it is a *medium of exchange*, which means that it can be used in transactions; it is a *unit of account*, in that economic values are typically measured in units of money (e.g. euros); and it is a store of value, a means by which people can hold wealth. In practice it is difficult to measure the money supply since many assets have some money-like features. A relatively narrow measure of money is M1, which includes currency and chequing accounts. Broader measures of money, such as M2 and M3, include all the assets in M1 plus additional assets that are somewhat less convenient to use in transactions.

- Because bank deposits are part of the money supply, the behaviour of commercial banks and of bank depositors affects the amount of money in the economy. A key factor is the *reserve–deposit* ratio chosen by banks. *Bank reserves* are cash or similar assets held by commercial banks, for the purpose of meeting depositor withdrawals and payments. The reserve–deposit ratio is bank reserves divided by deposits in banks. A banking system in which all deposits are held as reserves practises *100 per cent reserve banking*. Modern banking systems have reserve–deposit ratios less than 100 per cent, and are called *fractional-reserve banking systems*.

- Commercial banks *create money* through multiple rounds of lending and accepting deposits. This process of lending and increasing deposits comes to an end when banks' reserve–deposit ratios equal their desired levels. At that point, bank deposits equal bank reserves divided by the desired reserve deposit ratio. The money supply equals currency held by the public plus deposits in the banking system.

- The *Eurosystem* consists of those EU member states that use the euro as their currency. The original 11 countries were Austria, Belgium, Finland, France, Germany, Ireland, Italy, Luxemburg, the Netherlands, Portugal and Spain. Greece joined in January 2001, but the United Kingdom, Sweden and Denmark decided to opt out of the euro and retain their national currencies.

- The central bank of the Eurosystem is called the *European Central Bank* (or the ECB). The ECB is part of the *European System of Central Banks* (ESCB), which includes the ECB and the national central banks (NCBs) of member states of the European Union, although non-euro countries do not participate in policy decisions. The ESCB was established by the Maastricht Treaty and became fully operational on 1 January 1999. The ECB's main responsibilities are formulating monetary policy for the Eurosystem and regulating financial markets, especially banks. The *Governing Council* is the ECB's supreme decision-making body and is made up of the President and Vice-President of the ECB, other members of the *Executive Board* and the governors of the NCBs. The Executive Board consists of the President and Vice-President of the ECB plus four others appointed on the basis of their expertise and experience in financial matters.

- The ECB can affect the money supply indirectly through its control of the supply of *bank reserves*. The principal method the ECB uses to control the money supply is called a *main refinancing operation* in which the ECB lends reserves to the commercial banks. The main refinancing rate is the interest rate that banks pay to borrow from the ECB. The *main refinancing rate* is regarded as the key interest rate in the Eurosystem and is set by the ECB's *Governing Council*.

- The central bank of the United States is called the *Federal Reserve System* (or the Fed). The Fed's two main responsibilities are making monetary policy (which means determining how much money will circulate in the economy), and overseeing and regulating financial markets, especially banks. Created in 1914, the Fed is headed by a *Board of Governors* made up of seven governors appointed by the President of the United States. One of these seven governors is appointed chairman. The *Federal Open Market Committee* (FOMC), which meets about eight times a year to determine monetary policy, is made up of the seven governors and five of the presidents of the regional Federal Reserve Banks.

▶

▶
> ■ The central bank of the United Kingdom is called the *Bank of England*. The *Monetary Policy Committee* (or MPC) is the Bank's policy decision-making body and consists of the Governor of the Bank of England, two Deputy Governors, the Bank's Chief Economist and four members appointed by the government. The Bank of England Act 1998 gives the Bank a mandate for price stability and grants the MPC operational independence in formulating monetary policy. However, the inflation target or definition of price stability is set by the government rather than the MPC.

Review questions

1. What is *money*? Why do people hold money even though it pays a lower return than other financial assets?

2. Suppose that the introduction of debit cards means that the public reduces its currency holdings by 50 per cent. If the central bank takes no action, what will happen to the national money supply? Explain.

3. The central bank wants to reduce the economy's money supply. Describe the various actions it might take, and explain how each action would accomplish the bank's objective.

4. What would you expect to happen to the Eurosystem's money supply if the ECB raised its main refinancing rate?

5. What are the main policy-making bodies in the ECB, the Fed and the Bank of England?

6. What is the ECB's definition of price stability in the Eurosystem?

7. How does the ECB use its marginal lending and deposit facilities to control interest rates in the Eurosystem?

connect Problems

1. During the Second World War, an Allied soldier named Robert Radford spent several years in a large German prisoner-of-war (POW) camp. At times, more than 50,000 prisoners were held in the camp, with some freedom to move about within the compound. Radford later wrote an account of his experiences. He described how an economy developed in the camp, in which prisoners traded food, clothing and other items. Services, such as haircuts, were also exchanged. Lacking paper money, the prisoners began to use cigarettes (provided monthly by the Red Cross) as money. Prices were quoted, and payments made, using cigarettes.

    a. In Radford's POW camp, how did cigarettes fulfil the three functions of money?

    b. Why do you think the prisoners used cigarettes as money, as opposed to other items of value such as squares of chocolate or pairs of boots?

    c. Do you think a non-smoking prisoner would have been willing to accept cigarettes in exchange for a good or service in Radford's camp? Why or why not?

2. Using the ECB website (www.ecb.int), obtain recent data on M1, M2 and M3 (see Table 22.1). By what percentage have the three monetary aggregates grown over the past year?

3. Redo the example of Euroland in the text (see Tables 23.2–23.6), assuming that (a) initially, the Euroland Central Bank puts €5,000,000 into circulation, and (b) the commercial banks desire to hold reserves of 20 per cent of deposits. As in the text, assume that the public holds no currency. Show the consolidated balance sheets of Euroland commercial banks after the initial deposits (compare with Table 22.2), after one round of loans (compare with Table 22.3), after the first redeposit of euros (compare with Table 22.4), and after two rounds of loans and redeposits (compare with Table 22.5). What are the final values of bank reserves, loans, deposits and the money supply?

4. a. Bank reserves are 100, the public holds 200 in currency and the desired reserve–deposit ratio is 0.25. Find deposits and the money supply.

   b. The money supply is 500, and currency held by the public equals bank reserves. The desired reserve–deposit ratio is 0.25. Find the currency held by the public and bank reserves.

   c. The money supply is 1,250, of which 250 is currency held by the public. Bank reserves are 100. Find the desired reserve–deposit ratio.

5. When a central bank increases bank reserves by €1, the money supply rises by more than €1. The amount of extra money created when the central bank increases bank reserves by €1 is called the *money multiplier*.

   a. Explain why the money multiplier is generally greater than 1.

   b. The initial money supply is €1,000, of which €500 is currency held by the public. The desired reserve–deposit ratio is 0.2. Find the increase in money supply associated with increases in bank reserves of €1, €5 and €10. What is the money multiplier in this economy?

Online **LearningCentre**

To help you grasp the key concepts of this chapter check out the extra resources posted on the Online Learning Centre. There are chapter summaries, self-test questions, an interactive graphing tool, weblinks and a glossary, all for free!

Visit the Online Learning Centre at: www.mcgraw-hill.co.uk/textbooks/mcdowell for information on accessing all of these resources.

23

The IS-LM Model

Chapter 21 introduced the Keynesian model and defined short-run equilibrium as a position in which the level of output Y equals planned aggregate expenditure PAE. Chapter 22 took the analysis a step further by introducing the money market, and established that for a given level of output the equilibrium rate of interest is determined by equality between the demand for and supply of money. Hence, in this expanded model, the economy consists of two markets: the market for goods and services and the market for money.

These markets are interlinked. For a given rate of interest, as determined in the money market, we can use the Keynesian model in Chapter 21 to determine the equilibrium level of output. Conversely, for a given level of output, as determined in the market for goods and services, we can use the money market model in Chapter 22 to determine the equilibrium value of the rate of interest. Furthermore, a change in equilibrium in one market will lead to a change in equilibrium in the other market. For example, as we saw in Chapter 21 an increase in autonomous expenditure leads, via the income–expenditure multiplier, to an increase in the level of output. However, as explained in Chapter 22, an increase in aggregate income increases the demand for money and, given the supply of money, leads to a higher equilibrium interest rate. Likewise, an increase in the money supply reduces the equilibrium rate of interest, which stimulates consumption and investment and, via the multiplier, increases the equilibrium level of output.

In short, we cannot determine equilibrium in one market independently from equilibrium in the other. Rather, we must determine the equilibrium values of income and the interest rate simultaneously. This task is achieved by the IS-LM model, which uses the equilibrium conditions in each market to simultaneously determine the equilibrium values for the level of output and the rate of interest. To simplify matters we shall assume inflation is constant and equal to zero so that the real rate of interest r equals the nominal rate of interest i in the short run. (We deal with inflation and differences between the real and nominal rates of interest in Chapter 26.)

The IS curve

The IS curve plots combinations of the rate of interest and the level of output for which the market for goods and services is in equilibrium. Figure 23.1 illustrates the derivation of the IS curve. The top panel of the figure illustrates the determination of equilibrium Y and is similar to the Keynesian cross diagram (Figure 21.8 in Chapter 21). With a rate of interest equal to i_1 the expenditure line is PAE_1 and equilibrium output is determined at point A on the 45° line $(Y = PAE)$ with $Y = Y_1$. The bottom part of Figure 23.1 has the interest rate on the vertical axis and output on the horizontal. Point C defines the interest rate, output combination (i_1, Y_1), which gives equilibrium in the market for goods and services. If the interest rate were to fall to a lower level i_2 then, as illustrated in Figure 23.1, the expenditure line shifts up to PAE_2 and equilibrium output is determined at the point B on the 45° line $(Y = PAE)$ with $Y = Y_2$. In the bottom panel of Figure 23.1, point D defines a second interest rate, output combination (i_2, Y_2), which also gives equilibrium in the market for

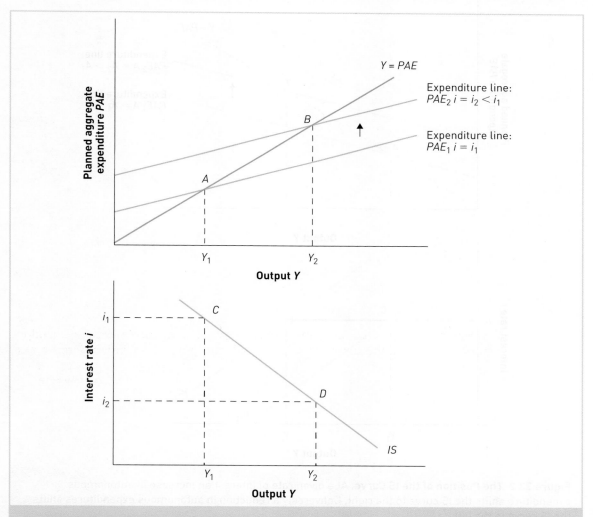

Figure 23.1 The IS Curve. The IS curve traces interest rate and output combinations, which give equilibrium in the market for goods and services.

IS curve defines combinations of the rate of interest and aggregate output, which determine equilibrium in the market for goods and services

goods and services. Points C and D are (i, Y) combinations that determine equilibrium in the market for goods and services. The line joining these points is known as the **IS curve**.[1] The IS curve has a negative slope because a reduction in the interest rate stimulates planned aggregate expenditure and via the multiplier leads to a higher equilibrium level of output. That is, to maintain equilibrium in the market for goods and services, i and Y must change in opposite directions.

The position of the IS curve

As illustrated by Figure 23.2, the position of the IS curve will shift when autonomous expenditures change. The top panel of Figure 23.2 is similar to Figure 23.1 except that

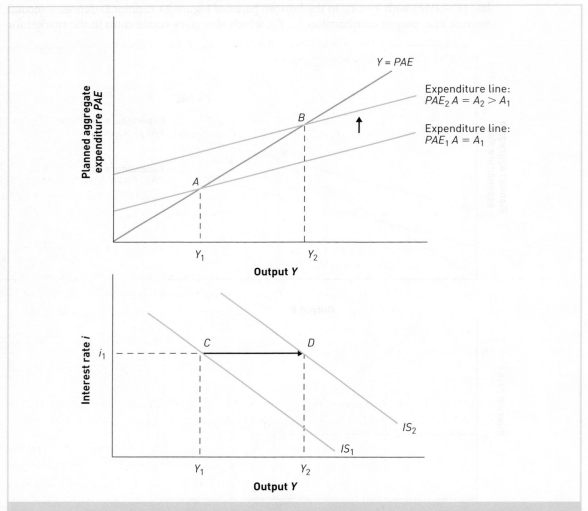

Figure 23.2 The Position of the IS Curve. At a given rate of interest an increase in autonomous expenditure shifts the IS curve to the right. Conversely a reduction in autonomous expenditures shifts the IS curve to the left.

---

1 The IS, or investment–saving, curve gets its name from the fact that in a closed economy without international trade and capital flows, the equilibrium level of Y also corresponds to equality between domestic saving and investment.

the rate of interest is now held constant at i_1. With a rate of interest equal to i_1 and autonomous expenditures equal to A_1 the expenditure line is PAE_1 and equilibrium output is determined at the point A on the $45°$ line ($Y = PAE$) with $Y = Y_1$. In the bottom panel of Figure 23.2, point C defines the interest rate, output combination (i_1, Y_1), which gives equilibrium in the market for goods and services when autonomous expenditures are A_1. As we saw in Chapter 21 (Figure 21.9) *at a given value for the rate of interest* a change in autonomous expenditures shifts the PAE line. Hence an increase in autonomous expenditure to A_2 shifts the PAE line up to PAE_2 establishing a new equilibrium at point B with $Y = Y_2$. In the bottom panel of Figure 23.2, point D defines a second interest rate, output combination (i_1, Y_2), which also gives equilibrium in the market for goods and services. As this result will hold at any given level of the interest rate it follows that an increase in autonomous expenditures shifts the IS curve to the right. Conversely, a reduction in autonomous expenditures shifts the IS curve to the left.

This section has presented a diagrammatic derivation of the IS curve. Box 23.1 gives an equivalent algebraic derivation.

Maths Box 23.1 The IS curve

In Chapter 21 we saw that the market for goods and services can be described as follows:

$$C = \bar{C} + c(Y - T) - ar \tag{1}$$

$$I^P = \bar{I} - br \tag{2}$$

$$PAE = C + I^P + \bar{G} + \overline{NX} \tag{3}$$

$$Y = PAE \tag{4}$$

Equation (1) is an extended consumption function, Equation (2) relates planned investment to the real rate of interest r, Equation (3) defines planned aggregate expenditures and Equation (4) is the equilibrium condition in the market for goods and services. As in the text we shall continue to assume that inflation is zero so that the real rate of interest r equals the nominal rate i. Substituting for C and I^P in Equation (3) gives

$$PAE = [\bar{C} - c\bar{T} + \bar{I} + \bar{G} + \overline{NX}] - (a + b)i + cY$$

or:

$$PAE = \bar{A} - fi + cY$$

where $\bar{A}$ = autonomous expenditures and $f = (a + b)$, which measures the responsiveness of consumption and investment expenditures to changes in the rate of interest. Substituting for PAE in the equilibrium condition (4) and collecting the terms in Y gives:

$$Y = \left(\frac{1}{1 - c}\right)[\bar{A} - fi] \tag{5}$$

Because Equation (5) defines (i, Y) combinations which give equilibrium in the market for goods and services ($Y = PAE$) it is the equation for the IS curve. To derive the slope of the IS curve we can rewrite Equation (5) as:

$$i = \left(\frac{1}{f}\right)\bar{A} - \left(\frac{1 - c}{f}\right)Y \tag{6}$$

Letting the Greek letter delta, or Δ, denote the phrase 'change in', then, for a constant level of autonomous expenditure $\bar{A}$:

$$\Delta i = -\left(\frac{1-c}{f}\right)\Delta Y$$

and the slope of the IS curve is:

$$\left(\frac{\Delta i}{\Delta Y}\right)_{IS} = -\left(\frac{1-c}{f}\right) \tag{7}$$

Hence given the value of the marginal propensity to consume c the slope of the IS curve depends on the parameter f, which measures the response of consumption and investment to the rate of interest. Other things being equal, the greater is f, or the greater the responsiveness of consumption and investment to interest rate changes, the smaller the slope and the flatter the IS curve.

Example 23.1 The IS curve

In a certain economy, $c = 0.8$, $f = 1,000$ and $\bar{A} = 1,010$. Derive the IS curve when $i = 0.05$, or 5 per cent, and when $i = 0.01$, or 1 per cent.

Using Equation (2) in Box 23.1 for:

$$i = 0.05 : Y = \left(\frac{1}{0.2}\right)[1,010 - 1,000(0.05)] = 4,800$$

$$i = 0.01 : Y = \left(\frac{1}{0.2}\right)[1,010 - 1,000(0.01)] = 5,000$$

Hence in Figure 23.1, point C corresponds to an (i, Y) combination $(0.05, 4,800)$ and point D to a combination $(0.01, 5,000)$. As both combinations give equilibrium in the market for goods and services both lie on the IS curve.

Exercise 23.1   In Euroland the components of planned aggregate expenditure are given as:

$$C = \bar{C} + c(Y - T) - ai$$
$$I^P = \bar{I} - bi$$
$$\bar{G} = 200\ T = 320\ NX = 0$$

If $\bar{C} = 1,245$, $\bar{I} = 310$, $a = 1,000$, $b = 500$ and $c = 0.75$, derive the equation for Euroland's IS curve and find the equilibrium values of Y when $i = 0.01$ and when $i = 0.03$.

We have seen that the IS curve plots combinations of the rate of interest and the level of output for which the market for goods and services is in equilibrium and that an increase in autonomous expenditures will shift the IS curve to the right. This, however, cannot be the end of the story because, as explained in Chapter 22, an increase in income will increase the demand for money and given the money supply will lead to an increase in the equilibrium rate of interest which in turn will lead to a fall in equilibrium income. Hence to complete the story we need to incorporate the money market in the model.

The LM curve

Figure 23.3 illustrates the derivation of the LM curve. The LM curve plots combinations of the rate of interest and the level of output for which the money market is in equilibrium. The left-hand panel of Figure 23.3 illustrates the market for money. The money supply is fixed by the central bank at MM and the demand for money is negatively related to the interest rate. At a given level of income $Y = Y_1$ the demand for money curve is L_1 and the money market equilibrium is at point A. The right-hand panel of Figure 23.3 has the interest rate on the vertical axis and output on the horizontal, and point C defines an interest rate, output combination (i_1, Y_1), which gives equilibrium in the money market. If income were to rise to a higher level Y_2 then as explained in Chapter 22 the demand for money curve shifts up to L_2 and as the money supply is fixed the increase in the demand for money forces an increase in the rate of interest to i_2. Hence equilibrium in the money market is now at the point B with $i = i_2$. In the right-hand panel, point D defines a second interest rate, output combina-

LM curve defines combinations of the rate of interest and aggregate output, which determine equilibrium in the money market

tion (i_2, Y_2), which also gives equilibrium in the money market. Hence points such as C and D are (i, Y) combinations, which determine equilibrium in the market for money. The line joining these points is known as the **LM curve**.[2] The LM curve has a positive slope because, as explained in Chapter 22, an increase in Y increases the demand for money which given the money supply shifts the demand for money curve to the right, resulting in a higher interest rate. That is, to maintain equilibrium in the money market i and Y must change in the same direction.

The position of the LM curve

As illustrated by Figure 23.4 the position of the LM curve will shift when the central bank changes the money supply. The left-hand panel of Figure 23.4 is similar to Figure 23.3 except that income is now held constant at Y_1. With the money supply set

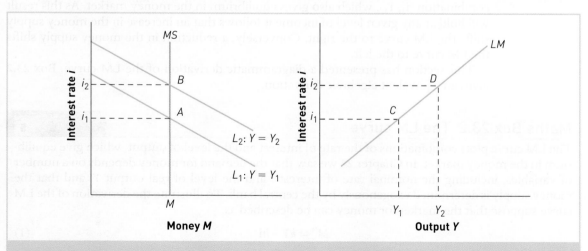

Figure 23.3 The LM Curve. The LM curve traces interest rate and output combinations, which give equilibrium in the money market.

---

2 The LM curve gets its name from the money market equilibrium condition in which the demand for money, or in Keynesian terminology liquidity preference (L), equals the money supply (M).

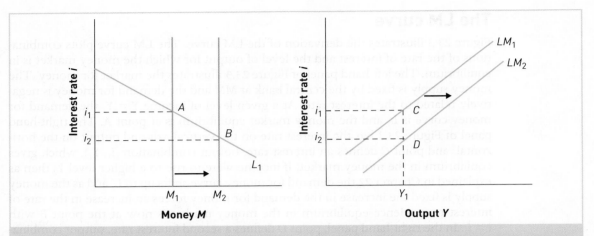

Figure 23.4 The Position of the LM Curve. At a given level of income an increase in the money supply shifts the LM curve to the right. Conversely, a reduction in the money supply shifts the LM curve to the left.

at M_1 and money market equilibrium determined at the point A, the equilibrium interest rate is i_1. In the right-hand panel of Figure 23.4, point C defines the interest rate, output combination (i_1, Y_1), which gives equilibrium in the money market when the money supply is set at M_1. Now suppose the central bank conducts an open-market purchase that increases the money supply to M_2. As we saw in Chapter 22 (Figure 22.5) *at a constant level of income* Y_1 the rate of interest must fall for the public to hold the increased money supply. Hence in the left-hand panel of Figure 23.4, we move down the demand for money curve L_1 to the point B and the equilibrium interest rate falls to i_2.

In the right-hand panel of Figure 23.4, point D defines a second interest rate, output combination (i_2, Y_1), which also gives equilibrium in the money market. As this result will hold at any given level of income it follows that an increase in the money supply shifts the LM curve to the right. Conversely, a reduction in the money supply shifts the LM curve to the left.

This section has presented a diagrammatic derivation of the LM curve. Box 23.2 gives an equivalent algebraic derivation.

Maths Box 23.2 The LM curve

The LM curve plots combinations of the rate of interest and the level of output, which give equilibrium in the money market. In Chapter 22 we saw that the demand for money depends on a number of variables, including the nominal rate of interest i and the level of real output Y, and that the money supply is determined exogenously by the central bank. To illustrate the derivation of the LM curve suppose that the market for money can be described as:

$$M^D = kY - hi \tag{1}$$

$$M^S = \overline{M} \tag{2}$$

$$M^D = M^S \tag{3}$$

Equation (1) specifies the demand for money as a function of the level of income Y and the rate of interest i. The parameter k models the transactions demand for money. For example, if $k = 0.2$ then a 1,000 increase in income increases the demand for money by 200. Likewise the parameter h models the idea that the interest rate is the opportunity cost of money. Hence, if $k = 1,000$ then a 1 per cent increase in the interest rate, or a rise equal to 0.01, reduces the demand for money by 10. Equation (2) assumes that the money supply is exogenously determined by the central bank, and Equation (3) is the money market equilibrium condition. Substituting the first two equations into the equilibrium condition gives:

$$kY - hi = \overline{M}$$

Rearranging gives:

$$i = \frac{1}{h}\left[kY - \overline{M}\right] \tag{4}$$

Because Equation (4) defines (i, Y) combinations that give equilibrium in the money market $(M^D = M^D)$ it is the equation for the LM curve. Letting the Greek letter delta, or Δ, denote the phrase 'change in', then, for a constant level of the money supply $\overline{M}$:

$$\Delta i = \frac{k}{h} \Delta Y$$

and the slope of the LM curve is:

$$\left(\frac{\Delta i}{\Delta Y}\right)_{LM} = \frac{k}{h}$$

Hence given the value of the parameter k the slope of the LM curve depends on the parameter h, which measures the response of demand for money to the rate of interest. Other things being equal, the greater is h, or the greater the responsiveness of demand for money to interest rate changes, the smaller the slope and the flatter the LM curve.

Example 23.2 The LM curve

In a certain economy, $k = 0.2$, $h = 1,000$ and $\overline{M} = 910$. Derive the LM curve when $Y = 4,800$ and when $Y = 5,000$.

Using Equation (4) in Box 23.2 for:

$$Y = 4,800: i = \frac{1}{1,000}[960 - 910] = 0.05$$

$$Y = 5,000: i = \frac{1}{1,000}[1,000 - 910] = 0.09$$

Hence in Figure 23.3, point C corresponds to an (i, Y) combination $(0.05, 4,800)$ and point D to a combination $(0.09, 5,000)$. As both combinations give equilibrium in the market for goods and services both lie on the LM curve.

Exercise 23.2 Suppose Euroland's money market can be described by:

Demand	$M^D = kY - hi$
Supply	$M^S = \overline{M}$
Equilibrium	$M^D = M^S$

If $k = 0.2$, $h = 2,800$ and $\overline{M} = 972$, derive the equation for Euroland's LM curve and find the equilibrium values of i when $Y = 5,140$ and when $Y = 5,420$.

We have seen that the LM curve plots combinations of the rate of interest and the level of output for which the market for money is in equilibrium, and that an increase in the money supply will shift the LM curve to the right. As is the case with the IS curve this cannot be the end of the story because, as explained in Chapter 21, a lower rate of interest will increase planned aggregate expenditure and thus income, which in turn will shift the demand for money curve to the right, forcing a rise in the interest rate. To model these interactions we must bring the IS and LM curves together to establish a general or overall equilibrium for the economy.

Equilibrium | Equilibrium in the IS-LM model

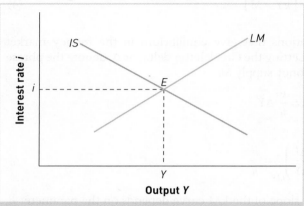

Figure 23.5 Equilibrium in the IS-LM Model. The intersection of the IS and LM curves at point *E* defines the (*i*, *Y*) combination, which gives simultaneous equilibrium in the market for goods and services (*Y* = *PAE*) and in the money market (*M^D = M^S*).

The IS and LM curves describe equilibrium in two interlinked markets. The IS curve traces (*i*, *Y*) combinations at which *Y = PAE*, the equilibrium condition in the market for goods and services, while the LM curve traces (*i*, *Y*) combinations at which $M^D = M^S$, the equilibrium condition in the money market. Hence together they determine the *general equilibrium* condition for the economy. That is, the (*i*, *Y*) combination, which gives simultaneous equilibrium in all markets. Figure 23.5 illustrates this overall or general equilibrium position. The IS and LM curves intersect at point *E*. As *E* lies on both curves it defines the (*i*, *Y*) combination, which gives simultaneous equilibrium in the market for goods and services (*Y = PAE*) and in the money market ($M^D = M^S$).

Box 23.3 presents a formal algebraic derivation of equilibrium in the IS-LM model.

Maths Box 23.3 Equilibrium in the IS-LM model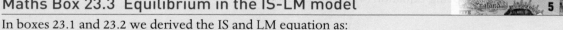

In boxes 23.1 and 23.2 we derived the IS and LM equation as:

$$IS: i = \left(\frac{1}{f}\right)\overline{A} - \left(\frac{1-c}{f}\right)Y \tag{1}$$

$$LM: i = \frac{1}{h}\left[kY - \overline{M}\right] \tag{2}$$

Equating the right-hand side of each equation gives:

$$\left(\frac{1}{f}\right)\overline{A} - \left(\frac{1-c}{f}\right)Y = \left(\frac{k}{h}\right)Y - \left(\frac{1}{h}\right)\overline{M}$$

Collecting the terms in *Y* gives:

$$\left[\frac{k}{h} + \frac{1-c}{f}\right]Y = \left(\frac{1}{f}\right)\overline{A} + \left(\frac{1}{h}\right)\overline{M}$$

or:

$$\left[\frac{fk + h\,(1 - c)}{hf}\right] Y = \left(\frac{1}{f}\right)\bar{A} + \left(\frac{1}{h}\right)\bar{M}$$

Hence equilibrium Y is given by:

$$Y = \frac{hf}{fk + h\,(1 - c)}\left[\left(\frac{1}{f}\right)\bar{A} + \left(\frac{1}{h}\right)\bar{M}\right]$$

$$= \frac{hf}{fk + h\,(1 - c)}\left[\frac{1}{hf}\left(h\bar{A} + f\bar{M}\right)\right] \tag{3}$$

$$= \frac{1}{fk + h\,(1 - c)}\left[h\bar{A} + f\bar{M}\right]$$

and given the value for Y from Equation (3) the equilibrium value for i can be determined from the LM Equation (2).

Example 23.3 Equilibrium in the IS-LM model

Suppose that, in a given economy, $\bar{A} = 1{,}010$, $\bar{M} = 910$, $c = 0.8$, $f = 1{,}000$, $h = 1{,}000$ and $k = 0.2$. Use the IS-LM model to find the equilibrium values for Y and i.

Using Equation (3) in Box 23.3 we get:

$$Y = \frac{1}{400}\left[(1{,}000)\,1{,}010 + (1{,}000)\,910\right] = 4{,}800$$

Substituting the equilibrium value for Y into the LM equation gives the equilibrium rate of interest:

$$i = \frac{1}{1{,}000}\left[0.2\,(4{,}800) - 910\right] = 0.05$$

Hence in equilibrium $i = 0.05$ and $Y = 4{,}800$. For example, in Figure 23.5, point E corresponds to an (i, Y) combination $(0.05, 4{,}800)$.

Exercise 23.3

Using the data in Exercises 23.1 and 23.2, find the equilibrium values for Y and i in the Euroland economy.

Examples 23.4 and 23.5 use the IS-LM model to illustrate the effects of changes in autonomous expenditure and the money supply.

Example 23.4 An increase in autonomous expenditure

Use the IS-LM model to illustrate the effect of an increase in autonomous expenditure on the equilibrium values of Y and i.

In Figure 23.6 the initial equilibrium is at point E_1 with $Y = Y_1$ and $i = i_1$. As shown in Figure 23.2 an increase in autonomous expenditure shifts the IS curve to the right. Hence in Figure 23.6 the new equilibrium is at point E_2 with $Y = Y_2$ and $i = i_2$. Income rises via the multiplier effect discussed in Chapter 21. However, as shown in Chapter 22, the increase in income leads to a higher demand for money. With the money supply fixed by the central bank the rate of interest must increase to i_2 to restore equilibrium in the money market.

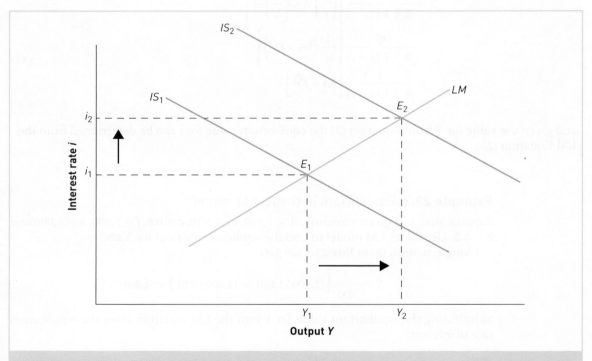

Figure 23.6 An Increase in Autonomous Expenditure. Starting from the equilibrium point E_1 an increase in autonomous expenditure shifts the IS curve from IS_1 to IS_2. The new equilibrium is at point E_2. Income increases to Y_2 but the higher level of Y leads to an excess demand for money and a higher equilibrium rate of interest.

Example 23.5 An increase in the money supply

Use the IS-LM model to illustrate the effect of an increase in the money supply on the equilibrium values of Y and i.

In Figure 23.7 the initial equilibrium is at point E_1 with $Y = Y_1$ and $i = i_1$. As shown in Figure 23.4 an increase in the money supply shifts the LM curve to the right. Hence in Figure 23.7 the new equilibrium is at point E_2 with $Y = Y_2$ and $i = i_2$. The interest rate falls because a lower interest rate is required for the public to willingly hold the increased money supply (a movement along the money demand curve). However, the lower rate of interest increases planned aggregate expenditure, leading to a higher level of income.

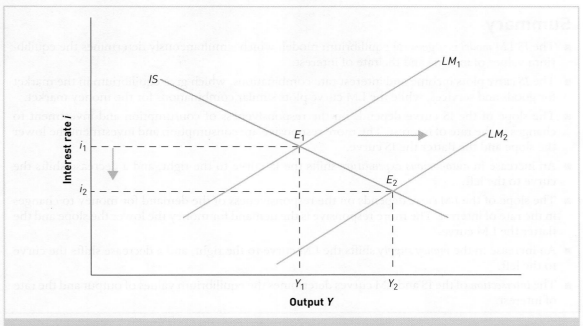

Figure 23.7 An Increase in the Money Supply. Starting from the equilibrium point E_1 an increase in the money supply shifts the LM curve from LM_1 to LM_2. In order for the public to hold the higher money supply the rate of interest must fall, which increases consumption and investment and, via the multiplier effect, increases income. The new equilibrium is at point E_2 with $Y = Y_2$ and $i = i_2$.

Summary

- The *IS-LM model* is a general equilibrium model, which simultaneously determines the equilibrium values of income and the rate of interest.
- The *IS curve* plots income and interest rate combinations, which give equilibrium in the market for goods and services, while the LM curve plots similar combinations for the money market.
- The slope of the IS curve depends on the responsiveness of consumption and investment to changes in the rate of interest. The more responsive are consumption and investment the lower the slope and the flatter the IS curve.
- An increase in *autonomous expenditure* shifts the IS curve to the right, and a decrease shifts the curve to the left.
- The slope of the *LM curve* depends on the responsiveness of the demand for money to changes in the rate of interest. The more responsive is the demand for money the lower the slope and the flatter the LM curve.
- An increase in the *money supply* shifts the LM curve to the right, and a decrease shifts the curve to the left.
- The *intersection* of the IS and LM curves determines the equilibrium values of output and the rate of interest.

Review questions

1. Explain how the market for goods and services and the market for money are interlinked. Why does this interdependency between the two markets require a general equilibrium model of income determination rather that the simple Keynesian model introduced in Chapter 21?

2. Explain why the slope of the IS curve depends on the responsiveness of consumption and investment to changes in the rate of interest. If consumption and investment become more responsive to changes in the rate of interest does this make the IS curve flatter or steeper?

3. Explain why the slope of the LM curve depends on the responsiveness of the demand for money to changes in the rate of interest. If the demand for money becomes less responsive to changes in the rate of interest does this make the LM curve flatter or steeper?

4. Explain how an increase in net exports shifts the position of the IS curve.

5. Explain how a reduction in the money supply shifts the position of the LM curve.

6. Using the IS-LM model explain how (a) a decrease in net exports and (b) a reduction in the money supply affect the equilibrium values for the level of income and the rate of interest. Problems

connect Problems

1. Suppose that in a given economy $\bar{A} = 1{,}200$, $\bar{M} = 1{,}000$, $c = 0.75$, $f = 800$, $h = 1{,}200$ and $k = 0.25$. What are the equilibrium values for Y and i?

2. Using the data in Problem 1, suppose the economy faced a recessionary gap of 360. By how much would the government have to increase purchases to close the recessionary gap?

3. Using the data in Problem 1, suppose the economy faced a recessionary gap of 360. By how much would the government have to cut net taxes to close the recessionary gap?

4. Using the data in Problem 1, suppose the economy faced an expansionary gap of 480. By how much would the government have to reduce the money supply to close the expansionary gap?

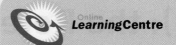

To help you grasp the key concepts of this chapter check out the extra resources posted on the Online Learning Centre. There are chapter summaries, self-test questions, an interactive graphing tool, weblinks and a glossary, all for free!

Visit the Online Learning Centre at: www.mcgraw-hill.co.uk/textbooks/mcdowell for information on accessing all of these resources.

24

Stabilising the Economy (1): the Role of Fiscal Policy

According to the Keynesian model, variations in aggregate spending are important causes of short-run fluctuations in economic activity. Policies that are used to affect planned aggregate expenditure, with the objective of eliminating output gaps, are called **stabilisation policies**. Policy actions intended to close a recessionary gap by increasing planned spending and output are called **expansionary policies**. Conversely, policy actions intended to close an expansionary gap by reducing planned spending are called **contractionary policies**.

The two major tools of stabilisation policy are *monetary policy* and *fiscal policy*. Recall that monetary policy refers to decisions about the size of the money supply, whereas fiscal policy refers to decisions about the government's budget – how much the government spends and how much tax revenue it collects. In this chapter we focus on how fiscal policy can be used to influence spending in the basic Keynesian model, as well as on some practical issues that arise in the use of fiscal policy in the real world. Monetary policy will be discussed in Chapter 25.

Fiscal policy is especially important in a European context. Recall from Chapter 22 that countries in the Eurosystem have transferred responsibility for monetary policy from their national central banks to the European Central Bank (ECB), based in Frankfurt. This sacrifice of policy independence means that individual countries can no longer use monetary policy to stabilise their domestic economies. Hence when countries such as France and Italy are faced with recession they cannot increase their domestic money supplies and reduce interest rates to offset a decline in aggregate spending. Likewise, when faced with inflationary pressures they cannot cool the economy by reducing the money supply and increasing interest rates. Rather, they must accept the monetary policy set by the ECB. While this policy may be appropriate for the Eurosystem as a whole there can be no guarantee that it will be appropriate for individual countries such as France, Italy and other members of the Eurosystem.

stabilisation policies
government policies that are used to affect planned aggregate expenditure, with the objective of eliminating output gaps

expansionary policies
government policy actions intended to increase planned spending and output

contractionary policies
government policy actions designed to reduce planned spending and output

Given that monetary policy is no longer an option, *fiscal policy* would appear to become much more important as it is now the only macroeconomic stabilisation policy available to national governments. However, although fiscal policy remains the responsibility of national governments we shall see that countries within the Eurosystem have placed limits on their fiscal independence through an agreement known as the *Stability and Growth Pact* (SGP). Later in this chapter we shall take a close look at the SGP, and ask why it is considered necessary and how successful it has been. There is, however, one important point that we should note at this stage. As stated above, fiscal policy refers to the government's budget, which we have defined as the difference between government purchases, G, and net taxes, T. Changes in the budget deficit $(G - T)$, can be taken as a key indicator of the strength and direction of fiscal policy. For example, a decision to increase the budget deficit by increasing G and/or reducing T would normally be seen as an indicator of an *expansionary* policy. Conversely, a decision to reduce the deficit by cutting G and/or increasing T can be interpreted as a *contractionary* policy.

These are *discretionary* policy changes. That is, the government takes decisions to spend more or less on specific projects (build new roads, increase the wages of public-sector workers, cancel plans to purchase new military equipment, etc.) or to cut or increase taxation. However, it is important to note that the deficit can change even if the government does not alter its spending and tax plans. Most government tax revenue comes from income taxes and taxes on expenditure, and as the economy moves into recession we would expect these revenues to fall as incomes and expenditures decline with output. Likewise, we would expect transfer payments such as unemployment benefits to increase as the *number claiming* these benefits grows during recession (remember that net taxes T are tax revenues less transfer payments). Conversely, we would expect tax revenues to increase and transfer payments to fall during an expansion as incomes rise and the *number claiming* unemployment benefits declines. That is, we would expect to observe *automatic* changes in the government's deficit as the economy moves from recession to expansion – increasing in recession, declining in an expansion. So long as tax revenues vary with the level of economic activity and transfer payments vary with the number claiming benefit, the deficit will automatically change over the course of the business cycle. When analysing the role and effectiveness of fiscal policy it will be important to distinguish between *discretionary* and *automatic* changes in the government's deficit. The next two sections discuss *discretionary* fiscal policy, or government decisions to change its purchases and taxation. The section after that discusses *automatic* changes in the government deficit and highlights their role in helping to stabilise the economy. Once we have dealt with the discretionary and automatic aspects of fiscal policy we can then analyse the SGP, which, as we shall see, limits government budget deficits to 3 per cent of a country's GDP.

Discretionary fiscal policy: changes in government purchases

Decisions about government spending represent one of the two main components of discretionary fiscal policy, the other being decisions about taxes and transfer payments. Keynes himself felt that changes in *government purchases* were probably the most effective tool for reducing or eliminating output gaps. His basic argument was straightforward: government purchases of goods and services, being a component of planned aggregate expenditure, directly affect total spending. If output gaps are caused by too much or too little total spending, then the government can help to guide the economy towards full employment by changing its own level of spending.

Example 24.1 An increase in the government's purchases eliminates a recessionary gap

Figure 24.1 uses the IS-LM model to show how increased government purchases of goods and services can help eliminate a recessionary gap. In the right-hand panel of Figure 24.1 the economy's initial equilibrium position is point E_1, at the intersection of IS_1 and LM_1. Equilibrium values for income and the rate of interest are Y_1 and i_1. The left-hand panel is the Keynesian cross diagram. With the rate of interest equal to i_1 the PAE line is PAE_1. Equilibrium $(Y = PAE)$ is at point A with $Y = Y_1$. Now suppose full employment or potential output is Y^*, which is greater than Y_1, giving a recessionary gap equal to $Y^* - Y_1$. Use Figure 24.1 to show how an increase in government expenditure can close the recessionary gap.

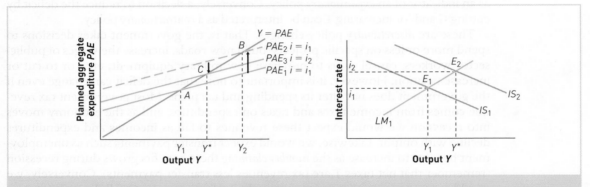

Figure 24.1 Using Fiscal Policy to Close a Recessionary Gap. An increase in government expenditure shifts the PAE line from PAE_1 to PAE_2 and the IS curve from IS_1 to IS_2, increasing the equilibrium rate of interest to i_2. The higher rate of interest reduces planned consumption and investment at each level of income, shifting the PAE line down to PAE_3. The new equilibrium is at E_2 with $Y = Y^*$ and $i = i_2$.

In Figure 24.1 an increase in government expenditure will shift the IS curve to the right to IS_2 (right-hand panel) and PAE line upwards to the dashed line PAE_2 (left-hand panel). Via the multiplier effect, income will initially increase from Y_1 to Y_2. However, as described in Chapter 22, the increase in income will also increase the demand for money, leading to a higher rate of interest which, via its effect on consumption and investment, reduces planned aggregate expenditures and partly offsets the positive effect of the rise in government expenditures. Hence as the rate of interest rises to i_2 consumption and investment will decline, shifting the PAE line down to PAE_3, establishing a new equilibrium at point C with $Y = Y^*$. The new overall equilibrium is at point E_2 in the right-hand panel of Figure 24.1 with $i = i_2$ $Y = Y^*$.

Exercise 24.1 Using the IS-LM model show how a reduction in government expenditures can be used to close an expansionary gap.

Crowding out

The key difference between this analysis and the basic or 'partial equilibrium' Keynesian model described in Chapter 21 is that the latter assumes that the rate of interest is constant at all levels of Y. In contrast, the IS-LM 'general equilibrium' model permits

crowding out effect the tendency of an increase in government expenditure to increase the rate of interest, and reduce consumption and investment

the market for goods and services to interact with the money market. Hence as income increases the demand for money increases, forcing a rise in the rate of interest, which in turn lowers consumption and investment spending and partially offsets the effect of the fiscal stimulus. This offsetting effect is called a **crowding out effect** because higher government expenditure replaces or 'crowds out' consumption and investment expenditures.

Using arrows to denote the direction of change, this sequence can be illustrated as:

$$\underbrace{\uparrow \bar{G} \to \uparrow Y}_{\text{Multiplier}} \to \underbrace{\uparrow M^D \to \uparrow i}_{\text{Money market}} \to \underbrace{\downarrow C, I \to \downarrow Y}_{\text{Crowding out}}$$

Because the crowding out effect dampens the expansionary impact of the fiscal stimulus (the first segment in the above sequence) it means that a greater increase in government purchases will be required to close a given recessionary gap. The strength of the crowding out effect will depend on two factors – the responsiveness of consumption and investment to interest rate changes (the third segment in the above sequence), and the responsiveness of the demand for money to changes in the rate of interest (the second segment in the above sequence). Clearly, for any given rise in the rate of interest the crowding out effect will be stronger the greater the resulting decline in consumption and investment. However, given the responsiveness of consumption and investment to interest rate changes the strength of the crowding out effect will also depend on the extent to which the increase in government expenditure changes the rate of interest. Other things being equal, the lower the rise in the equilibrium rate of interest the smaller the decline in consumption and investment, and the weaker the crowding out effect. As shown in the money market segment of the above sequence, the interest rate rises because the initial increase in income increases the demand for money. As the interest rate must rise to restore money market equilibrium the size of the increase will depend on the responsiveness, or elasticity, of the demand for money to interest rate changes. Other things being equal, the greater the responsiveness of the demand for money to interest rate changes the smaller the rise in the interest rate required to clear the money market. If, for example, the demand for money is highly responsive to changes in the interest rate (a given increase in i results in a relatively large change in M^D) then money market equilibrium can be restored with a relatively small interest rate rise and the crowding out effect will be relatively weak. Conversely, if the responsiveness of the demand for money to interest rate changes is low (a given change in i results in a relatively small change in M^D), then it will take a larger interest rate increase to restore money market equilibrium, and the crowding out effect will be correspondingly stronger. Figure 24.2 illustrates the relationship between the interest rate elasticity of the demand for money and the crowding out effect.

Figure 24.2 illustrates two alternative LM curves, LM_1 and LM_2. An increase in government expenditure shifts the IS curve to IS_2. If the LM curve is LM_1 the new equilibrium is at point E_2 and income rises from Y_1 to Y_2. Alternatively, if the LM curve is the flatter dashed curve LM_2 the new equilibrium is at point E_3 and income rises by more, from Y_1 to Y_3. Hence the flatter the LM curve, the weaker the crowding out effect and the greater the impact of a given increase in government expenditures (given shift in the IS curve) on output. The difference between the alternative LM curves is that LM_1 is drawn steeper than LM_2, implying a lower responsiveness of the demand for money to interest rate changes. To see this, consider a rise in income from Y_1 to Y_2. As income rises, the demand for money will increase and, at a constant money supply, the rate of

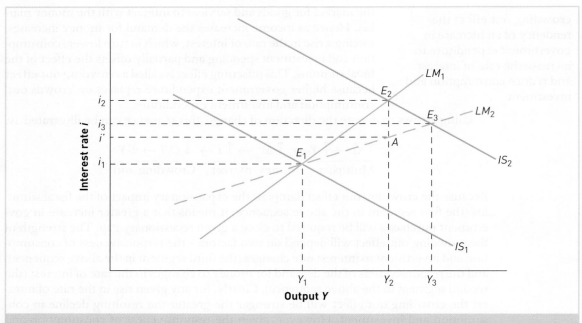

Figure 24.2 Crowding Out. The flatter the LM curve or the greater the responsiveness of the demand for money to interest rate changes, the weaker the crowding out effect.

interest must rise to maintain money market equilibrium. If the LM curve is LM_1 the rate of interest must rise to i_2 to maintain equilibrium in the money market. However, if the LM curve is LM_2, *the same increase in income Y_1 to Y_2 would require a lower interest rate increase, i_1 to i', to maintain money market equilibrium.* It follows that the responsiveness of the demand for money to interest rate changes is lower along the steeper curve LM_1. Hence, the greater the responsiveness of the demand for money to interest rate changes the weaker the crowding out effect and the greater the impact of a given fiscal stimulus. Put another way, the greater the interest elasticity of the demand for money the lower the increase in government expenditures needed to close a given recessionary gap.

Exercise 24.2 Suppose the LM curve is horizontal at the current equilibrium rate of interest. Would this property enhance or weaken the effectiveness of fiscal policy as a means to closing a recessionary gap?

Discretionary fiscal policy: changes in net taxes

Changes in net taxes are the second main component of discretionary fiscal policy. Changes in net taxes have the same qualitative effect as changes in government expenditures. To see this, recall that planned aggregate expenditure is the sum of consumption, planned investment, government purchases and net exports. That is:

$$PAE = C + I^P + \bar{G} + \overline{NX}$$

where:

$$C = \bar{C} + c(Y - \bar{T}) - ai$$

and

$$I^P = \overline{I} - bi$$

Hence:

$$PAE = \overline{A} - (a + b)\mathrm{i} + cY$$

where $\overline{A}$ is autonomous expenditure equal to $(\overline{C} + \overline{I} + \overline{G} - c\overline{T} + \overline{NX})$. Hence an increase in government purchases $\overline{G}$ or cut in net taxes $\overline{T}$ will increase PAE at any given level of income. Referring back to Figure 24.1, a cut in net taxes will also shift the PAE line to PAE_2 and the IS curve to IS_2. The only difference is that whereas a 100-unit increase in government purchases increases PAE by 100 units, a 100-unit cut in net taxes increases PAE by c (the marginal propensity to consume) times 100 at each level of Y. For example, suppose that in Figure 24.1 the shift in the PAE line to PAE_2 requires that government increase purchases by 100 units. If $c = 0.8$ same result can be achieved by a 125-unit cut in net taxes. That is, as 0.8 times $125 = 100$ a 125-unit cut in $\overline{T}$ has the same effect on PAE as a 100-unit increase in $\overline{G}$.

RECAP Fiscal policy and planned spending

Fiscal policy includes two general tools for affecting total spending and eliminating output gaps: (1) changes in *government purchases*, and (2) changes in *taxes or transfer payments*. An increase in government purchases increases autonomous expenditure by an equal amount. A reduction in taxes or an increase in transfer payments increases autonomous expenditure by an amount equal to the marginal propensity to consume times the reduction in taxes or increase in transfers. If the economy is in recession, an increase in government purchases, a cut in taxes or an increase in transfers can be used to stimulate spending and eliminate the recessionary gap. The effectiveness of fiscal policy can be reduced by the tendency of an increase in government expenditure or a cut in net taxes to raise interest rates and *crowd out* private consumption and investment expenditures.

Automatic stabilisers

So far, our discussion of fiscal policy has assumed that government takes *discretionary* decisions to increase or decrease the level of government purchases, transfer payments and taxation in order to stabilise the economy. Because they result from explicit policy decisions these changes in G and T are referred to as **discretionary fiscal policy**. However, as mentioned in the introduction to this chapter, under slightly more realistic assumptions the economy will have a built-in stabilisation mechanism that operates independently of discretionary policy changes. This mechanism works through changes in the *government budget deficit*, which dampen fluctuations in economic activity by automatically increasing in a recession and decreasing during an expansion. It is referred to as an **automatic stabiliser** effect.

discretionary fiscal policy
decisions by government to increase or decrease the levels of government purchases, transfer payments and taxation

automatic stabilisers
automatic changes in the government budget deficit, which help to dampen fluctuations in economic activity

The government budget deficit is defined government purchases G minus *net taxes* T:

$$\text{Government deficit} = G - T$$

Recall that *net taxes* were defined as tax revenues minus transfer payments (unemployment benefits, social welfare payments, etc.). We also assumed that both G and T were *autonomous*. That is, government sets G and T, and their levels do not vary as output Y changes. While this is a useful simplifying assumption it is unrealistic in most modern economies. For example, think what actually happens to tax revenues and transfer payments as the economy moves into recession. Most tax revenue comes from taxes on household incomes (income tax) and expenditures (value added tax) and from profits earned by firms (corporate taxes). During a recession some households will experience declining incomes and, given the consumption function, this will induce an automatic decline in consumption expenditures. Hence, we would expect revenue from income and expenditure taxes to fall during a recession. Company profits will also decline, resulting in reduced revenue from taxes on profits. Conversely, as the economy expands, revenues from income, expenditure and profits taxes will automatically rise. Transfer payments, on the other hand, will move in the opposite direction. If unemployment rises in recession, more households will be claiming unemployment benefit and total transfer payments will automatically increase. Conversely, as the economy recovers and unemployment falls, fewer households will claim unemployment benefits, leading to a decline in government expenditure on transfer payments. We can express this idea as

$$T = tY$$

where t can be thought of as the average rate of tax. If, for example, $t = 0.25$ then each time Y falls by €1, tax revenues will fall by €0.25, or 25 cents. Likewise if Y increases by €1, tax revenues will increase by €0.25. Note that these changes are completely automatic. They do not require any action by government such as a change in the rate of taxation, t. It also follows that at a constant level of government purchases the government deficit will automatically rise during recession and automatically fall during an expansion. Example 24.2 shows that this makes an important difference to our analysis of how changes in autonomous expenditures affect short-run equilibrium output.

Example 24.2 Automatic stabilisers

Suppose that, in a given economy, the market for goods and services can be described as follows:

Consumption function	$C = \bar{C} + c(Y - T) - ai$
Planned investment	$I^P = \bar{I} - bi$
Planned aggregate expenditure	$C + I^P + \bar{G} + \overline{NX}$

Use an IS-LM diagram to illustrate the changes in the equilibrium values of Y and i of a fall in autonomous expenditure when (a) net taxes are autonomous and (b) $T = tY$.

As we saw in Chapter 23 and in Example 24.1, a change in autonomous expenditures will shift the IS curve. We will now see that the extent of the shift will depend on whether net taxes are autonomous or vary with output.

(a) Net taxes are autonomous: $T = \bar{T}$: Substituting for consumption and investment in the equation for planned aggregate expenditures gives:

$$PAE = \bar{A} - (a + b)i + cY$$

where $\bar{A}$ is autonomous expenditure equal to $(\bar{C} + \bar{I} + \bar{G} - c\bar{T} + \overline{NX})$. In equilibrium $PAE = Y$. Hence:

$$Y = \bar{A} - (a + b)i + cY$$

Collecting terms in Y gives:

$$Y = \left(\frac{1}{1-c}\right)\left[\bar{A} - (a+b)\,i\right] \tag{24.1}$$

As Equation (24.1) is the equilibrium equation for the market for goods and services ($PAE = Y$) it is the equation for the IS curve when net taxes are autonomous.

(b) Net taxes vary with income $T = tY$. We can now write the consumption function as:

$$C = \bar{C} + c(Y - tY) - ai$$
$$= \bar{C} + c(1-t)Y - ai$$

Substituting into the definition of planned aggregate expenditure gives:

$$PAE = \bar{A} - (a+b)i + c(1-t)\,Y$$

where $\bar{A}$ is autonomous expenditure ($\bar{C} + \bar{I} + \bar{G} + \overline{NX}$). In equilibrium $PAE = Y$. Hence:

$$Y = \bar{A} - (a+b)i + c(1-t)\,Y$$

Collecting terms in Y gives:

$$Y = \left(\frac{1}{1 - c(1-t)}\right)\left[\bar{A} - (a+b)\,i\right] \tag{24.2}$$

As Equation (24.2) is the equilibrium equation for the market for goods and services ($PAE = Y$) it is also the equation for the IS curve when taxes vary with income.

Figure 24.3 illustrates the difference between these two cases.

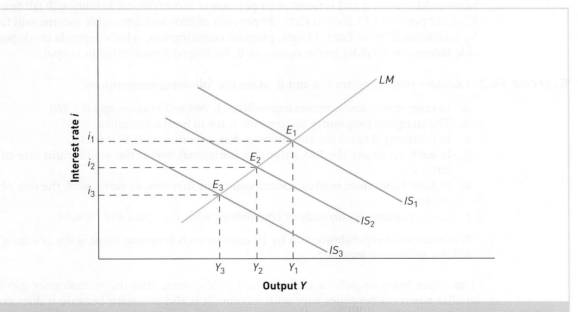

Figure 24.3 Automatic Stabilisers. For a given decline in autonomous expenditures the IS curve shifts by less and the fall in output is lower when taxes vary with income.

In Figure 24.3 the initial equilibrium is at point E_1 with $Y = Y_1$. At *any given rate of interest* a fall in autonomous expenditure will reduce the level of income necessary to maintain equilibrium in the market for goods and services. That is, the IS curve will shift to the left. We will now see that the extent of this shift and the fall in output depends on whether taxes are autonomous or vary with income.

(a) Net taxes are autonomous $T = \bar{T}$: from Equation (24.1) each unit change in autonomous expenditure will, *at a given rate of interest*, reduce Y by $1/(1 - c)$ units. In Figure 24.3 this is illustrated by the shift in the IS curve from IS_1 to IS_3, giving a new equilibrium at point E_3 with $Y = Y_3$.

(b) Net taxes vary with income $T = tY$: From Equation (24.2) each unit change in autonomous expenditure will, *at a given rate of interest*, reduce Y by $1/(1 - c(1 - t))$ units. In Figure 24.3 this is illustrated by the shift in the IS curve from IS_1 to IS_2 giving a new equilibrium at point E_2 with $Y = Y_2$.

Note that for a given decline in autonomous expenditures the IS curve shifts by less and the fall in output is lower when taxes vary with income. For example, if the marginal propensity to consume $c = 0.8$ and the tax rate $t = 0.25$ then $1/(1 - c) = 5$ and $1/(1 - c(1 - t)) = 2.5$. Why is the fall in output lower when taxes vary with income? The answer is that because less tax is paid to the government as income falls, disposable or after-tax income $(Y - T)$ falls by a smaller amount when taxes vary with income and consumption expenditure falls by less. To illustrate, consider two economies A and B. Assume that in A taxes are autonomous and each household pays €250 per week, but in B households are taxed at 25 per cent of their pre-tax income ($t = 0.25$). Suppose that in each economy the typical household earns €1,000 per week before tax. If the household lives in economy A it is taxed at €250 per week and its disposable income is €750. Suppose before-tax income falls to €900. As the household still has to pay €250 tax its disposable income will also fall by €100, to €650. However, if the household lives in B and is taxed at 25 per cent ($t = 0.25$) its tax liability will fall from €250 (25 per cent of 1,000) to €225 (25 per cent of 900) and disposable income will fall by less, from €750 to €675. Hence, planned consumption, which depends on disposable income, will fall by less in economy B, leading to a smaller fall in output.

Exercise 24.3 Consider two economies, A and B. Make the following assumptions.

   a. In economy A autonomous expenditure is 960 and in economy B 1,920.
   b. The marginal propensity to consume is 0.8 in both economies.
   c. In economy A taxes are autonomous but, in economy B, $T = 0.25Y$.
   d. In each economy the LM curve is a horizontal line at the equilibrium rate of interest.
   e. In both economies neither consumption nor investment varies with the rate of interest.
   f. Each economy is currently in equilibrium with $Y = 4,800$ and $i = 0.05$.

   If autonomous expenditure falls by 10 units in each economy what is the resulting fall in equilibrium income?

This effect helps to *stabilise* the economy in the sense that the recessionary gap is smaller when tax revenues vary with income. It is also *automatic* because it does not require any discretionary action by the government such as a change in government purchases G or the rate of taxation t. Hence, it is referred to as an *automatic stabiliser*. Another way to think of the automatic stabiliser effect is that the government deficit automatically increases as Y falls and partially offsets the contractionary impact of a fall in autonomous expenditure. Automatic stabilisers also work in the opposite direction. For example, if the economy experiences an increase in autonomous expenditures, tax revenues will increase as Y increases, thus reducing the increase in disposable income and planned consumption. Without automatic stabilisers, both expansionary and recessionary gaps would be larger and more prolonged. Hence, automatic stabilisers help to dampen the size and duration of cyclical fluctuations in economic activity. We shall see that one reason why countries in the Eurosystem have agreed to put limits on national government deficits is to ensure that automatic stabilisers can work effectively.

The problem of deficits

In this chapter we have seen that the government's budget deficit is a key indicator of the strength and direction of fiscal policy. Other things being equal, an increase in the deficit indicates an expansionary fiscal policy, while a decrease indicates a contractionary policy. We have also seen that changes in the deficit are partly the result of discretionary decisions taken by government to change taxes or purchases, and partly the result of automatic changes in net taxes as the economy moves from recession to expansion. While discretionary and automatic changes in the deficit are important stabilisation instruments, sustained government deficits can be harmful to the economy. As we saw in Chapter 20, higher government deficits reduce national saving, which in turn reduces investment in new capital goods – an important source of long-run economic growth. Also, deficits have to be financed by *borrowing* and if they persist over long periods the government's debt will increase continuously. Recall from Chapter 20 that the government deficit or surplus is a *flow* or the amount that the government borrows or saves in each year, but the government's outstanding debt is a *stock* resulting from the accumulation of previous deficits. For example, if government borrows €1 million in two consecutive years its stock of outstanding debt will be €2 million higher by the end of the second year. Hence a continuous flow of borrowing adds to the stock of *outstanding* debt and if governments continue to borrow year after year the stock of outstanding debt will continue to increase, creating the potential problem of *debt sustainability*.

Debt sustainability

The left-hand panel in Figure 24.4 shows the behaviour of government deficits in Belgium and Italy over the period 1990–2007, while the right-hand panel shows the outstanding debt of these countries. Both deficits and debts are expressed as percentages of each country's GDP. Figure 24.4 illustrates that continuous borrowing to finance large government deficits leads to an ever-increasing stock of outstanding debt.

Much the same was true of other countries, such as Greece and Ireland, whose debt ratios reached 100 per cent of GDP in the late 1980s, although the Irish debt ratio declined significantly over the 1990s. One way in which such countries can deal with an increasing debt ratio is to finance deficits by borrowing from their national central banks. Effectively, this means that, rather than borrowing from the private sector, the government prints the money necessary to finance its deficit, a policy known as *monetary financing*. Monetary financing typically leads to an increase in the money supply and rising inflation, which reduces the real value, and hence the burden, of the government's debt. However, Article 103 of the Maastricht Treaty explicitly prohibits the European System of Central Banks (ESCB) from lending to national governments.

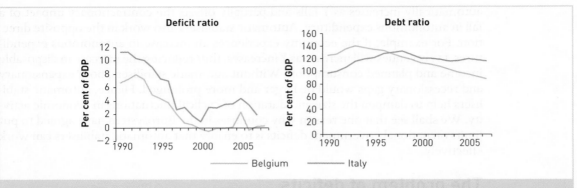

Figure 24.4 Deficit and Debt Ratios, Belgium and Italy, 1990–2007 (per cent of actual GDP).
Source: OECD, *Economic Outlook*.

no-bailout clause a provision in the Maastricht Treaty that prohibits the ESCB from lending to national governments

This Article is known as the **no-bailout clause**, and it means that responsibility for financing deficits and paying off debt remains at the *national* level.

The no-bailout clause implies that to stop their debt from rising, governments must reduce their deficits by cutting expenditures and/or increasing taxes. Unfortunately, such measures are politically unpopular and governments with time horizons focused on the next election are often unwilling to countenance such harsh fiscal measures. However, if deficits remain high and the debt continues to grow, then international financial markets may question the government's willingness to take the necessary corrective action and demand an interest rate premium to continue lending – or, in extreme cases, refuse to finance deficits by purchasing additional government debt. Such an outcome would not only force hard contractionary fiscal policies on the delinquent country but could also spill over into partner monetary union countries. One reason for this spillover is that, in the Eurosystem, all government debt is denominated in euros, which means that international investors may not distinguish between debt issues by different governments. German, French, Italian and Irish government bonds, etc. may simply be seen as *euro-denominated assets* rather than debt issued by different countries, with the consequence that a loss of confidence in bonds issued by one government may spill over into debt issued by the others. Once again, the actions of one country can affect its partners – the *externality effect*.

The authors of the Maastricht Treaty were very aware of the risks associated with large government deficits. Article 104 of the Treaty decrees that 'Member States shall avoid excess government deficits', and stipulates reference or target values for both government deficits and debt ratios. Specifically, to qualify for membership of the Eurosystem, a country's deficit could not exceed 3 per cent of GDP and its debt ratio could not exceed 60 per cent. These conditions were part of the Maastricht Convergence Criteria and became known as the *Excessive Deficit Procedure*. The condition for the debt ratio was, however, qualified. Countries with debt ratios above 60 per cent of GDP could be deemed to satisfy the criteria provided that the ratio was 'diminishing sufficiently and approaching the reference value at a satisfactory pace'.

While the Excessive Deficit Procedure proved to be successful in bringing deficits under control it would have been inconsistent with Article 104 of the Treaty if these restraints were removed once the monetary union actually started. As we have seen above, it is important that member countries avoid large deficits once they adopt the single currency. To prevent this the countries joining the Eurosystem agreed to control their deficits by negotiating the *Stability and Growth Pact* (SGP), discussed in Economic naturalist 24.1.

Economic naturalist 24.1 The Stability and Growth Pact

The SGP, more commonly known as the Stability Pact, was negotiated at the December 1996 European summit in Dublin and finally agreed six months later at the Amsterdam summit. As in the Excessive Deficit Procedure, the SGP establishes a 3 per cent reference value for government deficits. The European Commission monitors the fiscal positions of each country and reports to the Council of Economic and Finance Ministers, or Ecofin. If Ecofin rules that a country has breached the 3 per cent reference value it can issue recommendations and a deadline for corrective action. Countries that fail to comply with these recommendations can be subject to sanctions or fines. For example, if a country runs a deficit between 3 and 4 per cent of its GDP the fine is 0.2 per cent of GDP. If the deficit is between 4 and 5 per cent of GDP the fine is increased to 0.3 per cent of GDP, and so on. The maximum fine is 0.5 per cent and applies to countries whose deficit exceeds 6 per cent of GDP.

The Stability Pact ran into serious difficulties in 2002 when the two largest countries in the Eurosystem started to run deficits in excess of 3 per cent of GDP. In 2002 the French deficit was 3.3 per cent and the German deficit 3.5 per cent. The European Commission and Ecofin ruled that both countries were in breach of the Pact and recommended corrective action (expenditure cuts and/ or tax increases) with fines to be imposed if the deficits did not fall below 3 per cent by 2004. Put simply, both governments used their size to ignore these recommendations and their deficits continued to increase over 2003–04. In 2003 both governments had deficits of around 4 per cent of GDP and in 2004 the German deficit was 3.8 per cent and the French deficit 3.6 per cent.

The failure of France and Germany to comply with the Stability Pact led to a prolonged dispute between their governments, the European Commission and Ecofin, and as a result, in 2005, the European Council agreed to a series of revisions to the Pact. The most important revision was that Ecofin could extend deadlines for corrective action if it judged that an excessive deficit was caused by what is termed 'other relevant factors'. These factors include 'prevailing cyclical conditions' (a sudden downturn in the economy), spending on 'policies to foster R&D and innovation' 'and any other factors that in the opinion of the Member State concerned are relevant'.

Critics of the Stability Pact argued that these revisions were too liberal and gave greater flexibility to governments who wished to run deficits in excess of 3 per cent. This, however, has not been the case. By 2006 the overall deficit for the Eurosystem was 1.3 per cent, for France 2.4 per cent and for Germany 1.6 per cent.

The cyclically adjusted budget deficit

An alternative approach to measuring the deficit is to assess a government's fiscal policy on discretionary actions only. This, however, requires that we can decompose changes in the actual deficit into components due to *automatic* changes and *discretionary* policy. This is what the *cyclically adjusted budget deficit* attempts to do.

The cyclically adjusted budget deficit separates automatic from discretionary changes by evaluating each year's deficit at a *constant level of output*. Evaluating the deficit at a constant level of output means that automatic changes, which depend on output changes, are eliminated in the calculation, so that the measured change in the deficit reflects discretionary policy only. As automatic changes are the result of cyclical changes or year-to-year variations in output, the resulting measure is known as the cyclically adjusted budget deficit. Although the cyclically adjusted budget deficit can be calculated at any constant level of output, it is common to use the economy's full-employment or potential output $Y^\star$.

This approach is analogous to the calculation of the consumer price index discussed in Chapter 17. In that case we measured the cost of a fixed basket of goods at the prices prevailing in each year. As the quantities of goods are held constant, any change in their cost must be due to changes in prices. Likewise, evaluating the deficit at a constant level of output means that automatic changes, which happen only when output changes, are eliminated and the resulting change reflects changes in discretionary policy only. Economic naturalist 24.2 gives an example, while Economic naturalist 24.3 describes the UK's so-called golden rule of fiscal policy.

Economic naturalist 24.2 France, Germany and the Stability Pact

We have seen that increases in the French and German deficits over 2002–03 resulted in the threat of fines if their governments failed to comply with Ecofin's recommendations for corrective action. However, corrective action in the form of contractionary fiscal measures would have been inappropriate at a time when both economies were experiencing recession, and could have weakened or even disabled the automatic stabilisers. In France the recessionary gap increased from 0.1 per cent in 2002 to 1.8 per cent in 2003, and in Germany it increased from 1.3 per cent to 2.9 per cent at the same time. Given that both countries were stuck in recession there would have been little economic logic in forcing their governments to use contractionary fiscal policies designed to bring the deficits closer to the 3 per cent reference value but at the cost of further aggravating the underlying economic problem. Would Ecofin's decisions on France and Germany have been different if they had been judged on the cyclically adjusted rather than the actual deficit?

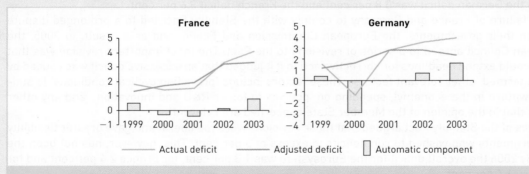

Figure 24.5 Actual and Adjusted Deficits, France and Germany, 1999–2003 (per cent of actual/potential GDP).

Source: OECD, *Economic Outlook.*

Figure 24.5 shows the actual and adjusted deficits for France and Germany over 1999–2003. The adjusted deficit measures the contribution of discretionary fiscal policy, and the automatic component, which is the difference between the actual and cyclically adjusted deficits, measures the contribution of automatic stabilisers. Note that the automatic component is positive when the actual deficit is greater than the adjusted deficit.

In 2003, the actual German deficit was 3.9 per cent of GDP, which can be broken down into a cyclical component equal to 2.3 per cent of GDP and an automatic component equal to 1.6 per cent. Without the automatic component, which was due to the widening recessionary gap, the German deficit would have been within the 3 per cent reference value as required by the SGP. By basing the reference value on the cyclically adjusted rather than the actual deficit there would have been no reason to recommend corrective action at a time when the German economy was moving further into recession. Hence, there is an obvious case for focusing on the adjusted rather than the actual budget deficit. France, on the other hand, was in a different position. The actual deficit was 4.1 per cent of GDP and the adjusted deficit was 3.3 per cent, leaving an automatic component of 0.8 per cent. The relatively large adjusted deficit was mostly the result of President Chirac fulfilling his election pledge to cut taxes, a discretionary change. Hence, based on the cyclically adjusted deficit there was still a case for recommending corrective action by reversing the tax changes or cutting government expenditures. However, the correction needed to bring the adjusted deficit into line with the reference value would have been less severe than that required to reduce the actual deficit to below 3 per cent.

Basing the 3 per cent reference value on the cyclically adjusted rather than the actual deficit has the advantage of reducing the need to take corrective action in the form of tax hikes and expenditure cuts at a time when the economy is in recession. Should the SGP be reformed in this way? To date, the European Commission and most economists seem to favour a move in this direction. There is, however, one important caveat. Like many other concepts in applied economics, calculating the cyclically adjusted deficit is far from a precise science and there is a danger that governments, the Commission and Ecofin could become embroiled in arguments about estimation methods. Unless there is a binding agreement on how cyclically adjusted deficits are to be estimated it would be difficult to classify deficits as excessive and requiring corrective action. What, for example, would have happened in 2003 if France had argued that using an alternative, and perhaps equally valid, estimator its adjusted deficit was actually 2.3 rather than 3.3 per cent of GDP?

Fiscal policy as a stabilisation tool: two qualifications

The basic Keynesian model might lead you to think that precise use of fiscal policy can eliminate output gaps. But, as is often the case, the real world is more complicated than economic models suggest. We close the chapter with two qualifications about the use of fiscal policy as a stabilisation tool.

Fiscal policy and the supply side

We have focused so far on the use of fiscal policy to affect planned aggregate expenditure. However, most economists would agree that *fiscal policy may affect potential output as well as planned aggregate expenditure* (PAE). On the spending side, for example, investments in public capital – such as roads, airports and schools – can play a major role in the growth of potential output, as we discussed in Chapter 19. On the other side of the ledger, tax and transfer programmes may well affect the incentives, and thus the economic behaviour, of households and firms. For example, a high tax rate on interest income may reduce the willingness of people to save for the future, while a tax break on new investment may encourage firms to increase their rate of capital formation. Such changes in saving or investment will in turn affect potential output. Many other examples could be given of how taxes and transfers affect economic behaviour, and thus possibly affect potential output as well.

Some critics of the Keynesian theory have gone so far as to argue that the *only* effects of fiscal policy that matter are effects on potential output. This was essentially the view of the so-called *supply-siders*, a group of American economists and journalists whose influence reached a high point during President Reagan's first term of office (1981–85). Supply-siders focused on the need for tax cuts, arguing that lower tax rates would lead people to work harder (because they would be allowed to keep a larger

Incentives
Matter

share of their earnings), to save more, and to be more willing to innovate and take risks. Through their arguments that lower taxes would substantially increase potential output, with no significant effect on planned spending, the supply-siders provided crucial support for the large tax cuts that took place under the Reagan administration. Supply-sider ideas were also used to support the long-term income tax cut passed under President George W. Bush in 2001.

A more balanced view is that fiscal policy affects *both* planned spending *and* potential output. Thus, in making fiscal policy, government officials should take into

Economic naturalist 24.3 The UK's golden rule for fiscal policy

Following its election victory in 1997 the new Labour government announced two important economic initiatives. One, as discussed in Chapter 22, was to grant policy independence to the Bank of England, while the second established a new guideline for fiscal policy which committed the government to borrowing only to finance productive investment, but not to finance current expenditures. This guideline became known as the *golden rule* and required that, net of investment, the government deficit should balance in the medium term. Hence the deficit could rise during recessions and fall during expansions, but should balance over the course of the business cycle. Has the government adhered to its so-called golden rule?

Year	Output gap % of potential GDP	Actual deficit % + deficit, – surplus	Adjusted deficit % + deficit, – surplus
2000	1.1	–4.0	–1.3
2001	0.7	–0.9	–0.5
2002	0.2	1.7	1.9
2003	0.2	3.3	3.5
2004	0.9	3.3	3.6
2005	–0.3	3.5	3.5
2006	–0.2	2.8	2.7
2007	0.2	3.0	3.1

Table 24.1 **UK Fiscal Policy 2000–2007**
Note: A positive output gap corresponds to an expansionary gap $(Y > Y^*)$.
Source: OECD, *Economic Outlook*, 2008.

Table 24.1 presents some evidence on the UK government deficit for the period 2000–2007. The first column gives the output gap in each year, the second column gives the actual deficit and the final column gives the cyclically adjusted deficit. Several points are worth noting about the data in Table 24.1. First, there is no evidence to suggest that the deficit balances over the business cycle. For example, when the economy moves from an expansionary gap in 2004 to a recessionary gap in 2005 and 2006, and then recovers in 2007, the deficit remains positive (expenditures exceed revenues) and averages to just over 3 per cent of GDP. Second, actual GDP exceeded potential output over 2000–2004, indicating an expansionary gap. If fiscal policy followed the golden rule we would expect the deficit to be in surplus over this period. However, as indicated by the third column, the actual deficit moved from a strong surplus to a significant deficit between 2000 and 2004. Further, the automatic component (actual minus adjusted) was negative in these years, indicating that the rise in the actual deficit can be attributed to discretionary fiscal policy. Hence it would be difficult to conclude that the UK fiscal authorities have adhered to the golden rule.

account not only the need to stabilise planned aggregate expenditure but also the likely effects of government spending, taxes and transfers on the economy's *productive capacity*.

The relative inflexibility of fiscal policy

The second qualification about the use of fiscal policy is that *fiscal policy is not always flexible enough to be useful for stabilisation*. Our examples have implicitly assumed that the government can change spending or taxes relatively quickly in order to eliminate output gaps. In reality, changes in government spending or taxes must usually go through a lengthy legislative process, which reduces the ability of fiscal policy to respond in a timely way to economic conditions. Another factor that limits the flexibility of fiscal policy is that fiscal policy makers have many other objectives besides stabilising aggregate spending – from ensuring an adequate national defence to providing income support to the poor. What happens if, say, the need to strengthen the national defence requires an increase in government spending, but the need to contain planned aggregate expenditure requires a decrease in government spending? Such conflicts can be difficult to resolve through the political process.

This lack of flexibility means that fiscal policy is less useful for stabilising spending than the basic Keynesian model suggests. Nevertheless, most economists view fiscal policy as an important stabilising force, for two reasons. The first is the presence of automatic stabilisers. These automatic changes in government spending and tax collections help to stabilise the economy by increasing planned spending during recessions and reducing it during expansions, *without the delays inherent in the legislative process*. The second reason that fiscal policy is an important stabilising force is that although fiscal policy may be difficult to change quickly, it may still be useful for dealing with prolonged episodes of recession: the Great Depression of the 1930s and the Japanese slump of the 1990s are two cases in point. However, because of the relative lack of flexibility of fiscal policy, in modern economies aggregate spending is more usually stabilised through *monetary policy*. The stabilising role of monetary policy is the subject of Chapter 25.

Summary

- To eliminate output gaps and restore full employment, the government employs *stabilisation policies*. The two major types of stabilisation policy are monetary policy and fiscal policy. Stabilisation policies work by changing planned aggregate expenditure (PAE) and hence short-run equilibrium output. For example, an increase in government purchases raises autonomous expenditure directly, so it can be used to reduce or eliminate a recessionary gap. Similarly, a cut in taxes or an increase in transfer payments increases the public's disposable income, raising consumption spending at each level of output by an amount equal to the marginal propensity to consume times the cut in taxes or increase in transfers. Higher consumer spending, in turn, raises short-run equilibrium output.

- *Fiscal policy* can be expansionary or contractionary. An *expansionary* policy is one that increases planned spending and output, while a *contractionary* policy has the opposite effect. The government budget deficit is the key indicator of the strength and direction of fiscal policy. An increase in the deficit indicates an expansionary policy, while a fall indicates a contractionary policy.

- The effectiveness of fiscal policy can be reduced by the tendency of an increase in government expenditure or a cut in net taxes to raise interest rates and *crowd out* private consumption and investment expenditures.

- The greater the elasticity of the demand for money with respect to the rate of interest (or the flatter the LM curve) the weaker the crowding out effect.

- Decisions to change government purchases and tax rates are types of *discretionary* fiscal policy. However, as net taxes vary with economic activity the budget deficit will automatically rise during recessions and fall during expansions. This is the *automatic stabiliser effect*, which helps to dampen cyclical fluctuations in economic activity. In the absence of automatic stabilisers recessions would be deeper and more prolonged.

- Persistent government deficits are harmful to the economy because they can reduce national saving and investment. In a monetary union such as the Eurosystem, high deficits in one or a group of countries can result in negative externality effects, which can lead to a loss of confidence and offset the benefits of a common currency. Hence countries in the Eurosystem have agreed a *Stability and Growth Pact* (SGP), which limits government deficits to 3 per cent of GDP.

- Two qualifications must be made to the use of fiscal policy as a stabilisation tool. First, fiscal policy may affect *potential output* as well as *aggregate spending*. Second, because changes in fiscal policy must go through a lengthy legislative process, fiscal policy is not always flexible enough to be useful for *short-run stabilisation*. However, *automatic stabilisers* can overcome the problem of legislative delays and contribute to economic stability.

Review questions

1. Define *stabilisation policies*. Distinguish between expansionary and contractionary stabilisation policies.

2. The government wishes to stimulate planned aggregate expenditure and is considering two alternative policies: a €50 million increase in government purchases and a €50 million tax cut. Which policy will have the greatest impact on planned aggregate expenditure? Why?

3. Explain why the *crowding out effect* may weaken the effectiveness of fiscal policy as a stabilisation instrument.

4. Explain the concept of an *automatic stabiliser*, and distinguish between automatic and discretionary changes in the government budget deficit.

5. Suppose the LM curve is perfectly inelastic (vertical) at the current level of income. What would this imply for the effectiveness of fiscal policy as a means to close output gaps?

6. What are the principal features of the *Stability and Growth Pact* (SGP)?

7. Define the concept of the *cyclically adjusted budget deficit*. How does the adjusted deficit differ from the actual deficit?

8. Explain how fiscal policy can affect potential output as well as aggregate spending.

9. Explain why fiscal policy may not be sufficiently flexible to deal with short-run stabilisation problems.

 ## Problems

Problems marked with an asterisk ($\star$) are more difficult.

1. Given the following equation for the IS curve:

$$Y = \left(\frac{1}{1-c}\right)\left[\bar{A} - (a+b)\,i\right]$$

assume that $\bar{A} = 1{,}040$, $a + b = 1{,}000$ and $c = 0.75$, and the rate of interest is constant at $i = 0.04$.

a. Find the equilibrium level of Y.

b. Find the change in equilibrium output if net exports fall by 40.

c. By how much would government have to increase its expenditures to stabilise output if net exports fall by 40?

d. By how much would government have to cut net taxes to stabilise output if net exports fall by 40?

2. Given the following equation for the IS curve:

$$Y = \left(\frac{1}{1 - c\,(1-t)}\right)\left[\bar{A} - (a+b)\,i\right]$$

if $\bar{A} = 1{,}640$, $a + b = 1{,}000$, $t = 0.2$ and $c = 0.75$, and the rate of interest is constant at $i = 0.04$:

a. find the equilibrium level of Y

b. find the change in equilibrium output if net exports fall by 40.

c. By how much would government have to increase its expenditures to stabilise output if net exports fall by 40?

3. Compare your answers to parts b and c in Problems 1 and 2. Explain the differences.

4.$\star$ Suppose that in a particular economy the consumption function, planned investment and the demand for money can be described as follows:

Consumption function	$C = \bar{C} + c(Y - \bar{T}) - ai$
Planned investment	$I^P = \bar{I} - bi$
Demand for money	$M^D = kY - hi$
	$c = 0.8$, $a = 400$, $b = 600$, $k = 0.2$, $h = 1{,}000$

Total autonomous expenditures are $\bar{A} = 1{,}010$, government expenditure $\bar{G} = 500$ and the money supply $\bar{M} = 910$. The economy is currently in short-run equilibrium with $i = 0.05$ and $Y = 4{,}800$. Suppose the full employment or natural level of output is $Y^\star = 5{,}000$, implying a recessionary gap $Y^\star - Y = 200$. By how much would the government have to increase its expenditure to close the recessionary gap?

25

Stabilising the Economy (2): the Role of Monetary Policy

Individuals charged with responsibility for monetary policy, such as the ECB's Governing Council or the Bank of England's Monetary Policy Committee, are often subjected to close public scrutiny aimed at ascertaining their views on the state of the economy and how they might react to current and future developments. The reason for the intense public interest in ECB or Bank of England decisions about monetary policy – and especially the level of interest rates – is that those decisions have important implications both for financial markets and for the Eurosystem economy in general. Decisions taken by the ECB's Governing Council can affect returns to small savers, the financial plans of large corporations and whether you change your car this year or next. Regardless of whether an individual is the chief executive of a large Dutch electronics company or owns a small restaurant in the west of Ireland, the deliberations of the Governing Council can have important implications for business success and financial well-being. Hence, it is not surprising that every speech and interview from a member of the Governing Council is closely analysed for clues about the future course of policy.

In this chapter we examine the workings of monetary policy, one of the two major types of *stabilisation policy*. (The other type, fiscal policy, was discussed in Chapter 24.) As we saw in Chapter 24, stabilisation policies are government policies that are meant to influence *planned aggregate expenditure (PAE)*, with the goal of eliminating *output gaps*. Both types of stabilisation policy – monetary and fiscal – are important and have been useful at various times. However, monetary policy, which can be changed quickly by a decision of the ECB's Governing Council, is more flexible and responsive than fiscal policy. Also, within the Eurosystem there is, as yet, no central fiscal authority equivalent to the ECB. As we saw in Chapter 24, national governments have, subject to the provisions of the Stability and Growth Pact (SGP), freedom to change tax and expenditure levels depending on the conditions in their own economies. Under normal circumstances, therefore, monetary policy is used more actively than fiscal policy to help stabilise the Eurosystem's economy.

When we introduced the ECB in Chapter 22, we focused on the Bank's tools for controlling the Eurosystem's *money supply*. Unlike the United States or the United

Kingdom, the Eurosystem is not a single country with a national government. While each country in the Eurosystem retains its own national central bank (NCB) these banks are now part of the European System of Central Banks (ESCB), headed by the Frankfurt-based ECB. As the policy set by the ECB's Governing Council prevails in all participating countries we can, from a monetary policy perspective, think of the Eurosystem as a single country. In short, because the Eurosystem is a full monetary union with a single currency and a unified central bank we can think of the Eurosystem's money supply in the same way as we think of the US or the UK money supply. Likewise, because it has a single monetary policy, interest rates are equal in all Eurosystem economies, from Finland to Greece, just as the same interest rates are common to all American states, from North Dakota to Texas. In this sense, and perhaps only in this sense, we can think of the Eurosystem, but not the European Union, as a single political and monetary entity. Hence, for the purpose of analysing monetary policy we shall treat the Eurosystem as a single country.

Determining the *money supply* is the primary task of central banks. But if you follow the economic news regularly, you may find the idea that the central bank's job is to control the money supply a bit foreign, because the news media nearly always focus on the bank's decisions about *interest rates*. Indeed, the announcement the ECB makes after each meeting of the Governing Council nearly always concerns its decisions on the *refinancing rate*, which, as we saw in Chapter 22, is the key interest rate in the Eurosystem. However, as explained in Chapter 22 there is no contradiction between the two ways of looking at monetary policy – as control of the money supply or as the setting of interest rates. As we shall see in this section, controlling the money supply and controlling the nominal interest rate are two sides of the same coin: any value of the money supply chosen by the central bank, whether it is the ECB, the Bank of England or the Fed, implies a specific setting for the nominal interest rate, and vice versa. The reason for this close connection is that the nominal interest rate is effectively the 'price' of money (or, more accurately, its *opportunity cost*). So, by controlling the quantity of money supplied to the economy, the ECB, or any central bank, also controls the 'price' of money (the *nominal interest rate*).

How central banks can fight a recession

We have seen that central banks can control the interest rate, and that the interest rate in turn affects planned spending and short-run equilibrium output. Putting these two results together, we can see how central bank actions may help to stabilise the economy. Note that, as in Chapter 24, we are assuming inflation is constant at zero so that the real rate of interest, which influences consumption and investment decisions, equals the nominal rate of interest set by the central bank. Chapter 26 deals with inflation and how it can be controlled by the central bank.

Suppose the economy faces a *recessionary gap* – a situation in which real output is below potential output, and planned spending is 'too low'. To fight a recessionary gap, the central bank should reduce the interest rate, stimulating consumption and investment spending and, according to the theory we have developed, this increase in planned spending will cause output to rise, restoring the economy to full employment. Example 25.1 uses the IS-LM model to illustrate how the central bank can close a recessionary gap.

Example 25.1 An increase in the money supply eliminates a recessionary gap.

Figure 25.1 uses the IS-LM model to show how an increase in the money supply can help eliminate a recessionary gap. In the right-hand panel of Figure 25.1 the economy's initial equilibrium position is point E_1 at the intersection of the IS_1 and LM_1. Equilibrium values for income and the rate of interest are Y_1 and i_1. The left-hand panel illustrates the money market. The money demand curve is L_1 and the money supply is set at M_1, giving money market equilibrium at point A with the interest rate at i_1. Now suppose full employment or potential output is Y^*, which is greater than Y_1, giving a recessionary gap equal to $Y^* - Y_1$. Use Figure 25.1 to show how an increase in the money supply can close the recessionary gap.

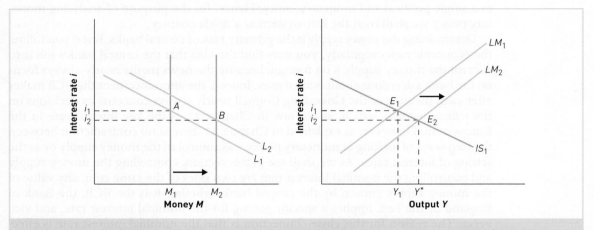

Figure 25.1 Using Monetary Policy to Close a Recessionary Gap. Starting from points A (left-hand panel) and E_1 (right-hand panel), an increase in the money supply shifts the LM curve from LM_1 to LM_2. For the public to hold the increased money stock the rate of interest must fall. As the rate of interest falls, consumption and investment increase leading to an increase in income, which in turn shifts the demand for money curve to L_2. The new equilibrium is at E_2 with $Y = Y^*$ and $i = i_2$.

As shown in Chapter 22 an increase in the money supply to M_2 will shift the LM curve to the right to LM_2 (right-hand panel) leading to a lower rate of interest. Remember that the rate of interest is the opportunity cost of holding money so it must fall for the public to hold the increased stock of money. As a fall in the rate of interest reduces the cost of borrowing and makes saving less attractive it stimulates consumption and investment, which leads to a rise in aggregate output and closes the recessionary gap. However, as income rises the demand for money will increase at any given rate of interest. This is illustrated by the shift in the money demand curve to L_2 in the left-hand panel of Figure 25.1. The new overall equilibrium is at point E_2 in the right-hand panel of Figure 25.1, with $i = i_2$ and $Y = Y^*$.

Exercise 25.1 Using the IS-LM model, show how a reduction in the money supply can be used to close an expansionary gap.

Exercise 25.2   Refer to Figure 25.1. Suppose at the initial equilibrium point E_1 output $Y_1 = 4,800$ and that Y_2 is potential or full employment output $Y^\star$ equal to 5,000. If the money supply is initially set at 910 and the demand for money is $M^D = 0.2Y - 1,000i$:

a. find the equilibrium rate of interest at E_1.
b. If the lower interest rate $i_2 = 0.01$, by how much would the central bank have to increase the money supply to close the recessionary gap?

How effective is monetary policy?

In Chapter 24 we saw that the effectiveness of fiscal policy in closing output gaps depends on the responsiveness of the demand for money to interest rate changes. Other things being equal, the greater the responsiveness, or elasticity, of the demand for money the flatter the LM curve and the greater the effectiveness of fiscal policy. We can now derive an equivalent result for monetary policy. Other things being equal, effectiveness in closing output gaps will depend on two factors: the interest rate elasticity of the demand for money and the responsiveness of planned aggregate expenditure to changes in the rate of interest. To illustrate, consider the following sequence of how changes in the money supply lead to changes in output.

$$\uparrow M \rightarrow \downarrow i \rightarrow \uparrow PAE \rightarrow Y$$

The first link in the sequence runs from changes in the money supply to changes in the rate of interest, and the second from interest rate changes to changes in planned aggregate expenditure.

Link 1: money supply to interest rates

Other things being equal, monetary policy is likely to be more effective if a given increase in the money supply results in a relatively large fall in the rate of interest. The extent to which the rate of interest will fall is determined by the interest rate elasticity of the demand for money. If, for example, the demand for money is very responsive to interest rate changes (high elasticity) then a given increase in the money supply will result in a relatively small fall in the interest rate and a weak stimulus to planned aggregate expenditure. Conversely, if the demand for money curve is relatively inelastic with respect to the interest rate it will require a larger decline in the rate of interest to induce the public to hold the higher money stock, giving a stronger stimulus to planned aggregate expenditure.

This result is illustrated by Figure 25.2, which shows two alternative demand for money curves, L_1 and L_2. The difference between them is that L_1 is much steeper than L_2, indicating a lower elasticity or responsiveness to interest rate changes. Starting from an initial equilibrium point A with $i = i_1$ consider an increase in the money supply from M_1 to M_2. If the demand for

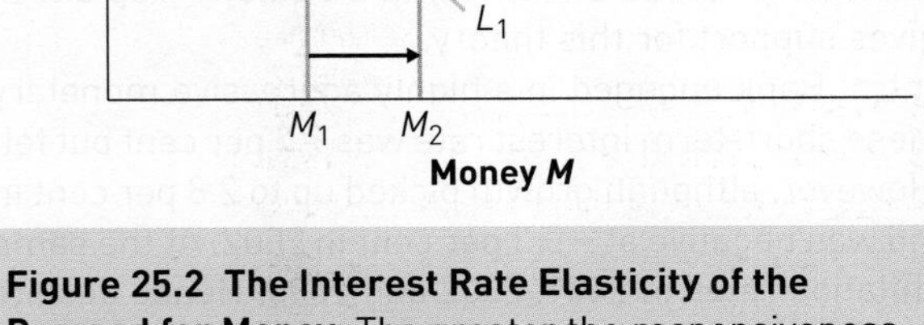

Figure 25.2 The Interest Rate Elasticity of the Demand for Money. The greater the responsiveness of the demand for money to changes in the rate of interest, the smaller the fall in the equilibrium rate of interest.

money curve is L_1 the interest rate must fall to i_3 for the public to hold the higher money stock. Alternatively, if the demand for money curve is L_2 the interest rate will fall to i_2. The difference is that the greater elasticity of L_2 means that it requires a smaller decline in the rate of interest for the public to hold the higher money stock. Hence, other things being equal, the lower the interest rate elasticity of the demand for money, the greater the interest rate decline and the greater the effectiveness of a given monetary expansion in closing a recessionary gap. Conversely, monetary policy will be less effective the greater the interest rate elasticity of the demand for money. An extreme case of the latter is where the demand for money is perfectly elastic with respect to the rate of interest. That is, the public are willing to hold any amount of money at the prevailing rate of interest. In this case the demand for money curve will be a horizontal line at the prevailing rate of interest and an increase in the money supply will have no effect on the equilibrium rate of interest. This situation is known as a

liquidity trap a situation in which changes in the money supply do not change the rate of interest

liquidity trap. Liquidity traps can occur when interest rates are at or close to zero.

When this is the case, the opportunity cost of holding money becomes very low or even zero, and the public have little to gain by holding essentially zero-interest-rate government bonds rather than money. Hence if the central bank attempts to increase the money supply by buying government bonds the public are simply swapping one more-or-less zero interest rate asset (bonds) for another (money) and, as nominal interest rates cannot be negative, the open-market purchase cannot reduce the rate of interest. Hence monetary policy becomes totally impotent in a liquidity trap situation.

Exercise 25.3 Draw a diagram illustrating the money market in a liquidity trap situation. What would the LM curve look like?

Monetary economists have tended to treat the idea of the liquidity trap as a theoretical curiosity – possible in theory but unlikely in the real world. However, as explained in Economic naturalist 25.1 the recent experience of Japan has led economists to take the idea of a liquidity trap more seriously.

Economic naturalist 25.1 Japan's liquidity trap

In the mid-1990s the Japanese economy started to experience a severe recession. Economic growth as measured by the annual percentage change in real GDP was 5.2 per cent in 1990 but fell to 1.9 per cent in 1995, and was actually negative at – 1.1 per cent in 1998. While economists are still divided on the reasons for the Japanese recession, most agree that the banking crisis and the collapse of a speculative asset-price bubble in the early 1990s was an important factor. Some economists have argued that, by the end of the 1990s, the Japanese economy was effectively in a liquidity trap situation, and the evidence presented in Figure 25.3 gives support for this theory.

As illustrated by Figure 25.3, the Japanese Central Bank engaged in a highly aggressive monetary expansion throughout the 1990s. In 1990 the Japanese short-term interest rate was 7.7 per cent but fell to 0.2 per cent by 1999 and reached zero in 2003. However, although growth picked up to 2.8 per cent in 2000 it subsequently fell to 0.4 per cent in 2001, and was negative at – 0.3 per cent in 2002. At the same time, Japan experienced deflation with negative inflation rates in 2001, 2002 and 2003. Hence despite the Central Bank's aggressive actions, which reduced interest rates to zero, the real economy did not respond and the monetary expansion failed to close Japan's recessionary gap.

The American economist Paul Krugman has argued that the Japanese experience is consistent with a liquidity trap situation in which monetary policy is an ineffective means to stabilising the

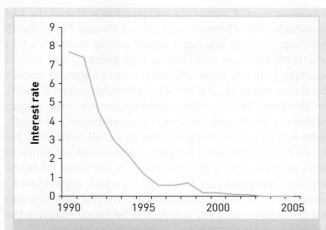

Figure 25.3 Japanese Short-Term Interest Rate, 1990–2005.

economy.[1] Krugman uses two bits of evidence to support his argument. First, the Japanese economy did not respond to a very aggressive monetary expansion despite the fact that interest rates were reduced to zero. Second, Krugman shows that the stock of high-powered money, or the monetary base (see Chapter 22), increases by 25 per cent between 1994 and 1997 but bank lending did not increase at all. Hence very low interest rates and a rapid expansion of the monetary base did nothing to stimulate aggregate expenditure and the Japanese economy remained in recession as would be predicted in a liquidity trap situation.

Link 2: interest rates to expenditure

The second link in the monetary policy sequence depends on the responsiveness of consumption and investment to changes in the rate of interest. As illustrated by Figure 25.4, monetary policy will be most effective when consumption and investment are responsive to interest rate changes.

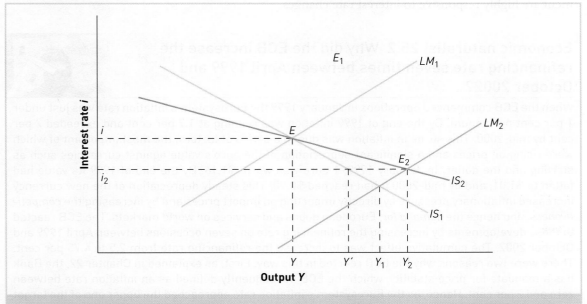

Figure 25.4 The Effectiveness of Monetary Policy. Monetary policy will be most effective when consumption and investment are responsive to interest rate changes and the IS curve is relatively flat.

1 Krugman (1998). Further articles can be found on Krugman's website: http://web.mit.edu/krugman/www.

Starting from an initial equilibrium at point E a monetary expansion will shift the LM curve from LM_1 to LM_2. Now consider the alternative IS curves IS_1 and IS_2. If the IS curve is IS_1 the new equilibrium is at point E_1 and equilibrium output rises from Y to Y_1. Alternatively, if the IS curve is IS_2 the new equilibrium is at point E_2 and output rises from Y_1 to Y_2. Hence monetary policy is more effective, or has a greater impact on output, if the IS curve is the flatter curve IS_2. To see why, consider points E and E_2 on IS_2. As these points are on the same IS curve they identify interest rate–output combinations at which the market for goods and services is in equilibrium ($Y = PAE$). Hence when output increases from Y to Y_2 the rate of interest must fall from i to i_2 for planned aggregate expenditure to match the rise in output and maintain equilibrium in the market for goods and services. However, if the IS curve is IS_2 the same fall in the rate of interest would increase planned expenditure from Y to Y', which is less than Y_2. Hence along IS_2 planned expenditures are more responsive to interest rate changes than along IS_1. It follows that a given monetary expansion will be more effective the greater the response of consumption and investment to interest rate changes.

RECAP Monetary policy and the economy

Monetary policy works through the effect of interest rate changes on planned aggregate expenditure and, by controlling the interest rate, the central bank can influence planned spending and short-run equilibrium output. To fight a *recession* (a recessionary output gap), the central bank should *lower* the interest rate, stimulating planned spending and output. Conversely, to fight the threat of *inflation* (an expansionary output gap), the central bank should *raise* the interest rate, reducing planned spending and output. Monetary policy tends to be most effective when the interest rate elasticity of the demand for money is relatively low, and when consumption and investment are highly responsive to interest rate changes.

Economic naturalist 25.2 Why did the ECB increase the refinancing rate seven times between April 1999 and October 2002?

When the ECB commenced operations in January 1999 the Eurosystem's inflation rate was just under 1 per cent per annum. By the end of 1999 inflation was running at 1.7 per cent and exceeded 2 per cent by mid-2000. This surge in inflation was due to a series of factors, the most important of which were rising oil prices and a significant depreciation of the euro's value against currencies such as sterling and the dollar. In January 1999, 1 euro was worth $1.16. By the end of 1999 its value had fallen to $1.01, and by mid-2000 it had reached $0.90. This steady depreciation of the new currency increased inflationary pressure by directly impacting on import prices and by increasing the *competitiveness*, and hence the *demand for*, European goods and services on world markets. The ECB reacted to these developments by increasing the refinancing rate on seven occasions between April 1999 and October 2002. The cumulative effect was to increase the refinancing rate from 2.5 to 4.75 per cent. There were two reasons why the ECB reacted in this way. First, as explained in Chapter 22, the Bank has a mandate for price stability, which the ECB subsequently defined as an inflation rate between zero and 2 per cent. Hence, as the Eurosystem's inflation rate approached the upper end of the target range, the ECB honoured its mandate and increased interest rates in an attempt to moderate the inflationary surge. Second, by late 1999 the Bank had become increasingly concerned about the growth of the money supply, which was above 6 per cent in early 2000. In the view of the Governing Council, this monetary expansion was seen as excessive and associated with a surge in bank lending to the private sector to finance consumption, which further intensified inflationary pressures.

By increasing interest rates the ECB aimed at moderating these pressures by making bank loans more expensive and less attractive as a means of financing consumption.

Despite these actions by the ECB, inflation continued to rise, and peaked at 3.1 per cent in May 2001. This, however, was largely due to increases in food prices related to animal diseases and not to underlying monetary conditions. Indeed, the growth rate of the broad money supply, M3, declined towards 4 per cent in late 2000, which, along with lower growth forecasts for the Eurosystem's economy, convinced the Governing Council to reduce the refinancing rate by 25 basis points in both May and August 2001. Inflation subsequently declined to 2 per cent by the end of 2001. However, by that date the ECB, along with other central banks, was primarily concerned with the onset of recession and the economic effects of the 11 September terror attacks on the United States (see Economic naturalist 25.3).

Monetary policy making: art or science?

In this chapter we have used the IS-LM model to analyse the basic economics underlying monetary policy. As part of the analysis we worked through some examples showing how monetary policy can be used to close output gaps. While those examples are useful in understanding how monetary policy works – as with our analysis of fiscal policy in Chapter 24 – they overstate the precision of monetary policy making. The real-world economy is highly complex, and our knowledge of its workings is imperfect. For example, though we assumed in our analysis that the central bank knows the exact value of potential output, in reality potential output can be estimated only approximately. As a result, at any given time the central bank has only a rough idea of the size of the output gap. Similarly, central bank policy makers have only an approximate idea of the effect of a given change in the interest rate on planned spending, or the length of time before that effect will occur. Because of these uncertainties, the central bank tends to proceed cautiously. In most cases central bank policy makers avoid large changes in interest rates and rarely raise or lower the refinancing rate more than one-half of a percentage point (from 3.50 per cent to 3.00 per cent, for example) at any one time. Indeed, the typical change in the interest rate is one-quarter of a percentage point.

Is monetary policy making, then, an art or a science? In practice, it appears to be both. Scientific analyses, such as the development of detailed statistical models of the economy, have proved useful in making monetary policy. But human judgement based on long experience – what has been called the 'art' of monetary policy – plays a crucial role in successful policy making, and is likely to continue to do so.

Economic naturalist 25.3 Why did the Bank of England cut interest rates seven times between December 2007 and January 2009?

In December 2007 the Bank of England's Monetary Policy Committee announced a 25 basis points reduction in its official interest rate from 5.75 per cent to 5.50 per cent. Over 2008 and into the early months of 2009 the Bank announced a further six interest rate reductions which brought the official bank rate down to an historical low of 1.5 per cent by January 2009, a cut of 4 per cent compared to December 2007. Over approximately the same period the European Central Bank cut its refinancing rate from

4.25 per cent in July 2007 to 2 per cent in January 2009. Why did the Bank of England and other central banks act so aggressively?

In late 2007 and throughout 2008 the global economy was hit by the onset of the banking crisis and the so-called credit crunch. Commercial banks, especially in the United States and the United Kingdom, were heavily exposed to assets based on sub-prime mortgage lending and derivative products (assets tied to loans to people who could not afford to repay them), which threatened bank solvency and led to direct government intervention to keep the commercial banks in business. As the crisis intensified the inter-bank market froze, the supply of bank lending to households and firms tightened dramatically and the credit crunch eventually spilt over into the real economy. In the UK economic growth slowed dramatically. The growth of real GDP, which had been around 3 per cent in 2007, slowed throughout 2008 and became negative at the end of the year. At the same time unemployment increased to 6 per cent (an 11-year high) and inflation slowed to such an extent that the CPI actually fell by 0.4 per cent in December 2008.

In short the UK, along with most other industrialised nations, was moving rapidly into recession with declining investment and consumer expenditure. One way to think about this is a leftward shift in the IS curve leading to lower output and higher unemployment. Hence the Bank of England's aggressive interest rate cutting can be seen as an attempt to stabilise the economy – remember that a cut in interest rates is the same as an increase in the money supply or a rightwards shift in the LM curve. Whether this policy will succeed is still open to question. However, there can be little doubt that if the Bank of England had not responded in this way the recession would be deeper and more prolonged.

Summary

■ *Monetary policy* is one of two types of stabilisation policy, the other being fiscal policy. In the Eurosystem there is no central fiscal authority that has the ability to conduct fiscal policy for all participating economies. Hence, monetary policy as determined by the ECB is the principal stabilisation instrument. Although the ECB, like other central banks, operates by controlling the money supply, the media's attention nearly always focuses on the ECB's decisions about interest rates, not the money supply. There is no contradiction between these two ways of looking at monetary policy, however, as a central bank's ability to control the money supply is the source of its ability to control interest rates.

■ Monetary policy works through the effect of interest rate changes on planned aggregate expenditure. By controlling the interest rate, the central bank can influence planned spending and short-run equilibrium output. To fight a *recession* (a recessionary output gap), the central bank should *lower* the interest rate, stimulating planned spending and output. Conversely, to fight the threat of *inflation* (an expansionary output gap), the central bank should *raise* the interest rate, reducing planned spending and output.

■ Monetary policy tends to be most effective when the interest rate elasticity of the demand for money is relatively low, and when consumption and investment are highly responsive to interest rate changes.

■ Monetary policy is least effective when the demand for money is very responsive (has a high elasticity) to interest rate changes. When this is the case, a monetary expansion may result in a relatively small fall in interest rates.

■ Monetary policy will be totally ineffective when the demand for money is perfectly elastic with respect to interest rate changes. When this is the case an increase in the money supply cannot change the rate of interest, making monetary policy impotent. This situation is known as a *liquidity trap*. Although considered by many to be a theoretical curiosity there is some evidence to suggest that the Japanese economy may have experienced a liquidity trap situation in recent times.

■ In practice, the ECB's information about the level of potential output, and the size and speed of the effects of its actions is imprecise. Monetary policy making is thus as much an art as a science.

Review questions

1. Why does the rate of interest affect planned aggregate expenditure? Give examples.

2. The ECB faces a recessionary gap. How would you expect it to respond? Explain step by step how its policy change is likely to affect the economy.

3. Under what circumstances is monetary policy likely to be most effective in closing a recessionary gap?

4. The ECB decides to take a *contractionary* policy action. What would you expect to happen to the rate of interest and the money supply?

5. Explain what you understand by a liquidity trap, and review the evidence that the Japanese economy may have experienced a liquidity trap situation in recent times.

6. Discuss why the analysis of this chapter may overstate the precision with which monetary policy can be used to eliminate output gaps.

Problems

Problems marked with an asterisk (*) are more difficult.

1. In a particular economy, the demand for money is $M^D = 0.2Y - 1,000i$, potential output is $Y^\star = 4,200$ and the corresponding equilibrium interest rate is 0.02. The equation for the IS curve is:

$$Y = \left(\frac{1}{1-c}\right)[\bar{A} - fi]$$

The parameter f measures the response of consumption and investment to changes in the rate of interest. Assume that $\bar{A} = 1,040$, $f = 1,000$ and $c = 0.75$, and the current equilibrium rate of interest is 0.04.

    a. What is the size of the current output gap?

    b. By how much would the central bank have to change the money supply to close the output gap?

2. As in Problem 1 the demand for money is $M^D = 0.2Y - 1,000i$, potential output is $Y^\star = 4,200$ and the corresponding equilibrium interest rate is 0.03. The equation for the IS curve is:

$$Y = \left(\frac{1}{1-c}\right)[\bar{A} - fi]$$

Assume that $\bar{A} = 1,160$, $f = 4,000$ and $c = 0.75$, and the current equilibrium rate of interest is 0.04.

    a. What is the size of the current output gap?

    b. By how much would the central bank have to change the money supply to close the output gap?

3. Compare your answers to Problems 1 and 2 and explain the differences.

4.* Suppose that a particular economy can be modelled as follows:

          Consumption: $C = \bar{C} + 0.8(Y - \bar{T}) - 400i$

          Investment: $I^P = \bar{I} - 600i$

          Money demand: $M^D = 0.2Y - 1,000i$

Total autonomous expenditures are $\bar{A} = 1,010$ and the money supply is $\bar{M} = 910$.

    a. Find the equilibrium values for output and the rate of interest.

    b. If potential output is 5,000 by how much would the central bank have to change the money supply to close the output gap?

References

Krugman, P. (1998) 'It's baaack: Japan's slump and the return of the liquidity trap', *Brookings Papers on Economic Activity*, 2, pp. 137–205.

To help you grasp the key concepts of this chapter check out the extra resources posted on the Online Learning Centre. There are chapter summaries, self-test questions, an interactive graphing tool, weblinks and a glossary, all for free!

Visit the Online Learning Centre at: www.mcgraw-hill.co.uk/textbooks/mcdowell for information on accessing all of these resources.

26

Aggregate Demand, Aggregate Supply and Inflation

In Chapter 22, we saw that, under the terms of the Treaty on European Union (TEU, 1993), commonly known as the Maastricht Treaty, the European Central Bank (ECB) has a primary mandate for the maintenance of price stability in the Eurosystem. Although the Treaty does not offer a precise definition of price stability it is generally understood to mean the maintenance of low inflation, which the ECB has defined as a medium-term inflation rate below but close to 2 per cent. Hence the ECB's primary objective is to achieve an inflation rate of approximately 2 per cent over the medium term. Likewise the Bank of England has an inflation target, set by the government, of 2 per cent per annum. In this chapter we will analyse the causes of inflation, while the following chapter will discuss the policies that the central banks use to achieve inflation targets and how they might react to sudden surges in the inflation rate.

In Chapters 21–25 we made the assumption that firms are willing to meet the demand for their products at pre-set prices. When firms simply produce what is demanded, the level of planned aggregate expenditure determines the economy's real GDP. If the resulting level of short-run equilibrium output is lower than potential output, a *recessionary* output gap develops, and if the resulting level of output exceeds potential output, the economy experiences an *expansionary* gap. As we saw in Chapters 24 and 25, policy makers can attempt to eliminate output gaps by taking actions that affect the level of autonomous expenditure, such as changing the level of government spending or taxes (fiscal policy) or using the central bank's control of the money supply to change the real interest rate (monetary policy).

The basic Keynesian model is useful for understanding the role of spending in the short-run determination of output, but it is too simplified to provide a fully realistic description of the economy. The main shortcoming of the basic Keynesian model is that it does not explain the behaviour of *inflation*. Although firms may meet demand at pre-set prices for a time, as assumed in the basic Keynesian model, prices do *not* remain fixed indefinitely. Indeed, sometimes they may rise quite rapidly – the phenomenon of high inflation – imposing significant costs on the economy in the process. In this chapter we shall extend the basic Keynesian model to allow for ongoing inflation. As we shall show, the extended model can be conveniently represented by a new diagram, called the *aggregate demand–aggregate supply diagram*. Using this extended analysis, we shall be able to show how macroeconomic policies affect inflation as well as output, illustrating in the process the difficult trade-offs that policy makers sometimes face.

aggregate demand (AD) curve shows the relationship between short-run equilibrium output Y and the rate of inflation π; the name of the curve reflects the fact that short-run equilibrium output is determined by, and equals, total planned spending in the economy: increases in inflation reduce planned spending and short-run equilibrium output, so the aggregate demand curve is downward-sloping

The aggregate demand curve

To begin incorporating inflation into the model, our first step is to introduce a new relationship, called the **aggregate demand curve**, which is shown graphically in Figure 26.1. The aggregate demand (AD) curve is a relationship between *rate of inflation*, denoted π, and the total demand for output.

The name of the curve reflects the fact that short-run equilibrium output is determined by total planned spending, or aggregate demand, in the economy. Indeed, by definition, short-run equilibrium output *equals* planned aggregate expenditure, so that we could just as well say that the AD curve shows the relationship between inflation and spending.[1] As shown in Figure 26.1, the aggregate demand curve has a negative slope, implying that demand and inflation are assumed to change in opposite directions.

Why does the aggregate demand curve have a negative slope? As we shall see next, one important reason is the manner in which the central bank responds to *changes in inflation*.

Inflation, the central bank and the *AD* curve

One of the primary responsibilities of any central bank is to maintain a low and stable rate of inflation. For example, following its mandate for price stability the ECB has tried to keep inflation in the Eurosystem below but close to 2 per cent. By keeping inflation low, the Bank tries to avoid the costs that high inflation imposes on the economy. What can a central bank do to keep inflation low and stable? One situation that is likely to lead to increased inflation is an *expansionary output gap*, in which short-run equilibrium output exceeds potential output. When output is above potential output, firms must produce at above-normal capacity to meet the demands of their customers. Like Bill's ice cream parlour, described in Chapter 21,

Figure 26.1 The Aggregate Demand Curve. The aggregate demand curve AD shows the relationship between short-run equilibrium output Y and the rate of inflation π. Because short-run equilibrium output equals planned spending, the AD curve also shows the relationship between inflation and planned spending. The downward slope of the AD curve implies that an increase in inflation reduces short-run equilibrium output.

---

1 It is important to distinguish the AD curve from the expenditure line, introduced as part of the Keynesian cross diagram. The upward-sloping expenditure line shows the relationship between planned aggregate expenditure and output. Again, the AD curve shows the relationship between short-run equilibrium output (which equals planned spending) and inflation.

firms may be willing to do this for a time but eventually they will adjust to the high level of demand by raising prices, contributing to inflation. To control inflation, then, the central bank needs to dampen planned spending and output when they threaten to exceed potential output.

How can the central bank avoid a situation of economic 'overheating', in which spending and output exceed potential output? As we saw in Chapter 21, if the central bank can engineer an increase in the *real interest rate* it can reduce planned expenditures and ease inflationary pressures. However, we must be careful to maintain a distinction between the real rate of interest (r) and the nominal rate of interest (i). Remember that the real rate is defined as the nominal rate minus the real rate, or

central bank reaction function describes how central banks react to changing economic conditions

$r = i - \pi$. This distinction is important because the central bank controls the nominal rate but it is the real rate of interest that influences consumption and investment decisions. To be sure that central bank decisions on the nominal rate are translated into changes in the real rate, we will introduce a new concept known as the **central bank reaction function**.

To explain the reaction function we will simplify things by assuming that the central bank has only one policy target, the rate of inflation, and that each time the inflation rate increases, the central bank conducts an open-market sale designed to increase the *real rate of interest*. Formally, we can express this idea by the following simple equation:

$$r = \alpha + \beta(\pi - \pi^\star) \qquad (26.1)$$

where π is the actual rate of inflation and $\pi^\star$ is the bank's target rate. In Equation (26.1) the parameter β measures the amount by which the bank would like the real rate of interest to increase when the inflation rate increases by 1 per cent. For example, if $\beta = 0.25$ then the bank would want the real rate of interest to increase by 0.25 per cent if the actual inflation rate rises by 1 per cent above the target. The parameter α, on the other hand, is the real rate of interest that the central bank would wish if inflation is exactly on target, $\pi = \pi^\star$. Using the definition of the real rate of interest $r = i - \pi$ we can write Equation (26.1) as:

$$i - \pi = \alpha + \beta(\pi - \pi^\star)$$

or:

$$i = \alpha + (1 + \beta)\pi - \beta\pi^\star \qquad (26.2)$$

So long as the reaction parameter β is positive then the real rate of interest will rise each time the nominal rate increases. For example, if $\beta = 0.25$ then the bank will increase the nominal rate of interest by 1.25 and the real rate of interest by 0.25 if the actual inflation rate rises by 1 per cent. Given the assumption that β is positive, Equation (26.2) tells us that when the central bank changes the nominal rate of interest the real rate will change in the same direction. Hence an increase in the rate of inflation leads to an increase in the real rate of interest, which reduces aggregate demand. Because higher inflation leads, through the central bank's actions, to a reduction in output, the *AD* curve is downward-sloping, as Figure 26.1 shows. We can summarise this chain of reasoning symbolically as follows:

AD curve: $\pi \uparrow \Rightarrow \uparrow i \Rightarrow \uparrow r \Rightarrow \downarrow$ aggregate demand

The central bank reaction function is illustrated by Figure 26.2. From Equation (26.2) we can see that when the actual inflation rate equals the target rate, the bank will set

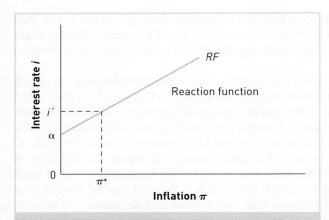

Figure 26.2 The Central Bank Reaction Function.
The *RF* shows the nominal rate of interest set by the central bank at each rate of inflation.

the nominal rate at $i' = \alpha + \pi^\star$. That is, setting $\pi = \pi^\star$ Equation (26.2) reduces to:

$$i = \alpha + \pi^\star \qquad (26.3)$$

Figure 26.3 illustrates the link between the central bank reaction function and aggregate demand.

In Figure 26.3, the bank's reaction function is drawn in panel (a) and the IS-LM diagram (see Chapter 23) in panel (b). With an initial inflation rate of π_1 the central bank sets the nominal rate of interest at i_1 – point A on its reaction function. In panel (b) the short-run equilibrium is at point A with $Y = Y_1$, which also equals planned aggregate expenditure *PAE*. Hence, point A in panel (c) plots the equilibrium inflation–output combination (π_1, Y_1). That is, when inflation equals π_1 aggregate demand, or *PAE*, equals Y_1. Now suppose inflation increases to π_2. The central bank reacts by increasing the nominal rate of interest from i_1 to i_2 – a

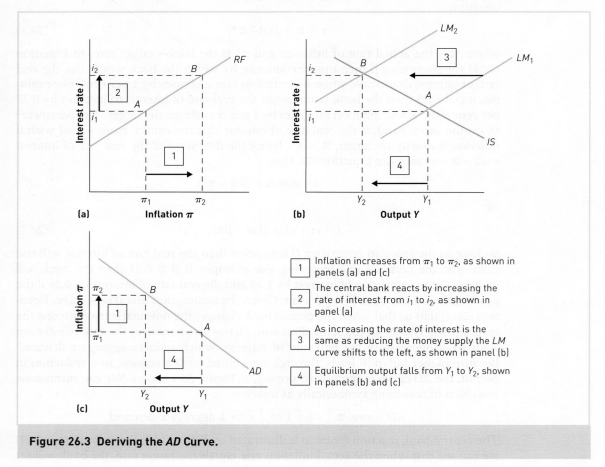

1 Inflation increases from π_1 to π_2, as shown in panels (a) and (c)

2 The central bank reacts by increasing the rate of interest from i_1 to i_2, as shown in panel (a)

3 As increasing the rate of interest is the same as reducing the money supply the *LM* curve shifts to the left, as shown in panel (b)

4 Equilibrium output falls from Y_1 to Y_2, shown in panels (b) and (c)

Figure 26.3 Deriving the *AD* Curve.

movement along the reaction function from point A to point B. However, as we have seen in Chapter 22, to increase the rate of interest the central bank must simultaneously reduce the money supply, which shifts the LM curve to the left, establishing a new short-run equilibrium at point B in panel (b) of Figure 26.3 with $Y = Y_2$. Hence, point B in panel (c) plots a second equilibrium inflation–output combination (π_2, Y_2) at which inflation equals π_2 and aggregate demand, or PAE, equals Y_2. As the points A and B in panel (c) give PAE, or short-run equilibrium output, the line going through them is the aggregate demand curve.

Why do aggregate demand and equilibrium output fall as inflation rises? There are two parts to the answer. First, as the central bank is assumed to increase the nominal rate of interest by more than the increase in inflation the real rate of interest increases (β is greater than zero in Equation (26.2), and planned expenditure falls at each level of Y). Second, via the multiplier effect (see Chapter 21) the decline in aggregate expenditure leads to a decline in equilibrium output. The AD curve thus embodies everything that you learned in the previous chapters (the basic Keynesian model, the multiplier process, the IS-LM model and the central bank's monetary policy) in one graph.

Other reasons for the downward slope of the *AD* curve

Although we focus on the behaviour of central banks as the source of the AD curve's downward slope, there are other channels through which higher inflation reduces planned spending and thus short-run equilibrium output. Hence the downward slope of the AD curve does not depend on the central bank behaving in the particular way just described.

One additional reason for the downward slope of the AD curve is the effect of inflation on the *real value of money* held by households and businesses. At high levels of inflation, the purchasing power of money held by the public declines rapidly. This reduction in the public's real wealth may cause households to restrain consumption spending, reducing short-run equilibrium output.

A second channel by which inflation may affect planned spending is through *distributional effects*. Studies have found that people who are less well off are often hurt more by inflation than are wealthier people. For example, retirees on fixed incomes and workers receiving the minimum wage (which is set in euro terms) lose buying power when prices are rising rapidly. Less affluent people are also likely to be relatively unsophisticated in making financial investments and hence less able than wealthier citizens to protect their savings against inflation.

People at the lower end of the income distribution tend to spend a greater percentage of their disposable income than do wealthier individuals. Thus, if a burst of inflation redistributes resources from relatively high-spending, less-affluent households towards relatively high-saving, more-affluent households, overall spending may decline.

A third connection between inflation and aggregate demand arises because higher rates of inflation generate *uncertainty* for households and businesses. When inflation is high, people become less certain about what things will cost in the future, and uncertainty makes planning more difficult. In an uncertain economic environment, both households and firms may become more cautious, reducing their spending as a result.

A final link between inflation and total spending operates through the *prices of domestic goods and services sold abroad*. As we shall see in Chapter 28, the foreign price of domestic goods depends in part on the rate at which the domestic currency, such as the euro, exchanges for foreign currencies, such as the dollar or sterling. However, for constant rates of exchange between currencies, a rise in domestic inflation causes the prices of domestic goods in foreign markets to rise more quickly. As domestic goods become relatively more expensive to prospective foreign purchasers, export sales decline. Net exports are part of aggregate expenditure, and so once more we find that increased inflation is likely to reduce spending. All these factors contribute to the downward slope of the *AD* curve, together with the behaviour of the ECB.

Shifts of the *AD* curve

The downward slope of the *AD* curve reflects the fact that, *all other factors held constant*, a higher rate of inflation will lead to lower planned spending (a movement along the *AD* curve). However, even if inflation is held constant, various factors can affect planned spending and lead to a shift in the *AD* curve at any given rate of inflation. We shall focus on two sorts of changes that shift the aggregate demand curve: (1) changes in spending caused by factors other than output or interest rates, which we shall refer to as *exogenous* changes in spending; and (2) changes in the central bank monetary policy, as reflected in a shift in the policy reaction function.

Examples 26.1 and 26.2 show how these factors will cause the *AD* curve to shift.

Example 26.1 Exogenous changes in spending

At given levels of output and inflation, an increase in government purchases will increase aggregate demand. Likewise, a rise in consumer confidence may lead to higher consumption spending and new technologies may cause firms to increase their planned investment at the current real rate of interest. How can exogenous changes such as these shift the *AD* curve?

Figure 26.4 illustrates how exogenous changes in spending can shift the aggregate demand curve.

Imagine, for example, that a rise in the stock market or house prices makes consumers more willing to spend (the wealth effect) at the current levels of income. Then, for each level of inflation, aggregate spending will be higher, as shown by the shift of the *AD* curve to the right, from *AD* to *AD*₁. Similarly, at a given inflation rate, an exogenous decline in spending – for example, a fall in government purchases resulting from a more restrictive fiscal policy – causes aggregate demand to fall as shown by the shift of the *AD* curve to the left, from *AD* to *AD*₂.

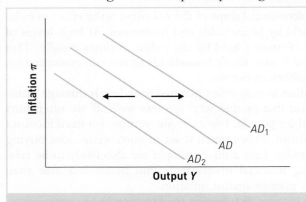

Figure 26.4 Shifts in the Aggregate Demand Curve.
Increases in autonomous expenditures will shift the aggregate demand curve to the right (AD₁).
Conversely, decreases in autonomous expenditures will shift the aggregate demand curve to the left (AD₂).

Exercise 26.1 Determine how the following events will affect the *AD* curve:

a. due to widespread concerns about future weakness in the economy, businesses reduce their spending on new capital
b. a reduction in income taxes by governments in the Eurosystem.

Example 26.2 Changes in the central bank's policy reaction function

Suppose that the central bank announces that it will set a higher interest rate at each rate of inflation. How will this announcement affect the *AD* curve?

Recall that the central bank's policy reaction function describes how the central bank sets the interest rate at each level of inflation. This relationship is built in to the *AD* curve – indeed, it accounts for the curve's downward slope. As long as the central bank sets the interest rate according to an unchanged reaction function, its policy will not cause the *AD* curve to shift. For example, in Figure 26.3 the central bank reacts to an increase in inflation by moving *along* its reaction function from point *A* to *B* in panel (a) and, as a higher nominal interest is assumed to lead to a higher real interest rate, planned expenditure will fall as illustrated by the movement *along* the aggregate demand curve from point *A* to *B* in panel (c) of Figure 26.3.

However, suppose that inflation does not increase but the central bank decides that the current rate is excessive and wishes to reduce it.

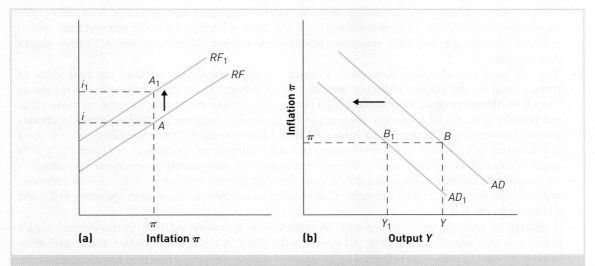

Figure 26.5 A Shift in the Central Bank's Policy Reaction Function. An upward shift in the reaction function increases the rate of interest at any given rate of inflation. As the real rate of interest increases, aggregate demand falls at the current inflation rate and the *AD* curve shifts to the left.

This decision is illustrated by Figure 26.5. With inflation running at π, aggregate demand is Y, point *B* in panel (b). With inflation at π the central bank will set the rate of interest at i, point *A* on the reaction function. If the bank decides that the current inflation rate is too high it will increase the rate of interest *without any change in the rate of inflation*. For example, the bank may decide to reduce its target rate of inflation or to increase the parameter α (the real rate of interest that the bank would wish when inflation is on target) in Equation (26.2). In both cases the bank will increase the nominal rate of interest *at the current rate of inflation*. This is illustrated by the move from point *A* to A_1 in panel (a) of Figure 26.5, and the leftward shift in the policy reaction function from *RF* to RF_1. This move to a tighter monetary policy means that the bank will now set a higher interest rate at any given inflation rate and is illustrated by the upward shift in the policy reaction function in Figure 26.5. However, as the nominal interest rate has increased, the real rate of interest will also increase and aggregate demand will fall at the current rate of inflation. Hence the *AD* curve will shift to the left, as shown in panel (b) of Figure 26.5. Conversely, if the economy is in a recession and the central bank decides to reduce the rate of interest at the current inflation rate, the policy reaction function will shift downwards and the *AD* curve will shift to the right.

Exercise 26.2   What is the difference, if any, between the following?

    a. an upward shift in the central bank's policy reaction function
    b. a response by the central bank to higher inflation, for a given policy reaction function.

How does each scenario affect the *AD* curve?

RECAP The aggregate demand (*AD*) curve

- The *AD* curve shows the relationship between *planned aggregate expenditure* or *short-run equilibrium output* and *inflation*. Higher inflation leads the central bank to raise the interest rate, which reduces expenditure and thus short-run equilibrium output. Therefore, the *AD* curve slopes downwards.

- The *AD curve may also slope downwards* because (1) higher inflation reduces the real value of money held by the public, reducing wealth and spending; (2) inflation redistributes resources from less affluent people, who spend a high percentage of their disposable income, to more affluent people, who spend a smaller percentage of disposable income; (3) higher inflation creates greater uncertainty in planning for households and firms, reducing their spending; and (4) for a constant rate of exchange between the euro and other currencies, rising prices of domestic goods and services reduce foreign sales and hence net exports (a component of aggregate spending).

- An exogenous *increase* in spending raises short-run equilibrium output at each value of inflation, and so shifts the *AD* curve to the right. Conversely, an exogenous *decrease* in spending shifts the *AD* curve to the left.

- A change to an *easier* monetary policy, as reflected by a downward shift in the central bank's policy reaction function, shifts the *AD* curve to the right. A change to a *tighter*, more anti-inflationary monetary policy, as reflected by an upward shift in the policy reaction function, shifts the *AD* curve to the left.

- Assuming no change in the central bank's reaction function, changes in inflation correspond to movements *along* the *AD* curve; they do not *shift* the *AD* curve.

The aggregate supply curve

short-run aggregate supply curve (*SRAS*) shows the relationship between short-run equilibrium output *Y*, *which firms wish to supply*, and the rate of inflation π; the *SRAS* curve has a positive slope, indicating that inflation and aggregate supply change in the same direction

Aggregate demand is of course only one side of the story. As we are interested in understanding how inflation is determined, what causes it to change and how it can be brought under control, we need to introduce the other side of the picture: aggregate supply. Figure 26.6 introduces a second relationship between output and inflation called the **short-run aggregate supply curve** or *SRAS*.

We shall see in the following sections why this relationship is labelled a 'short-run' supply curve. In Figure 26.6 the *SRAS* curve is drawn as a positive relationship between output and inflation. That is, along the *SRAS* curve output and inflation change in the same direction. Why does the *SRAS* curve have a positive slope? To answer

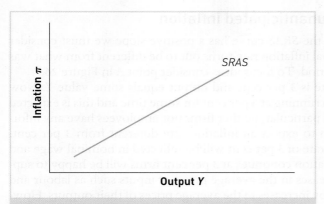

Figure 26.6 The Short-run Aggregate Supply Curve.
The short-run aggregate supply curve shows the relationship between the equilibrium output that firms plan to supply and the rate of inflation π. The upward slope of the *SRAS* curve implies that aggregate supply and inflation change in the same direction.

this question, we must consider two closely related factors that play an important role in determining the inflation rate: the behaviour of the public's *inflation expectations* and the existence of *fixed-term wage and price contracts*. First, consider the public's expectations about inflation. In negotiating wages and prices, both buyers and sellers take into account the rate of inflation they expect to prevail in the future. As a result, today's *expectations* of future inflation may help to determine the future inflation rate. To explain, suppose that nominal wage increases are set for a specific period called the contract period. If, for example, the contract period is one year then firms and their employees, or their representatives, will meet each year to agree a wage increase for the coming 12 months. Ignoring productivity gains, which would justify increases in real wages, it seems reasonable to assume that the agreed wage increase will reflect what each side *expects inflation to be* over the contract period. If both sides agree that they expect inflation to be, say, 3 per cent over the contract period then both sides should be happy to agree a 3 per cent wage increase. From an employee's viewpoint, a 3 per cent increase would compensate for expected inflation and, if the expectation is realised, prevent real wages and worker's real living standards from falling. Likewise, as employers expect the average price of their output to increase by 3 per cent, granting a 3 per cent wage increase will not increase the real cost of hiring labour or erode their profits. On the other hand, if inflation is expected to be 6 per cent, then firms agree to pay 6 per cent more, knowing that a nominal wage increase of 6 per cent will not change the real cost of its labour input. Hence it seems reasonable to assume that wage inflation, or the percentage increase in money wages, will reflect the *expected rate of inflation*.

A similar dynamic affects the contracts for production inputs other than labour. For example, if a manufacturer is negotiating with a company supplying components, the prices the manufacturer will agree to pay for next year's deliveries will depend on what it expects the inflation rate to be. If the firm anticipates that the price of components will not change relative to the prices of other goods and services, and that the general inflation rate will be 3 per cent, then it should be willing to agree to a 3 per cent increase in the price of components. Hence we will assume that wage and other nominal price contracts reflect the inflation rate that is expected to prevail over the contract period.

Exercise 26.3 Assume that employers and workers agree that real wages should rise by 2 per cent next year.

a. If inflation is expected to be 2 per cent next year, what will happen to nominal wages next year?

b. If inflation is expected to be 4 per cent next year, rather than 2 per cent, what will happen to nominal wages next year?

c. Use your answers from parts (a) and (b) to explain how an increase in expected inflation will tend to affect the following year's actual rate of inflation.

Aggregate supply and unanticipated inflation

To answer the question why the *SRAS* curve has a positive slope we must consider what might happen if the actual inflation rate turns out to be different from what was expected over the contract period. To focus ideas consider point A in Figure 26.7.

At point A the inflation rate is 3 per cent and output equals some value Y. Now assume that inflation has been running at 3 per cent for some time and this is expected to continue into the future. In particular, neither firms nor employees have any information that would lead them to expect an inflation rate different from 3 per cent. Hence the expected inflation rate of 3 per cent will be reflected in nominal wage and price contracts. So long as inflation continues at 3 per cent firms will be happy to supply the output Y because increases in the average prices of inputs such as labour and components will be matched by increases in the average prices of their outputs. However, suppose that, due to unexpected events, inflation actually turns out to be 4 per cent rather than 3 per cent. For example, the central bank may have taken a sudden and unexpected decision to ease monetary policy and reduce interest rates, with the resulting surge in aggregate demand leading to higher inflation. Whatever the reason, firms will now be paying 3 per cent more for labour and other inputs but the average price of their outputs will be increasing at 4 per cent, creating a profitable opportunity to increase supply, and aggregate output will increase to Y_1, as illustrated by the move from point A to A_1 in Figure 26.7. Conversely, suppose that actual inflation turns out to be lower than expected, say 2 per cent. Firms will now have agreed to pay their workers and suppliers a 3 per cent nominal increase but the average price of their outputs will be increasing by less. Because the real cost of labour and other inputs is greater than expected, continuing to produce at point A will mean that firms will have lower profits than they anticipated and will cut back on production. In Figure 26.7 this eventuality is illustrated by the move from point A to A_2 and a fall in output from Y to Y_2.

Unanticipated inflation explains why the *SRAS* curve has a positive slope. When actual inflation is greater than expected the real cost of labour and other inputs will be falling and firms have a profitable opportunity to increase production. Conversely, when actual inflation is lower than expected the real cost of labour and other inputs will be increasing and firms have an incentive to cut their losses by reducing production.

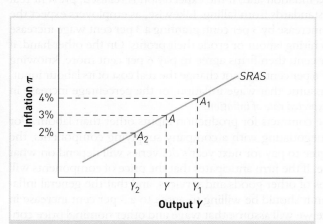

Figure 26.7 Unanticipated Inflation and Aggregate Supply. With wage and other input price contracts reflecting expected inflation at 3 per cent, aggregate supply will be at point A. An unanticipated increase in inflation to 4 per cent reduces the real cost of labour and other inputs, and production is increased to Y_1. Conversely, an unanticipated fall in inflation to 2 per cent increases the real cost of labour and other inputs, and production is cut back to Y_2. Hence the *SRAS* curve has a positive slope.

Shifts of the *SRAS* curve

The positive slope of the *SRAS* curve reflects the fact that *given the expected rate of inflation*, an unanticipated increase in the *actual rate of inflation* creates a profitable opportunity for firms to increase production. For example, the move from point A to A_1 in Figure 26.7 is due to the fact that the increase in inflation from 3 to 4 per cent is unanticipated and not reflected in wage and input contracts. Likewise the move from point A to A_2 is due to the fact that the fall in actual inflation to 2 per cent was unexpected when wage and other contracts were agreed. This, however, is not the end of the story. As illustrated by Example 26.3, when actual inflation differs from expected inflation it is reasonable to assume that, at some point, inflationary expectations will be revised.

Example 26.3 Why the *SRAS* curve may shift over time

Firms and their suppliers including labour are negotiating new contracts. They know that last period's inflation rate was 1 per cent higher than anticipated and expect the higher inflation rate to persist into the next contract period. How will this affect the *SRAS* curve?

As illustrated by Figure 26.8, inflationary expectations will be revised upwards and the *SRAS* will shift to the left.

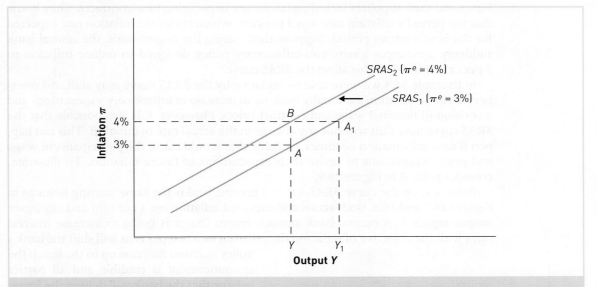

Figure 26.8 A Shift in the *SRAS* Curve. A higher expected rate of inflation shifts the *SRAS* curve to the left.

In Figure 26.8, points A and A_1 are the same as in Figure 26.7. At each of these points the expected rate of inflation is 3 per cent and the fact that output is higher at point A_1 is due to the unanticipated rise in inflation to 4 per cent. Hence the supply curve going through these points is labelled $SRAS_1$ ($\pi^e = 3$ per cent) where π^e denotes the expected rate of inflation. That is, at all points on $SRAS_1$ the expected rate of inflation is 3 per cent. However, when inflation rises to 4 per cent, workers will realise that their real wage is lower than expected when the wage contract was agreed, and will attempt to renegotiate nominal wages for the next contract period. Likewise, firms supplying components and raw materials etc. will eventually realise that the relative price of their products has fallen. Provided that inflation stays at 4 per cent, expected inflation will be revised upwards and firms will have to increase money wages and contract prices to reflect the higher actual and expected inflation. This, however, means that the real cost of labour and other inputs will revert to the level they were at, at point A, before the rise in inflation. When this happens firms will no longer find the increases in output profitable and will cut production back to Y, *but at the higher inflation rate of 4 per cent*. This is illustrated by a move from point A_1 to point B in Figure 26.8. Hence the upward revision of expected inflation shifts the $SRAS$ curve to the left, to $SRAS_2$ ($\pi^e = 4$ *per cent*). Along this new curve expected inflation is 4 per cent. Likewise, a downward revision in expected inflation will shift the aggregate supply curve to the right. Hence we can think of the short run as the period of time over which the expected inflation rate does not change.

In Example 26.3 we were able to explain that the $SRAS$ curve will shift if an unexpected rise in inflation leads to an increase in inflationary expectations and a revision of nominal wage and contract prices. However, as illustrated by Example 26.4, the $SRAS$ curve may shift without any change in the actual rate of inflation.

Example 26.4 The importance of new information

Firms and their suppliers including labour are negotiating new contracts. They know that last period's inflation rate was 3 per cent, which is also the inflation rate expected for the new contract period. Suppose that, during the negotiations, the central bank suddenly announces a new anti-inflationary policy designed to reduce inflation to 2 per cent. How will this affect the $SRAS$ curve?

In Example 26.3 we were able to explain why the $SRAS$ curve may shift. An unexpected rise in inflation eventually leads to an increase in inflationary expectations and a revision of nominal wage and contract prices. However, it is also possible that the $SRAS$ curve may shift without any change in the actual rate of inflation. This can happen if new information becomes available that would cause the participants in wage and price negotiations to revise their expectations of future inflation. To illustrate, consider point A in Figure 26.9.

Point A is on the curve $SRAS_1$ ($\pi^e = 3$ *per cent*) and is the same starting point as in Figures 26.7 and 26.8. Both actual and expected inflation are 3 per cent and aggregate output equals Y. A central bank announcement that it is going to increase interest rates with the objective of reducing the inflation rate to 2 per cent will shift the bank's policy reaction function up to the left. If the announcement is credible and all parties believe that the bank will deliver the lower inflation rate over the contract period then inflationary expectations may be revised down to 2 per cent. Firms, workers and suppliers will accept a 2 per cent increase because they now expect future inflation to fall to 2 per cent. In Figure 26.9 this is illustrated by a move from point A to point B, and a shift in the $SRAS$ curve to $SRAS_2$ ($\pi^e = 2$ *per cent*). As in Example 26.3, the shift in the $SRAS$ curve is caused by a revision in inflationary expectations but, in this case, expectations are revised without a change in the actual inflation rate.

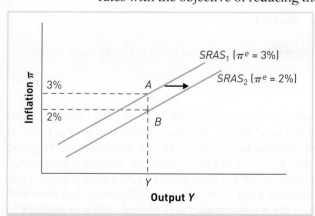

Figure 26.9 New Information Causes the Aggregate Supply Curve to Shift. New information such as an anti-inflationary monetary policy may lead to a downward revision of inflationary expectations and shift the $SRAS$ curve.

RECAP The short-run aggregate supply (*SRAS*) curve

- The *SRAS* curve shows the relationship between *aggregate output* and *inflation*.
- Unanticipated changes in inflation are a key reason explaining why the *SRAS* curve slopes upwards. When an increase in inflation is unanticipated and not reflected in nominal contracts firms find it profitable to increase output and employment.
- A revision in inflationary expectations and new information leads to shifts in the *SRAS* curve. Higher expected inflation or an announcement of an easier monetary policy will shift the *SRAS* curve to the left. Conversely, lower expected inflation or an announcement of a tighter monetary policy will shift to the *SRAS* curve to the right.
- Assuming no change in expected inflation, changes in the actual inflation rate correspond to movements *along* the *SRAS* curve; they do not *shift* the *SRAS* curve.

Short- and long-run equilibrium

We now have the components necessary to determine the equilibrium inflation rate and explain why inflation varies over time. As illustrated by Example 26.5, the short-run equilibrium inflation rate is determined by the intersection of the aggregate demand short-run aggregate supply curves.

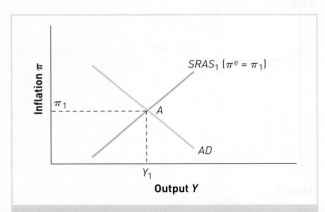

Figure 26.10 Short-run Equilibrium. The short-run equilibrium inflation rate is determined by the intersection of the *AD* and *SRAS* curves at point *A*.

Example 26.5 Short-run equilibrium

In Figure 26.10, short-run equilibrium is at point *A*. The equilibrium inflation rate is π_1 and output is Y_1, and along the *SRAS* expected inflation π^e equals the actual inflation rate. If there are no exogenous shocks that shift the position of the *AD* curve, is this situation likely to persist into the future?

The answer depends on the relationship of actual output Y_1 to full employment or potential output $Y^\star$. If the equilibrium position in Figure 26.10 corresponds to a *recessionary* gap with Y_1 less than $Y^\star$ firms will be selling an amount less than their capacity to produce, and they will have an incentive to cut their *relative* prices so they can sell more. Alternatively, if the equilibrium position in Figure 26.10 corresponds to an *expansionary gap* with Y_1 greater than $Y^\star$, firms will find that their sales exceed their normal production rates and, as we might expect in situations in which the quantity demanded exceeds the quantity firms desire to supply, firms will ultimately respond by trying to increase their *relative* prices. Hence in a recessionary gap the pressure of excess supply will lead to a downward revision of inflationary expectations, whereas excess demand will increase expected inflation in an expansionary gap. Finally, if Y_1 in Figure 26.10 equals $Y^\star$, sales will equal normal production levels and firms will have no need to change their relative prices. These results are summarised in Table 26.1.

Relationship of output to potential output	Behaviour of expected inflation
1. Recessionary gap $Y < Y^*$	π^e falls
2. Expansionary gap $Y > Y^*$	π^e rises
3. No output gap $Y = Y^*$	π^e remains unchanged

Table 26.1 **The Output Gap and Inflation**

Example 26.6 Long-run equilibrium

If the economy is in short-run equilibrium with Y less than Y^* how will the economy adjust in the long run? How will it adjust if Y is greater than Y^*?

Figures 26.11 and 26.12 illustrate the long-run adjustment of inflation to output gaps.

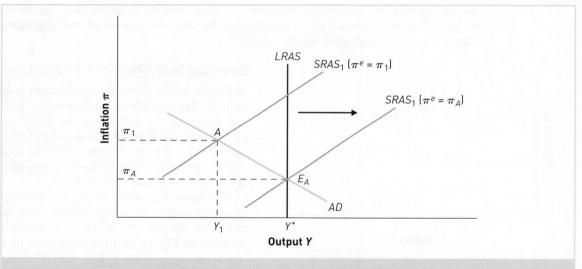

Figure 26.11 Adjustment to a Recessionary Gap. The recessionary gap leads to a downward revision in expected inflation and shifts the *SRAS* curve to the right. Long-run equilibrium is at point E_A with $Y = Y^*$ and $\pi = \pi_A$.

In Figure 26.11 the equilibrium at point A corresponds to a recessionary gap with actual output Y_1 less than potential output Y^*. Firms will have agreed to wage and input price contracts that reflect the expected rate of inflation π_1. However, as they are operating below capacity they will reduce the rate of price increase (inflation). Actual inflation will start to fall and will eventually be reflected in lower expected inflation, which shifts the *SRAS* curve to the right. Note that as the actual inflation rate declines, the central bank will follow its reaction function and reduce the rate of interest, which stimulates aggregate demand leading to an increase in short-run equilibrium output (a movement along and down the *AD* curve). This process will continue until firms are producing at full capacity and actual output equals potential output Y^*, as illustrated by point E_A in Figure 26.11. When point E_A is reached, firms will be operating at full

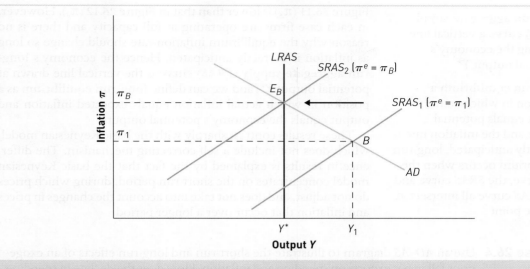

Figure 26.12 Adjustment to an Expansionary Gap. The expansionary gap leads to an upward revision in expected inflation and shifts the *SRAS* curve to the left. Long-run equilibrium is at point E_B with $Y = Y^*$ and $\pi = \pi_B$.

capacity and there will be no further incentive to reduce the rate of price increase. Hence point E_A is a long-run equilibrium position with $\pi = \pi_A$ and $Y = Y^*$.

Figure 26.12 illustrates the opposite scenario. The equilibrium at point *B* corresponds to an expansionary gap with actual output Y_1 greater than potential output Y^*. Firms will be operating above full capacity and will react to high demand by increasing prices at a rate greater than their costs are rising (expected inflation π_1). Actual inflation will start to rise and will eventually be reflected in higher expected inflation, which shifts the *SRAS* curve to the left. Note that as the actual inflation rate increases the central bank will follow its reaction function and increase the rate of interest, which reduces aggregate demand leading to a decline in short-run equilibrium output (a movement along and up the *AD* curve). As in the case of a recessionary gap the adjustment will continue until firms are producing at full capacity and actual output equals potential output Y^*, as illustrated by point E_B in Figure 26.12. Hence point E_B in Figure 26.12 is also a long-run equilibrium position with output equal to potential output Y^* and an equilibrium inflation rate equal to π_B.

short-run equilibrium a situation in which inflation equals expected inflation and output equals the level of short-run equilibrium output that is consistent with that inflation rate; short-run equilibrium occurs at the intersection of the *AD* and *SRAS* curves

Figures 26.11 and 26.12 enable us to distinguish between short- and long-run equilibrium. The intersection of the *AD* curve and the *SRAS* curve (point *A* in Figure 26.11 and point *B* in Figure 26.12) is referred to as the point of **short-run equilibrium**. When the economy is in short-run equilibrium, inflation equals the value determined by expected inflation and short-run equilibrium output equals the level of planned aggregate expenditure that is consistent with that inflation rate.

Our analysis of Figures 26.11 and 26.12 predicts that the economy will be *self-correcting* in the long run. Regardless of the starting point (*A* in Figure 26.11 or *B* in Figure 26.12), the economy will always converge to its potential output level Y^*. In Figures 26.11 and 26.12 the only difference is that the long-run equilibrium inflation rate in

long-run aggregate supply (LRAS) curve a vertical line showing the economy's potential output $Y^\star$

long-run equilibrium a situation in which actual output equals potential output and the inflation rate is correctly anticipated; long-run equilibrium occurs when the AD curve, the SRAS curve and the LRAS curve all intersect at a single point

Figure 26.11 (π_A) is lower than that in Figure 26.12 (π_B). However, in each case firms are operating at full capacity and there is no reason why the equilibrium inflation rate should change so long as inflation is correctly anticipated. Hence the economy's **long-run aggregate supply (LRAS) curve** is the vertical line drawn at potential output $Y^\star$, and we can define **long-run equilibrium** as a position in which actual inflation equals expected inflation and output equals the economy's potential output.

These results contrast sharply with the basic Keynesian model, which does not include a self-correcting mechanism. The difference in results is explained by the fact that the basic Keynesian model concentrates on the short-run period, during which prices do not adjust, and does not take into account the changes in prices and inflation that occur over a longer period.

Exercise 26.4   Use an AD–AS diagram to illustrate the short-run and long-run effects of an exogenous fall in net exports on spending and inflation. How does the decline in spending affect output in the short run and in the long run?

RECAP *AD–AS* and the self-correcting economy

- The economy is in short-run equilibrium when inflation equals expected inflation and output equals the level of short-run equilibrium output that is consistent with that inflation rate. Graphically, short-run equilibrium occurs at the intersection of the AD curve and the SRAS curve.
- The economy is in long-run equilibrium when actual output equals potential output (there is no output gap) and the inflation rate is stable. Graphically, long-run equilibrium occurs when the AD curve, the SRAS curve and the LRAS curve intersect at a common point.
- Inflation adjusts gradually to bring the economy into long-run equilibrium (a phenomenon called the economy's *self-correcting* tendency). Inflation rises to eliminate an expansionary gap and falls to eliminate a recessionary gap. Graphically, the SRAS curve moves up or down as needed to bring the economy into long-run equilibrium.

Sources of inflation

demand shocks events that lead to unanticipated changes in planned aggregate expenditure

supply shocks unanticipated events that lead to firms changing their planned output levels

We have seen that inflation can rise or fall in response to an output gap. But what creates the output gaps that give rise to changes in inflation? And are there factors besides output gaps that can affect the inflation rate? To answer these questions it is useful to think of sudden changes in demand and supply as either **demand shocks** or **supply shocks**. By a demand shock we mean an unanticipated event that causes consumers to change their planned expenditure at given levels of income and the rate of interest. By supply shocks we mean unanticipated events that change the output behaviour of firms.

Demand shocks

Demand shocks are unanticipated changes in aggregate spending. For example, if the economy is at or close to full capacity output, a sudden rise in consumer confidence will lead to increased expenditure at each level of income and higher inflation – or, in more colloquial terms, 'too much spending chasing too few goods'. Positive demand shocks, or increases in planned expenditure at the current rate of inflation, shift the aggregate demand curve to the right, whereas negative demand shocks, or decreases in planned expenditure, shift the curve to the left. Example 26.7 illustrates a positive demand shock.

Example 26.7 Government deficits and inflation

Excessive government budget deficits are sometimes associated with increased inflation. Explain why, using an AD–AS diagram.

A government's budget deficit is the *excess of government spending over tax revenues*. In Figure 26.4 we saw that higher government expenditures shift the AD curve to the *right*. The same is true for reductions in net taxes, which increase disposable incomes, leading to higher consumption expenditures. As consumption is a key component of total expenditure in the economy, aggregate demand will increase at any given level of inflation – that is, the AD curve will shift to the *right*. Hence higher government deficits are potentially inflationary because increased spending and lower taxation raise total demand relative to the economy's productive capacity. In the face of rising sales, firms increase their prices more quickly, raising the inflation rate.

Figure 26.13 illustrates this process. Suppose that the economy is initially in long-run equilibrium at point A, where the aggregate demand curve AD intersects both the short-run and long-run aggregate supply curves, $SRAS_1$ and $LRAS$, respectively. Point A is a long-run equilibrium point, with output equal to potential output and equilibrium inflation equal to π_1. Now suppose that without any preannouncement the government suddenly decides to start increasing its budget deficit. We saw earlier

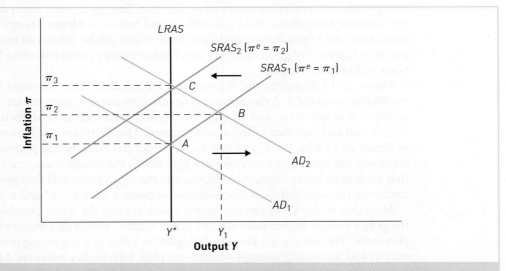

Figure 26.13 A Demand Shock. An unanticipated increase in government budget deficit shifts the AD curve to the right, from AD_1 to AD_2. At the new short-run equilibrium point B, actual output has risen above potential output Y^*, creating an expansionary gap. This gap leads to a rise in inflationary expectations, shown as an upward movement of the SRAS line from $SRAS_1$ to $SRAS_2$. At the new long-run equilibrium point C, actual output has fallen back to the level of potential output, but inflation is higher at π_3.

that, for a given level of inflation, an exogenous increase in spending raises short-run equilibrium output, shifting the AD curve to the right. Figure 26.13 shows the aggregate demand curve shifting rightwards, from AD_1 to AD_2, as a result of the increased deficit. The economy moves to a new, short-run equilibrium at point B, where AD_2 intersects $SRAS_1$. At point B actual output has risen to Y_1, creating an expansionary gap, and inflation has increased to π_2. Note that along the short-run supply curve $SRAS_1$ the expected inflation rate is π_1 but the actual inflation rate is higher at π_2. That is, the rise in inflation is unanticipated and firms are willing to increase output because the prices of their outputs are now increasing faster (π_2) than their input costs (π_1). The process doesn't stop there, however, because inflationary expectations will eventually be revised upwards and, as in Figure 26.12, the $SRAS$ will shift to the left. The new long-run equilibrium is at point C with $Y = Y^\star$ and inflation higher at π_3. Hence, the increase in output created by a higher government deficit is temporary. In the long run output returns to potential output but at a higher equilibrium rate of inflation.

Supply shocks

Supply shocks are unanticipated events that lead to changes in the output that firms are willing to supply at each rate of inflation. Like demand shocks, supply shocks can be positive or negative. A positive supply shock means that firms are willing to increase output at the current rate of inflation and the $SRAS$ will shift to the right. Conversely a negative, or adverse, supply shock causes firms to reduce output, shifting the $SRAS$ to the left. Example 26.8 illustrates an adverse supply shock.

Example 26.8 An increase in oil prices

Oil is an input into many production processes; it is also a major source of generating energy, which is crucial to nearly all production. Energy in some form drives machinery, powers computers, and lights offices and factories. Hence energy prices are an important cost of production and a rise in oil prices can be seen as an increase in input prices to suppliers of goods and services. Higher energy prices therefore lead to higher costs and reduced output.

Figure 26.14 illustrates the implications for inflation. The economy is in long-run equilibrium at point A. A rise in energy, or other production costs, means that firms will supply less at any given rate of inflation. Hence the $SRAS$ curve shifts to the left, and both actual and expected inflation will increase. The short-run equilibrium is at point B in Figure 26.14 with $Y = Y_1$ and $\pi = \pi_2$. As output has fallen below potential output the economy has moved to a recessionary gap, which eventually leads to a fall in inflation that feeds in to lower expected inflation, and the $SRAS$ curve will drift back to the right until long-run equilibrium is re-established at point A with $Y = Y^\star$ and $\pi = \pi_1$.

Note that in the short run the supply shock creates the worst possible scenario for the policy maker: higher inflation *and* lower output, which also implies higher unemployment. This situation is known as *stagflation* – that is, a stagnating economy (falling output and increasing unemployment) coupled with higher inflation. Many Western economies experienced this phenomenon in the mid-1970s following the quadrupling of oil prices in 1973. In the long run the economy will self-correct and return to full employment but at the possible cost of a protracted recession and sustained high unemployment. Hence policy makers might be tempted to shorten the recession by pursuing an expansionary monetary policy. The following chapter will explain the consequences of such a response by the central bank.

stagflation a situation in which the economy is experiencing low growth and rising unemployment coupled with higher inflation

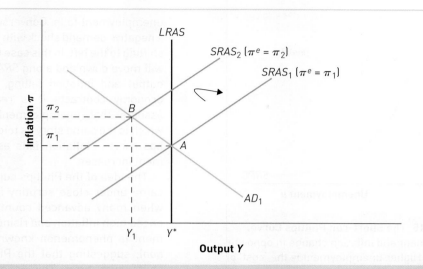

Figure 26.14 A Supply Shock. An unanticipated increase in energy or other costs shifts the *SRAS* curve to the left, from *SRAS*₁ to *SRAS*₂. At the new short-run equilibrium point *B*, actual output has fallen below potential output *Y**, creating a recessionary gap. If the central bank does not intervene, this gap leads to a fall in inflationary expectations, shifting the *SRAS* curve back towards *SRAS*₁ and the economy will revert to the initial long-run equilibrium point *A*, with *Y* = *Y** and π = π₁.

Economic naturalist 26.1 The Phillips curve

In 1958 the New Zealand-born economist Bill Phillips published a paper in which he studied the relationship between wage inflation (the annual percentage change in the average money wage) and unemployment in the United Kingdom over the period 1861 to 1957. Phillips found that in years when wage inflation was high, unemployment tended to be low, and in years when wage inflation was low, unemployment tended to be high. In other words, wage inflation and unemployment tended to change in opposite directions. In the years following the publication of Phillips' research, economists identified similar relationships in data for other advanced countries, and were also able to show that the same relationship held between price inflation and unemployment. This negative or inverse relationship between inflation and unemployment subsequently become known as the Phillips curve. Figure 26.15 gives a stylised picture of the Phillips curve relationship.

We shall see presently why the curve in Figure 26.15 is labelled a 'short-run' Phillips curve (*SRPC*). As drawn in Figure 26.15 the Phillips curve appears to present the policy maker with a trade-off or choice between inflation and unemployment. For example, if policy makers wish to lower the rate of inflation they have to pay a 'price' in terms of higher unemployment (a move down the Phillips curve). Conversely, if lower unemployment is the objective, policy makers have to accept higher inflation (a move up the Phillips curve).

The idea of the Phillips curve trade-off is totally consistent with the short-run aggregate demand–aggregate supply models used in this chapter. To explain, consider Figure 26.13. Starting from the long-run equilibrium point *A*, suppose a demand shock shifts the *AD* curve out to *AD*₂. In the short run, defined as the period over which expected inflation does not change, the economy will move up and along *SRAS*₁ towards point *B*, and both output and inflation will increase and, as the economy expands, it is reasonable to assume that unemployment declines. Hence, as along the Phillips curve, inflation rises as

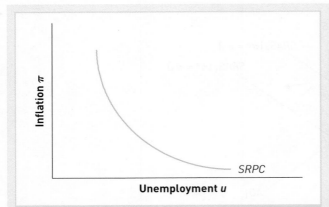

Figure 26.15 The Short-run Phillips Curve.
Unemployment and inflation change in opposite directions. Higher unemployment is the 'cost' of lower inflation.

unemployment falls. Conversely, consider a negative demand shock with the AD curve shifting to the left. In this case the economy will move down and along $SRAS_1$ with both output and inflation falling, and as the economy contracts it is reasonable to assume that unemployment increases, which is the same story as told by the Phillips curve – inflation falls as unemployment increases.

The idea of the Phillips curve trade-off came under close scrutiny in the 1970s when many advanced countries experienced high inflation *and* rising unemployment (a phenomenon known as *stagflation*), suggesting that the Phillips curve shifts over time. This is explained by Figure 26.16.

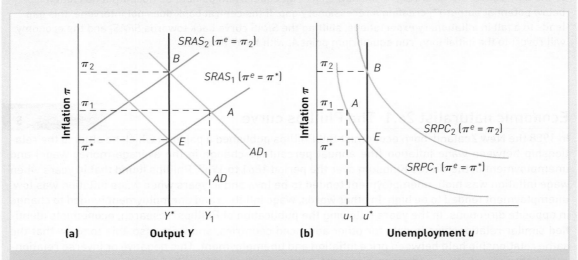

Figure 26.16 The Long-run Phillips Curve. In the long run the Phillips curve trade-off disappears and the long-run Phillips curve is a vertical line at the natural rate of unemployment u^*.

In panel (a) of Figure 26.16 the economy is assumed to be in an initial long-run equilibrium at point E where the AD curve intersects $SRAS_1$ and the $LRAS$ curve. Output equals potential output Y^* and the equilibrium inflation rate is π^*, which is also the expected rate of inflation. The corresponding point in panel (b) is point E on the Phillips curve, labelled $SRPC_1$. The equilibrium rate of unemployment is the natural rate u^* defined as the rate of unemployment that prevails when the economy is operating at its potential output. As was explained in Chapter 21, when $u = u^*$ all unemployment is either frictional or structural and cyclical unemployment is zero. Now consider a demand shock that shifts the AD curve out to AD_1. In the short run the economy will move towards point A in panel (a). Output will increase, unemployment will fall and inflation will increase to π_1. In panel (b) the corresponding move is from E to point A on $SRPC_1$. Consistent with the Phillips curve story, unemployment falls to u_1.

However, we know that output has increased because the rise in inflation is unanticipated and, as inflationary expectations are revised to reflect the higher inflation rate, the *SRAS* curve will shift to the left, establishing a new long-run equilibrium at point *B* in panel (a). Output will have returned to its potential level and the equilibrium rate of inflation is π_2. However, as output contracts towards Y^*, unemployment will revert back to its natural level u^* but at the higher rate of inflation π_2. Hence in panel (b) the new long-run equilibrium is at point *B* with $u = u^*$ and $\pi = \pi_2$, and the short-run Phillips curve shifts up to $SRPC_2$. The reason for the shift is that once the higher rate of inflation is reflected in wage and other nominal contracts, firms will no longer find it profitable to produce an output greater than Y^*. As real wages and relative input prices are the same at points *E* and *B* in both panels, output and unemployment must also be the same. Hence the increase in the expected inflation rate shifts the Phillips curve to the right.

We can conclude that the Phillips curve trade-off is at best a short-run phenomenon, which vanishes once expected inflation catches up with actual inflation and that, in the long run, the Phillips curve is a vertical line at the natural rate of unemployment u^*.

RECAP Sources of inflation

- Inflation may result from *demand shocks*, which create an expansionary output gap and put upward pressure on inflation. An example is an increase in government deficits, which shift the *AD* curve to the right and intensify inflationary pressures. Monetary policy can be used to offset excessive deficits, preventing higher inflation from emerging.
- Inflation may also arise from *supply shocks*, such as an increase in oil and energy costs. In the absence of policy intervention, supply shocks dissipate and do not lead to changes in the equilibrium rate of inflation. However, if the central bank accommodates the shock it can shorten the recession, but only at the cost of higher inflation.

Shocks to potential output

In analysing the effects of higher energy prices in Example 26.8 we assumed that potential output remained unchanged. However, as energy prices increase, firms may scrap energy-inefficient equipment, leading to a lower capital stock, which reduces the economy's productive capacity and its potential output Y^*. Figure 26.17 illustrates the effects on the economy of a sudden decline in potential output.

Suppose that the economy is in long-run equilibrium at point *A* and potential output falls unexpectedly from Y^* to $Y^{*\prime}$, shifting the long-run aggregate supply line leftwards from $LRAS_1$ to $LRAS_2$. After this decline in potential output, is the economy still in long-run equilibrium at point *A*? The answer is no, because output now exceeds potential output at that point. In other words, an *expansionary gap* has developed. This gap reflects the fact that although planned spending has not changed, the capacity of firms to supply goods and services has been reduced. As we have seen, an expansionary gap leads to rising inflation. In Fig. 26.17, increasing inflation leads to higher expected inflation and shifts the *SRAS* curve to the left to $SRAS_2$, and the economy reaches a new long-run equilibrium at point *B*. (Why is point *B* a long-run, and not just a short-run, equilibrium?) At that point, output has fallen to the new, lower level of potential output, $Y^{*\prime}$ and inflation has risen to π_2.

Exercise 26.5 What effect would improvements in technological progress have on output and inflation?

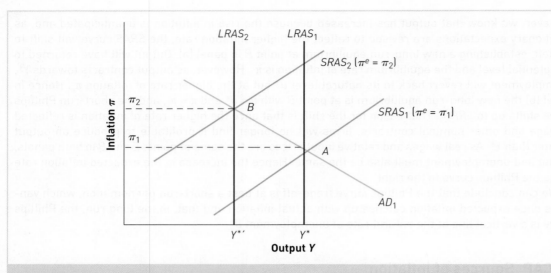

Figure 26.17 The Effects of a Shock to Potential Output. The economy is in long-run equilibrium at point A when a decline in potential output, from Y^* to $Y^{*\prime}$, creates an expansionary gap. Expected inflation is revised upwards and the short-run aggregate supply line shifts upwards from $SRAS_1$ to $SRAS_2$. A new long-run equilibrium is reached at point B, where actual output equals the new, lower level of potential output, $Y^{*\prime}$, and inflation has risen to π_2. Because it is the result of a fall in potential output, the decline in output is permanent.

Real and nominal shocks

Shocks to potential output differ from the type of demand and supply shocks discussed in earlier sections because they lead to a change in both the equilibrium inflation rate and the economy's long-run equilibrium output. In contrast, the demand shock discussed in Example 26.7 leads to a higher equilibrium rate of inflation but did not change long-run output. Likewise the supply shock discussed in Example 26.8 does not imply a change in long-run output. For this reason, we often refer to the type of shock illustrated by Examples 26.7 and 26.8 as **nominal shocks** because they only affect inflation and not output. Shocks to potential output, on the other hand, are referred to as **real shocks** because they change the economy's productive capacity and long-run equilibrium output.

nominal shocks demand and supply shocks that may change the equilibrium rate of inflation but do not change long-run equilibrium output

real shocks shocks that lead to a change in the economy's productive capacity and its long-run potential output

Economic naturalist 26.2 The policy maker's dilemma

Both real and nominal supply shocks can lead to sharp changes in output. The key difference between the two types of supply shock is that the output losses associated with an adverse nominal shock are temporary (because the economy self-corrects and will ultimately return to its initial level of potential output), but those associated with a real shock are permanent (output remains lower even after the economy has reached a new long-run equilibrium).

The distinction between adverse real and nominal shocks can create a dilemma for the policy maker. If the shock is temporary then, as we have seen, the central bank may respond by easing monetary policy and shifting the *AD* line to the right in order to stabilise output at its potential level. If the shock is permanent then the appropriate response may be to adopt a 'do-nothing' approach and let the economy stabilise at the lower level of permanent output. However, those responsible for policy may simply observe a fall in actual output followed by a rise in inflation. As both are consistent with each type of shock it may not be clear whether they are the result of a shock to permanent output or an adverse inflation shock. Hence, the policy maker's dilemma is to decide if the observed fall in output and rise in inflation are the result of an adverse inflation shock or a decline in permanent output, a decision that will determine the appropriate policy reaction.

Suppose the shock is actually the result of a decline in potential output but the central bank misinterprets it as temporary. In order to offset what it thinks is a recession, the central bank may attempt to stabilise output by lowering the rate of interest. This, however, would simply stimulate demand at a time when the economy's potential output is falling, leading to a greater expansionary gap and higher inflation. In the long run the equilibrium output will fall back to its new lower potential level but at a higher equilibrium inflation rate. Hence, by misinterpreting the data the policy maker runs the risk of failing to reverse the decline in output and pays a price in terms of higher equilibrium inflation.

This example also illustrates the point made in Chapter 25, that policy making is both an art and a science. Although we have classified aggregate supply shocks as either temporary or permanent, most shocks, such as the oil price increases of the 1970s, probably contain elements of both. Unfortunately, shocks do not come labelled 'permanent' or 'temporary', and the policy maker's task is to decide which component is the most important. While statistical models and economic analysis (science) may be of considerable help, the complexity and uncertainty surrounding the real-world economy will always require judgement on the part of the policy maker (art).

Summary

- This chapter has extended the basic Keynesian model to include *inflation*. First, we showed how planned spending and short-run equilibrium output are related to inflation, a relationship that is summarised by the *aggregate demand (AD) curve*. Second, we discussed how inflation itself is determined. In the short run, inflation is determined by past expectations and pricing decisions, but in the longer run, inflation adjusts as needed to eliminate output gaps.

- The *aggregate demand (AD) curve* shows the relationship between short-run equilibrium output and inflation. Because short-run equilibrium output is equal to planned spending, the aggregate demand curve also relates spending to inflation. Increases in inflation reduce planned spending and short-run equilibrium output, so the aggregate demand curve is downward-sloping.

- The *inverse relationship* of inflation and short-run equilibrium output is the result, in large part, of the behaviour of the central bank. To keep inflation low and stable, the central bank reacts to rising inflation by increasing the real interest rate. A higher real interest rate reduces consumption and planned investment, lowering planned aggregate expenditure and hence short-run equilibrium output. Other reasons that the *AD* curve slopes downwards include the effects of inflation on the real value of money, distributional effects (inflation redistributes wealth from the poor, who save relatively little, to the more affluent, who save more), uncertainty created by inflation and the impact of inflation on foreign sales of domestic goods.

- For any given value of inflation, an *exogenous increase in spending* (that is, an increase in spending at given levels of output and the real interest rate) raises short-run equilibrium output, shifting the *AD* curve to the right. Likewise, an *exogenous decline in spending* shifts the *AD* curve to the left. The *AD* curve can also be shifted by a change in the central bank's policy reaction function. If the central bank gets 'tougher', shifting up its reaction function and thus choosing a higher real interest rate at each level of inflation, the *AD* curve will shift to the left. If the central bank gets 'easier', shifting down its reaction function and thus setting a lower real interest rate at each level of inflation, the *AD* curve will shift to the right.

- The *SRAS* curve shows the relationship between *aggregate output* and *inflation*. Unanticipated changes in inflation are a key reason explaining why the *SRAS curve slopes upwards*. When an increase in inflation is unanticipated and not reflected in nominal contracts firms find it profitable to increase output and employment.

- A revision in inflationary expectations and new information leads to shifts in the *SRAS* curve. Higher expected inflation or an announcement of an easier monetary policy will shift the *SRAS* curve to the left. Conversely, lower expected inflation or an announcement of a tighter monetary policy will shift the *SRAS* curve to the right.

- The economy is in short-run equilibrium when inflation equals the value determined by expected inflation and output equals the level of short-run equilibrium output that is consistent with that inflation rate. Graphically, short-run equilibrium occurs at the intersection of the *AD* curve and the *SRAS* curves.

- The economy is in long-run equilibrium when actual output equals potential output (there is no output gap) and the inflation rate is stable. Graphically, long-run equilibrium occurs when the *AD* curve, the *SRAS* curve and the *LRAS* curve intersect at a common point. The *LRAS* curve is a vertical line at the economy's potential output $Y^\star$.

■ Inflation adjusts gradually to bring the economy into long-run equilibrium (a phenomenon called the economy's *self-correcting* tendency). Inflation rises to eliminate an expansionary gap and falls to eliminate a recessionary gap. Graphically, the *SRAS curve* moves up or down as inflationary expectations are revised. The more rapid the self-correction process, the less need for active stabilisation policies to eliminate output gaps.

■ *Demand and supply shocks* are important sources of inflation. They can lead to a change in the equilibrium inflation rate but they do not lead to permanent output changes. For this reason they are referred to as *nominal shocks*.

■ Shocks to potential output lead to changes in both the equilibrium rate of inflation and the economy's productive capacity and are referred to as *real shocks*.

Review questions

1. Define the aggregate demand (*AD*) curve and explain why it has a negative slope.

2. State how each of the following affects the *AD* curve, and explain:
   a. an increase in government purchases
   b. a cut in taxes
   c. a decline in planned investment spending by firms
   d. a decision by the central bank to lower the real interest rate at each level of inflation.

3. Define the short-run aggregate supply curve (*SRAS*) and explain why it has a positive slope.

4. State how each of the following affects the *SRAS* curve, and explain:
   a. an increase in the expected rate of inflation
   b. a fall in the expected rate of inflation
   c. an announcement by the central bank to lower its target inflation rate.

5. Discuss the relationship between output gaps and inflation. How is this relationship captured in an aggregate demand–aggregate supply (*AD–AS*) diagram?

6. Sketch an aggregate demand–aggregate supply (*AD–AS*) diagram depicting an economy away from long-run equilibrium. Indicate the economy's short-run equilibrium point. Discuss how the economy reaches long-run equilibrium over a period of time. Illustrate the process in your diagram.

connect Problems

1. Suppose that the central bank's target inflation rate is 2 per cent, or 0.02. When the target is met the bank sets the nominal rate of interest at 4 per cent, or 0.04, and if the actual inflation rate increases by 0.01 (1 per cent) the bank increases the nominal interest rate by 0.0025. If inflation is 0.05 (5 per cent) what nominal interest rate will be set by the bank? What is the real rate of interest?

2. Suppose that the central bank reaction function is $i = \alpha + (1 + \beta)\,\pi - \beta\pi^\star$ and the relationship between short-run equilibrium output or planned expenditure and the real interest rate r is given by $Y = 1,000 - 1,000r$. If $\alpha = 0.02$ and $\beta = 0.25$ and the bank's target inflation rate is 0.02 find short-run equilibrium output when equilibrium actual inflation is 0.04 or 4 per cent.

3. Using the information in Problem 2 what is the change in planned aggregate expenditure if the central bank decides to set a real rate of interest equal to 0.01 when inflation is on target?

4. For each of the following, use an *AD–AS* diagram to show the short-run and long-run effects on output and inflation. Assume the economy starts in long-run equilibrium.

   a. An increase in consumer confidence that leads to higher consumption spending

   b. A reduction in taxes

   c. An easing of monetary policy by the central bank (a downward shift in the policy reaction function)

   d. A sharp drop in oil prices

   e. A war that raises government purchases

5. An economy is initially in recession. Using an *AD–AS* diagram, show the process of adjustment:

   a. if the central bank responds by easing monetary policy (moving its reaction function down)

   b. if the central bank takes no action.

   What are the costs and benefits of each approach, in terms of output loss and inflation?

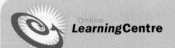

To help you grasp the key concepts of this chapter check out the extra resources posted on the Online Learning Centre. There are chapter summaries, self-test questions, an interactive graphing tool, weblinks and a glossary, all for free!

Visit the Online Learning Centre at: www.mcgraw-hill.co.uk/textbooks/mcdowell for information on accessing all of these resources.

27

Controlling Inflation

As discussed in Chapter 17, high and variable inflation is economically costly. These costs include the costs of economising on holding cash, distortions of the tax system, unexpected redistributions of income and wealth, interference with long-term planning and reduced efficiency of the price mechanism. To minimise these costs central banks such as the European Central Bank (ECB) and the Bank of England set explicit low inflation targets. In this chapter we will use the aggregate demand–aggregate supply model to analyse how central banks can achieve and maintain low inflation. We start by asking how monetary policy can be used to secure a permanent reduction in inflation and then ask how the central bank might respond if a demand or supply shock causes the actual rate of inflation to deviate from the target rate. We will see that, in each case, the central bank has an option of taking a do-nothing approach or responding by changing its policy to speed up the adjustment process. We will also consider possible central bank reactions to real shocks, which lead to a change in the economy's potential output $Y^\star$. An important conclusion of this chapter is that in the long run monetary policy can only determine the equilibrium rate of inflation; it cannot determine the long-run equilibrium level of output.

Using monetary policy to achieve low inflation

In Chapter 26 we saw that inflation changes in response to the emergence of output gaps, and that these gaps are caused by demand and supply shocks. Suppose that the economy is in a long-run equilibrium position but the central bank considers the equilibrium inflation rate too high and wishes to reduce it. Example 27.1 describes how anti-inflationary policy can reduce the equilibrium rate of inflation.

Example 27.1 Anti-inflationary monetary policy

Consider an economy in long-run equilibrium output equal to potential output $Y^\star$. Suppose the central bank decides to aim for an inflation target lower than the current rate of inflation. How can the bank achieve the inflation target? What are the implications for output and unemployment?

Figure 27.1 combines the central bank reaction function (panel (a)) with the IS-LM model of Chapter 23 (panel (b)) and the *AD–AS* model developed in Chapter 26 (panel (c)).

In panel (b) the economy is in equilibrium at point *A* where the IS curve intersects the LM curve. Point *A* in panel (c) is the corresponding long-run equilibrium position where the aggregate demand, short-run aggregate supply and long-run aggregate supply all intersect. Output equals potential output Y^* and the inflation rate is π_1, which implies that the central bank sets the rate of interest at i_1 on its reaction function RF_1 in panel (a). To achieve a lower equilibrium rate of inflation, the central bank will increase the rate of interest at the current inflation rate π_1. That is, the bank's reaction function will shift up to RF_2 in panel (a) and the bank sets the rate of interest at i_2 on its new reaction function. Recall from Chapter 22 that increasing the nominal rate of interest is exactly the same as reducing the money supply, which shifts the LM curve to the left as shown by LM_2 in panel (b) of Figure 27.1. When the central bank increases the nominal rate of interest at the current inflation rate the real

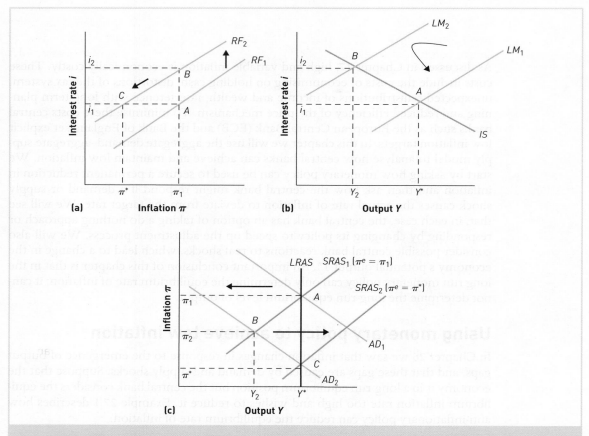

Figure 27.1 Anti-inflationary Monetary Policy. The economy is in long-run equilibrium at point *A* with $\pi = \pi_1$. To reduce inflation to the new lower target rate at π^* the central bank increases the rate of interest and reduces the money supply at the current rate of inflation. In panel (b), the *LM* curve shifts to LM_2. In panel (c) the *AD* curve shifts to AD_2, inflation falls and expectations are revised down. The *SRAS* curve shifts to the right, establishing the new long-run equilibrium at point *C* with $\pi = \pi^*$.

rate of interest will increase. As a consequence, consumption and investment will fall and the aggregate demand curve will shift to the left to AD_2 in panel (c), establishing a short-run equilibrium at point B. However, as output has fallen below potential output, point B in panel (c) corresponds to a recessionary gap $(Y_2 < Y^\star)$ leading to a downward revision in expected inflation and a leftward shift in the SRAS curve to $SRAS_2$. The new long-run equilibrium is at point C in panel (c) with inflation equal to the target rate $\pi^\star$. Note that as inflation falls the central bank reduces the rate of interest by moving down its reaction function RF_2. However, to reduce the rate of interest the bank must simultaneously increase the money supply, which shifts the LM curve back to the right, re-establishing the long-run equilibrium at point A in panel (b).

However, the adjustment to the new long-run equilibrium will not be instantaneous. As aggregate demand starts to fall, the economy will initially move along the supply curve $SRAS_1$ in Figure 27.1. Both inflation and output will decline and a recessionary gap will open as Y falls below $Y^\star$. Eventually the recessionary gap will lead to a lower expected inflation rate, shifting the SRAS to the right and establishing the new long-run equilibrium at point C. The key question is how long will it take for expected inflation to be revised downwards? If expectations change slowly then the recessionary gap will persist and the economy will experience a prolonged period of lower output and higher unemployment. Alternatively, if expectations adjust rapidly, the recession will be short-lived and the adjustment rapid. The speed with which expectations adjust will depend on factors such as the prevalence of long-term contracts, and the efficiency and flexibility of product and labour markets. However, as explained in Economic naturalist 27.1, it may also depend on central bank credibility.

Economic naturalist 27.1 Inflation adjustment and central bank credibility

Example 27.1 illustrates that anti-inflationary monetary policies may succeed in achieving a lower equilibrium inflation rate but only at the cost of a short-term increase in unemployment and lower output. Looking at Figure 27.1, it should be clear that the extent and persistence of this recessionary gap will depend on the speed at which the inflationary expectations fall. The faster expectations are revised, the faster the SRAS curve shifts down towards $SRAS_2$ in Figure 27.1, the shorter the duration of the recession and the faster the adjustment of Y back to Y^*. Hence, a key question is: What determines the *speed* with which actual inflation adjusts?

While many factors may influence inflationary expectations, the *credibility* the public attaches to the central bank and its policies is among the most important. By 'credibility' we simply mean the confidence the public has in the central bank's ability and willingness to see its policy through to fulfilment. If the public are confident that the central bank will, despite a short-term rise in unemployment, maintain its anti-inflationary policy, then we can expect inflationary expectations to be revised rapidly. Alternatively, if – say, on the basis of its past record – the public expect that the central bank may weaken or reverse its policy once a recessionary gap emerges then inflationary expectations may be revised slowly, if at all. In terms of Figure 27.1 maintaining the policy means that the central bank will stay on the higher reaction function RF_2 and keep the interest rate high enough to hold the AD curve at AD_2, despite the fall in output. Weakening the policy means that, as output starts to decline, the central bank will revert back to its original reaction function RF_1 and ease policy, letting the AD curve drift back to its initial position at AD_1. In the first case, it is reasonable to assume that the public will become convinced that the equilibrium inflation rate will fall in the near future, leading to a more rapid downward revision of inflationary expectations and a faster adjustment to the new equilibrium at *C*. In the second case, the public may be much less convinced that the new policy will be maintained, with the consequence that inflationary expectations may not be revised downwards and the recession will persist.

The credibility that the public attaches to central bank policy is therefore critical to the revision of expectations and the speed at which the economy adjusts to the lower equilibrium inflation rate. What characteristics should central banks have to ensure that the public has confidence in their ability and willingness to maintain a tight anti-inflationary policy even when output is falling and unemployment rising? We give two answers, both relevant in a European context: central bank independence and pre-commitments to other objectives.

An independent central bank is a bank that is free to decide monetary policy without interference from government. Suppose the central bank is not independent but takes policy instructions from politicians. Governments are elected by voters who become concerned when economic activity slows down and unemployment starts to rise. As government may be more concerned with its short-term popularity and the need to get re-elected than with the long-run equilibrium inflation rate, it may instruct the central bank to relax monetary policy when a temporary recessionary gap emerges. Conversely, policy makers in politically independent central banks normally have fixed terms of office and do not need to get re-elected or be concerned with their short-term popularity. Hence it is possible that the public may, other things being equal, place greater confidence in the anti-inflationary policies of independent central banks. Given the ECB's mandate for price stability and its high level of independence, this is perhaps one reason why the Maastricht Treaty required governments of all EU member states to introduce legislation designed to increase the political independence of their national central banks prior to the start of full monetary union in 1999.

Central bank credibility may also be enhanced if the bank has a pre-commitment to other targets that require a lower equilibrium inflation rate. The Maastricht Convergence Criteria provide one possible example. To be admitted to the new monetary union in 1999, member states of the European Union were required to satisfy a number of criteria, which became known as the Maastricht Convergence Criteria. One of these criteria was convergence to a low and stable inflation rate. Specifically, a country would be deemed eligible if its annual inflation rate was not more than 1.5 per cent higher than the average of the three lowest inflation rates in the European Union. This posed a problem for several countries, such as Italy, whose inflation rate was approximately twice the European average for most of the 1980s and into the early 1990s. Hence, to satisfy the Maastricht criteria, Italy and several other countries had to introduce tough anti-inflationary policies of the type illustrated by Figure 27.1. Italy's problem was that because of its high inflation history the public was unlikely to attribute much credibility to a new policy that, following many that had failed in the past, promised to deliver a lower equilibrium inflation rate. Other things being equal, this low credibility implied that Italy might have to pay a high price in terms of slower economic growth and higher unemployment in order to reduce its equilibrium inflation rate. However, the Italian government and its central bank now had an overriding objective, which was to be admitted to the new monetary union. Success in achieving this objective meant that the benefits from a tight monetary policy would be much greater than those normally associated with lower inflation. They would also include the political advantages of being at the forefront of a major European initiative with a seat 'at the table' and full voting rights on the Governing Council of the new ECB. The firm commitment of the Italian government and the majority of its electorate to monetary union may have enhanced the credibility of monetary policy in the 1990s because the primary commitment was not low inflation per se, but qualification for the new monetary regime, which required a strong anti-inflationary policy.

The stance of Italian monetary policy over this period may be gauged from the annual rate of growth of the money supply, which fell from 9 per cent in 1991 to under 1 per cent in 1998, and was actually negative in 1995. Over the same period, unemployment increased from 8 to 12 per cent but the inflation rate declined from 7 to under 3 per cent, which enabled Italy to satisfy the Maastricht criteria. In short, without its firm commitment to monetary union and its effects on policy credibility, Italian inflation, judged on previous performance, might have declined more slowly and, if the policy had been pursued, resulted in even higher unemployment.

Responding to nominal shocks

In the previous section we saw how the central bank can achieve a given inflation target. However, as we saw in Chapter 26, demand and supply shocks can cause the actual inflation rate to deviate from the target rate. Recall that a demand shock is an unanticipated change in planned aggregate expenditure, which shifts the aggregate demand curve. Likewise, a supply shock is an unanticipated change in output which shifts the short-run aggregate supply curve. Both demand and supply shocks will cause the inflation rate to differ from the central bank's target rate. Examples 27.2 and 27.3 discuss possible policy responses to demand and supply shocks.

Example 27.2 Responding to a demand shock

In Example 26.7, we analysed the manner in which the economy adjusts to a positive demand shock such as an unanticipated increase in the government deficit. In that example we saw that starting from long-run equilibrium with $Y = Y^\star$ an unanticipated increase in the deficit shifts the AD curve to the right, leading to an increase in both inflation and short-run equilibrium output (Figure 26.13). However, in the absence of a policy change, higher inflation leads to higher expected inflation, which shifts the $SRAS$ to the left establishing a new long-run equilibrium with output returning to $Y^\star$ but at a higher equilibrium rate of inflation – point C in Figure 26.13. Does the central bank have the power to prevent the increased inflation induced by the demand shock?

As illustrated by Figure 27.2 the answer is yes. Starting from a long-run equilibrium at point A with $Y = Y^\star$ and inflation equal to the target rate π_1 an unanticipated increase in planned expenditure shifts the AD curve to the right, from AD_1 to AD_2. At the new short-run equilibrium point B, actual output has risen above potential output $Y^\star$, creating an expansionary gap leading to a rise in inflationary expectations that shifts the $SRAS$ line from $SRAS_1$ to $SRAS_2$. At the new long-run equilibrium point C, actual output has fallen back to the level of potential output, but inflation is higher at π_3. However, as we saw in Example 27.1, a decision by the bank to set a higher interest rate at any given level of inflation – an upward shift in the policy reaction function – will shift the AD curve to the left. Hence if the central bank aggressively tightens monetary policy (shifts its reaction function) it can reverse the rightward shift of the AD curve caused by increased government spending. As illustrated by Figure 27.2, offsetting the rightward shift of the AD curve restores equilibrium at point A and avoids the development of an expansionary gap, with its inflationary consequences. The bank's policy works because the higher interest rate it sets at each level of inflation acts to reduce consumption and investment spending. The reduction in private spending offsets the increase in demand by governments, eliminating the inflationary impact of the higher deficits.

We should not conclude that avoiding the inflationary consequences of higher deficits is *costless* to society. As we have just noted, inflation can be avoided only if

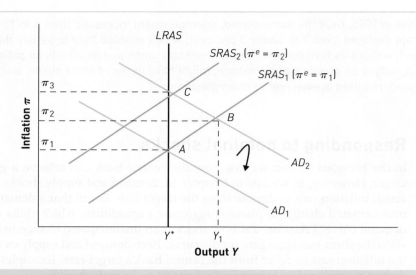

Figure 27.2 Responding to a Demand Shock. An unanticipated increase in planned expenditure shifts the AD curve to the right, from AD_1 to AD_2. At the new short-run equilibrium point B, actual output has risen above potential output Y*, creating an expansionary gap. If the central bank does not react, this gap leads to a rise in inflationary expectations, shown as an upward movement of the SRAS line from $SRAS_1$ to $SRAS_2$. At the new long-run equilibrium point C, actual output has fallen back to the level of potential output, but inflation is higher at π_3. If the bank reacts by increasing interest rates, the AD curve shifts back to AD_1 re-establishing the long-run equilibrium at A, and the target rate of inflation is maintained at π_1.

consumption and investment are reduced by a policy of higher interest rates. Effectively, the private sector must give up some resources so that more output can be devoted to public purposes. This reduction in resources reduces both current living standards (by reducing consumption) and future living standards (by reducing investment). Also, one reason behind the Eurosystem's Stability and Growth Pact (SGP), as discussed in Chapter 24, is to prevent national governments from running excessive deficits that would require the ECB to undertake the type of contractionary monetary policy discussed above.

Exercise 27.1 Starting from a position of long-run equilibrium, increased uncertainty about the world financial system causes firms to cut back on planned investment. Explain how inflation and output will adjust in the short and long run. Can the central bank maintain the initial long-run inflation rate?

Economic naturalist 27.2 How was UK inflation conquered in the 1980s?

As shown in Table 27.2, UK inflation rose to over 13 per cent in 1979 and to 18 per cent in 1980, but had declined to under 5 per cent by 1983. What led to this fall in inflation?

Year	Growth in real GDP (%)	Unemployment (%)	Inflation (%)	Nominal interest rate (%)	Real interest rate (%)
1978	3.5	5.0	8.3	11.9	3.6
1979	2.7	4.6	13.4	16.5	3.1
1980	−1.6	5.6	18.0	13.4	−4.6
1981	−1.3	8.8	11.9	15.4	3.5
1982	1.5	10.1	8.6	10.0	1.4
1983	3.5	10.8	4.6	9.0	4.4
1984	2.5	10.9	5.0	9.3	4.3

Table 27.2 **UK Macroeconomic Data, 1978–1984**

The data in Table 27.2 fit our analysis of anti-inflationary policy quite well. When inflation started to increase over 1978–79 the monetary authorities tightened policy by increasing nominal interest rates and maintaining the real rate of interest at a relatively high level. Although the real rate of interest was negative in 1980 the economy moved into recession, and experienced negative growth and rising unemployment in 1980–81. Despite this slowdown in activity, real interest rates were kept relatively high, perhaps reflecting factors other than monetary policy, and inflation eventually declined to less than 5 per cent by 1983. Since then British inflation has, apart from a brief period in the early 1990s, remained at relatively low levels.

These results are broadly consistent with the short-run analysis of Figure 27.2. Increasing interest rates and tightening policy initially leads to a recessionary gap followed by a decline in the rate of inflation.

Example 27.3 Responding to a supply shock

In Example 26.8 we saw that, in the absence of policy intervention, adverse supply shocks dissipate in the long run and do not lead to changes in the equilibrium rate of inflation or the level of output (Figure 26.14). However, during the adjustment period the economy may experience stagflation, a combination of recession and rising inflation. Suppose the central bank attempts to close the recessionary gap by relaxing monetary policy and setting a lower interest rate at each inflation rate. What will happen to inflation and output in the long run?

Figure 27.3 illustrates the long-run behaviour of output and inflation when the central bank relaxes monetary policy following an adverse supply shock.

In Figure 27.3 the adverse supply shock is illustrated by the leftward shift in the SRAS curve from $SRAS_1$ to $SRAS_2$. As a result the economy moves from the initial long-run equilibrium at point A, establishing a short-run equilibrium at point B. A recessionary gap opens and inflation increases to π_2. A decision by the central bank to close the recessionary gap by setting a lower interest rate at any given level of inflation – a downward shift in the policy reaction function – will increase planned aggregate expenditure and shift the AD curve to the right, as illustrated by the shift from AD_1 to AD_2 in Figure 27.3. As aggregate demand increases output will revert back towards $Y^\star$, but

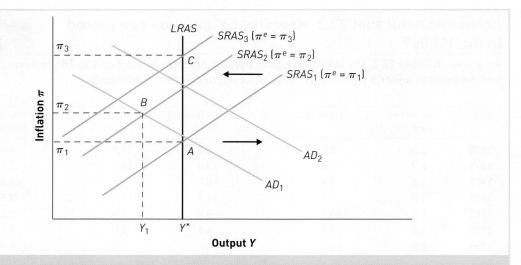

Figure 27.3 Accommodating a Supply Shock. An adverse supply shock shifts the *SRAS* curve to the left, from *SRAS₁* to *SRAS₂*. At the new short-run equilibrium point *B*, actual output has fallen below potential output *Y**, creating a recessionary gap. If the central bank does not react this gap leads to a fall in inflationary expectations and the *SRAS* curve shifts back to *SRAS₁* re-establishing long-run equilibrium at point *A*. If the central bank accommodates the shock by increasing the money supply, the *AD* curve will shift out to *AD₂*, inflation will increase, which leads to higher expected inflation, and shifts the *SRAS* curve further to the left to *SRAS₃* establishing a new long-run equilibrium at point *C* with *Y* = *Y** and with inflation higher at π₃.

inflation will also increase leading to higher expected inflation, which shifts the *SRAS* curve further to the left towards *SRAS₃*. The new long-run equilibrium is at point *C* with *Y* = *Y** but with inflation higher at π₃. Note that a decision by the central bank to reduce the rate of interest is exactly the same as a decision to increase the monetary supply. Hence the policy illustrated by Figure 27.3 is referred to as *monetary accommodation*. That is, the bank accommodates the shock by a policy of monetary expansion. Monetary accommodation may shorten the recession and speed up the adjustment back to full employment but at the cost of higher equilibrium inflation.

There is an important lesson to be learned from Examples 27.2 and 27.3. In the long run monetary policy can only determine the equilibrium rate of inflation; it cannot determine the level of output. In both examples the central bank has a choice of doing nothing or reacting to the shock. In each case a 'do-nothing' approach means that the bank allows the economy to self-correct in the long run. In Example 27.2 this means that the economy will converge to point *C* in Figure 27.2 with an equilibrium inflation rate equal to π₃. But if the bank reacts to the demand shock by tightening monetary policy, the *AD* curve shifts back to *AD₁*, giving a long-run inflation rate of π₁. Likewise, in Example 27.3, a 'do-nothing' approach means that the economy will revert back to point *A* in Figure 27.3 with inflation at π₁. On the other hand, if the bank accommodates the supply shock, the long-run equilibrium is at point *C* in Figure 27.3 with inflation higher at π₃. However, in all cases output will always revert to potential output *Y** irrespective of the bank's policy. Hence, in the long run, the central bank (or monetary policy) can determine the rate of inflation but not the equilibrium level of output.

Exercise 27.2 Assume that the economy is in long-run equilibrium. The central bank is not independent and the government is facing an election. In an attempt to gain popularity the government orders the bank to cut interest rates. Explain how inflation and output will adjust in the short and long run.

Economic naturalist 27.3 Inflation and money in the long run: the quantity theory

Examples 27.2 and 27.3 demonstrate that changes in aggregate expenditure and increases in input prices can result in a surge in inflation but, over the longer run, inflation depends on the behaviour of the money supply. The American economist Milton Friedman summarised the long-run relationship between money and inflation by saying that 'inflation is always and everywhere a monetary phenomenon'. To explore the relationship of money growth and inflation in a bit more detail, it is useful to introduce the concept of **velocity**. In economics, *velocity* is a measure of the speed at which money circulates. For example, a given euro might pass from your hand to the grocer's when you buy a litre of milk. The same euro may then pass from the grocer to his supplier, from the supplier to the dairy farmer who produced the milk, from the farmer to the feed supply store owner, and so on. More formally, velocity is defined as the value of transactions completed in a period of time divided by the stock of money required to make those transactions.

> **velocity** a measure of the speed at which money circulates

The higher this ratio, the faster the 'typical' euro is circulating. As a practical matter, we usually do not have precise measures of the total value of transactions taking place in an economy so, as an approximation, economists often measure the total value of transactions in a given period by nominal GDP for that period. That is, letting V denote velocity:

$$V = \frac{PY}{M} \tag{27.1}$$

where P = the average price level, Y = real GDP and M = the quantity of money in circulation. Note that as Y is real GDP P times Y is nominal or money GDP. A variety of factors determines velocity. A leading example is advances in payment technologies, such as the introduction of credit cards and debit cards, or the creation of networks of automatic teller machines (ATMs). These new technologies and payment methods have allowed people to carry out their daily business while holding less cash, and have thus tended to increase velocity over time.

We can use the definition of velocity to see how money and prices are related in the long run. First, rewrite the definition of velocity, Equation (27.1), by multiplying both sides by the money stock M. That is:

$$MV = PY \tag{27.2}$$

> **quantity equation** money times velocity equals nominal GDP: $M \times V = P \times Y$

Equation (27.2), a famous relationship in economics, is for historical reasons called the **quantity equation**. The quantity equation states that the money supply times velocity equals nominal GDP. Because the quantity equation is simply a rewriting of the definition of velocity it always holds exactly.

The quantity equation is historically important because late nineteenth- and early twentieth-century monetary economists used this relationship to theorise about the relationship between money and prices. We can do the same thing here. To keep things simple, imagine that velocity V is determined by current payments technologies and thus is approximately constant over the period we are considering. Likewise, suppose that real output Y is constant at its long-run potential value. If we use a bar over a variable to indicate that the variable is constant, we can rewrite the quantity equation as:

$$M\bar{V} = P\bar{Y} \tag{27.3}$$

where we are treating $\bar{V}$ and $\bar{Y}$ as fixed numbers. If we use a dot (•) over a variable to indicate its percentage change

$$\dot{M} = \dot{P} \tag{27.4}$$

suppose that for some reason the central bank increases the money supply M by 10 per cent per year, or $\dot{M}$ = 10 per cent. Because V and $\bar{Y}$ are assumed to be fixed, Equation (27.4) can continue to hold only if the price level P also rises by 10 per cent. That is, inflation or $\dot{P}$ = 10 per cent. Hence, according to the quantity equation, a 10 per cent increase in the money supply M should cause a 10 per cent increase in the price level P – that is, an inflation of 10 per cent. Thus high rates of money growth will tend to be associated with high rates of inflation. Figure 27.4 shows this relationship for ten countries in Latin America during the period 1995–2001. You can see that countries with higher rates of money growth tend also to have higher rates of inflation. The relationship between money growth and inflation is not exact, in part because – contrary to the simplifying assumption we made earlier – velocity and output are not constant but vary over time.

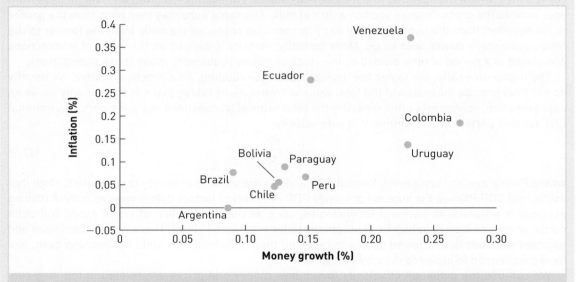

Figure 27.4 Inflation and Money Growth in Latin America, 1995–2001. Latin American countries with higher rates of growth in their money supplies also tended to have higher rates of inflation between 1995 and 2001. (The data for Argentina and Uruguay end in 2000 and the data for Ecuador end in 1997. In 1997 Ecuador abandoned its currency, the *sucre*, and began using US dollars instead.)

Stabilisation policy and the self-correcting economy

Examples 27.2 and 27.3 make an important point: the economy tends to be *self-correcting* in the long run. In other words, given enough time, output gaps that result from demand and supply shocks tend to disappear without changes in policy (other than the change in the interest rate and money supply embodied in the central bank's policy reaction function). Expansionary output gaps resulting from positive demand shocks are eliminated by rising inflation, while recessionary output gaps resulting from adverse supply shocks are eliminated by falling inflation.

Does the economy's tendency to self-correct imply that macroeconomic policies are not needed to stabilise output? The answer to this question depends crucially on the *speed* with which the self-correction process takes place. If self-correction takes place very slowly, so that actual output differs from potential output for protracted periods, then active use of policy can help to stabilise output. But if self-correction is rapid, then active stabilisation policies may not be required. The speed with which a particular economy corrects itself depends on a variety of factors, including the prevalence of long-term contracts, and the efficiency and flexibility of product and labour markets. Most importantly the speed with which the economy adjusts to output gaps will depend on how fast inflationary expectations are revised as economic conditions change. For example, in Figure 27.3, the downward revision of expected inflation shifts the *SRAS* to the right and output converges to potential output. During this process actual inflation is falling and, given our explanation of the negative relationship between inflation and aggregate demand, planned aggregate expenditure and hence output are increasing. But the speed of this process depends on how fast lower inflation is reflected in lower expected inflation and in the fixed-term contracts that determine wage and other input price increases. If inflationary expectations are revised very slowly then the adjustment will be prolonged and the recessionary gap will be eliminated slowly. If this is the case then there may be an important role for active stabilisation policy to speed up the adjustment to full employment.

Exercise 27.3   Assume that the economy is in long-run equilibrium. The economy experiences a beneficial nominal supply shock and a downward revision in the expected rate of inflation. Explain (a) how output will adjust if the central bank maintains its existing policy, and (b) how the central bank might take advantage of this shock to secure a permanent reduction in the rate of inflation.

RECAP Using monetary policy to maintain low inflation

- To achieve a low inflation target the central bank must tighten monetary policy by increasing interest rates and shifting the aggregate demand curve to the left. In the short run, the main effects of an anti-inflationary policy may be lower output and higher unemployment.
- In the long run, output will revert to its full employment or potential level. The speed of adjustment to long-run equilibrium depends on how fast inflationary expectations are revised to reflect the lower inflationary environment.
- Positive demand shocks lead to an expansionary gap and higher inflation in the short run. In the long run, the economy returns to its potential output level but at a higher inflation rate. However, tighter monetary policy can offset the inflationary effects of demand shocks resulting in a lower equilibrium inflation rate.
- Adverse supply shocks lead to a recessionary gap and higher inflation in the short run. In the long run, the recessionary gap lowers inflationary expectations and the economy returns to its potential output level but at the initial inflation rate.
- If the central bank accommodates an adverse supply shock by a policy of monetary expansion, the equilibrium inflation rate will increase without any gain in terms of higher output.
- In the long run, monetary policy can only control the equilibrium rate of inflation.

Responding to real shocks

A real shock is a shock that leads to a change in long-run potential output. As explained in Chapter 26, an increase in oil and other energy prices may cause firms to scrap energy-inefficient equipment, leading to a lower capital stock, which reduces the economy's productive capacity and its potential output $Y^{\star}$. How should monetary policy respond to an adverse real shock? Should the central bank ease or tighten policy, or should it take a 'do-nothing' approach. Example 27.4 explores these alternatives.

Example 27.4 Responding to a real shock to potential output

Figure 27.5 illustrates the effect of a real shock to potential output.

In Figure 27.5 the economy is in long-run equilibrium at point A. As we saw in Chapter 26 (Figure 26.17), a decline in potential output, from $Y^\star$ to $Y^{\star\prime}$, creates an expansionary gap leading to higher expected inflation, which shifts the short-run aggregate supply curve upwards from $SRAS_1$ to $SRAS_2$. If the central bank takes a 'do-nothing' approach, the new long-run equilibrium is reached at point B, where actual output equals the new, lower level of potential output, $Y^{\star\prime}$, and inflation has risen to π_2. However, suppose the central bank announces that it is going to maintain inflation at π_1, and tightens monetary policy accordingly by increasing interest rates and shifting the aggregate demand curve to the left to AD_2 in Figure 27.5. Provided that the bank's announcement is credible, inflationary expectations will not be revised upwards but the $SRAS$ curve will shift to the left to $SRAS_3$ because firms now face higher relative energy prices and their profit-maximising output will be lower at any given rate of inflation. Hence the new long-run equilibrium will be at point C with $Y = Y^{\star\prime}$ and π_1. Once again we have seen that, in the long run, monetary policy can determine the equilibrium inflation rate but not the equilibrium level of output.

What if the central bank responds to a shock to potential output by easing policy and reducing interest rates? The consequences of this approach are illustrated by Figure 27.6.

Figure 27.6 is similar to Figure 27.5 except that in this case the bank cuts interest rates, which stimulates planned expenditures and shifts the aggregate demand curve

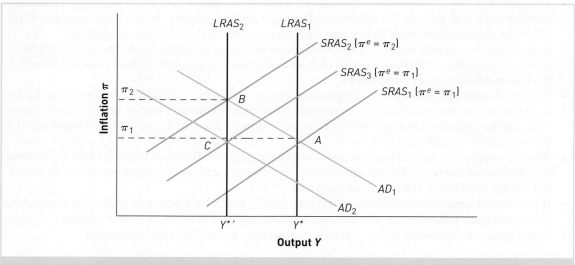

Figure 27.5 Responding to a Real Shock. The economy is in long-run equilibrium at point A when a decline in potential output, from Y^* to $Y^{*\prime}$, creates an expansionary gap. Expected inflation is revised upwards and the short-run aggregate supply line shifts upwards from $SRAS_1$ to $SRAS_2$. If the central bank takes no action, the new long-run equilibrium is reached at point B, where actual output equals the new, lower level of potential output, $Y^{*\prime}$, and inflation has risen to π_2. If the bank tightens policy, the AD curve shifts to the left to AD_2 lowering actual and expected inflation, which shifts the $SRAS$ curve to the right, giving a new long-run equilibrium at point C with inflation at π_1.

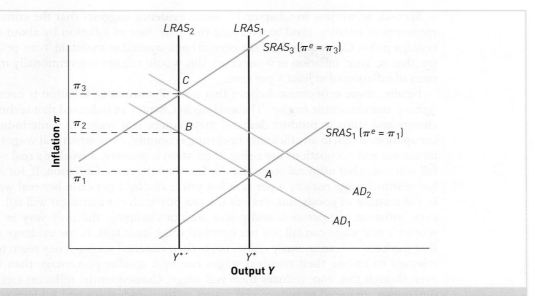

Figure 27.6 Accommodating a Real Shock. The economy is in long-run equilibrium at point *A* when a decline in potential output, from *Y** to *Y*'*, creates an expansionary gap. Expected inflation is revised upwards and the short-run aggregate supply line shifts upwards from *SRAS*₁ to *SRAS*₂. If the central bank takes no action, the new long-run equilibrium is reached at point *B*, where actual output equals the new, lower level of potential output, *Y*'*, and inflation has risen to π_2. If the bank eases policy, the *AD* curve shifts to the right to *AD*₂ increasing the expansionary gap and both actual and expected inflation, which shifts the *SRAS* curve further to the left giving a new long-run equilibrium at point *C* with inflation at π_3.

to the *right*. However, as aggregate demand has increased, the expansionary gap will widen leading to a greater upward revision in expected inflation and a greater leftward shift in the *SRAS* curve. In Figure 27.6 the final equilibrium is at point *C* with inflation at π_3, which is greater than the inflation rate that would prevail if the bank took a 'do-nothing' approach, π_2.

Should the inflation target be zero?

Because central banks often state that they are in favour of stable prices, it would seem that the logical long-run target for inflation is 0 per cent. However, most economists believe that an inflation target of zero is too low, and central banks that announce an explicit inflation target usually choose values that are low but above zero. Why shouldn't the inflation target be zero?

Several reasons have been offered. First, because hitting the target at all times is impossible in practice, an inflation target of 0 per cent increases the risk that the economy will experience periods of deflation (negative inflation). The deflationary experiences of industrialised economies in the 1930s and, more recently, in Japan (see Chapter 17), illustrate that deflation can be difficult to stop once it starts, and can lead to painful and persistent declines in real GDP, especially if people expect it to continue. Many policy makers prefer to reduce the risk of deflation by choosing an inflation target above 0 per cent.

Second, as we saw in Chapter 17, some evidence suggests that the conventional measures of inflation tend to overstate the 'true' rate of inflation by about one percentage point. Consequently, if the central bank wanted to maintain 'true' price stability (that is, 'true' inflation of 0 per cent), this would require conventionally measured rates of inflation of at least 1 per cent.

Finally, some economists believe that a small amount of inflation is necessary to 'grease' our economic engine. The analysis in Chapter 18 indicated that technological change and shifts in product demand may require real wages in some industries or occupations to fall in an efficiently operating economy, even when real wages in other industries and occupations are rising. If inflation is positive, a worker's real wage will fall whenever her nominal wage rises by less than the rate of inflation. If, for example, her nominal wage rises by 4 per cent but prices rise by 5 per cent, her real wage (that is, the amount of goods and services she can buy with her earnings) will fall. If, however, inflation is 0 per cent and prices are not changing, the only way in which a worker's real wage can fall is if her nominal wage itself falls. Some evidence suggests that workers will strenuously resist cuts in their nominal wages. They seem to be less resistant to having their nominal wages rise by a smaller percentage than inflation even though this, too, reduces their real wage. Consequently, inflation can provide the 'grease' required to reduce real wages in some industries and achieve economic efficiency. Critics of the 'grease' theory, however, argue that workers will become less resistant to nominal wage cuts at very low or zero rates of inflation. In a low-inflation environment, nominal wage cuts would, of necessity, be more common and workers would get used to the idea.

Should the central bank announce a numerical inflation target?

Some economists believe that expectations are more firmly anchored and the central bank is perceived as more credible in those countries in which the central bank announces an explicit numerical target for inflation. We have already introduced the idea of a target rate of inflation in our discussion of the monetary policy rule. Generally speaking, central banks must have an idea of the inflation rate they would like to achieve in order to make sensible policy. The more controversial question is whether central banks should announce their target inflation rate to the public. Proponents argue that announcing a numerical target for long-run inflation, and then sticking to it, will increase credibility and better anchor inflation expectations.

Many central banks publicly announce their inflation target. The Bank of Canada, for example, began announcing its inflation target in 1991. Since 1995, that target has been 2 per cent. In March 2008, the Bank of England's inflation target was 2 per cent, and the Central Bank of Brazil's target was 4.5 per cent. For the European Central Bank the target rate is below but close to 2 per cent over the medium term. Other central banks provide a range for their target rather than, or in addition to, a single number. The Bank of Israel and the Reserve Bank of New Zealand, for example, both had a 1–3 per cent target range as of March 2008; in Chile the range was 2–4 per cent. Central banks that announce their targets typically provide additional information to the public. This information may include their forecasts of inflation, real GDP and other variables, as well as some discussion of the specific policies that will be needed to meet their targets. For example, the Bank of England's *Quarterly Inflation Report* explains the Bank's inflation forecast, its monetary policy actions and how these actions can achieve the target rate of inflation. Advocates believe that announcing inflation targets and accompanying them with supporting information enhances the credibility of the central bank and reduces uncertainty among households and firms. This helps to anchor inflationary expectations, keep inflation low and maintain full employment. Note that it makes sense for a central bank to announce a long-run inflation target, in that the central bank is able to control the rate of inflation in the long run. It would *not* make sense for a central bank to announce a long-run target for real GDP or employment because these variables are determined by a host of factors (such as productivity and the supply of labour) that are not under the control of the central bank.

Once an inflation target is announced, the central bank may choose to adhere to it strictly, or it may be more flexible. A central bank that sets a strict target tries to meet the target all the time without regard for the consequences for output. As we have seen, this policy keeps output at potential when the economy is beset by spending shocks, but it may result in a recession if the central bank acts to eliminate even the initial surge in inflation following a shock to aggregate supply such as an inflation shock. In practice, virtually all central banks that announce an inflation target are flexible inflation targeters – they try to hit their inflation target in the long run or on average over a long period while responding to short-term shocks to aggregate supply in a way that takes account of both output gaps and inflation. In these cases, the announced inflation targets correspond to the target inflation rate in the monetary policy rule. Advocates of announcing explicit numerical targets believe that this practice reduces uncertainty in financial markets and among the public. Reduced uncertainty allows people to plan more effectively, save the resources used to protect themselves from unexpected inflation, and improve market functioning. By putting the prestige of the central bank behind its commitment to meet the target, the advocates also believe that explicit inflation targets enhance the central bank's credibility and anchor inflation expectations. Supporters of inflation targets emphasise that it has been successful in both developing and industrialised countries. They believe that explicit targets in Brazil, Chile, Mexico and Peru are one important reason why the central banks in nine of the most populous Latin American countries were able to reduce their inflation rates from 160 per cent per year in the 1980s and 235 per cent during the first half of the 1990s to only 13 per cent per year in 1995–1999 and less than 8 per cent in the period 2000–2004.[1] Those central banks, such as the Federal Reserve, that do not announce an explicit target to the public still may have a target or range in mind when making policy. Instead of announcing a specific number to the public, however, these banks typically state that they are interested in keeping inflation low, without defining exactly what that means. Proponents of this approach believe that a system of publicly announced targets is too rigid and may reduce the flexibility of the central bank to deal with unexpected circumstances. They worry that having an explicit inflation target may lead the central bank to pay too much attention to inflation and not enough attention to stabilising output and maintaining full employment. Finally, opponents of explicit inflation targeting for the United States emphasise that the Fed has achieved good results without having a publicly announced target. They suggest following the adage, 'if it's not broke, don't fix it'.

---

1 Bernanke (2005).

Summary

- This chapter has looked at ways in which monetary policy can be used to control the rate of inflation. The central bank can achieve a lower target rate of inflation by shifting its reaction function upwards and increasing the rate of interest. In the short run this results in lower aggregate expenditure, which shifts the aggregate demand curve to the left, opening a recessionary gap leading to lower inflation and a downward revision in inflationary expectations, which shifts the short-run aggregate supply curve to the right, closing the recessionary gap and establishing a lower equilibrium inflation rate.

- In the short run, the main effects of an anti-inflationary policy may be reduced output and higher unemployment, as the economy experiences a recessionary gap. These short-run costs of *disinflation* must be balanced against the long-run benefits of a lower rate of inflation. Over time, output and employment will return to normal levels and inflation declines. Both the extent and persistence of these short-run costs may be determined by the speed with which *inflationary expectations* are revised.

- The effectiveness of an anti-inflationary monetary policy is related to the *credibility* the public attaches to central bank policy announcements. If, on its past record, the central bank is deemed highly credible then the public will believe that the bank will deliver its target inflation rate and inflationary expectations will be revised rapidly.

- Demand and supply shocks may cause the actual inflation rate to diverge from the central bank's target rate.

- A positive demand shock shifts the aggregate demand curve to the right, opening an expansionary gap leading to higher inflation. If the central bank does not change its policy, expected inflation will be revised upwards, shifting the short-run aggregate supply curve to the left resulting in a higher long-run equilibrium rate of inflation. The central bank can prevent this by increasing interest rates (upward shift in its reaction function) and shifting the aggregate demand curve back to the left.

- An adverse supply shock shifts the short-run aggregate supply curve to the left, opening a recessionary gap leading to lower inflation. If the central bank does not change its policy expected inflation will be revised downwards, shifting the short-run aggregate supply curve back to the right and re-establishing the initial long-run equilibrium rate of inflation. If the central bank accommodates the shock by monetary expansion the equilibrium inflation rate will increase without any compensating gain in terms of a permanent increase in output.

- An adverse shock to potential output opens an expansionary gap and results in higher equilibrium inflation unless the central bank closes the gap by tighter monetary policy.

- In the long run, monetary policy can determine the equilibrium rate of inflation. It cannot determine long-run output, which following a shock will revert to its potential level $Y^\star$. Monetary policy can, however, influence the speed with which the economy adjusts to a new long-run equilibrium.

Review questions

1. Suppose the central bank lowers its target inflation rate. How will this decision affect inflation and output in the short and long run?

2. What do you understand by 'central bank credibility'? What role might credibility play in helping the central bank achieve a lower target rate of inflation?

3. What, if any, are the benefits of having an independent central bank?

4. If the central bank's sole policy objective is to maintain its target inflation rate, how might it react to (a) a rise in net exports, and (b) an increase in energy prices?

5. How should the central bank react to a fall in the economy's potential output?

6. Do you agree with the following statement? 'In the long run, monetary policy can determine the equilibrium inflation rate but not the equilibrium level of output.' Explain.

Problems

1. Starting from a position of long-run equilibrium, the central bank decides to raise its target inflation rate. Use the IS-LM and *AD–AS* models to explain:

    a. how the bank can achieve the new target inflation rate

    b. the adjustment of inflation and output in the short and long run.

2. Starting from a position of long-run equilibrium, the economy experiences a favourable supply shock such as a fall in raw material prices. Use an *AD–AS* model to explain the short- and long-run adjustment of output and inflation if:

    a. the central bank accommodates the shock

    b. the central bank does not accommodate the shock.

3. Draw diagrams to illustrate the movements, if any, of the IS and LM curves in your answers to Problem 2.

4. Suppose that several governments of large countries in the Eurozone decide to cut taxes. Use an *AD–AS* diagram to illustrate how this might impact on Eurozone inflation. If the ECB maintains its target inflation rate how might inflation and output adjust in the long run?

5. Suppose the economy is initially in long-run equilibrium. Due to a fall in house prices consumers decide to consume less at each level of income. Explain the short- and long-run adjustment of inflation and output if:

    a. the central bank maintains its existing target inflation rate

    b. the central bank reduces its target inflation rate.

6. What are the long-run consequences for inflation if the central bank decides to accommodate an adverse shock to potential output?

References

Bernanke, B. (2005) 'Inflation in Latin America: a new era?', 11 February (http://www.federalreserve.gov/boarddocs/speeches/2005/20050211/default.htm).

To help you grasp the key concepts of this chapter check out the extra resources posted on the Online Learning Centre. There are chapter summaries, self-test questions, an interactive graphing tool, weblinks and a glossary, all for free!

Visit the Online Learning Centre at: www.mcgraw-hill.co.uk/textbooks/mcdowell for information on accessing all of these resources.

Part 8
The International Economy

One of the defining recent economic trends is the 'globalisation' of national economies. Since the mid-1980s, the value of international trade has increased at nearly twice the rate of world GDP, and the volume of international financial transactions has expanded at many times that rate. From a long-run perspective, the rapidly increasing integration of national economies we see today is not unprecedented: before the First World War, Great Britain was the centre of an international economic system that was in many ways nearly as 'globalised' as our own, with extensive international trade and lending. But even the most far-seeing nineteenth-century merchant or banker would be astonished by the sense of *immediacy* that recent revolutionary changes in communications and transportation have imparted to international economic relations. For example, teleconferencing and the internet now permit people on opposite sides of the globe to conduct 'face-to-face' business negotiations and transactions.

We have introduced international dimensions of the economy at several points in this book already. For example, in Chapter 15 we drew attention to the increasing economic interdependence among nations, and stressed the importance of this trend for the European Union, which now consists of 27 countries. Working together these countries have progressively dismantled barriers to trade and formed a unified trading bloc called the European single market. As explained in Chapter 22 , many of these countries have also eliminated their national currencies and adopted the euro as their common currency, with responsibility for monetary policy transferred from national central banks (NCBs) to the European Central Bank (ECB). Hence, while globalisation has increased interdependence between Europe and other regions, such as North America and Asia, the process of economic integration has also increased interdependence among European economies.

In Part 8 we shall look at the monetary aspects of this integration process. Chapter 28 focuses on a particularly important variable: the *exchange rate*, or the price of one currency in terms of another. The exchange rate plays a key role in determining *patterns of trade* and has important implications for the effectiveness of macroeconomic policies. Understanding what the exchange rate is, how it is determined and how it can – or, in some cases, cannot – be controlled will help us to understand why some European countries have decided to adopt a single currency that completely eliminates exchange rates between them.

28

Exchange Rates, Capital Flows and the Balance of Payments

Dealing with exchange rates and different currencies can be confusing. A New York couple approaching retirement decide to buy a dream holiday home in Europe. After extensive research on the internet they whittle the options down to two houses, one in the west of Ireland and one in the Scottish highlands. After visiting both properties they cannot decide which they prefer. 'It's easy,' said the wife, 'let's choose the cheapest.' Her husband agrees and checks the prices. The Irish property is on offer at 500,000 euros and the Scottish at 450,000 pounds. Finding the comparison difficult the husband says, 'Which is the cheapest in real money?' (by which he means the American dollar). 'I haven't a clue,' replies the wife, 'but I have just read that since our trip the dollar has appreciated against the euro and the pound has depreciated against the dollar, what does that mean?' To which her husband replies, 'It means we are moving to Florida!'

Regardless of whether they are interested in a foreign property, negotiating a business deal or simply chilling out in another country, dealing with unfamiliar currencies is a problem every international traveller faces. These problems can be further complicated by the fact that *exchange rates* may change unpredictably. Thus the number of Russian rubles, Japanese yen, Australian dollars or US dollars that one euro can buy may vary over time, sometimes quite a lot.

The economic consequences of variable exchange rates are much broader than their impact on travel and tourism. For example, the competitiveness of European exports depends in part on the prices of European goods in terms of foreign currencies, which in turn depend on the *exchange rate* between the euro and those currencies. Likewise, the prices Europeans pay for imported goods depend in part on the value of their currency relative to the currencies of the countries that produce those goods. Exchange rates also affect the value of financial investments made across national borders. For countries that are heavily dependent on trade and international capital flows – the majority of the world's nations and certainly most European countries – fluctuations in the exchange rate may have a significant economic impact.

This chapter discusses exchange rates and the role they play in open economies. We will start by distinguishing between the *nominal exchange rate* – the rate at which one national currency trades for another – and the *real exchange rate* – the rate at which one country's goods trade for another's. We shall show how exchange rates affect the prices of exports and imports, and thus the pattern of trade.

Next we shall turn to the question of how exchange rates are determined. Exchange rates may be divided into two broad categories, flexible and fixed. The value of a *flexible* exchange rate is determined freely in the market for national currencies, known as the *foreign exchange market*. Flexible exchange rates vary continually with changes in the supply of and demand for national currencies. In contrast, the value of a *fixed* exchange rate is set by the government at a constant level.

Although most large industrial countries have a flexible exchange rate, many small and developing economies fix their exchange rates, so we shall consider the case of fixed exchange rates as well. We shall explain first how a country's government (usually, its central bank) goes about maintaining a fixed exchange rate at the officially determined level. Though fixing the exchange rate generally reduces day-to-day fluctuations in the value of a nation's currency, we shall see that, at times, a fixed exchange rate can become severely unstable, with potentially serious economic consequences. We shall also see that the choice of exchange rate regime has important implications for the effectiveness of monetary and fiscal policies as a means to close output gaps.

Exchange rates

The economic benefits of trade between countries in goods, services and assets are similar to the benefits of trade within a country. In both cases, trade in goods and services permits greater specialisation and efficiency, whereas trade in assets allows financial investors to earn higher returns while providing funds for worthwhile capital projects. However, there is a difference between the two cases, which is that trade in goods, services and assets *within* a country normally involves a single currency – euros, sterling, dollars, yen or whatever the country's official form of money happens to be – whereas trade *between* nations usually involves dealing in different currencies. So, for example, if a Dutch resident wants to purchase an automobile manufactured in South Korea, she (or, more likely, the automobile importer) must first trade euros for the Korean currency, called the won. The Korean car manufacturer is then paid in won. Similarly, a British pension fund wishing to purchase shares in an American company (a US dollar financial asset) must first trade sterling for dollars and then use the dollars to purchase the shares. The price the Dutch importer or the British pension fund must pay for won or dollars is known as the exchange rate. When discussing exchange rates we must take care to distinguish between the nominal exchange rate and the real exchange rate.

Nominal exchange rates

nominal exchange rate the rate, or price, at which two currencies can be traded for each other

The **nominal exchange rate** is simply the price of one currency in terms of another currency, and is normally expressed as the amount of 'foreign' currency that can be bought with one unit of the 'domestic' currency.

For example, suppose we treat the euro as the domestic currency and sterling as the foreign currency. Then if €1 can be exchanged for £0.80 the nominal exchange rate between the euro and pound is 0.80 pounds per euro. Alternatively, if we think of sterling as the domestic currency we could express the same nominal exchange rate as 1.25 euros per pound (1.25 = 1/0.8). Table 28.1 gives nominal exchange rates between the euro and six other currencies, as published by the ECB on 8 August 2008.

Country	Foreign currency/euro (1)	Euro/foreign currency (2)
United States (dollar)	1.5074	0.6634
United Kingdom (pound)	0.7841	1.2753
Japan (yen)	165.61	0.0060
Denmark (krone)	7.4601	0.1340
Sweden (krona)	9.3945	0.1064
Poland (zloty)	3.2645	0.3063

Table 28.1 **Nominal Exchange Rates for the Euro, 8 August 2008**
Source: ECB (www.ecb.int).

Table 28.1 shows that exchange rates can be expressed either as the amount of foreign currency needed to purchase one euro (column (1)) or as the number of euros needed to purchase one unit of the foreign currency (column (2)). These two ways of expressing the exchange rate are equivalent: each is the *reciprocal* of the other. For example, on 8 August 2008, the exchange rate between the euro and the dollar could have been expressed either as 1.5074 dollars per euro or as 0.6634 euros per dollar, where $0.6634 = 1/1.5074$.

Example 28.1 Nominal exchange rates

Based on Table 28.1, find the exchange rate between the British and American currencies. Express the exchange rate in both dollars per pound and pounds per dollar.

From Table 28.1, we see that 0.7841 pounds will buy one euro, and that 1.5074 dollars will also buy one euro. Therefore 0.7841 pounds and 1.5074 dollars are equal in value:

$$£0.7841 = \$1.5074$$

Dividing both sides of this equation by 0.7841 we get

$$£1 = \$1.9224$$

In other words, the British–American exchange rate can be expressed as 1.9224 dollars per pound. Alternatively, dividing by 1.5074 gives

$$\$1 = £0.5202$$

That is, one dollar buys 0.5202 pounds.

Figure 28.1 shows the nominal exchange rates for the euro against the US dollar and the British pound from the euro's launch in 1999 to the end of 2007. The exchange rate is measured as the number of dollars or pounds per euro. You can see from Figure 28.1 that the euro's value fluctuated over these eight years. Starting from a value of approximately 1.16 dollars per euro in January 1999 the exchange rate fell consistently, reaching a low of just over 0.80 dollars per euro in early 2002. However, since then the exchange rate has increased

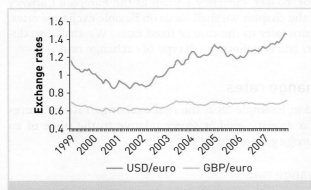

Figure 28.1 Euro Nominal Exchange Rates. US dollars and British pounds per euro, January 1999 to December 2007.

appreciation an increase in the value of a currency relative to other currencies

depreciation a decrease in the value of a currency relative to other currencies

steadily to over 1.50 dollars per euro by mid-2008. (If you are interested in more recent changes, use an online source such as ECB, at www.ecb.int, or Pacific Exchange Rate Service, at http://fx.sauder.ubc.ca, to check movements in exchange rates.)

An increase in the value of a currency relative to other currencies is known as **appreciation**; a decline in the value of a currency relative to other currencies is called **depreciation**. As can be seen from Figure 28.1 the euro depreciated against the dollar in 1999 and 2001, and has appreciated since 2002. We shall discuss the reasons a currency may appreciate or depreciate later in this chapter.

Flexible versus fixed exchange rates

flexible (floating) exchange rate an exchange rate whose value is not officially fixed but varies according to the supply of and demand for the currency in the foreign exchange market

foreign exchange market the market on which currencies of various nations are traded for one another

fixed exchange rate an exchange rate whose value is set by official government policy

As we saw in Figure 28.1, the exchange rate is not constant but varies continually. Indeed, changes in the exchange rates between currencies occur daily, hourly and even minute by minute. Such fluctuations in the value of a currency are normal for countries such as the United Kingdom, the United States and the Eurosystem, which have a **flexible** or **floating exchange rate**. When exchange rates are flexible the value of a currency varies according to the supply of and demand for the currency in the **foreign exchange market** – the market on which currencies of various nations are traded for one another. We shall discuss the factors that determine the supply of and demand for currencies shortly.

Some countries do not allow their currency values to vary with market conditions but instead maintain a **fixed exchange rate**. The value of a fixed exchange rate is set by official government policy. A government that establishes a fixed exchange rate typically determines the exchange rate's value independently, but sometimes exchange rates are set according to an agreement among a number of governments. Between the end of the Second World War and the early 1970s most of the world's currencies operated within the *Bretton Woods* exchange rate system, which required a fixed value against the US dollar. From 1979 to 1999 countries in the European Union attempted to fix the value of their currencies against a composite or 'basket' currency known as the *European Currency Unit*, or ECU. In the next part of the chapter we shall focus on flexible exchange rates, but shall return later to the case of fixed rates. We shall also discuss the costs and benefits of each type of exchange rate.

real exchange rate the price of the average domestic good or service *relative* to the price of the average foreign good or service, when prices are expressed in terms of a common currency

Real exchange rates

As explained in Example 28.2, the **real exchange rate** measures the price of a *domestic good or service* relative to the price of an equivalent *foreign good or service*.

Example 28.2 The real exchange rate

Suppose an Irish-made computer costs €1,500 and an equivalent British-made computer costs £1,000. Which computer is the cheapest?

As the computers are priced in different currencies we cannot make a direct comparison to decide which is the cheapest. To convert the prices to the same currency we can use the nominal exchange rate. For example, if Ireland is the domestic country and €1 currently buys £0.8 then the price of the British computer is $1{,}000/0.8 = €1{,}250$ and the real exchange rate is just the price of the Irish computer relative to the price of the British computer when both prices are measured in euros. That is, $1{,}500/1{,}200 = 1.2$, indicating that the Irish computer is 20 per cent more expensive. Alternatively, we could convert the Irish price into sterling and compare it to the British price. At a nominal exchange rate of 0.8 pounds per euro, €1,500 is equivalent to £1,200 ($1{,}500 \times 0.8$) and the real exchange rate is $1{,}200/1{,}000 = 1.20$ as before.

More generally if we denote the nominal exchange rate as e (pounds per euro), the domestic price level as P (in euros) and the foreign price as P^f (in pounds) then, as shown in Example 28.2, the real exchange rate can be expressed as:

$$\frac{P}{P^f/e} \quad \text{or} \quad \frac{eP}{P^f} \tag{28.1}$$

The real exchange rate has important implications for a country's competitiveness. In Example 28.2 the Irish-made computer is 20 per cent dearer than the British computer, putting Irish manufacturers at a competitive disadvantage on export markets. Likewise, the higher the real exchange rate the greater the incentive for Irish firms and households to import computers from the UK. Conversely, if the real exchange rate is low, then the home country will find it easier to export while domestic residents will buy fewer imports. Hence, other things being equal, we would expect net exports to be lower when the real exchange rate is relatively high but to increase as the real exchange rate falls.

A decrease in the real exchange rate is known as a *real depreciation of the domestic currency*. As a lower real exchange rate makes domestic goods more competitive relative to foreign goods, a real depreciation will, other things being equal, lead to an increase in net exports. Conversely, an increase in the real exchange rate is known as a *real appreciation of the domestic currency*. As a higher real exchange rate makes domestic goods less competitive relative to foreign goods, a real appreciation will, other things being equal, lead to a decline in net exports.

Exercise 28.1 In 1999 the average sterling–euro exchange rate was €1 = £0.6587 and in 2007 the average rate was €1 = £0.6843. Based on 2005 = 100 the Harmonised Consumer Price Index (*HCPI*) for the Eurosystem was 87.85 in 1999 and 104.4 in 2007. The equivalent UK price index rose from 92.3 to 104.7 over the same period. Has the euro experienced a real depreciation or a real appreciation against sterling over this period?

Economic naturalist 28.1 Does a strong currency imply a strong economy?

Politicians and the public sometimes take pride in the fact that their national currency is 'strong', meaning that its value in terms of other currencies is high or rising. Likewise, policy makers sometimes view a depreciating ('weak') currency as a sign of economic failure. Does a strong currency necessarily imply a strong economy?

Contrary to popular impression, there is no simple connection between the strength of a country's currency and the strength of its economy. For example, Figure 28.1 shows that the value of the euro relative to the US dollar rose steadily throughout most of 2002 and 2003. However, in both years, US economic growth exceeded growth in the Eurosystem. In 2003, for example, real US GDP increased by 3.1 per cent compared with only 0.4 per cent in the Eurosystem. The following sections will analyse how exchange rates are determined, and why they change over time.

RECAP Exchange rates

- The *nominal exchange rate* between two currencies is the rate at which the currencies can be traded for each other. More precisely, the nominal exchange rate *e* for any given country is the number of units of foreign currency that can be bought for one unit of the domestic currency.
- An *appreciation* is an increase in the value of a currency relative to other currencies (a rise in *e*); a *depreciation* is a decline in a currency's value (a fall in *e*).
- An exchange rate can be either *flexible* – meaning that it varies freely according to supply of and demand for the currency in the foreign exchange market – or *fixed*, meaning that its value is established by official government policy.
- The *real exchange rate* is the price of the average domestic good or service relative to the price of the average foreign good or service, when prices are expressed in terms of a common currency. A useful formula for the real exchange rate is *eP*/*Pf*, where *e* is the nominal exchange rate, *P* is the domestic price level, and *Pf* is the foreign price level.
- An *increase* in the real exchange rate implies that domestic goods are becoming more expensive relative to foreign goods, which tends to reduce exports and stimulate imports. Conversely, a *decline* in the real exchange rate tends to increase net exports.

Determination of the nominal exchange rate

Countries that have flexible exchange rates, such as the United Kingdom, the United States and those that use the euro as their common currency, see the international values of their currencies change continually. What determines the value of the nominal exchange rate at any point in time? In this section, we shall try to answer this basic economic question. Again, our focus for the moment is on flexible exchange rates, whose values are determined by the foreign exchange market. Later in the chapter, we shall discuss the case of fixed exchange rates.

Determination of the exchange rate: a supply and demand analysis

In this section, we shall analyse the behaviour of nominal exchange rates by using a simple demand and supply model. However, in this case the market is the *foreign exchange market*, which, as we have seen, is a market on which different currencies (euros, dollars, sterling, yen, etc.) are traded for one another and the price is the nominal exchange rate or the value of one currency in terms of another. To focus our attention on Europe we shall concentrate on the market for euros. For convenience we shall use the terms 'Eurosystem' and 'Europe' as meaning the same thing, even though many European countries do not use the euro as their currency. This is a simplifying assumption that enables us to focus on the fundamentals of the foreign exchange market. As we shall see, euros are demanded in the foreign exchange market by foreigners who seek to purchase European goods and assets, and are supplied by European residents who need foreign currencies to buy foreign goods and assets. The *equilibrium exchange rate* is the value of the euro that equates the number of euros supplied and demanded in the foreign exchange market. Our aim is to analyse the supply of and demand for euros, and thus the euro exchange rate.

The supply of euros

Anyone who holds euros – from an international bank to a Russian citizen whose euros are buried in the back garden – is a potential *supplier of euros* to the foreign exchange market. In practice, however, the principal suppliers of euros to the foreign exchange market are European households and firms. Why would a European household or firm want to supply euros in exchange for foreign currency? There are two major reasons. First, a European household or firm may need foreign currency to *purchase foreign goods or services*. For example, a Dutch automobile importer may need yen to purchase Japanese cars, or an Italian tourist may need dollars to make purchases in New York. In each case the European household or firm must supply euros to buy the foreign currency. Second, a European household or firm may need foreign currency to *purchase foreign assets*. For example, an Irish pension fund may wish to acquire shares issued by American companies. Because American assets are normally priced in dollars, the pension fund will need to trade euros for dollars to acquire these assets.

The supply of euros to the foreign exchange market is illustrated in Figure 28.2. We shall focus on the market in which euros are traded for US dollars, but bear in mind that similar markets exist for every other pair of traded currencies. The vertical axis of Figure 28.2 shows the dollar–euro exchange rate as measured by the number of dollars that can be purchased with each euro. The horizontal axis shows the number of euros being traded in the market.

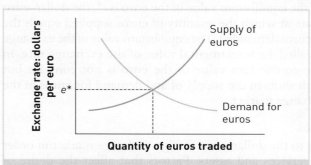

Figure 28.2 The Supply and Demand for Euros in the Dollar–Euro Market. The supply of euros is upward-sloping because an increase in the number of dollars offered for each euro makes US goods, services and assets more attractive to European buyers. Similarly, the demand for euros is downward-sloping because holders of dollars will be less willing to buy euros the more expensive they are in terms of dollars. The equilibrium rate e*, also called the *fundamental value of the exchange rate*, equates the quantities of euros supplied and demanded.

Note that the supply curve for euros is *upward-sloping*. In other words, the more dollars each euro can buy, the more euros people are willing to supply to the foreign exchange market. Why? At given prices for American goods, services and assets, the more dollars a euro can buy, the cheaper those goods, services and assets will be in euro terms. For example, if a computer game costs $55 in the United States, and a euro can buy $1.00, the euro price of the computer game will be €55. However, if a euro can buy $1.10, then the euro price of the same computer game will be €50 (or $55/$1.10). Assuming that lower euro prices will induce Europeans to increase their expenditures on American goods, services and assets, a higher dollar–euro exchange rate will increase the supply of euros to the foreign exchange market. Thus the supply curve for euros is upward-sloping.

The demand for euros

In the dollar–euro foreign exchange market, demanders of euros are those who wish to acquire euros in exchange for dollars. Most demanders of euros in the dollar–euro market are American households and firms, although anyone who happens to hold dollars is free to trade them for euros. Why demand euros? The reasons for acquiring euros are analogous to those for acquiring dollars. First, households and firms that hold dollars will demand euros so that they can *purchase European goods and services*. For example, an American importer who wants to purchase French wine needs euros to pay the French exporter, and an American student studying in a European university must pay tuition fees in euros. The importer or the student can acquire the necessary euros only by offering dollars in exchange. Second, households and firms demand euros in order to *purchase European assets*. The purchase of a French factory by an American company, and the acquisition of German bonds by an American bank are two examples.

The demand for euros is represented by the *downward-sloping* curve in Figure 28.2. The curve slopes downwards because the more dollars an American citizen must pay to acquire a euro, the less attractive European goods, services and assets will be. Hence the demand for euros will be low when euros are expensive in terms of dollars and high when euros are cheap in terms of dollars.

The equilibrium value of the euro

As mentioned earlier, the Eurosystem maintains a flexible, or floating, exchange rate, which means that the value of the dollar–euro exchange rate is determined by the forces of supply and demand in the foreign exchange market. In Figure 28.2 the equilibrium value of the euro is $e^\star$, the dollar–euro exchange rate at which the quantity of euros supplied equals the quantity of euros demanded. The equilibrium value of the exchange rate is also called the **fundamental value of the exchange rate**. In general, the equilibrium value of the euro is not constant but changes with shifts in the supply of and demand for euros in the foreign exchange market.

fundamental value of the exchange rate (or equilibrium exchange rate) the exchange rate that equates the quantities of the currency supplied and demanded in the foreign exchange market

Changes in the supply of euros

Recall that people supply euros to the dollar–euro foreign exchange market in order to purchase American goods, services and assets. Factors that affect the desire of European households and firms to acquire American goods, services and assets will therefore affect the supply of euros to the foreign exchange market. Some factors that will *increase* the supply of euros, shifting the supply curve for euros to the right, include the following.

- An *increased preference for American goods*. For example, suppose that Californian wine becomes more popular in Europe. To acquire the dollars needed to buy more Californian wine, European wine importers will increase their supply of euros to the foreign exchange market.
- An *increase in European real GDP*. An increase in European real GDP will raise the incomes of Europeans, allowing them to consume more goods and services (recall the *consumption function*, introduced in Chapter 21). Some part of this increase in consumption will take the form of goods imported from the United States. To buy more American goods, Europeans will supply more euros to acquire the necessary dollars.
- An *increase in the interest rate on American assets*. Recall that European households and firms acquire dollars in order to purchase American assets as well as goods and services. Other factors, such as risk, held constant, the higher the interest rate paid by American assets, the more American assets Europeans will choose to hold. To purchase additional American assets, European households and firms will supply more euros to the foreign exchange market.

Conversely, reduced demand for American goods, a lower European GDP or a lower interest rate on American assets will *reduce* the number of dollars Europeans need, in turn reducing their supply of euros to the foreign exchange market and shifting the supply curve for euros to the left. Of course, any shift in the supply curve for euros will affect the equilibrium exchange rate, as Example 28.3 shows.

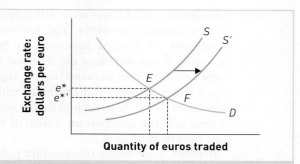

Figure 28.3 An Increase in the Supply of Euros Lowers the Value of the Euro. To buy more American computer games Europeans must supply more euros to the foreign exchange market to acquire the dollars they need to buy the games. The supply curve for euros shifts from S to S', lowering the equilibrium value of the euro from e^* to $e^{*'}$.

Example 28.3 Computer games, the euro and the dollar

Suppose American firms come to dominate the computer game market, with games that are more exciting and realistic than those produced in Europe. All else being equal, how will this change affect the relative value of the euro and the dollar?

The increased quality of American computer games will increase the demand for the games in Europe. To acquire the dollars necessary to buy more American computer games, European importers will supply more euros to the foreign exchange market. As Figure 28.3 shows, the increased supply of euros shifts the supply curve to the right and reduces the equilibrium value of the euro: in other words, the euro will depreciate against the dollar. At the same time, the value of the dollar will appreciate against the euro: a given number of dollars will buy more euros than it did before.

Exercise 28.2 The United States goes into a recession, and real GDP falls. All else being equal, how is this economic weakness likely to affect the value of the euro?

Changes in the demand for euros

The factors that can cause a change in the demand for euros in the foreign exchange market, and thus a shift of the euro demand curve, are analogous to the factors that affect the supply of euros. Factors that will *increase* the demand for euros include the following.

- An *increased preference for European goods*. For example, airlines in the United States might find that planes built by the French company Airbus are superior to others such as the US-built Boeing, and decide to expand the number of Airbus planes in their fleets. To buy the European planes, US airlines would demand more euros on the foreign exchange market.
- An *increase in real GDP abroad*, which implies higher incomes abroad, and thus more demand for imports from Europe.
- An *increase in the interest rate on European assets*, which would make those assets more attractive to foreign savers. To acquire additional European assets, foreign savers would demand more euros.

Example 28.4 Monetary policy and the exchange rate

Suppose that the European Central Bank decides to increase euro interest rates. How might this decision affect the euro's equilibrium exchange rate?

The effects of this policy change on the value of the euro are shown in Figure 28.4. Before the policy change, the equilibrium value of the exchange rate is e^*, at the intersection of supply curve S and demand curve D. Higher euro interest rates make

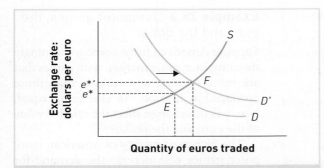

Figure 28.4 A Tighter Monetary Policy Strengthens the Euro. Tighter monetary policy in Europe raises euro interest rates, increasing the demand for euro assets by foreign savers. An increased demand for European assets increases the demand for euros. The demand curve for euros shifts from D to D', increasing the equilibrium value of the euro from e^* to $e^{*'}$.

euro-denominated assets more attractive to foreign financial investors. The increased willingness of foreign investors to buy European assets increases the demand for euros, shifting the demand curve rightwards from D to D' and the equilibrium point from E to F. As a result of this increase in demand, the equilibrium value of the euro rises from e^* to $e^{*'}$.

In short, a tightening of monetary policy by the ECB raises the demand for euros, causing the euro to *appreciate*. By similar logic, an easing of monetary policy, which reduces the real interest rate, would weaken the demand for the euro, causing it to *depreciate*.

Exercise 28.3 Suppose the US Federal Reserve cuts dollar interest rates. What is the likely effect on the dollar–euro exchange rate?

RECAP Determining the exchange rate

- Supply and demand analysis is a useful tool for studying the short-run determination of the exchange rate. European households and firms supply euros to the foreign exchange market to acquire foreign currencies, which they need to purchase foreign goods, services and assets. Foreigners demand euros in the foreign exchange market to purchase European goods, services and assets. The *equilibrium exchange rate*, also called the fundamental value of the exchange rate, equates the quantities of euros supplied and demanded in the foreign exchange market.
- An increased preference for foreign goods, an increase in European real GDP or an increase in the interest rate on foreign assets will increase the supply of euros on the foreign exchange market, *lowering* the value of the euro. An increased preference for European goods by foreigners, an increase in real GDP abroad or an increase in the interest rate on European assets will increase the demand for euros, *raising* the value of the euro.

Fixed exchange rates

So far, we have focused on the case of flexible exchange rates, the relevant case for most large industrial countries such as the United Kingdom, the United States and the Eurosystem. However, the alternative approach, *fixing the exchange rate*, has been quite important historically. Prior to the introduction of the euro in 1999 most European countries had a strong preference for fixed exchange rates between their currencies. One reason is that exchange rate flexibility and volatility is often seen as a threat to trade between European countries and the continuing process of economic integration. In this section we shall see how our conclusions change when the nominal exchange rate is fixed rather than flexible.

How to fix an exchange rate

In contrast to a flexible exchange rate, whose value is determined solely by supply and demand in the foreign exchange market, the value of a fixed exchange rate is determined by the government (in practice, usually the finance ministry with the cooperation of the central bank). Today, the value of a fixed exchange rate is usually set in terms of a major currency (for instance, several countries in Central and Eastern Europe (CEE) link their currency to the euro and China pegs its currency to the US dollar), or relative to a 'basket' of currencies, typically those of the country's trading partners. Historically, currency values were often fixed in terms of gold or other precious metals, but in recent years precious metals have rarely if ever been used for that purpose.

devaluation a reduction in the official value of a currency (in a fixed exchange rate system)

revaluation an increase in the official value of a currency (in a fixed exchange rate system)

overvalued exchange rate an exchange rate that has an officially fixed value greater than its fundamental value

undervalued exchange rate an exchange rate that has an officially fixed value less than its fundamental value

Once an exchange rate has been fixed, the government usually attempts to keep it unchanged for some time. However, sometimes economic circumstances force the government to change the value of the exchange rate. A reduction in the official value of a currency is called a **devaluation**; an increase in the official value is called a **revaluation**. The devaluation of a fixed exchange rate is analogous to the *depreciation* of a flexible exchange rate; both involve a reduction in the currency's value. Conversely, a revaluation is analogous to an *appreciation*.

When the officially fixed value of an exchange rate is *greater* than its fundamental value, the exchange rate is said to be **overvalued**. The official value of an exchange rate can also be *lower* than its fundamental value, in which case the exchange rate is said to be **undervalued**.

Example 28.5 An overvalued exchange rate

Suppose the Bank of England decides to fix the value of sterling against the euro. Assuming that the official exchange rate is greater than the fundamental rate, explain what actions the Bank must take to maintain the official exchange rate.

Figure 28.5 uses the demand and supply model to illustrate how exchange rates are fixed and the problems associated with maintaining an official exchange rate at a level different from its fundamental value.

In Figure 28.5 the exchange rate is measured as euros per pound. The foreign exchange market is in equilibrium at point E and the equilibrium exchange rate is $e^\star$. Suppose the Bank of England decides to fix the exchange rate at e_1. As the official value is greater than the fundamental value the currency is overvalued. The problem this creates is that the currency will be

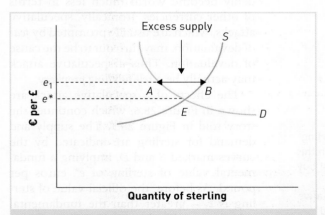

Figure 28.5 An Overvalued Exchange Rate. Market equilibrium is at E and the initial value of the fundamental exchange rate is e^*. Fixing the exchange rate at e_1 creates an excess supply equal to AB per period. To maintain the official value, the central bank must use its foreign exchange reserves to continuously purchase AB of its own currency in each period.

over-supplied. At the exchange rate e_1 demand is at point A and supply at point B, implying excess supply equal to the quantity AB. If the Bank does not interfere the excess supply will force the exchange rate (price) down and the market will clear at point E. Hence to keep the exchange rate at its official value e_1 the Bank must *continuously purchase* sterling equal to the quantity AB per period. To purchase its own currency the Bank must hold foreign currency assets called **foreign exchange reserves**.

foreign exchange reserves foreign currency assets held by a central bank for the purpose of purchasing the domestic currency in the foreign exchange market

For example, the Bank of England may hold euro deposits in German banks or German government debt, which it can sell for euros to buy sterling in the foreign exchange market as needed. Because a country with an overvalued exchange rate must use part of its reserves to support the value of its currency in each period, over time its available reserves will decline. However, as we shall see in the next section, this is not a sustainable strategy for the central bank.

Speculative attacks

speculative attack a massive selling of domestic currency assets by financial investors

Attempts to maintain an overvalued exchange rate can be ended quickly and unexpectedly by the onset of a **speculative attack**. A speculative attack involves massive selling of domestic currency assets by both domestic and foreign financial investors. For example, in a speculative attack on sterling, financial investors would attempt to get rid of any *financial assets* – stocks, bonds and deposits in banks – *denominated in sterling*. A speculative attack is most likely to occur when financial investors fear that an overvalued currency will soon be devalued, since in a devaluation, financial assets denominated in the domestic currency suddenly become worth much less in terms of other currencies. Ironically, speculative attacks, which are usually prompted by *fear* of devaluation, may turn out to be the cause of devaluation. Thus a speculative attack may actually be a *self-fulfilling prophecy*.

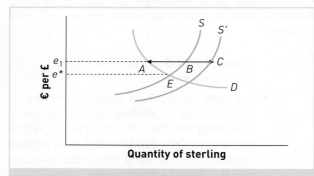

Figure 28.6 A Speculative Attack. Initially, sterling is overvalued at e_1 euros per pound. To maintain this official exchange rate the Bank of England must buy sterling in the amount AB per period. Fearing devaluation, financial investors launch a speculative attack selling sterling-denominated assets, and supply additional sterling to the foreign exchange market. As a result, the supply curve for sterling shifts from S to S', lowering the fundamental value further and forcing the central bank to buy sterling in the amount AC to maintain the official exchange rate at e_1. This more rapid loss of reserves may lead the central bank to devalue sterling.

The effects of a speculative attack are shown in Figure 28.6, which continues the story told in Figure 28.5. The supply and demand for sterling are indicated by the curves marked S and D, implying a fundamental value of sterling of $e^\star$ euros per pound. As before, the official value of sterling is e_1 – greater than the fundamental value – so sterling is *overvalued*. To maintain the official rate at e_1, the Bank of England must use its foreign exchange reserves to *continually* buy back sterling, in the amount corresponding to the line segment AB in Figure 28.6.

Unfortunately, the Bank of England's stock of foreign exchange reserves is finite.

As reserves continue to fall financial markets will realise that the Bank cannot continue to buy its own currency indefinitely and will start to anticipate a sterling devaluation, which reduces the excess supply and moves e closer to e^*. When this expectation takes hold, financial investors will sell sterling in the belief that it can be bought back at a lower price once the devaluation happens. For example, suppose that in Figure 28.6, $e_1 =$ €1.60 and $e^* =$ €1.50. Hence if sterling were to be devalued from its official value of £1 = €1.60 to its fundamental value of £1 = €1.50, then a £1 million sterling investment, worth €1.6 million at the official exchange rate, would suddenly be worth only €1.5 million. To try to avoid these losses, financial investors will sell their sterling-denominated assets and offer the sterling proceeds on the foreign exchange market to buy assets denominated in other currencies. The resulting flood of sterling into the market will shift the supply curve of sterling to the right, from S to S' in Figure 28.6. Effectively, speculators are being offered a one-way bet. If sterling is devalued they gain by repurchasing sterling assets at the lower exchange rate. If sterling is not devalued, the value of assets in their portfolios will not change. For example, if a speculator sells assets worth £1 million, or €1.60 million, at the official exchange rate they can repurchase these assets for €1.50 million if the exchange rate is devalued to £1 = €1.50. Alternatively, if the devaluation does not happen, the value of the speculators' investment remains constant at €1.60 or £1 million.

This speculative attack creates a serious problem for the British authorities. Prior to the attack, maintaining the value of sterling required the central bank to spend each period an amount of international reserves corresponding to the line segment AB. Now suddenly the central bank must spend a larger quantity of reserves, equal to the distance AC in Figure 28.6, to maintain the fixed exchange rate. These extra reserves are needed to purchase the sterling being sold by panicky financial investors. In practice, such speculative attacks often force devaluation by reducing the central bank's reserves to the point where further defence of the fixed exchange rate is considered hopeless. Thus a speculative attack ignited by fears of devaluation may actually end up producing the very devaluation that was feared.

Exchange rate systems

Historically, relatively small countries have independently fixed the values of their currencies against the currency of a major trading partner. Argentina and Hong Kong have pegged against the US dollar while CEE transition economies have attempted to maintain stable currency values against the German mark and now the euro. Likewise, between the foundation of the State in 1922 and 1979 the Irish authorities maintained a fixed one-to-one exchange rate between the Irish pound and sterling. In these cases the responsibility for maintaining the fixed exchange rate normally rests with the smaller country and the fixed exchange rate policy is rarely the result of a cooperative agreement between the two countries concerned. To protect international trade and promote economic integration, countries in Western Europe have also favoured fixed exchange rates between their currencies. However, rather than follow independent exchange rate policies European countries attempted to maintain stable currency values by collectively agreeing to operate a *fixed-exchange system*. Economic naturalist 28.2 discusses the most successful and long-lived attempt by European countries to achieve stable exchange rates – the European Monetary System (EMS), which lasted from 1979 to the introduction of the euro in 1999.

Economic naturalist 28.2 The European Monetary System  5

The 1970s was a turbulent decade on world and European financial markets. Over the six years following the quadrupling of oil prices in 1973 the French franc depreciated by approximately 30 per cent against the German mark and the Italian lira by more than 50 per cent. Fearing that this exchange rate instability could damage international trade and threaten the process of European integration, France and Germany proposed a new exchange rate system designed to restore order and stability to the foreign exchange markets and establish a *zone of monetary stability* in Europe. In 1978, the nine member states of the then EC reached agreement and the new *European Monetary System (EMS)* was launched in March 1979. The key features of the EMS were the *European Currency Unit (ECU)*, the *Exchange Rate Mechanism* (ERM) and *realignments*.

- *The European Currency Unit* The ECU was a composite or 'basket' currency that included specific amounts of all EMS currencies (German mark, French franc, Irish pound, etc.). The contribution of each currency reflected the economic importance of the different countries. Hence, the German mark accounted for over 30 per cent of the ECU, while the Irish pound contributed just over 1 per cent. Each currency was assigned a central value against the ECU, which was used to fix *bilateral central values* between pairs of currencies.

- *The Exchange Rate Mechanism* Participation in the ERM required countries to maintain their bilateral exchange rates within an agreed band of fluctuation around the central rate. For most countries this band was set at ±2.25 per cent around the central rate. Hence, if the FF–DM central rate is 1 DM = 2.4 FF, then Germany would be required to maintain the actual exchange within the range 2.4 + 2.25 per cent (2.2414) and 2.4 − 2.25 per cent (2.34). Belgium, Denmark, France, Germany, Ireland, the Netherlands and Luxemburg adopted the ±2.25 per cent fluctuation band, while Italy operated in a wider ±6 per cent band. The United Kingdom, while a member of the EMS and a contributor to the ECU basket, opted out of the ERM and maintained a flexible exchange rate throughout the 1980s.

- *Realignments* Realignments were the method by which countries could change their central rates against the ECU and therefore against other currencies in the ERM. In effect realignment usually meant a *devaluation* or *revaluation* of the currency or currencies concerned.

The history of the EMS can be divided into three distinct periods, which we shall label 'soft', 'hard' and 'flexible'.

- *The soft EMS: 1979–86* The early years of the EMS were characterised by a lack of policy coordination among the participating countries. Germany, committed to price stability, favoured tight monetary policies while other countries, such as France and Italy, were more concerned with unemployment and followed more expansionary monetary policies. This lack of coordination resulted in large inflation differentials. Between 1979 and 1985 German inflation averaged 4 per cent per annum compared with 10 per cent for France and 15 per cent for Italy. As a result the high-inflation countries experienced continuous balance of payments difficulties, requiring frequent realignments to correct for the competitive losses resulting from excess inflation. Between September 1979 and August 1986 the Italian lira was devalued five times and the French franc four times. The low-inflation DM, on the other hand, was revalued on six occasions. The cumulative effect was that the lira lost almost 50 per cent of its value against the DM and the franc 30 per cent. Also, the financial markets were quick to learn that persistent inflation differentials would lead to realignments, and launched frequent attacks against the high-inflation currencies. Over these years, the EMS was far from being the zone of monetary stability intended by its designers.

- *The hard EMS: 1987–92* By 1986 there was common agreement that the EMS could deliver stability only if the participating countries could agree on a high level of policy coordination. A major problem in finding a cooperative solution was that Germany was unlikely to moderate its strong anti-inflationary policies to accommodate more inflation-prone countries such as France and Italy. Germany may have wanted a more stable EMS but not at the price of weakening its commitment to price stability. The solution, although not publicly announced, was to grant Germany leadership of the EMS. Germany was free to determine its own monetary policy and the other countries followed. Effectively the other central banks acted as 'Bundesbank clones'. The move to German leadership resulted in a much greater convergence of inflation rates within the EMS. Over 1987–91 the average German inflation rate was just over 2 per cent per annum but the average French rate fell to 3 per cent and the Italian rate to 5.6 per cent. Realignments and speculative attacks became very infrequent and even the British joined the ERM in 1991. Anchored on German monetary policy the ERM appeared to be fulfilling its potential as a zone of monetary stability. However, things were not what they seemed and, in mid-September 1992, speculators launched a series of massive attacks against several EMS currencies, and especially against sterling and the lira. These attacks were largely prompted by a growing policy conflict between Germany and its partner ERM countries. The fall of the Berlin Wall and German reunification were accompanied by a dramatic increase in government spending and an inflationary surge. Committed to price stability the Bundesbank increased German interest rates to offset the rise in inflation. As Germany had effective leadership of the EMS, higher DM interest rates were transmitted across the other participating countries. This, however, coincided with recession in the United Kingdom and Italy. These countries required lower interest rates to combat recession and increasing unemployment, but their commitment to maintain a stable exchange rate with Germany meant that they had to accept higher rather than lower interest rates. International financial markets became convinced that the United Kingdom and Italy would have to choose between using monetary policy to stabilise their economies and their commitment to maintaining a stable exchange rate. They bet heavily on the first, and massive speculation forced sterling and the lira to leave the ERM and depreciate against the DM. At least two important lessons can be learned from this period.

1. First, a fixed exchange rate system can work properly only if all countries *face the same problems and require the same policies*. Once these problems differ, with some countries requiring high interest rates to fight inflation and the others needing lower interest rates to offset recession, the resulting policy conflict will eventually lead to one of the groups breaking free and following the monetary policy best suited to their own economies.
2. Second, if the goal is to achieve full monetary integration and an end to exchange rate instability the obvious path is to *full monetary union*, which completely eliminates national currencies and, by definition, exchange rates.

• *The flexible ERM: 1993–99* The speculative attacks that started in mid-1992 continued periodically throughout the first half of 1993. In order to reduce the incidence of these attacks, the EMS countries agreed to replace the narrow ±2.25 per cent fluctuation band with a much wider ±15 per cent band in August 1993. The introduction of these wider bands greatly reduced incentives for speculative attacks. For speculators to gain, the currency must be devalued, which in the ERM meant that the actual exchange rate would jump from its initial fluctuation band into a lower band. However, the wider the band the greater the probability that the new equilibrium value will be within the initial fluctuation band. When this is the case, the central bank does not have to defend the currency. It can simply let the exchange rate depreciate towards the lower fundamental value and speculators are not presented with an incentive to sell the currency in the expectation that it will have to be realigned.

The EMS vanished on 31 December 1998 and was replaced by the European Monetary Union, with the previous members of the ERM choosing to eliminate their national currencies and replace them with a common currency called the euro.

Exchange rates and stabilisation policy

The choice between fixed and flexible exchange rates has important implications for stabilisation policy. In this section we shall see that monetary policy is most effective when exchange rates are flexible and least effective when they are fixed. Conversely, we shall see that fiscal policy is least effective when exchange rates are flexible and most effective when they are fixed. In Chapters 24 and 25 we used the IS-LM model to analyse how fiscal and monetary policies can be used to close output gaps. However, in these chapters we assumed that the economy was 'closed', and ignored international trade and capital flows. To incorporate these factors into the model we will first modify the IS and LM curves to account for exchange rate changes and capital movements and then introduce a new curve called the balance of payments, or *BP*, curve to control for equilibrium in the foreign sector.

The IS curve in an open economy

In Chapter 23 we defined the IS curve as combinations of interest rate and output combinations at which the market for goods and services is in equilibrium. We also saw that changes in autonomous expenditures such as a change in net exports will cause the IS curve to shift. In this chapter we have introduced the real exchange rate and shown that a fall in the real exchange rate, a real depreciation, will increase net exports. Conversely, a rise in the real exchange rate, a real appreciation, leads to a fall in net exports. Hence a fall in the real exchange rate leads to higher net exports (an increase in autonomous expenditure) and shifts the IS curve to the right (see Figure 23.2). Likewise, an increase in the real exchange rate leads to lower net exports (a decrease in autonomous expenditure) and shifts the IS curve to the left. Note that we have defined the real exchange rate as eP/P^f, where e is the nominal exchange rate and P and P^f are the domestic and foreign price levels. To simplify things we shall assume, for the moment, that prices do not change in the short run and that changes in the nominal exchange rate are reflected by changes in the real exchange rate. Hence a fall in the nominal exchange rate increases net exports and shifts the IS to the right, whereas an increase in the nominal exchange rate shifts the IS curve to the left.

The LM curve in an open economy

In Chapter 23 we defined the LM curve as combinations of interest rate and output combinations at which the market for money is in equilibrium. We also assumed that the money supply was exogenous and controlled by the central bank via open-market operations. We shall now see that opening the economy to international trade and capital movements has important implications for this assumption. To see why, we will construct simplified balance sheets for the commercial banks and the central bank. To simplify things we make the following assumptions.

- Commercial banks hold two assets – loans to the public and government (L) and reserves (RES) – and one liability, deposits held by the public (DEP).
- Commercial banks hold their reserves as deposits with the central bank.
- The economy's stock of foreign exchange reserves (FXR) are held by the central bank.
- The central bank holds two assets: FXR and a portfolio of government bonds (B).
- The central bank's liabilities are commercial bank reserves, RES, and currency in circulation with the public (CUR).

- The money supply (MS) is the sum of commercial bank deposit liabilities, DEP, and currency in circulation with the public, CUR.

Putting these assumptions together we can write the commercial and central bank balance sheet identities as:

Commercial banks: $DEP = L + RES$

Central bank: $RES + CUR = B + FXR$

From the central bank balance sheet $RES = B + FXR - CUR$ and substituting for reserves in the commercial bank balance sheet gives:

$$DEP = L + B + FXR - CUR$$

As the money supply is defined as $MS = DEP + CUR$ we can rewrite this expression as:

$$MS = L + B + FXR$$

Hence the money supply is defined as being equal to the sum of commercial bank loans and the central bank's holding of government bonds plus the stock of foreign exchange reserves. As L (commercial bank lending to the public and government) and B (central bank lending to government) account for total bank lending to the public and government it is sometimes referred to as domestic credit, denoted DCR. Hence the money supply identity can be written as:

$$MS = DCR + FXR \qquad (28.2)$$

Example 28.6 explains these linkages.

Example 28.6 The money supply in an open economy

Suppose a German wine importer signs a contract to import wine from California at a cost of $1.5 million. If the nominal exchange rate is €1 = $1.50 how does this transaction affect the Eurosystem's money supply?

To pay for the wine the German importer must purchase 1.5 million dollars from a German or Eurosystem commercial bank. At an exchange rate of €1 = $1.50 the cost will be €1 million. The following sequence explains how this transaction leads to a decline in the Eurosystem's money supply.

- The importer orders $1.5 million from its commercial bank and pays by a €1 million reduction in its bank deposits.
- The commercial bank purchases the dollars from the central bank and pays by an equivalent reduction in its reserve assets held at the central bank.

These transactions imply that commercial bank deposit liabilities and reserve assets both fall by €1 million while the central bank's stock of foreign exchange reserve assets and its liability to the commercial banks in the form of reserves also fall by €1 million. Note that the balance sheets of the commercial banks and the central bank remain in balance (liabilities = assets). Further, the decline in commercial bank reserves will, by the process described in Chapter 22, lead to a multiple contraction in deposits and bank lending. Hence we can conclude that, other things being equal, a fall in central bank foreign exchange reserves leads to a decline in the money supply, which shifts the LM curve to the left. Likewise an increase in the stock of central bank foreign exchange reserves leads to an increase in the money supply, which shifts the LM curve to the right.

The foreign sector

The IS-LM model developed in Chapter 23 established equilibrium conditions in two markets or sectors – the market for goods and services (or the real sector) and the market for money (or the monetary sector). We now wish to incorporate a third sector, the foreign sector, into the model. By the foreign sector we mean all transactions that involve the sale or purchase of the domestic currency for another currency. We will classify these transactions into two types – net exports, denoted NX, and net **capital flows**, denoted KF. As in other chapters net exports are defined as the export of goods and services minus imports of goods and services. Exports are purchases of domestic goods by foreigners, while imports are purchases of foreign goods and services by domestic residents. Hence on the foreign exchange market exports generate a demand for the domestic currency while imports generate a supply of the domestic currency. *Net capital flows*, denoted KF, are defined as purchases of domestic assets by foreign households, firms and institutions minus the purchase of foreign assets by domestic households, firms and institutions. For example, if an American financial institution purchases a euro-denominated German bond it must purchase (demand) euros on the foreign exchange market. Conversely, if a German financial institution purchases a dollar denominated bond it must sell (supply) euros on the foreign exchange market.

capital flows purchases of domestic assets by foreigners less purchases of foreign assets by domestic residents

Net exports and net capital flows lead to changes in the economy's stock of foreign exchange reserves, FXR. For example, if net exports are positive, the demand for the domestic currency will exceed supply (or the supply of the foreign currency will exceed demand) and FXR will be increasing. Likewise if net capital flows are negative the supply of the domestic currency on the foreign exchange market will exceed demand (or the demand of the foreign currency will exceed supply) and FXR will be decreasing. Hence the change in foreign exchange reserves equals the sum of net exports and net capital flows. That is, using the Greek delta Δ as shorthand for the phrase 'the change in':

$$\Delta FXR = NX + KF$$

We can think of the change in the stock of foreign exchange reserves as the balance of payments, or the total demand for the currency on the foreign exchange market minus the total supply. If the stock of foreign exchange reserves is falling, the country is experiencing a **balance-of-payments deficit**. Conversely, if the stock of foreign exchange reserves is increasing, the country is experiencing a **balance-of-payments surplus**.

balance-of-payments deficit a net decline in a country's stock of foreign exchange reserves

balance-of-payments surplus a net increase in a country's stock of foreign exchange reserves

Hence the foreign sector will be in equilibrium when the stock of foreign exchange reserves is constant. That is:

$$NX + KF = 0 \tag{28.3}$$

The BP curve

The IS curve plots combinations of income and the rate of interest at which the market for goods and services (or the real sector) is in equilibrium. Likewise, the LM curve plots combinations of income and the rate of interest, at which the market for money (or the monetary sector) is in equilibrium. We can now introduce a third relationship between income and the rate of interest, called the BP curve. The BP curve plots combinations of income and the rate of interest at which the balance of payments (or the foreign sector) is in equilibrium. To derive the BP curve we first consider the determinants of net exports and net capital flows. Net exports are the difference between the value of goods and services exported by a country and the value of goods and services imported by the country. Hence net exports will depend on the following factors.

- *Domestic income (Y)* The higher is domestic income the greater are consumption and imports. Hence we would expect net exports to fall (imports increase) as domestic income rises. Conversely, we would expect net exports to rise (imports fall) as domestic income falls.
- *Foreign income (Y^f)* As the domestic country's exports are the foreign country's imports, we would expect net exports to increase (exports increase) as foreign income rises. Conversely, we would expect net exports to fall (exports fall) as foreign income falls.
- *The real exchange rate (eP/P^f)* A fall in the real exchange rate (a real depreciation) leads to an increase in net exports. Conversely, a rise the real exchange rate (a real appreciation) leads to a fall in net exports.

Net capital flows represent the difference between purchases of domestic assets by foreigners and purchases of foreign assets by domestic residents. Hence net capital flows will depend on the following factors.

- *The domestic rate of interest (i)* The higher the domestic rate of interest the greater the demand for domestic currency assets and the lower the domestic rate of interest the lower the demand for domestic assets. Hence we would expect net capital flows (inflows minus outflows) to increase as the domestic rate of interest rises.
- *The foreign rate of interest (i^f)* The higher the foreign rate of interest the greater the demand for foreign currency assets and the lower the foreign rate of interest the lower the demand for foreign assets. Hence we would expect net capital flows (inflows minus outflows) to fall as the foreign rate of interest increases.

the BP curve plots combinations of income and the rate of interest at which the balance of payments is in equilibrium

perfect capital mobility a situation in which there are no restrictions on the free movement of capital and investors treat assets denominated in different currencies as perfect substitutes

The **BP curve** plots combinations of income and the rate of interest at which the balance of payments (or the foreign sector) is in equilibrium.

To simplify matters, we will assume that international financial markets are characterised by **perfect capital mobility**, which means that there are no restrictions on the free movement of financial capital between currencies and that investors treat assets denominated in different currencies as perfect substitutes.

The absence of restrictions on capital movements means that billions of euros, pounds or dollars can be bought or sold on the world's foreign exchange markets in a few minutes, normally by computer without any physical transaction actually taking place, and the assumption that different assets are perfect substitutes means that investors are concerned with rates of interest only when deciding which currencies to buy or sell. For example, if the domestic interest rate were to fall below the foreign interest rate we would expect to see large-scale selling of domestic assets matched by large-scale purchases of foreign assets, which will force an increase in the domestic interest rate and/or a fall in the foreign interest rate. Alternatively, if the domestic interest rate were to rise above the foreign interest rate we would expect to observe the reverse,

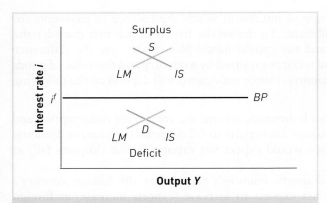

Figure 28.7 The BP Curve. Assuming perfect capital mobility the BP curve is horizontal with $i = i^f$. Points above the BP curve are positions of balance-of-payments surplus, and points below the BP curve are positions of balance-of-payments deficit.

with large capital inflows to the domestic currency, which will force a fall in the domestic interest rate and/or a rise in the foreign interest rate. Hence in equilibrium the gap between the domestic and foreign interest rate will be closed and i will equal i^f, as illustrated by the horizontal BP curve in Figure 28.7.

What happens if the economy is not on the BP curve? For example, suppose the IS and LM curves intersect at an interest rate–output combination that is above or below the BP curve. If this is the case the two domestic markets (goods and money) will be in equilibrium but the balance of payments will not be in equilibrium. Remember that for any given level of income the BP curve gives the rate of interest necessary for balance of payments equilibrium. Hence if the IS and LM curves intersect at a point above the BP curve, such as S in Figure 28.7, the rate of interest will be greater than the foreign rate of interest and, as net capital flows increase with the rate of interest, the balance of payments will be in surplus. Conversely, if the IS and LM curves intersect at a point below the BP curve, such as D in Figure 28.7, the rate of interest will be lower than the foreign rate of interest and the balance of payments will be in deficit. We will see shortly that the way in which the economy adjusts to surpluses and deficits depends on whether the exchange rate is fixed or flexible, and is crucial for the effectiveness of fiscal and monetary policies in an open economy.

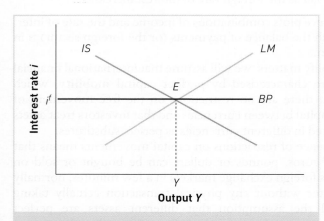

Figure 28.8 Equilibrium in the IS-LM-BP Model. The intersection of the IS, LM and BP curves at point E defines the (i, Y) combination that gives simultaneous equilibrium in the market for goods and services $(Y = PAE)$, the money market $(M^D = M^S)$ and in the external sector $(\Delta FXR = 0)$.

Equilibrium in the IS-LM-BP model

Overall equilibrium in the IS-LM-BP model is illustrated by Figure 28.8.

Equilibrium is at point E, where all three curves intersect. Hence the interest rate–output combination at point E gives equilibrium in the market for goods and services $(Y = PAE)$, the money market $(MD = MS)$ and the foreign sector $(\Delta FXR = 0)$. We will now use this model to analyse fiscal and monetary policy in the open economy.

Fiscal policy in the open economy

Figure 28.9 illustrates how fiscal policy works in the open economy. The nominal exchange rate is assumed to be flexible in panel (a) and fixed in panel (b).

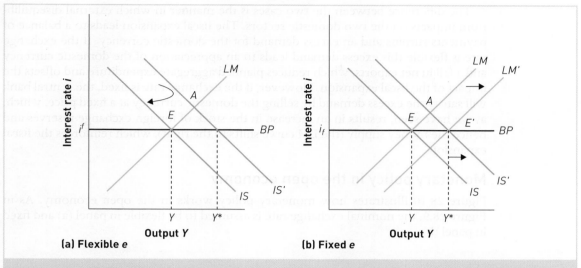

Figure 28.9 Fiscal Policy. A fiscal expansion leads to an increase in short-run equilibrium output, under a fixed exchange rate, panel (b), but is ineffective when the exchange rate is flexible, panel (a).

In both panels of Figure 28.9, initial equilibrium is at the point E with output equal to Y and the domestic interest rate equal to the foreign interest rate. Full employment or potential output is $Y^\star$ and the economy is experiencing a recessionary gap.

Example 28.7 Fiscal policy

Can fiscal policy be used to close the recessionary gap in Figure 28.9?

Flexible exchange rate, panel (a): a fiscal expansion such as an increase in government purchases or a cut in net taxes shifts the IS curve to the right, to IS'. In the short run, the economy moves along the LM curve to a point such as A. As A is above the BP curve the balance of payments will be in overall surplus and, as a surplus implies an excess demand for the domestic currency, it will force an increase in the nominal exchange rate that, at given prices, leads to an increase in the real exchange rate (eP/P^f) and, as the real exchange rate appreciates, net exports will decline. Other things being equal, the fall in net exports reduces planned aggregate expenditure at each level of income and shifts the IS curve back to the left, re-establishing the initial equilibrium at point E. Hence fiscal policy is ineffective when the exchange rate is flexible.

Fixed exchange rate, panel (b): as in the case of a flexible exchange rate a fiscal expansion shifts the IS curve to the right, to IS', and in the short run, the economy moves along the LM curve to a point such as A, which, as we have seen, corresponds to a balance-of-payments surplus and an excess demand for the domestic currency. A fixed exchange rate means that the central bank will satisfy any excess demand for the domestic currency. That is, the central bank will sell the domestic currency in exchange for foreign currency at the official exchange rate. As a result, the stock of foreign exchange reserves (*FXR*) will increase and, using Equation (28.2), the money supply will increase, shifting the LM curve to the right, to LM', and establishing a new equilibrium at point E' with $Y = Y^\star$. Hence fiscal policy is effective when the exchange rate is fixed.

The difference between the two cases is the manner in which external disequilibrium impacts on the two domestic sectors. The fiscal expansion leads to a balance of payments surplus and an excess demand for the domestic currency. If the exchange rate is flexible this excess demand leads to an appreciation of the domestic currency and a fall in net exports, which reduces planned aggregate expenditure and offsets the impact of the fiscal expansion. However, if the exchange rate is fixed, the central bank will satisfy the excess demand by selling the domestic currency at a fixed price, which, as we have seen, results in an increase in the stock of foreign exchange reserves and hence the money supply (the LM curve shifts to the right), which reinforces the fiscal expansion.

Monetary policy in the open economy

Figure 28.10 illustrates how monetary policy works in the open economy. As in Figure 28.9, the nominal exchange rate is assumed to be flexible in panel (a) and fixed in panel (b).

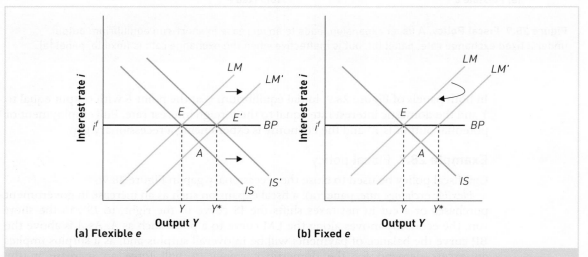

Figure 28.10 Monetary Policy. A monetary expansion leads to an increase in short-run equilibrium output, under a flexible exchange rate, panel (a), but is ineffective when the exchange rate is fixed, panel (b).

In both panels of Figure 28.10, initial equilibrium is at point E with output equal to Y and the domestic interest rate equal to the foreign interest rate. Full employment or potential output is $Y^\star$ and the economy is experiencing a recessionary gap.

Example 28.8 Monetary policy

Can monetary policy be used to close the recessionary gap in Figure 28.10?

Flexible exchange rate, panel (a): an increase in the money supply will shift the LM curve to the right, to LM'. In the short run, the economy moves along the IS curve to a point such as A. As A is below the BP curve, the balance of payments will be in overall deficit and as a deficit implies an excess supply of the domestic currency it will force a fall in the nominal exchange rate, which at given prices leads to a lower real exchange rate (eP/P^f) and, as the real exchange rate depreciates, net exports will increase. Other things being equal, the rise in net exports increases planned aggregate expenditure at each level of income and shifts the IS curve to the right, to IS', establishing a new equilibrium at point E' with $Y = Y^*$. Hence monetary policy is effective when the exchange rate is flexible.

Fixed exchange rate, panel (b): as in the case of a flexible exchange rate, a monetary expansion shifts the LM curve to the right, to LM'. In the short run, the economy moves along the IS curve to a point such as A, which, as we have seen, corresponds to a balance-of-payments deficit and an excess supply for the domestic currency. When the exchange rate is fixed the central bank will satisfy any take-up of any excess supply of the domestic currency. That is, the central bank will sell foreign exchange for the domestic currency at the official exchange rate. As a result, the stock of foreign exchange reserves (*FXR*) will fall and, using Equation (28.2), the money supply will also fall, shifting the LM curve back to the left, re-establishing the initial equilibrium at point E. Hence monetary policy is ineffective when the exchange rate is fixed.

As in the case of fiscal policy the difference between the two cases is the manner in which external disequilibrium impacts on the two domestic sectors. A monetary expansion leads to a balance-of-payments deficit and an excess supply of the domestic currency. If the exchange rate is flexible this excess supply leads to a depreciation of the domestic currency and a rise in net exports, which increases planned aggregate expenditure (IS shifts to the right) and reinforces the impact of the monetary expansion. However, if the exchange rate is fixed, the central bank will stop the excess supply from reducing the exchange rate by buying the domestic currency at a fixed price, which, as we have seen, results in a fall in the stock of foreign exchange reserves, leading to a contraction in the domestic money supply.

Monetary policy and the nominal exchange rate

In Example 28.8 we saw that monetary policy is most effective when the exchange rate is flexible and ineffective when the exchange rate is fixed. We can state this result in a different way; monetary policy can be used to stabilise the economy or it can be used to fix the exchange rate but it cannot be used for both. This can be illustrated by the case of the United Kingdom, which, to date, has retained its own currency and opted for a flexible exchange rate against other currencies such as the euro and the dollar. Because it operates under a flexible exchange rate the Bank of England can use active monetary policy to stabilise the economy. For example, if a recessionary gap opens, the Bank can stimulate aggregate demand by increasing the money supply, which reduces interest rates. Conversely, if an expansionary gap opens, the Bank can react by reducing the money supply and increasing interest rates. Now suppose the UK changes policy and decides to fix the value of sterling against the euro. If a recessionary gap opens, any move by the Bank of England to reduce interest rates by increasing the money supply would lead to capital outflows and, as the stock of foreign exchange reserves falls, the money supply would decline as shown in panel (b) of Figure 28.10. Conversely, if an expansionary gap opens and the Bank of England reduces the money supply to increase interest rates, the resulting capital inflows will increase the stock of foreign exchange reserves, reversing the fall in the money supply (Equation 28.3). Hence with a fixed exchange rate, the central bank must set interest rates, and hence the money supply, at a level consistent with maintaining the fixed exchange rate. Given this constraint, maintaining a fixed exchange rate predetermines domestic monetary policy and it cannot be used to stabilise the economy.

The conclusion that, in a world of capital mobility, a country must choose between fixed and flexible exchange rates is sometimes called the 'impossible trinity', which means that a country can choose *only two* of the following three types of policy: free capital mobility, an independent monetary policy, which requires a flexible exchange rate, and a fixed exchange rate, which requires a sacrifice of monetary policy independence. Given capital mobility, the impossible trinity means that a country must choose to use monetary policy to either stabilise the economy or fix the exchange rate. Economic naturalist 28.3 gives a famous example of the impossible trinity in action.

Economic naturalist 28.3 Breaking the Bank of England: sterling and the 1992 ERM crisis

When the European Monetary System (EMS) commenced operation in early 1979 the United Kingdom was the only member state to opt out of the ERM, which, as we have seen, was a system designed to limit fluctuations between participating currencies. However, in October 1990 the British Prime Minister Margaret Thatcher gave in to pressure from her more pro-European cabinet colleagues and agreed that sterling should participate in the ERM. Sterling entered the ERM at a central rate of 2.95 DM per pound sterling (which was probably overvalued) and operated in the wide band, which permitted the exchange rate to fluctuate by ±6 per cent around the central rate. However, less than two years later, on Wednesday, 16 September 2002, a series of massive speculative attacks forced sterling and the Italian lira not just to be devalued but to leave the ERM completely. What caused the 1992 ERM crisis and prompted such speculation against these currencies?

Somewhat ironically, the background to the crisis lay in the United States, which had started to experience a severe recession in the late 1980s. The recession spread to several European countries and especially the United Kingdom, where unemployment increased from 7.3 per cent to over 10 per cent between 1989 and 1992. The Federal Reserve (Fed) reacted to the US recession by aggressively cutting interest rates, which resulted in a decline in the three-month money market rate from 8.4 per cent in 1989 to 3.5 per cent in 1991. However, because the British authorities had sacrificed policy independence by joining the ERM they were unable to respond to recession in a similar manner. This situation was further complicated by German reunification, which dramatically increased government spending and created an inflationary surge in the German economy. To moderate the rise in inflation, Germany's central bank, the Bundesbank, followed an opposite path to the Fed and sharply increased short-term interest rates. As the other EMS currencies were linked to the DM via the ERM this rise in interest rates spread across the system. The widening differential between European and American interest rates increased the attractiveness of European assets, leading to a higher demand for European currencies and a steady appreciation against the dollar. As the United States accounted for approximately 12 per cent of UK exports, this loss of competitiveness against the dollar was a further blow to the British economy.

By mid-1992, the United Kingdom could be described as a country facing recession and rising unemployment combined with high interest rates and an overvalued currency. Germany, on the other hand, was experiencing an expansionary gap and rising inflation. Maintaining high interest rates and a strong currency may have been the appropriate policy for Germany but not for the United Kingdom, which required lower interest rates and a more competitive exchange rate. However, so long as the United Kingdom maintained its currency link with Germany it could not deviate far from German monetary policy. Britain was now caught on the horns of the impossibility trinity. Given capital mobility, it had to choose between maintaining a fixed exchange rate and using monetary policy to stabilise the domestic economy. As the recession deepened, financial markets became convinced that the British authorities would opt for the latter and launched a massive speculative attack against sterling. At first the Bank of England attempted to defend the exchange rate by buying sterling in the foreign exchange market and, on Wednesday 16 September, increased its key lending rate, called the *base interest rate*, from 10 to 12 per cent, and threatened a further 3 per cent increase as an incentive for speculators to stop selling sterling. The markets were not convinced and continued to sell large amounts of the British currency in anticipation of devaluation. With reserves falling rapidly the United Kingdom had little choice but to abandon its fixed exchange rate policy and, at 7 pm that evening, the government announced that Britain would leave the ERM and float against the other European currencies. The announced increases in interest rates were reversed and, by the end of 1992, sterling had depreciated by 16 per cent against the dollar and by 11 per cent against the DM.

Having driven sterling out of the ERM, the speculators turned their attention to other European economies such as Belgium, France, Italy and Spain, which, like the United Kingdom, were experiencing low growth and required lower interest and more competitive exchange rates. The Italian lira was also forced out of the ERM and the Spanish peseta was devalued twice. Speculative attacks continued throughout the first half of 1993 and, in August, the narrow ±2.25 ERM fluctuation band was abandoned and replaced with a much wider ±15 per cent band. Given this wide range of permitted fluctuation, the ERM was now a closer approximation to a flexible exchange rate system than to a fixed exchange rate system.

The attempt to circumvent the impossible trinity by defending the exchange rate is estimated to have cost the Bank of England £4 billion in reserves. One of the most prominent speculators, George Soros, is thought to have earned up to £0.5 billion from the crisis and became known as 'the man who broke the Bank of England'. Wednesday, 16 September 1992 is sometimes referred to as 'Black Wednesday'. However, for the remaining years of the decade and into the new century the UK economy generally outperformed those of countries such as France and Germany, leading proponents of flexible exchange rates to call that day 'Golden Wednesday'.

Summary

■ The *nominal exchange rate* between two currencies is the rate at which the currencies can be traded for each other. A rise in the value of a currency relative to other currencies is called an *appreciation*; a decline in the value of a currency is called a *depreciation*.

■ Exchange rates can be flexible or fixed. The value of a *flexible exchange rate* is determined by the supply and demand for the currency in the *foreign exchange market*, the market on which currencies of various nations are traded for one another. The government sets the value of a *fixed exchange rate*.

■ The *real exchange rate* is the price of the average domestic good or service *relative* to the price of the average foreign good or service, when prices are expressed in terms of a common currency. An increase in the real exchange rate implies that domestic goods and services are becoming more expensive relative to foreign goods and services, which tends to reduce exports and increase imports. Conversely, a decline in the real exchange rate tends to increase net exports.

■ Supply and demand analysis is a useful tool for studying the determination of exchange rates in the short run. The equilibrium exchange rate, also called the *fundamental value of the exchange rate*, equates the quantities of the currency supplied and demanded in the foreign exchange market. A currency is supplied by domestic residents who wish to acquire foreign currencies to purchase foreign goods, services and assets. An increased preference for foreign goods, an increase in the domestic GDP, or an increase in the real interest rate on foreign assets will all increase the supply of a currency on the foreign exchange market and thus lower its value. A currency is demanded by foreigners who wish to purchase domestic goods, services and assets. An increased preference for domestic goods by foreigners, an increase in real GDP abroad, or an increase in the domestic real interest rate will all increase the demand for the currency on the foreign exchange market, and thus increase its value.

■ The value of a *fixed exchange rate* is officially established by the government. A fixed exchange rate whose official value exceeds its fundamental value in the foreign exchange market is said to be *overvalued*. An exchange rate whose official value is below its fundamental value is *undervalued*. A reduction in the official value of a fixed exchange rate is called a *devaluation*; an increase in its official value is called a *revaluation*.

■ For an overvalued exchange rate, the quantity of the currency supplied at the official exchange rate exceeds the quantity demanded. To maintain the official rate, the country's central bank must use its *international reserves* (foreign currency assets) to purchase the excess supply of its currency in the foreign exchange market. Because a country's international reserves are limited, it cannot maintain an overvalued exchange rate indefinitely. Moreover, if financial investors fear an impending devaluation of the exchange rate, they may launch a *speculative attack*, selling their domestic currency assets and supplying large quantities of the currency to the foreign exchange market. Because speculative attacks cause a country's central bank to spend its international reserves even more quickly, they often force a devaluation.

■ The choice of exchange rate regime has important implications for stabilisation policies. Monetary policy is most effective when the exchange rate is flexible and least effective when the exchange rate is fixed. Conversely, fiscal policy is least effective when the exchange rate is flexible and most effective when the exchange rate is fixed.

■ The 'impossible trinity' teaches us that in a world characterised by free capital mobility countries must choose between *domestic stabilisation* and *fixed exchange rates*. If they opt for the latter they cannot use macroeconomic policies to stabilise their domestic economies.

Review questions

1. Japanese yen trade at 110 yen per dollar and Mexican pesos trade at 10 pesos per dollar. What is the nominal exchange rate between the yen and the peso? Express it in two ways.

2. Define the *nominal exchange rate* and the *real exchange rate*. How are the two concepts related? Which type of exchange rate most directly affects a country's ability to export its goods and services?

3. Why do German households and firms supply euros to the foreign exchange market? Why do Americans demand euros in the foreign exchange market?

4. Define an *overvalued exchange rate*. Discuss four ways in which government policy makers can respond to an overvaluation. What are the drawbacks of each approach?

5. Use a supply and demand diagram to illustrate the effects of a speculative attack on an overvalued exchange rate. Why do speculative attacks often result in a devaluation?

6. Suppose that Poland decides to fix the value of the zloty against the euro. What are the implications for monetary and fiscal policies as means of stabilising the domestic economy?

7. The UK has decided to opt out of the euro and follow a flexible exchange rate policy. What does this decision imply for the effectiveness of monetary and fiscal policies?

connect Problems

1. Using the data in Table 28.1, find the nominal exchange rate between the yen and zloty. Express it in two ways. How do your answers change if the yen appreciates by 10 per cent against the euro while the value of the zloty against the euro remains unchanged?

2. A British-made automobile is priced at £20,000. A comparable US-made car costs $26,000. One pound trades for $1.50 in the foreign exchange market. Find the real exchange rate for automobiles from the perspective of the United States and from the perspective of Great Britain. Which country's cars are more competitively priced?

3. Between last year and this year, the CPI in Blueland rose from 100 to 110, and the CPI in Redland rose from 100 to 105. Blueland's currency unit, the blue, was worth €1 last year and is worth 90 cents this year. Redland's currency unit, the red, was worth 50 cents last year and is worth 45 cents this year. Find the percentage change from last year to this year in Blueland's *nominal* exchange rate with Redland and in Blueland's *real* exchange rate with Redland. (Treat Blueland as the home country.) Relative to Redland, do you expect Blueland's exports to be helped or hurt by these changes in exchange rates?

4. How would each of the following be likely to affect the value of the euro, all else being equal? Explain.

    a. Shares in European companies are perceived as having become much riskier financial investments.

    b. American households decide to purchase less French, Spanish and Italian wine, and more Australian, Chilean and South African Wine.

c. As East Asian economies recover from recession, international financial investors become aware of many new, high-return investment opportunities in the region.

d. The US government imposes higher tariffs on imported European goods.

e. Faced with rising inflation, the ECB decides to increase interest rates.

f. European consumers increase their spending on imported goods.

5. The demand for and supply of Polish zlotys in the foreign exchange market are

$$Demand = 30,000 - 8,000e$$
$$Supply = 25,000 + 12,000e$$

where the nominal exchange rate is expressed as euros per zloty.

a. What is the fundamental value of the zloty?

b. The zloty is fixed at 0.30 euros. Is the zloty overvalued, undervalued, or neither? Find the balance-of-payments deficit or surplus in both zlotys and euros. What happens to the country's international reserves over time?

c. Repeat part (b) for the case in which the zloty is fixed at 0.20 euros.

6. The annual demand for and supply of zlotys in the foreign exchange market is as given in Problem 5. The zloty is fixed at 0.30 euros per zloty. The country's international reserves are €600. Foreign financial investors hold chequing accounts in the country in the amount of 5,000 zlotys.

a. Suppose that foreign financial investors do not fear a devaluation of the zloty, and thus do not convert their zloty chequing accounts into euros. Can the zloty be maintained at its fixed value of 0.30 euros for the next year?

b. Now suppose that foreign financial investors come to expect a possible devaluation of the zloty to 0.25 euros. Why should this possibility worry them?

c. In response to their concern about devaluation, foreign financial investors withdraw all funds from their chequing accounts and attempt to convert those zlotys into euros. What happens?

d. Discuss why the foreign investors' forecast of devaluation can be considered a 'self-fulfilling prophecy'.

To help you grasp the key concepts of this chapter check out the extra resources posted on the Online Learning Centre. There are chapter summaries, self-test questions, an interactive graphing tool, weblinks and a glossary, all for free!

Visit the Online Learning Centre at: www.mcgraw-hill.co.uk/textbooks/mcdowell for information on accessing all of these resources.